ENCYCLOPEDIA OF FORENSIC SCIENCES

SECOND EDITION

EDITORS-IN-CHIEF

JAY A SIEGEL

Professor Emeritus, Michigan State University and
Adjunct Professor, Indiana University
Purdue University, Indianapolis, USA

PEKKA J SAUKKO

Professor and Chairman, Department of Forensic Medicine
University of Turku, Turku, Finland

SENIOR EDITOR

MAX M HOUCK

Department of Forensic Sciences
Consolidated Forensic Laboratory
Washington, D.C., USA

ELSEVIER

AMSTERDAM BOSTON HEIDELBERG LONDON NEW YORK OXFORD
PARIS SAN DIEGO SAN FRANCISCO SINGAPORE SYDNEY TOKYO
Academic Press is an imprint of Elsevier

ACADEMIC PRESS

Academic Press is an imprint of Elsevier
32 Jamestown Road, London NW1 7BY, UK
225 Wyman Street, Waltham, MA 02451, USA
525 B Street, Suite 1900, San Diego, CA 92101-4495, USA

First edition 2000

British Library Cataloguing in Publication Data
A catalogue record for this book is available from the British Library

Library of Congress Cataloging-in-Publication Data
A catalog record for this book is available from the Library of Congress

ISBN: 978-0-12-382165-2

For information on all Elsevier publications
visit our website at store.elsevier.com

Printed and bound in Poland

13 14 15 16 17 18 10 9 8 7 6 5 4 3 2

EDITORS-IN-CHIEF: BIOGRAPHIES

Jay Siegel holds a Ph.D. in analytical chemistry from George Washington University. He worked for 3 years at the Virginia Bureau of Forensic Sciences, analyzing drugs, fire residues, and trace evidence. He was then professor of chemistry and forensic science at Metropolitan State College for 3 years. From 1980 to 2004, he was professor of forensic chemistry and Director of the forensic science program at Michigan State University in the School of Criminal Justice. In 2004, he moved to Indiana University–Purdue University, Indianapolis, to become Director of the Forensic and Investigative Sciences Program. In 2008, he also became the Chair of the Department of Chemistry and Chemical Biology at IUPUI. He retired from IUPUI in July 2012.

Dr. Siegel has testified over 200 times as an expert witness in 12 states, Federal Court, and Military Court. He is the Editor-in-Chief of the *Encyclopedia of Forensic Sciences* and has over 20 publications in forensic science journals. He has published a college textbook entitled *Fundamentals of Forensic Science*, which is into its 2nd edition. In 2009, he was named Distinguished Fellow by the American Academy of Forensic Sciences. In April 2009, he was given the Distinguished Alumni Scholar Award by his alma mater, George Washington University.

Pekka Saukko is currently professor of forensic medicine and Head of the Department of Forensic Medicine of the University of Turku, Finland.

He graduated in medicine from the University of Vienna, Austria, in 1975 and was certified as a specialist in forensic medicine in 1981 by the National Board of Health, Finland. In 1983, he received a Doctorate in medical science (MD) for his thesis in forensic pathology from the University of Oulu, Finland, and was appointed adjunct professor of forensic medicine in the same University in 1986. From 1978 to 1989, he held the position of the provincial medical officer, medico-legal expert, provincial government of Oulu. In 1989, he was appointed as the professor of forensic medicine of the University of Tampere, Finland, and since 1992, he has been holding the current position at the University of Turku.

He has published widely as an author or coauthor in scientific journals, books, and encyclopedia and is the coauthor of 'Atlas of Forensic Medicine' (CD-ROM) (Elsevier Science, 2003), 'Knight's Forensic Pathology' (Arnold, 2004), and 'Forensic Medicine in Europe' (Schmidt-Römhild, 2008).

Dr. Saukko is the recipient of the Ajtai K. Sandor Medal and an Honorary Doctorate in Medicine (Dr. h.c.) from the Semmelweis University, Budapest, Hungary. His expert work as consultant includes needs assessment of the forensic facilities in Cambodia for the UNDP (1996) and the Working Party on the Harmonization of Autopsy Rules for the Council of Europe (1997–98), and quality assessment of the Portuguese Departments of Forensic Pathology; he has worked as a member of an international team of experts (2001), the external case review panel for the Office of the Chief Coroner, Toronto, Canada (2006), and the consultant panel, and was an expert witness for the Inquiry into Pediatric Forensic Pathology in Ontario, Canada (2007), and forensic expert for the UNDP/NHRC in Kathmandu, Nepal (2008).

Since 1993, he has been the Editor-in-Chief of the journal *Forensic Science International*, published by Elsevier, and an Editorial Board member of a number of other national and international scientific journals of forensic medicine and science.

He is a member of the German National Academy of Sciences Leopoldina and an honorary member of the Hungarian Forensic Science Society, the Royal Belgium Society of Forensic Medicine, the German Society of Legal Medicine, and the Japanese Society of Legal Medicine, and a founding and honorary fellow of the faculty of forensic and legal medicine, Royal College of Physicians (London).

SENIOR EDITOR: BIOGRAPHY

Max M. Houck is an internationally recognized forensic expert with research interests in anthropology, trace evidence, education, and the fundamentals of forensic science, both as a science and as an enterprise. He has worked in the private sector, the public sector (at the regional and federal levels), and in academia. Dr. Houck has published in a wide variety of areas in the field, in books, book chapters, and peer-reviewed journals. His casework includes the Branch Davidian Investigation, the September 11 attacks on the Pentagon, the D.B. Cooper case, the US Embassy bombings in Africa, and the West Memphis Three case. He served for 6 years as the Chair of the Forensic Science Educational Program Accreditation Commission (FEPAC). Dr. Houck is a founding coeditor of the journal *Forensic Science Policy and Management*, with Jay Siegel; he has also coauthored a major textbook with Siegel, *Fundamentals of Forensic Science*. Dr. Houck lives and works in the Washington, DC area.

SECTION EDITORS

Jay A Siegel
Professor Emeritus, Michigan State University and Adjunct Professor, Indiana University Purdue University, Indianapolis, USA

Pekka J Saukko
Professor and Chairman, Department of Forensic Medicine, University of Turku, Turku, Finland

Max M Houck
Department of Forensic Sciences, Consolidated Forensic Laboratory, Washington, D.C., USA

Cristina Cattaneo
Sezione di Medicina Legale e LABANOF – Laboratorio di Antropologia e Odontologia Forense, Dipartimento di Morfologia Umana e Scienze Biomediche, Università degli Studi di Milano

Bruce Arrigo
Department of Criminal Justice and Criminology, University of North Carolina at Charlotte, Charlotte, NC, USA

John M Butler
National Institutes of Standards and Technology, Biochemical Science Division, Gaithersburg, MD, USA

Angel Carracedo
Institute of Forensic Science, University of Santiago de Compostela, Spain

Claude Roux, Ph.D.
Professor of Forensic Science and Director, Centre for Forensic Science, University of Technology Sydney, Broadway, NSW, Australia

Niamh Nic Daeid
Professor of Forensic Science, Centre for Forensic Science, Department of Pure and Applied Chemistry, University of Strathclyde, Glasgow, Scotland, UK

Frank Crispino
Gendarmerie National Criminal Center, Fort de Rosny, Rosny sous Bois, France; Université du Québec à Trois-Rivières (UQTR), Département de Chimie-Biologie, Trois-Rivières, Québec, Canada

James Fraser
Centre for Forensic Science, Department of Pure and Applied Chemistry, University of Strathclyde, Glasgow, Scotland, UK

Barry AJ Fisher, M.S., M.B.A.
Retired Crime Laboratory Director, Los angeles County Sheriff's Department, Los Angeles, CA, USA

Jules Epstein
Widener University School of Law, Wilmington, DE, USA

James Robertson
Professorial Fellow and Director, National Centre for Forensic Studies, University of Canberra, Canberra, ACT, Australia

Simon W Lewis
Department of Chemistry, Curtin University, Perth, Western Australia, Australia

Glenn Langenburg
Minnesota Bureau of Criminal Apprehension, St. Paul, MN, USA

Robin T Bowen
MA, Morgantown, WV, USA

Olaf H Drummer
Head (Forensic Scientific Services), Victorian Institute of Forensic Medicine, Head of Department of Forensic Medicine, Monash University, Victoria, Australia

Stefan Pollak
Institute of Legal Medicine, University of Freiburg, Freiburg/Br., Germany

Michael Pollanen
Chief Forensic Pathologist, Ontario Forensic Pathology Service, Director, Centre for Forensic Science and Medicine, University of Toronto, Toronto, ON, Canada

Marcus Rogers
Professor, University Faculty Scholar, Department of Computer and Information Technology, Purdue University, West Lafayette, IN, USA

Bryan Found
Chief Forensic Scientist, Victoria Police Forensic Services Department, Macleod, VIC, Australia

Scott Batterman, Ph.D., P.E.
Batterman Engineering LLC, Cherry Hill, NJ, USA

CONTRIBUTORS

J Adamec
Institute of Legal Medicine, Munich, Germany

G Aitchison
Skills for Justice, Edinburgh, UK

C G G Aitken
The University of Edinburgh, Edinburgh, UK

R W Allen
Oklahoma State University, Tulsa, OK, USA

A Alonso
Instituto Nacional de Toxicología y Ciencias Forenses, Servicio de Biología, Madrid, Spain

V Alunni
Université de Nice Sophia Antipolis, Nice, France

A Amorim
University of Porto, Porto, Portugal

B A Arrigo
UNC Charlotte, Charlotte, NC, USA

E Baccard
International Criminal Court, The Hague, The Netherlands

E Baccino
Hopital Lapeyronie, Montpellier, France

T Bajanowski
University of Duisburg-Essen, Essen, Germany

J Ballantyne
University of Central Florida, Orlando, FL, USA

K N Ballantyne
Victoria Police Forensic Services Centre, Macleod, VIC, Australia

S C Batterman
Batterman Engineering, LLC, Cherry Hill, NJ, USA

S D Batterman
Batterman Engineering, LLC, Cherry Hill, NJ, USA

L (Brun-Conti) Bender
National Laboratory Center, Ammendale, MD, USA

H Y Bersot
UNC Charlotte, Charlotte, NC, USA

P Betz
University of Erlangen-Nuremberg, Erlangen, Germany

A D Beveridge
Burnaby, BC, Canada

J Beyer
Monash University, Southbank, VIC, Australia

A Biedermann
The University of Lausanne, Lausanne-Dorigny, Switzerland

R A C Bilo
Netherlands Forensic Institute, The Hague, The Netherlands

C L Bird
Forensic Science SA, Adelaide, SA, Australia

S Black
University of Dundee, Dundee, UK

W J Bodziak
Bodziak Forensics, Palm Coast, FL, USA

M Bohnert
University of Würzburg, Würzburg, Germany

M S Bonfanti
University of Lausanne, Lausanne-Dorigny, Switzerland

C Børsting
University of Copenhagen, Copenhagen, Denmark

J Brandi
National Institute of Forensic Science, ANZPAA, Melbourne, VIC, Australia

M Breadmore
University of Tasmania, Hobart, TAS, Australia

M Brión
Xenética de enfermidades cardiovasculares e oftalmolóxicas. Instituto de Investigación Sanitaria de Santiago-CHUS, Spain

H Buchannan
University of Strathclyde, Glasgow, UK

Z M Budimlija
Office of Chief Medical Examiner of the City of New York, New York, NY, USA

E Buel
State of Vermont Forensic Laboratory, Waterbury, VT, USA

R K Bullis
Forensics and communication consultant and adjunct, Averett University, Virginia, USA

S G Bunch
Forensic Firearms Consultants, LLC, Dumfries, VA, USA

E Burton
Greater Manchester Police Forensic Services Branch, Manchester, UK

F Busetti
Curtin University of Technology, Perth, WA, Australia

J M Butler
National Institute of Standards and Technology, Gaithersburg, MD, USA

R W Byard
Forensic Science SA, Adelaide, SA, Australia

J Cali, CPA, CFF, CGMA

T Caragine
Office of Chief Medical Examiner of the City of New York, New York, NY, USA

A Carracedo
University of Santiago de Compostela, Santiago de Compostela, Spain

M Carter
Las Vegas Metropolitan Police Department Forensic Laboratory, Las Vegas, NV, USA

C Cattaneo
Università degli Studi di Milano, Milano, Italy

C Champod
University of Lausanne, Lausanne, Switzerland

B-L Chang
Department of Health, Taipei, Taiwan

W-C Cheng
Government Laboratory, Hong Kong Special Administrative Region

W J Chisum
Elk Grove, CA, USA

D R Christian Jr.
Professional Business Solutions, Lake St Louis, MO, USA

J G Clement
The University of Melbourne, Melbourne, VIC, Australia

M D Coble
National Institute of Standards and Technology, Gaithersburg, MD, USA

S A Cole
University of California, Irvine, CA, USA

K A Collins
Emory University School of Medicine, Atlanta, GA, USA

S L Cooper
Birmingham City University School of Law, Birmingham, UK

K Corbin
US Secret Service, Washington, DC, USA

S Coulson
Institute of Environmental Science and Research Ltd (ESR), Auckland, New Zealand

J Coumbaros
ChemCentre, Bentley, WA, Australia

J B Crippin
Western Forensic Law Enforcement Training Center, Pueblo, CO, USA

F Crispino
Université du Québec à Trois-Rivières, Trois-Rivières, QC, Canada

P A Cross
University of Central Lancashire, Preston, UK

D J Crouch
Center for Human Toxicology, University of Utah, Department of Pharmacology and Toxicology, Salt Lake City, UT, USA

E Cunha
University of Coimbra, Coimbra, Portugal

J M Curran
University of Auckland, Auckland, New Zealand

K Currie
Office of Chief Medical Examiner of the City of New York, New York, NY, USA

F Daoust
Institut de recherche criminelle de la gendarmerie nationale, Paris, France

J de Koeijer
Netherlands Forensic Institute, The Hague, The Netherlands

R Decorte
University Hospitals Leuven, Leuven, Belgium; KU Leuven, Leuven, Belgium

V J Desiderio
United States Postal Inspection Service Forensic Laboratory Services, Dulles, VA, USA

S Doyle
Linked Forensic Consultants Ltd, Wellington, New Zealand

O H Drummer
Monash University, Southbank, VIC, Australia

G Edmond
The University of New South Wales, Sydney, NSW, Australia

W Eisenmenger

E Elaad
Ariel University Center of Samaria, Ariel, Israel

J Epstein
Widener University School of Law, Wilmington, DE, USA

L A Farwell
Brain Fingerprinting Laboratories, Seattle, WA, USA

A A Fatah
Office of Law Enforcement Standards, National Institute of Standards and Technology, Gaithersburg, MD, USA

P D Felgate
Forensic Science Centre, Adelaide, SA, Australia

T W Fenton
Michigan State University, East Lansing, MI, USA

K A Findley
University of Wisconsin Law School, Madison, WI, USA

D S Fisher
King's College Hospital NHS Foundation Trust, London, UK

R W Fitzpatrick
CSIRO Land and Water, Glen Osmond, SA, Australia

R J Flanagan
King's College Hospital NHS Foundation Trust, London, UK

D Franklin
The University of Western Australia, Crawley, WA, Australia

I Freckelton
Monash University, Melbourne, VIC, Australia

A A Frick
Curtin University, Perth, WA, Australia

P Fritz
Curtin University, Perth, WA, Australia

T Fritz
IRCGN, Rosny Sous Bois, France

S Fu
University of Technology Sydney, Broadway, NSW, Australia

P Gabriel
University Clinic Düsseldorf, Düsseldorf, Germany

C Gabrielle Salfati
John Jay College of Criminal Justice, New York, NY, USA

R J Garrett
Denver, NC, USA

Z Geradts
Netherlands Forensic Institute, Den Haag, The Netherlands

D Gerostamoulos
Monash University, Southbank, VIC, Australia

D Gibelli
Università degli Studi di Milano, Milano, Italy

J V Goodpaster
Indiana University Purdue University Indianapolis, Indianapolis, IN, USA

W H Goodwin
University of Central Lancashire, Preston, UK

T Grant
Aston University, Birmingham, UK

M Graw
Institute of Legal Medicine, Munich, Germany

C Grigoras
University of Colorado Denver, Denver, CO, USA

K Grimwood
University of Technology Sydney, Sydney, NSW, Australia

V L Grose
US National Transportation Safety Board, Washington, DC, USA

L Gueissaz
Université de Lausanne, Lausanne, Switzerland

R Guijt
University of Tasmania, Hobart, TAS, Australia

L Gusmão
IPATIMUP, Porto, Portugal

C Haas
University of Zürich, Zürich, Switzerland

S Hales
NSW Police Force, Pemulwuy, Australia

R W Halstead
IronWood Technologies, Inc., Syracuse, NY, USA

I Hamilton
Glasgow Fingerprint Unit, Forensic Services, Scottish Police Services Authority, Glasgow, UK

L Hammer
Hammer Forensics, Anchorage, AK, USA

D L Hammond
U.S. Army Criminal Investigation Laboratory, Forest Park, GA, USA

A J Hansen
University of Copenhagen, Copenhagen, Denmark

E Hanson
University of Central Florida, Orlando, FL, USA

B R Harris
Alliant International University, Fresno, CA, USA

K C Harris
US Secret Service, Washington, DC, USA

J Hebrard
Forensic and Criminal Intelligence Agency of the French Gendarmerie, Paris, France

S Heide
University of Halle-Wittenberg, Halle, Germany

B J Heidebrecht
Maryland State Police, Forensic Sciences Division, Pikesville, MD, USA

J M Hemmings
Australian Federal Police, Forensic and Data Centres, Canberra, ACT, Australia

C Henderson
Stetson University College of Law, Gulfport, FL, USA

E W Hickey
Alliant International University, Fresno, CA, USA

T Hicks
Institut de police scientifique and Formation continue UNIL-EPFL, Lausanne-Dorigny, Switzerland

M-C Hofner
University Center of Legal Medicine, Lausanne, Switzerland

S Hofstadler
Ibis Biosciences Inc., Carlsbad, CA, USA

H Hollien
University of Florida, Gainesville, FL, USA

C R Hollin
University of Leicester, Leicester, UK

J Horswell
Approved Forensics Sendirian Berhad, Selangor, Malaysia

M M Houck
Consolidated Forensic Laboratory, Washington, DC, USA

H-M Hsieh
Central Police University, Taoyuan, Taiwan ROC

M-C Huang
Department of Health, Taipei, Taiwan

W Huckenbeck
University Clinic Düsseldorf, Düsseldorf, Germany

J R Hunter
University of Birmingham, Birmingham, UK

C V Hurst
Michigan State University, East Lansing, MI, USA

L A Hutchins
United States Secret Service, Washington, DC, USA; US Government, Washington, DC, USA

K Inman
California State University, Hayward, CA, USA

T Ishikawa
Osaka City University Medical School, Osaka, Japan

R L Jantz
University of Tennessee, Knoxville, TN, USA

S H Johns
Peoria, IL, USA

D Johnson
Las Vegas Metropolitan Police Department, Las Vegas, NV, USA

G R Jones
Alberta Medical Examiners Office, Edmonton, AB, Canada

P Jones
Purdue University, West Lafayette, IN, USA

R Julian
University of Tasmania, Hobart, TAS, Australia

C Jurado
National Institute of Toxicology and Forensic Sciences, Sevilla, Spain

T Kanchan
Kasturba Medical College (affiliated to Manipal University), Mangalore, Karnataka, India

W A Karst
Netherlands Forensic Institute, The Hague, The Netherlands

D H Kaye
Penn State School of Law, University Park, PA, USA

M Kayser
Erasmus MC University Medical Center, Rotterdam, The Netherlands

S F Kelty
University of Tasmania, Hobart, TAS, Australia

R B Kennedy
Orleans, ON, Canada

T Kent
University of Lincoln, Lincoln, UK

G Kernbach-Wighton
University of Bonn, Bonn, Germany

G C Kessler
Embry-Riddle Aeronautical University, Daytona Beach, FL, USA

M Kettner
Saarland University Medical School, Homburg/Saar, Germany

J De Kinder
National Institute voor Criminalistiek en Criminologie, Brussels, Belgium

P Kintz
X-Pertise Consulting, Oberhausbergen, France

U Klopfstein
Bern University of Applied Sciences, Bern, Switzerland

K Krishan
Panjab University, Chandigarh, India

R Labonte
University of New Haven, West Haven, CT, USA

R F Lambourn
Transport Research Laboratory, Wokingham, UK

N E I Langlois
Forensic Science SA, Adelaide, SA, Australia

M Lareu
University of Santiago de Compostela, Santiago de Compostela, Spain

X Laroche
Special Tribunal for Lebanon, Leidschendam, The Netherlands

G Lau
Health Sciences Authority, Singapore, Republic of Singapore

J C-I Lee
Institute of Forensic Medicine, New Taipei, Taiwan ROC; National Taiwan University, Taipei, Taiwan ROC

S-A Legrand
Ghent University, Ghent, Belgium

C E Lenehan
Flinders University, Adelaide, SA, Australia

C Lennard
University of Canberra, Canberra, ACT, Australia

J J Lentini
Scientific Fire Analysis, LLC, Big Pine Key, FL, USA

K W Lenz Esq.
Saint Petersburg, FL, USA

G B Leong
Center for Forensic Services, Western State Hospital, Tacoma, WA, USA

B Levine
Office of the Chief Medical Examiner, Baltimore, MD, USA

S W Lewis
Curtin University, Perth, WA, Australia

C H Liao
Department of Health, Taipei, Taiwan

K F Lim
Deakin University, Burwood, VIC, Australia

J G Linville
University of Alabama at Birmingham, Birmingham, AL, USA

R H Liu
University of Alabama, Birmingham, AL, USA

T E Lockhart
Virginia Tech, Blacksburg, VA, USA

A Loll
Phoenix Police Crime Laboratory, Phoenix, AZ, USA

B Ludes
Institut de Médecine Légale, Strasbourg, France

A Maceo
Las Vegas Metropolitan Police Department Forensic Laboratory, Las Vegas, NV, USA

B Madea
University of Bonn, Bonn, Germany

H Maeda
Osaka City University Medical School, Osaka, Japan

P Margot
University of Lausanne, Lausanne, Switzerland

M K Marks
The University of Tennessee, Knoxville, TN, USA

J H C Martin
Institut de Police Scientifique et de Criminologie, Université de Lausanne, Lausanne, Switzerland

P Martin
CRAIC Technologies, San Dimas, CA, USA

S L Massey
Campbell River, BC, Canada

G Massonnet
Université de Lausanne, Lausanne, Switzerland

V M Maxwell
University of New Haven, West Haven, CT, USA

W D Mazzella
University of Lausanne, Lausanne, Switzerland; Forensic Document Examination Services Inc., Vancouver, BC, Canada

B R McCord
Florida International University, Miami, FL, USA

J McGinn
Department of Immigration and Citizenship, Perth, WA, Australia; Document Examination Solutions, Perth, WA, Australia

J R Meloy
University of California, San Diego, CA, USA

A Mendlein
Indiana University Purdue University Indianapolis, Indianapolis, IN, USA

A D Micheals
San Jose State University, San Francisco, CA, USA

P Millen
Paul Millen Associates, London, UK

H Miller Coyle
University of New Haven, West Haven, CT, USA

J J Miller
York Archaeological Trust for Excavation and Research Limited, York, UK

C M Milroy
University of Ottawa, Ottawa, ON, Canada

R P Mislan
RP Mislan, DeTour, MI, USA

L A Mohammed
Cherry Avenue, San Bruno, CA, USA

M Morelato
University of Technology Sydney, Broadway, NSW, Australia

N Morling
University of Copenhagen, Copenhagen, Denmark

R D Morrison
Hawi, HI, USA

C Muehlethaler
Université de Lausanne, Lausanne, Switzerland

B Muir
ChemCentre, Bentley, WA, Australia

S G Murray
Cranfield University, Royal Military College of Science, Shrivenham, UK

E Mützel
Institute of Legal Medicine, Munich, Germany

S H Neal
Morgantown, WV, USA

S Nekkache
IRCGN, Rosny Sous Bois, France

C-S Ng
Government Laboratory, Hong Kong Special Administrative Region

N NicDaéid
University of Strathclyde, Glasgow, UK

R G Nichols
Bureau of Alcohol, Tobacco, Firearms and Explosives, Walnut Creek, CA, USA

H G T Nijs
Netherlands Forensic Institute, The Hague, The Netherlands

C O'Connor
Office of Chief Medical Examiner of the City of New York, New York, NY, USA

S Olinder
Australian Federal Police, Canberra, ACT, Australia

C L O'Neal
Center for Human Toxicology, University of Utah, Department of Pharmacology and Toxicology, Salt Lake City, UT, USA

D L Ortiz-Bacon
US Army Criminal Investigation Laboratory – Expeditionary Forensic Division, Forest Park, GA, USA

V Otieno-Alego
Australian Federal Police Forensic and Data Centres, Canberra, ACT, Australia

T M Palmbach
University of New Haven, West Haven, CT, USA

R Palmer
Northumbria University, Newcastle Upon Tyne, UK

W Parson
Innsbruck Medical University, Innsbruck, Austria

J P Pascali
University of Verona, Verona, Italy

R S Pepler
Institut de Police Scientifique et de Criminologie, Université de Lausanne, Lausanne, Switzerland

D B Peraza
Exponent, Inc., New York, NY, USA

M Große Perdekamp
University of Freiburg, Freiburg, Germany

V Pereira
IPATIMUP, Porto, Portugal

R Perkins
Aston University, Birmingham, UK

D D Perlmutter
University of Pennsylvania, Philadelphia, PA, USA

O Peschel
Institut für Rechtsmedizin, München, Germany

C Phillips
University of Santiago de Compostela, Galicia, Spain

J Pinheiro
Instituto Nacional de Medicina Legal, Coimbra, Portugal

A Polettini
University of Verona, Verona, Italy

S Pollak
University of Freiburg, Freiburg, Germany; Universitätsklinikum Freiburg, Freiburg, Germany

F Poole
Forensic Services Group, New South Wales Police Force, Parramatta, NSW, Australia

N-L Poon
Government Laboratory, Hong Kong Special Administrative Region

D C Purdy
University of Lausanne, Lausanne, Switzerland; Forensic Document Examination Services Inc., Vancouver, BC, Canada

G Quatrehomme
Université de Nice Sophia Antipolis, Nice, France

E Quayle
University of Edinburgh, Edinburgh, UK

K Ramsey
Greater Manchester Police Forensic Services Branch, Manchester, UK

B W J Rankin
Teesside University, England, UK

R T Ratay
Columbia University, New York, NY, USA

L P Raymon
NOVA Southeastern College of Osteopathic Medicine, Fort Lauderdale, FL, USA

M A Raymond
NSW Police Force, Sydney, NSW, Australia

M Reznicek
Federal Bureau of Investigation – Latent Print Units, Quantico, VA, USA

O Ribaux
University of Lausanne, Lausanne, Switzerland

K Ritchie
Forensic Explosives Laboratory, DSTL Fort Halstead, Sevenoaks, UK

L Rivier
Laurent Rivier Scientific Consulting, Lausanne, Switzerland

J Robertson
University of Canberra, Canberra, ACT, Australia

L R Rockwell
Forensic and Intelligence Services, LLC, Alexandria, VA, USA

L Roewer
Charité – Universitätsmedizin Berlin, Berlin, Germany

P Roffey
Forensic and Data Centres, Australian Federal Police, Canberra, ACT, Australia

M K Rogers
Purdue University, West Lafayette, IN, USA

F S Romolo
SAPIENZA Università di Roma, Rome, Italy

W Rosenbluth
Reston, VA, USA

C Roux
University of Technology, Sydney, NSW, Australia

W F Rowe
The George Washington University, Washington, DC, USA

N Rudin
Forensic DNA Consultant, Mountain View, CA, USA

A Ruffell
Queen's University, Belfast, UK

R M Ruth
Federal Bureau of Investigation – Latent Print Units, Quantico, VA, USA

M J Saks
Sandra Day O'Connor College of Law, Tempe, AZ, USA

P Saukko
University of Turku, Turku, Finland

K A Savage
University of Strathclyde, Glasgow, UK

B Saw
Australian Federal Police, Canberra, ACT, Australia

D M Schilens
Federal Bureau of Investigation – Latent Print Units, Quantico, VA, USA

A Schmeling
Institute of Legal Medicine, Münster, Germany

P H Schmidt
Saarland University Medical School, Homburg/Saar, Germany

U Schmidt
Freiburg University Medical Center, Freiburg, Germany

W M Schneck
Spokane, WA, USA

P M Schneider
University of Cologne, Cologne, Germany

Y Schuliar
Forensic Sciences Institute of National Gendarmerie, Rosny-sous-Bois, France

K S Scott
Arcadia University, Glenside, PA, USA

N Scudder
Australian Federal Police, Canberra, ACT, Australia

A Shallan
University of Tasmania, Hobart, TAS, Australia

S A Shappell
Embry-Riddle Aeronautical University, Daytona Beach, FL, USA

T P Shefchick
Sunnyvale, CA, USA

R A Shellie
University of Tasmania, Hobart, TAS, Australia

Y Shor
Jerusalem, Israel

J A Siegel
Indiana University Purdue University Indianapolis, Indianapolis, IN, USA

J A Silva
VA Outpatient Clinic, San Jose, CA, USA

T Simmons
University of Central Lancashire, Preston, UK

G Skopp
University Hospital, Heidelberg, Germany

J M Smith
Missouri State Highway Patrol Crime Laboratory, Jefferson City, MO, USA

J M Smith
University of Colorado Denver, Denver, CO, USA

R Waddell Smith
Michigan State University, East Lansing, MI, USA

W S Smock
University of Louisville, Louisville, KY, USA

B Sobrino
Grupo de Medicina Xenomica-USC. Instituto de Investigación Sanitaria de Santiago, Spain

A Soler
Pima County Office of the Medical Examiner, Tucson, AZ, USA

N Speers
Australian Federal Police Forensic and Data Centres, Canberra, ACT, Australia

C Sperling
Arizona State University, Tempe, AZ, USA

M Stangegaard
University of Copenhagen, Copenhagen, Denmark

E Stauffer
Commissariat d'Identification Judiciaire, Police Cantonale Fribourg, Fribourg, Switzerland

H Steffan
Graz University of Technology, Graz, Austria

C N Stephan
Central Identification Laboratory, Hawaii, USA

M Steyn
University of Pretoria, Hatfield, South Africa

N Stojanovska
University of Technology Sydney, Broadway, NSW, Australia

A Stowell
Environmental Science and Research Limited, Porirua, New Zealand

B Stromback
Las Vegas Metropolitan Police Department Forensic Laboratory, Las Vegas, NV, USA

B Stuart
University of Technology Sydney, Broadway NSW, Australia

C Sturdy Colls
Forensic and Crime Science, Stoke-on-Trent, Staffordshire, UK

L Swann
University of Western Australia, Crawley, WA, Australia

C L Swanson
US Army Criminal Investigation Laboratory – Expeditionary Forensic Division, Forest Park, GA, USA

C Szkudlarek
Indiana University Purdue University Indianapolis, Indianapolis, IN, USA

F Tagliaro
University of Verona, Verona, Italy

T Tamiri
Division of Identification and Forensic Science (DIFS), Israel National Police, Jerusalem, Israel

F Taroni
The University of Lausanne, Lausanne-Dorigny, Switzerland

S C Thaman
Saint Louis University School of Law, St. Louis, MO, USA

A Thierauf
University of Freiburg, Freiburg, Germany

D S K Thurley
York Archaeological Trust for Excavation and Research Limited, York, UK

L Tierney
Gaithersburg, MD, USA

T Trubshoe
Department of Immigration and Citizenship, Perth, WA, Australia; Document Examination Solutions, Perth, WA, Australia

T Tsach
Jerusalem, Israel

L-C Tsai
Central Police University, Taoyuan, Taiwan ROC

S C Turfus
Victorian Institute of Forensic Medicine, Southbank, VIC, Australia

B E Turvey
Forensic Solutions, LLC, Sitka, AK, USA

D H Ubelaker
Smithsonian Institution, NMNH, Washington, DC, USA

R A H van Oorschot
Victoria Police Forensic Services Centre, Macleod, VIC, Australia

M Vennemann
University of Münster, Münster, Germany

A Verstraete
Ghent University, Ghent, Belgium

H Vogel
University Hospital Eppendorf, Hamburg, Germany

Ted Vosk
Criminal Defense Law Firm, Kirkland, WA, USA

S J Walsh
Australian Federal Police, Canberra, ACT, Australia

M Wang
Health Sciences Authority, Singapore, Republic of Singapore

J Was-Gubala
Institute of Forensic Research, Krakow, Poland

R Weinstock
University of California, Los Angeles, USA; and West Los Angeles Veterans Affairs Medical Center, Los Angeles, CA, USA

B S Weir
University of Washington, Seattle, WA, USA

J D Wells
Florida International University, Miami, FL, USA

C Welsh
Skills for Justice, Edinburgh, UK

R Wennig
Université du Luxembourg-Campus Limpertsberg, Avenue de la Faïencerie, Luxembourg

D J Wescott
Texas State University, San Marcos, TX, USA

R Wickenheiser
Montgomery County Police Crime Laboratory, Gaithersburg, MD, USA

D A Wiegmann
University of Wisconsin, Madison, WI, USA

S Wiesner
Jerusalem, Israel

J G Wigmore
Toronto, ON, Canada

S Wilkinson
ChemCentre, Bentley, WA, Australia

L Wilson-Wilde
National Institute of Forensic Science, ANZPAA, Melbourne, VIC, Australia

C Winskog
University of Adelaide, Adelaide, SA, Australia

Y Yekutieli
Jerusalem, Israel

S Zitrin
Division of Identification and Forensic Science (DIFS), Israel National Police, Jerusalem, Israel

GUIDE TO USE OF THE ENCYCLOPEDIA

Structure of the Encyclopedia

The material in the Encyclopedia is arranged as a series of entries in alphabetical order. Some entries comprise a single article, whilst entries on more diverse subjects consist of several articles that deal with various aspects of the topic. In the latter case the articles are arranged in a logical sequence within an entry.

There are three features to help you easily find the topic you are interested in: an alphabetical contents list, cross-references to other relevant articles within each article, and a full subject index.

1. Contents Lists

Your first point of reference will probably be the contents list. The complete contents list appearing in each volume will provide you with both the volume number and the page number of the entry. On the opening page of an entry a contents list is provided so that the full details of the articles within the entry are immediately available.

Alternatively you may choose to browse through a volume using the alphabetical order of the entries as your guide.

To assist you in identifying your location within the Encyclopedia a running headline indicates the current entry and the current article within that entry.

2. Cross-References

All of the articles in the Encyclopedia have been extensively cross referenced. The cross references, which appear at the end of an article, have been provided at three levels:

1. To indicate if a topic is discussed in greater detail elsewhere.
2. To draw the reader's attention to parallel discussions in other articles.
3. To indicate material that broadens the discussion.

Example

The following list of cross references appear at the end of the entry entitled **Foundations** | Principles of Forensic Science:

See also: **Foundations:** Forensic Intelligence; History of Forensic Sciences; Overview and Meaning of Identification/Individualization; Semiotics, Heuristics, and Inferences Used by Forensic Scientists; Statistical Interpretation of Evidence: Bayesian Analysis; The Frequentist Approach to Forensic Evidence Interpretation; **Foundations/Fundamentals:** Measurement Uncertainty; **Pattern Evidence/Fingerprints (Dactyloscopy):** Friction Ridge Print Examination – Interpretation and the Comparative Method.

3. Index

The index will provide you with the volume number and page number of where the material is to be located, and the index entries differentiate between material that is a whole article, is part of an article, or is data presented in a table or figure. Detailed notes are provided on the opening page of the index.

4. Contributors

A full list of contributors appears at the beginning of each volume.

PREFACE TO THE SECOND EDITION

In 2000, Academic Press, an imprint of Elsevier, published the first major multivolume work on forensic science that covered the many disparate disciplines that make up this field in a manner that ensured both depth and breadth. This encyclopedia enjoyed worldwide acceptance and acclaim and garnered the prestigious honorable mention award for reference works from Dartmouth University. Only one of these is given each year.

Why then did the publisher and editors decide that it was time for a second edition? Forensic science has made incredible leaps in technology, popularity, and notoriety in the ensuing years. The National Academy of Sciences weighed in with its controversial and far reaching report on the present state and future of forensic science. The world of forensic science has shrunk even further – it touches people virtually all over the world. There have been numerous books published on various aspects of forensic science, some more comprehensive than others, but the need still remains for a work that covers the whole depth and breadth of this multifaceted group of scientific endeavors. The editors have brought the encyclopedia up to date with the latest developments in virtually all areas of forensic science, with information that is easy to locate and read. This new multivolume set contains more than 300 articles, written by more than 300 lead authors and many coauthors. They hail from 20 countries in nearly every continent in the world. The field was divided into 20 sections, each with a section editor. They made up our Editorial Board. Our heartfelt thanks go out to all of them. They did a terrific job of commissioning and editing the articles.

Special thanks are due to Max Houck, who chaired the Editorial Board. Max not only provided the second level of editing but was also the 'traffic cop' that kept everyone on task and handled the difficult situations with aplomb. Special thanks also go to Kate Mittell of the Elsevier Major Works staff. Kate has been a marvelous 'chaser.' She kept everyone at it and made the trains run on time. Without the efforts of Max and Kate, this encyclopedia could not have happened.

Jay A Siegel
Pekka J Saukko

INTRODUCTION

A scant two decades ago there was no *Encyclopedia of Forensic Sciences*, there were hardly any textbooks that covered the field, even at an introductory level, and there were almost no books that covered specific areas of forensic science in any depth. There was no CSI on television and hardly any other TV shows or movies that brought publicity and knowledge to the general public about the forensic sciences. In those days, many people, in and outside of science, would describe forensic science as a collection of techniques and methods that were begged, borrowed, and stolen from 'legitimate' science.

One could argue that the landmark Supreme Court case, *Daubert v. Merrill Dow*, changed the whole landscape. The Court said that in order for scientific (and later, other technical information) techniques, methods, and analyses to be admitted into court, they had to be proven to be scientifically valid. This case caused an explosion of research manuscripts and books on the scientific aspects of forensic science to be published for high school and college students, attorneys and judges, and forensic and other scientists. With all of these in hand, there was still no comprehensive source of scholarly material that spanned the breadth and depth, or which could explain the practice and the philosophy of this emerging science, which could be easily located and readable for a wide variety of audiences. Then came the *Encyclopedia of Forensic Sciences*, published by Academic Press, an imprint of Elsevier Sciences. The Encyclopedia was embraced by scientists, scholars, and students, and was the benchmark for timely information about virtually any forensic science.

Now, a decade later, comes the 2nd edition of the Encyclopedia. It has been updated, revised, and expanded with 50% more articles covering even more areas of forensic science, while retaining easy location of articles, each written in an accessible and readable style. Other improvements have also been made. Instead of having separate sections for photographs and illustrations, they are integrated into the articles. The Encyclopedia is now modern and mobile, available online as well as in traditional hardback. The online edition will make it easier for the editors to keep the Encyclopedia current and relevant with timely coverage of emerging areas of forensic science.

The 2nd edition of *Encyclopedia of Forensic Sciences* was written to be an indispensable resource for scientists, students, attorneys, judges, and the public. It is hoped that one will find it to be a valuable resource for their interests in this fascinating field of science.

CONTENTS

VOLUME 4

C

CHEMISTRY/TRACE

Stomach Contents Analysis

WM Schneck, Spokane, WA, USA

Glossary

Alternate light source (ALS) An instrument that delivers a high intensity light of an adjustable wavelength.

Cotyledons Botanically, a food storage organ in seeds. The embryos of flowering plants usually have either one cotyledon or two. Seeds of gymnosperms, such as pines, may have numerous cotyledons. In some seeds, the cotyledons are flat and leaf like; in others, such as the bean, the cotyledons store the seed's food reserve for germination.

Dichotomous plant cell key A dichotomous key is a method for determining the identity of something (e.g., the name of a plant cell) by going through a series of choices that lead the user to the correct name of the item. Dichotomous means 'divided in two parts.'

Entomology (ical) The scientific study of insects.

Formaldehyde An organic compound with the formula CH_2O with a characteristic pungent odor. An aqueous solution of formaldehyde can be used as a disinfectant and preservative as it kills most bacteria and fungi including spores.

Histology The study of the microscopic anatomy of cells and tissues of plants and animals. It is performed by examining a thin section of tissue using a light microscope or electron microscope. Histological stains are often used to visualize and identify microscopic structures.

Masticate Chewing, crushing, and grinding of food in the mouth prior to swallowing.

Neolithic Period A period in the development of human technology, beginning about 9500 B.C.E.

Polarized light microscope A specialized type of light microscope employing a set of polarizing filters typically set below and above a round specimen stage. When an object is viewed in polarized light, observable optical properties inherent within the object are used in characterization and identification.

Titanium dioxide A white inorganic material, TiO_2, that occurs naturally as the mineral anatase and rutile and is used extensively in industrial applications and sometimes as a food colorant.

The process of digestion begins in the mouth where enzymes in saliva begin to break down starch products as food is chewed. Food is then swallowed and travels to the stomach, where the physical action of peristalsis churns and kneads the food into a semisolid amorphous mass called chyme. Gastric juices secreted from the walls of the stomach add hydrochloric acid, mucus, and the gastric enzymes pepsin and rennin. These enzymes start the break down of proteins into amino acids. Food normally resides in the stomach for up to 6 h; although when an individual becomes ill or is violently attacked; physiologic reactions may occur which discharge food from the stomach and out through the mouth.

One of the earliest recorded scientific experiments involving gastric contents and digestive processes occurred in 1822. William Beaumont, M.D., a surgeon stationed at Fort Mackinac, performed the first experiments on gastric digestion on an unfortunate individual by the name of Alexis St. Martin, a Canadian voyageur. An accidental discharge from a shotgun lacerated St. Martin's diaphragm and perforated his stomach, reportedly with stomach contents oozing into the wound site. Dr. Beaumont dressed his wounds and after 3 years of convalescence began conducting digestion experiments on St. Martin's still open stomach wound. Beaumont inserted different foods directly into St. Martin's stomach in cloth sacks with an attached string and recorded the time taken for the food to digest in his stomach. In 1833, Beaumont published, *Experiments and Observations on the Gastric Juice and the Physiology of Digestion*, a book based on his experiments on St. Martin. His observations laid the groundwork for future study on the human stomach and the digestive process.

 http://dx.doi.org/10.1016/B978-0-12-382165-2.00322-6

Procedures for the Examination of Gastric Contents and Vomit Stains

The stereomicroscope, polarizing light microscope (PLM), and the scanning electron microscope (SEM) are the instruments used to characterize and identify food traces. The identification of vomit stains is based on the characterization of partially digested and masticated food ingredients and the presumptive presence of gastric enzymes. Samples submitted to the forensic laboratory may include stomach contents from postmortem examinations, dried stains collected at crime scenes, or stains found on materials such as clothing. The presence of drips, projected patterns, and transfer stains are important to document in sketches and photographs (**Figures 1** and **2**). Large vomit stains are recognized by all the too familiar gross appearance and attendant unpleasant odor. When stain size is small, further microscopical and enzymatic tests are conducted to identify the stain as vomit. Dried stains can be collected by scraping and particle picking with forceps to a small paper envelope. In the laboratory, suspected vomit stains can be examined visually and documented as part of a routine clothing or materials examination. An alternate light source or a hand-held long-wave/short-wave ultraviolet (UV) lamp can be used to search for stains. Many vomit stains glow, allowing rapid detection using the UV lamp (**Figure 3**). This type of illumination may have deleterious effects on nucleated cells useful in deoxyribonucleic acid (DNA) analysis as well as the DNA itself; therefore, consultation with DNA scientists is required prior to its use. When a stain has been located, a stereo binocular microscope is used to magnify the area up to approximately 100 times. Individual particles within the stain can be particle picked to a microscope slide for further analysis by PLM. A portion of the stain can be removed and tested for the presence of gastric enzymes common in gastric fluids.

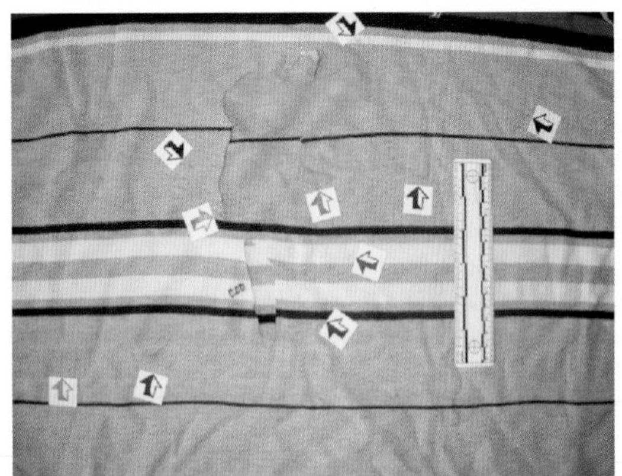

Figure 1 Gastric content stains on a shirt. Arrows point to stains. Note the scale in the photograph to document the size of stains.

Figure 2 Food particles embedded on the outsole of a restaurant worker's shoe.

Microscopic Examinations

When autopsy specimens of gastric contents are received, a small amount of formaldehyde may be added as a disinfectant and preservative. If the vomit or gastric contents are received in the liquid state, a representative portion can be wet sieved through a variety of fine, progressively smaller screens, catching food particles of known size ranges on the various screens. The screened particles can be identified directly on the screen or applied to a microscope slide by gently smearing a small quantity across the slide with a drop of distilled water. If a dry vomit stain is received, a portion of the stain can be gently particle picked to a microscope slide and resuspended in distilled water or a variety of other mounting media such as Norland Optical Adhesives, Cytoseal™, Cargille refractive index liquids, or Permount®. Stains can be used to improve contrast and aid in the identification of food products. Some of the more common stains used in the examination of food products include toluidine blue, aqueous iodine solutions, safranin, trypan blue, and Oil Red 'O' (**Figures** 4(a)–4(d)).

The microscopist should have available dichotomous plant cell keys, commercially prepared microscope slide sets, and prepared food standards (e.g., starches and spices) prior to undertaking the identification of food particles. Vomit may contain food particles from meat, grains, vegetables, dairy products, fruits, nuts, candy, and fats. Large fragments of food, such as seeds, pieces of meat, and leafy vegetables, often can be identified visually and with a stereo binocular microscope. The stereo binocular microscope can also be used to examine vomit stains in situ, showing the relationship of food particles as they were applied to the substrate.

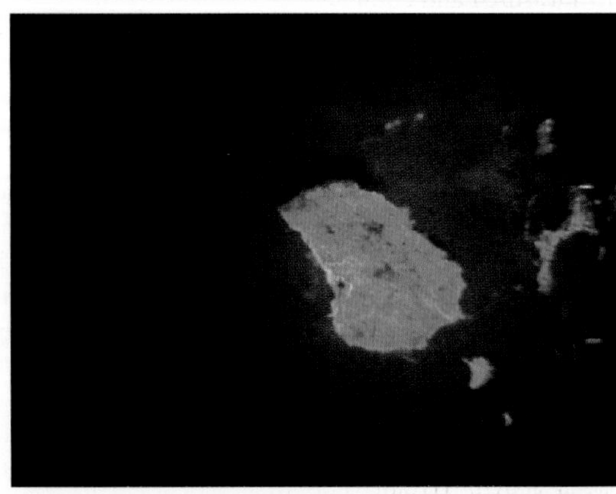

Figure 3 Ultraviolet fluorescence of a vomit stain on a shoe.

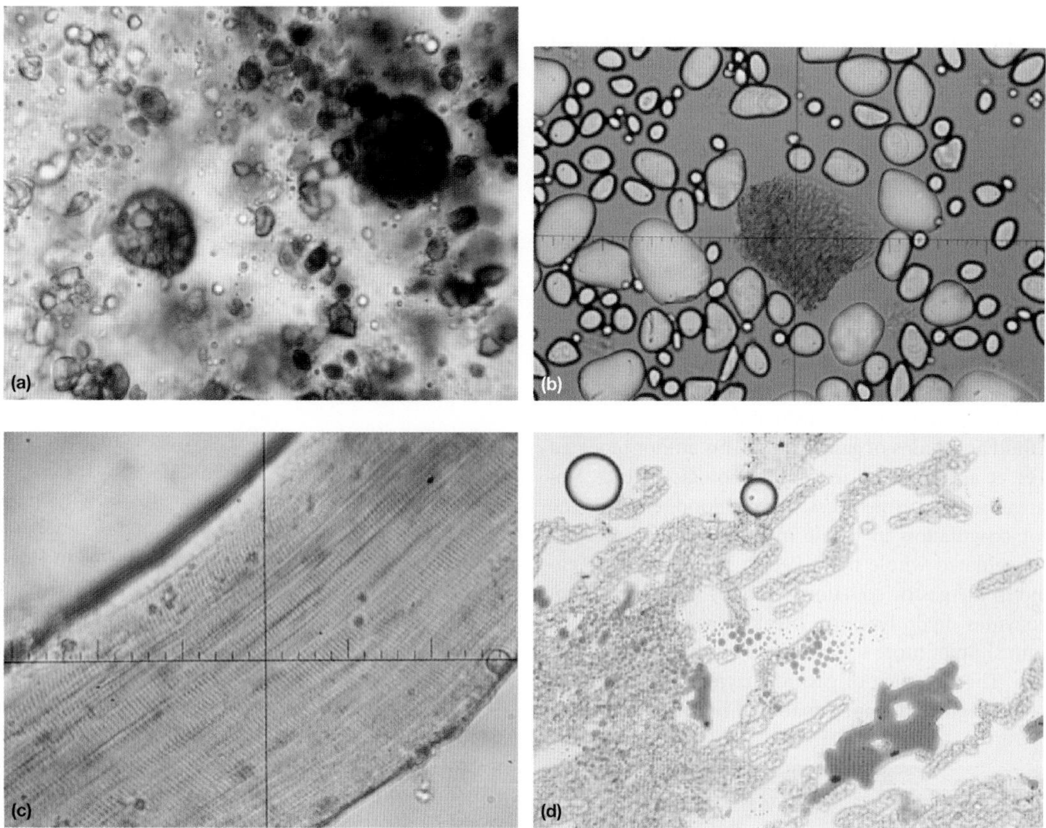

Figure 4 (a) Oat starch stained using an aqueous iodine solution. Unprocessed starch will stain various shades of purple. Image taken using plane polarized light microscopy. (b) Processed starch is stained blue using Trypan Blue, whereas the unprocessed potato starch is unaffected by the stain. Image taken using plane-polarized light microscopy. (c) Skeletal muscle stained blue–green using toluidine blue. The cell nuclei are stained blue. Image taken using plane-polarized light microscopy. (d) Lipids are stained red using Oil Red O. Image taken using plane-polarized light microscopy.

Smaller food particles may contain particles such as starch grains that require closer scrutiny using polarized light microscopy (PLM). Starch is a carbohydrate storage product and is common in many foods. Starch occurs as insoluble granules stored primarily in the roots, tubers, and seeds of plants but may also occur in the leaves and stems. Important commercial sources of starch are derived from the cereals (corn, wheat, and rice) and the root tubers (potato and cassava-tapioca). The starch granule develops stratified layers that is formed around a nucleus, called the hilum. The size of starch grains can be readily measured and compared to known standards of starch using the PLM. The shape of starch grains can vary from near perfect spheres to polygons, flattened spheroids, elongated disks, and many others. In crossed-polarized light, unprocessed starch grains have a characteristic 'Maltese cross' extinction pattern, with the hilum often near the center of the cross (**Figure 5**). The size and shape of each starch grain is characteristic of the plant from which it is derived.

At elevated temperatures in the presence of water, starch undergoes a process called gelatinization. This process can be observed microscopically beginning with granule swelling and progressing at higher temperature to the loss of the Maltese cross-birefringence pattern observed in polarized light. The stain trypan blue is recommended for the examination of processed starch. Trypan blue will only stain damaged or cooked grains, leaving the intact uncooked grains clear.

Figure 5 Using crossed-polarized light microscopy, intact starch grains show a black a 'maltese cross' pattern. This image is potato starch.

The informative textbooks *Food Microscopy*, *Identifying Plant Food Cells in Gastric Contents for Use in Forensic Investigations: A Laboratory Manual*, *The Particle Atlas*, and *The Atlas of Microscopy of Medicinal Plants Culinary Herbs and Spices* are excellent references when characterizing food particles. SEM is also useful in the characterization of minute structural features such as cell walls (**Figure 6**). Many older textbooks in the field of analytical vegetable histology are recommended for anyone interested in studying food products. These textbooks include *The Structure and Composition of Foods*, *The Microscopy of Vegetable Foods*, and *The Microscopical Examination of Foods and Drugs*.

Gastric Enzyme Screening Test

The literature contains only a few references concerning the identification of gastric fluid and in particular vomit stains. Simon describes a test for the presence of gastric enzymes. If a specific quantity of gastric juice coagulates in the presence of milk, the enzymes chymosin (also known as rennin) and chymosinogen are present. Lee et al. modified these clinical assay procedures to test for the pepsin and rennin-like activity on gastric fluid and stains of gastric fluid. This author repeated some of Lee et al.'s work by testing physiological fluids (including saliva, semen, urine, feces, whole blood, etc.) for the presence of coagulation in whole milk. None of the tested materials coagulated whole milk. Pepsin is a proteolytic enzyme found in the gastric secretions of many vertebrates. Proteolytic enzymes hydrolyze, or break down, proteins or peptides into simpler more soluble products during the digestion process. The presence of gastric enzymes in a stain indicates that it originated from a mammal but not necessarily a human. A quick screening test for the presence of gastric fluid can be used to identify stains that are suspected to be vomit. Known vomit samples as small as 0.75 mm in diameter have tested positive using this procedure. A small portion of the suspected stain is removed to a black porcelain spot plate along with a dried recently obtained vomit control. Several drops of whole cow's milk are pipetted into each well. The spot plate is placed in a humidity chamber at 38 °C for approximately 30 min. The spot plate wells are then examined with a stereo binocular microscope. The occurrence of coagulation or curdling indicates gastric enzymes are present in the sample (**Figure** 7(a) and 7(b)). The known vomit sample should also exhibit the same reaction. The reactions on the spot plate should then be documented.

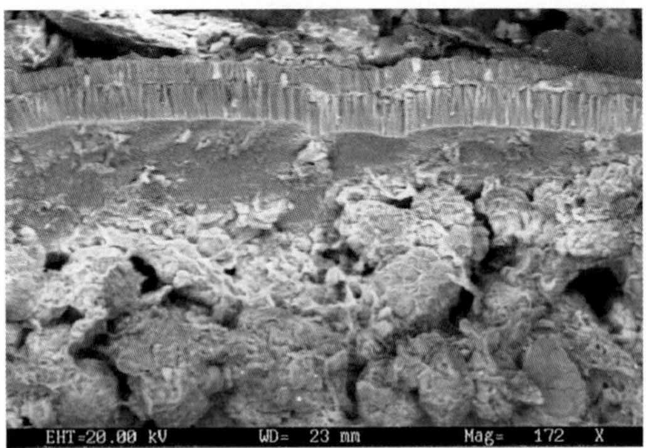

Figure 6 Cell wall structure of a Pinto bean is shown by using a scanning electron microscopy.

Case Studies

Case 1: The frozen well-preserved remains of an elderly gentleman were recovered in a wheat field. A suspect vehicle was searched, and a date and time stamped restaurant receipt was found. The receipt did not identify what menu items were selected, but it did have the total dollar amount purchased. Due to the absence of entomological evidence, the time of death could not be determined. The investigators requested the examination of gastric contents to determine if the stomach contents would reveal food from the victim's last meal and if it could be the food from the restaurant on the receipt. If so, an approximate time of death could be determined.

The stomach contents consisted of approximately one-fourth of a cup of viscous semiliquid material with a light brown solid component. Approximately 60 ml of formaldehyde solution was added to the mass as a preservative. A representative portion of the gastric contents was stirred and sieved through 12 mesh (1.7 mm), 20 mesh (850 μm), and 40 mesh (425 μm) screens to separate particles into varying sizes for examination. The particles were rinsed with alcohol and placed into a Petri dish for stereomicroscopic examination (**Figure** 8). Selected particles were transferred to microscope slides for examination and identification via light microscopy

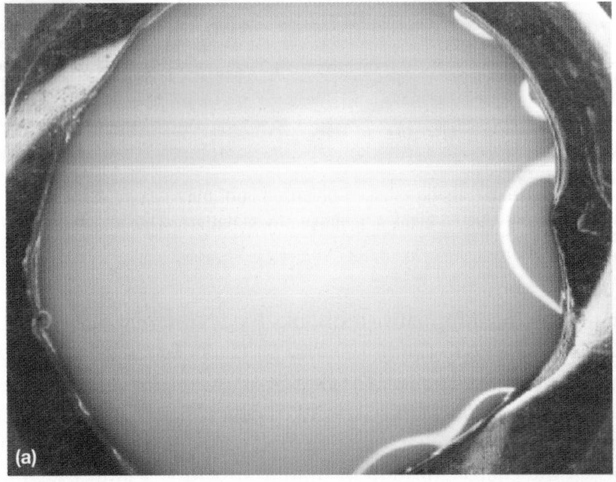

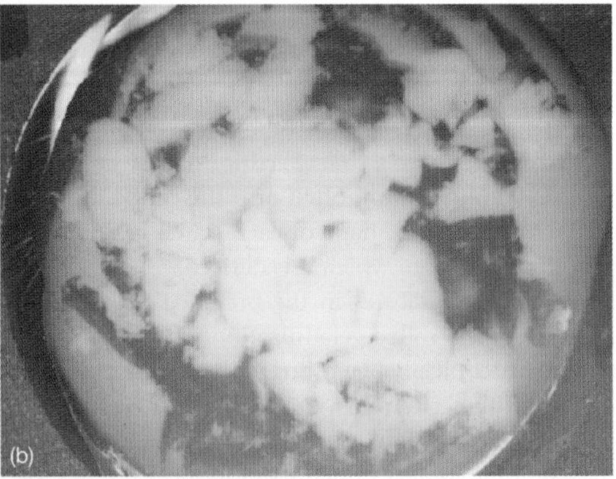

Figure 7 (a) Spot plate well with whole cow's milk and a known dried vomit control sample prior to incubation. (b) Spot plate as seen in **Figure** 7(a) after 30 min incubation showing curdling, a positive test for the presence of gastric enzymes.

with magnification up to 400 times. Additional particles were selected and characterized using SEM.

The author visited the restaurant and narrowed down the menu choices from the receipt and purchased a crisp taco shell with refried brown pinto beans, lettuce, chopped red tomatoes, and yellow shredded cheese and 'Mexi-fries'. Samples of soft and hard taco shell, crisp burrito shell, and four varieties of salsa condiments were sampled. Packets of 'hot' and 'original' sauce were also collected. A portion of the refried bean component was chewed and discharged into a separate Petri dish for comparison to the gastric contents. In addition, one yellow bell pepper was purchased to microscopically compare the distinctive yellow food particles found in both the gastric contents and the 'hot' and 'original' sauce packets for similarities.

Figure 8 Screened gastric stomach contents.

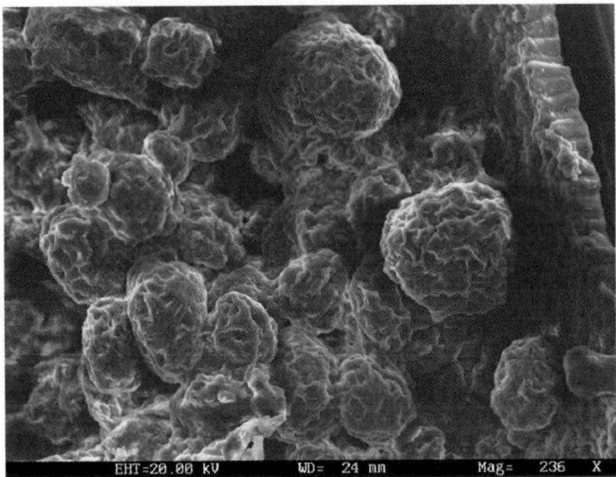

Figure 9 Pinto bean cotyledons imaged using a scanning electron microscope.

Identifiable food particles in the gastric contents consisted primarily of light brown Pinto beans showing outer shell/seed coat with a double-walled (~50 μm) columnar structure. Internal bean cotyledons containing starch were white in color and prune-like in structure (**Figure 9**). The outer skin of yellow bell pepper, light reddish-brown red pepper particles, pepper seeds, corn starch, and wheat starch were identified in the gastric contents. Other menu choices at the restaurant contained skeletal muscle/meat, red tomato, green spices, and yellow cheese. These items were not seen in the gastric contents.

Food products purchased at the suspected chain restaurant contained refried pinto beans in many of their meals. Yellow bell pepper particles, pepper seeds, and possible red pepper were found in the 'original' and 'hot' sauce packets. Wheat and corn starch flour were used in their soft taco shells. Menu items that can be purchased with primarily refried Pinto beans were half a pound soft taco (beans only), an original crisp (bean) burrito, and a soft (bean) burrito. The food ingredients found in the victim's stomach probably originated from a nonmeat, bean taco or burrito, with an added condiment such as 'original' or 'hot' sauce. The food was found to be consistent with a Mexican-style meal and could have been the one purchased at the date and time stamped on the receipt, thus indicating the approximate time of his demise within 1 day.

Case 2: During dinner and drinks at an upscale restaurant, a patron broke an arm in several locations as she reportedly slipped and fell in the restroom. This action initiated a civil lawsuit against the establishment. Opposing experts found a small oil stain on the back of her pants; unfortunately they missed the vomit stains on her shoes, pants, and blouse (**Figure 10(a)** and **10(b)**). The food particles in the stains matched the food ingredients that comprised the dinner she was eating. Further investigations revealed that she historically

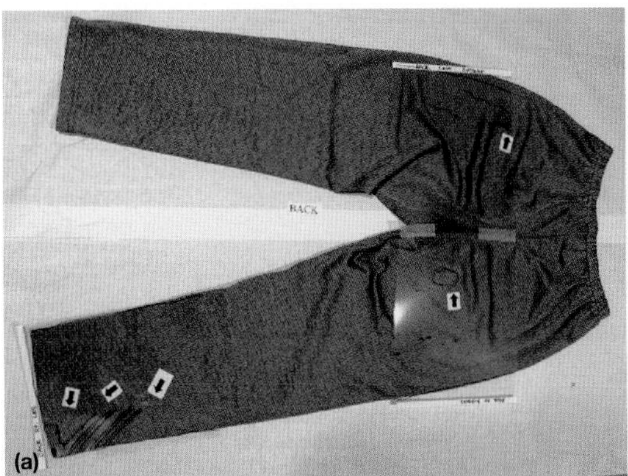

Figure 10 (a) The back of a pair of ladies slacks showing clear film overlays with stain locations labeled on them. (b) Food particles trapped within the fabric of the slacks are imaged using a stereomicroscope.

had an adverse reaction to alcohol – projectile vomiting. She likely slipped on her own vomit and fell in the restroom. The plaintiff dropped the case when confronted with the evidence.

Case 3: A parent left his infant unattended in a car seat for 20 min. On arrival, the infant was lifeless and unresponsive. The autopsy was inconclusive and cause of death determined as unknown. The infants and the father's clothing were examined for physical evidence. Several minute red stains were observed on the infant and the fathers clothing, which were not blood. The stains were similar to each other containing sucrose, titanium dioxide, red pigment, and a positive gastric enzyme test. Further investigations recovered a red candy ball under the front driver's seat, which exhibited similar color and ingredients as the stains on the clothing of the infant and father and car seat straps. The infant likely choked on the candy and obstructed his airway. During the resuscitation attempt and subsequent removal from the car seat by his father, the candy may have been expelled from his trachea.

Case 4: The Ice Man (also known as Otzi), a 5200-years-old well-preserved mummy was discovered in 1991 in the Tyrolean Alps at the Austrian/Italian border. Microscopic examination of the Iceman's last meal was reconstructed from a tiny piece of transverse colon dissected from the mummy. Particles of semi-digested einkorn, an important agricultural wheat of the Neolithic Period, were discovered by particle analysis. It was determined that the einkorn was ground to a fine meal and was probably eaten like a cracker. Electron microscopy revealed charcoal attached to the einkorn bran. The presence of charcoal was thought to represent remnants of a baking process.

See also: **Methods:** Analytical Light Microscopy; Microscopy (Electron).

Further Reading

Bechtel DB (ed.) (1983) Varriano–Marston E, Polarization microscopy: Applications in cereal science, ch. 3, pp. 71–108; Hood LF and Liboff M, Starch ultrastructure, ch. 11, pp. 341–370. In: *New Frontiers in Food Microstructure*. St. Paul, MN: American Association of Cereal Chemists.

Bisbing RE and Schneck WM (2006) Particle analysis in forensic science. *Forensic Science Review* 24(2): 119–143.

Bock JH, Lane MA, and Norris DO (1988) *Identifying Plant Food Cells in Gastric Contents for the Use In Forensic Investigations: A Laboratory Manual*. Washington, DC: U.S. Department of Justice, National Institute of Justice.

Dickson JH, Oeggl K, Holden TG, Handley LL, O'Connell TC, and Preston T (2000) The omnivorous Tyrolean iceman: Colon contents (meat, cereals, pollen, moss, whipworm) and stable isotope analysis. *Philosophical Transactions of the Royal Society of London* 355: 1843–1849.

Edwards M (ed.) (2004) *Detecting Foreign Bodies in Food*. Boca Raton, FL: CRC Press LLC.

Essery RE (1922) The value of fish scales as a means of identification of the fish used in manufactured products. *The Analyst* 47: 163–165.

Fast RB and Caldwell EF (eds.) (2000) *Breakfast Cereals and How They Are Made*, 2nd edn. St Paul, MN: American Association of Cereal Chemists.

Flint O (1984) Applications of light microscopy in food analysis. *The Microscope* 32: 133–140.

Flint O (1994) *Food microscopy: A manual of practical methods, using optical microscopy. Microscopy Handbooks 30*. Oxford, UK: Bios Scientific Publishers.

Gantner GE, Dwyer JD, and Lynch E (1976) *Identification of Food Materials in Gastric Contents (Emphasizing Microscopic Morphology)*. Forensic Science Foundation.

Greenish HG (1923) *The Microscopical Examination of Foods and Drugs*. Philadelphia, PA: Blakiston's Son and Co.

Hanausek TF (1907) *The Microscopy of Technical Products*. New York: Wiley.

Jackson BP and Snowdon DW (1990) *Atlas of Microscopy of Medicinal Plants, Culinary Herbs and Spices*. Boca Raton, FL: CRC Press.

Lee HC, Gaensslen RE, Galvin C, and Pagliaro EM (1985) Enzyme assays for the identification of gastric fluid. *Journal of Forensic Sciences* 30: 97–102.

Makowski J, Vary N, McCutcheon M, and Veys P (eds.) (2010) *Microscopic Analysis of Agricultural Products*. Urbana, USA: AOCS Press.

McCrone WC and Delly JG (1973) *The Particle Atlas*, vol. II. Ann Arbor, MI: Ann Arbor Publishers.

McCrone WC, Delly JG, and Palenik SJ (1979) *The Particle Atlas*, vol. V. Ann Arbor, MI: Ann Arbor Publishers.

Platek SF, Crowe JB, Ranieri N, and Wolnik KA (2001) Scanning electron microscopy determination of string mozzarella cheese in gastric contents. *Journal of Forensic Sciences* 46: 131.

Radley JA (1976) *Examination and Analysis of Starch and Starch Products*. England: Applied Science Publishers LTD.

Schneck WM (2004) Cereal murder in spoken. In: Houck M (ed.) *Trace Evidence Analysis, More Cases in Mute Witnesses*, pp. 165–190. Burlington, MA: Elsevier Academic Press Chapter 6.

Schoch TJ and Maywald EC (1956) Microscopic examination of modified starches. *Analytical Chemistry* 28: 382–387.

Simon Charles E (1897) *A Manual of Clinical Diagnosis by Means of Microscopic and Chemical Methods, for Students, Hospital Physicians, and Practitioners*, pp. 141–146. Philadelphia: Lea Brothers and Co..

Vaughan JG (ed.) (1979) *Food Microscopy*. London: Academic Press.

Whistler RL, Bemiller JN, and Paschall EF (eds.) (1984) *Starch: Chemistry and Technology*, 2nd edn. Orlando, FL: Academic Press.

Winton AL, Moeller J, and Winton KB (1916) *The Microscopy of Vegetable Foods*. New York, NY: Wiley.

Winton AL and Winton KB (1932) *The Structure and Composition of Foods*, vol. 1. New York, NY: Wiley.

Yahl KR (1984) Starch pasting for industrial applications and some problems. *The Microscope* 32: 123–140.

Yahl KR (1992) Utilization of a polarization color technique for the identification of starch composition. *The Microscope* 40: 247–250.

CHEMISTRY/TRACE/ADHESIVE TAPES

Adhesive Tapes

JM Smith, Missouri State Highway Patrol Crime Laboratory, Jefferson City, MO, USA

Glossary

Adhesive A material that will hold two or more objects together solely by intimate surface contact.

Backing A thin, flexible material to which adhesive is applied.

Biaxially oriented polypropylene (BOPP) Same as MOPP below except that BOPP films are stretched in two directions.

Elastomer A material that can be deformed but will return to its original form when the forces are removed. Serves as the base material for pressure-sensitive adhesives.

Fill yarns Fibers in the scrim fabric of reinforced tape that run crosswise, perpendicular to the warp direction. Also called *weft yarns*.

Monoaxially oriented polypropylene (MOPP) A polymer film manufactured in a controlled melting, cooling, and stretching cycle that results in an alignment (orientation) of the polymer chains along the direction of the stretch. This imparts strength to the films. MOPP films are stretched in only one direction.

Plasticizer Material added to plastics to impart flexibility by creating spaces between the polymer chains and lowering the inter- and intrachain attractive forces, allowing freer movement of the chains. It is used in pressure-sensitive backings (particularly polyvinylchloride (PVC)), as well as in some adhesives to lower glass transition temperatures, and allows use at subambient temperatures.

Reinforcement Cloth, scrim, glass filaments, or plastic filaments added to tape for stability and strength.

Scrim A loosely woven, gauze-type cloth added to duct tape for reinforcement and strength.

Warp yarns Fibers in the scrim fabric of reinforced tape that run lengthwise, in the machine direction.

Tape products are often used in the commission of crimes, and therefore they are frequently collected by law enforcement officials as part of their investigations. Tapes may be used as ligatures, restraints, or blindfolds; they may also be used in the construction of improvised explosive devices and in illegal drug packaging (**Figure 1**). Tape evidence is therefore often submitted to crime laboratories for analysis. This involves the comparison of a questioned piece of tape to a known source either to determine whether a physical match showing an individualizing relationship can be found or to determine whether a class relationship exists. Where there is no known source for comparison, the crime lab may be asked to source the tape to the probable manufacturer or distributor of the questioned tape. Aside from analysis of the tape itself, the forensic examiner should always be alert to other exams that could be necessitated by the tape evidence such as DNA, latent prints, hairs, fibers, and other trace evidence that may be adhering to the tape.

The examination of tape products in the forensic laboratory involves an extensive analysis of the physical construction and the chemical components.

The more variable a commercial product, the more valuable it is as evidence. Studies have shown that tape products are highly variable between manufacturers and even within a given manufacturer. In general, the more complex a tape product, the more variable it is. For example, duct tape is more complex and variable than office tape.

Differences between tapes of the same class made by different companies can often be detected with the naked eye.

The variability within the same manufacturing plant is due to the ever-changing supply-and-demand market of the components used to construct the tape. For example, a lower bid for a minor component could lead to its substitution from one batch to the next.

In their simplest form, tape products consist of a flexible backing and an adhesive (**Figure 2**). When a pressure-sensitive tape is applied to a surface with slight pressure, it forms a bond that can generally be broken/removed without damage to the surface. The most commonly encountered pressure-sensitive tapes submitted to the crime lab are duct tapes, electrical tapes, and packaging tapes.

There is a wide range of materials used in the flexible backing of tapes depending upon their commercial end use. Common materials used for tape backings include low-density polyethylene (PE), polypropylene, polyvinylchloride (PVC), saturated paper, cloth, and polyester. Fillers, colorants, release coats, primer coats, plasticizers, and preservatives may be added to the backing, adding to the complexity.

The adhesive formulations that make tape 'sticky' vary widely but basically consist of an elastomer with which a tackifying resin has been blended. Some of the more common elastomers include natural rubber, polybutadiene, styrene butadiene copolymer, styrene isoprene copolymer (SIS), and

 http://dx.doi.org/10.1016/B978-0-12-382165-2.00117-3

Figure 1 Tape is used in the commission of many different crimes, such as illicit drug packaging.

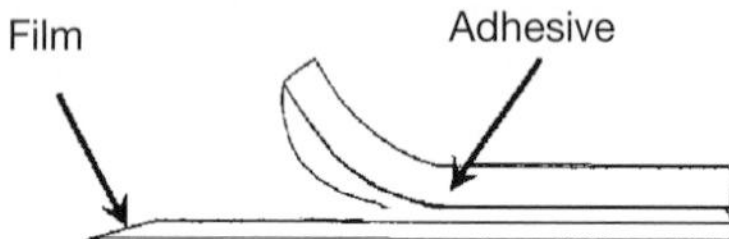

Figure 2 Basic construction of tapes.

ethyl or butyl acrylate. These elastomers are solid at room temperature, but on blending with a tackifying resin such as a C-5 hydrocarbon, they provide freer movement to polymer chains, thus lowering the glass transition temperature and making the elastomer sticky at room temperature.

While both the elastomer and tackifying resin can vary in a given formulation, further complexity comes with the addition of colorants, inorganic fillers, and stabilizers, all of which vary from one manufacturer to another.

Duct Tape

The industry name for duct tape is 'polycoated cloth tape.' It can come in any color, but most typically it comes in gray and in 2-in. rolls. Duct tape consists of three basic components: the high-density PE backing, the scrim cloth reinforcement fabric, and the adhesive (Figure 3). The two main manufacturing methods for duct tape are coextrusion and lamination. Coextruded tapes may have a dimpled surface and multiple layers, while the laminates have a smooth surface and, usually, one layer (Figures 4 and 5). Inorganic fillers, such as calcium carbonate, may be added to the backing. The gray color of the backing comes from aluminum powder. The thickness of the backing layer is usually related to its quality.

The reinforcement cloth in duct tape is a scrim fabric usually made of either cotton and polyester or polyester alone. There are several different possible weaves of the scrim. The 'scrim count' is a measure of the number of yarns in both the warp (lengthwise) and fill (crosswise) direction per inch and is typically related to the strength and quality of the tape. The shape and delustering of the polyester fibers within the scrim add still more variability to this feature.

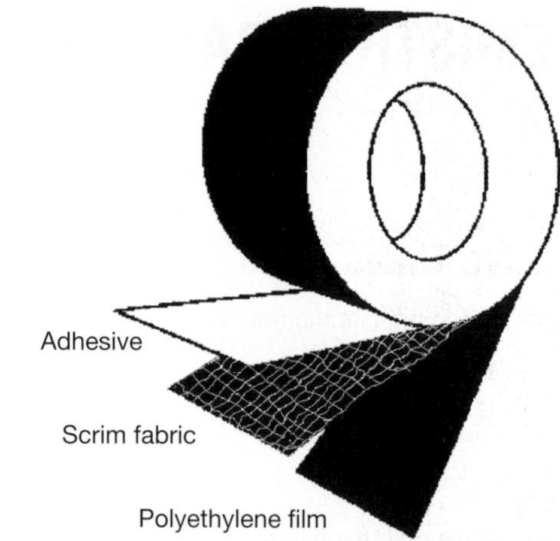

Figure 3 Duct tape has a reinforcement (scrim) fabric.

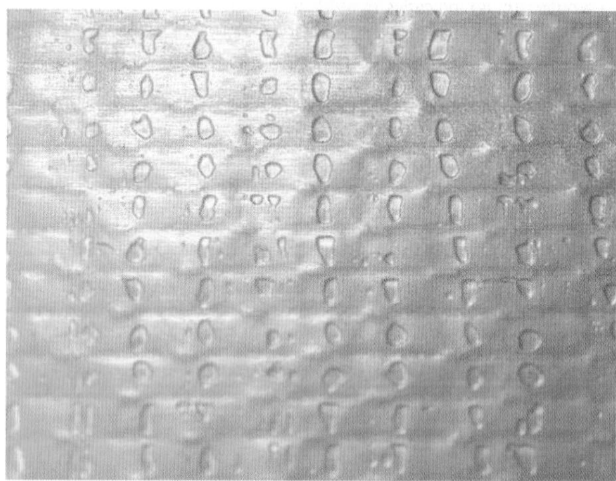

Figure 4 Dimpled surface of a co-extruded duct tape.

Figure 5 Smooth surface of a laminate duct tape.

The most common elastomer found in duct tape is natural rubber. Fillers are added for bulk or to impart color; thus, these adhesives are opaque. Calcite, dolomite, kaolinite, talc, zincite, and titanium dioxide are common fillers.

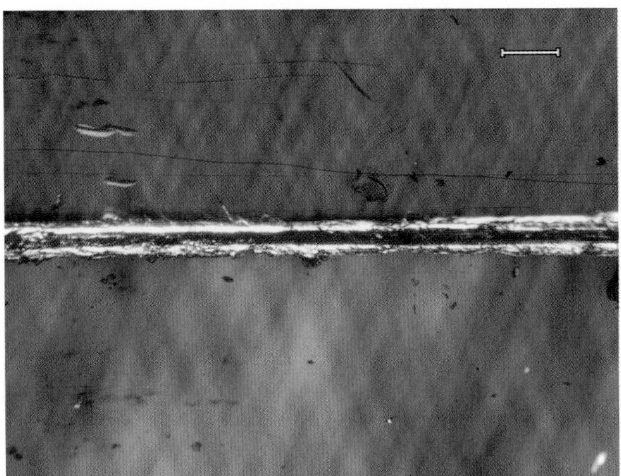

Figure 6 Clear packaging tape under polarized light at 100x magnification showing the two-directional stretching (the XXXs) and the retardation (blue) indicative of the tape's thickness.

Packaging Tape

Packaging tape typically comes in brown or clear 2-in. rolls. The backing is polypropylene. Fillers, such as calcium carbonate, iron oxide, and titanium dioxide, may be added. In brown packaging tapes, the ratio of Fe and Ti may be highly variable, giving the tapes variable shades of brown. The strength of these tapes comes from the manufacturing process, whereby controlled cooling and stretching of the polymer films gives biaxially oriented polypropylene (BOPP) films or monoaxially oriented polypropylene (MOPP) films. BOPP films are stretched in two directions and cannot be torn by hand. MOPP films are stretched in one direction and can be torn by hand. The BOPP tape is more common (**Figure 6**).

The adhesive commonly encountered in packaging tape is SIS or acrylate. It is typically clear; in brown tape, the color may be either in the backing or in the adhesive.

Electrical Tape

The end use of electrical tape is to insulate electric wires. PVC, which has good insulation properties, is typically used for the backing. PVC is naturally hard at room temperature, but the addition of a plasticizer gives it flexibility. To this may be added flame retardants, UV stabilizers, fillers, and colorants.

The adhesive may be any of the aforementioned elastomers: natural rubber, SIS, or acrylate. Plasticizer from the PVC backing almost invariably will be found to have migrated into the adhesive. Common plasticizers are dioctyl phthalate and dioctyl adipate.

Forensic Analysis of Tape Components

The first task for the forensic analyst when comparing a questioned and a known tape is to look for a physical match. If a match is not found, a stepwise physical and chemical analysis can demonstrate whether the tapes share class characteristics.

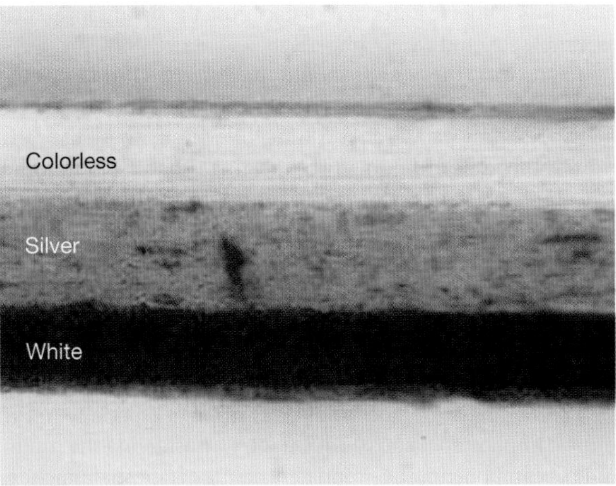

Figure 7 Cross section of a duct tape backing under 100x magnification showing three layers.

This analysis would begin with macroscopic and stereoscopic characteristics, comparison of colors and textures, followed by physical features such as tape width and thickness. Cross-sectioning of tapes, particularly the coextruded duct tapes, is recommended, as the number of layers and the fillers in those layers may vary (**Figure 7**). In duct tape, a scrim count might require separation of the adhesive from the backing. Polarized light microscopy (PLM) can identify and compare the fibers within the scrim. PLM can also tentatively identify the fillers in the adhesive. A complete examination should include Fourier transform infrared (FTIR) and elemental analysis of both the backing and adhesive to confirm the elastomer and fillers and also to identify the polymer in the backing.

In clear tapes such as clear packaging tapes, PLM may be very useful to identify MOPP and BOPP tapes, to assess the tape thickness, and to observe manufacturing features that are not otherwise detectable by FTIR or elemental analysis.

Pyrolysis gas chromatograph–mass spectrometer (CG–MS) might be useful, particularly in black electrical tapes.

Interpretation

A physical match between a known and questioned piece of tape is of utmost significance. However, due to the stretchy nature of polymer films, broken tapes will never go back together perfectly, for example, like glass does. The quality of the fit and number of points of similarities across a break may vary depending on the quality of the tape (thickness and scrim) and on whether it was cut by scissors or torn by hand or teeth.

Where there is no physical match, and at the same time no significant physical or chemical differences are found between the known and questioned tape, a class relationship can be reported. This can be determined only after a systematic examination, which includes macro- and stereoscopic, polarized light, physical characteristics, FTIR, and elemental analysis. A class relationship means that the tapes were manufactured by the same company and the possibility that the known and questioned samples are from the same roll cannot be ruled out. The significance of this relationship also varies. Some features may enhance the significance, such as manufacturing marks, striations, or anomalies. Other features may detract from the significance, such as sample size and weathering effects.

In any case, the analyst should make every effort to express in his report the significance of the positive relationship. There are no data available at the time of writing to statistically express the odds of finding two indistinguishable but random and unrelated tapes. Databases are useful for both sourcing commercial products and for significance assessment. However, databases for commercial products are inherently difficult to assemble and to keep updated because of the ever-changing market. An added complication is that the same tape product might be distributed under different brand names and sold in different outlets.

The variability of tape products is striking, especially in the more complex tapes such as duct tapes. Considering the multitude of components, the proprietary nature of tape manufacture, and the fluctuations in the market, the end product has endless variation both between manufacturers and within the same manufacturer. It is this variability that makes the forensic analysis of evidentiary tapes worthwhile.

See also: **Behavioral**: Interpretation; **Methods**: Analytical Light Microscopy; Spectroscopic Techniques; Spectroscopy: Basic Principles; **Pattern Evidence**: Physical Match.

Further Reading

Bradley MJ, Kaegy RL, Lowe PC, Rickenbach MP, Wright DM, and LeBeau MA (2007) A validation study for duct tape end matches. *Forensic Science Communications* 9(3).

Bradley MJ, Gauntt JM, Mehltretter AH, Lowe PC, and Wright DM (2011) A validation study for vinyl electrical tape end matches. *Journal of Forensic Science* 56(3): 606–611.

Hobbs AL, Gauntt J, Keagy R, Lowe PC, and Ward D (2007) A new approach for the analysis of duct tape backings. *Forensic Science Communications* 9(1).

Johnson JJ (2003) *Pressure Sensitive Adhesive Tapes: A Guide to Their Function, Design, Manufacture, and Use*, revised edn. Northbrook, IL: Pressure Sensitive Tape Council.

Johnston JJ and Serra J (2005) The examination of pressure sensitive adhesive tapes. *IAMA Newsletter* 5(1): 19–31.

Mehltretter AH, Bradley MJ, and White DM (2011) Analysis and discrimination of electrical tapes: Part 1. Adhesives. *Journal of Forensic Science* 56(1): 82–94.

Merrill RA and Bartick EG (2000) Analysis of pressure sensitive adhesive tape: I. Evaluation of infrared ATR accessory advances. *Journal of Forensic Science* 45(1): 93–98.

Noble W, Wheals BB, and Whitehouse MJ (1974) The characterization of adhesives by pyrolysis gas chromatography and infrared spectroscopy. *Forensic Science* 3: 163–174.

Rappe R (1991) Microscopical examination of polymer films. Presented at the INTER/MICRO 91 Meeting, 19–21 August, Chicago, IL.

Smith J (1998) The forensic value of duct tape comparisons. *Midwestern Association of Forensic Scientists Newsletter* 27(1): 28–33.

Smith JM (2007) Forensic examination of pressure sensitive tape. In: Blackledge RD (ed.) *Forensic Analysis on the Cutting Edge: New Methods for Trace Evidence Analysis*, 1st edn., pp. 291–332. New York: Wiley.

Smith J and Weaver R (2004) PLM examinations of clear polymer films. *Microscope* 52: 113–118, 3rd and 4th quarter.

Snodgrass H (1991) Duct tape analysis as trace evidence. In: *Proceedings of the International Symposium on Trace Evidence*, pp. 69–73. Quantico, VA: FBI Academy.

Relevant Websites

http://swgmat.org – Scientific Working Group for Materials Analysis (SWGMAT).

Decomposition Chemistry: Overview, Analysis, and Interpretation

B Stuart, University of Technology Sydney, Broadway, NSW, Australia

Glossary

Adipocere The wax-like substance formed due to the transformation of lipids.
Autolysis The destruction of a cell due to the action of intrinsic enzymes.
Diagenesis The processes responsible for the changes to the chemical and structural properties of an organic material.
Hydroxyapatite The naturally occurring mineral form of a calcium phosphorus compound.
Volatile fatty acids Fatty acids with a carbon chain of six or less carbon atoms.
Volatile organic compounds Organic chemical compounds with significant vapor pressures.

Abbreviations

ATP	Adenosine triphosphate
CE	Capillary electrophoresis
DSC	Differential scanning calorimetry
GC	Gas chromatography
HPLC	High-performance liquid chromatography
LC	Liquid chromatography
MS	Mass spectrometry
SEM	Scanning electron microscopy
TD-GCMS	Thermal desorption gas chromatography mass spectrometry
TGA	Thermogravimetric analysis
VFA	Volatile fatty acid
VOC	Volatile organic compound
XRD	X-ray diffraction

Introduction

Decomposition involves a number of postmortem processes, with the first processes beginning immediately after death. Decomposition involves the disintegration of soft tissue to ultimately leave skeletonized remains. An understanding of the processes occurring during decomposition can provide an insight into the fate of human remains, including the important issues of the estimation of the postburial interval and the location of clandestine graves.

The chemistry of decomposition is complex and depends very much on environmental conditions. Factors such as temperature, moisture, oxygen availability, the presence of clothing or other coverings, soil or water chemistry, the method of burial, and the types of microorganisms present all can influence the decomposition process. The body is predominantly comprised of water, with lipids, proteins, and carbohydrates being the other main structures present. During decomposition, reactions occur as a result of the breakdown of lipids, proteins, and carbohydrates into components including, for example, fatty acids, amino acids, and glucose, respectively. Knowledge of the chemistry of the compounds present in decomposition fluids and when they are produced is the goal in this field.

The application of a range of analytical techniques to the characterization of decomposition products is an emerging field in forensic science. Various spectroscopic and separation techniques have been widely adopted in forensic analysis, with the application of such techniques to drug, toxicological, fiber, and paint analysis, for instance. The ability of these analytical techniques to characterize complex mixtures, combined with continuing improvements in instrument sensitivity and sophistication, means that they are suitable for the investigation of decomposition products. The application of this analytical approach has been somewhat limited until recent times, but the field is expanding with the developments in technology.

Decomposition Stages

Decomposition in mammals is characterized by two main stages: pre- and postskeletonization. Preskeletonization may be further divided into four stages: fresh, bloated, decay, and dry. During the fresh stage, the first recognizable process is autolysis. This process involves the disintegration of cellular membranes and the release of cellular fluids in the body, with tissues containing cells with the highest rate of adenosine triphosphate (ATP) production decomposing first. Autolysis results in the appearance of blisters on the skin and skin slippage.

 http://dx.doi.org/10.1016/B978-0-12-382165-2.00120-3

During the bloated stage, usually occurring at a time 36–72 h after death, the destruction of soft tissues by microorganisms, such as bacteria and fungi, begins. In a predominantly anaerobic environment, putrefaction causes lipids, proteins, and carbohydrates to undergo a variety of reactions. The resulting gases and fluids produce bloating in the body. Putrefaction may also manifest itself by a dark discoloration of the skin as a result of pigments released by pancreatic cells.

After bloating has ceased, the active stage begins. A large amount of bacteria and insect activity occurs during this stage. The continuing decay of soft tissue during active decay produces an array of compounds.

The final stage of decomposition is the dry stage. The remaining skin and tissue can be mummified in dry conditions at this stage. Bone also becomes exposed at this stage. During skeletonization, the more chemically resistant bones and teeth remain. The slower process of diagenesis occurs to bones – this process involves the exchange of ionic species between the bones and the surrounding environment.

Lipid Degradation

Lipids are a major component of adipose tissue, comprising approximately 60–85% of the tissue. The predominant types of lipid present are triacylglycerols (also known as triglycerides) making up 90–99% of the lipid composition of adipose tissue, with diglycerides, phospholipids, and cholesterol esters present in smaller amounts. Triacylglycerols are triesters of glycerol with three fatty acids attached and the type of fatty acid composition is dependent on factors such as diet. The major fatty acids present in adipose tissue are oleic, lineoleic, palmitoleic, and palmitic acids. The chemical structures of the fatty acids of interest are illustrated in **Table 1**.

Following death, the lipids undergo hydrolysis due to the presence of intrinsic tissue lipases, producing a mixture of unsaturated and saturated fatty acids. The hydrolysis reaction results in the formation of free fatty acids and a glycerol molecule. As the decomposition process continues, the concentration of the neutral lipids decreases while the concentration of fatty acids increases.

The nature of the reaction depends on the type of environment in which the decomposition occurs. In an aerobic environment, oxidation of unsaturated fatty acids can occur due to bacteria, fungi, or atmospheric oxygen. Oxidation of lipids is a reaction in which oxygen attacks the double bond in a fatty acid to initially yield peroxide bonds. The final products of this process are aldehydes and ketones. However, hydrolysis of the fatty acids is more likely than oxidation to occur because the decomposing body is exposed to reducing conditions. In an anaerobic environment, the mixture of unsaturated and saturated fatty acids produced during the postmortem hydrolysis process undergoes further hydrolysis and hydrogenation (the addition of a hydrogen bond to change an unsaturated bond to a saturated bond). The hydrogenation process transforms the unsaturated fatty acid bonds into single bonds. For example, the hydrogenation of oleic and palmitoleic acids will yield stearic and palmitic acids, respectively.

Volatile fatty acids (VFAs) are useful products of the decomposition process. VFAs are short-chain fatty acids (C_2–C_5) that can be detected during mid- and late postmortem times. The VFAs of interest in decomposition are propionic, butyric, valeric, isobutyric, and isovaleric acids, the structures of which are listed in **Table 2**. The concentrations of certain VFAs can be potentially correlated with the rate of decomposition.

Protein Degradation

Bacterial enzymes are responsible for the degradation of proteins into their component amino acids. The process is known as proteolysis. Proteolysis occurs at the different rates for the different types of proteins present in the body. Soft-tissue proteins degrade first, while the hard-tissue proteins, such as collagen and keratin, are more resistant. Certain amino acids that are produced during protein degradation, including tryptophan, tyrosine, and phenylanaline, can be used as biomarkers for the estimation of the postmortem interval. Continuing proteolysis leads to the production of phenolic compounds such as indole and gases including carbon dioxide, hydrogen sulfide, ammonia, and methane.

The amino acids produced as a result of protein degradation can undergo deamination. This process results in the loss of an amine group and a hydrogen atom from the amino acid to produce ammonia, which can be used by plants or microbes in the surrounding environment. Amino acids may also undergo decarboxylation by bacterial enzymes. Decarboxylation results

Table 2 Structures of VFAs of interest in decomposition

Common name	*Systematic name*	*Structure*
Propionic acid	Propanoic acid	CH_3CH_2COOH
Butyric acid	Butanoic acid	$CH_3(CH_2)_2COOH$
Valeric acid	Pentanoic acid	$CH_3(CH_2)_3COOH$
Isobutyric acid	2-Methylpropanoic acid	$(CH_3)_2CHCOOH$
Isovaleric acid	3-Methylbutanoic acid	$(CH_3)_2CHCH_2COOH$

Table 1 Structures of fatty acids of interest in decomposition

Common name	*Systematic name*	*Structure*	*Carbon atoms:double bonds*
Palmitic acid	Hexadecanoic acid	$CH_3(CH_2)_{14}COOH$	16:0
Palmitoleic acid	9-Hexadecenoic acid	$CH_3(CH_2)_5CH{=}CH(CH_2)_7COOH$	16:1
Stearic acid	Octadecanoic acid	$CH_3(CH_2)_{16}COOH$	18:0
Oleic acid	9-Octadecenoic acid	$CH_3(CH_2)_7CH{=}CH(CH_2)_7COOH$	18:1
Linoleic acid	9,12-Octadecadienoic acid	$CH_3(CH_2)_4CH{=}CHCH_2CH{=}CH(CH_2)_7COOH$	18:2

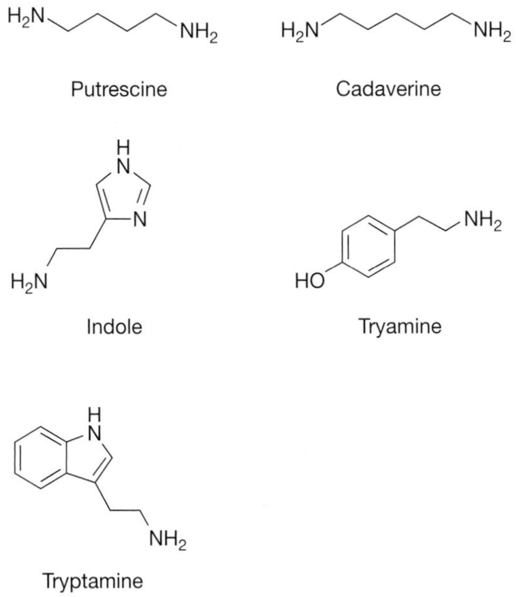

Putrescine Cadaverine Indole Tryamine Tryptamine

Figure 1 Structures of some common biogenic amines detected during decomposition.

in the loss of a carbonyl group and the production of carbon dioxide. The biogenic amines that can form as a result of decarboxylation include putrescine, cadaverine, indole, tyramine, and tryptamine. **Figure 1** illustrates the structures of some of the common biogenic amines formed during decomposition.

The amino acids that contain sulfur, such as cysteine and cystine, can undergo desulfhydralation (the removal of sulfur) and decompose to produce hydrogen sulfide, other sulfides, ammonia, thiols, and pyruvic acid. If iron is present in the environment, the black ferrous sulfide can be precipitated by reaction with hydrogen sulfide.

Carbohydrate Degradation

During early decomposition, microorganisms cause polysaccharides such as glycogen to break down into the component sugars, such as glucose. Fungi can decompose sugars into organic acids including glucuronic, citric, and oxalic acids. Under aerobic conditions, bacteria are responsible for the decomposition of sugars into organic acids such as lactic and pyruvic acids. The sugars may then be further decomposed into carbon dioxide and water. Under anaerobic conditions, bacteria can decompose sugars into organic acids including lactic, butyric, and acetic acids. These are responsible for the acidic environment associated with decomposing bodies. Bacterial carbohydrate fermentation can also occur and produces the alcohols ethanol and butanol and the gases methane, hydrogen sulfide, and hydrogen.

Volatile Organic Compounds

Volatile organic compounds (VOCs) are a class of compound comprising molecules with significant vapor. VOCs are of interest in decomposition chemistry as they occur as intermediate products of the decomposition of lipids, proteins, and carbohydrates. Lipids produce hydrocarbons, nitrogen, phosphorus, and oxygenated compounds. Proteins give rise to nitrogen and phosphorus compounds. Carbohydrates produce a range of oxygenated compounds including alcohols, aldehydes, ketones, esters, and ethers. VOCs are the compounds used to train cadaver dogs to detect human remains and clandestine graves.

Preservation of Soft Tissue

When environmental conditions are suitable, soft tissue can be preserved. The types of preservation that may be observed are adipocere formation and mummification by desiccation. Adipocere has a wax-like appearance and can preserve facial features and wounds in remains, for instance. Hydrogenation of free fatty acids yields saturated fatty acids that may transform into adipocere under appropriate conditions (recognized as a moist anaerobic environment). Adipocere is chiefly comprised of the saturated fatty acids, palmitic and stearic acids. Salts of fatty acids and hydroxy- and oxo-fatty acids have also been identified as constituents of adipocere.

Mummification is the result of the dehydration of soft tissue and occurs in dry environments. The consequence of mummification is preserved skin with a leathery appearance. The desiccation process inhibits the decomposition reactions by preventing the normal actions of microorganisms. Over time, changes will occur to the proteins and lipids present in skin. Proteins denature and triacylglycerols eventually decompose into the component fatty acids.

Vitreous Humor

The vitreous humor is the fluid located behind the lens of the eye. As the vitreous humor is isolated by membranes from the remainder of the decomposing body, attempts have been made to use the chemistry of the fluid to estimate the postmortem interval. The concentrations of both potassium ions and hypoxanthine have been used. Vitreous potassium increases in concentration after death. Hypoxanthine is a degradation product of adenosine and increases due to hypoxia before death. Although various attempts to correlate the concentrations of these components to the postmortem interval have been attempted, the conditions of death such as environment, body temperature, and cause of death can cause deviation from a simple relationship between concentration and time; so, this approach must be used with caution.

Bone Degradation

Bone is composed of three main phases: a protein phase mainly comprised of collagen (with a triple-helical structure), a mineral phase comprised of hydroxyapatite ($Ca_5(PO_4)_3OH$), and a phase comprising organic compounds including polysaccharides and glycoproteins. The hydroxyapatite crystals are embedded within the collagen fibers and the strong bonding between collagen and hydroxyapatite contributes to the long-term stability of bone.

During bone decomposition, collagen can initially be broken down by bacterial collagenases into peptides and then further to the constituent amino acids. Following the elimination of the protein phase, hydroxyapatite is lost or modified by inorganic mineral weathering. In a burial environment, the loss and/or substitution of hydroxyapatite calcium ions result in changes to bone structure. For instance, the uptake of fluoride or carbonate ions can affect the crystalline structure of bone. The mineral leaching of bone depends on environmental factors including temperature, pH, moisture, bacteria, fungi, and soil type. For example, hydroxyapatite is stable of neutral pH and has low solubility in alkaline environments, but solubility is higher in acidic environments. A consequence of mineral dissolution is an increase in the porosity of bones.

Analytical Methods

An understanding of decomposition chemistry requires the identification of the compounds produced in the resulting complex of products formed. Knowledge of the stage at which particular compounds are produced is vital to the story. Despite the often complex mixtures produced during decomposition, there is a range of established analytical techniques suitable for the study of such specimens.

Spectroscopic techniques, including infrared spectroscopy and ultraviolet–visible spectroscopy, can be used to study decomposition products. Infrared spectroscopy is used to identify lipids, proteins, and carbohydrates and the compounds that result from their decomposition. The infrared spectra of mixtures of decomposition products can be used to identify the types of compounds present and to observe changes with time. For example, the transformation of triacylglycerols into the constituent free fatty acids can be monitored using this technique by monitoring changes to the carbonyl band. Infrared spectroscopy has the advantage of being nondestructive, enabling recovery for future analyzes. The use of this method for the quantitative analysis has been limited in the field of decomposition chemistry due to the lack of perceived sensitivity. Another spectroscopic technique, ultraviolet–visible spectroscopy, can be employed in some cases for quantitative analysis. For instance, ultraviolet–visible spectroscopy can be used to measure the concentrations of nitrogen compounds produced during decomposition.

Analytical techniques such as gas chromatography (GC), liquid chromatography (LC), and capillary electrophoresis (CE) provide a means of separating individual decomposition products. Quantitative analysis can be carried out using separation techniques. GC is usually employed in combination with mass spectrometry (MS) and is used to determine the concentration of fatty acids, VFAs, and VOCs. The technique is widely used because it enables a range of mixtures to be separated and the individual components to be quantified. Consideration should be given to the need for a derivatization procedure prior to analysis for decomposition products. Derivatization enables nonvolatile compounds to be converted into volatile derivatives suitable for GC analysis. For example, trimethylsilyl esters are commonly used derivatives for fatty acids. For the analysis of compounds such as VOCs, thermal desorption GCMS (TD-GCMS) is an established technique. This method allows volatiles to be directly analyzed without the need for a solvent and has an increased sensitivity.

High-performance liquid chromatography (HPLC) can be used to study the components of decomposition products that are potentially nonvolatile or too thermally unstable for GCMS analysis. LC has thus far been mostly limited to the analysis of fluids extracted from the vitreous humor. However, with improvements in instrumentation, LC shows great promise as a technique for the quantification of products. Current LCMS instrumentation avoids the use of a large volume of solvent in an experiment and has been used, for instance, for the quantitative analysis of the fatty acid composition of adipocere.

CE is widely used for the study of nitrogen-based compounds and is an established technique for the separation of proteins and nucleic acids. CE with ultraviolet–visible detection enables fast and efficient separations of complex mixtures to be carried out. The technique is capable of analyzing thermally unstable compounds not suitable for GC analysis. CE can also provide better resolution and faster analysis than LC for certain systems. CE can be used to identify amino acids and biogenic amines in decomposition samples and is also useful for determining the potassium ion concentration in the vitreous humor.

There are a number of recognized techniques for the characterization of both the mineral and protein components of bone. Infrared spectroscopy is an established technique for studying the changes to bone due to degradation. Alterations to the inorganic and organic phases can be quantified using specific spectral bands. The organic content, the carbonate content, and the degree of crystallinity are all measurable using infrared spectroscopy. X-ray diffraction (XRD) enables changes to the crystallinity of bone to be determined and correlated with diagenetic changes. Thermal analysis, including the techniques thermogravimetric analysis (TGA) and differential scanning calorimetry (DSC), can be used to monitor changes to both the inorganic and organic components of bone. Scanning electron microscopy (SEM) enables the crystalline structures of bone to be observed and the porosity to be examined.

See also: **Forensic Medicine/Pathology**: Early and Late Postmortem Changes; Estimation of the Time Since Death; **Methods**: Capillary Electrophoresis: Basic Principles; Capillary Electrophoresis in Forensic Biology; Capillary Electrophoresis in Forensic Chemistry; Gas Chromatography; Gas Chromatography–Mass Spectrometry; Liquid and Thin-Layer Chromatography; Liquid Chromatography–Mass Spectrometry; Spectroscopic Techniques.

Further Reading

Carter DO, Yellowless D, and Tibbett M (2008) Using ninhydrin to detect gravesoil. *Journal of Forensic Sciences* 53: 397–400.

Dent BB, Forbes SL, and Stuart BH (2004) Review of human decomposition processes in soil. *Environmental Geology* 45: 576–585.

Forbes SL (2008) Decomposition chemistry in a burial environment. In: Tibbett M and Carter DO (eds.) *Soil Analysis in Forensic Taphonomy*, pp. 203–223. Boca Raton, FL: CRC Press.

Forbes S (2008) Forensic chemistry: Application to decomposition and preservation. In: Oxenham M (ed.) *Forensic Approaches to Death, Disaster and Abuse*, pp. 233–242. Brisbane: Australian Academic Press.

Gill-King H (1999) Chemical and ultrastructural aspects of decomposition. In: Haglund WD and Sorg MH (eds.) *Forensic Taphonomy: The Postmortem Fate of Human Remains*, pp. 93–108. Boca Raton, FL: CRC Press.

Hedges REM (2002) Bone diagenesis: An overview of processes. *Archaeometry* 44: 319–328.

Janaway RC, Percival SL, and Wilson AS (2009) Decomposition of human remains. In: Percival SL (ed.) *Microbiology and Aging*, pp. 313–334. New York: Springer.

Nielsen-Marsh C, Gernaey A, Turner-Walker G, Hedges R, Pike A, and Collins M (2000) The chemical degradation of bone. In: Cox M and Mays S (eds.) *Human Osteology in Archaeology and Forensic Science*, pp. 439–454. Cambridge: Cambridge University Press.

Swann LM, Forbes SL, and Lewis SW (2010) Analytical separations of mammalian decomposition products for forensic science: A review. *Analytica Chimica Acta* 682: 9–22.

Vass AA, Barshick SA, Sega G, Caton J, Skeen JT, Love JC, and Synstelien JA (2002) Decomposition chemistry of human remains: A new methodology for determining the postmortem interval. *Journal of Forensic Sciences* 47: 542–553.

CHEMISTRY/TRACE/DRUGS OF ABUSE

Contents

Clandestine Laboratories

DR, Christian Jr., Professional Business Solutions, Lake St Louis, MO, USA

Glossary

Adulterant A substance used to increase the mass of a controlled substance. These substances produce a physiological effect on the body and are used to give the illusion that there is more controlled substance present than actually is present.
Controlled substance Any substance, commonly drugs, whose possession or use is regulated.
Conversion process Changing a raw material into the finished product through minor changes in the molecule or its salt form.
Diluent An inert substance used to increase the mass of the controlled substance. These substances have no physiological effect on the body and are used to give the illusion that there is more controlled substance present than actually is present.
Distillation The separation of a liquid from a solid or other liquid using evaporation followed by condensation.
Drug A substance other than food intended to affect the structure or function of the body.
Extraction The act of separating a constituent from the whole.
Extraction process Removes raw material from a mixture without chemically changing the material being extracted.
Hydrogenation A chemical reaction that adds hydrogen to a substance through the direct use of gaseous hydrogen.
Manufacture (21 CFR 1300.01) "... the producing, preparing, propagating, compounding or processing of a drug or other substance or the packaging or repackaging of such substance or labeling or relabeling of the commercial container of such ..."
Precursor chemical A raw material that becomes a part of the finished product.
Reagent chemical A chemical that reacts with one or more of the precursor chemicals, but does not become part of the finished product.
Reflux A controlled boiling process in which the evaporated liquid is condensed and returned to the reaction mixture.
Solvent A chemical that is used to dissolve solid precursors or reagents, to dilute reaction mixtures, and to separate or purify other chemicals. They do not react with precursor or reagent chemicals.
Synthesis process A chemical reaction or series of chemical reactions in which molecules or parts of molecules are combined to create a new molecule.
Tableting process The act of placing the finished product into dosage forms or into smaller saleable units for distribution.

Introduction

The investigation of clandestine labs can be one of the most challenging efforts of law enforcement. The successful investigation and prosecution of this illicit activity can utilize forensic science at every stage. Traditional investigative techniques require forensic input to develop information concerning the location of the lab and the identity of the lab operators. Forensic science is used to establish the identity of the final product as well as the manufacturing process. Forensic experts combine and present the information from the various stages of the investigation into a cohesive understandable written report or orally to a jury whose members possess varying levels of scientific knowledge and understanding.

All clandestine laboratories share the same basic principles. The end product of the clandestine lab is immaterial. The manufacture of contraband drugs and explosives utilize the same basic processes. This article will focus on the clandestine

 http://dx.doi.org/10.1016/B978-0-12-382165-2.00075-1

manufacture of drugs of abuse. Although not specifically addressed in text, the manufacture of other weapons of mass destruction, that is, chemical and biological weapon, also share the same principles of clandestine manufacture and as such the same forensic investigative techniques can be utilized during their investigation and prosecution.

The goal of this article is to provide the reader the information required to guide them through the process of establishing the existence of a clandestine lab beyond a reasonable doubt. This will be accomplished by dividing the forensic aspects of a clandestine lab investigation into its component parts. These parts include recognition of the potential manufacturing process, processing the site of a clandestine lab, analysis of the evidence and generating opinions that can be rendered from the physical evidence, and their relationship to the crime scene.

Scope of the Problem

What a clandestine lab is must be defined before the scope of the problem can be established. In its simplest form, a clandestine lab is a hidden (clandestine) place where drugs and chemicals are manufactured (laboratory). The end product of the manufacturing process is irrelevant. It can be illicit drugs, explosives, weapons of mass destruction, or alcohol beverages. The common thread in these operations is the desire of the operators to avoid detection by the government.

Manufacture is the operative word in the definition. The Code of Federal Regulations 21 CFR 1300.01 defines manufacture as "... the producing, preparing, propagating, compounding or processing of a drug or other substance or the packaging or repackaging of such substance or labeling or relabeling of the commercial container of such substance ..." This definition relates more directly to the production of drugs of abuse and is applicable in one form or another throughout the United States. Most states have adopted a version of this wording into their own criminal codes.

The definition of manufacture is less specific when associated with the production of explosives. 27 CFR 555.11 and 40 of Title 18 of the United States Code (18 USC 40) defines the person not the process. The statute defines manufacturer as "any person engaged in the business of manufacturing explosive materials for purposes of sale or distribution or for his own use." This statute relies on the accepted meaning of manufacture to define the activity.

Clandestine drug labs have been a concern for law enforcement since the 1960s. At the time, outlaw motorcycle gangs began producing methamphetamine for distribution within the United States. The Drug Enforcement Administration (DEA) has reported the number of clandestine laboratory seizures steadily increasing over time. The first clandestine drug lab was seized in Santa Cruz, California, in 1963. DEA statistics show the number of clandestine lab seizures has increased to 41 in 1973, 187 in 1983, 286 in 1993, and 2155 in 1999.

Dramatic increases in the number of clandestine drug laboratory-related seizures were observed in the subsequent 10 years. The National Seizure System reported 17 194 clandestine drug lab incidences in 2004 and 10 068 in 2009. Changes in manufacturing methods as well as the reporting criteria influenced the increase. However, the amount of final product produced by domestic laboratories has reduced over time. Reduction in the availability of precursor chemicals and shifts in the manufacturing methods utilized by clandestine lab operators are contributing factors to this decrease. These factors have forced the domestic clandestine lab operators to shift toward small-scale operations focused on personal use qualities using the rapid production of small usable qualities of methamphetamine using items that can be purchased over the counter.

Although clandestine drug laboratories can be used to produce a wide variety of illicit drugs (i.e., phencyclidine (PCP), methylenedioxymethamphetamine (MDMA), lysergic acid diethylamide (LSD), etc.), methamphetamine has always been the primary drug manufactured in the vast majority of labs seized by law enforcement. The manufacture of 'crack' or 'rock' cocaine is generally not accounted for in these statistics. If they were, the numbers would be significantly larger.

The scope of the clandestine lab problem is far reaching and no community is exempt. It is advisable that every law enforcement or emergency services agency have a clandestine lab expert on staff. These agencies should have staff with the knowledge required to recognize the potential of a clandestine lab operation and where to find the resources to handle the situation if one identified. A clandestine lab may create a larger potential hazard without this ability.

Recognition

Recognition of clandestine lab activity is the first step in the process. Numerous clandestine labs are unwittingly discovered every year by police patrol officers, fire fighters, and emergency responders such as emergency medical technicians (EMTs), paramedics, and parole officers. These individuals should be provided forensic training in the recognition of the physical signs of clandestine lab activity.

Clandestine labs come in a variety of shapes and sizes. Their sophistication is limited only by the education and imagination of the operator. Complicated equipment and exotic chemicals are not required to manufacture drugs of abuse or explosives. Most of the equipment and chemicals found in a clandestine lab have legitimate uses and can be obtained from a variety of legitimate retail outlets. Therefore, the forensic clandestine lab investigator must be able to recognize the combinations of equipment and chemicals that are used to manufacture controlled substances and to determine whether the combination is coincidental or intentional.

Manufacturing Processes

There are a number of different processes that can be used to manufacture a controlled substance. The one employed will depend on the starting materials used and the end product desired. Each process may be encountered alone or in combination with one or more of the others. One clandestine lab may incorporate multiple manufacturing processes to obtain the end product. The four basic manufacturing processes used in clandestine labs are extraction, conversion, synthesis, and tableting.

Extraction labs (**Figure 1**) isolate raw materials from a mixture. This is accomplished by using the component's

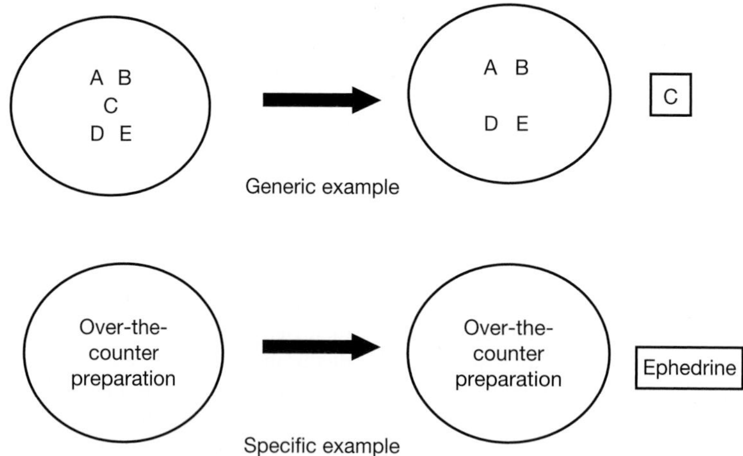

Figure 1 Extraction lab chemistry.

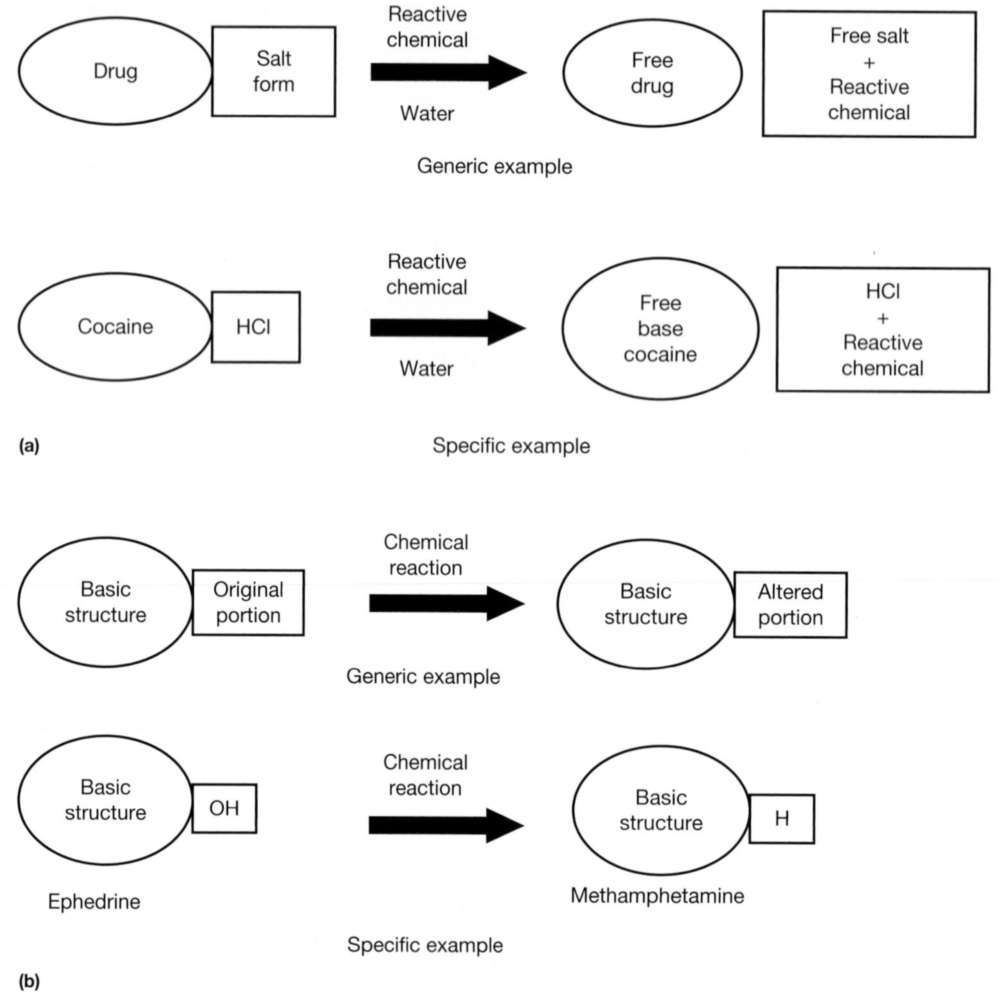

Figure 2 (a and b) Conversion lab chemistry.

physical and chemical properties to separate it from the mixture. The chemical structure of the raw material is not changed during the process. Examples of extraction labs include hashish production, coca paste productions, and extractions of the active ingredients from pharmaceutical preparations.

The conversion process takes a raw material and changes it into the desired product. This involves minor structural changes within the molecule of the compound, or of the chemical's salt form. Functional groups may be added or removed from the molecule, somewhat like pieces on a tinker toy (**Figure 2(b)**). The drug of

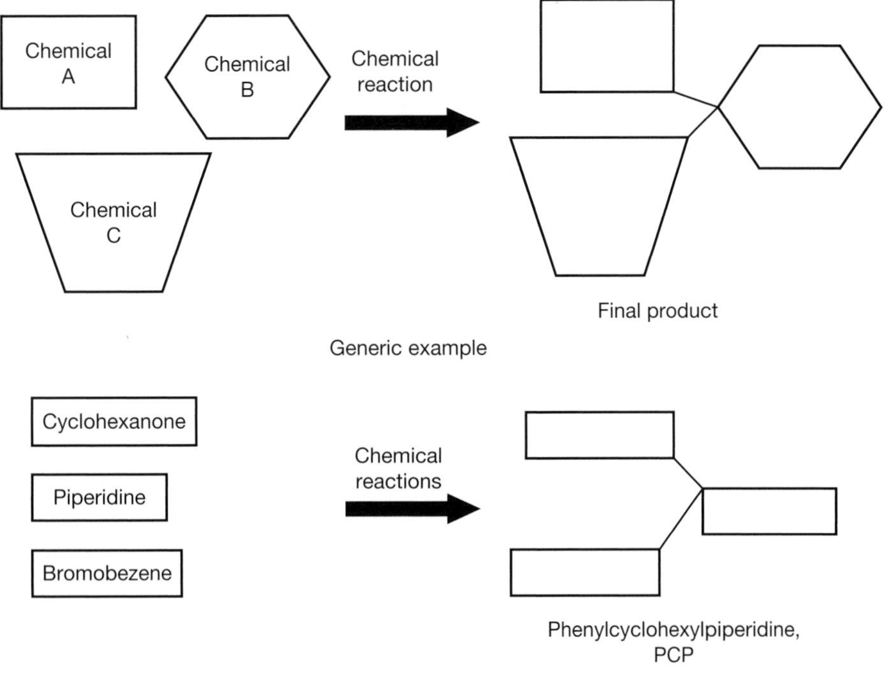

Figure 3 Synthesis lab chemistry.

interest can be changed from its salt form to the freebase form or from the freebase form to the salt form (**Figure 2(a)**). Examples of the conversion process include the conversion of cocaine hydrochloride into freebase or 'crack' cocaine and the conversion of ephedrine or pseudoephedrine into methamphetamine.

The synthesis process (**Figure 3**) is a chemical reaction or series of chemical reactions in which molecules or parts of molecules are combined to create a new molecule. This process can be equated to a chemical erector set. It differs from the conversion process in that the skeleton of the resulting molecule is a sum of the molecules or significant parts of the molecules involved in the reaction. LSD, PCP, phenylacetone, and certain methamphetamine reactions are examples of drugs produced using the synthesis process.

Clandestine labs that are involved in the tableting process are placing the finished product into dosage forms or into smaller, more salable units for distribution. The tableting process derives its name from operations that place controlled substances into tablet form. The tableting process often includes pressing corporate logos onto the tablets to simulate legitimate pharmaceuticals.

A combination of processes is used to manufacture a controlled substance. It is not uncommon for more than one process to be observed at any given clandestine lab site. The size and scope of the operation will often determine exactly how many processes are seen at the site. The following sequence demonstrates the multiprocess nature involved in the manufacture of methamphetamine.

- Step 1: Pseudoephedrine is *extracted* from over-the-counter pharmaceutical tablets
- Step 2: Pseudoephedrine is *converted* into methamphetamine base using one of a number of methods commonly used by clandestine lab operators
- Step 3: Methamphetamine base is *extracted* from the reaction mixture used to convert the pseudoephedrine into methamphetamine
- Step 4: Methamphetamine base is *converted* into methamphetamine hydrochloride
- Step 5: Methamphetamine hydrochloride is *extracted* from the solvent used to extract the methamphetamine base from the reaction mixture
- Step 6: Methamphetamine hydrochloride is packaged for distribution and sale in what is referred to as the *tableting* process.

Needs Triangle

Clandestine labs need equipment, chemicals, and knowledge to be complete. This 'Needs Triangle' (**Figure 4**) theme is recurrent in many areas of science and life. As in any triangle, if any one of the three elements is eliminated, the system will not be complete. The amount of each component may vary, but each must be present for the operation to exist.

Equipment

The manufacturing methods used by clandestine lab operators include reflux, distillation, and extractions. Understanding the mechanics of the scientific equipment used in the various manufacturing processes will allow the investigator to recognize the alternative equipment that is frequently encountered in clandestine labs.

Reflux

Refluxing is one of the most common methods used in the synthesis and conversion processes. This is a controlled boiling process in which the evaporated liquid is condensed and then returned to the reaction mixture. **Figure 5(a)** represents the

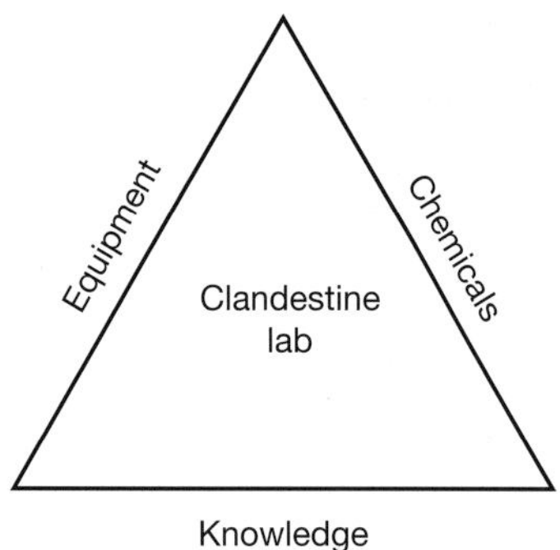

Figure 4 Clandestine lab needs triangle.

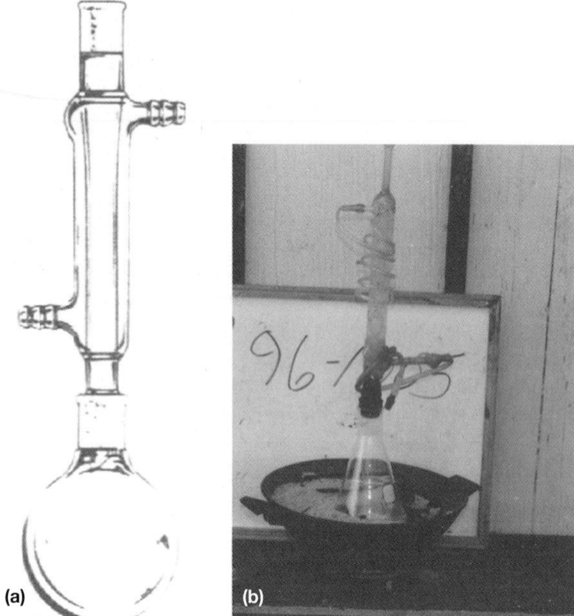

Figure 5 (a) Reflux apparatus and (b) clandestine reflux apparatus.

scientific equipment that has been specifically designed for this process.

Clandestine lab operators commonly create reflux apparatus utilizing ordinary household items (**Figure 5(b)**). Hot plates have been used as a heating mantel. Countertop deep fryers have been used as an oil bath. Glass cookware has been used as reaction vessels. Condensers have been fabricated from copper or polyvinyl chloride (PVC) pipes. The only limitation is the operator's imagination, so the clandestine lab investigator must also be thinking creatively in order to recognize things for what they really are.

Distillation

Distillation is the separation of a liquid from a solid or other liquid using evaporation followed by condensation. It is a modification of refluxing. It can be used as a technique to synthesize and separate compounds, or used solely as a separation technique.

Distillation and reflux utilize the same equipment, configured in a slightly different manner (**Figure 6(a)**). The individual components of the apparatus are rearranged to allow gravity to separate the condensing liquid from the boiling mixture rather than return it. As with a reflux apparatus, the distillation apparatus requires a heating mantle (stove), a boiling/reaction flask (pot), and a lid (condenser). The heating mantle provides the heat required to boil the ingredients in the reaction vessel. The vapors from the boiling ingredients then condense in the condenser. The orientation of the condenser is changed to allow gravity to separate the condensing liquid away from the boiling liquid instead of returning it to the mixture. It may then be collected in a reception flask. Clandestine lab operators have also designed distillation apparatus that do not require the use of traditional scientific glassware (**Figure 6(b)**).

Hydrogenation

Hydrogenation is a chemical reaction that adds hydrogen to a substance through the direct use of gaseous hydrogen. Under high pressure, in the presence of a catalyst and hydrogen, ephedrine can be converted into methamphetamine in a commercial vessel similar to **Figure 7(a)**. As with all scientific

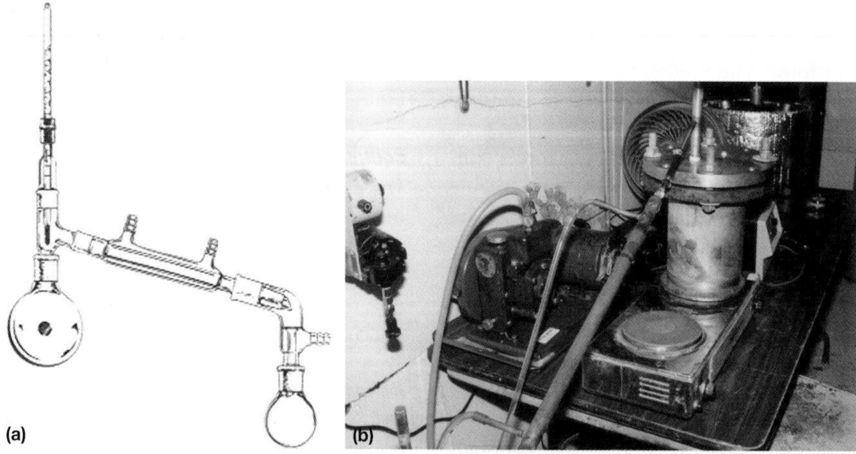

Figure 6 (a) Distillation apparatus and (b) clandestine distillation apparatus.

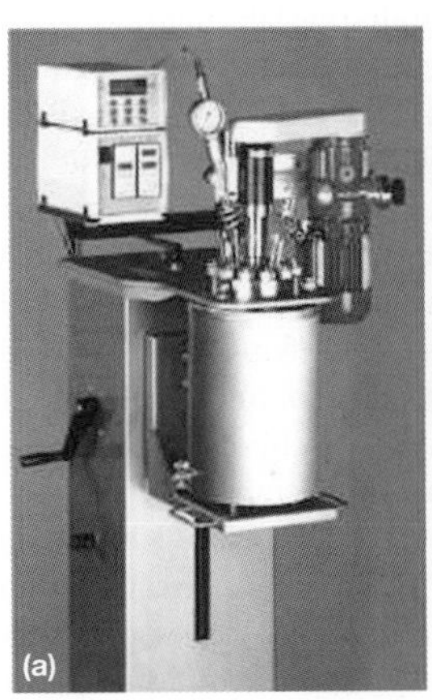

Figure 7 (a) Commercial hydrogenator. (b) Clandestine hydrogenator

Figure 8 Bucket chemistry.

equipment, the clandestine lab operators have developed alternatives for this specialized piece of equipment as well (**Figure** 7(b)).

Bucket chemistry

There are certain manufacturing methods that do not require traditional scientific apparatus. 'Bucket' chemistry is an appropriate term in this situation because the reactions literally can take place in a plastic bucket (**Figure** 8). The chemicals are placed into the container and allowed to react. At some point in time, an extraction process is undertaken to separate the final product from the reaction mixture. No heat is necessary, but cooling may be required. Phencyclidine and methamphetamine can be produced using nothing more than plastic containers.

Extractions

Extraction is the act of separating a constituent from the whole. It may be performed a number of times during the manufacturing process. Clandestine lab operators rely on the component's physical and chemical properties to isolate it from the rest of the substances.

Chemical extractions use a component's ability to dissolve in a liquid (solubility) to separate it from the bulk substance. The component being extracted may be the compound of interest or some unwanted by-product(s). The process does not require sophisticated equipment. All that is required is a container to hold the original mixture and a liquid that the desired material will not dissolve in.

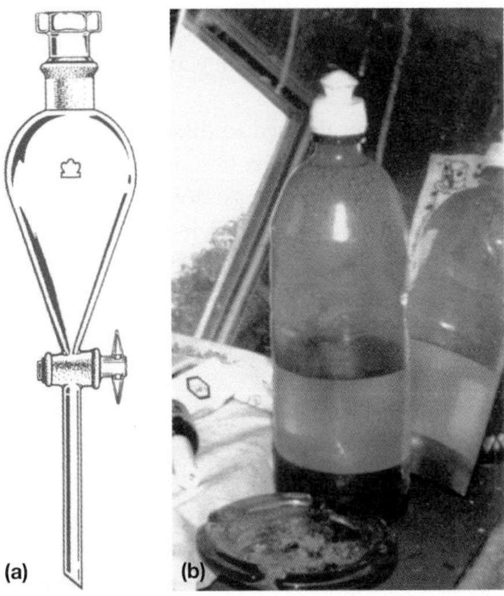

Figure 9 (a) Separatory funnel and (b) clandestine separatory funnel.

Physical extractions physically separate the component(s) of interest. In many instances, the act of chemically separating the desired component is only half the battle. In one form or another, the two chemically incompatible components still need to be physically separated. Specialized equipment has been developed to perform this task (**Figure** 9(a)). However, clandestine alternatives have been developed with this portion of the process as well (**Figure** 9(b)).

Chemical needs

The second leg of the triangle is the chemical needs of a clandestine lab. Chemicals are the bricks and mortar of the manufacturing process. Drugs cannot be manufactured without the chemical building blocks and the glue used to combine the parts.

Most of the chemicals used in the manufacture of controlled substances and explosives have legitimate uses. Some have legitimate home and hobby uses and may be found in anyone's kitchen, medicine cabinet, garage, or workshop. Many can be obtained without restrictions through chemical suppliers or from grocery, drug, or hardware stores. Legitimate alternatives or sources that do not have restrictions on their distribution exist as alternatives to the chemicals that do have restrictions on their sale or distribution. The key to a successful forensic clandestine lab investigation is the ability to recognize combinations of chemicals that together can potentially form a controlled substance.

The three types of chemicals used in the manufacture of controlled substances are precursors, reagents, and solvents. All three types are used at some point during the manufacturing process. Some of the chemicals perform dual roles.

A precursor chemical is a raw material that becomes a part of the finished product. It is the building block(s) with which the final product is constructed. In a conversion reaction, a precursor's chemical skeleton is altered to create the final product. In the synthesis process, precursors are chemically bonded together to produce the final product.

Reagent chemicals react chemically with one or more of the precursor chemicals, but do not become part of the final product. During the process, a portion of the reagent may be part of an intermediate product, but is removed prior to the formation of the final product. They are the catalyst that helps drive the reaction process.

Solvents are chemicals used to dissolve solid precursors or reagents, to dilute reaction mixtures, and to separate or purify other chemicals. A solvent does not chemically react with precursor or reagent chemicals. Their purpose is to provide a place for a chemical reaction to take place or facilitate the extraction of a chemical from one environment to another.

Knowledge needs

Knowledge is the final leg of the manufacturing triangle. Knowing how to combine the equipment and chemicals to produce a controlled substance is a necessary element. Knowledge is necessary to establish both capability and criminal intent. Knowledge may come from education (schooling or professional training), mentoring/apprenticeship, underground literature, and often even simply handwritten recipes that are bought and sold as property. The Internet has unfortunately become a source for many 'recipes' as well. Original methods have been taken from academic chemical literature and translated into simple recipes that can be followed by someone with no chemical training.

Forensic Components

The Chemist

A forensic science is utilized in every portion of the clandestine lab investigation. As such a forensic chemist should participate in every phase. Forensic science is utilized to argue how common household chemicals and kitchen utensils can be used to manufacture drugs of abuse. Forensic principles are used at the crime scene to determine relevance of the items located at the scene as well as establishing the sampling protocols required to establish the elements of the crime. Forensic chemistry is used in the analysis of the samples recovered from the crime scene. Forensic experts are used to render opinions concerning the association of the crime scene information and the analytical data as related to the existence of a clandestine laboratory. Each of these roles should be assumed by a forensic clandestine lab chemist.

The clandestine lab chemist's role in a clandestine lab investigation requires a different thought process when approaching his analysis. As such, all clandestine lab chemists are forensic chemists. However, not all forensic chemists are clandestine lab chemists. They should specialize in the analysis of samples from clandestine labs. They should have training in clandestine manufacturing techniques as well as in inorganic analysis. Their function is identifying the manufacturing process, not just the identification of the controlled substance involved.

There are two schools of thought concerning which forensic clandestine lab chemist analyzes the samples once they enter the laboratory. One school has a single chemist process the crime scene, analyzing the samples and rendering opinions in a cradle to approach. The other school has an independent chemist analyze the samples once they reach the laboratory. This school theorizes that it should not matter who does the analytical work as long as the person is trained in clandestine lab analysis. Arguments can be made in favor of each situation.

Utilizing a single chemist to process the scene and subsequently analyze the samples can streamline the analytical process. The scene chemist understands the relationship between samples and the importance of each in the investigation. This broad understanding produces an intuitive prioritization of the samples based upon the direct knowledge of the sample's origin. If a sample's analytical results are consistent with the chemist's on-scene theories, analysis of similar subsequent samples may not be necessary. If they are not, theories, analytical schemes, and opinions may need to be modified to follow the direction the evidence leads.

Some level of examiner bias is introduced into the examination process when a single individual performs all aspects of the forensic examination process. The bias may be conscious or subconscious. However, it does exist.

Multiple forensic chemists can be used to minimize bias. Independent forensic chemists do not have specific knowledge concerning the history of the samples from a clandestine lab operation. They can provide objective analytical results. As such they would not be inclined to skew the analysis to meet the opinions formed at the scene.

The case management philosophy of the forensic laboratory will dictate the use of the single or multiple forensic chemists to process clandestine lab evidence. The proper processing of a clandestine lab scene is a time-consuming process. Utilizing a laboratory chemist to process clandestine lab scenes can remove a chemist from the bench effectively one day or more per scene. The skills required to process a clandestine lab scene are different than those required to analyze the samples. Having chemists trained in specific areas of forensic clandestine lab investigation may provide for a more efficient flow of the case through the forensic system.

Crime Scene Support

The amount and type of crime scene support provided to clandestine labs seizures varies from forensic laboratory to forensic laboratory. Some laboratories provide a full range of support, with a group of chemists dedicated to providing crime scene and analytical support for clandestine lab investigations. Other laboratories provide support by sending crime scene chemists who may or may not have specialized training in clandestine labs. Other laboratories opt to train nonlaboratory personnel to provide forensic support at crime scene and relegate the scientists to laboratory analysis duties.

The on-scene forensic personnel provide a variety of technical support. They identify the chemicals and equipment that can potentially be used in the manufacturing of illicit drugs. They assist in the sampling process. They can also provide preliminary opinions as to the proposed final product and the manufacturing method used by the operation. Their scene report is used by laboratory examiners as a guide to devise the analytical scheme used to identify the controlled substance and associated chemicals. Additionally, the crime scene information combined with the laboratory data is used to establish the manufacturing method used.

Laboratory Analysis

The laboratory analysis of samples taken from the scene of a clandestine lab is the link between the investigation and the opinions that leads to prosecution. It provides the scientific foundation that corroborates the investigator's theories and is used to support the opinions rendered in reports, legal depositions, and court testimony. Without complete and thorough laboratory analysis, the case may remain unresolved.

The analysis of exhibits from clandestine labs involves the use of a variety of scientific techniques. Some examinations use techniques outside of those normally associated with drug identification. These techniques range from simple chemical color tests to the use of X-ray and infrared energy to elicit the compound's chemical fingerprint. The type of test used depends upon the information desired from the sample and the burden of proof required to establish its identity.

The laboratory analysis of clandestine lab exhibits is more complex than the simple identification of a controlled substance. The identification of the components of the sample matrix may be just as important. A complete analysis is essential to establish the manufacturing method. Yet in some instances, it may not be absolutely necessary.

Ramifications outside the laboratory should be considered when the examiner maps out his analysis. The lack of a complete analysis may affect aspects of the investigation or prosecution of which the examiner is not aware. If the examiner is asked to render opinions concerning the manufacturing operation, he must have documentation to support his opinion. A complete laboratory analysis is one source of the information he needs to support his opinions.

It is not sufficient to say that the clandestine lab operator was using a particular method simply because some or all of the ingredients were found at the site. The presence or absence of a particular precursor or reagent chemical cannot be established beyond a reasonable doubt without laboratory examination. The relabeling of ingredients by the lab operator or lack of labels on the containers at the scene often makes the actual identity of the chemicals at the location questionable.

The same holds true with reaction mixtures. The chemist should identify the ingredients within the reaction mixture. The fact that a chemical or chemical container was located at the scene does not establish its presence in a reaction mixture. It only provides the chemist information he can utilize in developing his analytical scheme.

Expert Opinions

A clandestine lab is a Pandora's box of illegal activities. Controlled substances are produced using household chemicals mixed in ordinary utensils in what some have called a 'kitchen of death.' What appears at first glance to be simply atrocious housekeeping or even just a hobby gone awry may actually be the final step in the production of many of the drugs sold on the street or the explosives used in various forms of domestic terrorism.

The clandestine lab chemist provides the expert opinions that draw calm from the chaos. He couples his clandestine lab training and experience with his deductive reasoning ability and laboratory examination results to develop a plausible scenario concerning the clandestine manufacturing operation in question. The clandestine lab chemist combines the black and white answers of the laboratory analysis with the crime scene information to provide answers to the investigation's and prosecution's 'who, what, when, where, why, and how' questions.

Many types of opinions can only be generated from the laboratory analysis of evidentiary samples. Some opinions are a result of generalities that do not require the support of analytical data. For example, just because a red powder is found at the scene of a suspected ephedrine reduction lab does not make the powder the critical red phosphorus. It is absolutely essential for an analytical chemist who is going to render an opinion concerning a clandestine lab to have the analytical data ready to support that opinion.

As with laboratory analysis, opinions concerning clandestine lab operations should be able to withstand peer review. A component chemist or other forensic expert should be able to review the facts of the case or the laboratory data and draw the same conclusion the original expert did. Alternative opinions can and do exist, as is evidenced by prosecution and defense differences. But the information must support the opinion or the opinion is worthless.

See also: **Chemistry/Trace/Drugs of Abuse:** Analysis of Controlled Substances; **Chemistry/Trace/Explosives:** Clandestine Explosive Laboratories.

Further Reading

Christian DR (2003) *Forensic Investigation of Clandestine Laboratories*. Boca Raton, FL: CRC Press.
Christian DR (2004) *Field Guide to Clandestine Laboratory Identification and Investigation*. Boca Raton, FL: CRC Press.
Christian DR (2009) Analysis of controlled substances. In: *Forensic Science: An Introduction to Scientific and Investigative Techniques*, 3rd edn., ch. 23. Boca Raton, FL: CRC Press.
Christian DR (2010a) *Clandestine Drug and Terrorist Lab, First Responder and Investigator Guide*. O'Fallon, MO: Professional Business Solutions, Inc.
Christian DR (2010b) Forensic chemistry. In: *The Forensic Laboratory Handbook: Procedures and Practice*, 2nd edn. New York, NY: Springer Science and Business Media.
Khan J, Kennedy TJ, and Christian DR (2011) *Basic Principles of Forensic Chemistry*. New York, NY: Springer Science and Business Media.

Analysis of Controlled Substances

N NicDaéid and H Buchannan, University of Strathclyde, Glasgow, UK

Abbreviations

BSIA	Bulk stable isotope analysis
CF-IRMS	Continuous flow isotope ratio mass spectrometry
CSIA	Compound-specific isotope analysis
EA-IRMS	Elemental analyzer isotope ratio mass spectrometry
GC-IRMS	Gas chromatography isotope ratio mass spectrometry
GCMS	Gas chromatography mass spectroscopy
HPLC	High-performance liquid chromatography
IRMS	Isotope ratio mass spectrometry
NMR	Nuclear magnetic resonance spectroscopy
TC/EA-IRMS	Temperature conversion/elemental analyzer isotope ratio mass spectrometry
TLC	Thin-layer chromatography

Introduction

One of the main activities in a forensic chemical laboratory is the examination of powders, pills, and plant materials thought to be illicit or controlled substances. The analysis of suspected drugs of abuse occurs over a number of stages. These involve a physical examination of the item, including its packaging, followed by sampling, and subsequent presumptive and confirmatory testing. A variety of analytical tests are used in drug analysis, and the analytical test is selected according to the nature of the suspect material and the ultimate question being asked about it: that is, identification, quantification, or chemical profiling. This article explores, in brief, the analytical techniques used in conventional drug analysis. The data derived from the analysis of such substances are used in the production of forensic science reports for use within the criminal justice system and/or used by the police in the development of intelligence information for disrupting dealer user networks and clandestine manufacture at national and international levels.

Analytical Strategy

The strategy chosen by the drug analyst in the investigation of drug samples will depend upon the ultimate question at issue balanced by the resource and time implications. Within the laboratory, this may involve decisions in relation to the necessity to identify, quantify, or profile the drug sample in question. In general circumstances, samples will be physically examined (including examination of the packaging materials), will undergo presumptive and/or thin-layer chromatographic analysis, and be analyzed using a variety of confirmatory tests.

Physical Examination

Once a drug sample is presented for examination, its packaging should be checked to ensure that it is intact. Any breech of the packaging should be recorded and a decision taken as to whether the analysis of that item should continue.

The physical description of an item, as well as the analyses undertaken, depends upon whether that item is considered a bulk or trace sample. Each item should be described fully (with diagrams if appropriate), including a description of color, smell, and packaging materials. Any logos (e.g., on tablets) or marks (such as stamp marks on blocks of resin or packages of drugs) must also be fully described and recorded. Microscopic examination may also be required to examine the morphological characteristics of the material, particularly for plant-based substances.

Specific analysis of packaging material also is beneficial. In particular, such examinations can provide intelligence information for case-to-case linkages. Examination of packaging material not only can include a general physical characterization of the materials used but may also include DNA, fingerprint, and specific chemical analysis of materials such as plastic and duct tape using, for example, isotope ratio mass spectrometry (IRMS).

Presumptive Tests

A sample is initially subjected to presumptive colorimetric tests to give an indication of the class of drug which may be present in the sample. These tests are widely accepted. Presumptive tests are also used extensively as field tests where various commercial kits are available. In the laboratory, presumptive tests are generally performed on clean porcelain tiles, in solution, or on adsorbent substrates. The most common type of presumptive test involves the addition of reagents to the sample to produce a color. Other tests utilize microscopy to identify plant components (e.g., trichomes in suspected cannabis samples) or microcrystalline tests in which the formation of specific crystals is indicative of the class of drug present. In all cases, appropriate positive and negative control samples must be used. Although presumptive tests are cheap, quick, and easy to use, they may be subjective in nature and prone to spurious positive results when drug mixtures are encountered. Furthermore, 'false positive' results may be obtained when a color change occurs due to the presence of certain noncontrolled substances within the drug sample.

 http://dx.doi.org/10.1016/B978-0-12-382165-2.00076-3

Fourier Transform Infrared Spectroscopy

Infrared (IR) spectroscopy is a technique available for the identification of functional groups within molecules. When IR light is passed through an organic compound, some wavelengths of light are absorbed. This absorption of light causes an energy transition in the form of vibrational excitation of bonds within the molecule. One example of this vibrational excitation is the stretching and bending of bonds. Light of wavelength λ will only be absorbed if there is an energy transition (ΔE) according to the following equation:

$$\Delta E = \frac{hc}{\lambda}$$

where h is Planck's constant (6.626×10^{-34} J s), c is the speed of light (3.0×10^{8} m s^{-1}), and λ is the wavelength of light in meters.

After the light has passed through the sample, the frequencies which have been absorbed are detected due to their absence, and the intensities are recorded as troughs in the resultant spectrum.

Different types of bonds have different vibrational frequencies, so the presence or absence of characteristic frequencies in the spectrum can provide information about the functional groups present in an organic molecule; most useful for functional group identification are the absorptions above 1400 cm^{-1} and below 900 cm^{-1}. [The per cm unit, or 'wavenumber,' is the reciprocal of wavelength (λ).] For example, carbonyl compounds generally absorb IR at 1670–1780 cm^{-1}, alkenes (nonterminal) at 1640–1680 cm^{-1}, and amines at 3300–3500 cm^{-1} (for N–H) and 1030–1230 cm^{-1} (for C–N). The range from 1400 to 900 cm^{-1} is termed the 'fingerprint region' and contains a complex pattern of absorptions which can be characteristic of the analyzed molecule. This region is valuable for direct comparison between two spectra, but it is generally of little use for determining the presence or absence of functional groups. Fourier transform infrared is often used in the confirmation of the identity of a pure drug substance or the determination of functional groups in an unknown drug compound.

Nuclear Magnetic Resonance Spectroscopy

'Nuclear magnetic resonance' occurs because nuclei of certain atoms spin, thus creating a weak magnetic field around the nucleus. The instrument applies an external magnetic field to the sample, which causes the spinning nuclei to reorient themselves. In the case of proton (^{1}H) and carbon (^{13}C) nuclear magnetic resonance spectroscopy (NMR), the nuclei become aligned with or against the external magnetic field. The former is the lower energy state, and the latter is the higher energy state. When radiofrequency radiation of the appropriate frequency is applied, nuclei in the lower energy state can jump to the higher energy state; that is, nuclei which are parallel to the applied magnetic field can invert so that they are antiparallel. When this occurs, NMR has been induced. The nuclei in the higher energy state then relax to the lower energy state, and a very small amount of energy is released. This small pulse of radiofrequency electromagnetic radiation is detected and converted to an intensity against frequency signal.

A nucleus is surrounded by circulating electrons, each of which creates a magnetic field that acts in opposition to the external magnetic field; thus, the nucleus is shielded from the applied magnetic field by the electron cloud. Different degrees of shielding require different frequencies in order to attain resonance, and, in this way, the different chemical environments can be discriminated. Nuclei which are deshielded resonate at higher frequencies, and nuclei which are shielded resonate at lower frequencies.

The frequency differences between nuclei in different chemical environments are plotted in an NMR spectrum as chemical shift. Chemical shift (δ) is a relative measure of frequency (v) in parts per million:

$$\delta = \frac{v - v_{\text{ref}}}{v_{\text{ref}}}$$

where the reference compound for proton and carbon NMR is tetramethylsilane, and the chemical shift for this compound is defined arbitrarily as 0.0 ppm.

Both ^{1}H and ^{13}C NMR are routinely used for the identification of organic compounds. ^{1}H is more powerful than ^{13}C NMR for two reasons: first, ^{1}H NMR is more sensitive than ^{13}C NMR because ^{13}C is not the dominant isotope of carbon and only exists in 1.1% abundance. ^{1}H is, however, the dominant isotope and naturally occurs in >99% abundance. Second, the signal intensity in ^{1}H NMR relates to the number of nuclei in a particular chemical environment, but this does not hold true for ^{13}C NMR.

NMR is increasingly used in the forensic analysis of unknown drug samples, particularly to elucidate the structure of the compound.

Chromatography

The International Union of Pure and Applied Chemistry (IUPAC) defines chromatography as 'a physical method of separation in which the components to be separated are distributed between two phases, one of which is stationary while the other moves in a definite direction.' Three different types of chromatography techniques are most commonly used in the analysis of drugs of abuse. Thin-layer chromatography (TLC), in which the stationary phase is coated onto an inert support and the mobile phase is a solvent or mixture of solvents, gas chromatography (GC), in which the mobile phase is a carrier gas and the stationary phase is a thin coating on the inside of a capillary column, and high-performance liquid chromatography (HPLC), in which the mobile phase is a liquid and the stationary phase a packed column containing silica. The choice of method normally depends on the laboratory procedure, analytical efficiency, and cost. Some drug compounds are susceptible to thermal degradation and are derivatized (i.e., their chemical structure is modified to impart greater stability) prior to analysis by GC. Derivatization is not required for analysis by HPLC.

Thin-Layer Chromatography

TLC is a technique which has the advantages of being both rapid and cheap. With TLC, the sample is separated according to the relative strength of interaction of the sample analytes with a stationary phase (often a silica plate) and a mobile phase (composed generally of a solvent mixture). The sample is prepared by dissolution in a small volume of a suitable solvent (often methanol). An ideal solvent for drug analysis is one in which the drug of interest is freely soluble, does not react with the drug or catalyze breakdown, and is volatile for easy concentration of the sample. The sample to be analyzed, together with positive and negative controls, should all be spotted onto the same TLC plate and developed in the usual manner.

After development, the plate is viewed under UV light and any visible spots recorded. Depending on the suspected class of drug present in the sample, other visualization techniques are commonly used, usually involving spraying the plates with reagents. The R_f values of the sample are compared with the controls run on the same plate, and they may also be compared with literature values using the same solvent system (though these should be interpreted with care).

High-Performance Liquid Chromatography

HPLC systems are generally comprised of a pump, an injector to introduce the sample, a column containing the stationary phase, a detector, and a recorder or other data handling system. The pump delivers the mobile phase through the system at high pressure. The sample is introduced into an injection port equipped with a fixed volume sample loop which ensures that the injection volume remains constant and reproducible for every injection. The column, usually 5–25 cm long with an internal diameter of 2–5 mm, is packed with adsorbent. In normal-phase chromatography, the stationary phase is polar and the mobile phase is less polar; in reversed-phase chromatography, the stationary phase is nonpolar and the mobile phase is polar.

UV detectors are the most commonly used type of HPLC detector. UV spectrophotometers monitor the light absorbed by the solute molecules from the incident beam. Absorbance in solution is proportional to concentration according to the Beer–Lambert law:

$$A = \log\left(\frac{I_0}{I_t}\right) = \varepsilon cl$$

where A is the absorbance (dimensionless), I_0 and I_t are the intensities of the incident and transmitted radiation, respectively, ε is the absorptivity (L cm^{-1} mol^{-1}), c is the concentration (mol L^{-1}), and l is the pathlength through the absorbing volume (cm).

Flow cells, which are of small volume and avoid excessive band broadening, are required. Typically, flow cells have a pathlength of 10 mm and a bore of 1 mm, resulting in a volume of 8 μl. There are two general types of UV detector in use for drug analysis: fixed wavelength and variable wavelength. Fixed-wavelength detectors use mercury vapor lamps to produce radiant energy which is passed through the sample. Variable-wavelength detectors utilize deuterium and tungsten lamps combined with manually adjustable diffraction grating monochromators to allow the user to choose the optimum wavelength. Photodiode array detectors (DADs) allow continuous scanning of the absorbance spectrum of the eluant. With this setup, all of the light (rather than single wavelengths) is passed through the sample. The transmitted light is then dispersed into single wavelengths which are simultaneously focused onto an array of up to 1056 photodiode detectors.

Gas Chromatography

In GC, the vaporized sample is transported by a carrier gas (the mobile phase) through a column containing the stationary phase. The column, which is heated in an oven, is where separation of the components of the injected sample occurs, and each component is detected when it elutes from the column. A variety of detectors can be used, but increasingly a mass spectrometer (MS) is favored.

In the injection port, the sample (usually 1–2 μl) is injected onto the column through a self-sealing rubber septum. The temperature of the injection port is such that the sample is immediately vaporized, ideally without thermal decomposition of the sample. Injections can be split or splitless. In both cases, a glass liner is positioned between the injection port and top of the column with a needle valve positioned between the liner and top of the column. The liner may also contain a plug of glass wool to trap nonvolatile components. In a split injection, the valve is opened to allow the majority of the sample to be vented to waste. Typically, only 1–2% of the sample enters the column with split ratios ranging from 1:10 to 1:100. Splitless injections require the split needle valve to be fully closed initially.

Normally, capillary columns are used for drug analysis consisting of a long length of tubing, typically 10–100 m, with a small internal diameter, 0.1–0.7 mm, which is coated with a thin layer of the stationary phase. Introduction of the GC effluent into the high vacuum of the MS can be achieved relatively easily when capillary columns are in use. Due to the narrow bore of the column, mobile phase flow rates are low (generally <2 ml min^{-1}) and the end of the column can be directly connected to the ion source of the MS. The interface between the GC and MS consists of a transfer line of glass or glass-lined metal which is also heated to prevent condensation of the analytes. The carrier gas is then pumped away by the vacuum system of the MS.

Quantitative Chromatographic Analysis

The area under a component peak is proportional to the concentration of the component in the sample. A simple method of quantification requires the peak area of a component to be expressed as a percentage of total peak area of all the components in the sample. The accuracy of this method, however, depends on all the components being detected with the same sensitivity.

The use of external standards allows precise and rapid quantification of an unknown component, so long as the detector has a linear response for the encountered concentration(s) of the unknown component. An internal standard can be added to the sample matrix itself to achieve quantification as well as compensate for slight variations in injection volumes. Component peak areas are then divided by the internal standard's peak area and the resulting 'normalized' peak area used for quantification or comparison of components between samples.

HPLC and gas chromatography mass spectroscopy (GCMS) are both commonly used for quantitative analysis of drugs of abuse, and GCMS is generally used for impurity identification in drug profiling.

Mass Spectrometry

MS is a technique used for the identification of compounds by determination of molecular weight as well as detection of positions within the molecule at which fragmentation can occur during ionization. MSs have three main components: an ion source for ionizing the sample, a magnetic sector for separating the ionized particles according to mass-to-charge ratio (m/z), and a detector. Two methods are used for the ionization of molecules: electron impact (EI) and chemical ionization. EI is most commonly used, so only this method will be addressed here. In EI MS, an organic molecule is bombarded with electrons and converted to a positively charged ion; loss of an electron from this starting molecule leads to a radical cation, which is called the molecular ion or parent ion and is denoted by $M^{+\bullet}$. The molecular ion is then broken apart into fragment or daughter ions. The molecular ion usually breaks up into a pair of fragments:

$$M^{+\bullet} \rightarrow m_1^+ + m_2^\bullet \quad \text{or} \quad m_1^{+\bullet} + m_2.$$

All of these ions are subjected to a variable magnetic field where they are separated according to their mass and charge (which is usually one) in a high vacuum. At the collector, each ion generates a current in proportion to its relative abundance. This current is then converted and plotted as relative abundance against the mass-to-charge ratio (m/z) of the ion. Neutral particles, such as $m^\bullet$ or m, cannot be detected.

The electrons used to fragment the sample molecule are produced by a heated tungsten filament. The number and energy of electrons emitted are dependent on the temperature and potential of the filament, respectively. At low potential (10 V), fragmentation does not occur so readily, which is useful for determination of molecular weight since the molecular ion tends to dominate the spectrum. At higher potential (70 V), structural determination is better achieved due to extensive fragmentation.

The ion source, which is heated at 200–250 °C, is kept at low pressure. This helps prevent collisions between sample molecules and ions, reduces background spectra, and maintains the mean free path of the ions within the source.

The mass analyzer, which separates ions according to their m/z ratio, is commonly a quadrupole consisting of four conducting rods positioned parallel to the direction of travel of the ions. Adjacent rods are of opposite charge. By application of a fixed direct current (DC) potential and an oscillating radio frequency (rf) field, an electric field is generated within the region bound by the four rods. This causes the ions to travel in spiral paths, and the DC:rf ratio is set so that the ions within a narrow m/z range, typically 0.8 m/z, reach the detector without colliding with the rods. Ions outside this narrow range collide with the rods and are not detected. In scanning mode, the DC:rf ratio is varied so that ions with increasing m/z reach the detector. In a technique such as GCMS, the quadrupole mass analyzer has a fast scan rate of up to 780 mass units per second which achieves the full mass spectrum for each eluted component.

After separation of ions according to m/z, they are detected and their relative abundance recorded. The detector consists of a glass tube drawn out into multiplication tubes with ring-shaped electrodes, called dynodes, along the length of the tube. These dynodes are coated with a substrate, typically PbO, which readily emits secondary electrons. The ion beam from the mass analyzer is attracted to the multiplication tube by application of a high voltage (−2600 to −3500 V). Ions collide with the dynodes, thus causing emission of one or more secondary electrons. These electrons are accelerated along the tube and further collisions occur, resulting in the emission of more secondary electrons. In this way, the original low-intensity ion beam is amplified, usually in the order of 10^5–10^7.

Isotope Ratio Mass Spectrometry

In recent years, considerable attention has been paid to the applications of IRMS in forensic science, including the analysis of drugs of abuse.

Isotopes of an element have different mass numbers (i.e., the same number of protons but a different number of neutrons in their nuclei). The lighter isotope (lower mass number) usually dominates in natural abundance, with one or more heavier isotopes existing in less than a few percent. The dominant isotope is often referred to as the major isotope, with the heavier isotope(s) called the minor isotope(s). Normally, IRMS analysis of drugs of abuse involves the determination of the relative isotope abundances of hydrogen (^1H and ^2H), carbon (^{12}C and ^{13}C), nitrogen (^{14}N and N^{15}), and oxygen (^{16}O, ^{17}O, and ^{18}O). The terrestrial isotope ratios were determined when the earth was formed and are, for the most part, fixed. Compartmentally (e.g., between species or climatic regions), isotope ratios vary constantly as a result of biological, biochemical, chemical, and physical processes. Any such process which changes the relative abundances of an element's isotopes is called isotopic fractionation. Two different types of effects result in isotopic fractionation: kinetic isotope effects (KIEs) and thermodynamic isotope effects (TIEs).

KIEs, or mass discriminating effects, are due to differences in reaction rates as a result of different bond strengths between heavier and lighter elements. Statistical models predict that lighter isotopes form weaker bonds; therefore, lighter isotopes are more reactive and will be concentrated in the products, while the heavier isotopes will be concentrated in the reactants. When this occurs, the effect is said to be *normal*. If, on the other hand, the products are enriched with the heavier isotopes and the reactants with the lighter ones, the effect is termed *inverse*.

Isotope fractionation is associated with differences in melting point, boiling point, vapor pressure, IR absorption, and other physicochemical properties. In contrast with KIEs, TIEs are evident in processes in which chemical bonds are neither broken nor formed.

IRMS measures natural-abundance isotope ratios *relative* to a standard; it does not measure absolute natural abundance.

Data are generally quoted as delta values, δ, which can be calculated by the following equation:

$$\delta^{13}C = 1000\left(\frac{R_{samp}}{R_{std}} - 1\right),$$

where R_{samp} is the ratio of the number of atoms of the heavy isotope to the number of atoms of the light isotope of an element and R_{std} is the equivalent ratio corresponding to the standard. Because differences in isotope abundance ratios between the sample and the standard are typically only 0.001–0.05%, δ values include multiplication by 1000 for ease of discussion and are therefore quoted 'per mill' (‰). A negative δ value indicates the sample is enriched in the light isotope relative to the standard, and a positive δ value indicates the sample is enriched in the heavy isotope relative to the standard.

Natural abundances of isotopes vary constantly despite fixed whole earth isotope abundances. Given that the synthesis of most illicit substances starts with a natural product (e.g., safrole from the sassafras tree in the case of 3,4-methylenedioxymethylamphetamine (MDMA), coca leaf in the case of cocaine, and opium from poppies in the case of heroin), the isotopic fractionation occurring in these plants may play an important role in determining the final isotopic composition of a specific product.

Analysis of a plant's natural carbon isotope abundance can allow determination of the pathway by which the plant fixes (or assimilates) atmospheric CO_2 into carbohydrate. For example, plants that assimilate CO_2 by the Calvin cycle, that is, they convert CO_2 into carbohydrates via the three-carbon-chain molecule phosphoglyceric acid, are called C_3 plants. These plants generally have $\delta^{13}C$ values of −34‰ to −24‰. Plants that assimilate CO_2 by the Hatch–Slack cycle, that is, they convert CO_2 into carbohydrates via the four-chain molecule oxaloacetic acid, are called C_4 plants. Plants with this type generally have $\delta^{13}C$ values of −16‰ to −9‰. Humidity, temperature, isotopic composition of the soil, and isotopic composition of CO_2 also affect these $\delta^{13}C$ values.

Hydrogen and oxygen isotope abundances of terrestrial waters are affected by evaporation. For example, citrus trees growing in subtropical climates may be subjected to extensive evaporation which causes ^{2}H enrichment in the cellular water of the fruit. Variation in nitrogen isotope abundance is caused by many chemical and physical processes, resulting in variable isotope ratios of common materials.

The IRMS system can be interfaced with different sample preparation techniques, which allow either bulk stable isotope analysis (BSIA) or compound-specific isotope analysis (CSIA) to be undertaken. BSIA measures the isotope ratios for the sample as a whole. If carbon is the target element for analysis, then the $^{13}C/^{12}C$ ratio returned by the instrument will represent *all* of the carbon atoms in *every* compound present in the sample. CSIA measures the isotope ratio for one compound in the sample. The separation of the sample can be achieved by the coupling of the IRMS to a GC instrument. In this case, the sample is dissolved in an organic solvent and injected onto the first GC column. Baseline separation of the peaks is essential, as accurate determination of isotope ratios cannot be achieved from a partial GC peak.

Conclusions

Most analysis of drugs of abuse is undertaken using conventional analytical techniques. The implementation of techniques such as IRMS has specific values in drug profiling but is not used for routine analysis. In selecting the appropriate analytical regime, a balance must be struck between required laboratory efficiencies and desired scientific result to the specific task at hand (e.g., identification, quantification, and intelligence).

See also: **Chemistry/Trace/Drugs of Abuse**: Clandestine Laboratories; Classification; Designer Drugs.

Further Reading

Besacier F, Chaudron-Thozet H, Rousseau-Tsangaris M, Girard J, and Lamotte A (1997) Comparative chemical analyses of drug samples: General approach and application to heroin. *Forensic Science International* 85(2): 113–125.

Braithwaite A and Smith FJ (1996) *Chromatographic Methods*, 5th edn. Glasgow: Blackie Academic & Professional.

Carter JF, Titterton EL, Grant H, and Sleeman R (2002) Isotopic changes during the synthesis of amphetamines. *Chemical Communications* 21: 2590–2591.

Carter JF, Titterton EL, Murray M, and Sleeman R (2002) Isotopic characterisation of 3,4-methylenedioxyamphetamine and 3,4-methylenedioxymethylamphetamine (ecstasy). *Analyst* 127: 830–833.

Casale J, Casale E, Collins M, Morello D, Cathapermal S, and Panicker S (2006) Stable isotope analyses of heroin seized from the merchant vessel Pong Su. *Journal of Forensic Sciences* 51(3): 603–606.

Desage M, Guilluy R, Brazier JL, et al. (1991) Gas-chromatography with mass-spectrometry or isotope-ratio mass-spectrometry in studying the geographical origin of heroin. *Analytica Chimica Acta* 247(2): 249–254.

Kurashima N, Makino Y, Sekita S, Urano Y, and Nagano T (2004) Determination of origin of ephedrine used as precursor for illicit methamphetamine by carbon and nitrogen stable isotope ratio analysis. *Analytical Chemistry* 76(14): 4233–4236.

Lurie IS and Wittwer JD Jr. (1983) *High-Performance Liquid Chromatography in Forensic Chemistry*, vol. 24. New York: Marcel Dekker.

Mas F, Beemsterboer B, Veltkamp AC, and Verweij AMA (1995) Determination of common-batch members in a set of confiscated 3,4-(methylendioxy) methylamphetamine samples by measuring the natural isotope abundances – A preliminary study. *Forensic Science International* 71(3): 225–231.

Meier-Augenstein W and Liu RH (2004) Forensic applications of isotope ratio mass spectrometry. In: Yinon J (ed.) *Advances in Forensic Applications of Mass Spectrometry*, pp. 149–180. Boca Raton, FL: CRC Press.

Palhol F, Lamoureux C, Chabrillat M, and Naulet N (2004) $^{15}N/^{14}N$ isotopic ratio and statistical analysis: An efficient way of linking seized ecstasy tablets. *Analytica Chimica Acta* 510(1): 1–8.

Willard HH, Merritt LL Jr., Dean JA, and Settle FA Jr. (1988) *Instrumental Methods of Analysis*, 7th edn. Belmont, CA: Wadsworth Publishers.

Classification

N NicDaéid and KA Savage, University of Strathclyde, Glasgow, UK

Introduction

Drugs can be classified depending upon how they are derived. This classification is as natural products, semisynthetic drugs, synthetic drugs, and designer drugs. Natural drugs are active ingredients and/or secondary metabolic products of plants and other living systems that may be isolated by extraction (e.g., morphine). Semisynthetic drugs are products from natural sources, which are subject to some chemical process to modify their structure (e.g., diamorphine or cocaine). Synthetic drugs are artificially produced substances for the licit or illicit market that are almost wholly manufactured from chemical compounds in a laboratory (e.g., amphetamine and benzodiazepines). Designer drugs are substances, either natural or synthetic, whose molecular structure has been modified in order to optimize their effect, on the one hand, and in order to bypass laws and regulations governing the control of substances, on the other hand.

Natural Drugs

Cannabis

Cannabis is the most consumed illicit drug in the world, and therefore the subject of the most illegal trafficking in one form or another. The botanical name of cannabis is *Cannabis sativa* and it is referred to as marijuana (herbal cannabis) and hashish (cannabis resin), terms associated with cannabis grown for its illicit use, or as hemp, a term usually associated with *Cannabis* plants grown for their fiber content.

Cannabis is native to the mountainous areas of central and south Asia and the plant has been used by man for over 6000 years. *Cannabis* grows over a wide variety of geographic terrains, altitudes, and latitudes. It is grown in many countries and on all continents. Although it prefers the higher temperatures and longer growing seasons of the equatorial areas of the world, it has been cultivated as far north as 60° latitude. With the more recent prevalence for hydroponic growth, *Cannabis* is known to be grown in 172 countries around the globe.

Cannabis and its related products comprise over three quarters of the drug materials submitted to Forensic Science Laboratories in the United Kingdom for analysis. A number of forms of the drug may be encountered, including plant material, resin, and 'hash oil.' The active ingredient in all of these is Δ^9-tetrahydrocannabinol (THC). Also found is Δ^9-tetrahydrocannabinolic acid (THCOOH), which is converted to THC through smoking. Also present are the compounds Δ^8-tetrahydrocannabinol (an isomer of the active ingredient), cannabidiol (CBD – the precursor), and cannabinol (CBN – the metabolite), as well as upward of 50 minor cannabinols. The chemical structures of these compounds are presented in **Figure 1**.

Fresh plant material

Cannabis plant material can occur as live plants, or as dried plant material. It is important when examining plant material that it should be in the dried state as water content will affect any weight measurements, a crucial factor in determining the seriousness of any charges. Male and female *Cannabis* plants are separate, with the male plant flowering before the female to ensure cross-pollination. The plant grows between 30 cm and 6 m in height and grows from seed to maturity in about 3 months, though harvesting can occur after 2 months. The leaves are palmate with serrated edges and are opposite and alternate around a hollow four-cornered stem. The leaves are coated with upward-pointing unicellular hairs called trichomes. Nonglandular trichomes are found on the stems and leaves together with a few glandular trichomes, which contain the THC. The greatest concentration of glandular trichomes are in the flowering tops of the plants and those of the female plant have a greater concentration of THC. Material prepared from the flowering tops or leaves is commonly called marijuana and usually contains 0.5–5% THC. *Cannabis* plants grown under controlled hydroponic conditions, which are predominantly female plants (skunk), generally have a higher quantity of THC (9–25%) and can reach full maturity in about 13 weeks.

Dried plant material

This may occur in various ways. Low-quality products contain stalks, seeds, leaves, and flowering tops. This may be compressed into blocks (West African and Caribbean material) as loose material or rolled up and wrapped in vegetable leaves (Central and Southern Africa). High-quality material contains mostly flowering tops and can be found rolled up or wrapped around bamboo sticks ('Buddha' or 'Thai' sticks) or sieved ('Kif') and generally originates from South East Asia or parts of Africa.

Resin

This is also produced directly from the plant material. The glandular trichomes produce a resin, which is scraped from the surface of the plant and pressed into blocks. Hashish contains about 2–10% by weight of the active constituent, Δ^9-THC. Most resin is produced either in the Indian subcontinent or parts of the Mediterranean. Usually between 100 and 400 mg of resin are used in a joint, though this varies from user to user. Mediterranean resin is made by threshing the herbal material, sieving to remove seeds and stems, and the remainder compressed into slabs. The final material is light in color and quite brittle. Indian subcontinent resin is quite sticky and is removed from the plant by rubbing the plant and then molded into slabs. The final material is dark brown and sticky. When examining resin, several facts are recorded, including

 http://dx.doi.org/10.1016/B978-0-12-382165-2.00077-5

whether or not the blocks seized fit together, any striation marks (cutting marks) which may be present, and whether these can they be linked to a cutting instrument. The color and different layers within the resin block should also be examined and recorded. Packaging material (commonly cling film) can also be examined for physical fits linking blocks together.

Hash oil

This is a manufactured product of cannabis and is produced by extracting the whole plant material using an organic solvent (usually alcohol, ether, or benzene). On extraction the resulting oil can contain between 10 and 30% by weight of Δ^9-THC. The oil is used in various ways including smoking in special pipes with tobacco.

The effect caused by cannabis depends largely on the expectations, moods, and motivations of the user. The most sought after effects are pleasurable sensations and greater sensory awareness, though inexperienced users on high doses can experience psychological distress. In general, *Cannabis* is recognized by the characteristics of the plant including odor, shape, and presence of trichomes.

Mushrooms and Cacti

Psilocybin and *psilocin* are found in at least 15 species of mushrooms – so-called 'magic mushrooms' – belonging to the genera *Psilocybe*, *Panaeolus*, and *Conocybe*. If a seizure contains whole or parts of mushrooms, the examination should include a description of the shape, size, and color of the fungus, as well as information regarding the gills, spores, cap, and stalk. Identification of fungi is difficult and should be performed by experts in that field. Illicit trafficking of cacti, which contain the psychoactive agent, mescaline, is also known. This drug occurs in at least three species of cacti. The most common illicit form of mescaline is produced as dried disk-shaped cuttings taken from the tops of the cacti and called 'mescal buttons.' The main compounds are presented in **Figure 2**.

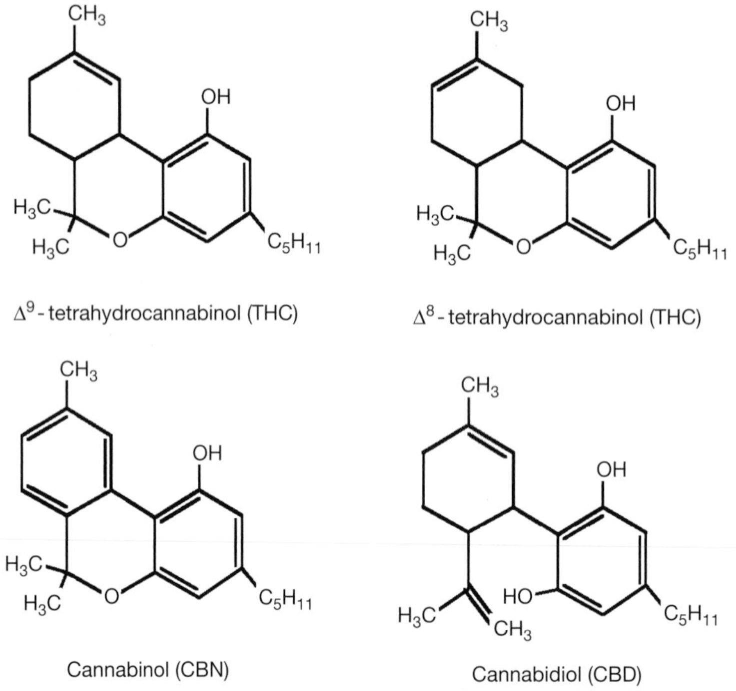

Δ^9 - tetrahydrocannabinol (THC)

Δ^8 - tetrahydrocannabinol (THC)

Cannabinol (CBN)

Cannabidiol (CBD)

Figure 1 Chemical structures of the main cannabinoids.

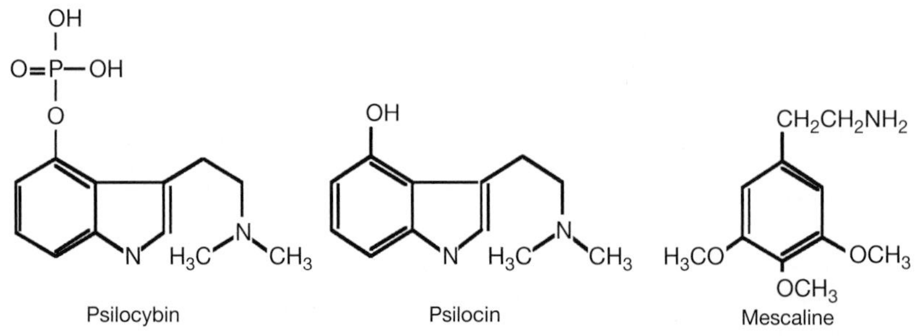

Psilocybin

Psilocin

Mescaline

Figure 2 Chemical structure of psilocybin, psilocin, and mescaline.

Semisynthetic Drugs

Opiates

Opium is a natural product obtained from unripe poppy capsules. There are over 100 species of the genus *Papaver* (or poppy) known; however, only two, *Papaver somniferum* and *Papaver setigerum* D.C., are known to produce opium.

An incision is made in the poppy capsule, and the latex which oozes from the incision is scraped-off and collected to produce a raw opium gum. When fresh, the material is a sticky tar-like brown substance with a liquorice-like odor, which becomes brittle as it dries. Raw opium is a complex mixture containing sugars, proteins, lipids, and water, as well as the active alkaloid compounds (10–20%). About 40 alkaloids are known and fall broadly into two categories:

- Phenanthrene alkaloids such as morphine, codeine, and thebaine
- Isoquinoline alkaloids such as papaverine and noscapine

The relative amounts of these alkaloids vary and are dependent on factors such as climate, soil fertility, altitude, available moisture, and age of the plant.

Raw opium can be used for smoking but must first be extracted most commonly with water. Morphine can still be detected in the leftover dross that remains in the opium pipe. Several purification processes can be used in the preparation of crude morphine from raw opium. Morphine-free base is further refined to produce diamorphine. Because of the nature of the raw opium starting material, the production process, and the addition of excipients to produce 'street' heroin samples, there can be a considerable intersample variation. The main alkaloids encountered in heroin street samples are presented in Figure 3.

Cocaine

Cocaine is derived from ecgonine alkaloids in the leaf of the coca (*Erythroxylon*) plant. There are various varieties of plant which produce leaves of different size and appearance. In all

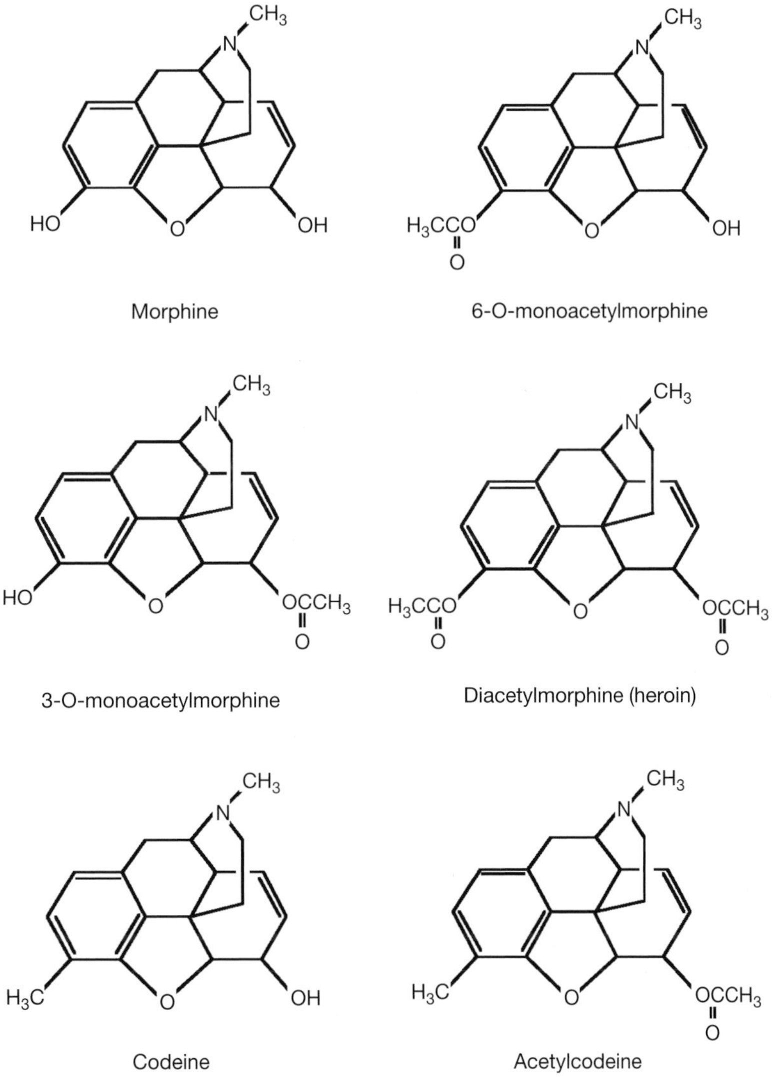

Figure 3 Chemical structures of common opiates.

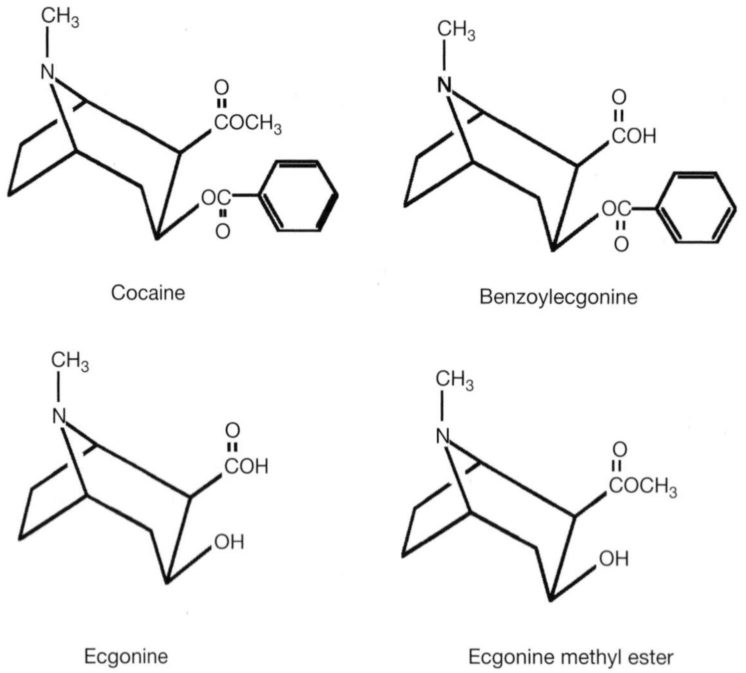

Cocaine

Benzoylecgonine

Ecgonine

Ecgonine methyl ester

Figure 4 Chemical structures of cocaine and analogs.

species, the upper side of the leaf is darker in color. The underside of the leaf has two lines running parallel to the midrib of the leaf and is considered characteristic of the coca leaf. The production of cocaine from the plant is via an intermediate stage producing coca paste.

Coca leaves are mixed with calcium hydroxide (lime) and water. The mixture is crushed and stirred in a hydrocarbon solvent, usually kerosene. The extracted coca leaf residue is removed and the kerosene extracted with acidified water. The cocaine alkaloids (presented in **Figure** 4) are extracted into the aqueous layer and coca paste is precipitated by the addition of base. This paste contains crude cocaine as well as a mixture of inorganic salts and is further refined to extract cocaine.

Tryptamines

Tryptamines (**Figure** 5) are naturally occurring alkaloids found in a variety of plants and life forms around the world and exist in more than 1500 natural varieties. The basic element of tryptamine is the indol-structure and tryptamine itself is an endogenous amine found in the human brain; for example, serotonin and melatonin are two essential tryptamines present as neurotransmitters in the brain. Tryptamines can also be produced either completely synthetically or semisynthetically.

The main tryptamines found on the illicit market are dimethyltryptamine (DMT) and bufotenin. DMT is an active component of various South American snuff products, such as 'COHOBA' and 'YOPO' and has been produced synthetically for a number of years. Its abuse has been restricted to a small number of dedicated users. Bufotin is chemically very similar to DMT and can be found either in the skin secretions of toads or in combinations with DMT in different trees in South America (e.g., the YOPO tree).

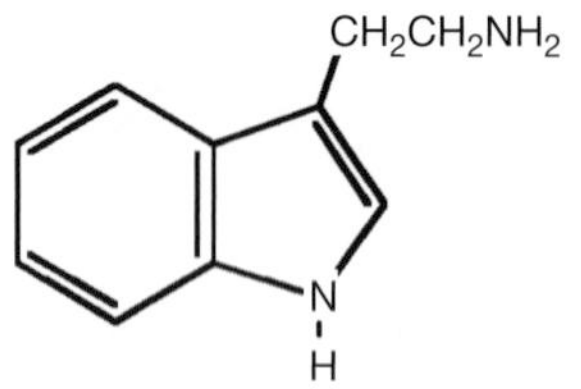

$CH_2CH_2NH_2$

Figure 5 Tryptamine structure.

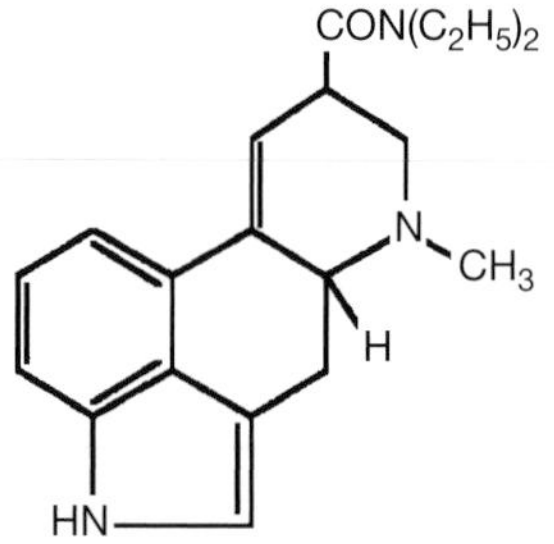

$CON(C_2H_5)_2$

Figure 6 Chemical structure of LSD.

Lysergic acid diethylamide (LSD) (**Figure** 6) is a semisynthetic drug incorporating the tryptamine structure and first synthesized by Albert Hofmann in 1938. The starting materials are lysergic acid compounds derived from ergot spores of some mushrooms. On the illicit drug market, LSD has been sold impregnated as an alcohol solution onto paper (blotters acids 'trade marked' with various designs), microdots, thin squares of gelatine (window panes), or impregnated on sugar cubes.

Synthetic Drugs

Amphetamine and Amphetamine-Type Stimulants

Amphetamine-type stimulants (ATS) drugs are generally divided into two groups, the amphetamines group (amphetamine sulfate and methylamphetamine) and the ecstasy group (methylenedioxy methyl amphetamine (MDMA), methylenedioxy amphetamine (MDA), methylenedioxy ethyl amphetamine (MDEA), MDE). ATS precursor and pre-precursor chemicals are also controlled. From a chemical point of view, all ATS are related to β-phenethylamine, which is the basic element of neurotransmitters in the body (such as dopamine and adrenaline).

The most common amphetamine derivatives (**Figure 7**) available on the illicit drug market include amphetamine sulfate, methylamphetamine, MDA, MDMA, and MDEA. Dosages in powders and tablets vary considerably but are generally in the range of 10–110 mg of drug in a single dose. Street samples of amphetamine sulfate typically contain as little as 5% drug, whereas ecstasy tablets can be up to 56–60% pure. Most, if not all, amphetamine and related compounds are synthesized in clandestine laboratories by various synthetic routes.

Ecstasy group

When the term Ecstasy was first used in the early 1970s, it was an American street name for preparations containing the active agent MDMA. Now the term describes tablets or capsules predominantly containing one or more (or combinations) of psychotropic active agents derived from the β-phenethylamine group. It is becoming more and more common to compress amphetamine/methamphetamine into tablets which are then also marketed as ecstasy. In more recent years, other relatively new ATS are appearing in tablets. These include para-methoxymethamphatamine and PMA (3,4-methylenedioxy-phenylpropan-2-ol), ketamine (an anesthetic used in veterinary medicine), and even gamma-hydroxybutyric acid (GHB).

Amphetamine group

Amphetamine was first synthesized in 1887 but was not used for medical purposes until the early 1930s, when it was found that it increased blood pressure, stimulated the central nervous system, was effective against asthma, and useful in treating epileptic seizure disorders. On the illicit drug market, amphetamines have been sold in the form of powders, liquids, crystals, tablets, and capsules.

Barbiturates

Barbiturates (**Figure 8**) are therapeutically used as sedatives, hypnotics, anesthetics, and anticonvulsants. Virtually all barbiturates on the illicit drug market come from licit sources. There are 12 barbiturates recognized and scheduled by the United Nations and occur mainly as capsules and tablets and in some cases as injectable solutions. Illicit compounds occur as mixtures of barbiturates, or mixed with other drugs such as caffeine, aspirin, codeine, or, in some cases, heroin.

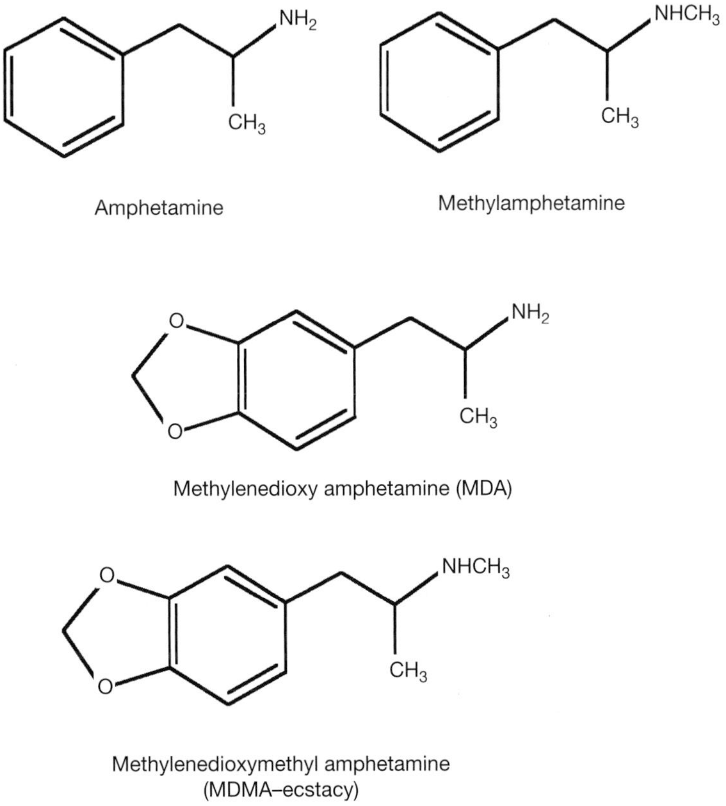

NH_2 CH_3

Amphetamine

$NHCH_3$ CH_3

Methylamphetamine

O O NH_2 CH_3

Methylenedioxy amphetamine (MDA)

O O $NHCH_3$ CH_3

Methylenedioxymethyl amphetamine
(MDMA–ecstacy)

Figure 7 Amphetamine and related compounds.

Methaqualone and Meclaqualone

Methaqualone was first synthesized in 1951 and introduced as a new drug that produced sedation and sleep in 1956. Methaqualone has been initially designed to counter the nervous damage caused by long-term consumption of barbiturates and to reduce the risk of dependency on barbiturates. Methaqualone and meclaqualone were also prepared as nonbarbiturate sleeping tablets, though they have also legally been used as hypnotics in some European countries. Interest in methaqualone has risen dramatically in recent years. Its popularity was due to its undeserved reputation as an 'aphrodisiac' often in combination with diphenhydramine. Methaqualone was effectively removed from the market in 1984 because of its strong addiction-forming properties. Their structures are presented in Figure 9.

They appear on the illicit drug market either through diversion from the legitimate pharmaceutical trade or through illicit synthesis. The illicit samples are usually brown or gray powders with varying degrees of purity. Methaqualone is also used sometimes as a cutting agent for heroin.

Benzodiazepines

Benzodiazepines (**Figure 10**), therapeutically used as tranquillizers, hypnotics, anticonvulsants, and centrally acting muscle relaxants, rank among the most frequently prescribed drugs. In 1960, the first benzodiazepine, chlordiazepoxide, was introduced. To date, more than 50 benzodiazepines have been marketed in over 100 different preparations. They appear mainly as capsules and tablets; however, some are marketed in other forms such as injectable solutions or powders. Benzodiazepines were introduced to replace barbiturates and methaqualone as tranquillizers, hypnotics, anticonvulsants, and muscle relaxants. Currently, there are 33 benzodiazepines on the control list all of which appear as tablets or capsules, though some also appear as vials or powders for preparation for injection.

On the illicit drug market, diazepam ('Valium'), temazepam (often referred to as 'jellies'), and flunitrazepam ('Rohypnol') are used as drug substitutes, as additives in drug preparations, or in combination with alcohol, as methods of incapacitating individuals ('Rohypnol' is sometimes known as a 'date rape drug'). Virtually all benzodiazepines on the illicit market result from diversion from legitimate sources and there is no evidence of clandestine manufacture.

Phencyclidine and Analogues

Phencyclidine (PCP) was synthesized and tested in the early 1950s and recommended for clinical trials as an anesthetic in humans in 1957. In 1965, further human clinical investigation of PCP was discontinued and the compound was marketed commercially as a veterinary anesthetic. PCP became available through the drug culture in the late 1960s, referred as 'PeaCePill,' commonly sold as 'angel dust,' 'crystal,' or 'hog' in powder, tablet, leaf mixture, and 1 g 'rock' crystal forms, usually taken orally, by smoking, snorting, or intravenous injection. The laboratory synthesis of PCP and approximately 120 related substances, such as Eticyclidin (PCE) or Tenocyclidin (TCP), is cheap but also work intensive and time consuming.

A structurally related anesthetic, ketamine ('special K'), has been developed and has gained popularity in recent years.

Gamma-Hydroxybutyric Acid

GHB is a drug that is very similar to a natural chemical in the human brain called gamma-aminobutyric acid. GHB is a simple sodium (or potassium) salt of 4-gamma-hydroxybutyric acid. The street names are 'liquid E,' 'liquid ecstasy,' or 'fantasy' and is currently not listed as a controlled substance. The forms of use are tablets, white powder, or dissolved in water or other liquids. GHB (like Rohypnol) is sometimes added to alcoholic drinks as methods of incapacitating individuals and is also known as a 'date rape drug.'

H N O O NH R1 R2 O

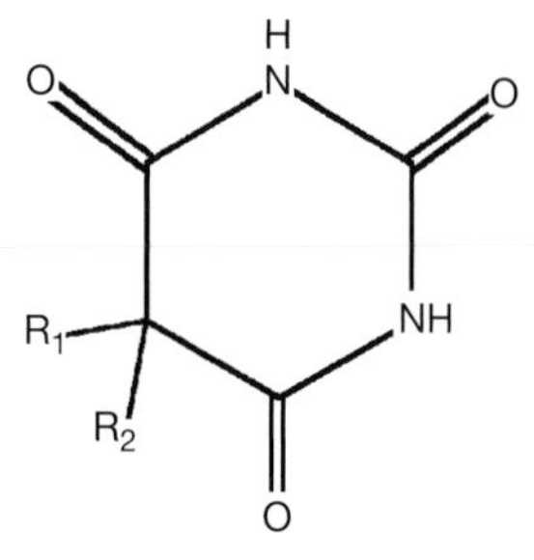

Figure 8 Barbiturate structure.

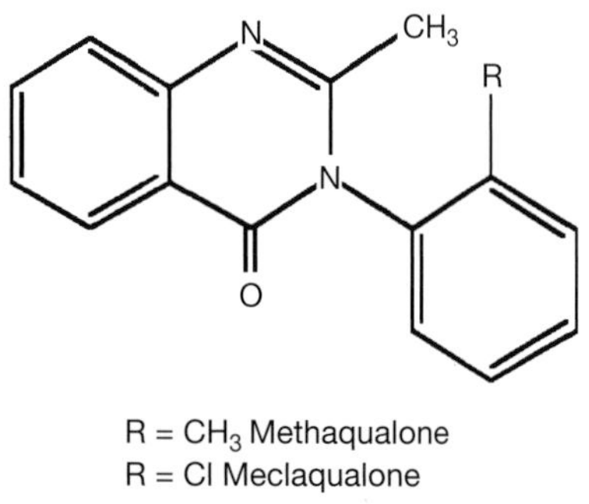

N CH3 R N O

R = CH_3 Methaqualone
R = Cl Meclaqualone

Figure 9 Methaqualone and meclaqualone.

R2 R3 N R4 R1 N R5

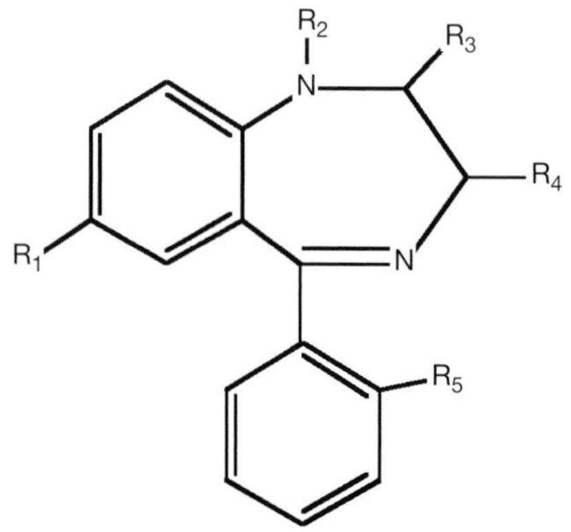

Figure 10 Benzodiazapine structure.

Originally GHB was marketed as a supplement replacement for L-tryptophan (an amino acid). Since the early 1990s, it has been illicitly used by athletes and bodybuilders believing that its growth hormone releasing effects contribute to anabolism and lipolysis, or misused as a sleep aid and for weight control.

GHB can be very easily prepared from gamma butyrolactone – a common industrial chemical for paint removers – by alkaline hydrolysis. The clandestine manufacture of GHB requires no prior chemical expertise as evidenced by the simplistic instructions given in the underground publications or on the Internet.

'Legal Highs'

'Legal highs' have the same or similar effects as illegal drugs, but are structurally different enough from the drugs that they mimic to avoid control under the Misuse of Drugs Act. In order to circumvent the Medicines Act, they are sold as, for example, plant food or bath salts. Legal highs are widely available over the Internet and may be known as, for example, 'legal marijuana,' Spice, NRG, Ivory Wave.

Mephedrone is a synthetic compound similar to methcathinone, the active ingredient in Khat, and has been found in some legal high substances. Mephedrone may be known as M-Cat, Miew-miew, among other names. Mephedrone has recently been classified as an illegal Class B drug.

See also: **Chemistry/Trace/Drugs of Abuse:** Analysis of Controlled Substances; **Chemistry/Trace/Fire Investigation:** Interpretation of Fire Debris Analysis.

Further Reading

Karch SB (2007) *A Drug Abuse Handbook*. Boca Raton, FL: CRC Press.

King LA (2009) *Forensic Chemistry of Substance Misuse*. Cambridge: Royal Society of Chemistry.

Laing R (ed.) (2003) *Hallucinogens a Forensic Drug Handbook*. London: Academic Press.

Moffat AC, Osselton MD, and Widdop B (2004) *Clarke's Analysis of Drugs and Poisons*, 3rd edn. London: Pharmacutical Press.

Designer Drugs

S Fu and N Stojanovska, University of Technology Sydney, Broadway, NSW, Australia

Glossary

Adulterant Any material that lessens the purity or effectiveness of a substance, especially a pharmacologically active drug.

Date-rape An act of sexual intercourse regarded as tantamount to rape, especially if the victim was under the influence of alcohol or other drugs.

Designer drug A drug with properties and effects similar to a known illicit or prohibited drug but having a slightly altered chemical structure, especially such a drug created in order to evade legislative controls.

Herbal High A recreational drug mixture consisting mainly of natural and/or synthetically derived compounds producing drug-like effects.

Smart Shops/Head Shops Retail outlets specializing in drug paraphernalia (e.g., pipes to smoke cannabis) used for the consumption/ingestion of recreational drugs.

Spice A mixture of plant materials fortified with synthetic chemicals that mimic the effect of cannabis when smoked by users.

Introduction

The term designer drug is used to describe drugs that are modified in an attempt to circumvent legislative controls. This is usually done by modifying the chemical structure of current illegal drugs or by finding drugs with entirely different chemical structures that have similar subjective effects to current recreational/illicit drugs. Besides the classic examples of amphetamine (AP)-type designer drugs such as 3,4-methylenedioxyamphetamine (MDA) and 3,4-methylenedioxymethamphetamine (MDMA), which have been widely abused for decades, a number of new drug classes have appeared on the illicit drug market in recent years. These new drug classes include 2,5-dimethoxy amphetamines, 2,5-phenylamines (2C drugs), β-keto amphetamines (cathinones), phencyclidines, piperazines, pyrrolidinophenones, fentanyls, piperidines, and tryptamine derivatives. A number of 'Herbal Highs' such as 'Kratom,' a *Mitragyna* plant native to Thailand and other southeast Asian countries, and more recently 'Spice,' which contains added synthetic cannabinoids, have also been encountered in many illicit drug markets. Some designer steroids have emerged and are particularly popular among athletes seeking to avoid detection of steroidal abuse in order to gain unfair performance enhancement advantages. The chemical structures of some of these designer drugs are presented in **Figure 1** and **Table 1**.

The continual emergence and rapid spread of novel designer drugs not only pose a serious health risk to consumers due to the limited pharmacokinetics and toxicological data available but also present an ongoing challenge to forensic chemists, forensic toxicologists, and law enforcement agencies. To effectively combat the problems associated with designer drugs, a collective effort needs to be in place from forensic scientists, health professionals, and law enforcement authorities. It is important to stay at the forefront of drug detection techniques and strategies to allow speedy identification of new substances as they emerge. Metabolism and toxicity data need to be collected to facilitate diagnosis and treatment of designer drug-induced intoxication. At the same time, drug scheduling authorities need to schedule these drugs promptly to enable laws to be applied to the production, distribution, and consumption of these illicit substances to safeguard society.

Designer Drugs of Various Structural Types

AP-Type Designer Drugs

There are many designer drugs that are structural analogs of AP and methamphetamine (MA). The most common way for the construction of an AP-type designer drug is the introduction of *N*-alkyl substituents of a different size into the molecule of a parent drug of known activity. Consequently, a number of MDA homologues, such as MDMA, 3,4-methylenedioxyethylamphetamine (MDEA), *N*,*N*-dimethyl-3,4-methylenedioxyamphetamine (DMMDA), *N*-propyl-3,4-methylenedioxyamphetamine (*N*-propyl-MDA), and *N*-isopropyl-3,4-methylenedioxyamphetamine (*N*-isopropyl-MDA), were synthesized and introduced into the illicit drug market. In addition, benzodioxolylbutanamine (BDB) and *N*-methylbenzodioxolylbutanamine (MBDB) have also been encountered in recent years. *N*-Hydroxy analogs, such as *N*-hydroxy-MDA and *N*-hydroxy-MDMA, have recently been distributed as new designer drugs in some drug markets. These psychoactive drugs produce emotional and social effects similar to those of MDMA. Despite mostly producing stimulant effects, these drugs can commonly result in feelings of empathy, love, and emotional closeness to others.

A number of *N*-alkyl homologues of 4-methylthioamphetamine (4-MTA), including 4-methylthiomethamphetamine (4-MTMA), 4-methylthioethylamphetamine (4-MTEA), 4-methylthiodimethamphetamine (4-MTDMA), 4-methylthiopropylamphetamine (4-MTPA), and 4-methylthiobutylamphetamine (4-MTBA), some of which have been encountered as early as in the 1990s as research chemicals, are becoming more prevalent as designer drugs of abuse. In addition, the modification of *p*-methoxyamphetamine (PMA) to its *N*-methyl homologue, *p*-methoxymethylamphetamine (PMMA), has been performed several years ago. The presence of *N*-ethyl-4-methoxyamphetamine has also been identified in illicit samples in the United States. The effects resulting from the homologues of

 http://dx.doi.org/10.1016/B978-0-12-382165-2.00078-7

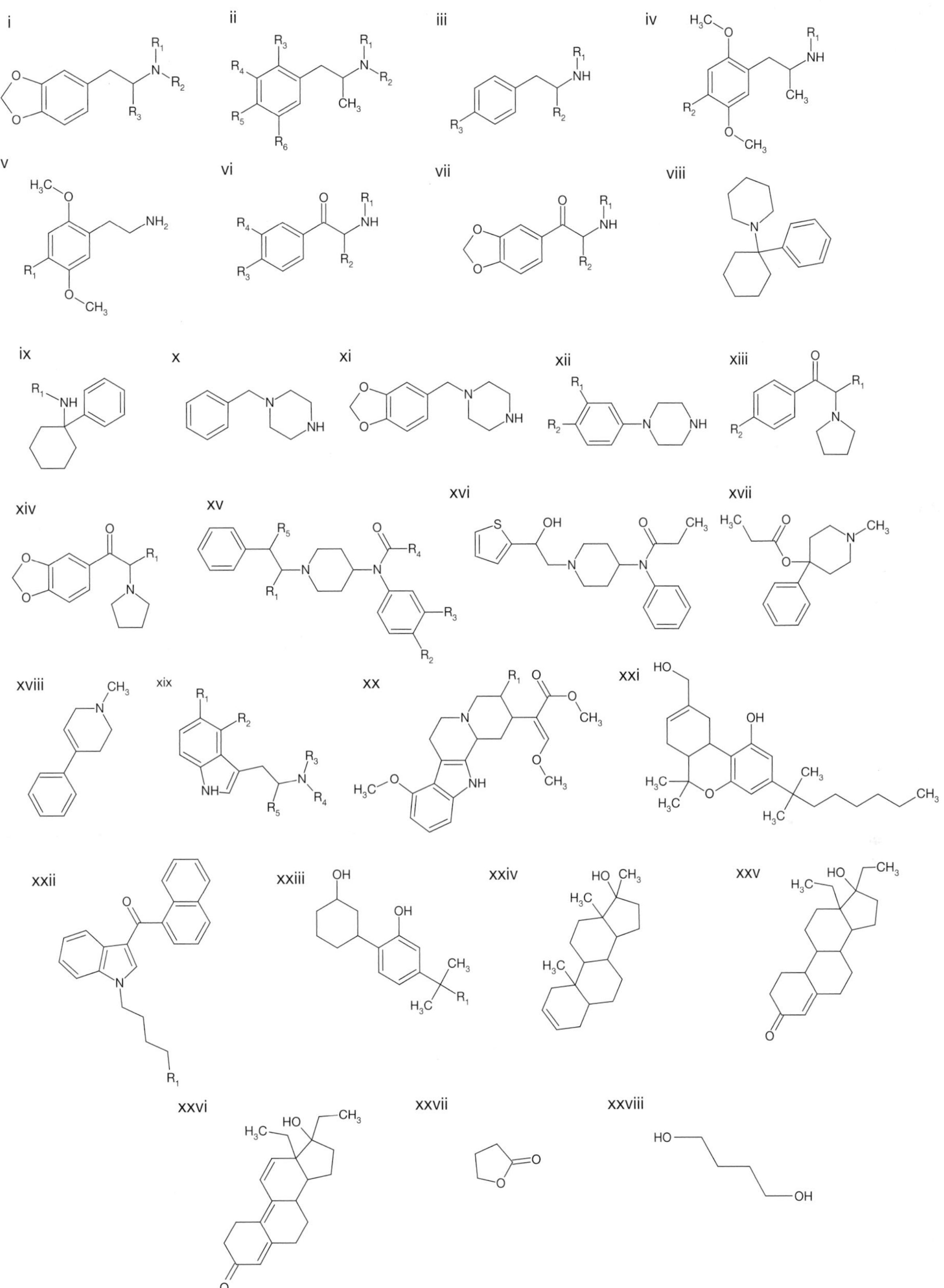

Figure 1 Structures of some common designer drugs. Amphetamine types (i–iii); 2,5-dimethoxy amphetamines (iv); 2,5-phenethylamines (v); β-keto amphetamines (vi, vii); phencyclidines (viii, ix); piperazines (x–xii); pyrrolidinophenones (xiii, xiv); fentanyls (xv, xvi); piperidines (xvii, xviii); tryptamines (xix); 'Kratom' alkaloids (xx); synthetic cannabinoids (xxi–xxiii); synthetic steroids (xxiv–xxvi); GHB-related substances (xxvii, xxviii).

Table 1 Names and chemical structures of common designer drugs with parent molecular features illustrated in **Figure 1**

Drug Name	*Parent structure*	*Substituents*					
		R_1	R_2	R_3	R_4	R_5	R_6
3,4-Methylenedioxyamphetamine (MDA)	i	—H	—H	—CH_3	–	–	–
3,4-Methylenedioxymethamphetamine (MDMA)		—CH_3	—H	—CH_3	–	–	–
3,4-Methylenedioxyethylamphetamine (MDEA)		—CH_2CH_3	—H	—CH_3	–	–	–
N,*N*-Dimethyl-MDA (DMMDA)		—CH_3	—CH_3	—CH_3	–	–	–
N-Propyl-MDA		—$CH_2CH_2CH_3$	—H	—CH_3	–	–	–
N-Isopropyl-MDA		—$CH(CH_3)_2$	—H	—CH_3	–	–	–
Benzodioxolylbutanamine (BDB)		—H	—H	—CH_2CH_3	–	–	–
N-Methylbenzodioxolylbutanamine (MBDB)		—CH_3	—H	—CH_2CH_3	–	–	–
N-Hydroxy-MDA		—OH	—H	—CH_3	–	–	–
N-Hydroxy-MDMA		—OH	—CH_3	—CH_3	–	–	–
4-Methylthioamphetamine (4-MTA)	ii	—H	—H	—H	—H	—S—CH_3	—H
4-Methylthiomethamphetamine (4-MTMA)		—CH_3	—H	—H	—H	—S—CH_3	—H
4-Methylthioethylamphetamine (4-MTEA)		—CH_2CH_3	—H	—H	—H	—S—CH_3	—H
4-Methylthiodimethamphetamine (4-MTDMA)		—CH_3	—CH_3	—H	—H	—S—CH_3	—H
4-Methylthiopropylamphetamine (4-MTPA)		—$CH_2CH_2CH_3$	—H	—H	—H	—S—CH_3	—H
4-Methylthiobutylamphetamine (4-MTBA)		—$CH_2CH_2CH_2CH_3$	—H	—H	—H	—S—CH_3	—H
p-Methoxyamphetamine (PMA)		—H	—H	—H	—H	—O—CH_3	—H
p-Methoxymethylamphetamine (PMMA)		—CH_3	—H	—H	—H	—O—CH_3	—H
2-Fluoroamphetamine		—H	—H	—F	—H	—H	—H
3-Fluoroamphetamine		—H	—H	—H	—F	—H	—H
4-Fluoroamphetamine		—H	—H	—H	—H	—F	—H
5-Fluoro-2-methoxyamphetamine		—H	—H	—O—CH_3	—H	—H	—F
3-Fluoro-4-methoxyamphetamine		—H	—H	—H	—F	—O—CH_3	—H
N-Methyl-4-fluoroamphetamine		—CH_3	—H	—H	—H	—F	—H
N-Ethyl-4-fluoroamphetamine		—CH_2CH_3	—H	—H	—H	—F	—H
N-Ethyl-4-methoxyamphetamine	iii	—CH_2CH_3	—CH_3	—O—CH_3	–	–	–
1-(4-Fluorophenyl)-butan-2-amine		—H	—CH_2CH_3	—F	–	–	–
4-Bromo-2,5-dimethoxyamphetamine (DOB)	iv	—H	—Br	–	–	–	–
4-Iodo-2,5-dimethoxyamphetamine (DOI)		—H	—I	–	–	–	–
4-Chloro-2,5-dimethoxyamphetamine (DOC)		—H	—Cl	–	–	–	–
2,5-Dimethoxy-4-methyl-amphetamine (DOM)		—H	—CH_3	–	–	–	–
4-Bromo-2,5-dimethoxymethamphetamine (MDOB)		—CH_3	—Br	–	–	–	–
2,4,5-Trimethoxyamphetamine (TMA)		—H	—O—CH_3	–	–	–	–
4-Bromo-2,5-dimethoxyphenethylamine (2C–B)	v	—Br	–	–	–	–	–
4-Iodo-2,5-dimethoxyphenethylamine (2C–I)		—I	–	–	–	–	–
4-Methyl-2,5-dimethoxyphenethylamine (2C–D)		—CH_3	–	–	–	–	–
4-Ethyl-2,5-dimethoxyphenethylamine (2C–E)		—CH_2CH_3	–	–	–	–	–
4-Chloro-2,5-dimethoxyphenethylamine (2C–C)		—Cl	–	–	–	–	–
4-Ethylthio-2,5-dimethoxyphenethylamine (2C-T-2)		—S—CH_2CH_3	–	–	–	–	–
4-(n)-Propylthio-2,5-dimethoxyphenethylamine (2C-T-7)		—S—$CH_2CH_2CH_3$	–	–	–	–	–
4-(2-Fluoroethylthio)-2,5-dimethoxyphenethylamine (2C-T-21)		—S—CH_2CH_2—F	–	–	–	–	–
Cathinone	vi	—H	—CH_3	—H	—H	–	–
Ephedrone (methcathinone)		—CH_3	—CH_3	—H	—H	–	–
Mephedrone (bk-MMA)		—CH_3	—CH_3	—CH_3	—H	–	–
3-Fluoromethcathinone		—CH_3	—CH_3	—H	—F	–	–
Butylone (bk-MBDB)	vii	—CH_3	—CH_2CH_3	–	–	–	–
Ethylone (bk-MDEA)		—CH_2CH_3	—CH_3	–	–	–	–
Methylone (bk-MDMA)		—CH_3	—CH_3	–	–	–	–
Phencyclidine (PCP)	viii	–	–	–	–	–	–
N-(1-Phenylcyclohexyl)propanamine (PCPPA)	ix	—$CH_2CH_2CH_3$	–	–	–	–	–
N-(1-Phenylcyclohexyl)-3-methoxypropanamine (PCMPA)		—$CH_2CH_2CH_2$—O—CH_3	–	–	–	–	–
N-(1-Phenylcyclohexyl)-2-methoxyethanamine (PCMEA)		—CH_2CH_2—O—CH_3	–	–	–	–	–
N-(1-Phenylcyclohexyl)-2-ethoxyethanamine (PCEEA)		—CH_2CH_2—O—CH_2CH_3	–	–	–	–	–

Table 1 (Continued)

Drug Name	*Parent structure*	*Substituents*					
		R_1	R_2	R_3	R_4	R_5	R_6
N-Benzylpiperazine (BZP)	x	–	–	–	–	–	–
1-(3,4-Methylenedioxybenzyl)piperazine (MDBP)	xi	–	–	–	–	–	–
Trifluoromethylphenylpiperazine (TFMPP)	xii	—CF_3	—H	–	–	–	–
m-Chlorophenylpiperazine (mCPP)		—Cl	—H	–	–	–	–
Methoxyphenylpiperazine (MeOPP)		—H	—O—CH_3	–	–	–	–
Fluorophenylpiperazine (FPP)		—H	—F	–	–	–	–
α-Pyrrolidinopropiophenone (PPP)	xiii	—CH_3	—H	–	–	–	–
4-Methoxy-α-pyrrolidinopropiophenone (MOPPP)		—CH_3	—O—CH_3	–	–	–	–
4-Methyl-α-pyrrolidinopropiophenone (MPPP)		—CH_3	—CH_3	–	–	–	–
4-Methyl-α-pyrrolidinohexanophenone (MPHP)		—$CH_2CH_2CH_2CH_3$	—CH_3	–	–	–	–
3,4-Methylenedioxy-α-pyrrolidinopropiophenone (MDPPP)	xiv	—CH_3	–	–	–	–	–
3,4-Methylenedioxypyrovalerone (MDPV)		—$CH_2CH_2CH_3$	–	–	–	–	–
α-Methylfentanyl	xv	—CH_3	—H	—H	—CH_2CH_3	—H	–
p-Fluorofentanyl		—H	—F	—H	—CH_2CH_3	—H	–
α-Methylacetylfentanyl		—CH_3	—H	—H	—CH_3	—H	–
3-Methylfentanyl		—H	—H	—CH_3	—CH_2CH_3	—H	–
β-Hydroxyfentanyl		—H	—H	—H	—CH_2CH_3	—OH	–
β-Hydroxy-4-methylfentanyl		—H	—CH_3	—H	—CH_2CH_3	—OH	–
β-Hydroxythiofentanyl	xvi	–	–	–	–	–	–
1-Methyl-4-phenyl-4-piperdyl propionate (MPP)	xvii	–	–	–	–	–	–
1-Methyl-4-phenyl-1,2,5,6-tetrahydropyridine (MPTP)	xviii	–	–	–	–	–	–
N,*N*-Diisopropyl-5-methoxy-tryptamine (5-MeO-DIPT)	xix	—OCH_3	—H	—$CH(CH_3)_2$	—$CH(CH_3)_2$	—H	–
5-Methoxy-*N*,*N*-dimethyltryptamine (5-MeO-DMT)		—OCH_3	—H	—CH_3	—CH_3	—H	–
α-Methyltryptamine (AMT)		—H	—H	—H	—H	—CH_3	–
N-Isopropyl-5-methoxy-*N*-methyltryptamine (5-MeO-MIPT)		—OCH_3	—H	—$CH(CH_3)_2$	—CH_3	—H	–
5-Methoxy-α-methyltryptamine (5-MeO-AMT)		—OCH_3	—H	—H	—H	—CH_3	–
N,*N*-Diisopropyl-4-acetoxytryptamine (4-Acetoxy-DIPT)		—H	—$OCOCH_3$	—$CH(CH_3)_2$	—$CH(CH_3)_2$	—H	–
α-Ethyltryptamine (AET)		—H	—H	—H	—H	—CH_2CH_3	–
N,*N*-Diisopropyltryptamine (DIPT)		—H	—H	—$CH(CH_3)_2$	—$CH(CH_3)_2$	—H	–
N,*N*-Dipropyltryptamine (DPT)		—H	—H	$CH_2CH_2CH_3$	$CH_2CH_2CH_3$	H	–
Mitragynine (MG)	xx	—CH_2CH_3	–	–	–	–	–
Paynantheine (PAY)		—CH═CH_2	–	–	–	–	–
HU-210	xxi	–	–	–	–	–	–
JWH-018	xxii	—CH_3	–	–	–	–	–
JWH-073		—H	–	–	–	–	–
CP 47,497	xxiii	—C_6H_{14}	–	–	–	–	–
CP 47, 497–C_8 homolog		—C_7H_{16}	–	–	–	–	–
Desoxymethyltestosterone	xxiv	–	–	–	–	–	–
Norbolethone	xxv	–	–	–	–	–	–
Tetrahydrogestrinone (THG)	xxvi	–	–	–	–	–	–
γ-Butyrolactone (GBL)	xxvii	–	–	–	–	–	–
1,4-Butanediol	xxviii	–	–	–	–	–	–

4-MTA appear to mimic the sympathomimetic effects of PMA. However, their potency appears to decrease with the increasing size of the *N*-alkyl substituent – for example, *N*-propyl 4-MTA was found to be less potent than *N*-methyl 4-MTA.

In January 2003, a series of clandestinely prepared fluoro-α-methoxy-substituted phenylalkylamines were seized in Germany, which were unknown on the illicit market at the time of their appearance. They include 2-fluoroamphetamine sulfate and hydrochloride salts of 3-fluoroamphetamine, 4-fluoroamphetamine, 5-fluoro-2-methoxyamphetamine, 3-fluoro-4-methoxyamphetamine, *N*-methyl-4-fluoroamphetamine, *N*-ethyl-4-fluoroamphetamine, and 1-(4-fluorophenyl)butan-2-amine. These materials were marketed as white powders with very high purities.

2,5-Dimethoxy Amphetamine Designer Drugs

The most common drugs of this class include 4-bromo-2,5-dimethoxyamphetamine (DOB), 4-iodo-2,5-dimethoxyamphetamine (DOI), 4-chloro-2,5-dimethoxyamphetamine (DOC), 2,5-dimethoxy-4-methyl-amphetamine (DOM), 4-bromo-2,5-dimethoxymethamphetamine (MDOB), and 2,4,5-trimethoxyamphetamine (TMA).

Most of these drugs are sold in 'Smart Shops' either alone or as mixtures with other designer drugs in tablets, powder, liquids, and blotters. The 2,5-dimethoxy amphetamines exhibit hallucinogenic-like activity. It is thought that the methyl group in the α position is responsible for increased *in vivo* potency and duration of action.

2,5-Phenethylamine Designer Drugs (2C drugs)

The 2,5-dimethoxy phenethylamines are analogs of the just-mentioned 2,5-dimethoxy amphetamines. Some common 2C drugs include 4-bromo-2,5-dimethoxyphenethylamine (2C–B), 4-iodo-2,5-dimethoxyphenethylamine (2C–I), 4-methyl-2,5-dimethoxyphenethylamine (2C–D), 4-ethyl-2,5-dimethoxyphenethylamine (2C–E), 4-chloro-2,5-dimethoxyphenethylamine (2C–C), 4-ethylthio-2,5-dimethoxyphenethylamine (2C-T-2), 4-(*n*)-propylthio-2,5-dimethoxyphenethylamine (2C-T-7), and 4-(2-fluoroethylthio)-2,5-dimethoxyphenethylamine (2C-T-21). The synthesis of 2C–I was published first in 1991 and the drug became popular in tablet form as a club drug in the United Kingdom around 2003.

The name 2C comes from the two carbon atoms that separate the amine from the phenyl ring. These drugs have hallucinogenic properties and are sometimes sold as MDMA. Little is known about the pharmacological and toxicological properties of the 2C drugs, but their affinity to type-2 serotonin receptors has been demonstrated.

β-Keto Amphetamine Designer Drugs

Some common β-keto designer drugs include cathinone, ephedrone (methcathinone), mephedrone (2-methylamino-1-*p*-tolylpropane-1-one, 4-methylmethcathinone, bk-methylmethamphetamine, bk-MMA), butylone (2-methyl-amino-1-(3,4-methylenedioxyphenyl)butan-1-one, bk-MBDB), ethylone (3,4-methylenedioxyethylcathinone, bk-methylenedioxyethylamphetamine, bk-MDEA), and methylone (3,4-methylenedioxymethcathinone, bk-MDMA).

Cathinone can be extracted from *Catha edulis* or synthesized from α-bromopropiophenone, a compound that can be made from propiophenone. Methcathinone can be prepared from oxidation of ephedrine. Even the chiral synthesis of these materials has been reported, using amino acids as precursors, with ease. The ease of preparation of these materials has contributed to the emergence of an increasing number of cathinone analogs in the illicit market.

Despite being relatively new as drugs of abuse, these β-keto designer drugs have been around since the 1930s. Ephedrone, originally used as an antidepressant in the 1930s, went on to be used recreationally in the Netherlands and in the United States during the 1970s–90s. Similarly, mephedrone was first synthesized in the late 1920s but did not become widely known until early 2000s. Intelligence from Australia Customs and Border Protection Service has identified China and the United Kingdom as being the principal sources of mephedrone. The compound 3-fluoromethcathinone has been identified in capsules marketed as plant feeders available from Internet suppliers in the United Kingdom. Other materials were also identified in the tablet and include caffeine and methylamine salt. Methylone was found in street drugs in the Netherlands in 2004 and is the main ingredient of a new liquid designer drug that appeared on the Dutch drug market, called 'Explosion.'

When administered to experimental animals, methcathinone and cathinone were found to cause hyperactivity, with methcathinone being $\sim$10 times more potent than cathinone. The subjective effects of methylone exhibit subtle differences with those of MDMA. A vast majority of the drugs in this class, particularly those recently introduced, do not have any pharmacological and toxicological data recorded thus far.

Phencyclidine-Derived Designer Drugs

Developed in the 1950s as an intravenous anesthetic, phencyclidine (1-(1-phenylcyclohexyl)piperidine, or PCP) was never approved for human use because of its side effects, including intensely negative psychological effects observed during clinical studies. Illicit use of this classical designer drug is in the form of tablets, capsules, or powder. It can be snorted, smoked, or ingested.

Several PCP-derived designer drugs have been encountered in Germany in recent years. These designer drugs include *N*-(1-phenylcyclohexyl)propanamine (PCPPA), *N*-(1-phenylcyclohexyl)-3-methoxypropanamine (PCMPA), *N*-(1-phenylcyclohexyl)-2-methoxyethanamine (PCMEA), and *N*-(1-phenylcyclohexyl)-2-ethoxyethanamine (PCEEA). Due to the lack of information on the pharmacological properties of these substances, their psychotomimetic and anesthetic properties are only assumed based on their structural similarities with PCP and ketamine.

Piperazine-Derived Designer Drugs

N-Benzylpiperazine (BZP) and its analogs such as 1-(3,4-methylenedioxybenzyl)piperazine (MDBP), trifluoromethylphenylpiperazine (TFMPP), *m*-chlorophenylpiperazine (mCPP), methoxyphenylpiperazine (MeOPP), and fluorophenylpiperazine (FPP) have been found to be the active ingredients of some recently encountered 'party pills.' They are used extensively as recreational drugs globally despite their prohibition in several countries.

These piperazines became known as drugs of abuse in the United Kingdom in early 2008. A few nonfatal and fatal cases have been published and typically involve other drugs. In the United Kingdom, in recent years, the presence of BZP and TFMPP have been confirmed in three fatalities (road traffic deaths and a fatal fall off a building), with two of these involving both drugs. Research has shown that drug users are ingesting piperazine analogs, like BZP and TFMPP, in order to mimic the psychoactive effects of MDMA. It has been demonstrated that BZP/TFMPP and MDMA share the ability to evoke monoamine release, but dangerous drug synergism may occur when piperazines are coadministered in high doses.

Pyrrolidinophenone-Derived Designer Drugs

Pyrrolidinophenone-type drugs such as α-pyrrolidinopropiophenone (PPP), 4-methoxy-α-pyrrolidinopropiophenone (MOPPP), 3,4-methylenedioxy-α-pyrrolidinopropiophenone (MDPPP), 4-methyl-α-pyrrolidinopropiophenone (MPPP), and 4-methyl-α-pyrrolidinohexanophenone (MPHP) have gained popularity and notoriety as 'rave' drugs. Very little experimental data on pharmacology and toxicology of this drug class has been published. Pyrrolidinophenones are thought to possess AP-like effects. 3,4-Methylenedioxypyrovalerone (MDPV) is the methylenedioxy derivative of pyrovalerone. In 2008, MDPV was seized in the United States and is thought to be a drug of abuse. MDPV is a white or light tan powder and is commonly described as boosting a user's libido; however, it is also associated with extreme anxiety at higher dosages.

Fentanyl-Derived Designer Drugs

'China White' as it has become known on the heroin market is an opioid analgesic designer drug called α-methylfentanyl. 'China White' was encountered as early as 1979 and it was significant as the first example of a designer drug that had been developed entirely by clandestine chemists for sale as an illicit recreational drug rather than as a product of legitimate scientific research. Following the appearance of α-methylfentanyl on the market, several new analogs of fentanyl have been reported, including *para*-fluorofentanyl, α-methylacetylfentanyl, and the highly potent 3-methylfentanyl. 3-Methylfentanyl was allegedly used as a chemical warfare agent by the Russian army. Subsequently, many other fentanyl derivatives have been encountered, including β-hydroxyfentanyl, β-hydroxythiofentanyl, and β-hydroxy-4-methylfentanyl. There have been a significant number of reported fatalities associated with the use of fentanyl derivatives in the past.

Piperidine Analogs

One of the representative compounds for this class of designer drugs is 1-methyl-4-phenyl-4-piperdyl propionate (MPP). Despite being a powerful analgesic, MPP has never been used in clinical medicine. Its synthesis was solely for the purpose of recreational drug use. One MPP product that was sold as 'synthetic heroin' on the black market caused what was termed by clinicians as a 'designer drug disaster' in the 1980s. Many of the individuals who used the product developed irreversible Parkinsonism. It was later found that the toxic properties of the product were attributable to 1-methyl-4-phenyl-1,2,5,6-tetrahydropyridine (MPTP), a by-product formed during the synthesis of MPP. MPTP is known to cause permanent Parkinsonism by destroying neurons in the brain of the subject.

Tryptamine-Derived Designer Drugs

Hallucinogenic tryptamines are derivatives of indoleethylamine with substitutions on the indole ring and ethylamine side chains that are responsible for its hallucinogenic properties. *N*,*N*-Diisopropyl-5-methoxy-tryptamine (5-MeO-DIPT), also known as 'Foxy,' emerged as a drug of abuse in 1999 and has been used increasingly since its appearance. Some effects that have been encountered by users of 'Foxy' include euphoria, visual and auditory hallucinations, loss of inhibition, and feelings of empathy for others. In general, the effects of 'Foxy' mimic the effects of MDMA. 5-MeO-DIPT is several times more potent than *N*,*N*-dimethyltryptamine and is widely available over the Internet.

Some other designer tryptamines that have been encountered include 5-methoxy-*N*,*N*-dimethyltryptamine (5-MeO-DMT), α-methyltryptamine (AMT), *N*-isopropyl-5-methoxy-*N*-methyltryptamine (5-MeO-MIPT), 5-methyoxy-α-methyltryptamine (5-MeO-AMT), *N*,*N*-diisopropyl-4-acetoxytryptamine (4-Acetoxy-DIPT), α-ethyltryptamine (AET), *N*,*N*-diisopropyltryptamine (DIPT), and *N*,*N*-dipropyltryptamine (DPT).

Herbal Drug 'Kratom'

'Kratom' is the Thai name for the plant *Mitragyna speciosa* Korth., which is native in Thailand and other southeast Asian countries and contains several alkaloids including mitragynine (MG) and paynantheine (PAY). 'Kratom' has been used as a traditional medicine to treat illnesses, including coughing, diarrhea, muscle pain, and hypertension. It is also effective in relieving opiate withdrawal symptoms for heroin or morphine addicts. 'Kratom' is misused as an herbal drug of abuse mainly because of its stimulant and euphoric effects. The herbal drug has been controlled in Thailand since 1946 and in Australia since 2005.

Synthetic Cannabinoids in 'Spice'

Since 2004, herbal mixtures such as 'Spice' (also known as 'K2' or 'Spice Gold') have been sold in Switzerland, Austria, Germany, and other European countries in 'Head Shops' or 'Smart Shops' and over the Internet. These products are marketed as 'Incense' as a result of their rich aromas, although users utilize them in the same way as cannabis, by inhaling the smoke. 'Spice' is said to contain ingredients of natural origin (inactive herbs) mixed with other synthetically derived cannabinoids (active component of mixture). Some inactive herbs that have been encountered in mixtures of 'Spice' include *Canavalia maritime, Nymphae caerulea, Scutellaria nana, Pedicularis densiflora, Leonitis leonurus, Zornia latifolia, Nelumbo nucifera, and Leonurus sibiricus*. Synthetic cannabinoids have received a lot of attention recently due to their ability to mimic the effects of cannabis. Synthetic cannabinoids bind to cannabinoid-like receptors, producing effects that are stronger than natural cannabis with users typically ingesting less than 1 mg. The main synthetic cannabinoids found in 'Spice' include HU-210, JWH-018, JWH-073, CP-47,497 and the C_8 homolog of CP-47,497, among hundreds of their analogs. Some 'Spice' products contain only a single cannabinoid, while others may contain multiple cannabinoid compounds.

Users have reported addiction syndrome and withdrawal effects that parallel those resulting from natural cannabis use. Accidental overdosing may lead to severe psychiatrical complications and life-threatening conditions in the case of cannabinoid receptor agonist. However, pharmacological and toxicological studies of these 'Spice' mixtures in human are rare; therefore, potential health risks or possible psychoactive effects of these products cannot be clearly defined. It remains unclear where and how actual production of the herbal mixtures takes place; however, it is clear that producers are purposely risking the health of consumers for high profits.

Designer Steroids

Several designer steroids such as desoxymethyltestosterone, norbolethone, and tetrahydrogestrinone (THG) have appeared either in confiscated powders or in urine samples of elite athletes in recent years. While many anabolic steroids abused by athletes are pharmaceuticals intended for veterinary or human use, or discontinued, designer steroids are typically those that were given to athletes without toxicity or teratogenicity assessment and thus pose greater health risks to users.

Norbolethone was first detected in urine of athletes in competition in the early 2000s. It is an anabolic steroid agent that was synthesized and trialed clinically in the 1960s to encourage weight gain and for the treatment of short stature. Norbolethone was never marketed commercially, possibly due to its toxicity concerns. Detection of norbolethone in athletes' urine after three decades of its abandonment by the pharmaceutical industry suggests strongly that a clandestine source may exist.

THG was identified in the residue of a spent syringe provided anonymously to the United States Anti-Doping Agency (USADA) in 2004. THG is considered the first true 'designer steroid,' as the substance was designed, synthesized, and distributed only to beat the test. THG as a sports doping agent reflects both an alarmingly sophisticated illicit manufacturing facility and an underground network of androgen abusers in sports. Since the implementation of testing methods for THG by anti-doping laboratories, THG has never been detected again in sport drug testing programs up until this date.

Desoxymethyltestosterone (or madol) was first discovered in 2005 and is another steroid (never commercially marketed) to be found in the context of performance-enhancing drugs in sports. Desoxymethyltestosterone was synthesized in the early 1960s. There is very limited data on the safety and efficacy of the substance and the drug has never been approved for human use.

Other Designer Drugs

Other designer drugs which are rarely mentioned in literature and fall outside the groups discussed above include 1, 4-butanediol and γ-butyrolactone (GBL). Both drugs are metabolized to γ-hydroxybutyric acid (GHB) in the human body, thus producing symptoms that parallel those of GHB ingestion alone. Some common effects of these drugs include euphoria, enhanced sensuality, and empathy toward others. GHB, GBL, and 1,4-butandiol are commonly used as 'date-rape' drugs due to their profound sedative effects. Determination of these drugs or their metabolites in a victim's urine is challenging due to firstly their short detection windows and secondly the presence of a low level of endogenous GHB in the testing samples.

Forensic Relevance

Forensic Chemistry

Driven by burgeoning appetite for profit, clandestine industries are constantly developing new illicit products for street sale. They are well aware of the legal framework of drug control legislations and are more aware of the drug market and thus may have sophisticated drug synthesis and release strategies in place. They market new drugs in the form of tablets, powder, liquids, or blotters, as research chemicals, fertilizers, and more recently as 'Spice' or 'Incense' products and sell via the Internet and other distribution channels.

Since the black market changes more quickly than testing reference standards can be developed legitimately, effective identification of these new designer drugs becomes an ongoing challenge for forensic chemists. First, many new designer drugs may be present at a low concentration and coexist with many masking interfering substances such as in the case of 'Herbal Highs,' and correct identification of these minor illicit drug components will not be easy. Secondly, some designer drug preparations contain many structural isomers, which make structural identification difficult. For instance, TFMPP, mCPP, and MeOPP have structural isomers relating to substitution at the 2-, 3-, and 4- positions relating to ortho-, meta-, and para-positions, respectively. The existence of these structural isomers complicates identification of these piperazines. And thirdly, due to lack of reference materials, reference spectra of mass spectrometry, ultraviolet, and infrared will not be available in the respective reference libraries, therefore rendering these spectroscopy-based drug screening techniques inadequate.

To keep up with the dynamic and changing market of the designer drugs, it is important not only to utilize and adapt existing analytical methods but also to develop new ones that allow determination of these new drugs. Gas chromatography–mass spectrometry (GC-MS) and liquid chromatography–mass spectrometry (LC-MS) have been very useful in analyzing illicit drugs in the past and will continue to be so in the future. Direct coupling of LC with high-resolution nuclear magnetic resonance (NMR) or coupling novel techniques such as desorption electrospray ionization with mass spectrometry may become the methods of choice in speedy screening and identification of novel drugs and drug analogs.

Forensic Toxicology

Although many toxicokinetic studies have been recorded in the literature on some classic designer drug classes such as the AP-type drugs, they are scarce or not existent for newer designer drugs. For instance, only little information is available on toxicological properties of the 2C series. Even less is known about the toxicokinetics of synthetic cannabinnoids recently encountered in 'Spice' preparations. Due to the growing global interest in 'Spice' and related 'Herbal High' products, a number of certified reference materials including JWH-018, JWH-073, and their deuterated counterparts have been made available commercially. Availability of these standards allows accurate determination of these species in biological fluids such as blood. However, for many designer drugs, toxicological analyses, especially urine analyses, are difficult, as urinary metabolites are unknown and reference standards do not exist. Therefore, it is important that forensic toxicologists conduct metabolic studies in order to better understand the metabolic pathways and search for appropriate metabolites as markers for urine analysis. The importance of these studies also lies in the belief that many metabolites may contribute to some of the toxic effects of the parent drugs, including life-threatening serotonin syndrome, hepatotoxicity, neurotoxicity, and psychopathology. For example, demethylenation of MDMA gives rise to a toxic catechol, which can be further metabolized into a neurotoxin following aromatic hydroxylation. Thus, knowledge of their metabolism is a prerequisite for toxicological risk assessment of these designer drugs of abuse.

Drug monitoring in nonconventional biological matrices (e.g., oral fluid, hair, nails, and sweat) has recently gained much attention because of its possible applications in clinical and forensic toxicology. An individual's past history of medication, compliance, or drug abuse can be obtained from testing of hair and nails, whereas data on current status of drug use can be provided by analysis of sweat and oral fluid. Countries such as Australia have been testing oral fluid at the roadside by police for the presence of MDMA along with other drugs such as MA and tetrahydrocannabinol (THC). Oral fluid testing for the presence of synthetic cannabinoids, for example, JWH-018 and JWH-073, is anticipated to take place in the near future should the problem of 'Spice' drug abuse continue to grow.

Clinical Intoxication

Unlike therapeutical substances, new designer drugs enter the black market without any safety testing and thus pose a serious health risk. Emergency physicians have had to deal with overdoses and symptoms, the characteristics of which they may not have seen before. Since studies for risk assessment of these drugs are limited for ethical reasons, corresponding metabolic and especially toxicokinetic data for humans can only be obtained from authentic clinical or forensic cases. Undesired side effects of using these drugs may also be gathered from Internet sites such as drug user forums.

History has seen many severe or fatal poisoning cases as a result of designer drug abuse. 4-MTA has led to several fatal poisonings in the past. No deaths have been reported following the sole ingestion of BZP; however, there have been at least two reported deaths from the combination of BZP and MDMA. Co-ingestion of ethanol and BZP increases the likelihood of common and distressing symptoms related to BZP ingestion; however, it reduces the incidence of BZP seizures. Some fatal intoxications involving 2C-T-7 and PMA have also been reported. There have been dozens of reported fatalities during the period of 2008–10 in the United Kingdom and other European countries in which mephedrone has been implicated. Over 150 deaths resulted from the use of α-methylfentanyl ('China White') and other fentanyl derivatives in late 1970s and early 1980s. There have been only a limited number of clinical emergency cases in the literature so far related to the use of the synthetic cannabinoids of 'Spice.' The health risks, especially the risks at developing 'Spice' drug-associated dependence and psychosis, are yet to be further assessed.

5-MeO-DIPT as well as other tryptamine-derived designer drugs are increasingly common drugs of abuse and are not detectable by routine toxicology screening. The possibility of intoxication with these agents should be noted, and clinicians should be aware of the potentially serious morbidity and mortality associated with their use. In addition, it should be realized that possible health risks may depend on individual users and their behavior; therefore, each case of intoxication should be treated individually, keeping in mind any known health risks associated with the drug taken.

Legislation

Different countries have different drug control legislations. A drug controlled in one country may not necessarily be controlled in others. For example, BZP is illegal in many countries, including the United States, Australia, and New Zealand; however, it remains legal in other countries such as Canada and the United Kingdom.

Synthetic cannabinoids are controlled substances in Australia, Europe, the United States, and Canada. In the United States, MDPV is currently unscheduled, while 5-MeO-DIPT, also known as 'Foxy,' is classified as a Schedule 1 Drug of the Controlled Substances Act.

Some countries such as Germany, Canada, the United States, and the United Kingdom ban new drugs as they become a concern. Other countries such as Australia and New Zealand ban drugs together with their structural analogs, including those that may have never been made. Regardless of the difference in drug scheduling acts, fast and accurate detection and identification of designer drugs are the key to effective drug control and law enforcement. Nonscheduling of a drug in a country does not necessarily mean that the drug poses less health concerns to the community, but might be attributable to the inability of toxicologists to detect the drug substance. It is therefore necessary for scientists and authorities to promote the availability of relevant standards, validated assays, and scientific knowledge regarding these designer drugs of abuse.

Conclusions

Designer drugs of abuse exist in a dynamic market with new drugs appearing all the time. They pose a serious health risk to society and present an ongoing challenge to forensic chemists, forensic toxicologists, health professionals, and law enforcement agencies. Scientists and authorities must keep a close eye on the drug trends as in-depth investigations on chemical, analytical, toxicological, and metabolic properties of these emerging drugs are critical in combating the problem of drug abuse.

See also: **Chemistry/Trace/Drugs of Abuse:** Clandestine Laboratories; **Toxicology/Drugs of Abuse:** Validation of Twelve Chemical Spot Tests for the Detection of Drugs of Abuse.

Further Reading

Antia U, Lee HS, Hydd RR, Tingle MD, and Russell BR (2009) Pharmacokinetics of 'party pill' drug N-benzylpiperazine (BZP) in healthy human participants. *Forensic Science International* 186: 63–67.

Archer RP (2009) Fluoromethcathinone, a new substance of abuse. *Forensic Science International* 185: 10–20.

Baumann MH, Clark RD, Budzynxki AG, et al. (2005) *N*-Substituted piperazines abused by humans mimic the molecular mechanism of 3,4-methylenedioxymethamphetamine (MDMA, or 'Ecstasy'). *Neuropychopharmacology* 30: 550–560.

Blachut D, Wojtasiewicz K, Czarnocki Z, and Szukalski B (2009) The analytical profile of some 4-methylthioamphetamine (4-MTA) homologues. *Forensic Science International* 192: 98–114.

Bossong MG, Van Dijk JP, and Niesink RJM (2005) Methylone and mCPP, two new drugs of abuse? *Addiction Biology* 10: 321–323.

Drees JC, Stone JA, and Wu AHB (2009) Morbidity involving the hallucinogenic designer amines MDA and 2C-I. *Journal of Forensic Sciences* 54: 1485–1487.

Elliott S and Smith C (2008) Investigation of the first deaths in the United Kingdom involving the detection and quantitation of the piperazines BZP and 3-TFMPP. *Journal of Analytical Toxicology* 32: 172–177.

Glennon RA (1990) Phenylalkylamine stimulants, hallucinogens, and designer drugs. *NIDA Research Monograph* 105: 154–160.

Maurer HH (2010) Chemistry, pharmacology, and metabolism of emerging drugs of abuse. *Therapeutic drug monitoring* 32: 544–549.

Peters FT, Schaefer S, Staack RF, Kraemer T, and Maurer HH (2003) Screening for and validated quantification of amphetamines and of amphetamine- and piperazine-derived designer drugs in human blood plasma by gas chromatography/mass spectrometry. *Journal of Mass Spectrometry* 38: 659–676.

Rosner P, Quednow B, Girreser U, and Junge T (2005) Isomeric fluoro-methoxy-phenylalkylamine: A new series of controlled-substance analogues (designer drugs). *Forensic Science International* 148: 143–156.

Shulgin A and Shulgin A (1991) *Pihkal: A Chemical Love Story*. Berkley, CA: Transform Press.

Takahashi M, Nagashima M, Suzuki J, et al. (2008) Analysis of phenethylamines and tryptamines in designer drugs using gas chromatography–mass spectrometry. *Journal of Health Science* 54: 89–96.

Relevant Websites

http://www.justice.gov/dea: DEA United States Drug Enforcement Administration

http://www.emcdda.europa.eu: European Monitoring Centre for Drugs and Drug Addiction

http://www.rednetproject.eu: ReDNet Research Project

http://www.crimecommission.gov.au/publications: Australian Crime Commission Publications

http://www.unodc.org/unodc/en/scientists/smart.html: United Nations Office on Drugs and Crime Global SMART Programme

http://www.drugs-forum.com: Drugs Forum

http://www.mixmag.net/drugssurvey: Mixmag | MIXMAG'S DRUG SURVEY: THE RESULTS

CHEMISTRY/TRACE/ENVIRONMENTAL ANALYSIS

Overview, Analysis, and Interpretation of Environmental Forensic Evidence

RD Morrison, Hawi, HI, USA

Glossary

Chemical profiling The use of diagnostic chemical features in a sample that allow detailed compositional comparisons between samples.
Chlorinated solvent An organic compound containing chlorine atoms.
Environmental forensics The systematic and scientific evaluation of physical, chemical, and historical information for the purpose of developing defensible scientific and legal conclusions regarding the source or age of a contaminant released into the environment.
Surrogate chemical analysis The use of coincident chemical or physical evidence present with a contaminant of concern to identify the date or source of a contaminant release.

Introduction

Identification of the origin of a contaminant release, the timing of the release, and its distribution in the subsurface are common issues in environmental litigation, whether civil or criminal. Given the circumstances of a particular contaminant release, one or more environmental forensic approaches are usually available to identify its origin and age. While many environmental investigative techniques are available, the selection of an appropriate method(s) and the decision to use one or more approach in concert requires a comprehensive understanding of the techniques and their respective evidentiary advantages and limitations. This article describes four unrelated forensic methodologies as illustrative of the range of techniques available and their potential applications. The four forensic techniques are:

- age dating the release of contaminants from a leaking underground storage tank using corrosion models;
- use of solvent stabilizers and feedstock impurities in trichloroethylene (TCE) to age date the release;
- the use of compound-specific isotopic analysis (CSIA) to distinguish the source of a TCE release; and
- the use of chemical surrogate analysis to age date a contaminant release.

Dating the Release of Contaminants from Underground Storage Tanks

A common environmental forensic question regarding the allocation of responsibility for a contaminant release arises when potential contaminants such as gasoline, diesel, chlorinated solvents, alcohols, and waste liquids stored in an underground storage tank are detected in the surrounding soil. The application of tank corrosion models is one approach used to examine this question. In most instances, tank corrosion models provide the ability to associate probability statistics to produce a range of likely release dates, as corrosion pitting and perforation leak data are normally distributed.

Two variables governing the corrosion rate for an underground storage tank and associated piping are (a) the thickness of the metal and (b) the electrical resistivity of the soil. The thicker the tank or piping wall is, the longer it takes for corrosion to occur. Soil resistivity is a property defined as the resistance or ability of an electrical current to flow in soil. The lower the resistivity of the soil is, the easier it is for an electric current to flow through soil, resulting in a higher corrosion rate of the metal and perforation of the tank or pipe wall. Soil corrosivity therefore increases proportionally with a decrease in soil resistivity. Soil with resistivity values below 10 000 ohm-cm is considered corrosive, respective to steel, while soil with resistivity values of 2000 ohm-cm are five times more corrosive. Soil with resistivity values below 1000 ohm-cm are considered extremely corrosive, although rarely encountered.

In addition to the thickness of the metal wall and the soil resistivity, additional soil measurements used in underground storage tank corrosion models include the following:

- soil moisture content,
- water-soluble chloride and sulfate,
- pH, and
- bicarbonate concentration.

Soil with high chloride and sulfate content increases the corrosion rate of steel tanks. Generally, the evaluation of these six soil parameters along with information specific to the tank construction and materials provide the analytical framework for determining the likely corrosion rate.

Examples of corrosion models for underground storage tanks include the mean time to corrosion failure, the tank

 http://dx.doi.org/10.1016/B978-0-12-382165-2.00118-5

environmental profiling and the tank suitability study methods, and the Rossum pitting model. Of these models, the Rossum pitting model is frequently used in environmental forensic investigations and is therefore described in greater detail, although all these models share common elements.

In 1969, John R. Rossum proposed the following expression to estimate when pitting of an underground storage tank would result in leakage.

$$T_{\mathrm{L}} = (\rho/10 - \mathrm{pH})(z/K_n K_a)^{1/n}(1/A)^{a/n} \qquad [1]$$

where T_{L} is the time for the first leak to occur (years); ρ, resistivity in ohms-centimeter; pH, a measure of acidity or alkalinity of the soil; z, wall thickness of the metal (mils); K_n, an empirical constant (dimensionless) equal to 170 for soil with good aeration, 222 for soil with fair aeration, and 355 for soil with poor aeration; K_a, relative pit depth, equal to 1 for wrought iron, 1.06 for steel, and 1.4 for cast iron; A, area of exposed pipe or underground storage tank surface (sq. ft); a, an empirical constant, equal to 0.13 for wrought iron, 0.16 for steel, and 0.22 for cast iron; and n, an empirical constant, equal to 1/6 for soils with good aeration, 1/3 for soil with fair aeration, and 1/2 for poor aeration.

Rossum also provided a solution for the number of leaks that can occur at any time as expressed by eqn [2]:

$$L = A(K_n K_a/z)^{1/a}\,[t(10 - \mathrm{pH})/\rho]^{n/a} \qquad [2]$$

where L is the number of leaks and t, the time.

Given that the parameter values used in the Rossum model are available or are reasonably estimated, the forensic scientist can estimate when a leak first occurred. The ability to provide a range of values for eqns [1] and [2] also provides the ability to use probability statistics to assign confidence levels to estimate when a release first occurred.

The Rossum corrosion model presents a simplified expression for estimating when an underground storage tank began leaking and the number of leaks. Other considerations influencing the corrosion rate include

- the presence of cathodic protection, which can retard the corrosion rate and result in underestimating the time when the tank or piping fails;
- the presence of interconnected tanks and piping of different composition and wall thickness;
- the presence of a surface coating on the exterior of the tank, often similar to asphalt, will retard the actual corrosion rate estimated by the model;
- the historical presence of a fluctuating groundwater table in contact with the tank and associated piping for some portion of time each year, potentially resulting in accelerated corrosion, especially if saline; and
- evidence that contamination in soil or groundwater occurred from tank overfilling/spills as opposed to tank corrosion.

The final consideration is examined by identifying whether soil at the ground surface, and especially near the fill port of the underground storage tank, indicates the presence of the same contaminants identified at depth in samples adjacent to or below the underground storage tank. In such cases, care must be exercised when reaching conclusions regarding the source of the contaminants detected in soils adjacent to the underground storage tank and piping and whether the contaminant distribution reflects a combination of surface and tank failure releases.

Additives for Age Dating TCE

Chlorinated solvents, including TCE, perchloroethylene (PCE), carbon tetrachloride (CT), and 1,1,1-trichloroethane (TCA) are a group of organochlorine compounds frequently of interest in forensic investigations. TCE is the most common chlorinated solvent of concern in forensic investigations. Two forensic approaches used to age date a TCE release include (1) the presence of stabilizers added to TCE and (2) formulation impurities in TCE. Both approaches assume that the stabilizers and formulation impurities are present at detectable concentrations in environmental samples along with TCE.

Stabilizers Used for Age Dating a TCE Release

Stabilizers detected in environmental samples with TCE may be diagnostic indicators for when the TCE was manufactured or possibly its application. Stabilizers are chemicals added to TCE to enhance its performance and longevity and include acid inhibitors (amines, epoxides, phenols, pyridines, trimethylamine, alcohols, alkyl halides, and azo-aromatic compounds), metals, antioxidants, and light inhibitors. Without stabilizers, degradation occurs, especially when TCE is used as a vapor degreasing solvent, in the presence of aluminum. Typical TCE stabilizer formulations include an acid acceptor, a metal stabilizer, and/or an antioxidant. These additives typically comprise about 0.1–0.5% of the TCE solvent, but concentrations can range as high as 2%. In vapor degreasing grades of TCE, concentrations at the higher end of the range are typical, and additional compounds are added to enhance thermal stability. Some stabilizers such as butylene oxide, epichlorohydrin, ethyl acetate, and methyl pyrrole are often present within 35% of their initial concentrations in spent or distilled TCE, thus offering the ability to detect them even if they are present initially at concentrations less than 1%.

Gasoline and other unsaturated hydrocarbons were the earliest TCE stabilizers. Until 1954, the most common TCE stabilizers were acid acceptors and included amines, including trimethylamine, triethylamine, triethanolamine, aniline, and diisopropylamine. Of these acid acceptors, trimethylamine was often the dominant additive with initial concentrations in the TCE of about 20 parts per million (ppm). The presence of these stabilizers in a sample with TCE may, therefore, indicate a pre-1954 release. In the mid-1950s, amines were replaced by nonalkaline formulations, particularly a pyrrole-based, six-to-seven component mixture developed by DuPont de Nemours. The presence of pyrrole compounds with TCE may, therefore, indicate a manufactured date post mid-1950s. An example is methyl pyrrole that appears to accumulate in spent and distilled TCE relative to its concentration in virgin TCE and is therefore likely to be analytically detected, although its initial concentration in new TCE is less than about 1.6×10^4 by weight.

Metal inhibitors added to TCE include cyanide, esters, ketones, olefins, thiophene, peroxides, 1,2-butylene oxide, and epichlorohydrin. The use of epichlorohydrin was discontinued in the 1980s in the United States due to its toxicity and therefore provides a potential diagnostic marker when found with TCE. Another advantage to the use of epichlorohydrin as a diagnostic marker is that its concentration in reclaimed TCE remains similar to its initial concentration.

Examples of antioxidants include alkyl pyrroles, boranes, thiocyanates, and aromatic carboxylic acids. Light inhibitors include esters, guanidine, organometallic compounds, and hydroxyl-aromatic compounds. Additives for thermal stability include cyclohexane, diisobutylene, and amylene, although many others were used; the presence of these thermal additives may be indicative of high-temperature applications of TCE.

Table 1 summarizes additives used in TCE and PCE, as many stabilizers are common to both solvents.

Presence of Impurities in TCE for Age Dating

Impurities present in TCE originating from the manufacturing process can provide a means to age date when the TCE was produced. The historical commercial production of TCE used either acetylene or ethylene as the initial feedstock. The chlorination of acetylene yields 1,1,2,2 tetrachloroethane ($CHCl_2CHCl_2$) which is dehydrochlorinated by alkaline hydrolysis with calcium hydroxide or via pyrolysis with mixed metallic chlorides at 300–500 °C to yield TCE. The TCE yield from acetylene is approximately 94% of the theoretical available amount or about 4.8 pounds of TCE per pound of acetylene. Chlorination of ethylene yields 1,2-dichloroethane (1,2-DCA), which is then oxychlorinated with chlorine and oxygen to yield TCE. The production of TCE from acetylene and ethylene is shown in Figure 1.

Table 1 Stabilizers used in TCE and PCE

Description	*Trichloroethylene (TCE)*	*Additives in TCE and PCE*
Acid inhibitor	Olefins	Acetylenic alcohols
	Oxirane	Alcohols
	Phenols	Aliphatic amines
	Pyridines	Aliphatic monohydric alcohols
	Pyrrole	
	Quaternary ammonium compounds	Hydroxyl aromatic compounds
	Terpenes	Nitroso compounds
	Alkaloids	Azo-aromatic compounds
	Alky halides	
	Azines	
	Aziridines	
Metal inhibitor	Thiophene	Alcohols
	Ethers	Aromatic hydrocarbons
	Ketones	Cyclic trimers
	Olefins	Esters
	Peroxides	Oximes
	Pyridines	Sulfones
	Amides	Sulfoxide
	Amines	
	Complex ethers and oxides	
	Cyanide	
	Cyclic ethanes	
	Epoxides	
Antioxidant	Amides	Pyrrole
	Amines	Thiocyanates
	Aromatic carboxylic acids	Phenols
	Aryl stibine	
	Boranes	
	Butylhydroxyanisole	
Light inhibitor	Aromatic benzene nuclei	Hydroxyl aromatic compounds
	Boranes	
	Ethers	Organometallic compounds
	Guanidine	

Reproduced from Morrison R (2009) Age dating the release of PCE, TCE and TCA using stabilizers and feedstock. Environmental Forensics. *Proceedings of the 2009 INEF Annual Conference*, 298. UK: RSC with permission from the Royal Society of Chemistry (RSC).

Prior to 1950, TCE was produced almost exclusively from acetylene. Between 1963 and 1967, it is estimated that 85% of all the TCE produced in the United States was manufactured using acetylene as the starting material. In 1966, it is estimated that 85% of the TCE in the United States was produced from acetylene and 15% from ethylene. In 1968 and 1969, acetylene accounted for 65% and 55% of the feedstock used to produce TCE; by 1970–71, it was 51%. By 1972, only 15% of the operating capacity of manufacturers in the United States used acetylene. By 1973–74, acetylene as a feedstock for TCE production decreased to about 8% primarily due to the cost differential between acetylene and the less expensive ethylene. By 1978, acetylene was no longer used as a feedstock for the commercial scale production of TCE.

As shown in Figure 1, 1,1,2,2-trichloroethane (1,1,2,2-TeCA) is an intermediate product in the formation of TCE when produced from acetylene, while 1,2-DCA is an ethylene feedstock intermediary. Given that TCE production using acetylene as feedstock was not used on a commercial scale by 1978 in the United States, the presence of 1,1,2,2-TeCA along with TCE in an environmental sample is suggestive that the TCE was formulated prior to 1978. Conversely, the presence of 1,2-DCA with TCE in an environmental sample is suggestive of a post-1978 release.

The premise of using the presence of feedstock impurities (1,1,2,2-TeCA and/or 1,2-DCA) when detected in conjunction with TCE in an environmental sample to age date a TCE release as prior or post about 1978 is based on the following assumptions:

- no reasonable sources of 1,1,2,2,-TeCA and/or 1,2-TCA exists other than as an impurity in the TCE, and
- the presence of 1,2-DCA with TCE is not attributable to other sources of 1,2-DCA, such as its origin as a lead scavenger in leaded gasoline or as an auxiliary solvent for pesticides, such as DDT (1,1,1-trichloro-2,2-bis(p-chlorophenyl)ethane).

If these assumptions are met then when TCE is detected with 1,1,2,2-TeCA and/or 1,2-TCA, it is probable that the released material was manufactured prior to or after 1978. The presence of 1,2-DCA when detected with TCE may indicate that it was formulated as early as 1960s, with an increasing probability that it was produced by the late 1970s.

Compound Specific Isotope Analysis for Source Identification of TCE

Compound-specific isotope analysis (CSIA) is a powerful tool for studying the source and environmental distribution of

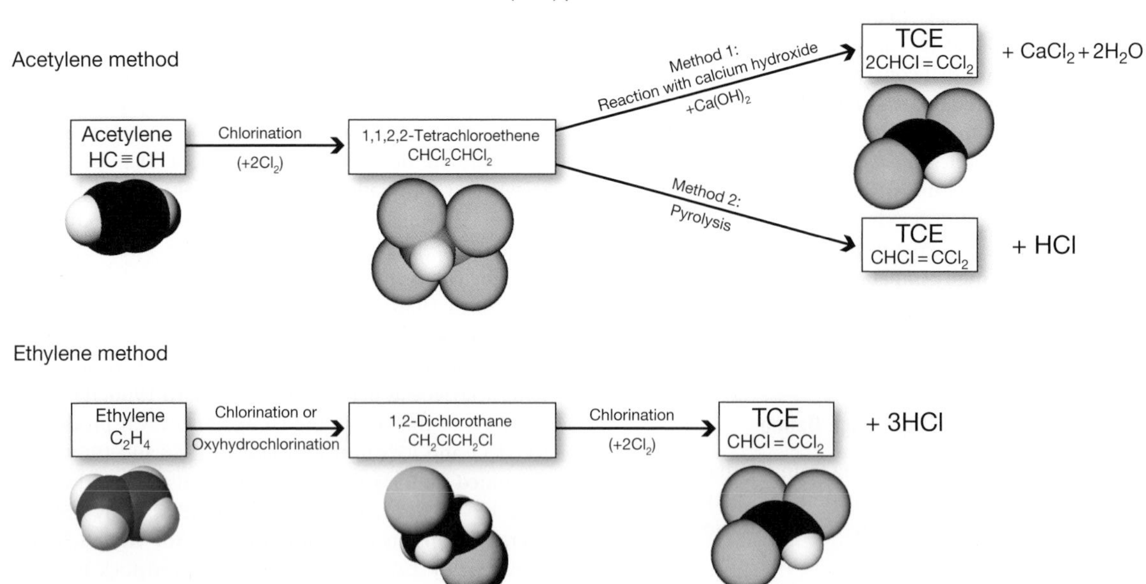

Figure 1 Production of TCE from acetylene and ethylene. Reproduced with permission from Morrison RD and Hone JR (2010) Age dating the release of PCE, TCE and TCA using stabilizers and feedstock impurities as indicators. In: Morrison RD and O'Sullivan G (eds.) *Environmental Forensics Proceedings of the 2009 INEF Annual Conference*. 295. Cambridge, UK: Royal Society of Chemistry Publishing.

contaminants. The ability to measure the isotopic composition of TCE is facilitated by gas chromatography–isotope ratio mass spectrometry, which allows for the measurement of the isotopic composition of individual compounds within a complex contaminant mixture. Rather than measuring a 'true ratio,' measuring its 'apparent ratio' is obtained by gas source mass spectrometry. The ratios of elements, such as oxygen, hydrogen, chlorine, sulfur, or nitrogen, are expressed in the same way relative to their specific standards. For oxygen and hydrogen isotopes, the accepted reference is standard mean ocean water (SMOW); for chlorine isotopes, it is standard mean ocean chloride; for sulfur, it is the troilite (ferric sulfide) phase of the Canon Diablo meteorite, and for the nitrogen isotope, it is atmospheric nitrogen (air). To cancel the instrumental error due to operational variations in different laboratories and instruments, a known reference is measured on the same instrument at the same time. Differences between the measured ratios of the sample and reference are expressed by the delta (δ) notation. δ values are expressed as parts per thousand or per mill (‰) difference from a reference as described in eqn [3] for hydrogen.

$$\delta^2\mathrm{H}_{\mathrm{sample}} = \left[\left({}^2\mathrm{H}/{}^1\mathrm{H}_{\mathrm{sample}}\right)/\left({}^2\mathrm{H}/{}^1\mathrm{H}_{\mathrm{reference}}\right) - 1\right] \times 1000‰\ \mathrm{SMOW} \qquad [3]$$

where SMOW is the name of the reference used, in this case standard mean ocean water.

In the case of carbon, a similar expression is used but for a different reference.

$$\delta^{13}\mathrm{C}_{\mathrm{sample}} = \left[\left({}^{13}\mathrm{C}/{}^{12}\mathrm{C}_{\mathrm{sample}}\right)/\left({}^{13}\mathrm{C}/{}^{12}\mathrm{C}_{\mathrm{reference}}\right) - 1\right] \times 1000‰\ \mathrm{PDB} \qquad [4]$$

where PDB is the name of the reference used, in this case Pee Dee Belemnite, a belemnite rostrum from the Cretaceous Peedee formation of South Carolina.

A δ‰ value that is positive (~+5‰) signifies that the sample has 5‰ or 0.5% more ^{13}C than the reference or is enriched by 5‰. Similarly, a sample that is depleted from the reference by this amount would be expressed as δ^{13}C equal to −5‰ PDB.

An alternative approach to measure only the carbon isotope is to measure the hydrogen isotopic compositions of individual molecules. Because of the larger relative mass difference between deuterium and hydrogen as compared with that between ^{13}C and ^{12}C, hydrogen isotopes fractionate significantly more during natural processes than carbon isotopes. The use of carbon and hydrogen is therefore a useful first approximation as to whether TCE sources can be discriminated based only on these two isotopic signatures. When appropriate, the use of ^{37}C and ^{35}Cl can be used with carbon and hydrogen isotopes. The most effective use of CSIA is a combination of carbon, hydrogen, and/or chlorine isotopic signatures where multiple sources of TCE are suspected but cannot be discriminated using concentration gradients. In these situations, the use of CSIA can provide a basis for distinguishing between different sources and approximate contributions.

Another potential use for chlorine isotope analysis is to discriminate between manufacturers when virgin TCE samples are available. The ability to use this technique is because ^{37}C is bound more tightly to the carbon than ^{35}Cl due to the differences in the temperature and pressure used to manufacture TCE. For example, in one study, the isotopic range of four samples of technical grade TCE (>99% TCE) from different manufacturers for carbon chlorine and hydrogen isotopes were δ^{13}C = −48.0 to −27.8‰, δ^{37}Cl = −2.54 to +4.08‰, and δ^2H = −30 to +530‰. These differences have been used to distinguish between different chlorinated solvent manufactures when pure-phase TCE was available for analysis.

A forensic question that arises regarding a comingled contaminant plumes containing TCE and PCE is whether the TCE

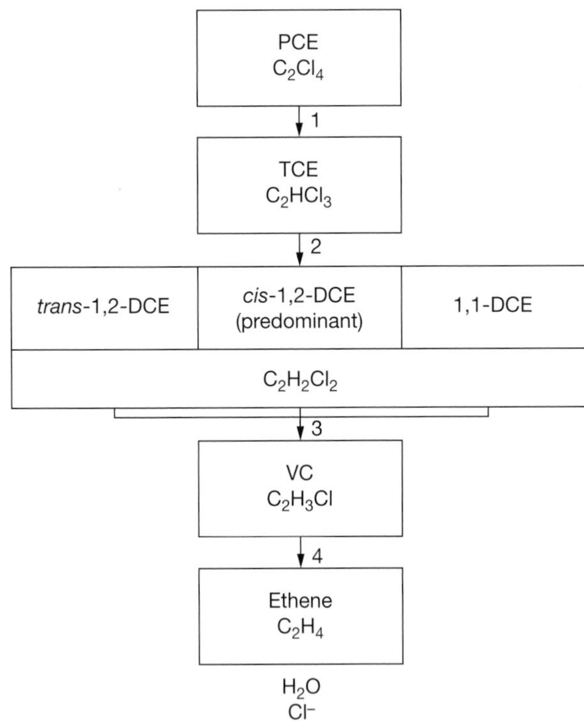

Figure 2 Degradation pathways for PCE and TCE.

is a degradation product of PCE or was released as TCE. As shown in **Figure 2**, TCE may originate from the degradation of PCE. This forensic question is resolved by using CSIA for hydrogen, and potentially for carbon.

The ability to use CSIA to ascertain whether TCE is a degradation product of PCE is because the hydrogen and carbon isotopic composition of manufactured TCE has been characterized for the fairly limited number of companies that historically produced TCE. For example, the ^{2}H for a range of manufactured TCE varies between +466.9 and +681.9‰, 31.57 and −27.37‰ for δ^{13}C, and −3.19 and +3.90‰ for δ^{37}Cl. TCE originating from the dechlorination of PCE is significantly depleted, generally with ^{2}H values less than 300‰. The hydrogen isotope composition of manufactured TCE is therefore a function of fractionation associated with synthesis reactions used to produce TCE with values less than 300‰, while the lighter hydrogen isotope composition of dechlorinated TCE in the environment is from the lighter hydrogen isotope from the surrounding soil water or groundwater.

Figure 3 depicts the range of isotopic values for carbon and hydrogen for manufactured TCE and TCE dechlorinated from PCE.

If the CSIA test results for hydrogen and carbon are inconclusive or if additional confirmation of the results is necessary, the isotopic value for chlorine can be measured, although values for δ^{37}Cl from PCE and manufactured TCE tend to overlap.

Surrogate Analysis

Surrogate analysis is the use of coincident physical or chemical evidence that provides information regarding the source and/or age of a contaminant release. Surrogate forensics consists of many techniques whose selection depends on the specifics of

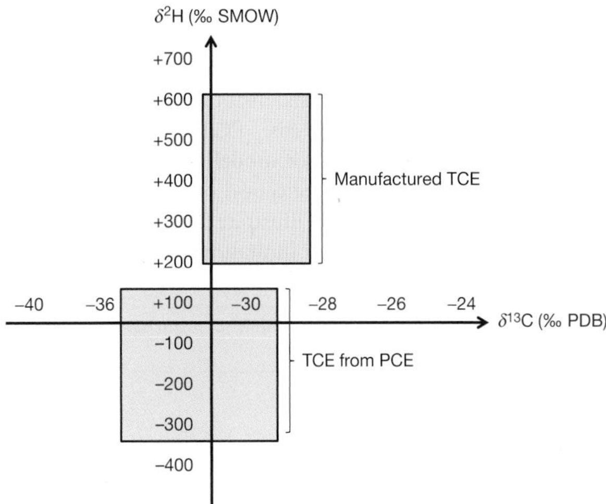

Figure 3 Compound specific isotopic analysis signatures for hydrogen and carbon for determining the origin of TCE.

the investigation and their chemical associations with a contaminant of concern. Surrogates can also be physical evidence that is diagnostic of a particular time frame.

Examples of surrogates techniques used to age date or identify the source of a contaminant include the following:

- The presence of trihalomethanes, including chloroform, bromodichloromethane, dibromochloromethane, tribromomethane, trifluoromethane, high TDS, elevated bacteria counts relative to background, and detergents in a sample with PCE is an indicator of a release from an underground septic pipe, likely from a dry cleaning establishment.
- Dating the release of PCBs via the presence of combustion debris from a fire whose date is known in conjunction with elevated furans to dioxins congeners that indicate a combustion source.
- The presence of methyl-tertiary butyl ether (MTBE) with BTEX (benzene, toluene, ethylbenzene, and xylene) in an environmental sample can be used as a surrogate for a gasoline release after 1986 when MTBE was introduced as a gasoline oxygenate in the United States.
- The presence of Aroclor 1016 and PCE in the same environmental sample. Aroclor 1016 was manufactured by Monsanto Company from 1971 through 1974, indicating a post-1971 release, while PCE was used for a limited time in transformers in the United States.
- The presence of 1,4-dioxane, a stabilizer used extensively in the United States with 1,1,1-TCA beginning in the late 1960s, as an indicator of its use after late 1960s for vapor degreasing.

The effective use of surrogate techniques requires an understanding of forensic approaches, along with their respective attributes and limitations, and a decision to use those that are scientifically defensible evidence regarding the source and date of a contaminant release.

Conclusion

Environmental forensics includes a multitude of forensic techniques available for contaminant age dating and source identification including chemical associations with discrete chemical processes, identification of the manufacturer of a particular product, chemical additives and/or impurities, chemical profiling, degradation models, contaminant transport modeling, surrogate analysis, historical changes in chemical processes, isotopic analysis, PCB and dioxin/furan congener analysis, mass balance modeling, and degradation product ratio analysis. The application of four of these techniques presented in this article illustrate how they are applied in actual cases, along with their limitations and advantages.

See also: **Foundations:** History of Forensic Sciences; Principles of Forensic Science.

Further Reading

Doherty RE (2000a) A history of the production and use of carbon tetrachloride, tetrachloroethylene, trichloroethylene and 1,1,1-trichloroethane in the United States: Part 1: Historical background, carbon tetrachloride and tetrachloroethylene. *Journal of Environmental Forensics* 1: 69–81.

Doherty RE (2000b) A history of the production and use of carbon tetrachloride, tetrachloroethylene, trichloroethylene and 1,1,1-trichloroethane in the United States: Part 2: Trichloroethylene and 1,1,1-trichloroethane. *Journal of Environmental Forensics* 1: 83–93.

Hunkeler DJ, Aravena RS, and Butler BG (1999) Monitoring microbial dechlorination of tetrachloroethene (PCE) in groundwater using compound-specific stable carbon isotope ratios: Microcosm and field studies. *Environmental Science and Technology* 33(16): 2733–2738.

Hunkeler DJ, Chollet N, Pittet X, Aravena RS, Cherry JA, and Parker BL (2004) Effect of source variability and transport processes on carbon isotope ratios of TCE and PCE in two sandy aquifers. *Journal of Contaminant Hydrology* 74: 265–282.

Mohr TKG (2001) Solvent stabilizers. White Paper. Prepublication Paper. June 14, 2001. Santa Clara Valley Water District. Underground Storage Tank Program, Water Supply Division, p. 52.

Mohr TKG (ed.) (2010) *Environmental Investigation and Remediation 1,4-Dioxane and Other Solvent Stabilizers*. Boca Raton, FL: CRC Press.

Morrison RD (2000a) Critical review of environmental forensic techniques: Part I. *Environmental Forensics* 1: 157–173.

Morrison RD (2000b) Critical review of environmental forensic techniques. Part II. *Environmental Forensics* 1(4): 175–195.

Morrison RD (2001) Chlorinated solvents and source identification. *Environmental Claims Journal* 13(3): 95–104.

Morrison RD and Hone JR (2010) Age dating the release of PCE, TCE and TCA using stabilizers and feedstock impurities as indicators. In: Morrison RD and O'Sullivan G (eds.) Environmental Forensics Proceedings of the 2009 INEF Annual Conference, pp. 289–304. Cambridge, UK: Royal Society of Chemistry Publishing.

Morrison RD and Murphy BL (eds.) (2006) *Environmental Forensics Contaminant Specific Guide*. Oxford, UK: Academic Press.

Morrison RD and O'Sullivan G (eds.) (2010) Environmental Forensics Proceedings of the 2009 INEF Annual Conference, Cambridge, UK: Royal Society of Chemistry Publishing.

Murphy BL and Morrison RD (eds.) (2004) *Introduction to Environmental Forensics*. Oxford, UK: Elsevier Academic Press.

Murphy BL and Morrison RD (eds.) (2007) *Introduction to Environmental Forensics*, 2nd edn. Oxford, UK: Academic Press.

Rossum J (1969) Prediction of pitting rates in ferrous metals from soil parameters. *Journal of American Water Works Association* 305–310.

Shouakar-Stash O, Frape SK, and Drimmie RJ (2003) Stable hydrogen, carbon and chlorine isotope measurements of selected chlorinated organic solvents. *Journal of Contaminant Hydrology* 60: 211–228.

Slater GF, Lollar BS, Sleep BE, and Edwards EA (2001) Variability in carbon isotopic fractionation during biodegradation of chlorinated ethenes: Implication for field applications. *Environmental Science and Technology* 35: 901–907.

Van Warmerdam EM, Frape SK, Aravena RS, Drimmie RJ, Flatt HR, and Cherry JA (1995) Stable chlorine and carbon isotope measurements of selected chlorinated organic solvents. *Applied Geochemistry* 10(5): 547–552.

Contents

Clandestine Explosive Laboratories

N Speers and V Otieno-Alego, Australian Federal Police Forensic and Data Centres, Canberra, ACT, Australia
K Ritchie, Forensic Explosives Laboratory, DSTL Fort Halstead, Sevenoaks, UK

Glossary

Bulk explosives Explosives and/or their components that are visible to the naked eye, including with the use of a low-power (up to ×20) optical microscope.
Clandestine Secret and concealed, often in order to conceal an illicit or improper purpose.
Contamination Unintended presence, or introduction, of particles, chemicals, and other substances.
Explosive A substance in a metastable state that is capable of undergoing a rapid chemical reaction without external reactants to produce predominately gaseous reaction products.
Fuel A substance capable of reacting with oxygen and oxygen carriers with the evolution of heat.
Nanogram One-billionth (10^{-9}) of a gram.
Oxidizer Substance that yields oxygen readily to stimulate combustion. Or a substance that accelerates the burning of other materials.
Picogram One-trillionth (10^{-12}) of a gram
Swabbing Sampling using a dry or solvent-wetted solid substrate such as cotton wool, fabric, or synthetic fibers.
Synthesis The formation of one chemical compound from another.
Trace explosives Explosives and/or their components that are invisible to the naked eye, including with the use of a low-power (up to ×20) optical microscope.
Vacuuming/vacuum sampling Sampling using a high-powered vacuum pump coupled to a filter.

Introduction

Safety warning: Clandestine explosive laboratories present significant safety issues. A scene suspected of being a clandestine explosive laboratory should not be entered without a safety assessment by a suitably qualified individual(s). Only after safety issues have been addressed, the examination of a scene can proceed. Safety also must be continually considered during an examination.

The examination of clandestine explosive laboratories presents many challenges for an explosives chemist. First and foremost are the issues of safety for those involved, including first responders, forensic scientists, and the general public. A scene suspected of being a clandestine explosive laboratory should not be entered without a safety assessment by a suitably qualified individual(s), including checks for booby trap devices within the premises.

For the purposes of this article, clandestine explosive laboratories will be taken to have a broad meaning and will encompass sites in which explosives are being manufactured (either by synthesis or mixing), sites in which devices have been/are being manufactured, and sites where explosive caches have been located. **Figure 1** shows an example of a site setup to manufacture explosives. All of these scenes present similar challenges, including safe entry to the scene, safe collection of samples, safe destruction of explosives and hazardous materials, and the location of evidence to determine what was occurring within the scene and to potentially link the scene with people, explosive devices, and/or other scenes.

 http://dx.doi.org/10.1016/B978-0-12-382165-2.00081-7

Figure 1 Example of clandestine explosive laboratory in kitchen. Crown Copyright 2010: Source CPNI.

While the nature of some clandestine explosive laboratories will be easily identified, in others it will be more difficult to determine exactly what is or has been occurring. It is possible that scenes that are initially believed to be clandestine explosive laboratories will turn out to be associated with drugs, chemical warfare agents, or biological agents instead of, or as well as, explosives. Any person entering or examining a potential clandestine explosive laboratory needs to be aware of this possibility and not be blinkered into only considering explosives. This is equally true in reverse; examiners of potential drug, chemical warfare agent, or biological warfare agent scenes should be alert to the possibility that explosives may be present and could even be manufactured (intentionally or inadvertently) in the scene.

Recognition of Clandestine Explosive Laboratories

External indicators of a clandestine explosive laboratory will be common to other types of clandestine laboratories and illegal activities. These can include covered windows, extra security, chemical smells, and the discoloration of pavements and soil. These external indicators are more valuable to the investigators and intelligence analysts in identifying potential clandestine explosive laboratory locations than to the explosives chemist.

Once a clandestine laboratory has been located, the next issue is the determination of the type of material being manufactured. There are a number of indicators that will aid in differentiating clandestine explosive laboratories from those manufacturing drugs, chemical agents, or biological agents. These include the chemicals, equipment, documentation, and other materials present.

The chemicals present in a scene should give an indication of the type of materials being manufactured. Although there are chemicals that are common to the manufacture of drugs, chemical warfare agents, and explosives, the combination of chemicals present in a scene should direct a chemist who is knowledgeable in this field to the material being manufactured. It is important to note that many of the chemicals utilized to manufacture explosives also have innocent and even domestic uses. Legitimate uses of chemicals must be considered, and an explosives chemist should provide balanced advice on both explosives and legitimate uses of chemicals.

The equipment required to manufacture explosives can vary from minimal to more extensive ones. The equipment used may be laboratory-type equipment or could be household items that can be adapted to serve the same purpose. The presence of cooling equipment is an indicator that explosives rather than drugs are being manufactured. The equipment present will be determined by the method of manufacture being employed.

Explosives can be manufactured by a number of methods. Simply mixing a fuel and oxidizer in the correct ratio can create an explosive material. If the fuel or oxidizer are solid materials, then a fine powder is generally desired to enable more intimate mixing and so a more efficient and powerful explosive. For this reason, grinding and mixing equipment may be present in a location. Equipment such as a kitchen blender or mortar and pestle could be used. Equipment to contain, mix, and store the chemicals and explosive materials will also be required.

Other explosives are manufactured by chemical synthesis. Equipment required will include a vessel in which the reaction will occur. This could be a household item such as glass jar or laboratory equipment such as a beaker, reaction vessel, or flask. Equipment to measure different amounts of chemicals will also be required. This could include scales, measuring cups/spoons/cylinders, and syringes. Explosive synthesis may require that reactants and products be kept cool either to encourage a desired reaction or for safety reasons, as heat is a potential initiator for explosives. Conversely, heating may also be required by some processes such as concentrating a liquid and so the presence of heating equipment does not necessarily indicate that explosives are not being manufactured.

Other materials such as documentation and device construction materials present in a scene may also give significant information about what has been occurring at a site. Documentation may be physical or electronic and both forms of documentation should be extensively searched for. Documentation could include recipes/directions for the manufacture of explosives, directions for device construction, information on chemicals and equipment that have been sought, information about intended targets, and modes of attack. Materials related to device construction can be varied depending on the method of delivery and initiation intended. They could include initiators (electronic or not), containers, shrapnel, soldering equipment, and electrical circuitry and componentry. It is noteworthy that a device can be constructed without electrical components.

It should be considered that the site at which the explosive is manufactured and the site where a device is constructed may not be one and the same. The presence of device components in the absence of precursor chemicals and chemical equipment may indicate that the location is one in which a device was constructed, but that the explosive utilized was obtained ready to use or the explosive manufacture occurred at a different location.

A storage location for explosives may contain explosives with no or very little other materials. A potential explosive cache will be identified by chemical analysis and physical examination of the materials present.

Objectives of Clandestine Explosive Laboratory Examination

There are two distinct and potentially competing objectives when a clandestine explosive laboratory is located. The first is the safe removal and disposal of hazardous materials located within the scene. The second is the investigation of the suspected illegal activity.

Safety for all affected, who may include first responders, forensic personnel, investigators, and the general public must be given priority; when the two objectives are competing safety will always take precedence. In some instances, this may mean that materials are destroyed without a sample being taken. This will occur if the risks of taking a sample are too great even though the investigation and prosecution may suffer in the absence of a sample. An explosives chemist can have valuable input to decisions about the safe removal and destruction of materials by identifying the chemicals and explosives present and advising about the hazards associated with the materials located.

Once safety issues have been addressed then the second objective, the investigation of the suspected illegal activity, can be considered. There will be multiple objectives within this which forensic examination and analysis can contribute to. These will include the identification of materials present, the identification of the processes underway or previously undertaken, the identification of the people involved, the linking of the scene to other scenes, and the linking of the scene to explosive devices.

The Examination of Clandestine Explosive Laboratories

The examination of a clandestine explosive laboratory will be a difficult and time-consuming task. Each situation will be unique, but certain issues will need to be considered in every situation. Safety will be the paramount consideration, but consideration will also need to be given to contamination concerns, sampling of the materials present, the potential for other forensic evidence, and the use of on-site analysis.

Safety at a Clandestine Explosives Laboratory

The hazards associated with a clandestine explosives laboratory increase the complications of processing such scenes and require that only people with specialized training be involved. The risk of explosion is the greatest concern because it can potentially do the greatest amount of harm to responding personnel in the shortest amount of time. Thus, when a clandestine explosive laboratory is identified, it is paramount that bomb disposal (BD) officers first attend the scene and assess the situation. If required, the BD officers are able to use robots as a remote method to enter such premises, relaying back live videos that can allow the responding teams to undertake scene appreciation from a safe distance.

The priority of the first search by the BD experts is to locate any improvised explosive devices (IEDs) or booby-traps, which could be linked to explosives, firearms, or other devices. If IEDs are identified, this danger needs to be mitigated first. The BD officers can utilize specialized equipment to interrogate and render safe such devices. In some instances, the robots may be used to remove and/or relocate the IED to a safe location for destruction. When destroying such devices, the recovery of forensic evidence including the type of explosive contained in the IED should be considered. Given the potential for encountering explosives and/or IEDs during the scene processing, the BD officers should remain active participants during the entire scene processing.

Once safe entry has been established, the explosives chemists, in liaison with the BD experts, commence processing the scene for physical evidence. A clandestine explosive laboratory is a unique scene in that it requires both the protocols to process a crime scene and a hazardous materials incident. In particular, the dynamics of the hazardous materials involved must be taken into account, and the safety of the personnel processing the scene must be paramount. Each responder on-site should continually be evaluating the scene for potential hazards or situations that could present a hazard, and how the hazard can be abated. The responding team must use appropriate personal protective equipment (PPE), which may change during the various stages of the processing operation. Nothing should be taken for granted in a clandestine explosive laboratory. For example, it is not unusual to find incompatible chemicals (e.g., strong acids and strong bases) stored together in such premises. Such chemicals can accidentally combine and create a more hazardous situation.

If the site is a manufacturing site, the initial task of the explosives chemist is to establish the nature of chemicals at the scene. This allows for their safe handling and transport. The identification of chemicals on-site can be aided by the use of portable instruments (see section 'On-Site Analysis'). The greatest challenge to the explosives chemist is the identification of chemicals in unlabeled containers. Extreme caution should be exercised when handling such containers because they could contain sensitive explosive substances. Chemical containers should not be opened unless the process is fully assessed and deemed safe. For example, the sensitive homemade explosive triacetone triperoxide (TATP) if stored in a bottle can sublime and recrystallize on the top of the bottle. Opening such a container may provide enough friction to initiate the explosive.

Depending on the nature and amount of precursor chemicals, their safe transportation and destruction can be undertaken by the explosives chemist or commercial chemical disposal companies. If bulk explosives are found on-site, only small amounts of the materials are collected for analysis. The bulk of the explosive is transported by the BD experts to a magazine for storage or to a safe location for disposal. Where possible, samples of the chemicals analyzed on-site can be taken for further examination and confirmation in the central laboratory.

Most common precursor chemicals used in explosives manufacture are often household products. Such chemicals are expected to have less impact and persistence in the environment. The common homemade explosives mixtures (such as the nitrate- or chlorate-based mixtures) also have less persistence in the environment. Thus, unlike a typical clandestine drug laboratory, site remedial for toxic chemicals is not a common occurrence. In any case, once all chemicals are removed from the site, inspection of the premise by suitable experts is warranted to facilitate any site remediation if required.

The safety of those who will examine items collected from the scene must also be considered. The safety aspect will be significant if bulk quantities (i.e., amounts that are visible to the naked eye) are present on items. Ideally, any such contamination should be physically removed by collecting the explosive for storage and/or cleaning of the item. Cleaning will likely affect other evidence that may be present on an item, such as fingerprints and DNA; however, the primary consideration must be for the safety of those who will subsequently collect, package, transport, and examine the item.

Contamination

When processing a clandestine explosive laboratory scene, the protocols adopted should demonstrate anti-contamination measures to ensure that any evidence gathered meets the burden of proof required in a criminal investigation. From an evidential point of view, the contamination of items that are known or suspected to be significant to an investigation must be avoided if at all possible. If contamination accidentally takes place, it is imperative that it is recorded and reported to anyone whom it may later affect. The consequences of external interference with explosives samples can be very serious, particularly, if their presence (or indeed absence) eventually forms part of a criminal prosecution or defense.

Demonstrably robust anti-contamination measures are especially important if trace levels of explosives (i.e., invisible to the naked eye) are involved. Modern laboratory analytical techniques can detect explosives traces at nanogram or even picogram levels. Even at such minute quantities, the presence or absence of explosives can be key issues to the investigators, the prosecution, and the defense in a criminal trial. At best contamination can lead to wasted time by investigators who may follow false leads or theories. At worst, it can lead to a miscarriage of justice.

Minimizing the risk of trace explosives contamination is primarily best achieved by the first responders, and subsequent scene examiners, being suitably equipped and having an awareness of trace explosives issues. An important general principle is to keep the number of people who enter a scene to an absolute minimum; anyone who does not need to be there to do a specific job should not be allowed to enter, including the press and other visitors who may wish to enter 'for a look.' Similarly, anyone who does enter ideally should neither have recently been in contact with explosives nor have been in a bulk explosives environment.

An exception to this is the potential need for inherently and unavoidably contaminated personnel, such as BD officers or military/police officers carrying firearms, to enter a scene. Wherever possible, they should be encouraged to take as many anti-contamination measures as reasonably possible. Before trace explosives sampling being done, they should be asked to keep their time and contact with items in the scene (including any suspects) to an absolute minimum; however, most certainly not to the point that it hinders their very important tasks. Even simple precautions such as the wearing of disposable, brand new outer protective Tyvek suits and plastic gloves will greatly reduce the likelihood of them introducing contamination. If this is not reasonably possible, for example, because it hinders their movement or use of their equipment, then the investigators and other scene examiners will need to be aware of this and will then have to be appropriately cautious with the subsequent interpretation of the significance of any positive trace explosives results. In some jurisdictions, pre-entry swabs are collected from these officers, as it is considered that analysis of these swabs can aid interpretation of the scene by identifying the specific explosives traces that these members may have introduced to the scene. Other jurisdictions take a different view and have alternate procedures in place, which take into account and mitigate any concerns about the possible contamination of a scene by those who enter as part of the investigation. A careful and comprehensive record of the nature and locations of the activities within the scene of the known or suspected contaminated person will also be required. With such measures in place, it should be possible to minimize the impact on the integrity of any trace work conducted at the scene.

The fundamental principle in the prevention of explosives contamination is to keep a series of clean, physical barriers between a suspect item and anything that it comes to physical contact with. This includes the use of pristine gloves, over-suits, and scene examination equipment such as bags and other packaging. Packaging materials that will prevent cross-transfer must be used, particularly for explosives with relatively high vapor pressure such as nitroglycerine and TATP.

Sampling of a clandestine laboratory for explosives traces should be carried out as soon as reasonably possible after the explosive safety of the scene has been assessed and determined. Completion of that work at an early stage will minimize the chances of contamination, which will become virtually inevitable as the scene examination proceeds and deepens.

Sampling

All examinations of a clandestine laboratory will be done under unique, potentially unknown, dangerous, and highly variable circumstances. Therefore, careful consideration and evaluation by scene investigators of the most appropriate and necessary samples and items to collect is essential.

As in all work involving energetic materials, particularly any close manual handling of improvised explosives and devices, safety is the first priority. Initially, expert advice from appropriately trained and experienced advisors should be sought on what is, or more importantly is not, reasonably safe to touch and manipulate.

While the specifics of each situation will need to be considered before decisions can be made about appropriate sampling, some general principles will apply. Samples collected for analysis should contain only a sufficient amount for analysis and not considerably more than this. Samples that present the least risk should be collected first for initial analysis. Factors that affect the eventual sampling strategy could include the amount of material in a particular container/location, the nature of the material (e.g., liquid, powder, or solid), and available access to the sample (e.g., container open or closed).

If substances particularly sensitive to initiation by heat, spark, impact, or friction are known or suspected to be present, great care must be taken to avoid accidental initiation. For example, the likelihood of electrical sparks can be significantly reduced by the use of anti-static packaging, tools, and clothing.

All transmitting electrical devices should be switched off to mitigate any potential electrical spark and radio frequency hazards. The risk of accidental initiation by impact and friction can be minimized by careful handling, avoiding the use of screw-capped containers, and by ensuring that any samples collected are packaged in suitably rigid and strong vessels.

In the vast majority of instances, it will be appropriate to securely seal samples in a padded metal box. However, some improvised explosives, such as mixtures containing hydrogen peroxide, can spontaneously react and off-gas or even ignite. In those cases, a fire-proof, vented container will be necessary.

If it is evident that explosives have been manufactured, but bulk suspect materials are not present, consideration can be given to swabbing/vacuuming the suspect area for explosive traces and/or their precursors. For example, during the investigation following the Bali 2002 bombings in Indonesia, a house in which the bomb was alleged to have been assembled was examined 6 months after the event. Despite an apparent attempt to clean the site, vacuuming of the floor revealed valuable forensic evidence on the nature of the explosive mixture used in the bombing. Figure 2 shows part of the scene and examples of the crystals recovered from the floor vacuumings. Furthermore, the collection of plumbing fixtures and fittings and subsequent analysis of them for traces of explosives may yield important forensic evidence. This was the case during the investigation of the failed London bombings on the 21st July 2005 in which traces of TATP were recovered from sink drainage pipes in one of the bomb factories.

Other potentially explosives-related equipment or items are likely to be present too. This can include, but is not exclusive to, batteries, timers, electrical/electronic equipment, chemicals, scientific/chemistry equipment, beakers, funnels, hot plates, PPE, and documents. Most items will have legitimate nonexplosive-related uses; therefore, it is important to consider whether or not they are likely to be significant in the context and circumstances of a particular investigation. If in doubt, it is best to seize an item, as there may only be one chance to examine it in the condition in which it was first found.

Figure 2 Alleged device construction location for the Bali 2002 bombing in Indonesia. Forensic examination of the floor vacuuming revealed the presence of tiny conglomerates (see inset) containing a fine mixture of potassium chlorate, sulfur, aluminum flakes, and charcoal.

On-Site Analysis

Field-portable analytical instruments are often deployed to provide rapid on-site sample triage, screening, and identification of unknown chemicals during clandestine laboratory investigation. The instruments are set up in a forward location close to, but not within, the scene itself. The forward location can be a van fitted out appropriately (e.g., a 'mobile laboratory'), a room within a hotel or office, or a makeshift location with appropriate facilities such as power and benches or tables. Figure 3, for example, shows portable instruments deployed in a fitted-out mobile laboratory.

Portable analytical instruments offer a number of advantages in any clandestine laboratory investigation where immediate data are required to facilitate critical decisions in the field and/or to avoid issues with field sampling and transportation. In the context of explosives manufacture, the instruments can provide critical information in the identification of suspected explosive material, thereby enabling informed decisions to be made concerning render-safe procedures and the relevant transportation requirements. This is of particular importance when extremely sensitive explosives, such as the homemade organic peroxides, are suspected. On-site identification of precursor chemicals can also direct the chemist to the type of explosive likely to be at the scene. Furthermore, knowing the nature of the chemicals allows the chemist to separate and segregate them as required, thereby minimizing any risk due to chemical incompatibilities during storage or transportation.

Figure 3 Mobile laboratory showing (a) sample submission area and (b) interior with portable instrument setup.

When examining a location previously used to assemble explosive devices, one of the challenges facing the explosives chemist is knowing what to collect and/or swab. This has often led to a 'take and/or swab-all approach.' With the availability of field testing, a more targeted approach is possible. Swabs taken from different surfaces can be examined on-site using the portable instruments. The preliminary results not only give insight into the type(s) of explosive(s) that was utilized at the scene but also the positive results used to inform further sample collection for additional testing in the central laboratory.

Currently, a suite of portable analytical techniques are in use by the forensic science community. The techniques utilized for explosive detection and identification include ion mobility spectrometry (IMS), Fourier transform infrared (FTIR) spectroscopy, Raman spectroscopy, gas chromatography (GC) coupled to different detection systems (e.g., mass spectrometry (MS), chemiluminescence (CL), and surface acoustic wave (SAW)), and ion chromatography. Of these techniques, FTIR and Raman spectroscopy have emerged as the two most common analytical techniques for characterizing unknown chemicals recovered from clandestine laboratories. FTIR and Raman spectroscopy are similar insofar as they both produce spectra based on the vibrational transitions within the molecules of the sample. The particular combination of the infrared and/or Raman bands provide identification of an unknown substance (inorganic or organic) normally by means of comparison of the band characteristics of the unknown substance with those of standard materials stored in a database. For example, **Figure 4** shows an explosive cache with FTIR and Raman spectra from portable instruments, which were used to identify the materials.

In several respects, FTIR and Raman spectroscopic techniques are well suited for the analysis of unknown chemicals recovered from clandestine laboratories. The spectrometers can be considered as being 'universal detectors'; the two techniques can be used to analyze virtually anything – solids, liquids, or gases, and organic and inorganic samples. This is a big advantage in clandestine laboratory investigations, where a myriad of unknown chemicals are often recovered. On-site analysis features that make FTIR and Raman portable spectrometers attractive include their ease of use, short warm-up times, short analysis times, minimal sample preparation (if any), and limited requirements for field maintenance and consumables. The techniques are also nondestructive, thus, any sample analyzed can be reserved for the later laboratory analysis, if required.

When compared to FTIR, Raman spectroscopy has additional advantages as a portable technique in that Raman spectra (unlike Infrared) can be obtained through the walls of sealed clear plastic bags, transparent bottles, and vials without opening the container. The Raman's 'point-and-shoot' sampling is important, especially when attempting to identify unlabeled sealed chemicals from clandestine laboratories. In addition, Raman spectrometers can be coupled with fiber-optic probes of various lengths, which can be mounted onto remote-controlled robots, allowing potentially hazardous materials to be identified at a safe distance.

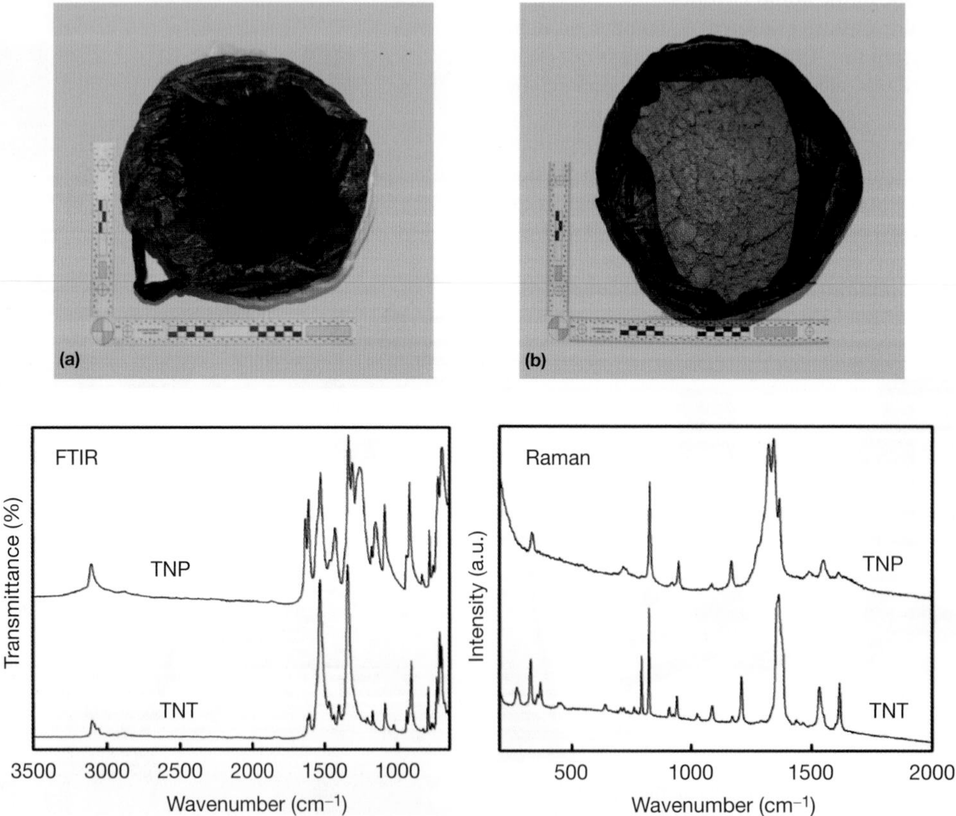

Figure 4 Examples of unknown suspect explosive chemicals identified using both portable FTIR and Raman. The chemicals were positively identified as being (a) trinitrophenol (TNP) and (b) trinitrotoluene (TNT).

It is noteworthy, however, that the high-powered (785 nm) lasers typically used with many commercially available portable Raman instruments have sufficient power to burn solid samples. The potential to burn samples raises concerns when identifying unknown chemicals, especially in a clandestine explosive laboratory. In particular, darkly colored energetic materials (e.g., black powder or chlorate/sulfur/aluminum/carbon explosive mixture) can absorb sufficient heat to self-initiate when irradiated with the Raman laser. Thus, as a safety guide, caution should be taken when using a Raman instrument to interrogate unknown dark/gray colored solids. Raman's 'point-and-shoot' method is safe for liquid samples because any laser heating is easily dispersed though the solution (by convention).

Other Evidence Types

Forensic examination of a clandestine explosive laboratory needs to be far broader than only the chemistry. A team of forensic specialists, not solely an explosives chemist, are required to fully examine a scene. It will generally not be possible for other specialists to conduct their examinations until after the explosives chemist's examination, so it is essential that the explosives chemist has an awareness of other potential forensic evidence, and how their examinations could impact on other evidence types.

There is a potential for many other forms of forensic evidence to be present in a clandestine explosive laboratory. There will be instances in which examinations for one evidence type will negatively impact on another evidence type, and advice will need to be sought from investigators on which evidence type should take priority.

Other evidence types that should be considered include (but are not limited to) DNA, fingerprints, electronic evidence, documents, other forms of chemical trace evidence, and marks evidence. DNA and fingerprint examinations will be important to identify the people involved. Electronic evidence and physical documents could both contain important information such as explosive recipes or details of plans. Examinations to determine the sources of electronic information may provide links to other people or organizations. Physical documents could link people through handwriting examinations, printers through ink, and paper analysis and could also reveal extra information through examinations for indentations. Other forms of chemical trace evidence (such as paint, fibers, tapes, and plastics) and marks evidence (such as shoe marks and tool marks) could provide valuable links to explosive devices or other scenes.

Case Study – The Explosions in London on 7 July 2005

The terrorist bombings of the London transport system in July 2005 involved the examination of a series of crime scenes, one of which was an address in Leeds, northern England. Within it was a clandestine laboratory where the explosives had been manufactured.

A forensic scientist from the UK Forensic Explosives Laboratory (FEL) was asked to attend and assist. On entering the premises, accompanied by a military Explosive Ordnance Disposal (EOD) Officer and an investigating police officer, he was faced with a variety of unknown substances. Figure 5 shows one of the bedrooms in the location with equipment and unknown substances.

Within the address were observed approximately 25 open-topped plastic containers, each 3–6 L in volume, that contained quantities of a yellow/brown sludge. Figure 6 shows some of these containers located in bedroom 1. There were also various plastic trays, funnels, and filter papers that were all heavily coated with a white powder.

Initial assessments of the sludge and powder were made by carrying out some carefully executed field tests. Those tests indicated that the sludge was an energetic substance but that it was not particularly sensitive, and therefore, it was not an immediate safety concern. Tests on the white powder indicated that it was also an energetic substance and that it was very sensitive. The initial assessment was that it could be a primary high explosive.

Therefore, the white powder was considered to be a serious safety hazard, and it was dealt with as a priority. Subgram samples of the powder were very carefully taken and desensitized in an appropriate solvent for transportation to FEL.

The main initial concern at the scene was to ensure that the powder, and anything with the white powder on it, were dealt

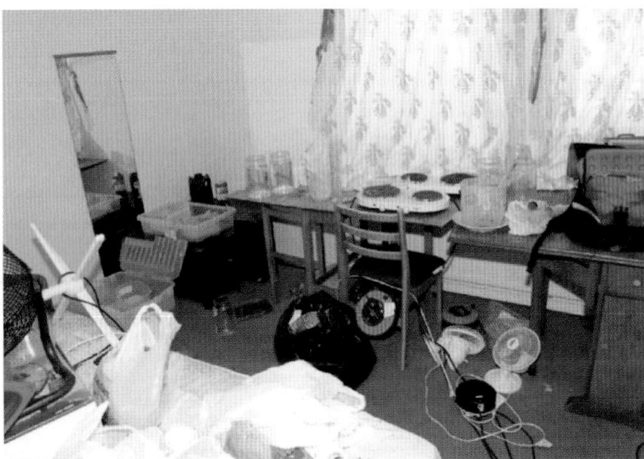

Figure 5 Bedroom in clandestine laboratory associated with bombings in London on 7th July 2005.

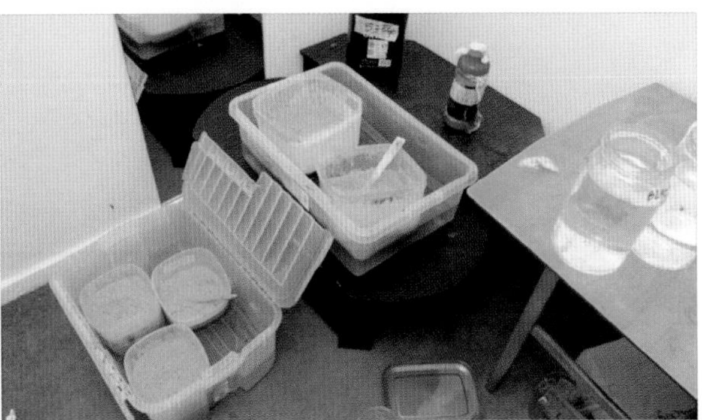

Figure 6 Containers of yellow/brown sludge located in bedroom of clandestine laboratory associated with bombings in London on 7th July 2005.

with safety while preserving as far as possible any other forensic evidence that may have been present. This was done by systematically collecting the powder and carefully cleaning anything that had the powder on it. The cleaning materials were disposed of safely.

In instances where items could not be cleaned satisfactorily, they were taken outside to a suitable location nearby and destroyed by the EOD officers, along with the collected bulk quantities of white powder. It later became clear that the white powder was the primary high explosive, hexamethylene triperoxide diamine (HMTD).

During the scene examination, it was observed that the sludge was spontaneously reacting and generating a gas. The sludge was collected; the containers that it was put into were vented to prevent a significant pressure build up. Small samples of the sludge were sent for urgent analysis by various specialists, including chemical and biological agents. It was soon discovered that the sludge was a high explosive mixture of concentrated hydrogen peroxide and ground black pepper.

The examination of this scene demonstrates the complexity involved in the examination of clandestine explosive laboratories. As discussed in this article, safety issues were the primary concern and had to be addressed first before other examinations could proceed. Forensic examination and processing of the address took several weeks, which is typical for a complex scene where improvised high explosives are suspected or known to be present.

Conclusions

Clandestine explosive laboratories are very challenging crime scenes for explosives chemists and other forensic examiners. Safety must always be the primary consideration at a clandestine explosive laboratory and must be constantly considered during an examination. Major safety hazards are explosions from devices (including booby-traps) or explosive materials and chemical hazards. Explosives chemists have a significant role in these examinations by providing chemical information, safety advice, and an assessment of what has occurred within the site. An explosives chemist will also consider the contamination concerns, the safe collection of samples, and the potential for other forensic evidence. When processed safely and systematically, valuable forensic evidence can be recovered from the clandestine explosive laboratories.

See also: **Chemistry/Trace/Drugs of Abuse:** Clandestine Laboratories; **Chemistry/Trace/Explosives:** Explosives: Analysis; Improvised Explosive Devices; Improvised Explosives; **Investigations:** Explosions.

Further Reading

Benson S, Speers N, and Otieno-Alego V (2012) Portable explosive detection instruments. In: Beveridge A (ed.) *Forensic Investigation of Explosions*, 2nd edn. Boca Raton, FL: CRC Press.

Christian DR (2004a) *Field Guide to Clandestine Laboratory Identification and Investigation*. New York: CRC Press.

Christian DR (2004b) *Forensic Investigation of Clandestine Laboratories*. New York: CRC Press.

McMahon G (2007) Portable analytical instrumentation. In: McMahon G (ed.) *Analytical Instrumentation, A Guide to Laboratory, Portable and Miniaturised Instruments*, pp. 173–216. UK: John Wiley & Sons, Ltd.

Rhykerd CL, Hannum DW, Murray DW, and Parmeter JE (1999) Guide for the selection of commercial explosives detection systems for law enforcement applications. *NIJ Guide 100-99, National Institute of Justice, Office of Science and Technology*, Washington, DC 20531, September 1999, NCJ 178913. http://www.ojp.usdoj.gov/nij/pubs-sum/178913.htm (accessed 1 October 2008).

Relevant Website

http://publicintelligence.net/ – Department of Homeland Security. Identifying and Differentiating among Clandestine Biological, Chemical, Explosives, and Methamphetamine Laboratories.

Improvised Explosive Devices

AD Beveridge, Burnaby, BC, Canada

Introduction

Improvised explosive devices (IEDs), commonly known as 'bombs,' are designed to produce explosions that result in property damage, bodily injury, or death, and sow fear and uncertainty in the affected population. IEDs are distinguished from commercial and military explosive devices by incorporating components which are 'home-made' in clandestine laboratories or are manufactured items applied to IED construction for a purpose for which they were not originally intended. IEDs have no legitimate uses and may be unpredictable in sensitivity, power, and stability.

IEDs are weapons of choice for criminals and for insurgent and terrorist groups targeting transportation, military, and civilian targets. IEDs range from small pipe bombs containing propellant powders through hidden devices like roadside bombs or devices in luggage to vehicles loaded with multiple kilograms of blasting agents. The nature of each device is determined by the nature of the target, the ingenuity and skill of the bomb maker, and access to components. However, all IEDs have common elements which in turn provide important physical evidence for forensic science examinations.

Elements of IEDs

IEDs require two basic elements:

- Explosive
- Initiation system

Additional components may include:

- Container
- Binding material
- Shrapnel; other hazardous material

Explosives

Any legitimate or improvised explosive can be used in an IED, and will be either a high explosive or a low explosive. The distinguishing property is the speed with which the chemical reaction occurs as the reaction front moves through the unreacted explosive. Low explosives react by deflagration – very fast particle-to-particle burning in which the reaction front travels at less than the speed of sound. High explosives detonate, with the reaction front propagated by a shock wave traveling at greater than the speed of sound. Mechanisms of explosions are discussed in detail elsewhere in this encyclopedia.

Low explosives are propellant powders and chemical mixtures. This class of explosive must be confined in order to explode. The most common form is a pipe with threaded end caps (pipe bomb). Propellant powders are black powder (potassium nitrate, sulfur, charcoal) and smokeless powders (single base: nitrocellulose; double base: nitrocellulose, nitroglycerin). Chemical mixtures consist of an oxidizer (contains oxygen) and a suitable fuel with which the oxidizer will react in an oxidation–reduction reaction. Examples are improvised flash powder (oxidizer and powdered metal) and a chlorate/sugar mixture. Smokeless powder propellants, black powder, and many black powder substitutes such as Pyrodex® are widely available commercial products for hand-loading and other than black powder are rarely improvised.

Initiation of the explosive reaction of confined propellant powders and many chemical mixtures may be achieved by the relatively low energy of a flame. Chemical mixtures like black powder are also very susceptible to initiation by friction and sparks.

High explosives do not require confinement in order to explode. They are divided into two classes – primary and secondary. Primary high explosives may be initiated by flame whereas secondary high explosives require initiation by detonation.

The principal commercial use of primary high explosives is in detonators. Examples are lead styphnate and lead azide. Secondary high explosives are the most commonly encountered legitimate commercial and military high explosives: nitroglycerine and ethylene glycol dinitrate, pentaerythritol tetranitrate, trinitrotoluene, cyclotrimethylene trinitramine, cyclotetramethlene tetranitramine, tetryl, and emulsion and slurry explosives (ammonium nitrate based; detonator initiated). There is a further subclass of secondary high explosives for which the shock wave from a detonator usually is insufficient to induce an explosive reaction. These are the blasting agents that require both a detonator and a booster secondary explosive to produce a reliable explosive reaction. The most commonly used blasting agent is ammonium nitrate/fuel oil (ANFO). Further details about commercial and military explosives are given elsewhere in this encyclopedia.

Some improvised explosive formulations have a long history which has been documented in anarchist literature. Books available by mail order and online also cover the subject, but the prime accessible source of information on improvised explosives and IEDs is the Internet. The most commonly encountered improvised explosives are

- fertilizer based
- inorganic salt based
- peroxide based

Improvised fertilizer explosives typically are based on ammonium nitrate and urea. Improvised ANFO can be made by mixing ammonium nitrate fertilizer with fuel oil. Also, a mixture of ammonium nitrate with a fuel like sugar can create an improvised blasting agent. Urea nitrate is synthesized from the fertilizer urea, and has been widely used in illegal acts in the Middle East, including Israel, and reportedly was used in the World Trade Center bombing in New York in 1993.

 http://dx.doi.org/10.1016/B978-0-12-382165-2.00082-9

Inorganic salt-based explosives are physical mixtures of oxidizers (salts of chlorates and perchlorates; permanganates; nitrates and nitrites) mixed with fuels such as sugar, metal powders, sulfur, carbon, and hydrocarbons. Chlorate mixtures were used in large vehicle-borne IEDs (VBIEDs) in Northern Ireland in the 1980s and 1990s and in Bali (2002). Most salt-based explosive mixtures, however, tend to be used as pipe bomb fillers.

Peroxide explosives are improvised high explosives, the use of which has increased during the 1990s and through the last decade. Peroxide explosives are synthesized from hydrogen peroxide and other chemicals. An example is TATP (triacetone triperoxide). Impure peroxide explosives are notoriously unstable and TATP has been named the 'Mother of Satan' by bomb makers on account of this property. Peroxide explosives were used in IED attacks on the London transportation system in 2005.

Many of the secondary high explosives listed above have been used in IEDs, and although recipes exist for improvised synthesis, such products are not often encountered. Theft or other illegal acquisition is preferred. Another source of secondary high explosives is the main charge in artillery shells. But all explosives used in IEDs, be they commercial, military, or improvised, may survive an explosion. Both unreacted explosives and products of their reaction may be identified by forensic chemists using sophisticated and highly sensitive analytical instruments.

Initiation System

In order to initiate the explosive charge in an IED, energy must be supplied to activate the chemical reaction. As discussed above, the IED initiator will be selected according to the nature of the explosive – flame for primary high explosives and contained low explosives and a shock wave for secondary high explosives. Some smokeless powder propellants in pipe bombs may also be initiated with a shock wave. Flame may be supplied by a burning fuse, an electrical circuit which ignites incendiary chemicals by way of a glowing filament and by a hypergolic mixture (chemicals, which when mixed, react to produce flames). Shockwaves are produced by detonators, also known as blasting caps. These may be initiated by flame, an electrically heated resistance wire or a shock wave (shock tube). Detonator function is described elsewhere in this encyclopedia. Improvised detonators can be made from improvised primary explosives such as mercury fulminate and TATP.

Three primary modes of initiator activation which may be selected by the bomb maker are

1. delay initiation
2. victim initiation
3. command initiation.

Delay initiation

IEDs with delay initiation are often referred to as 'time bombs.' Such IEDs allow the placer of the IED to be remote from the explosion location. The delay mechanism can be any kind of timer which, after a preset time interval, produces a mechanical or electronic action that completes an electrical circuit between the energy source (battery) and the initiator (detonator). A measured length of burning commercial or military fuse can also supply a short-term delay, as can hypergolic chemical reactions such as an acid eating through a rubber condom to combine with an appropriate chemical to produce flame.

Victim initiation

Victim-initiated IEDs often are referred to as 'booby traps.' They take many forms.

Some are hidden and will be initiated by application of pressure as with roadside bombs or devices planted on pathways or trails. Others may be operated by tripwire, by light or movement, by touching or lifting a device, or by opening a parcel. The safety rule is that if something could be an IED, assume that it is and do not approach or touch it. Booby traps are designed to kill. These triggering mechanisms are variations of an on–off switch with no delay.

Command initiation

Command initiation is normally undertaken by a third party who activates the switch from a remote location. One method is by hidden hard wires; another is by a cell phone in which activation of the ringer completes the circuit. These triggers are further examples of nondelayed on–off switches. Another variation is the simple on–off switch used in suicide bombings where the bomber is willing to sacrifice his or her life to deliver an IED directly to a target.

Forensic evidence

Most components of initiation devices survive an explosion albeit in altered form caused by the effects of the explosion. Skillful crime scene investigators, postblast experts, and forensic scientists can combine to reconstruct the initiation system, track the components, and relate these to a suspect. The greater the complexity of an initiation device, the greater is the quantity of physical evidence. An example is an IED design including a simple on–off switch to arm the system once the device has been transported to and placed at a specific location.

Examples of physical evidence of initiation systems include:

- timer parts
- switch parts
- battery parts
- electronic parts
- wires
- electrical connectors
- fuse remains
- monofilament line (trip line)
- cell phone parts

Any of these items could also be sources of residue from explosives due to their proximity in the IED.

Containers

As discussed above, containment is required for low explosives to function effectively. Containers are also used for packaging, transportation, and concealment. For example, relatively small IEDs can be transported in commonly used products like suitcases, back packs or parcels; larger IEDs can be transported by air, water, or land and as the size of the carrying capacity of the transportation increases, so too does the potential size of the primary charge. Charges in latter instances usually are fertilizer-based improvised explosives. Containers can also be used as shrapnel, and can be modified to direct a blast and fragments in a specific direction (improvised Claymore antipersonnel mine).

Containers which are manufactured products can yield very important physical evidence such as numbers stamped onto vehicle parts recovered postblast which, with the cooperation of manufacturers and business records, can enable a vehicle to be identified and traced to retail and rental outlets. Such evidence was an important part of the investigation into the VBIED attack on the Alfred Murrah Federal Building in Oklahoma City in 1983 and the investigation into the World Trade Center bombing in New York in 1995. Containers also may bear such important personal evidence as fingerprints, DNA, and handwriting. Portable containers such as backpacks might also aid identification of individuals via CCTV images and eyewitnesses.

Binding Material

Another application of materials in IED construction is to hold components together. Examples are

- glue
- adhesive tapes
- wire
- cordage
- paper
- cardboard
- wood
- plastic
- textiles

Each material will typically survive an explosion and constitute both forensically pertinent physical evidence and a probable source of explosive residue.

Additional Components

IEDs may contain further material to enhance a specific effect. These components could be shrapnel, incendiary chemicals, and hazardous chemical, biological, and radiological material. Metal plates can also be added to create a directed charge effect.

Effects of IEDs

The primary effects of an explosion on its surroundings are produced by pressure, fragmentation, and heat. IED damage falls broadly into these three categories.

1. In blast damage, the primary explosive effect on the surroundings is produced by the shock wave from an uncontained high explosive; examples are a stick of dynamite or emulsion explosive initiated by a detonator and a light container of blasting agent detonated by a booster charge. Blast damage may be accompanied by secondary fragmentation from the blast effect on the environment.
2. Fragmentation blast damage is an intentional effect in which a contained low or high explosive or an uncontained high explosive is employed to propel high-velocity particles at a target; examples are the pipe of a pipe bomb and added shrapnel. IEDs can be configured to direct fragments in linear (shaped charge) or arced configurations (Claymore).
3. The intended thermal effect of an IED is to induce fire by adding a fire accelerant to be ignited and spread by the explosion. This effect is distinct from fires which may be caused by an explosion itself – such fires are a frequently encountered side effect of explosions.

Detection and Countermeasures to IEDs

Numerous steps are taken by counter terrorist and intelligence agencies and other branches of government and private agencies to counter threats posed by IEDs, with much, often unheralded, success. Methods range from control, substitution, and rendering inert of precursors which could be used to make improvised explosives through detection of hidden explosives to disruption of terrorist plans. A prime example was a major plot foiled in the United Kingdom in 2006 that involved a plan to coordinate suicide attacks on transatlantic flights using liquid explosives. Convictions resulted and airport security measures were enhanced.

Some of the more visible protocols to detect hidden explosives are particularly apparent to air travelers. The most commonly used systems are physics-based radiation, chemistry-based trace detection instrumentation, and biological detection, most commonly by dogs. Any detection system has to optimize the combination of sensitivity (detect small quantities of explosive), specificity (minimize false alarms), and efficiency (rapidity of operation and reporting).

The ingenuity of bomb makers is constantly being challenged by countermeasures of detection and deactivation aimed at both the explosive charge and the initiation system.

Both sides constantly innovate. IEDs containing non-nitrated explosives such as peroxides and other home-made explosives, and also detonator-sensitive ammonium nitrate-based emulsion explosives have required new methods of detection to be researched and implemented. Use of suicide bombers as part of the initiation system has increased the application of a human factor approach to detection of IED carriers.

Forensic Science and IEDs

Because many parts of an IED survive an explosion and can be recovered with skill and persistence, forensic scientists from many disciplines may become involved in IED investigations. Forensic science can contribute to an investigation by identifying the explosive, initiator, initiation system, container, and binding material of an IED. These data provide lists of material for a search warrant for a suspect's premises, vehicles, etc. and can be significant circumstantial evidence at a trial. Once IED components are identified at a scene, they may be sourced from databases and through cooperation with industry and compared with items seized from a suspect. Information gleaned about an IED can be used to corroborate or cast doubt on statements, possibly link explosives to incidents, and provide intelligence to counterterrorism authorities. Some applications of forensic science to investigation of a clandestine explosives laboratory, an intact IED, and a postblast situation follow.

Clandestine Laboratories

A forensic chemist will normally be part of a clandestine explosives laboratory investigation team along with explosive incident investigators and forensic identification specialists. Once the laboratory is declared safe to enter, the chemist's role is to give an opinion on the potential significance and relevance to IED construction of specific chemicals, recipes, work in progress, literature, work notes, and equipment. The foundation of the chemist's opinions lies in having the same currency in literature and Internet information as the bomb makers plus access to comprehensive databases on precursor chemicals, improvised initiation systems, improvised explosives, and their residues. Exhibits will be seized, collected, and transported on the advice of the chemist. Chemicals will largely be bulk (visible) except for materials bearing residues from test explosions. Methods used to identify the chemicals probably will be drawn from infrared spectroscopy (IR), elemental analysis (e.g., energy dispersive X-ray analysis) used in conjunction with a scanning electron microscope (SEM/EDX), and gas and/or liquid chromatography with a mass spectrometry detector (GC/MS or LC/MS). Clandestine laboratories are discussed in detail elsewhere in this encyclopedia.

Intact IEDs

Forensic examination of a safely recovered and deactivated intact IED requires more diverse expertise. After photography and X-ray imaging, the design of the IED is ascertained by skilled and experienced IED investigators and typically provides important intelligence. Each component is physical evidence and all necessary precautions such as protective clothing, gloves, footwear, etc. must be taken to ensure that no contamination occurs. Identification of the explosive is the responsibility of the chemist as is analysis of manufactured products making up the initiation system. The analytical results aid in sourcing and provide a database for future comparisons once a suspect(s) has been identified. Each item is also examined for foreign chemical or biochemical material which may be related to the bomb maker such as fingerprints (fingerprint experts) and hair and DNA (biologists). Examination also is made for material which may relate to where the IED was constructed, such as fibers and detritus which may be entrapped in adhesives. Foreign markings such as tool marks are examined and recorded by experts in that field and if a clandestine laboratory is identified the marks will be compared to tools at that location.

Analytical methods for components will depend on the materials used in their construction. Some typical classifications are polymers: paint, fibers, adhesives, glues, plastic, rubber; metal: wires, electrical connectors, solder, shrapnel; hydrocarbons: tar; chemicals: explosives, battery cores. Methods for polymers include microscopy, IR, pyrolysis GC, MS, and elemental analysis. Metals are analyzed by elemental analysis, and hydrocarbons by IR and GC/MS. Methods for chemicals are noted above and methods for explosives are presented and discussed elsewhere in this encyclopedia.

Postblast Investigation

Once an IED explodes, its components are altered by the effect of the explosion and may be widely dispersed. Depending on the size and location of the explosion, postblast scenes on land may be as small as a high school washroom in the case of a small pipe bomb or as large as many city blocks in the case of a VBIED. Aircraft sabotage by explosives at cruising altitude may have wreckage fields extending over many square kilometers on land or under water.

Postblast scene examinations are optimally undertaken or assisted by highly trained national expert teams. The composition of a team varies with the circumstances but the core usually consists of postblast investigators, forensic identification specialists, and a forensic chemist. The forensic chemist's primary role at the scene is as a consultant with respect to recognition, preservation, and collection of physical evidence from the IED components initiation system and residues from explosives. Once the scene has been declared safe to enter, the chemist will walk through with the team leader and postblast experts to get a collective overview and conduct a damage assessment of the effects explosion – blast pressure, fragmentation and heat, and distribution of debris. The seat of the explosion will be determined, optimal scene examination protocols put in place, and teams deployed. Canine search units usually are part of the teams. Searchers must know what pertinent physical evidence looks like and will have honed this skill on explosives ranges.

Contamination prevention procedures must be employed and documented and anything worn or taken onto the scene must be demonstrably free of explosives and this must be documented. If contamination with explosives occurs or could have occurred at any stage – scene, packaging, transportation, storage, or analysis –then any findings with respect to explosives' residues may be of no significance and all of the work in recovering and identifying such traces may be for naught. Quality control procedures at a scene are as important as quality control in a forensic laboratory.

The forensic chemist plays an important role in evidence selection, preservation, and packaging, and may perform a useful triage function in selecting material for expedited analytical examination of evidence for his or her own or other disciplines. Explosives' residues typically are found on parts of the ignition system and container remains as well as on material surrounding the seat of the explosion. Immovable objects showing potential evidence of residues should be swabbed and floor sweepings should be taken. Fragments which have penetrated inanimate objects and victims should be recovered as should the clothing of victims. In all instances of recovery, a control sample of uncontaminated matrices should be taken for comparison and elimination purposes. Likewise anything added to the scene like dry chemical fire extinguisher powder and other contaminants must be sampled as controls. With air crash underwater scenes, the search is conducted by remote equipment and appropriate recovery technology. Postblast specialists, structural engineers, and chemists on the investigation team decide what should be recovered.

In appropriate circumstances, a forensic chemist may examine recovered material by application of chemical tests and portable instrumental analysis in a temporary or mobile laboratory in order to provide preliminary results to quickly advance the direction of an investigation. Preliminary results need to be confirmed in the home laboratory.

In large-scale disasters like aircraft sabotage, finding physical evidence typically involves highly sophisticated searching and recovery equipment such as possessed by military organizations. Likewise, large VBIEDs which cause massive structural failures and building collapses require heavy equipment and industrial scale sieving techniques as part of a comprehensive search.

Secondary Scenes

Secondary scenes also can provide very important links in an investigation. These include evidence present in hospitals and morgues, clandestine laboratories and suspects' residences, possessions, and transportation. Retrieval of exhibits from hospitals and morgues normally falls to investigators rather than scientists.

Forensic Examinations

Examination of postblast exhibits and controls and exhibits for comparison from suspects may require many more forensic disciplines than examination of intact IEDs. Examples are pathology, anthropology, serial number restoration, metallurgy, structural engineering, and documents examination.

A high level of communication between disciplines and investigators is vital. For example, if a piece of evidence is suspected of bearing fingerprints, DNA, and explosives' residue, then a conference should be held by the involved experts to determine the optimal sequence of examination to ensure that the maximum pertinent information can be gained from the analysis.

Analysis of residues from explosives is one of the more demanding applications of analytical chemistry given that only trace quantities may survive an explosion, and may be in or on any type of matrix. The analytical expertise and forensic opinions of chemists involved in this trace chemistry analysis has a foundation built from analyses of intact explosives, postblast residues recovered from test explosions conducted under clean conditions and then under 'real world' conditions.

When exhibits from the scene are compared to exhibits seized from a suspect or to manufactured products linked to the suspect, further very demanding analytical chemistry is required using methods proven to detect small differences in composition of the materials in question. Many of these methods have been noted above. A notable case example is the Narita Airport explosion in 1985 in Japan when a suitcase being interlined from a Canadian flight to an Air India flight exploded killing two baggage handlers and seriously injuring two others. Nine items of physical evidence found at the scene in Japan were related by forensic examinations to the suspect in Canada: dynamite, smokeless powder, detonator, electronic timer, electrical relay, battery, ether can, adhesive tape, and a stereo tuner which housed the IED. The trial judge concluded that the combination of items in the bomb was unique and that the suspect was in possession of "that unique combination of exactly corresponding materials" shortly before the bomb must have been fabricated. The bomb maker was convicted. This case and numerous other cases emphasize that meticulous evidence recovery at the scene and meticulous forensic science combined with meticulous police investigation and prosecution lead to justice.

The Courts

Once the forensic laboratory work is complete, scientists determine the significance of the results and give their forensic opinions and reports to the investigators. If the matter goes to trial, scientists will consult with the prosecution on the significance of their opinions, organize their testimony, and testify as expert witnesses. In the adversarial legal system of common law countries, an expert witness for the defense goes through the same type of consultation and preparation steps. On the witness stand, regardless of whichever side calls him or her as an expert, a forensic scientist must be completely objective and demonstrate that the role of the expert witness is to assist the court and not to advocate for either side. The court will ascertain the weight to be given to an expert opinion by its scientific foundation.

See also: **Chemistry/Trace/Explosives**: Clandestine Explosive Laboratories; Commercial; Explosions; Explosives: Analysis; Improvised Explosives; **Investigations**: Explosions.

Further Reading

Beveridge A (2012) *Forensic Investigation of Explosions*, 2nd edn. Boca Raton, FL: CRC Press, Taylor and Francis.

Beveridge AD and Benson SJ (2010) Investigation of explosions. In: Freckelton I and Selby H (eds.) *Expert Evidence*, ch. 84. Sydney: Thomson Reuters.

National Research Council (1998) *Containing the Threat from Illegal Bombings*. Washington, DC: National Academy Press.

National Research Council (2007) *Countering the Threat of Improvised Explosive Devices*. Washington, DC: National Academy Press.

National Research Council (2008) *Disrupting Improvised Explosive Device Terror Campaigns*. Washington, DC: National Academy Press.

Thurman JT (2006) *Practical Bomb Scene Investigation*, chs. 3 and 4. Boca Raton, FL: CRC Press, Taylor and Francis.

Explosives: Analysis

T Tamiri and S Zitrin, Division of Identification and Forensic Science (DIFS), Israel National Police, Jerusalem, Israel

Glossary

AN ammonium nitrate
APCI atmospheric pressure chemical ionization
API atmospheric Pressure Ionization
CE capillary electrophoresis
CI chemical ionization
CID collision-induced dissociation
DA diode array
DESI desorption electrospray ionization
DNT dinitrotoluene
DPA diphenylamine
DSC differential scanning calorimetry
ECD electron capture detector
EGDN ethylene glycol dinitrate
EI electron ionization
EOF electroosmotic flow
ESI electrospray ionization
FTIR Fourier Transform infrared
GC gas chromatography
HMTD hexamethylene triperoxide diamine, 3,4,8,9,12,13-hexaoxa-1,6-diazabicyclo[4.4.4.]tetradecane
HMX octogen, 1,3,5,7- tetranitro-1,3,5,7-tetrazacyclooctane
HPLC high pressure liquid chromatography
IC ion chromatography
IR infrared
LC high pressure liquid chromatography
MS mass spectrometry
NC nitrocellulose, cellulose nitrate
NG nitroglycerine, glycerol trinitrate
NMR nuclear magnetic resonance
PETN pentaerythrithol tetranitrate
RDX hexogen, 1,3,5-trinitro-1,3,5-triazacyclohexane
R_f rate of flow
R_t retention time
SEM/EDX scanning electron microscopy-energy dispersive X-ray spectroscopy
SPE solid phase extraction
SPME solid phase microextraction
TATP triacetonetriperoxide, 3,3,6,6,9,9-hexamethyl-1,2,4,5,7,8-hexaoxacyclononane
TEA 'thermal energy analyser'
TLC thin layer chromatography
TNT trinitrotoluene
TOF time of flight
UN urea nitrate
UV ultraviolet
XRD x-ray diffraction
XRF x-ray fluorescence

Caution!

Some explosives are extremely sensitive to spark, heat, shock, or friction; therefore, necessary precautions should be taken by the analyst while handling explosives.

Introduction

An explosive is defined as a substance or a mixture of substances that may be made to undergo a rapid chemical change with the liberation of large quantities of energy, generally accompanied by the evolution of hot gasses. An explosive mixture usually contains an oxidizing agent and a reducing agent.

Explosives are used legally in industry and in the military and also illegally in terrorist and criminal activity. Some explosive compounds (e.g., some nitrate esters) are used in medicine or in the paint industry (cellulose nitrate).

Forensic analysis of explosives deals with the identification of explosives both preblast (when no explosion occurred) and postblast.

The aim of forensic analysis of unexploded explosives is often to prove their illegal possession. Sometimes, it is also important to identify the starting materials for the preparation of explosives (e.g., acetone and hydrogen peroxide for the synthesis of triacetone triperoxide (TATP)).

In postblast analysis, because the explosion has already occurred, it may seem unnecessary to analyze the explosive, but such analyses have high priority in most forensic laboratories. One reason is that information about the explosives involved can be of great assistance to the investigation.

Sometimes, it is not unequivocally clear whether the explosion was initiated by the ignition of a fuel–air mixture ('vapor explosion') or by other explosives. When an explosive is identified in the debris, it may be assumed that this explosive caused the explosion. On the other hand, if no explosive is identified in the debris, it may indeed suggest a vapor explosion but it may also be that the explosive, which had caused the explosion, was not identified.

In addition, the type of the explosive may sometimes direct the investigator as to whether the explosion was carried out by terrorists or by criminals unrelated to terrorist activity. An explosion could also be the result of a prank or an accident.

Another reason to pursue postexplosion analysis is the need for law enforcement agencies to know what explosives are used by criminals or terrorists. In the case of improvised explosives, this information may alert law enforcement agencies to look for the corresponding starting materials. This information may also help to connect different cases, and in rare cases even to point to a certain criminal group, as well as to connect a suspect to the scene of crime. The latter case includes the

 http://dx.doi.org/10.1016/B978-0-12-382165-2.00083-0

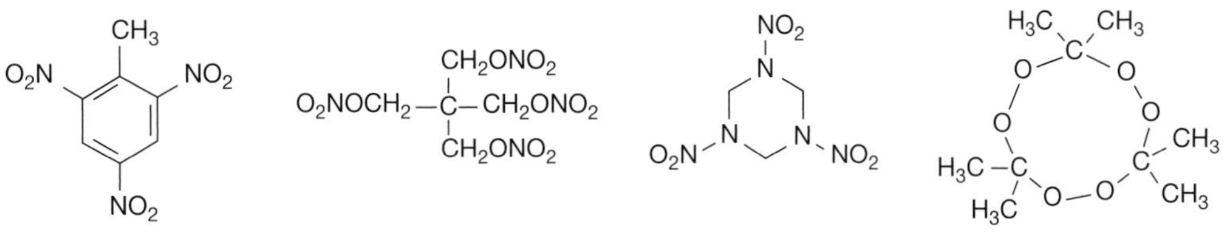

2,4,6-TNT PETN RDX TATP

Figure 1 Structural formulas of some organic explosives.

trace analysis of explosives on suspects' hands, and on items and premises which can be connected to suspects. Although not a postexplosion situation, the procedures used in such analysis are similar to those employed in postexplosion analysis. In both cases, the analysis usually involves trace amounts of unreacted explosives mixed with large amounts of interfering materials.

An ultimate goal of a forensic analyst is to provide an expert opinion for a court of law. Wrong results may lead to a gross injustice, where innocent people can be found guilty. This dictates the need to adhere to extremely strict criteria for a safe identification of explosives.

Classification of Explosives

Many compounds, which may be classified as explosives, are mentioned in the literature. In practice, the forensic analyst routinely encounters only few of them.

Common classifications of explosives have been done according to their chemical structure, their use, their explosive properties, and their place in the explosive train (triggering sequence). These classes along with few examples are listed below.

Chemical structure

- Organic compounds containing a nitro group:
  1. Nitro compounds in which the nitro group is bonded directly to a carbon atom ($C{-}NO_2$). These include nitroaromatic compounds such as 2,4-dinitrotoluene (2,4-DNT), 2,4,6-trinitrotoluene (TNT) or picric acid, and nitroaliphatic compounds such as nitromethane.
  2. Nitrate esters in which the nitro group is bonded to an oxygen atom that is connected to a carbon atom ($C{-}O{-}NO_2$). Examples are ethylene glycol dinitrate (EGDN), glycerol trinitrate (nitroglycerine, NG), pentaerythrithol tetranitrate (PETN), and cellulose nitrate (nitrocellulose, NC).
  3. Nitramines in which the nitro group is bonded to a nitrogen atom that is connected to a carbon atom ($C{-}N{-}NO_2$). Examples are 1,3,5-trinitro-1,3,5-triazacyclohexane (hexogen, RDX) and 1,3,5,7- tetranitro-1,3,5,7-tetrazacyclooctane (octogen, HMX).
- Organic peroxides containing O—O bonds: 3,3,6,6,9,9-hexamethyl-1,2,4,5,7,8-hexaoxacyclononane (TATP), 3,4,8,9,12,13-hexaoxa-1,6-diazabicyclo[4.4.4.]tetradecane (hexamethylene triperoxide diamine, HMTD).
- Inorganic salts: ammonium nitrate (AN).
- Mixtures of oxidizing and reducing agents: black powder (potassium nitrate, sulfur, and charcoal), black powder substitutes (e.g., Pyrodex), potassium chlorate/sugar.

Structural formulas of some organic explosives are shown in Figure 1.

Use

- Military explosives: TNT, PETN, and RDX.
- Industrial or commercial explosives: dynamites, AN, and emulsion explosives.
- Illegally manufactured improvised explosives: TATP, urea nitrate (UN), potassium chlorate/sugar mixtures.

Explosive properties

- High explosives: PETN and RDX.
- Low explosives (propellants): smokeless powder and black powder.

Place in explosive train (for high explosives)

- Primary explosives: mercury fulminate, lead styphnate, and lead azide.
- Boosters: PETN.
- Main charge: TNT and RDX.

Explosive formulations usually contain other compounds such as sensitizers, desensitizers, stabilizers (e.g., diphenylamine (DPA) and ethyl centralite), plasticizers (e.g., phthalate and sebacate esters), and other additives.

Methods and Procedures

The analytical procedures used in forensic laboratories for the analysis of explosives are based on conventional analytical methods. Naturally, a procedure for trace analysis is different from the analysis of bulk explosives. The latter case may include intact explosives (before an explosion) and also observable explosive particles in the postexplosion debris. The identification, as in many areas in forensic analysis, may start with presumptive tests (usually spot tests) followed by suitable confirmation methods.

It is essential for the forensic laboratory to have a library of spectral data of all common explosives and related compounds and – preferably – authentic samples of the explosives. The analysis usually includes identification of the sample, though quantitation may also be required.

Postexplosion analysis, including a general flow chart, is discussed in section 'Postexplosion and Trace Analysis of Explosives' of this article.

The choice of identification methods may be derived from the properties of the explosives. Some explosives are highly volatile (e.g., EGDN) or sublime easily (e.g., TATP), whereas some are nonvolatile (e.g., HMX) or thermally labile (e.g., tetryl). For example, analytical methods which involve evaporation of compounds may be unsuitable for nonvolatile explosives.

In addition, information from the scene and from the investigation as to the possible type of explosive may be highly relevant to the scheme of analysis.

Other factors that may influence the procedures in a specific laboratory are budget restrictions, professional skill of the staff, and even adherence to methods, which had been routinely used in that laboratory.

The commonly used analytical methods in the analysis of explosives are listed below:

Preliminary Tests

Burning and calorimetric tests

When an unknown material is submitted for analysis, it is sometimes useful to try to burn it in order to find out if it is an energetic material. This should be performed with extreme care, using a few milligrams of the sample. Differential scanning calorimetry (DSC) is sometimes used in order to obtain data on the heat capacity and the phase transitions of the sample.

Chemical tests

Chemical tests, often referred to as spot tests or color tests, are based on a color produced by a reaction between a reagent and an analyte. Some well-known color reactions (sometimes in modified versions) are used in the analysis of explosives. These color reactions are widely used by forensic laboratories as presumptive tests for screening and for field tests.

Some spot tests mentioned in this article are listed here according to the type of explosives. Di- and trinitroaromatic compounds react with an alkali (e.g., 3% KOH in ethanol) to produce a purple-brown color in the case of TNT and an yellowish color in the case of 2,4-DNT and 2,6-DNT. The colors developed in the reaction between polynitroaromatic compounds and bases are sometimes attributed to the formation of 'Meisenheimer complexes.'

Griess reaction is a well-established, highly specific color reaction for the identification of nitrite ions. In this reaction, nitrite ion reacts with an aromatic amine such as sulfanilamide in an acidic medium to form a diazonium ion. This ion is then coupled with a suitable active aromatic compound, such as *N*-1-naphtylethylenediamine, to produce an azo compound, which has a characteristic pink or purple color. The application of the Greiss test to explosives is based on the formation of nitrite ions by the action of an alkali on nitrate esters and nitramines. Nitrate ions produce the nitrite ions by reduction (e.g., by zinc powder). It should be noted that the Greiss reaction, though highly specific for nitrite ions, is not specific for explosives; any compound which releases nitrite ions in the presence of an alkali would produce the typical color even if it is not an explosive.

Another spot test is based on the oxidation of a reagent by an explosive or an oxidizing constituent of an explosive mixture. Examples are DPA, which develops a blue color with TATP; aniline sulfate, which develops a blue color with chlorates; and *p*-dimethylaminocinnamaldehyde, which develops a red color with uronium cation.

The reactions mentioned above are the basis of some commercially available kits, used for field tests, often carried out in border crossings to screen persons suspected to have been in contact with explosives or items suspected as explosives. An example is the ETK, an Israeli-produced kit, which is capable of detecting some polynitroaromatic compounds, nitrate esters, nitramines, inorganic nitrate salts, and peroxides. The ETK has been successfully used in real cases.

In general, the sensitivity of many spot tests used in the analysis of explosives is in the microgram range.

Spot tests are fast, inexpensive, simple (do not need instrumentation), and may be performed by technicians in the field. In general, spot tests are not specific enough to be the basis for unequivocal identification. Another problem is that most color tests are destructive by nature and, therefore, the explosive may be lost. Nevertheless, their value in a forensic explosive laboratory should not be underestimated; when correctly used, they may constitute a strong indication about the chemical class. They are also useful in preselecting relevant exhibits from the scene of explosion, subsequently to be analyzed in the laboratory.

Separation Methods

Separation methods are used to separate a mixture to its components. Almost all separation methods used nowadays are chromatographic, utilizing differences in the affinity of the components of a mixture toward stationary and mobile phases. Chromatographic behavior of a compound in given stationary and mobile phases is expressed by its migration rate, usually called rate of flow (R_f) or retention time (R_t). The retention data may also depend on other conditions such as temperature (e.g., in gas chromatography (GC)). Though originally used to separate a mixture, chromatographic methods have often been used to tentatively identify a compound by analyzing the analyte and the authentic sample under the same conditions and comparing their retention data. It is widely accepted that the identification of a single compound cannot be based only on chromatographic methods. Some common chromatographic methods in the analysis of explosives are described:

Thin layer chromatography

In thin layer chromatography (TLC), the stationary phase consists of an adsorbent, such as silica gel, coated on aluminum or glass plates. Solutions of samples are spotted near one end of the plate, which is then placed in a chamber containing the developing solvent (the mobile phase). The developing solvent is allowed to ascend to a certain distance on the plate. Different compounds are carried by the solvent with different rates, resulting in a separation. The plate is then removed from the container and dried. Visualization of the spots is done by ultraviolet (UV) light or by spraying reagents, usually based on the chemical tests mentioned above. Both the R_f and the color developed by spraying, if similar to those of an authentic sample, may indicate the identity of a compound. TLC can also be used in a preparative mode in which the separated compound is extracted and its identity confirmed by other methods.

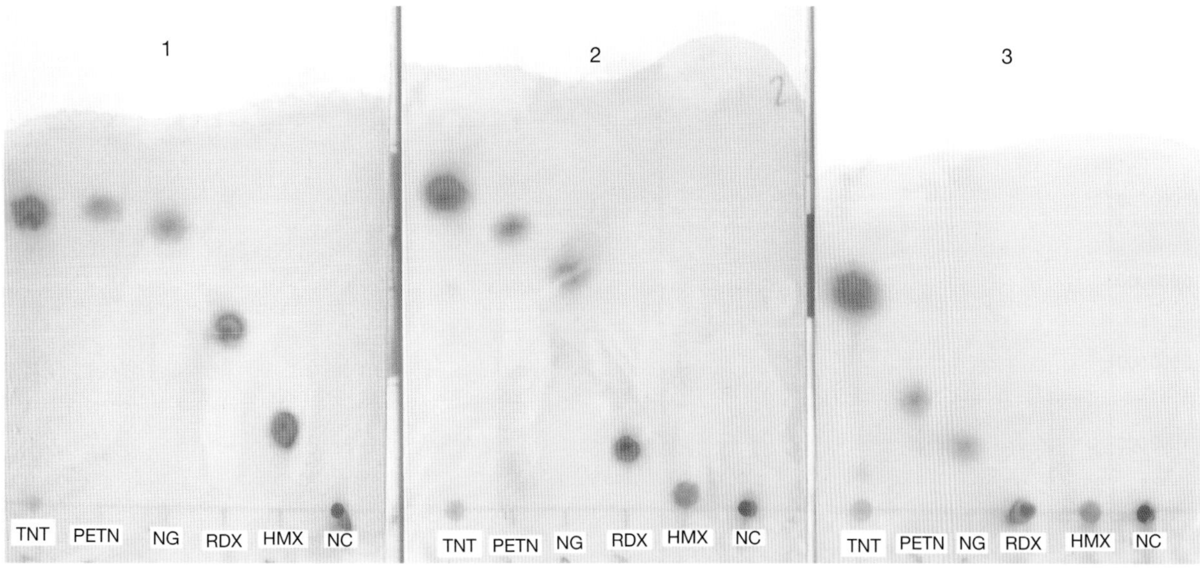

Figure 2 Military explosives (TNT, PETN, NG, RDX, HMX, and NC) separated on three TLC solvent systems: (1) 1,2-dichloroethane:acetonitrile (90:10), (2) trichloroethylene:acetone (80:20), and (3) petrol ether (b.p. 60–80 °C):ethyl acetate (90:10) spray reagents: 3% ethanolic KOH followed by Griess reagent (DIFS collection).

Sensitivity of TLC is generally in the microgram to submicrogram range, depending on the type of visualization used.

Although there are many reports describing different TLC systems for the separation of explosive compounds, no single system has been known to separate all organic explosives, and a combination of several systems is usually used. Some examples of TLC systems used in the analysis of explosives are (1) 1,2-dichloroethane:acetonitrile (90:10), (2) trichloroethylene:-acetone (80:20), and (3) petrol ether (b.p. 60–80 °C):ethyl acetate (90:10). Figure 2 shows some organic explosives separated by these TLC systems.

A TLC plate often deteriorates after spraying; therefore, it is recommended that documentation by camera or by a scanner should be carried out immediately after spraying.

TLC is a simple, inexpensive, and fast method allowing analysis of several samples in a single run. TLC is considered a low-resolution method and, in addition, separation is susceptible to contaminants, especially when present in large amounts. Despite these limitations, TLC serves as a valuable tool in explosives laboratory.

Gas chromatography

Modern GC utilizes capillary columns in which the stationary phase is chemically bonded to the fused silica wall. A sample, dissolved in a suitable solvent, is injected into an injection port. The compounds are evaporated and pushed along the coated column (usually at elevated temperatures) toward a detector by the flow of a mobile phase (carrier gas, e.g., helium). Different compounds having different affinities to the stationary phase are separated, usually with a good resolution. GC is also suitable for quantitative analysis. GC is a simple, high-speed, and high-resolution method for the analysis of organic mixtures.

A typical column used in the analysis of explosives is the nonpolar diphenyl (5%)-dimethylsiloxane copolymer (e.g., DB-5, HP-5, Rtx-5), 25 μm coating and 15 m long. Typical GC conditions are injector temperature 180 °C and column temperature programmed from 50 to 250 °C at a rate of 25 °C min^{-1}.

GC is especially suitable for the analysis of thermally stable explosives such as many nitroaromatic explosives. When analyzing thermally labile compounds (e.g., some nitrate esters and nitramines), some loss in sensitivity is observed. Sometimes, decomposition products of explosives (e.g., tetryl, nitrate esters) are produced in the injector or in the column. Nonvolatile explosives (e.g., NC, inorganic ions) cannot be analyzed by GC. The organic peroxides TATP and HMTD can be analyzed by GC.

Several common detectors are used in GC analysis of explosives:

- Electron capture detector: In electron capture detector (ECD), the eluent coming from the gas chromatographic column passes through a slow electron beam. An analyte containing electronegative atoms, such as nitrogen, 'captures' electrons from the constant electron current, producing a signal by decreasing this current. Sensitivity is usually in the range of picograms. The ECD is quite selective, being highly sensitive toward nitrogen-containing compounds but insensitive to hydrocarbons.
- Chemiluminescence detector: In this detector, the eluent from the gas chromatographic column passes through a furnace which pyrolizes the compounds at elevated temperatures (e.g., 500–900 °C). Compounds containing nitro- and nitroso-groups produce nitrogen oxide, which is then allowed to react with ozone to produce nitrogen dioxide in an excited energy level. Decaying of the excited NO_2 to its ground state is accompanied by emission of light at the infrared (IR) region, which is monitored by a detector. Sensitivity is in the picogram range. Commercial instruments (e.g., 'thermal energy analyzer' (TEA)) are available and are very sensitive and

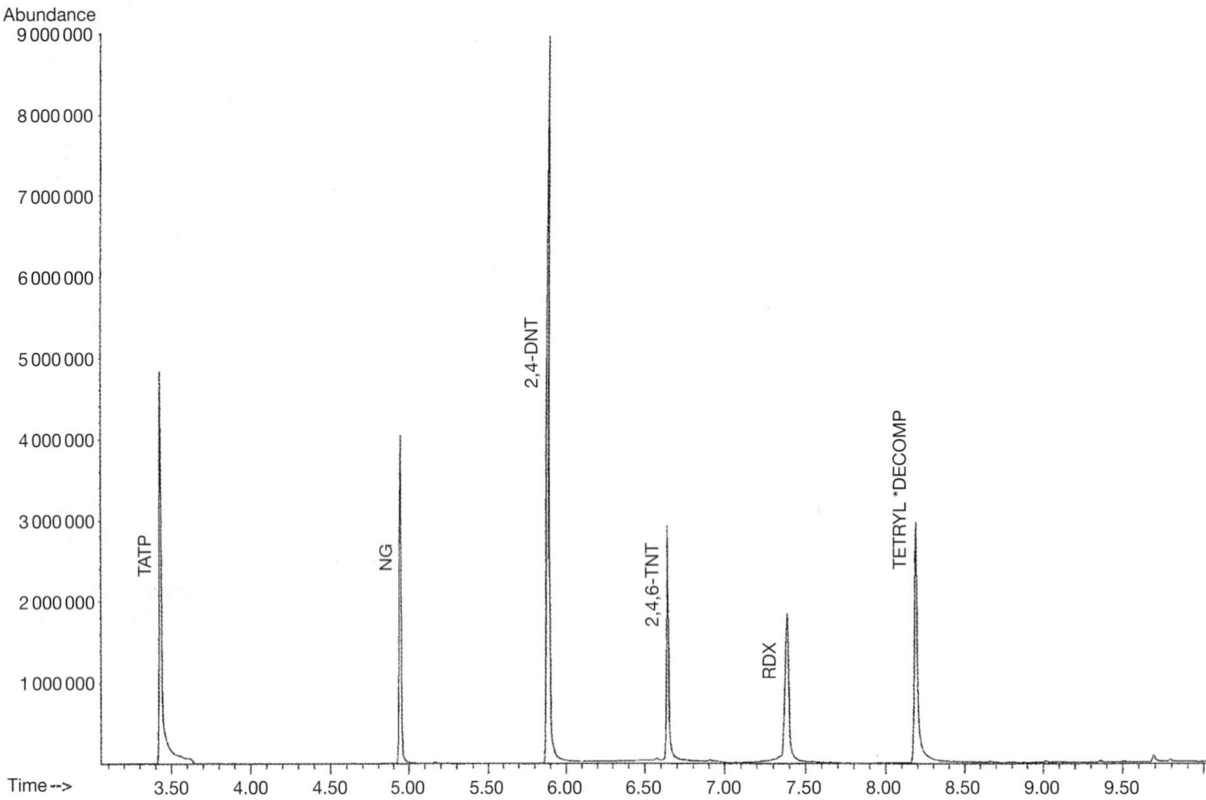

Figure 3 Total ion current (TIC) of some explosives, obtained by GC/MS. *Tetryl decomposes in GC to *N*-methylpicramide (the mechanism is discussed below) (DIFS collection).

highly specific for the analysis of compounds containing nitro- and nitroso-groups. Explosives containing no nitro- or nitroso-groups (e.g., peroxides) are usually not detected. GC/TEA is useful for the analysis of postexplosion residues mainly because many contaminants, having no nitro- or nitroso-groups, are usually not observed. GC/TEA is therefore widely used in the forensic analysis of explosives.

- Mass spectrometer: Mass spectrometry (MS) (discussed below) is widely used as a detector for the gas chromatographic analysis of explosives. A chromatogram of some explosives is shown in **Figure 3**.

High pressure liquid chromatography

In liquid chromatography (LC, HPLC), the stationary phase is often a 'reversed phase' type, such as octadecylsiloxane. The mobile phase is a solvent or a mixture of solvents, which is pumped into the column at relatively high pressure, usually at room temperature. An advantage of LC is that it is suitable for the analysis of thermally labile or nonvolatile compounds, which is highly relevant to the analysis of many explosives (e.g., HMX and PETN).

LC may also be used in a preparative mode by collecting the desired fraction and confirming its identity by other methods. Some widely used detectors in explosives analysis are the following:

- UV and diode array: The eluent from the column passes through a cell irradiated by UV light. In the UV detector, the source is set at a fixed wavelength or scanned over the UV range. In the diode array (DA), a multiwave radiation is applied. The UV spectrum obtained by the DA may be subjected to a computerized library search. The sensitivity of these detectors is in the nanogram range but their selectivity is rather low, detecting only UV-absorbing explosives.
- TEA – see above.
- Mass spectrometer – see below.

Ion chromatography

This method is suitable for the separation of ions. It utilizes an ion-exchange resin as the stationary phase and a solution of salts as the mobile phase. Examples of functional groups attached to the stationary phase are quaternary ammonium cations in anion analysis and sulfonate anions in cation analysis.

In some instruments, a second column ('suppressor column') is situated after the ion-exchange column. This enhances the sensitivity by lowering the background noise of the detector.

Ion chromatography (IC) is widely used in the analysis of explosives and related materials. It is used to separate inorganic ions present in black powders (e.g., K^+, Na^+, and NO_3^-), commercial explosives (e.g., NH_4^+ and NO_3^-), home-made explosives (e.g., K^+ and ClO_3^-), and pyrotechnical mixtures (e.g., Sr^{2+}, Ba^{2+}, and ClO_4^-). IC is also used to analyze products from burning or explosion of explosives and propellants (e.g., SO_4^{2-} and CNS^-). Organic ions can also be analyzed by this method. Sensitivity is in the nanogram range.

The common detection modes employed in IC are the following:

- Conductivity detector: In this detector, a signal is produced when an eluted ion reaches the detector and changes the conductivity of the solution.
- UV/Visible detector: Since most inorganic ions do not absorb UV or visible light, this detector is used in IC in an indirect mode by using a UV-absorbing mobile phase.
- Mass spectrometer (see below).

Capillary electrophoresis

In capillary electrophoresis (CE), it is possible to analyze both organic and inorganic explosive compounds. Chromatography is performed on a capillary column, immersed at its two ends in a buffer solution. Negatively charged SiO groups are formed near the capillary wall in the aqueous medium, leading to accumulation of solvated cations. Application of a suitable electric field on the capillary results in the migration of the solvated cations toward the cathode, generating electroosmotic flow (EOF). Analytes introduced to the capillary column move in different directions and mobilities; negatively charged species move toward the anode, positively charged species move toward the cathode, and neutral compounds move with the EOF. As the EOF is usually faster than the migration velocity of the anions, all species are swept toward the detector, which is usually situated near the cathode. Compounds with different mobility are usually separated with high efficiency. Detection is usually by UV where the capillary itself serves as the cell. In some laboratories, CE is applied as a confirmation method for results obtained in IC. Coupling to a mass spectrometer was also reported. Sensitivity is in the picogram range.

Spectroscopic and Spectrometric Methods

IR and Raman spectroscopy

Molecules irradiated by IR light (4000–500 cm^{-1}) absorb energy at certain wavelengths, which correspond to intramolecular vibrations.

Absorbing bands in the range ~4000–1300 cm^{-1} are usually associated with specific functional groups, whereas absorption bands below ~1300 cm^{-1} are usually characteristic of the molecule as a whole. Therefore, the region below 1300 cm^{-1} is sometimes called the 'fingerprint' region of the IR spectrum. Modern IR instruments, used by most laboratories, are Fourier Transform IR (FTIR). IR may be used to identify a pure compound by comparing its spectrum to the spectrum of an authentic sample. In addition, absorption bands characteristic of certain functional groups may be useful in the analysis of unknown samples. Sensitivity is in the microgram range but it can be increased by using a microscope FTIR. FTIR is sometimes coupled to an attenuated total reflectance device. This sampling technique does not require any sample preparation.

Mixtures may require chemical separation of components before the analysis in order to obtain IR spectra of the pure components. Another possibility is to perform a mathematical 'subtraction' of a spectrum of one component to obtain an IR spectrum of a second component. This may reduce the need for chemical separation.

Symmetric and asymmetric stretching vibrations of the NO_2 group give rise to two distinct absorption bands, which have a highly diagnostic value in the analysis of explosives. In nitroaromatic compounds, these bands appear at 1390–1320 and 1590–1510 cm^{-1}, respectively. They can be clearly observed in the IR spectrum of 2,4,6-TNT, as shown in **Figure** 4.

The two NO_2 stretching vibrations in nitrate esters appear at 1285–1270 and 1660–1640 cm^{-1}, respectively, as can be seen in the IR spectrum of PETN, shown in **Figure** 5. The spectra of some nitrate esters could be similar, which calls for special care in their interpretation.

The two NO_2 stretching vibrations in nitramines appear at 1310–1270 and 1590–1530 cm^{-1}, respectively.

An IR spectrum of TATP (which lacks nitro groups) is shown in **Figure** 6.

Inorganic anions related to explosives have highly characteristic absorption bands. Nitrate ions absorb at two bands: 1380–1350 and 840–815 cm^{-1}; chlorates absorb at 980–910, 630–615, and 510–480 cm^{-1}. The IR spectrum of potassium chlorate is shown in **Figure** 7.

The IR spectrum of UN (shown in **Figure** 8) is very informative, including absorption bands of nitrate ions.

Raman spectroscopy is based on inelastic scattering of monochromatic light, usually from a laser source. The sample absorbs photons from the laser light and then emits them in frequencies, which are different from the original frequency of the incident light. The spectrum obtained often has a 'fingerprint' value and thus may be used for identification of a compound. Vibrations which are inactive in the Raman are usually active in the IR, which means that the two spectra are complementary. Some works on the analysis and detection of explosives by Raman spectroscopy were reported.

Nuclear magnetic resonance

Nuclei, whose nuclear spin is not zero (e.g., ^{1}H, ^{13}C, and ^{14}N), behave as small magnets. When such nuclei are put in an external magnetic field, they may align with the magnetic field, having a low-energy orientation, or against it, having a high-energy orientation. Transition between these two energy levels takes place by absorption of suitable radiofrequency radiation called the resonance frequency.

The energy absorbed at such transition depends on the chemical environment of the nucleus; thus, various protons in a molecule resonate at different frequencies. The nuclear magnetic resonance (NMR) spectrum is highly characteristic and may be used for the identification of a compound by comparing its spectrum to that of an authentic sample. NMR is especially useful for structure elucidation of unknown samples even when no authentic sample is available. Most work in NMR has been done on protons. Sensitivity of NMR is usually in microgram to milligram range. NMR has not been widely used in routine analysis of explosives.

Mass spectrometry

In this technique, the sample is usually introduced into an ion source where it is ionized to form molecular and fragment ions according to its structure. The ions pass through an analyzer (e.g., magnet, quadrupole, ion trap, and time of flight (TOF)), which separates the ions according to their mass-to-charge ratio (m/z). The ions are detected and recorded, producing a

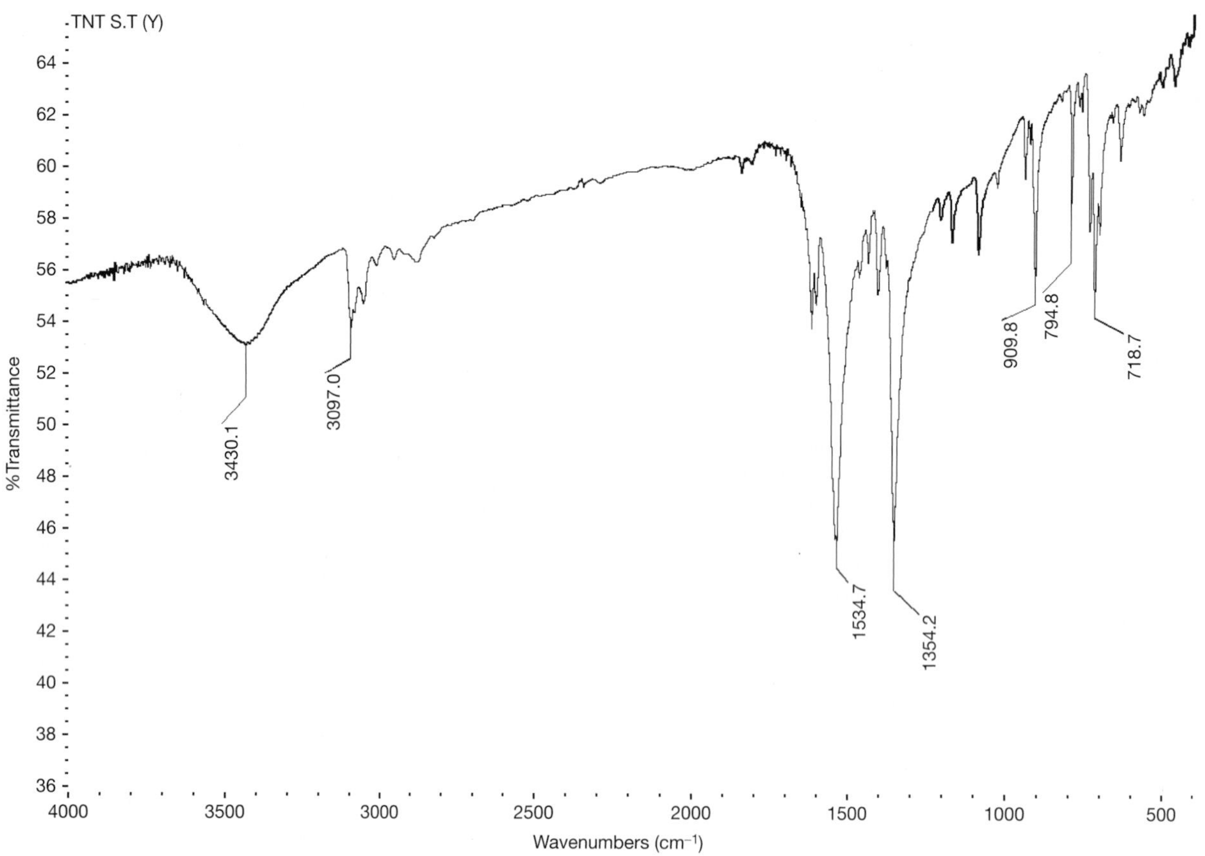

Figure 4 IR spectrum of 2,4,6-TNT (DIFS collection).

mass spectrum. The information obtained from a mass spectrum usually reflects the structure of a molecule, often including its molecular weight. Sensitivity is usually in the range of picogram to nanogram depending on the operation mode.

As it is highly reliable as well as specific and sensitive, MS is considered to be an excellent method for the identification of organic compounds. It is especially useful for the identification of unknown compounds.

Introduction techniques include inlets for gasses, liquids, and solids. Solid probe is usually used for the insertion of nonvolatile compounds and is usually unsuitable for the analysis of mixtures. The most common introduction techniques are the on-line combination with GC (GC/MS) and LC (LC/MS).

GC/MS: The technical possibility to connect a highly efficient separation method (GC) with a highly sensitive and reliable identification method (MS) was a breakthrough in analytical chemistry. GC/MS enables the separation of complex mixtures with the subsequent rapid identification of each of the separated components. Therefore, GC/MS is the method of choice in organic analysis in many forensic laboratories. As aforementioned (see section 'Gas Chromatography') some explosives are easily analyzed by GC (hence by GC/MS) while with others some difficulties are encountered.

LC/MS: This technique requires an interface between high output of liquids and sometimes nonvolatile buffers, and the high vacuum of the mass spectrometer. This enables analysis of nonvolatile or thermally labile explosives that cannot be analyzed by GC/MS (see section 'High Pressure Liquid Chromatography'). This method is widely used in forensic laboratories.

- Common ionization methods in MS:
  1. Electron ionization (EI)

     In EI, or electron impact, electrons are ejected from a filament and accelerated, usually by a voltage of 70 eV. The sample molecules are bombarded by these electrons, to produce mainly positively charged ions. Data bases, containing more than 600 000 spectra, enable a useful library search.
  2. Chemical ionization (CI)

     In this method, the ionization of the sample molecules takes place by reactions with ions derived from reagent gasses (e.g., methane, isobutane) present in the ion source at relatively high pressure (~1 torr). This method usually produces $[M+H]^+$ ions, where the proton is transferred from the reagent ions to the sample molecule M. The $[M+H]^+$ ions have less energy than the molecular ions obtained in EI, resulting in less fragmentation. CI is usually more suitable than EI to obtain molecular weight information and it is best used as a complementary method to EI.
  3. Negative-ion mass spectrometry

     Although less common than MS of positive ions, this has some relevance to the analysis of explosives.

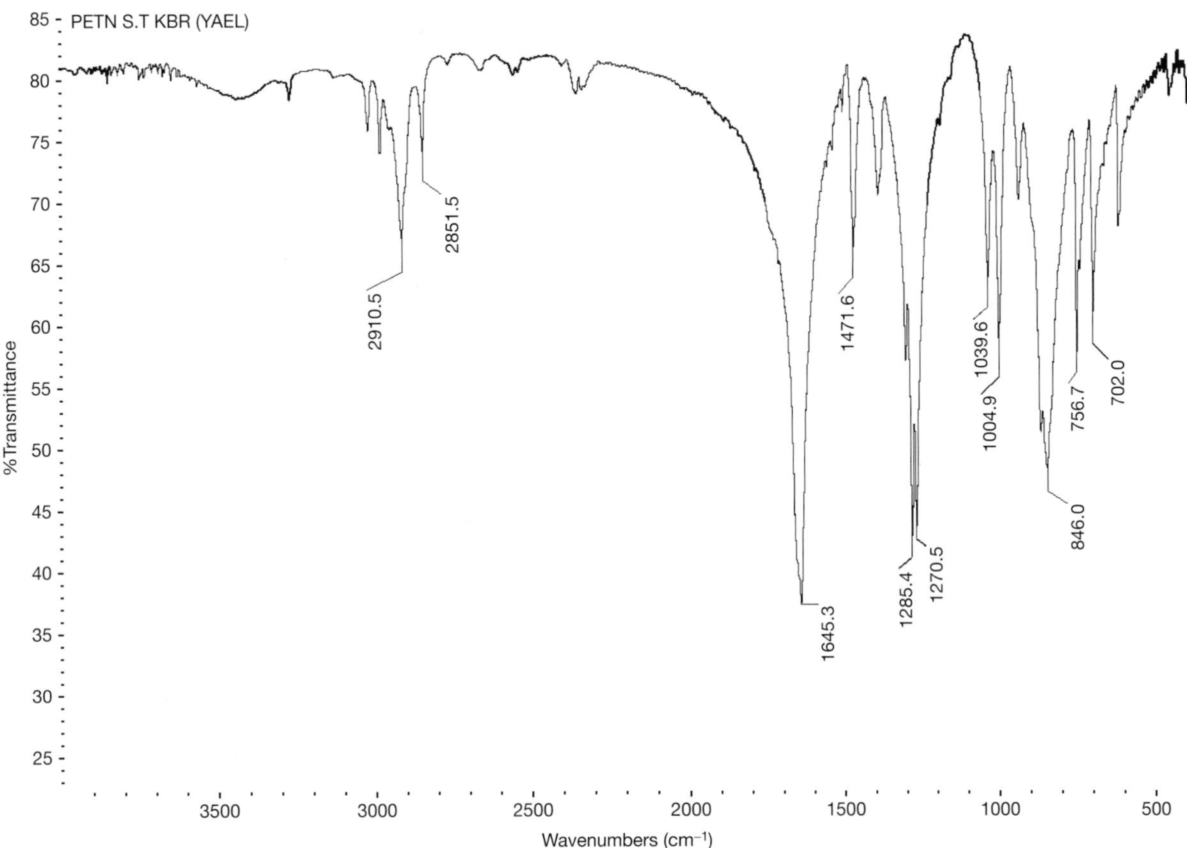

Figure 5 IR spectrum of PETN (DIFS collection).

Formation of negative molecular ions in EI is usually less efficient than formation of the positive ions. CI may also be used in the negative mode.

4. Atmospheric Pressure Ionization (API)
   - Electrospray ionization (ESI): This ionization technique takes place at atmospheric pressure. The eluent from the separation device (e.g., liquid chromatograph) passes through a stainless steel capillary to which a high-positive (or -negative) potential (e.g., 3–5 kV) is applied. Charged droplets containing solvent and analytes are produced. Evaporation of the solvent leaves behind charged analytes.
   - Atmospheric pressure CI (APCI): In APCI, the solvent eluted from the liquid chromatographic column is evaporated by a nebulizing gas (e.g., nitrogen). Molecules from the gas and the mobile phase are ionized by a corona discharge and form ionized species. These species ionize the analyte molecules via ion–molecule reactions similar to CI.

   Ions at m/z values higher than the molecular weights are often observed in the ESI and APCI mass spectra. They are formed by the addition of ionic species to molecules in the analyte and are often called 'adduct ions.' The added species may often be chloride, nitrate, formate, or acetate (in the negative mode) and H^+, NH_4^+, Na^+, or K^+ (in the positive mode).

   The mass spectra obtained by API usually contain a small number of ions. Unlike EI spectra, API spectra are different when measured in different instruments. Parameters such as instrument configuration, working conditions, type of mobile phase, and sample composition may affect the mass spectra. It is a common practice for laboratories to have a collection of authentic compounds and to create their own library in given conditions on a given instrument.

   Other insertion and ionization methods were reported for the analysis of explosives. An example is desorption ESI (DESI), introduced by Cooks and his coworkers, which was applied for direct analysis of common explosives. In this method, a spray of charged droplets ionizes the sample, which is located on a surface. The resulting ions are then introduced to the analyzer. No sample preparation is required, and the limits of detection are usually in the picogram range.
5. MS/MS

   In tandem mass spectrometry or MS/MS, ions at a selected m/z value (precursor ions) are separated by the first analyzer and enter a collision cell where they collide with atoms of an inert gas such as argon. The resulting fragment ions (product ions) are then mass analyzed by a second mass spectrometer to produce a product-ion

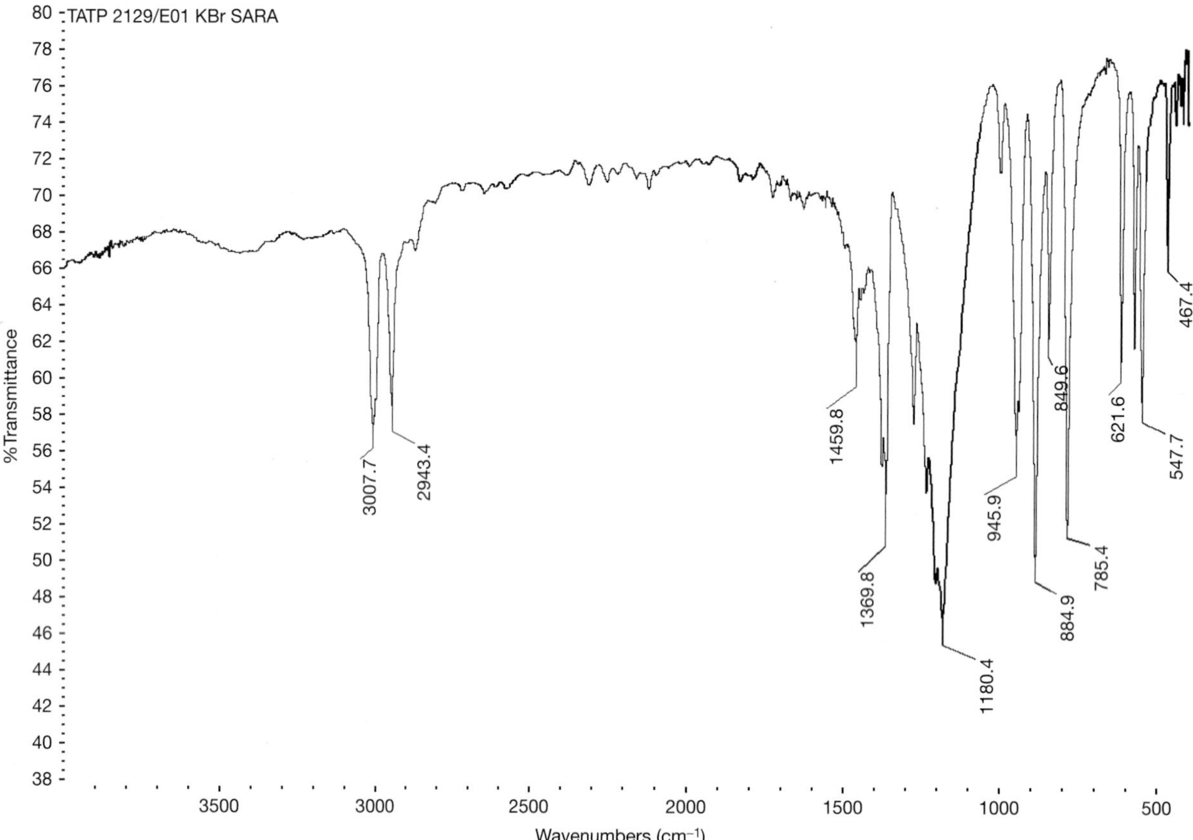

Figure 6 IR spectrum of TATP (DIFS collection).

mass spectrum, often called collision-induced dissociation (CID) spectrum. MS/MS can also be carried out in ion-trap instruments, where a precursor ion is selected and then undergoes fragmentation in the same ion trap to form product ions.

CID spectra of ions are often highly diagnostic. They have been extensively used in the analysis of explosives mainly in LC/MS whose spectra often contains little information.

- Mass spectrometry of explosives
  1. Nitroaromatic explosives

     EI mass spectra of nitroaromatic compounds are highly informative. A loss of NO_2 groups from the molecular ion is an important process, leading to characteristic $[M\text{-}xNO_2]^+$ ions. Unlike nitrate esters, the abundance of NO_2^+ ions in the spectra of nitroaromatic compounds is low. The abundant ion ('base peak') in the EI spectrum of 2,4,6-TNT (m/z 210) is attributed to an unusual loss of a hydroxyl group from the molecular ion ('ortho' effect) and the molecular ion is hardly observed. The EI mass spectrum of 2,4,6-TNT is shown in Figure 9.

     The CI mass spectra of nitroaromatic compounds contain highly abundant $[M+H]^+$ ions and usually very few fragment ions. The characteristic major ions in negative-ion ESI or APCI of nitroaromatic compounds are $[M\text{-}H]^-$ or M^-. Adduct ions are usually not observed, even when salts are present. ESI and APCI mass spectra of TNT are shown in Figure 10(f) and 10(c), respectively. The M^- ion of TNT obtained in ESI was reported to produce in CID mainly m/z 210 corresponding to the loss of OH group.

     Most nitroaromatic compounds may be analyzed by both GC/MS and LC/MS.
  2. Nitrate esters

     EI spectra of common nitrate esters are usually similar, containing highly characteristic ions at m/z 30, 46, and 76, attributed to $[NO]^+$, $[NO_2]^+$, and $[CH_2ONO_2]^+$, respectively, and no molecular ions. Therefore, the identification of most nitrate esters cannot be based only on their EI spectra. A suitable method to confirm the identity of a nitrate ester is CI where its molecular weight is clearly observed. The CI spectra of nitrate esters contain not only molecular weight information ($[M+H]^+$ ion), but also characteristic abundant ions at m/z $[M+H-63]^+$, attributed to the loss of $HONO_2$ from the protonated molecule. EI and CI mass spectra of NG are shown in Figure 11.

     The negative-ion ESI or APCI spectra of common nitrate esters are usually characterized by the presence of adduct ions. When acetate or formate are present in the liquid chromatographic eluent, abundant $[M+\text{acetate}]^-$ or $[M+\text{formate}]^-$, respectively, are observed in the spectra. This is an important difference

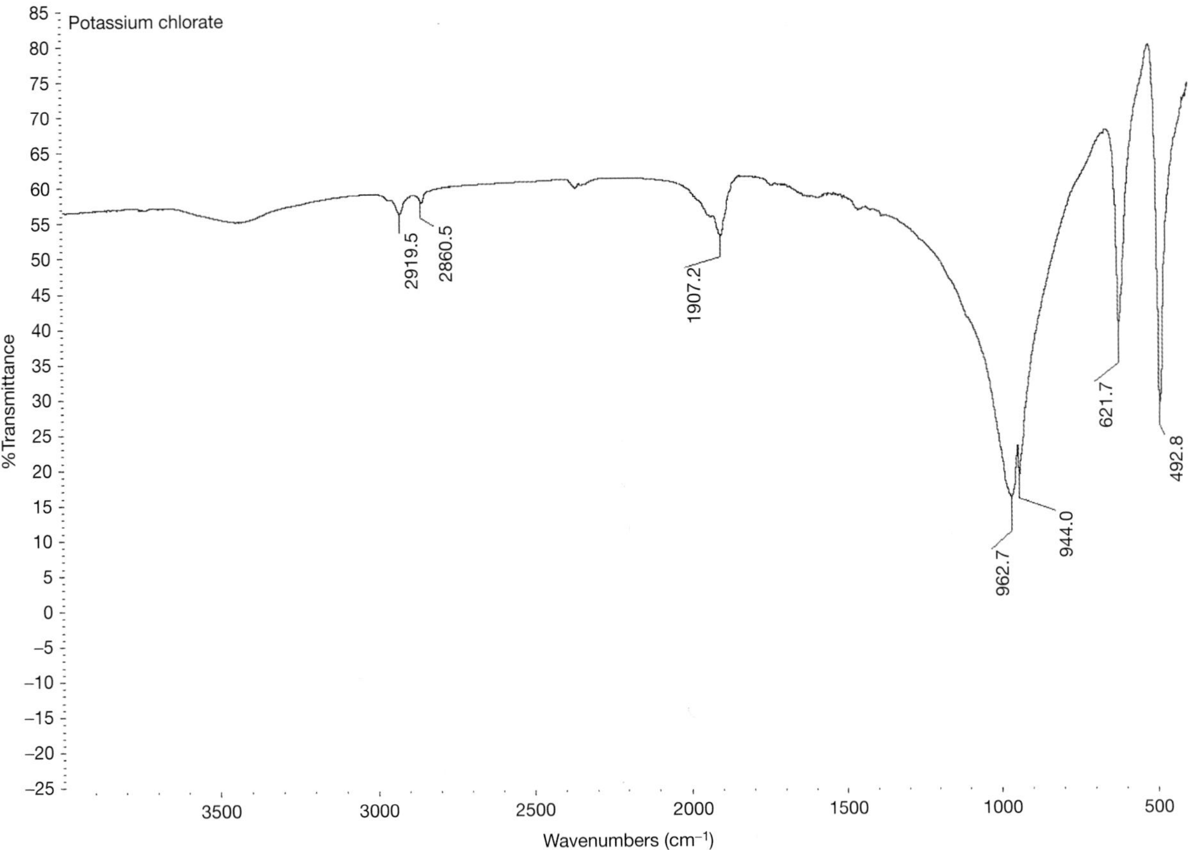

Figure 7 IR spectrum of potassium chlorate (DIFS collection).

between nitroaromatic compounds and nitrate esters or nitramines. ESI and APCI mass spectra of PETN are shown in **Figure 10(d)** and **10(a)**, respectively.

The CID spectrum of the $[M+acetate]^-$ in ESI of PETN was reported to produce the nitrate anion at *m/z* 62.

Most nitrate esters may be analyzed by both GC/MS and LC/MS, though some explosives, such as NG and PETN, may partially decompose under GC conditions.

3. Nitramines

EI spectra of the two heterocyclic nitramines, RDX and HMX, are similar and usually lack the molecular ion. The EI spectrum of RDX is shown in **Figure 12**.

In the CI spectra of RDX and HMX, $[M+H]^+$ ions can be observed.

Negative-ion ESI and APCI spectra of RDX and HMX are usually characterized by abundant adduct ions (e.g., $[M+acetate]^-$ and $[M+formate]^-$). ESI and APCI mass spectra of RDX are shown in **Figure 10(e)** and **10(b)**, respectively.

The CID spectrum of the $[M+acetate]^-$ in ESI of RDX was reported to produce the nitrite anion at *m/z* 46.

HMX, being nonvolatile, can be analyzed by LC/MS but not by GC/MS. RDX can be analyzed by both GC/MS and LC/MS, though it may partially decompose under GC conditions.

Tetryl, a nitramine with a trinitroaromatic nucleus, can be analyzed by GC/MS and LC/MS. Tetryl was found to undergo hydrolysis in the presence of water, to produce *N*-methylpicramide, identified by EI and CI. This process, which occurs in GC (and to a lesser extent in LC), may lead to erroneous interpretation in the analysis of tetryl. This hydrolysis is shown in **Figure 13**. The EI mass spectrum of *N*-methylpicramide is shown in **Figure 14**.

ESI spectrum of tetryl includes the $[M-H]^-$ ion and some adduct ions. Ions reported in APCI of tetryl were attributed to fragment ions of tetryl but their formation from *N*-methylpicramide could not be excluded.

The CID spectrum of the $[M-H]^-$ ion of tetryl was reported to produce an ion at *m/z* 240, possibly due to the loss of nitro group.

4. Peroxides

The two frequently encountered peroxide explosives, TATP and HMTD, can be analyzed by both GC/MS and LC/MS. The EI spectrum of HMTD is highly informative, including a clearly observed molecular ion. The EI spectrum of TATP (**Figure 15**) contains mainly ions in the low-mass range and a low-abundant molecular ion at *m/z* 222, which is not always observed. CI mass spectra of both peroxides contain the corresponding $[M+H]^+$ ions.

The analysis of TATP by ESI using postcolumn addition of sodium acetate was reported. $[M+H]^+$ or

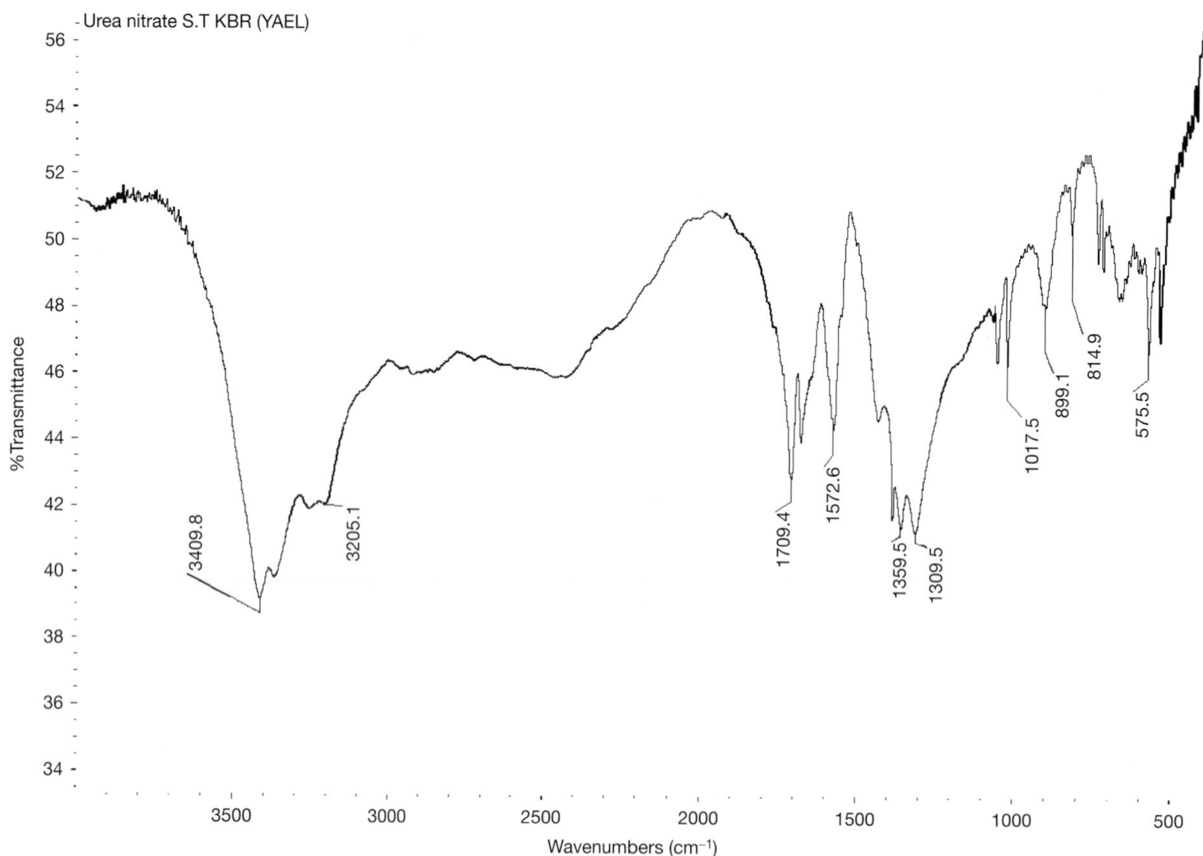

Figure 8 IR spectrum of UN (DIFS collection).

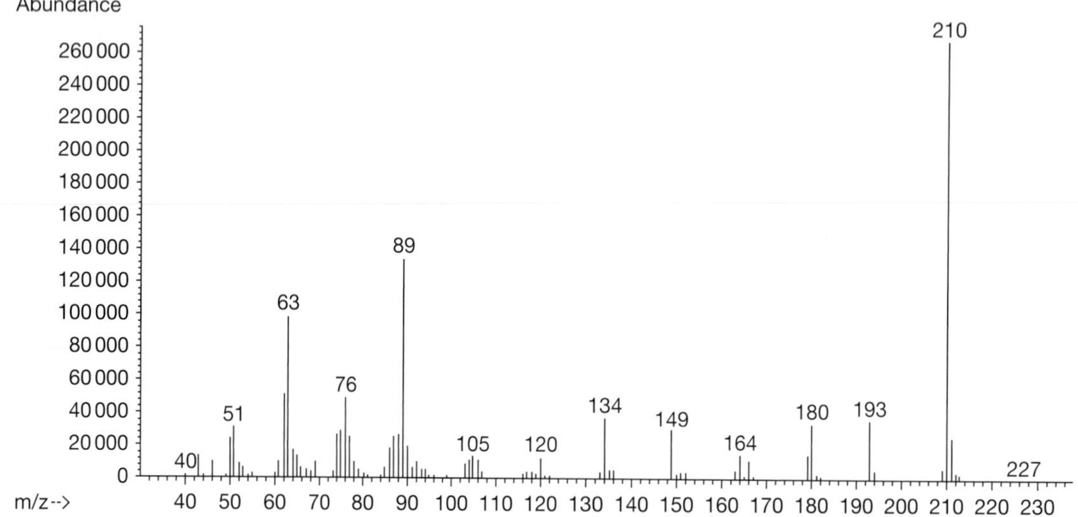

Figure 9 EI mass spectrum of 2,4,6-TNT (DIFS collection).

$[M-H]^+$ ions were observed in the APCI of HMTD, whereas $[M+NH_4]^+$ was observed in the APCI of TATP.

The CID spectrum of the $[M+NH_4]^+$ ion of TATP was reported to produce ions at m/z 74 and 91.

5. UN

UN cannot be analyzed by GC/MS. LC/MS (ESI and APCI) has been tried for its analysis. The results included ions corresponding to species containing UN. However, unequivocal identification of the original presence of UN could not be made since these ions appeared also when analyzing mixtures such as ammonium nitrate and urea.

6. Inorganic ions

While LC/MS can be used for the analysis of anions, GC/MS cannot be applied directly to the identification

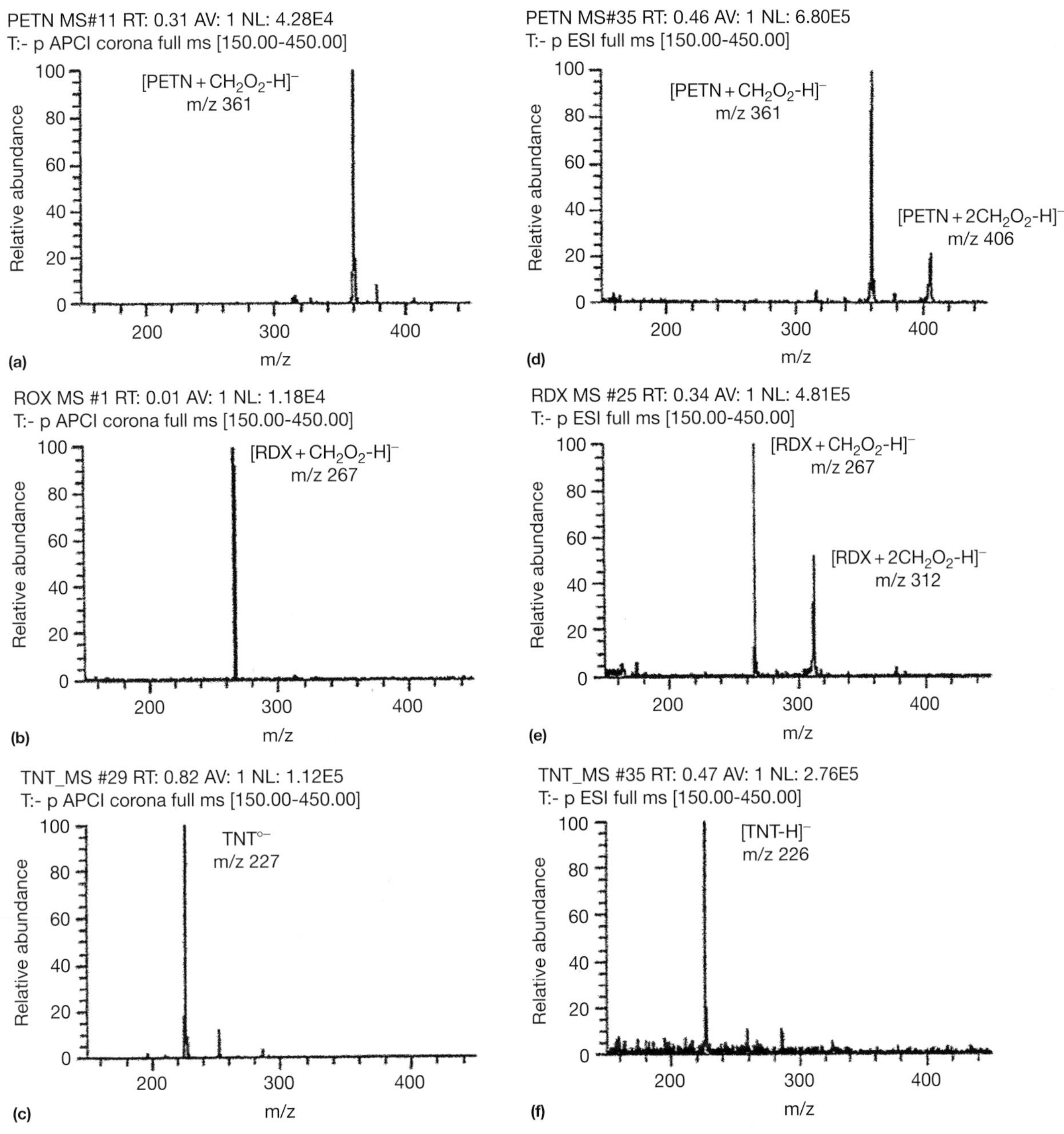

Figure 10 Spectra of PETN, RDX, and TNT recorded in APCI (a–c) and ESI (d–f). Reproduced from Tachon R, Pichon V, Barbe Le Borgne M, and Minet J-J (2007) Use of porous graphitic carbon for the analysis of nitrate ester, nitramine and nitroaromatic explosives and by-products by liquid chromatography-atmospheric pressure chemical ionization-mass spectrometry. *Journal of Chromatography A* 1154(1–2): 174–181, with permission from Elsevier.

of inorganic anions. A possible way to rectify this would be the incorporation of inorganic ions into organic molecules, which would then be identified by GC/MS. One example is the substitution of a halogen atom in an organic molecule (e.g., pentafluorobenzyl bromide) by the relevant anion. In these analyses, the inorganic anions have to be transferred from an aqueous solution into a nonaqueous phase, where the substitution reactions take place. This is done by phase-transfer catalysts such as quaternary ammonium salts. Among the ions analyzed were cyanide, nitrite, sulfide, cyanate, thiocyanate, azide, and nitrate. EI mass spectrum of pentafluorobenzyl nitrate is shown in Figure 16.

Direct-insertion negative-ion ESI was employed for analysis of some inorganic anions: HSO_4^-, ClO_3^-, ClO_4^-, NO_3^-, and CNS^-. Perchlorate ions were successfully detected by this method in the water extract from a postblast residue of Pyrodex, a commercial propellant common in the United States. When LC preceded the ESI ionization, the two inorganic anions in Pyrodex, nitrate and perchlorate, were detected as their free ions and their

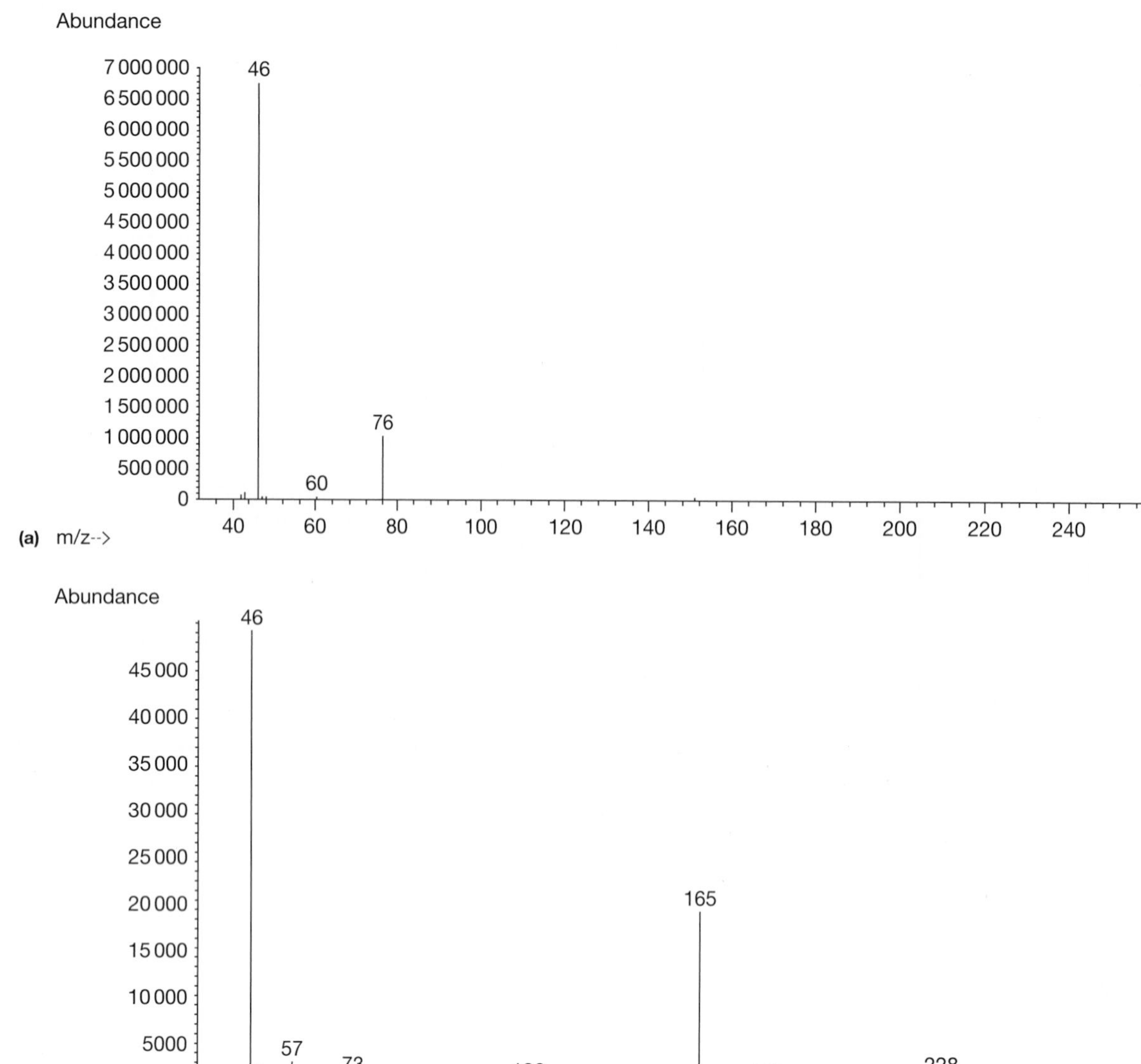

Figure 11 (a) EI and (b) CI-methane mass spectra of NG (DIFS collection).

acetate adduct ions. These ions, along with CNS^-, were also detected when the method was applied to a postexplosion analysis of Pyrodex. **Figure 17** shows the analysis of some ions related to explosives using LC/ESI/TOF/MS.

ESI in both positive- and negative-ion modes, followed by MS/MS, was used for the analysis of some salts (ammonium, sodium, and potassium nitrates; sodium and potassium chlorates; and ammonium and sodium perchlorates).

7. Other compounds

   Mass spectrometry is widely used in the analysis of explosives-related compounds such as plasticizers and stabilizers. Sugars were analyzed by GC/MS (as methyl or silyl derivatives) or by LC/MS.

x-Ray diffraction

x-Ray diffraction (XRD), or x-ray powder diffraction, utilizes x-ray radiation on crystalline organic and inorganic samples. The rays are diffracted in a pattern determined by the position, arrangement, and size of the constituents of the crystal. Scattered photons, which may undergo subsequent interference, lead to a characteristic diffraction pattern, which is specific to the crystalline powder and may serve as its 'fingerprint'. Sensitivity is usually in the microgram to milligram range.

XRD is widely used in the analysis of explosives. Its advantage over IC or CE is that it identifies a compound as a whole, where in the latter methods anions and cations are identified separately.

Scanning electron microscopy/energy-dispersive x-ray

Scanning electron microscopy/energy-dispersive x-ray (SEM/EDX) enables analysis and morphological characterization of surfaces of organic and inorganic samples. The sample is bombarded by a high-voltage electron beam. An interaction between the sample and the electron beam causes emission of radiation in the x-ray range, which is characteristic of an

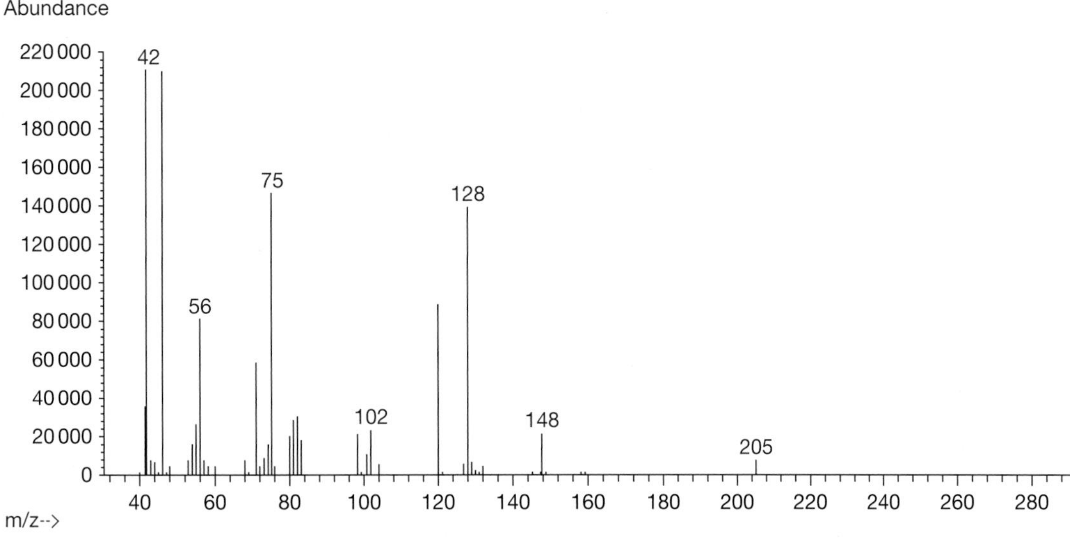

Figure 12 El mass spectrum of RDX (DIFS collection).

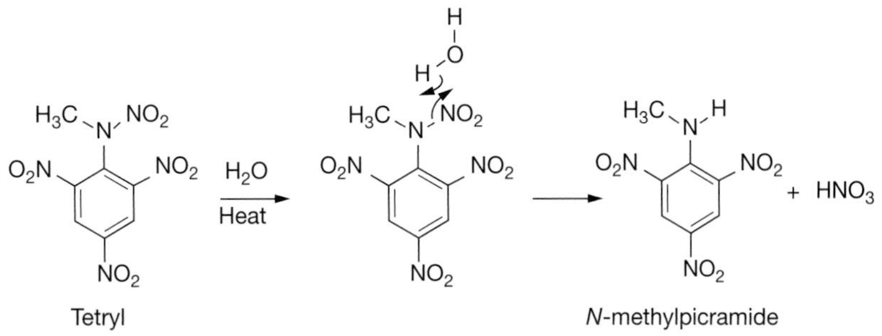

H_2O

Heat

$+ HNO_3$

Tetryl

N-methylpicramide

Figure 13 Hydrolysis of tetryl to *N*-methylpicramide.

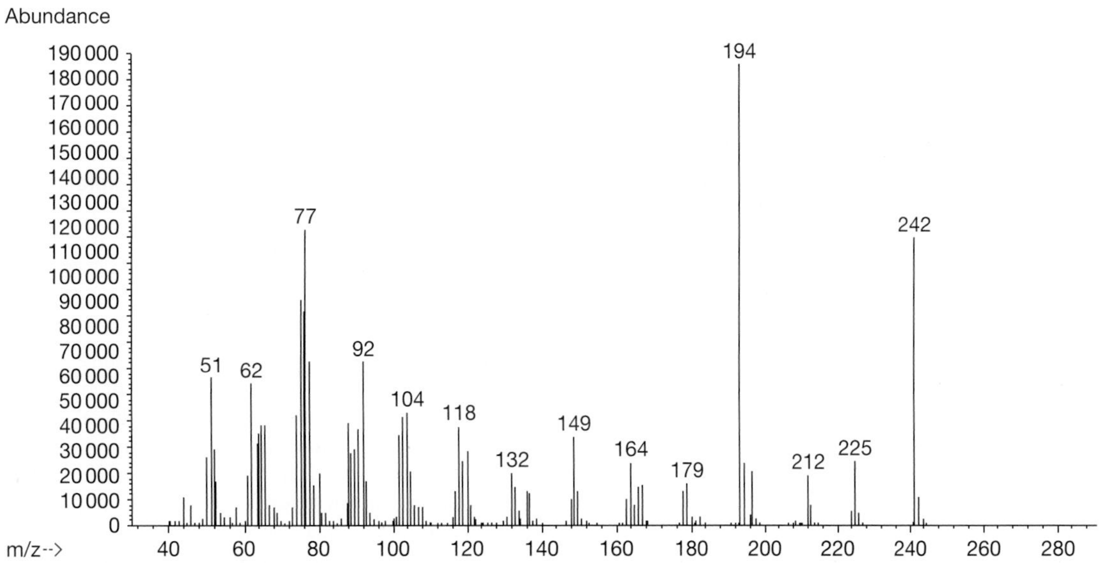

Figure 14 The El mass spectrum of *N*-methylpicramide (DIFS collection).

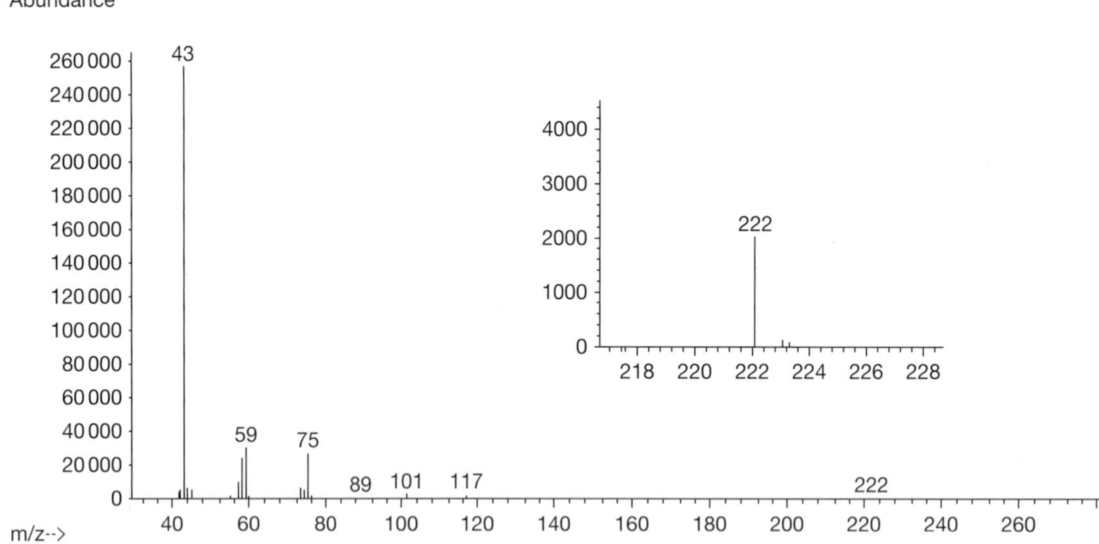

Figure 15 The EI mass spectrum of TATP. Zoom-in on the molecular weight region (inset) (DIFS collection).

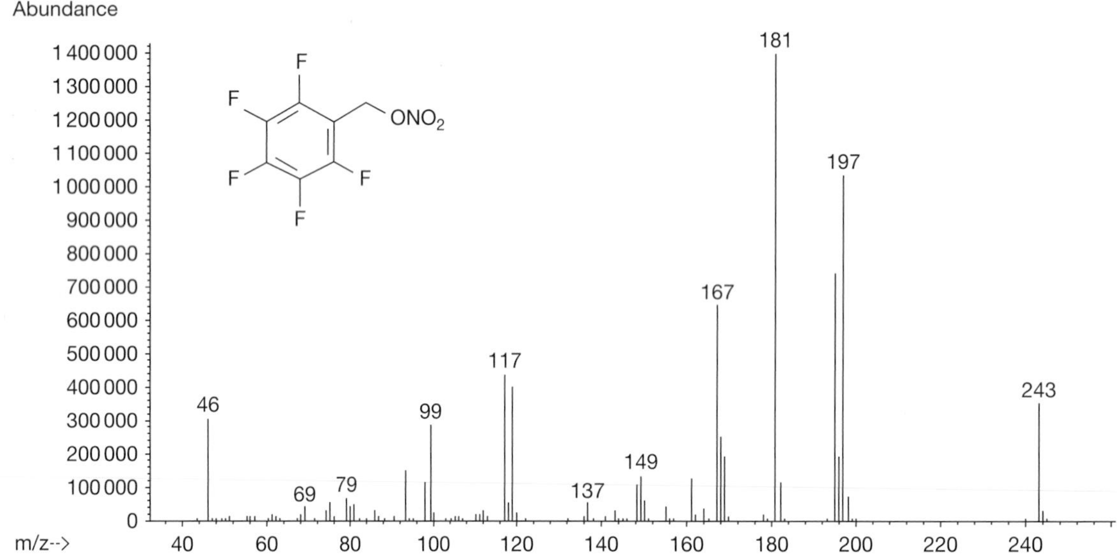

Figure 16 EI mass spectrum of pentafluorobenzyl nitrate (DIFS collection).

element. This technique allows high-speed qualitative elemental analysis. Quantitation can also be made according to the intensity of the energy emitted by the sample. SEM/EDX is usually suitable for the analysis of elements having atomic number 11 (sodium) and higher. When equipped with special light-element detector, the method enables the identification of elements having atomic number 5 (boron) and higher. This may have relevance to the identification of explosive molecules, which often contain nitrogen atoms. SEM/EDX is suitable for the identification of metals present in primary explosives such as lead azide, lead styphnate, and mercury fulminate.

Other methods such as x-ray fluorescence (XRF), atomic absorption spectroscopy, and inductively coupled plasma emission are sometimes used for elemental analysis of explosives.

Postexplosion and Trace Analysis of Explosives

Postexplosion analysis is normally based on the identification of the unreacted explosive which 'survived' the explosion. When the explosion is nearly complete, usually only trace amounts of the unexploded explosives are present. In cases of incomplete explosions, relatively large amounts of the original explosive may be recovered. The other alternative, that is, analyzing decomposition products is rarely carried out. This is because the explosion products (e.g., common gasses and salts) have often little diagnostic value. A noteworthy exception is the thiocyanate ion (CNS^-) whose formation is characteristic to the burning of black powder.

Procedures for trace analysis of postexplosion debris are usually much more complicated than those employed in bulk

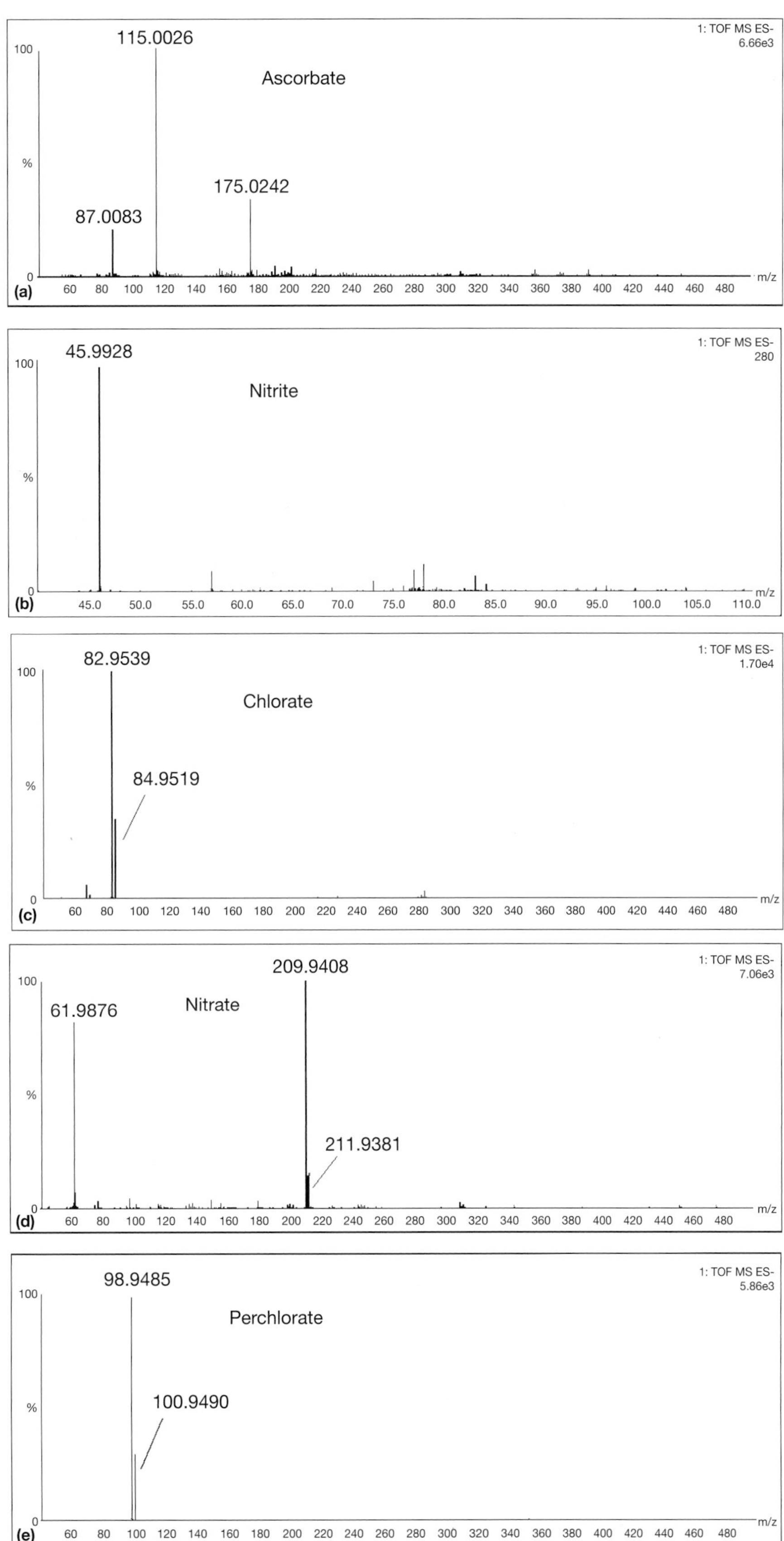

Figure 17 Analysis of (a) ascorbate, (b) nitrite, (c) chlorate, (d) nitrate, and (e) perchlorate using LC/ESI/TOF/MS. Reproduced from Bottegal M, Lang L, Miller M, et al. (2010) Analysis of ascorbic acid based black powder substitutes by high-performance liquid chromatography/electrospray ionization quadrupole time-of-flight mass spectrometry. *Rapid Communications in Mass Spectrometry* 24: 1377–1386, with permission from John Wiley and Sons.

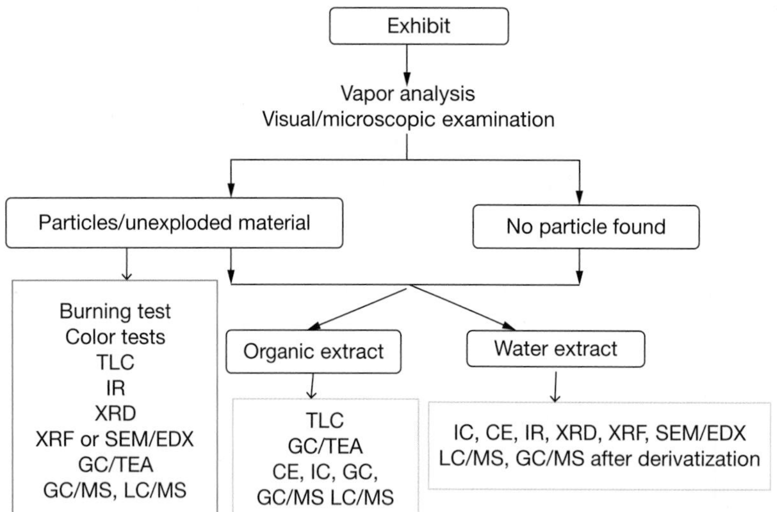

Figure 18 Example of a flowchart of analysis of postexplosion debris.

analysis, including recovery techniques as well as methods of identification.

Exhibits from bomb scene may be wet or oily and should be treated accordingly, taking into account different properties of explosives (e.g., preanalysis drying of wet exhibits might lead to evaporation of volatile explosives).

Extraction and cleaning procedures are especially important in postexplosion analysis where trace amounts of the explosives are often mixed with large amounts of interfering materials (such as plasticizers and oily compounds), which may complicate the analysis.

A typical flowchart for postexplosion analysis is given in Figure 18.

The expert may choose suitable procedures and methods according to the circumstances. These could include information from the investigation and the condition of the exhibit (e.g., wet, oily).

The investigator should consider the necessity of other forensic tests (e.g., fingerprints, DNA) on a recovered item and should determine the sequence of the required tests.

Caution should be exercised when blood is present in the scene due to possible biohazards.

Sampling Methods

Modern analytical methods may detect extremely small amounts of material, but no method, however sensitive, can detect an explosive if it is not present on the exhibit. Therefore, the collection of exhibits is a critical step in postexplosion analysis. It is not unknown that explosives are not identified on exhibits collected from the site of explosion, even in controlled experiments. Much work has been done to establish a methodology for the collection of exhibits according to their distribution around the bomb seat, that is, the site where the device was located when exploded. Often this site is characterized by a crater, which is a recommended place to start collecting exhibits. Protocols for comprehensive collection of evidence have been suggested according to distances from the bomb seat and to the types of surfaces. It seems that the chance to recover explosives is greater on distorted or charred debris. The type of the collected material (i.e., metal, plastic, upholstery, cloth, concrete, and soil) may affect the recovery method and the yield. Nevertheless, it seems that luck plays an important role in collecting the 'right' exhibit. When there is a large number of exhibits, field screening may help to decide which items should be transferred to the laboratory and which items should have priority in the subsequent analysis. This screening may be carried out either by chemical kits or by mobile instrumentation based on methods such as chemiluminescence, ion mobility spectrometry, or DESI. It should be emphasized that most field tests are of presumptive nature and, therefore, their results are indicative and cannot be considered an unequivocal identification.

Visual Examination

It is highly recommended that the analysis of an exhibit begins with visual examination. As is usual in routine forensic work, nondestructive methods should be applied before destructive methods in order to avoid loss of information by the latter. Such information may include morphological appearance of a particle. This could help in the identification of an explosive and also may connect a suspect to a scene if similar particles are found both in the scene and in the suspect's possession. Particles such as black powder, smokeless powder, or unconsumed material may be retrieved by physical separation carried out by the naked eye, a low-power stereoscope or sieving.

Vapor Analysis

Volatile explosives such as TATP or NG may be detected by direct headspace, or by adsorption on a suitable adsorbent. Examples of common adsorbents are resins such as Amberlite XAD-7 and Tenax. A widely used method is solid phase microextraction (SPME) where analytes are adsorbed on a fiber and then directly injected to the gas chromatograph or liquid chromatograph. A typical fiber used in explosives analysis by SPME is polydimethylsiloxane/divinylbenzene.

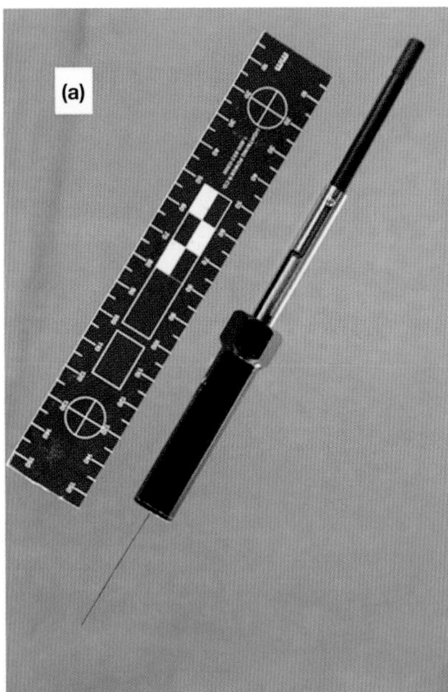

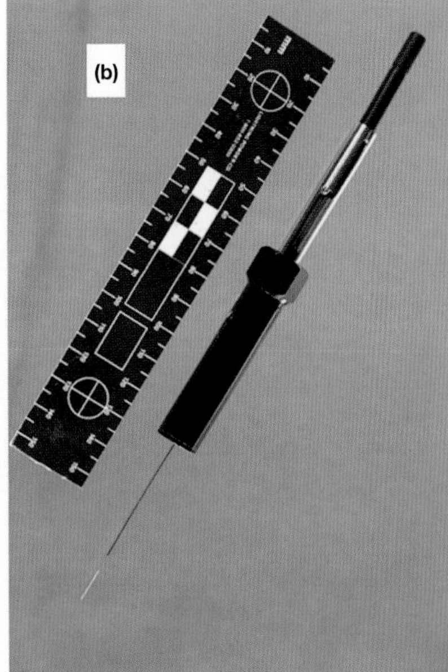

Figure 19 (a) SPME holder, (b) SPME holder with the adsorbent fiber exposed, and (c) SPME of nails, recovered from explosion of a suicide bomber in Jerusalem, wrapped in a nylon 66 bag (photograph by Yehuda Gabbay, DIFS).

In controlled experiments and in a real case carried out in the DIFS, it seemed that addition of water to soil or ashes improved the recovery of TATP by SPME. The use of SPME is demonstrated in Figure 19.

Organic Extraction

Organic extraction is usually performed by washing the exhibits with an organic solvent such as acetone, which is a common solvent for organic explosives. The solvent is then evaporated, preferably under a stream of nitrogen, rather than by heating, in order to minimize loss of volatile explosives. Unfortunately, acetone also dissolves nonexplosive materials from the debris such as hydrocarbons, fatty acids, phthalates, and even some more polar compounds. These materials, often present in large amounts, may coelute with the explosives in the chromatography and even change the R_t of the explosives. These coeluting compounds may also cause significant decrease in instrumental performance. For example, contamination of the injection port, column, and ion source in GC/MS results in decrease in sensitivity and resolution. This problem may be partly overcome by the use of ethanol:water mixtures rather than acetone. Normally a mixture of ethanol:water is used to extract both organic and inorganic components (instead of separate organic and aqueous extractions).

In another laboratory procedure, exhibits are being swabbed by dry or wet cotton wool (or another suitable cloth) and the swabs are subsequently extracted and analyzed. The use of swabs is especially relevant to large exhibits and exhibits that cannot be transferred to the laboratory from the explosion site.

Cleaning procedures

In order to reduce the amounts of contaminants in the extract, cleaning procedures may be carried out before the analysis. They include liquid/liquid extraction, preparative TLC or LC, and solid-phase extraction (SPE). SPE employs a suitable adsorbent packed in a column or in commercially available cartridges. After the extract is mounted on the adsorbent, the elution starts with nonpolar solvents (e.g., hexane), where the hydrophobic compounds (e.g., hydrocarbons) are washed out. The subsequent, more polar solvents elute polar compounds including the explosives. Another way to reduce the amounts of contaminants is to use aqueous extraction. Although water is not the ideal solvent for organic explosives, the amounts dissolved are usually compatible with many analytical methods especially LC and LC/MS.

Analysis

Analysis of the extract often starts with chromatographic methods (e.g., TLC) followed by a suitable confirmation method (e.g., GC/MS, LC/MS). GC/TEA may also serve as a confirmation method when several chromatographic columns are employed. As TEA detector is highly specific, it often leads to 'cleaner' chromatograms. Figure 20 shows the analysis of traces of RDX from a real case, by GC/TEA (in the upper trace) and by GC/MS (in the lower trace). RDX could not be clearly observed in the chromatogram obtained by GC/MS while the chromatogram obtained by GC/TEA could be safely interpreted.

IR is usually unsuitable for postexplosion analysis due to the large amount of contaminants which interfere with the spectrum. However, it is possible to apply FTIR-microscope when a discrete particle can be observed in the debris. The application of NMR to postexplosion extracts has had limited success.

Aqueous Extraction and Analysis

Hydrophilic, water-soluble species, including inorganic explosive-related anions, cations, and other compounds (e.g., sugars), are extracted by water and subjected to further

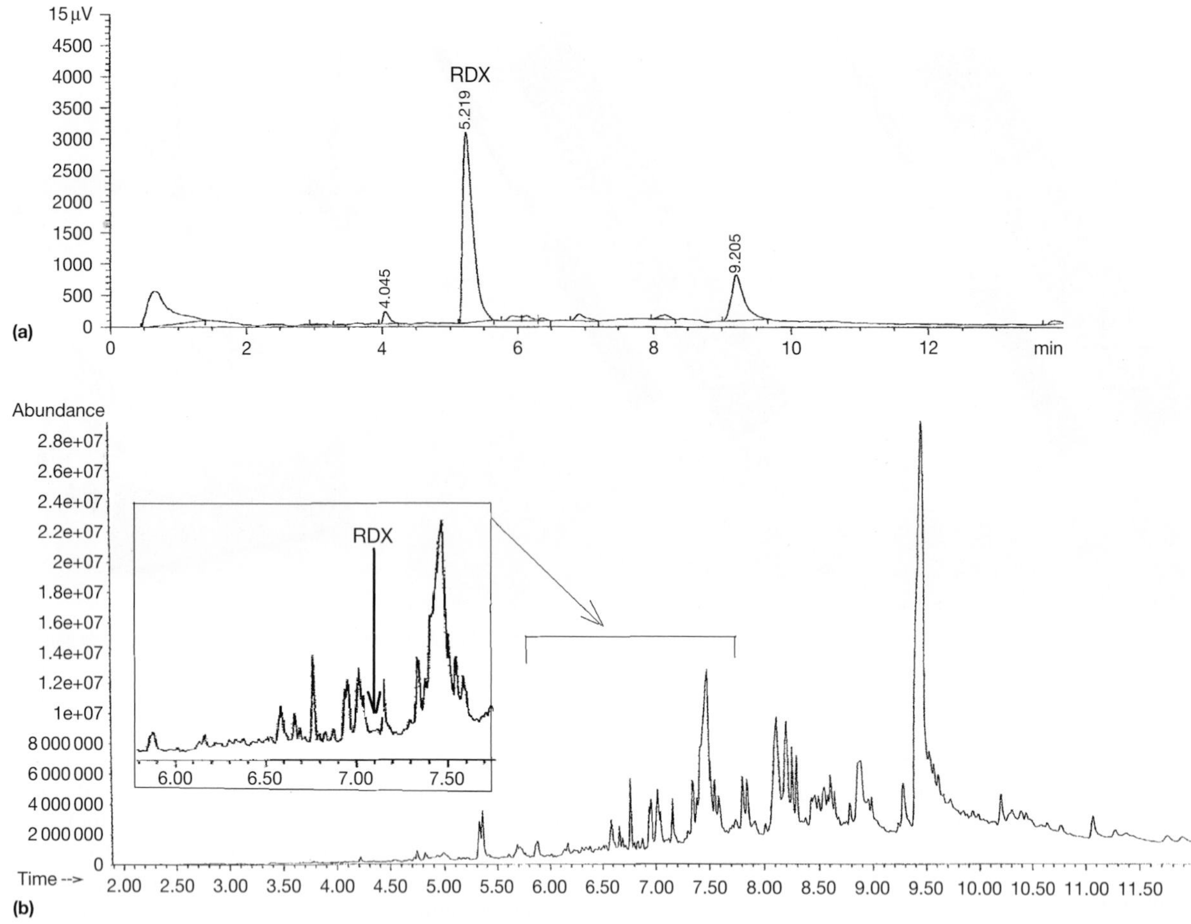

Figure 20 (a) GC/TEA and (b) GC/MS of RDX from postexplosion debris. The RDX chromatographic peak in (b) is hardly observed (marked by an arrow in the inset) while it is clearly observed in (a) (DIFS collection).

analysis. They may then be analyzed by methods such as spot tests, IC, IC/MS, CE, LC/MS, IR, SEM/EDX, and XRD. Unequivocal identification of some explosive-related inorganic anions may be carried out by GC/MS following their derivatization (see inorganic ions in section 'Mass Spectrometry' of this article). **Figures** 21 shows the EI mass spectrum of the derivatization product of thiocyanate, obtained from a real case where a pipe bomb containing black powder had been exploded. The molecular ion of pentafluorobenzyl thiocyanate is clearly observed at m/z 239.

Sometimes, when the aqueous or organic extracts are filtered, undissolved material remains on the filter paper (or cotton). This material should be tested for explosive-related species such as metals (e.g., Al and Mg).

Criteria of Identification

In forensic analysis where the results may affect the verdict in a court of law, a mistake must be avoided at all costs. Hence, an identification of an explosive should be reported only if strict criteria are met.

It is generally accepted that unequivocal identification cannot be based on spot tests alone, as the results are presumptive and can at best indicate the chemical class to which the explosive belongs. The situation is more complex with chromatographic methods. The conservative view has been that the identification of a single organic compound could not be based on chromatographic methods alone. Results from spectroscopic methods such as IR, MS, XRD, and NMR are required because they are highly reliable, being more directly related to the molecular structure of the analyte than chromatographic methods. This criterion may pose problems in postexplosion analysis. The chromatographic results cannot always be confirmed by spectrometric methods because of the extremely small amounts of unreacted explosives mixed with the large amounts of contaminants.

It was suggested that the introduction of highly specific detectors to chromatographic methods could suffice for a safe identification.

An example is the introduction of the TEA for gas chromatographic and liquid chromatographic analysis of nitro-containing explosives. A prerequisite for a positive response of the TEA is the presence of nitro (or nitroso) group. Normally, without their presence there would be no response.

This enhanced specificity has led some forensic analysts to regard chromatographic retention data combined with a positive TEA response as adequate for the identification of nitro-containing explosives (when at least two chromatographic systems with different polarities were used).

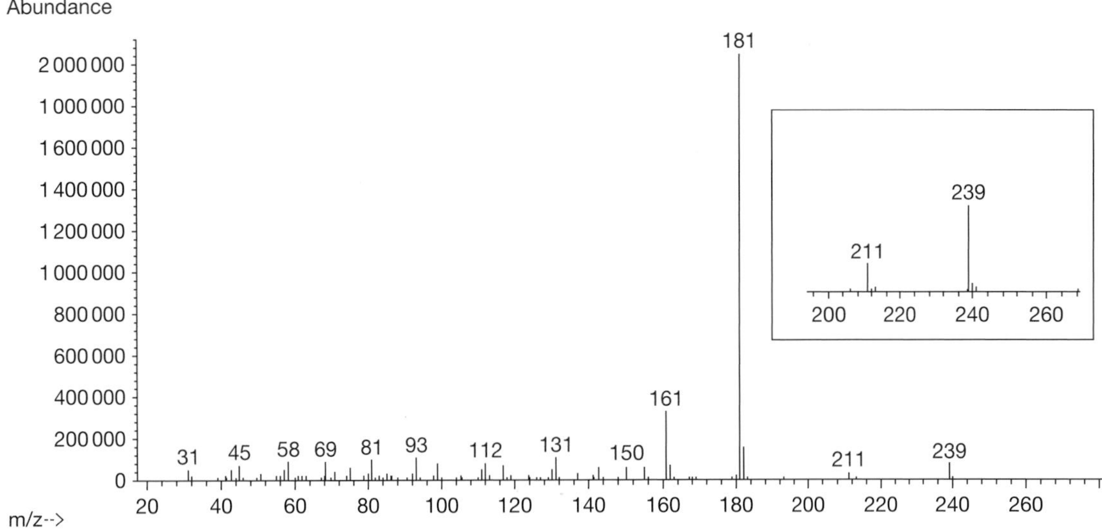

Figure 21 EI mass spectra of the derivatization product of thiocyanate, from an explosion of a pipe bomb containing black powder. Zoom-in on the molecular weight region (inset) (DIFS collection).

Guidelines regarding criteria for a safe identification of a single organic compound were suggested (e.g., by the European Commission in the case of pesticides residues).

Interpretation

Some problems related to the interpretation of the analytical results are given here.

- Some species, which appear in explosives, may also be found in the environment where they are not connected to the explosion. Detection of nitrate ions is not necessarily evidence for their presence in the original explosive as they are abundant in the environment. NC is abundant in the paint industry, so clearly its identification in the debris does not necessarily prove its presence in the explosive device.
- A special case is when the identified species is an explosive but from a source unrelated to the investigated explosion. An example is a case when NG is detected but originates from propellants present in the bomb scene (e.g., from ammunition possessed by soldiers or policemen), and not from the explosive device. Another example is the use of some nitrate esters in medicine.
- The identification of two species in the debris does not necessarily prove that they were chemically connected in the original explosive. Identification of a cation (e.g., ammonium) and an anion (e.g., nitrate) does not prove that the explosion was caused by the corresponding salt (e.g., ammonium nitrate). Independent identification of nitrate ions and urea in the debris does not necessarily prove the original presence of UN.
- Hydrolysis of polynitrate esters to lower nitrate esters is a process which, if unrecognized, may lead to erroneous results. Hydrolysis products of NG and PETN are sometimes observed in postexplosion extracts. These include the mono- and dinitrates of glycerol and the mono-, di-, and trinitrates of pentaerythrytol.
- Explosives could also originate from people present in the scene such as bomb-squad personnel. A good practice for anyone collecting exhibits is to submit swabs of himself, taken before the sampling, to reveal a possible contamination. These swabs are sent to the laboratory and processed by the same procedures used for the exhibits.
- Another important problem is cross-contamination in the laboratory itself. Avoiding errors resulting from contamination in the laboratory is an important issue in quality assurance procedures.
- When computerized databases are employed, a chemist should not rely only on computer results but should exercise his or her own judgment.

As demonstrated in this article, the analysis of explosives in forensic laboratories involves modern and sophisticated instrumentation. The human factor, however, remains an important element in forensic science. It is the skill, experience, intelligent judgment, and integrity of the chemist, which determine the quality of the analytical results.

See also: **Chemistry/Trace/Drugs of Abuse:** Clandestine Laboratories; **Chemistry/Trace/Explosives:** Commercial; Improvised Explosive Devices; Improvised Explosives; Military; **Chemistry/Trace/Firearm Discharge Residues:** Overview, Analysis, and Interpretation; **Management/Quality in Forensic Science:** Principles of Quality Assurance; **Methods:** Capillary Electrophoresis in Forensic Chemistry; Chromatography: Basic Principles; Gas Chromatography; Gas Chromatography–Mass Spectrometry; Liquid and Thin-Layer Chromatography; Mass Spectrometry; Presumptive Chemical Tests; Spectroscopic Techniques.

Further Reading

Beveridge AD (1992) Development in the detection and identification of explosives residues. *Forensic Science Review*, vol. 4, 18–49.

Beveridge AD (ed.) (2012) *Forensic Investigation of Explosions*, 2nd edn. Boca Raton, FL: CRC/Taylor & Francis Group.

Cotte-Rodriguez I and Cooks RG (2006) Non-proximate detection of explosives and chemical warfare agent simulants by desorption electrospray ionization mass spectrometry. *Chemical Communications* , vol. 28, 2968–2970.

European Commission Decision (2002) Implementing Council Directive 96/23/EC concerning the performance of analytical methods and the interpretation of results (2002/657/EC). *Official Journal of the European Communities* 221: 8, (17.8.2002). Chapter 2.3. Available at http://faolex.fao.org/docs/pdf/eur49615.pdf (accessed 24 July 2011).

Fedoroff BT, Aaronson HA, Reese EF, Sheffield OE, and Clift GD (1960). *Encyclopedia of Explosives and Related Items*, vol. 1, PATR 2700. Dover, NJ: Picatinny Arsenal (volumes 2–10, different authors and years of publication).

Lancaster SL, Marshall M, and Oxley JC (2009) Explosion debris: Laboratory analysis of. In: Jamieson A and Moenssens A (eds.) *Wiley Encyclopedia of Forensic Science*, pp. 1028–1060. Chichester, West Sussex: Wiley.

Marshall M and Oxley JC (eds.) (2009) *Aspects of Explosives Detection*. Oxford: Elsevier.

McCord BR, Hargadon KA, Hall KE, and Burmeister SG (1994) Forensic analysis of explosives using ion chromatographic methods. *Analytica Chimica Acta* 288: 43–56.

Saferstein R (1998) Criminalistics: An Introduction to Forensic Science, 6th edn., pp. 326–360. Englewood Cliffs, NJ: Prentice-Hall.

Urbanski T (1964) *Chemistry and Technology of Explosives*, vol. 1–3. and (1984) vol. 4. Oxford: Pergamon Press.

Yinon J and Zitrin S (1981) *The Analysis of Explosives*. Oxford: Pergamon Press.

Yinon J and Zitrin S (1993) *Modern Methods and Applications in Analysis of Explosives*. Chichester: Wiley.

Commercial

SG Murray, Cranfield University, Royal Military College of Science, Shrivenham, UK

This article is reproduced from the previous edition, volume 2, pp. 750–758, © 2000, Elsevier Ltd., with an updated Further Reading section supplied by the Editor.

Introduction

To secure the best value from this article it is recommended that the article entitled 'Mechanism of Explosion' be read first.

The first use of explosives for commercial enterprises dates back to the seventeenth century, for example, for mineral mining in Hungary, tin mining in Cornwall in the UK and civil engineering in France with the building of the Languedoc tunnel. In all of these cases the explosive used was black powder. Even today black powder still finds limited commercial use for example in slate quarrying where the shattering effect of a high explosive would be too damaging to the fragile slate.

The true potential of explosives for mining and quarrying began with the development of nitroglycerine-based explosives in the nineteenth century and the advent of the detonator. This created a much more efficient method of using chemical energy both in breaking rock and for lift and heave in trenching or cratering to move earth. These dynamites or gelignites were the mainstay of commercial explosives until the 1950s, by which time explosives based on ammonium nitrate began to develop. This has led to the development of slurry and emulsion explosives and these are now displacing the nitroglycerine explosives in the commercial sector.

In comparison to military high explosives, commercial explosives are driven by cost. This is because the explosive is a significant component in the costs of a commercial enterprise such as quarrying or tunneling. It may be more cost effective, particularly in recent times, to use mechanical methods instead of explosives. The Channel Tunnel between the UK and France was excavated without the use of any explosives. Furthermore, in relation to costs, as the shattering ability or brisance of the explosive increases, so does the cost of the explosive. This means that there is a need for a range of explosives with different properties, particularly their detonation pressure but also their power, that is gas expansion effects.

Performance Parameters

Indication of Performance

For commercial explosives, the ability to create lift and heave (power) is usually described by strength. This is a comparison of a particular explosive with a standard. The comparison may be with the same weight (mass) or the same volume of the standard giving the 'weight strength' or 'bulk strength', respectively. For nitroglycerine-based explosives, strength is usually compared to blasting gelatine, the most powerful of the type. More recently, strength may be compared to other standards and thus the literature must be scrutinized carefully to assess the actual performance. The method of conveying the information either in the literature or on the wrapping or container of the explosive charge is to quote the strength as a percentage, e.g. 80% strength.

The manufacturer rarely gives the detonation pressure; however, the literature will give the density and the detonation velocity. Together, these will indicate the shattering ability as high velocity of detonation and high density (relative) give high-detonation pressure. This is indicated in the description of the various types of explosive in the following text.

Fume Characteristics

One of the hazards of using explosives in confined spaces such as tunneling is the production of toxic fumes. Commercial explosives are mixtures of various ingredients and it is possible to vary the ratio of fuel elements to available oxygen. This means that the manufacturer can create explosive formulations that minimize the production of carbon monoxide, thus making them much safer for use in confined situations.

For some explosives it is possible to create toxic products by having an excess of oxygen relative to the fuel that is present. This is particularly true for ammonium nitrate/fuel oil where a deficiency of fuel may lead to the production of oxides of nitrogen, seen as a brown gas cloud after detonation.

Water Resistance

Another property of commercial explosives that is important to the user is the ability to use the explosive in the presence of water, for example in wet boreholes. Thus, the details provided for a particular product would state the water resistance from 'none' to 'excellent'. This water resistance may be due to the packaging in more recent times with the advent of plastic containers. However, in earlier times it was a property of the actual formulation. For example, ammonium nitrate/fuel oil as a loose material has no water resistance, whereas the gelignites with a high nitroglycerine content, have excellent water resistance.

Shock Sensitivity

An important factor in the use of commercial explosives is the knowledge of the ability to reliably detonate the explosive charge with a detonator. This is known as detonator or cap sensitiveness. The formulations containing nitroglycerine are detonator sensitive; however, many of the bulk borehole charges are not. These include ammonium nitrate/fuel oil and certain slurries and emulsions. However, it is possible to formulate slurries and emulsions that are detonator sensitive.

For charges that are not detonator sensitive, a booster (or primer) is employed. This is an explosive charge that will reliably detonate from a detonator and amplify the shock wave which then detonates the insensitive column of explosive.

Critical Diameter

Critical diameter is the minimum diameter of a bare charge of explosive that will sustain a detonation shock wave. For military explosives this value is very small, often 1–2 mm. However, for commercial explosives the value can be much greater, perhaps as much as 50 mm. This requires a matching of explosive type to borehole diameter. In practice, the manufacturer will supply cartridged explosives in diameters that are guaranteed to detonate fully. If, however, the explosive is to be bulk loaded into a borehole, it is imperative that the hole diameter is well above the critical diameter for the explosive.

Nitroglycerine-containing Explosives

From the mid-nineteenth century to the mid-twentieth century, nitroglycerine (NG) (**Figure 1**) was the most important energetic ingredient and sensitizer for commercial explosives. The early developments were attributed to the Nobel family in Sweden with Immanuel Nobel being the first to realize the potential of nitroglycerine and then his son Alfred who has now been immortalized through his efforts in developing modern explosives and the introduction of the Nobel Prizes. The oily liquid is manufactured by the reaction of glycerine (glycerol, propane-1,2,3-triol) with a mixture of concentrated nitric and sulfuric acids, during which the temperature must be carefully controlled to avoid a rise in temperature that could cause a runaway decomposition of the explosive that has formed resulting in an explosion. Modern synthesis uses a continuous nitration process where the maximum quantity of explosive in the reaction vessel is limited.

Pure nitroglycerine has a melting point of 13 °C and is undesirable for the explosive to freeze when mixed in a formulation. Partly thawed nitroglycerine is dangerously sensitive; this is thought to be due to the presence of triclinic crystals that may rub together if the charge is handled. To overcome this, another explosive molecule, ethyleneglycoldinitrate (EGDN, nitroglycol) (**Figure 1**) is mixed with the nitroglycerine to lower the freezing point. EGDN is manufactured at the same time as the nitroglycerine by using a mixture of glycerine and glycol (ethane-1,2-diol) in the nitration reaction. The ratio of these explosive types is usually around 50/50 and lowers the freezing point of the mixed liquid explosives to around −10 °C. Pure nitroglycol freezes at −22 °C.

The range of explosives described below is manufactured worldwide; however, in recent years the development of commercial explosives that do not contain nitroglycerine is causing a serious decline in the use and therefore production of this type of explosive. It is estimated that in the very early part of the twenty-first century, the production of dynamites will cease.

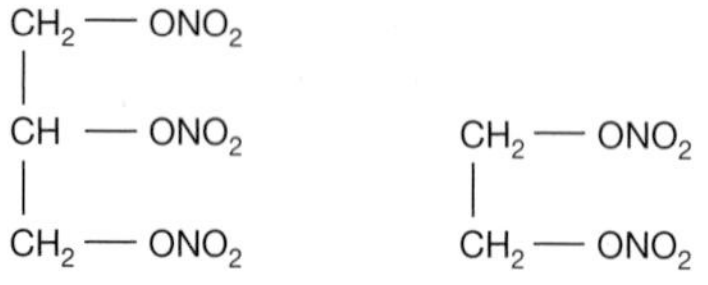

$$\begin{array}{l} CH_2 - ONO_2 \\ | \\ CH - ONO_2 \\ | \\ CH_2 - ONO_2 \end{array} \qquad \begin{array}{l} CH_2 - ONO_2 \\ | \\ CH_2 - ONO_2 \end{array}$$

(1) (2)

Figure 1 The structure of nitroglycerine (1) and ethyleneglycoldinitrate (2).

Dynamite Explosives

This group of explosives was developed from the original dynamite of Nobel that was simply nitroglycerine absorbed into kieselguhr, a dry powdered clay. This significantly reduced the extreme sensitivity of the nitroglycerine to shock initiation. There were two major developments that followed: (1) the addition of nitrocellulose (NC) that gelled with the nitroglycerine (and nitroglycol as mentioned above); (2) the inclusion of a fuel/oxidizer mixture in the formulation. The use of nitrocellulose allowed the liquid nitroglycerine/nitroglycol to form a gelatinous mixture giving useful physical properties and minimizing the separation of the liquid explosives from the mixture. Also, it significantly reduced the sensitivity of the pure liquid explosives. This led to a range of explosives known as gelatine dynamites or gelignites with the NC content being approximately in the ratio 1:20 with the NG/EGDN. The original dynamite as described above is no longer found.

The use of a fuel/oxidizer mixture gave the extra dynamites or extra gelatine dynamites although it should be noted that these are often simply called gelignites. The fuels are usually cellulose based, such as sawdust or wood meal (fine sawdust), and the oxidizer is either sodium or, more usually, ammonium nitrate. In some countries the term 'straight gelatine dynamite' may be used to differentiate the use of sodium rather than ammonium nitrate and 'ammon' or 'special' to denote the use of ammonium nitrate.

This allows a large range of explosive formulations to be produced depending on the ratio of gelled nitroglycerine/nitroglycol to fuel/oxidizer mixture. Those with a reasonable gelled nitroglycerine/nitroglycol content are rigid in form and are the true gelatine explosives. They can be deformed by pressing with a tamping rod when loading shot holes. As this ingredient is reduced in the formulation then the consistency becomes more crumbly. These are known as semigelatines and will have reduced performance. Finally, the content may be reduced so much that the consistency is a powder; at this stage it is unlikely that nitrocellulose is present. These low performance explosives are the nitroglycerine powders. In some countries it is possible to find formulations that have the same NG/EGDN content as a gelatine or semigelatine explosive but without the NC as a gelling agent. Confusion may occur as these have been called 'straight' dynamites in some texts.

Other additives may be found in these formulations. Both barium sulphate and manganese dioxide can be added to increase the density and achieve maximum velocity of detonation. Sodium chloride and calcium oxalate are added to act as flame suppressants (see below) and often naturally occurring gums are present to aid consolidation of the mixtures. Calcium carbonate may be added to act as a stabilizer to minimize the risk of autocatalytic decomposition of the nitroglycerine/nitroglycol. On rare occasions, dinitrotoluene may be present.

Permitted Explosives

When blasting in coalmines, there is always the risk of secondary explosions and fire from ignition of either methane/air or suspended coal dust/air mixtures. To overcome this problem permitted explosives were developed. These must pass rigorous national testing to ensure that such ignitions cannot occur and are categorized for particular uses. These are given designations such as P1-P4/5 in the UK.

The source of ignition for the fuel/air mixtures that may be present could be one of the following:

1. A long lasting flame as would be produced from a black powder explosion;
2. A secondary burn of hydrogen/carbon monoxide produced by an explosive that had a negative oxygen balance;
3. An intense shock wave from a high-detonation pressure explosive causing shock heating of the surrounding air.

To overcome these possible mechanisms, formulations have been devised that have relatively low shock pressure and a positive oxygen balance. Furthermore, sodium chloride is added in significant quantity, as much as 30% by weight, as this acts as a flame suppressant by interfering with the flame propagation process.

Performance

Nitroglycerine is a very powerful explosive producing an energy release of 6275 J g^{-1} and 740 cm^3 g^{-1} of gas. This ranks with the highest performing explosive molecules for power output. Nitroglycol has an even higher energy output at 6730 J g^{-1} but the same gas production. It is clear that a high percentage of these ingredients will produce an explosive with good lift and heave. Also, the velocities of detonation and densities suggest a high-detonation pressure. However, as discussed above it is usual to find these explosive liquids absorbed into a nitrate/wood meal mixture and this will significantly reduce the density and velocity of detonation.

The most energetic formulation of this group of explosives is blasting gelatine, which contains 92–94% nitroglycerine/nitroglycol together with 6–8% nitrocellulose. This is used as the standard against which the strength of other gelatine dynamites is measured. This explosive is rarely used in practise, as the level of performance is hardly ever required. As the percentage of nitroglycerine/nitroglycol decreases the detonation pressure falls quite rapidly. However, although the power also falls, the percentage reduction is not as great as for the detonation pressure.

Typical percentages of nitroglycerine/nitroglycol for the various types described above will be:

Blasting gelatine	92–94%
Gelatine dynamites	75–25%
Semigelatines	20%
NG powders	10%
Permitted	30–10% (being gelatines, semigelatines or NG powders)

The weight strength, bulk strength, density, and velocity of detonation for typical examples of the various types are given in **Table 1**. The velocity of detonation is the maximum as achieved by a strong shock initiation. These types of explosives have an unusual feature if initiated with a relatively weak shock. They will detonate with a velocity of detonation of ~2500 m s^{-1} irrespective of the NG/EGDN content. Thus a gelatine, semigelatine, or NG powder can have two quite different values for a stable velocity of detonation.

Table 1 Performance figures for nitroglycerine-based explosives

Explosive type	*Weight strength vs BG (%)*	*Bulk strength vs BG (%)*	*Density (g cm^{-3})*	*Velocity of detonation (ms^{-1})*
Blasting gelatine	100	100	1.6	7500
Gelatine dynamite	80–65	80–65	1.5–1.4	6600–5500
Semigelatine	65–50	60–50	1.3	6000–5000
NG powder	80	65	1.15	4000

Table 1 also shows that the bulk strength is often lower than the weight strength. This is because in those cases the density of the explosive is much lower than the blasting gelatine standard.

Military Dynamites

It should be noted that in the United States, military dynamites are not based on nitroglycerine but contain trinitrotoluene (TNT) and cyclotrimethylene trinitramine (RDX) as the explosive molecular components.

Ammonium Nitrate-based Explosives

Ammonium Nitrate Fuel Oil (ANFO)

Any carbonaceous material mixed with ammonium nitrate (AN) will produce a possible explosive mixture. In fact AN, as a pure material is not classified as an explosive for transportation and storage unless it contains >0.4% carbonaceous material. However, there have been many apparent incidences of pure AN being transported in bulk that has caught fire and ultimately transitioned to a detonation. In all cases where an explosion followed an AN fire, the mass of AN was confined, for example in the hold of a ship, and it is contested was almost certainly contaminated with combustible materials to some extent. The infamous incident at Oppau, in the Rhineland of Germany, was caused by the explosive blasting of an approximately 50/50 mixture of AN and ammonium sulfate. Although it was found that there had been around 20 000 blasts carried out previously, a procedure used to break up the hard consolidated mass of AN/ammonium sulfate, in this instance it is likely that the condition of the material had altered from the norm and probably contained less moisture and was of slightly lower density. The ensuing explosion killed 500, injured 1900 and caused damage in a town at 1.5 km distance. Most of Oppau was completely destroyed. The explosion was estimated to be equivalent to around 500 tonnes of TNT.

Ammonium nitrate (NH_4NO_3) has been manufactured as a fertilizer at least since the turn of the twentieth century. Developments in the 1950s led to a form of AN known as prills. These were small spherical or ovoid beads, 2–3 mm in diameter, manufactured by passing concentrated AN solution droplets down a drying tower against a rising stream of hot air. Control of the conditions gave prills of differing densities. The crystal density of AN is 1.7 g cm^{-3}. For agricultural use, a high density prill is favorable at ~1.1 g cm^{-3}; however, for use in the manufacture of an explosive, a lower density is better at 0.8–0.9 g cm^{-3}. This is because the porosity of the lower density material allows the liquid fuel (fuel oil or diesel) to absorb readily into the prills. Thus, an intimate fuel/oxidizer mixture is achieved. These lower density prills are somewhat prone to physical breakage, which at first appeared to be a disadvantage. However, with some modern methods of use it may actually be advantageous as described below.

The commercial explosive is known as ANFO (AN fuel oil) and the correct proportions of AN to diesel, a commonly used fuel oil, are 94/6 based on pure AN. If it is known that the AN is not pure then the diesel percentage should be adjusted to give the same ratio of the AN content to the diesel. It is important to ensure that the fuel/oxidizer balance is correct as variance may give large quantities of carbon monoxide if fuel rich, or of nitrogen dioxide, if oxidizer rich. Most explosives manufacturers will sell both readymade ANFO and bags of AN prills for the user to manufacture the ANFO on site. For large-scale use it is mixed on site in a purpose-built vehicle and poured directly into vertical boreholes. ANFO can be loaded into horizontal or vertically inclined boreholes by pneumatic loading. This is carried out at a pressure of ~4 bar which causes the density to rise from the 0.8–0.9 g cm^{-3} to ~1.1 g cm^{-3}. This provides an explosive fill that has more power and a higher velocity of detonation.

Performance of ANFO

ANFO is a very insensitive explosive, which makes it extremely safe to use. However, it is not detonator sensitive and therefore requires the use of a booster to provide reliable detonation. When poured loose into a borehole or pneumatically loaded, there will be maximum filling of the hole. This does not occur when cartridged charges are used.

On the other hand, ANFO has no water resistance unless packaged in waterproof containers. It cannot be loaded directly in to wet boreholes as this makes the column of explosive insensitive even to a booster. Also, ANFO has a large critical diameter and is not likely to propagate a detonation shock wave successfully in boreholes of less than 50 mm in diameter. Figure 2 indicates how the velocity of detonation varies with borehole diameter. As the value increases, so will the shock pressure. A commonly used borehole size is 100 mm (4 inches).

Typical values quoted for the weight strength and bulk strength of ANFO are 70% BG (blasting gelatine) and 30% BG, respectively. The bulk strength is so low because of the very low density of poured ANFO. Addition of aluminum powder increases the energy in the mixture and gives weight and bulk strengths of 77% BG and 40% BG, respectively. The shock pressure of these explosives will be in the region of 10–30 kbar. The higher values will be for large diameter boreholes as the velocity of detonation is higher or for the pneumatically loaded ANFO where the density is higher. A typical value for

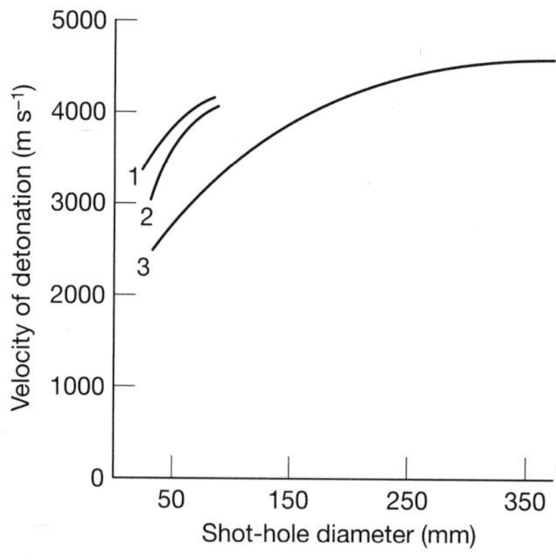

Figure 2 Velocity of detonation for ANFO (poured and pneumatically loaded) versus borehole diameter. 1, Pneumatically loaded, 1.1 g cm^{-3}; 2, pneumatically loaded, 0.95 g cm^{-3}; 3, poured ANFO, 0.8 g cm^{-3}.

velocity of detonation for poured ANFO in a standard borehole of 100 mm would be <3000 m s^{-1}.

Slurry Explosives

A slurry explosive is based on AN as oxidizer mixed with a fuel as with ANFO. However, they have as part of the formulation, a significant percentage of water, usually 10–25% by weight. The water, together with the presence of guar gum or equivalent as a gelling agent, produces an explosive superior in many ways to ANFO. The basic formulation is ammonium nitrate solid together with either a carbonaceous fuel or aluminum powder or both held in suspension in a gelled saturated solution of ammonium nitrate. Over the years many types of carbonaceous fuels have been used, ranging from solid hydrocarbons, powdered coal, carbohydrates (e.g. sugars), bagasse (sugar cane cellulose) to paint-grade aluminum. When aluminum is present in the mixture it is usual to include an additive to buffer the pH against the acidity caused by the presence of the ammonium nitrate. The pH is held at about 5 to prevent reaction with the aluminum that would evolve hydrogen.

To provide sensitivity to shock initiation it is usual to introduce very small (40–50 μm) air pockets or bubbles, which act as centers that create hot spot initiation when a shock wave passes. This is done in one of several ways, the simplest of these being to use a beating process and the air bubbles are trapped as the gel sets. Other methods are to add glass or plastic microballoons or expanded polystyrene beads. These are favored if it is thought that the pressure in a borehole may squeeze the explosive increasing the density and reducing the number of air pockets or if the shock pressure from an adjacent borehole creates a similar effect. A recent chemical reaction method has been used to create the bubbles. This is the reaction between sodium nitrite and acetic acid which produces nitrogen gas bubbles. The presence of aluminum powder also leads to hot spot creation and in some cases actual explosive molecular types are added such as smokeless powder (propellant) or 20-mesh TNT. The most recent developments have led to the use of nitrated chemical sensitizers that introduce both sensitivity and fuel, examples being isopropyl nitrate or the now favored methylamine nitrate.

Until relatively recent times, the manufacture of these complex mixtures could be achieved only under factory conditions. Thus, slurry explosives were supplied cartridged in flexible plastic tubing similar to that used to package meat products such as liver sausage. Current cartridge sizes have diameters of 25–200 mm and weigh between 200 g and 5 kg. In more recent times systems have become available for on-site manufacture and mixing trucks are available that manufacture and pump the product directly into the borehole. A further development has been the use of blends of slurry with ANFO (see below).

Performance of Slurry Explosives

At first, slurry explosives were detonator insensitive and required a booster as for ANFO. Developments have now led to compositions that are detonator sensitive, but the majority still require boosting. Due to their physical nature as water-containing gelled systems, they are quite insensitive to accidental initiation. The use of gelling agent gives these explosives a reasonable degree of water resistance if loaded unpackaged into a wet borehole and thus is a superior explosive to ANFO. Most slurry compositions have reasonably large critical diameters and are employed in boreholes greater than 75 mm in diameter although as noted above, the smallest size is a 25 mm diameter cartridge.

As explosives, they are superior to ANFO, largely due to the higher densities that are achieved. Densities are in the range of 0.9–1.4 g cm^{-3} and this, together with the higher energies give velocities of detonation in the range 3500–5500 m s^{-1} and this will give shock pressures in the range 50–100 kbar. Depending on the formulation, weight strengths are in the range of 50–100% BG and bulk strengths from 30–75% BG. The much higher density than ANFO produces bulk strengths that are relatively not as low compared to the weight strength as is seen for ANFO.

Emulsion Explosives

At first sight the formulation of an emulsion explosive appears very similar to a slurry being based on ammonium nitrate, water, hydrocarbon oil, aluminum powder, and a sensitizer. However, there is a fundamental difference in the physical nature of the two explosives. A slurry has a continuous aqueous phase, whereas the emulsion consists of aqueous droplets containing the ammonium nitrate held in true emulsion with a hydrocarbon continuous phase. The hydrocarbon layer may be as little as 3 μm in thickness. Depending on the properties of the hydrocarbon, from a mobile oil to a wax at ambient temperatures, the consistency of an emulsion explosive ranges from toothpaste to putty.

Other than this, there are a number of similarities between emulsions and slurries. The sensitization is achieved by exactly the same methods as described above. Both factory cartridged and truck-mixed versions are used and the critical diameter considerations are about the same although those with higher densities are detonator sensitive and maintain the detonation in small diameter, e.g. 25 mm.

A current technique in the use of emulsion explosives is to use a mixture with ANFO. This fills the void in the standard ANFO fill creating not only a denser material but also one of higher energy. The mixtures range from 70/30 emulsion/ANFO to 30/70 emulsion/ANFO. The former can be pumped but the latter is like thick porridge and is augered into the boreholes.

Table 2 Performance comparison between ANFO, an emulsion and an ANFO/emulsion blend

Property	*ANFO*	*Emulsion*	*ANFO/emulsion blend*
Density (g cm^{-3})	0.8	1.25	1.3
Energy (kJ g^{-1})	3.8	2.9	3.6
Energy (kJ cm^{-3})	3.1	3.6	4.5
Velocity of detonation (m s^{-1})	3000	4500	5500

Performance of Emulsion Explosives and Emulsion/ANFO Blends

The range of emulsion explosives is very similar to the slurries in explosive performance for velocity of detonation, weight strength, and bulk strength. However, advantage is gained by using the blend technique. Table 2 indicates the change in density and energy between ANFO, an emulsion, and a typical blend. The velocity of detonation tends to be higher for the blend than either component and can approach 6000 m s^{-1} at a density of ~1.4 g cm^{-3}.

Miscellaneous Types

There are two types of ammonium nitrate-based explosives that are available but are peripheral to the mainstream commercial production of explosives. In one, the AN is mixed with the liquid nitromethane (CH_3NO_2), perhaps up to 15% of the liquid to produce an explosive with a velocity of detonation of ~5500 m s^{-1} and shock pressure of ~90 kbar. In the other, the AN in mixed with hydrazine (N_2H_4) to produce a trade product known as ASTRO-PAK or Astrolite T. The explosive is a liquid with a density of ~1.4 g cm^{-3} and a velocity of detonation of 8000 m s^{-1} if initiated by a strong shock. This will give a detonation shock pressure of >200 kbar and thus the ability to break metal.

Detonating Cords

Essentially, detonating cord is a plastic tube, sometimes reinforced with wound or woven fibers and filled with powdered explosive. It is used to transmit a detonation shock wave for multiple charge initiation, that is to link charges together, or to lead a detonation shock wave from a detonator to a booster that may be in a borehole. Also, it may be used as an explosive charge in its own right.

There are three parameters relevant to the description of a particular cord. One is the tensile strength, which is important if any load may be applied to the cord. This tends to be relevant only for use in oil wells. The second is the type of explosive used to fill the cord and the third, the loading of explosive per unit length. Obviously, as the loading increases so will the

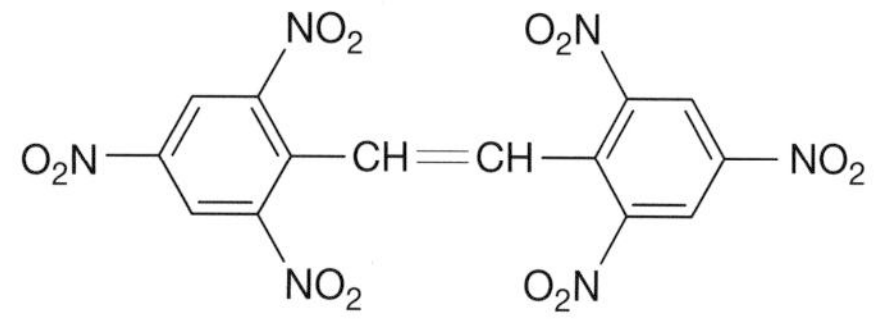

(1)

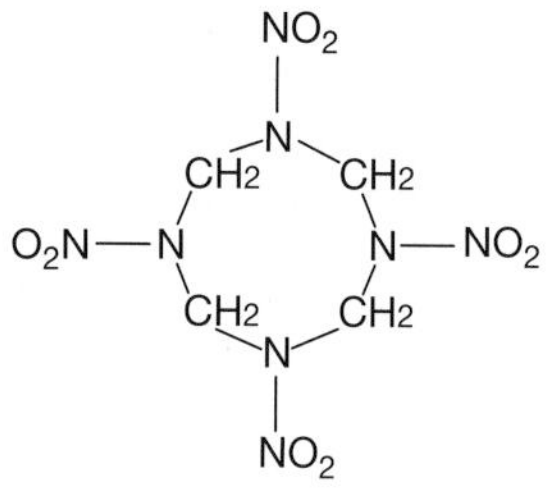

(2)

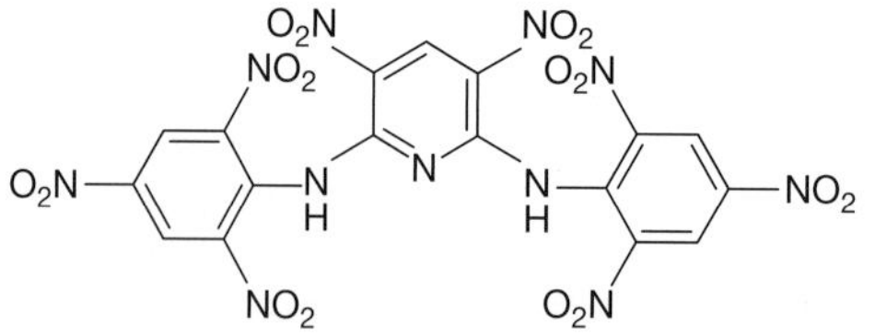

(3)

Figure 3 Structures of some explosives used at high temperatures. 1, hexanitrostilbene; 2, cyclotetramethylenetetranitramine; 3,3,5-dinitro-2,4-di (picrylamino)pyridine.

Table 3 Approximate maximum operating temperatures for prolonged residence times

Explosive	*Maximum operating temperature (°c)*
Pentaerythrytoltetranitrate (PETN)	125
Cyclotrimethylenetrinitramine (RDX)	165
Cyclotetramethylenetetranitramine (HMX)	180
Hezanitrostilbene (HNS)	300
3,5-dinitro-2,4-di(picrylamino)pyridine (PYX)	>300

diameter of the cord. The smallest commercial cord contains 1 gm^{-1} of explosive and the largest 100 g m^{-1}.

In general use, cords containing 5–8 g m^{-1} are used to lead a detonation to a booster or to initiate shock tube (see below). The cords used for linking multiple charges contain 10–12 g m^{-1} and the cords with 40 g m^{-1} upward are used for engineering operations such as presplitting of rock or for demolitions.

The general explosive filling is pentaerythrytol tetranitrate (PETN) as this explosive has a small critical diameter of ~1 mm and thus will propagate a detonation shock wave reliably in very small columns. However, when cords are used in oil wells there may be a problem associated with the temperature in the deeper wells. In down-hole operations it is necessary to have the explosive charges in the hole for some time before firing. The cords filled with PETN can be used at a maximum temperature of 135 °C for 1 h or 121 °C for 24 h. For higher temperatures different explosives are used, structures of which are given in **Figure 3** and approximate maximum operating temperatures in **Table 3**.

Boosters (Primers)

As discussed above, many commercial explosives are not detonator sensitive. Reliable initiation is achieved through the use of booster charges that provide an intense shock wave to the column of explosive in the borehole. The most commonly used explosive in a booster is Pentolite, a 50/50 mixture of PETN and TNT. This has a detonation shock pressure of ~250 kbar and reliably detonates ANFO, slurries, and emulsions.

Detonators

Standard Demolition Detonators

For commercial use it is normal for electric detonators to have a time delay from the firing current initiating the fuze head to the detonator providing the shock output. This is done by introducing a delay element consisting of a column of pyrotechnic between the fuze head and the lead azide pellet. The concept of delay detonators is to allow one firing signal to be sent to multiple detonators that will initiate all the fuze heads; however, for different delay times this will give different firing times for the detonators. This reduces ground shock when quarrying by separating borehole detonations at intervals of ~25 ms. In tunneling it allows some charges to fire first to create a face towards which the next row of charges firing, some time later can work. Finally, for demolitions it is necessary for some parts of a structure to be blasted first giving a controlled collapse or a direction for toppling. There are two delay series; the millisecond series separated by 25 ms intervals up to 850 ms for some manufacturers and the half-second series usually up to a maximum of 6 s.

Delay detonators can be identified and are classified by the delay number stamped on the end of the detonator body or on a plastic or paper tag attached to the leg wires. This is usually a number that must be related to the literature of the manufacturer to ascertain the delay time. This literature will describe the color of the leg wires and the type of wire (iron, copper, etc) and the material for the body, normally copper or aluminum.

There are nonelectric detonators known as 'plain' detonators. These are essentially an electric detonator without the fuze head and associated leg wires. To initiate this a delay fuze is inserted into the open end of the tube and crimped in place with a special tool immediately before use. The delay fuze usually contains black powder and burns at a steady rate of ~300 mm in 40 s. The flash output from the fuze initiates the lead azide pellet and fires the detonator. These are commonly used for single shots such as breaking a large rock on the quarry floor or in tree stump removal.

Special Initiating Systems

There have been several examples of developments aimed at improving the safe use of detonators. The Magnadet detonator was developed in the UK by ICI Explosives Ltd as a system that was immune from induced current initiation caused by electromagnetic radiation. This problem exists for fuse head-containing detonators, as the majority will fire from a current as low as 0.5 amp. This can be induced if an electric detonator is used near a powerful radio, radar, or under electric power cables. The Magnadet is a normal electric detonator with very short leg wires which form a continuous circuit with several loops wrapped around a ferrite toroid. The firing cable is not attached electrically to this circuit but passes through the hole in the toroid. When a special firing signal is sent down the firing cable it induces a current in the detonator circuit and fires the detonator.

Perhaps the most important development in recent years has been the shock tube detonator. This system relies on the initiating signal being transmitted to a detonator via a small hollow plastic tube ~2 mm in diameter the inside of which is coated with a mixture of the explosive cyclotetramethylene-tetranitramine (HMX) and aluminum powder at a loading of ~20 mg m^{-1}. This layer propagates a shock wave at ~2000 m s^{-1} which on reaching the detonator initiates the delay element if present or the lead azide pellet directly. There is so little explosive present that the tube is not disrupted and indeed could be held as the shock wave passes down the tube. The shock tube is factory fitted to the detonator and is available in various lengths. Systems are available to link tubes to create bunch firing. The advantage of this system is that it is completely immune to initiation from stray electric currents or induced current from electromagnetic radiation.

A recent development has been the introduction to the market, of detonators that do not contain lead azide. It has been replaced with a finely powdered secondary explosive, PETN, which in a confined metal collar burns to detonation. The advantage of using a secondary explosive instead of the primary explosive, lead azide, is that the detonator is much more difficult to initiate accidentally. Trials in which rocks and weights were dropped on to both types of detonator demonstrated this insensitivity.

See also: **Chemistry/Trace/Explosives:** Explosions; Explosives: Analysis; Military.

Further Reading

Agrawal JP (2007a) *High Energy Materials: Propellants, Explosives and Pyrotechnics*. Wiley-VCH.

Agrawal JP (2007b) *Hodgson, Organic Chemistry of Explosives*. Wiley-VCH.

Akhavan J (2011) *The Chemistry of explosives*. Royal Society of Chemistry.

Atlas Powder Co. (1987) *Explosives and Rock Blasting, Field Technical Operations*. Dallas: Atlas Powder Co.

Beveridge A (2011) *Forensic Investigation of Explosives*. CRC press.

Dolan JE and Langer SS (1997) *Explosives in the Service of Man, the Nobel Heritage*. Cambridge: Royal Society of Chemistry.

Gregory CE (1993) *Explosives for Engineers*, 4th edn. Zurich: Clausthal-Zellerfeld.

Hopler RB (1998) *Blasters Handbook*, 17th edn. Cleveland: International Society of Explosives Engineers.

Kubota N (2007) *Propellants and explosives*. Wiley-VCH.

Meyer R, Köhler J, and Homburg A (2007) *Explosives*. Wiley-VCH.

Olofsson SO (1991) *Applied Explosives Technology for Construction and Mining*. Arla, Sweden: Applex.

Persson P-A, Holmberg R, and Lee J (1994) *Rock Blasting and Explosives Engineering*. Boca Raton: CRC Press.

Teipel U (2005) *Energetic Materials*. Wiley-VCH.

Wang X (1994) *Emulsion Explosives*. Beijing: Metallurgical Industry Press.

Military

SG Murray, Cranfield University, Royal Military College of Science, Shrivenham, UK

This article is reproduced from the previous edition, volume 2, pp. 764–771, © 2000, Elsevier Ltd., with an updated Further Reading section supplied by the Editor.

Introduction

To secure the best value from this article it is recommended that the article entitled 'Mechanism of Explosion' be read first.

Until the nineteenth century, the military use of explosives was limited to black powder, also known as gunpowder when used in muskets and cannon, as the only available material. The advent of nitrated molecules opened the way to explosives with far better energetic properties and also the ability to create detonations. Thus, two families of military explosives were born: those that burned explosively and were used to replace the obsolete gunpowder and those that could detonate, which became known as 'high explosives'. The burning type of explosives were called 'low explosives', but in general were for use in guns and later rockets and so became classified as propellants.

Within the various sections below, consideration is given to some historic military explosives as old ammunition is still found in collections or recovered from battlefields such as those in France and Belgium from the 1914–1918 conflict.

High Explosives

Historical

The discovery of the mercury fulminate detonator in the 1860s allowed the full potential of the newly developed nitroglycerine/nitrocellulose explosives to be exploited. However, these new formulations invented by the Nobel family were not suitable for military use in explosive ordnance. However, at the turn of the nineteenth century, other researchers were applying the concept of detonation to some different explosive molecules, some of which had been known for almost 100 years. One of the first to be developed into fillings for ordnance was picric acid (2,4,6-trinitrophenol), either as a pure material or mixed with dinitrophenol (mixed isomers) to lower the melting point of the mixture to aid melt casting.

At the same time the explosive 2,4,6-trinitrotoluene (TNT) (**Figure 1(a)**) was also being developed and was found to be superior to explosives based on picric acid. The disadvantages of picric acid were that it reacted with metals to give very impact-sensitive compounds and was at times difficult to detonate reliably. Thus, although picric acid formulations survived until the 1940s, after this time they became completely obsolete. The use of TNT was highly successful, not only as a pure filling but, by the end of World War I, as a mixture with ammonium nitrate to give the explosive known as amatol which could contain as much as 80% ammonium nitrate. The main driving force towards the use of amatol was that the requirement for explosives during the war could not be met solely by production of TNT, whereas ammonium nitrate could be produced in large quantities thereby supplementing the TNT when mixed in a formulation.

By the beginning of World War II, research into other explosives had identified another group of explosive molecules that could be used for the filling of ordnance. One of these was tetryl (**Figure 1(b)**), which had ideal explosive properties to be a booster in a detonating explosive train. Thus, from that time tetryl has been used worldwide as the most commonly used booster explosive. It is only recently that the toxicity of this explosive, causing severe dermatitis, has provided the impetus to find replacements. Even so, it is still in use today. The other major developments were based around three explosive molecules, pentaerythrytoltetranitrate (PETN) (**Figure 1(c)**), cyclotrimethylenetrinitramine (RDX) (**Figure 1(d)**) and cyclotetramethylenetetranitramine (HMX) (**Figure 1(e)**). These, together with TNT are the basis for all modern explosives.

Requirements for a Military High Explosive

Military high explosives are required to provide the following effects:

- Fragmentation of metal casings as in grenades, shells, mines, etc.;
- Blast (pressure wave in air created by the expanding gases from the explosion);
- Underwater bubble pulse for mines and torpedoes;
- Lift and heave for cratering;
- Shaped charge phenomenon.

Fragmentation is created by the shock wave in the detonating explosive breaking the casing, a phenomenon called brisance, and then accelerating the fragments. Thus, to achieve this requires an explosive with a reasonably good detonation shock pressure. Blast, underwater bubble pulse and lift and heave are all created by the expanding gases from the detonation and are not affected by the detonation shock pressure. Thus, it would be beneficial to increase the gas expansion effects at the expense of brisance. The shaped-charge phenomenon is the creation of a metal jet from a hollow metal cone backed by the explosive (**Figure 2**). The jet tip can be traveling at a velocity of approximately 10 000 ms^{-1} and can penetrate armor, the design requirement of this type of ordnance. The best explosive for this is one with the highest detonation pressure. The gas expansion is not relevant to the jet formation.

The above requirements are based on the explosive performance. There are other requirements that are important for military explosives, which must also be considered. These are:

- Safety during storage, transportation, and use;
- Long shelf life;
- Reliability;
- Ease of filling into ordnance.

This has led to a series of compositions capable of fulfilling all of these requirements based almost entirely on the explosive

 http://dx.doi.org/10.1016/B978-0-12-382165-2.00327-5

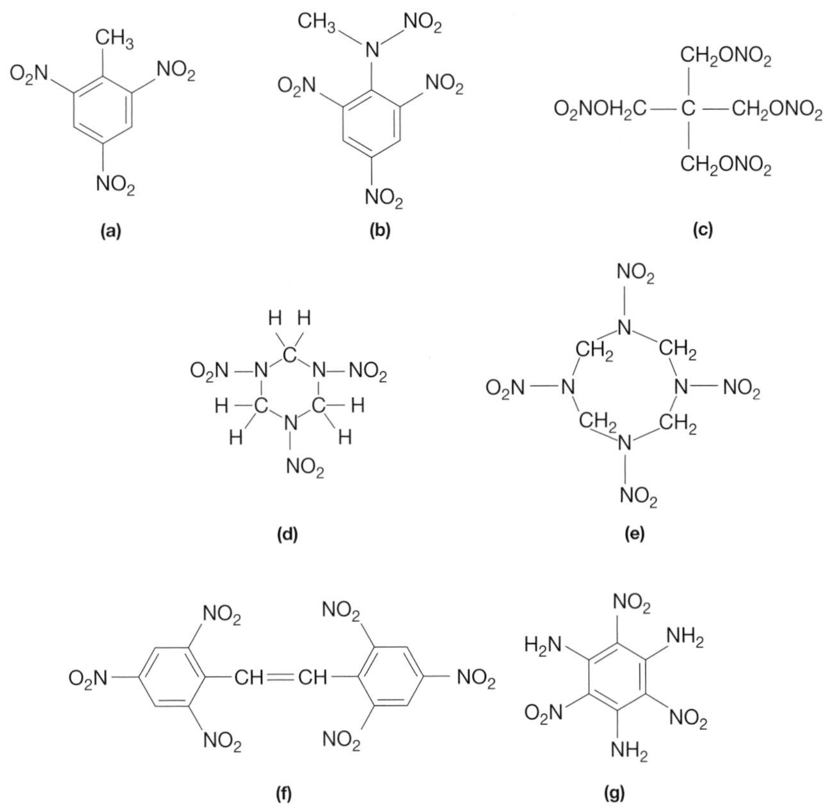

Figure 1 Structure of 2,4,6-trinitrotoluene (TNT) (a), tetryl (b), pentaerythrytoltetratrinitrate (PETN) (c), cyclotrimethylenetrinitramine (RDX) (d), cyclotetramethylenetetranitramine (HMX) (e), HNS (f), TATB (g).

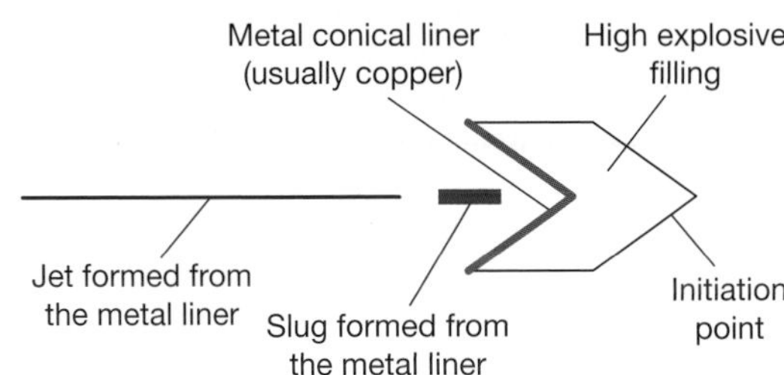

Figure 2 Shaped-charge warhead design and function.

molecules RDX, HMX, and TNT together with a limited use of PETN and a few highly specialized compounds such as HNS (**Figure 1(f)**) and TATB (**Figure 1(g)**). The performance of these as pure compounds together with some safety related data are given in **Table 1**.

Formulations

Table 1 shows that RDX, HMX, and PETN are all capable of providing very high shock pressures with HMX being the best. However, PETN is significantly more sensitive than RDX and this has led to the preference of RDX over PETN where safety is an issue in such uses as artillery and cannon rounds where the set-back forces on launch may cause premature initiation. As the performances of RDX and PETN are very similar, many countries have chosen to use RDX in preference to PETN in most other cases. HMX is slightly more sensitive than RDX but significantly more expensive. It is used where very high shock pressures are required.

Thus, military high explosives are based on RDX, HMX and to a lesser extent PETN to provide the necessary performance. However, for safety it is considered that they are too sensitive to be used on their own except when used as booster pellets. To provide a formulation that is acceptable for both safety and performance, they are mixed with either TNT or an inert phlegmatizer, both of which reduce the sensitivity. The choice of these binders is governed to some extent by their ability to provide practical methods of filling ordnance. For example, the presence of TNT aids the filling process due to its low melting temperature (see **Table 1**). The TNT is melted with low pressure steam and held at ~90 °C. The other components are then added and mixed to form a slurry, which can then be poured into the ordnance. The only drawback to this process is that the TNT contracts by 10% as it solidifies and this necessitates the use of equipment that can give a filling with no voids. This is important as the presence of voids in the filling of an artillery shell may cause premature initiation of that filling as the round is fired. This is caused by rapid compression of the air-filled voids creating adiabatic heating, thus igniting the explosive and causing an explosion in the barrel of the gun.

The other method used to desensitize the RDX, HMX, or PETN is with an inert material. This may be a wax that has a melting point around 140 °C and can be used to cast/press into a warhead. Another method is to mix it with a plasticizer-type material, which imparts a moldable consistency. A third

Table 1 Performance data for some compounds used in military explosive formulations

Compound name	*Melting point (°C)*	*Detonation velocity (m/s^{-1})*	*Detonation pressure (kbar)*	*Power*[a]	*Impact sensitivity (N m)*
RDX	205[b]	8700 @ 1.77 g cm^{-3}	338 @ 1.77 g cm^{-3}	480	7.5
HMX	285	9110 @ 1.89 g cm^{-3}	390 @ 1.89 g cm^{-3}	480	7.4
PETN	140	8260 @ 1.76 g cm^{-3}	335 @ 1.77 g cm^{-3}	523	3
TNT	80.9	6900 @ 1.60 g cm^{-3}	210 @ 1.63 g cm^{-3}	300	15
TATB	452[c]	7760 @ 1.88 g cm^{-3}	291 @ 1.88 g cm^{-3}	250[d]	50

[a]Expansion volume for a 10 g sample in the lead block test.
[b]With decomposition.
[c]Decomposes above 325 °C if heated slowly.
[d]Calculated value as a 10 g sample does not fully detonate.

Table 2 Components of some typical moldable explosives

Name	*RDX (%)*	*PETN (%)*	*Desensitizer*
C4	91		Di(2-ethylhexyl) sebacate Polyisobutene Motor oil
PE4	88		Lithium stearate Paraffin oil
Semtex A		83.5	Rubber Oil
Semtex H		85.5 (mixture)	Rubber Oil
Semtex 10		85	Rubber Dibutylformamide

method is to mix with a plastic, giving a range of plastic bonded explosives (PBX). And lastly, a recent development has been to set the explosive powder in a cross-linked polymer. These types are described below.

Moldable Explosives

Moldable explosives are sometimes known generically as plastic explosives. This may lead to some confusion, as there are PBX and cross-linked polymer-bound explosives. However, the term 'plastic explosive' is generally taken to mean one that is capable of being molded into shape by hand and used for demolition purposes. Some of the more well-known examples of this type of formulation are C4 (USA), PE4 (UK) and the Semtex family A, H, and 10 (Czech Republic). The compositions are given in **Table 2**.

Castable Explosives

As described above, molten TNT can be utilized as a vehicle for casting formulations that include solid powders. These powders include the explosives RDX, HMX, PETN, and tetryl together with a variety of other materials such as ammonium nitrate, barium nitrate, and aluminum. This has led to a range of explosives developed for various reasons.

The first castable explosives based on TNT were the amatols in which the TNT was mixed with ammonium nitrate. The main driving force behind this was the shortage of TNT during wartime periods. Since ammonium nitrate is oxygen rich and TNT oxygen deficient, the formulations gave a more oxygen balanced mixture with good explosive properties. Similarly, a range of explosives was developed based on barium nitrate mixed with TNT, the baratols. A range of formulations based on tetryl/TNT mixtures called tetrytols also developed. All of these are now obsolete and were replaced by mixtures containing RDX, HMX, and PETN. The RDX/TNT mixtures that developed ranged from 50/50 to 75/25 RDX/ TNT and are known by the US name of cyclotols. The most commonly used type is nominally 60/40 RDX/ TNT, often called Composition B. Those containing HMX are known as octols with high percentages of HMX and those with PETN, the pentolites.

Another major component mixed into these castable explosives is aluminum powder. This undergoes further chemical reaction with the gaseous products of explosion (CO_2, H_2O, and CO) to form aluminum oxide by extraction of oxygen from the gases at the temperature of the explosion. This creates more heat and at modest aluminum contents, no loss of gas volume. The overall effect is to increase the power of the explosive, that is the gas expansion effect. In the UK these RDX/TNT/aluminum formulations are the Torpex series of explosives and in the US, H-6 and HBX-1 to -3. Tritonal contains only TNT and aluminum. An obsolete explosive of this type is Ammonal containing ammonium nitrate/ TNT/ aluminum.

Compositions for the castable explosives are given in **Table 3**.

Plastic Bonded Explosives (PBX)

Plastic bonded explosives utilize plastics to bind and desensitize RDX and HMX or to act simply as a binder with TATB, an explosive compound that is very insensitive. A typical preparation of a PBX would be to suspend the explosive powder, e.g. RDX, in water and add the plastic dissolved in an organic solvent that does not dissolve the explosive but wets the surface. The plastic is then precipitated from the solution either by

Table 3 Formulations of some typical castable military explosives

Name	*TNT (%)*	*RDX (%)*	*Other components (%)*
Amatol	20		Ammonium nitrate 80
Baratol	24		Barium nitrate 76
Composition B	39.5	59.5	Wax 1
Cyclotol	25	75	
H-6	30	45	Aluminum 20 Wax 4.5 Calcium chloride 0.5%
Minol	40		Ammonium nitrate 40 Aluminum 20
Octol	25		HMX 75
Pentolite	50		PETN 50
Tritonal	80		Aluminum 20

Table 4 Some polymers used in the manufacture of PBX

Name	*Description*
Viton A	Vinylidine fluoride/hexafluoropropylene copolymer 60/40 wt%
PolyDNPA	2,2-Dinitropropyl acrylate polymer
Estane	Polyurethane
Kel-F 800	Chlorotrifluoroethylene/vinylidine fluoride copolymer (3:1)
Polystyrene	Polymerized styrene monomer

addition of another solvent or by evaporation of the solvent that dissolves the plastic. Thus, the plastic coats the explosive crystals and forms what is called the molding powder. This powder can then be pressed directly into the ordnance or isostatically in a rubber membrane followed by machining to shape. This pressing is carried out at high vacuum and achieves up to 97% of the theoretical maximum density. Details of the plastics used are given in **Table 4**.

There are several reasons why this technique is favored over TNT casting to provide formulations. One is to obviate the necessity to have TNT in the filling as the low melting point may be disadvantageous and also TNT is prone to cracking. However, the main reason is that it is possible to obtain formulations with very high RDX or more significantly HMX, content. To produce warheads that require very high detonation pressure it is necessary to have such high explosive loading but still be acceptable from a sensitivity standpoint. This is achievable with PBX. The majority of PBX formulations are from the US Armed Forces with designations LX-, PBX-, PBX (AF), PBXC-, PBXN- and PBXW- followed by a number. Some examples are given in **Table 5**.

A recent development in the manufacture of PBX has been the use of thermosetting polymer systems to form a matrix of solid powders in the polymer by polymerization after a mixture of ingredients plus liquid prepolymer has been formed. The polymerization is induced by gentle heating and the polymer forms without any volume change and can thus occur with the prepolymer mixture already in the warhead. One such system utilizes the reaction between hydroxy-terminated polybutadiene crosslinked with a di-isocyanate, producing a polyurethane. The products are rigid, have the

Table 5 Some typical PBX formulations

Name	*Explosive component*	*Plastic (%)*
LX-09-0	HMX 93	PolyDNPA 4.6 FEFO 2.4
LX-10-0	HMX 95	Viton A 5
LX-11-0	HMX 80	Viton A 20
LX-14-0	HMX 95.5	Estane 4.5
LX-15	HNS 95	Kel-F 800 5
LX-17-0	TATB 92.5	Kel-F 800 7.5
PBX-9205	RDX 92	Polystyrene 6 DIOP2
PBX-9604	RDX 96	Kel-F 800 4

physical properties controlled by choice of polymer system and cannot be melted by heat.

Other chemicals that might be present in PBX formulations are energetic plasticizers. These include mixtures of di- and tri-nitroethylbenzenes, bisdinitropropylacetal/bisdinitropropylformal (BDNPA/F) and bis(2-fluoro-2,2-dinitroethyl)formal (FEFO). At times it appear that an explosive is classed as a PBX by the presence of these energetic plasticizers. Examples can be found within the PBXN formulations of the US Department of Defense. Also, there are a few aluminized PBX formulations.

Recent Developments

Irrespective of the method of formulation, there are some recent additions to explosive compounds that will be used in future explosives. Probably the two most important additions are 3-nitro-1,2,4-triazol-5-one (NTO) and hexanitrohexaazaisowurtzitane (HNIW or CL20). These are currently being developed into ordnance fillings. Other new contenders include 1,3,3-trinitroazetidine (TNAZ). The chemical structures are shown in **Figure 3**.

Propellants

Gun Propellants

The discovery of nitroglycerine and nitrocellulose led to the invention of 'smokeless powders' by workers such as Vieille, Nobel, Abel, and Dewar. These were far superior to the gunpowder that they replaced. Thus, at the beginning of the twentieth century the use of gunpowder for military use had ceased.

The early forms of these new propellants were as extruded strands sometimes called cords, indeed, they were known generically as cordites. Otherwise they were spheres or flakes, the propellant powders, an example being ballistite. As the science of gun ballistics rapidly developed and these new propellants were used in large caliber guns, the geometries of the propellant pieces, or 'grains', developed leading to tubular, stick, and multitubular granular propellants. Some of these shapes are shown in **Figure 4**.

Propellant formulations have developed since the early days, initially into three basic types and more recently with the addition of a fourth type. They are differentiated by the explosive components:

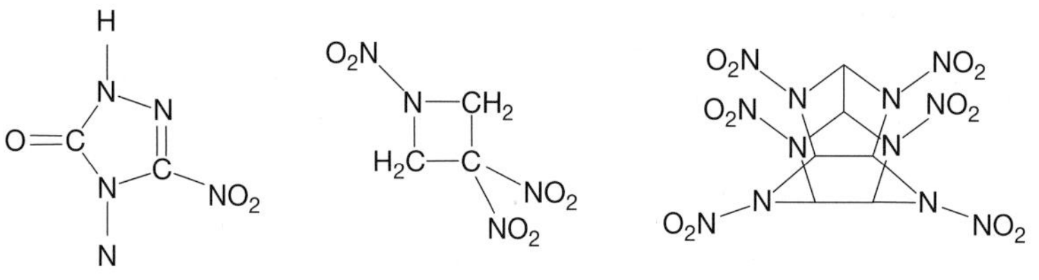

NTO TNAZ CL20

Figure 3 Some new compounds of relevance to military high explosives. NTO, 3-nitro-1,2,4-triazol-5-one; CL20, hexanitrohexa-azaisowurtzitane; TNAZ, 1,3,3-trinitroazetidine.

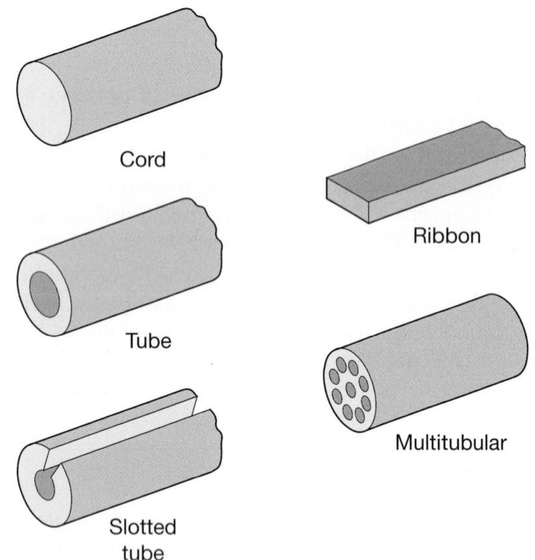

Figure 4 Grain shapes of gun propellant.

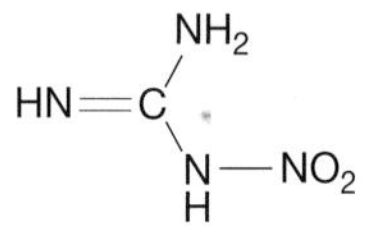

Figure 5 Structure of nitroguanidine (picrite).

- Single-base propellant which contains nitrocellulose (NC);
- Double-base propellant which contains NC and nitroglycerine (NG);
- Triple-base propellant which contains NC, NG, and nitroguanidine (picrite);
- High-energy propellant which contains NC, NG, picrite, and RDX (or HMX).

Nitrocellulose can be nitrated to differing amounts and thus can have different energies but, being polymeric, one of its main functions is to provide physical properties that resist grain cracking and also gel with NG, if present. The NG is a highly energetic explosive and thus its presence increases the energy of the propellant formulation. Nitroguanidine (Figure 5) contains a large percentage of nitrogen in the molecule. It is present in triple-base propellant in significant quantities, typically 55%. Thus, the gases that exit the barrel of the gun are extremely rich in nitrogen gas. This prevents the other gaseous products rich in hydrogen and carbon monoxide from spontaneous ignition thus acting as a muzzle flash suppressant. The RDX in high-energy propellant increases the performance without an unacceptable increase in flame temperature. High flame temperatures lead to barrel erosion.

These formulations also contain additives to aid safety, performance, and manufacture. The most important of these is the stabilizer. Both NC and NG are inherently unstable and very slowly decompose to release acidic species based on nitrogen and oxygen. If left unchecked, these decomposition products attack unreacted molecules, thus accelerating further decomposition. To prevent such a runaway situation, additives such as diphenylamine or ethyl centralite (carbamite) are included in the formulation. They do not prevent the slow decomposition; rather they chemically remove the decomposition products, preventing attack on unreacted molecules. Thus, during the life of a propellant this stabilizer additive is slowly consumed. Surveillance programs for stored ammunition monitor the depletion and it is usual to destroy the stock when the stabilizer falls to 50% of the original content.

Other additives include plasticizers such as dibutylphthalate, diethylphthalate, and glycerol triacetate (triacetin) to modify physical properties, dinitrotoluene as a moisture repellent and cryolite as another type of flash inhibitor. The small grains as found in small arms propellants are likely to be coated with a graphite glaze. This is to aid filling by acting as a lubricant, to increase moisture resistance, to dissipate electrostatic charge and to modify the initial burning reaction. For the triple base and high-energy propellants a dye may be added for color coding.

As for the use of these propellants, they tend to be grouped as follows:

- Single base – small arms and large caliber guns;
- Double base – small arms, machine pistols, small cannon, and mortars;
- Triple base – large caliber artillery and tank guns;
- High energy – high velocity tank guns.

Table 6 gives the components of typical examples of these propellants.

Rocket Propellants

With the development of the new gun propellants based on NC and NG, it was a logical progression that rocket propellants would follow a similar path. Indeed, a range of rocket propellant formulations exist based on these explosives and are known as double-base rocket propellants. There are two basic types: extruded and cast.

Table 6 Typical formulations of some gun propellants

Propellant type	*NC (%)*	*NG (%)*	*Picrite (%)*	*Nitramine (%)*	*Other[a] (%)*
Single base	85–95				DPA 1 DNT 0–10
Double base	60–90	8–50			EC 1–3
Triple base	16–22	16–22	~55		EC 2–7 Cryolite 0.3 K_2SO_4 1–2
High energy[b]	20	20	30	25	EC 2

[a]DPA (diphenylamine), DNT (dinitrotoluene), EC (ethylecentralite).
[b]These are classified and therefore the values given are an estimate by the author.

Extruded rocket motor grains are made from a colloid of nitrocellulose and nitroglycerine. As with the gun propellants, a stabilizer is required, usually carbamite and a plasticizer such as diethylphthalate. A typical formulation might contain over 40% nitroglycerine, a level no longer found in gun propellants due to erosion problems and over 50% nitrocellulose. Other ingredients may be potassium sulphate, carbon powder and wax.

Cast double-base rocket motor grains are manufactured by first filling a mold with a casting powder based on nitrocellulose grains containing some of the additives such as stabilizer, plasticizer, and a platonizing agent, normally a lead salt. A casting liquid is then added consisting of nitroglycerine mixed with a desensitizer such as triacetin. This is absorbed in to the casting powder creating a solid mass, which is cured for a few days at ~60 °C. The platonizing agent influences the relationship between burning rate and pressure such that at the working pressure of the motor, the burning rate is virtually independent of pressure.

The alternative type of rocket propellant is called a composite propellant. This is based on a fuel–oxidizer mixture. The oxidizer is ammonium perchlorate and the fuel a plastic or polymer, also acting as binder. Early versions in the 1950s and 1960s were known as plastic composites and contained polyisobutene or polyvinylchloride. A simple process using a plasticizer and heat allowed mixing of the plastic with the oxidizer followed by extrusion. This type of composite propellant is now obsolete.

The preferred composite is often called a rubbery composite and is based on the concept of polymerizing a liquid prepolymer mixed with the ammonium perchlorate. Several polymer systems have been used including:

- Polyurethane (PU) based on the di-isocyanate/glycol reaction;
- Polybutadiene (PB) polymers using hydroxy- or carboxy-terminated PB with a di-isocyanate;
- Polybutadiene–acrylic acid–acetonitrile (PBAN) with epoxide or aziridine crosslinking.

The favored system appears to be that based on hydroxy-terminated polybutadiene (HTPB).

Various hybrids also exist, designed to improve either the performance or the physical properties over the two types described above. Thus, there are formulations containing nitroglycerine, nitrocellulose, ammonium perchlorate, aluminum and even HMX. These are prodigious energy producers with a heat of burning as high as 7700 J g^{-1} compared to pure nitroglycerine at 6300 J g^{-1}.

See also: **Chemistry/Trace/Explosives:** Commercial; Explosions; Explosives: Analysis; **Pattern Evidence:** Shotgun Ammunition on a Target.

Further Reading

Akhavan J (2011) *The chemistry of explosives*, 3rd edn. Royal Society of Chemistry paperbacks, RSC paperbacks.
Bailey A and Murray SG (1989) *Explosives, Propellants and Pyrotechnics*. London: Brassey's (UK) Ltd.
Beveridge A (2011) *Forensic Investigation of Explosions*, 2nd edn. CRC Press.
Cooper PW (1996) *Explosives Engineering*. New York: Wiley-VCH.
Dobratz BM and Crawford PC (1985) *LLNL Explosives Handbook*. CA: Lawrence Livermore National Laboratory.
Kohler J and Meyer R (1993) *Explosives*, revised and extended edn. Weinheim: VCH.
Meyer R, Kohler J, and Homberh A (2007) *Explosives*, 6th edn. Wiley and sons.
Picatinny Arsenal (1960–1982) *Encyclopaedia of Explosives and Related Items*, vols. 1–10. Dover, NJ: Picatinny Arsenal (US AARADCOM).
Urbanski T (1964–1967) *Chemistry and Technology of Explosives*, vol. 4. Oxford: Pergamon Press.

Improvised Explosives

S Doyle, Linked Forensic Consultants Ltd, Wellington, New Zealand

Abbreviations

ESD	Electrostatic discharge
HMTD	Hexamethylene diamine triperoxide
IED	Improvised explosive device
PETN	Pentaerythritol tetranitrate
RDX	Research department explosive
R-Salt	1,3,5-trinitroso-1,3,5-triazacyclohexane
TATP	Triacetone triperoxide
TBC	Twist-boat-chair conformation
TCC	Twist-chair-chair conformation
TNT	Trinitrotoluene
VoD	Velocity of detonation

Introduction

The forensic treatment of explosives would be incomplete without consideration of improvised or homemade explosives. In terms of the forensic investigation of explosive-related crime, improvised explosives constitute a major focus.

Many terrorist attacks involve the use of improvised explosives. Improvised explosive devices (IEDs) in the United States, United Kingdom, Iraq, Afghanistan, Israel, Indonesia, and elsewhere have relied on improvised explosives for their destructive effects. IEDs including large charge weights of over 0.5 tonnes, for example, London (St Mary Axe) 1992 and Bali 2002, must exclusively rely on improvised explosives for practical reasons.

This article begins with some warnings. Improvised explosives are often extremely sensitive to all stimuli (shock, impact, friction, heat, and electrostatic discharge (ESD)) and there are many examples of recreational experimentation leading to tragic results. Furthermore, in many jurisdictions the preparation or storage of, or even retaining information about, improvised explosives exposes individuals to the risk of criminal prosecution.

Improvised explosives, as the name suggests, refer to explosives that are 'homemade' and not produced for military or commercial purposes.

As explained in the other articles, explosives are essentially mixtures of fuels and oxidizers. In most cases, they react either by deflagration (rapid burning) or by detonation. The fuel–oxidizer concept is particularly important for the consideration of improvised explosives. In simple terms, oxidizers provide a source of oxygen to produce rapid combustion-like reactions with fuels. An improvised explosive requires two constituents: one that can act as a source of oxygen and the other that can burn. Fuels are mostly carbonaceous materials. Therefore, it is easy to appreciate that the number of potential improvised explosives is very large. What follows is a consideration of those previously encountered in the commission of crime, and are thus of forensic interest. Frequently encountered oxidizers are listed in **Table 1** and fuels in **Table 2**.

While criminals do make use of low explosives to harm people and damage property, most improvised explosives are high explosives, that is, capable of detonation in their normal state. Such detonable improvised explosives will be the main subject of this article.

Explosives are useful in that they do work by releasing large amounts of energy (kJ g^{-1}) in very short periods of time (μs). In addition, the volume of the products is much greater than the reactants generating very high pressures (GPa). These properties are attractive to terrorists and other criminals needing to damage property and/or harm people.

Of course, terrorists and other criminals have used and continue to use commercial and military explosives in their weapons and devices. Pentaerythritol tetranitrate (PETN) was the main charge in the recent (2010) airline attacks and dynamite in the Madrid bombings of 2004. However, this article will focus on explosives that are not commercially available or used for military purposes. Nevertheless, commercial and military explosives will be mentioned in passing when necessary for the sake of completeness.

Improvised explosives are mainly used in terrorist weapons and devices. An IED comprises the main components of an explosives train. When considering an improvised explosive, the concept of an explosives train is important. An explosives train includes a means of initiation such as a detonator, sometimes a booster, and a main charge.

In the preparation of improvised explosives, there are essentially only two processes: mixing and synthesizing. Either ingredients are mixed to produce the explosive, for example, the oxidizer ammonium nitrate and the fuel sugar, or the explosive is synthesized from appropriate starting materials, for example, urea and nitric acid to produce urea nitrate.

It should be borne in mind that many of the explosives referred to in other articles and classified as either commercial or military may be synthesized using appropriate starting materials, the requisite knowledge, and equipment. Therefore, all explosives may potentially be classified as improvised. However, the main focus of this article will be those improvised explosives commonly used by criminals and particularly terrorists.

The chemistry, physics, and hence the performance of improvised explosives are highly variable and hard to predict. For mixtures, critical diameters tend to be large and the explosives are nonideal. Therefore, in addition to stoichiometry, mixing, and packing density, performance will also depend on charge weight and confinement. Large charge weights of intimately mixed and confined improvised explosive mixtures will tend to detonate more reliably. Nonideal explosives that are unlikely to reliably detonate are termed tertiary explosives as they require a booster.

 http://dx.doi.org/10.1016/B978-0-12-382165-2.00328-7

Table 1 Typical oxidizers

Oxidizer anion	*Typical cations*	*Salts*
ClO_4^-	Na^+	NH_4ClO_4
ClO_3^-	K^+	$NaClO_3$
NO_3^-	NH_4^+	NH_4NO_3
MnO_4^-		$KMnO_4$

Table 2 Typical fuels

Organic	*Metal*	*Nonmetal*	*Energetic*
Diesel fuel oil (FO)	Al	C	Nitromethane
Sugar	Mg	S	Nitrobenzene
Wax			
Sawdust			
Ethanol			
Ethylene glycol			

History

One of the most infamous and earliest recorded criminal acts involving explosives was that by Guido (Guy) Fawkes and his coconspirators. He attempted to blow up the Palace of Westminster in 1605 and assassinate the then King of England, James I. The explosive was black powder: a mixture of the oxidizer potassium nitrate and the fuels carbon and sulfur. The explosive mixture used was not improvised but may be easily prepared.

In the 1880s, Irish republican terrorism in the United Kingdom of Great Britain and Ireland saw the use of dynamite. Indeed, the criminal misuse of explosives in the nineteenth century tended to involve dynamite in its various forms.

It was not until the latter half of the twentieth century that improvised explosives began to be employed routinely by criminals, particularly terrorists.

In the late 1960s, Irish republican terrorism on the United Kingdom mainland began afresh prompted by the so-called Troubles in the province of Northern Ireland. The initial campaign used a mixture of the oxidizer ammonium nitrate with nitrobenzene, an energy-rich fuel. Later improvised explosives used by Irish republican terrorists included the oxidizer sodium chlorate and nitrobenzene; sodium chlorate with sugar as the fuel; and ammonium nitrate and fuel oil – which is a commercially available high explosive. Toward the end of the campaign in the 1990s, the terrorists turned to ammonium nitrate and sugar for large charge weight (>0.5 tonnes) vehicle-borne IEDs.

While not an improvised explosive, Semtex H should be mentioned in passing. It is one of the most infamous explosives used by terrorists. Semtex H was a commercially available plastic high explosive of variable composition but usually containing research department explosive (RDX), PETN, plasticizers, binders, and a dye, Sudan 1. It was used in the attack that brought down Pan Am Flight 103 in 1989, most commonly known as the Lockerbie bombing. Semtex H was manufactured by Synthesia, Pardubice, in what is now the Czech Republic. One of the first occurrences of Semtex H was in 1972 in connection with 'Black September.'

Returning to improvised explosives, one of the most significant developments in the field occurred in Israel in 1980. That was the first recorded synthesis of a highly sensitive, primary explosive used by terrorists, now most commonly known as triacetone triperoxide (TATP).

This was followed by the appearance of a second, even more sensitive, primary explosive known as hexamethylene triperoxide diamine (HMTD).

The first attack against the World Trade Centre in New York occurred in 1993. Based on circumstantial evidence, the explosive used was considered to be urea nitrate and was estimated to be about 1 tonne in weight. Urea nitrate is prepared by reacting urea fertilizer with nitric acid, both freely available materials with entirely legitimate uses. Urea nitrate is also frequently encountered in the Middle East.

The Alfred P. Murrah Federal Building in Oklahoma City was bombed by Timothy McVeigh in 1995. Until the tragedy of 9/11, this attack resulted in the largest loss of lives in a terrorist incident on the United States mainland. It was also one of the largest single IEDs ever assembled and was estimated to be the equivalent of 2.5 tonnes of trinitrotoluene (TNT). While each explosive component of the IED (established by circumstantial evidence) was commercially available, the overall explosive charge constituted an improvised explosive. The device was thought to comprise ammonium nitrate, fuel oil, nitromethane, and water gel explosives. Initiation was probably by means of an igniferous fuse and a shock tube detonator.

The year before the millennium saw one of the first incidents involving HMTD. Ahmed Rassam was arrested while crossing into the United States from Canada. Around 15 g of HMTD was found in his possession along with other explosives items.

In 2001, Richard Reid, the 'shoe bomber,' employed TATP as part of the initiatory system of the IED concealed in his shoe as he attempted to bring down American Airlines Flight 63.

In the Bali bombings of 2002, the main charge in the vehicle-borne IED was probably the oxidizer potassium chlorate mixed with the inorganic fuels aluminum and sulfur. The charge weight was estimated to be around 1 tonne.

The series of suicide bombings which took place in Casablanca in 2003 probably used a mixture of TATP and ammonium nitrate as the main charge.

In 2009, Umar Farouk Abdulmutallab, the 'underpants bomber,' probably employed TATP as part of the initiatory system in the IED used in his attempt to bring down Delta Flight 253. In addition to TATP, ethylene glycol and potassium permanganate were also thought to be part of the initiatory system – a rare use of permanganate as an oxidizer.

Most recently, in the United Kingdom in 2005, we witnessed the advent of mixtures of concentrated hydrogen peroxide and carbonaceous materials. Such mixtures have also been encountered in the Middle East.

Why terrorists choose to use particular improvised explosives or rely on commercial or military explosives is not clear but ease of procurement is probably a factor. What does seem clear is that no matter what barriers are placed in their way, terrorists always seem to find a way of either acquiring or manufacturing explosives for their weapons and devices.

Classifications

From a forensic perspective, explosives may be usefully classified under the following headings.

Conventional Organic Explosives

This includes, for example, RDX, TNT, and PETN. The chemistry, physics, and performance of these high explosives are covered in the article on military explosives. However, as already stated, they all may be synthesized from appropriate starting materials using the requisite knowledge and resources and in such circumstances would be considered improvised explosives.

It is worth noting some properties of these explosives which are of forensic significance. They all contain the nitro group, such as nitroaromatics, nitrate esters, or nitramines, and many detection systems rely on this property. In addition, they are all molecular explosives in that the oxidizer and fuel are in the same molecule. They are all high explosives and, although of varying sensitivity, they are all secondary explosives. Finally, they are all relatively stable both chemically and thermally. In one or more of these respects, they differ from improvised explosives.

Inorganics

This covers explosives that contain inorganic oxidizers such as ammonium nitrate and potassium perchlorate together with fuels such as sulfur and aluminum. These include pyrotechnics and other low explosives which are covered in other articles.

Peroxides

In practical terms, this includes only TATP and HMTD.

Concentrated Peroxides

These are mixtures of carbonaceous fuels and concentrated hydrogen peroxide.

In considering the chemistry, physics, and performance of improvised explosives, the most important distinction is that between those prepared by mixing and those prepared by synthesis.

Mixtures

Improvised explosive mixtures comprise a mixture of an oxidizer and a fuel, the performance of which depends on the chemical and physical properties of the oxidizer and fuel, the stoichiometry, the degree of mixing, the charge weight, the packing density, the degree of confinement, and the means of initiation.

Many mixtures are nonideal and are classified as tertiary explosives, that is, those requiring a booster for efficient detonation.

Oxidizers

Ammonium nitrate

Ammonium nitrate, in terms of quantity at least, is the most commonly used oxidizer in improvised explosive mixtures. The salt has been used in many terrorist attacks, particularly those involving large charge weights of over half a tonne. Ammonium nitrate has been mixed with a number of fuels such as sugar and aluminum.

Ammonium nitrate is the main component of slurry explosives used for mining. However, the source of ammonium nitrate used for improvised explosive mixtures is often fertilizer. Fertilizer-grade ammonium nitrate can be powdered or in the form of prills. Fertilizer-grade prills are usually coated to reduce hygroscopicity. However, as prills or powder, fertilizer-grade ammonium nitrate can be mixed with suitable fuels, such as sugar or fuel oil, to produce an effective high explosive. The detonability and explosive power of ammonium nitrate-based improvised explosives is dependent on the particle size, the fuel, stoichiometry, degree of mixing, the packing density, and the degree of confinement. In prill form, the explosive is not usually detonable and requires a booster charge for efficient detonation and complete reaction. It acts as a tertiary explosive. In powdered form, it is often detonable.

Explosive mixtures incorporating ammonium nitrate have large critical diameters and are therefore nonideal explosives, whose energy release during detonation occurs in a time scale insufficient for the majority of it to keep up with the shock front. The loss of energy from the system exceeds the rate of generation and a self-sustaining reaction cannot be maintained. The explosive fails to react completely and can fail to detonate; therefore, large charge weights are often necessary for reliable detonation. Furthermore, in contrast to ideal explosives, confinement has a significant effect on detonation, increased confinement resulting in an increased velocity of detonation (VoD).

Improvised explosives incorporating ammonium nitrate have detonation velocities in the range of 1400–6000 m s^{-1}. The TNT equivalence of ammonium nitrate-based improvised explosives ranges from 25% to 100% depending on the factors referred to earlier, for example, packing density and degree of confinement.

Fuels mixed with ammonium nitrate to produce effective improvised high explosives have included sugar, fuel oil, aluminum, nitromethane, and nitrobenzene.

Research has shown that most ammonium nitrate-based improvised explosives are chemically and thermally stable and insensitive to stimuli, friction, impact, and ESD in normal conditions. However, mixtures with aluminum have been found to be sensitive to ESD.

The potential for ammonium nitrate to decompose at temperatures above 200 °C and, as a result of the heat generated by decomposition, to then undergo a runaway reaction is well known. While many fuels have been shown to lower the decomposition temperature, mixtures have, nevertheless, been shown to be relatively thermally stable during storage and handling.

Chlorate and perchlorate salts

These oxidizers mostly find application in pyrotechnic and other low explosive mixtures. The explosives' chemistry, physics, and performance of these mixtures are covered in other articles.

Some mixtures, for example, perchlorates with metal fuels, have linear reaction rates approaching the speed of sound in the medium, particularly when confined. However, these mixtures tend to deflagrate rather than detonate, particularly at low charge weights or when unconfined.

Perchlorates have rarely been used as components in improvised high explosives, whereas chlorates, particularly potassium chlorate, have been used. Sodium chlorate is hygroscopic and tends to be tightly controlled in most jurisdictions and as a result has rarely been used in recent times.

Detonable chlorate mixtures tend to be more sensitive than detonable perchlorate mixtures. These oxidizers in detonable mixtures produce a VoD in the range of 1300–4100 m s^{-1} and TNT equivalences between 40% and 80%.

The decomposition of chlorates to liberate oxygen is a highly exothermic reaction, the heat of decomposition being −49.3 kJ mol^{-1}, which means that when mixed with fuels, they tend to be more sensitive than perchlorates.

It should be noted that mixtures of chlorates and some fuels are particularly sensitive to ignition by all stimuli.

Permanganate salts

This is encountered as potassium permanganate, which is a well-known oxidizer but rarely finds use in improvised explosive mixtures. However, when mixed with liquid fuels containing alcohol groups, it forms a hypergol (a mixture which spontaneously combusts). Such a hypergol appears to have been part of the initiatory system used by the 'underpants bomber'.

Permanganate mixtures tend to be highly sensitive to stimuli but not as sensitive as chlorate-based mixtures. They do not seem to form detonable mixtures.

Nitrate salts

We have already discussed perhaps the most important nitrate in improvised explosive mixtures; ammonium nitrate. Of the other nitrates, potassium is most commonly encountered. Calcium nitrate is not widely available and sodium nitrate is hygroscopic.

Nitrate mixtures, other than those with ammonium salt, do not tend to detonate under any circumstances and therefore should be treated as low explosives.

Hydrogen peroxide

Hydrogen peroxide in a concentrated form has been used as an oxidizer in a number of terrorist attacks, most notably in London in 2005. It has been mixed with readily available carbonaceous fuels such as flour. Research on this explosive mixture is in its early stages and its chemistry, physics, and performance are still being studied. However, the failure of the devices in London on 21 July 2005, and information released at the trial suggested that the concentration of peroxide is important for reliable detonation.

Fuels

As already stated anything that can burn, or combust, may be mixed with an oxidizer to produce an improvised explosive. A complete list of fuels would be very long indeed. However, the most commonly encountered fuels in improvised explosives used by criminals are listed in **Table 2**.

The amount of energy supplied by the fuel is an important consideration. The heat of explosion can be increased by using a fuel which has a high heat of combustion. Elemental fuels with high heats of combustion can be found toward the lighter end of the periodic table. Two such elements that are used as fuels in improvised explosive mixtures are aluminum with a heat of combustion of −834.3 kJ mol^{-1} and sulfur, −295.3 kJ mol^{-1}. Therefore, sulfur does not increase the heat of explosions to the extent of aluminum. In addition to aluminum and sulfur, highly energetic fuels such as nitrobenzene and nitromethane can significantly increase the sensitivity and power output of improvised explosive mixtures.

Sulfur is a very reactive element especially at elevated temperatures, which facilitate the cleavage of the S–S bond. Sulfur when added to any oxidizer produces an extremely sensitive explosive mixture. Improvised explosive mixtures incorporating sulfur should be treated with extreme caution.

Synthetics

Urea Nitrate

Urea nitrate is a colorless crystalline material produced through a chemical reaction between urea, the fuel, and nitric acid, the oxidizer. Both materials have legitimate uses and can be easily obtained. Its structure is shown in **Figure 1**. The nitrate ion is only loosely bonded to the molecule and therefore urea nitrate is corrosive. The salt is strongly acidic and the chemical stability is poor. However, it is thermally stable and relatively insensitive to friction, impact, and ESD.

Urea nitrate is detonable and considered more reliably so than ammonium nitrate. The detonation velocity at 0.7 g cm^{-3} is around 3500 m s^{-1}. However, it should still be considered a tertiary explosive, requiring a booster for reliable detonation.

A TNT equivalence of 90% has been reported but experiment has shown that this varies between 50% and 75%. This variation is to be expected from nonideal improvised explosives.

R-Salt

The structure of R-Salt (1,3,5-trinitroso-1,3,5-triazacyclohexane) is shown in **Figure 2**. It was first synthesized in 1888. It is a secondary high explosive that has found use in Middle Eastern terrorist attacks. It is easy to prepare requiring no concentrated

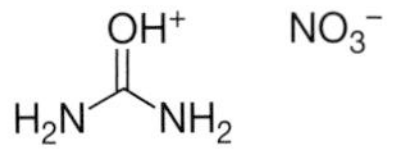

Figure 1 Urea nitrate.

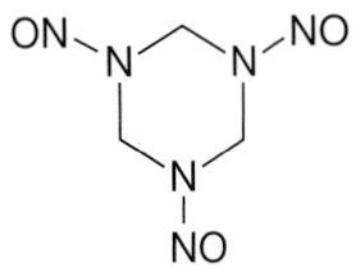

Figure 2 Structure of R-Salt.

acid. Large-scale production was considered during World War II. However, its poor chemical and thermal stabilities have prevented its commercial production and military use. The pure form occurs as light yellow crystals. It is highly brisant with a VoD of 7300 m s^{-1} at a charge density of approximately 1.5 g cm^{-3}. It has a TNT equivalence of around 130%. It has a melting point of 102 °C and a heat of explosion of 5427 kJ kg^{-1}.

Peroxides TATP and HMTD

While explosives including the peroxide group are not limited to TATP and HMTD, these two explosives have been by far the most commonly encountered in criminal use. Therefore, this section will be limited to consideration of these very sensitive primary explosives. Both have been known since the nineteenth century. However, due to their extreme sensitivity, they have never found commercial or military use.

Experiment has demonstrated that they are at least as sensitive as lead azide to all stimuli and should be treated with extreme caution.

Triacetone Triperoxide

The peroxide explosive TATP (3,3,6,6-tetramethyl-1,2,4,5-tetraoxane) is also known as acetone peroxide. It was first synthesized in 1895. The structure of the most stable conformer is shown in **Figure 3**. TATP is one of the most important improvised explosives. It may be synthesized from readily available materials. It is a highly sensitive explosive which has found use as a primary explosive in initiatory systems, as part of improvised detonators, and as a main charge.

Its physical form is that of a white crystalline material, the exact appearance of which depends on the synthetic process used.

Its melting point falls in the range of 91–98.5 °C but can be depressed by impurities which are often present in the synthesized product. The vapor pressure has been determined by experiment to be in the region of 6–7 Pa at normal temperatures. Therefore, it is highly volatile and easily detected by canines and vapor detection systems. This property also facilitates headspace sampling using a variety of sorbents. TATP sublimes at slightly elevated temperatures (60 °C). Its heat of sublimation has been calculated to be 109 kJ mol^{-1}.

As might be expected with synthesized improvised explosives, sensitivity data vary but it is clear that TATP should be considered at least as sensitive as lead azide to all stimuli. The detonation velocity of TATP has been recorded as 5300 m s^{-1} at 1.2 g cm^{-3} and around 1430 m s^{-1} at the more realistic density of 0.47 g cm^{-3}. Studies have shown that the relationship between VoD and density is linear in the range of 0.35–1.2 g cm^{-3}, the equation of the line being

$$y = 5405.1x - 1149 \text{ with } R^2 = 0.09983$$

The heat of explosion of TATP has been experimentally determined as 2803 kJ kg^{-1}. In terms of TNT equivalence TATP has been found to be as much as 88%, but given realistic charge densities, TNT equivalence is more likely to be in the region of 50%.

A number of studies have demonstrated that TATP exists as an equilibrium between two conformers at normal temperatures and pressures. The most stable conformer has a twist-boat-chair (TBC) structure with D_3 symmetry (**Figure 3**) and the least stable is a twist-chair-chair (TCC), which possesses C_2 symmetry. Studies have shown that the energy barrier between the two conformers in solution is 110 kJ mol^{-1} and that the TCC conformer is only 8 kJ mol^{-1} less stable.

The existence of these conformers has assisted in the analysis and detection of this thermally labile and highly volatile molecule.

Studies have shown that an explosion is not a thermodynamically favorable event for TATP. Its explosive mechanism, or thermal decomposition, has been shown to be entropic. That is, rather than undergo an oxidation reaction, the molecule falls apart in an entropy burst to give acetone and carbon dioxide as products. Thermal decomposition has been found to take place in the gas phase. Like sodium azide-based mixtures in early car airbags, TATP does not generate any heat or flame upon detonation. These effects come later as the acetone molecules ignite upon friction with air.

It should be noted that there have been many attempts, particularly in the Middle East, to stabilize TATP with a variety of carbonaceous liquids and waxes.

Hexamethylene Triperoxide Diamine

The peroxide explosive HMTD (3,4,8,9,12,13-hexaoxa-1,6-diazabicyclo[4.4.4]tetradecane) was first synthesized in 1885. The structure of this chemically stable compound is shown in **Figure 4**. HMTD has also become popular with terrorists for use as a primary explosive in initiatory systems and rarely, if ever, as a main charge. Like TATP, it may be synthesized from readily available materials. It is even more sensitive than TATP. One researcher found HMTD too sensitive to measure and recorded its friction sensitivity as 0 N.

Like TATP, its physical form is that of a white crystalline material, the exact appearance of which depends on the synthetic process used. The melting point of HMTD is 158 °C and its vapor pressure is much lower than that of TATP. Despite its explosive sensitivity, the molecule is more chemically stable

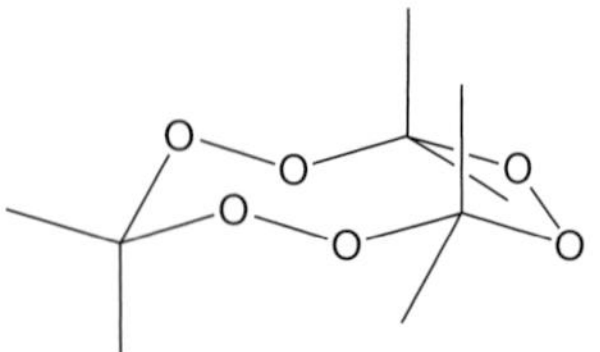

Figure 3 Structure of TATP–TBC conformer.

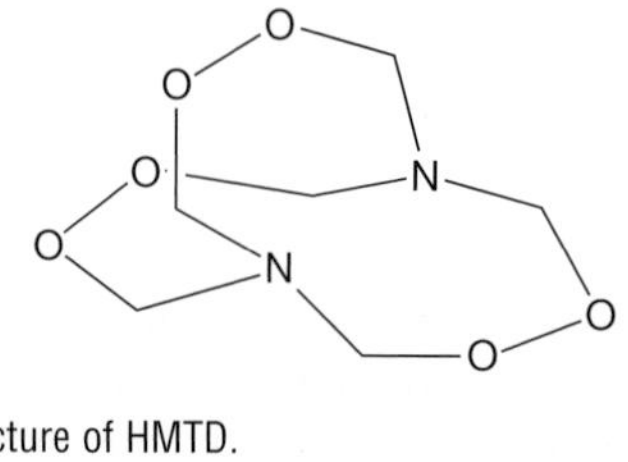

Figure 4 Structure of HMTD.

than TATP and is therefore far easier to sample and analyze than TATP.

Its detonation velocity is recorded as 4511 m s^{-1} at 0.88 g cm^{-3} and around 2820 m s^{-1} at the more realistic density of 0.38 g cm^{-3}. As with TATP, the same study has found a linear relationship between VoD and charge density between 0.35 and 1.2 g cm^{-3}, the equation of the line being

$$y = 3199.8x + 1622.8 \text{ with } R^2 = 0.9979$$

The heat of explosion has been experimentally determined as 5079 kJ kg^{-1} but doubts have been expressed about this figure, that it may be too high. In terms of TNT equivalence, HMTD has been found to be as much as 60%. Thermal decomposition has been found to take place in the condensed phase.

There are a number of other organic peroxides that are detonable and may be synthesized from readily obtainable materials. However, they have not been encountered as yet.

See also: **Chemistry/Trace/Explosives:** Commercial; Explosions; Improvised Explosive Devices.

Further Reading

Beveridge A (ed.) (2011) *The Forensic Investigation of Explosions*, 2nd edn. London: Taylor & Francis.

Damour PL, Freedman A, and Wormhoudt J (2010) Knudsen effusion measurement of organic peroxide vapour pressures. *Propellants, Explosives, Pyrotechnics* 35(6): 514–520.

Danekamp C, Gottlieb L, Tamiri T, Tsoglin A, Shilav R, and Kapon M (2005) Two separable conformers of TATP and analogues exist at room temperature. *Organic Letters* 7(12): 2461–2464.

Dubnikova F, Kosloff R, Almog J, et al. (2005) Decomposition of triacetone triperoxide is an entropic explosion. *Journal of the American Chemical Society* 127: 1146–1159.

Felix-Rivera H, Ramirez-Cedeno ML, Sanchez-Cuprill RA, and Hernadez-Rivera SP (2011) Triacetone triperoxide thermogravimetric study of vapor pressure and enthalpy of sublimation in 303–338 K temperature range. *Thermochimica Acta* 514: 37–43.

Kuzmin V, Solovev M, and Tuzkov Y (2008) Forensic investigation of some peroxides explosives. *Central European Journal of Energetic Materials* 5: 77–85.

Matyas R and Selesovsky J (2009) Power of TATP based explosives. *Journal of Hazardous Materials* 165: 95–99.

Oxley JC, Smith JL, Chen H, and Cioffi E (2002) Decomposition of multi-peroxidic compounds: Part II. Hexamethylene triperoxide diamine (HMTD). *Thermochimica Acta* 388: 215–225.

OxleyJC,SmithJL,ShindeK,andMoranJ(2005)Determinationofthevapourdensityof triacetonetriperoxide(TATP)usingagaschromatographyheadspacetechnique. *Propellants,Explosives,Pyrotechnics*30:127.

Explosions

JB Crippin, Western Forensic Law Enforcement Training Center, Pueblo, CO, USA

Glossary

Brisance The shattering power associated with high explosives.

Combustion Any type of exothermic oxidation reaction, including, but not limited to, burning, deflagration, and/or detonation.

Deflagration An exothermic reaction that occurs particle to particle at subsonic speed.

Detonation An exothermic reaction that propagates a shockwave through an explosive at supersonic speed (>3300 ft s^{-1}).

Explosion A rapid expansion of gases resulting from a chemical or physical action that produces a pressure wave.

Explosive A chemical substance or mixture capable of producing an explosion.

Explosive compound A single chemical compound capable of causing an explosion.

Explosive mixture A mixture of chemical compounds capable of causing an explosion.

Fuel Any substance capable of reacting with oxygen or oxygen carriers (oxidizers).

Oxidizer A chemical compound which supplies the oxygen in a chemical reaction.

Pyrotechnic mixtures An oxidizer/fuel mixture which produces bright or colored lights, heat, fogs, or acoustic effects.

Report A loud sound produced by an explosion.

Shrapnel Objects which are attached to the outside or included inside a device to increase the blast damage and/or injure/kill personnel. The device/container walls themselves can also function in this manner.

Probably the simplest definition of an explosion is a loud boom and a sudden going away of things from where they have just been. Under the fire and explosion investigation definition, an explosion is a physical reaction characterized by the presence of four major elements or criteria:

- Rapid increase in gas pressure (gas dynamic)
- Confinement of the pressure
- Rapid release of that pressure
- Damage or change to the confining structure of the vessel

The above definition is more in tune with defining an explosion from a low explosive source. A better definition might be the following:

- A rapid expansion of gases resulting from a chemical or physical action that produces a pressure wave.

This definition would encompass all types of explosions whether they would be the result of an energetic material (i.e., explosive) or some other source.

Explosives Effects

On detonation, high-order explosives will combust almost instantaneously. This near-instantaneous chemical reaction produces heat, light, sound, and a highly compressed region of gas, generating pressures of up to 150 000 atm and temperatures rising to 3000 °C. This highly compressed region of gas propagates outwards through a medium at supersonic speed, creating an overpressure shock wave known as a blast wave with a shattering force known as brisance. Examples of high explosives that produce these effects include trinitrotoluene (TNT), C4, Semtex, nitroglycerin, dynamite, and ammonium nitratolute fuel oil.

By contrast, low explosives combust on ignition/initiation in a process known as deflagration. These explosions lack the highly compressed region of gas generated by high explosives, hence the brisance and supersonic blast wave. These types of explosion occur at 'slower' speeds for the want of a better term. Examples of low explosive include pipe bombs, gunpowder, and Molotov cocktails.

Types of Explosions

Explosions can be broken down into four basic types:

1. Mechanical – Results from a buildup pressure that results in the failure of the containment vessel's structure integrity. Some examples are a boiler explosion, a dry-ice bomb, or even a balloon popping.
2. Chemical – A chemical explosion occurs when a material or compound undergoes a chemical reaction. This reaction results in the production of heat, light, and gases. These are what people normally think of when they are referring to an explosion. If one looks at the three things that are produced by a chemical explosion, it is easy to see that a chemical explosion is simply a combustion reaction.
3. Nuclear – A nuclear explosion entails either the splitting or fusing of atoms. One is a fission reaction, while the other is a fusion reaction. Both produce enormous amounts of energy in various forms such as heat and x-rays.
4. Electrical – In an electrical explosion, high-energy electrical arcs may generate sufficient heat to cause an explosion. The energy of the reaction energizes the atoms of the target

 http://dx.doi.org/10.1016/B978-0-12-382165-2.00085-4

material to a point they literally fly apart. Another theory is that the resultant heating of the surrounding gases by the electrical energy results in a mechanical explosion. As one can imagine, this is a somewhat controversial classification but it is becoming more accepted by the explosives community. Some examples are lightning strikes or electrical short circuits.

Primary Effects of an Explosion

The primary effects of an explosion can be divided into three basic types. They consist of a blast wave/pressure, fragmentation, and an incendiary/thermal component.

The blast wave (i.e., overpressure) component consists of the pressure wave that radiates outward from the seat of the explosion. This pressure wave may be produced by expanding gases produced by combustion (i.e., an explosion) or by gases already compressed and then released by the failure of the containment vessel (i.e., a boiler explosion or balloon popping). In any case, it is the pressure wave that does the most damage. The blast wave radiates outward rapidly but as distance increases the speed and pressure drop off rapidly (Figure 1).

Another interesting fact is that at the seat of the explosion, a near vacuum is created as all the air is 'pushed' away by the pressure wave. This characteristic is used in snuffing out oil-well fires. The fire is put out by placing explosives in the center of the fire and 'blowing' away all of the oxygen supporting the flame (Figure 2).

The fragmentation effect occurs when the device casing is broken into pieces by the blast or when objects are attached to the outside or included inside a device to increase the blast damage and/or injure/kill personnel. The device/container walls themselves can also be designed to function in this manner. This is particularly true in antipersonnel types of devices such as aerial bombs and hand grenades as well as improvised explosive devices (IEDs). Different types of explosives can cause different sizes and shapes of fragments or shrapnel (Figure 3).

- Low explosives generally cause large, rectangular/square fragments (Figure 4).

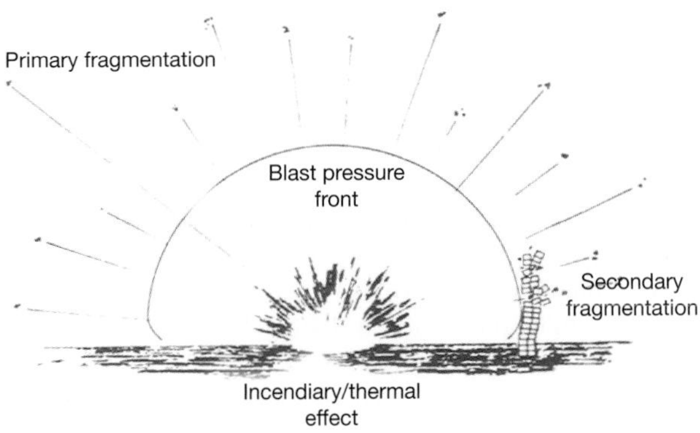

Figure 1 Demonstration of primary blast effects.

- High explosives generally cause small, triangular-shaped fragments. Additionally, these fragments appear much thinner because of the 'plasticizing' effect attributed to high explosives (Figure 5).

Fragments from an explosion can be split into two types/classes: primary fragmentation and secondary fragmentation. Primary fragmentation is defined as shrapnel or fragments produced as a direct result of the initial explosion (device casing or objects attached to the outside of the device casing). Secondary fragmentation is produced when primary fragments strike something and impart directional energy to that object. It is also caused by the pressure wave as it radiates outward striking 'frangible' objects. One of the most common types of secondary fragments is shards of glass from windows broken by the blast.

The incendiary/thermal effect is the high temperatures produced by an explosion. This effect may be localized at the seat of an explosion. In some instances, it can be caused remotely by hot fragments hurled out from the seat of the explosion (i.e., white phosphorus). Most chemical explosions will result in an incendiary/thermal effect of some type.

In addition to the primary effects, there are some secondary effects of an explosion that should be noted. They are focusing, shielding, and reflection/deflection. These effects are most notable when looking at the blast wave and, in some cases, fragmentation. The blast wave can be reflected and focused as well as shielded against. Shrapnel can be shielded against or deflected.

Results of Explosions

When talking about explosions, one must give thought to what they can do with the various effects/factors they produce. Some of these are structural damage, broken gas lines, broken water

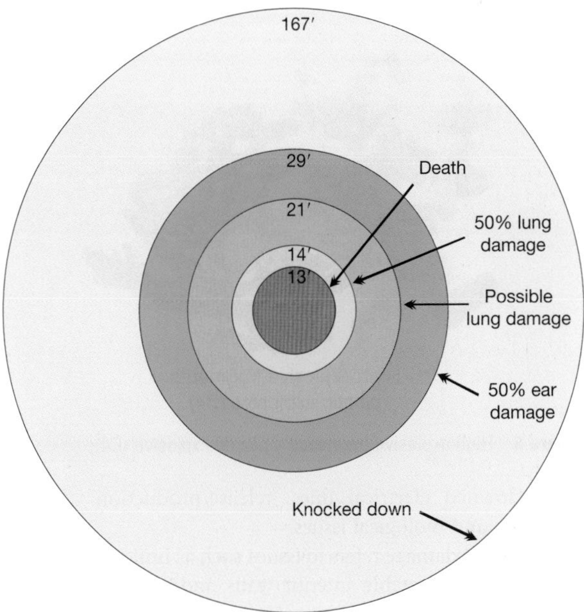

Figure 2 50 lb TNT airburst effects.

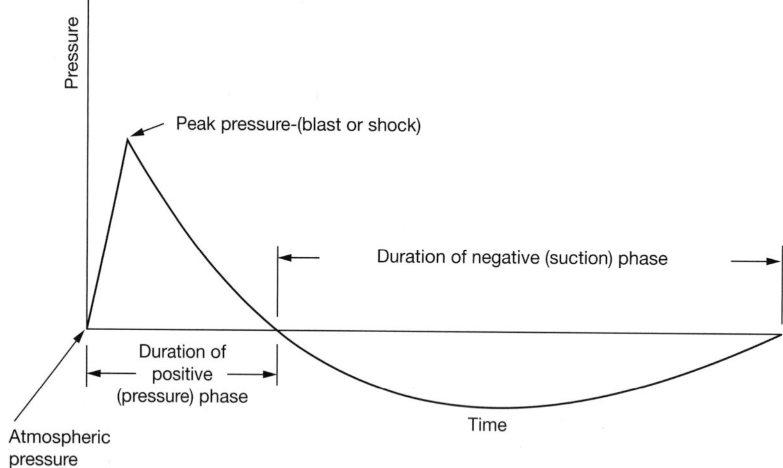

Figure 3 Time line of an explosion.

Figure 4 Low explosive fragments – Commercial black powder.

Figure 5 High explosive fragments – plastic explosive (C4).

lines, downed electrical lines, release/production of toxic materials, and biological issues.

Structural damage refers to issues such as building collapse, falling debris, unstable interior walls and/or floors, as well as fire(s).

Table 1 Blast pressure effects on structures

PSI	*Structure material*
0.5–1	Shatter single pane glass
1–2	Crack plaster walls, shatter asbestos siding, buckle steel sheeting, knock down wooden walls
2–3	Crack nonreinforced cinder block/concrete block walls
2–8	Crack nonreinforced brick walls
5–10	Shatter autosafety glass
16.5–35.8	Snap telephone poles
60	Reinforced concrete cracked

Broken water lines can cause further structural damage. They can also spread toxic and flammable materials. The water will fill in the low spots and can cause drowning when individuals fall into them (Table 1).

Broken gas lines can ignite causing fires and explosions. Another danger with broken gas lines is that the gas can displace air and cause asphyxiation in unprotected personnel.

Downed electrical lines constitute electrocution hazards. Additionally, they can be responsible for igniting flammable liquids or gases causing fires or explosions.

Explosions and the resulting fires can result in the release/production of toxic materials. The materials can be varied. Examples are asbestos and soot/smoke. Various burning clothing and plastics can produce extremely toxic smokes containing cyanide, polychlorinated biphenyls (PCBs) and/or polyvinyl chlorides (PVCs) for example.

Biological issues entail the release of *Escherichia coli* and pathogens that cause AIDS, hepatitis, gangrene, etc. into the area surrounding the explosion. These pathogens can contaminate everything they touch, including the emergency personnel responding to the explosion.

An explosive/energetic event can cause injuries to personnel in several ways. These injuries will be pressure, puncture, or thermally related. These injuries can be broken down into four categories.

Primary Blast Injuries

Primary blast injuries (PBIs) are caused by the large pressure differential of the blast wave, which leads to shearing, spalling, implosion, and acceleration/deceleration injuries. As pressure differentials are more pronounced at medium borders, hollow-medium-filled tissues and organs, such as the ears, lungs, and gastrointestinal system, are at a higher risk of injury than solid organs. Examples of PBIs include total body disruption (TBD), tympanic perforation, amputation, lung injury, and bowel contusion/perforation. TBD is uncommon and usually only occurs to victims in close proximity to the explosion. Suicide bombers wearing explosives and persons in proximity to blasts of great magnitude are the ideal candidates for TBD. Tympanic membrane perforation is the most common PBI. It can serve as an indicator of exposure to blast overpressure. Traumatic amputation tends to occur through the shaft of long bones and not at the site of articulate joints, as might be expected. It is therefore not surprising to find that massive coronary or cerebral air embolism in patients with PBI is often the cause of death. Blast lung is a term used to describe a combination of pulmonary symptoms caused by blast wave exposure. Because the blast wave attenuates exponentially in relation to distance, PBIs are normally sustained by patients in close proximity to the explosion. However, the amplification of blast waves in confined spaces, indoors, in car parks, and in buses are associated with a higher incidence of PBI, severe injury, and mortality rate. Often, PBIs prove incompatible with life. Because of this and other aspects associated with explosions, the majority of wounds carried by survivors of a bomb blast are secondary blast injuries (SBIs).

Secondary Blast Injury

SBIs are caused by objects accelerated by the explosion. The velocity and injury potential of these projectiles are based on the magnitude of the explosion, the weight of the projectile, and the distance from the source of explosion. Some of these projectiles reach sufficient velocity to cause injury on impact and this is the mechanism behind SBI. This projectile effect is often utilized in military explosive fragmentation devices such as grenades. IEDs often utilize a variety of additives (nails, metal fragments, glass, etc.) to achieve a similar effect. In addition to these additives, an unlimited number of other items can be propelled by the blast wind to become missiles, including bricks, plaster fragments, wood, and biological remains. Even dust and dirt can be propelled sufficiently to leave a fairly uniform characteristic tattooing and dusky purple discoloration of exposed skin. While PBI is likely to be fatal, in the absence of building collapse SBIs account for the majority of injuries to survivors. For example, 95% of survivors of the Khobar Towers bombing in Dhahran, Saudi Arabia, had penetrating foreign-body (mostly glass) injuries. In general, the closer to an explosion the patient is, the greater the number and severity of injuries.

Tertiary Blast Injury

Tertiary blast injury (TBI) is a result of displacement of the patient by the blast wind. Often, patients are propelled along the ground, resulting in abrasive, contusive, and blunt trauma. Occasionally, patients are launched through the air and may collide or impale themselves on stationary objects. Once again, the severity of TBIs depends greatly on the proximity and magnitude of the blast. Tertiary injuries are common as demonstrated in the 1995 Oklahoma City bombing where 135 (33%) people reported as being pushed or pulled against an object by the force of the blast.

Quaternary Blast Injury

Quaternary blast injuries result from a variety of blast effects, including burns, chemical and toxic dust poisoning/inhalation, radiation exposure, and crush injury due to building collapse. Burns sustained from the action of the primary blast are known as flash burns and are caused by the brief but intense spike in temperature associated with detonation. Flash burns are cutaneous burns of uniform thickness to exposed skin, from which tight clothing (underwear, footwear, etc.) may protect. Full- and partial-thickness burns are more likely to result from fires ignited by the blast, rather than the blast itself. These burns are relatively uncommon as demonstrated in the Oklahoma City bombing where 9 of 592 persons had thermal burns covering up to 70% of their body. Chemical or toxic inhalation/exposure may result either from the inclusion of weaponized toxins into the explosive device or from the partial combustion of ignited materials postblast. The onset and presentation of symptoms vary greatly, depending on the substance in question. Although nuclear explosives have not been utilized since Nagasaki was bombed in August 1945, there exists the possibility that a so-called radiological 'dirty bomb' may cause widespread radiological contamination. Symptoms of whole-body exposure to low levels of radiation include nausea and vomiting and may develop over hours to days. Sufficient radiation exposure can lead to death through organ failure or cancer and widespread onset of these symptoms should be cause for alarm. Building collapse contributes significantly to the seriousness of a bombing incident and can immediately kill the majority of its occupants. In the Oklahoma City bombing, persons located in the collapsed region of the building were significantly more likely to die (87%) than persons in noncollapsed regions (5%). Problems for emergency personnel associated with building collapse include increased difficulty in communications, site access/ egress, patient retrieval, and a higher incidence of crush injury. Crush injury poses unique challenges for rescue personnel and is associated with complications, including limb loss and death.

See also: **Chemistry/Trace/Explosives:** Clandestine Explosive Laboratories; Commercial; Explosives: Analysis; Improvised Explosive Devices; Improvised Explosives; Military.

Further Reading

Beveridge A (1998) *Forensic Investigation of Explosions*, p. 512. Boca Raton, FL: CRC Press.

Cooper P and Kurowski SR (1996) *Introduction to Technology of Explosives*, p. 224. New York: Wiley.

Crowl DA (2003) *Understanding Explosions*, p. 220. Hoboken, NJ: Wiley.

NFPA (2011) *NFPA 921: Guide for Fire and Explosion Investigations*, p. 347. Quincy, MA: National Fire Protection Agency.

Thurman JT (2011) *Practical Bomb Scene Investigation*, 2nd edn., p. 519. Boca Raton, FL: Taylor & Francis.

TWGFEX/NCFS (2000) *A Guide for Explosion and Bombing Scene Investigation*, p.64. Washington, DC: DOJ.

CHEMISTRY/TRACE/FIBERS

Contents

Fibers: Overview

J Robertson, University of Canberra, Canberra, ACT, Australia
C Roux, University of Technology, Sydney, NSW, Australia

Introduction

In the modern world, our environment brings us into contact with a wide variety of textiles and other surfaces composed of fibers. Textiles are used in clothing, home furnishings, upholstery, carpets, automobile seats, and in numerous technical and other end products. The fibers from which textiles are constructed may be of natural or man-made origin and a wide variety of methods can be used to turn fibers into fabrics. Hence, the forensic examiner needs to have a good understanding of fabric construction as well as a detailed knowledge of the fibers most commonly encountered in forensic work.

Fibers are encountered in forensic work because they have a tendency to be shed and transferred between surfaces during contact. The work of the forensic examiner is to first find potentially transferred fibers, and then, conduct a range of qualitative and quantitative tests to identify and classify these fibers and to compare them with possible donor items to establish their possible origin. Fibers cannot directly identify an individual, but they can provide circumstantial and corroborating evidence that an individual was not only present but also involved in the commission of a crime by assisting in the interpretation of 'what happened.'

Fiber examination may also be useful as forensic intelligence, for example, by providing a link between a number of incidents.

Classification of Fibers

Technically, a fiber is defined as being an elongate structure whose length exceeds its breadth. Fibers can be grouped according to their origin as either natural or man-made fibers. In textile technology terms, a fiber is also the most fundamental unit of a fabric.

Natural fibers may be subdivided into animal, mineral, or vegetable fibers. Animal fibers include keratin-based fibers such as sheep wool and fibers of similar use such as alpaca, angora, cashmere, camel, and mohair. Other keratin-based animal fibers include 'fur' type fibers and even human hair. Non-keratin-based animal fibers include cultivated silk and wild silk (Tussah). Asbestos fibers are of mineral origin. Fibers of vegetable origin include bast (flax, hemp, jute, and ramie), leaf (obaca, phormium, and sisal), seed (akund, cotton, and kapok), and others (coconut or coir).

Man-made fibers conprise those that originate from natural substances and those that are truly synthetic. Man-made fibers are polymers comprising elongated chains of basic chemical units. For example, an acrylic fiber is made up of not less than 85% by mass of acrylonitrile units or of acrylonitrile copolymers.

Rayon is an example of a man-made fiber 'regenerated' from a natural substance. In this case, the basic building block is cellulose in which substituents have replaced not more than 15% of the hydrogens of the hydroxyl groups. Viscose is one form of rayon.

Although there are a very large number of man-made fiber types, in practice, only a small number of actual generic fiber types are commonly encountered in forensic work and these roughly parallel global textile fiber production. The most common fiber type is polyester, accounting for close to one-third of the global production. Cotton is a close second and thereafter no fiber type exceeds a few percent of global production with polypropylene, polyamide (nylon), polyacryconitriles

 http://dx.doi.org/10.1016/B978-0-12-382165-2.00088-X

(acrylic), and wool, in that order. Notwithstanding, the fiber examiner needs to have a good knowledge of a broader range of fibers, as global production aside, many fibers find application in specific end product uses.

Fiber Properties and Textile Fabrics

Textile fibers generally fall within the range of 10–50 μm in diameter and individual fibers can vary in length from less than 1 cm to thousands of meters. Natural fibers vary in length depending on the source. Manufactured fibers can be continuous filaments but these are often cut to specific lengths and are then called staple fibers.

Textile fabrics are rarely manufactured from individual fibers but rather from a yarn. A yarn is defined as "a strand of textile fiber in a form suitable for wearing, knitting, braiding, felting, webbing, or otherwise fabricating into a fabric" (US Federal Trade Commission).

A fabric refers to "any material woven, knitted, felted, or otherwise produced from, or in combination with, any natural or manufactured fiber, yarn, or substitute" (US Federal Trade Commission).

Fabrics are generally defined by the method of assembly, with the three major types being woven, knitted, and nonwoven fabrics. It is outside the scope of this article to describe fabric types in any detail. However, a forensic fiber expert would be expected to have a working knowledge of fabric construction, sufficient to be able to recognize and compare basic construction. If evidence consists of torn or damaged fabric, and a possible source is also available, then it may be possible to point to a common source through a physical (mechanical) fit. In the absence of a physical fit, comparison of fabric samples can be conducted, which may establish the nature of the fabric, point to a garment or fabric type, and, in rare instances, identify a fabric.

In cases of textile damage, knowledge of fabric construction is an essential prerequisite to interpret the nature and cause of the damage.

Transfer and Persistence

The basis for fiber examination lies in the fact that fibers may be transferred between items during contact and that they can be subsequently recovered and examined. This is based on Locard's exchange principle, which, simply stated, says 'every contact leaves a trace.' If fibers are to be recovered, their evidential value needs to be understood by crime scene examiners and others, who may be responsible for the collection of clothing and other items where there is the potential for transfer. This evidence 'recognition phase' is critical as is the subsequent recording and recovery of items relevant for meaningful examination and interpretation. As soon as fibers have been transferred, they may be moved, relocated, and lost. Fiber transfers may be primary or secondary. Secondary transfers are where fibers are transferred from an item, say a person sitting in a car seat, and then subsequently from the car seat to a second individual. It is often not easy to determine whether transfer is primary or secondary.

Hence, consideration should always be given to recovery of fibers at the scene of an alleged crime. For example, while the body of a deceased person is at the crime scene, recovery of fibers from the body will provide a more accurate picture of contact than when the body is taken to a morgue, the clothing removed, packaged, and sent to the laboratory. Similarly, fibers recovered from the bedding at the scene of an alleged sexual assault are likely to eventuate in potentially more useful evidence. The key is that the forensic examination of fibers is not merely an exercise in identifying and comparing fibers but also an exercise in interpreting what may have happened through the location of the recovered fibers.

Crime scene examiners and forensic fiber examiners need to be alert to the significant potential for fiber loss and also for fiber cross-contamination, which may render subsequent examination meaningless. The fiber examiner also needs to be aware of the potential for other forms of physical trace materials being present, including biological traces from which DNA may be recovered.

To avoid contamination, strict rules involving protective clothing recovery and examination protocols need to be in place as part of an overall quality system.

As far as is practical, potential evidence should be collected at the first possible opportunity following the GIFT (get it first time) principle. Many factors interact to influence the transfer of fibers and their subsequent persistence and these are discussed in more detail in the relevant entries in this Encyclopedia. The important thing to remember is the transient nature of physical traces and the need to collect it at the earliest opportunity and to protect items against further loss.

Recovery of Fibers

The nature of the items or scene to be examined will influence the choice of the most appropriate method, or sequence of methods, for the recovery of physical evidence. Consideration needs to be given to all forms of physical evidence to determine the sequence of recovery. Where there is the potential for biological traces to be present, these should usually be the first traces to be considered as they can identify potential suspects or persons of interest. Where any physical materials are visible to the naked eye, they should be recovered by hand (always wearing protective gloves) or using fine forceps. Some form of low magnification or even the use of specialist light sources may be helpful, as many fibers exhibit fluorescence. For fibers, the use of druggist paper folds is strongly recommended as this facilitates subsequent examination.

As most transferred fibers are not readily visible to the naked eye (being in the range of mm or less), the use of tape lifting is common. Here, pieces of clear adhesive tape are pressed onto the surface of the item being examined and the whole item systematically searched in a grid fashion. In some circumstances, the so-called 'one-to-one' tape lifting may be warranted; however, a zonal search pattern is more common.

The use of scraping techniques is not recommended, as it will disturb the location of the transferred fibers and also create more background fibers from the item under examination. Vacuuming would be a technique of last resort for the recovery of fibers, although it may have value in difficult-to-reach or large areas.

Case Management

All serious and many less serious cases should be considered for their potential to yield fiber evidence and scenes/items must be processed accordingly. Thereafter, the items worth searching can only be decided when case information becomes available. It is essential that the scientist has all relevant information, as this will result in resources being channeled where they are needed with more effective case management and use of available resources.

Thus, it is very important to evaluate the case history before starting laboratory examinations. A case conference involving the scientist as well as crime scene and investigating officers can be invaluable. There is no point in conducting a lengthy search to show that fibers are present in a location where they may reasonably be expected to be as a result of a legitimate transfer. Equally futile is a lengthy search, which fails to reveal the presence of fibers only for it to turn out that there is good reason to believe that the suspect's clothing was not involved or not worn during an incident under investigation. The type of information sought could include the following:

- What is alleged to have taken place, who is involved and how?
- Where is the incident said to have taken place? If it was in a house or in a car, who was the occupier or owner?
- With a sexual assault, did it occur on a bed or on the floor? Is it possible to reconstruct the sequence of events? Were bed covers present and were they moved?
- When did the incident take place and was there any delay in the scene being examined?
- Did any person involved have legitimate access to the scene or legitimate contact with the other person or persons prior to the incident?
- Are reliable descriptions available of what was being worn by the offender? Were items of clothing removed during the incident?
- Consideration should be given to possible CCTV capture of images, which may provide information about clothing.

This type of information will enable the scientist to concentrate on what is likely to be productive. Once a decision has been made to proceed on the basis of the case information available, it becomes necessary to evaluate which possible transfers are worth following up, through subsequent laboratory examinations and analysis.

Laboratory Examinations and Analysis

These aspects are covered in detail in other articles in this Encyclopedia. Broadly speaking, the aim of laboratory examination and analysis is to characterize fibers using the most discriminating techniques available. The usual scenario would be to compare fibers recovered from the clothing of a suspect with fibers comprising the fabric of clothing worn by an alleged victim. Of course, the reverse potential transfer from victim to suspect would also be investigated.

Hence, the first step in the laboratory examination of fibers is to examine all relevant items for their potential to transfer fibers. Items with transfer potential are then sampled to determine their construction and fiber composition. It is important to consider construction parameters to ensure that all the fiber types in a fabric are sampled. Preliminary examination using low-power microscopy will usually enable the fiber examiner to gain a good understanding of the variation in a fabric and ensure that all the fiber types are presented for subsequent testing. This preliminary examination would usually involve looking at yarns and tape lifts. Representative yarns and fibers are then prepared in a suitable microscopic mountant for a more detailed microscopic examination using low- and high-power microscopy. The use of polarizing microscopy can be very informative with respect to fiber type.

The examiner builds a complete picture of the fabric and fiber composition of each relevant item, which provides an understanding of the fibers likely to be transferred from each item.

Typical features assessed will include:

- fiber diameter and variation along fiber length;
- fiber shape;
- surface features may be seen, depending on the refractive index of the fiber surface relative to that of the mountant;
- internal details including the presence, amount, size, shape, and distribution of delustrant (titanium dioxide is used as a delustrant, the effect being a reduction in the brightness of man-made fibers);
- color; and
- fluorescence.

Once the examiner has a good understanding of the potential fibers that may transfer, all recovered fibers (usually on tape lifts) are then searched for the presence of 'target' fibers using low-power microscopy. Usually, the primary guide for this search will be fiber color, although an experienced examiner can usually determine generic categories of fibers even at this level of magnification (up to ×40 or ×50). Each 'potential' transfer is marked on the tape lift.

All 'potential' transfers are subsequently removed from the tape lifts or other recovered material and individually mounted (see **Figure 1**).

Further, detailed examination depends on the nature of the recovered and known fibers and this is covered in the protocols for examination. Broadly, known fibers are further characterized at a microscopic level with respect to color, generic fiber type, and fluorescence. Usually, fibers are identified using Fourier transform infrared spectroscopy, although other techniques such as mass spectrometry may also be used. Color is analyzed using visible, and/or visible–UV, microspectrophotometry, and, where available and appropriate, Raman spectroscopy. Dyes may be extracted and analyzed using thin-layer chromatography.

The same techniques are then applied to the recovered fibers. At a microscopic level, this culminates in one-to-one comparisons using a comparison microscope.

The driving principle in this comparative examination is looking for meaningful differences between recovered fibers and a known source or item. When one or more recovered fibers show no meaningful difference, then the examiner needs to interpret what this may mean in the context of the case circumstances.

Interpretation of Fiber Evidence

This is considered in detail in the article on interpretation of fiber evidence in this Encyclopedia.

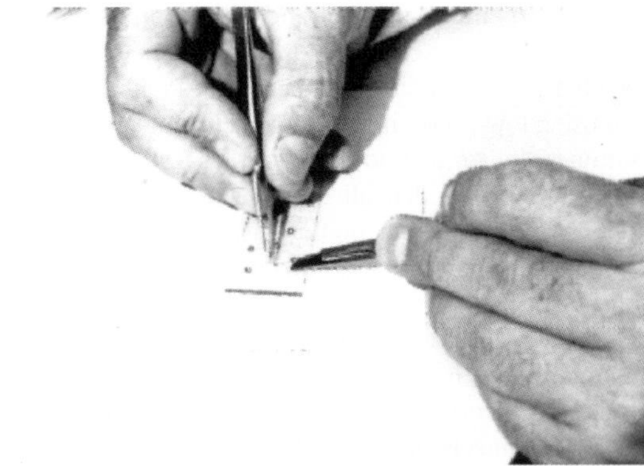

(a) Window being cut in tape lift.

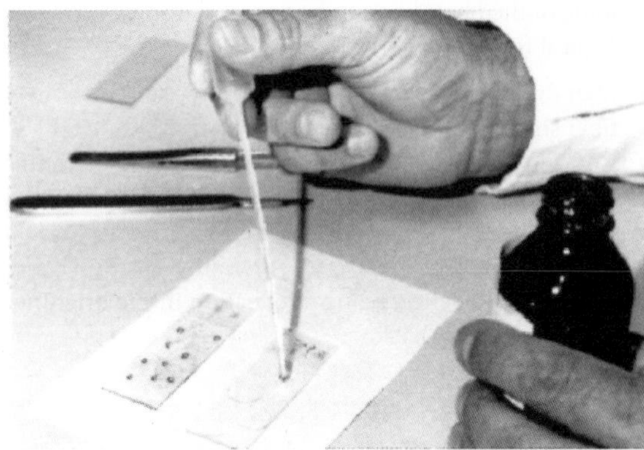

(b) Recovered fiber being placed in a mountant on a slide.

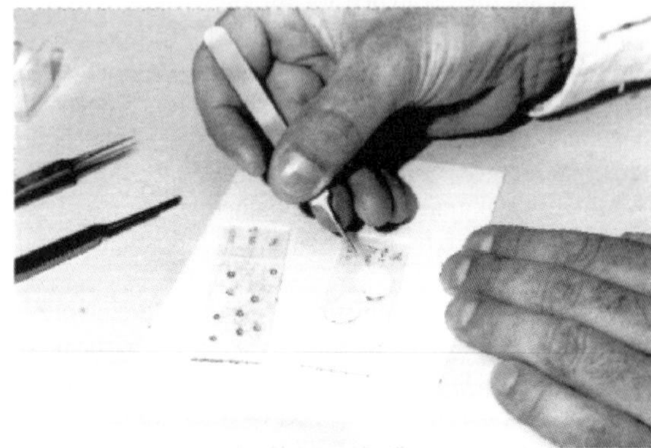

(c) Fiber and mountant being covered with a glass coverslip.

Figure 1 The preparation of 'questioned' fibers for further examination. Note: Gloves are not being worn as this is post evidence recovery for DNA testing.

Interpreting the value of fiber evidence is the most difficult challenge facing the fiber examiner. This is because there are so many variables that will influence the number of fibers recovered and their location. There are three broad levels that the fiber examiner needs to consider. First, there is the interpretation of macro aspects such as tufts of fabric, fabric impressions, and damage to fabric. Not all fiber examiners will have specific expertise in textile damage interpretation.

Second, there is the interpretation of the actual fibers recovered – are they common, rare, or somewhere in between? Third, there is the interpretation of where the recovered fibers were located – does this assist in answering questions as to what happened?

The fiber examiner requires an in-depth knowledge of not only the identification of fiber types but also factors such as:

- transfer studies;
- studies on differential shedding;
- experiments on the alteration of fiber characteristics in a manner consistent with localized conditions specific to a case;
- manufacturer inquiries;
- use of data collections; and
- statistical treatment.

Conclusion

As long as humans use textiles and fabrics there will be the potential for the transfer of fibers, especially during significant, forceful contacts such as the ones that occur in violent crime. Fiber examination starts with investigators and crime scene examiners understanding the potential for fiber transfer and the subsequent examination of fibers to provide useful information to attempt to answer questions of value to the investigation and, ultimately, questions of interest to the court in determining guilt or innocence. Hence, fiber examination often depends on the crime scene examiner recognizing the potential for fiber transfer and conducting appropriate investigations at the crime scene. Fiber examination in the laboratory is not merely a technical exercise of description, analysis, and comparison, although they are all essential components. The ultimate aim of the fiber examiner is to evaluate and interpret what meaning can be attached to recovered fibers in the context of what is alleged to have occurred. As a result, fibers can be considered as the ultimate type of trace evidence, which is as valuable, if not more valuable, to answer activity questions compared to source questions.

See also: **Chemistry/Trace/Fibers:** Color Analysis; Fiber Microscopy; Fiber: Protocols for Examination; Identification and Comparison; Interpretation of Fiber Evidence; Persistence and Recovery; Textile and Fiber Damage; Transfer.

Further Reading

Catling D and Grayson J (1982) *Identification of Vegetable Fibres*. London: Chapman and Hall.

Deadman HA (1984a) Fibre evidence and the Wayne Williams Trial (Part 1). *FBI Law Enforcment Bulletin* 53(3): 12–20.

Deadman HA (1984b) Fibre evidence and the Wayne Williams Trial (Conclusion). *FBI Law Enforcment Bulletin* 53(5): 10–19.

Gaudette BD (1988) The forensic aspects of textile fibre examination. In: Saferstein R (ed.) *The Forensic Examination of Fibres*, vol. 2. Englewood Cliffs, NJ: Prentice Hall.

Gordon Cook J (1984a) *Handbook of Textile Fibres. I. Natural Fibres*, 5th edn. Durham, NC: Merrow.

Gordon Cook J (1984b) *Handbook of Textile Fibres. II. Synthetic Fibres*, 5th edn. Durham, NC: Merrow.

Grieve MC (1990) Fibres and their examination in forensic science. In: Maehly A and Williams RL (eds.) *Forensic Science Progress*, vol. 4. New York: Springer.

Robertson J and Grieve M (eds.) (1999) *Forensic Examination of Fibres*. Oxford: Taylor & Francis.

Textile Institute (1975) *The Identification of Textile Materials*, 7th edn. Manchester: Textile Institute.

Transfer

C Roux, University of Technology, Sydney, NSW, Australia
J Robertson, University of Canberra, Canberra, ACT, Australia

Glossary

Differential shedding A phenomenon by which fabrics composed of two or more fiber types do not necessarily shed fibers proportionate to their representation in the donor fabric.

Primary transfer A direct fiber transfer from a donor item to a recipient item.

Secondary transfer (or *n* transfer) Fibers previously transferred on a recipient item are re-transferred to another surface during a second contact (or subsequent contacts).

Introduction

Since the invention of textiles, the potential for the transfer of fibers has existed. The recognition that it may have forensic value was little recognized until the twentieth century. Although no one individual can actually be credited as the first to single out textiles as a source of trace evidence, the much-quoted Locard's exchange principle is generally accepted as the starting point of the modern era of criminalistics based on the ubiquitous nature of the transfer of trace materials. More generally, traces are increasingly seen as central to forensic science as they are remnants of the presence of one of several individuals and of an activity. As such, they can be considered as the most fundamental 'physical' information about the crime itself. For this reason, it is important to the forensic fiber expert to understand fundamentals about fiber transfer and how this information impacts on the interpretation of fiber evidence.

Transfer

Studies since the 1970s by a number of key groups of workers including Pounds and Smalldon, Grieve, Robertson, and Roux have provided a sound basis for an understanding of the factors to be considered in the interpretation of the transfer and persistence of fibers in forensic investigations.

Textile fabrics used in upholstery, carpets, and clothing are manufactured using a wide variety of mechanisms and many different types of fibers. The transfer of fibers will be under the influence of the latter factors, fabric construction, and fiber type as well as the nature of the contact. Typically, contact will be between individuals wearing items of clothing or between an individual and an item such as a seat or a carpet.

Factors Affecting Transfer

In the general situation, the following factors have been shown to be important in determining the number of fibers which will transfer during a contact.

Fiber Type

This is important for both the 'donor' item and the 'recipient' item. Some fabrics can be expected to transfer more fibers than others. For example, fabrics made of wool and acrylic will shed more fibers than fabrics made of polyester fibers. Sometimes, the potential for a fabric to transfer fibers is called its 'shedability'. In a case situation, it may be useful to assess the shed potential of a donor item. Simple tape lifts may only provide a very rough guide to shed potential. Several authors have proposed the use of simulated contact devices. A rough order for shed potential would be wool $\geq$ acrylic $\geq$ cotton $>$ viscose $>$ polyester $>$ nylon.

Shed potential does not depend solely on the fiber type. Construction and state of wear of fabrics are also key factors.

Fiber Morphology and Thickness

There is evidence that within one fiber type, finer fibers will transfer in greater numbers than coarser fibers. This probably relates to the greater fragmentation of finer fibers compared to their coarser counterparts. Studies have shown that fabrics constructed of microfibers can generate up to seven times more fibers than cotton under the same conditions (they are, however, more difficult to detect and collect than cotton, for example).

Fabric Texture and Construction

As a general rule for the same fiber type, more fibers will transfer from a coarse than from a smooth fabric. This is, however, a gross simplification. Fabric construction is also important. This involves a wide range of factors. As discussed above, the shed potential is determined by a complex interaction of fiber type, fabric construction, and the condition of an item, that is, how well it wears.

Area of Contact

As a general rule, the greater the area in contact the more the fibers can be expected to transfer.

 http://dx.doi.org/10.1016/B978-0-12-382165-2.00089-1

Number of Contacts

The number of fibers transferred increases with the number of contacts where the number of contacts is small. With increasing contacts, some fibers will transfer back to the donor item.

Force of Pressure or Contact

The number of fibers transferred increases with the force or pressure of contact until a plateau is reached beyond which increased force has no further effect. The force of contact also influences the size of fibers transferred, with higher pressure resulting in a greater proportion of short fibers.

Differential Shedding

Most studies have shown that with fabrics composed of two or more fiber types they do not necessarily shed fibers proportionate to their representation in the donor fabric. A complicating factor which is sometimes forgotten is that a manufacturer's label may give proportions in terms of weight and not fiber or yarn numbers. The underlying reasons for differential shedding include fabric construction, in which only one fiber/yarn type is on the external, exposed surface of the fabric, and the shed potential of different fiber types. The need to consider differential shedding has been demonstrated in a number of published case studies. Where the proportion of recovered fibers in a case situation is clearly different from that found (by direct observation) in the putative donor, it is incumbent on the forensic scientist to explain this apparent discrepancy. This will usually involve simulation experiments. A further factor complicating the interpretation will be the influence of fiber persistence.

Primary and Secondary Transfer

In the discussion thus far, it has been assumed that the transfer is a primary transfer, that is, a direct transfer from a donor item to a recipient item. Primary, direct contacts can result in the transfer of hundreds and even thousands of fibers. It is well understood that it is then possible for these transferred fibers to be transferred 'on' during subsequent contacts. A good example would be a person sitting in a cinema seat. The first person leaves behind thousands of fibers on the cinema seat, a second person then sits on the same seat and some of those fibers are transferred on to the clothing worn by the second person. This is a secondary transfer. At least in theory, tertiary and subsequent lower-order transfers are a possibility. In a case scenario, the forensic scientist must remain alert to the possibility of such transfers. It is often the situation that a suspect will be part of an interconnected group of associates and may have been exposed to the potential for fibers to have arrived on their clothing through a nondirect contact. The interpretation of the location and the number of fibers require caution. A complicating factor is that there is no minimum number of fibers below which one can identify a secondary or subsequent transfer.

Special Cases

Most published studies have been conducted using garments. However, fibers may be transferred from any fibrous surface such as upholstery and carpets. The factors influencing fiber transfer from items such as blankets, bed sheets, and seat covers are no different from those outlined for the general case. Transfer from carpets has some different considerations, especially where the recipient surface is a shoe. Carpets are only a subcategory of any other fabric, although their construction is perhaps the major factor in determining their shed potential. Shoes are obviously a special case as a recipient surface. The composition and roughness of the sole are important parameters to consider. The mechanism of fiber transfer to a shoe surface is not identical to the mechanism of transfer between clothing fabrics. In some ways, fiber transfer to a shoe may be more comparable to transfer to any other physical object. **Figure 1** shows an example of results obtained by experiments re-enacting the contact between shoe soles and a car carpet. These data were pivotal to solve a murder case. Fiber persistence on shoes is discussed elsewhere in this encyclopedia.

Another special case of fiber transfer is the transfer of fibers from a fabric to the individual wearing the item. The best example of this is from a mask or balaclava often worn in a robbery. Sometimes, a robber may discard other clothing. It may be possible through a study of fiber transfer to establish contact between the clothing and a suspect. Fiber recovery from the body of a deceased or an alleged victim and its potential to provide evidence is considered too infrequently.

Mechanism of Fiber Transfer

There has been considerable theorizing with regard to the underlying mechanisms of fiber transfer but only limited attempts at providing experimental proof. It has been proposed that in the general fabric-to-fabric situation, three mechanisms may be involved:

- transfer of loose fragments already on the surface of the fabric;
- loose fibers being pulled out of the fabric by friction; and
- transfer of fiber fragments produced by the contact itself.

It is accepted that electrostatic attraction of fibers is not an important factor in the general case. However, electrostatic attraction may be a factor in special circumstances. This discussion has focused on the transfer of fiber fragments and not on the transfer of yarns or pieces of fabric torn or removed from a fabric by physical means.

Fiber transfer: A Dynamic Process

It will often be the case that there will be a time gap between the commission of an offense and the apprehension of a suspect. There is evidence to show that the transfer properties of items can alter with the passage of time. This may be due to wear, washing, or other treatments. As a general rule, garments will shed less through time. Caution should be exercised where

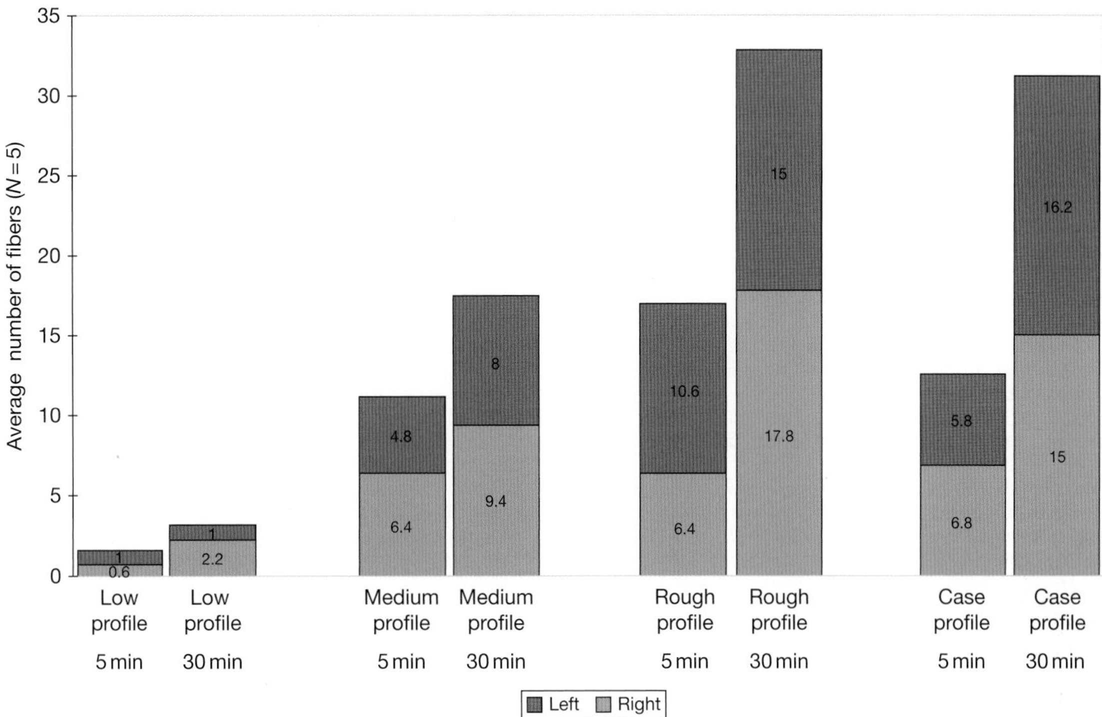

Figure 1 Typical example of comparison of case data with transfer experiments data (transfer of car carpet fibers on different shoe soles in this case).

there is a lengthy time gap between the commission of an offense and suspect items being submitted for examination. This factor also needs to be considered when making a decision as to whether or not to conduct simulation experiments.

Fiber Transfer Modeling

Knowledge of fiber transfer (along with other factors) is crucial to interpret fiber evidence correctly. In particular, such knowledge is necessary if one wishes to answer the question as to whether or not the number of fibers and the number of fiber types found in a given case are likely under the allegation of contact. In other words, knowledge on transfer (and persistence) assists to answer the typical competitive questions 'what is the probability of finding the number of fibers and fiber types found in a given case if there was a contact?' and 'what is the probability of finding the number of fibers and fiber types found in a given case if there was no contact?'

Since 1975, numerous transfer and persistence studies involving fibers have been undertaken. While it is still difficult to completely and accurately model the results, a wealth of information and data is available. General findings and information on how these assessments can be combined in a Bayesian framework are presented elsewhere in this encyclopedia.

Concluding Comments

Ultimately, the type of information that the forensic scientist seeks through fiber transfer should include:

- What is alleged to have taken place – who is involved and how?
- Where is the incident said to have taken place? If it was in a house or in a car, who was the occupier or owner?
- With a sexual assault, did it occur on a bed or on the floor? Is it possible to reconstruct the sequence of events? Were bed covers present and were they moved?
- When did the incident take place and was there any delay before the scene was examined?
- Did any person involved have legitimate access to the scene or legitimate contact with the other person or persons before the incident?
- Are reliable descriptions available of what was being worn by the offender?
- Were items of clothing removed during the incident?

This type of information is necessary if the scientist is to conduct meaningful experiments aimed at reconstructing the events of an alleged incident. There will rarely, if ever, be simple and easy answers to the interpretation of fiber evidence. This will also have to consider aspects described elsewhere in this encyclopedia.

See also: **Chemistry/Trace/Fibers:** Fibers: Overview; Identification and Comparison; Interpretation of Fiber Evidence; Persistence and Recovery.

Further Reading

Bresee RR and Annis PA (1991) Fibre transfer and the influence of fabric softener. *Journal of Forensic Sciences* 36(6): 1699–1713.

Burch HJ (2008) The transfer and persistence of fibres on bare skin. *Thesis Submitted to Centre of Forensic Science*. University of Strathclyde.
Cordiner SJ, Stringer P, and Wilson PD (1985) Fibre diameter and the transfer of wool fibres. *Journal of the Forensic Science Society* 25: 425–426.
Coxon A, Grieve M, and Dunlop J (1992) A method of assessing the fibre shedding potential of fabrics. *Journal of Forensic Sciences* 32(2): 151–158.
De Wael K and Gason F (2008) Microfibre transfer experiments. *Global Forensic Science Today* 4: 31–37.
Grieve MC and Biermann TW (1997) Wool fibres – transfer to vinyl and leather vehicle seats and some observations on their secondary transfer. *Science & Justice* 37(1): 31–38.
Kidd CBM and Robertson J (1982) The transfer of textile fibers during simulated contacts. *Journal of Forensic Science Society* 22: 301–308.
Merciani P, Monard Sermier F, Buzzini P, Massonnet G, and Taroni F (2003) A study of the cross transfer of fibers. *Forensic International* 136(1): 123.
Palmer R and Burch HJ (2009) The population, transfer and persistence of fibres on the skin of living subjects. *Science & Justice* 49(4): 259–264.
Parybyk AE and Lokan RJ (1986) A study of the numerical distribution of fibres transferred from blended products. *Journal of the Forensic Science Society* 26: 61–68.
Pounds CA and Smalldon KW (1975a) The transfer of fibers between clothing materials during simulated contacts and their persistence during wear – part 1: Fibre transference. *Journal of Forensic Science Society* 15: 17–27.
Pounds CA and Smalldon KW (1975b) The transfer of fibers between clothing materials during simulated contacts and their persistence during wear – part 3: A preliminary investigation of mechanisms involved. *Journal of Forensic Science Society* 15: 197–207.
Robertson J and Grieve MC (eds.) (1999) *The Forensic Examination of Fibers*. London: Taylor and Francis.
Robertson J and Lim M (1987a) Fibre transfer and persistence onto car seats and seatbelts. *Canadian Society of Forensic Science Journal* 20(3): 140–141.
Robertson J and Lim M (1987b) Fibre transfer and persistence onto car seats and seatbelts. *Canadian Society of Forensic Science Journal* 20(3): 140–141.
Roux C (1997) *La Valeur Indiciale des Fibers Textiles Decouvertes sur un Siege de Voiture: Problemes et Solutions*. PhD Thesis, University of Lausanne.
Roux C, Chable J, and Margot P (1996) Fibre transfer experiments on to car seats. *Science and Justice* 36: 143–152.
Roux C, Langdon S, Waight D, and Robertson J (1998) The transfer and persistence of automotive carpet fibers on shoe soles. *Science and Justice* 39: 239–251.
Salter M and Cook R (1996) Transfer of fibres to head hair, their persistence and retrieval. *Forensic Science International* 81: 211–221.
Salter MT, Cook R, and Jackson AR (1984) Differential shedding from blended fabrics. *Forensic Science International* 33: 155–164.
Salter MT, Cook R, and Jackson AR (1987) Differential shedding from blended fabrics. *Forensic Science International* 33(3): 155–164.
Siegel JA (1997) Evidential value of textile fibre – transfer and persistence of fibers. *Forensic Science Review* 9: 81–96.
Szewcow R, Robertson J, and Roux CP (2011) The influence of front-loading and top-loading washing machines on the persistence, redistribution and secondary transfer of textile fibres during laundering. *Australian Journal of Forensic Sciences* 43(4): 263–273.
Technical Working Group for Materials Analysis (1997) *Forensic Fiber Examination Guidelines*. Washington DC: Federal Bureau of Investigation.

Persistence and Recovery

C Roux, University of Technology, Sydney, NSW, Australia
J Robertson, University of Canberra, Canberra, ACT, Australia
R Palmer, Northumbria University, Newcastle Upon Tyne, UK

Glossary

Differential loss The rate of loss of different fiber types in a fabric blend may not be the same.
Fiber contamination Contact or fiber transfer between two items, which are alleged to have an association, after the alleged association has occurred.
Method of recovery Method used to recover extraneous fibers on a relevant exhibit.

Introduction

In its most simplistic expression, the Locard exchange principle is usually stated as 'every contact leaves a trace.' It follows that if all traces from a crime were available, one could reconstruct the steps of the events and follow a trail leading back to an individual or a location. In the real world, even when a transfer has taken place, it may not be detected. There are a number of reasons why this may be the case. The amount of material transferred may be so small that it cannot be detected or identified by current techniques. Furthermore, immediately after a transfer the trace material will be subject to loss. The persistence of transferred fibers may be so poor that a transfer cannot be detected at a very short time after transfer. It follows that, in normal circumstances, it is generally only possible to propose that a contact has taken place; it is not possible to prove that a contact has not taken place. This article provides an overview of fiber persistence and the significance of this topic in the interpretation of fiber evidence.

The assumption is, however, that every effort has been made to recover fibers after transfer. As a result, this article also provides an overview of the methods available and the approaches used for the recovery and preservation of fiber evidence from items submitted to the laboratory and those present at a crime scene. The methods and approaches to the recovery of fiber evidence outlined in this section should enable the reader to gain an appreciation of the practical issues and problems faced by the forensic fiber examiner in this primary, but crucial, aspect of fiber examination.

Persistence

Studies since the 1970s by a number of key groups of workers including Pounds and Smalldon, Grieve, Robertson, and Roux have provided a sound basis for an understanding of the factors to be considered in the interpretation of the transfer and persistence of fibers in forensic investigations.

Persistence is the part of the equation contributing to whether or not fibers will be found following a transfer. Whatever may be the number of fibers transferred, and almost irrespective of the nature of the recipient surface, there is an initial rapid loss of fibers. This can be as high as 80% in the first few hours with as little as only a few percent remaining after 24 h (Figure 1). Hence, it is essential that every effort be made to collect relevant items from complainants and suspects as soon as possible after an alleged incident.

In some circumstances, fiber loss may not follow the classic loss curve. For example, fibers transferred to car interiors will display the classic curve but the time frame is extended and fibers may be retained for weeks as compared to hours or days with garment-to-garment contacts. Fibers have also been shown to have been retained for longer periods in open-air settings and indefinitely on the bodies or clothing of a homicide victim. In both the latter examples, the weather can play an important role. Other special situations include persistence of fibers transferred to hair, where grooming, including hair washing, is the key factor, and persistence on shoes. In the last example, persistence is normally very poor and fibers persist for only minutes unless there are special reasons such as the presence of a sticky substance or deposit on the shoe sole.

Factors Affecting Persistence

The loss of transferred fibers will start immediately after the contact which resulted in the transfer. A number of factors have been shown to have an influence on the rate of this loss. These include the following:

- force or pressure of contact – persistence is poorer when the contact is light;
- the location of the contact – fibers are lost more rapidly from areas which are more prone to contact with other surfaces;
- wearing of the recipient garment – fibers are lost more rapidly when the wearer moves after contact; and
- placement of other clothing in contact with area of transfer – fibers are lost more rapidly when other clothing is worn over or on top of the recipient.

Effect of Fiber Size and Morphology

Persistence of short fibers under 2.5 mm in length is greater than longer fibers. A special case is that of microfibers. These show the same overall pattern of fiber loss but have greater persistence compared with 'natural' fibers. This is especially the case with the transfer of microfibers to microfiber garments.

 http://dx.doi.org/10.1016/B978-0-12-382165-2.00090-8

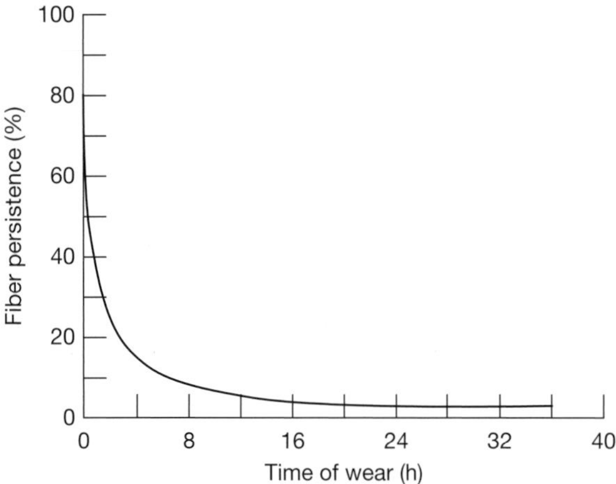

Figure 1 General persistence of fibers on clothing.

Differential Loss

Smooth polyester fibers have been shown to be lost more rapidly than viscose fibers. In general, it cannot be assumed that the rate of loss of different fiber types in a fabric blend will be the same. Hence, over a period of time, this factor will add to the potential difference in the ratio of transferred fibers noted earlier. In an extreme example, it may be that one or more type(s) of fiber from a blend may not be recovered. This makes the interpretation of the source fabric difficult unless an explanation can be demonstrated.

Effect of Garment Cleaning

Studies on the effect of a variety of forms of cleaning have shown that cleaning results in the loss of fibers, but of more importance it is still possible to recover fibers after cleaning. In general, caution needs to be exercised in interpreting the significance of a contact based on the location of recovered fibers because of their potential for redistribution. This is especially the case when a garment may have been cleaned.

Fiber Binding

Three states of binding have been proposed to explain the persistence of fibers after garment-to-garment contact. These are loosely bound, bound, and strongly bound states. It is suggested that loosely bound and bound fibers are lost first and strongly bound fibers become physically trapped in the weave of recipient fabrics. The method of recovery should be selected to maximize the chances of recovering fibers of evidential significance.

Fiber Redistribution

It is important to note that persistence may also involve transferred fibers moving from the point of transfer and being redistributed. The potential for this to occur clearly depends on the amount of movement the recipient garment or item experiences. In the case of a static deceased person redistribution, for example, fiber redistribution will be minimal (although this may happen when a body is removed to the morgue). In other case scenarios, there may be considerable potential for fiber redistribution. As indicated above, a classic situation would be where clothing is washed. Hence, while the location of recovered fibers should be considered, caution needs to be exercised where the circumstances post-transfer are not clear.

Methods of Recovery

There are various methods of fiber recovery available, the choice of which may be determined by the circumstances of the case, condition and nature of the exhibit, and personal preference of the examiner. Whatever methods of recovery are employed, they should be

- simple (easy to use);
- rapid (time efficient);
- efficient (optimal recovery);
- preserve the evidence (prevent contamination); and
- allow easy subsequent searching (time efficient).

Arguably, some of the methods available may fit these criteria better than others. The relative merits and disadvantages of each are considered here. Fiber examiners should also be reminded about the potential for the recovery of trace biological materials when developing a search strategy.

Visual Search

This method is clearly the simplest method of fiber recovery. A visual search of an item may often reveal transferred textile material, whether in the form of tufts or single fibers. Such a search can often be performed using a simple hand lens and is well suited to situations, such as burglary, where the perpetrator has left fibers at a point of entry, such as a broken window. This can also be considered when dealing with weapons such as knives, or with clothing from a body which has been transported in an item, such as a carpet, and subsequently dumped. Such material can be removed using forceps and then placed in a sealed, labeled container, pending further examination. The advantage of this approach is that the recovered fibers can be rapidly removed from the container for subsequent examination without having to be searched for amidst 'background' debris. This method is particularly useful where the item in question (such as a shoe) which, although poorly retentive in itself, may have fibers trapped in crevices or on some adhering medium, such as chewing gum. The detection and recovery of fibers in such circumstances can be greatly aided by the use of low-power stereomicroscopy. This method should be considered before any other is attempted.

Since fibers are mainly transferred in the form of single tiny fragments, rather than visible tufts or threads and are, therefore, not usually obvious to the unaided eye, other methods of recovery and searching of general fiber debris from an item have to be employed.

Surface Debris Tapings

Extraneous fibers can be recovered from the surface of a garment or other item by the use of transparent adhesive tape. This is achieved by taking the length of such a tape, holding it adhesive side down, and systematically dabbing the surface of the item in question (**Figure 2**). The tape is then stuck down onto a clear plastic sheet, effectively preserving the recovered debris. This process is repeated until all of the surfaces in question have been covered. Completed tapings are then clearly labeled and placed in an appropriately labeled grease-proof envelope or similar receptacle. As an alternative, the tape can be attached to a 'roller' (available from hardware stores and normally used to press down wallpaper edges) which is systematically rolled across the garment, replacing the tape as necessary. This method allows a greater degree of control of the pressure applied to the taping and hence the efficiency of recovery.

In addition to providing an efficient means of preserving the collected fiber debris, surface debris taping also allows easy subsequent searching using low-power stereomicroscopy. The area of tape around any potential fiber match is marked and a 'window' cut around the fiber in question using a scalpel (**Figure 3**).

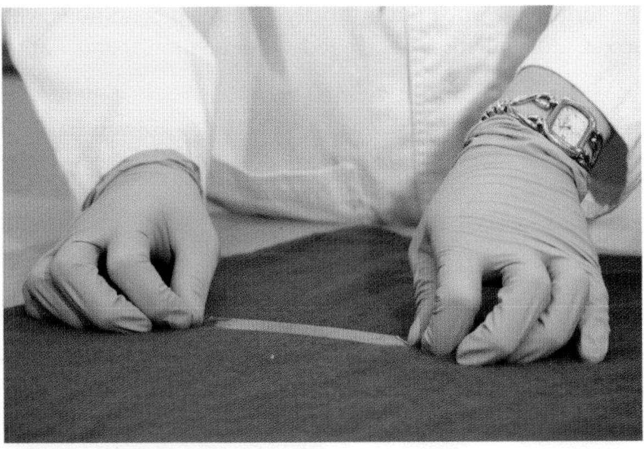

Figure 2 Recovering fiber debris from a garment using clear adhesive tape.

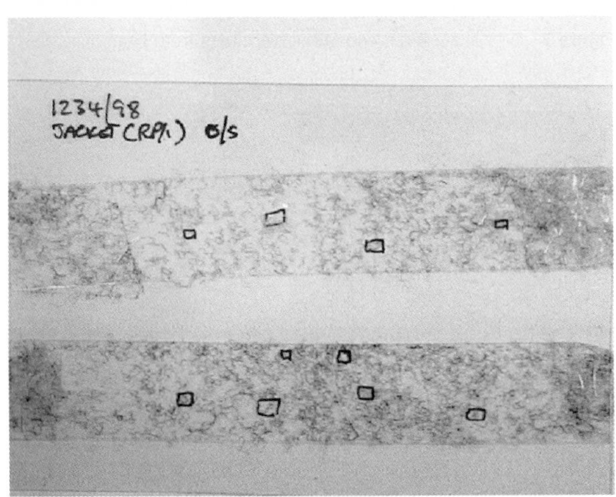

Figure 3 Tapings bearing fiber debris stuck onto acetate sheet. Note marked areas indicating potential 'matches.'

Using an appropriate solvent, the fiber is removed and mounted directly onto a microscope slide using a suitable mounting medium (**Figures** 4 and 5). The microscope slide is appropriately labeled and placed in a covered slide tray, again which has been appropriately labeled.

Care should be taken to prevent overloading the tape, that is, picking up too many 'background' fibers ('background' fibers refer to fibers which are part of the construction of the recipient garment, or any other extraneous fibers present on the item's surface which are not targeted). In addition to making it more difficult to search (as one has to search through all the 'background' fibers), this also reduces the adhesive ability of the tape and therefore seriously compromises the efficiency of recovery. It is, therefore, better to use many tapes on a given item, as this will optimize the efficiency of recovery by reducing 'overloading' and, in turn, aid subsequent searching. This problem can also be alleviated to a certain extent by using a low-adhesive tape on items which readily shed their constituent fibers, or where a high applied pressure of taping using 'rollers' is employed.

Scraping

This technique involves suspending the item in question above a collection funnel or sheet of paper and scraping the debris from the item onto the recipient item. The debris is

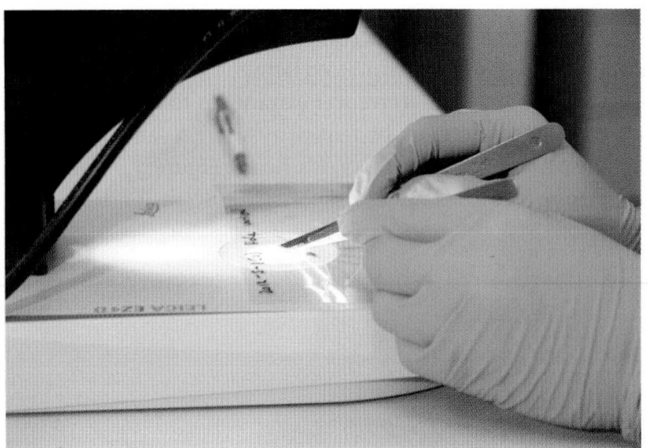

Figure 4 Searching for and removing matching fibers from surface debris tapings using stereomicroscopy.

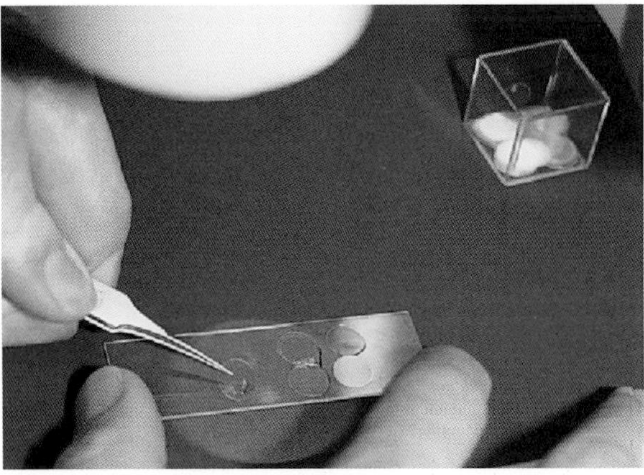

Figure 5 Mounting recovered fibers onto a microscope slide.

subsequently transferred to a Petri dish or a similar receptacle. Where a collection funnel is used, the debris falls directly into the receptacle. This method of collection can be useful for items which are soiled, or where several types of trace evidence are to be recovered simultaneously. However, some concerns have been raised over the efficiency of this method and its high risk for contamination. In addition, this method also removes any potential for location interpretation. As a result, this method is not universally regarded as best suited for the recovery of fiber evidence.

Vacuuming

This technique uses a modified vacuum cleaner with a collection filter incorporated into the hose system. This method is useful for items with large surface areas such as carpets, and items which are soiled with particulate debris, such as car footwells. The main disadvantages with this method are that the apparatus must be scrupulously cleaned to prevent contamination and the fact that it tends to be (ironically) too efficient, in that it indiscriminately recovers large masses of irrelevant debris, making searching for target fibers difficult. The efficiency of this method of collection also varies between different machines.

Combing

This method uses a 'seeded' comb, that is, a hair comb to which cotton wool has been introduced between the teeth (Figure 6). This is used primarily to recover extraneous fibers from hair in cases of armed robbery or terrorism where a fabric mask has been worn over the perpetrator's head (Figure 7). The introduction of cotton wool between the teeth of the comb increases the efficiency of collection by introducing a highly retentive collection surface to the recovery system. Studies have shown that such fibers transferred from such garments can persist on the head hair for considerable periods of time, even after washing. This method can also be applied in cases of rape, where it is suspected that fibers may have been transferred to the pubis of the victim or assailant.

Once the comb has been passed through the suspect's hair, the cotton wool (and the comb) is examined for the presence of fibers using stereomicroscopy. Since cotton wool is (generally) white, this also aids detection of transferred fibers. Any such fibers found are removed directly and mounted onto a microscope slide (Figure 8).

Care must of course be taken to ensure that the comb and cotton wool used are free from contaminants. The comb should be provided in a sealed tamper-evident bag and not used if the packaging appears compromised.

Figure 6 The seeded comb.

Choice of Recovery Method

In considering the various methods of recovery of fiber evidence, it is important to distinguish between a laboratory environment and that encountered at the crime scene. Whereas the former is carried out in strictly controlled conditions with access to microscopes, good illumination, and other

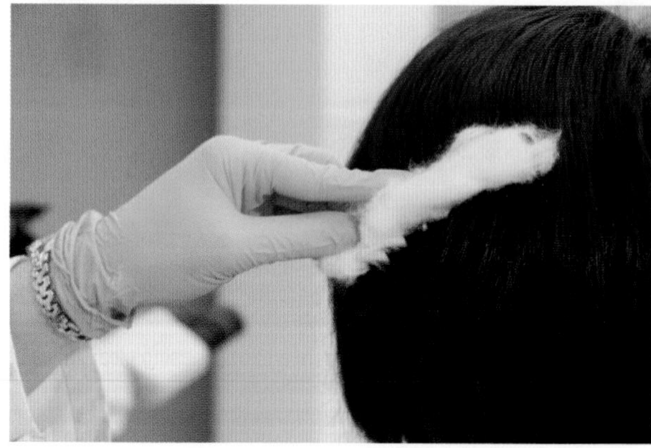

Figure 7 Use of seeded comb to recover fibers from head hair.

Figure 8 Searching for recovered fibers on the seeded comb.

instrumentation, the latter is often performed under difficult circumstances, where the environment is unpredictable, dirty, and poorly illuminated, with limited access to specialist equipment. Although many crime scenes are outdoors, and weather conditions may not be conducive to the recovery of trace evidence, experience and data from published studies have nevertheless shown that significant evidence can still be recovered in these circumstances. In such situations, the analyst will be confronted with what is essentially a damage limitation exercise, using whatever methods are appropriate to the conditions – even though they may not be (under ideal conditions) the most efficient.

Given a crime scene indoors and sheltered, the opportunity presents itself to recover fibers immediately, minimizing any potential losses and contamination. In cases of murder, it is appropriate to take surface debris tapings from the clothing and skin of the deceased *in situ*. A close visual search of the body (particularly the hands) prior to taping may also reveal fibers which can be removed by forceps. This approach minimizes any potential losses and/or contamination that may occur as a result of the body being removed from the scene to the morgue.

The so-called 'one to one' (1:1) taping may be employed. This is a method whereby surface debris tapings are placed over the exposed surfaces of the body and clothing. The position of each of these tapings is cataloged. Any recovered fibers subsequently recovered from these tapings can therefore be associated with a particular location on the deceased's body, allowing a 'distribution map' of any transferred fibers to be built up. This may provide useful additional evidence in certain circumstances. However, 1:1 taping is very time-consuming. For this reason, some forensic organizations have introduced a more pragmatic recovery method called 'zonal taping.' In this method, tapings are used and cataloged according to the location of the garment; for example, one taping is used for the front left sleeve, another one for the front right sleeve, etc. Zonal taping appears to be a good compromise between workload accurate information about the fibers' location on the recipient. It should be pointed out that fiber mapping using 1:1 or zonal taping is only appropriate when the body has been relatively undisturbed and has not been deposited from the primary murder scene (i.e., fibers likely to have been redistributed). In all cases, caution must be exercised when interpreting data obtained through these methods. Clothing removed from an individual is usually packed in a bag prior to submission to the lab, and, hence, fibers may be redistributed from one area of the garment to another during transit.

It can be seen then, that although the crime scene can present some technical difficulties in the recovery of fiber evidence, it can, in certain circumstances, present opportunities to maximize recovery and provide additional information. Although it may be the case that one particular method of fiber recovery is routinely employed by a particular laboratory, it may be that the circumstances of a particular case (whether at the crime scene or in the lab) dictate that a method other than the particular 'norm' is more appropriate. It is important that each of the above methods of recovery is not seen in isolation, as it is not unusual that a combination of some or all of the above methods becomes appropriate in certain circumstances. Given that the object is to recover and preserve fiber evidence, there is nothing to be gained and literally everything to be lost through blinkered thinking and an inflexible approach.

Documentation and Packaging

Whichever method of fiber recovery is employed, it is imperative that the recovered material is preserved in a manner which prevents loss and contamination until such times that it can be examined. We cannot stress enough the importance of handling items to ensure minimal redistribution and loss of fibers.

Since it is often the case that material is recovered by an individual other than the analyst, it is vital that any such material is clearly and unambiguously labeled as this information may become vital in demonstrating to the court the continuity, integrity, and significance of its recovery. Even where the analyst is the person recovering the material, the same scrupulous approach must be taken for the same reasons. Since it is not unusual for fiber debris to be recovered from many items in a given investigation, a meticulous approach to this aspect of documentation will have the added benefit that it is easier for the analyst to develop an examination strategy when it is known exactly what there is to work with.

The debris should be packaged using a suitable receptacle (ranging from a simple envelope to a brown paper sack) which should be securely sealed, preferably with some form of tamper-evident system. Such a system can simply be achieved by a signed label stuck underneath a clear sealing tape. The label, bearing the relevant information regarding the sample, should be securely attached to the outside of the packaging. This, of course, also applies to clothing and other items.

Where fiber debris is recovered and packaged at a scene, details should be recorded in a register by a designated exhibits officer. Since the significance of the material recovered from a scene of a crime may not become evident for many weeks or even years after a crime, it is vital to be able to establish what was actually recovered, from where, and by whom. Details of where and when a particular item was stored prior to its examination should also be recorded. The meticulous cataloging of a recovered exhibit can make the difference between a breakthrough being made in a long-running investigation and the investigation coming to a 'dead end' due to a crucial item being left on a shelf in a store somewhere, with its existence and significance long forgotten.

On receipt at the laboratory, the condition of the packaging and labeling should be noted and any problems likely to compromise any potential evidence should result in the item in question being rejected for examination. The examiner should also document the location, time, and date at which the item was examined and a detailed description of the item and recovered debris should be made in his/her notes. Again, this is crucial in demonstrating to the court the continuity and integrity of any evidentially significant findings.

Contamination Issues

Since fibers can be readily transferred, care must be taken to insure that this does not work against the examiner in the form of inadvertent contamination. 'Contamination' in this context refers to contact or fiber transfer between two items which are alleged to have an association, after the alleged association has occurred. Clearly, if contamination can be demonstrated, then any subsequent demonstration of fiber transfer between the items in question will have no evidential value. In addition to preventing contamination by keeping questioned items separate, care must also be taken to prevent the secondary transfer of fibers between items. An example of the secondary transfer of fibers might be when a victim of a crime has been transported in a police car, which is subsequently used to transport a suspect. In such a situation, there is a distinct possibility that fibers from the victim could be transferred to the car seat and these in turn transferred to a suspect's clothing.

It is of utmost importance to implement measures to prevent contamination before the recovery of fibers begins. The following are examples of such measures:

- victim and accused should be transported in separate cars;
- victim and accused should be interviewed and/or examined in separate rooms;
- clothing should be packaged in separate rooms by different individuals; and
- protective clothing (such as paper boiler suits) should be used at crime scenes to avoid the introduction of fiber material to the scene and/or to prevent transfer of material to items potentially associated with that particular scene.

Once at the laboratory, care must again be taken by the examiner to prevent primary or secondary fiber transfer between questioned items before any potential fiber evidence has been recovered and preserved. Methods to prevent such contamination at the laboratory are:

- the integrity of the labeling and packaging of items received at the laboratory should be checked;
- questioned items should be examined and material recovered from each in separate rooms, ideally in different parts of the laboratory;
- instruments such as forceps, etc., lab coats, and other items involved in the examination should be peculiar to each room and be left there after each examination;
- adhesive tapes used in recovery should be kept packaged;
- examination benches, collection funnels, and vacuum equipment should be thoroughly cleaned before and after use;
- examiners should also wash their hands before entering and leaving a room where fiber recovery is about to be, or has been performed; and
- since fibers are minute entities, care should be taken that any air handling/conditioning system does not potentially blow these away from or around the recovery area.

It is also important to note the clear distinction between these 'genuine' contaminations which may be introduced due to less-than-perfect handling contaminations and inevitable background fibers coming from the recipient fabric.

Conclusion

An understanding of the factors which impact on the persistence of fibers is critical if the forensic scientist is to interpret what meaning should be attached to the finding of fibers thought to be of evidential significance. As the circumstances of each case are different, each case must be considered on its own merits.

Once fibers have been transferred to a particular area of a garment they can also be redistributed over the garment and indeed onto other garments. All of the clothing worn may not have been submitted for examination. If only a small number of fibers are found on items, it may be because:

- there has been a long time gap between contact/transfer and examination;
- the fibers have arrived on these garments by redistribution;
- of a secondary or subsequent transfer;
- the recovery method was not efficient; or
- transfer is coincidental and not real.

It follows that:

- because fibers are so readily lost and retransferred, undue significance should not be placed on the exact distribution of a small number of fibers;
- unless a suspect is apprehended fairly quickly, subsequent to an incident, failure to find fibers matching the complainant's clothing does not necessarily imply lack of contact;
- evidence of contact and hence association found through comparison of transferred fibers will generally be of recent ones;
- it is vital to the integrity of fiber evidence that good contamination prevention procedures are in place; and
- as the time of wear increases, those fibers which do remain will be very persistent and difficult to remove, hence efficient methods of recovery need to be used.

It cannot be overemphasized that the subsequent analysis and interpretation of fiber evidence is dependent on getting this relatively simple aspect of fiber examination correct the first time, as mistakes during recovery cannot be rectified later.

See also: **Chemistry/Trace/Fibers:** Fibers: Overview; Identification and Comparison; Interpretation of Fiber Evidence; Transfer.

Further Reading

Akulova V, Vasiliauskiene D, and Talaliene D (2002) Further insights into the persistence of transferred fibres on outdoor clothes. *Science and Justice* 42(3): 165–171.

Ashcroft CM, Evans S, and Tebbett IR (1988) The persistence of fibres in head hair. *Journal of the Forensic Science Society* 28: 289–293.

Burch HJ (2008) *The Transfer and Persistence of Fibres on Bare Skin. Thesis Submitted to Centre of Forensic Science*, University of Strathclyde.

Chewning DD, Deaver KL, and Christensen AM (2008) Persistence of fibers on ski masks during transit and processing. *Forensic Science Communications* 10(3).

Fisher BAJ and Svensson W (1987) *Techniques of Crime Scene Investigation*, 4th edn. New York: Elsevier.

Krauss W and Doderer U (2009) Fibre persistence on skin under open-air conditions. *Global Forensic Science Today* 9: 11–16. www.global-forensic-science-today.net.

Lowrie CN and Jackson G (1991) Recovery of transferred fibres. *Forensic Science International* 50: 111–119.

Moore J, Jackson G, and Firth M (1984) The movement of fibres between working areas as a result of routine examination of garments. *Journal of the Forensic Science Society* 24: 394.

Nehse K (1999) Fibre investigation in the Berlin lab – Significance and use of 1:1 taping seen in examples of different cases. In: *Proceedings of the 7th European Fibres Group Meeting*, Zurich, June, pp. 51–57.

Palmer R (1998) The retention and recovery of transferred fibers following washing of recipient clothing. *Journal of Forensic Sciences* 43(3): 502–504.
Palmer R and Burch HJ (2009) The population, transfer and persistence of fibres on the skin of living subjects. *Science and Justice* 49(4): 259–264.
Palmer R and Polwarth G (2011) The persistence of fibres on skin in an outdoor deposition crime scene scenario. *Science and Justice* 51(4): 187–189.
Pounds CA (1975) The recovery of fibres from the surface of clothing for forensic examinations. *Journal of the Forensic Science Society* 15: 127–132.
Pounds CA and Smalldon KW (1975a) The transfer of fibers between clothing materials during simulated contacts and their persistence during wear – Part 2: Fiber persistence. *Journal of the Forensic Science Society* 15: 29–37.
Pounds CA and Smalldon KW (1975b) The transfer of fibers between clothing materials during simulated contacts and their persistence during wear – Part 3: A preliminary investigation of mechanisms involved. *Journal of the Forensic Science Society* 15: 197–207.
Robertson J and Grieve MC (eds.) (1999) *The Forensic Examination of Fibers*. London: Taylor and Francis.
Robertson J, Kidd CBM, and Parkinson HMP (1982a) The persistence of textile fibers transferred during simulated contacts. *Journal of the Forensic Science Society* 22: 353–360.
Robertson J, Kidd CBM, and Parkinson HMP (1982b) The persistence of textile fibres transferred during simulated contacts. *Journal of the Forensic Science Society* 22: 353–360.
Robertson J and Lim M (1987) Fibre transfer and persistence onto car seats and seatbelts. *Canadian Society of Forensic Science Journal* 20(3): 140–141.
Robertson J and Olaniyan D (1986) Effect of garment cleaning on the recovery and redistribution of transferred fibres. *Journal of Forensic Sciences* 31(1): 73–78.
Roux C, Huttunen J, Rampling K, and Robertson J (2001) Factors affecting the potential for fibre contamination in purpose-designed forensic search rooms. *Science and Justice* 41: 135–144.
Roux C, Langdon S, Waight D, and Robertson J (1998) The transfer and persistence of automotive carpet fibers on shoe soles. *Science and Justice* 39: 239–251.
Salter M and Cook R (1996) Transfer of fibres to head hair, their persistence and retrieval. *Forensic Science International* 81: 211–221.
Scott HG (1985) The persistence of fibres transferred during contact of automobile carpets and clothing fabrics. *Journal of the Canadian Forensic Science Society* 18(4): 185–199.
Siegel JA (1997) Evidential value of textile fibre – Transfer and persistence of fibers. *Forensic Science Review* 9: 81–96.
Szewcow R, Robertson J, and Roux CP (2011) The influence of front-loading and top-loading washing machines on the persistence, redistribution and secondary transfer of textile fibres during laundering. *Australian Journal of Forensic Sciences* 43(4): 263–273.
Technical Working Group for Materials Analysis (1997) *Forensic Fiber Examination Guidelines*. Washington, DC: Federal Bureau of Investigation.

Fiber: Protocols for Examination

J Robertson, University of Canberra, Canberra, ACT, Australia
C Roux, University of Technology, Sydney, NSW, Australia

Introduction

The search for extraneous fibers is based on the proposition that contact has or has not occurred between a suspect, a victim, and/or a scene relevant to what is alleged to be a crime. Where contact is established, this will rarely be at a level where there are no alternative explanations and, hence, the role of the fiber examiner extends beyond technical and scientific analysis to that of interpretation in the context of an investigation, perhaps as a component of forensic intelligence, and ultimately in the resolution of legal dispute, in the court.

In order for the fiber 'evidence' to contribute to any of the above elements, the potential for fibers must firstly be recognized at the crime scene. This responsibility usually falls on the crime scene examiner (CSE). As fibers are a form of physical evidence, and are most often essentially not visible to the naked eye, the CSE must have a knowledge of the potential value of fiber examination, of the ways in which fibers may 'present' or be found at various types of scene, and of the correct way to recover and maintain the integrity of potential fiber evidence. The role of the CSE in the recognition, recording, and recovery of fibers is considered elsewhere in this encyclopedia. The importance of the work done by the CSE to the success or failure of subsequent laboratory examinations simply cannot be overstated.

Laboratory Protocols for Fiber Examination

In order to conduct a complete and meaningful examination, the laboratory fiber examiner may have to visit the crime scene or request the collection of additional samples. In more complex matters, it is highly recommended that the fiber examiner visits the crime scene, or, at the very least, has an early and full discussion with the investigator about the case circumstances. Fiber examinations can be complex and very time consuming and it is essential that fiber examinations are considered and managed in the context of other forensic examinations and the likelihood fiber examination can answer questions of relevance. Decisions regarding fiber examination need to be taken in case context and these decisions need to be taken at the earliest possible time and frequently reviewed. Active case management is essential for successful and meaningful fiber examinations.

It is a relatively rare event for the fiber examiner to actually receive 'fibers,' rather, the examiner is usually presented with a number of items of clothing, bedding, tape lifts, or other samples collected at the scene(s). The fiber examiner needs to carefully consider the nature of the items received, liaise with forensic disciplines as to what other forensic examination are to be conducted, and then determine the sequence of forensic examinations. As fibers are most often too small to be readily seen by the naked eye (80% are under 2 mm), and they are subject to loss and relocation, it is important that where a decision is made to recover fibers, fiber examination should be one of the first, if not the first, examinations in the overall examinations strategy.

As modern DNA analysis is capable of producing a profile from trace biological material, the fiber examiner and the biological criminalist need to work together to first take samples for trace biological material. This may involve taking a tape lift or sometimes a swab.

Guiding rules for fiber recovery include:

- follow the GIFT principle, or 'get it first time' – this includes scene recovery;
- treat items to be searched gently to minimize loss or disturbance of trace materials;
- if trace materials are visible, remove by hand or using forceps;
- systematically tape lift items using a grid search pattern;
- do not shake or scrape items as these techniques have been shown to be inefficient and will also destroy location evidence; and
- as a final technique, vacuuming may be considered but this is normally only used for large and difficult-to-access areas.

In many circumstances, clothing will be involved. Here, damage interpretations may be required. This is a specialist area and is considered elsewhere in this encyclopedia. Textile damage should not be conducted until the relevant item has been examined for trace physical materials.

Relevant items of clothing should be searched and physical materials recovered as above. For fibers, most often, this will mean tape lifts being taken and, hence, tape lifts will be the starting point in the protocol for examination. For known items (an item from a known source such as an alleged victim or suspect), both yarns and tape lifts should be taken to ensure that the full fiber composition of the item is known. A tape lift is insufficient, as some fabrics will have surface and backing yarns, which are not usually available for transfer. However, the tape lift is more likely to show what fibers are available for transfer.

Figure 1 shows a typical flow diagram for fiber examination.

Initial examination of fibers from known samples is aimed at describing the fiber types, comprising the fabric from which fibers may have transferred. This examination uses both low- and high-power microscopy. This preliminary examination is capable of establishing the number of fiber types present in an item, an assessment of the generic fiber types present (at least natural vs. man-made), and the colors of fibers present. In order to fully identify the types of fibers present, samples of each fiber type should be placed in a suitable microscopic mountant with a refractive index in the order of 1.48–1.49.

 http://dx.doi.org/10.1016/B978-0-12-382165-2.00091-X

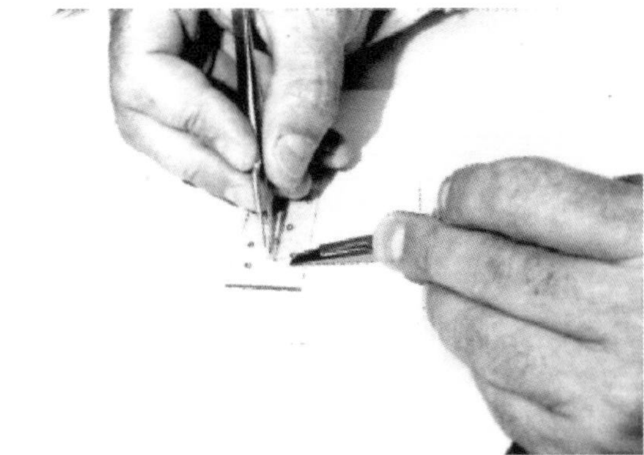

(a) Window being cut in tape lift.

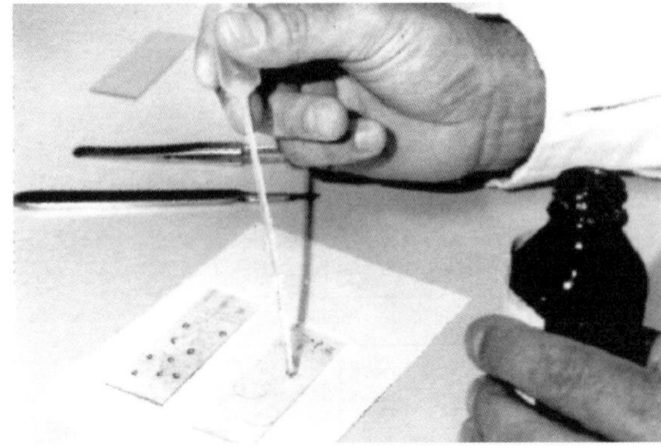

(b) Recovered fiber being placed in mountant on a slide.

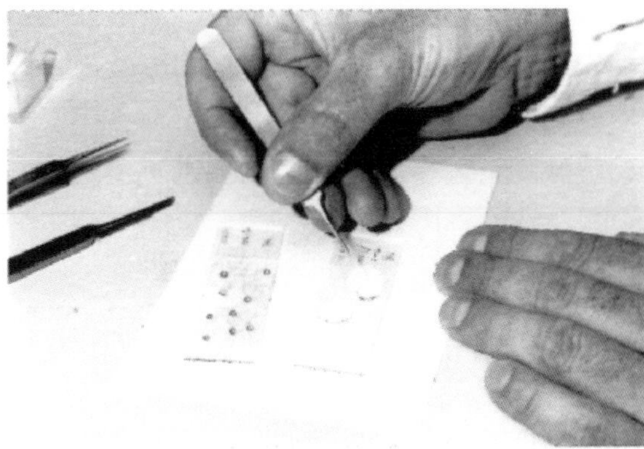

(c) Fiber and mountant being covered with a glass coverslip.

Figure 1 The preparation of 'questioned' fibers for further examination. Note: Gloves are not being worn as this is post evidence recovery for DNA testing.

Mounted fibers can then be examined using transmitted light microscopy and polarized light microscopy (PLM). An experienced microscopist can identify many, if not all, fiber types based on PLM examination. In many laboratories, PLM is only used as a method to differentiate fibers with low and high optical activity, with Fourier transform infrared (FTIR) spectroscopy being used to 'identify' fiber types. FTIR spectroscopy is not actually able to provide absolute identity for a fiber (e.g., it cannot identify different types of animal and, respectively, vegetable fibers, and this is still a comparison technique).

The fiber examiner armed with a knowledge of the various fiber types, comprising known and questioned items, then selects the best target fibers. Target fibers are those, which are sheddable and are of a color, which make them amenable for searching. This is not to say that there are no circumstances in which a fiber type not meeting these criteria will not have forensic value, as each case needs to be assessed with its own unique circumstances. For example, there are situations where a colorless fiber may have evidential value, especially if it is an uncommon fiber type. Conversely, a common fiber type such as blue denim cotton, generally considered a poor target fiber, may be significant in the specific context of a case.

Once target fiber types have been selected, recovered fibers, usually on tape lifts, are then searched with the aid of low-power microscopy. Fibers in the color range of the known target, and of the same microscopic appearance, are marked so that they can be individually removed and prepared for a more detailed examination. As this searching process can be time consuming and tedious, a number of commercial fiber finders were developed in the 1980s and 1990s. Mostly, fiber finders have fallen out of favor as they do not work well with many of the fibers types' color combinations commonly encountered in real casework. Figure 2 shows the preparation of individual 'questioned' fibers for further examination.

Subsequent examination of recovered/questioned fibers consists of three aspects:

- more detailed microscopic examination;
- color analysis; and
- fiber identification.

All three aspects are considered in three separate articles elsewhere in this encyclopedia and hence only considered in outline in this treatment.

Microscopic Examination

As previously stated, a full description of the microscopic feature of fibers can only be achieved with fibers placed in a suitable mountant. With a combination of transmitted light microscopy and PLM, it is possible to reach a high degree of certainty as to the type of fiber present and variation in color in a representative fiber sample. An additional valuable feature is fluorescence. Fluorescence is detected when the absorbing fiber is excited with energy of a given wavelength and emits light of equal or longer wavelength (equal or lower energy). Fluorescence can arise from a number of different sources: from the fiber itself, from dyes, or from optical brighteners and other finishing agents added to the fiber. It is important to recognize that the fluorescent properties of fibers may also be altered, for example, by the use of optical brighteners from detergents or due to wear. For this reason, differences in fluorescence intensity are generally not considered to be meaningful, unlike differences of emission (i.e., color or fluorescence vs. no fluorescence at all).

Animal fibers and vegetable fibers require specialist knowledge and expertise, which may not be possessed by all fiber examiners. However, the identification of wool and cotton at

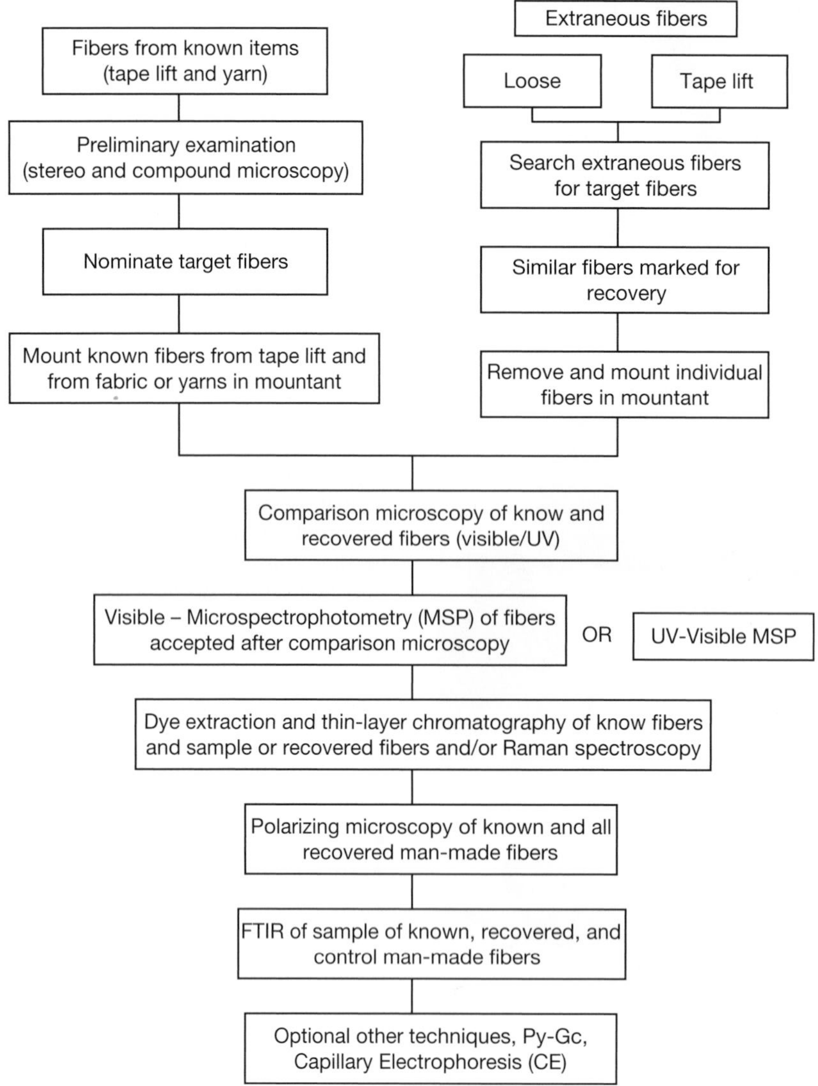

Figure 2 Flow diagram for forensic fiber examination.

the generic level is relatively straightforward. There are specific protocols for the examination of both animal and vegetable fibers, which are beyond the scope of this article. The reader is referred to Robertson and Grieve for a more detailed treatment.

Color Analysis

Color is assessed at the visual microscopic level using low- and high-power microscopy. This is a qualitative assessment and relies to some extent on the examiner's perceptions. Color can be quantitatively analyzed either using *in situ* techniques, such as microspectrophotometry (MSP) or Raman spectroscopy, or following extraction of the dye components with a variety of chromatographic techniques.

Microscopic assessment of color remains an important part of color assessment and, in particular, is used at the selection stage for recovered/questioned fibers. It is also used to select known fibers to ensure that color variation is represented.

Where possible, the fiber examiner would always prefer to assess color *in situ* and not have to extract the dye components. This is preferable because it does not alter or destroy the recovered fiber. MSP is used to assess color and can achieve high levels of discrimination for many colors. However, it has less discrimination for some common colors such as gray or black. Raman spectroscopy has great promise for fiber examination. This technique provides information about the chemical composition of the fiber (complimentary to FTIR spectroscopy) and can also reveal information about the dye components. Raman has some limitations including problems with fluorescence and the need for multiple lasers to produce the Raman excitation.

Finally, extraction protocols exist for fiber dyes, which can give a guide to the class of dyestuff and provide an extract for chromatographic analysis. Commonly, the latter involves thin-layer chromatography (TLC). Historically, attempts made to use high-performance liquid chromatography and capillary electrophoresis have met with disappointing results. However, newer instrumentation still holds out the hope that either, or both, techniques may still play a role in the analysis of dye components. This is especially the case when the chromatographic technique is hyphenated with the newest generation of mass spectrometers (e.g., time-of-flight mass spectrometers).

In summary, forensic laboratories today still rely on a combination of microscopic assessment, MSP, and, where practical, dye extraction and TLC analysis.

Fiber Identification

As previously discussed, microscopy, transmitted or bright field and polarized light, is a core technique in the identification of fibers. For fibers of animal and vegetable origin, microscopic examination is central to their identification. The latter requires significant experience and practice. For fibers of man-made origin, microscopy can be used to identify many fibers to at least generic class. In experienced hands, PLM can achieve very high levels of individualization and fiber identity. However, many forensic laboratories now only use polarizing microscopy as a screening tool to differentiate man-made fibers into those with low optical activity (less crystalline) and those with high optical activity (more crystalline). Optical activity is measured by the birefringence value of fibers.

By using a first-order red plate, it is possible to separate fibers with low birefringence from those with high birefringence. Low-birefringence fibers appear blue or orange, depending on their orientation relative to the first-order plate and polarize light. Fibers with low birefringence include acrylic, cellulose acetate, and viscose fibers. In fact, acrylics have a negative birefringence which, used with caution, is a valuable generic identification feature.

Fibers with high birefringence include nylon and polyester fibers. Viewed with a first-order plate, these fibers have a range of colors across their breadth. More accurate determination of birefringence can then be calculated, if necessary, using a compensator.

Before the introduction of modern instrumental techniques, solubility tests were commonly used to assist in identifying fibers. These are now used to a much more limited degree. However, solubility tests can still provide useful backup data to instrumental techniques and can be a very simple method to differentiate fibers having similar microscopic features. Solubility test is still worth considering in any protocol for fiber identification.

Infrared spectroscopy is a well-established technique for identification of organic materials. Its limitation for the examination of fibers historically had been the size of sample required for the analysis. With dispersive instruments, the use of anvil-type diamond cells meant that it was possible to work with individual fibers of about 0.5 cm in length. With the advent of FTIR spectroscopy, with associated infrared microscope attachments, sample preparation became simpler although use may still be made of a microdiamond cell. With the current technology, sample size is determined by what is large enough to be recovered and handled successfully. Thus, it is possible to remove a millimeter or less from a larger fragment of several millimeters, leaving the rest of the fiber for further testing.

It is important to understand that, while IR spectroscopy is considered to be a technique, which can be used to identify a fiber, there are limitations. Primarily, IR spectroscopy gives information about molecular structure, particularly the recognition of functional groups (such as OH, CH_3, and NH_2) and their molecular environment. The way in which a fiber is prepared does influence the fine detail of the spectra obtained. The main consideration here is in the extent to which the fiber is flattened. Some flattening is essential to get sufficient energy transmitted through the fiber substance. To obtain reproducible results, the technique of squashing needs to be reproducible. Thus, in one of the laboratories, it will be necessary to build up a library of spectra from known fiber types which can be used to compare against case fibers.

With FTIR spectroscopy, it is possible to go further than identifying the generic class of fiber, that is, acrylic, nylon, and polyester. It is now possible to separate or differentiate fibers based on difference in copolymer composition.

Other techniques, which have been applied to fiber identification, include pyrolysis gas chromatography with, or without, mass spectrometry. Although not widely used, with the added specificity of mass spectrometry and increased sensitivity, allowing smaller sample size, pyrolysis GC–MS may be worth reconsideration in fiber protocols.

Comparative Examinations

Microscopic examination remains central to protocols for fiber examination, identification, and comparison. Ultimately, the forensic fiber examiner must decide whether or not a recovered/questioned fiber and a fiber or fibers within a known source could have a common origin. Direct side-by-side examination using a comparison microscope remains central in determining that there are no meaningful visual differences between two fibers under comparison. If two fibers are different, then the recovered/questioned fiber is eliminated and no further testing is required. Other techniques to analyze color have the potential to add further discrimination, which is important when it comes to interpreting the weight and substance, which ought to be properly attached to the finding of fiber(s). Clearly, fibers being compared need to be identified as being of the same type.

Conclusion

Protocols for the forensic examination of fibers need to start at the crime scene and not be restricted to the laboratory. The ultimate aim of fiber examination is to assist and resolve issues before the court. It would be extremely rare for fibers to reach a level of individualization where, for all intents and purposes, there could only be one realistic source. Hence, the fiber examiner needs to adopt a protocol, which first develops a comprehensive description of the fibers in question and then seeks to eliminate fibers, which are different using techniques of increasing or complimentary discrimination ability. Essential in any protocol are microscopic techniques culminating in direct side-by-side comparisons. When recovered/questioned fibers cannot be eliminated as having a common origin with a known source, the fiber examiner must interpret what this means at two distinct levels. First, the examiner needs to assess how individual the fiber/dye combination is, and, second, the examiner should consider from where the questioned fibers have been recovered and in which quantity, and what this may reveal about the nature of the contact which resulted in a transfer of fibers. These matters are explored further in the interpretation of fiber evidence in this encyclopedia.

See also: **Chemistry/Trace/Fibers:** Color Analysis; Fiber Microscopy; Fibers: Overview; Identification and Comparison; Interpretation of Fiber Evidence; Persistence and Recovery; Textile and Fiber Damage; Transfer.

Further Reading

Biermann TW (1999) Fibre finder systems. In: Robertson J and Grieve M (eds.) *Forensic Examination of Fibres*. London: Taylor & Francis.

Catling D and Grayson J (1982) *Identification of Vegetable Fibres*. London: Chapman and Hall.

Challinor JM (1999) Fibre identification by pyrolysis techniques. In: Robertson J and Grieve M (eds.) *Forensic Examination of Fibres*. London: Taylor & Francis.

Cook JG (1984a) *Handbook of Textile Fibres. I. Natural Fibres*, 5th edn. Durham, NC: Merrow.

Cook JG (1984b) *Handbook of Textile Fibres. II. Synthetic Fibres*, 5th edn. Durham, NC: Merrow.

Gaudette BD (1988) The forensic aspects of textile fibre examination. In: Saferstein R (ed.) *The Forensic Examination of Fibres*, vol. 2. Englewood Cliffs, NJ: Prentice Hall.

Goodpaster JV and Liszewski EA (2009) Forensic analysis of dyed textile fibers. *Analytical Biochemistry* 394: 2009–2018. http://dx.doi.org/10.1007/s00216-009-2885-7.

Grieve MC (1990) Fibres and their examination in forensic science. In: Maehly A and Williams RL (eds.) *Forensic Science Progress*, vol. 4. New York: Springer.

Massonnet G, Buzzini P, Jochen G, et al. (2005) Evaluation of Raman spectroscopy for the analysis of colored fibers: A collaborative study. *Journal of Forensic Sciences* 50(5): 1028–1038.

Robertson J (1999) Transfer, persistence and recovery of fibres. In: Robertson J and Grieve M (eds.) *Forensic Examination of Fibres*. London: Taylor & Francis.

Robertson J and Grieve M (eds.) (1999) *Forensic Examination of Fibres*. London: Taylor & Francis.

Stefan AR, Dockery CR, Baguley BM, et al. (2009) Microextraction, capillary electrophoresis, and mass spectrometry for forensic analysis of azo and methine base dyes from acrylic fibers. *Analytical and Bioanalytical Chemistry* 394. 2087–2094. http://dx.doi.org/10.1007/s00216-009-2897-3.

Textile Institute (1975) *The Identification of Textile Materials*, 7th edn. Manchester: Textile Institute.

Wiggins KG and Drummond P (2007) Identifying a suitable mounting medium for use in forensic fibre examination. *Science and Justice* 47: 2–8.

Identification and Comparison

R Palmer, Northumbria University, Newcastle Upon Tyne, UK

Introduction

The perpetrator of a crime may transfer fibers from his/her clothing to a victim, or vice versa; therefore, the subsequent identification of fiber type(s) comprising a target garment, and the comparison of these with any suspect fibers, is a potentially invaluable method of demonstrating associations between individuals and/or places. Where fibers have been transferred during the commission of a crime, but no suspect has been identified, the identification of fiber types can be of immense intelligence value.

The scheme of analysis and types of comparison performed on fibers within the forensic context are crucial in that each level of comparison performed should provide a progressive degree of confidence in any matches found. The number and nature of the comparisons performed will therefore have a profound effect on the evidential value of the findings.

There are many different methods of analysis that can be employed in the identification and subsequent comparison of textile fibers. The selection of these should be made so as to provide the greatest degree of discrimination early on, thereby providing the best possibility of excluding material and making the best use of the analyst's time (see 'Scheme of Analysis'). The methods of analysis employed by a modern forensic science laboratory are normally nondestructive, as it is often the case that the fibers themselves become a court exhibit in their own right and/or may be scrutinized for the purposes of a second opinion.

It is not the purpose of this article to provide a comprehensive coverage of all the theoretical and practical considerations associated with these methods, but rather to provide an overview of the methods and practices currently employed (or at least available) in the modern forensic science laboratory where the identification and comparison of fibers are carried out.

Where further detailed information regarding the theoretical and practical aspects of these techniques is required, reference should be made to the supplied 'Further Reading' list.

It should also be pointed out that, although all the methods and techniques described are certainly desirable, it may be that, due to financial constraints and/or the lack of suitable expertise in a given laboratory, they may not all be available to the analyst. Where such constraints on resources are a factor, the most discriminating techniques affordable should clearly be the ones employed.

Identification

The types of fibers used in the manufacture of textiles can be broadly defined as naturally occurring (e.g., wool, cotton) or synthetic (e.g., nylon, acrylic). There are many methods of identification of the various fiber types, ranging from simple microscopic appearance to much more complicated instrumental methods. In the past, it has often been the case that destructive techniques, such as solubility tests, melting point analysis, flaming tests, etc., were employed. Although undoubtedly useful (and relatively inexpensive), such tests have fallen out of favor in the modern laboratory because (a) they are often cumbersome and messy, (b) they require relatively large sample sizes, and (c) they are destructive. Most modern methods of analysis have the advantage of combining high levels of discrimination with few (if any) of the disadvantages of the more 'classical' methods. It is these methods that will be of primary consideration.

Microscopy

White-Light (Bright-Field) Microscopy

This is the simplest yet the most useful method of fiber identification and comparison. Under simple white-light high-power microscopy, some naturally occurring fibers can be readily and speedily identified. Cotton (the most commonly encountered vegetable fiber), for instance, is characterized by its highly convoluted appearance caused by the collapse of the lumen cell wall during drying. Other types of vegetable fibers, such as those employed in cordage material (e.g., hemp, jute, sisal), are more problematic, often requiring a combination of microscopy and chemical/physical tests for conclusive identification. Wool, being a hair, is readily identified by the presence of scales. Synthetic fibers, on the other hand, are more difficult to identify using white-light microscopy alone, as they are often fairly featureless. In such situations, the differences in the chemistry between generic fiber types (e.g., nylon, acrylic, polyester, etc.) may be exploited using polarized light microscopy, in particular, by measuring the fiber's birefringence.

Birefringence

Since synthetic fibers are polymeric entities, they exhibit a pseudocrystalline structure and are anisotropic (i.e., possess different physical properties along different directions of the structure). The anisotropic behavior of synthetic fibers utilized by this technique is that of the difference in refractive index between the parallel axis ($n_{||}$) and the perpendicular axis ($n_{\perp}$) of the fiber, producing interference colors corresponding to the degree of difference between these two refractive indices, when viewed under polarized light. This difference is known as 'retardation,' or 'path difference' (i.e., $n_{||}-n_{\perp}$). Where $n_{||}>n_{\perp}$, a fiber is said to possess a positive elongation, and when $n_{||}<n_{\perp}$, a negative elongation. Since retardation is also a function of the diameter or thickness of the fiber, birefringence can be defined as

$$\Delta n = \left(n_{||} - n_{\perp}\right)/\text{diameter}$$

 http://dx.doi.org/10.1016/B978-0-12-382165-2.00092-1

In practice, the path difference is measured not by measuring $n_{||}$ and $n_{\perp}$ directly, but by the use of a tilting compensator or a quartz wedge. These devices introduced into the polarized light path between the sample and the observer produce a graduated effect opposite to the path difference of the fiber. Once the effect is opposite and equal to the path difference of the fiber, the interference colors are extinguished – this is known as the 'extinction point' (when a fiber is very intensely dyed, it may be difficult to establish this). The point at which this occurs can be read directly from the tilting compensator, and the path difference of the fiber (in nanometers) extrapolated from a calibration table. It is therefore a simple matter to determine the thickness of the fiber using a calibrated graticule to complete the equation

$$\Delta n = \text{Path difference(nm)/diameter(\mu m)} \times 1000$$

Given that not all synthetic fibers are round, an approximation of the thickness may be made by inferring the cross-sectional shape by viewing it longitudinally (optical sectioning) and taking the measurement between the appropriate points, as indicated in **Figure 1**.

In circumstances where the fiber has a very low Δn (e.g., acetate fibers) or a negative elongation (e.g., acrylic), then what is known as a 'first-order red tint' may be introduced in place of the compensator or wedge. This produces an increase in the path difference sufficient to distinguish between these fibers. Triacetate fibers generally have a path difference of zero, and therefore exhibit no anisotropy.

Birefringence measurement is therefore a useful technique for determining the generic class of fiber. Typical birefringence values obtained from the various generic fiber types are shown in **Table 1**.

Since textile manufacturers often introduce copolymers in the production of a fiber to improve, say, its fire-retardant properties, subtypes of fiber within a given generic class can be demonstrated. The technique of birefringence is not sensitive enough to distinguish between these. In such circumstances, an alternative method of identification/comparison is required.

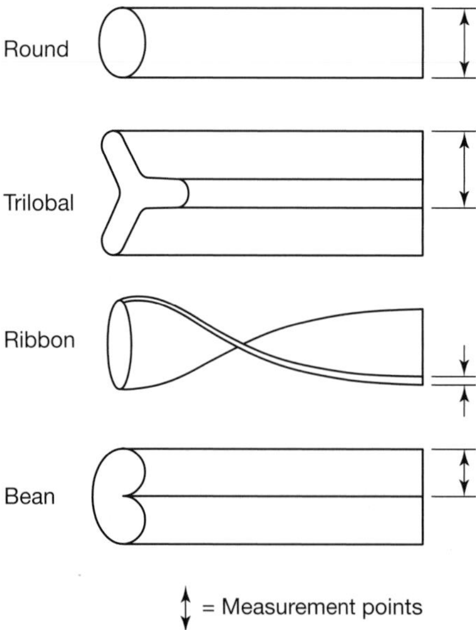

Figure 1 Typically encountered fiber cross-sections with fiber thickness measurement points indicated via optical (inferred) sectioning.

Infrared Spectroscopy

In any protocol designed for the identification and/or comparison of textile fibers, the technique of infrared spectroscopy is invaluable for identifying the polymers and copolymers employed in the production of a given fiber. Within the last decade or so, the availability of small, powerful, yet relatively inexpensive, computers has allowed this technique to evolve into Fourier transform infrared spectroscopy (FTIR), and such instruments have almost exclusively replaced dispersive instruments. It is beyond the scope of this article to describe the technical and theoretical issues concerning such instruments; however, they have the following advantages over the traditional dispersive instruments:

- They require minimal sample preparation
- They afford a more favorable signal-to-noise ratio
- They provide higher precision
- They give cleaner spectra
- They can be used on very small samples

As this technique identifies the constituent polymers present in a fiber, the generic type of the fiber can be readily identified. As already stated, textile manufacturers often employ copolymers within a process to alter some physical property of the fiber (e.g., flame retardation, increased tenacity), and so the identification of these chemical groups using FTIR allows a subclassification within a given generic type. In some circumstances, it may be possible to use this information (perhaps combined with other information such as cross-sectional shape) to identify a particular brand name of textile and its manufacturer. Examples of spectra of two easily identifiable subclasses of acrylic fibers (acrylonitrile copolymerized with vinyl acetate and methyl acrylate, respectively) are shown in **Figure 2**.

Because of its ability to identify and subclassify synthetic fibers, FTIR can also provide a means of additional potential discrimination in any subsequent scheme of comparison.

Pyrolysis

Pyrolysis can be defined as the decomposition of a molecule by high temperature within a nonreactive atmosphere. This decomposition produces molecular fragments that are

Table 1 Typical birefringence values obtained from different generic classes of fiber

Fiber type	Δn
Acrylic	Negative
Triacetate	0
Acetate	Positive
Viscose	0.025
Nylon	0.050
Polyester	0.195

characteristic of the original material and can subsequently be analyzed and identified by techniques such as gas chromatography, mass spectrometry, or FTIR. These techniques produce a pyrogram of the original material, which is used for identification and comparison purposes. Although this technique can potentially provide a high degree of discrimination, it is by nature destructive and requires relatively large samples. Questions have also been raised about the reproducibility of the resulting pyrograms. For these reasons, this technique is not one that is universally employed in the identification and comparison of synthetic fibers within the modern forensic science laboratory.

An example of a scheme for fiber identification using the methods outlined in this section is given in **Figure 3**.

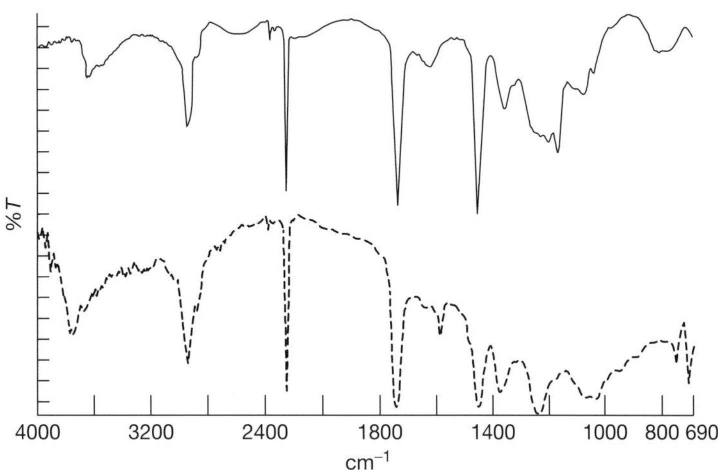

Figure 2 Examples of FTIR spectra of two subclasses of acrylic (polyacrylonitrile) fiber: acrylonitrile copolymerized with methyl acrylate (top) and acrylonitrile copolymerized with vinyl acetate (bottom).

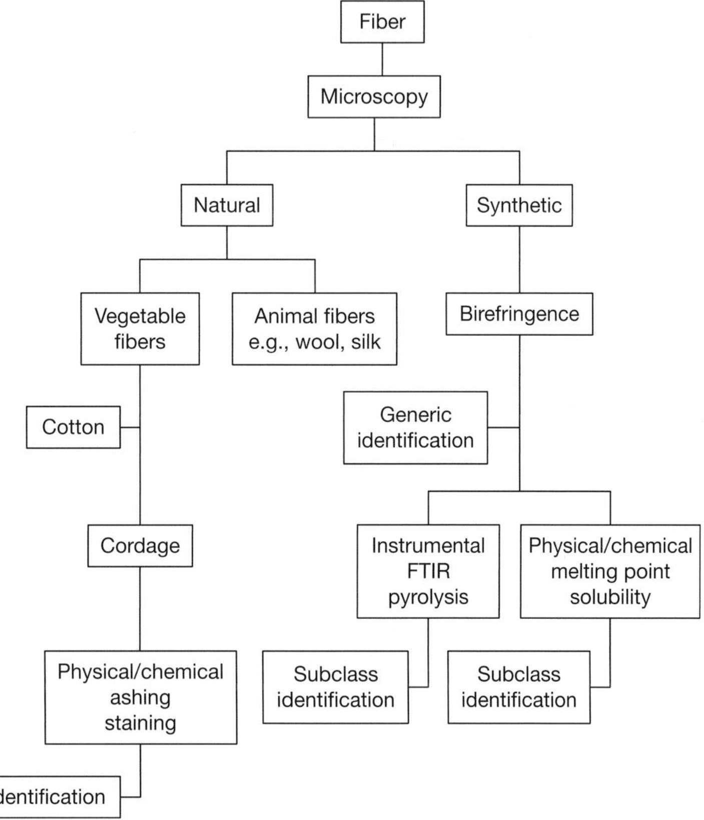

Figure 3 Flowchart showing scheme of fiber identification.

Comparison

As with any comparison, care must be taken to ensure that the reference (control) samples are as representative of the target item as possible.

The comparison of suspect fibers with those comprising the target garment or item begins with the initial searching of the surface debris tapings (or other methods of collection) using low-power stereomicroscopy. At this point, only general color and gross morphology are considered and therefore the search window is very wide. Over the past 10 years, there have been a number of attempts to automate this arduous part of the process; however, at the time of writing, none of the systems developed have been shown to be as reliable as the human operator. As technology continues to advance, it may be that such a system will eventually be perfected.

Any fibers not excluded by the initial search are removed and mounted using suitable media and cover slip onto a microscope slide for a more detailed comparison. There are numerous suitable types of mounting media available, and the choice of which one to use should consider aspects such as ease of removal of the fiber (for nonmicroscopic comparison), stability of background color over time, and nonreactivity with the fiber and its dye. The removal of a fiber from a microscope slide for subsequent analysis is usually done by breaking/cracking the cover slip and using a suitable solvent to liberate the fiber from the mountant. The fiber should then be thoroughly washed before analysis/comparison. Where a solvent-based mountant is used, care should be taken that, on removal and subsequent washing of the fiber, leaching of the dye does not occur.

In any scheme of analysis/comparison, it is important that the most rapid discriminating techniques are performed first, as this will serve to maximize the time efficiency of the examiner by quickly identifying exactly which fibers are required for further comparison and which can be excluded.

Such a scheme of analysis/comparison can be represented in a flowchart form, as in Figure 4.

Where the size of a given fiber is optimal, the maximum number of tests possible should be carried out. Where this is not possible due to the limiting factor of the size of a single fiber, it may be more appropriate to carry out each of these tests on a selection of different fibers. Clearly, the more the number of comparative tests performed on a given fiber, the greater the confidence of any subsequent match. In situations where the examiner is confronted by, say, dozens of good microscopically matching fibers, then it may be acceptable to select a random sample from among them for further testing.

Microscopic Appearance

Without doubt, the most widely used piece of equipment in the forensic laboratory is the comparison microscope. In its basic form, it consists of two identical optically balanced microscopes that have been linked via an optical bridge to allow the simultaneous viewing of two separate samples under white light. Features such as the presence or absence of a delustrant can be inferred, or direct observation of cross-sectional shape and color determined and directly compared. By introducing polarizers within the light path, direct comparison of birefringence interference colors can also be carried out. The direct visualization of the cross-section of a fiber (as opposed to inferred) can be achieved using various sectioning techniques and can provide useful comparative information, particularly where the modification ratio of a lobed fiber is determined. Briefly, the modification ratio can be defined as the ratio between the diameter of a circle subscribed by the outer tips of a lobed fiber and the inner circular core. Such measurements, in addition to providing comparative information, can, when combined with other information (e.g., infrared spectra), be used to identify a specific brand of fiber.

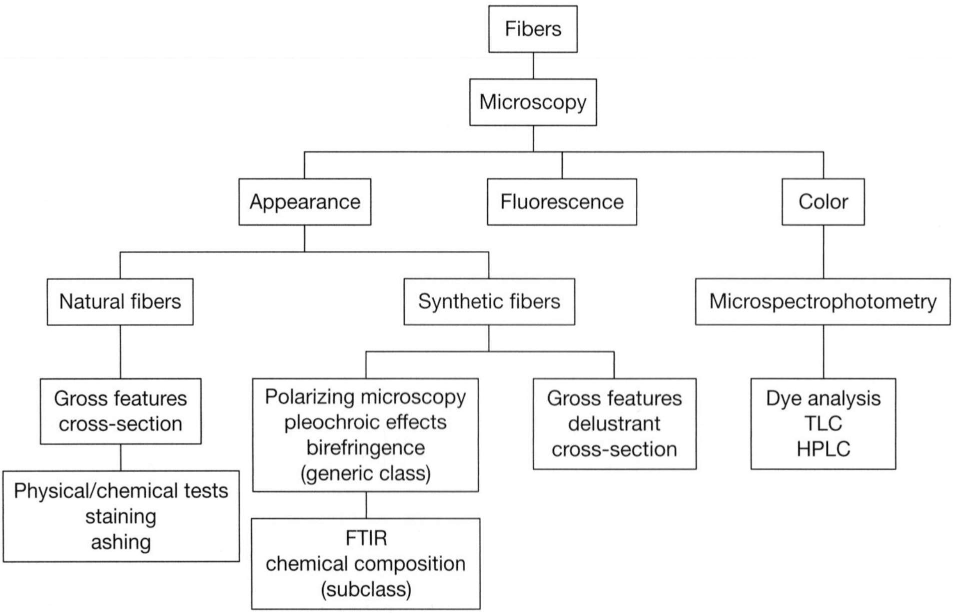

Figure 4 Flowchart showing generalized scheme of fiber analysis/comparison.

Direct cross-sectioning is also extremely useful in the identification and comparison of plant fibers used in cordage materials.

Many (most) modern comparison microscopes possess various accessories such as specialized light sources and filter systems, which allow the fluorescent characteristics of fibers to be compared using differing wavelengths of light. This is particularly useful in detecting the presence of optical brighteners.

Color Comparison

The comparison of color using the comparison microscope is undertaken after ensuring that each microscope is correctly adjusted via Kohler illumination, the background color is neutral and balanced, the intensities are the same, and the same magnification is employed. Pleochroic (or diochroic) effects, that is, the apparent differences in fiber color when viewed at different orientations under plane polarized light, can also be compared.

Considerable intrasample variation (both quantitative and qualitative) in the color of fibers from a given garment may exist because of differences in dye intensity and dye uptake, especially where a multicomponent dye has been employed. This type of intrasample variation is predominately seen in naturally occurring fibers such as cotton and wool and is a function of the individual fiber's affinity with a particular dye. Similar variation can also be observed in synthetic fibers, where part of a garment has been disproportionately worn, bleached, or exposed to sunlight. It is therefore crucial that a reference sample taken from a target garment be as representative as possible, taking features of wear and tear into consideration. If the reference sample is not truly representative, the chance of false exclusions is increased.

Although the human eye can discriminate between subtle differences in color, the color of two fibers can appear identical under one illuminant condition but different under another. This is known as 'metamerism' and, because of this and the fact that color comparison is essentially subjective, this aspect of fiber comparison is augmented by the use of objective analytical methods.

Microspectrophotometry

As the name suggests, this is an adaptation of a standard visual-range spectrophotometric analysis whereby spectra from small analytes can be obtained. In practical terms, such instruments consist of a microscope integrated into the light path of a single-beam-configuration spectrophotometer. The detector of the system is linked to a computer for data acquisition, output, and instrumental control. In addition to visible-range microspectrophotometry (MSP), many forensic science laboratories are now using instruments (UV–vis MSP) capable of operating into the ultraviolet (UV) range of the electromagnetic spectrum, thereby increasing the discrimination of the analysis. Over the past decade, various published studies have demonstrated and defined the increased discrimination afforded by these instruments in potentially distinguishing between fibers that had otherwise been indistinguishable using visible-range MSP alone.

For visible-range MSP, no special preparation of the fiber is required. In order to avoid any pleochroic effects, care should be taken to orient the reference and suspect fibers in the same way for analysis. With UV–vis MSP, the fibers need to be presented to the instrument using glycerine as a mountant and slides and coverslips of quartz instead of glass.

Over the past 10 years, the development of these instruments has moved from scanning dispersive technology towards multichannel scanning technology (MSC) using diode array configuration and more recently toward systems employing charge coupled device (CCD) technology.

MSP provides two types of comparative information: color matching and spectral comparison.

Spectral Comparison

The color of a fiber is determined by which parts of the visible electromagnetic spectrum are absorbed by its dye. A blue dye, for example, absorbs predominantly the red part of the spectrum. A plot of relative absorbance against wavelength can therefore produce a graph of the absorption spectrum of a particular color. In the practical comparison situation, the spectra obtained from suspect fibers are compared against the spectral range observed in the fibers from the target item, which can be performed by overlaying the spectral traces from the reference and suspect fibers on a light box or similar item and determining the closeness of fit. Most computer data acquisition software allow direct overlaying of spectra on the computer screen, often with the ability to 'zoom in' on specific parts of the spectrum under observation. Such displays can also be printed (**Figure 5**) for hard-copy inclusion in a case file. Where the spectrum of the suspect fiber falls within the qualitative and quantitative range observed in the reference sample, the fibers are said to match (i.e., are indistinguishable) in terms of color.

As with the microscopic visual comparison of color, care must be taken to ensure that the reference sample is as representative of the target garment as possible.

Many data acquisition software packages have the ability to carry out mathematical differentiation of absorption spectra, which can be very useful for exacerbating any subtle differences between the spectra of reference and recovered fibers, where incongruence is suspected.

While various mathematical procedures may be employed to differentiate spectral data, the first derivative has been found to be the most appropriate for MSP data. When data is recorded at evenly spaced intervals along the wavelength (λ), or other x-axis, the simplest method to produce the first derivative spectrum is by calculating the difference between two points i and $i+1$, that is,

$$\frac{\partial y}{\partial \lambda} = \frac{y_{i+1} - y_i}{\lambda_{i+1} - \lambda_i}$$

This function allows the rate of change of gradient of data presented in a graphical format (such as the absorbance spectra from MSP) to be visualized, and the first-derivative spectrum is

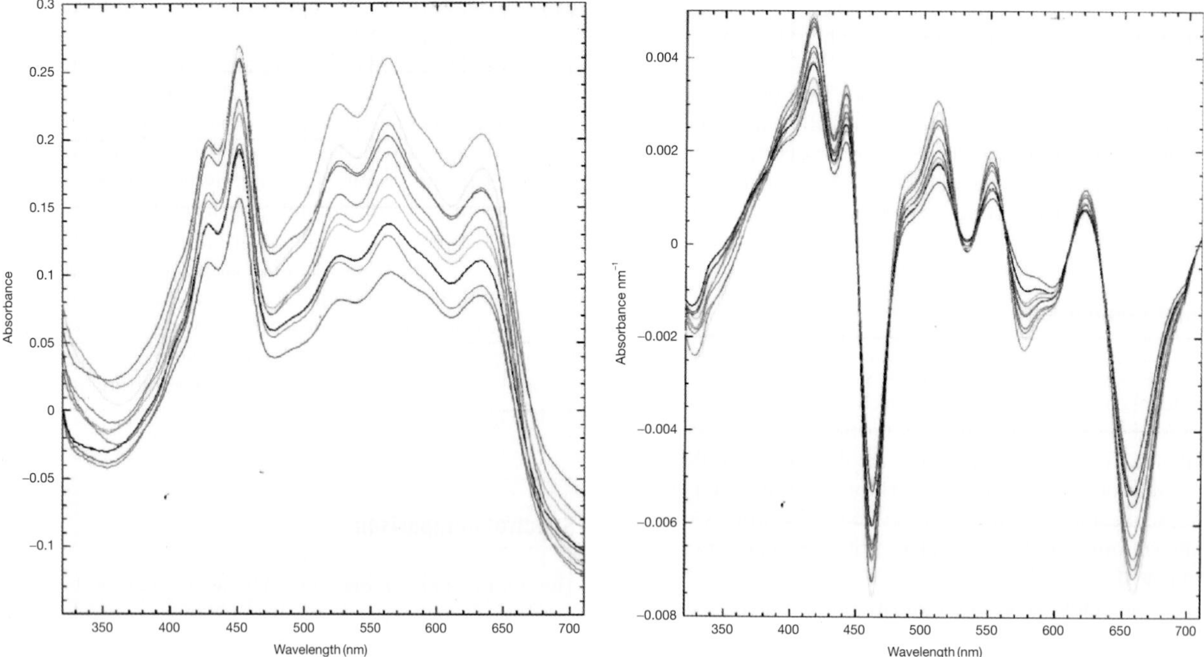

Figure 5 Microspectrophotometry output showing overlaid spectra of colored fibers.

produced when the results of such a calculation are plotted from the absorbance data.

While this function can provide a useful additional tool in evaluating MSP results, it should never be used in isolation from the original absorption spectra. In addition, published work over the past 10 years has shown that its use can lead to false exclusions in cases where there is high intra- and intersample variation in the constituent fibers of a garment. Caution should therefore be employed in its use, and as with other comparative methods, the degree of variation in the sample in question should be fully understood.

Color Matching

In addition to comparing the spectra of fibers directly, the spectral information can be used by the computer software to generate color data, that is, to describe the color within the parameters of a particular mathematical model. This can be useful as a means of databasing fiber color/type combinations for either estimation of prevalence of color/type combination or for intelligence purposes in an ongoing large inquiry.

Because of the prevalence of relatively inexpensive and powerful desktop computers, and their ability to perform complex comparisons on spectral data, the use of 'color matching' for the above purposes is very much on the decline. However, given that it is still employed in some laboratories, it is worth elaborating on its use.

Perhaps the most widely used model employed in calculating such color data is the CIE (Commission International Eclairage) system, which is based on the Young–Helmholtz theory of trichromatic color vision. Essentially, this model describes a color in terms of how much of each of the three primary colors of light (red, green, and blue) is absorbed by the dye. Each of the primary colors is present in equal quantities in white light. The value of red is denoted as X, green as Y, and blue as Z. These values are known as 'tristimulus values,' and hence, in the case of white light

$$X + Y + Z = 1$$

These values are calculated using transmission data.

These values can vary according to viewing conditions and type of illuminant used. In the case of the CIE model, the conditions are defined as 'Illuminant C' – equal to that experienced on a bright overcast day.

Since tristimulus values have been shown to be nonlinear due to their derivation from transmission values, and textile fibers vary in width and dye uptake, different values for these can be obtained from fibers of the same color. The way around this is to calculate these values using absorbance data (= log (100/T)) and to normalize them as follows:

$$x' = (X/X + Y + Z)$$
$$y' = (X/X + Y + Z)$$
$$z' = (Z/X + Y + Z)$$

As the wavelength of light transmitted is equivalent, but not identical to, the color absorbed, the color observed is complementary to the color absorbed. Hence these values are known as 'complementary color coordinates.' By using these values, the color of a fiber can be defined and compared, ignoring the perceived effect of intensity.

Dye Comparison

Thin-Layer Chromatography

Where a fiber is too opaque for meaningful MSP analysis, or as an additional comparative technique providing a further degree of discrimination, thin-layer chromatography (TLC) can be carried out on dye extracts from textile fibers. Given that the chemistry of the fiber–dye interaction can be complex, certain classes of dyes (based on their chemistry) are used with particular fiber types (basic dyes, for instance, are often used to color acrylic fibers).

The extraction of a dye from a fiber is usually achieved by placing the fiber in a sealed, labeled capillary tube along with a suitable extractant. The extractant tube is then heated. Since this is a semidestructive treatment, a portion of the fiber should be preserved on the microscope slide for any future scrutiny. The choice of the extractant solvent depends on the nature or class of the dye present, as these can have very varied solubility characteristics. Over the years, various sequential extraction schemes have been developed that not only provide the means of determining the best extractant solvent for a particular fiber–dye combination but also determine the class of dye employed. Once the class of dye has been determined, the optimum eluent system can be used. The best choice of eluents for a given dye class has been determined by various studies performed over the years. Ideally, an eluent should provide good separation of well-defined dye components. (It is beyond the scope of this article to list the various extractant and eluent systems for the various fiber type–dye class combinations. This information can be gained from the supplied bibliography.)

Once extracted, the dye is spotted onto a silica plate and placed in a chamber with the appropriate eluent. Components of the dye are selectively adsorbed as the eluent is drawn over the plate, causing the dye components to be separated out. The solvent front of the eluted plate should be marked and the plate itself quickly dried. If appropriate standards and controls are applied to the same plate as the questioned material, a direct means of visual comparison of the dye components can be carried out. The retardation factor (RF) values for each of the separated components can also be calculated. The eluted plate should also be visualized under UV light, in order to determine whether any fluorescent component bands are present. Since the success of visualizing all the components of a dye depends on the amount of material extracted and applied to the plate, care should be taken to ensure that broadly similar amounts of reference and questioned dyes are applied.

Where it is not possible to extract the dye from a particular fiber due to a high fiber–dye affinity (e.g., wool/reactive dye), then a similar behavior with a questioned fiber, although by no means as conclusive as the production of a chromatogram, may indicate a common origin and serve as a means of excluding nonmatching fibers.

High-Performance Liquid Chromatography

The technique of high-performance liquid chromatography (HPLC) has also been applied to the comparison of dyes from textile fibers. Although this technique is useful in terms of increased sensitivity, it does present some technical and practical difficulties when used for this application. The main difficulty is that, as fiber dyes are extracted in organic solvents, these are not easily compatible with aqueous-based HPLC eluent columns. This means that it is difficult (if not impossible) to obtain a specific instrumental configuration that will be optimal for the separation of dye components for every dye class. The provision of an expensive instrument of dedicated configuration (and therefore limited use) is not cost effective, especially where any advantage gained in its use, over TLC, is questionable. Until these practical difficulties are overcome, it is bound to remain a technique not normally employed on a routine basis.

Raman Spectroscopy

Raman spectrometry is a method of analysis providing information on the rotational, vibrational, and other energetic qualities of a molecule through the scattering of light from a laser source. It provides information complementary to that of FTIR and can therefore be used to assist in the identification and comparison of dyes associated with fiber polymers. There are a number of advanced methods applicable to Raman spectroscopy. These include resonance Raman spectroscopy or surface-enhanced Raman spectroscopy, but the details of these are outside the scope of this article.

Despite its potential, there are a number of practical 'problems' associated with this technique when it is applied to fiber analysis, as given below:

- Different wavelengths of lasers are required for particular fiber–dye combinations (increasing its cost).
- It relies on a comprehensive database for a meaningful interpretation of its results.
- Numerous studies have shown that it is yet to demonstrate any clear advantages in terms of discrimination over the combination of analytical techniques already carried out in most operational laboratories (e.g., MSP, FTIR, TLC).

For these reasons, Raman spectroscopy has not been widely employed as a routine technique for fiber dye analysis in operational forensic science laboratories. Consequently, there is no wide supporting data or experience with its application in this evidence type as there is for infrared analysis or MSP.

Chemical Composition

Fourier Transform Infrared Spectroscopy

Where the recovered fibers are of sufficient length, part of an individual fiber can be used for FTIR analysis. As with TLC, it is important to leave a portion of the fiber on the slide in order that it can be examined microscopically if required. As with all comparison techniques, it is important that the preparation of the reference and recovered samples for analysis be the same. The fibers should be flattened before analysis, as this minimizes variation in beam path length through the fiber, giving better spectra. Flattening can, however, cause minor variations in peak position and intensity, and therefore the compared fibers should be identically treated.

Once flattened, the fibers can be presented to the instrument by mounting them across a suitable aperture or IR window. Each sample should be aligned in the same direction in order to avoid any polarization bias effects that can occur with these instruments. Sample and background scans should be run under identical conditions.

Most FTIR instruments use data management packages that not only display individual spectra but can also overlay spectra for direct visual comparison purposes.

In addition, such software packages usually have 'tools' for the manipulation of the spectral data, specifically for functions such as noise reduction, normalization, etc. It is important that, if these functions are used, the original data is saved in a separate file from the 'treated' data. As well as displaying and manipulating spectra, many such software packages have a library of reference spectra with which the questioned spectra can be compared for rapid identification. These also allow the analyst to add further spectra to the library and so, over time, a comprehensive reference collection can be built up.

Chemical/Physical Tests

In situations where infrared spectroscopy yields limited information in the identification and subsequent comparison of very closely chemically related fiber types (e.g., acetate/triacetate, polyolefins), there may be little choice but to use destructive tests such as melting point analysis and/or solubility tests. Clearly, in circumstances where these tests are employed, it is important that they are performed on the reference material first and that as little of the questioned material is used as is practically possible.

Scheme of Analysis

Conventional dogma regarding the scheme of comparative analysis dictates that the most rapid discriminatory test be employed first. In terms of fiber examinations, this is conventionally the high-power microscopic visual comparisons. In the event that suspect and control fibers cannot be excluded at this stage, instrumental analyses are performed. However, over the past number of years, published work has shown that the discrimination power of the comparative tests employed varies according to the fiber type/color combination in question. For example, the discriminating power of microscopy for blue and black cotton fibers has been shown to be poor, whereas the discrimination of these fibers using UV–vis MSP has been very high. This means that, for this particular fiber type/color combination, it is more logical to perform UV–vis MSP as initial comparison, before microscopy. While the generalized scheme of analysis shown in **Figure** 4 may be appropriate for most fiber comparisons, current literature shows that the order of this scheme may need revising depending on the analyte in question.

Documentation

As with any analysis, it is important that all the work relating to the identification and comparison of fibers is properly documented. All fibers should be given a unique number/slide allocation, and the number and types of analysis performed on a given fiber, as well as the results, should be recorded. The record should also reflect the number of fibers recovered from a questioned source and the number of matches. In providing a clearly auditable record of work, the tasks of summarizing the work, interpreting the results, and external scrutiny/review of the case file are made easier.

Resources

As already mentioned, the given resources available to a particular laboratory and examiner in this field may preclude the use of some or all of the methods outlined in this article. Where the identification and comparison of fiber trace evidence is to be practiced within financial or other resource constraints, The European Fibers Group's recent revision of its "Manual of Best Practice in Fiber Examinations" provides a wealth of details concerning the 'minimum requirements' for this type of analysis.

See also: **Chemistry/Trace/Fibers:** Fibers: Overview; Fiber Microscopy; Persistence and Recovery; Transfer; **Foundations:** Evidence/Classification; **Methods:** Analytical Light Microscopy; Microscopy (Electron); Spectroscopy: Basic Principles.

Further Reading

Appleyard HM (1978) *Guide to the Identification of Animal Fibers*, 2nd edn. Leeds: WIRA.

Biermann T (2007) Blocks of colour IV: The evidential value of blue and red cotton fibers. *Science and Justice* 47: 50–68.

Buzzini P and Massonnet G (2008) The discrimination of coloured acrylic, cotton and wool fibers using raman spectroscopy. *Proceedings of the16th meeting of the European Fiber Group, Budapest.*

Catling DL and Grayon J (1982) *Identification of Vegetable Fibers*. London: Chapman and Hall.

Challinar JM (1992) Fiber identification by pyrolysis techniques. In: Robertson J (ed.) *Forensic Examination of Fibers*. New York: Ellis Horwood.

Chamberlin GJ and Chamberlin DG (1980) *Colour – Its Measurement*. Heyden, London: Computation and Application.

Deforest PR (1982) Foundations of forensic microscopy. In: Saferstein R (ed.) *Forensic Science Handbook*. Englewood Cliffs: Prentice Hall.

European Fiber Group (2011) *The Manual of Best Practice in the Forensic Examination of Fibers*. ENFSI.

Ferraro JR and Basile LJ (1979) *Fourier Transform Infra Red Spectroscopy Applications to Chemical Systems*, vol. 2. New York: Academic Press.

Gohl EPG and Vilensky LD (1985) *Textile Science – an Explanation of Fiber Properties*, 2nd edn. Melbourne: Longman Cheshire.

Grieve MC (1995) Another look at the classification of acrylic fibers using FTIR microscopy. *Science and Justice* 35: 179–190.

Grieve MC (2002) Black cellulosic fibers - a bete noir? *Science and Justice* V42(2): 81–88.

Grieve MC, Biermann TW, and Davignon M (2001) The evidential value of black cotton fibers. *Science and Justice* V41(4): 245–260.

Grieve MC and Cabirers LR (1985) The recognition and identification of modified acrylic fibers. *Forensic Science International* 20: 121–146.

Hamilton R and Hamilton S (1987) *Thin Layer Chromatography*. Chichester: Wiley.

Hartshorne A, Wild F, and Babb N (1991) The discrimination of cellulose di and tri acetate fibers by solvent test and melting point determination. *Journal of the Forensic Science Society* 31: 457–461.

Johri MC and Jatar DP (1979) Identification of some synthetic fibers by their birefringence. *Journal of Forensic Sciences* 24: 692–697.

Lepot L, De Wael K, Gason F, and Gilbert B (2008) Application of Raman spectroscopy to forensic fiber cases. *Science and Justice* V48(3): 109–117.

Palmer R, Hutchinson W, and Fryer V (2009) The discrimination of (non-denim) blue cotton. *Science and Justice* 49(1): 12–18.

Robertson J (1999) *The Forensic Examination of Fibers*, 2nd edn. London: Taylor and Francis.

Stoeffler SF (1996) A flowchart system for the identification of common synthetic fibers by polarised light microscopy. *Journal of Forensic Sciences* 41: 297–299.

Technical Working Group for Materials Analysis (1997) *Forensic Fiber Examination Guidelines*. Washington, DC: Federal Bureau of Investigation.

The Textile Institute (1985) *The Identification of Textile Materials*, 7th edn. Manchester: The Textile Institute.

Tungol MW, Bartick EG, and Mortimer A (1990) The development of a spectral database for the identification of fibers using infrared microscopy. *Applied Spectroscopy* 44: 543–549.

Wiggins K, Palmer R, Hutchinson W, and Drummond P (2007) An investigation into the use of calculating the first derivative of absorbance spectra as a tool for forensic fiber analysis. *Science and Justice* 47: 9–18.

Textile and Fiber Damage

J Was-Gubala, Institute of Forensic Research, Krakow, Poland

Glossary

MSP Microspectrophotometry in visible/UV light.
Scissor cut A type of cut created with a sharp two-bladed implement.
Slash cut A type of cut produced through contact along the surface of a material by the sharp edge of an implement.
Stab cut A type of cut produced by penetration of an implement through the material.
Tear A fabric separation caused by physical stress exerted in opposing directions.
Thermoplastic fiber A fiber made of polymer that turns into a liquid when heated.
Thermoset fiber A fiber made of cross-linked polymer that is cured or set using heat or heat and pressure.
Wear and tear Damage caused to garments in the course of normal use.

Introduction

Textile products are a part of people's everyday lives. The most important articles made from textiles include clothes, components of furnishings and equipment in homes, workplaces, and means of transport, for example, packaging. As they are part of the immediate surroundings of humans, textile products also 'coparticipate' in incidents of a criminal nature. From the point of view of the user and the producer of textiles, any damage that occurs in the course of their use is detrimental because it reduces their usefulness and esthetic value. However, for the forensic sciences, the value of a trace in the form a damaged textile product or of a fiber that is a component of such a product is great, because the sometimes observable characteristic physical and chemical features reflect the conditions in which the product has been. Scientific studies carried out by textile centers on the kinetics of destruction processes, the effects of the action of particular destructive factors on textiles and fibers, and the cause-and-effect relation are very important for the forensic science examination. They provide a basis for making more objective inferences about the circumstances of an event and its participants on the basis of analysis of damage to fibers and textiles.

In forensic casework, experts deal first and foremost with mechanical damage to textiles, especially cutting by sharp-edged objects; they also deal with textile damage connected with normal use (environmental, laundering effects) and with the influence of high temperature (and pressure) and of microorganisms (bacteria and fungi).

The above aspects of forensic casework relating to fibers and textile products are also currently the subject of numerous analyses and investigations. A summary of the results of selected studies carried out in the last couple of decades is presented below.

Mechanical Damage

Various forms of mechanical damage of textiles and fibers may be related to a crime. 'Normal wear and tear' damage resulting from routine use of textiles usually takes the form of a thinning of the fabric prior to a hole forming, pilling, and unraveling of hems and seams, or there may even be a tear. In a violent scuffle, a fabric may be torn, the seams often fail, and the structure of the fabric is distorted. It is often a difficult task for the forensic expert to distinguish between the effects of 'normal wear and tear' and other kinds of mechanical damage, which may be related to the crime in question.

Textiles may be neatly cut, either with scissors (scissor cut) or by slashing with a knife, a scalpel, a razor blade, and so on (slash cut). They may also be punctured by a relatively sharp (e.g., a screwdriver) or blunt (e.g., a hammer) object, and the nature of the damage will depend on the supporting material (if any) beneath the textile. The stabbing action of a knife may have features of both puncturing and cutting.

Pure tensile failure may occur, especially in ropes and webbing (seat belts), although this can often be precipitated by some other form of damage that has weakened the textile.

Abrasive damage, normally considered to be due to 'normal wear and tear' and caused by the material rubbing against another surface, can also be of forensic importance.

Mechanical damage may be inflicted by insects, such as moths, microorganisms such as some forms of bacteria and fungi, or caused by the jaws and/or claws of a larger animal (dog, wolf, mouse, rat, etc.).

Analysis of mechanical damage to textiles is a complex problem as there are a large number of variables associated with fabric manufacture and use, including fiber type, yarn structure, fabric structure, applied finishes, fabric orientation, garment construction, fit, and some kind of degradation.

Information such as blade type and size may be estimated when analyzing damaged textiles; this generally involves the observation of severance and fiber end morphologies, and the measurement of severance dimensions. The more distinctive the weapon, the more unique the characteristics in any damaged clothing. In general, a blunt tip results in more fabric distortion around the point of penetration, as individual fibers fail under tension rather than by cutting. A sharp blade will cut fibers and yarns as it passes through fabric, with little or no distortion; in contrast, a blunt blade increases fabric distortion and the disorder of yarn and fiber ends. The presence of scallops, serrations, and imperfections on a blade has also been reported to increase fabric fraying and distortion. Severance dimensions, in stabbed fabrics, do not accurately reflect the dimensions of the knife

 http://dx.doi.org/10.1016/B978-0-12-382165-2.00094-5

blade; the accuracy of such determinations is detrimentally affected by elastic recovery, depth of penetration, and 'slashing' (movement of the knife parallel to the fabric plane).

Characteristic features of sharp force fabric damage are typically assessed at varying levels of magnification, and therefore the results are at least partly subjective. Examination at the fabric level concentrates on the degree of distortion in the fabric surrounding the severance, changes to the 'normal' yarn spacing, the direction of the severance line relative to the yarn direction, and the relative position of severed yarn ends. At the yarn level, the relative position of the fiber ends within each yarn (planar array) and the presence of short segments of yarn are noted. Characteristic damage to fiber ends may be observed depending on the fiber type and the weapon used (Figure 1). Generalizations can be made about the cause of damage from single fiber fracture models:

(i) scissor cuts create pinched ends,
(ii) knife cuts produce flat tops with or without a lip, and
(iii) impact tears produce a mushroom (bulbous) cap.

Damage to clothing as a result of stabbing has also been studied in particular with respect to the ease of penetration of fabrics and underlying skin as a factor of function of the sharpness of the weapon, and the general characteristics of the damaged edges depending on the weapon type. The mark on the fabric is usually smaller than the mark on the skin, in some cases by upwards of 70%. The fabric type has an effect on the difference between corresponding marks on fabric and underlying skin, with a greater difference occurring in the case of natural fiber garments.

Environmental and Laundering Effects

Textiles and fibers are subjected to a variety of environmental stresses and a number of authors have researched into the effect of environmental conditions on textiles and fibers. For example, damage due to natural environmental factors (mainly sunlight, water, and burial in soil) in Australia has been studied. Changes were observed mainly with traditional methods (brightfield and fluorescence microscopy, microspectrophotometry, Fourier transform infrared microspectroscopy). Raman spectroscopy was also used for the analysis of fibers that had undergone environmental degradation.

Investigating the morphological changes of environmentally stressed fiber surfaces and changes in their physical (e.g., adhesion to a surface) and mechanical (e.g., elasticity) properties can turn out to be essential for understanding where and when a crime was committed. Examinations focussed on two natural (cotton and wool), and a regenerated cellulose (viscose) textile fiber exposed to various environmental stresses for different lengths of time. They were studied with the use of an atomic force microscope, allowing quantitative measurement of the surface texture parameters of the environmentally stressed fabrics as a function of the exposure time. It was also possible to visualize at the nanoscale level, the finest details of the surfaces of the three weathered fabrics and clearly distinguish between the detrimental effects of the imposed environmental conditions.

Multifaceted studies have been carried out in textile centers into changes in the structure of fibers, including polyamide fibers, under the influence of UV light. In the applied conditions, UV exposure evoked changes in the molecular structure of the material making up the fiber, and the size of these changes was dependent, among other things, on the amount of matting agent introduced into the material and the nature of the cross section of the fiber.

Laundering has been reported to be responsible for up to 90% of the deterioration (loss of tensile strength) observed with use. The effects of laundering include shrinkage, distortion, fading, cross-staining, stiffening of fibers, and fiber damage. Issues linked with changes in the color of individual fibers as a result of laundering products have not been thoroughly studied yet: the methods proposed in standards for assessing color fastness of textiles subjected to home and commercial laundering concern analysis of changes in color and degree of soiling of white textiles, and thus cannot be applied in the forensic field in analyses of single fibers.

Color changes that occur in several types of textiles and their fibers (blue, red, and gray/black cotton, wool, acrylic, and polyester) resulting from the long-term (14 days) effects of various solutions of popularly used laundry detergents were assessed. The experiment encompassed a wide variety of chemical compositions of detergents, but temperature and mechanical factors of the washing process remained at a fixed level. Color changes of the textile samples were evaluated through the visual comparison of their color against that of the untreated (control) material, while color changes of the fiber samples were evaluated by

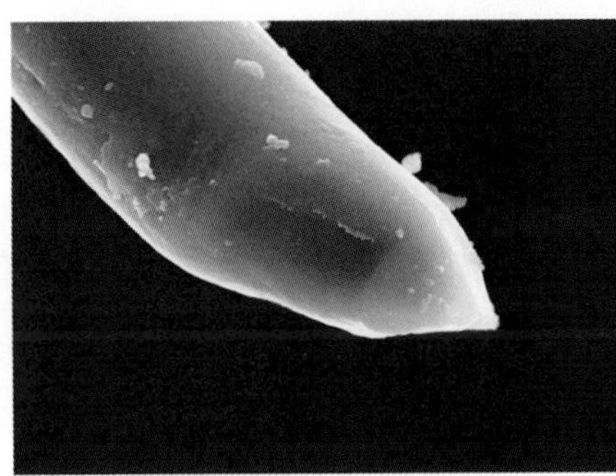

Scissors cut

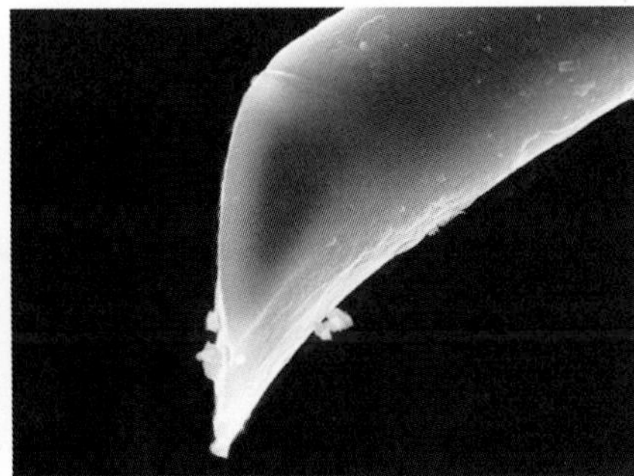

Knife cut

Figure 1 SEM images of polyester fibers cutting by scissors and knife (secondary electron image, magnification 1500x).

fluorescence microscopy (UV excitation filter) together with microspectrophotometric measurements. The most significant changes in fiber color – regardless of the type of detergent used – were achieved with natural fibers, that is, cotton and wool. Consequently, the type of dyed fiber – and mainly the heterogeneous nature of the microstructure of cotton and wool fibers – has a decisive influence on the extent of color variation in fibers treated with superficially active agents. The differences between the detergents in terms of the way they act stem from their differing chemical composition. The type of dye used in fibers has a bearing on the process as well. The degree of color change in the tested textiles and fibers was mainly contingent upon the amount of time the samples had been treated with the detergent solutions. This study shows that in many forensic cases, for instance, when a suspect has been identified sometime after a crime has been committed and his clothes may have been laundered, a comparison with fibers recovered from the victim's clothes, body etc. could mistakenly exclude a match between the suspect's sample and the evidential sample. It should be assumed that in the conditions present during the actual laundering of apparel, other factors such as mechanical action (intensive movement within the washing machine) and washing at temperatures of over 104 °F/40 °C may even intensify the effects observed in the above-mentioned experiment.

The Influence of Heat

The presence of thermal damage on a garment may be significant in an arson, other types of fire, explosion, and road accident cases and may be helpful in determining the cause of the events and – where applicable – in determining whether or not the physical evidence supports a link between a suspect and the scene of crime. Identification of evidential textiles and fibers often encompasses those subjected to the action of different types of heat coming from flames (from a large fire, or cigarette smoking-related burns), those that have come into contact with a hot plate (ironing) or direct blast effects resulting from the immediate action of an explosive shock wave (damage to textiles by high pressure and temperature).

The process of thermal degradation is different for the various kinds of polymer from which the fibers are made. Thermoplastic fibers, which include most synthetics (e.g., nylon, polyester, and polyolefine), change primarily in terms of their physical state as temperature increases (contracting and melting), while chemical degradation (decomposition and burning) occurs only after their melting point has been exceeded. In the case of fibers that are thermosets – natural (vegetable and animal), regenerated (cellulosic and protein), and certain synthetic fibers (some acrylics) – the primary effect of the action of high temperature in the course of heating is a change in the chemical structure of the polymer, whereas the progression of changes in their physical structure is less rapid (**Figure 2**).

The chemical structure of a fiber-forming polymer has a decisive influence on the thermal transformation process of a final fiber product. Other relevant factors that have a bearing on this process are textile product parameters such as the linear mass of a thread, thickness, tenacity, surface characteristics, and plait. The most important forensic aspects of the thermal behavior of fibers are structural changes with temperature, melting-point determination, and burning behavior.

A selection of clothing and household textiles differing in color, type, fiber composition, and construction were directly exposed to a vapor cloud explosion caused by the ignition of a mixture of explosive gases (about 1832 °F/1000 °C), and damaged by contact with a hot metal plate (about 662 °F/350 °C) and with a flame (about 2372 °F/1300 °C). The characteristic changes were studied by optical microscopy and scanning electron microscopy (SEM), which indicated that the vapor cloud explosion caused very specific, mainly superficial, damage to textiles and fibers (**Figure 3**). Damage caused by a flame proved to be the most intense for cellulose fibers, while the effect of a hot plate proved to be so for synthetic thermoplastic fibers. In the cases of wool and synthetics, the formation of conglomerations of fibers was observed following contact with a heating plate, whereas this phenomenon does not occur in degradation caused by vapor cloud explosions. Furthermore, following direct exposure to a flame, the morphological characteristics of all the types of single fibers analyzed were different from those of fibers exposed to the shock wave that

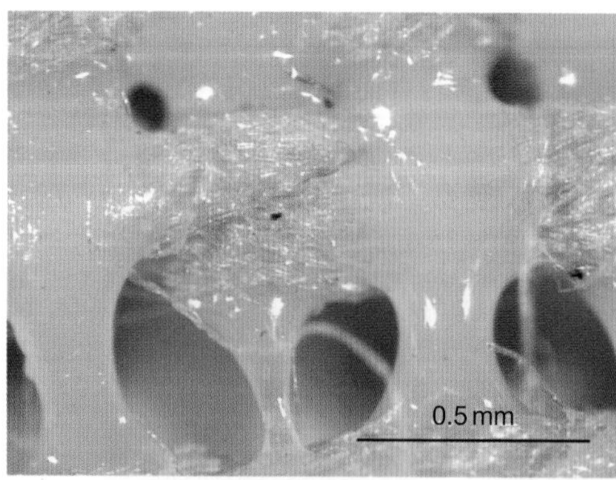

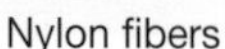

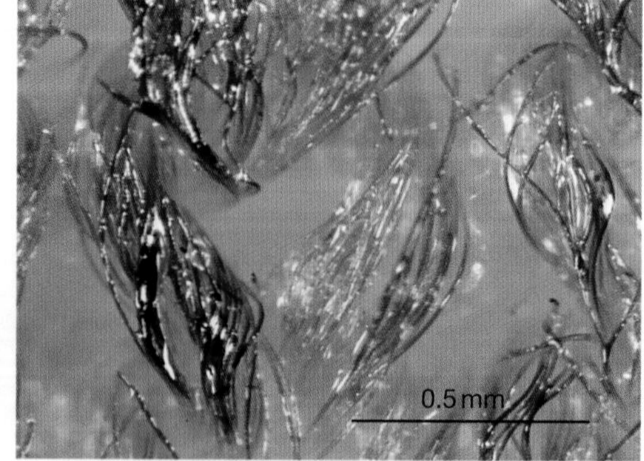

Viscose fibers

Figure 2 Stereomicroscopic images of damage to thermoplastic (nylon) and thermoset (viscose) fibers in mixed fabrics after brief contact with a hot metal plate at a temperature of about 572 °F/300 °C (magnification 50x).

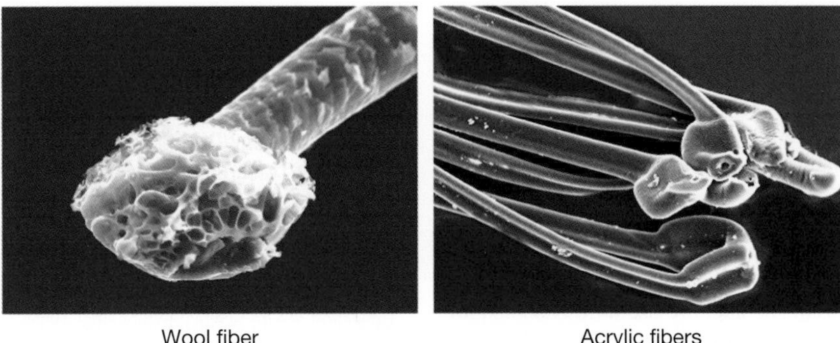

Figure 3 SEM images of different kinds of fibers coming from the area of a vapor cloud explosion (secondary electron image, magnification 200–500x).

accompanies a vapor cloud explosion. One of the most important factors that needs to be analyzed in order to determine the nature of the damage to the observed garment is the textile structure – areas of affected and unaffected fiber material alternate according to areas of different textile and yarn structure.

The concept of flashburning, the laboratory methodology used to identify it, and how an assessment of the overall distribution of such damage may allow a scientist to evaluate its evidential significance were studied based on two anonymized casework examples, demonstrating how this information had been interpreted and used in evidence in courts of law in the United Kingdom.

Materials that are capable of smoldering can be ignited by lighted cigarettes, but commonly encountered solid materials cannot be ignited directly by such a source. The mechanism of ignition of solid material by cigarettes was studied, as well as the smoldering process and the transition from smoldering to flaming combustion.

The prevalence of singed hairs on hands was examined in a representative sample comprising primarily Hamburg LKA staff members to determine the evidential value of such traces in criminal cases. Hair samples were taken from the hands of 160 subjects and examined under a microscope. Evidence of singeing was found in 53 of the samples. These traces were largely restricted to a limited number of areas. Distribution of singed hairs over a wide area was observed in just three subjects, all of whom reported contact with an open flame. The presence of singed hair on the back of the hand can be of great evidential value, though the corresponding distribution pattern must be carefully interpreted.

Microbiological Damage

This kind of damage is often seen in cases of examining textile materials coming from exhumations. Microorganisms may destroy fibers; cellulose fibers are more often damaged by fungi than by bacteria, but bacterial damage to animal fibers is observed more often than fungal damage. Both types of microorganisms can feed on natural fibers and on many types of textile and fiber additives based on natural substances (e.g., dyes, spinning oils, and softeners). Synthetic fibers are more resistant to microorganisms. Most of the bacteria and fungi, which play an important role in the process of organic material biodegradation, grow in a temperature of about 86 °F/ 30 °C. Fungi grow best in an acid habitat (pH 5.6–6.0) while the best conditions for bacterial growth are in an alkaline habitat (pH 7.0–8.0). In forensic practice, when damp evidential textile material is stored without access of air, one can observe the influence of humidity on this kind of damage.

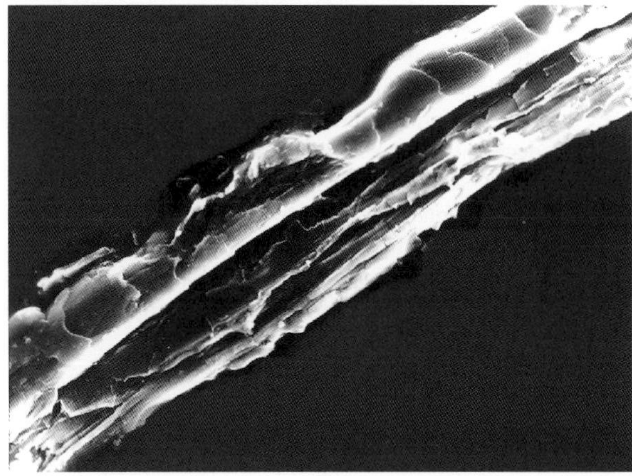

Figure 4 SEM image of wool fibers of the grey military fabric after 4 weeks of storing in biologically active soil (secondary electron image, magnification 1000x).

In another study, determination of changes in the morphological structure of woolen fabric and fibers of military uniforms after burial in biologically active soil for a particular period of time indicated that fungal and bacterial attacks led to changes in the color of the fabric and its looseness. The final decay, that is, the decomposition of the structure of the fabric of soldiers' uniforms took place 5–6 weeks after they had been buried in standardized, bioactive soil (literally, nothing was left of the textiles), and the observed changes in the morphological structure of fabric and fibers depended mainly on the duration of their burial in the soil. The scales on the surface of wool fibers became deformed and shredded; they merged and formed an almost undivided whole. They also decayed and internal parts of the fibers were exposed. Occasionally, a degradation of over half of the fibers was observed (**Figure 4**). The fibers situated on the external part of the thread were more quickly attacked by the microorganisms than were fibers located inside the thread. Taking into consideration the fact of the varying intensity of the process of biodegradation of particular fibers in the thread, one should be careful about the interpretation of the time of fabric decay based only on a microscopic examination. In order to ascertain the duration of decay, another kind of estimation of the degree of biodegradation, for example, chemical analysis or durability tests, should be applied.

Protocols for photography of archeological textiles to detect components of differing chemistry that are indicative of colorants were developed. Parameters of light source, camera distance, filter type, film type, film speed, and aperture size were evaluated for visible, UV reflectance, UV fluorescence, and infrared photography. Using these techniques facilitates selective sampling for further analysis that maximizes critical data acquisition, while minimizing destruction of the artifacts. Hence, forensic photography of archeological perishable materials should be regarded as a precursor to destructive analytical methods.

Characterization of metal threads (nine different metal fibers) on historical textile materials, chemical analysis of originally applied materials, the nature of their chemical and physical degradation, the sample constitution, morphology, topology, and chemical composition have been studied. A combination of methods encompassing SEM equipped with energy dispersive spectroscopy detector, inductively coupled plasma-optical emission spectroscopy, and atomic absorption spectrometry has proven to be very useful in analysis of such historical samples.

Conclusion

The assessment of textile and fiber damage is a complex, multifaceted, and challenging issue. These types of examinations can be undertaken only by experts with vast knowledge, great experience, and ability, and with the right combination of logic and intuition in their approach, depending on the given problem. The expert assessing textile and fiber damage must possess much additional information linked not only with the properties of the textile or the fiber, but also with the type and properties of the factors (mechanical, thermal, environmental, microbiological, etc.) that caused this damage. Sometimes, an appropriate simulation experiment must be carefully considered, but there will always be difficulties in attempting to simulate a scenario as accurately as possible. Unfortunately, a number of variables of damage processes may be unknown or cannot be replicated in laboratory conditions at a given time; consequently, great care must be exercised in drawing conclusions.

In spite of the complexity of the issues and the difficulties in interpreting observed changes, studies linked to textile and fiber damage are currently being undertaken in many laboratories throughout the world. They offer the possibility of greater individualization of results of analyses of textiles and fibers and/or of linking them with an incident, person, or object.

The study carried out in the field of damaged textiles and fibers, particularly in the area of interpretation of analytical results, will lead to better comparability and repeatability of examinations conducted for forensic purposes in different countries and to an increase in the evidential value of fiber and textile traces.

See also: **Biology/DNA:** Microbiology and Bioterrorism; **Chemistry/Trace/Fibers:** Color Analysis; Fiber Microscopy; Identification and Comparison; Interpretation of Fiber Evidence; **Chemistry/Trace/Fire Investigation:** Thermal Degradation; **Forensic Medicine/Clinical:** Airplane Crashes and Other Mass Disasters; Traffic Injuries and Deaths; **Investigations:** Evidence Collection at Fire Scenes; Explosions; Types of Fires; **Methods:** Analytical Light Microscopy; Microscopy (Electron); Spectroscopic Techniques.

Further Reading

Appel O and Kollo I (2010) The evidential value of singed hairs in arson cases. *Science and Justice* 50: 138–140.

Baldia CM and Jakes KA (2007) Photographic methods to detect colourants in archaeological textiles. *Journal of Archaeological Science* 34: 519–525.

Canetta E, Montiel K, and Adya AK (2009) Morphological changes in textile fibres exposed to environmental stresses: Atomic force microscopic examination. *Forensic Science International* 191: 6–14.

Healer JWS, Lomas B, and Cooke WD (1998) *Atlas of Fibre Fracture and Damage to Textiles*. Cambridge: Woodhead Publishing and The Textile Institute.

Holleyhead R (1999) Ignition of solid materials and furniture by lighted cigarettes. A review. *Science and Justice* 39(2): 75–102.

Kemp SE, Carr DJ, Kieser J, Niven BE, and Taylor MC (2009) Forensic evidence in apparel fabrics due to stab events. *Forensic Science International* 191: 86–96.

Leung EH and Halliday DX (2010) 'Flashburning' – Interpreting the presence of heat damage to a suspect's clothing and footwear in the investigation of fires. *Science and Justice* 50: 187–191.

NicDaeid N, Cassidy M, and McHugh S (2008) An investigation into the correlation of knife damage in clothing and the lengths of skin wounds. *Forensic Science International* 179: 107–110.

Rezic I, Curkovic L, and Ujevic M (2010) Simple methods for characterization of metals in historical textile threads. *Talanta* 82: 237–244.

Roux C, Favaloro K, Doble P, Robertson J, and Lennard C (2002) Implications of environmental impact for the forensic examination of textile fabrics and fibres. *Proceedings of the 16th Meeting of the International Association of Forensic Sciences, Montpellier, 38.*

Schindler WD (2009) Identifying and analyzing textile damage in the textile industry. In: Houck M (ed.) *Identification of Textile Fibres*, pp. 275–334. Cambridge: Woodhead Publishing and The Textile Institute.

Taupin J and Cwiklik ChJ (2011) Damage. *Forensic Examination of Clothing*, pp. 97–122. Boca Raton: CRC Press; Taylor and Francis.

Taupin J, Adolf F-P, and Robertson J (1999) Examination of damage to textiles. In: Robertson J and Grieve M (eds.) *Forensic Examination of Fibres*, 2nd edn., pp. 65–87. London, Philadelphia: Taylor & Francis Forensic Science Series.

Was-Gubala J (2009) The kinetics of colour change in textiles and fibres treated with detergent solutions. Part I – Colour perception and fluorescence microscopy analysis. *Science and Justice* 49: 165–169.

Was-Gubala J and Grzesiak E (2010) The kinetics of colour change in textiles and fibres treated with detergent solutions. Part II – Spectrophotometric measurements. *Science and Justice* 50: 55–58.

Was-Gubala J and Krauß W (2004a) Damage caused to fibres by vapour cloud explosions. *Forensic Science International* 141: 77–83.

Was-Gubala J and Krauß W (2004b) Textile damage caused by vapour cloud explosions. *Science and Justice* 44: 209–215.

Was-Gubala J and Krauß W (2006) Damage caused to fibres by the action of two types of heat. *Forensic Science International* 159: 119–126.

Was-Gubala J and Salerno-Kochan R (2000) The biodegradation of the fabric of soldiers' uniforms. *Science and Justice* 40(1): 15–20.

Fiber Microscopy

JM Hemmings, Australian Federal Police, Forensic and Data Centres, Canberra, ACT, Australia

Glossary

Anisotropic A difference when measured along different axes (for fibers it is the difference between along the fiber and across the fiber).
Birefringent The difference between the refractive indices in the perpendicular and horizontal plane of the fiber.
Dye A soluble colorant, usually organic, used to impart color.
Monochromatic Light of a narrow (or single) frequency.
Pigment A substance in particulate form, that is predominantly insoluble, used to modify color of light-reflecting properties.
Polarized light Orientation of light into a wave of a single direction.
Polarizer A device used to obtain plane-polarized light.
Questioned fiber/s Fiber/s recovered from a surface that are visually similar to the target fiber and may have been transferred by the known textile.
Refractive index Measure of the speed of light in a medium.
Stereoscopic The illusion of depth.
Target fibers Fibers collected from a known textile that will be used in the screening and comparison process.

Introduction

One of the inherent disadvantages of fiber evidence is its small size (fiber diameters are usually measured in microns). Aside from the issues of contamination and loss that this raises, there is also the necessity to visualize this microscopic evidence (even before analyzing it). The role of magnification through microscopy is therefore an essential aspect of any fiber examination and time has seen the incorporation of various microscopic instruments (such as the polarizing light microscope) to determine the physical and optical properties of fibers for comparison and identification purposes. Microscopes have also been used as attachments to analytical equipment (such as the infrared (IR) and Raman spectrometers) to enable the chemical characterization that these instruments provide for fibers and their dyes/pigments.

The skill of utilizing the types of microscopes encountered in the laboratory is essential for any fiber examiner. This article aims to introduce the range of microscopes commonly used in the forensic fiber examiner's laboratory and to discuss the value of microscopy.

Instruments Used for Fiber Microscopy

Microscopy is used during the collection, recovery, and analysis of fibers. The purpose of microscopy in these various processes is to primarily visualize fibers and subsequently to examine and compare the physical, optical, and chemical features of different fibers. In order to achieve this, various types of microscopes are used (and at different stages of the fiber examination). **Figure 1** shows the general comparison examination scheme for fibers and the types of microscopes that can be used at each stage.

Summarized below are the main types of microscopes encountered in the laboratory of a fiber examiner; other types may be utilized (such as hot stage microscopy) but are not used routinely.

Stereomicroscope

This is a low-powered microscope that has a typical magnification range of 2.5 times to 100 times. It combines two aligned compound microscopes to give the examiner a stereoscopic view of the fibers (refer to **Figure 2** for an example of a stereomicroscope, observe the long working distance). The stereomicroscope can be set up as reflected light or transmitted light (reflected light is the most common for fiber examinations) to compare physical properties and can have various imaging attachments such as cameras. Some stereomicroscopes can also include polarized light as well as incident fluorescence to compare optical properties at a relatively low magnification.

Comparison Microscope

Comparison microscopy allows for the real-time comparison of the physical and some optical characteristics of two fiber samples (typically a target and a questioned fiber). This is achieved by having two compound microscopes joined by an optical bridge (refer to **Figure 3** for an example of a comparison microscope). Typically, comparison microscopes allow for transmission bright-field microscopy as well as polarizing light and incident fluorescence microscopy at varying magnifications (up to 1500 times).

The comparison microscope is one of the most powerful techniques in the fiber comparison/identification process as the side-by-side comparison allows for the discrimination of fibers based on color and the high magnification allows for the resolution of microscopic physical features.

In order for the features of both fibers to be compared using this setup, it is critical that both samples are mounted under the same conditions and viewed using the same illumination.

Fluorescence Microscope

A fluorescence microscope is an optical microscope that exploits the fluorescent properties, if present, of a fiber (of fiber substrate as well as any dyes, pigments, or surface treatments

 http://dx.doi.org/10.1016/B978-0-12-382165-2.00095-7

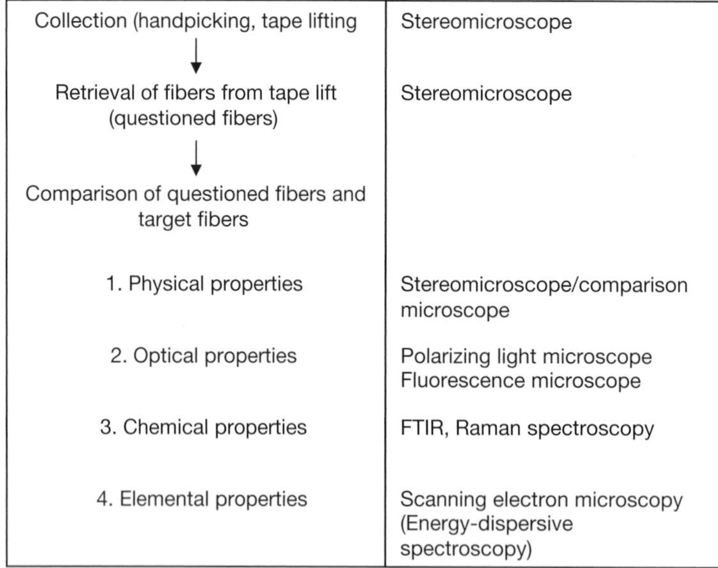

Examination	Microscope
Collection (handpicking, tape lifting ↓	Stereomicroscope
Retrieval of fibers from tape lift (questioned fibers) ↓	Stereomicroscope
Comparison of questioned fibers and target fibers	
1. Physical properties	Stereomicroscope/comparison microscope
2. Optical properties	Polarizing light microscope Fluorescence microscope
3. Chemical properties	FTIR, Raman spectroscopy
4. Elemental properties	Scanning electron microscopy (Energy-dispersive spectroscopy)

Figure 1 General flowchart of fiber examination (left) and associated microscopes (right).

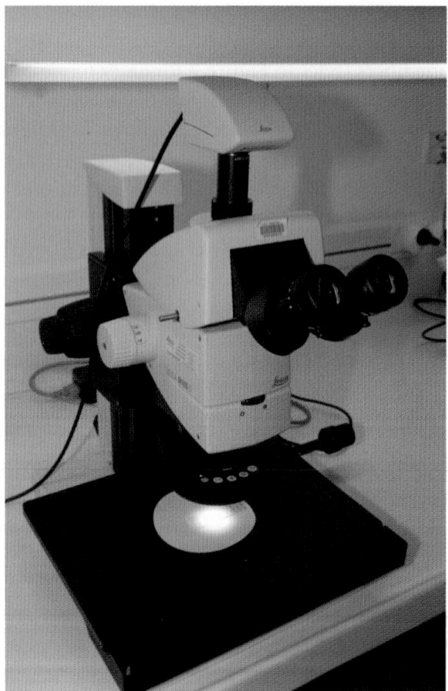

Figure 2 Stereomicroscope with camera attachment.

present). This microscope impinges light of a known wavelength onto the fiber; if the sample is fluorescent, it will emit light at a longer wavelength that will be detected through the microscope objective. For each wavelength tested, two filters are required: the excitation (or illumination) filter, which is used to ensure that the light emitted is at the desired wavelength and is as near monochromatic as possible, and the second is the emission filter, which filters out the light at the excitation wavelength (which is much stronger than the emitted light) after it has interacted with the fiber. Modern fluorescent microscopes allow for multiple filter sets to examine a range of wavelengths from ultraviolet to red. As previously mentioned, modern comparison microscopes are equipped with accessories to view and compare the fluorescent characteristics of fibers and the need for a separate fluorescence microscope is diminishing.

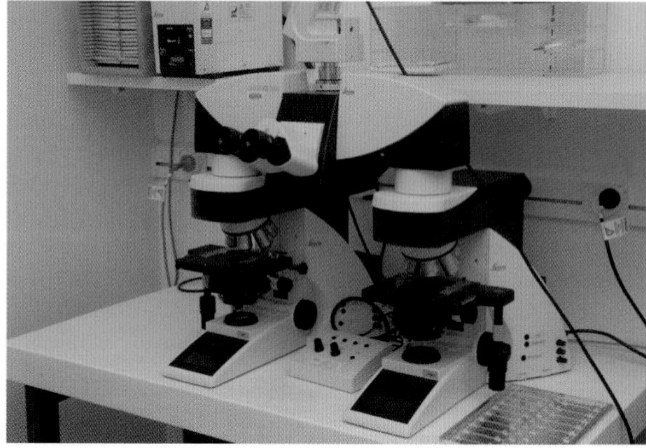

Figure 3 A comparison microscope.

Polarizing Microscope

A polarizing light microscope uses two polarizing filters (termed the polarizer and the analyzer), one placed below the specimen and the other placed above the specimen. When the filters are at right angles to each other, they are considered 'crossed'. This type of microscope is designed to visualize fibers based on their anisotropic properties. As the plane-polarized light interacts with the fiber, two individual wave components are created with one along the fiber and one across the fiber. The velocities of these wave components are different and are based on the crystalline structure of the fiber. This contrast technique, in the hands of an experienced microscopist, is useful in discriminating between manmade fibers.

Microscopes as Attachments

Most stand-alone microscopes in the laboratory will provide information in relation to the physical and optical properties of fibers. However, in order to determine the chemical, color, or elemental properties, it is necessary to utilize analytical equipment such as an IR spectrometer, spectrophotometer, Raman spectrometer, and/or scanning electron microscope–electron dispersive spectrometer (SEM–EDS). As fibers are generally microscopic in nature, these analytical instruments require microscopes as attachment to be functional for a fiber examiner. IR and Raman spectrometers and spectrophotometers utilize light microscopes and SEM–EDS utilize electron microscopes.

Role of Microscopy in Fiber Examinations

The role of microscopy varies depending on the stage of the fiber examination (summarized in **Figure 1**). The following section outlines the role of microscopy for each of the fiber examination processes.

Collection and Recovery

Unless fibers are discovered at the crime scene as a clump of fibers or a torn section of fabric, they will require some level of collection prior to any detailed examination. Collection can be precise with the use of a low-powered stereomicroscope and handpicking from the textile surface (very time consuming and therefore rarely used for a whole textile surface) or it may be more generalized with the use of adhesive tape applied to the surface of a textile to gather any loosely adhered fibers. If a stereomicroscope is used as a tool during collection, a boom arm with the microscope attached is ideal, as this enables the examiner to move the microscope over an item without touching it (and thereby disrupting or possibly contaminating evidence).

Once fibers are collected, they need to be screened for the presence of fibers that are visually similar to the target fiber/s. This is one of the most time-consuming steps of the fiber examination process, while there have been some steps toward automating this process it is still largely manual. Typically, the examiner compares the fibers of interest (i.e., the target fibers) against the fibers on a tape-lift using a stereomicroscope. The examiner will mark those fibers on the tape-lifts that are visually similar to the target fibers for removal. These marked and recovered fibers are the 'questioned fibers.'

The large working distance and wide field of view of the stereomicroscope enable the examiner to screen large amounts of fibers at this stage. The relatively low magnification and inability to do a direct side-by-side comparison of the target and questioned fibers mean that the range of fibers marked is generally wider (and therefore more in number) than the range of the target fiber.

At the screening stage of the fiber examination process, the use of a stereomicroscope enables an examiner to discriminate fibers based on color, relative diameter, crimp, and, in most cases, whether the fiber is manmade or natural.

Comparison

At the comparison stage of the fiber examination process, the examiner needs to determine if the fibers recovered and mounted from the screening stage show no significant differences from the known fiber/s. This requires a comparison of physical, optical, and chemical characteristics. This is achieved through the use of bright-field microscopy with attachments for examining under polarized light and incident fluorescent light for physical and optical properties. The determination of chemical properties is through the use of additional instrumental techniques such as IR and Raman spectroscopy (with microscope attachments).

Physical properties

The majority of the physical features of a fiber are created during the growing process for a natural fiber or the extrusion process for a manmade fiber (additional physical features are introduced during the processing of a fiber into a textile, such as color). The comparison of physical features is predominantly undertaken by the comparison microscope which requires that the samples being compared are mounted and lit in the same manner.

Physical features that can be compared at this stage are:

1. *Color*: Color can be imparted to textiles at the fiber, yarn, fabric, or garment/textile product stage through the use of dyes or pigments. Color, due to its high variability, is one of the most important characteristics for comparison. The color observed by the forensic fiber examiner can be described approximately in terms of hue (i.e., predominantly red, green, brown, blue, etc.), saturation (the nearness of the color observed, in purity, to the associated spectral color), and lightness (the intensity of the color). Natural fibers will tend to show a greater variability of color, predominantly due to the irregular uptake of dye (i.e., variation of lightness), than the variability observed for manmade fibers. It is important for the fiber examiner to know the variability of the known fibers when comparing the recovered/questioned fibers.
2. *Diameter*: The fiber diameter is a function of the fiber type and growing conditions for natural fibers and the extrusion process for manmade fibers. Once again, the range of diameter for natural fibers is more variable than that observed for manmade fibers due to the controlled conditions for the manufacture of manmade fibers.
3. *Delustrant*: This is a material (predominantly the anatase form of titanium dioxide) that is added to the polymer composition of manmade fibers prior to extrusion. Delustrant is added to reduce the luster of fibers and it can vary with respect to quantity, shape, size, and distribution. Refer to **Figure 4** for examples of delustrant in manmade fibers.

4. *Cross-sectional shape*: The shape of the transverse cross-section of a manmade fiber is a result of the shape of the spinneret/s used during extrusion. The cross-sectional shape of the fiber is determined by the end use of the particular fiber (i.e., trilobal fibers are useful for carpet as they 'hide' the dirt in the three channels produced by the lobes, thereby making carpet appear cleaner for longer). Refer to **Figure 5** for some longitudinal views of fibers with different cross-sections.
5. *Draw marks (or fish eyes)*: If insoluble material is present on the surface of the fiber (either purposely there, such as delustrant, or as a result of surface contamination), then as the fiber is 'drawn' after the extrusion process the fiber polymer is pulled away (in both directions) from the surface material. This can produce what looks like an 'eye' on the surface of the fiber. Refer to **Figure 6** (far left image) for an example of draw marks.
6. *Fine striations*: These are fine lines that generally run along a fiber. Striations are most obvious in rayon fibers (and are used and identifying characteristic) that occur as the fiber shrinks from the removal of solvent causing the 'skin' of the fiber to wrinkle.
7. *Twist/convolutions/crimp*: These are features that can be added to a manmade fiber during the spinning process. These are added to improve the manmade fiber for its end use. Refer to **Figure 6** for an example of crimp.

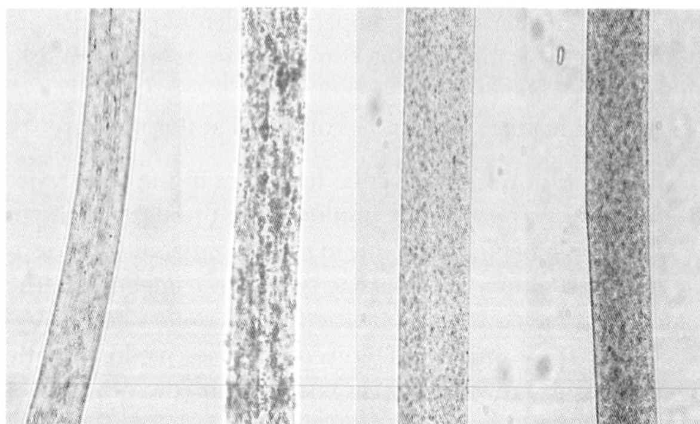

Figure 4 Varying density and fineness of delustrant in some colourless manmade fibers.

8. *Voids*: These are irregular air spaces within the fiber polymer itself.
9. *Internal channels*: These are regular, intentional air spaces that run the internal length of a fiber. These are usually created to a produce a fiber with a specific end use such as a technical textile used for sports apparel.

If the comparison microscope is fitted for fluorescence and polarizing microscopy, these optical properties can also be compared; if not, separate bright-field microscopes will need to be used.

Optical properties

Most fibers will exhibit some level of fluorescence whether it is from the fiber substrate (such as the dull green of cotton with ultraviolet excitation), the dyes or pigments, optical brighteners, and/or contaminants. The best result is achieved by using a number of excitation filters that will cover the range of wavelengths from ultraviolet to green. The observation of a fiber's fluorescent properties is useful in discriminating fibers, as color in fibers is usually achieved through combination of two or more dyes/pigments. Dyes and pigments are generally fluorescent and will fluoresce in a range colors and with different excitation wavelengths.

The arrangement of molecules is generally aligned along the length of the fiber which means that for all fibers polarized light will travel at different speeds along the fiber compared to across the fiber (i.e., fibers are anisotropic). This results in different refractive indices in each direction (with the higher refractive index generally along the length of the fiber). The difference between the two refractive indices for a fiber can be measured and is referred to as the birefringence. The birefringence of a fiber can be calculated by determining the refractive indices in each direction through the immersion method (using oils of known refractive indices) or by calculating, from the known thickness of the fiber, the retardation of the light (amount by which the light wave in one direction is slowed down in comparison with the other). This requires the aid of a Michel-Lévy chart. For comparison purposes, this will provide a good indication of the fiber subtype as follows:

1. Acrylic, modacrylic, or acetate – first order (gray colors)
2. Nylon, polypropylene, or rayon – second order (bright)
3. Polyester, specialized fiber – high order (white)

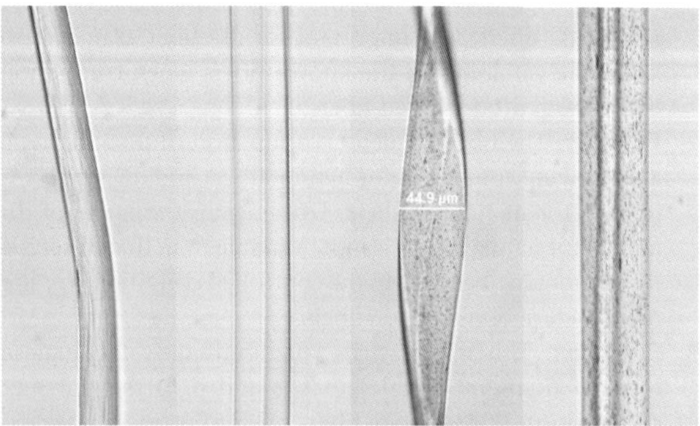

Figure 5 Indication of cross-section from optical microscopy in some manmade fibers (from left to right) – round, dogbone (or bilobal), ribbon, and multilobal (most likely trilobal).

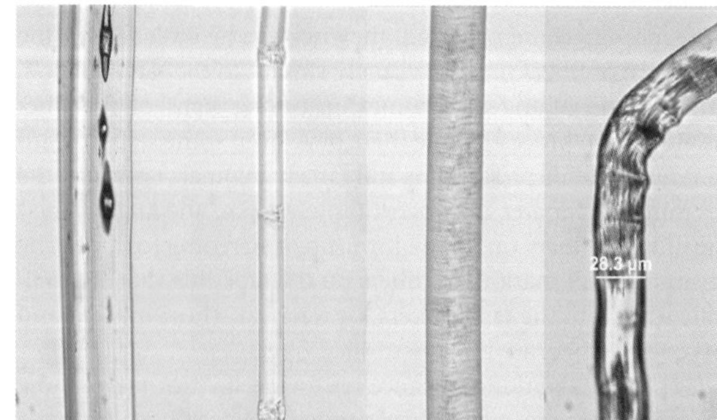

Figure 6 Some physical features that may be present in manmade fibers (from left to right) – draw marks (also known as fisheyes), false nodes, surface texture, and crimp.

Table 1 Comparison of the microscopical features of cotton and flax

Vegetable fiber	*Microscopic features*
Cotton	• Ribbon like with twists (convolutions) at intervals along fiber • Lumen (central canal) is flattened and large and may not be very visible
Flax	• Nodes at interval along fiber length (in the shape of V, X, or I) • Width varies • Small lumen (typically less than half the fiber width) • Often seen as bundles o fibers

Table 2 Comparison of the microscopical features of wool and silk

Protein fiber	*Microscopic features*
Wool (fine)	• Presence of scales giving rough appearance to outer surface • Minimal to no medulla (may appear as row or dots)
Silk (cultivated)	• Cylindrical cross-section (slightly triangular) • Periodic bulges • Possible faint striations

Identification

The identification of the generic fiber type is important for the fiber examiner; not only is it necessary as a feature for comparison, but it may also be important in determining the possible end use of a fiber for intelligence purposes. Microscopy can be used to identify a fiber type either as a stand-alone technique or when attached to an analytical instrument. The following will outline the role of microscopy as a stand-alone technique for identifying fibers, as analytical techniques such as IR spectroscopy are covered in other areas of this text. It must be noted that for manmade fibers, microscopy will give an indication of fiber subtype through the observation of physical features and the estimation of birefringence; however, complete identification requires the use of an analytical technique such as IR spectroscopy.

The identification of natural fibers is almost exclusively the domain of microscopy (sometimes microchemical or burn testing is also required for confirmation). The physical characteristics imparted during the growing process (be it a cotton fiber or a wool fiber) generally enable the microscopist to discriminate between fibers of similar origin such as the bast fibers, ramie, and hemp. Table 1 outlines some of the microscopic features that can be used to discriminate between the vegetable fibers of cotton and flax origin and Table 2 outlines some of the microscopic features that can be used to discriminate between the protein fibers, wool, and silk.

Examiners must be aware that a large amount of processing can lead to changes in the features of a fiber and can hinder identification. The use of a comprehensive reference collection will help with the identification of a natural fiber as well as the facilities to undertake burn or other microchemical testing.

Conclusion

Microscopy is a quick, accurate, and nondestructive tool that is used in the recovery, identification, and comparison of fiber evidence. It is a key element in fiber examinations, whether it is utilized as a stand-alone technique or as an accessory to an analytical instrument such as the Raman spectrometer. A knowledge of the broad range of microscopes available is important for the forensic fiber examiner and this knowledge must include an understanding of theory, the types of microscopes available, their respective advantages and disadvantages, and, importantly, when to utilize which microscope during the fiber examination process.

When microscopy is utilized effectively by the forensic fiber examiner, a large amount of information is available for the comparison and identification of fiber evidence.

See also: **Chemistry/Trace/Fibers:** Fiber: Protocols for Examination; Identification and Comparison; Color Analysis; **Methods:** Analytical Light Microscopy; Microscopy (Electron).

Further Reading

Cook JG (1968a) *Handbook of Textile Fibres. Natural Fibres*, vol. 1. England: Merrow.
Cook JG (1968b) *Handbook of Textile Fibres. Man-Made Fibres*, vol. 2. England: Merrow.
Greaves PH and Saville BP (1995) *Microscopy of Textile Fibers.* Oxford: BIOS Scientific Publishers.
Palenick SP (1999) Microscopical examination of fibres. In: Robertson J and Grieve M (eds.) *Forensic Examination of Fibres*, 2nd edn., pp. 153–177. London: Taylor and Francis.
Petraco N and Kubic T (2004) *Colour Atlas and Manual of Microscopy for Criminalists, Chemists and Conservators.* Boca Raton, FL: CRC Press.
The Textile Institute (1975) *Identification of Textile Materials*, 7th edn. Manchester: The Textile Institute.
The Textile Institute (2002) *Textile Terms and Definitions*, 11th edn. Manchester: The Textile Institute.
Wheeler BP and Wilson LJ (2008) *Practical Forensic Microscopy: A Laboratory Manual.* Sussex: Wiley.

Relevant Websites

http://www.olympusmicro.com/index.html – Olympus Microscopy Resource Centre.

Color Analysis

P Martin, CRAIC Technologies, San Dimas, CA, USA

Glossary

Light The portion of the electromagnetic spectrum detectable by the human eye.

Microspectrophotometer An instrument used for measuring the photometric intensity of each wavelength in the ultraviolet, visible, and near-infrared regions from a microscopic sampling area.

Standard illuminant In color science, the standard illuminant is a theoretical source of light with a defined spectral power distribution.

Introduction

Color is part of our daily life. We perceive different colors, in all their shades and hues, and these impressions are an important part of our lives. Our brains are conditioned genetically and since birth so that color serves to differentiate and identify objects and even affects our moods. As such, color has become an important part of the way we communicate with one another and interact with our surroundings.

Sir Isaac Newton, in his treatise *Opticks*, stated: "For the Rays to speak properly are not coloured. In them there is nothing else than a certain Power and Disposition to stir up a Sensation of this or that Colour." Simply put, color is a subjective physical experience and not a property of electromagnetic energy. When we perceive color, our brains are interpreting the signals generated by our eyes after they have interacted with specific wavelengths of electromagnetic energy. As such, color is not a measurable phenomenon but only something that we perceive and describe.

In this section, we discuss electromagnetic energy and color and how it is related to human vision. The discussion continues with how trace evidence is analyzed instrumentally by the way it interacts with ultraviolet (UV), visible, and near-infrared (NIR) energy. Techniques for the preparation and analysis of trace evidence are also discussed, as are the basics of spectral interpretation.

What is Color?

The color of an object, as we perceive it, arises from how that object affects the light with which it interacts and the wavelength of that light. The effects can be broken down into two categories: chemical and structural. The chemical effects range from reflectance, absorbance, or the various forms of emission. The structural effects are many, with some common ones being surface roughness relative to illuminating light wavelength or the 'rainbow' from interference effects, as seen with a layer of oil on water.

The human eye perceives electromagnetic energy from approximately 400 to 700 nm. Of course, normal biological variation means that this spectral range varies from person to person, but in general this is the range. Electromagnetic energy in this region is called 'light' and this region is called the 'visible range.' The visible range is a very small part of the entire electromagnetic spectrum, which spans gamma rays to long radio waves. For a human to perceive colors, four basic conditions are to be met. The first is that there must be a source of light. Second, the object should have color. Third, an observer has to be present and, lastly, the human brain has to decode the signals from the observer.

The source is a physically realizable source of light. It is something whose spectral power distribution can be experimentally determined. A 'standard source' is a light source that has been measured with a high degree of accuracy and has been specified. An example of a standard source would be a tungsten halogen lamp. Illuminants that are used in color science are not sources. The 'standard illuminant' is light defined by a theoretical spectral power distribution. The concept of illuminants provides the basis for comparing colors under theoretically identical conditions. The experimenter measures the emission from a standard source and compares it with the published spectra for a particular illuminant. By removing the spectral characteristics of the light source and substituting it with that of an illuminant, color comparisons may be made with a greater degree of accuracy.

The perception of color also requires that the object must interact with light and we must detect that light. Photons that impinge upon the object may be reflected, transmitted, or emitted, or there may be some physical characteristic of the object that causes a change in the light. Examples of reflection would include the red of an apple, while that of transmission would be the colors from a stained glass window. Emission would be the color of light from a light emitting diode (LED). An example of a physical characteristic causing the effect of color would be a thin film of oil on water. The film appears to have different colors depending upon the source and viewing angle, thickness of the film, and the types of oil involved.

The last two components required for color to be perceived are the human eye and the brain to process the nerve signals from the eye. In the eye, light is focused by the eye's lens onto the retina, which is a thin layer on the inside of the eye and includes rods and cones. Rods are primarily sensitive to changes in the light intensity. On the other hand, there are three types of cones in the human visual system. Each type has an optimal sensitivity to light at a different range of wavelengths. One type is most sensitive at 420 nm, another at 534 nm, and the third at 564 nm. This corresponds to optimal sensitivity in the blue,

 http://dx.doi.org/10.1016/B978-0-12-382165-2.00096-9

green, and red regions, in that order. Additionally, the rods have an optimal sensitivity at 498 nm, which we perceive as green. Signals from each of these cells travel by nerves to the brain, which processes the signal for us to perceive color.

Microspectroscopy Techniques

Microspectrophotometers are used for ultraviolet (UV), visible, and NIR analysis of microscopic samples because they avoid many artifacts of the human visual system while providing more information than possible by the eye. The microspectrophotometer integrates a spectrophotometer with a microscope so that it can acquire spectra of microscopic samples of evidence such as fibers, dyed hair, paint chips, and glass fragments. Depending upon the instrument configuration, commercial microspectrophotometers can have spectral sensitivity ranging from the deep UV (200 nm) all the way to the NIR (2100 nm) (**Figure 1**). They can be configured to measure samples by absorbance or reflectance microspectroscopy, as well as by polarization, fluorescence, and other types of luminescence microspectroscopy. While microspectrophotometers can be configured to measure sampling areas smaller than a micrometer, most recovered trace evidence is larger than 10 μm because of the fact that recovery tools such as stereomicroscopes do not generally have the magnification to locate smaller pieces.

The microscope portion of a UV–visible–NIR microspectrophotometer has a special optical design that allows for an effective spectral range over the entire region. This is important for accurate color measurements because most commercially available microscopes do not transmit even the entire visible range, leading to inaccuracies in color measurements. In order to achieve a broad spectral range, a UV–visible–NIR microscope uses a combination of lenses and mirrors that are optimized for this range. Such microscopes also feature light sources that emit energy from the UV to the NIR region.

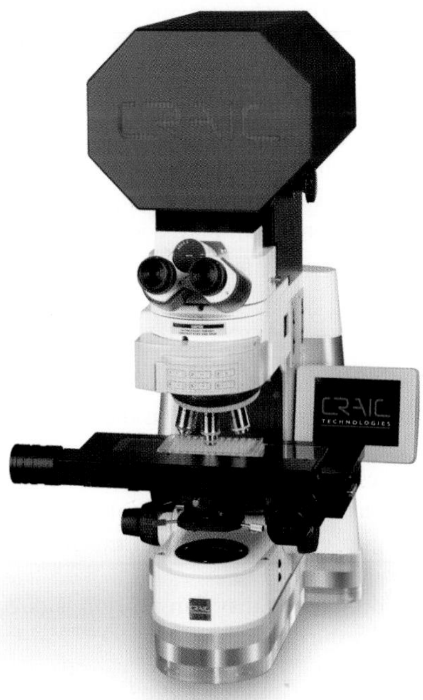

Figure 1 A UV–visible–NIR microspectrophotometer.

The spectrophotometer portion of the microspectrophotometer is designed to work with the optical and spectral characteristics of the microscope. As with the microscope, the spectrophotometer is optimized to work in the UV–visible–NIR by using appropriate optical materials, optical design, and detectors. Modern microspectrophotometers use a static optical path, combined with an array detector containing thousands of individual light sensors or pixels. For the spectral range from 200 to 1000 nm, charge coupled devices (CCDs) are favored because of their sensitivity and speed. For the NIR, indium gallium arsenide (InGaAs) arrays are generally used for the region from 900 to 2200 nm. The use of array detectors offers several advantages. Speed is the most obvious; spectra can be measured in terms of milliseconds for the entire spectral range. Second, spectrometers can be designed with rigidly mounted optical components and will remain calibrated for longer periods. Third, multiple scans may be averaged in order to improve the signal-to-noise ratio, resulting in higher quality spectra.

The microspectrophotometer consists of light sources, optics to illuminate the sample and to collect light from the sample, imaging apparatus to view the sample and to align it, optics to guide the light from the microscope into the spectrophotometer, the spectrophotometer, and, of course, the software to control it all. The basis behind the microspectrophotometer is that white light illuminates the sample and, depending upon the molecular structure of the sample, different wavelengths interact in different ways with the sample. Light of all wavelengths is then collected from the sample and directed into the spectrophotometer where a grating serves to separate the white light into each wavelength and focus each wavelength onto a different pixel on the detector. The intensity of each wavelength is then measured by each pixel and the result is plotted as an *XY* graph. Traditionally, the *X*-axis is in nanometers while the *Y*-axis varies depending upon the type of illumination. Color analysis of fiber evidence is done with transmission and fluorescence microspectroscopy.

Transmission Microspectroscopy

When the microspectrophotometer is used to measure transmission or absorbance spectra, the light source illuminates the sample from below. Depending upon the sample's molecular structure, it will absorb some frequencies and transmit the rest. The portion transmitted is collected by the objective and then focused onto the entrance aperture of the spectrophotometer. As this entrance aperture is mirrored, most of the field of view is imaged by a digital camera. This provides the user with the ability to see the entrance aperture in the same focal plane as the sample, making it very simple to ensure that the spectrophotometer is actually measuring the sample and not something else. The light from the sample also enters the spectrophotometer through the entrance aperture where it is separated by wavelength, and each wavelength is focused onto

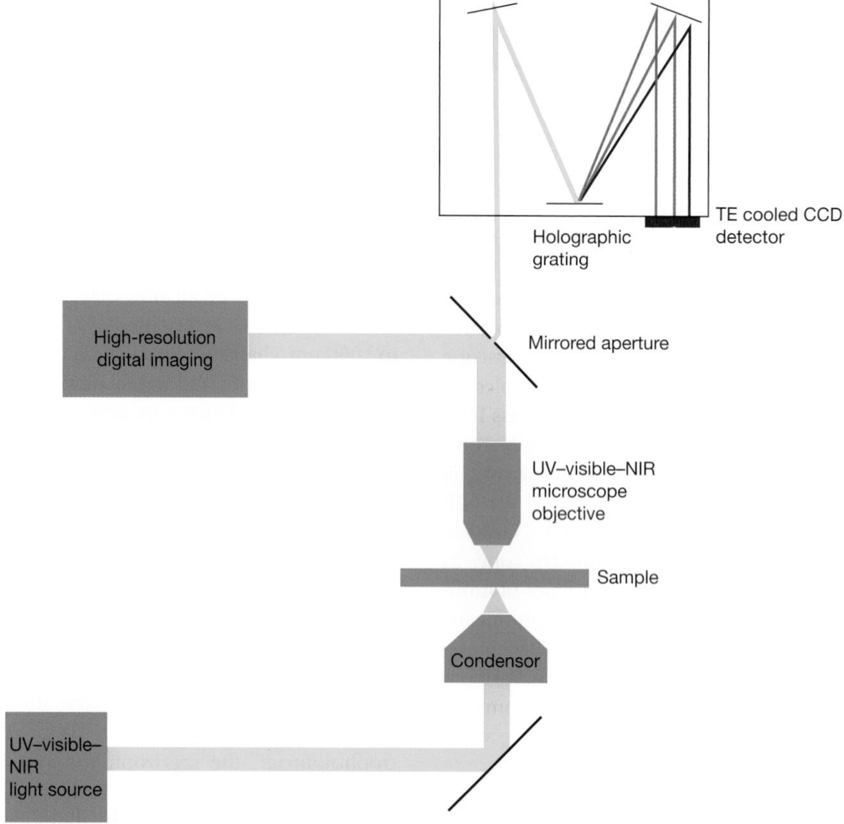

Figure 2 Optical path for a modern UV–visible–NIR microspectrophotometer configured for transmission microspectroscopy.

a separate pixel on the array detector. Each pixel measures the intensity of the light and the results are reported as an *XY* graph with the *Y*-axis in units of either transmission or absorbance and the *X*-axis in units of nanometers (**Figure 2**).

Acquiring a transmission or absorbance spectrum consists of a series of steps. The reason is that each component of the microspectrophotometer has its own optical characteristics. If these characteristics are not taken into account, then the final spectrum will consist of not only the spectrum from the sample but also the spectral response of the light sources, optics, and even the detector. This is one of the problems with the human visual system: we are unable to eliminate the spectral characteristics of light sources and the eye itself, so our brain has evolved compensation mechanisms. However, the microspectrophotometer eliminates this issue in that it can measure the optical characteristics of its light source, optics, and even the detector, and eliminate them from the final result.

The process begins by locating the sample to be measured, such as a fiber, and focusing the microscope on the sample. The optical path is then adjusted so that the sample is Kohler-illuminated. The sample is then moved with the microscope stage so that the entrance aperture of the spectrophotometer, as visualized on the computer, is just off the edge of the sample. The spectrophotometer is then optimized in terms of the required spectral range and integration time. Next, a dark scan is acquired. This is simply a measurement of the electronic noise of the system across the spectral range of interest. A reference spectrum, with the aperture just off the sample, is then acquired. The reference spectrum contains the optical response of the light source, the optics, the detector, the sample slide and cover slip, as well as the mounting media. The microscope stage is then moved so that the spectrophotometer aperture covers the area of the sample to be measured, and the sample spectrum is acquired. The computer then performs the following calculation so that only the spectral response of the sample of interest is displayed in what is called a 'corrected spectrum'

$$C_t = \frac{S - D}{R - D}$$

where C_t is the corrected spectrum, *S* is the sample spectrum, *R* is the reference spectrum, and *D* is the dark scan. The result is either a transmission or absorbance spectrum of just the sample of interest. The instrumental spectral response has been eliminated, giving much more accurate data about the sample and helping to eliminate potential experimental errors from the sample data.

It should be noted that transmission is directly related to absorbance by the equation

$$A = -\log T$$

where *A* is the absorbance and *T* is the transmittance. Which type of scale is displayed in spectra is usually a matter of preference or laboratory policy.

Fluorescence Microspectroscopy

For fluorescence microspectroscopy, incident illumination is also used. This means that a light source is used to illuminate the sample from above. But while fluorescence does use an incident light path, it does not utilize a white-light source but a line source able to illuminate the sample at specific wavelengths with high energy. In most forensic microspectroscopy instruments, this is accomplished by having the light pass through a cube-shaped holder containing three filters. The filter set serves to isolate a single wavelength of light and focus that onto the sample via the objective. If the sample fluoresces when excited by the illuminating photons, the emitted light is collected by the objective and passed again through the filter cube. At this point, the filter cube is being used to block the exciting light that has been reflected, as the intensity of the reflected light is generally much greater than the intensity of the fluorescent emission. The fluorescent emission passes into the spectrophotometer, which measures its intensity relative to wavelength. The spectrum consists of an *XY* graph with the *Y*-axis being intensity in counts, which is a unitless value, and the *X*-axis in nanometers (Figure 3).

The operation for measuring the fluorescence spectra is similar to that of reflectance microspectroscopy except that a reference scan is not required. The first step is to locate, and focus on, the sample. The sample is then moved with the microscope stage so that the entrance aperture of the spectrophotometer, as visualized on the computer monitor, is on the sample. The spectrophotometer is then optimized in terms of the required spectral range and the integration time. Next, a dark scan is acquired, which is a measurement of the electronic noise of the system at each point in the spectral range of interest. And, as this is a unitless measurement, a reference spectrum is not required. At this point, a fluorescence emission spectrum of the sample is acquired. The computer then performs the following calculation so that fluorescent intensity relative to the wavelength relative to wavelength is displayed

$$C_f = S - D$$

where C_f is the uncorrected emission spectrum, S is the sample spectrum, and D is the dark scan. The result is a fluorescence spectrum but with no correction across the spectral range displayed for variations in detector sensitivity, optics, and light source. The spectrum allows for comparison of the fluorescent emission between samples by the wavelengths of the peaks as well as by their relative intensities. While corrections are possible, they are laborious and limited in spectral range and therefore not done for most forensic work.

Sample Preparation

Trace evidence sample preparation for microspectroscopy is similar to the techniques used for standard microscopy and microscale imaging. However, as the spectral range is beyond that of a standard microscope, different materials may have to be used. Commonly found glass microscope slides and coverslips do not transmit UV light very well.

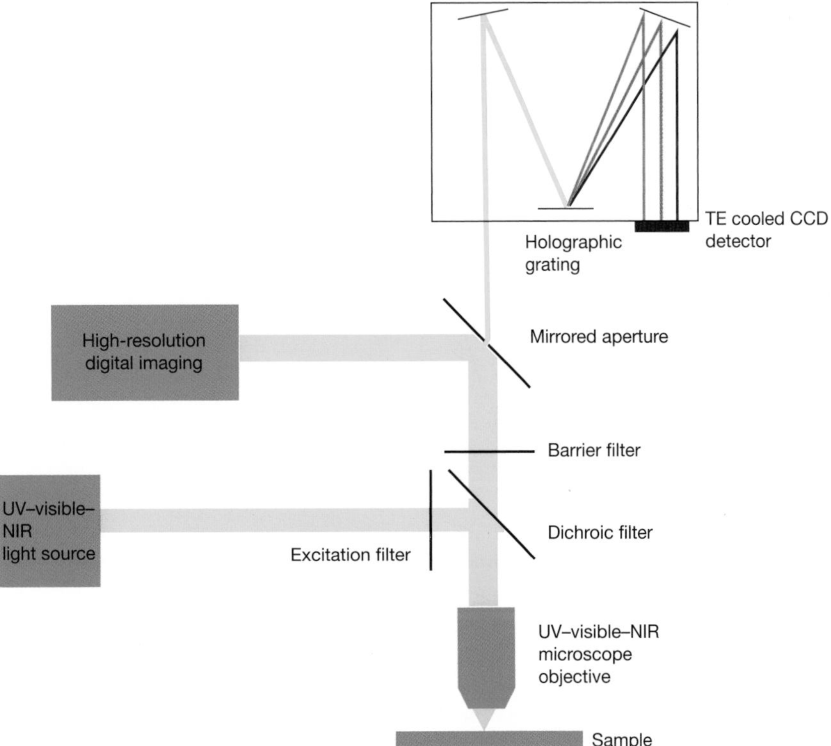

Figure 3 Optical path for a modern UV–visible–NIR microspectrophotometer configured for fluorescence microspectroscopy.

Similarly, most commercially available mounting media contain compounds that strongly absorb the UV, and many media also exhibit a low-intensity fluorescent emission that can interfere with any fluorescence emission from an evidentiary sample.

When preparing samples for transmission microspectroscopy, sample preparation must take into account the experimental parameters. If measurements are to be made in the UV range, synthetic quartz slides and coverslips must be used, as they have a high level of UV transmissivity. Care should also be taken in selecting the type of quartz material, as certain types of synthetic quartz have superior deep-UV transmissivity. The slides must also be of high optical quality in their manufacture to avoid artifacts due to defects in their construction. Slides of this quality do not exhibit any optical emission that can interfere with fluorescence microspectroscopy.

The mounting medium of choice for this type of microspectroscopy is fresh high-purity glycerol. Glycerol is a water-soluble and nonpermanent medium with a high level of UV transmissivity with no fluorescent emission. The medium should be fresh, of high purity, and uncontaminated. As it is water soluble, trace evidence samples can easily be washed with water after microspectral analysis. This also allows the quartz slides to be reused.

Transmission microspectroscopy is commonly used for fiber trace evidence. Fiber and hair evidence is prepared in the same manner as for standard microscopy with the exception of using quartz slides, coverslips, and glycerol if attempting to measure the spectra in the UV region.

Fluorescence microspectroscopy usually uses the same samples as those analyzed by reflectance or transmission microspectroscopy. However, it is important to use a nonfluorescent mounting medium as well as nonfluorescent slides and coverslips when preparing the samples.

Spectral Analysis

Analysis of trace evidence by UV–visible–NIR spectroscopy is especially challenging because almost nothing is known about the samples. Unlike other fields of research or manufacturing, forensic samples are obtained from many sources and there is rarely a link to the manufacturer and much less an idea of the compounds contained in the sample or how they may change over time or as a result of exposure. Forensic UV–visible–NIR spectroscopy in the traditional sense is a qualitative method. However, with the advent of advanced statistical analytical techniques, microspectroscopy is becoming a quantitative method.

As a comparative method, the UV–visible–NIR spectra of the known and questioned samples of trace evidence are compared. The comparison is generally done by observing wavelength shifts in peaks as well as the relative intensities of various peaks and shoulders to one another. **Figure 4** is the absorbance spectrum of a blue textile fiber. It strongly absorbs in the UV region as well as absorbing yellow, orange, and red light. This fiber appears blue to us because it is mainly transmitting blue light but absorbing most of the rest of the visible range. And while it transmits strongly in the NIR, the human eye cannot perceive that region well.

Figure 5 shows the absorbance spectrum of a red textile fiber. In this spectrum, most of the light in the blue and green regions is being absorbed while red light is transmitted through the fiber. Hence, we observe a red color.

When a sample fluoresces under the microscope, it appears as a bright object on a dark background. This holds true with the spectra because one is observing the emission of the light only from the sample (**Figure 6**). The textile fiber was excited with 365-nm light and the emission observed from 400 to 700 nm. The sharp drop in the peak at 400 nm is due to the cutoff of the filter cube and not due to the fiber. This spectral artifact is common in filter-based fluorescence

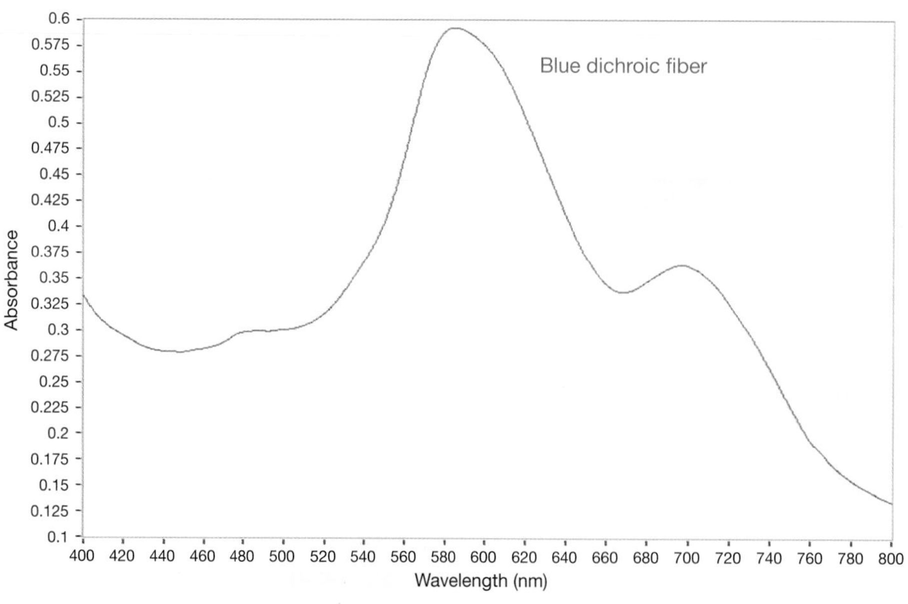

Figure 4 UV–visible–NIR absorbance spectrum of a single blue textile fiber.

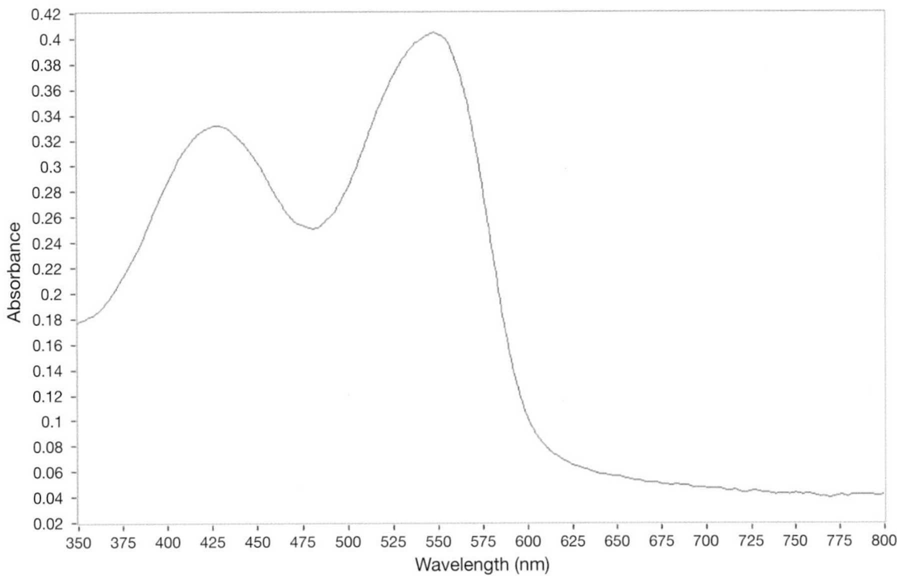

Figure 5 Absorbance spectrum of a red textile fiber.

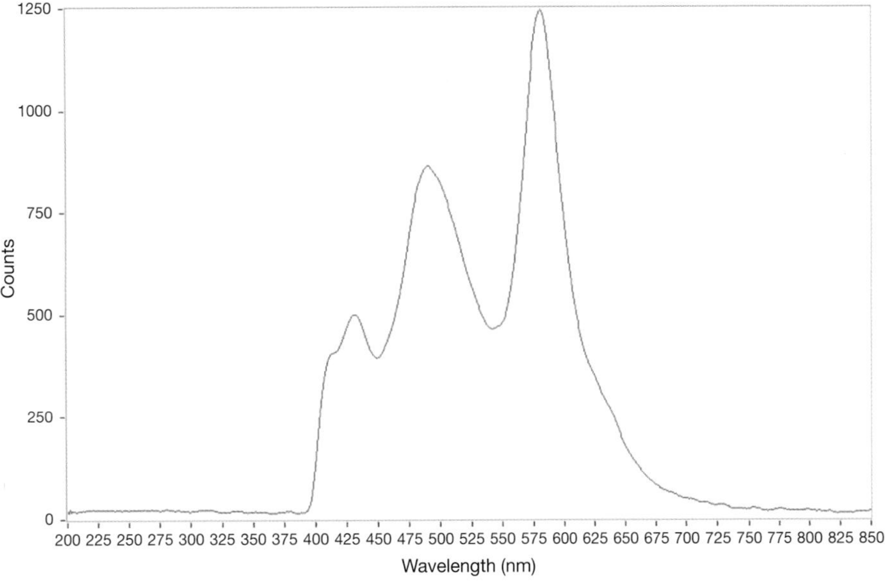

Figure 6 Fluorescent emission spectrum of a textile fiber with 365-nm excitation.

microspectroscopy and is therefore worthy of note. In the case of this sample, the fiber contains three emitters: violet, green, and yellow.

Conclusion

Color analysis is a vital step in the forensic analysis of trace evidence. While visual analysis, both with and without a microscope, is an important first step, it is also prone to error. Instrumental analysis of trace evidence is done with a UV–visible–NIR microspectrophotometer, which is able to eliminate many optical artifacts as well as perceive well beyond the range of the human eye and therefore aid in evidentiary comparisons. Most trace evidence is analyzed by transmission and fluorescence microspectroscopy, and multiple techniques aid in differentiation of samples.

See also: **Chemistry/Trace/Fibers:** Fiber Microscopy; Persistence and Recovery.

Further Reading

20/20 PV™ User Manual (2011). San Dimas: CRAIC Technologies.
ASTM E2228–10 Standard Guide for Microscopic Examination of Textile Fibers.
ASTM E2808–11 Standard Guide for Microspectrophotometry and Color Measurement in Forensic Paint Analysis.

Begunov BN, Zakaznov NP, Kiryushin SI, and Kuzichev VI (1988) *Optical Instrumentation: Theory and Design*. Moscow: MIR Publishers.
James J (2007) *Spectrograph Design Fundamentals*. Cambridge: Cambridge University Press.
Newton I (1730) *Opticks: Or a Treatise of the Reflexions, Refractions, Inflexions and Colours of Light*, 4th edn. London, London: Printed for William Innys at the West-End of St. Paul's.
Wyszecki G and Stiles WS (1982) *Color Science: Concepts and Methods, Quantitative Data and Formulae*, 2nd edn. New York: Wiley.

Relevant Websites

http://www.swgmat.org/Forensic%20Fiber%20Examination%20Guidelines.pdf – Scientific Working Group-Materials: Forensic Fiber Examination Guidelines.
http://en.wikipedia.org/wiki/Spectrophotometry,_ultraviolet – Wikipedia, Ultraviolet Spectrophotometry.
http://en.wikipedia.org/wiki/Color – Wikipedia, Color.

Interpretation of Fiber Evidence

C Roux, University of Technology, Sydney, NSW, Australia
J Robertson, University of Canberra, Canberra, ACT, Australia

Glossary

Fiber population studies Studies in which relevant surfaces are examined for extraneous fibers (generally using tapings) and these fibers or a random subset of these fibers are characterized according to their color, type, etc. These studies assist to obtain general statistics about the most common types of fibers (i.e., 'what is out there in general?').
Persistence studies Similar experiments to transfer studies, but where the persistence of transferred fibers on selected recipients is studied instead of the transfer. They assist to answer questions such as: Is it possible for these fibers to persist on this recipient given this situation? In that number? In this location?, etc.
Target fiber studies Studies in which fibers coming from a very common piece of fabric (with known sales statistics) are selected as target. A large number of extraneous fibers from a group of surfaces are subsequently collected and compared to this target, and the number of coincidental 'matches' with the target can be eventually assessed. These studies assist the scientist to answer questions such as 'how common is it to find these fibers by chance?'
Transfer studies Experiments in which different pieces of fabric are put in contact with each other mimicking the context under investigation. Transferred fibers are subsequently counted, collected, and characterized with the view to assist to answer questions such as: Is it possible for these fibers to be transferred given this situation? In that number? In this location?, etc.

Introduction

In a case where, after thorough laboratory examination and where there are no meaningful differences and two or more fiber samples cannot be distinguished, the question remains as to how best this result can be interpreted? In some laboratories or jurisdictions, this finding may be reported using a 'could have could come' statement. One ought to ask the question: What is the value of this type of statement? This is probably the most difficult challenge faced by the forensic fiber examiner.

Unlike glass or paint evidence where a proof of common source can sometimes be achieved through a physical fit, fibers (excluding pieces of fabrics and some exceptional cases) are always considered as class evidence. In other words, there is probably always more than one item in the world that shares some common characteristics with a specimen of evidential fibers.

However, this does not mean that fibers have little or no value. The evidential value of fibers depends upon a multitude of parameters and often is stronger than a layperson would expect. Fibers can even constitute primary evidence under some circumstances. Their main strength resides in their ability to reconstruct an event or a series of events. The interpretation and value of fiber evidence are presented and discussed in this article.

Factors Influencing the Value of Fiber Evidence

While the fundamental parameters such as relevance of the trace, transfer/persistence, and frequency in the population of interest are similar to those related to other trace evidence such as glass or paint, the problems associated with fibers are more difficult. For example, it is not possible to build and maintain a database of clothing types in the same way than one would do with a database of glass types. In most cases, the questions raised in relation to the significance of fibers are extremely complex.

Since the mid-1980s different aspects of the evidential value of fibers have been studied by key researchers such as Gaudette, Grieve, Robertson, and Roux, and there is now a clearer view on the significance of fiber evidence. It is generally accepted that the value of fiber evidence depends on many factors that are often complex and interacting. These factors can be classified as known (or usually determinable) or unknown (or difficult to determine).

Factors That Are Known (or That Are Usually Determinable)

- *The circumstances of the case*: The discovery of fibers may be more or less significant depending on the circumstances. The forensic scientist needs to consider whether or not fibers can be explained by an alternative hypothesis, that is, by coincidence, by a real transfer but one which has an explanation which is not incriminating or the latter but where the explanation may be incriminating. In order to attempt to select between these options the scientist needs to know relevant and often detailed information about the circumstances of the case and details relevant to the individuals allegedly involved.
- *The time that has elapsed before collection of the evidence*: The longer the time between the transfer event and the collection, the weaker the evidence. The risk that the relevant fibers are being lost and replaced by nonrelevant fibers via secondary or a higher degree transfer is increased with time.
- *The suitability of the fiber types for recovery and comparison*: Some fibers are highly colored or luminescent, which means that they not only are easier to find and collect, but

 http://dx.doi.org/10.1016/B978-0-12-382165-2.00097-0

also have more features to examine and to compare with each other. This increases the probability to discriminate fibers which do not have a common origin, and, therefore, enhance the significance.

- *The extent of the comparative information derived from the samples*: This information may be limited by the laboratory resources or by the size and type of fibers. It is obvious that a 'fiber match' is much more significant when complementary and highly discriminating techniques have been used in comparison to simple screening tests.
- *The number of types of matching fibers*: Garments often contain more than one fiber type. This means that a 'multiple match' increases the significance of fibers. It should be noted that, in cases involving a blended fabric, the absence of one or more fiber types in the pool of recovered fibers does not necessarily preclude the blended fabric from being the source of the questioned fibers. Different components of a blended fabric may have different shed potential, and the number of fibers transferred of the different types is not necessarily proportional to the stated composition of the garment. This phenomenon is well known and called 'differential shedding'.
- *Whether or not there has been an apparent cross-transfer of fibers*: This situation arises where, for example, fibers found on the victim's garment are not distinguishable from the fibers of the suspect's garment and fibers found on the suspect's garment are not distinguishable from the fibers of the victim's garment. The demonstration of a cross-transfer constitutes the ideal situation following the Locard exchange principle. In this case, the significance of fiber evidence is dramatically increased, because the chance of finding 'matching fibers' in both samples by pure coincidence is remote.
- *The number of matching fibers recovered*: In general, the larger the number of fibers, the smaller the chance of finding these fibers by chance only. The discovery of a small or an unexpected number of fibers is difficult to interpret and requires good knowledge of transfer and persistence theories.
- *The location of the recovered fibers*: Some locations are more prone to secondary (nonrelevant) fiber transfer than others. In a break-in case, for example, fibers found at the edge of a smashed window are more significant than fibers found on the ground. The link between the perpetrator and the evidence in the latter case is quite unclear, which decreases the significance. Similarly, fibers found on undergarments in a sexual case may be more significant than fibers found on outer garments, for example.
- *The methods used to conduct the examinations*: More discriminating and complimentary methods will bring more significant comparative features and will decrease the risk of coincidental match.

Factors That Are Unknown (or That Are Difficult to Determine)

- *The extent and force of contact*: These factors influence fiber transfer and persistence with respect to both the number of fiber types and the number of fibers.
- *The degree of certainty that specific items were definitely in contact*: In some cases, there is a higher degree of certainty that the items submitted are those involved in the alleged incident. For example, there may be good eyewitness accounts or the suspect was apprehended quickly. In other cases, it is quite possible that the clothing is not relevant to the incident. For example, there might have been an opportunity to dispose of the clothing or eyewitness statements might be unclear.
- *Donor fiber shed potential*: Some fabrics shed more fibers than others, and this must be considered when assessing the significance of the number of fiber types and the number of fibers. This means that it is impossible to give a simple rule which would define a cutoff number of fibers beyond which the primary transfer is certain, as opposed to secondary or higher transfers.
- *Frequency of occurrence of the matching fiber types*: The significance is weighted by the frequency of occurrence of the matching fibers. It is obvious that a match involving common fibers is less significant than that involving rare fibers. It should be noted that, owing to the high degree of variability of fibers, this frequency is generally much smaller than one might expect in the first instance.

Information Available to Assist the Interpretation of Fiber Evidence

The interpretation of fiber evidence requires a systematic study of the different factors described above in light of the context of the case and the hypotheses alleged by the different parties (generally defense and prosecution). This process requires a great deal of experience and logical reasoning. Some valuable information exists through specialized literature or unpublished research projects, and can be used as an aid by the fiber expert during the interpretative process. However, in some cases, the lack of relevant information may prompt the set up of simulation experiments in order to confirm or deny some hypotheses that remain unresolved. Although interpretation problems have engendered great debates within the forensic community in these past 25 years, significant advances have been made in interpretation modeling (see section 'Statistical Treatment (Probabilistic Model)').

Most of the information currently available in the area of the interpretation of fiber evidence is related to the following issues (see Further Reading for detailed information):

- fiber transfer and persistence;
- frequency of occurrence of fiber types or chance of a coincidental match; and
- statistical interpretation.

Fiber Transfer and Persistence

Knowledge of fiber transfer and persistence assists to answer the question as to whether or not the number of fibers and the number of fiber types found in a given case are likely under the allegation of contact. In other words, knowledge on transfer and persistence assists to answer the competitive questions 'what is the probability of finding the number of fibers and fiber types found in a given case if there was a contact?' and 'what is the probability of finding the number of fibers and fiber types found in a given case if there was no contact?'

This area of investigation includes the following topics:

- transfer studies;
- studies on differential shedding;
- experiments on the alteration of fiber characteristics in a manner consistent with localized conditions specific to a case; and
- persistence studies.

Since 1975, numerous transfer and persistence studies involving fibers have been undertaken. The results give general guidance when assessing the number of fibers expected to be found under a given set of circumstances. It is beyond the scope of this article to examine these results in fine detail, but the most important findings are given below.

The number of fibers to be found mostly depends on:

- the area of contact;
- the kind of physical contact (number of contacts, pressure, friction, time, etc.);
- the construction of the fabrics involved (donor and recipient);
- the fiber types (generic class, density, diameter, etc.);
- the length of the fiber fragments; and
- whether or not, and how, the recipient is mobile after the transfer event has occurred.

Small fiber fragments on the outer surface of a garment are more likely to be transferred and generally are more persistent on the recipient. Transferred fibers are more or less rapidly lost and redistributed on other locations (on the same recipient or not). Experimental studies have shown that fibers transferred at the time of contact may range from only a few to many hundreds or thousands. When the recipient is mobile, it has been shown that there is a rapid loss of fibers (typically 80% of loss within the first 4 h and 5–10% remaining after 24 h). On the other hand, fibers can persist for periods of many days and even weeks when transferred to a recipient which remains subsequently relatively undisturbed such as a car seat or a dead body.

As already stated, in blended fabrics, the number of fibers transferred of the different types are not necessarily proportional to the stated composition of the garment. This issue, called 'differential shedding', is important when interpreting findings involving a fabric of blended composition.

The presence of only a few matching fibers may mean that they have been deposited by means of a secondary or subsequent transfer as opposed to a primary one (secondary transfer is the first indirect transfer after primary transfer, taking place via an intermediary object – common in contacts involving seating). Other reasons may also account for this situation, including a long time gap between contact/transfer and examination, a redistribution of fibers (e.g., due to the washing of the garment), the use of an inefficient method for fiber recovery, and a coincidental transfer. In all cases, caution is necessary when interpreting the finding of a small number of fibers, especially to items such as underclothing.

In real life, the variables which will contribute to the number of fibers which may be transferred are so numerous and unknown that the most reliable assessment of the number of fibers to be found is done by the simulation of the suspected contact with the actual fabrics in the case under investigation. However, the pressure of casework in most laboratories would make this type of research work impossible in all but the most critical cases.

Frequency of Fibers

'Fibers are mass produced; they are not like fingerprints or DNA, are they?' This question is typically asked by the defense in court. It is therefore necessary to consider fiber frequencies. Knowledge of these frequencies helps the assessment of the relative rarity of the fiber features observed during the examination. In other words, knowledge on the frequency of fibers assists to answer the competitive questions 'what is the probability of finding the fiber features observed in a given case if there was a contact?' and 'what is the probability of finding the fiber features observed in a given case if there was no contact?' A large number of studies have been achieved over the past 15 years in this area. Crucial information comes from the following sources:

- population studies;
- target fiber studies;
- data collections; and
- trade enquiries.

The population studies have analyzed examples of the normal fiber population that may be expected on a given surface. This is vital information to have at hand when trying to answer the defense question 'well surely you would expect this type of fiber to be present on any such surface?' Fiber population studies involve sampling the given surface and classifying the recovered fibers into fiber type and color categories.

Conclusions which can be drawn from the studies which have been carried out so far have shown that:

- synthetic fibers form only a low percentage (13–20%) of any population yet studied;
- the majority of color/morphology/generic type combinations (~65%) are represented by a single fiber type only. Synthetic fibers exhibit a very high degree of polymorphism; and
- the chance of one type representing >1% of the total population is remote. A collection of synthetic fibers (same type, same morphology, and same color) can therefore be said to be the result of a recent contact with a specific textile and can be considered highly significant.

Target fiber studies give some idea of what proportion of the population has fibers of a particular type on their clothing (or car seat, cinema seat, pub seat, etc.). These data incidentally will automatically take into account not only the rarity of a fiber type, but also the tendency for this fiber to be transferred or to persist on the receiving fabric. Without being comprehensive, a list of target fiber studies that have been carried out to date include:

- a blue wool nylon pullover from Mark & Spencer with sales over 1 million;
- red wool from ladies pullover and brown polyester of men trousers on car seats;

- green cotton fibers from Mark and Spencer's leggings and red acrylics from a pullover on car and cinema seats;
- red acrylics from a scarf sold over a 5-year period in quantities of 5–10 000 annually in nine European countries;
- blue wool fibers on seats in public houses throughout the United Kingdom; and
- blue wool, gray and black polyester (all common) as well as blue acrylic (less common) on outer clothing from English households.

Findings of similar studies in different parts of the world regularly appear in the literature. So far, target fiber studies suggest that it is a rare event to find a fiber, even from a very common garment, on clothing (or a seat) without the donor recently having been in close contact with the garment in question.

Databases are generally built using garments received in forensic laboratories for examination. They yield very detailed information, such as the:

- frequency of morphological characters within a fiber type;
- frequency of a certain polymer composition within a fiber type;
- frequency of uncommon fiber types in the general population;
- frequency of usage of fiber types in different textiles divided into different categories; and
- frequency of certain fiber type combinations in different textiles.

One of the criticisms of databases is that the collection of materials takes too long to accumulate and, hence, the data quickly become out of date. However, this criticism only really applies where the measurement of color data is involved. To overcome this problem, some authors have built up a comprehensive and easily updated database using data on garments offered for sale in mail order catalogs. However, this approach is feasible only in countries where mail order is popular.

Trade enquiries involve tedious and time-consuming investigative work. However, such enquiries can bring extremely valuable information on the relative frequency of a given type of fiber, including sales figures and manufacture figures such as quantity of items dyed using the same dye batch, for example.

Statistical Treatment (Probabilistic Model)

The interpretative process is not entirely free from subjective opinion when dealing with fiber evidence because of the number of interactive factors that must be considered. Taking note of the fact that the decision process at the time of the trial is based on inference, it appears that the logical rules for thinking about facts in legal cases are those of probability. As a result, a probabilistic model has been proposed as an aid to this process.

During the past 25 years, many researchers have shown increasing interest for a probabilistic model based on the Bayes theorem. This model describes how the elements of proof are combined and evolve during the decision process of the trial, avoiding distortion based on inappropriate use of intuition. The Bayesian framework, or more precisely on the likelihood ratio approach, can help to formulate and assess the most relevant questions faced by the forensic scientist. The relevant questions are dependent upon the circumstances of the case, but they are all derived from two fundamental questions:

- what is the probability of the evidence if the alleged story is true?
- what is the probability of the evidence if the alleged story is not true (or the complementary story is true)?

The ratio of these two probabilities is called a likelihood ratio. The latter measures the value of the evidence in terms of a pair of hypotheses, indicating if the given set of observations supports one hypothesis more than the other. It clearly shows that the concept of evidence, including fiber evidence, is relative.

The main challenge of a probabilistic model is the fact that such a model uses data that, in the fibers context, are incomplete and difficult to quantify. Ideally, for each case, a target fiber study and transfer and persistence experiments should be carried out using relevant materials to the context of the case. Of course, such an approach is not practical and the assessment relies rather on the accumulated knowledge derived from experimental studies.

However, many scientists argue that the Bayesian approach can still be used as a logical framework to provide the most accurate guide to interpretation currently possible. Conservative estimates that can be seen as 'measures of belief' and simulations can also help to go through the process. In other words, this approach greatly minimizes the subjective component of the interpretation process. It is also worth noting that the Bayesian approach has been the initiator of numerous experimental studies which brought crucial data for the interpretation of fiber evidence, regardless of whether the scientist applies the Bayesian framework or not. **Figure 1** shows how various factors affecting the interpretation of fiber evidence are taken into consideration in a Bayesian framework.

Examples

Various examples of the application of the Bayesian approach to the assessment of the evidential value of fibers were developed by key researchers such as Aitken, Champod, and Taroni. Inferential guidelines can be extracted from these scenarios. They ultimately assist the forensic scientist in the evaluation of fiber evidence.

The main points are:

- Evaluation of the evidential value of forensic evidence (including fiber evidence) is a matter of probability assessment.
- For the assessment of the strength of the evidence (E) it is necessary to consider the probability of the evidence under two given competing explanations for its occurrence, respectively, presented by the prosecutor and by the defense (H_p and H_d). The value of the evidence is estimated using a likelihood ratio $LR = P(E|H_p)/P(E|H_d)$. Hence, the likelihood ratio is defined not only by the evidence but also by the strategy chosen either by the prosecution or by the defense.
- Evidence (recovered trace and known material) may be to some extent incompatible with the offense. Hence, $P(E|H_p)$

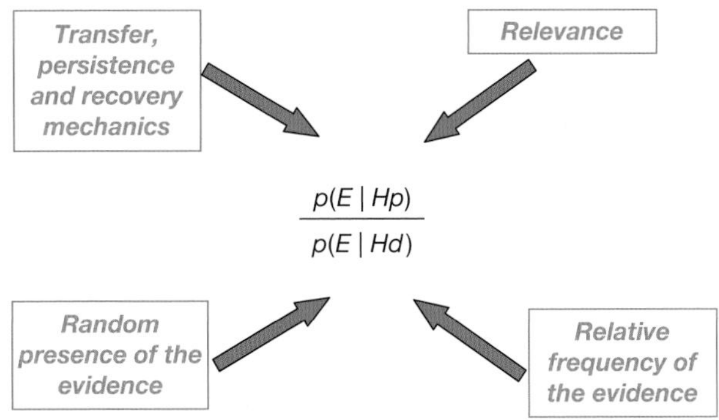

Figure 1 Various factors affecting the interpretation of fiber evidence combined in a Bayesian framework. Adapted from Champod C and Taroni F (1999) The Bayesian approach. In: Robertson J and Grieve M (eds.) *Forensic Examination of Fibres*, 2nd edn., pp. 379–398. London: Taylor & Francis.

is not always equal to 1, because of their number and position, and because of the phenomena of transfer, persistence, and recovery. There is a need to consider transfer probabilities.

- When traces (recovered evidence and known material) are supposed to be associated with the offense, we also have to allow for the probability of their absence before the commission of the offense. The corollary of this is that if traces are supposed to be unrelated to the offense, the probability of their presence by chance is also to be considered. There is a need to consider background probabilities.
- The evaluation of trace evidence has to consider all potential recovered traces and not only the concordant evidence. This number of groups has to be considered.
- The number of declared offenders has a significant impact on the likelihood ratio.
- The definition of H_d excludes the implication of the defendant. Thus, the scientist has to specify the relevant population in which adequate forensic surveys have to be made. There is a need to estimate frequencies correctly.
- In all investigation and evaluation of transfer traces, all possible exchanges have to be investigated including extreme situations in which expected evidence has either not been found or not been produced.

Conclusions

Background data available to the forensic fiber examiner to assist in interpreting the significance of fiber findings have increased greatly in the past 25 years. There is also a deeper understanding of the factors that need to be considered, and acceptance that it is incumbent on the practitioners to assist the court in assessing significance.

Given the circumstances facing forensic fiber examiners in different climatic and socioeconomic environments, local databases and research to put available data in a local context are essential. This type of data is now emerging.

The Bayesian approach has been studied and proposed in the area of fiber evidence. It is seen by many as a useful logical framework to provide the most accurate guide to interpretation currently possible. However, it is fair to say that the complexity of fiber evidence (when compared to other evidence categories such as glass, for example) remains a challenge.

Ultimately, it is worth pointing out that the value of fibers is more in their ability to reconstruct an event or a series of events (i.e., 'fibers can tell a story') rather than necessarily uniquely identify the source at the origin of a transfer.

See also: **Chemistry/Trace/Fibers:** Fibers: Overview; Identification and Comparison; Persistence and Recovery; Transfer.

Further Reading

Aitken C and Taroni F (2004) Fibres. In: Aitken C and Taroni F (eds.) *Statistics and evaluation of evidence for forensic scientists*, 2nd edn., pp. 381–398. Chichester: John Wiley & Sons.

Biermann TW and Grieve MC (1996a) A computerized data base of mail order garments: A contribution toward estimating the frequency of fiber types found on clothing. Part 1: The system and its operation. *Forensic Science International* 77: 65–73.

Biermann TW and Grieve MC (1996b) A computerized data base of mail order garments: A contribution toward estimating the frequency of fiber types found on clothing. Part 2: The content of the data bank and its statistical evaluation. *Forensic Science International* 77: 75–91.

Biermann TW and Grieve MC (1998) A computerized data base of mail order garments: A contribution toward estimating the frequency of fiber types found on clothing. Part 3: The content of the data bank-is it representative. *Forensic Science International* 95: 117–131.

Bruschweiler W and Grieve MC (1997) A study on the random distribution of a red acrylic target fiber. *Science & Justice* 37: 85–89.

Cantrell S, Roux C, Maynard P, and Robertson J (2001) A textile fibre survey as an aid to the interpretation of fibre evidence in the Sydney region. *Forensic Science International* 123: 48–53.

Champod C and Taroni F (1997) Bayesian framework for the evaluation of fiber transfer evidence. *Science & Justice* 37: 75–83.

Champod C and Taroni F (1999) Interpretation of fibres evidence – The Bayesian approach. In: Robertson J and Grieve M (eds.) *Forensic Examination of Fibres*, 2nd edn., pp. 379–398. London & Philadelphia: Taylor & Francis.

Cook R and Wilson C (1986) The significance of finding extraneous fibers in contact cases. *Forensic Science International* 32: 267–273.

Cresswell SL, Cunningham D, and NicDaeid N (2003) Textile survey of cinema seats in Glasgow. *Forensic Science International* 136(1): 117.

Dignan SJ and Murphy KJ (2002) Fibre evidence from fingernail clippings. *Canadian Society of Forensic Science Journal* 35(1): 17–21.

Gaudette BG (1988) The forensic aspects of textile fiber examination. In: Saferstein R (ed.) *Forensic Science Handbook*, vol. 2, pp. 209–272. Englewood Cliffs, NJ: Prentice Hall.

Grieve M (1999) Interpretation of fibres evidence – Influencial factors, quality assurance, report writing and case examples. In: Robertson J and Grieve M (eds.) *Forensic Examination of Fibres*, 2nd edn., pp. 343–378. London & Philadelphia: Taylor & Francis.

Grieve MC and Biermann T (1997) The population of coloured textile fibers on outdoor surfaces. *Science & Justice* 37: 231–239.

Grieve MC and Biermann TW (2003) The individuality of blue polyester fibers used to provide forensic evidence. *Forensic Science International* 136(1): 121–122.

Grieve MC, Biermann TW, and Davignon M (2003) The occurrence and individuality of orange and green cotton fibres. *Science & Justice* 43(1): 5–22.

Grieve M, Biermann T, and Schaub K (2005) The individuality of fibres used to provide forensic evidence – Not all blue polyesters are the same. *Science & Justice* 45(1): 13–28.

Home JM and Dudley RJ (1980) A summary of data obtained from a collection of fibers from casework material. *Journal of the Forensic Science Society* 20: 253–261.

Houck MM (2003) Inter-comparison of unrelated fiber evidence. *Forensic Science International* 135: 146–149.

Jackson G and Cook R (1986) The significance of fibers found on car seats. *Forensic Science International* 32: 275–281.

Kelly E and Griffin RME (1998) A target fiber study on seats in public houses. *Science & Justice* 38: 39–44.

Kidd C and Robertson J (1982) The transfer of textile fibers during simulated contacts. *Journal of the Forensic Science Society* 22: 301–308.

Marname R, Elliot D, and Coulson S (2006) A pilot study to determine the background population of foreign fibre groups on a cotton/polyester T-shirt. *Science & Justice* 46(4): 215–220.

Marshall L, Griffin RME, and Robinson K (2003) Recovery of transferred carpet fibres from shoes, their persistence on the outer surface and the value of fibres recovered from the inner surfaces of the shoes. *Forensic Science International* 136(1): 123–124.

Merciani P, Monard Sermier F, Buzzini P, Massonnet G, and Taroni F (2003) A study of the cross transfer of fibers. *Forensic International* 136(1): 123.

Palmer R and Banks M (2005) The secondary transfer of fibres from head hair. *Science & Justice* 45(3): 123–128.

Palmer R and Chinherende V (1996) A target fiber study using cinema and car seats as recipient items. *Journal of the Forensic Science Society* 41: 802–803.

Palmer R and Oliver S (2004) The population of coloured fibres in human head hair. *Science & Justice* 44(2): 83–88.

Pounds CA and Smalldon KW (1975a) The transfer of fibers between clothing materials during simulated contacts and their persistence during wear. Part III: A preliminary investigation of the mechanisms involved. *Journal of the Forensic Science Society* 15: 197–207.

Pounds CA and Smalldon KW (1975b) The transfer of fibers between clothing materials during simulated contacts and their persistence during wear. Part I: Fiber transference. *Journal of the Forensic Science Society* 15: 17–27.

Pounds CA and Smalldon KW (1975c) The transfer of fibers between clothing materials during simulated contacts and their persistence during wear. Part II: Fiber persistence. *Journal of the Forensic Science Society* 15: 29–37.

Robertson J and Grieve M (1999) *Forensic examination of fibres*, 2nd edn. London & Philadelphia: Taylor & Francis.

Robertson J, Kidd CBM, and Parkinson HMP (1982) The persistence of textile fibers transferred during simulated contacts. *Journal of the Forensic Science Society* 22: 353–360.

Roux C, Chable J, and Margot P (1996) Fiber transfer experiments onto car seats. *Science & Justice* 36: 143–151.

Roux C, Langdon S, Waight D, and Robertson J (1999) The transfer and persistence of automotive carpet fibres on shoe soles. *Science & Justice* 39(4): 239–251.

Roux C and Margot P (1997) The population of textile fibers on car seats. *Science & Justice* 37: 25–30.

Salter MT, Cook R, and Jackson AR (1987) Differential shedding from blended fabrics. *Forensic Science International* 33: 155–164.

Siegel JA (1997) Evidential value of textile fiber-transfer and persistence of fibers. *Forensic Science Review* 9: 81–96.

Szewcow R, Robertson J, and Roux CP (2011) The influence of front-loading and top-loading washing machines on the persistence, redistribution and secondary transfer of textile fibres during laundering. *Australian Journal of Forensic Sciences* 43(4): 263–273.

Was-Gubala J (2004) Comparative population studies of fibres secured in Poland, Czech Republic and Germany. *Zagadnien-Nauk-Sadowych* 60: 58–77.

Watt R, Roux C, and Robertson J (2005) The population of coloured textile fibres in domestic washing machines. *Science & Justice* 45(2): 75–83.

Wiggins KG and Allard JE (1987) The evidential value of fabric car seats and car seat covers. *Journal of the Forensic Science Society* 27: 93–101.

Wiggins K, Drummond P, and Hicks Champod T (2004) A study in relation to the random distribution of four fibre types on clothing incorporating a review of previous target fibres studies. *Science & Justice* 44(3): 141–148.

CHEMISTRY/TRACE/FIRE INVESTIGATION

Contents

Chemistry of Fire

E Stauffer, Commissariat d'Identification Judiciaire, Police Cantonale Fribourg, Fribourg, Switzerland
N NicDaéid, University of Strathclyde, Glasgow, UK

Glossary

Autoignition Ignition in the absence of an external source of ignition, also known as nonpiloted ignition. This can result from the ambient temperature or from a self-heating process of the fuel (known as spontaneous ignition) bringing the fuel to its autoignition temperature.
Autoignition temperature The minimum temperature to which a substance must be heated in air to ignite independently of the heating source.
Combustion An oxidation reaction that occurs at a rate sufficient to produce heat and light.
Conduction Process of transferring heat through a material or between materials by direct physical contact from a region of higher temperature to a region of lower temperature.
Convection Process of transferring heat by movement of a fluid.
Evaporation The physical change of state of a liquid into a vapor at a temperature below the boiling point of a liquid.
Exothermic reaction A chemical reaction that releases heat.
Fire point The minimum temperature, generally a few degrees above the flash point, at which a liquid produces a sufficient quantity of vapors to sustain continuous flame when ignited.
Fire triangle A symbol used to describe the necessary requirements for fire to occur in which the three sides represent fuel, oxidizer, and a source of ignition. The connection of the sides to form a triangle symbolizes the chain of reaction.
Flash point The lowest temperature at which a substance will give off a vapor that will flash or burn momentarily when ignited.
Glowing combustion The rapid oxidation of a solid fuel directly with atmospheric oxygen creating light and heat in the absence of a flame.
Ignition The initiation of combustion.
Pyrolysis A process by which a solid (or a liquid) undergoes chemical decomposition into smaller molecules due to heat, without interaction with oxygen or any other oxidizer.
Spontaneous heating An exothermic chemical or biological process that may generate enough heat to ignite the reacting material (spontaneous ignition).
Vapor The gaseous phase of a substance simultaneously present with its liquid and/or solid state at a temperature below its boiling point.

Introduction

Fire has always fascinated people. It can be beautiful, like the lighting of the Olympic flame at the opening ceremony. It has definitely been useful since the first Cro-Magnon man discovered it and used it to cook food. It can occur as part of a natural phenomenon, as with a volcano eruption or a lightning strike. Nevertheless, it can be dangerous, destructive, and even deadly, as the Great Fire of London in 1666 for example.

Because fires are often the result of negligence or criminal activity, and because they lead to the destruction of property and the loss of lives, many fires are investigated by law enforcement. The goal of such an investigation is usually twofold: determining (1) the origin and (2) the cause of the fire. This is performed by observing the fire scene, tracing the fire back to its point or points of origin through the study of fire patterns, and, finally, identifying the first fuel ignited and the ignition source. In order to do so, the underlying theories developed in fire

 http://dx.doi.org/10.1016/B978-0-12-382165-2.00098-2

chemistry and physics are used. The transfer of heat, the ignition of a combustible material, the way fire propagates, and its interaction with fuels are all examples of events that are regulated through fire chemistry and physics. This phenomenon is actually much more complicated than it may first appear.

Fire investigators and fire debris analysts must fully understand the underlying chemistry and physics of fire. Without that knowledge, it is impossible to conduct a sound fire investigation, or to perform a sound fire debris analysis. The full understanding of the phenomenon regulating the birth of a fire and its subsequent propagation is fundamental. This article provides an introduction to fire chemistry. It starts with the basic conditions necessary for a fire to exist and develops the interactions between these conditions.

Conditions for a Fire

Fire is the result of combustion that occurs at a rate high enough to generate heat and light. There are other combustion reactions, such as rusting for example, that are not considered as 'fire' because they do not provide heat and light. Combustion is an exothermic chemical reaction between a combustible substance (called fuel) and an oxidizer. In order for a fire to occur, three conditions must be present and interacting together:

- Fuel (combustible material)
- Oxidizer
- Source of heat (activation energy)

These conditions are usually represented in a graphic called the fire triangle (see Figure 1). Each side of the triangle represents one condition and the fact that the triangle is assembled symbolizes the interaction between the three conditions and, thus, the birth of a fire.

Other graphical representations exist, such as the fire tetrahedron (where the fourth side is the chemical chain reaction); however, they are not as widespread as the fire triangle. If the fire triangle symbolizes the birth of a fire, it is also used to explain fire extinguishment. As a matter of fact, extinguishing a fire simply consists of suppressing one of the sides, or breaking the interaction between two sides. By using water on a fire, one removes the heat, and thus the fire dies. By using a carbon dioxide fire extinguisher, one suppresses the oxidizer, and the fire extinguishes.

Fuel comprises any material that can be oxidized when in the presence of a suitable ignition source as well as sufficient oxidizer. Fuels are almost everywhere, such as in wood, plastics, paper, gasoline, and propane. However, it is important to realize that many substances that are not thought of as fuels at first are actually very good fuels. For example, some metals or some other inorganic materials can greatly contribute to a fire, once ignited. Combustibles are found in all three phases (gaseous, liquid, and solid), which can seriously complicate a fire investigation.

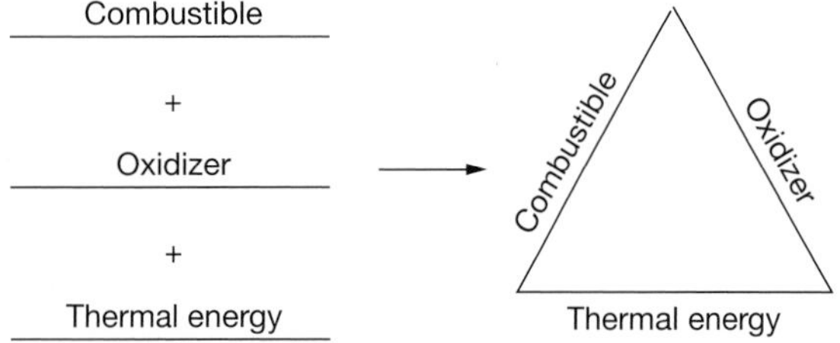

Figure 1 Fire triangle. When the three sides interact together, fire occurs. Reproduced from Stauffer E, Dolan JA, and Newman R (2008) *Fire Debris Analysis*, p. 86. Burlington, MA: Academic Press. © Elsevier.

The oxidizer is readily available through the oxygen contained in the air (21%). However, oxygen is not the only oxidizer that can be used to feed a fire. For example, chlorine is also an excellent oxidizer, and it is possible to start a fire without any oxygen by using chlorine and methane. However, in almost all fires that a fire investigator will be called upon to investigate, oxygen will be the oxidizer involved. The few exceptions that exist are typically found in chemical plants, where particular chemical substances are used. As a result, the presence or absence of an oxidizer is often not a decisive factor in the determination of the cause of a fire. However, it highly influences the fire's development.

The source of heat is the activation energy that raises the temperature of the fuel high enough so that it will ignite under the appropriate circumstances. While this statement appears simple, the issue of the source of energy is quite complex and is often the key element in a fire investigation. As a matter of fact, combustibles are in constant contact with oxygen in everyday life, and things do not catch fire spontaneously: The missing element is the source of energy on, which the fire investigator often will focus. It is also important to understand that not all sources of energy are suitable for all fuels. Even if they contain sufficient energy, some are not capable of transferring their energy to the fuel in question. As an example, although it is possible to light a newspaper with a lit cigarette, it is impossible to ignite gasoline with a lit cigarette. Conversely, an electrical spark can readily ignite a proper gasoline/air mixture, but it will be relatively inefficient in igniting a book.

Fire as a Chemical Reaction

As previously indicated, combustion is a chemical reaction between a combustible material and an oxidizer. It is actually a redox reaction during which the oxidizer is reduced and the combustible material is oxidized. The formula, as follows, provides an example of such a redox reaction, with the combustion of ethane:

$$2C_2H_6 + 7O_2 \rightarrow 4CO_2 + 6H_2O$$

In this example, the oxidation number of carbon goes from −III (in ethane) to +IV (in carbon dioxide) and in oxygen goes from 0 (in molecular oxygen) to −II (in carbon dioxide and water). Thus, carbon is oxidized and oxygen is reduced.

The above formula shows the stoichiometric reaction between ethane and oxygen and is referred to as a complete combustion. In practice, few fires lead to a proper stoichiometric ratio. As a result, the chemical reaction does not go to completion. Two types of reactions, complete and incomplete, are thus possible.

In a complete reaction, the stoichiometric ratios are reached and, thus, enough oxidizer is available to fully oxidize the fuel into the most simple products: carbon dioxide and water in this example. In real life, it is almost impossible for a fire in an uncontrolled environment to reach the stoichiometric ratio. Complete combustion is the result of a controlled burn, such as with an oxyacetylene torch, where it is possible to provide sufficient oxygen to guarantee the stoichiometric ratio of the reaction. This is shown as an example in the following equation:

$$2C_2H_2 + 5O_2 \rightarrow 4CO_2 + 2H_2O$$

In such a case, the flame will be blue, as no carbon particles are generated. This is shown in **Figure 2**.

If the amount of oxygen available is lower, an incomplete reaction will occur, such as

$$2C_2H_2 + 3O_2 \rightarrow 4CO + 2H_2O$$

In this example, carbon monoxide is produced instead of carbon dioxide. Carbon monoxide is a colorless and odorless toxic gas. It is extremely dangerous to human beings and is often the cause of asphyxiation in fires. Additionally, carbon monoxide is a combustible gas, since it can burn with oxygen to produce carbon dioxide. As such, carbon monoxide has resulted in explosions.

If even less oxygen is available, carbon will be produced:

$$2C_2H_2 + O_2 \rightarrow 4C + 2H_2O$$

In this situation, a heavy release of soot will be seen, because there is not enough oxygen to oxidize carbon.

The well-known orange color of the flame is a typical indicator of incomplete combustion. This indicates clearly that incomplete combustion is much more common than complete combustion, since the orange color is almost always associated with flaming combustion. A complete combustion usually leads to a blue flame (depending on the fuel), such as the one shown in **Figure 2**.

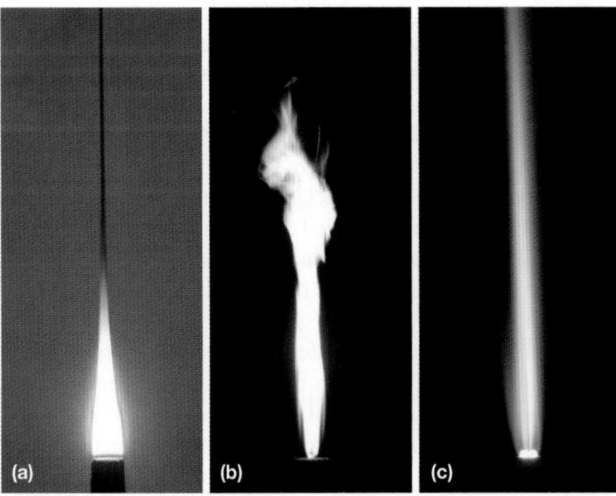

Figure 2 Example of incomplete, partial, and complete combustion with an oxyacetylene torch where the availability of oxygen is increased from left to right. (a) Notice the generation of heavy soot, indicative of an incomplete combustion. (b) The bright yellow flame also indicates an incomplete combustion, however without the release of soot. (c) A complete combustion is shown as a blue flame. Reproduced from Stauffer E, Dolan JA, and Newman R (2008) *Fire Debris Analysis*, p. 92. Burlington, MA: Academic Press. © Elsevier.

If oxygen is completely removed from the equation (and given that there are no other oxidizers), then fire will extinguish. This situation is called an oxygen-controlled fire as opposed to a fuel-controlled fire, where the fire is controlled according to the available supply of fuel. The availability of oxidizer is an important factor in the development of a fire. When the fire is in its initial growing phase, it consumes more and more oxygen. When the concentration of oxygen is of least 10%, it is possible to have a flaming fire (i.e., a fire with visible flames). If the concentration drops below 10%, it is no longer possible to have flames, and the fire smolders. In a smoldering fire, the reaction between the combustible material and the oxidizer is a solid-to-gas reaction, meaning that the combustible material is a solid and the oxidizer is a gas in its surroundings. One can thus deduct that a smoldering fire can only occur with solids. A typical example of a smoldering fire is glowing charcoal on a grill. In a flaming fire, a gas-to-gas chemical reaction occurs. This means that only gases can burn in flames; thus, solids and liquids must first transform into gas.

If a flaming fire is in a confined environment, it will run out of oxygen relatively quickly and the amount of soot produced will greatly increase. Eventually, the level of oxygen will drop below 10%, at which point the flames will die and the fire will smolder. At that point, the fire is oxygen-controlled, because it is a lack of oxygen that prevents it from spreading further. If one creates an opening and a sudden supply of oxygen is provided, the fire will consequently burst into flames. This phenomenon is known as backdraft and is extremely dangerous to fire fighters.

In practice, a fire is an extremely complex chemical reaction with many different reactants and many levels of incomplete combustion, which generates many different radicals, as shown in **Figure 3**.

Phase Change and Pyrolysis

As stated previously, a fuel must be in a gaseous form in order to burn in a flaming fire. This means that because solids (except for smoldering fire) and liquids do not burn, they must be transformed into a gaseous phase. This is an important point in fire investigation, because one must determine how the fuel got in its proper form before it was ignited.

In order to achieve a gaseous state, liquids and solids can undergo different physical transformations as shown in **Figure 4**.

Besides physical phase changes, a solid (or a liquid, less often) can also undergo a chemical change, called pyrolysis, to become a gas. Pyrolysis is the decomposition of a larger molecule into smaller molecules as a consequence of exposure to heat, without undergoing any oxidation.

Pyrolysis is a very important phenomenon in fire investigation and, more importantly, in fire debris analysis. As a matter of fact, pyrolysis is the main way by which a solid gives off ignitable gases. As such, pyrolysis products can be found in fire debris samples, thus rendering their interpretation much more complex. There are three main pyrolysis mechanisms: random scission, side-group scission, and monomer reversion. Often, a substance is subjected to more than one mechanism. This is dictated by the strengths of the bonds where the

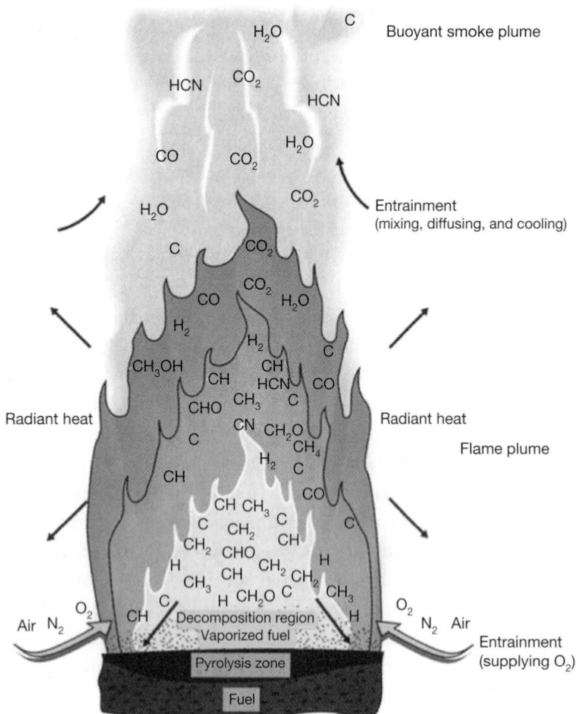

Figure 3 Representation of a fire plume with the presence of many different molecules and radicals. Reproduced from DeHaan JD and Icove DA (2011) *Kirk's Fire Investigation*, 7th edn. Upper Saddle River, NJ: Pearson Education. © Prentice Hall.

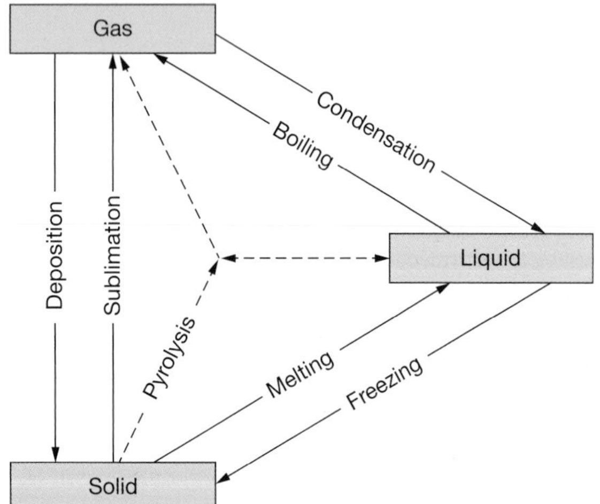

Figure 4 Passage of a solid or liquid to the gaseous phase by chemical and physical changes. Reproduced from Stauffer E, Dolan JA, and Newman R (2008) *Fire Debris Analysis*, p. 96. Burlington, MA: Academic Press. © Elsevier.

bond with the lowest bond dissociation energy will often break apart first.

In random scission, the carbon-to-carbon bonds are randomly broken, thus creating smaller molecules. With the example of polyethylene, random scission will create a series of saturated and unsaturated hydrocarbons (alkanes, alkenes, and alkadienes). In the side-group scission mechanism, the carbon-to-side element bond is broken, thus leaving an unsaturated carbon chain that rearranges into a series of aromatic compounds, such as benzene, toluene, and styrene. Polyvinylchloride is a perfect example of a polymer undergoing mainly side-group scission. In monomer reversion, the polymer undergoes a reverse phenomenon, thus decomposing into its monomeric form. Polymethylmetacrylate is a typical example of a polymer undergoing monomer reversion. This pyrolysis mechanism usually results in one molecule; thus, it does not produce a significant interference in fire debris analysis.

Heat Source and Transfer

Fundamentally, only five heat sources exist:

- Electrical, as with the heat produced by an electrical arc between two conductors
- Mechanical, as with the heat generated by the friction of a stone on metal, such as in a lighter
- Chemical, as with the heat generated when sodium is mixed with water
- Biological, as with the biological activity in hay
- Nuclear, as with the reaction of fissile material

Thus, all heat sources found on earth are derived from one of these five fundamental sources. Once ignition has occurred, an open flame is available.

Heat can be transferred through three different modes: convection, conduction, and radiation. Convection is the mode of transfer occurring with fluids (liquids and gases). Energy transfers from one place to another through the motion of fluids. Hot gases released by a fire are a good example of convection. Because a fluid's density usually decreases with the increasing temperature, a fluid warmer than its environment moves upward. In the case of a typical room fire, convection is the phenomenon that creates the hot layer of gas located at the ceiling of the compartment.

In conduction, heat is transferred within a solid, such as through a copper wire through the interaction of vibrating atoms from particle to particle. By heating one end of the wire, the other end experienced an increase in temperature. If a solid is a good conductor, conduction will occur with significant intensity. If the solid is a poor conductor, the phenomenon of conduction will barely take place.

In radiation, heat is transferred through electromagnetic waves. The main difference in this heat transfer mode is that it does not require matter in order to take place. With convection, heat can only rise upward. With conduction, heat can only go through the conductor in contact. With radiation, heat can be transferred in all directions. In a typical room fire, it is the radiant heat that increases the temperature of the objects on the floor. The body of hot gases at the ceiling (created through convection) reaches a temperature high enough to radiate all the way down to the floor and bring the nearby objects to their autoignition temperature. As the fire develops, radiative heat becomes the dominant heat transfer mechanism.

Flammability Limits, Flash Point, and Fire Point

While a combustible material is represented by one side of the fire triangle, its mere presence is not a sufficient condition for fire to exist. The combustible material must be present in a sufficient concentration so that it can be ignited. This is called the lower flammability limit (LFL). Conversely, one cannot have too much fuel; otherwise, it will not ignite either. This is called the upper flammability limit (UFL). **Figure 5** shows the concept of LFL and UFL with the examples of gasoline and acetylene. Each fuel exhibits its own LFL and UFL.

When a liquid is at equilibrium, a given vapor concentration is found at its surface, known as the vapor pressure. This vapor pressure is highly dependent on the temperature of the liquid. When the vapor pressure equals the LFL, ignition can occur. At that point, the temperature of the liquid is defined as the flash point. In other words, it is the temperature at which a liquid gives off a sufficient vapor concentration so that it can be ignited using a piloted ignition source. At the flash point, when ignition occurs, the air/vapor mixture above the substance will burn very quickly (flash flame); however, fire will not sustain.

Flash points vary greatly from one substance to another and are very relevant in terms of both fire safety and fire investigation. The flash point of a material is the lowest temperature at which an ignition can occur if a suitable ignition source is brought within the ignitable vapor/oxidizer mixture. As a practical example, gasoline, with a flash point of approximately $-40\,^{\circ}\mathrm{C}$, will readily ignite when a lighter is swept above its surface. However, diesel fuel, with a flash point of approximately $40\,^{\circ}\mathrm{C}$, will not ignite when sweeping a lighter above its surface.

For a fire to sustain once initial ignition has occurred, one would have to reach the fire point of the substance. The fire point can thus be defined as the lowest temperature at which a material will generate a sufficient concentration of vapors so as to form an ignitable mixture that will sustain combustion, once ignited. In general, the fire point is a few degrees above the flash point.

Ignition

Similarly to the presence of a combustible material, the mere presence of a heat source in the fire triangle does not imply that ignition will occur. The heat source must be suitable to the combustible material and have sufficient energy for fire to occur.

Ignition of a material can be reached through different modes. The material can be heated to the point at which it ignites, which is called autoignition. Alternatively, the material can be brought to its flash point or fire point, and its vapors then ignited (piloted ignition). The flash point, fire point, and the autoignition temperature are three parameters that characterize a material and with which a fire investigator must be familiar.

When a material is heated, in an oven, for example, at some point, the material will ignite by itself. This is called autoignition, or nonpiloted ignition, which is the ignition of a material without the addition of a piloted source, such as a flame. As an example, with an autoignition temperature of approximately $100\,^{\circ}\mathrm{C}$, carbon disulfide will ignite when in contact with boiling water.

Autoignition occurs quite often in fires. For example, the phenomenon of flashover, where a compartment suddenly bursts into flames, is the result of the autoignition of materials. The small original fire gives off hot gases that accumulate at the ceiling. They produce radiant heat that increases the temperature of the material on the floor. At some point, the material on the floor reaches its autoignition temperature, at which point it ignites. Because the autoignition temperatures of most common goods found in a household are in the same range, the entirety of the room bursts into flames.

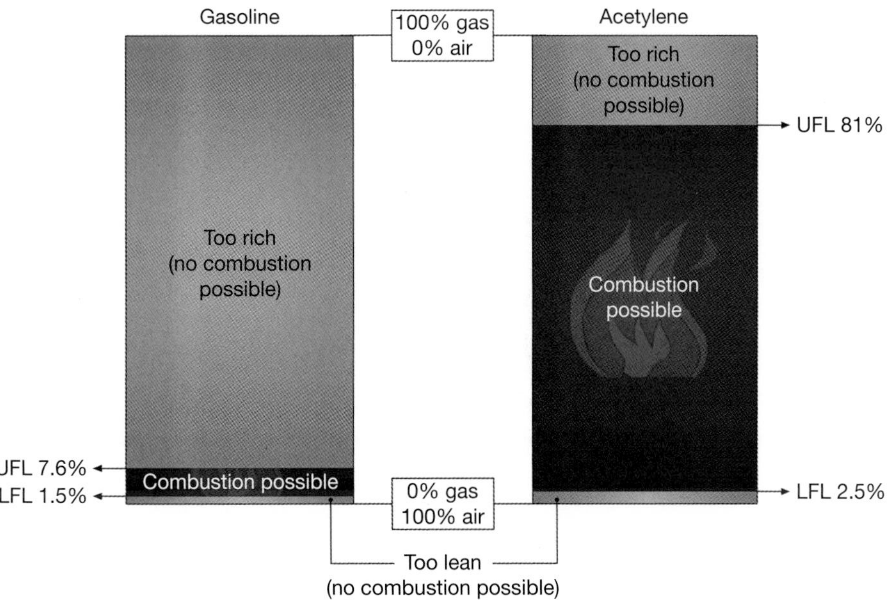

Figure 5 Illustration of the concepts of lower flammability limit (LFL) and upper flammability limit (IFL). Reproduced from Stauffer E, Dolan JA, and Newman R (2008) *Fire Debris Analysis*, p. 117. Burlington, MA: Academic Press. © Elsevier.

Another important phenomenon is spontaneous ignition, which is the autoignition of a material through the heat generated by itself. This means that it does not receive energy from an external source, but it produces the increase of heat by itself. A typical example of spontaneous ignition is the ignition of a rag due to the exothermic reaction of drying linseed oil present on it. Spontaneous ignition is a specific type of autoignition, for which the production of heat is particular; however, it does not change the fact that the material must reach its autoignition temperature before it ignites.

Finally, piloted ignition is the ignition of a material through a direct external source (piloted source), such as a flame or a spark. Practically, the application of this ignition source to the material brings a portion of the material to its autoignition temperature; however, the rest of the material may be of much lower temperature.

Conclusion

The chemistry of the fire phenomena is a complex interaction of many physical and chemical characteristics of the materials involved. We have attempted to discuss the most important of these factors in this brief article. It is essential that those involved in the investigation of fires fully understand these properties to ensure that correct interpretation of postfire indicators can be made.

See also: **Chemistry/Trace/Fire Investigation:** Analysis of Fire Debris; Interpretation of Fire Debris Analysis; Physics/Thermodynamics; Thermal Degradation.

Further Reading

Babrauskas V (2003) *Ignition Handbook*. Issaquah, WA: Fire Science Publishers.
Bond J (1991) *Sources of Ignition: Flammability Characteristics of Chemicals and Products*. Jordan Hill, England: Butterworth-Heinemann.
DeHaan JD and Icove DJ (2011) *Kirk's Fire Investigation*, 7th edn. Upper Saddle River, NJ: Pearson Education.
Drysdale D (1985) *An Introduction to Fire Dynamics*. Chichester, England: Wiley.
Ettling BV and Adams MF (1971) Spontaneous combustion of linseed oil in sawdust. *Fire Technology* 7(3): 225–236.
Faraday M (1993) *The Chemical History of a Candle*. Atlanta, GA: Cherokee Publishing Co.
Haessler WM (1974) *The Extinguishment of Fire*. Quincy, MA: National Fire Protection Association.
Holleyhead R (1996) Ignition of flammable gases and liquids by cigarettes: A review. *Science and Justice* 36(4): 257–266.
Lentini JJ and Waters LV (1991) The behavior of flammable and combustible liquids. *Fire and Arson Investigator* 42(1): 39–45.
National Fire Protection Association (2011) *NFPA 921 Guide for Fire and Explosion Investigation*, 7th edn. Quincy, MA: National Fire Protection Association.
Nic Daéid N (2004) *Fire Investigation*. Boca Raton, FL: CRC Press.
Quintiere JG (1997) *Principles of Fire Behavior*. Albany, NY: Delmar Publishers.
Simmons RF (1995) Fire chemistry. In: Cox G (ed.) *Combustion Fundamentals of Fire*, pp. 403–473. San Diego, CA: Academic Press.
Stauffer E (2003) Basic concept of pyrolysis for fire debris analysts. *Science and Justice* 43(1): 29–40.
Stauffer E, Dolan JA, and Newman R (2008) *Fire Debris Analysis*. Burlington, MA: Academic Press.

Physics/Thermodynamics

JHC Martin and RS Pepler, Institut de Police Scientifique et de Criminologie, Université de Lausanne, Lausanne, Switzerland

This article is reproduced from the previous edition, volume 2, pp. 928–933, © 2000, Elsevier Ltd.

Introduction and Overview

Within the various domains of criminalistics, the investigator compares traces found at the scene of a crime with those recovered from a person, tool, or place. By contrast, the work of the fire investigator is not purely comparative in nature; extensive practical experience of the examination of as many fire scenes as possible combined with a sound scientific knowledge, especially in the areas of physics and thermodynamics, is paramount to the success of the investigation. These two criteria enable him or her to identify the origin of the fire and determine its cause despite having to work on sites that have been destroyed by the fire and further disrupted during the extinguishing process.

This article explores: the relevant background areas of physical thermodynamics; the role of thermodynamics in fire investigation; fire ignition and propagation; thermodynamic classification of ignition sources; and the phenomena of smouldering and flaming combustion.

Physical Thermodynamics: The Relevant Background

Before considering the role of thermodynamics in fire investigation, it is essential to remember that the fundamental subject under scrutiny is concerned with the transformation of a macroscopic system which is dependent on one of the basic elements of physics: temperature. It is also important to understand that an intensive thermodynamic variable is one which is dependent on the amount of a chemical substance in the system, whereas an extensive variable does not.

Physical Systems

A physical system is defined as that part of the universe under the influence of thermodynamics which has been identified for study. It can be:

- isolated: no exchange of heat, work, or matter with the surroundings is possible. The system is said to be ideal and can be assumed in various situations;
- closed: exchange of heat and work, but not matter, is possible with the surroundings;
- open: exchange of heat, work, and matter is possible with the surroundings.

Thermodynamic Principles

Two of the fundamental laws of thermodynamics can be described in the following manner:

The first law of thermodynamics

All systems possess an internal energy U, which is a state variable, signifying that U is independent of the history of the system. When a system undergoes a change from state 1 to state 2, the difference in thermodynamic energy, ΔU is:

$$\Delta U = U_2 - U_1$$

While respecting the principle of the conservation of energy, the ΔU of a closed system can be expressed as:

$$\Delta U = \Delta Q + \Delta W$$

where ΔQ and ΔW are, respectively, the applied heat and work.

For an isolated system, U is constant; in keeping with the conservation of energy, U_1 is therefore equal to U_2. There is no energy change between the system and its surroundings therefore:

$$\Delta Q = \Delta W = 0$$

The second law of thermodynamics

This law concerns change and entropy. Entropy, S, is an extensive state variable which denotes the degree of disorder of the system. During reversible changes, the system and surroundings are in constant equilibrium. When considering such a change from a state 1 to a state 2, the entropy of a system is:

$$S = \int dQ/T$$

irrespective of the pathway taken.

However, energy dissipated in the form of heat is not an ideal process; it is spontaneous and irreversible which consequently means that the entropy of such a system increases.

The Role of Thermodynamics in Fire Investigation

An understanding of fundamental thermodynamics is important in fire investigation in considering possible ignition processes. The most important factors are identified below.

Temperature

Temperature is an intensive state variable which can be measured for any given system by the use of a thermometer. The Celsius, or centigrade, scale of temperature is governed by the triple point and the boiling point of water. At 0 °C, under standard pressure, water exists simultaneously in solid, liquid, and gaseous states; at 100 °C only the existence of the liquid and gaseous states is possible. There are two other temperature scales which are extensively used: Kelvin (K) and Fahrenheit (F).

The conversion formulae between the three scales are as follows:

$$0^\circ C = 273.15\,K = 32^\circ F$$

$$T(K) = T(^\circ C) + 273.15$$

$$T(^\circ F) = 9/5T(^\circ C) + 32$$

At any given atmospheric pressure there are certain temperature values, which are specific to a particular substance, that indicate whether the ignition of this substance is possible.

- Flash point: the lowest temperature at which a sufficient quantity of vapor is produced above a solid or liquid which can be ignited by a flame, spark, or localized heat source. At this temperature combustion does not endure;
- Point of inflammation: the lowest temperature at which the production of flammable vapors above a solid or liquid is such that a flame, spark, or other localized heat source will cause their ignition; combustion, and its accompanying flames are sustained;
- Point of auto-ignition: the lowest temperature at which a solid or liquid will spontaneously ignite without the presence of an additional heat source (flame, spark, or other).

Heat

Heat is a form of energy which has a number of effects on a system. It can be generated by the transformation of energy, be it mechanical, electrical, chemical or other, into calorific energy. A temperature gradient exists between two systems at different temperatures, along which calorific energy (heat) is transferred in order to reach a state of thermal equilibrium.

The fundamental unit of calorific energy is the Joule (J); however, a more widely recognized terminology is the calorie (cal) or kilocalorie (kcal). These units are defined as the quantity of heat required to raise 1 g, or 1 kg respectively, of water from 14.5 °C to 15.5 °C.

$$1\ \text{kcal} \equiv 10^3\ \text{J} \quad 1\ \text{cal} \equiv 4.185\ \text{J}$$

Physical Properties

Heat capacity, C, is the heat transferred to a body in order to raise its temperature by one degree (K):

$$C = \frac{dQ}{dT} \quad \text{units: J K}^{-1}$$

Specific heat capacity, c, is the heat capacity of 1 kg of a substance which, in general, is dependent on temperature:

$$c = \frac{1}{M}\frac{dQ}{dT} \quad \text{units: J kg}^{-1}\ \text{K}^{-1}$$

One of the fundamental laws of physical chemistry is the Ideal Gas Law:

$$pV = nRT$$

where p=pressure, in Pa (1 atm=101325 Pa) V=volume, in m^3; n=moles; T=temperature, in K; R=gas constant=8.315 J K^{-1} mol^{-1}.

When an ideal gas makes the transition from state 1 to state 2, the following combined gas law applies:

$$\frac{p_1V_1}{T_1} = \frac{p_2V_2}{T_2}$$

This expression can be used for real gases on the understanding that the data obtained will only be an indication of and not the exact values desired.

Fire: Ignition and Propagation

Fire is an oxidation–reduction (redox) reaction accompanied by the production of heat and light. The two chemical requirements are an oxidizing agent (or combustive agent) – usually the oxygen in air – and a reducing agent (or fuel), which must be in a gaseous state in order to mix with the air. An activation energy, always in the form of heat, is required to ignite the gaseous mixture and combustion is maintained by the calorific energy produced during the exothermic reaction.

Activation Energy

The limit of flammability of a gas (or gaseous mixture) is expressed as a percentage which indicates the proportion of gas present in the air. The ignition of a homogeneous mixture of air and a gas is possible when the lower limit of flammability has been attained; however, ignition is impossible above the upper limit of flammability as the air is too saturated. Understanding and establishing the activation energy that is required for ignition of a gas/vapor (other than autocombustion) is fundamental to fire and explosion investigations. The scene examination is often complex as several calorific energy producing systems can be present, of which some could be weak heat producers and others situated some distance from the combustible material. In any situation, the means of ignition has to originate from one of these sources. In order to eliminate each ignition possibility until left with the most probable, a second factor must be taken into consideration: the thermal or calorific power.

Thermal Power and Reaction Temperature

The thermal or calorific power of a system is the calorific energy produced over a period of time. The investigator can only estimate the thermal power which is at the origin of and aids the development of a fire. The relationship between the thermal power of the heat source, W_T, and that dissipated in the surrounding environment, w_T, constitute the thermodynamic foundation of the whole investigation. This can be seen from the following equation derived from the Arrhenius expression:

$$W_T = \Delta H_c nA \exp\left(-E_a/RT\right)$$

where: ΔH_c=enthalpy of combustion; A=pre-exponential factor, E_a=activation energy and:

$$w_T = hA\Delta T$$

where: h=convective heat transfer coefficient; A=surface area.

The thermal power of a heat source is exponentially dependent on temperature, and the only circumstances when a body will not emit heat is at absolute zero temperature (0 K); $W = 0$ if, and only if, $T = 0$.

This observation is important in that any system not at $T = 0$ K will produce calorific energy. If the energy dispersion into the surrounding environment is restricted, the system's temperature will inevitably increase. Ignition frequently occurs where the temperature of a combustible material has been augmented to the point of autocombustion.

The possibility of a given heat source (spark, flame, fermentation, etc.) igniting a specific material (wood, insulation, paper, etc.) in a certain environment (quasi-isolated, closed or open) must always be considered before the source can be eliminated from the investigation. However, calculations of W_T and w_T for real systems are impractical and inexact, except for certain types of heating; instead, the essential factor that should be taken into consideration when examining possible ignition sources is the influence of W_T and w_T on the system. Therefore, the first step of a fire/explosion investigation is to locate the place where the activation energy was produced; in other words, to determine the foyer, or seat, of the fire/ explosion. Once a potential heat source has been identified, the implications of the thermal power produced and the heat dissipated in its immediate vicinity should be estimated. This enables the investigator to verify whether or not the proposed source is a plausible source of ignition of the material situated at the (presumed) foyer.

Combustion Speed

The phenomena of smouldering fires, flaming fires, and explosions differ only in their rate of combustion.

- Smoldering is a flameless combustion involving the slow oxidation of a porous combustible material, which occurs in an environment where oxygen can easily penetrate, yet is sufficiently isolated so that heat dissipation to the surroundings is minimal.
- The speed of combustion of a flaming fire can vary enormously. The chemical reaction occurs without a perceptible pressure increase within the immediate vicinity.
- An explosion is an extremely rapid combustion. When occurring in a confined environment, it is accompanied by a considerable augmentation of pressure. The reactants are present within their limits of flammability and are usually in a gaseous state; however, very fine droplets of liquid, such as those produced by an aerosol, or fine powders/dust can also combust explosively. After ignition, the entirety of the explosive material undergoes the exothermic reaction of combustion almost instantaneously; the ambient air subsequently expands very quickly resulting in a pressure increase in the immediate environment.

Thermodynamic Classification of Ignition Sources

Fires can be classified according to their ignition source, whether due to a spark, naked flame, or localized heat source.

Heating

Heating is a transfer of calorific energy to a physicochemical system without the presence of a spark or flame. If the system generates heat by itself to augment its temperature to the point of inflammation and subsequently to autoignition, this is known as spontaneous combustion. With the exception of this latter form of heating, heat is transferred to the material via the methods outlined below.

Conduction

This is the mode of heat transfer without displacement of matter, due to electronic movement within a solid. Where two faces of a solid are at different temperatures, T_1 and T_2, the heat flux, q', through the material is:

$$q' = \frac{k}{x}(T_1 - T_2) \quad T_1 > T_2$$

where: x = thickness of material; k = thermal conductivity.

If a steady state heat flux traverses two (or more) layers of material:

$$q'_1 = q'_2 = q'_{1,2}$$

$$q'_{1.2} = \frac{T_1 - T_2}{x_1/k_1 + x_2/k_2}$$

Convection

Convection occurs in liquids and gases and is a transfer of heat via mechanical movement due to changes in density. This process can, however, transfer heat to a solid. For example, if a solid surface of area A is in contact with a liquid/gas at temperature T, the heat flux, q'', transferred to the surface is:

$$q'' = hAdT \quad \text{units: Watts}$$

where: h = convective heat transfer coefficient; A = surface area.

Radiation

Electromagnetic radiation in the visible and infrared regions is radiated from all bodies with a temperature above absolute zero. When a system is in thermal equilibrium, its components emit and absorb radiated heat at the same rate. Although this radiation is rarely quantified it is important to note that:

- radiation is the prevalent mode of heat transfer between flames and combustible material; it is therefore the principal cause of vaporization and consequently the main means of the ignition of fresh material;
- before suspecting human intervention after a large fire where several foyers have been identified, it is essential to verify that the separate ignition sites are not a consequence of thermal radiation. Fire may have spread in this manner from one combustible material to another despite the lack of an apparent physical link.

When a body has two identical surface areas, A, respectively at temperatures T_1 and T_2, a heat flux, f, flows from surface 1 to surface 2 if $T_1 > T_2$:

$$f = a_1 a_2 \sigma A(T_1{}^4 - T_2{}^4)$$

Where: a = heat absorption or reflection factor; σ = Boltzmann constant.

Heating appliances

When a heating appliance is identified as being the origin of a fire, any of the three modes of heat transport can constitute the transfer of calorific energy to the combustible material. As the correct use of these devices is for the generation of heat, the cause of the fire has to be a result of an inappropriate usage or a malfunction of the apparatus.

Electrical sources

Fires of electrical origin are often complex to investigate and difficult to prove. Heat is produced when an electrical current, I, passes through a conductor with resistance, R, over a time period, t, according to Joule's Law:

$$\Delta E_{\text{electric}} = I^2Rt \quad \text{units:} \quad A^2 \cdot \Omega \cdot \text{sec} = \text{J}$$

The electrical power is therefore:

$$W = I^2R \quad \text{units:} \ \Omega A^2 = W$$

Friction

The generation of heat by the friction between two objects is proportional to the speed at which the two bodies move against each other and their respective weights. The nature of the surfaces in contact, which is indicated by the friction coefficient, will also have a bearing on the quantity of calorific energy produced; those with a high friction coefficient generating more heat.

Sparks

Material sparks

Material sparks are produced when solid particles with a mass of milligram magnitude are emitted into an open system existing at high temperature. These tiny fragments of incandescent or burning matter can constitute the origin of a fire if:

- when smoldering, the distance between the source and the combustible material is very short; due to their miniscule mass the particles lose heat rapidly;
- the spark enters into contact with a highly flammable material or one with a small heat capacity in which a smoldering fire can manifest.

A spark of mass m, and heat capacity c, emitted with a temperature T_2, into an environment at temperature T_1, produces heat, Q, according to:

$$Q = mc(T_2 - T_1)$$

For example, when grinding a metal, the metallic fragments produced are of milligram mass, which generate an approximate heat of $Q \approx 1.3$ J; this is of sufficient magnitude to ignite a flammable gas/ vapor. Another example is the fusion of a metal/metal oxide when welding; the resulting droplets have a diameter of 2–5 mm and generate heat between the values of: $37 < Q < 578$ J. The first value is more than sufficient for the ignition of a gaseous mixture, whereas the second can initiate the combustion in a nearby combustible material such as plastic isolation or wood, provided that it is within the boundaries of the quasi-isolated system.

Electrical sparks and arcs

In the space separating two charged objects, there is an electrical field. If an avalanche of electrons occurs due to this field, it is visible (to the naked eye) as a spark. Because of its short lifetime, an electric spark produces a relatively small amount of heat; nevertheless, the millijoules of energy generated can ignite a homogeneous air/flammable gas mixture resulting in an explosion.

The difference between an electrical arc and spark is the duration of the electrical discharge: that of an arc being markedly longer than a spark, which can be said to be instantaneous. Logically, it follows that the energy produced by an arc is of greater magnitude and can subsequently inflame a combustible material rather than uniquely gaseous mixtures as for a spark.

The above phenomena will occur under the following conditions.

- A defective contact (of a switch, relay unit, etc.) in an electric circuit, with or without a coil, will result in an increase in resistance and will thus generate heat. This default can also occur with the use of adapters and extension cables.
- In the presence of an electrolyte (water, humid air, etc.), a defective insulation of a cable will enable the passage of an electric current between two conducting wires at different electric potentials. An augmentation in resistance will subsequently generate calorific energy at a precise point which can be sufficient to ignite the insulation or a combustible material in close proximity.

Smoldering

In a smoldering solid, the heat conduction is difficult to calculate, as are the speed and propagation of combustion. This type of fire obviously still requires an ignition source, however the thermal power of the source can vary enormously. For example:

- after most fires, smoldering is the natural progression of flaming combustion. This latter form of combustion can be reinitiated when a great quantity of smoldering material is remnant after a large fire. This eventuality only applies to one aspect of fire investigation: that where flames are rekindled from smoldering remains, even after extinction by the fire brigade;
- when the heat source is weak, smoldering combustion commences at the surface of the material. In this case the only conceivable progression of combustion is to the interior of the material, otherwise self-extinction will occur.

Smoldering combustion is self-maintained if an equilibrium is established between the thermal power of the exothermic (combustion) reaction and that dissipated into the surroundings:

$$\Delta W = W_T - w_T$$

If the difference, ΔW, between the former thermal power values is small, the fire will neither self-extinguish nor reach an open flame state; the smoldering combustion will simply continue to burn fresh material with a random progression that is due to the inhomogeneous environment. In order to maintain a constant value of ΔW, or one that varies within a very narrow range, the oxygen supply must be adequate; nevertheless, it must be noted that even in an oxygen-deficient environment (proportion of O_2 in the air $<16\%$), it is possible for this type of combustion to be sustained.

Smoldering material will burst into flames if there is sufficient heat build-up and enough oxygen available. For example, smoldering combustion will progress to the flaming stage if the burning material gets into contact with air. A pertinent example of this is when the exterior surface temperature of a material is increased by heat transferred from internal smoldering combustion; when the surface, which is in contact with the ambient air, reaches the point of inflammation, flaming combustion will result and will spread at a rapid rate.

Flames

If a combustible material is exposed to prolonged contact with a flame its temperature will eventually reach the point of inflammation and ignition will occur. The resulting flames will subsequently raise the temperature of the surrounding material which will also attain its inflammation point and start to burn. The propagation of fire by direct flame contact is a natural progression which does not require further explanation.

Hot gases produced by burning material are propelled upwards. Due to their inferior density the buoyancy forces within the smoke plume cause the hot gases to rise with a speed that is dependent on the temperature of the fire. At high temperatures, for example directly above the flames, the gases are dispersed vertically very rapidly and have little sideways diffusion into the ambient air. This effect diminishes as the ambient temperature decreases, thus the gases have greater horizontal convection the further they are from the flames. They can therefore be seen to rise in the form of a three-dimensional 'V' (an inverted cone). This plume of hot gases transport soot particles which are deposited on vertical nonflammable supports; the characteristic triangular pattern of these deposits can often be used to locate the seat of a fire.

The smoke resulting from a fire contains combustion products and small unburned residues which are, by definition, nonoxidized vapors that are transported by the diffusion of the other hot gases. These vapors can accumulate in enclosed spaces and spontaneously ignite, under the right conditions, even at considerable distances from the original foyer.

Fire spread can often be deduced with relative ease if the initial heat source has been identified and there is evidence of the presence of combustible material throughout the entire burned area. However, when justifying a source of ignition, problems can arise when the heat source is found to be separated from the combustible material by nonflammable material such as walls, floors and ceilings.

With an open fire, the vertical flame movement and the air supply are practically limitless. At the exterior of a stone or brick building, a fire situated at ground level can extend to roof height. If the roof is constructed from combustible material such as wood or thatch, it will eventually catch fire (due to the prolonged contact with the flames and hot gases) even if separated from the seat of the fire by several floors of nonflammable material.

If the fire is restricted by a wall or other incombustible barrier, the supply of air may well be limited. The flames will consequently spread towards the direction of the air source. When vertically extending flames are hindered by the ceiling of a room, the plume of hot gases is redirected along its surface. The horizontal spread can be of considerable distance as the area directly below the ceiling is at a highly elevated temperature, thus sustaining the capacity of the gases to ignite fresh combustible material. Therefore:

- if the entrainment of air and the diffusion of flammable gases/vapors in the vertical part of the flame is sufficient, there will be limited flame spread: combustion will occur at ceiling level;
- with a low ceiling or a vapor-rich smoke plume, the hot gases will spread out beneath the ceiling and the flames can spread to material situated some distance from the original fire seat.

It must be remembered that a corridor, ventilation shaft, or other form of passageway can aid the propagation of fire between rooms, apartments, or even separate buildings.

Conclusion

This article does not attempt to list each and every possible heat source capable of initiating a fire. Instead it indicates the most significant sources and analyzes them thermodynamically, consequently highlighting the role of thermodynamics and that of fundamental physics in verifying the conclusions of the fire investigator. Nevertheless, it must be noted that numerical values are rarely calculated when considering the various exchanges of heat or the laws of thermodynamics, as the fires under investigation are not performed in the laboratory under controlled conditions. The equations and mathematics are simply used to give an indication of the magnitude of the process in question. The work of the fire investigator is therefore to identify the origin of a fire and to report its cause by exploiting an extensive practical experience and intricate knowledge of the laws of physics and chemistry.

See also: **Chemistry/Trace/Fire Investigation:** Chemistry of Fire; **Investigations:** Fire Patterns and Their Interpretation; Major Incident Scene Management; Types of Fires; **Management/Quality in Forensic Science:** Risk Management.

Further Reading

Atkins PW (1990) *Physical Chemistry*, 6th edn. Oxford: Oxford University Press.

Bush LS and McLaughlin J (1996) *Introduction to Fire Science*. Fire Engineering. Tulsa, USA: Penn Well.

Chaussin C, Hilly G, and Barralis J (1969) *Chaleur et Thermodynamique*. Paris: Dunod.

Clavin P and Linau A (1985) *Theory of Gaseous Combustion*. NATO ASI SER; SER B 116: 291–338.

DeHaan J (1991) *Kirk's Fire Investigation*, 3rd edn. Brady: Prentice Hall.

Drysdale D (1986) *An Introduction to Fire Dynamics*, 2nd edn. Chichester: John Wiley & Sons.

Noon R (1992) *Introduction to Forensic Engineering*. Boca Raton: CRC Press Ltd..

Phillipps CC and McFadden DA (1986) *Investigating the Fireground*. Fire Engineering. Tulsa, USA: Penn Well.

Schultz N (1985) *Fire and Flammability Handbook*. New York: Van Nostrand.

Yallop HJ and Kind SS (1980) *Explosion Investigation*. Harrogate: The Forensic Science Society and Scottish Academic Press.

Yereance RA (1989) *Electrical Fire Analysis*. Springfield, IL: Charles C. Thomas.

Thermal Degradation

K Grimwood, University of Technology Sydney, Sydney, NSW, Australia

Introduction

Thermal degradation describes the chemical decomposition of materials via the application of heat. In fire investigation, the terms thermal degradation, thermal decomposition, and pyrolysis are often used interchangeably; however, this is not wholly correct. Generally, pyrolysis is the thermal degradation of solid fuels and describes the stage without which flaming combustion cannot occur, while evaporation is the thermal degradation of liquid fuels. There are exceptions, however, with some ignitable organic liquid fuels undergoing pyrolysis, rather than evaporation.

In fire investigation, thermal degradation occurs in an oxygenated or reduced oxygen environment, although thermal degradation is not a phenomenon specific to fire investigation. In chemistry, materials are pyrolyzed, or undergo thermal degradation, in air as well as in inert atmospheres, such as nitrogen. The mechanism of thermal degradation of materials can be monitored with the use of thermogravimetric instrumentation and pyrolysis products can be identified using analytical techniques such as gas chromatography coupled with mass spectrometry.

There is extensive representation of materials in structures or vehicles that will undergo thermal degradation in elevated temperatures. A broad range of examples has been provided in this section that may be commonly encountered in fire investigation. It is also pertinent to understand that not all materials commonly found in structures or vehicles undergo thermal degradation according to the description provided here. Glass, for example, undergoes state transition at elevated temperatures and so has not been discussed in this section.

Thermal Degradation Effects

Wood

Wood is a composite material consisting of cellulose, lignin, and hemicelluloses. Wood can undergo thermal degradation and combustion; however, the extent of thermal degradation is dependent on a number of conditions. The species of wood, its pH, and water content, in addition to the degree of thermal assault the wood is exposed to will dictate the extent of degradation. A flaming fire will occur when combustible pyrolysis products are ignited and can independently sustain flame.

Experiments on the thermal degradation of chemically untreated wood have demonstrated the following general trends:

1. From 65 to 100 °C, the strength of wood can be significantly and irreversibly affected. The reduction in strength is most likely due to depolymerization in the form of carbohydrate loss. However, this is dependent on the species, duration of exposure to heat, and thickness of the wood.
2. Between approximately 100 and 200 °C, pyrolysis yields water vapor (H_2O), carbon dioxide (CO_2), and formic and acetic acid as well as additional noncombustible liquids and gases. At this temperature, significant char can be produced if the exposure period is sufficient.
3. The progression of events occur from 200 to 300 °C that are initiated, in part, at lower temperatures but continue throughout this temperature range and potentially into the next. Dehydration early in this temperature gradient leads to the significant pyrolysis of hemicelluloses and lignin, producing further noncombustible liquids and gases. Most notable is the significant generation of carbon monoxide (CO) and tar. Toward the end of this temperature gradient, the depolymerization of cellulose occurs more readily and results in the formation of volatile pyrolysis products that are combustible in addition to significant char.
4. Temperatures of 300–450 °C result in the generation of the majority of the combustible volatiles. These are produced from the depolymerization of cellulose.
5. At temperatures in excess of 450 °C, the phenomenon referred to as afterglow occurs, where further thermal degradation of the wood, now in the form of char, yields CO_2, CO, and H_2O.

Wood that has been chemically treated to inhibit ignition, heat release, and flame spread has, for this reason, an alternative thermal degradation mechanism compared to untreated wood. There are different chemical compounds in use to aid flame retardation; however, the fundamental goal of each is the same. The period during thermal degradation when noncombustible gases and H_2O are the major pyrolysis products is maintained for a longer time. The result of flame retardation is an increase of smoke production and a higher char yield.

Wood char is a product of the thermal degradation, pyrolysis, of chemical components in wood. Historically, deep charring on wood was widely accepted as an indicator of rapid and intense fire. Considerable research regarding wood char has shown that the level of char is dependent on several factors including but not limited to the extent of thermal exposure, ventilation, density of the wood, its specific chemical composition, grain size, and moisture content. Recognizing that char yields differ depending on a number of variables is essential in fire investigation as the extent of char is often employed as a tool to compare fire spread within a scene.

Polymeric Materials

The term polymeric material refers to the repetition of many monomeric units linked together to form a chain. Polymeric materials are abundant in nature and examples include silk, latex, cellulose, and wood. Polymers can also be synthesized to produce different materials that display a vast range of physical and chemical properties. Synthesized polymeric materials include polyurethane (PU), polyvinyl chloride (PVC), and polystyrene. The diversity in the physical properties of polymeric

 http://dx.doi.org/10.1016/B978-0-12-382165-2.00100-8

materials ensures that their use in building and vehicle construction is prolific. In addition to construction, polymeric materials are widely used for the internal coverings and furnishings of buildings and vehicles. Furthermore, polymeric materials play an important role in the textiles industry.

Pyrolytic thermal degradation of polymeric materials generally occurs in elastomeric and thermoplastic materials to produce noxious gaseous products. This is of particular interest during a fire investigation as inhalation of the toxicants can impact on the occupants' ability to self-egress, or ultimately could lead to death. Considerable amounts of noxious gases are produced by the pyrolysis (or combustion) of polymeric materials that include, but are not limited to, CO_2, CO, hydrogen cyanide (HCN), oxides of nitrogen, hydrocarbons as well as nitrogen or oxygen-containing organic compounds. There has been significant research regarding the production and toxic effects of CO as a toxicant in fires. More recently, since the advent and subsequent prolific use of nitrogen-containing polymeric materials, there has been an increase in the investigation of the production and toxic effects of HCN.

In addition to the toxic effects of the thermal degradation of polymeric materials, the evolution of pyrolysis gases in a compartment can contribute to the onset of flameover, a phenomenon that can lead to flashover. Factors that should also be considered during a flameover or flashover include ventilation, fuel load, and compartment size.

Human Remains

The discovery of human remains at a fire scene can occur during the course of suppression or investigation. Recognizing that remains will have been impacted thermally, and the potential for thermal degradation to have occurred, is essential to how the remains are treated and interpreted. Most agencies will have specialized personnel to process this type of evidentiary material; however, having an understanding of what information can be gathered and how its destruction can be avoided can aid the progress of the investigation. The effects of thermal degradation on human remains can be viewed at a macro- and microscopic level, although at the scene a macroscopic interpretation will be more achievable.

At a fire scene, human remains can range from appearing unaffected by heat and flame to being so completely desecrated that recognition and subsequent recovery become the domain of specialized personnel.

Visual indicators that may occur as a result of thermal degradation can mimic those caused by other means. Appreciating that different causes can produce similar results is vital to avoid inaccurate assumptions pertaining to the state of the remains prior to the fire.

Soft tissue

The soft tissue of humans includes, but is not limited to, skin (epidermal and dermal layer) connective tissue, adipose, muscle, veins, nerves, and hair follicles. Post-mortem blistering can occur on the surface of skin due to thermal degradation of soft tissue. This type of blister is gas filled, unlike liquid blisters formed ante mortem from heat or chemical burns or post mortem from heating. Their presence, in the absence of other blisters, can potentially help determine the victim's state at the time of the fire when considered contextually.

Thermal degradation in the form of dehydration contributes to the contraction of tendons and muscles. Uneven relative contraction between the flexor and extensor muscles results in characteristic posturing widely known as the pugilistic pose. Formation of this pose can cause the victim to move during the fire from their original position prior to the fire. This is a fact that needs to be taken into consideration by the investigator when documenting and assessing the position of the remains.

Bone

Bone is a composite material consisting of both organic and inorganic components. The structural stability of bone is reliant on the interaction of these phases, and as the thermal degradation of the bone progresses, the structural stability decreases. It is important for those investigating the fire scene to recognize the fragility of the remains in order to ensure they are suitably protected prior to removal. The analysis of bone that has undergone thermal degradation can benefit fire investigation as the morphological change associated with the degree of thermal degradation can potentially present a temperature guide to the level of exposure.

The extent of thermal degradation of bone is dependent on a number of variables, including the health, age, and type of bone in addition to the degree of protection from thermal assault, temperature, and length of exposure of the bone to thermal interference. Further, the composite nature of bone ensures that thermal degradation is a nonuniform process meaning different degrees of degradation may be expressed on a single piece of bone.

During the progression of a fire, bones undergo a change in color and stability due in part to the thermal degradation of the bones organic and inorganic components.

Experiments involving the thermal degradation of bones have demonstrated the following general trends:

1. From 50 to 220 °C, the dehydration of bones occurs marking the initial stages of reduced stability.
2. At temperatures up to 600 °C, organic components of the bone are undergoing thermal degradation. The result is further loss of stability, and the characteristic coloration of the bone is reported as gray to blue-gray. It is worth noting that in an oxygen-deficient environment, the pyrolysis of organic components in the bone leads to carbonization of the bone, which is recognizable from its black appearance.
3. Between 600 and 900 °C, the thermal degradation of the remaining organic components comes to an end. In addition, the calcium hydroxyapatite component of the bone degrades and produces CO_2. The resultant calcinated material is white in appearance and has lost significant stability.

Although it is not within the scope of this article, it is worth noting that other color changes to the bone have been recorded such as pink, red, green, and yellow. These color changes are most likely associated with the presence of metals and alloys in the surrounding environment at the time of the fire.

In addition to the alteration in color and stability from thermal degradation of bone, other morphological aspects undergo modification as well. The length and width of bone are reduced as a result of thermal degradation. Bone shrinkage and deformation are dependent, like other items present in a fire, on a number of variables. In this instance, the variables associated with bone include, but are not limited to, the age, sex, type and health of the bone, the mineral content, and the degree of protection in addition to the temperature and length of thermal exposure.

The multiple variants associated with shrinkage in bone mean that the literature data lack standardization. The reduction reported is between 1 and 18% for the length measurements and up to 27% for diameters. There is, however, general agreement with regard to bone that has been subjected to temperatures in excess of 800 °C that suggests that the shrinkage is significant (reported in places as greater than 30%) and hinders the visual estimation of sex and age.

When the visual analysis has been exhausted at the scene and during the post-scene investigation, complementary forms of bone analysis can be used to yield useful information. In addition to the existing methods, significant work using Fourier transform infrared spectroscopy has been undertaken to estimate the temperature that individual bones have been subjected to based on the thermal degradation of water and collagen present in the bone. X-ray diffraction has also been used in recent research to investigate the possibility of differentiating between species of bone that has been burned based on the level of thermal degradation of the mineral component of bone, calcium hydroxyapatite.

While some of the techniques discussed in this section require specialist knowledge and training that may not be available to those in the position of physically investigating a fire, the knowledge that they exist and how the techniques can be used to attain information is crucial. It is the responsibility of those in fire investigation to be aware of the tools available to them, which could aid in determining cause and origin.

Blood

Accepted methods exist to test for trace amounts of blood in an evidentiary capacity. Blood is a nonhomogeneous substance and testing methods target different components of blood. The tests, the majority of which are colorimetric, focus on the protein and enzymatic portions of blood. Although the testing methods have been developed for use at ambient temperatures, some may be applied post suppression to aid in the detection of blood at a fire scene.

At temperatures below 50 °C, thermal degradation effects are insignificant and will not hinder the use of accepted testing mediums on recently created stains. Colorimetric tests that target the enzymatic portion of blood are generally still effective when the stain has not been subjected to temperatures in excess of 100 °C, as the degradation of the enzyme has not been extensive enough. Prior to 200 °C, protein-specific dyes, such as phenolphthalein, can remain effective as the proteins' response has not been stopped by degradation due to heat.

It is generally accepted that if a stain is subjected to temperatures in excess of 200 °C, thermal degradation of the target components will have been significant enough for conventional mediums used to test for blood to yield positive results. However, like many aspects of evidentiary material, and especially material exposed to elevated temperatures, variables exist, such as length of exposure, that contribute to the degree of thermal degradation.

It should be considered that protein in bodily fluids such as semen and deoxyribonucleic acid (DNA) will follow a similar thermal degradation pathway as blood.

Trace Evidence

It is thought, often by the criminal element, that fire will destroy all evidence of a crime having been committed. This is not the case, and the recovery of trace evidence including, but not limited to, fingermarks and ignitable liquid residue is possible.

Fingermarks

Fingermarks are secretions that include a combination of water, proteins, and sebaceous and eccrine elements, which are deposited when a finger touches a surface. Latent fingermarks (those that require enhancement to view) and patent fingermarks (those that are visible in white light) are susceptible to thermal degradation, but can still be present, located, and enhanced post suppression of a fire.

When a fingermark is subjected to elevated temperatures, thermal degradation of the proteins in the mark occurs to yield amino acids. Existing chemical enhancement techniques for the detection of latent fingermarks, such as ninhydrin, work by reacting with the protein and amino acid components in the fingermark. Therefore, this method of detection may still yield useful information if the mark has not undergone extensive thermal degradation. The remaining components of the fingermark, sebaceous and eccrine secretions, will maintain their integrity to higher temperatures than proteins. Consequently, accepted methods to detect this portion of latent fingermarks can still be used. Accepted techniques for the detection of latent fingermarks can generally be used at a fire scene when the fingermark has not been subjected to temperatures in excess of 200 °C. In scenarios where the temperature reaches between 200 and 600 °C, the number of methods available to detect the mark declines in response to the increase of thermal degradation of the components in the fingermark. The detection of latent fingermarks at a fire scene is dependent on a number of variables including the substrate the mark is on, the level of thermal assault, and thermal degradation the mark has been subjected to, in addition to the water solubility of the remaining components of the fingermark.

Research has been conducted, and is gaining greater acceptance, regarding the development of latent fingermarks on specific substrates via the application of heat. Latent finger marks can undergo development to produce patent finger marks on substrates such as paper exposed to heat. The mechanism of development is thought to be due to the thermal degradation of the substrate itself, which is accelerated in areas where fingermark residue is present, producing contrast between the fingermark and the substrate. Some researchers claim that the thermal degradation of the fingermark itself also contributes to the development.

Patent fingermarks may be observed as a depression in another substance, such as dust or paint, a deposit made from a combination of finger secretions and other substances, such as blood or paint, or a deposit of another substance, such as soot deposits, onto a latent fingermark so that it becomes patent. In cases such as this, the potential for thermal degradation is dependent not only on the nature of the fingermark secretions, but also on the other substance(s) present. The development or enhancement of these fingermarks using existing methodology is subject to the degree of thermal degradation the mark, adhering substance, and other substance(s) present have undergone.

The most significant challenge hindering the recovery of fingermarks at a fire scene, apart from heat and flame, is the excessive use of water during the suppression effort, residual condensation post suppression and physical destruction of the mark during the overhaul and investigation process. Preserving the areas where the least amount of thermal degradation of the fingermark is paramount to aid the collection and further development of this type of trace evidence. Areas of the scene that have been protected from direct flame and least exposure are the most likely to yield exploitable fingermarks. It is worth noting that similar observations and considerations are applicable to alternative marks such as palm, lip, ear, and foot marks.

Ignitable liquids

The term ignitable liquid includes organic and inorganic liquids that are flammable or combustible as well as substances that can be liquefied and ignited. In some cases of arson, ignitable liquids are used as accelerants to aid the initiation of flame and the propagation of fire. For this reason, it is beneficial for the fire investigator to be aware of the effect of thermal degradation on ignitable liquids to aid the collection and possible identification of the unknown liquid or residue.

The thermal degradation of ignitable liquids involves pyrolysis, evaporation, or a combination of both. The portion of the ignitable liquid that remains after thermal degradation is significant for the fire investigation when trying to determine the likelihood of the residual components detected being present at that specific location. If it is suspected that ignitable liquids are present at a fire scene and the reason for their presence cannot be satisfactorily explained, then further investigation is warranted. The amount of residue remaining will depend on the level of thermal degradation the liquid has undergone. The residue will mimic a sample that has been weathered, partially evaporated, and will be compared with known weathered samples accordingly.

Ignitable liquid residue may be found in fire debris located in areas that have been protected from thermal impact, and potentially at the seat or seats of fire. It should also be noted that ignitable liquids can absorb into substrates including, but not limited to, carpet, fabric, and soil. Collecting substrates in and around areas that are suspected to have had ignitable liquids poured can help establish, via analytical methods, if ignitable liquid residues are present. It is possible that the degradation of the liquid will be sufficiently extensive that the detection of ignitable residues, if detectable at all, will be below the detection limits of accepted analytical methods. It is worthwhile noting that there has been significant research, and subsequent discussion, regarding the use and ability of accelerant detection canines to identify thermally degraded ignitable liquids at fire scenes.

Summary

The purpose of this section was to provide an overview of materials commonly encountered at fire scenes that may have been affected by thermal degradation. While the provision of an exhaustive list of thermally degradable materials would potentially be beneficial as an additional tool, without discussion the list alone could lead to misinterpretation of the material being investigated. It should be noted that the majority of the aforementioned temperature ranges have been experimentally derived in a controlled environment. Consequently, when materials are thermally impacted in a fire scenario, the extent of thermal degradation will depend heavily on a number of factors.

See also: **Chemistry/Trace/Fire Investigation:** Analysis of Fire Debris; Chemistry of Fire; Interpretation of Fire Debris Analysis; Physics/Thermodynamics; **Investigations:** Evidence Collection at Fire Scenes; Fire Patterns and Their Interpretation.

Further Reading

Bradshaw G, Bleay SM, Deans J, and Nic Daeid N (2008) Recovery of fingerprints from arson scenes: Part 1 – Latent Fingerprints. *Journal of Forensic Identification* 58: 54–82.

Brown AG, Sommerville D, Reedy BJ, Shimmon RG, and Tahtouh M (2009) Revisiting the thermal development of latent fingerprints on porous surfaces: New aspects and refinements. *Journal of Forensic Sciences* 54: 114–121.

DeHaan JD (2007) *Kirk's Fire Investigation*, 6th edn. Upper Saddle River, NJ: Prentice-Hall.

Dominick AJ, Nic Daeid N, Bleay SM, and Sears V (2009a) The recovery of fingerprints on paper exposed to elevated temperatures – Part 1: Comparison of enhancement techniques. *Journal of Forensic Identification* 59: 325–339.

Dominick AJ, Nic Daeid N, Bleay SM, and Sears V (2009b) The recovery of fingerprints on paper exposed to elevated temperatures – Part 21: Natural fluorescence. *Journal of Forensic Identification* 59: 340–355.

Mark P and Sandercock L (2007) Fire investigation and ignitable liquid residue analysis – A review: 2001–2007. *Forensic Science International* 176: 93–110.

Mayne Correia PM (1996) Fire modification of bone: A review of the Literature. In: Haglund WD and Sorg MH (eds.) *Forensic Taphonomy: The Postmortem Fate of Human Remains*, pp. 275–293. Boca Raton, FL: CRC Press.

Moore J, Bleay SM, Deans J, and Nic Daeid N (2008) Recovery of fingerprints from arson scenes: Part 2 – Fingerprints in blood. *Journal of Forensic Identification* 58: 83–108.

National Fire Protection Association (2011) *NFPA 921 – Guide for Fire and Explosion Investigations*, 2011 edn. Quincy, MA: National Fire Protection Association.

Raja S, Thomas P, Stuart B, Guerbois J, and O'Brien C (2009) The estimation of pig bone age for forensic application using thermogravimetric analysis. *Journal of Thermal Analysis and Calorimetry* 98: 173–176.

Song DF, Sommerville D, Brown A, Shimmon R, Reedy B, Tahtouh M, et al. (2011) Thermal development of latent fingermarks on porous surfaces – Further observations and refinements. *Forensic Science International* 204: 97–110.

Stauffer E (2003) Concept of pyrolysis for fire debris analysts. *Science & Justice* 43: 29–40.

Analysis of Fire Debris

N NicDaéid, University of Strathclyde, Glasgow, UK
E Stauffer, Commissariat d'Identification Judiciaire, Police Cantonale Fribourg, Fribourg, Switzerland

Introduction

When a fire investigator suspects the presence of an ignitable liquid at a fire scene, he/she will proceed to the collection of fire debris in order to obtain a confirmation through a laboratory analysis. The analysis tests for the presence of ignitable liquid residues (ILR) within the sample; however, the presence of such ILR may not necessarily be correlated to the use of an ignitable liquid. In addition, despite the enormous variety of ignitable liquids available on the market, the analysis performed focuses mostly on petroleum-based ignitable liquids. Thus, it may not detect other, less commonly used ignitable liquids unless the analyst is advised to look for them. This emphasizes the importance of a clear communication between the fire debris analyst and the fire investigator at the scene.

Laboratory-based analyses require the appropriate skill and knowledge of relevant scientific instrumentation, proper laboratory practice in dealing with crime scene evidence, and an understanding of the nature of flammable materials and their pyrolysis and combustion products as well as an ability to interpret the results of their analysis. Knowledge of the nature of fire and the mechanisms of combustion is also essential.

ILR cannot be analyzed *in situ* from the fire debris sample. They must first be extracted from the sample and prepared into a suitable form for injection and analysis by gas chromatograph–mass spectrometry (GC–MS). **Figure 1** indicates the different steps taken during the examination of a fire debris sample.

The examination steps are preceded by the work of the fire investigator at the fire scene, in particular by the collection of the debris.

Evidence Collection – Sampling Containers

The correct collection of evidence for laboratory examination (specifically for the identification of any ignitable liquids that may have been used to accelerate the fire) from a fire scene is of great importance. However, not every scene will require the collection of fire debris for such analysis. Specifying how to gather fire debris from every scene is difficult because each scene will differ in its nature. However, in general, samples must be placed in sealable, gas-tight containers of which there are various types in common use around the world.

Unused tin cans (similar to paint cans) predominate in the United States and Australia/New Zealand. The cans come in a variety of sizes and types and can be unlined or lined with an epoxy coating (designed for the storage of water-based paints). When a lining is present, it can interfere with the chromatographic response of some ignitable liquids.

The sample is placed in the can and the lid firmly shut in place. It is then sealed and labeled. Cans have the advantage of not being permeable to any vapor and are generally very durable and resistant to puncture. However, sample size is restricted by the size of the can, which may become problematic with large samples. Given certain samples or conditions, corrosion and rusting can also be a problem, which may occur relatively quickly.

In many countries around Europe, glass jars as well as tin cans are used. Glass jars have the obvious disadvantages of fragility as well as constraining sample size but otherwise prove to be effective containers. They have the advantage of being able to see the sample without opening the container.

Also in Europe, and elsewhere in the world, a popular method of sample storage involves the use of solvent-free nylon bags. Samples are placed within the bag, which is sealed by a variety of means including knotting the neck tightly, tying with a cable tie, or heat sealing. Adhesive tape is not generally used to seal such containers because of poor sealing efficiency. Bags have the obvious disadvantage of being easily punctured although this is minimized by 'double bagging.' These containers have, however, been shown to be permeable to alcohols. Research has demonstrated that from time to time hydrocarbon residues are detected within nylon bags, which may lead to erroneous results.

Some European countries, particularly Germany and Scandinavia, use different types of bags for fire debris. These include Kapak bags (polyethylene/polyolefin composite material, manufactured in the US), laminated bags (polyethylene–aluminum/polyamide), duo bags (polypropylene/polyethylene), and CLS bags (polypropylene/polyamide, manufactured by CLS, Israel). Duo bags are preferred in Sweden although they have been shown to leak decane and branched alkanes after about a week. Similar to nylon bag, the seal also has an effect on leakage rates with aluminum tie seals showing leakage within 6 h, cable tie seals allowing leakage after 24 h, and heat seals showing leakage only after about 6 weeks.

Whatever container is chosen, the procedure for sample gathering is the same. In a best-case situation, three samples should be collected for laboratory analysis:

- A container control sample – this shows any volatiles that may be within the container itself (sometimes known as a negative control sample). Often, a few containers by batch are analyzed, thus suppressing the need to send an empty container with every sample.
- A comparison sample – this is the same material as that of the sample but taken from an area away from the one suspected to contain ignitable liquid. Such sample is used in the interpretation of the data to discriminate between the interfering products and the possible ILR from the original sample. A comparison sample is always difficult to choose because one never knows the history of the substrate and, in many cases, the investigator may not be able to find a suitable comparison sample.
- The fire debris sample.

 http://dx.doi.org/10.1016/B978-0-12-382165-2.00101-X

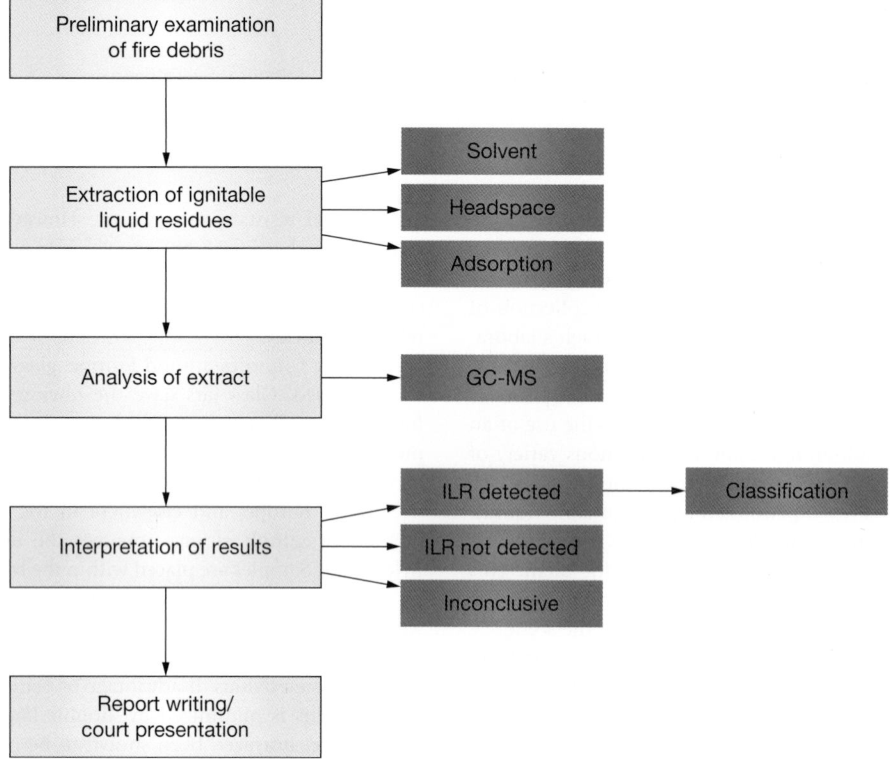

Figure 1 The different steps in the examination of fire debris samples. Adapted from Stauffer E, Dolan JA, Newman R (2008) Fire Debris Analysis, Academic Press, Burlington, MA, p. 10. © Elsevier.

Each sample should be clearly labeled with the case name, location, date of recovery, and person responsible for recovery.

Occasionally, positive control samples are prepared for a particular case. These contain a sample spiked with a volatile flammable liquid packaged and treated in the same manner as the other samples pertaining to the case. These samples allow the fire debris analyst to evaluate the influence of the matrix against the content of the ILR. The positive control is generally analyzed at the end of the analytical sequence to reduce the risk of contamination.

Preliminary Examination of Fire Debris Samples

Items sent for analysis should be recorded and signed into the laboratory. It is essential that correct record keeping is carried out to ensure that the continuity of evidence is complete.

Before conducting an extraction, the analyst must take a first look at the sample. The goal of this step is to gather information about the nature of the sample, which is very important for the interpretation of the data. Likewise, observing the sample allows the analyst to choose the best extraction technique. Finally, fire debris samples may contain other forensic evidence, which may need to be separated prior to extraction.

Contrary to some popular beliefs, one will not lose all the ILR of a fire debris sample by opening the container, spreading some of its content on a clean sheet of paper, and examining it. Alternatively, it may not be necessary to remove the content from the container if one can see through. However, in any case, it is crucial that the fire debris analyst has a clear understanding of the sample's content.

In some laboratories, a preliminary sample of the headspace gases associated with the fire debris sample is taken. This gives a first indication of the presence of ILR and their relative quantity. Instruments such as portable flame ionization detectors (FIDs) are sometimes used for this purpose.

Extraction and Sampling Techniques

Among the many different techniques used to extract ILR from fire debris samples, three are most commonly used: direct headspace, dynamic headspace concentration, and passive headspace concentration. These are also the only techniques that still have valid standards through ASTM International. Distillation was widely used in the past; however, because of the efficiency and, most importantly, nondestructive nature of the adsorption techniques, it has been abandoned and is not described here. Solvent extraction entails soaking the debris in a given solvent, so that the analytes of interest will preferentially migrate into the solvent rather than remain adsorbed on the matrix. ASTM standard E1386 describes this technique. Solvent extraction is destructive and can co-extract matrix compounds. As such, solvent extraction is not routinely used, but rather when a particular application is required.

Direct Headspace Analysis

Direct headspace analysis is commonly used especially for samples thought to be rich in volatile components. This technique requires that the sample be contained within a vessel such as a nylon bag and heated to some degree to release volatile components from the sample into the headspace above the sample (see **Figure 2**). A sample of this headspace is directly analyzed using GC–MS. Heating of the sample is essential as higher molecular weight compounds such as long-chain hydrocarbons have lower vapor pressures and are less likely to be detected without heating the samples first.

The general procedure, described in ASTM standard E1388, for direct headspace analysis requires the sample in its packaging container to be placed in an oven heated to 60–90 °C for about 30 min. A sample of the headspace is then extracted using a gas syringe (previously flushed with air and heated). The gas sample is then injected directly into the analytical instrument. This method is easily susceptible to contamination and should be monitored by the injection of air blanks between each sample. Because of the sampling procedure, low concentrations of volatile materials may not be detected and a technique allowing for sample concentration may be required. Fire debris may also (and often do) contain water, which influences the vapor pressure of other compounds and results in lower detection levels of ILR.

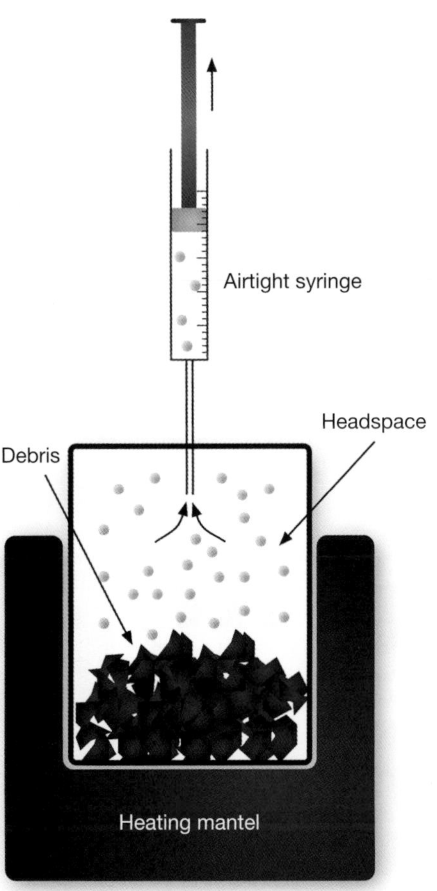

Figure 2 Principle of direct headspace extraction. Source: Stauffer E, Dolan JA, Newman R (2008) Fire Debris Analysis, Academic Press, Burlington, MA, p. 398. © Elsevier.

Passive/Dynamic Headspace Analysis

These methods of sampling are among the most commonly used. They involve the extraction and concentration of vapors onto a solid phase by either an active or passive adsorption method involving heating of the sample to facilitate release of volatile components. Once extracted on the adsorbing medium, this one is desorbed using a solvent or heat before injection into the GC–MS.

Two main adsorption media are commonly used in fire debris analysis: Tenax and activated charcoal. Tenax is an organic polymer (2,6-diphenyl-*p*-phenylene oxide), which has a high affinity for hydrocarbons and low affinity for water. Tenax must be thermally desorbed because it resists very little to solvents. Activated charcoal is most commonly desorbed using pentane, carbon disulfide (although this is very toxic), or diethyl ether. Alternatively, it can also be thermally desorbed.

Passive headspace analysis, which is described in ASTM standard E1412, involves placing the adsorbent within the sample container, which is heated to 80–100 °C for a number of hours. Extraction time varies depending on laboratory practice but is usually set between 12 and 16 h. Following this, the sample is removed and the adsorption media desorbed with the solvent. The sample's extract is then injected into the GC–MS with appropriate solvent controls and blanks.

Dynamic headspace analysis, which is described in ASTM standard E1413, involves drawing the heated headspace vapors through the adsorbent by use of a vacuum over a set period of time (see **Figure 3**). Desorption is accomplished as described before.

Solid-phase microextraction (SPME) techniques have also been increasingly used. In this case, volatiles are adsorbed onto the surface of a fiber and thermally desorbed within the injection port of the instrument. Unfortunately, in addition to SPME fibers being extremely fragile, SPME exhibits a serious problem of displacement, thus rendering the extraction of ILR extremely inefficient. As such, SPME has not yet become a routine technique in fire debris analysis and cannot be used as a standalone extraction technique according to ASTM standard E2154.

Effectiveness of Extraction/Concentration Methods

Each of the methods described has advantages and disadvantages. Overexposure of the adsorbent materials to debris containing volatile hydrocarbons will usually favor the adsorption of heavier components through the displacement of lower molecular weight components. Conversely, underexposure can result in the nonappearance of the heavier end of any volatile materials that may be present in the debris. This is why the preliminary examination of the fire debris must be thoroughly conducted, so that the analyst can determine which technique and parameters will result in the most efficient extraction.

Analysis

Instrumental Analysis

The analysis of fire debris samples is carried out by gas chromatography–mass spectrometry (GC–MS). Because an ignitable liquid is usually composed of tens or hundreds of different compounds, it is necessary to first separate them before they can be identified. Because ILR are volatile compounds, gas chromatography is the most suitable separation technique available. Mass spectrometry, which is a detector commonly hyphenated to GC, provides the necessary structural information to identify most compounds encountered in fire debris analysis. Thus, the hyphenation of GC and MS results in a powerful analytical technique that can separate, characterize, and identify volatile components within complex mixtures, such as the ones encountered in fire debris analysis.

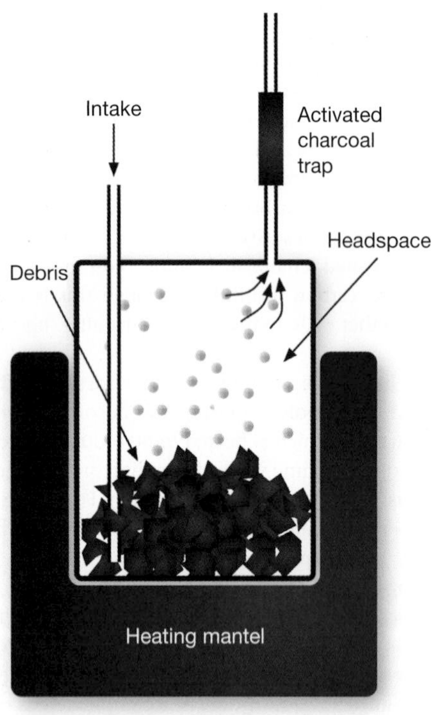

Figure 3 Principle of passive headspace concentration. Source: Stauffer E, Dolan JA, Newman R (2008) Fire Debris Analysis, Academic Press, Burlington, MA, p. 404. © Elsevier.

The proper functioning of the instrument may be checked using a standard mixture of compounds before and after analysis of samples when necessary. It is essential to ensure (and be able to prove) that the instrument is clean and that the observed peaks are due to the sample being analyzed, and not carried over from previous injections. A record of the order in which samples are injected, with the negative container control being injected first, should be kept.

While GC–FID was widely accepted in the past for fire debris analysis, the evolution of technology and the wide availability of inexpensive GC–MS led to the demise of GC–FID. GC–MS is now promoted as the gold standard for fire debris analysis. As such, ASTM has withdrawn its standard on fire debris analysis by GC–FID and only analysis by GC–MS has a valid ASTM standard (E1618).

Gas Chromatography

The sample is introduced into the gas chromatographic system through the injector port, is then swept through the column by the carrier gas, and ends up in the detector. **Figure 4** shows the general GC set-up.

Fire debris analysts often use helium as a carrier gas. In order to guarantee an effective separation, it is important to choose the right column and the correct temperature settings. A bonded, nonpolar capillary column (100% dimethylpolysiloxane or 5% phenylpolysiloxane/95% dimethylpolysiloxane) or equivalent is required for ignitable liquid analysis

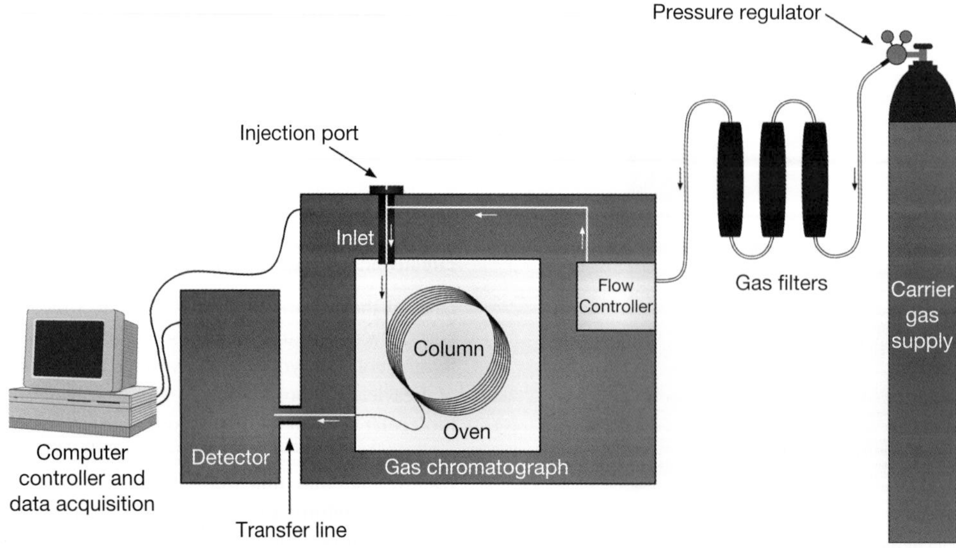

Figure 4 A chromatograph and its main components. Source: Stauffer E, Dolan JA, Newman R (2008) Fire Debris Analysis, Academic Press, Burlington, MA, p. 246. © Elsevier.

as recommended in ASTM E1618. Automated temperature programming allows the oven to gradually increase its temperatures within a specified time so that the analytes separate at different rates.

Mass Spectrometer

The mass spectrometer is comprised of three major elements, which are the ionizer for ionizing and fragmenting the sample, the mass analyzer for separating the ionized particles, and the electron multiplier, which detects the ionized particles.

Electron impact (EI) is the ionization technique of choice in fire debris analysis. EI produces a charged molecule or radical cation known as the molecular ion or parent ion and denoted as $M^{+\bullet}$.

$$M(g) + e^- \rightarrow M^{+\bullet} + 2e^-$$

Continuous bombardment causes the molecular ion to break down further producing more fragment ions or daughter ions.

$$M^{+\bullet} \rightarrow m_1{}^+ + m_2{}^\bullet \ldots \text{or}$$

$$M^{+\bullet} \rightarrow m_1{}^+ + m_2$$

All of these ions are then separated according to their mass to charge ratio (m/z ratio) by the mass analyzer and detected in proportion to their abundance. Mass spectral data are usually collected in scan acquisition mode, which provides a wide range of ion detection, commonly set between 10 and 400 amu in fire debris analysis. This results in a total ion chromatogram (TIC). Alternatively, it is possible to use selected ion monitoring (SIM), which only scans for preselected ions to detect compounds of interest. SIM mode increases the detector sensitivity.

GC–MS Data

GC–MS typically generates data under the form of a TIC. The characterization and identification of ILR are based on visual pattern recognition. The TIC pattern and relative peak ratio obtained from the sample are visually compared to the TIC from an ignitable liquid reference collection or database to identify the class of ignitable liquid present.

In order to properly interpret the chromatograms, the fire debris analyst must be very familiar with the types of compounds found in ILR, as shown in Table 1.

Most ignitable liquids are composed of various aliphatic components such as octane or trimethylpentane and aromatic components such as trimethylbenzenes, xylenes, and toluene.

The use of selective ion monitoring (SIM) and extracted ion chromatograms (EIC) to distinguished ignitable liquid

Table 1 Compounds commonly found in ILR

Type of compounds	*Specific structure*	*Description*	*Examples*
Alkane	Normal alkanes (*n*-alkanes)	Straight chain hydrocarbons (C_nH_{2n+2})	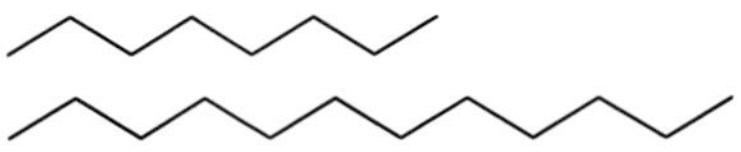
	Isoalkanes (isoparaffins)	Branch chained hydrocarbons (C_nH_{2n+2})	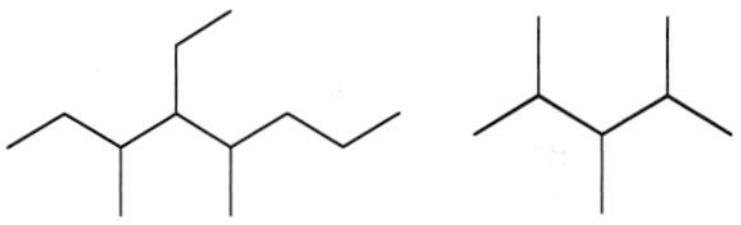
	Cycloalkanes (cycloparaffins, naphthenics)	Cyclic hydrocarbons (C_nH_{2n})	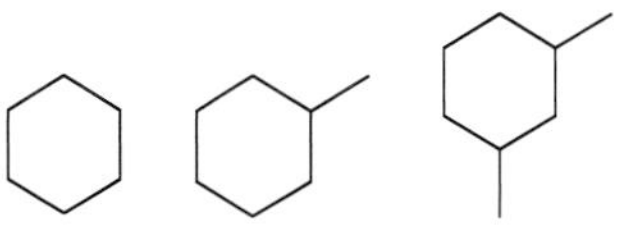
Aromatic	Simple	Alkyl-substituted benzenes	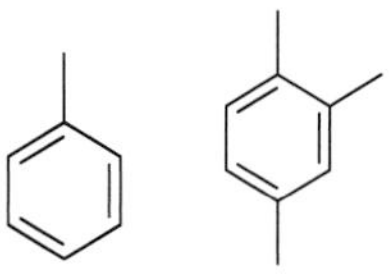
	Polynuclear (naphthalenes)	Multiple fused benzene ring compounds	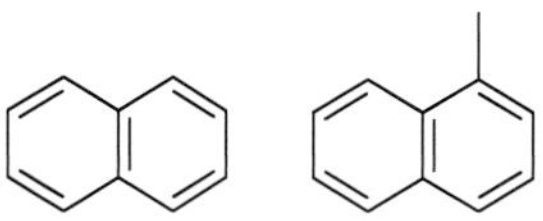
	Indane	Benzene ring fused to a cyclopentane	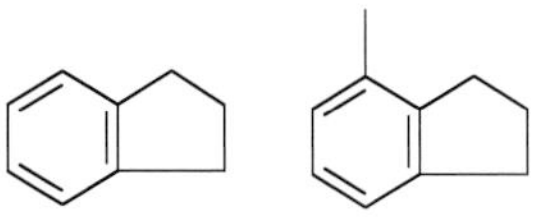

Table 2 Ions representative of ILR compounds

Hydrocarbon class	*Ions*				
Alkanes (iso and normal)	43	57	71	85	99
Cycloalkanes and alkenes	55	69	83	97	
Simple aromatics	91	105	119	133	
Polynuclear aromatics	128	142	156		
Indanes	117	118	131	132	

samples, ILR, and interfering products also brings undeniable advantages. By looking at the single ions rather than the TIC, it is possible to filter the pattern, which greatly facilitates the comparison. Table 2 shows the ions most representative of the different types of compounds present in ILR.

Once ILR analysis is performed, the interpretation of the results starts. This is the most difficult part of fire debris analysis and it is briefly described in other articles of this encyclopedia.

See also: **Chemistry/Trace/Fire Investigation:** Chemistry of Fire; Interpretation of Fire Debris Analysis; Physics/Thermodynamics.

Further Reading

ASTM International (2010) ASTM E1618-10 standard test method for ignitable liquid residues in extracts from fire debris samples by gas chromatography-mass spectrometry. West Conshohocken, PA: ASTM International. Annual book of ASTM standards 14.02.

DeHaan JD and Icove DJ (2011) *Kirk's fire investigation*, 7th ed. Upper Saddle River, NJ: Pearson Education.

Newman R, Gilbert M, and Lothridge K (1997) *GC-MS guide to ignitable liquids*. Boca Raton, FL: CRC Press.

Nic Daéid N (2004) *Fire investigation*. Boca Raton, FL: CRC Press.

Stauffer E, Dolan JA, and Newman R (2008) *Fire Debris Analysis*. Burlington, MA: Academic Press.

Interpretation of Fire Debris Analysis

E Stauffer, Commissariat d'Identification Judiciaire, Police Cantonale Fribourg, Fribourg, Switzerland
N NicDaéid, University of Strathclyde, Glasgow, UK

Glossary

Aliphatic An organic compound which is not aromatic; organic compounds that are alkanes, alkenes, and alkynes and their derivatives.
Alkane A saturated hydrocarbon compound having the general formula C_nH_{2n+2}.
Aromatics A class of unsaturated organic compounds that have a benzene ring or that have chemical properties similar to benzene as part of their structure.
Combustion products The set of products that are released during the combustion reaction of materials. These products are the result of both complete and incomplete combustion but not of the pyrolysis process.
Crude oil Naturally occurring oil consisting primarily of hydrocarbons with some other elements such as sulfur, oxygen, and nitrogen. Source material of nearly all petroleum products.
Fire debris A generic term commonly used to describe material collected at a fire scene and submitted to the laboratory for ignitable liquid residue analysis.
Gasoline A mixture of several hundreds of volatile hydrocarbons ranging from C_4 to C_{12} used in an internal combustion engine.
Ignitable liquid A liquid fuel that is either flammable or combustible.
Ignitable liquid residues The remaining portion of an ignitable liquid on a substrate after undergoing physical and/or chemical changes.
Interfering products The set of chemicals found in a sample that interferes with the proper identification of ignitable liquid residues.
Isoparaffinic products An ASTM class of petroleum distillate almost exclusively composed of branched alkanes.
Microbial degradation The decomposition of petroleum products by bacterial action that can diminish some components relative to others resulting in an altered chromatographic pattern that may not allow for a definitive characterization.
Petroleum distillates An ASTM class of products obtained primarily from the fractionation of crude oil.
Pyrolysis products The set of products generated by the process of pyrolysis only.
Substrate The sample material from which a substance of interest (analyte) is removed for analysis.

Abbreviations

GC Gas chromatography or gas chromatograph
IL Ignitable liquid
ILR Ignitable liquid residues
MS Mass spectrometry or mass spectrometer

Introduction

Once the chromatogram has been obtained, it is time to conduct the most difficult part of fire debris analysis: the interpretation of the results. It is necessary to distinguish the interpretation of chromatograms obtained from neat liquids from the ones obtained from fire debris samples. In the first case, the neat liquid is simply diluted and injected. As such, there are almost no influences to take into account in the interpretation. In the second case, the debris is first subjected to an extraction (passive headspace, solvent, etc.) and then analyzed. In addition, interfering products are coextracted with ignitable liquid residues (ILRs). Thus, the interpretation of the chromatogram is much more complicated.

The goal of the interpretation of the results is to determine whether or not ILRs are present in the fire debris sample. In order to achieve this, one will have to study the chromatogram for patterns exhibited by known ignitable liquids (ILs).

Because thousands of different ILs with different components exist, a system of organizing them into groups and finding common patterns exhibited within each group had to be devised. This led to a classification system, now described in the ASTM standard test method for ILR in extracts from fire debris samples by gas chromatography–mass spectrometry (GC–MS) E1618. As a result, these patterns are well known and the process of interpretation is clearly described.

Classification

While one may think that hundreds of thousands of different ILs potentially used at fire scenes may exhibit as many different patterns, this is not the case. First of all, most ILs are petroleum based, that is, they are derived from crude oil. As such, most of them are composed exclusively of aliphatic and/or aromatic compounds. Second, because the processes of transforming crude oil into refined products are not very diverse, patterns exhibited by petroleum-based ILs can be placed into six different classes of ILs, each with a characteristic set of patterns. Finally, when dealing with nonpetroleum-based ILs, even though all possibilities

 http://dx.doi.org/10.1016/B978-0-12-382165-2.00102-1

Table 1 ASTM E 1618–10 ignitable liquid classification scheme

Class	*Light (C_4–C_9)*	*Medium (C_8–C_{13})*	*Heavy (C_8–C_{20+})*
Gasoline	Fresh gasoline is typically in the range of C_4–C_{12}		
Petroleum distillates (including dearomatized)	Petroleum ether Some cigarette lighter fluids Some camping fuels	Some charcoal starters Some paint thinners Some dry cleaning solvents	Kerosene Diesel fuel Some jet fuels Some charcoal starters
Isoparaffinic products	Aviation gas Some specialty solvents	Some charcoal starters Some paint thinners Some copier toners	Some commercial specialty solvents
Naphthenic paraffinic products	Cyclohexane-based solvents/products	Some charcoal starters Some insecticide vehicles Some lamp oils	Some insecticide vehicles Some lamp oils Industrial solvents
Aromatic products	Some paint and varnish removers Some automotive parts cleaners Xylene-based products Toluene-based products	Some automotive part cleaners Specialty cleaning solvents Some insecticide vehicles Fuel additives	Some insecticide vehicles Industrial cleaning solvents
Normal alkane products	Solvents: pentane, hexane, heptane	Some candle oils Some copier toners	Some candle oils Carbonless forms Some copier toners
Oxygenated solvents	Alcohols Ketones Some lacquer thinners Fuel additives Surface preparation solvents	Some lacquer thinners Some industrial solvents Metal cleaners/gloss removers	
Others/miscellaneous	Single-component products Some blended products Some enamel reducers	Turpentine products Some blended products Some specialty products	Some blended products Some specialty products

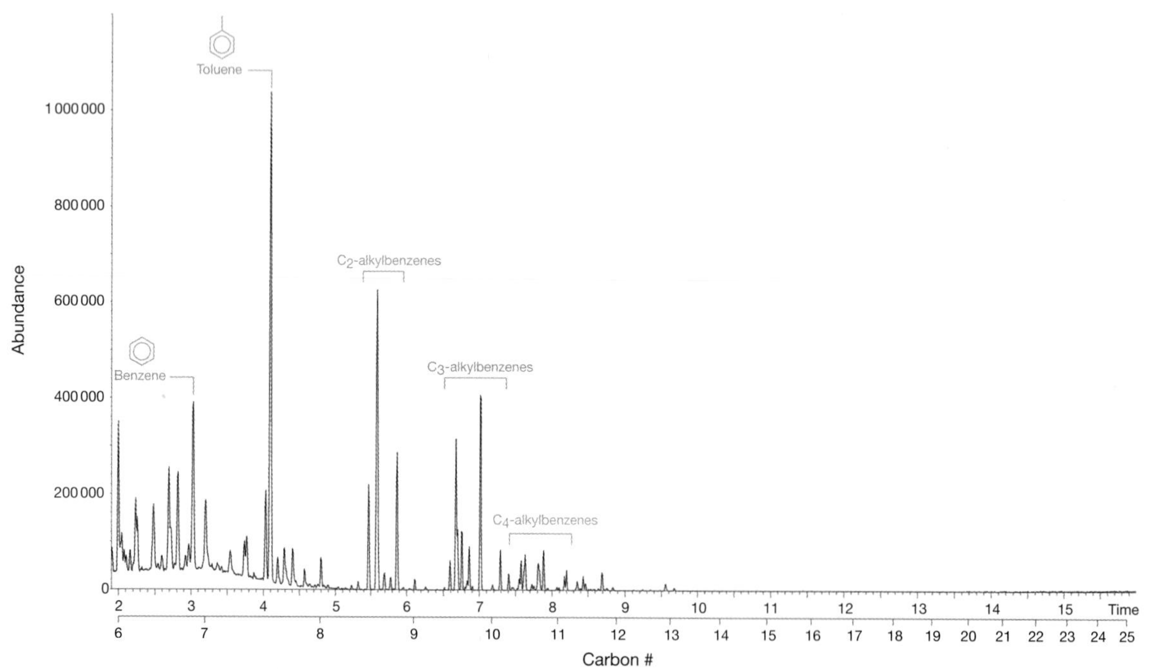

Figure 1 Chromatogram of a neat gasoline (unweathered). Time in minutes. Reproduced from Stauffer E, Dolan JA, and Newman R (2008) *Fire Debris Analysis*, p. 323. Burlington, MA: Academic Press. © Elsevier.

are open, these liquids usually consist of only a few different components. Thus, the resulting chromatograms are not as complicated as those from petroleum-based ILs, which can exhibit several hundreds of components.

ASTM standard E1618 proposes a classification system based on eight different classes, as shown in Table 1.

The examples for each class are not exhaustive; they are just the most commonly encountered products found in each

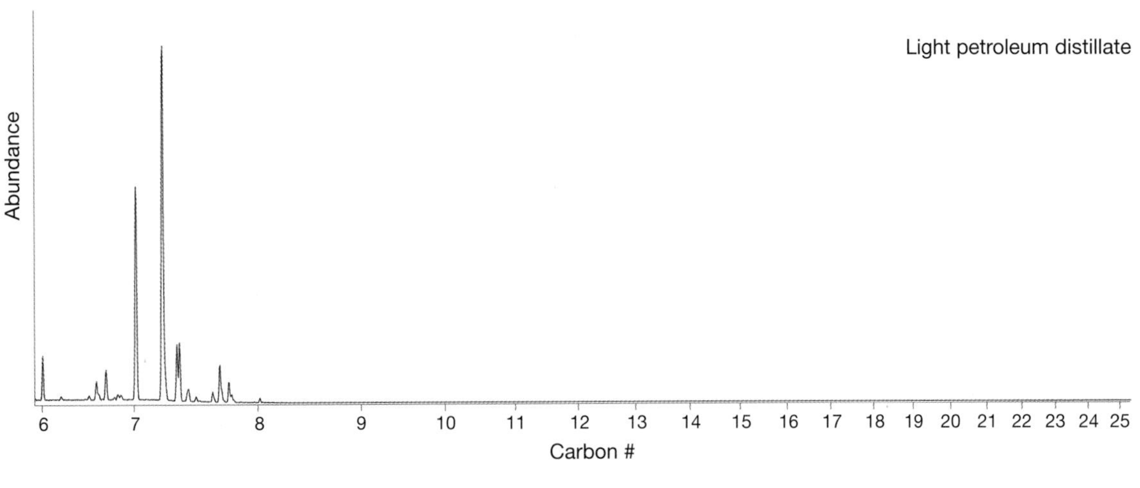

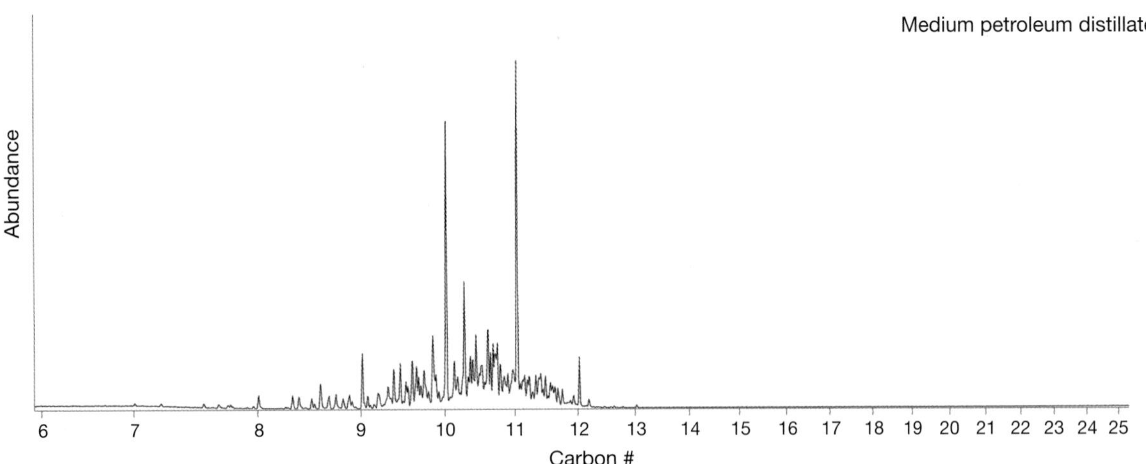

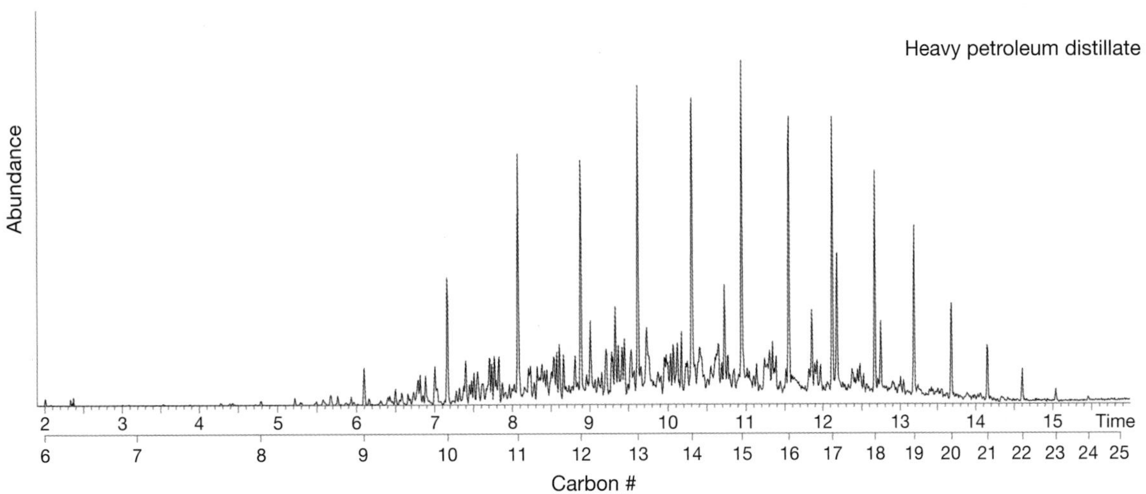

Figure 2 Chromatograms of light, medium, and heavy petroleum distillates. Time in minutes. Reproduced from Stauffer E, Dolan JA, and Newman R (2008) *Fire Debris Analysis*, p. 328. Burlington, MA: Academic Press. © Elsevier.

particular class. In his/her findings, the fire debris analyst does not report a finished product itself, but rather the ASTM class. Then, products found in that class can be cited as examples, to guide the fire investigator.

Because the difference between the classes relies on the chemical composition of the IL, the ASTM system introduces a second dimension of classification to refine the different categories: the boiling point range. By using the boiling point range, one can

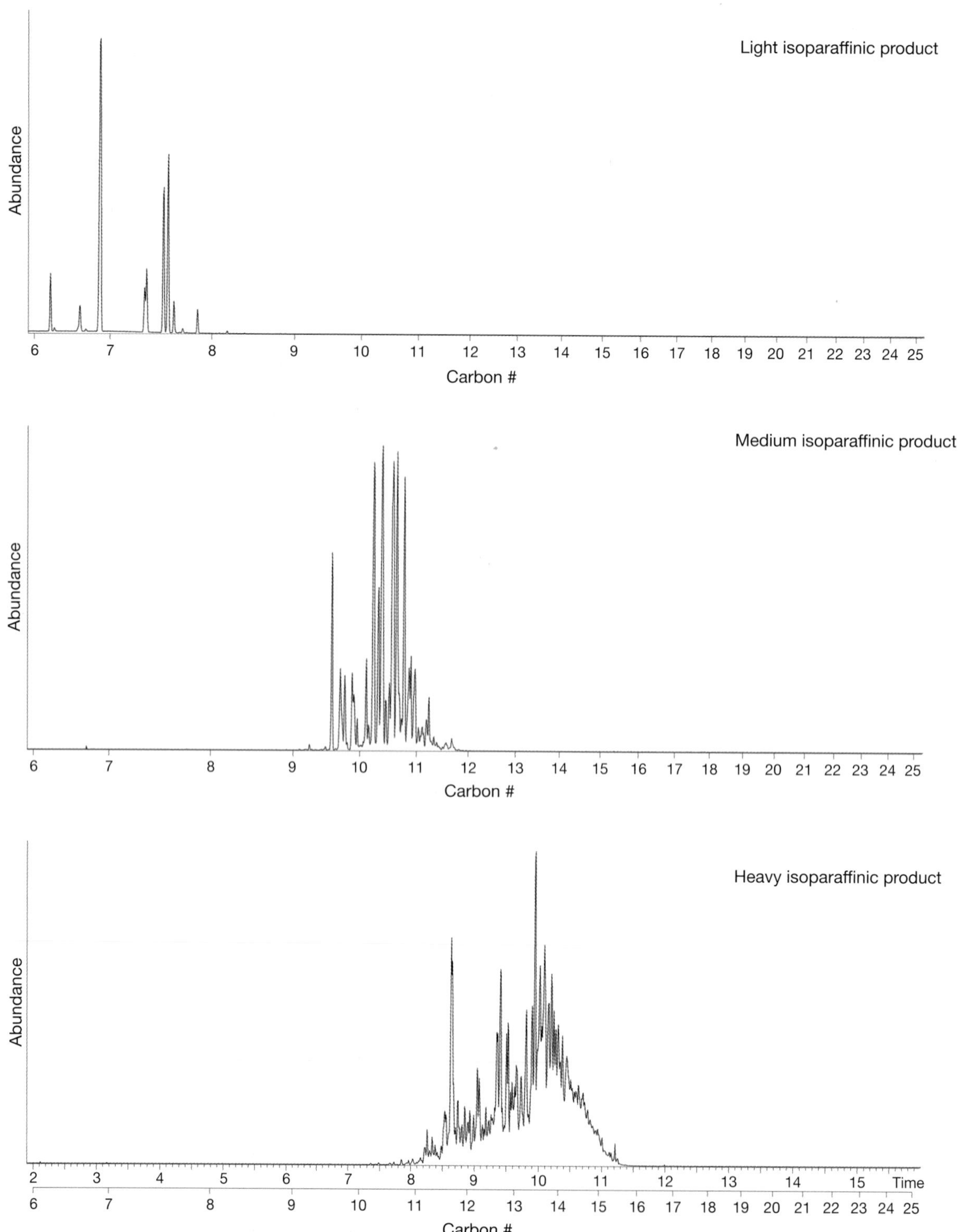

Figure 3 Chromatograms of light, medium, and heavy isoparaffinic products. Time in minutes. Reproduced from Stauffer E, Dolan JA, and Newman R (2008) *Fire Debris Analysis*, p. 332. Burlington, MA: Academic Press. © Elsevier.

refine the different classes and create more pertinent categories. In practice, the light subclass ranges approximately from 0 to 150 °C, the medium from 120 to 240 °C, and the heavy from 120 °C to more than 350 °C. The only exception to that subclassification is gasoline, whose boiling point range does not vary greatly. This classification system works perfectly well with the separation and analysis obtained by GC–MS as this instrument separates the compounds based on their boiling points and the MS provides identification of their chemical nature.

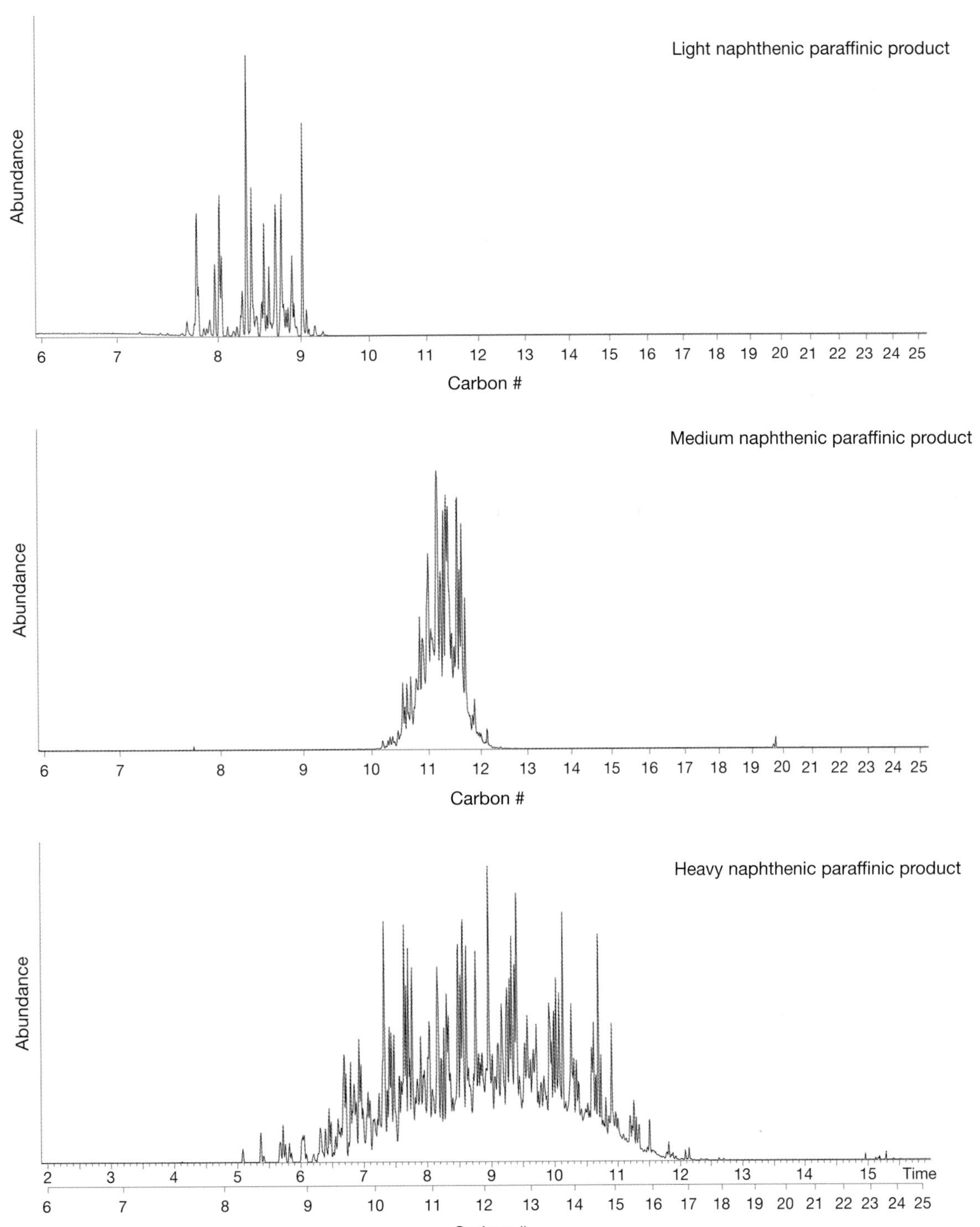

Figure 4 Chromatograms of light, medium, and heavy naphthenic paraffinic products. Time in minutes. Reproduced from Stauffer E, Dolan JA, and Newman R (2008) *Fire Debris Analysis*, p. 335. Burlington, MA: Academic Press. © Elsevier.

Interpretation of Neat Liquids

With petroleum-based products, the basic principle of interpretation is to evaluate the chromatogram for the presence, distribution, boiling point range, and relative abundance of all saturated aliphatics and all aromatics. With nonpetroleum-based products, the analyst looks at all compounds present in the chromatogram and evaluates whether or not they could originate from an IL.

While an advanced knowledge of crude oil-refining processes is necessary to fully understand the reasons behind the chemical compositions of the different ASTM classes, this goes beyond the

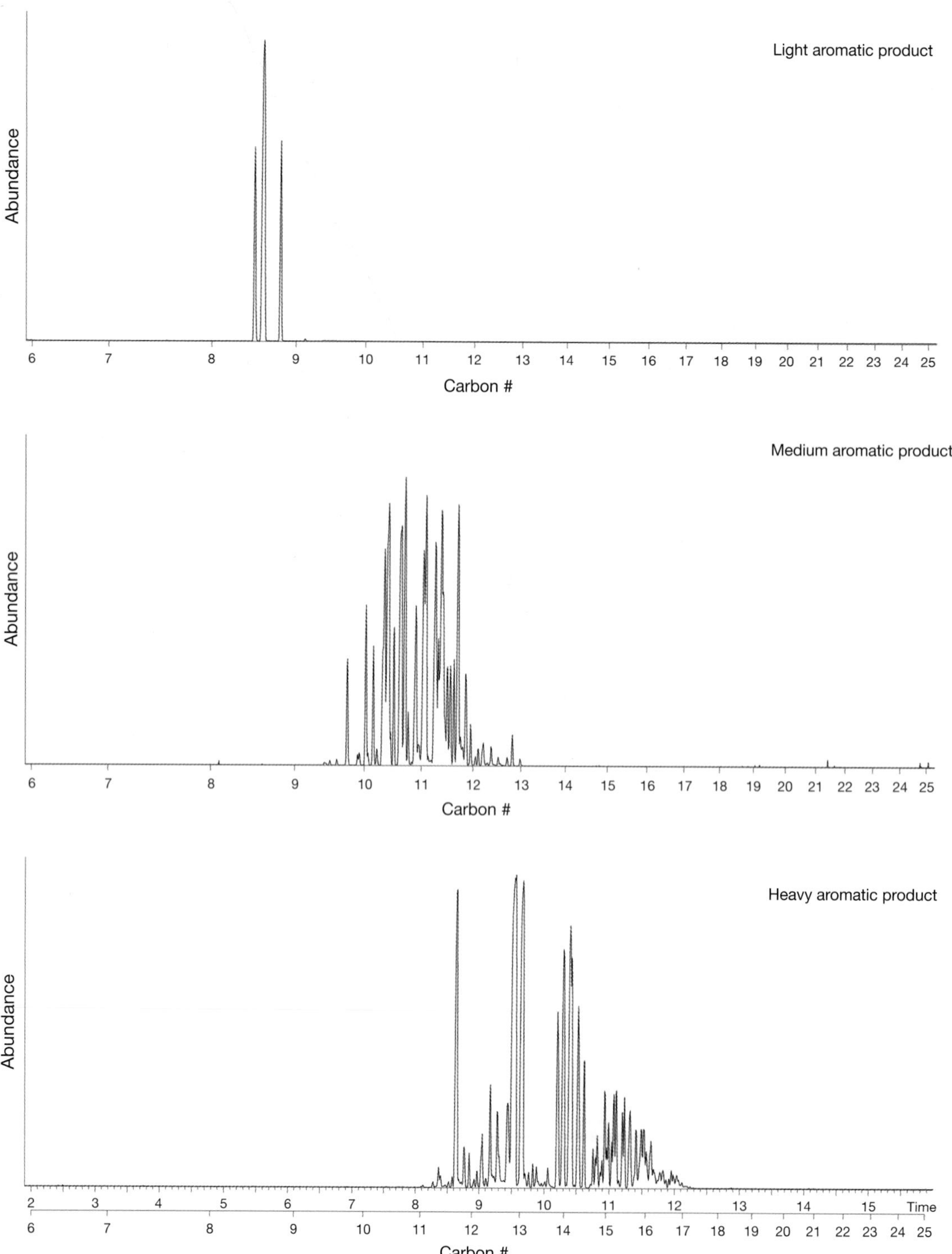

Figure 5 Chromatograms of light, medium, and heavy aromatic products. Time in minutes. Reproduced from Stauffer E, Dolan JA, and Newman R (2008) *Fire Debris Analysis*, p. 339. Burlington, MA: Academic Press. © Elsevier.

scope of this chapter. Nevertheless, it is possible to provide a rapid overview of the different classes and their compositions.

Gasoline is mostly composed of aromatic compounds ranging from C4 (4-carbon'long chain) to C12 (12-carbon'long chain). It also contains some alkanes; however, they are normally not abundant. **Figure 1** shows an example of a chromatogram of gasoline.

Petroleum distillates are the closest products to crude oil, as they have undergone a minimum of refinement. They contain both aliphatics and aromatics in a normal (Gaussian) distribution with spiking *n*-alkanes. Some petroleum distillates said to be dearomatized have no aromatic content. **Figure 2** shows examples of light, medium, and heavy petroleum distillates.

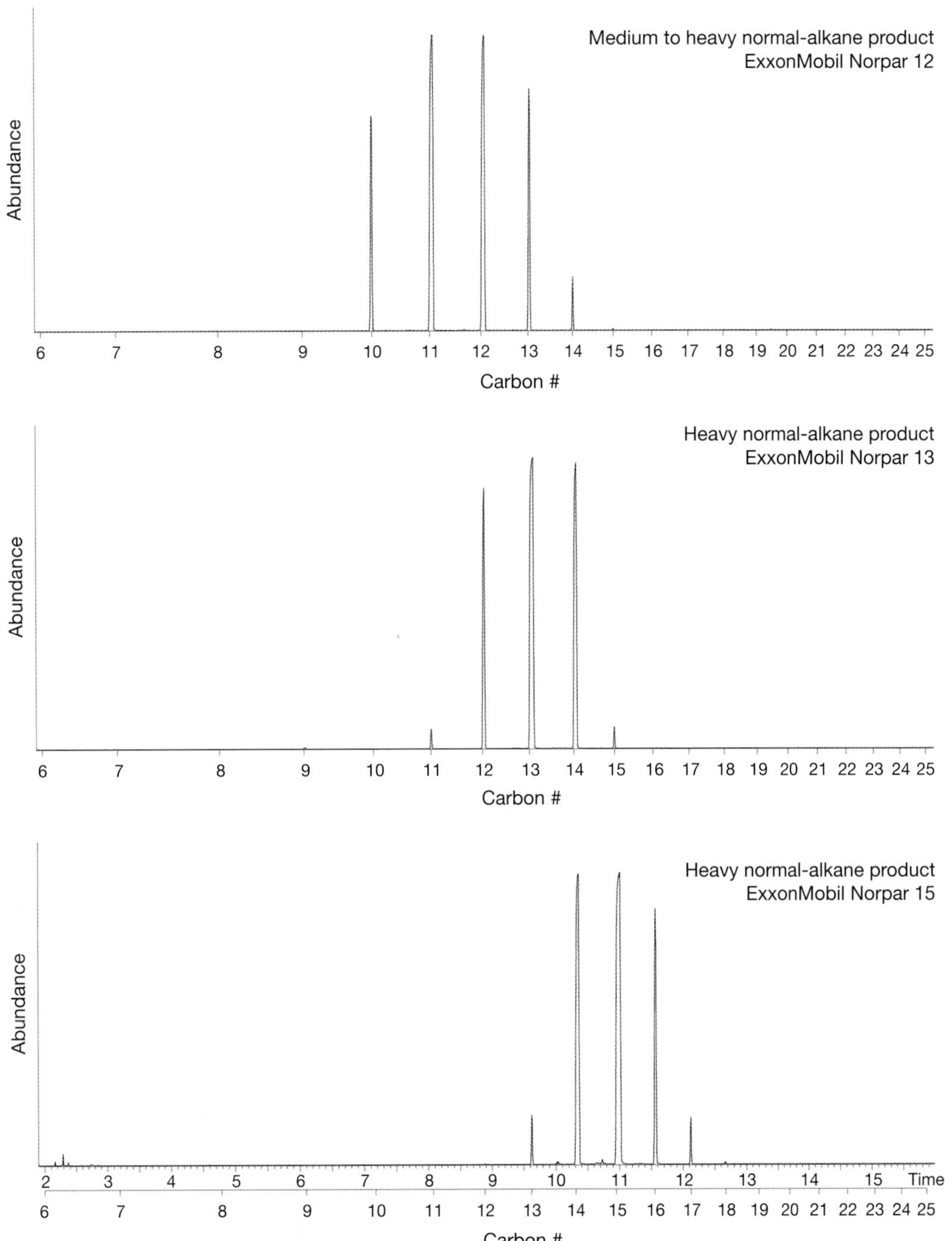

Figure 6 Chromatograms of light, medium, and heavy *n*-alkanes. Time in minutes. Reproduced from Stauffer E, Dolan JA, and Newman R (2008) *Fire Debris Analysis*, p. 337. Burlington, MA: Academic Press. © Elsevier.

Isoparaffinic products are exclusively constituted of isoalkanes as shown in **Figure** 3. They have no aromatics, *n*-alkanes, or cycloalkanes.

Naphthenic paraffinic products are comprised of cycloalkanes and isoalkanes (see **Figure** 4). Basically, a naphthenic paraffinic product is a petroleum distillate in which the *n*-alkanes and the aromatic content have been removed.

Aromatic products are composed exclusively of aromatic compounds. As a matter of fact, such a product is constituted of the aromatic fraction that was isolated from crude oil. In general, they exhibit a narrow boiling point range, as shown in **Figure** 5.

n-Alkane products represent the simplest pattern: a narrow fraction of *n*-alkanes (usually not spanning more than four or five carbons). **Figure** 6 shows an example of light, medium, and heavy *n*-alkane products.

Oxygenated solvents include all ILs containing at least one oxygenated compound in large excess of the rest of the components (at least one order of magnitude in the chromatogram). Oxygenated solvents may also contain other ILs such

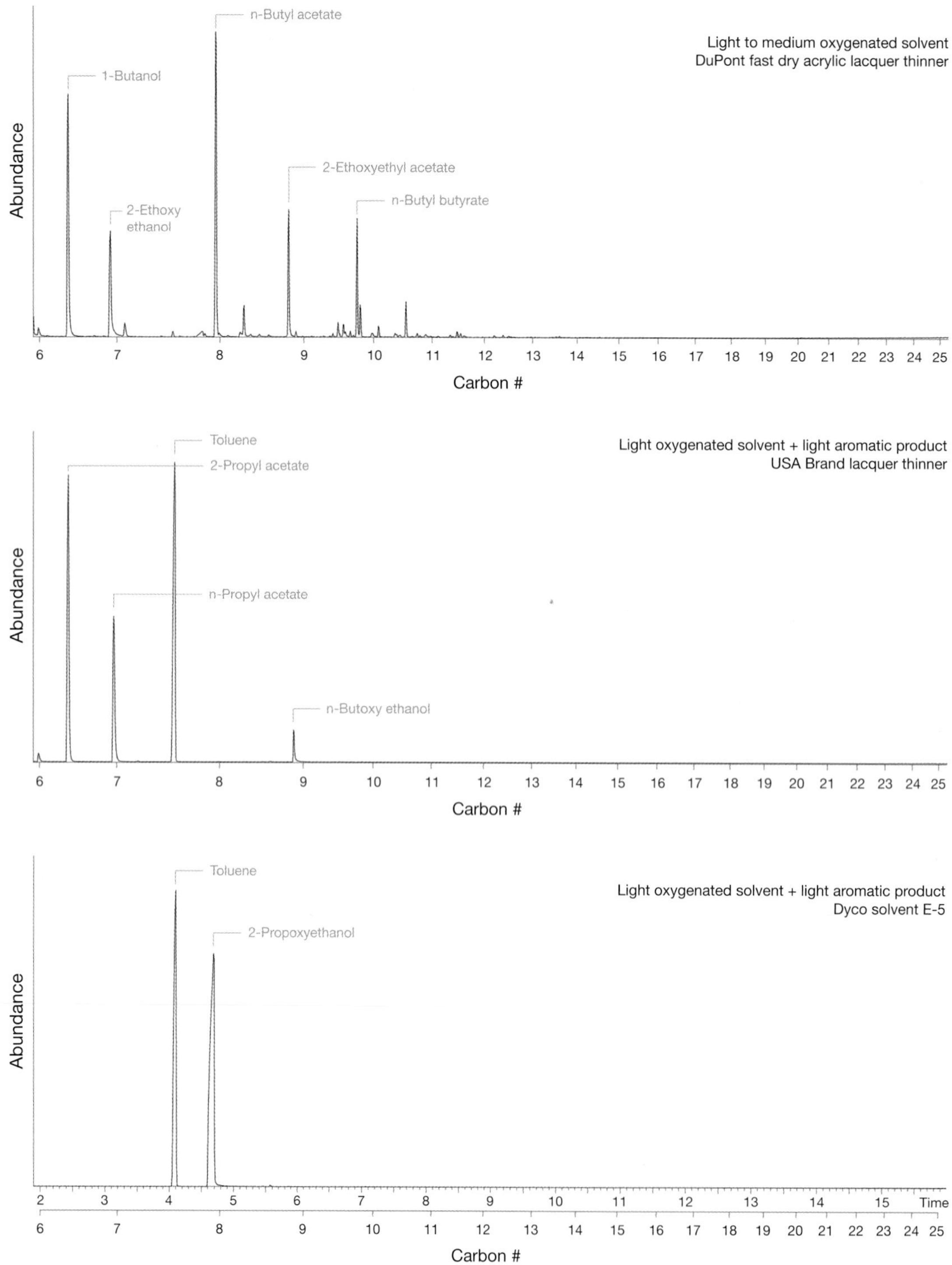

Figure 7 Chromatograms of light, medium, and heavy oxygenated solvents. Time in minutes. Reproduced from Stauffer E, Dolan JA, and Newman R (2008) *Fire Debris Analysis*, p. 342. Burlington, MA: Academic Press. © Elsevier.

as medium petroleum distillates. **Figure** 7 shows three examples of oxygenated solvents.

Miscellaneous products include ILs that do not fit in any of the categories previously described. **Figure** 8 shows an example of a turpentine, which is classified as miscellaneous.

In summary, **Table** 2 shows the different components found in each ASTM class and subclass.

While the interpretation and classification of chromatograms may appear relatively complex at first, it is in fact quite easy with neat liquids. **Figure** 9 provides a guide to the proper interpretation of chromatograms. If the analyst follows this guide, there should be no problem in correctly identifying neat liquids. Unfortunately, it is a whole other story with ILR from fire debris samples.

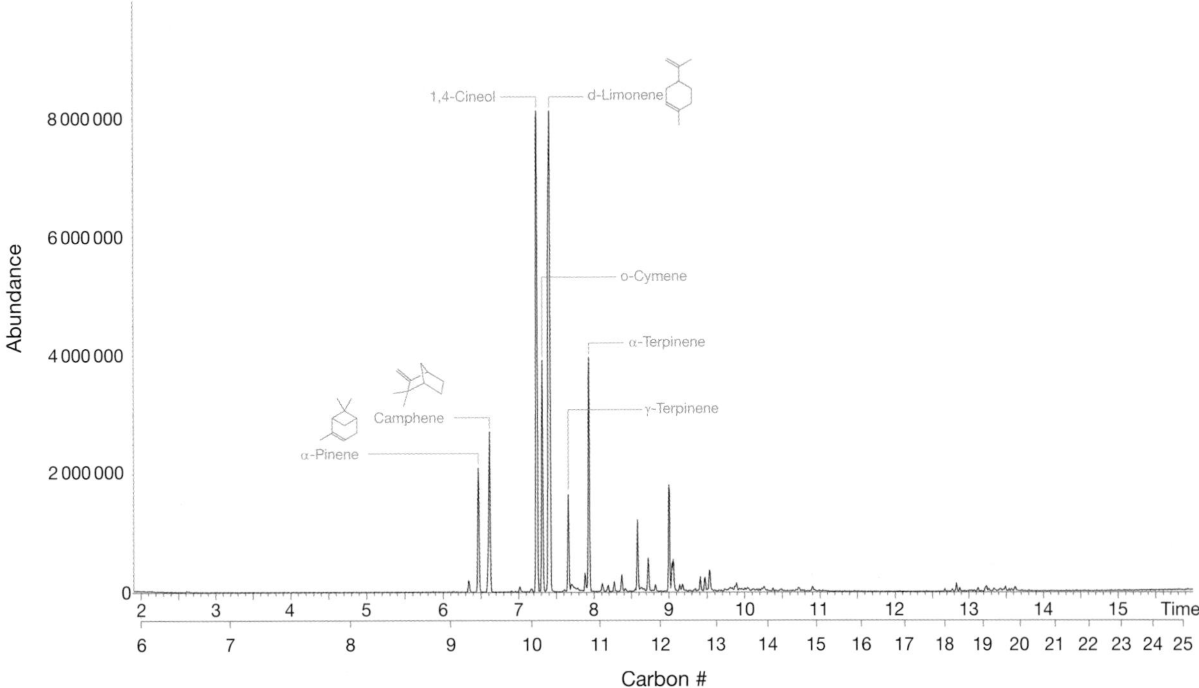

Figure 8 Chromatogram of turpentine product, classified as miscellaneous. Time in minutes. Reproduced from Stauffer E, Dolan JA, and Newman R (2008) *Fire Debris Analysis*, p. 344. Burlington, MA: Academic Press. © Elsevier.

Table 2 The different components found in each ASTM class and subclass

Class	*Alkanes*	*Cycloalkanes*	*Aromatics (including indanes)*	*Polynuclear aromatics*
Gasoline	Present, less abundant than aromatics	Present, less abundant than aromatics	Abundant	Present
Petroleum distillates	Abundant, normal (Gaussian) distribution	Present, less abundant than alkanes	Present, less abundant than alkanes (absent in dearomatized distillates)	Present (depending on boiling point range), less abundant than alkanes (absent in dearomatized distillates)
Isoparaffinic products	Branched alkanes abundant, *n*-alkanes absent or strongly diminished	Absent	Absent	Absent
Naphthenic paraffinic products	Branched alkanes abundant, *n*-alkanes absent or strongly diminished	Abundant	Absent	Absent
Aromatic products	Absent	Absent	Abundant	Abundant (depending on the boiling point range)
Normal alkanes products	Abundant	Absent	Absent	Absent
Oxygenated solvents	Composition may vary, presence of oxygenated organic compounds			

Interpretation of Ignitable Liquid Residues

When an IL is poured onto a substrate, and then set on fire, extinguished, collected, and finally extracted, one can easily imagine that it no longer exhibits the same chromatographic pattern as when it was neat. This is the reason why the interpretation of ILR is much more complicated than that of mere IL, in addition to the fact that the analyst does not know at first whether or not ILR are present in the debris.

There are several parameters influencing the composition of the ILR extract from a fire debris as shown in **Figure 10**.

First, the substrate itself may already contain some IL, or at least some compounds that are found in IL. These are called precursory products and they may be due to the raw material constituting the substrate, to its manufacturing process, to the setup in its final position/use, and to some natural or accidental contaminations. For example, some woods contain terpenes, compounds typically found in

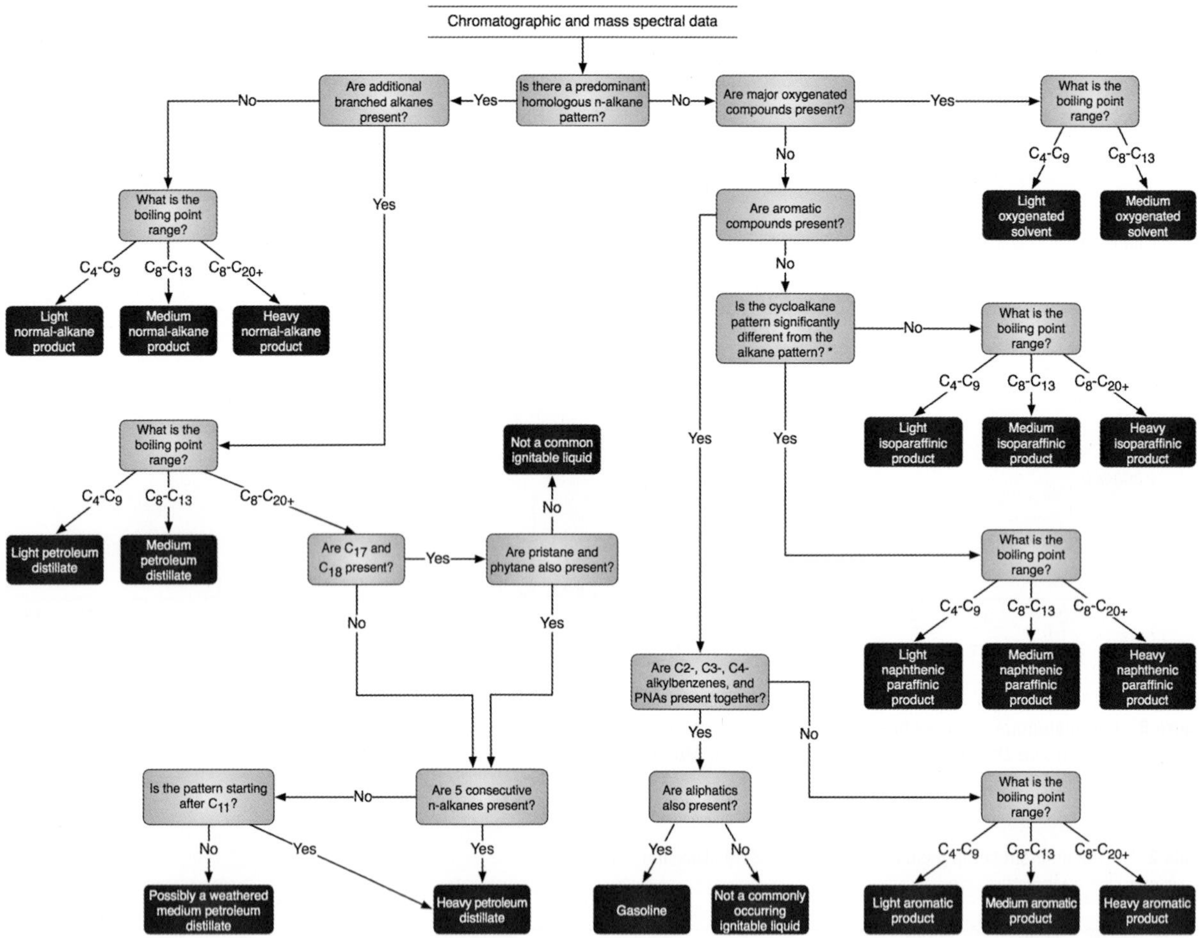

Figure 9 Petroleum-based ignitable liquid flow chart. Every question related to the presence of specific compounds implies that these compounds must be present in the proper pattern (as compared to a pattern of these compounds from a reference liquid analyzed on the same system). * Or "Are cycloalkanes distinctively present in the extracted ion chromatograms"? Reproduced from Stauffer E, Dolan JA, and Newman R (2008) *Fire Debris Analysis*, p. 345. Burlington, MA: Academic Press. © Elsevier.

thinners. Most outsoles are glued to the shoe and this glue usually contains an aromatic compound, such as toluene. A carpet is also often glued to the floor; however, this glue usually contains a medium petroleum distillate. When one sprays insecticides around a baseboard, these become contaminated with a naphthenic paraffinic or an aromatic product. These are all examples of precursory products that may be found on a substrate before it is even deliberately contaminated with an IL used as an accelerant.

Second, once an IL is poured onto a substrate, it will undergo three effects, which will influence its composition: weathering, diminution, and degradation. Weathering is the effect of the evaporation of an IL. Because an IL is commonly made of many different compounds of different boiling points, not all compounds will evaporate at the same rate. As such, the chromatographic pattern of a neat IL (unweathered) is different from that of its 50% evaporated version. As a matter of fact, as the weathering increases, the chromatogram moves to the right, meaning that the light compounds disappear and the heavy compounds become more and more dominant. Diminution represents the uniform loss of the different compounds of an IL. In practice, it occurs simultaneously with weathering, but it may also be due to poor evidence collection or to fire suppression activities. Finally, degradation occurs when the substrate, mostly soil, contains proteobacteria, which are capable of degrading petroleum-based IL. These bacteria, depending on their type, will selectively degrade aliphatics or aromatics. As a result, the composition of an IL may drastically change, not based on its boiling point range, but rather on its chemical characteristics.

Third, when a substrate burns, pyrolysis and combustion products are created. Pyrolysis products consist of compounds that are often the same as the ones found in petroleum products. As a result, they strongly interfere with the chemical composition of an IL, making it impossible in some instances to properly identify an ILR. Most commonly encountered pyrolysis products are toluene, styrene, naphthalene, benzaldehyde, ethylbenzene, indene, phenylethyne, *m*,*p*-xylenes, 1- and 2-methylnaphthalene, acetophenone, and the series of alkane–alkene–alkadiene ranging from C10 to C16. **Figure 11** shows an example of pyrolysis products created with burned polyethylene.

Combustion products usually do not interfere as much as pyrolysis products with ILR because they are oxidized products, which are not often found as IL components. Because they are very light compounds, they tend not to be trapped in substrates.

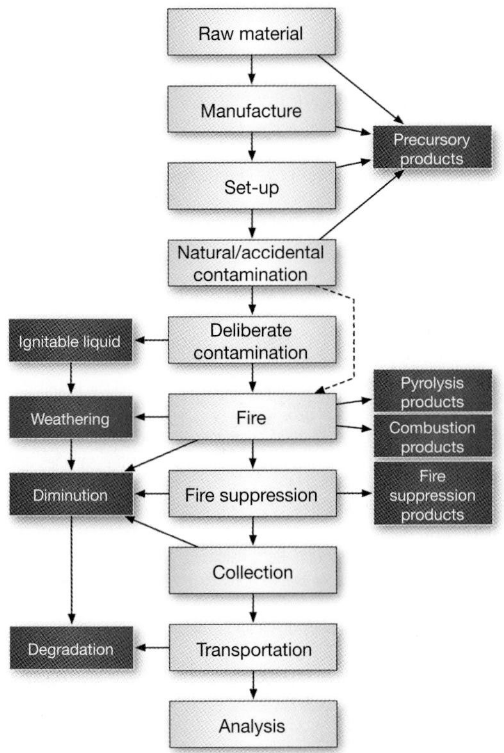

Figure 10 The different steps (in the middle) to which the fire debris sample is subjected from its creation to its analysis, along with the influences (on the left) on the potential ignitable liquid present in the debris and the different interfering products created (on the right). Reproduced from Stauffer E, Dolan JA, and Newman R (2008) *Fire Debris Analysis*, p. 443. Burlington, MA: Academic Press. © Elsevier.

Finally, fire suppression agents may also be used by the intervening fire department. Some of these agents may also contribute to the fire debris extract, such as some foams that use D-limonene or some alcohol-based compounds.

Interfering products, then, are a set of products comprising precursory, pyrolysis, combustion, and fire suppression products. When interpreting chromatograms of extracts from fire debris samples, one must account for the presence of these interfering products. In addition, one must not forget the different effects occurring directly on the IL. This is why a systematic approach was developed.

Systematic Approach

Because the interpretation of chromatograms for ILR identification is quite complicated, it is important to follow a systematic approach, which is constituted of the six following steps:

1. Identify the sample and its substrate.
2. Estimate the typical contribution from that substrate.
3. Determine to which influences the substrate was subjected.
4. Estimate the effect of these influences.
5. Study the chromatogram from start to finish, including peak identification.
6. Study extracted ions in the regions of interest, including peak identification.

Even if the fire debris analyst did not work on the fire scene, he/she must have some clear basic knowledge about the sample in question, particularly in regard to its composition, its environment at the time of the fire, and the different steps it underwent. Knowledge of the sample's history is crucial, too.

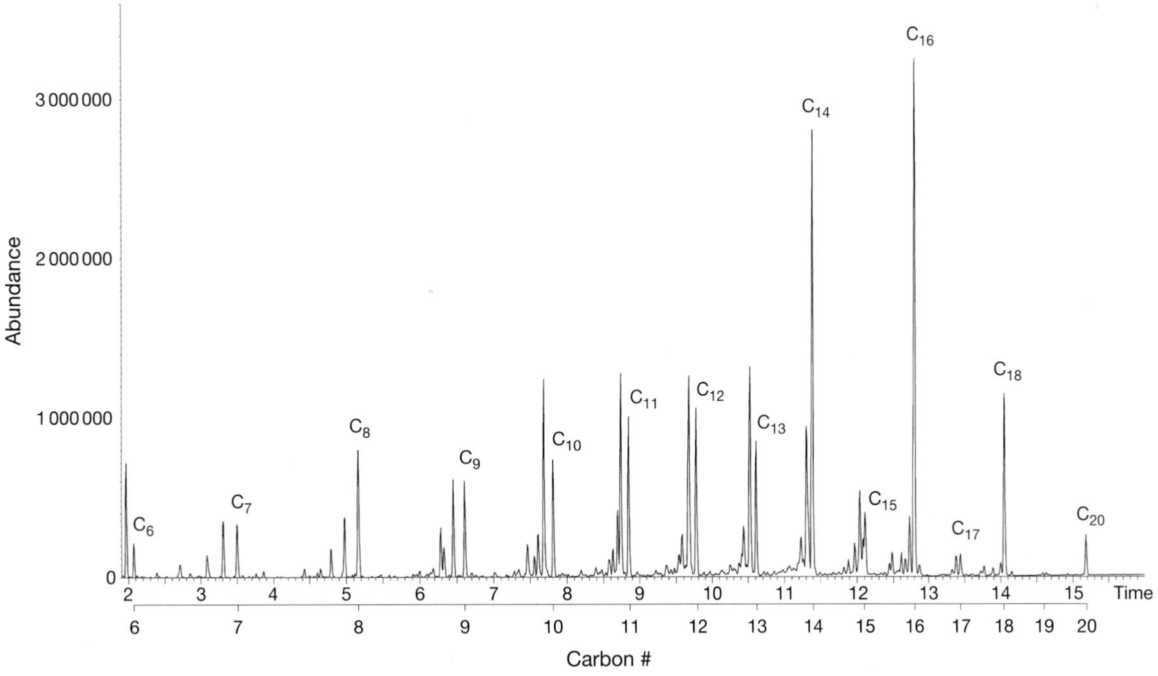

Figure 11 Chromatogram of polyethylene pyrolysis products. Time in minutes. Reproduced from Stauffer E, Dolan JA, and Newman R (2008) *Fire Debris Analysis*, p. 459. Burlington, MA: Academic Press. © Elsevier.

The preliminary examination of fire debris samples is, thus, a very crucial step that should never be undermined.

Significance of Findings

Fire debris analysis is an extremely complex science and the reason is twofold. First, the interpretation of chromatograms is rendered very difficult due to the numerous components of many different IL and the presence of interfering products. The second reason is that the simple presence of ILR in a debris does not imply at all that it was used as an accelerant in the fire. This last determination requires the experience of both the fire debris analyst and the fire investigator, as well as a very good knowledge of the fire scene and the circumstances surrounding the fire.

See also: **Chemistry/Trace/Fire Investigation:** Analysis of Fire Debris; Chemistry of Fire; Thermal Degradation; **Methods:** Gas Chromatography; Gas Chromatography–Mass Spectrometry; Mass Spectrometry.

Further Reading

ASTM International (2010) *ASTM E1618-10 Standard Test Method for Ignitable Liquid Residues in Extracts from Fire Debris Samples by Gas Chromatography-Mass Spectrometry*, Annual Book of ASTM Standards 14.02. West Conshohocken, PA: ASTM International.

Byron DE (2002) The effects of surfactants and microbes on the identification of ignitable liquids in fire debris analysis. *Fire and Arson Investigator* 53(1): 50ss.

DeHaan JD, Brien DJ, and Large R (2004) Volatile organic compounds from the combustion of human and animal tissue. *Science and Justice* 44(4): 223–236.

DeHaan JD and Icove DJ (2011) *Kirk's Fire Investigation*, 7th edn. Upper Saddle River, NJ: Pearson Education.

Gilbert MW (1998) The use of individual extracted ion profiles versus summed extracted ion profiles in fire debris analysis. *Journal of Forensic Sciences* 43(4): 871–876.

Leffle WL (2000) *Petroleum Refining in Nontechnical Language*, 3rd edn. Tulsa, OK: PennWell Corporation.

Lentini JJ, Dolan JA, and Cherry C (2000) The petroleum-laced background. *Journal of Forensic Sciences* 45(5): 968–989.

Mann DC and Gresham WR (1990) Microbial degradation of gasoline in soil. *Journal of Forensic Sciences* 35(4): 913–923.

McGee E and Lang TL (2002) A study of the effects of a micelle encapsulator fire suppression agent on dynamic headspace analysis of fire debris samples. *Journal of Forensic Sciences* 47(2): 267–274.

Newman R, Gilbert M, and Lothridge K (1997) *GC-MS Guide to Ignitable Liquids*. Boca Raton, FL: CRC Press.

Nic Daéid N (2004) *Fire Investigation*. Boca Raton, FL: CRC Press.

Spreight JC (1999) *The Chemistry and Technology of Petroleum*, 3rd edn. New York, NY: Marcel Dekker.

Stauffer E (2003) Basic concept of pyrolysis for fire debris analysts. *Science and Justice* 43(1): 29–40.

Stauffer E, Dolan JA, and Newman R (2008) *Fire Debris Analysis*. Burlington, MA: Academic Press.

Trimpe MA (1991) Turpentine in arson analysis. *Journal of Forensic Sciences* 36(4): 1059–1073.

CHEMISTRY/TRACE/FIREARM DISCHARGE RESIDUES

Overview, Analysis, and Interpretation

FS Romolo, SAPIENZA Università di Roma, Rome, Italy

Abbreviations

ASTM	American Standard and Testing Materials
DDNP	Diazodinitrophenol
DPA	Diphenylamine
EDS or EDX	Energy dispersive x-ray spectrometry
GC	Gas chromatography
HPLC	High-performance liquid chromatography
IBA	Ion beam analysis
MS/MS	Tandem mass spectrometry
NAA	Neutron activation analysis
NCNM	Noncorrosive, nonmercuric
NG	Nitroglycerine
PDME	Pendant drop mercury electrode
SEM	Scanning electron microscopy
SPME	Solid phase microextraction
TEA	Thermal energy analyzer

Introduction

Firearms discharge residue (FDR) is composed of materials produced during the discharge of a firearm due to the explosion of the cartridge. Chemical substances in the FDR come not only from all the components of the cartridge but also from the firearm itself. These materials are projected through any possible openings in the firearm, including the muzzle, the breach area, and the ejection port. Most FDR exits through the muzzle and may be deposited onto the target, but a significant amount can also be deposited on the surfaces around the firearm, including the shooter's hands or clothes. FDR can be useful during criminal investigations to get information about several aspects of a shooting incident, but the vast majority of forensic analyses of FDR are carried out for detection and identification of FDR on surfaces such as the hands or clothes of a suspect.

FDR is not the only definition adopted; the American Standard and Testing Materials (ASTM) "Standard Guide for Gunshot Residue Analysis by Scanning Electron Microscopy/Energy Dispersive X-Ray Spectroscopy" does not use FDR, but refers to gunshot residue (GSR), while some articles make reference to other definitions, such as cartridge discharge residue, primer discharge residue, potential FDR, or full GSR. Given that a definition is a 'statement of meaning,' the term 'FDR' is used in the present article for consistency reasons.

The Ammunition for Firearms from the Chemical Point of View

Modern cartridge cases are generally made of brass, which is an alloy made of copper and zinc, but other metals, such as steel or, as shown in **Figure 1**, aluminum, can also be used.

The case of a cartridge contains two explosive charges: the primer, which is contained in a cup, and the propellant.

The primer is a small charge that initiates the explosive reaction following a mechanical shock. It is a mixture containing not only the explosive compound (called the initiator) but also different substances with specific functions. The sensitizer helps the ignition process of the initiator when the firing pin hits the primer. The fuel helps to sustain the flame and to ensure adequate time for the propellant to be lighted. The oxidizer supplies an oxygen source for both the fuel and the initiator. Other substances such as binding agents or dyes may be added to the mixture during the production.

Mercury fulminate is one of the most important initiating explosives in the history of primers, its first preparation being published in 1690 by Kunkel. Other initiating explosives are lead styphnate, which was patented for use in primers in 1914 by von Herz, and diazodinitrophenol (DDNP), which was discovered by Griess in 1858 and patented in 1922 for use in primers and detonators by Dehn. The primer contains several compounds. The primer of Frankford Arsenal (mercury fulminate 35%, potassium chlorate 15%, black powder 40%, glass powder 5%, and gum Arabic 5%) was the usual mixture for rifle ammunition used when the propellant was black powder. In 1928, Rheinisch-Westfälischen Sprengstoff (RWS) developed the first practical, noncorrosive, nonmercuric (NCNM) primer, called SINOXID. Subsequently, the mixture of lead styphnate with tetracene as sensitizer began replacing the former primers based on mercury fulminate and potassium chlorate. By the 1950s, the NCNM primer had shown such good stability that all US military small arms primers were converted to that type. The presence of lead styphnate, barium nitrate, and antimony sulfide in NCNM primers is the main reason for the successful use of scanning electron microscopy (SEM) in FDR analysis.

 http://dx.doi.org/10.1016/B978-0-12-382165-2.00116-1

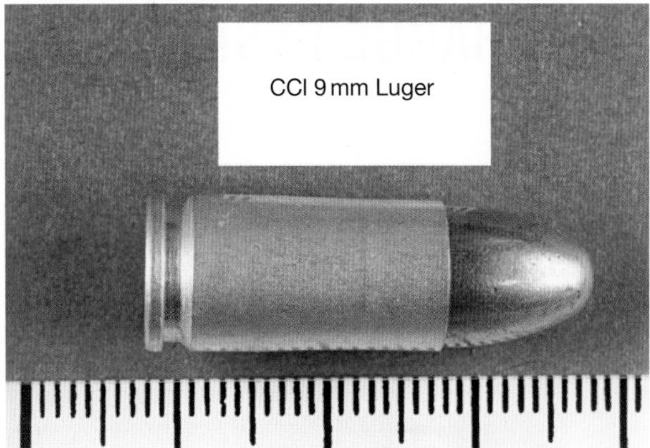

Figure 1 Cartridge CCI 9 mm Luger.

Figure 2 Internal surface of a primer cup disassembled from the cartridge case of a CCI 38 Special + P. The three holes trough the anvil allow the flame due to the explosion of the primer to ignite the propellant.

In 1982, Hagel and Redecker patented a primer used in the manufacture of a new ammunition which was developed to minimize airborne lead levels and possibly other metallic residues such as barium and antimony. The primer contained DDNP, tetrazene, zinc peroxide, and titanium powder. Other examples of primers developed to decrease the toxic impact of the residue produced by shooting on human health are CCI Blazer® Lead free (0.38 SPL + P), containing tetracene, DDNP, smokeless powder, and strontium nitrate; and Winchester Winclean™ (9 mm and 0.45ACP), containing DDNP, potassium nitrate, boron, and nitrocellulose. When the firing pin strikes the primer cup, the primer is crushed against the anvil (see Figures 2 and 3) and detonates.

The temperature and pressure go from ambient to about 1500–2000 °C and 10^4 kPa, respectively, in about 0.1 ms. The explosion of the primer ignites the propellant charge, causing its deflagration and increasing the temperature and pressure to about 3600 °C and 3×10^5 kPa, respectively. The bullet is pushed up into the barrel and the pressure is vented to the atmosphere when the bullet leaves the muzzle of the firearm. Bullets are commonly made with lead, generally alloyed with varying quantities of antimony, and can be covered with a thin layer of a much harder material, including a copper/zinc alloy, a copper/nickel alloy, or steel.

Following the invention of nitrocellulose by Schonbein in 1846, attention was rapidly drawn to its explosive properties, and research led to the invention of a new propellant to replace the black powder in firearms. The work of Paul Vieille and Alfred Nobel in the following years resulted in a propellant that has been used exclusively for a long time in conventional military weapons: smokeless (or, more accurately, low smoke) powder. With reference to the actual composition, it is possible to distinguish between single-base powders (e.g., nitrocellulose powder), double-base powders (e.g., nitrocellulose + nitroglycerine (NG) powder), and triple-base powders (e.g., nitrocellulose + NG or diglycol dinitrate + nitroguanidine powders). Several additives are added to smokeless powders during their manufacture, such as stabilizers, gelatinizers, and phlegmatizers. Stabilizers exert their stabilizing effect by binding the decomposition products, such as the free acids and nitrous gases, the stabilizers themselves being converted into relatively stable compounds at the same time. Pure stabilizers include diphenylamine (DPA) and akardite I (as diphenylurea). Stabilizers with a gelatinizing

Figure 3 The same primer cup from **Figure 2**, disassembled: the anvil on the left, the cup containing the primer on the right, (yellowish). The edges of the squares on the paper in the background **are 1 mm long**.

effect include centralite I (diethyldiphenylurea), centralite II (dimethyldiphenylurea), centralite III (methylethyldiphenylurea), akardite II (methyldiphenylurea), akardite III (ethyldiphenylurea), ethylphenylurethane, methylphenylurethane, and diphenylurethane. Gelatinizers are chemical substances having a softening effect and are incorporated into the powders for ease in their manufacture. Pure gelatinizers (plasticizers) without a stabilizing effect include dibutylphthalate, diamyl phthalate, and camphor. Phlegmatizers are combustion-retarding substances (such as centralite, dibutyl phthalate, camphor, and dinitrotoluene), which are used to modify the burning rate of the external layers of the powder grains. The propellant charge is the larger explosive charge in a cartridge (Figure 4), while the amount of primer composition is very small.

Looking for FDR on Surfaces

Sampling Techniques for FDR

The choice of a correct sampling technique plays a critical role in the detection and identification of chemical traces. Any analytical procedure needs to be planned, starting with the

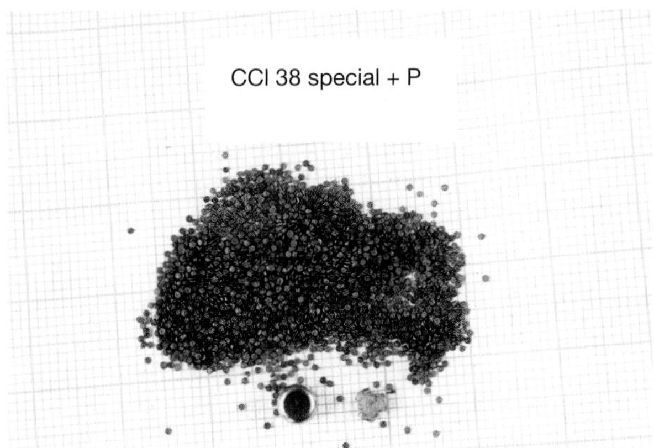

Figure 4 The same primer cup as in **Figure 3** and the smokeless powder contained in the cartridge case of a CCI 38 Special + P. The edges of the squares on the paper in the background are 1 mm long.

sampling method, taking several factors into consideration, including the surface to be sampled (e.g., skin surfaces, hair, clothes), the nature of the compounds being searched for, and the techniques that will be used for the analyses.

Tape lifting

The favorite sampling approach for collecting FDR particles before SEM analysis is called 'tape lifting.' It is carried out using an SEM aluminum sample holder (stub) covered with an adhesive layer. Stability under vacuum and an electronic beam, elemental composition, and adhesive properties of the adhesive need to be tested to ascertain its suitability for use. The adhesive may be conductive or non-conductive, but because of the probable presence of nonconductive materials collected during sampling, the sample is generally coated with a thin film of carbon to ensure electrical conductivity and to prevent its charging during SEM analysis. During tape lifting, the adhesive stub is pressed several times against the surface to be sampled (e.g., hands, hair, clothing). Zeichner and Levin studied the collection efficiency of FDR particles from hair and hands using double-sided adhesive tape and found that 50–100 dabbings are necessary to achieve maximum collection efficiency from hands, while 200–300 dabbings are necessary to achieve maximum collection efficiency from hair.

Vacuum lifting

Particles cannot be collected by swabbing if they are trapped in a fabric, but they can be lifted by an airflow and stopped in a sampling device, generally an inert filter, using a technique called 'vacuum lifting.' An apparatus for vacuum lifting can be made using a vacuum cleaner, or a vacuum pump, connected by a flexible plastic tube to a sampling unit. This unit can be a disposable syringe barrel containing a filter, or a filter holder designed for this purpose. The sampling procedure published by Wallace and McKeown in 1993 and adopted by the Forensic Science Agency of Northern Ireland is an efficient vacuum-lifting procedure, used for the recovery of explosive traces as well as organic and inorganic FDR particles. The sampling unit consists of a 25-mm diameter inline Delrin® filter holder and a 25-mm diameter Fluoropore™ membrane filter. The choice of the appropriate filter and filter holder needs to be based on the desired sampling capability and the subsequent analytical steps, keeping in mind the solvents and the analytical techniques used. Disposable and single-sealed sampling units are recommended for casework to minimize the possibility of contamination.

Swabbing

'Swabbing' is a sampling technique carried out by firmly rubbing the surface to be sampled several times using a piece of swabbing material such as cotton wool, synthetic wool, paper, nonwoven cotton cloth, or Acrilan®. The swabbing material can be used on its own or after wetting with a solvent system. Particles can be trapped in the swab or, when a solvent system is used, chemical traces can be dissolved in it. The swabbing technique is effective to treat skin surfaces (e.g., hands), work surfaces, floors, and smooth fabrics such as leather or plastic. It is difficult to evaluate which is the best swabbing system: as principal criteria, the swab should efficiently remove the traces from the surface with as few coextracted interfering compounds as possible. If a wet swab is used, the sampled compounds must remain stable in the solvent system used. The choice of the material of the swab and the solvent system, if any, should be based on considering the traces searched for and the analytical techniques to be used. After dissolving the soluble chemical substances with a suitable solvent system, insoluble FDR particles can be dispersed in a liquid, filtered through a coarse filter, trapped on a membrane filter, and analyzed by SEM. Single-sealed swabs are recommended for casework to minimize the possibility of contamination.

Vapor trapping

Chemical substances having high vapor pressure, such as NG, can be trapped by drawing a known volume of air through a trap. The trap can be a sampling tube containing a suitable material. The trapping material can be heated later, giving the trapped molecules the opportunity to return to the vapor phase and allowing chemical analysis. A special type of vapor trapping can be carried out using a fiber covered with a suitable phase (solid-phase microextraction, SPME). The SPME fiber can trap molecules in the vapor phase and release them later for analysis by heating. The item to be sampled by SPME must be closed in a sealed vessel (e.g., a piece of cloth in a multilayered bag, or a cartridge case in a vial). 'Vapor trapping' efficacy is increased with higher analyte vapor pressure.

Other sampling techniques

The first test for the presence of FDR on hands was called 'paraffin glove' because of the sampling procedure developed by Teodoro Gonzalez of the Mexico City police. This procedure involved taking a cast of the hand using molten paraffin wax. After solidifying, the cast was sprayed with a solution of *N,N'*-diphenylbenzidine in concentrated sulfuric acid, resulting in blue areas where the oxidizing residue was present. The same sampling procedure was used later with different color tests (e.g., DPA) or before neutron activation analysis (NAA). A modern version of the 'paraffin glove' is based on polyvinyl alcohol (Polyviol®). This kind of sampling procedure is promising only on cadavers, because it takes 45 min to produce the film to be analyzed. In 1995, Schwartz and Zona proposed a method for detecting airborne GSR retained in human nasal mucus. In 2003, MacCrehan et al. published a procedure to collect FDR from hair by combing and to analyze the organic FDR by micellar electrokinetic chromatography.

Any Police Force or Forensic Science Institute generally follows a very standardized sampling procedure for casework, especially for hands, but there are cases where large surfaces or many items need to be sampled, requiring a carefully planned sampling strategy. It is important to keep in mind that increasing the number of samples causes an increase of time needed to get analytical results, and an increase of the overall cost of the analyses. Topographic information from a piece of cloth can be useful, but only if the item is properly collected and packed before arrival in the lab. Samples must be packed properly in order to avoid transfer of materials from one surface to another of the same item and between different items, and to prevent the possible transfer of foreign matter from external sources during transport and storage. Particles can be transferred by a simple contact between surfaces, or can be lost from packages that are not properly sealed. Volatile compounds (e.g., NG) may evaporate if the containers are not airtight. The overall procedure of packaging items, transferring them to the laboratory, and storing them must also respect the so-called chain of custody.

Inorganic Techniques for FDR Analysis

Color tests and instrumental bulk analysis

Several color tests have been used in FDR analysis in the past; for example, *N,N′*-diphenylbenzidine in concentrated sulfuric acid gives a blue color where oxidizers are present (e.g., the residue produced by smokeless powder). Later, DPA was used, but it produced the same reaction and suffered from the same lack of selectivity. The Griess test and the procedure based on using triphenylmethylarsonium iodide and sodium rhodizonate to detect lead, barium, and antimony published by Harrison and Gillroy in 1959 are more selective, but they also give many false positives when used to answer the question: 'Is there FDR on this surface?' Despite the limited selectivity, these tests can provide very useful information on victims and targets (e.g., determining the shooting distance).

In 1964, Ruch et al. published their procedure to quantify the amount of barium and antimony by NAA in samples collected from the hands of shooters and nonshooters. In 1971, Krishnan reported the levels of Pb in hand samples using atomic absorption spectroscopy. Jones and Nesbitt in 1975 proposed a photoluminescence technique to analyze lead and antimony in FDR. In 1999, Woolever et al. published a procedure for the simultaneous detection of lead and antimony in FDR by differential pulse anodic stripping voltammetry. Koons et al. proposed the use of inductively coupled plasma atomic/emission spectroscopy in 1988, and in 1998, Koons published an article describing the use of inductively coupled plasma/mass spectrometry in the analysis of FDR.

All the instrumental techniques listed above allow bulk analysis but lack the specificity required for FDR analysis in forensic science. They are only able to determine that *some* elements (e.g., lead, antimony, barium) are present in a sample collected from a surface. The detected elements can be transferred separately, in different moments, from the environment to the surface, where they are collected before the analysis. There are many materials containing lead, such as plumbing materials, battery plates, type metal, solder, glass, and paint. Alloys containing lead often contain antimony too, and antimony oxide is a fire retardant used in fibers. Barium can be present in paint, in automobile grease, and in paper. For these reasons, bulk instrumental techniques give too many false positives when used to answer the question: 'Is there FDR on this surface?'

Particle analysis of FDR

A scanning electron microscope equipped with an x-ray detector does not suffer from the limitations of color tests and instrumental bulk analysis: it can examine the shape of a single particle in a size range down to less than 1 μm and analyze the x-rays emitted by the same particle, allowing elemental analysis. Metallic elements used in ammunition manufacture can vaporize as a result of the explosion of the primer and of the propellant and condense later, producing particles whose chemical composition is related to the exploded ammunition and firearm used. The use of a beam of electrons rather than visible light allows the study of these FDR particles by SEM. A scanning electron microscope has a greater depth of field compared to an optical microscope, an extremely high resolution, and a magnification capability in excess of 100 000. Electrons strike the sample and are collected by detectors, producing the image on a screen. If the detector is close to the plane through the sample, perpendicular to the electron beam, it collects the secondary electrons and the image shows details of the surface of the sample. If the detector is close to the electron beam, it collects the backscattered electrons (BSE), and the intensity of the BSE signal increases with the increase in the atomic number of the element. Using the BSE approach, particles containing lead, antimony, and/or barium are very easy to detect because their images are much brighter than particles normally diffused in the environment, containing atoms with low atomic number. The scanning electron microscope is not only particularly suitable for the detection and identification of FDR particles (if they contain atoms with high atomic number), but it can also be equipped with detectors able to determine the energy of the x-rays emitted by the atoms excited by the electron beam. The spectra of the emitted x-rays allow elemental analysis of a few cubic micrometers of the material examined (**Figure 5**).

The technique generally used in FDR elemental analysis is energy dispersive x-ray spectrometry (EDS or EDX), but wavelength dispersive x-ray spectrometry (WDX) can also be used. WDX is particularly useful when dealing with the problem of overlapping peaks (e.g., calcium and antimony or titanium and barium).

The pioneering work on the forensic use of SEM/EDS in FDR forensic analysis was carried out both in Europe and the United States by scientists from the Aerospace Corporation, the Federal Bureau of Investigation, the Swedish National Laboratory of Forensic Science, the Metropolitan Police Forensic Laboratory in London, and the Forensic Science Agency of Northern Ireland in Belfast. In 1979, Wolten et al. proposed a classification system based on compositional criteria, morphology, and size, and listed some compositions observed only in FDR and therefore considered 'characteristic,' and other compositions 'consistent' with FDR considered useful but less important in

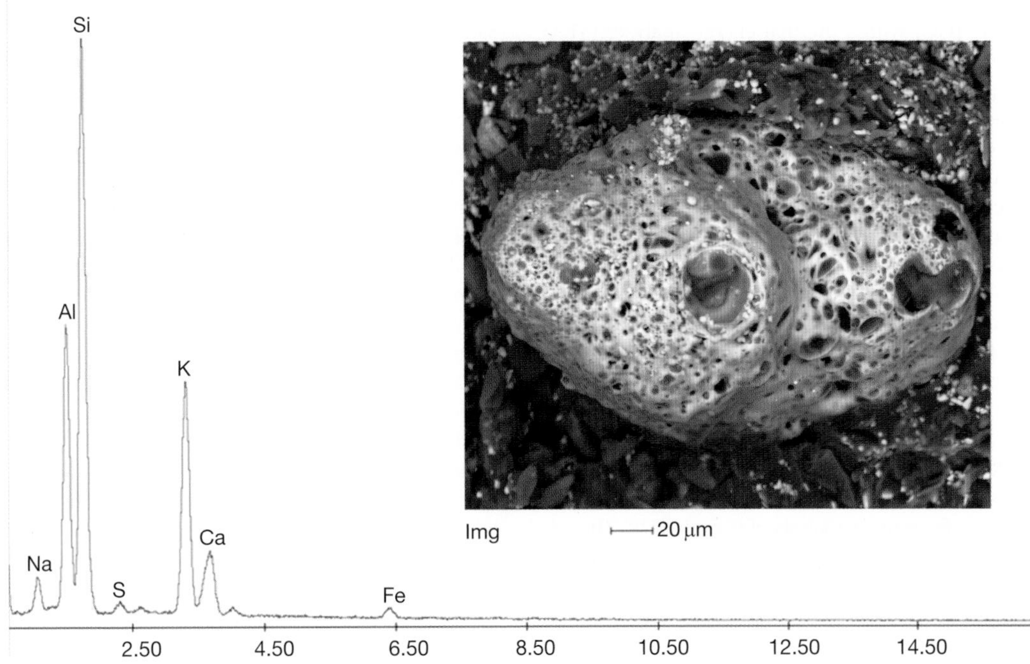

Figure 5 Backscattered electron image (on the right) and the EDS spectrum (red line beginning on the left) of a particle produced by a Fiocchi ZP 9 mm Luger. Courtesy of Major Matteo Donghi, Head, Firearms Laboratories, Raggruppamento Investigazioni Scientifiche Carabinieri, Parma, Italy.

forensic investigations. In 1984, Wallace and McQuillan suggested that the classification of FDR should consider only two particles coming specifically from the explosion of a primer (so-called unique particles): particles containing lead, antimony, and barium, and particles containing antimony and barium. 'Unique' particles could contain other elements if their presence and the height of their peaks obeyed a system of rules. In the latest version of the ASTM "Standard Guide for Gunshot Residue Analysis by Scanning Electron Microscopy/Energy Dispersive X-Ray Spectroscopy," corrected in July 2010, the classification system considers that particles containing lead, antimony, and barium are 'characteristic of GSR (i.e., most likely associated with the discharge of a gun).' The Standard Guide also lists several elemental profiles 'consistent' with FDR, from both primers containing lead and lead-free primers, such as particles containing titanium and zinc or particles containing strontium (**Figure 5**).

In the initial years of the use of SEM/EDS to look for FDR, the main issue was the time needed to manually search the stub. This problem became less important with automated SEM/EDS systems; however, when analyzing stubs containing many particles with elements having high atomic number, the analysis still takes several hours per square centimeter.

An important contribution to the field was made by Niewoehner et al., who developed a strategy to produce several copies of the same sample containing 'synthetic' FDR particles. In the proficiency test organized by the European Network of Forensic Science Institutes in 2011 (GSR2011), the sample was a silicon chip of 8×8 mm^2, with an exactly defined number of 'synthetic' FDR particles: circular areas having a diameter between 0.5 and 2.4 μm, containing lead, antimony, barium, and fluorine. The laboratories had the opportunity to compare their results with known information about the total number, locations on the stub, and size of the 'synthetic' FDR particles. This test allowed the comparison of the performances of the equipment used and of the settings adopted by different laboratories and the optimization of the parameters to maximize the number of FDR particles detected.

SEM/EDS is not the only approach to get both morphological and analytical information. X-ray microfluorescence is based on optical microscopy and can scan larger areas, but it is unsuitable for the small particles that can be detected by SEM/EDS in routine cases. Raman microscopy was also used to analyze FDR, showing evidence of a particular crystal structure and stoichiometry (e.g., orthorombic PbO), but it is still far from routine use. A microbeam of protons, having a similar diameter of electron beams as used by SEM/EDS but with higher energy, is used in ion beam analysis (IBA). An IBA technique particularly promising in FDR analysis is particle-induced x-ray emission. X-rays emitted as a result of the protons striking the sample allow a more sensitive detection of elements compared to SEM/EDS, and can excite higher energy emissions, such as signals due to antimony called 'L lines.'

Organic Techniques for FDR Analysis

The organic FDR is mainly the residue of the explosion of smokeless powder contained in the cartridge. A large number of procedures to analyze organic FDR were extensively reviewed by Meng and Caddy in 1997, but are nowadays used only in a limited number of laboratories. Analysis of organic FDR in casework was started at the beginning of the 1990s in the Forensic Science Service Laboratory in Birmingham and in the Northern Ireland Forensic Science Laboratory, using swabbing for skin surfaces and vacuum lifting for clothing. In both laboratories, high-performance liquid chromatography

(HPLC) with pendant drop mercury electrode (PDME) plus gas chromatography (GC) with a thermal energy analyzer (TEA) was used to detect NG and other nitrocompounds. When both analyses gave positive results for a nitrocompound, the overall procedure was considered sufficiently selective for forensic identification of that chemical substance. Organic analysis can be faster than SEM/EDS analysis. The screen-up method for explosives used in the Forensic Science Service Laboratory in Birmingham takes around 3 h for swabs and around 1 h for examination of an item of clothing. The Division of Identification and Forensic Science of the Israeli Police began analyzing organic GSR on clothes from real cases at the end of 2002: garments are first sampled by tape lifting for inorganic FDR particles, then vacuum lifting is used for the collection of organic FDR. Analyses are carried out by ion mobility spectrometry, and GC/TEA. GC/TEA is suitable only for nitrocompounds. Romolo in 2004 and Laza et al. in 2007 showed that HPLC coupled to tandem mass spectrometry (MS/MS) can be effectively used for routine analysis of organic FDR. The advantage of the HPLC/MS/MS system is its capability to analyze not only NG or dinitrotoluenes but also additives, such as methyl centralite, ethyl centralite, and DPA, and degradation products such as *N*-nitrosodiphenylamine, 4-nitrodiphenylamine, and 2-nitrodiphenylamine, during the same chromatographic run. Interesting results were also obtained using micellar electrokinetic capillary electrophoresis by MacCrehan et al., who demonstrated the possibility of analyzing organic FDR after hair combing.

Interpretation of Analytical Results

There are two possible interpretative approaches in FDR analysis: a 'formal' approach and a 'case-by-case' (or 'case-specific') approach. If a formal approach is adopted, the shape and the chemical composition of the particles examined by SEM/EDS are considered following some rules to evaluate whether they were'characteristic,' or 'consistent' with FDR, or whether they were products unrelated to the explosion of a firearm cartridge.

In 1984, the word 'unique' was proposed by Wallace and McQuillan, meaning that the only possible source of some particles was the explosion of a firearm cartridge. Since the publication of their article, several scientists have criticized this search for 'uniqueness.' Moreover, the Bayesian approach has become more and more important in forensic science: specialists are more used to always considering at least a second explanation for any possible evidence. Recently, several publications have posed serious problems to the 'formal' approach, suggesting that stud guns, fireworks, brake linings, and airbags can be alternative sources of 'unique,' 'characteristic,' or 'consistent' FDR-like particles. Finally, with the increasing use of heavy-metal-free primers, the definition of 'unique' FDR for heavy-metal-based particles has become quite useless, giving rise to the need for a different approach to the interpretation of the results.

The 'case-by-case' approach can be used with both organic and inorganic FDR, and is based on comparing the residue from an unknown source found on a specific surface (e.g., the hands or the clothes of a suspect) with FDR from a known source (e.g., a firearm, a cartridge case, a bullet, or a bullet hole). At this level of interpretation, called 'source,' the pairs of propositions considered for the interpretation are (a) the two samples of residue examined come from the same source; or (b) the two samples of residue examined come from different sources. During this comparison, it is important that the particles are considered as a group, composed of several chemical classes. The FDR particles are formed during a very rapid process under kinetic control, resulting in great variability in their chemical composition. The population of FDR particles found on a known source is generally larger than that found on the hands of the shooter (there are cases where only one interesting particle is found). Moreover, Brozek-Mucha recently showed that the number of GSR and the proportions of their chemical classes as well as their sizes depend on the shooting distance. The differences in the composition of FDR particle population found in the cartridge case compared to that of particles exiting from the firearm is another problem to consider. The reason is the 'memory effect': residue from previous firings with different cartridges stays in the firearm and mixes with the FDR produced by the last ammunition used. The ASTM standard guide for GSR analysis prescribed the formal approach procedure in the 1995 version. Starting from the 2007 version, to the latest (2010) one, the guide considers the possibility of comparing the elemental composition of the particles of unknown origin with case-specific known source items, such as the weapon, cartridge cases, or victim-related items.

When the organic FDR are considered, the most important compound is NG. The finding of NG in the sample from the clothes or from the hands of a suspect can be related to different sources, such as dynamites or cardioactive drugs containing NG. Possible sources of DPA are apples, tires, solid rocket fuels, pesticides, dyes, and pharmaceuticals.

Interpretation of FDR is not limited at the 'source' level: the evaluation of evidence can be carried out at the 'activity' level too. The conflicting hypotheses to be considered can be (a) the suspect has fired, or (b) the suspect is not related to the shooting incident. It is always important to consider that it is not possible to discriminate between the presence of FDR on a surface resulting from proximity to a discharging firearm and that resulting from contact with a surface rich in FDR (e.g., spent cartridge case, firearm, or target hole). At the 'activity' level, the probability of transfer and the persistence of FDR play an important role. For example, FDR particles stay much longer on clothes than on hands, where the larger particles are lost more quickly than the small ones. For this reason, it is very important to consider the time between the shooting incident and the collection of a sample for interpretation at the 'activity' level. It is also important to consider at this level the possibility of a secondary transfer from police officers or police cars. The modern sampling procedure adopted by many police forces is based on kits developed to minimize this possibility (e.g., kits containing disposable sampling equipment) and to demonstrate the absence of contamination (e.g., by taking blank samples from the police officers who collected the sample).

Some activities can be inferred after finding NG: proximity to an exploding charge containing NG; contact with a source of NG (primary transfer); or contact with a surface where NG is present (secondary or subsequent transfer). Only limited data are available to assess the likelihood that a suspect might have become contaminated with organic FDR without being involved in criminal activities. Some 'population studies,' have been carried out to determine the background levels of explosive residues, including NG, in public places; however, more population studies, as well as more research, are needed to statistically evaluate the population of FDR particles and to calculate the likelihood ratio at both 'source' and 'activity' levels. Despite the difficulties involved, what has happened in the last 10 years in the field of FDR clearly shows that the 'case-by-case' or 'case-specific' approach will be the one allowing the best use of scientific information related to FDR in criminal investigations.

See also: **Chemistry/Trace/Explosives:** Commercial; Explosives: Analysis; Military; **Foundations:** Overview and Meaning of Identification/Individualization; Statistical Interpretation of Evidence: Bayesian Analysis; **Investigations:** Collection and Chain of Evidence; Contamination; **Methods:** Microscopy (Electron); **Pattern Evidence/Firearms:** Residues.

Further Reading

American Society for Testing and Materials (2010) Standard guide for gunshot residue analysis by scanning electron microscopy/energy dispersive X-ray spectroscopy. *Annual Book of ASTM Standards*. West Conshohocken, PA: ASTM International.

Bailey MJ, Kirkby KJ, and Jeynes C (2009) Trace element profiling of gunshot residues by PIXE and SEM-EDS: A feasibility study. *X-Ray Spectrometry* 38: 190–194.

Berk RE (2009a) Automated SEM/EDS analysis of airbag residue. I: Particle identification. *Journal of Forensic Sciences* 54: 60–68.

Berk RE (2009b) Automated SEM/EDS analysis of airbag residue. II: Airbag residue as a source of percussion primer residue particles. *Journal of Forensic Sciences* 54: 69–76.

Berk RE, Rochowicz SA, Wong M, and Kopina MA (2007) Gunshot residue in chicago police vehicles and facilities: An empirical study. *Journal of Forensic Sciences* 52: 838–841.

Brozek-Mucha Z (2009) Distribution and properties of gunshot residue originating from a Luger 9 mm ammunition in the vicinity of the shooting gun. *Forensic Science International* 183: 33–44.

Dalby O, Butler D, and Birkett J (2010) Analysis of gunshot residue and associated materials – A review. *Journal of Forensic Sciences* 55: 924–943.

Laza D, Nys B, Kinder JD, Mesmaeker AKD, and Moucheron C (2007) Development of a quantitative LC-MS/MS method for the analysis of common propellant powder stabilizers in gunshot residue. *Journal of Forensic Sciences* 52(4): 842–850.

MacCrehan WA, Layman MJ, and Secl JD (2003) Hair combing to collect organic gunshot residues (OGSR). *Forensic Science International* 135(2): 167–173.

Meng HH and Caddy B (1997) Gunshot residue analysis – A review. *Journal of Forensic Sciences* 42(4): 553–570.

Romolo FS (2004) *Organic Gunshot Residue from Leadfree Ammunition. Série Criminalistique*, XXIX, ISBN 2-940098-33-6, PhD thesis, Lausanne, Switzerland. http://doc.rero.ch/lm.php?url=1000,40,5,20081009102309-IJ/These_Romolo.pdf.

Romolo FS and Margot P (2001) Identification of gunshot residue: A critical review. *Forensic Science International* 119(2): 195–211.

Speers SJ, Doolan K, McQuillan J, and Wallace JS (1994) Evaluation of improved methods for the recovery and detection of organic and inorganic cartridge discharge residues. *Journal of Chromatography A* 674(1–2): 319–327.

Trimpe MA (2011) The current status of GSR examinations. FBI Law Enforcement Bulletin. http://www.fbi.gov/stats-services/publications/law-enforcement-bulletin/may_2011/The%20Current%20Status%20of%20GSR%20Examinations.

Wallace J (2008) *Chemical Analysis of Firearms, Ammunition, and Gunshot Residue*. Boca Raton, FL: CRC Press.

Wallace JS and McKeown WJ (1993) Sampling procedures for firearms and/or explosives residues. *Journal of the Forensic Science Society* 33(2): 107–116.

Wright DM and Trimpe MA (2006) Summary of the FBI Laboratory's Gunshot Residue Symposium, May 31–June 3, 2005. *Forensic Science Communications* 8(3). http://www2.fbi.gov/hq/lab/fsc/backissu/july2006/research/2006_07_research01.htm.

Zeichner A (2003) Recent developments in methods of chemical analysis in investigations of firearm-related events. *Analytical and Bionalytical Chemistry* 376: 1178–1191.

Relevant Websites

http://www.enfsi.eu/page.php?uid=60 – ENFSI Firearm Working Group.
http://quodata.de/en/interlaboratory-tests/gsr-quality-scheme.html – GSR Proficiency Tests.

CHEMISTRY/TRACE/FORENSIC GEOSCIENCES

Contents

Crime Scene Considerations

J Robertson, University of Canberra, Canberra, ACT, Australia

Introduction

Forensic soil science is defined elsewhere in this series as the study of soil that involves the application of a wide range of soil information to answer legal questions and problems of hypotheses. Up to the 1980s, in a pre-DNA forensic world, the examination of soils as a trace evidence material was quite commonplace to the extent that many forensic laboratories employed geology specialists for this type of work. DNA analysis of human biological materials resulted in a heavy emphasis on identity arguably at the expense of other areas of forensic examination in which discrimination of samples rather than 'identification' was the norm.

Expertise was largely lost from mainstream forensic laboratories and forensic capabilities in soil examination diminished in the 1990s. The more recent resurgence of interest in soil examination and forensic geology has come in the main from outside the government forensic sector with a number of sole traders or small company players and the involvement of non-forensic government organizations with broader core interest in soil. An International Union of Geological Sciences Initiative on Forensic Geology has been developed and they are working on a Guide to Forensic Geology and a Code of Conduct to address issues of competence and regulation.

These initiatives are important to ensure that individuals and organizations who apply their knowledge to address matters of a forensic nature in the criminal justice system do so by meeting relevant forensic standards.

One of the potential benefits of soil materials as a contact trace is that soil can be collected by nonspecialists at a locus from items being examined. However, as with any strength, the 'flip side' is that it can also be a weakness. Forensic soil examination is often comparative rather than being focused on identifying a particular soil (although the latter is *one* aspect of forensic soil examination). A comparison obviously requires two samples, one recovered from an item of investigative interest (a questioned sample) and one from a potential source or scene (a known or control sample). For a meaningful examination to be possible, both types of samples need to be recovered following acceptable protocols and procedures. The laboratory recovery of soil is relatively simple, although not always straight forward. The same cannot always be said for sampling at the locus of an alleged event or crime.

Although many soil scientists will be experienced field scientists well versed in sampling procedures and used to meeting scientific standards for packaging and labeling, these will not normal meet forensic standards. Furthermore, the forensic requirements for recording the scene and recovery of samples have forensic specific elements.

Most crime scene examiners (CSEs) will not have specialist knowledge of forensic soil examination nor will it be common for a soil scientist to have specialist expertise in scene examination. In an ideal world, and certainly for complex and major investigations, the soil science specialist should attend the scene and advise on sampling and work with the CSE to take appropriate samples. The proper recording of sampling is an important element of this process.

A Team Approach to Crime Scenes

The focus of this article is on forensic soil examinations and less so on broader forensic geology examinations, but it is not possible to deal with the first in isolation of the latter.

While a forensic soil scientist and a forensic geologist may be the same individual this will not always be the case. Furthermore, as soils in forensic context are often human made (or at least human influenced), they may contain a broad range of components of mixed origin, which may require even more specialist knowledge. In complex investigations (the complexity may be in the nature of the incident, the potential evidentiary material, or a combination of both), it will be usual for

 Encyclopedia of Forensic Sciences, Second Edition http://dx.doi.org/10.1016/B978-0-12-382165-2.00112-4

the forensic examinations to involve several individuals with specialist knowledge. These individuals should operate as a team under the direction of a senior CSE. Typically at a scene involving a deceased, such a team will involve a range or 'ologists' such as a pathologist, potentially an anthropologist and/or an archaeologist, and an entomologist. A forensic botanist and a forensic geologist may also be involved. Elsewhere in this series are papers on forensic botany and palynology. Careful consideration needs to be given to the sequence of examination and sampling by specialists to maximize the potential for each to ensure their work is not compromised and to minimize any potential negatives for other specialists. Fundamental to the successful processing of a crime scene is that specialists understand not only their potential contribution but also that they understand and respect the role of other specialists. It is often not clear at the crime scene which aspects of a forensic investigation will be the most important. The CSE needs to develop a crime scene strategy with the investigation team and specialists. The CSE will normally be responsible for the core crime scene examinations but should seek specialist advice and input especially in developing a search and/or sampling strategy.

Crime Scene Reminders

In an ideal world, specialists who attend scenes on more than an ad hoc basis should undertake at least basic crime scene awareness training aimed at ensuring they understand what is happening at a crime scene and why. It does not follow that a specialist needs to be a crime scene expert although over time a specialist may indeed gain considerable experience and a higher level of crime scene expertise. The principle responsibilities of the CSE can be summed up as the three 'R's, evidence RECOGNITION, evidence RECORDING, and evidence RECOVERY. Of these three responsibilities, evidence recording and recovery are obviously vital but these are essentially technical functions. Evidence recognition is not a technical function! A critical skill of a CSE, and any other forensic scientist, is to recognize anomalies or inconsistencies which may indicate that there is the potential for harvesting evidence. A useful analogy is to think of a crime scene as a radar screen with the role of the CSE to discern what is a meaningful signal against background noise.

A forensic geology example would be to interpret a locus for anomalies which might indicate an area of interest when searching for a buried body.

Any specialist attending a scene should be aware of scene protocols relevant to their jurisdiction. This would include wearing appropriate protective clothing, an awareness of any occupational health and/or safety issues at the scene and following the directions of the CSE or investigator when approaching, entering, or exiting the scene. It will not normally be the role of the specialist to record the scene for later court purposes but the specialist must make their own contemporaneous notes which may include diagrams, sketches, and even photographs. If the latter are to be used in court then they need to meet relevant standards for data recording, storage, and reproduction. As there is really no such thing as personal notes *all* notes, etc. should be to an appropriate standard working on the basis that anything which is recorded is subject to appropriate discovery.

The specialist may advise the CSE who then takes samples at the scene or the specialist may take their own samples. This

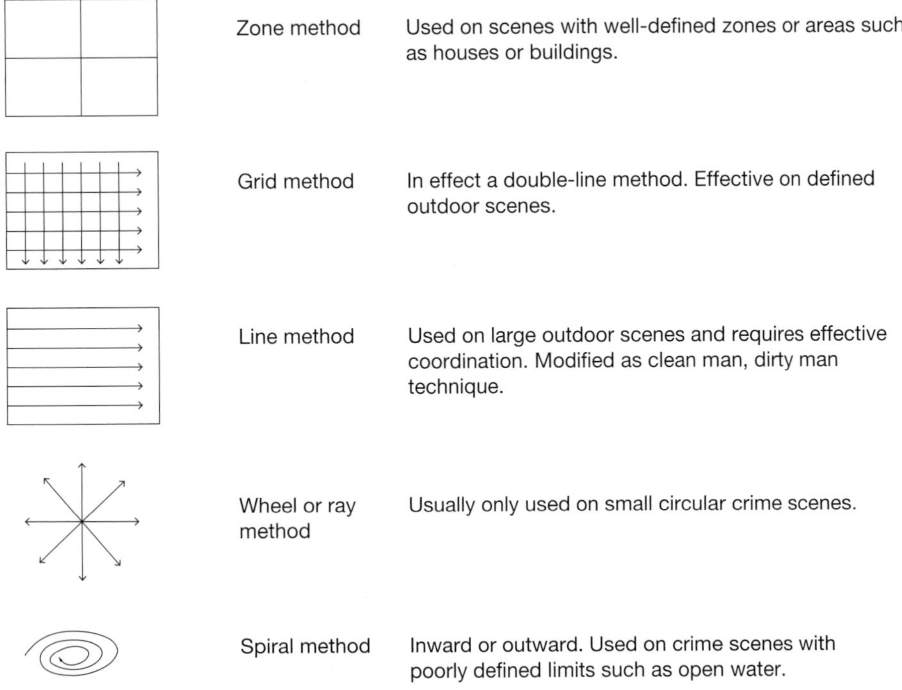

Figure 1 Crime scene search methods.

largely depends on local protocols and legal requirements. The specialist should always ensure samples are appropriately packaged, sealed and a chain of custody initiated. For soil samples specific consideration needs to be given to 'appropriate' packaging as soils may include vegetation and may themselves be moist. Moist material placed in plastic bags or glass jars can lead to very rapid deterioration of the sample. Depending on sample size it is often preferable to place samples in folded paper and then into a sealable plastic container. Samples which may be moist need to be passively dried at the

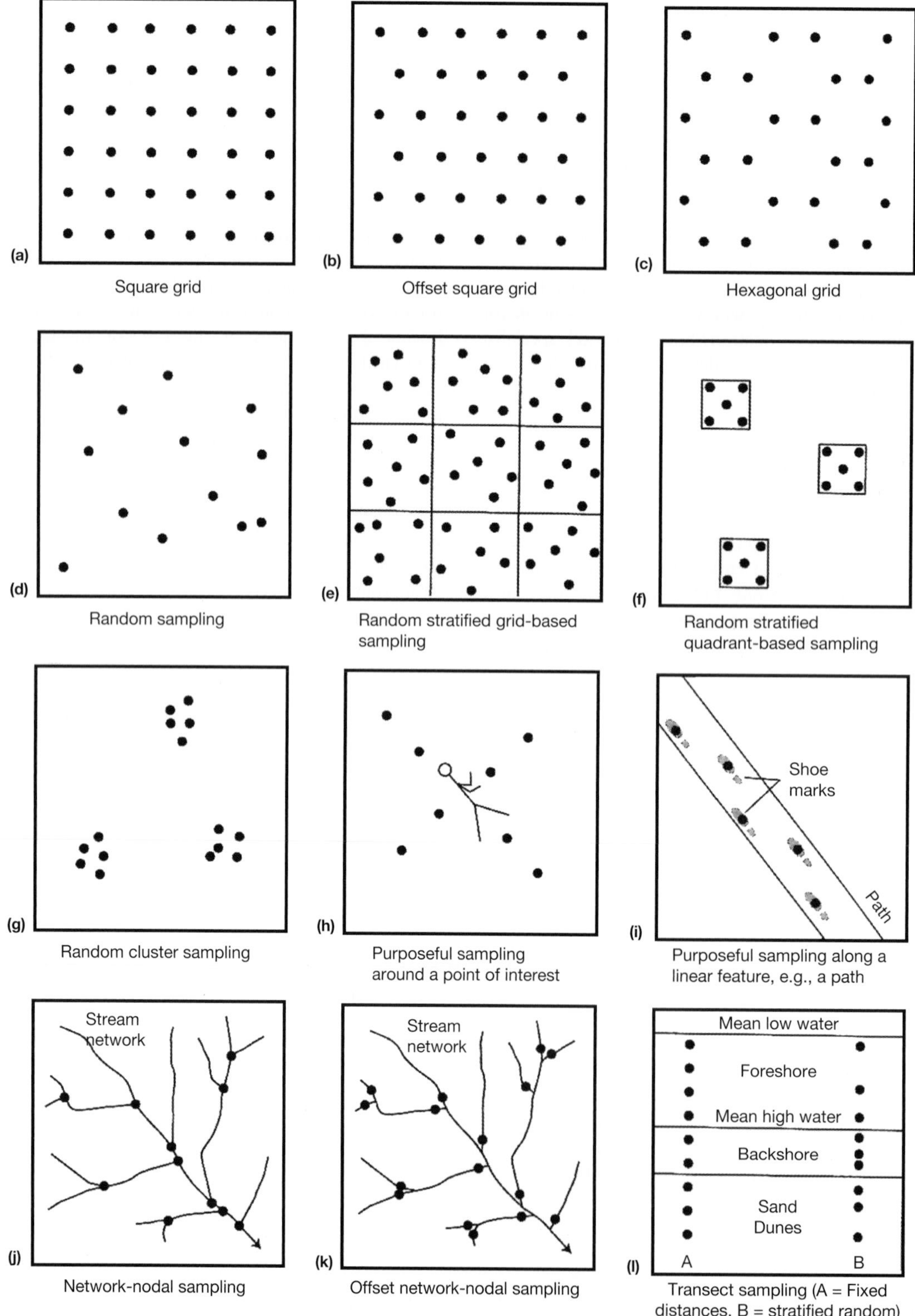

Figure 2 Crime scene sampling strategies. *Source:* Pye K (2007) *Geological and Soil Evidence: Forensic Applications*. Boca Raton, FL: CRC Press.

earliest opportunity in a contamination free environment. A specific sampling issue is where samples have to be recovered from a river, sea, or other aqueous environment where they will not just be 'moist' but will often be liquid. Appropriate plastic sample bottles should be used.

Soil Forensic Crime Scene Specifics

Arguably, the most significant forensic challenge facing the soil scientist is that of sampling. Crime scenes by their nature differ greatly and it would simply not be possible to dictate specific approaches for all possibilities. The principle is simple. Samples should be sufficient (adequate) and representative of possible variation.

The forensic soil scientist firstly needs to appreciate the concepts of *scale* and *spatial resolution* with respect to defining a search area, a search strategy and sampling strategies. Spatial scale refers to the geographical extent of an area. Spatial resolution deals with the resolution or spacing for a sampling strategy.

Clearly, if an actual location has been identified, due to a body being discovered, then the spatial scale is to a significant extent defined. Even in this simplest of cases, a 'closed' urban environment and a nonurban scene require fit for purpose strategies. One important role for forensic geology, to which soil analysis sometimes contributes, is the development of the potential location for an incident. For example, where soil recovered from a vehicle can be characterized to the point where an expert can identify possible locations for that soil type and hence potential search sites. However, these may be still very large spatial areas. The use of so-called *scenario-based* and *feature-based* search methods can further define the potential search area and direct appropriate search strategies. This may involve aerial examination, analysis of the geology of the area. The creation of national or local geodatabases is useful but usually only at the macro-spatial resolution level.

The geoforensic scientist needs to view a scene from the perspective of an ecologist and, indeed, there is much to be said for working with a specialist ecologist to target smaller areas which anomalies would indicate were worthy of more detailed examination.

Where a scene does involve human remains, either in a shallow grave or buried at a greater depth, these scenes are three dimensional and require careful sampling of each layer in a soil horizon.

There are *no* simple rules with respect to the number or size of samples which would meet the criteria of being adequate and representative as these will be determined by the specific circumstances at the scene. The specialist should consider the classic crime scene search patterns – see **Figure 1**, – although these will need to be adapted to the specific scene.

Pye proposes a number of alternative sampling strategies (see **Figure 2**).

Within reason, it is preferable to take more samples rather than less and to consider both macro and micro variation when sampling, especially with 'human made' soils where there is likely to be greater variation than with a relatively undisturbed geolocation. All samples should have their accurate geolocation recorded so that the location can be relocated, if necessary. Sample size will again depend on the case circumstances.

Conclusion

The examination of soils to assist in investigations and the criminal justice system is increasing after a 20-year period where forensic soil analysis reached a low point in government run forensic laboratories. As 'soil' in all its various forms is largely an outdoor material, there is a very significant chance that it will be transferred from a scene of an incident to a person or persons, a vehicle or other primary or secondary source which may later lead to an association relevant to the investigation. Soil examination may inform a search strategy and indicate a 'scene.'

Whether in an outdoor environment or not, like all forensic work, the locus of crime scene is paramount. The forensic soil specialist needs to have at least broad forensic awareness training and an understanding of fundamental concepts and practice at a crime scene. Most often a forensic soil specialist will be a member of a team attending a scene, under the direction of a CSE and as such, needs to understand and respect the role of all players at the scene. The value of all subsequent laboratory-based analysis hinges on the work done at the crime scene. If the correct advice is not given then the opportunity to locate a body may be lost. If sampling is inadequate at the scene, this will almost inevitably reduce the potential value of subsequent analysis. If the samples fail to meet the appropriate quality standards any analytical results may not be admissible evidence.

Hence, the importance of work done at the crime scene cannot be over emphasized. The soil scientist who becomes involved in forensic applications needs to fully appreciate the crime scene specifics of their work to fully realize laboratory potential.

See also: **Chemistry/Trace/Forensic Geosciences:** Botany; Forensic Geoscience; Soils.

Further Reading

Fitzpatrick RW and Raven MD (2011) *Guidelines for Conducting Criminal and Environmental Soil Forensic Investigations (version 3)*. Report No. CAFSS_076. Australia: Centre for Australian Forensic Soil Science. http://www.clw.csiro.au/cafss/.

Murray RC (2011) *Evidence from the Earth: Forensic Geology and Criminal Investigation*, 2nd edn. Missoula, MT: Mountain Press.

Pye K (2007) *Geological and Soil Evidence: Forensic Applications*. Boca Raton, FL: CRC Press.

Ritz K, Dawson L, and Miller D (eds.) (2008) *Criminal and Environmental Soil Forensics*. Amsterdam: Springer Science+Business Media BV.

Robertson J (2008) *Soils ain't soils*: Context and issues facing soil scientists in a forensic world In: Ritz KL, Dawson LS, and Miller D (eds.) *Criminal and Environmental Soil Forensics*, pp. 3–12. Amsterdam: Springer Science and Business Media BV.

Ruffell A and McKinley J (2008) *Geoforensics*. Chichester: Wiley.

Soils

RW Fitzpatrick, CSIRO Land and Water, Glen Osmond, SA, Australia

Glossary

Human-altered and human-transported (HAHT) soils Are soils formed through profound, intentional alteration or transportation of materials, and do not include soils altered unintentionally or chemically treated standard production agriculture practices.

Pedology (From the Greek *pedon* = soil) Is the soil science discipline concerned primarily with understanding the variety of soils and their distribution, and is most directly concerned with the key questions concerning sampling, descriptions, processes of soil formation including the quality, extent, distribution, spatial variability, and interpretation of soils from microscopic to megascopic scales. This description and interpretation of soils can be used in addressing the questions 'What is the soil like?' and 'Where does it come from?' (i.e., provenance determination) in studies relating to characterizing and locating the sources of soils to make forensic comparisons.

Introduction

Forensic soil science is the science or study of soil that involves the application of a wide range of soil information to answer legal questions, problems, or hypotheses. For soil scientists, soil is made up of different-sized mineral particles (sand, silt, and clay) including organic matter and has complex biological, chemical, physical, mineralogical, and hydrological properties that are always changing over time. Soil is ubiquitous and is dynamic, teeming with organisms, and is an integral part of both terrestrial and aquatic environments. But for farmers, gardeners, and agronomists, soil is just a medium for growing crops, pastures, and plants. And for engineers, soil is a material to build on and excavate. Thus soils can be both naturally occurring, comprising natural minerals and organic materials, and human-made, such as those that often contain very small amounts of manufactured materials, including brick fragments, explosive residues, or paint flecks. It is this soil diversity and heterogeneity that has enabled forensic soil examiners to distinguish between soils that may appear to be similar to the untrained observer.

The shift from traditional soil science and pedology to forensic soil science is not straightforward and requires a wide understanding of crime scene protocols, the evidential requirements of forensic workers, and the nature of legal constraints within which forensic work takes place. It is important to understand and know the different kinds of natural and human-made soils and how they form and especially how to carefully sample and analyze them because this helps to make accurate forensic comparisons.

Classification of Soils

Diversity of Natural Soils

To characterize the wide variety of soils that occur in the world, it is necessary to understand the purpose of the various kinds of soil classification systems used. Soil classifications help to organize knowledge about soils, especially in conducting soil surveys. The two international soil classification systems, which are used widely, are the World Reference Base (WRB) and Soil Taxonomy. Many countries also have national and specialized technical classifications. Soil surveys enable the depiction of soils across a landscape and soil maps are made to show the patterns of soils that exist and provide information on the properties of soils. Soil maps are produced at different scales to depict soils over: (1) large areas such as the world, countries, and regions (1:100 000 or smaller scale) and (2) detailed areas such as farms (1:10 000 or larger scale). A wide diversity of natural soils exists and each has its own characteristics (e.g., morphology, mineralogy, and organic matter composition). For example, according to the United States Department of Agriculture (USDA), which collects soil data at many different scales, there are over 50 000 different varieties of soil in the United States alone! Parent material, climate, organisms, and the amount of time it takes for these properties to interact will vary worldwide.

Diversity of Human-Made Soils

Human-made and urban soils are general terms used to indicate soils that are essentially under strong human influence in urban and suburban areas. However, various other terms are used in several soil classification systems (e.g., human-altered and human-transported soils (HAHT) in Soil Taxonomy, Technosols in WRB, and Anthroposols in The Australian Soil Classification). Human-made soils are characterized by a strong spatial heterogeneity, which results from the various inputs of manufactured materials (e.g., brick fragments, compost, or toxic wastes) and the mixing of the original (natural) soil material (e.g., gardens, parks, or cemeteries). Mine or quarry soils are another class of human-made soils, which are also strongly human-influenced soils but found away from cities.

In summary, human-made soils are characterized by diversity, heterogeneity, and complexity, which enables forensic soil examiners to distinguish between soils that may appear to be similar. Human-made soils usually contain a large array of known historical information, which has been proved very useful in understanding and quantifying soil differences in forensic soil comparisons.

 http://dx.doi.org/10.1016/B978-0-12-382165-2.00113-6

Soil Categories Used in Forensic Investigations

Soil forensic investigations usually involves collection of one or more soil samples followed by soil characterization. Collected samples are categorized as: (1) questioned soil samples whose origin is unknown or disputed (often from suspect or victim), (2) control samples whose origin is known and usually from specific sites directly related to the investigation such as the known or proposed crime scene, and (3) alibi samples whose origin is known and that provide a measure of the uniqueness of the questioned and control samples, hence providing a more comprehensive analysis of the targeted comparator samples to provide a more accurate picture of the within-site heterogeneity.

Why is Soil Evidence so Good?

Soil materials are a powerful 'contact trace' and may even be considered as approaching the ideal 'contact trace' for the following six reasons:

Soil is Highly Individualistic

There are thousands of different soil types in existence and it is this vast diversity and complexity that enables forensic examiners to distinguish between soil samples. The anthropogenic properties (e.g., brick or glass fragments) make the naturally occurring soils even more individualistic.

Soil has a High Probability of Transfer and Retention

In general, soil usually has a strong capacity to transfer and stick, especially the fine fractions in soils (clay and silt size fractions) and organic matter. The larger quartz particles (e.g., >2-mm size fractions) have poor retention on clothes, shoes, and carpets.

Soil is Nearly Invisible

The presence of fine soil materials, especially when they impregnate vehicle carpeting, shoes, or clothing, is often not visible by the naked eye and a suspect will often make little effort to remove soil materials. This is, for example, often unlike the more obvious bright transfer colors of blood, lipstick smears, and paint.

Soil can Quickly be Collected, Separated, and Concentrated

Soil materials are easily located and collected by police when inspecting crime scenes or examining items of physical evidence. Traces of soil particles can easily and quickly be located directly using hand lenses or light microscopes.

Soil Materials are Easily Characterized

Generally, soil materials are easily described (e.g., soil color) and characterized using various analytical methods such as X-ray diffraction (mineralogy) and mid-infrared and Raman spectroscopy (chemistry).

Computerized Soil Databases Capacity

The mapping of the surface and subsurface of both natural and anthropogenic soils provides crucial information as to the origin of a site's specific location, function, land degradation, and management. In many developed countries in the world, soil data has been encoded into computer-compatible form. In Australia, for example, a national database of soil profile data and maps can be readily produced by police or soil scientists by downloading information directly from the Internet via the Australian Soil Resources Information System (ASRIS) database.

Historical Perspective

Although forensic soil science has only recently seen increased interest and acceptance in the forensic sciences and in courts of law (since the early 1990s), the initial contributions of soil and geological materials in legal investigations dates back to about 150 years ago. Arguably, the first documented case of a forensic comparison of soils took place in Berlin and was used to help police solve a crime that took place on a Prussian railroad in April 1856. A barrel containing silver coins had been emptied and refilled with sandy soil during transit. Prof. Christian Gottfried Ehrenberg in Berlin acquired samples of the soil from all the stations along the line. Using a light microscope, he examined features of the soil particles, such as color and shapes, to compare the soil similarity in the barrel to the station from which the sand originated. Then, in 1887, Sir Arthur Conan Doyle published several fictional cases involving Sherlock Holmes where forensic soil comparisons were used. In October 1904, George Popp, a forensic scientist in Frankfurt, successfully examined soil, minerals, and dust from clothes for identification to help solve a criminal case.

Between 1905 and 1990, soil information was used extensively by police. However, by that point, soil analysis became too specialized and expensive for in-house use in most forensic laboratories and outside forensic agencies worldwide. As a consequence, critical soil forensic evidence was often missed or ignored completely, hidden among trace evidence and insufficiently analyzed. And new techniques in soil science and geology were not deployed on complex forensic cases.

The recent surge in research around the world into the pedology, mineralogy, geochemistry, and biology of forensically important soil materials has helped bring forensic soil science back to the forefront (**Figure 1**).

Basic Principles Used in Forensic Soil Criminal Investigations

Forensic soil science, as with any other forensic disciplines, is contemporary and pertains to matters of court. It normally involves working with police forces or environmental agencies in the resolution of serious crime, usually homicides. Soil input to crime investigation has been growing, especially where no human DNA evidence is available. A number of fairly typical case studies, illustrating the point at which soil has been

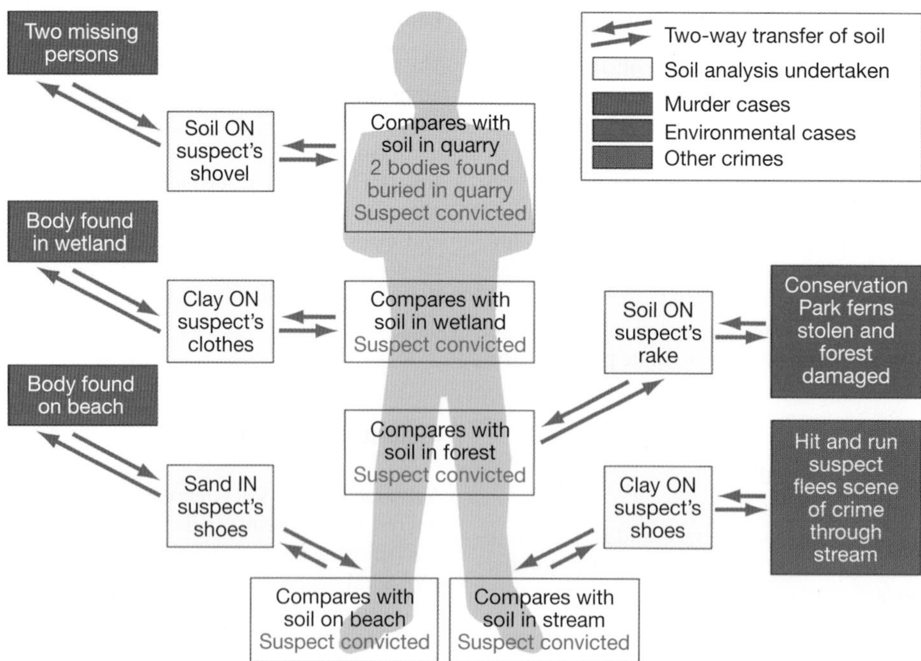

Figure 1 Case study examples of two-way soil transfer investigations varying in origin and complexity used to show associations of the transfer between various types of soil materials from questioned items (e.g., shovel, clothing, shoes, and rake) to control crime scene or alibi sites from a (1) gravel quarry, (2) clayey wetland site sampled 17 years after the crime, (3) sandy beach with shells, (4) stony/gravelly soil submerged under water in a stream, and (5) organic-rich soil in forest.

utilized are outlined in **Figure 1**, and the soil methodologies involved are discussed in the following sections.

Theory of Transfer of Soil Materials from One Surface to Another as a Result of Contact

The transfer of trace evidence is governed by what has become known as the Locard Exchange Principle, which states that when two surfaces come into physical contact there is a mutual exchange of trace evidence between them. For example, the exchange can take the form of soil material from a location transferring to the shoes of a person who walked through a particular area (**Figure 1**). These types of transfers are referred to as primary transfers (e.g., evidence is transferred from the soil surface to the shoe and later recovered from the shoe, such as in the treads of the sole or within the shoe). Once a soil material has transferred, any subsequent movements of that material, in this case from shoes, are referred to as secondary transfers. These secondary transfers of soil materials can be significant in evaluating the nature and source(s) of contact. Hence, the surface of soils can provide information linking persons to crime scenes, control sites, or alibi sites. Higher order transfers (tertiary transfers) of soil evidence can also occur, which can present interpretative problems for forensic soil scientists because the ultimate source of trace evidence may be extremely difficult to identify.

The vast majority of cases involve two-way or primary associations between questioned items such as shovels, shoes, and clothing to identify control and alibi locations of interest (**Figure 1**). Multiple soil transfer investigations can also be used to show associations between questioned items to identify control and alibi locations of interest. Very often, trace soil evidence can link an object or suspect to the scene of a crime, as well as rule out a suspect or support an alibi.

Soil Evidence Collection and Characterization

The aim of forensic soil analysis is to associate a soil sample taken from an item (e.g., shoes, clothing, shovel, or vehicle) by police or forensic soil scientists with a specific location. To achieve this aim, methods of sample collection and analyses chosen must be able to discriminate between soil samples from different locations as indicated in **Figure 1**. All sampling methods, sample storage security, soil characterization, and analytical methods must be subject to the most rigorous procedures of sample/data handling available so they can be discoverable and questioned in court.

The forensic investigation of soil usually involves the following two main activities:

1. Soil collection and sampling of one or more samples.
2. Soil characterization and evaluation.

Soil Collection and Sampling of One or More Samples

First and foremost, soil evidence must be recognized at the crime scene. Secondly, evidence must be well documented. Finally, collection and preservation must be maintained so as to preserve the integrity of the soil evidence. Knowing how many control samples to collect from the scene of a crime or alibi samples is difficult. The number, size, and type of samples to be taken are strongly dependent on the nature of the environment being investigated, especially the type of soil and nature of activity that may have taken place at the sampling location (e.g., suspected transfer of soil from the soil surface only or at depth in the case of a buried object or body – or both). A soil profile usually consists of a number of different soil layers or horizons each with different properties. Consequently, observation of depth changes in soil morphological characteristics is critical. A layer structure is also found in other forensic situations such as the soil accumulated on the soles of shoes or on shovels. Consequently, it is recommended that wherever possible each layer be carefully sampled and characterized. Soil sampling can be divided into two classes: (1) targeted sampling of localized areas where distinguishing features are evident in the soil (e.g., shoeprint) or on some other surface (e.g., flooring) and (2) random sampling should be used in cases where there is an absence of obvious features at or around a location of interest (i.e., conduct a systematic sampling of the location to obtain an unbiased sample).

It is critical to wear clean latex gloves when sampling. Do not use powdered gloves or talcum powder in the gloves because the layer silicate mineral talc will contaminate the soil sample. Always use clean tools (e.g., shovel, trowel, which are made of stainless steel). Plastic spades and trowels generally lack the strength required to dig soils, especially for most Australian soil conditions. Artist's palette knives are useful for sampling very thin layers of mud or dust on surfaces. Preferably, place samples in 'rigid plastic containers' rather than polythene bags or paper bags because the package must keep soil lumps intact. If the soil is wet/moist or adhering in a wet/moist condition to objects (e.g., tyres, vehicles, clothing, or shovels) first air dry and then package. However, as in the case of obvious sequential/chronologically deposited layers of soil being present, first remove the 'surface layer' and then air dry. Store dry samples at room temperature. If soil biological material is attached, package using clean cardboard box/paper bags because samples are prone to rapid deterioration.

Soil Sample Chain-of-Custody

Of paramount importance in both soil collection/sampling and soil characterization/evaluation is continuity of evidence or the sample chain-of-custody, which must be maintained and documented at all times throughout an entire soil forensic investigation. Secure sealing of dry soil samples in sample bags or bottles with tamper-indicating serrated evidence tape and sample storage is vital. Secure sample storage and rigorous procedures ensure that information about each sample is unambiguously retrievable and can be presented in court with absolute certainty.

Soil Characterization and Evaluation

Forensic soil comparisons of a questioned sample with one or more samples of known origin are usually based on several pedological, physical, mineralogical, and biological properties to evaluate the significance of observed similarities and differences in order to arrive at a conclusion regarding a possible association. Soil can be used to indicate or compare provenance, and therefore be used as *intelligence* and subsequently evidence to narrow areas of search during an investigation. Evaluative comparison of soil on one article of evidence compared to another, or compared to a known location, can and has been used as evidence in courts of law. However, forensic evidence is often available only as very small amounts of soil-regolith material, which may have trace amounts of mineral particles or organic materials. Consequently, the majority of forensic cases involving soil materials are usually complex and the challenges of associating relevant information from one source with another often requires the application of new, sophisticated field and laboratory methods. Importantly, the methods used for comparing the samples must be practical (use of standard methods), inexpensive, accurate, and applicable to small and large samples. To do this properly, the soil must first be systematically described and characterized using standard soil testing methods to deduce whether a soil sample can be used as evidence (i.e., Stage 1).

Methods for characterizing soils for a forensic comparison, broadly involves subdividing methods into four stages each comprising several steps and involving a combination of techniques (e.g., various descriptive or morphological and analytical methods listed in **Figure 2**). Consequently, soil characterization requires a multidisciplinary approach, which combines descriptive, analytical, and spatial information (e.g., mapping) steps in four stages (**Figure 2**). The progression of a soil examination through each of the four stages will depend on a number of factors such as the amount of sample available and the results from the early stages of the examination (**Figure 2**). Several forensic practitioners have suggested a similar sequence or succession approach of sediment/soil analysis for exclusionary/comparative forensic investigations. However, there is no 'authoritative scene of crime manual or laboratory methods manual' that prescribes approaches, stages, and steps for soil forensic examinations. The approach and method of each forensic situation has to be taken on its merits according to existing conditions but must involve using standard approaches to record, describe, and analyze materials.

Initial characterization for screening of samples (Stage 1)

Initial screening (i.e., morphological comparison examination) of whole soil samples is to visually compare samples (i.e., hand-held samples/specimens, soil profiles, and samples/specimens under a stereo-binocular light microscope). To do this properly, the soil must first be systematically described and characterized using standard soil morphological descriptors and tests such as color, consistency, structure, texture, segregations/coarse fragments (charcoal, ironstone, or carbonates), and abundance of roots/pores; to deduce whether a soil sample can be used as evidence. These soil morphological descriptions follow strict conventions whereby a standard array of data is described in a sequence, and each term is defined according to both International, (e.g., USDA Field book) and National standard systems for describing and sampling soils.

The use of petrography is a major and often precise method of studying and screening soils for discrimination in forensics (**Figure 2**). For example, nearly 50 common minerals (e.g., gypsum), as well as several less common minerals can easily be observed by the naked eye, but using a hand lens or low power stereo-binocular microscope enables the forensic soil scientist to better detect mineral properties (e.g., particle shape and surface texture) and provide more accurate mineral

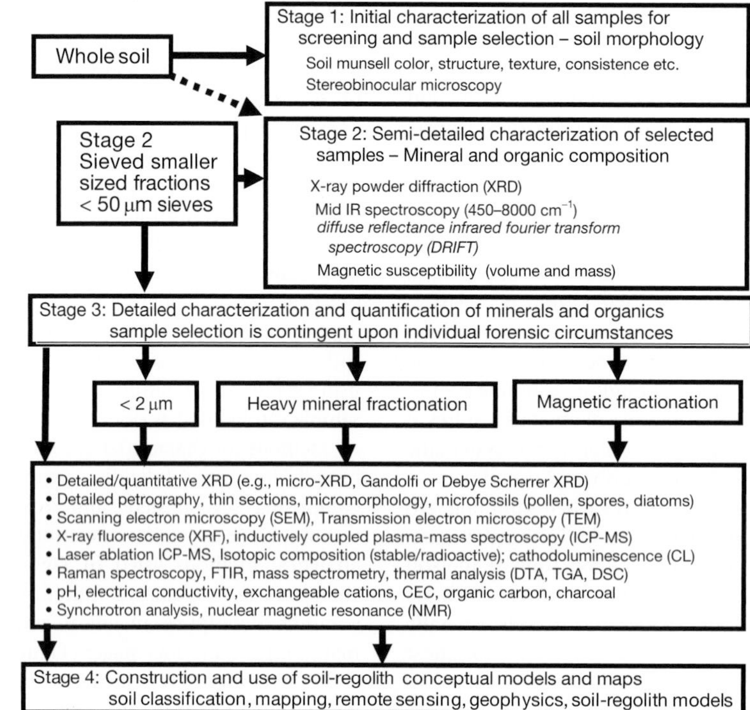

Figure 2 A systematic approach to discriminate soils for forensic soil examinations where, FTIR is Fourier transform infrared spectroscopy, DTA is differential thermal analysis, TGA is thermogravimetric analysis, DSC is differential scanning calorimetry, and CEC is cation exchange capacity.

identification. The petrographic microscope is also commonly used for characterizing microfossils (pollen grains, grass spores, opal phytoliths, diatoms).

Semi-detailed characterization (Stage 2)

Rapid identification, semi-detailed characterization and semi-quantification of minerals and organic matter in bulk samples and individual soil particles following sample selection and size fractionation (<50 μm) using selected methods, such as (1) X-ray powder diffraction (XRD), (2) diffuse reflectance infrared Fourier transform (DRIFT), and (3) mass and volume magnetic susceptibility methods (**Figure** 2).

XRD methods are arguably the most significant for identification, characterization, semi-quantitative, and quantitative analyses of minerals in forensic soil science. Extremely small sample quantities (e.g., a few tens of milligrams) as well as large quantities can be successfully analyzed using XRD. The critical advantage of XRD methods in forensic soil science is based on the unique character of the diffraction patterns of crystalline and even poorly crystalline soil minerals. Elements and their oxides, polymorphic forms (e.g., anatase and rutile polymorphic forms of TiO_2) and mixed crystals can be distinguished by this nondestructive examination. Part of the comparison involves identification of as many of the crystalline components as possible, either by reference to a database of XRD data or to a local collection of standard reference diffraction patterns, coupled with expert interpretation. XRD patterns can be likened to finger print comparisons between soil samples that delineate how closely the samples relate to each other. The main advantages of DRIFT spectroscopy are that the analysis is also nondestructive and can be rapidly applied. The mid-infrared portion of the electromagnetic spectrum is sensitive to organic materials, clay minerals, and quartz because of the absorption of infrared light at the vibrational frequencies of molecular functional groups constituting these materials. Added to the above two rapid methods and techniques are the use of magnetic susceptibility methods, which have become a very powerful tool to detect magnetic materials in soils (e.g., maghemite, magnetite) that are present at amounts below the detection limits of both XRD and DRIFT. Mineral magnetic techniques should always be used before moving to the more costly detailed methods (Stage 3), which generally require sample separation (**Figure** 2).

Detailed characterization (Stage 3)

Detailed identification, characterization, and quantification of minerals and organic matter in bulk samples and individual soil particles using additional analytical methods following sample selection, size, or magnetic or heavy mineral fractionation (see wide range of methods listed in **Figure** 2). For example, in many soil forensic investigations, the amount of soil available for analyses may be extremely small (e.g., thin coatings or single particles weighing of the order of 0.5–5 mg), which will preclude using pressed powders for XRD analyses. In such situations, it is essential to use an XRD that is fitted with a system for analysis that enables small soil samples to be (1) deposited onto Si wafer low background holders or (2) loaded into thin glass capillaries for XRD analysis.

Scanning electron microscopes (SEM) and transmission electron microscopes (TEM) are frequently used to examine the morphology and chemical composition (via energy dispersive spectroscopy) of particles magnified to over 100 000 times their original size making them very useful for discrimination. Soil minerals, fossils, and pollen spores that occur in soils can be described and analyzed in detail by SEM and TEM, and are therefore very useful indicators when studying soil samples. Fossil pollen grains and grass spores are preserved in many soils that are not strongly acidic (<pH 4) or alkaline (>pH 6). These reproductive particles are produced in large amounts by trees, shrubs, and grasses. Opal phytoliths (silica-rich) and calcium phytoliths are mineral deposits that form in and between plant cells and can be used to differentiate soils with similar mineralogy. Fourier transform infrared spectroscopy (FTIR) can be used to characterize soil organic constituents (fats, waxes, proteins, cellulose, hemicellulose, and lignin) in soils. Several soil forensic studies have been reported to show that a soil bacterial community DNA profile could be obtained from samples of soil recovered from potential crime scenes (e.g., shoes or clothing) with the profiles being representative of the site of collection.

Integration and extrapolation of soil information (Stage 4)

Landform and soil mapping should be used by forensic soil scientists to integrate and extrapolate soil information from one scale to next to build a coherent model of soil information from microscopic observations to the landscape scale (e.g., using soil/geological maps, terrain analysis, remote sensing, and geophysics). This combined information is used for geographic sourcing to identify the origin of a sample by placing constraints on the environment from which the sample originated.

Example Case Studies

Overcoming a potential recognition problem is best accomplished by making crime scene personnel aware of the possible value of soil evidence and sharing successful case examples such as those outlined in **Figure 1**. Several of these case studies, which have successfully used soil evidence to help solve legal cases, are likely attributed to the systematic methodology of crime scene sampling, processing, and soil characterization/ interpretation outlined in **Figure 2**. Investigators are trying to establish linkages or associations between the victim, suspect, crime scene, and individual items as with any form of evidence (**Figure 1**). To draw attention to this somewhat underutilized forensic tool, some important ways, which soil evidence has already proven useful in helping to solve criminal, civil, and environmental cases are presented in **Figure 1** and summarized below. These five case studies demonstrate how innovative ideas, methods, or applications of field and laboratory approaches have been critical in developing coherent, predictive, soil-regolith models from landscape to microscopic scales, to solve difficult soil-based investigations at a range of scales involving highly complex issues. As well, Dr. Raymond Murray in his book entitled 'Evidence from the Earth' presents several high-profile legal cases in which geological materials and methods have contributed significantly to solving cases from around the world.

Two Missing Persons

Neighbors reported disturbance at the home of two women, to the police. When the police arrived at the home in the Adelaide Hills, South Australia, the women and their car were missing. The missing vehicle and the suspect were found over 200 km away by police. A shovel with soil attached was found in the boot (trunk). The soil on the back of the shovel was found to be compacted and smeared indicating that the shovel was used to pat down moist soil. On the basis of the knowledge of local soils and geology, forensic soil scientists determined that the soil on the shovel came from one of the local industrial soil gravel quarries. The mineralogical composition of the soil on the shovel narrowed the search down to a small group of gravel quarries. Samples from these quarries were collected and one located in the sump or wet area of the quarry produced identical mineralogy to the soil on the shovel, which helped identify the burial site of the two bodies. The suspect was convicted and received a life sentence.

This case illustrates many of the issues regarding comparing soils, which involved the integration and understanding soil-landscapes, soil types, and the systematic implementation of field sampling, detailed soil characterization, especially XRD and use of soil/geological maps. The questioned and control samples were indistinguishable and the soil evidence was unequivocal in terms of all comparison criteria used, thus revealing the location of the two buried bodies. This success led to the establishment of the Centre for Australian Forensic Soil Science (CAFSS) in 2003. The Centre maintains a critical mass of expertise in soil forensics, to help protect Australia from crime, terrorism, and environmental pollution.

Body in Clayey Wetland (Cold Case)

The body of a drowned teenage girl was located by police in a wetland in 1988 but no suitable soil samples were analyzed. A suspect's tracksuit pants and shoes, which were kept by police since 1988 was re-examined by forensic soil scientists in 2005 (17 years later) to show traces of grey and yellowish clayey soil. These soil traces were removed and characterized. Samples of clayey grey soil from within the wetland and yellowish soil on the fringe were sampled in 2005. The morphology and mineralogy from XRD analyses of the two control samples taken from the suspects clothing were similar to the two samples from the wetland area – despite being sampled 17 years later. Soil evidence gathered indicated that the suspect had been present at the site where the victim drowned.

Body on Sandy Beach

The body of a teenage girl was located in shallow water on a beach (crime scene) in South Australia. Police located shoes from the two suspects on a beach in Victoria, which is approximately 1000 km from the crime scene. The morphology (color, size, and shape) of the sand grains and mineralogy of shell fragments from XRD analyses of the samples taken from within the shoes of both suspects were similar to beach samples at the crime scene. Equally, they do not resemble the sand samples collected from the beach in Victoria where the shoes were retrieved by the police, indicating the presence of both suspects at the crime scene. A man was found guilty of murder by a jury and sentenced to life imprisonment.

Hit-Run Suspect Flees Scene of Crime Through a Stream

A hit-and-run offender flees the scene of a fatal car collision and was later observed crossing a stream in Adelaide, South Australia. The suspect was apprehended by police. His shoes showed traces of dry yellow-brown clayey soil (questioned sample), which was tightly trapped in the grooves and treads of the rubber soles. Control samples of submerged wet black gravelly soil material were sampled from the alleged 'crime trail' in the stream, which comprised 95% alluvial stone and coarse gravel with only 5% clay and silt. However, after drying the control sample, a small amount of fine yellow-brown soil (<50 μm) was recovered by sieving. The morphology and mineralogy from XRD analyses of the sieved fine control soil material (<50 μm) closely resembled the questioned yellow-brown fine soil material from the suspect's shoe. The wet black control sample under typical viewing conditions by the naked eye did not readily show the yellow-brown color of the fine 5% clay and silt (<50 μm fraction) fractions hidden in the extremely stony/gravelly soil until the sample was dried and sieved and the fine fraction concentrated. The suspect was successfully prosecuted.

Conservation Park Ferns Illegally Stolen and Forest Damaged (US$ 13.5 Million Worth)

A rake with traces of questioned encrusted yellow soil was located by the police on a suspect's trailer in Tasmania. Control samples of yellowish soil were collected where clearance of native flora and tree ferns occurred in a Conservation Park in Victoria's south Gippsland (over 600 km from Tasmania). The morphology and mineralogy from XRD analyses of the control soil samples from the conservation park were similar to the questioned soils on the rake and trailer. Suspects were charged and jailed for criminal damage, theft, and conspiracy to defraud.

Conclusions

Recognition of the role of forensic soil science within criminal investigation has been a gradual process. As more and more crime enforcement agencies become aware of the potential value of forensic soil work, the need for trained personnel in the field will increase and will provide the emphasis needed to encourage the establishment of soil forensic training courses and centers. In many areas of the world, there is growing evidence that soil forensics use has a bright future. Five forensic cases in Australia have been solved with no work done because detectives have simply mentioned to the suspect or legal teams that soil samples have or will be compared/investigated by forensic soil scientists. Potentially, soil evidence could be used to help resolve a wide range of circumstances associated with criminal and environmental investigations.

See also: **Chemistry/Trace/Forensic Geosciences:** Botany; Crime Scene Considerations; Forensic Geoscience.

Further Reading

Donnelly LJ (2003) The applications of forensic geology to help the police solve crimes. *European Geologist. Journal of the European Federation of Geologists* 16: 8–12.

Fitzpatrick RW (2008) Nature, distribution and origin of soil materials in the forensic comparison of soils. In: Tibbett M and Carter DO (eds.) *Soil Analysis in Forensic Taphonomy: Chemical and Biological Effects of Buried Human Remains*, pp. 1–28. Boca Raton, FL: CRC Press.

Fitzpatrick RW (2009) Soil: Forensic analysis. In: Jamieson A and Moenssens A (eds.) *Wiley Encyclopedia of Forensic Science*, pp. 2377–2388. West Sussex, UK: John Wiley & Sons, Ltd.

Fitzpatrick RW (2012) Forensic earth science: Getting the dirt on crime. *e-Science* Faculty of Sciences, The University of Adelaide. Issue 2, pp. 6–13; 56–65. http://www.sciences.adelaide.edu.au/e-science/.

Fitzpatrick RW and Raven MD (2012) Guidelines for conducting criminal and environmental soil forensic investigations (Version 7). *Report No. CAFSS_076*. Australia: Centre for Australian Forensic Soil Science. http://www.clw.csiro.au/cafss/.

Fitzpatrick RW and Raven MD (2012) How Pedology and mineralogy helped solve a double murder case: Using forensics to inspire future generations of soil scientists. *Soil Horizons*. http://dx.doi.org/10.2136/sh12-05-0016.

Fitzpatrick RW, Raven MD, and Forrester ST (2009) A systematic approach to soil forensics: Criminal case studies involving transference from crime scene to forensic evidence. In: Ritz K, Dawson L, and Miller D (eds.) *Criminal and Environmental Soil Forensics*, pp. 105–127. New York: Springer.

Kugler W (2003) X-ray diffraction analysis in the forensic science: The last resort in many criminal cases. JCPDS – International Centre for Diffraction Data. *Advances in X-ray Analysis* 46: 1–16.

Murray RC (2011) *Evidence from the Earth: Forensic Geology and Criminal Investigation*, 2nd edn. Missoula, MT: Mountain Press Publishing.

Murray RC and Tedrow JCF (1992) *Forensic Geology*. NJ: Prentice Hall.

Pirrie D, Butcher AR, Power MR, Gottlieb P, and Miller GL (2004) Rapid quantitative mineral and phase analysis using automated scanning electron microscopy (QemSCAN); potential applications in forensic geoscience. In: Pye K and Croft DJ (eds.) *Forensic Geoscience: Principles, Techniques and Applications*, pp. 103–122. London: Geological Society of London Special Publication of the Geological Society of London, 232.

Pye K (2007) *Geological and Soil Evidence: Forensic Applications*. Boca Raton, FL: CRC Press.

Pye K and Croft D (eds.) (2004) *Forensic Geoscience: Principles, Techniques and Applications*. London: Geological Society of London Special Publication of the Geological Society of London, 232.

Ritz K, Dawson L, and Miller D (eds.) (2008) *Criminal and Environmental Soil Forensics*. Soil Forensics International, Edinburgh Conference Centre: Springer.

Ruffell A and McKinley J (2008) *Geoforensics*. Chichester: John Wiley & Sons, Ltd.

Schoeneberger PJ, Wysocki DA, Benham EC, and Broderson WD (eds.) (2002) *Field Book for Describing and Sampling Soils, Version 2.0*. Lincoln, NE: Natural Resources Conservation Service, National Soil Survey Center.

Relevant Websites

http://www.clw.csiro.au – Centre for Australian Forensic Soil Science (CAFSS).
http://www.geolsoc.org.uk – The Geological Society of London Forensic Geoscience Group.
http://www.forensicgeologyinternational.org/ – International Union of Geological Sciences (IUGS), Initiative on Forensic Geology (IFG).
http://www.forensicgeology.net/ – Raymond Murray forensic geology.

Forensic Geoscience

A Ruffell, Queen's University, Belfast, UK

Glossary

Anthropology Study of the origin, behavior, and physical, social, and cultural development of humans.
Archaeology Study of past human life through analysis of artifacts, skeletal remains, and past environments.
Geographic information science (GIS) Academic theory behind the development, use, and application of GIS.
Geology Study of earth materials (rocks, fossils, minerals) and processes (tectonics, volcanoes).
Geophysics Physics of Earth, often divided into deep or whole Earth and near-surface or shallow studies.
Hydrodynamics Study of the forces acting on, or exerted by, fluids, especially water.
Hydrogeology Subdiscipline of geology that studies the distribution and movement of groundwater in soils, sediments, and rocks, all commonly aquifers.
Mineralogy Study of minerals, their structure, habit, and use.
Pedology Soil science.
Petrography Study of the composition and properties of rocks.
Remote sensing Acquisition of information about the Earth or objects without need for direct contact. Examples include aerial photography, satellite imagery, and some areas that are included in geophysics (x-ray imaging).
Seismology Study of earthquakes.

Introduction

'Forensic geoscience' was first used as the title of a meeting of the Geological Society of London in 2003. Prior to this (since 1975), the term 'forensic geology' described the use of geological methods in assisting criminal investigations, especially the analysis of geological particles and rocks by petrography and mineralogy. Geology and other earth science methods had been in use (in criminal investigations) for nearly 100 years previously. The first documented use of geology in what we would now term forensics was in the 1880s by Christian Ehrenberg, a famous Berlin professor who analyzed sand that had been substituted for gold coins being transported in barrels on a railway in Prussia. Ehrenberg collected sand from each stop the train had made and indicated the station where the swop occurred, causing a railway worker to confess to the crime. Through the turn of the nineteenth and twentieth centuries, Sir Arthur Conan Doyle, author of the Sherlock Holmes adventures, was aware of a German judge named Hans Gross who used geology and geography in his investigations, and adapted his work to be included in the fictitious knowledge of his fictitious detective Sherlock Holmes. Subsequently, police forces increasingly used geology in their work, either through specialists such as Georg Popp in Germany, Edmond Locard in France, and later, Oscar Heinrich in the United States, or through government laboratories such as the FBI or the Central Research Establishment in the United Kingdom. However, from the 1930s onward, little or nothing was published on forensic geology, with one article in the 1960s on forensic pedology by Brooks and Newton and the book *Forensic Geology* by Murray and Tedrow in 1975. Amazingly, this brilliant and inspirational book did not cause a flood of articles; moreover, readers of the text were probably amazed at what the authors had been doing in using geological analyses in assisting criminal investigations. Subsequent to 2003, the term 'forensic geoscience' included more than forensic geology, with geophysics, remote sensing, hydrodynamics, geographic information science/systems included and with traditional geological techniques applied to unusual forensic scenarios (bone histology, study of impacts on spacecraft surfaces). The origin of the term is of interest, with a thematic meeting (at the Geological Society of London in 2003) and an edited book (of the same name, 2004) appearing coincidentally to an *Earth Science Reviews* article, also in 2004 and also with the same name. The main uses of forensic geology have been in assisting criminal investigations into where suspects or victims may have been, often using the exclusionary principle (aiming to exclude all other explanations, rather than associating someone with a location). The classic examples are mud/soil on a person's footwear or vehicle and the material at the scene of crime – does one compare with the other? Forensic geology, however, extends into the examination of substituted materials (see the work of Ehernberg above), the failure of structures, faked geological items (especially gems and mining fraud), and the use of geological materials in drug cutting or concealing graves/mass graves. Forensic geoscience includes the above examples, but widens the applications to geophysics, the geological aspects of anthropology, the understanding of bedrock geology, and the use of geostatistics. Geoforensics goes even further by including all of the above as well as remote sensing, geomorphology, and fossil organisms. With an increasing number of techniques included in forensic geology through to geoforensics, applications have also widened from assisting in criminal investigations to helping with humanitarian incidents, examining problems of pollution (especially hydrogeology), and working with military authorities. The latter is especially interesting, as geologists have long been employed by the army especially for testing the density of beaches for amphibious assaults, planning desert campaigns around the location of oases, and the location of firm ground for tank movement. In summary, forensic geoscience sits right at the heart of the application of earth science techniques in forensic science (or criminalistics in some countries), with the very specific forensic geology and forensic pedology (soil forensics) on one side, and the very broad geoforensics at the other, the latter incorporating all that has gone before, the former being the origin of these interesting applications to all sorts of problems, now far beyond the investigation of crime alone.

From the Macro- to the Microscale

The largest scale at which forensic geoscience operates would be the global analysis of seismology, wherein the networks of seismometers distributed across the world detect and locate major tremors on Earth. These devices were installed to monitor earthquake and volcanic activity, as well as to help enforce the Nuclear Test Ban Treaty. Subsequently, they have detected large explosions; allowed seismologists to state that the submarine Kursk exploded in two events, one small and the second a larger one, and that the Dar-es-Salaam and Nairobi bombings were accurately timed (making them likely to be the work of Al Qaeda); and located aircraft crashes remotely, thus assisting search and rescue. The next scale at which geoforensics assists in forensics and criminology would be in contributing to the search for buried objects. Geologists are trained to find things in the ground (water, oil, ores, aggregates, voids) and are thus highly competent in providing possible search locations for buried objects. Their methodology is often the same: given a search area, the geologist will make a desktop study of bedrock geology, surface deposits ('loose,' or drift geology), soils, topography, and past and present land use, possibly using aerial imagery. The above range of data will limit the search area prior to any field visit, as assessments of diggability, thickness of soil and sediment, access routes, areas of rock with voids, and places that have been altered will all have been identified. This significantly reduces the size of the area to be searched, saving time, effort, and cost. The desktop study also allows the geologist to advise on what remotely sensed imagery may be useful to collect, what hazards may be present for the search team, and what geophysical devices (if any) may be appropriate in locating a target of known makeup, size, and (from the above study) probable depth of burial. Thus, it maybe surprising that much of the work is done without stepping into the field. Before a field visit, a full-scale search is often undertaken to test desktop predictions of geology, soil, diggability, access, and hazards, and to consider the method of deployment of any recommended assets (geophysics, excavators). Once targets have been located, they may be subjected to further geological analysis (detailed geophysics, analysis of escaping gases) or the deployment of other specialists (search dogs, engineers, archaeologists) recommended. In the case of inhumations, the geologist does not dig: this is the job of the archaeologist/anthropologist (whose work also falls under the umbrella of forensic geoscience). The geologist is generally not trained to recover things such as ordnance, cadavers, or contraband, but he or she may be interested to know (either at the time or afterward) what was discovered on the dig as this would relate to the ground truths of their predictions. Excavated items are often examined by a geologist or a soil scientist in case any adhered soil or sediment is alien to the burial site. This occurred in the classic case of a USDEA officer, Agent Enrique Camarena. When Camarena went missing while working undercover in Mexico, the US government demanded that he be found; on visiting the subsequently discovered burial site, the attending geologist noticed that the soil on Camarena's clothes was different from that at the burial site. This raised questions about where he had been and who had killed him; eventually, the Mexican government was implicated, causing a major political argument. The Camarena case is a perfect example of where the macroscale application of forensic geoscience links to the medium and microscales.

The medium scale of soil and sediment examination from suspects, victims, scenes, and alibi locations is the most common application of forensic geoscience, and includes the famous cases of Gross, Popp, Heinrich, and Murray (mentioned above, so not repeated). The number of published cases in books, edited volumes, and journals is well over 200, many of which use standard methods of geological analysis (color, particle size, petrography). The traditional application of geological analysis in comparing soil, sediment, or rock from suspects and victims to that from possible scenes of crime has used both large quantities (sometimes boulders and slabs of concrete) and small amounts (a few grains of quartz sand). As Morgan et al. and Ruffell and McKinley (see their definition) demonstrate, trace geological evidence is assuming increasingly greater importance in all forensic investigations on account of the forensically aware perpetrator carrying out 'clean-up' operations. Likewise, questions such as (1) 'Where has the deceased been?' (2) 'Where has this illegal package or vehicle been?' and (3) 'What is this substance on a suspect, victim, or material?' are frequently being asked by investigators; the solutions often rely on trace amounts of evidence. A major concern with such small sample sizes is that conventional geological analyses cannot be carried out, the latter having been developed for outcrop- and borehole-derived samples of virtually unlimited quantity. The approach to trace evidence is far more akin to the analysis of meteorite, moon rock, or precious (or fake) materials. Developments in this field include a dual approach, starting with exhaustive nondestructive tests. These include automated color, visual description, in situ (i.e., dust and mud left on the seized item, such as clothing, footwear, and car floor mats) x-ray diffraction, and in situ Fourier transform infrared analysis. This allows for the retention of sample integrity, as well as the gaining of knowledge regarding what the trace material is, progressing to appropriate destructive testing. However, with all such approaches, an initial examination of the sample is paramount before any destructive analysis method is considered, not least to ensure that other physical evidence, such as hair, fibers, flakes of paint, etc. are recovered. An alternative approach is to choose, after examination, a sophisticated destructive technique that has a good track record in such trace evidence analysis and hope it proves appropriate, whether or not the makeup of the sample is known. Examination by scanning electron microscopy (SEM), especially that with automated chemical analysis (SEM– EDX (energy dispersive x-ray) or the QEMSCAN system), falls into this category. Nondestructive analysis provides a useful 'baseline' knowledge, after which samples may be split for destructive analysis by prosecution and defense, both of whose results can be referenced back to the nondestructive stage in order to test for intersample variations, analytical error, or contamination.

Geological trace evidence analysis protocols follow two general approaches. The first is to mimic the good practice already demonstrated with conventional geological samples, and then to adopt a multiproxy system. Trace evidence (often less than a gram of sample) presents a major problem in applying such good practice: larger sample amounts may be split and eventually destroyed, even allowing experimentation with new methods. With smaller sample sizes, the makeup of the material needs to be established in order to decide on what analyses are to be undertaken: sometimes, makeup is determined by destructive analysis, creating a major conundrum! What if the initial 'guess' (based on visual inspection) is incorrect, and the wrong method of analysis is chosen? The innocent could remain as suspects and the guilty escape punishment as a result of such error. A good approach is to first find out what the trace material is by nondestructive analyses, and then to follow it up with informed destruction. The range of appropriate nondestructive screening methods available are of course limited (see above), but they are expanding with new research and often provide enough information to determine what a material is, in order to inform what further destructive analysis is to be undertaken. The second approach is to look beyond the geological evidence base and consider what transferable particles, from the scene to the suspects and victims, exist in airborne particulates (aeolian dust, combustion products), precipitation residues (salts), and cosmic fallout (spherules). However, Ruffell and McKinley have expressed concern over this approach, stating that the use of isotope from water in comparing suspects to locations was all 'crazy conjecture,' when chlorine isotopes in rainwater (and its residue salts) are already being used as a tool in meteorology. The multiproxy use of both geological and nongeological methods can be subjected to geostatistical analysis, allowing testing of the 'strength' of some exclusions or connections and the weakness of others.

Besides providing crime scene evidence, geological trace material such as mud specks on clothing and vehicles plays an important role in assisting in the search for unknown locations. The challenge is in comparing such small amounts of material to large areas of the Earth's surface. However, Oscar Heinrich (The 'Wizard of Berkeley') did just this in 1921, using the diagnostic features of quartz grains found in a murder victim's hair. Rawlins et al. performed the same function on bulk samples but using a multiproxy approach. It seems rational therefore that multiproxy nondestructive testing of trace evidence will yield sufficient geological information for informed sampling and thus help to focus the search on where the person/vehicle/item had been. Gaining abundant knowledge about a sample is of low value without a sufficient database of the stratigraphy and distribution of soils and rock types with which to compare the questioned sample. The other challenge for the analysis of trace particulate evidence will be to exclude or compare samples in the urban environment, where less transferable mineral material of geological origin is available.

A common concern among forensic scientists is the need to have only appropriately trained experts working on specific material: the original concept of the 'expert witness.' This applies to geoscience applications in forensics; for example, geologists would be concerned about biologists comparing rock debris from scenes of crime to that found on suspects (and vice versa, with geologists handling plant material). However, two related issues compromise this statement: first, in the case where geoforensic techniques are more advanced than others, and, second, where there are no analytical methods previously devised for exclusion/comparison of the material. In the investigation of fraud, the need for nondestructive testing is paramount in order to preserve the evidence (it may not be a fake sculpture yet ends up a damaged real one!). Just as the geologist warns against the practitioners of other disciplines to stick firmly to their area of expertise, so engineers, chemists, and biologists/microbiologists use their methods in ways considered appropriate by them. However, some materials contain a mix of ingredients that can be analyzed (for exclusion/comparison to scenes of crime) by a number of methods. Recent examples in the literature include safety matches found at the scene of an attempted arson attack, concrete used to cover a murder victim, and manufactured goods with 'geological' materials involved (drugs, explosives). Instead of the scientist involved being partisan about the analysis of such materials, a more appropriate route would be the involvement of other disciplines in a team-based approach.

See also: **Anthropology/Odontology**: Biomechanics of Bone Trauma.

Further Reading

Block EB (1958) *The Wizard of Berkeley*, p. 254. New York: Coward-McCann.

Brooks M and Newton K (1969) Forensic pedology. *Police Journal (London)* 42: 107–112.

Brown AG, Smith A, and Elmhurst O (2002) The combined use of pollen and soil analyses in a search and subsequent murder investigation. *Journal of Forensic Sciences* 47: 614–618.

Bull P, Morgan RM, Wilson HE, and Dunkerely S (2004) Multi-technique comparison of source and primary transfer soil samples: An experimental investigation by Croft, D. and Pye, K. A comment. *Science and Justice* 44: 173–176.

Cosgrove D and Daniels S (1988) *The Iconography of Landscape, Cambridge Studies in Historical Geography*, 328 pp. Cambridge: Cambridge University Press.

Croft DJ and Pye K (2004) Multi-technique comparison of source and primary transfer soil samples: An experimental investigation. *Science and Justice* 44: 21–28.

Dawson L, Miller D, and Towers W (2007) Dirty work: New uses for soil databases. http://vector1media.com/article/feature/dirty-work-%96-new-uses-for-soil-databases/.

Donnelly LJ (2002a) Finding the silent witness, how forensic geology helps solve crimes. All-Party Parliamentary Group for Earth Science. The Geological Society of London. *Geoscientist* 12(5 May): 24.

Donnelly LJ (2002b) Finding the silent witness. The Geological Society of London. *Geoscientist* 12(5 May): 16–17.

Donnelly LJ (2002c) How forensic geology helps solve crime. All-Party Parliamentary Group for Earth Science. House of Lords & House of Commons, Westminster Palace, 12 March 2002.

Donnelly LJ (2003) The applications of forensic geology to help the police solve crimes. *European Geologist: Journal of the European Federation of Geologists* 16: 8–12.

Farmer NL, Ruffell A, Meier-Augenstein W, Meneely J, and Kalin RM (2006) Forensic analysis of wooden safety matches. *Science and Justice* 46(3): 88–98.

Harrison M and Donnelly LJ (2008) Locating concealed homicide victims: Developing the role of geoforensics. In: Ritz K, Dawson L, and Miller D (eds.) *Criminal and Environmental Soil Forensics*. Soil Forensics International, Edinburgh Conference Centre, 30 October–1 November 2008, Berlin: Springer.

Keaney A, Ruffell A, and McKinley J (2008) Geological trace evidence: Forensic and legal perspectives. In: Ritz K, Dawson L, and Miller D (eds.) *Criminal and Environmental Soil Forensics*. Soil Forensics International, Edinburgh Conference Centre, 30 October–1 November 2008, Berlin: Springer.
Kugler W (2003) X-ray diffraction analysis in the forensic science: The last resort in many criminal cases. *Advances in X-Ray Analysis* 46: 1–16.
Martin M (2007) *Earth Evidence (Forensic Crime Solvers)*, p. 32. Mankato, MN: Capstone Press.
Morgan R and Bull PA (2007) The nature, philosophy and practice of forensic sediment analysis. *Progress in Physical Geography* 31: 1–16.
Morgan RM, Wiltshire PEJ, Parker A, and Bull P (2006) The role of forensic geoscience in wildlife crime detection. *Forensic Science International* 162: 152–162.
Murray R (2004) *Evidence from the Earth*, p. 226. Missoula, MT: Mountain Press.
Murray R and Tedrow JCF (1975) *Forensic Geology: Earth Sciences and Criminal Investigation*, p. 240. New York: Rutgers University Press.
Pye K (2007) *Geological and Soil Evidence: Forensic Applications*, p. 335. Boca Raton, FL: CRC Press.
Pye K and Croft D (eds.) (2004) In: *Forensic Geoscience: Principles, Techniques and Applications*, vol. 232, p. 318. London: Geological Society Special Publication.
Rawlins BG, Kemp SJ, Hodgkinson EH, et al. (2006) Potential and pitfalls in establishing the provenance of earth-related samples in forensic investigations. *Forensic Science International* 51: 832–845.
Ritz K, Dawson L, and Miller D (2008) *Criminal and Environmental Soil Forensics*, p. 520. Amsterdam: Springer.
Ruffell A (2010) Forensic pedology, forensic geology, forensic geoscience, geoforensics and soil forensics. *Forensic Science International* 202: 9–12.
Ruffell A and McKinley J (2005) Forensic geology and geoscience. *Earth-Science Reviews* 69: 235–247.
Ruffell A and McKinley J (2008) *Geoforensics*, p. 332. Chichester, UK: Wiley-Blackwell.
Thorwald J (1967) *Crime and Science: The New Frontier in Criminology*. San Diego: Harcourt, Brace & Co.

Relevant Websites

www.forensicgeology.net/ – Forensic Geology
http://www.geolsoc.org.uk – The Geological Society of London
http://www.usgs.gov/ – United States Geological Survey

Botany

J Robertson, University of Canberra, Canberra, ACT, Australia

Introduction and Scope

Botany is the branch of biology concerned with the study of plants and plant life.

Hidden even in this simple definition is what classifies them as a plant. In simple terms, this is any member of the Kingdom Plantae. So are fungi plants? Fungi traditionally were included in the study of botany! However, it is now understood and recognized that in evolutionary terms, fungi are more closely related to the animal kingdom than the plant kingdom.

However, for the purposes of this short treatment, fungi will be included.

The modern emphasis on the study of biology is clearly at the molecular level, and as will be briefly considered later in this article, molecular approaches to the examination of forensic botanical exhibits and samples has its place. However, it is critical to emphasize that plants do not exist alone. They are part of a broader ecosystem with other organisms, and indeed, are subject to natural and imposed influences wherever they are found. In forensic context, human impact is often the dominant influence. The term forensic taphonomy attempts to consider all of the factors that create a complex, dynamic (living and changing), and interdependent chemical, physical, and biological environment.

When one considers that there are something around 400 000 angiosperms (seed bearing plants) alone, and possibly 1.5 million fungal species, is it possible for any one person to have the expert knowledge required of a forensic botanist? The answer to this question is that, of course, it is not possible for any one person to have a detailed knowledge of all aspects and all species within the plant group. In this article, a model will be presented for how forensic botany can be managed as part of a forensic investigation.

Forensic botany can contribute to all of the normal forensic functions such as associative evidence linking suspects, victims and/or scenes, individualizing/identifying samples, and helping reconstruct events. More specifically, it may also assist in investigating suspicious deaths, through ascertaining time of deposition, in time of death, in locating deceased persons, and in cause of death (for example, through poisonings). Plant material may also be the source of bioterrorism agents. Plants are the source of many licit and illicit drugs, and forensic botany plays a key role in the identification of suspicious materials and, through profiling, contributes to forensic intelligence. Less obvious is that drug seizures may have trace materials adhering, which could indicate geographic origin.

Another way of looking at the scope is to consider the types of plant material that may be encountered. The examples are as follows:

- partially digested food such as stomach contents, vomit, and feces;
- wood and wood fragments (these are considered to be very important in forensic botany found in the ballast material in older safes);
- pollen and spores;
- diatoms and other algae;
- licit and illicit drugs including poisonous plants;
- plant fibers used in the manufacture of paper and textiles; and
- nonspecific plant parts, or whole plants, often present as fragments or trace physical evidence.

Forensic Botany Starts at the Crime Scene

Forensic science has been described as information in context. The context in a forensic investigation starts at the scene or locus of an incident. Sometimes, it will be obvious that a crime has been committed, but this may or may not be determined for sometime and may depend on post-scene forensic analysis. For example, a body located in an outdoor location may be the victim of a crime or may be the result of death by natural causes. The role of the crime scene examiner (CSE) and investigator is to assess the circumstances at a scene and, in conjunction with police investigators, reach at least an initial view on whether or not the circumstances are suspicious warranting a higher level of forensic treatment. The police, and the broader criminal justice system (CJS), would not be well served if every natural death was treated as a murder case. Of course, the danger is that if a scene is not initially treated as a crime scene then the potentially valuable evidence may be lost. It would be possible to return to the scene to collect relevant botanical material, but it is unlikely that the scene will not have been disturbed, probably to the point where any evidence of entry and exit will have been compromised. It is unlikely that most CSEs will have a high degree of awareness of the potential role of a forensic botanist or, more broadly, a scene ecologist and may not give sufficient consideration to involving such a specialist. However, the early involvement of a specialist in a crime scene team could be the difference between a successful scene examination and a failed scene examination. For such a specialist to play this role, they too must possess the necessary skills and experience and a cognitive ability to recognize what may be important through understanding and reading anomalies and indicators that show something at the scene is unusual or unexpected. The specialist needs to be given relevant information about what is known (often very little at the early stages) in order to inform decisions. Often success or failure will depend on collecting the correct samples at the scene, which necessarily requires that the 'scene' is properly defined (how local, how extended).

The need for, or extent of, detailed examination of samples can only be decided as a part of broader case management and will be determined by other potential evidence and ultimately the key issues of identification and 'what happened.'

Hence, the appropriate use of forensic botany should involve a team approach, based on an appreciation by the CSE of the potential for forensic botany to contribute and the

 http://dx.doi.org/10.1016/B978-0-12-382165-2.00115-X

'specialist' understanding how their work can contribute to the investigation process.

On occasion, the forensic botanists attending a death scene will find themselves working with specialists such as geologists, anthropologists, entomologists, and others under the direction of a CSE. Specialists need to have a good understanding of a criminalistics approach to forensic science, but they will very rarely be specialized CSEs. The specialist is likely to be used to deal with what can be described as standard samples, whereas forensic work most often involves nonstandard and fragmented samples. The specialist needs to operate at the same standards as the CSE with respect to scene procedures, attention to contamination potential, making comprehensive systematic and contemporaneous records, and proper evidence handling and storage, otherwise potential evidence may be weakened or even may be inadmissible.

Typical Sample Types Encountered in Forensic Botany

Partially Digested Food, Feces, Stomach Contents, and Vomit

The examination of stomach contents may identify the last meal eaten by a deceased person, which may help establish the time of death or a timetable of recent events before death. Except in very rare instances, it is not possible to estimate the time of death with great accuracy, but it may place death in a window of time and corroborate other indicators of time since death. During violent crimes, victims may vomit and/or defecate and traces of this may be carried away by the offender. Offenders are also known to leave feces at a scene.

The examination of this type of material involves separation of food residues that may be plant or animal. Plant cells are resistant to digestion, especially fiber-containing plant materials. Through a systematic examination of recovered plant fragments, it is often possible to identify the types of foodstuffs present. This relies on the specialist having an excellent knowledge of the structure of common foods and usually will involve the use of key (old) reference works and the comparison with reference samples. Low- and high-power microscopy and 'old fashioned' histo-staining techniques are key competencies for this type of work. There are few botanists left with this type of background or training.

Wood and Other Plant Fibers

Wood may take many forms in forensic examinations and may include pieces of timber or timber products used as weapons, from built structures where there has been a forced entry or from sawdust/wood shavings used in older safes. Wood comes from two broad groups, softwood and hardwood. These two groups are easily distinguished even with small fragments because of very obvious differences in the major cell types present. The morphology and internal anatomy of woods are well described, and there are excellent keys available for commercial species.

As wood is laid down through an annual growth cycle, these annual 'rings' can be read to give a history of the parent tree. Hence, there are many documented cases, where growth rings have been used to associate stolen timber back to stumps where trees have been harvested. Theft and illegal logging of timber is a significant environmental crime type.

Perhaps the most famous case involving growth ring analysis is the well-documented Lindbergh kidnapping from the 1930s, where a piece of wood found in the suspect's home was linked to a homemade ladder used to gain access to the Lindbergh home.

Growth ring analysis may also associate recovered sawn off shotgun stocks with recovered weapons. Cases have also been reported where growth ring disruption has been used to date when a body may have been buried in a wooded environment.

Consideration should always be given to the possibility of a physical fit when timber is recovered.

The examination of very small fragments of wood down to individual cells requires significant specialist knowledge. Although rarely seen today, a significant component of the work of a forensic botanist at least until the 1970s was the examination and identification of small particles of wood emanating from the material comprising the ballast of older safes. When these safes were blown open, wood fragments were commonly transferred to the safe blower.

Wood cells or fibers are also found in paper, and their examination forms a part of the work of a document examiner.

Palynology

Strictly speaking, palynology is the subdiscipline of botany in which pollen grains are examined and identified. Once the pollen population or palynomorph is established, this can assist in areas as diverse as ancient environments, evolution and allergen studies, and even to assist in soil examination. As pollen samples will often include other plant spores and microscopic fragments, the expert palynologist will usually be able to describe and identify a wide range of microscopic entities.

Pollen and spores may persist for very long periods of time because of them being chemically robust.

It is beyond the scope of this article to attempt to describe the variation in microscopic features, which enables the palynologist to describe, differentiate, and identify the pollen. Pollen may be identified at species, at genus, or sometimes only at family level. The examination of fungal spores is a separate discipline and requires further specialist knowledge.

Identification to whatever extent possible is only one part of the role of a palynologist who needs to understand taphnomomy, production and dispersal patterns for distribution and transfer, and persistence in order to interpret and evaluate the significance of a pollen population. Critical to a meaningful evaluation will be appropriate sampling at the scene. This necessarily requires the palynologist to have knowledge of the taxa represented at a scene where comparative analysis is required. Palynology is the subject of a separate entry in this encyclopedia.

Plant Toxicology

Plants are widely used for medicinal purposes because of their natural pharmaceutical constituents. In addition, many plants contain toxin as products of normal metabolic processes. Poisoning may occur as a result of accidental ingestion, misidentification, or misadventure. Rapid identification of what has been ingested can be paramount in saving life by enabling the doctor to take appropriate medical action. The botanist may have to identify whole plants, plant parts, products such as herbal medicines, and gastric contents.

Plant materials may be intentionally ingested, where the plant has some drug effect or where the individual is attempting suicide.

Included in plants are fungi, where these may be consumed for hallucinogenic drug properties (so called 'magic mushrooms'). Unfortunately, there have been instances where highly poisonous mushrooms have been misidentified for edible species with fatal consequences.

A specific form of poisoning involves the poison ricin derived from the seed of the castor oil plant (*Ricinus communis*). Concerns over the use of ricin as a terrorism agent have increased in recent years.

Diatoms and Other Microalgae

Diatoms are the most common microalgae encountered as trace evidence. They occur in many habitats, including marine, freshwater, and terrestrial environments. There are various species that flourish in generally inhospitable environments, such as highly acidic habitats and thermal water bodies, where temperatures prevent the growth of most other life forms. Diatoms have extremely resilient siliceous cell walls termed frustules, which are composed of two valves. They are classified into two groups based on their symmetry: centric (with radial symmetry) and pennate (with bilateral symmetry). Their taxonomy is based on frustule morphology, including shape and surface ornamentation.

These frustules are highly resistant, and diatoms are found in the environment and in the manufactured products containing diatomaceous earth, such as cleaning agents, some paints, and some brands of match heads.

The examination of diatoms is most commonly associated with the investigation of drowning. There is still an ongoing debate as to how accurate diatoms are as an indicator of drowning, but it would appear that when applied in a conservative way, such analysis can have value.

Consideration should be given to other forms of 'aquatic' botanical evidence in any scene involving water such as ponds, rivers, or dams.

Cannabis and Other Plants Used as Illicit Drugs

By far the most common plant material examined in forensic laboratories is Cannabis. The identification of Cannabis plant material is straightforward, although requiring specialist knowledge. The combination of microscopic features of Cannabis is unique. Excellent descriptions of the microscopic features of Cannabis are to be found in older pharmacy books reflecting the fact that Cannabis used to be commonly known as a medicinal drug. Increasingly, many laboratories have adopted a minimalist botany approach relying on chemical tests (color spot tests and thin layer chromatography).

From a crime scene perspective, the forensic investigator is only likely to be involved in more serious cases involving cultivation. These may involve outdoor scenes, the use of glass houses; and increasingly indoor settings with non-soil-based hydroponic cultivation.

Other botanical evidence may also be valuable when an outdoor scene is involved, especially as pollen from surrounding plants will be trapped by the sticky surfaces of the Cannabis plant.

The forensic botanist may also be presented with other non-Cannabis drug plants, most commonly from plants suspected of being Papaver somniforum or poppies. Other plants or plant products may include coco leaf and khat (Figure 1).

Plant Fibers Used in Paper and Textiles

Plant fibers may be used in some specialist paper manufacture, although most commercial paper is made of fibers from wood sources. Although man-made fibers have replaced botanical sources of fibers, botanical fibers are still found in textile used as ropes and cordage.

Plant DNA Analysis

DNA analysis of plants and fungi is now commonplace for many applications and almost all of the techniques used for DNA analysis have been applied to plants.

For example, a short tandem repeat (STR) multiplex has been developed and validated for the forensic analysis of *Cannabis sativa*, along with a database of Australian seizures to inform the interpretation of STR profiles.

Another example is the development of a molecular identification system for grasses.

Summary and Conclusion

In this article, the range and scope of forensic botany have been outlined. There is a potentially exciting future to enhance the evidential value of botanical samples through the future of DNA analysis. This will only be achieved if investigators and crime scene examinations are open to the possibilities for forensic botany to contribute and to collect the necessary known and reference materials. Mostly, there is nothing unique from a crime scene investigation viewpoint for forensic botany as, generally speaking, these contact, physical materials are transferred or picked up at normal scenes. Hence, normal scene work is involved. Awareness to the environment is the key. In many cases, it will be within the scope of the crime scene investigator to record and take appropriate samples from the scene. The key is to ensure photographs record for not only the overview but also any necessary detail. The focus of the collection process should be twofold: first, what is necessary to identify the materials available for transfer, and second, how does the material present for transfer. Sampling needs to meet the basic requirements of being large enough (sufficient) and of being representative. There are some special requirements to be followed in dealing with gravesites. The key is to seek expert assistance if in doubt. It may be necessary to use academic or industry scientists. Here, the role of the crime scene investigator is critical, as many of these individuals cannot be expected

Figure 1 Examples of Cannabis cultivations. (a) Large single Cannabis plant, (b) example of outdoor cultivation, and (c) example of cultivation in a commercial green house.

to appreciate all facets of a forensic approach. In an effective relationship, there will be no sense of inappropriate role protection.

Plant materials should be carefully selected and packaged with the primary aim being the preservation of (what may be) the moist plant material.

With appropriate investment and proper application of forensic principles, forensic botany could play a larger role in the investigation of crime than is currently the case.

See also: **Chemistry/Trace/Drugs of Abuse**: Designer Drugs; **Toxicology**: Herbal Medicines and Phytopharmaceuticals – Contaminations; Herbal Psychoactive Substances.

Further Reading

Bock JJ and Norris DO (2012) *Handbook of Forensic Botany*. Berlin: Springer Science.

Cooper MR, Johnson AW, and Dauncey EA (2003) *Poisonous Plants and Fungi. An Illustrated Guide*, 2nd edn. London: HMSO.

Coyle HM (ed.) (2005) *Forensic Botany: Principles and Applications to Criminal Casework*. Boca Raton: CRC Press.

Hawksworth DR and Wiltshire PEJ (2011) Forensic mycology: The use of fungi in criminal investigations. *Forensic Science International* 206: 1–11.

Henry RJ (ed.) (2001) *Plant Genotyping. The DNA Fingerprinting of Plants*. New York: CABI.

Henry RJ (2008) *Plant Genotyping 11. SNP Technology*. Collingwood: CSIRO.

Howard C, Gilmore S, Robertson J, and Peakall R (2008) Developmental validation of a *Cannabis sativa* STR multiplex system for forensic analysis. *Journal of Forensic Sciences* 53: 1061–1067.

Howard C, Gilmore S, Robertson J, and Peakall R (2009) A Cannabis sativa STR genotype database for Australian seizures: Forensic applications and limitations. *Journal of Forensic Sciences* 54: 556–563.

Jackson BP and Snowdon DW (1968) *Powdered Vegetable Drugs. An Atlas of Microscopy for Use in the Identification and Authentication of Some Plant Materials Employed as Medicinal Agents*, 2nd edn. London: Churchill.

Mildenhall DB, Wiltshire PEJ, and Bryant VM (2006) Forensic palymology: Why do it and how it works. *Forensic Science International* 163: 163–172.

Moeller J, Winton AL, and Winton KCB (1916) *The Microscopy of Vegetable Foods: With Special Reference to the Detection of Adulteration and the Diagnosis of Mixtures*, 2nd edn. London: John Wiley & Sons (available as a reproduction from Nabu Public Domain Reprints).

Nelson LS, Shih RD, and Balick MJ (2007) *Handbook of Poisonous and Injurious Plants*, 2nd edn. New York: Springer.

Stormer BT and Sinol JP (eds.) (1999) *The Diatoms Applications for the Environmental and Earth Sciences*. Cambridge: Cambridge University Press.

Ward J, Gilmore S, Robertson J, and Peakall R (2009) A grass molecular identification system for forensic botany: A critical evaluation of the strengths and limitations. *Journal of Forensic Sciences* 54: 1254–1260.

Weising K, Nybom H, Wolff K, and Kahl G (2005) *DNA Fingerprinting in Plants. Principles, Methods, and Applications*, 2nd edn. Boca Raton: CRC Press.

Wiltshire PEJ (2009) Forensic ecology, botany, and palynology: Some aspects of their role in criminal investigation. In: Ritz K, Dawson R, and Miller D (eds.) *Criminal and Environmental Soil Forensics*, pp. 129–149. Dordrecht: Springer Science.

CHEMISTRY/TRACE/GLASS

Contents

Overview (Glass)

S Coulson, Institute of Environmental Science and Research Ltd (ESR), Auckland, New Zealand

Glossary

Annealing The removal of internal stresses in glass by controlled heating and cooling.
Devitrification To cause a glassy material to become crystalline and brittle.
Float glass Flat glass made using the float process, which involves floating molten glass on a bath of molten tin.
Glass A hard, brittle, and usually transparent product formed by the fusion of sand with soda or lime.
Laminated glass A type of safety glass made from a sheet of plastic (polyvinyl butyral) sandwiched between two sheets of flat glass.
Lehr A temperature-controlled kiln for annealing an object made of glass.
Likelihood ratio The probability of finding the evidence given the prosecution's hypothesis and the background information divided by the probability of finding the evidence given the defense's hypothesis and the background information.
Refractive index The ratio of the speed of light in a vacuum relative to the speed of light in a substance (e.g., glass). It can be measured using Snell's law, which takes the ratio of the sine of the angle of incidence to the sine of the angle of refraction of a light beam as it passes through a medium.
Tempered glass See toughened glass.
Toughened glass A type of safety glass. The glass has undergone a process after manufacture that involves cooling the surfaces of the glass more rapidly than the center to produce differential stress across the glass. Toughened glass forms small cubes of glass when broken. It is also called tempered glass.

Glass is defined as the inorganic product of fusion that has cooled to a rigid condition without crystallization. It is hard, brittle, and usually transparent and is used in a vast array of everyday products.

Glass fragments, as a form of trace evidence, can be encountered in a variety of crimes. These can involve 'break and enter' burglaries where a glass window or a glass pane in a door is broken to permit entry into a building; 'hit and run' cases where one or more vehicle windows are broken as a result of the impact of a vehicle with either a person or a second vehicle; or an assault where a glass object, such as a bottle, breaks while being used as a weapon. All these situations result in glass fragments being transferred from a breaking glass object to the clothes of a person (e.g., victim or offender) or to a recipient object (e.g., a vehicle or the road).

The forensic investigator's role in the examination of such crimes is to recognize the possibility that the transfer of glass fragments may have occurred during the event and to ensure that the relevant exhibits are seized and packaged appropriately.

The examination of glass objects for other types of evidence can also be undertaken. For example, fire investigators can examine the shape of broken windows to determine whether they were broken as a result of the heat of the fire or by an impact break prior to the fire.

The examination of ridges on the broken surfaces of glass can be used to determine which side the window was broken from. These ridges are called rib or hackle marks. Such an examination can be useful to determine whether a window was broken from the inside or outside of a building.

Collection and Packaging of Glass Exhibits

The glass fragments located at the scene should be collected and packaged to ensure their integrity. Packaging such as paper bags or plastic bottles is commonly used. Proper sealing of exhibits is vital to eliminate the possibility of contamination between items. Small glass fragments can pass through stapled seals or penetrate through layers of paper packaging. In

 Encyclopedia of Forensic Sciences, Second Edition http://dx.doi.org/10.1016/B978-0-12-382165-2.00103-3

practice, multiple layers of paper packaging combined with wide tape seals are sufficient to ensure the security of the exhibits.

Ideally, sampling of large broken glass objects, such as windows, must ensure that a representative sample is collected by removing pieces of glass from different areas of the broken glass object. Multiple pieces of glass need to be sampled to ensure that the true variation in analytical properties measured by the laboratory can be determined during testing.

Packaging of clothing and shoes should be carried out as soon as possible to minimize the loss of glass fragments from these items. Paper bags are routinely used for packaging these types of exhibits. Usually, different items of clothing from one person should be packaged separately to prevent transfer of glass between items during transport and storage.

Types of Glass

The types of glass submitted for forensic cases can generally be categorized as building glass, vehicle glass, and container glass (bottles and jars). Other types of glass such as glass fibers (insulation), domestic glass (tableware), automotive headlamps, and optical glass may also be encountered.

The most common type of glass is soda lime glass, which is manufactured by melting silica from sand (SiO_2), soda ash (Na_2CO_3), limestone (CaO), and varying other modifying components such as magnesium oxide, aluminum oxide, potassium oxide, and barium oxide (MgO, Al_2O_3, K_2O, and BaO). Cullet (recycled broken glass) can also be added. Building windows, automotive windows, and containers are commonly manufactured from soda lime glass.

Another commonly encountered type of glass is borosilicate glass, which contains boric oxide (B_2O_3) and silica. Borosilicate glass has excellent thermal shock resistance and is frequently encountered in headlamps and cookware.

Lead silicate glass contains lead oxide and silica and is used in a range of optical, crystal, and electrical glass products.

Glass Manufacture

The majority of glass products are produced in automated, large-scale plants where the manufacturing process usually follows five steps: (1) storage, weighing, and mixing of the raw materials; (2) melting of the raw materials, including refining and homogenizing; (3) forming the melt into the required shape; (4) annealing of glass; and (5) warehousing and/or secondary processing of the product.

The raw material specifications are designed to ensure that high-quality end products are produced. The raw materials are weighed and mixed thoroughly before being introduced to the furnace where the melting process occurs at temperatures in excess of 1500 °C. A continuous flow of molten glass is fed from the furnace to automatic glass-forming machines. Prior to being formed, the removal of gas bubbles (carbon dioxide and water) occurs during the refining stage as the molten glass passes through the furnace. Thermal, and sometimes mechanical, stirring of the molten glass facilitates the removal of gas bubbles and homogenizes the melt.

The molten glass is then slowly cooled, resulting in a gradual increase in viscosity that allows the molten glass to be formed into a range of products (flat glass, container, glass fiber). The speed at which the glass is cooled is crucial. Devitrification, which is the formation of crystals in the glass, can occur if the temperature of the molten glass is reduced too slowly. Once the glass is formed, the annealing stage slowly cools the product as it passes through kilns or continuous lehrs.

The manufacture of flat glass can be through either the float process or the rolled process.

The float glass process is the principal method for producing flat glass. It involves the homogenized glass passing on to a bath of molten tin in a float chamber. The glass forms a ribbon, which is drawn continuously along the tin bath. As the glass exits the float chamber, it is pulled by a series of rollers, the speed of which determines the thickness of the glass. After leaving the float chamber, the glass then passes through an annealing lehr where it is cooled. The glass is then cut and stored.

The rolling process involves passing the molten glass between two water-cooled rollers and is used to make patterned glass and wired glass.

Secondary processing of glass products such as toughening, coating, and coloring or decolorizing can also be carried out. Toughened glass (also called 'tempered glass') is glass that has undergone a toughening process after its manufacture. This process involves cooling the surfaces of the glass more rapidly than the center of the glass, producing differential stress across the glass object. Toughened glass is widely used in automotive windows because of its increased strength and ability to break safely into small cubes of glass.

Laminated glass is formed by placing a sheet of plastic (polyvinyl butyral) between two or more layers of flat glass. If a laminated window is broken, the sheet of plastic aids in keeping the broken glass bonded together. This feature of laminated glass makes it particularly useful for safety glass windows, such as automotive windscreens.

The modern manufacture of glass products is a highly automated international industry that produces uniform products on a large scale. However, minor variations in the properties of the glass products may still be present because of slight impurities or variations in the raw materials used. The final products can be shipped worldwide, meaning that any particular jurisdiction may contain both locally manufactured and imported products.

The Transfer and Persistence of Breaking Glass

When a glass object, such as a window or a bottle, is broken, minute fragments of glass can be transferred to the clothing of the breaker and any other person within close proximity. This transfer of glass is called 'backscatter' or 'backwards fragmentation.'

Numerous backscatter studies have shown that the main factors affecting the number of glass fragments transferred are the distance between the person and the breaking glass object, the manner in which the glass was broken, and the type and amount of glass that was broken. The principal finding of these studies shows that breaking of glass objects is highly variable, even under closely controlled laboratory conditions.

The majority of glass fragments transferred to the clothing of the breaker or bystander will be rapidly lost from the surfaces of the clothing; however, a small number of fragments can be retained for a number of hours. If any fragments become lodged inside pockets, cuffs, or turnups, or embedded in soles of shoes, then these fragments can be preserved for much longer periods.

The main factors that affect the persistence of glass fragments on clothing include the type of clothing worn, particularly the coarseness of the fabric and the construction of the garments, the length of time between when the glass object was broken and when the clothing was seized; the activity of the wearer, and whether the clothing was damp.

Secondary transfer refers to glass fragments being transferred from the primary recipient (e.g., the breaker) to a second person or object. Studies have shown that, while secondary transfer of glass fragments is possible, only a small percentage of the available fragments on the primary recipient are transferred to the receiving person or object.

Background Glass in the Population

While studies have shown that glass can be transferred and retained on the clothing of a person who has broken a glass object, it is also essential to understand how much glass is present on the clothing of people who have unknowingly had contact with a source of broken glass.

A number of studies have assessed the amount of glass on the clothing of members of the general population and of people suspected by the police of different crimes. Overall, these studies show that very little, if any, glass is found on the clothing from either of these two populations and, when a number of fragments are found, they are usually from multiple sources of glass.

Glass Analysis

The analysis of a forensic glass case involves three steps: (1) recovery of glass fragments from submitted items (e.g., clothing); (2) comparison of recovered glass fragments to the alleged source of broken glass (control sample); and (3) assessment of the evidential value of the results (**Figure 1**).

Glass evidence is usually submitted in the form of clothing, footwear, hair combings, and tools suspected of containing glass fragments. Recovery of glass fragments from these items is usually undertaken by shaking, brushing, or scraping the items and microscopically searching the resulting debris for fragments of glass. Items that may contain embedded fragments of glass, such as shoe soles or tools, can also be examined microscopically.

The only way that a conclusive association can be made between recovered and control glass samples is if a physical fit is found. This can occur in cases where larger pieces of glass are being compared: for example, pieces of a broken bottle. However, in the vast majority of cases, this is not possible because of the small size of the fragments available. This notwithstanding, modern analytical techniques are extremely sensitive and, depending on the circumstances of the case, very useful evidence can be obtained.

If relatively large pieces of glass are present in the recovered sample, then a number of macroscopic comparisons to the control sample can be undertaken. These comparisons include color, thickness, fluorescence characteristics, curvature, and any other surface features.

Small fragments of glass can then be compared using refractive index (RI) and elemental techniques.

RI has been the most commonly used technique for comparing fragments of glass in forensic laboratories. The RI of glass varies with its composition and the physical and thermal regimes of the manufacturing process and can be used to distinguish between glasses. However, with enhanced manufacturing quality controls, the range of RI for glass objects has diminished, resulting in RI having reduced discriminatory power.

If two fragments of glass have the same RI, then they may have come from the same source. However, there will be other glass objects that also share the same RI as the recovered fragments of glass. Databases are consulted to assess the commonness of RI for these recovered fragments.

Annealing can be used in conjunction with RI to determine whether small fragments of glass are from toughened or non-toughened sources of glass. The fragments are heated and cooled in a controlled manner to remove the internal stresses present in the fragment. The change in RI (ΔRI) can then be used to classify the source of the fragments.

Elemental analysis represents another approach to the discrimination of glass fragments. The composition of glass can vary as a result of (1) deliberate choice by the manufacturer, (2) variations in trace and minor components in the raw materials used, and (3) the interaction of the molten glass with the surfaces of the furnace during manufacture. Depending on the elemental technique employed, all, or some, of these compositional changes can be detected.

A variety of elemental techniques have been used for the analysis of glass fragments. Ideally, for forensic purposes, these techniques should be able to analyze multiple elements over a wide concentration range with accuracy and precision, able to analyze small fragments nondestructively, and economically realistic.

Elemental techniques capable of analyzing the major and minor elements in glass such as x-ray fluorescence spectrometry (XRF), micro-XRF, and energy dispersive x-ray spectroscopy (EDX) have historically been used to achieve greater discrimination than RI alone. While each technique has its own advantages and disadvantages, the emergence of inductively coupled plasma mass spectrometry (ICP-MS) has led to the ability to analyze trace elements in glass fragments, resulting in greater discrimination power. The main drawback of ICP-MS is the need to dissolve the glass fragments prior to analysis.

The addition of laser ablation (LA) permits solid samples to be directly analyzed by ICP-MS without the need to dissolve glass fragments, and therefore provides a simple, fast, and essentially nondestructive technique for the elemental analysis of glass. However, at present the cost of the LA-ICP-MS is prohibitive for many forensic laboratories.

Assessing the Evidential Value

In some instances, it may be desirable to determine the category of glass from which the recovered fragment came. In cases

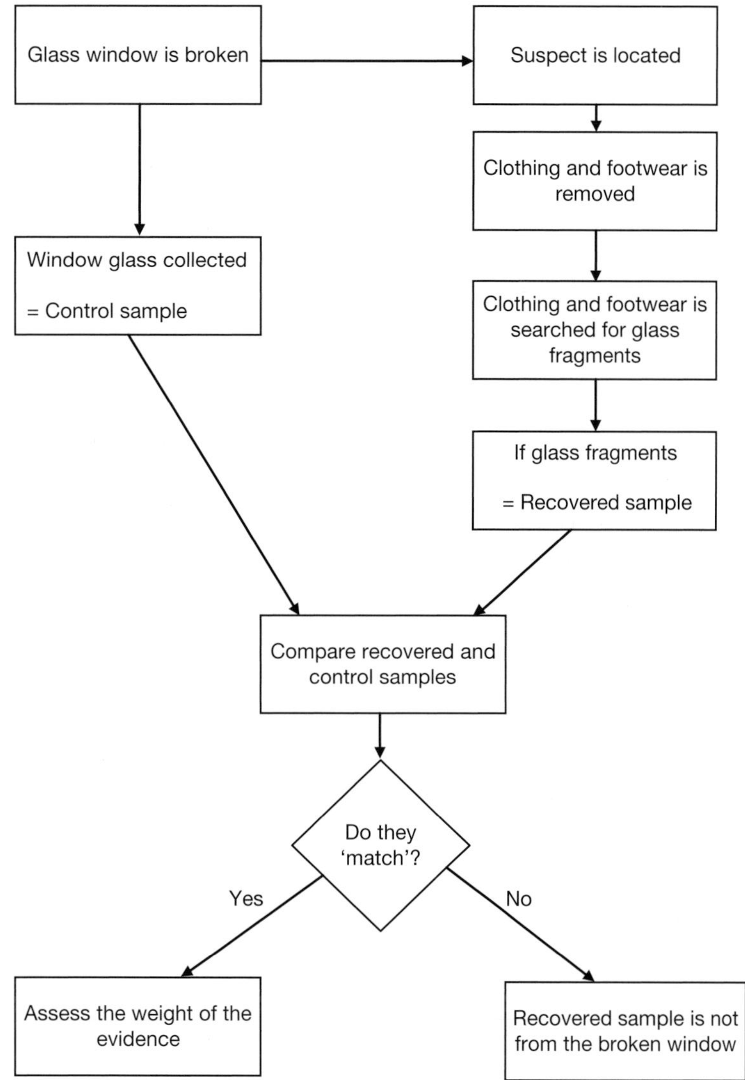

Figure 1 Flowchart depicting the steps in a forensic glass case.

Table 1 Approximate RI range for different types of glass

Glass type	*RI*
Borosilicate glass	1.46–1.49
Soda lime glass	1.51–1.53
Alumino-silicate glass	1.53–1.55
Lead silicate glass	>1.56
Silica	1.46

where the recovered sample contains large pieces of glass, this can be achieved from macroscopic observations. However, in general, the fragments are small and a combination of physical and elemental composition measurements is needed.

While RI is a useful discriminating tool, it allows only approximate classification into the basic chemical type (Table 1). As previously mentioned, glass fragments can also be classified as toughened or nontoughened by the measurement of RI before and after annealing.

Classification of glass fragments can usually be obtained by elemental analysis of the major and minor components. The range of components analyzed and the size of the database available to the laboratory will influence the ability to classify small fragments of glass.

Once the recovered and control glass samples have been analyzed, a comparison of the analytical results is required. Before these tests are applied, it is routine to assess whether the analytical results for the recovered fragments of glass indicate whether they have come from one or multiple sources of glass. A range of statistical tests can then be used to compare the analytical results (RI and/or elemental composition) to determine whether or not the recovered fragments could have come from the control glass.

If a 'matching' glass fragment is found, the final step is to assess the evidential value of the glass evidence. This assessment can be made in a subjective manner or by using a more formal approach, such as calculating a likelihood ratio (LR). The LR considers the probability of finding the evidence given the prosecutor's hypothesis (H_p) compared to the probability of finding the evidence given the defense's hypothesis (H_d).

There are many factors to be taken into account when assessing glass evidence. These include the following:

- Availability of physical fits
- The presence of original surfaces
- The number of glass items allegedly broken during the offense
- The number of glass fragments recovered from the suspect that match the controls
- The number of distinctly different sources of glass recovered from the suspect that do not match the controls
- The distribution of fragments of glass on the clothing, hair, and footwear
- The time interval between the alleged incident and the seizing of the items
- The commonness or frequency of the 'matching' recovered glass fragments in relation to a relevant database.

In summary, a number of factors need to be considered when interpreting the results of forensic glass cases. Nevertheless, glass evidence can be extremely useful in supporting or refuting allegations relating to the activity of breaking glass objects.

See also: **Chemistry/Trace/Glass**: Glass Analysis; Interpretation of Glass Evidence.

Further Reading

Almirall JR and Trejos T (2006) Advances in the forensic analysis of glass fragments with a focus on refractive index and elemental analysis. *Forensic Science Review* 18: 73–95.

Bottrell MC (2009) Forensic glass comparison: Background information used in data interpretation. *Forensic Science Communications* 11(2). Available at http://www.fbi.gov/about-us/lab/forensic-science-communications/fsc/oct2009/review/2009_04_review01.htm/.

Caddy B (ed.) (2001) Forensic Examination of Glass and Paint. *Analysis and Interpretation*. London and New York: Taylor & Francis Forensic Science Series.

Curran JM, Hicks TN, and Buckleton JS (2000) *Forensic Interpretation of Glass Evidence*. Boca Raton, Fl, London, New York, Washington DC: CRC Press.

Irwin M (2011) Transfer of glass fragments when bottles and drinking glasses are broken. *Science and Justice* 51: 16–18.

Koons RD, Buscaglia J, Bottrell M, and Miller ET (2002) Forensic glass comparisons. In: Saferstein R (ed.) *Forensic Science Handbook*, 2nd edn., pp. 161–214. Upper Saddle River, NJ: Prentice Hall.

Nelson DF and Revell BC (1967) Backward fragmentation from breaking glass. *Journal of the Forensic Science Society* 7: 58–61.

Pounds CA and Smalldon KW (1978) The distribution of glass fragments in front of a broken window and the transfer of fragments to individuals standing nearby. *Journal of the Forensic Science Society* 18: 197–203.

Trejos T, Castro W, and Almirall JR (2006) Elemental analysis of glass and paint materials by laser ablation inductively coupled plasma mass spectrometry (LA-ICP-MS) for forensic applications. NIJ Technical Report 2006. Available at http://www.ncjrs.gov/pdffiles1/nij/grants/232133.pdf.

Winstanley R and Rydeard C (1985) Concepts of annealing applied to small glass fragments. *Forensic Science International* 29: 1–10.

Glass Analysis

T Hicks, Institut de Police Scientifique and Formation Continue UNIL-EPFL, Lausanne-Dorigny, Switzerland

Glossary

Anisotropic Particles that are anisotropic have two refractive indexes, one for each light polarizing direction, respectively.
Annealing A process used in glass industry to remove thermal stress in glass products: the formed hot glass is gently cooled to enable cutting and processing of the glass.
ASTM American Society for Testing and Materials.
ENFSI European Network of Forensic Science Institutes.
ICP-AES Inductively coupled plasma atomic emission spectroscopy.
ICP-MS Inductively coupled plasma mass spectroscopy.
Reannealing In forensic science, reannealing refers to the process where the control and recovered glass are placed in a mini-furnace, heated to 590 °C and then slowly cooled to remove internal thermal stress. As toughened glass has more internal stress than nontoughened glass, this will reflect on its variation of refractive index.
SEM-EDX Scanning electron microscope with energy-dispersive x-ray analysis.
SWGMAT Scientific Working Group for Materials Analysis.
Toughened or tempered glass Glass that has gone through a heat (or chemical) treatment to improve its strength. This type of glass is also known as security glass, as it shatters into small-diced fragments avoiding therefore major injuries.
XRF x-Ray fluorescence.

Introduction

Glass is a material that can be valuable for investigation and evaluation. In investigation work, it can be used, for example, to help in the reconstruction of the facts (e.g., was the pane broken from the interior or the exterior?) or to search for the possible sources of the recovered glass (e.g., a type of vehicle). For evaluation purposes, a classic example would be an offense against property where the offender has broken a window and a person of interest arrested.

The choice of the techniques will depend on whether glass is to be used for investigation or evaluation. The case, the type of material recovered, and the results of previous examination (if any) will also play a role as to the choice of the methods. It therefore appears that although there are methods applied in routine, the exact choice of the examination sequence will be case dependent and ought to be devised when preassessing the case. Note that the remainder of this article will focus on glass used for evaluation.

Before presenting the techniques that are applied for the analysis of glass, although it may seem straightforward, it is useful to discuss why glass analysis is performed. The aim of the examination is to help the Court discriminate between two views, generally Defense's and Prosecution's. Example of hypotheses (or propositions) could be whether the person of interest is the person who broke the window as alleged by prosecution or if she/he has nothing to do with the incident as alleged by the defense. In the latter, the glass may be present as background or the presence of glass might be due to an alternative explanation, for example, the person of interest may work on a construction site and recently replaced a window or she/he may have broken a glass item at home. Depending on the alternative, one will need a technique that allows differentiating glass found as background from glass from windows or glass from different windows (the relevant population in the former alternative is windows from the construction site) and with the third alternative, we will need a technique that allows discriminating the control glass from tableware glasses such as those broken by the person of interest.

Therefore, depending on the alternative, the relevant population will change and so will the criteria that the techniques have to meet. This point is important because often very discriminating techniques will also be the very expensive and depending on the alternative, one might not need the most discriminative, thus the most expensive, technique.

It should be noted that although the analysed characteristics are an important factor when evaluating glass evidence, they are not the only one: the number, size, and emplacement of the fragments are equally important and should be evaluated in conjunction with intrinsic characteristics. The strategy that examiners will choose will therefore depend on a large number of factors and not only on the discriminating power of the techniques (see examples in **Table 1**).

In this article, first physical examinations that have been suggested for the comparison of recovered and control glass will be described, and then elemental analysis.

Physical Examination

Before examination, it is necessary first to recover the fragments and to determine if the particles are glass or some other material. A number of recovery methods have been reported: if the particles are sufficiently large (1 mm or greater), then they can be picked up with tweezers; if the particles are smaller and to be searched on a garment, then debris can be scrapped with a clean metal spatula over paper in order to collect the fragments; the garment can be shaken over a clean paper or a clean metal cone; the garment can be tapped (this allows one to know the geographical position of the fragments and also is the method of choice when both fibers and glass are relevant to

 http://dx.doi.org/10.1016/B978-0-12-382165-2.00104-5

Table 1 Example of factors influencing the choice of the techniques used for glass comparison

Example of factors influencing the choice of the techniques used for glass
Type of case (i.e., investigation/evaluation)
Propositions addressed by Prosecution and Defense
Discriminative power of the techniques for the relevant population
Size of the recovered fragments
Number and emplacement of the fragments (e.g., hair and shoe sole)
Destruction of the sample
Cost of the techniques and type of case
Possibility to store the analyzed characteristics in a database
Availability of the method

the case). For large areas, vacuuming has also been suggested. It should be noted that the noise induced by this method of collection will be higher than for other methods and is not often the technique of choice. It has been shown that when a person disrobes, fragments are lost: this suggests that the persons of interest should be asked to remove their garments over a clean sheet of paper in order to recover the fragments that fall while disrobing (the same applies to studies performed on the transfer and persistence of glass). Glass present in hair is usually recovered by combing.

Once the particles have been isolated, they can be observed under crossed polarized light conditions in order to determine if they are isotropic. Anisotropic particles such as quartz, other mineral crystals, or most other particles resembling glass (e.g., small fragment of clear plastic) will appear bright or colored at least in some orientations, and glass will remain dark. When measuring the refractive index, it will also be possible for the examiners to detect if they have picked up glass or quartz by its characteristic appearance in oil.

Physical examinations that can be performed on glass will depend on the size of the recovered fragments. We will begin with those that regard large fragments.

Examination Performed on Large Fragments

If the fragments are large and both surfaces are present, the examiner can compare the thickness of the recovered glass and the control glass (e.g., the broken window).

The color and UV fluorescence of large glass fragments, provided that the samples are of comparable size and thickness, can also be compared under a variety of lights or using a microspectrophotometer as it is done for the comparison of material such as paint, fibers, or inks (although unpublished results suggested limited discrimination). If performing such examinations, it is recommended that caseworkers are blind-tested in order for them to know their limitations, as the determination of color can be difficult. The main challenge of this examination is to evaluate the value of the results as the information on subjective color cannot be stored.

Sanger suggested the use of polarized light microscopy for the identification of toughened (or tempered) glass. The technique of polarized light microscopy is applicable to fragments larger than 20 mm^3, for smaller fragments laboratory re-annealing is the technique of choice.

When fragments are large, one can attempt a physical fit: although the chances of success are small, if the edges of the recovered and the control match or/and if the markings known as hackle marks are similar on both samples, then the evidence can provide extremely strongly support for the hypothesis that both fragments once formed a larger piece of glass.

Density comparisons

The density of glass (i.e., its mass per unit volume) will depend on its composition and thermal history. The same can be said about refractive index and these two physical characteristics are correlated. Authors have reported that the discrimination of the techniques is enhanced when both characteristics are used. However, if using elemental analysis, it has been suggested that the gain was minor. Because of this and the fact that the measurement of density requires large fragments for accurate measurements (2–3 mm in diameter), the examination is not commonly performed, and refractive index remains the property of choice.

If performing density measurements, fragments must be perfectly clean, have no inclusions or cracks, control and recovered have to be of approximate same size, and be either both from surfaces or both from bulk. Disadvantage of the technique is the time required for examination and the fact that recovered and control glass are sometimes placed in the same tube.

Several methods have been published in the literature and by working groups (e.g., SWGMAT or ENFSI): the densities of the recovered and control glass can be compared directly or both densities can be determined. Density can be performed at the same temperature or by varying the temperature. In order to assess the value of the examination, one needs to estimate the intra- and intervariation of this characteristic. Because there are not many recovered samples that are large enough for density measurement, it is difficult to have a good estimator for both of these (if the alternative hypothesis is that the glass is present as background). To be able to refer to databases, it would be necessary to determine the density of the fragments using a densitometer.

Examination Performed on Small Fragments (e.g., Less Than 1 mm)

The examination of the surface of the recovered fragments can be very useful in cases where the person is suspected of having broken a window. Indeed, breaking experiments have shown that a large number of fragments backscattered show an original surface. There are a few laboratories that look at surfaces: one can use the phenomenon of interference and/or fluorescence. Interference microscopy may help discriminate flat from curved glass objects (e.g., windows from containers), given that the fragments are larger than 0.4 mm^2 in size or if there are sets of fragments. UV fluorescence is useful as the surface of float glass that has been 'floating' on the bed of liquid tin exhibits UV visible fluorescence when excited at 254 nm. Casework-sized fragments can be observed using special equipment. Elemental analysis may also be used to detect the surface that was in contact with the molten tin.

Refractive index comparison

Refractive index comparison is the most common examination performed in casework: it provides a high degree of discrimination; the method can be performed on very small fragments, and is quick and relatively inexpensive. The European and North American scientific working groups specialized in forensic glass evidence have published guidelines on the techniques that allow the measurement of the refractive index of glass. When light passes through from one medium to the other, its velocity changes as well as its direction (i.e., it is refracted). The refractive index can either be described as the change of the wave's velocity in a vacuum to the wave's velocity in a transparent medium (e.g., glass) or the ratio of the sine of the incident angle to the sine of the angle of refraction (see eqn. [1]). The refractive index of a material will vary with wavelength and temperature: the standard wavelength is the sodium D line (589 nm) and the standard temperature 25 °C:

$$\mathrm{RI} = \frac{\sin \theta_I}{\sin \theta_R} \qquad \mathrm{RI} = \frac{V_{\mathrm{Vacum}}}{V_{\mathrm{Glass}}} \qquad [1]$$

In 1892, Friedrich Johann Karl Becke, an Austrian mineralogist, reported the observation of a bright line inside the edge of a mineral that had a refractive index different from its surroundings. By altering the RI of the medium with the addition of a miscible liquid with a different RI, it is possible to reach a point where this line is no longer visible, the refractive index of the two media being similar. With a refractometer, the RI of the oil can be measured and the RI of the glass is determined. This first method is time consuming and not very efficient. However, it is useful to remember that the Becke line will move to the medium with the highest RI when the distance from critical focus is increased.

Emmons double variation method consists in varying both the temperature and the wavelength of the light (three wavelengths are used: the sodium D line (589 nm), and the hydrogen C and F lines (656 nm and 486 nm)). This technique was accepted as an official method by the Association of Analytical Chemists (Method 973.65). Instrumentation includes a phase contrast microscope, a monochromator, and a controlled hot stage.

In the mid-1980s, Foster and Freeman in collaboration with forensic scientists developed a semiautomatic instrument that was called 'glass refractive index measurement' or GRIM. The glass fragment is immersed in silicon oil and observed using a phase contrast microscope at a fixed wavelength of about 589 nm (a narrow band filter is used). A hot stage allows the variation of the temperature of the microscope slide. Several studies have shown that the instrument is precise, accurate, and has long-term stability. It is a very popular instrument and, until recently, it was the only one on the market: now a few other companies offer similar equipment (e.g., Lucia Forensics, Craic Technologies).

The quality of the measurements can be monitored through the edge tracings and the edge counts (that depend on the contrast of the Becke line). Edge count ranges from 1 to 99, high scores indicating high contrast. The contrast of the Becke line will depend on the edge morphology of the fragment and the instrumentation. Debris contamination present on the recovered fragment will also influence the quality of measurements: large fragments will be cleaned, but smaller fragments (e.g., 200 μm in size) typically will not, as there would be a high risk of losing the fragment. Therefore, control fragments (that are larger and freshly broken) will typically show large edge counts and less variation than recovered fragments. An illustration from Newton and coworkers shows the aspect of a clean and a dirty fragment taken from patterned glass (**Figure 1**).

Although the GRIM manual suggests that fragments with edge count values below 10 should not be used or be repeated manually, Newton and collaborators showed that the limit was around 30 (the authors do not, however, suggest this value as a minimum edge count). Ultimately, it is the user's choice to reject or accept a measurement, as this will depend on different factors (e.g., the edge tracing, the Becke line aspect, the lamp, and the instrumentation). When edge counts are low, the mean of the refractive index of the glass remains stable, but the variance is larger. If one considers the added variance when comparing and assessing the glass evidence, then these measurements can still be used.

We have seen that the shape of the fragments, the presence of debris, the contrast of the Becke line, and the instrumentation will influence refractive index measurements to some degree. The intravariation of this physical characteristic also plays a major role, and studies have been performed in order to

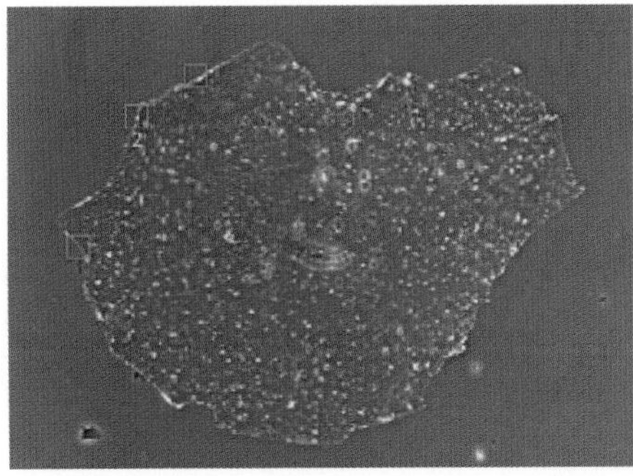

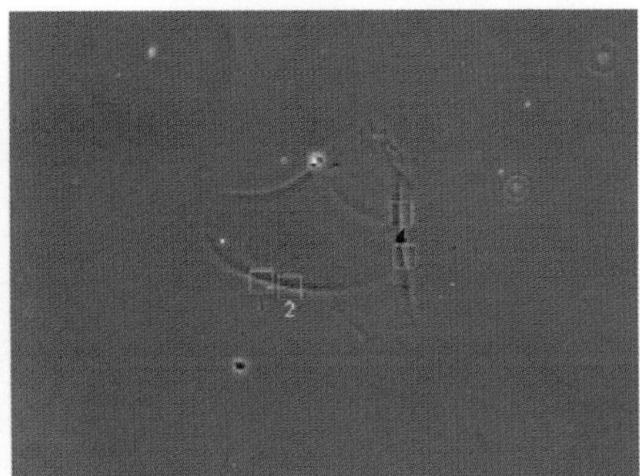

Figure 1 GRIM3 images of fragments of glass from the 'dirty' sample (left) and from the 'clean' sample (right). Reproduced from Newton AWN (2011) An investigation into the variability of the refractive index of glass: Part II – The effect of debris contamination. *Forensic Science International* 204: 182–185, with permission from Elsevier.

know how refractive index varies inside the same object. Bennett and coworkers concluded that their study "showed that although there was observable variation of refractive indices within a pane of [float] glass there was no evidence of systematic variation or patterning of refractive indices." The practical fallout is that in order to have a sample that is representative of the broken glass object, it is best to sample as much of the control window (or object) as feasible, taking samples from the frame and glass from the ground. It must be noted that the actual number of fragments to analyze will depend on the number of fragments recovered as shown by Curran et al.

Refractive index surface anomalies have also been reported in the literature and it has been described that float surfaces (enriched in SnO_2) have a different RI than the bulk of the glass. This can be observed when a fragment shows both a surface and a piece of the bulk: only parts of the fragment will then 'disappear' as they have different RI. For control fragments, it is possible to mark using different colors (e.g., red, green) both float and antifloat surfaces. One can then sample both surfaces and the bulk. Once cleaned, their refractive index will be measured.

Newton and collaborators showed that the RI of the float surface has on average a higher RI than the bulk and the antifloat surface an RI that is on average lower than the bulk. However, it does not seem that there are discrete RI surfaces. In addition, surface fragments are difficult to measure, and the use of surface fragment RI as a discrimination tool would be very difficult. Other types of glasses (container glass, tableware, nonfloat flat glass) also show surface anomalies. Again, this shows how important it is to have a representative sample (Figure 2).

Illustration of a float surface present on a glass fragment observed when measuring its RI from Newton and collaborators: the region on the left side is an original surface of float origin (higher RI); the remaining portion of the fragment is the bulk glass (lower RI).

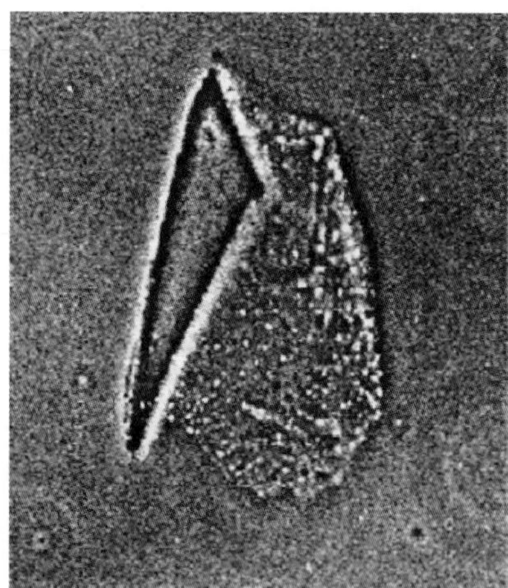

Figure 2 GRIM2® image of glass fragment. Reproduced from Newton AWN, Curran JM, Triggs CM, and Buckleton JS (2004) The consequences of potentially differing distributions of the refractive indices of glass fragments from control and recovered sources. *Forensic Science International* 140: 185–193, with permission from Elsevier.

Comparison of refractive index measurements

It is recommended to choose the number of control fragments according to the number of recovered fragments, to group the recovered fragments and compare them to the control using either a two-stage approach (first the data are compared using classical statistical tests such as the Welch test, then the results are assessed) or a continuous approach (results are assessed and compared in one stage). If several measurements are made on the same fragment, then only the mean of the measurements should be used. Once the RI of the recovered and control fragments has been determined, to assess the value of the characteristics, their frequency in the relevant population will be estimated.

Examination of tempered glass by reannealing

A useful examination of tempered glass has been described by Locke and collaborators: it consists in first measuring the refractive index of the glass, then reannealing the glass sample in the forensic laboratory (if particles are large enough, then the best is to divide the particle so that the examinations can be performed on the same fragment) according to a given procedure. The refractive index of the reannealed glass is then measured and the difference between both RIs noted (ΔRI). Large positive differences between the RI measurements after and before reannealing support the hypothesis that the glass is tempered (ΔRI are positive when the RI after reannealing is higher). ΔRI will depend on the annealing procedure used and cannot be generalized. Later studies in New Zealand confirm that laboratory reannealing is a valid means to classify glass as toughened or nontoughened. This classification may be useful when prosecution or defense suggests that the recovered glass is toughened glass.

Reannealing has also been suggested in order to reduce the internal variation of glass and, therefore, enable further discrimination. Results of studies on that topic differ, as some researchers report that the internal variation of nontempered glass is larger after reannealing and some smaller. It should be noted that the authors have used different reannealing procedures and different samples.

Refractive index measurements have shown to provide good discrimination in casework, but give, for example, limited information as to the class of the unknown. When this is of importance in the case at hand, one can use elemental analysis, as it will help achieve this task. It may also prove to be useful if one needs to differentiate glass that has the same end use.

Elemental Analysis

Depending on its purpose, glass will have different elemental composition. Different manufacturers will also have their own 'recipes'; methods of production and raw materials will vary in time. As glass composition varies depending on its end use and on its manufacture, elemental analysis of glass can serve two purposes:

(1) Classification according to its end use, that is to help evaluate if the recovered glass originated from a window or from a container, for example.

(2) Discrimination, that is to differentiate glass with the same end use, for example, glass from two different windows.

Classification will be based on the composition of major elements, whereas discrimination will rely on minor or trace elements.

A large number of techniques have been suggested for the analysis of glass as early as the 1970s and new applications of methods are regularly published. Recently, particle-induced x-ray emission has been suggested as an alternative method, as well as high-energy synchrotron radiation x-ray fluorescence spectrometry and laser-induced breakdown spectroscopy that has the advantage of being almost nondestructive. The choice of the method will depend on a number of criteria, the main one being – for evaluative work – given that the glass does not originate from the given control (e.g., a window), where does it originate from? Indeed, if the person of interest does not recall having broken glass, then we should look at techniques that enable us to differentiate glass from windows (one of the propositions is that the glass comes from the control, e.g., a window) from glass recovered as background on the item of interest (e.g., a jacket). However, if the alternative source is a container (i.e., the person remembers having recently broken a beer bottle), then a method allowing classification may be sufficient to help evaluate both propositions. If the alternative source is glass from a window, then we will need a method allowing discrimination among windows.

Other criteria important in the choice of the method of analysis will be cost, availability of the equipment, limit of detection, precision, accuracy, sample preparation; whether or not it is destructive, if it is adapted to small irregular fragments; whether it is a multielemental technique, possible applications of the method to other forensic evidence; and whether the data can be stored in a database in order to assess these results in casework (i.e., the frequency of the analyzed characteristics in the relevant population).

Methods that are currently used in casework and in research are x-ray and ICP techniques. Two well-documented x-ray methods suggested for the analysis of glass are SEM-EDX and μXRF. These techniques are considered nondestructive (although the fragments will often be embedded in a resin and polished to have more precise measurements) and rapid. They are less sensitive than ICP methods and are used for semi-quantitative analysis. They have been used for classification and discrimination. SEM-EDX is more sensitive to small atomic number elements, but XRF has better analytical capabilities for discriminating elements such as Mn, Sr, Zr, and Ba.

ICP methods have been extensively studied, again both for classification and discrimination purposes. Early publications on the analysis of glass using ICP-AES and ICP-MS began in the 1990s. A decade later, a project called NITE-CRIME (Natural Isotopes and Trace Elements in Criminalistics and Environmental Forensics) was initiated by the European Union (from 2001 to 2005) and allowed one to develop – among others – the use of laser ablation ICP-MS for the analysis of glass. Standard methods have been published by the NITE-CRIME group and other researchers. Glass fragments are either embedded or fixed on a small tray using double-sided transparent self-adhesive foil. Laser ablation has the great advantage of being faster, as it can be performed on a solid sample, whereas ICP-AES requires the dissolution of the glass fragments in hydrofluoric and hydrochloric acids. It is a sensitive and precise method that allows quantitative analysis. It has been compared to other available methods, and sampling strategy has been studied. From these studies, authors recommend to sample at least five different glass fragments of the known source and analyze the unknown at least by triplicates. When possible, authors avoid the tin side of float glasses as 'the interpretation of tin content should be addressed carefully.'

Interpretation of data, whatever the technique used, requires knowledge of the variation of the elements measured within and between relevant populations. Statistical approaches for classification and discrimination, as well as empirical approaches have been suggested, but this is still an area that would benefit from research. The two challenges that have been raised by Campbell and Curran are that a large number of elements, but a small number of fragments, are measured. The authors conclude: "Therein lies a far more complex and important problem than multivariate normality — that the number of variables exceeds the number of observations. This is a classical problem in statistics which is not limited to forensic applications."

Conclusion

In this article, the different methods of analysis applied to glass evidence have been presented. When choosing the technique, one of the key points is to know what is the relevant population of glass we wish to discriminate the unknown from. Generally, forensic scientists are asked to help with the issue of whether the person has broken a given window or has nothing to do with the incident. The methods of analysis should therefore help discriminate glass that originate from controls (e.g., windows) from glass recovered on clothing of persons having a similar lifestyle as the person arrested by the police. Where the glass is found and the quantity of glass recovered (i.e., the extrinsic characteristics) is of great importance, as it is an indicator of its relevance regarding the alleged activities. When assessing the value of glass evidence, these factors are of paramount importance. To be able to take them into account, forensic scientists need to help address activity level propositions and bring knowledge and expertise that otherwise would remain unavailable to the court.

There have been studies on the discriminative power of refractive index (and on the frequency of this characteristic) performed on glass fragments recovered on clothing of suspects. These studies show that refractive index is useful to differentiate glass recovered on clothing from glass originating from windows. Depending on the value of the extrinsic and intrinsic characteristics, the findings can help the judicial system. It is true that from an analytical point of view, elemental analysis may bring further discrimination. But, will elemental analysis be useful in that particular case? Will it be useful for casework, provided that an appropriate case strategy has been carried out? One can argue that when a large amount of glass (with a similar refractive index) is recovered on the surface of clothing, then – depending on the case – there might be no need for further analysis. In the last decade, there has been no published study on how useful is the elemental analysis in actual casework. What is needed is the most efficient technique that would allow discriminating glass from windows recovered on crime scenes from glass recovered on persons suspected of breaking windows (when indeed they have not broken the control window during the incident for which they were arrested). To test the efficiency of LA-ICP-MS, for example, we need to analyze glass recovered on suspects and not glass produced by the same plant. Monitoring how many times elemental analysis enables us to discriminate recovered glass in real cases would be very useful. A limited research on that aspect with μXRF (that is less discriminative than LA-ICP-MS) showed that the only extra discrimination in real cases was obtained when the fragments were recovered in pockets, and when, therefore, the recovered glass had low evidential value. This result supports the view that if appropriate sampling is done (if generally glass recovered in pockets has low evidential value, why analyze it?), then refractive index alone may be sufficient and one might not need to perform elemental analysis. A research testing the usefulness of promising techniques such as LA-ICP-MS or LIBS, taking into account the relevance of the recovered, as well as previous examinations using appropriate data comparisons would be very welcomed. However, in the end, the choice regarding the appropriate techniques to use will depend on the given case, on the value of the evidence, and on what the judicial system needs in that particular case.

See also: **Behavioral**: Interpretation; **Chemistry/Trace/Glass**: Interpretation of Glass Evidence; Overview (Glass); **Foundations**: Statistical Interpretation of Evidence: Bayesian Analysis; The Frequentist Approach to Forensic Evidence Interpretation.

Further Reading

Almirall JR and Trejos T (2006) Advances in the forensic analysis of glass fragments with a focus on refractive index and elemental analysis. *Forensic Science Review* 18: 73–96.

Bennett RL, Kim ND, Curran JM, Coulson SA, and Newton AWN (2003) Spatial variation of refractive index in a pane of float glass. *Science & Justice* 43: 71–76.

Berends-Montero S, Wiarda W, De Joode P, and Van Der Peijl G (2006) Forensic analysis of float glass using laser ablation inductively coupled plasma mass spectrometry (LA-ICP-MS): Validation of a method. *Journal of Analytical Atomic Spectrometry* 21: 1185–1193.

Buckleton JS, Walsh KAJ, and Evett IW (1991) Who is 'Random Man'? *Journal of the Forensic Science Society* 31: 463–468.

Buscaglia JA (1994) Elemental analysis of small glass fragments in forensic science. *Analytica Chimica Acta* 288: 17–24.

Curran JM, Hicks TN, and Buckleton JS (2000) *Forensic Interpretation of Glass Evidence*. Boca Raton, FL: CRC Press LLC.

Curran JM, Triggs CM, Almirall JR, Buckleton JS, and Walsh KAJ (1997) The interpretation of elemental composition measurements from forensic glass evidence: II. *Science & Justice* 37: 245–249.

Interpol publishes every three years a report on forensic material, see for example, http://www.interpol.int/Public/Forensic/IFSS/meeting16/Default.asp for proceedings.

Latkoczy C, Becker S, Dücking M, et al. (2005) Development and evaluation of a standard method for the quantitative determination of elements in float glass samples by LA-ICP-MS. *Journal of Forensic Sciences* 50: 1327–1341.

Locke J and Underhill M (1985) Automatic refractive index measurement of glass particles. *Forensic Science International* 27: 247–260.

Naes BE, Umpierrez S, Ryland S, Barnett C, and Almirall JR (2008) A comparison of laser ablation inductively coupled plasma mass spectrometry, micro X-ray fluorescence spectroscopy, and laser induced breakdown spectroscopy for the discrimination of automotive glass. *Spectrochimica Acta – Part B Atomic Spectroscopy* 63: 1145–1150.

Newton AWN (2011) An investigation into the variability of the refractive index of glass: Part II – The effect of debris contamination. *Forensic Science International* 204: 182–185.

Newton AWN and Buckleton JS (2008) An investigation into the relationship between edge counts and the variability of the refractive index of glass: Part I: Edge morphology. *Forensic Science International* 177: 24–31.

Newton AWN, Kitto L, and Buckleton JS (2005) A study of the performance and utility of annealing in forensic glass analysis. *Forensic Science International* 155: 119–125.

Rushton KP, Coulson SA, Newton AWN, and Curran JM (2011) The effect of annealing on the variation of glass refractive index. *Forensic Science International* 209(1–3): 102–107.

Saferstein R (2002) *Forensic Science Handbook*, 2nd edn. New Jersey: Prentice Hall.

Scientific Working Group for Materials Analysis (SWGMAT) (January 2005) Glass density determination, Forensic Science Communications (Online). Available: http://www.fbi.gov/about-us/lab/forensic-science-communications/fsc/jan2005/standards/2005standards8.htm/.

Relevant Websites

http://www.enfsi.eu – The European guidelines published by the European Network of Forensic Science Institutes (ENFSI).

http://www2.fbi.gov/hq – The North American guidelines.

Interpretation of Glass Evidence

S Coulson, Institute of Environmental Science and Research Ltd (ESR), Auckland, New Zealand

Glossary

Annealing Removal of internal stresses in glass by controlled heating and cooling.

Glass A hard, brittle, and usually transparent product formed by the fusion of sand with soda or lime.

Hypothesis testing Statistical tests used to make decisions about data comparisons. Examples of hypothesis tests include Hotelling's T^2 test, Student's t-test, and the Welch test.

Likelihood ratio The probability of finding the evidence, given the prosecution's hypothesis and the background information, divided by the probability of finding the evidence, given the defense's hypothesis and the background information.

Refractive index The ratio of the speed of light in a vacuum relative to the speed of light in a substance (e.g., glass). It can be measured using Snell's law which takes the ratio of the sine of the angle of incidence to the sine of the angle of refraction of a light beam as it passes through a medium.

Nomenclature

Alternative hypothesis (H_1) The hypothesis that there is a difference between the control and recovered means.

Defense's hypothesis (H_d) The assertion made by the defense. For glass cases, this could be that the suspect has no connection to the breaking crime.

Null hypothesis (H_0) The hypothesis that there is no difference between the control and recovered means.

Prosecution's hypothesis (H_p) The assertion made by the prosecution. For glass cases, this could be that the suspect broke the window.

Glass evidence is frequently encountered in a range of forensic cases that have involved the breaking of a glass object, such as a window in a burglary, a windscreen in a hit-and-run incident, or a bottle in an assault. The forensic analyst is tasked with comparing glass from the scene (control sample) to glass fragments recovered from either a suspect or a complainant (recovered sample).

A number of optical, physical, and chemical techniques are available for the comparison of glass fragments. This is the first question arising from the results of these analytical tests: Could the recovered glass fragments have come from the control glass object? This is followed by the second question: What is the evidential value of these results?

The majority of published work concerning the interpretation of glass evidence has focused on the scenario of finding glass on the clothing of a person accused of breaking a window. Other types of crimes where glass has been broken have been studied to a lesser extent. Therefore, this article focuses predominantly on the interpretation of glass evidence relating to crimes where a window has been broken.

Transfer of Glass Fragments

When a glass window is broken, approximately 30% of the broken glass will scatter backwards towards the breaker; this mechanism is called 'backscatter' or 'backward fragmentation.' The rest of the broken glass is dispersed in the direction of the breaking action. This backscattered glass can land on the breaker if he/she is within approximately 3 m of the breaking window. Furthermore, any other person, such as an accomplice, standing within 3 m of the breaking window, can also be showered with glass fragments from the breaking window.

A large number of factors affect the actual number of glass fragments that are transferred on to the breaker or the accomplice. These include the distance between the breaker and the window, the way the window was broken, the size of the window including the amount of glass that has been broken, the type of window glass, and the height of the window.

The most influential factor is the distance between the breaker and the window, with the number of transferred glass fragments decreasing with increasing distance.

Very few studies have looked at the transfer of glass fragments from other glass objects. One study on the transfer of glass from breaking bottles and drinking glasses showed that in all the instances, glass fragments were transferred to the upper clothing of the breaker.

In summary, there are a large number of factors that affect the amount of glass transferred in any particular situation and, even for experiments performed under closely controlled laboratory circumstances, the number of fragments transferred can vary considerably.

 http://dx.doi.org/10.1016/B978-0-12-382165-2.00105-7

Secondary or tertiary transfer can also be possible under certain circumstances. However, most experimental findings indicate that if secondary or tertiary transfer does occur, only a small number of fragments, at most, will be transferred.

Persistence of Glass Fragments on Clothing

A significant number of studies have examined the persistence of glass fragments on clothing. In general, these studies have shown that the majority of glass fragments that land on the clothing of a breaker will fall off his or her clothing within a few hours.

While time is a significant factor in determining the persistence of glass fragments on clothing, there are a number of additionally important factors to consider. These include the position of the glass fragments, the construction of the clothing worn, the activities of the breaker, and the damp or dry state of the clothing.

For example, glass fragments that land on the surfaces of the clothing will be lost much faster than any fragments that end up in cuffs, pockets, or shoe soles. In fact, fragments of glass that are transferred to pockets and shoe soles can be retained for long periods, such as weeks or months, or even until they are physically removed. This indicates that the surface of the clothing will contain only recently transferred glass fragments, whilst locations such as pockets and shoe soles may contain glass fragments from historic breaking events.

The type of fabric used to construct the clothing worn will also influence the persistence of glass fragments. In general, bulky garments, such as knitted sweaters, will retain glass fragments for longer periods than smooth fabrics, such as leather. Commonly submitted garments such as T-shirts, sweatshirts, and jeans have moderate retention characteristics.

The activities of the wearer of the clothing will also affect the persistence of any transferred glass fragments. Studies have shown that the more physically active the wearer, the faster the fragments of glass are lost from his/her clothing. For example, a person running will lose glass fragments at a faster rate from his/her clothing than a person walking, while the latter will lose fragments more quickly than a person sitting.

The weather conditions at the time the window is broken may also affect the persistence of glass on clothing since it has been suggested that damp or wet clothing can be more retentive to glass fragments than dry clothing.

Overall, the number of glass fragments transferred from a breaking window on to the clothing of the breaker can be variable and depends on a large number of factors. Most of the transferred fragments will be quickly lost from the clothing within a few hours. It is, therefore, ideal for the clothing of a person suspected of a breaking crime to be seized as quickly as possible. The likelihood of any glass fragments remaining on the clothing for subsequent recovery and analysis will be significantly affected by the time delay between when the window was broken and when the clothing was seized and packaged by the law enforcement personnel.

Presence of Background Glass

A large number of surveys have been undertaken to determine how much glass, if any, is present on the clothing of people unconnected with breaking glass crimes. Most members of the general public had no glass on the surfaces of their clothing and if any glass was found, it was usually only one fragment. A slightly larger number of fragments of glass were found in the pockets and shoe soles, but this was usually only a small number from different sources of glass.

Interpretation of Analytical Results

The forensic analyst is interested in determining whether the recovered glass fragments could have come from the same source as the control glass fragments. This is a question of discrimination. However, in some instances, classification of the source object from which a fragment has come may be needed.

The comparison and discrimination of glass samples can be performed using a number of different analytical methods. The choice of the analytical method used will frequently depend upon the number and size of the fragments recovered and the instrumentation available to the laboratory.

For large fragments of glass, classification of a potential source based on the shape, thickness, color, and original surfaces can be performed with relative ease. For smaller glass fragments, classification of a potential source usually requires knowledge of the elemental composition. Refractive index alone is frequently unable to identify the potential source of soda lime glass fragments.

Comparison of the color, thickness, and type of glass can be undertaken on relatively large fragments of recovered glass. However, the majority of fragments recovered from clothing are too small for such comparisons. Elemental composition and refractive index (including annealing) measurements are routinely carried out on small fragments of glass.

Grouping of Measurements

The first step in interpreting the analytical results is to determine the number of possible sources of glass present in the recovered glass sample. This grouping of fragments considers the expected within-source variation of a glass object and determines whether the analytical results for the recovered fragments are 'close enough' to be considered coming from one source of broken glass.

A number of grouping methods have been suggested, which include subjective grouping 'by eye,' agglomerative methods, and divisive methods.

Grouping by eye involves examining the data from the recovered glass fragments for clusters of fragments that show a variation less than or equal to that expected for a single source of glass. This subjective method is relatively easy to apply to cases where the fragments clearly form a small number of clusters, but can become complex where there are a large number of overlapping groups.

Agglomerative grouping employs a 'bottom-up' approach. Each fragment is compared to its closest neighbor and, if they are closer than the expected range for a glass object, they are grouped together. This process continues until the minimum number of groups of glass are identified, where the range of each group does not exceed the expected range for glass from one source. This method is straightforward for one-dimensional analytical results, such as refractive index, but can be complex for multivariate data, such as elemental composition.

The divisive approach to grouping utilizes a 'top-down' approach where the fragments are initially considered to have come from one group, and then consideration is given as to whether dividing the fragments into two groups would increase the homogeneity within each group.

Once the recovered fragments have been grouped, each group is compared to the control glass to determine whether the group of recovered glass could have come from the control glass sample. A number of different types of statistical tests have been used, including comparison of the range overlap, calculation of confidence intervals, hypothesis testing, and continuous methods.

Comparison of Refractive Indices

A hypothesis test, such as Student's *t*-test or Welch's modification to the *t*-test, is commonly used to compare the refractive index measurements for the recovered group of glass to the control glass.

Three assumptions are made by these tests:

1. The recovered and control measurements have the same mean and are representative of the distribution of the glass object (e.g., broken window). This also assumes that the standard deviations for the recovered and control measurements are estimates of the population standard deviation.
2. The RI measurements of glass fragments from a broken window have a normal distribution.
3. The recovered group of glass fragments is from one source of glass.

The first assumption can fail if either the recovered or control samples are not representative of the broken window. In particular, poor sampling of the control glass at the scene can have a detrimental effect on establishing the true mean and standard deviation for the broken glass object. The second assumption of normal distribution has been shown to be reasonable, and any deviation from a normal distribution would have only a limited effect on the performance of the test. The third assumption relies on the grouping stage being correctly performed.

Hypothesis testing involves proposing a null hypothesis (H_0) and an alternative hypothesis (H_1). For glass comparisons, the null hypothesis is that there is no difference between the recovered glass mean (μ_x) and the control glass mean (μ_y) H_0: $\mu_x-\mu_y=0$. The alternative hypothesis (H_1) is that there is a difference between the means; H_1: $\mu_x-\mu_y\neq 0$.

The Student's *t*-test determines the T statistic by calculating the difference between the means of the recovered and control groups of glass relevant to their pooled standard deviation (s_p).

$$T=\frac{(\bar{x}-\bar{y})}{s_p\sqrt{\frac{1}{n}+\frac{1}{m}}}$$

$$s_p^2=\frac{(n-1)s_x^2(m-1)s_y^2}{n+m-2} \qquad [1]$$

where recovered glass, $\bar{x}, s_x^2, n$; control glass, $\bar{y}, s_y^2, m$; degrees of freedom $=n+m-2$.

The T statistic is then compared to tables of critical values from a standard *t*-distribution at a particular significance level (e.g., 1%, 5%) and at a certain number of degrees of freedom. The significance level is also known as the Type I error rate, which is the theoretical probability of a false exclusion. As the Type I error rate is reduced, the Type II error rate (false inclusion) increases. Therefore, there is an inevitable compromise between setting the Type I and Type II error rates.

If the T statistic is less than the critical value, then the null hypothesis is true, and if the T statistic exceeds the critical value, then the null hypothesis is rejected.

Welch's modification makes the same assumptions as Student's *t*-test except that it allows for unequal variance for the recovered and control groups. The distribution of V is no longer exactly a *t*-distribution, but it can be approximated by a t_ψ distribution with ψ degrees of freedom.

$$V=\frac{(\bar{x}-\bar{y})}{\sqrt{\frac{s_x^2}{n}+\frac{s_y^2}{m}}}$$

$$\psi=\frac{\left(\frac{s_x^2}{n}+\frac{s_y^2}{m}\right)}{\left(\frac{s_x^4}{n^2(n-1)}+\frac{s_y^4}{m^2(m-1)}\right)} \qquad [2]$$

Both the Student's *t*-test and Welch's modification are discrete test methods and have a critical value at which the conclusion changes from 'match' to 'nonmatch.' This can be avoided by using a continuous approach that assigns a sequentially lower evidential value as the difference between the means of the recovered and control groups increases.

Comparison of Elemental Compositions

A number of different methods have been used to compare the elemental compositions of the recovered and control groups. Statistically straightforward methods such as determining whether the ranges of the different elements overlap or the use of matching criteria based on the 2σ or 3σ rule (mean ± 2 or ± 3 standard deviations) have been employed. One problem with these tests is that they fail to take into consideration any correlation between the elements measured.

One alternative method for the comparison of two multivariate samples is Hotelling's T^2 test. This test is the multivariate analog of the *t*-test and examines the standardized square distance between the two samples.

For the comparison of n recovered glass fragments to m control fragments, where $n+m>p+1$ and p is the number of elements analyzed, T^2 has a scaled *F*-distribution. The larger the value of T^2, the greater the evidence that the two samples have come from different populations.

$$T^2\sim\frac{(n+m-2)p}{(n+m-p-1)}F_{p,\,n+m-p-1} \qquad [3]$$

The formula for constructing Hotelling's T^2 statistic is

$$T^2=(\bar{x}-\bar{y})^{\mathrm{T}}\left[\left(\frac{1}{n}+\frac{1}{m}\right)S_{\text{pooled}}\right]^{-1}(\bar{x}-\bar{y})$$

where

$$S_{\text{pooled}} = \frac{(n-1)S_X + (m-1)S_Y}{n+m-2}$$

And the sample covariance matrices are

$$S_X = \frac{1}{n-1}\sum_{j=1}^{n}(x_j - \bar{x})(x_j - \bar{x})^T \quad \text{and}$$

$$S_Y = \frac{1}{m-1}\sum_{j=1}^{m}(y_j - \bar{y})(y_j - \bar{y})^T$$

The use of the *F*-distribution relies on two assumptions about the statistical distribution of the data:

1. Both samples have come from a multivariate normal distribution;
2. Both populations have the same covariance structure.

A number of researchers have questioned the validity of these two assumptions, and alternative permutation testing methods have been suggested that overcome these restrictions.

The Continuous Approach for the Comparison of Analytical Data

A significant disadvantage of hypothesis testing methods such as Student's *t*-test and Hotelling's T^2 test is their discrete conclusion options of either a 'match' or 'nonmatch.' A continuous approach to data comparisons provides a method of assigning greater value to a 'good match' compared to a 'poor match.' Therefore, for cases where the recovered and control glass fragments have 'closer' analytical results (i.e., a 'good match'), the evidential value is higher than for cases where there is more variation between the recovered and control glass fragments (a 'poor match').

Statistical methods are available for applying the continuous approach to both univariate data (e.g., RI) and multivariate data (e.g., elemental composition). However, in general, these techniques are considerably more complex than the hypothesis testing methods.

Evaluating the Evidential Value of the Results

Determining whether the recovered group of glass could have come from the control source of glass is only the first step in evaluating the glass evidence. The analyst now needs to consider the evidential value of these findings.

This evaluation can be carried out subjectively by assessing the factors relevant to a particular case or, in a more formalized framework, calculating, for example, the likelihood ratio (LR). Both approaches take into consideration a number of different factors, as described below.

1. The number of fragments of 'matching' glass found. In general, the more fragments found that 'match' the control glass, the stronger the evidential value.
2. The likelihood of multiple sources of broken glass. The finding of different recovered groups of glass that 'match' each of the sources of broken glass improves the evidential strength.
3. The position of the matching glass found on the suspect's clothing. For example, 'matching' glass found on the surfaces of a jacket will have higher evidential value than glass found embedded in a shoe sole.
4. An assessment of the transfer and persistence factors related to the case. This includes the time delay from when the window was broken to when the clothing was seized and the type of clothing submitted.
5. The frequency of the RI and/or elemental composition of the recovered group of glass. This is usually obtained from a database of glass samples and indicates the commonness of the recovered group of glass.
6. The number of groups of nonmatching glass found. The presence of groups of nonmatching glass increases the chance of a coincidental match to the control glass, and therefore decreases the evidential value.
7. The amount of glass expected to be found on a person who has not had any contact with broken glass. This type of information is taken from background surveys, sometimes called 'random man' surveys.

LR Approach

To evaluate the LR for a case, two competing hypotheses need to be considered.

$$\text{LR} = \frac{\Pr(E|H_p, I)}{\Pr(E|H_d, I)} \quad [4]$$

They can be phrased as follows:

What is the probability of finding the glass evidence (E) given that the prosecution's hypothesis (H_p) is true and given the background information (I)?

and

What is the probability of finding the glass evidence (E) given that the defense's hypothesis (H_d) is true and given the background information (I)?

The prosecution's hypothesis is usually clear-cut: for example, the suspect broke the window at the scene. However, the defense's hypothesis is usually unknown at the time of examining the case, and may be revealed only during the resulting court case. If the defense's hypothesis is unknown, then the opposite of the prosecution's hypothesis is normally considered, that is, that the suspect did not break the window and he/she has no connection to the case.

Two simple examples are presented to demonstrate how the LR approach can be applied to glass cases.

Case Example 1 Five fragments of glass are found on the jacket from the suspect. Four of these fragments match the broken window at the scene.

The numerator for the LR for this case is

$$\Pr\left(E\middle|H_p, I\right) = P_1 S_1 f_1 T_4 + 2P_2 S_1 f_1 S_4 f_2 T_0 \quad [5]$$

where P_x is the probability of finding x groups of glass on the suspect's clothing, S_x is the probability that a group of glass on the suspect's clothing will contain x number of fragments, f_x is the frequency of the group of glass, and T_x is the probability of x number of fragments being transferred from the breaking window on to the clothing and being retained long enough for their subsequent detection.

The P_x and S_x terms are taken from random man background surveys. The f_x term is taken from glass databases and will be influenced by the analytical techniques used. The T_x term relates to specific case factors, such as the time delay, the way the window was broken, and the type of clothing worn. Frequently, not all of these factors are known and therefore an estimate may be required. Statistical modeling programs are available to assist in predicting T_x values.

The first term in the numerator can be verbally explained as follows:

The probability of finding one group of glass (P_1) of size one fragment (S_1) with a certain frequency (f_1) on the clothing as background glass prior to the window being broken and then, when the suspect breaks the window, four fragments (T_4) being transferred and retained on the clothing.

Similarly, the second term in the numerator can be explained as follows:

The probability of finding two groups of glass (P_2) on the clothing: one group has one fragment (S_1) of a certain frequency (f_1) and the second group has four fragments (S_4) with a certain frequency (f_2), and then when the suspect breaks the window, no fragments of glass are transferred and retained (T_0).

The denominator for this case is

$$\Pr\left(E\middle|H_d, I\right) = 2P_2S_1f_1S_4f_2 \qquad [6]$$

The denominator assesses the probability of finding the glass evidence given that the suspect is unconnected with the breaking window. This term can be explained as follows:

The probability of finding two groups of glass (P_2) on the clothing: one group has one fragment (S_1) of a certain frequency (f_1) and the second group has four fragments (S_4) with a certain frequency (f_2).

Therefore, the LR for this case is

$$\mathrm{LR} = \frac{P_1T_4}{2P_2S_4f_2} + T_0 \qquad [7]$$

Using the values in **Table 1** for each of these terms, the LR is calculated as 252.

Case Example 2 Ten fragments of glass are found on the suspect's sweatshirt and jeans. Six of these fragments match one window broken at the scene, and the remaining four fragments of glass match the second window broken at the scene. The LR equation for this case is

$$\frac{\Pr(E|H_p, I)}{\Pr(E|H_d, I)} = \frac{P_0T_4T_6 + P_1S_4f_1T_0T_6 + P_1S_6f_2T_4T_0 + 2P_2S_4f_1S_6f_2T_0T_0}{2P_2S_4f_1S_6f_2}$$

$$\frac{\Pr(E|H_p, I)}{\Pr(E|H_d, I)} = \frac{P_0T_4T_6}{2P_2S_4f_1S_6f_2} + \frac{P_1T_0T_6}{2P_2S_6f_2} + \frac{P_1T_4T_0}{2P_2S_4f_1} + T_0^2 \qquad [8]$$

In this instance, there are four parts to the numerator to explain the following four alternative circumstances:

1. No glass was initially present on the clothing. The suspect then broke both windows, with four fragments transferred from window 1 and six fragments transferred from window 2.
2. One group of glass (four fragments) was already present on the clothing. The suspect broke window 1, but no glass fragments were transferred; then he/she broke window 2 with six fragments being transferred.
3. One group of glass (six fragments) was already present on the clothing. The suspect broke window 1, and four fragments of glass were transferred; then he or she broke window 2 with no fragments being transferred.
4. Both groups of glass were already present on the clothing. The suspect broke both windows with no glass fragments being transferred from either window.

Using the terms shown in **Table 2**, the LR for this case is 92 214. For this example, the first term in the LR is numerically the largest (92 178) and it is therefore standard practice to calculate only the first term.

Reporting of Glass Evidence

The results and conclusions from a glass case can be aimed at a number of different audiences, including law enforcement, lawyers, the judiciary, and the jury. Therefore, significant effort is spent in writing reports and statements to ensure that the evidence is appropriately presented.

The LR can be presented using either a numeric form, a verbal scale, or both. A verbal scale can be applied to different evidence types (e.g., DNA, paint, toolmarks) providing a

Table 1 Case example 1 – Suggested values for P_x, S_x, f_x, and T_x terms and LR

P_1	0.1276
P_2	0.0449
S_4	0.0236
f_2	0.02
T_4	0.0839
T_0	0.1450
LR	252

Table 2 Case example 2 – suggested values for P_x, S_x, f_x, and T_x terms and LR

P_0	0.6277
P_1	0.1506
P_2	0.0653
S_4	0.0236
S_6	0.0086
f_1	0.03
f_2	0.04
T_0	0.1100
T_4	0.0762
T_6	0.0614
LR	92214

Table 3 LR ratio scale with verbal equivalent phrases

LR	*Verbal equivalent scale*
1	Inconclusive
1–10	Slightly supports
10–100	Moderately supports
100–1000	Strongly supports
1000–1 000 000	Very strongly supports
1 000 000+	Extremely strongly supports

method to put the evidential value of these different findings in perspective. **Table 3** shows one version of a verbal scale.

For case example 1 above, the conclusion in a statement could read as follows:

'In my opinion, the evidence is approximately 250 times more likely if the jacket was close to the window when it broke than if the jacket had never been near this window.'

Or

'In my opinion, the glass evidence strongly supports the suggestion that the wearer of the jacket was close to the breaking window.'

Summary

Comparison of the analytical glass results is undertaken to determine whether the recovered and control glass fragments could have come from the same source. The evidential value of these findings is then assessed by considering a number of factors, including the transfer and persistence of glass, the amount of background glass present on a random person, and the frequency of the matching recovered glass. A number of statistical techniques can be used to assist with each of these steps.

See also: **Chemistry/Trace/Glass**: Glass Analysis; Overview (Glass).

Further Reading

Almirall JR and Trejos T (2006) Advances in the forensic analysis of glass fragments with a focus on refractive index and elemental analysis. *Forensic Science Review* 18: 73–95.

Bennett RL, Curran JM, Kim ND, Coulson SA, and Newton AWN (2003) Spatial variation of refractive index in a pane of float glass. *Science & Justice* 43: 71–76.

Bottrel MC (2009) Forensic glass comparison: Background information used in data interpretation. *Forensic Science Communications* 11(2) Available:http://www.fbi.gov/about-us/lab/forensic-science-communications/fsc/oct2009/review/2009_04_review01.htm/.

Caddy B (ed.) (2001) *Forensic Examination of Glass and Paint. Analysis and Interpretation*. London and New York: Taylor & Francis Forensic Science Series.

Campbell GP and Curran JM (2009) The interpretation of elemental composition measurements from forensic glass evidence III. *Science & Justice* 49: 2–7.

Coulson SA, Buckleton JSS, Gummer AB, and Triggs CM (2001) Glass on clothing and shoes of members of the general population and people suspected of breaking crimes. *Science & Justice* 41(1): 39–48.

Cox AR, Allen TJ, Barton S, Messam P, and Lambert JA (1996) *The Persistence of Glass Part 1: The Effects of Clothing Type and Activity*. Birmingham, England: Forensic Science Service.

Curran JM (2003) The statistical interpretation of forensic glass evidence. *International Statistical Review* 71(3): 497–520.

Curran JM, Hicks TN, and Buckleton JS (2000) *Forensic Interpretation of Glass Evidence*. Boca Raton, FL, London, New York, Washington DC: CRC Press.

Curran JM, Triggs CM, Almirall JR, Buckleton JS, and Walsh KAJ (1997a) The interpretation of elemental composition measurements from forensic glass evidence: I. *Science & Justice* 37: 241–244.

Curran JM, Triggs CM, Almirall JR, Buckleton JS, and Walsh KAJ (1997b) The interpretation of elemental composition measurements from forensic glass evidence: II. *Science & Justice* 37: 245–249.

Curran JM, Triggs CM, Buckleton JS, and Coulson SA (1998) Combining a continuous Bayesian approach with grouping information. *Forensic Science International* 91: 181–196.

Garvin EJ and Koons RD (2011) Evaluation of match criteria used for the comparison of refractive index of glass fragments. *Journal of Forensic Sciences* 56: 491–500.

Hicks T, Vanina R, and Margot P (1996) Transfer and persistence of glass fragments on garments. *Science & Justice* 36: 101–107.

Irwin M (2011) Transfer of glass fragments when bottles and drinking glasses are broken. *Science & Justice* 51: 16–18.

McIntee E, Viglino E, Kumor S, Rinke C, Ni L, and Sigman ME (2010) Non-parametric permutation test for the discrimination of float glass samples based on LIBS spectra. *Journal of Chemometrics* 24: 312–319.

Nelson DF and Revell BC (1967) Backward fragmentation from breaking glass. *Journal of the Forensic Science Society* 7: 58–61.

Pounds CA and Smalldon KW (1978) The distribution of glass fragments in front of a broken window and the transfer of fragments to individuals standing nearby. *Journal of the Forensic Science Review* 18: 197–203.

CHEMISTRY/TRACE/MISCELLANEOUS UNKNOWNS

The Forensic Analysis of Chemical Unknowns

VJ Desiderio, United States Postal Inspection Service Forensic Laboratory Services, Dulles, VA, USA

Glossary

DNA A common acronym for deoxyribonucleic acid, the polymeric biomolecule responsible for genetic inheritance.

Ignitable liquids Liquids that are capable of flaming combustion upon the addition of sufficient amounts of heat. Examples of such liquids include gasoline, kerosene, ethanol, and isopropanol, to name just a few.

Personal protective equipment (PPE) Equipment such as safety glasses, goggles, face shields, gloves, chemical-resistant suits, and so on that are worn or used to protect individuals from the dangerous effects of materials that they are handling or exposed to.

Universal precautions Measures taken to ensure safety under the assumption that any unknown materials or situations present the most dangerous scenario possible.

Introduction

The typical forensic laboratory is equipped to handle a wide array of evidence. For the most part, specific sections of any given laboratory are designed to handle the analysis of a specific subdiscipline of evidence. Examples of this model include the fact that the Drug Section analyzes samples suspected of containing illicit controlled and dangerous substances that are illegally sold for the purpose of consumption, and the DNA laboratory that examines suspected biological materials with the goal of identifying a possible contributor.

Chemical unknowns are materials that may be submitted to a laboratory for which there is no defined section that is designed to handle such evidence. They are materials, as their name would suggest, that are of unknown origin and composition. It is the job of the laboratory to attempt to identify these materials. This, of course, is no simple task.

In comparison to DNA (one molecule) and drugs (a large but somewhat well-defined set of molecules and their precursors), chemical unknowns can be any molecule made by either man or nature. As such, the analysis and identification of chemical unknowns presents a major challenge to the forensic laboratory.

Owing to the diverse analytical capabilities that many trace evidence sections possess, this is typically where such cases are submitted in most laboratories. Trace evidence sections are usually equipped with a broad range of instrumentation, and the staff members of such sections often contain knowledge of a broad range of materials. Considering what might be termed routine trace evidence classifications such as paint, glass, and fibers, even the specialist that contains expertise in one such area is required to possess knowledge of all the materials that are used to manufacture and treat such items. In addition to a broad knowledge of the raw materials involved, such a specialist would also possess the skills and instrumental prowess that are necessary to analyze and identify the various organic and inorganic compounds that might be found as a part of such 'routine' samples.

Common Submissions

Chemical unknowns may be submitted to the laboratory for a variety of reasons. Some common reasons for submission include: (1) outright identification of a suspicious material, (2) analysis of an item to determine if any tampering may have occurred, or (3) comparison of an unknown material found on or in the possession of a suspect to a similar material recovered from a crime scene.

Of the first type of submission discussed above, the most common request often involves the identification of white powders. After the anthrax scare in the United States during the fall of 2002, white powder examinations took on a new significance. Very often, the powders in question are benign materials such as talcum powder, starch, sugar, and so on. However, until someone takes the time to figure out exactly what it is, one should never underestimate the deleterious potential of an unknown powder.

In addition to white powders, unknown liquids are often submitted with the goal of identification. For some odd reason, some nefarious individuals seem to enjoy throwing dangerous liquids either at or on other people. Most often, in cases where actual harm was intended, these liquids turn out to be strong mineral acids or bleach. Other commonly encountered liquids may include ignitable liquids such as gasoline or kerosene.

Considering the second type of submission mentioned above, people are often accused of adding something to other people's foodstuffs. Typical situations include drinks or food that either look, smell, or taste funny. In actual cases of tampering with dangerous substances, the intended victim often

 http://dx.doi.org/10.1016/B978-0-12-382165-2.00119-7

realizes that something is wrong before ingesting the tampered item. In a worst-case scenario, the victim may have ingested some of the questionable material and either became sick or, worse yet, died as a result.

In the last type of submission discussed above, an investigator may discover some foreign material at the scene of a crime. The material in question may be recovered from the body of a victim or the scene at large. If a suspect is found, they may be in possession of a similar material or some of the material from the scene may have transferred to their clothing or possessions. Comparison of these materials may provide a link between the suspect and the scene in question.

It should be noted that these are just three common scenarios that may result in the submission of chemical unknowns to the laboratory. As with any other type of forensic evidence, the possible scenarios where any object in our environments might become an important piece of physical evidence are virtually limitless.

Safety Considerations and Presumptive Testing

As the name blatantly implies, chemical unknowns can contain any of a wide array of materials of either natural or man-made origin. The list of available chemicals and mixtures thereof is endless with many of these materials being dangerous to life in some form or another. Couple this inherent potential danger with the fact that they are usually being submitted because of questioned malfeasance, and the potential for a dangerous situation is amply multiplied.

The fact that the level of danger associated with such submissions is often unknown should lead those who are charged with handling, transporting, and analyzing such materials toward the use of universal precautions. That is to say that all chemical unknowns should be treated as though they are extremely dangerous and handled as such. Proper personal protective equipment should be used at all times, and it is recommended that these types of samples be handled in a fume hood and/or isolated areas whenever feasible.

It is often the case that some form of screening has been performed before submission to the laboratory. This screening may have been performed by a scientist, a highly trained HAZMAT unit, or someone who has little to no knowledge about the proper handling of the materials in question. Unfortunately, the level of expertise of those performing this screening is not always known. Taking this into consideration, any preliminary identifications that are made in the field should be viewed with a skeptical eye and the materials treated with the same level of caution as if they were of completely unknown origin. In the experience of the author, it has not been uncommon for something that was screened in the field to be preliminarily identified as something relatively benign when in fact it was a dangerous material.

As mentioned below, odor is a discriminating characteristic that can be used to great advantage. It should be noted at this point that 'observing' odors should be approached with due caution. By no means should an analyst ever put their face up to a sample and inhale vapors from an unknown compound. The general rule with odors should be to note anything obvious and leave the rest to your instruments.

Contextual Information

Although some may view the possession of background information as a potential bias, it is critical to obtain contextual information about the sample when it is received. In certain forensic circumstances, the possession of such information may be unnecessary and could potentially lead to a biased result; however, when facing the dangers associated with materials of unknown composition and attempting to narrow down the pool of potential compounds or products, it is critical to have such information.

Information obtained from the scene and/or the examination of a victim in the form of statements or medical reports can be used to help cautiously guide the forensic scientist. The presence of a strong odor, lachrymation due to exposure, causation of nausea and/or vomiting, causation of burns on exposure, or extreme flammability are all specific indicators of what may be present. These indicators can not only help to narrow down the list of possible compounds that might be involved but also help to avoid exposure situations in the laboratory.

Analytical Approach

The analytical methods that are employed will be highly dependent on the state of the material that is submitted for analysis. Chemical unknowns can be submitted to the laboratory as solids; liquids; gases; and homogeneous mixtures including solid–solid mixtures, solid–liquid solutions, liquid–liquid solutions, gas–liquid solutions, and heterogeneous mixtures including solid–solid mixtures, particulates in liquids, and slurries. The materials contained within can be natural or man-made, organic, inorganic, or mixtures thereof. In order to have any chance at identifying general unknowns, analytical protocols should be developed which take all such possibilities into consideration (Figure 1).

The best approach is one that can narrow down the possibilities as efficiently as possible. To this end, one should use general methods that are capable of providing large amounts of information in short amounts of time at the beginning of the scheme and progress toward more specific methods as the possibilities are narrowed.

The first thing one should consider is the state of the material in question. Is it a solid, a liquid, a slurry, or a gas? Depending on the state, one can then branch off into protocols that are designed to extract the most information out of the material in question given its state.

Solids

Solid unknowns can consist of a variety of different types. They can be organic, inorganic, crystalline, amorphous, they may contain color, they may be single component, or can be complex mixtures.

The first step with any unknown examination (after reviewing any and all information submitted with the case) is a visual examination. At this point, the general characteristics of the material in question should be noted. Are there any obvious

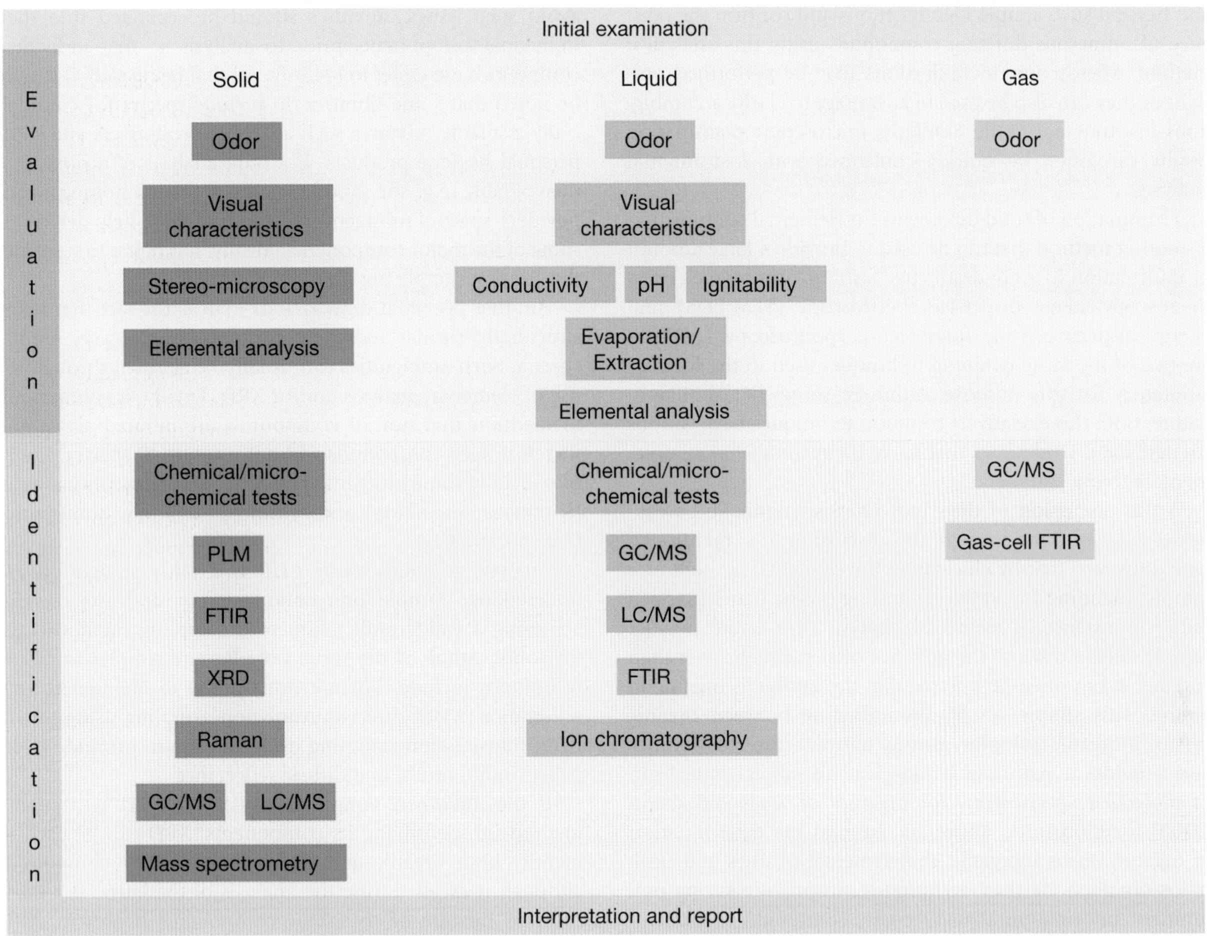

Figure 1 Chemical unknown abbreviated analysis matrix: Note – This matrix is intended for use as a general guide and includes the more common analytical methods that are used in most forensic laboratories. Additional methods are available that can be used based on availability.

features, is the material colored or tinted, does it look homogeneous, does it look familiar? At this point, although not a visual observation, obvious odors should be noted as well.

After documenting these general characteristics, a closer inspection of the material should be made using a stereomicroscope. The importance of this step cannot be stressed enough. This seemingly simple analysis can provide more information than any subsequent methods. Bulk materials look very different when viewed under a stereomicroscope. Observations as to the homogeneity of the material, the morphology of the particles contained therein (e.g., crystalline versus amorphous), and any other microscopic features can be noted. Some basic, yet important, information about the physical characteristics of the components being viewed can also be obtained at this point. A simple example along this line of inquiry would include probing individual particles with forceps or a needle to determine if the particle is hard, brittle, soft, or elastomeric.

During a thorough stereomicroscopic examination, it is often possible to make preliminary identifications of common materials based solely on their morphological characteristics. If crystalline, the morphology of the crystals can be noted. In some instances, the crystal morphology can be used as a presumptive identification. Examples might include the presumptive identification of table salt (NaCl) by the presence of clear cubic crystals and/or common sugar (sucrose) by the presence of clear rhombohedral crystals. This examination can easily be extended to include some basic microchemistry. To this end, various reagents may be used under the stereomicroscope to determine the chemical characteristics of the sample and any individual components. If a mixture is present, separation can be performed at this stage as well. By scanning the sample and separating particles, sufficient amounts of pure analyte may be obtained to perform confirmatory tests. This may be a tedious way of performing a separation, but it is certainly effective and context and particle morphology will be maintained.

In the hands of a skilled examiner, polarized light microscopy (PLM) is a very powerful, nondestructive analytical technique. It is a logical extension of the stereomicroscopic examination and can be used to great effect to complement any previously obtained information. A simple example of this would be the confirmation of sodium chloride by viewing the previously mentioned cubic crystals under crossed polars. If the crystals are isotropic, it is highly likely that the sample contains NaCl. This thought can be confirmed at this point with a simple refractive index measurement using suitable immersion oils. A skilled microscopist can often go above and beyond such simple identifications and confirm the presence of numerous different compounds using this analytical method. Microscopic identifications may be performed outright or they can also be used to advantage to clarify an ambiguous instrumental result. Similarly, microscopic examination results can often be quickly confirmed with instrumental analysis.

Examination of solid unknowns for elemental composition is another method that can be used to provide a large amount of information in a nondestructive fashion. Scanning electron microscopy-energy dispersive spectroscopy (SEM-EDS) and energy dispersive X-ray fluorescence spectroscopy (EDXRF) are two of the more common techniques used in the forensic laboratory for this purpose. Although somewhat similar in nature, both these relatively common techniques have various strengths and weaknesses that make them somewhat complementary to one another.

A full discussion of their individual strengths and weaknesses is beyond the scope of this discussion. It is mentioned here, however, that by elucidating the elemental content of a sample, planning for additional testing can be better mapped out. For instance, if elemental analysis of a white powder sample fails to disclose the presence of elements heavier than sodium, it can often be inferred that the sample is organic in nature. This simple act of discriminating between organic versus inorganic samples greatly narrows the possibilities and provides a path which may lead to either some form of molecular spectroscopy for organics or X-ray diffraction (XRD) for inorganics. Above and beyond the determination of organic versus inorganic, the elemental profiles and peak ratios obtained via these techniques can provide strong preliminary information that a certain compound is present. For example, if thin-window SEM-EDS is employed and carbon, oxygen, and calcium are detected and the oxygen to carbon ratio is approximately 3:1, it is a good bet that calcium carbonate is present.

Additional elemental analysis techniques that may be used include atomic absorption spectroscopy, atomic emission spectroscopy, inductively coupled plasma atomic emission spectroscopy (ICP-AES), inductively coupled plasma mass spectrometry (ICP-MS), and laser-induced breakdown spectroscopy (LIBS).

Fourier transform infrared spectroscopy (FTIR) is an important part of any analytical protocol. It can be used to characterize and/or to identify a large number of both organic and inorganic compounds. It is a relatively simple technique that can be used in a nondestructive manner to obtain a large amount of structural information. In the hands of a skilled spectroscopist, identifications can typically be made by a thorough analysis of the data. For the rest of us, numerous high-quality libraries exist to assist with identifications. As powerful a technique as FTIR is, it does have a few drawbacks. One major drawback to using FTIR for identifications of solid unknowns is that the sample being analyzed should ideally be fairly pure. Complex mixtures can produce complex spectra with various overlapping peaks that obfuscate the spectral interpretation process. Additionally, if a bulk sample is analyzed without homogenization of the sample, any replicate spectra that are obtained may differ significantly as different components of the mixture may be in the beam path at different times. To avoid such issues, mixtures should be separated into their individual components prior to analysis so that individual compounds are easier to identify. All that being said, it should be noted that some libraries do include spectra for commercially available mixtures such as carpet deodorizers and some personal hygiene products. If a bulk analysis of a mixture is unavoidable (e.g., the sample is a finely ground homogeneous powder), spectral subtractions could be used to help determine some of the major components. Ideally, it is better to start with the cleanest sample possible.

Another potential drawback of FTIR is the fact that many structurally similar inorganic compounds give very similar spectra. Such ambiguities can usually be clarified through the use of elemental analysis and/or XRD. Finally, it is important to mention that not all compounds are infrared active and therefore such compounds will not produce IR spectra. Examples include some inorganic salts (e.g., KBr, hence its use as an IR transparent matrix) and symmetric diatomic compounds (e.g., N_2 and Cl_2).

Analysis of solids using FTIR is a fairly straightforward undertaking. Sample preparation is a critical step toward achieving a valid result. Numerous sampling methods exist for solids. Some of the more popular and simpler sampling techniques include, but are not limited to attenuated total reflectance (ATR), direct transmission sampling using micro-FTIR, transmission sampling using potassium bromide (KBr) pellets, nujol mulls, and diffuse reflectance.

If the unknown sample is crystalline, XRD is a superb method for identifying its components. XRD can be used to identify both organic and inorganic crystalline compounds although it excels during the analysis of the latter. If a fairly complex mixture of crystalline components is present, XRD can often be used to identify each compound.

Both gas and liquid chromatography can be used to separate components of complex organic mixtures. This may require specific extractions or headspace analysis depending upon the type of sample encountered and the compounds that one is looking for. When combined with a mass spectrometer, these separation techniques can be used to provide an enormous amount of information about a sample.

Mass spectrometry on its own in its various forms may also be used to great effect. In addition to the typical forms of mass spectrometers routinely coupled to chromatographic systems such as quadrupole and ion trap mass analyzers, time of flight instruments can be of use as well. Time of flight instruments, when coupled to a soft ionization source can provide information on the complexity of a mixture and possibly provide tentative compound identifications based on the masses and isotope patterns that are observed. These instruments can also be used to analyze fairly large compounds especially when matrix-assisted laser desorption ionization (MALDI) techniques are employed.

Liquids

Unknown liquids may very well be the most challenging samples that are encountered in the forensic laboratory. This is especially true for product tampering situations where it is thought that a dangerous compound has been added to a complex matrix such as someone's soft drink. Although important with just about any forensic examination, it is imperative that proper controls be analyzed in conjunction with unknown liquid sample. This is especially true for product-tampering cases. If a specific brand of beverage has been submitted with the thought that something was added, an additional unopened/unadulterated sample of the same brand beverage should be submitted for parallel analysis.

As with solid unknowns, visual and microscopic examinations are a critical part of the analytical protocol for liquids. During the initial examination such features as the color and heterogeneity/homogeneity of the liquid should be noted. At this early stage, it may be possible to determine that something was in fact added to the liquid in question. If the color is off, particulates are observed either suspended or settled at the bottom, or multiple phases are observed, one would know right away that additional analyses should be pursued. If particulates are observed or a slurry is present, the sample can be filtered, the solid fraction can then be dried and analyzed as a solid unknown and the liquid analyzed according to the suggestions presented below.

After the initial visual examination of the questioned liquid, any aqueous fraction(s) should be tested for pH and conductivity. If an extreme pH is observed, it is very likely that a strong acid or base is present. Confirmation of either can be accomplished using a combination of various techniques including but not limited to elemental analysis (e.g., EDXRF at atmospheric pressure), gas-cell FTIR, ATR-FTIR, various chemical tests, and analysis of residual salts via PLM, FTIR, and/or XRD after neutralization.

If the liquid is strongly ionic, the presence of an inorganic solution would be indicated. Such solutions could be screened for elemental composition using EDXRF at atmospheric pressure and/or other solution-based atomic spectroscopy techniques (e.g., ICP-AES/MS).

If an organic fraction is observed or suspected, a simple flame test can be used to great advantage. This can be carried out by dipping a swab into the liquid, taking the swab to a location remote from the sample, and bringing a flame to the swab. If the sample on the swab readily ignites, an ignitable liquid is indicated and the sample should be analyzed according to standard liquid sample fire debris protocols.

In order to determine if a solid–liquid solution is present, a small aliquot of any original or filtered liquids could be evaporated on a clean glass slide. If a residue is observed, a solution is indicated and the residue can also be analyzed using the suggestions for solid samples as described above. If only a small amount of residue is recovered and sufficient sample is present, additional drops of the liquid can be evaporated off in the same location to concentrate the solid fraction.

While these preliminary examinations are being performed, any apparent odors should be noted. Again, one should take caution at this step to note only those odors which are obvious. Deliberately 'sniffing' a sample is ill advised and extremely dangerous. If an obvious odor is noted, however, this can be a very important piece of information.

Both gas and liquid chromatography are very useful for the analysis of liquid unknowns, especially when coupled to a mass spectrometer. At the very least, it should be possible to determine if a mixture is present. In an ideal situation, all components that are present can be identified. It should be noted that care should be exercised when analyzing unknown liquids using these techniques. If the samples are not prepared correctly, costly damage to the instrumentation used can result. Some possible clean-up procedures that may prevent such damage include liquid–liquid extractions using a suitable solvent, solid-phase extractions, and headspace sampling (either direct sampling or adsorption techniques). If an organic drug or poison is suspected to be present, it would be wise to consult with a drug chemist or toxicologist in order to determine the best course of action for separating any such compounds from the liquid.

If a relatively pure liquid is present, liquid cell or ATR-FTIR can be used. Along these lines, if a gas–liquid solution is thought to be present, a small amount of the liquid can be placed in a gas cell and light vacuum applied to pull any gaseous compounds into the vapor phase for analysis.

Gases

Although unknown gases are rarely encountered, such submissions are certainly not unheard of. One of the most common submissions along this line is the questionable gas cylinder that may have been found in someone's possession.

Such submissions present some perils of their own. Gases are often contained in pressurized vessels, which require specialized handling. In order to obtain samples from such vessels, proper pressure regulators must be used. If the laboratory does not have the correct regulator on hand, no analysis should be attempted without consulting an entity that is familiar with the specific fitting that is encountered. The vessels that are submitted may or may not be labeled. In the event that a vessel is labeled, and such a label may assist in your determination, it should in no way be relied upon. The cylinder may be labeled to contain something relatively benign when in fact; it has been refilled with something dangerous. With such dangers in mind, these containers should be handled with extreme care.

One of the best techniques available for analyzing gaseous unknowns is the use of a gas cell in an FTIR spectrometer. A word of caution here, as mentioned above, this technique is only reliable for asymmetric compounds. It is of no use for single-element diatomic gases such as hydrogen, chlorine, or fluorine which all have specific dangers yet are entirely undetectable using FTIR.

Gas chromatography is another valuable method for the analysis of unknown gases. For this purpose, concentrated gas samples can be injected and analyzed directly. Mass-spectrometric detection under such conditions would be the ideal way to identify any gaseous compounds that are present.

Interpretation of Results

As mentioned in the introduction above, general unknowns can consist of literally hundreds of thousands of pure compounds, mixtures, or manufactured products making it look like the analysis of these materials is an impossible task. In reality though, the situation is not so dire in that most materials that are encountered are relatively common. This is due to the fact that it is relatively difficult to obtain any chemical compound except for the most common types in the bulk amounts that are submitted.

Although the primary goal of these investigations is the identification of any and all compounds that are present, this is not always practical. Some mixtures that are encountered may present extraordinary complexity. This can be true of many manufactured products that may contain complex chemistries, dilute amounts of additives, and possibly proprietary compounds. If a full identification cannot be made, the best one can usually do is identify some of the components and attempt to narrow down the pool of possible products. Sometimes, enough of the material can be characterized to guide the interpretation in a more specific direction and a class of product can be named.

Unfortunately, there are situations where any semblance of an identification simply cannot be made. This may be due to limitations in instrumentation that is available, limitations in knowledge, or due to the nature of the material itself (e.g., highly complex mixture). If the scientist is stuck and has exhausted all possible avenues for information in-house, they should by all means reach out to others. It is often the case that some other colleague has encountered the same or a similar problem that you are facing. Various means for communication exist to facilitate exchange of information with other people in the field. Professional society meetings/webpages and on-line discussion groups are just a few examples of where such information can be obtained.

This leads to the point that a full identification may not be necessary in all situations. In cases where samples are submitted to the laboratory with the thought that a specific product was used to either damage property or cause harm, the analyst should either obtain or request potential comparison samples. If any suspect materials are obtained, they should be compared to the questioned material. If both the questioned and known samples are examined and analyzed in the exact same way using a thorough analytical protocol and all data are observed to correspond, a class identification can be effectively be made. If any significant differences are observed, the known source can be ruled out.

See also: **Chemistry/Trace/Fire Investigation:** Analysis of Fire Debris; Interpretation of Fire Debris Analysis; **Chemistry/Trace/Glass:** Glass Analysis; Interpretation of Glass Evidence; **Chemistry/Trace/Paint and Coating:** Architectural Paint; Automotive Paint; Forensic Paint Analysis; Interpretation of Paint Evidence; **Chemistry/Trace/Trace Evidence:** Microchemistry; **Foundations:** Interpretation/The Comparative Method; **Management/Quality in Forensic Science:** Health and Safety; **Methods:** Analytical Light Microscopy; Chromatography: Basic Principles; Field-Deployable Devices; Gas Chromatography; Gas Chromatography–Mass Spectrometry; Liquid Chromatography–Mass Spectrometry; Mass Spectrometry; Microscopy (Electron); Presumptive Chemical Tests; Spectroscopic Techniques; Spectroscopy: Basic Principles.

Further Reading

Bowen A (2010) Article identification of unknowns. *Journal of the American Society of Trace Evidence Examiners* 1: 73–100.
Chamot EM and Mason CW (1989) *Handbook of Chemical Microscopy: Chemical Methods and Inorganic Qualitative Analysis*, 2nd edn. Chicago: McCrone Research Institute.
Feigl F (1958) *Spot Tests in Inorganic Analysis*, 5th edn. NY: Elsevier Publishing Company.
Feigl F (1966) *Spot Tests in Organic Analysis*, 7th edn. NY: Elsevier Publishing Company.
Goldstein J, Newbury DE, Joy DC, and Lyman CE (2003) *Scanning Electron Microscopy and X-ray Microanalysis*, 3rd edn. NY: Springer.
Grob RL and Barry EF (eds.) (2004) *Modern Practice of Gas Chromatography*, 4th edn. NJ: John Wiley & Sons, Inc.
Houghton R (2008) *Emergency Characterization of Unknown Materials*. Boca Raton, FL: CRC Press.
Humecki H (ed.) (1995) *Practical Guide to Infrared Microspectroscopy*, 2nd edn. NY: Marcel Dekker, Inc.
Jenkins R (1999) *X-ray Fluorescence Spectrometry*, 2nd edn. NY: Wiley-Interscience.
Jenkins R and Snyder RL (1996) *Introduction to X-ray Powder Diffractometry*. NY: Wiley-Interscience.
McLafferty FW and Turecek F (1993) *Interpretation of Mass Spectra*, 4th edn. CA: University Science Books.
Pavia DL, Lampman GM, and Kriz GS (2001) *Introduction to Spectroscopy*, 3rd edn. NY: Brooks/Cole.
Smith B (1999) *Infrared Spectral Interpretation: A Systematic Approach*. NY: CRC Press.

Relevant Websites

http://riodb01.ibase.aist.go.jp – AIST Spectral Database for Organic Compounds.
http://webbook.nist.gov – NIST Chemistry WebBook.
http://householdproducts.nlm.nih.gov/ – US Department of Health Household Product Database.

CHEMISTRY/TRACE/PAINT AND COATING

Contents

Overview

L (Brun-Conti) Bender, National Laboratory Center, Ammendale, MD, USA

Published by Elsevier Ltd.

Glossary

Coating A generic term for paint, lacquer, enamel, or other liquid or liquefiable material that is converted to a solid, protective, or decorative film or a combination of these types of films after application.

Paint Commonly known as a pigmented coating.

Pigments Particles that impart color, opacity, effect (sparkle or sheen), bulk (filler and extender pigments), and/or desirable physical properties to paint. Pigment particles are suspended in place in the final dry film by the resin.

Polymerization A reaction where many small molecules unite to form a large or more complex molecule with a higher molecular weight and usually with different physical and chemical properties.

Resin or binder Any polymer that is dissolved in or suspended in a solvent that can be converted into a self-sustaining film.

Solvent Low-viscosity volatile liquids used in coatings allowing the polymer, pigments, and other components to remain in solution until the paint is ready to be applied to a substrate.

Paints and coatings have been used for thousands of years. The earliest evidence of paint was found in cave paintings from the Paleolithic period (~40 000 years ago). The 'paint' used for these consisted of sap from plants such as dandelions, tulips, and milkweed. Colorants of these coatings were made from blood, berries, and colored soils. It is even said that Noah's ark was painted with pitch, a high-solid water-resistant coating.

Basically, paints, or coatings, are a resin or binder that may or may not contain a solvent or pigment. Powder coatings do not include solvents, but just resin and pigments. Clear finishes contain a resin and a solvent, but no pigment. The list of painted objects is endless and includes items such as automobiles and other vehicles, interior and exterior surfaces of buildings, furniture, tools, fabrics, engine parts, roofs, works of art, and road surfaces, to name just a few. Each substrate will have different requirements regarding the durability, gloss, color, and chemical and/or mechanical resistance. There are two primary reasons why substrates are painted: for protection and for decoration.

Paint as Protection

The Resin or Binder System – The Cornerstone of Paint

The resin portion of the paint system is the part that holds everything together and imparts most of the physical characteristics, as well as the curing mechanism and the durability qualities, to the final coating. The curing mechanism is the way the wet paint or powder particle becomes a solid, continuous film. This can be done through polymerization or evaporation.

Evaporation is the simplest way for a dry film to form. It occurs when the solvent evaporates and the resin and pigments (if present) are left behind. This type of film can be made into a solution simply by the reintroduction of the solvent. Films formed by evaporation are called 'nonconvertible films' because of the fact that the resin does not 'convert' to a polymerized coating. Essentially, the resin remains the same in the wet or dry film.

Polymerization mechanisms are used to form covalent bonds in the resin, resulting in a film that is cross-linked and,

 http://dx.doi.org/10.1016/B978-0-12-382165-2.00106-9

therefore, not easily put back into solution. Oxidation polymerization involves the conversion of double bonds into free radicals, which are then available to form covalent bonds. Oxidation polymerization is at work in varnishes and alkyd coatings. Addition polymerization, sometimes referred to as 'coagulation,' occurs when a free radical is used to initiate and propagate polymerization without the creation of by products. Latex and nonaqueous dispersions (NADs) form films using this method. Condensation polymers form by products such as water, carbon dioxide, or hydrogen gas when the resin polymerizes. Urethane and epoxy films, as well as amino resins, when cross-linked with acrylic, alkyd, polyester, and epoxy resins, are condensation polymers.

When a hard film is formed by polymerization upon drying, it is considered a 'convertible' film. As opposed to the 'nonconvertible' film formed during evaporation, when a 'convertible' film is dried, the resin is cross-linked through oxidation and is 'converted' irreversibly into a hardened film. When a hard film is polymerized upon the application of heat, it is considered a 'thermoset' film. If the hard film can be softened by the addition of heat, it is considered to be a 'thermoplastic' film.

Resins can also be defined by how they are put into solution, or if they are in a solution at all. 'Solvent-borne' coatings refer to coatings in which the resin, pigments, and any other components are made fluid using a solvent other than water. Solvents, which are discussed later in this article, are used not only to put the solid portions of the paint into a liquid for ease of application but also to impart certain qualities to the drying film so that the coating does not dry too slowly or too quickly.

In 'waterborne' coatings, some or all of the solvent is water. Waterborne polymers, for the most part, are initially synthesized in a solvent and then finished using water. Usually, there is a small amount of a cosolvent, which is miscible in water present in waterborne coatings to help maintain the stability of the paint.

Emulsion coatings, also known as 'latex' coatings, are paints in which the resin is in the form of particles, usually about 0.1–0.5 μm in size, that are dispersed in an immiscible liquid. The film forms when the particles come together to coalesce, usually through an addition polymerization, while the immiscible liquid evaporates. In latex paints, the immiscible liquid is water. When the immiscible liquid is a solvent, then the coating is referred to as a NAD. NADs were used in the automotive industry for a number of years.

Finally, there is a type of coating that involves no liquid portion at all: powder coatings. Powder coatings usually consist of epoxy, polyester, or acrylic resin systems. Powder coatings can be cured by heat, by exposure to ultraviolet (UV) radiation, or by exposing the powder-coated item to a reactive vapor. All curing techniques are dependent upon the formulation of the resin system of the powder.

Resin types

The following are the resin types commonly found in coatings. It should be noted that this is not an exhaustive list.

Acrylic: Acrylic resins are made from monomers of acrylic and methacrylic acid esters. Acrylic polymers may be made of only acrylic monomers, or they may be modified with other materials such as alkyds and urethanes. Acrylic monomers may be modified with various functional groups that add qualities such as flexibility, durability, and chemical resistance to the final film.

Amino: Amino resins are formed by the polymerization of urea or melamine with formaldehyde. These resins can be blended with alkyd, polyester, acrylic, and epoxy resins to form a durable, cross-linked film upon baking, air-drying at room temperature, or with the aid of a catalyst.

Alkyd: Alkyd resins are formed by the condensation polymerization of a polyol and a dibasic acid, and are usually modified with the fatty acid from oils or the oils themselves. Alkyds can be modified with other substances, such as acrylic, urethane, silicone, and vinyl compounds, to obtain the desired properties in the final film.

Epoxy: Epoxy resins are usually made from epichlorohydrin and bisphenol A. All epoxy coatings contain a three-membered oxygen-containing ring called an 'oxirane,' or 'epoxide' group. Epoxies may be blended with acrylic resins, drying oil fatty acids, and amino resins, to name a few.

Polyester: Polyester resins are formed by combining a polyol with a polybasic acid. The difference between these and alkyd resins is the absence of the modifying oil common in alkyds. The film properties of polyesters are dependent upon the types of dibasic acid used (aliphatic for softer films, aromatic for harder films) and the extent of the polymerization with styrene.

Urethane: Urethane resins are based on isocyanate monomers reacted with other monomers, usually polyols, to form a urethane linkage. Urethane resins have active isocyanate groups that react with available hydroxyl groups on other monomers/polymers such as acrylics, alkyds, and vinyl resins, which have an active proton available to form a cross-linked film.

Vinyl: Vinyl resins are based on the vinyl chloride monomer that is frequently polymerized with monomers such as vinyl acetate. Vinyl resins are usually found in latex architectural coatings in the form of latex paint.

Solvents

Solvents do not provide the coating with any 'protection' qualities per se. However, the solvent is an important component of the paint, permitting ease of application to the surface or substrate it is designed to protect. With the exception of powder coatings, solvents are present in all other coatings. The current trend in the coatings industry is to use as little solvent as possible. Water is an exception to this, as the evaporation of water is not seen as harmful to the environment. One of the purposes of a solvent is to solubilize the resin and to adjust the viscosity of the paint. However, in some paint systems, emulsions and latex paints in particular, the solvent is a carrier for the resin particles and is used mostly as a diluent for ease of application.

The solvent, also referred to as a 'thinner' or 'reducer,' will also affect the appearance of the final film. The ability of the paint to remain on a vertical surface without dripping or 'tearing' is accomplished by using a faster evaporating solvent. Conversely, the ability of the paint to remain on a horizontal surface long enough to form a glossy film, and not dry too quickly to form a puckered or 'orange-peeled' appearance, is achieved by making use of a slower evaporating solvent. Paint chemists may use a number of different solvents in a formulation to achieve the aforementioned qualities of the wet paint. Solvents are also used to adjust paint for the environmental conditions in which the paint is to be used. The solvent package for an automotive paint which will be applied in a plant that is cool and dry may be very different than the solvent package for the same paint that is to be sprayed in a plant in a humid area of the country.

As stated previously, environmental concerns are causing a trend in the paint industry to use less solvent. Measuring the volatile organic components (VOCs) of paint is done by weighing a sample of paint before and after drying. The difference is the %VOC. Water is not considered a VOC. The %VOC is regulated by the Environmental Protection Agency (in the United States).

Solvents used in varying degrees in the paint industry are classified into the following groups: hydrocarbons, terpenes, oxygenated solvents, furans, nitroparaffins, and chlorinated solvents. Solvents are chosen for their solvency, volatility, odor, and toxicity. The solvency of a solvent is related to its ability to dissolve the film-forming resin into solution. Volatility is related to the rate of evaporation of a solvent. The odor of a solvent is critical for interior trade sales products since homeowners or office workers do not want a lingering 'solvent smell' from a newly applied coating. Odor has less of an impact in an industrial setting. Certain solvents, such as most chlorinated solvents and benzene, are considered toxic, and therefore are rarely used in coatings. Coating chemists endeavor to use as little solvent as possible when formulating paint.

Terpene solvents are obtained from pine trees and consist of mixtures of unsaturated cyclic compounds containing 10 carbon and 16 hydrogen atoms. They are currently used in limited amounts because of both their strong odor and the availability of solvents with better solvency. Hydrocarbon solvents consist of only carbon and hydrogen and come primarily from the petroleum industry. Classifications include aliphatics (consisting of normal paraffins and isoparaffins), naphthenes (cycloparaffins), aromatics, and olefins. Oxygenated solvents are those that contain not only carbon and hydrogen but also oxygen. The four types widely used in the coatings industry are alcohols, esters, ketones, and glycol ethers. Glycol ether is especially important because it is found to be a good substitute for aromatic hydrocarbons and is miscible in water, making it a vital solvent for the movement toward more environmentally friendly paints. Furans, nitroparaffins, and chlorinated solvents are used in limited amounts and in specialized situations.

Additives

Additives and additive packages are introduced into a coating to enhance the performance of the paint. Additive packages can be seen as treatment for issues encountered in the wet paint, or as treatment for environmental issues encountered in the dry film. While the paint is still in a liquid form, problems such as foaming, skinning, and sagging of the paint film can occur. Silicone products can be added to the liquid paint to act as antifoaming and defoaming agents (one prevents foam, the other breaks up the foam bubbles). Clays can be used to prevent the paint from sagging on a vertical surface. Because alkyd-based paints dry through oxidation, a skin will commonly form on the surface of the paint while it is in an opened container and exposed to atmospheric oxygen. Adding oximes to the alkyd paints can prevent skin formation.

Some additives are designed to improve the durability of the dried paint film. Coatings that are exposed to UV radiation from sunlight may contain UV absorbers and hindered amine light stabilizers (HALS) to prevent UV degradation. UV absorbers absorb the UV radiation and safely dissipate the energy, and HALS are designed to scavenge free radicals that are formed when a coating is exposed to UV radiation.

Biocides, algaecides, and fungicides are additives that benefit both the wet and dry films. Paints contain materials that are susceptible to microbial attacks. If the bacteria and/or yeasts begin to attack the coating in the can, the production of the resulting gases may cause lid-popping, can-bulging, offensive odors, or application problems. In the dried film, biocides, algaecides, and fungicides prevent mold, mildew, fungus, and algae growth.

Application

The most common form of application of paint is using a brush or roller. Paint may also be applied using a mitten or cloth. If specialized effects are desired, sponges, feathers, or other pattern-making application tools can also be used.

Spraying the paint onto the surface can be done in a number of ways. Spray paints in cans are commonly found in home-improvement stores. Industrial paint-spraying of an item is accomplished using various techniques and equipment. The air spray gun propels the paint in a stream of air. The airless spray gun produces a pressure that propels the paint onto a surface. An electrostatic spray method can be used in which the item to be coated is electrically grounded and the paint is given a negative charge. Therefore, the paint is attracted to the intended item.

Electrodeposition essentially 'electroplates' the item with paint. The part is dipped into a tank and a current is passed. The part, acting as either the cathode or anode, will receive a uniform coating of paint on all conductive areas. The thickness is determined by the electrical potential.

Powder coatings can be applied in many ways. Powder coatings may be applied by immersing the part in a fluidized bed of the powder. The powder may or may not be electrostatically charged. After the powder is applied to the part, the paint is cured. Another method of applying the powder to a part is the spraying of the electrostatically charged powder onto the part. In this method of coating, the powder that is not deposited onto the part is reclaimed and reused.

Paint as Decoration

Color has an effect on a person's mood, emotions, and behavior. A pleasing color in an office may increase morale, a change of color in packaging may cause an increase in sales, and the color of a kitchen or restaurant may increase or decrease the appetite. The color red can be seen as passionate or full of rage. Green is a sacred color to Muslims. The color blue is considered an appetite suppressant, and persons on a diet are encouraged to eat from blue plates. And some prison cells are painted pink because it is found that pink helps suppress anger, aggression, and anxiety in prisoners.

Color plays a large part in the marketing of products. Associations such as the Color Marketing Group meet and discuss trends in color. Formed in 1962, this international nonprofit organization comprises representatives from various industries in which color is an important part of the product, such as home interiors/exteriors, transportation, architectural/ building, communications/graphics, fashion, action/ recreation, and environments for office, health care, retail, and hospitality/entertainment. Another organization is the Inter-Society Color Council, Inc., which was founded in 1931 with the goal of advancing the knowledge of color as it relates to art, science, and industry. The fashion industry plays a major role in deciding the colors for automobiles. Automobile colors are about 2 years behind the fashion industry in color trends as it takes about 2 years for a color to move from conception to application.

Pigments – Color, Effect, and Extender

Pigments impart color, add bulk to liquid paint, or impart a desired physical quality to the wet and final film. However, not all coatings contain pigments. Colorless coatings are used to protect the substrate and usually add some kind of reflective finish (high gloss, low gloss, and matte) to the surface. Pigments consist of particles that are introduced into the paint by first incorporating them into an appropriate resin and/or solvent called a 'pigment dispersion.' The pigment dispersion is necessary to separate aggregated and agglomerated particles of the pigment and disperse the pigment into the chosen resin/ solvent with the use of a mill (ball mill, three-roll mill, or Netzsch mill) or by using the sheering action of a specialized spinner blade. This process will stabilize the pigment in the resulting resin system, preventing reaggregation, flocculation (formation of loose reaggregations of pigments), and settling of the pigment particles. Also, this process will reduce the size of the pigment particle so that it is smaller than the final film thickness. If the pigment particle size is greater than the film thickness, the pigment particles will protrude from the film. However, in some instances, pigment protrusion is a desired quality (such as in flat coatings in architectural paints or automotive primers) as it allows for a matte finish and/or better adhesion of subsequent coatings.

Color pigments

Color pigments are divided into organic and inorganic pigments. Of the inorganic pigments, white and some black pigments are considered 'hiding pigments.'

Hiding pigments

Hiding pigments are important in a coating because they obliterate or 'hide' any color variation in the previous coating or surface; therefore, all that is seen is the color of the top coating. The predominant white hiding pigment is titanium dioxide. The black pigments that have the best hiding power and tinting strength (less pigment is needed to impart color) are furnace black and channel black. The difference between furnace black and channel black is in the way they are produced. Furnace black is produced by injecting an oil with a high aromatic content into a hot (~2600 °F) refractory chamber. The minute carbon particles produced are then passed through a cooling zone and collected. Channel black is produced by burning natural gas and impinging the flame onto a metal surface. Other black pigments used for tinting or adding mechanical/ chemical properties to paint are graphite, bone, vegetable, mineral, and iron oxide blacks.

Organic colored pigments

Organic colored pigments provide a brighter, purer, and richer color than inorganic pigments; however, they are more susceptible to the destructive influences of UV radiation, chemical damage, and color bleeding. Organic pigments do not provide any hiding ability. They consist of azo-type compounds such as phthalocyanines and anthraquinones, to name a few generic types. They all have complex structures with a number of double-bond configurations.

Inorganic colored pigments

Inorganic pigments are considered hiding or semi-hiding pigments and are generally low in cost. Even though these pigments impart color, the colors of inorganic pigments tend to be earthy and muddy. Iron oxide can come in red, yellow, black, and brown colors. Some of the inorganic pigments, containing elements such as lead, mercury, and cadmium, are used in smaller amounts because of the potential toxic nature of the elemental composition.

Extender pigments

Extender pigments were first added to paint to increase volume or bulk and thereby lower the cost, as extender pigments are less expensive than the hiding pigments. However, it was found that some of the extender pigments impart certain desirable qualities on the final film. Some common extender pigments include calcium carbonate, magnesium silicate, barium sulfate, potassium aluminum silicate, and amorphous silicas.

Metallic pigments

Aluminum flake is the most widely used metal flake in automotive paint. The aluminum flakes can be of various size and appearance (smooth or rough edges to the flakes) and add a sparkle (larger flakes) or a subtle sheen (smaller flake) to the appearance of the paint surface. Other metallic flakes used in coatings are bronze, 'gold bronze' (an alloy of zinc and copper), and stainless steel.

Nacreous pigments

Nacreous pigments give a product a pearl-like finish. Nacreous pigments such as bismuth oxychloride, basic lead carbonate, lead hydrogen arsenate, and naturally pearlescence, obtained from shells and fish scales and skins, were used for a period but have been replaced by nacreous pigments made of mica (potassium aluminum silicate) coated with a metal oxide. A platelet of muscovite mica was coated on the broad face with titanium dioxide or other metal oxide. The content of the titanium dioxide varies from 20% to 50%. A thinner application of titanium dioxide results in a white or pearl effect. If a thicker application is made of the titanium dioxide, then a color is reflected from the pigment, which depends on the thickness of the titanium dioxide coating. These color-reflecting pigments are called 'interference pigments.' It should be noted that the color reflected from these pigments are complementary to the color seen using transmitted light (i.e., if the reflected color is green, the color seen using transmitted light is red). If the metal oxide used to coat the mica particle is iron oxide, the resulting colors range from bronze to copper-red and will have a more metallic quality.

New-effect pigments

New-effect pigments have come on the market and may be encountered more in the coming years. One of these consists of aluminum oxide coated with another metal oxide (such as titanium dioxide or iron oxide) to produce an appearance that is a bit flashier than the metal oxide-coated mica particles, which produce a satiny effect. There are also hue-shifting particles produced by coating aluminum with magnesium fluoride, or silicon dioxide coated with a metal oxide (titanium or iron oxide). The presence of the hue-shifting particles causes the color to shift when the coating is viewed at varying angles.

Holographic pigments are produced by embossing physical grooves on the surface of a solvent-inert material. This material is then coated with a metal, usually aluminum using vapor deposition, and sealed with a clearcoat. The resulting effect is a prismatic appearance.

See also: **Chemistry/Trace/Paint and Coating**: Architectural Paint; Automotive Paint; Forensic Paint Analysis; Interpretation of Paint Evidence; **Chemistry/Trace/Trace Evidence**: Microchemistry.

Further Reading

Patton TC (ed.) (1973) *Pigment Handbook*, vols. I–III. New York: Wiley.
Rodrigues F (1989) *Principles of Polymer Systems*, 3rd edn. New York: Hemisphere Publishing Corporation.
Thornton JI (2002) Forensic paint examination. In: Saferstein R (ed.) *Forensic Science Handbook*, 2nd edn., pp. 430–478. Upper Saddle River, NJ: Prentice Hall.
Tracton AA (ed.) (2007) *Coatings Materials and Surface Coatings*. Boca Raton, FL: CRC Press.
Weismantle GE (ed.) (1981) *Paint Handbook*. New York: McGraw-Hill book Company.

Relevant Websites

http://www.swgmat.org – Scientific working group for materials analysis (SWGMAT).
http://www.swgmat.org/paint.htm – SWGMAT forensic paint analysis and comparison guidelines.

Architectural Paint

L (Brun-Conti) Bender, National Laboratory Center, Ammendale, MD, USA

Published by Elsevier Ltd.

Glossary

Coating A generic term for paint, lacquer, enamel, or other liquid or liquefiable material that is converted to a solid, protective, or decorative film, or a combination of these types of films after application.

Convertible polymer A film in which the polymer undergoes a chemical change with drying and cannot be dissolved in the original solvent.

Emulsion Monomers are dispersed in an immiscible solvent and the resulting film is formed through coagulation. If the solvent is water, the coating is a *latex*; if the solvent is something other than water, the coating is a nonaqueous dispersion (NAD).

Enamel A term for a pigmented coating that forms a durable, glossy film. This term does not refer to any particular polymer or solvent system.

Known sample A coating sample of established origin.

Lacquer A clear or colored coating that forms a nonconvertible film through evaporation.

Nonconvertible polymer A coating that can be dissolved in the original solvent and forms a film by evaporation of the solvent.

Paint Commonly known as a pigmented coating.

Pigment Particles that impart color, opacity, effect (sparkle or sheen), bulk (filler and extender pigments), and other desired physical properties to the paint. Pigment particles are suspended in place in the final dry film by the resin.

Questioned sample A coating sample whose original source is unknown.

Resin or binder Any polymer that is dissolved or suspended in a solvent that can be converted into a self-sustaining film.

Solvent Low-viscosity volatile liquids used in coatings allowing the polymer, pigments, and other components to remain in solution until the paint is ready to be applied to a substrate.

Stain Pigments suspended in a vehicle that imparts color. It does not contain a binder.

Varnish A clear coating containing resins and oils that forms a convertible film through oxidation.

Vehicle The liquid-forming constituents of a coating. In general, the vehicle is comprised of the binder and any volatile solvents, driers, and other components. The nonvolatile portion is referred to as vehicle solids.

An architectural paint is defined, for this article, as any coating that imparts color and/or protection to surfaces (substrates) on or in buildings. These coatings can be pigmented or clear. Pigmented liquid paints or coatings consist of three basic components: the resin or binder, the particle portion (color pigments and extender pigments), and the solvents. The resin is the polymeric film-forming part of the paint. Pigments that form the particle portion of the paint consist of colored organic and inorganic pigments as well as extender pigments. Extender pigments do not add color but add bulk to the paint and may impart physical properties (e.g., film strength or water resistance) as well. Forensic scientists rarely encounter the solvent portion of the paint, but it is an integral part of the paint formulation. Solvents are used to control the paint flow and evaporation rate. Additives, in the form of driers, antisettling agents, and flatting agents, may also be added to the paint but are not necessary components of film formation.

Substrates such as drywall, masonry, concrete, metal, and wood are generally found in homes and buildings. Most of these substrates need to be primed in order to prepare them for coating with the top coat. The primer coat will improve adhesion between the substrate and the topcoat. Primers can also seal the substrate (if the substrate is porous), preventing excess moisture or dryness.

Substrates and Their Appropriate Primer and Coating

Table 1 lists some substrates commonly found in a structure or building, along with coatings and primers that are recommended for the substrates. It is not a comprehensive list, and real-world variations will occur.

Solvents

The first of the three components of coatings to be examined in this article is the one that most forensic paint examiners rarely encounter: the solvent. However, architectural paints are divided into two major categories depending on the solvents they use: 'solvent-thinned coatings' and 'water-thinned coatings'.

Solvent-thinned coatings are based on resins soluble in organic solvents. The coatings from **Table 1** that are generally made of such resins are alkyds, epoxies, varnishes, lacquers, and polyurethanes. Film formation occurs in organic solvent-thinned coatings by polymerization (alkyds, epoxies, polyurethanes, and varnishes) and evaporation (lacquers). Water-thinned coatings consist of two types of technology: an emulsion or latex system and a system based on water-soluble resins. The only water-thinned system in **Table 1** is latex, and

 http://dx.doi.org/10.1016/B978-0-12-382165-2.00107-0

Table 1 Examples of coatings and primers for various substrates

Substrate	*Topcoat/primer*
Drywall, sheetrock	Alkyd enamel/alkyd enamel or vinyl sealer Latex (acrylic, vinyl)/vinyl sealer
Woodwork (pigmented coating)	Alkyd enamel/enamel undercoat or mixture of enamel undercoat and alkyd enamel (optional) Acrylic latex/enamel undercoat
Wood floors, steps, or porches (pigmented coating)	Phenolic alkyd/thinned enamel undercoat thinned Acrylic latex/enamel undercoat
Woodwork (clear coating)	Lacquer/lacquer sanding sealer Varnish/thinned varnish Polyurethane/thinned polyurethane
Wood floors (clear coating)	Polyurethane
Masonry, plaster, brick, or concrete block	Alkyd enamel/alkyd enamel or vinyl sealer Acrylic latex/alkyd enamel or vinyl sealer
Concrete floors	Phenolic alkyd/thinned alkyd enamel Acrylic latex Two-component epoxy

Source: Weismantle GE (ed.) (1981) *Paint Handbook*. New York: McGraw-Hill book Company.

the film is formed by coagulation. Film-forming chemistry is discussed later in the article.

The primary function of solvents in paint is to keep the film-forming resins, pigments, and any other additives in a liquid form so that the coating can be applied to a surface with a brush, roller, mitt, or spraying device. Solvents are chosen on the basis of their solvency (the ability to dissolve the film-forming resin into solution), volatility (how fast the solvent evaporates), odor, and toxicity. The rate of evaporation, flow properties, and viscosity are all considered when a coating is formulated. Examples of solvents are hydrocarbon solvents (derived from petroleum and coal tar and consisting primarily of only carbon and hydrogen), terpene solvents (obtained from pine trees), oxygenated solvents (containing oxygen along with carbon and hydrogen), and water. All of the aforementioned solvents (except water) are considered volatile organic compounds (VOCs) by the Environmental Protection Agency (of the United States), and thus are regulated. Therefore, paint and coating manufacturers strive for paint formulations so as to minimize the VOC content of their products.

Resin or Binder: The Film-Forming Portion of the Paint

The resin portion of paint conveys properties to the final film such as resistance to acids, alkalis, solvents, water, or any other material that would mar the surface of the coating. It is also the component that imparts most of the physical properties such as hardness, flexibility, adhesion, abrasion resistance, and ease of cleaning. Additionally, the resin binds the particles (color pigments and extender pigments) in place. In architectural coatings, the ratio of binder to pigment affects the gloss of the coating. Interior paints come in gloss, semigloss, and flat, in relation to the light reflecting properties of the paint. In a gloss finish, the binder-to-pigment ratio is higher than in a semigloss finish, and a semigloss paint has a higher binder-to-pigment ratio than a flat paint. Gloss paint film is a hard, mar-resistant film that is easily cleaned and reflects light. However, adhesion of any subsequent coating on a gloss surface will be minimal; therefore, the gloss coating will have to be primed or sanded, or both, to effect adhesion between coatings. Semigloss paint has a bit more pigment than gloss film paint, and therefore causes the light to be reflected in slightly different directions, giving the film a silky appearance. In a flat paint, many of the pigment particles actually extend beyond the surface of the film, causing diffuse reflectance and no gloss. The adhesion between the flat film and any successive coating will be good, precluding any need for an additional primer. The following are the resins found in architectural coatings.

$CH_2{=}C(CH_3)CO_2R$

R=	
-H	Methacrylic acid
$-CH_3$	Methyl methacrylate
$-CH_2CH_3$	Ethyl methacrylate
$-CH_2CH_2CH_2CH_3$	Butyl methacrylate
$-CH_2CH_2OH$	Hydroxyethyl methacrylate

$CH_2{=}C(H)CO_2R$

R=	
-H	Acrylic acid
$-CH_3$	Methyl acrylate

$CH_2{=}C(H)CN$ Acrylonitrile

$CH_2{=}C(H)C_6H_5$ Styrene

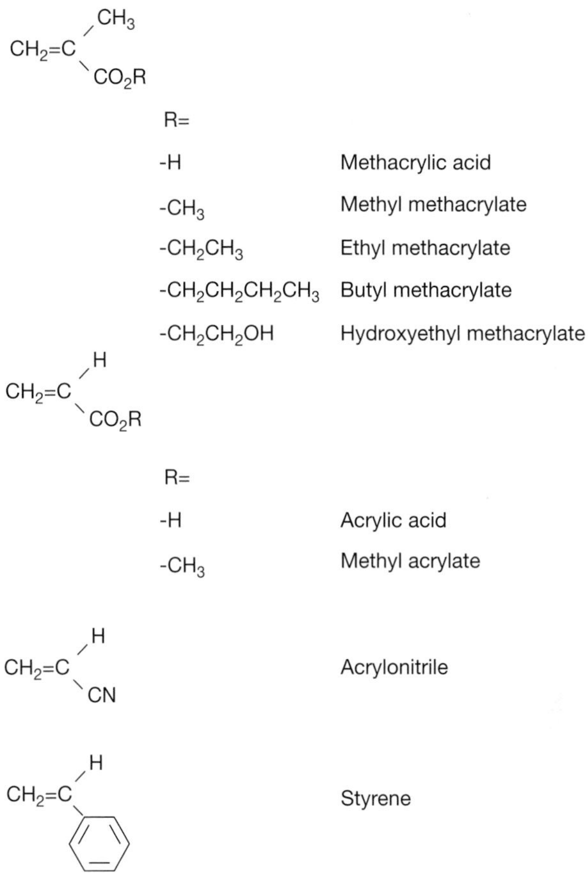

Figure 1 Monomers based on acrylic and methacrylic acids.

Acrylic

Acrylic resins are polymers made from monomers based on acrylic and/or methacrylic acid (**Figure 1**). Functional groups impart the desired properties (hardness, flexibility, mar resistance, etc.) to the final film (**Table 2**). Acrylic resins are used in architectural coatings primarily in the form of emulsions in water or latex paints. The monomers are introduced into the

Table 2 Examples of monomers and their effects on film formation

Film properties	*Monomers*
Exterior durability	Acrylates, methacrylates
Hardness	Styrene, methyl methacrylate
Mar resistance	Acrylonitrile, methacrylamide
Gloss	Styrene, aromatic constituents
Color retention	Ethyl acrylate, butyl actylate
Flexibility	Acrylonitrile, methacrylate
Solvent resistance	Styrene, methyl methacrylate
Water resistance	Styrene, vinyl toluene

Source: Allyn G (1971) *Acrylic Resins*. Philadelphia, PA: Federation of Societies for Paint Technology.

emulsions using two different methods: the redox method and the reflux method. In the redox method, the water, emulsifiers, and monomers are placed in a reactor. The air in the reactor is then displaced by an inert gas and then the initiators and reducing agents are added, resulting in a vigorous reaction. The reflux method starts with a part of the water containing the emulsifiers and initiators being placed in the reactor, which is then heated to a temperature near the reaction temperature. The monomers, along with the remaining quantity of water, are then added to the reactor and the solution is brought up to the reaction temperature.

Formulation of the emulsion coating begins with the dispersion of pigments in water. Next, the acrylic resin emulsion is added with any requisite additives. The final steps include tinting and testing of the finished film. Acrylic resins can be modified by blending them with other resins to impart additional properties to the final coating. For example, an alkyd emulsion could be added to an acrylic emulsion to improve adhesion and wetting over a chalky surface as well as intercoat adhesion between the topcoat and the primer.

Alkyds

Alkyd resins are a segment of a large class of polymers known as polyesters. Polyesters are, technically, any polymer produced by ester monomers. Alkyds are polyesters that contain drying oils and are formed with three basic components: fatty acids, polyols, and dibasic acids. Triglycerides (oils consisting of 3 moles of monobasic fatty acid and 1 mole of glycerol) can replace the polyol and fatty acid (**Figure 2**).

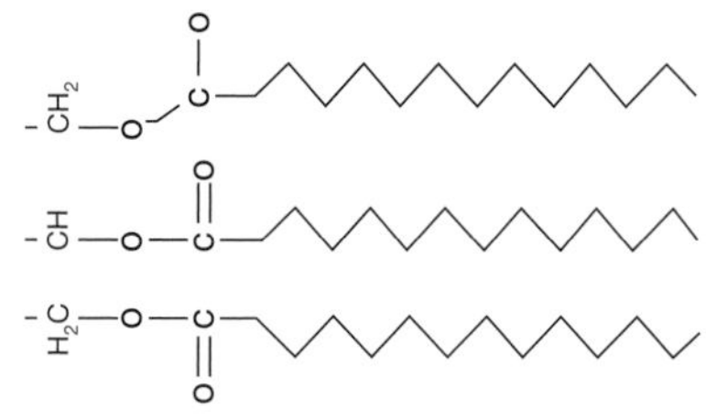

Polyols other than glycerol are ethylene glycol (two —OH), pentaerythritol (4 —OH), and sorbitol (6 —OH). The choice of polyols will affect the degree of branching in the subsequent polymer. Also, the distance between the hydroxyl groups will have an influence on the flexibility of the resulting film. For example, a polymer using diethylene glycol will produce a more flexible coating than one using ethylene glycol (**Figure 3**).

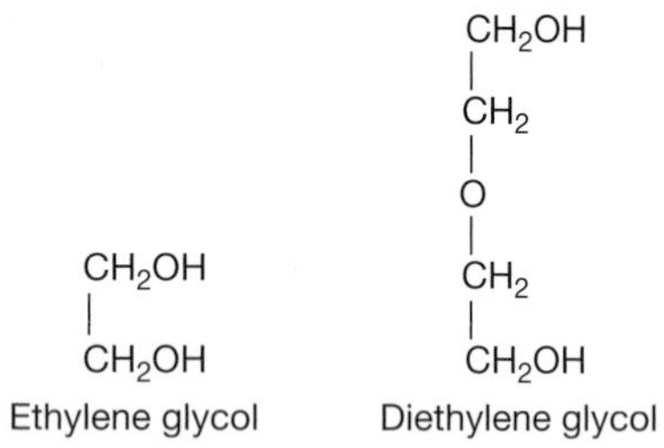

The fatty acids or oils used have a significant effect on the curing and physical properties of the final film (**Table 3**). The more unsaturated the fatty acid, the shorter it takes for the coating to dry. Alkyds are classified according to the percentage of fatty acid in the resin. Short oil alkyds contain <30% fatty acids, medium oil alkyds between 45 and 55%, and long oil alkyds >55%. The majority of fatty acids come from

Figure 2 Triglyceride.

Figure 3 Examples of polyols with varying lengths between the hydroxyl groups.

vegetable oils; soybean oil is the most utilized. Fish oils may be used, and rosins are employed occasionally to improve hardness. Some coatings containing short oil alkyd resins must be baked to form a solid film. In architectural coatings, the alkyd resin must cure through air drying and oxidation; therefore, medium and long oil alkyd resins are used for this purpose.

Orthophthalic acid is used primarily as the polybasic acid, and usually in the anhydride form (phthalic anhydride). Isophthalic acid is added to increase chemical resistance, resulting in faster drying and added toughness in the final film. Longer aliphatic dibasic acids can be added in small amounts to increase flexibility (**Figure 4**).

Urethane

Urethane coatings provide a highly durable film and are used primarily in architectural coatings for floors. The film is formed by the reaction of isocyanates and a compound containing an active proton (**Figure 5**). When the two components are kept separately, it is called a 'two-package' system. When they are combined, cross-linking begins right away; therefore, they should be mixed only immediately before application. A more convenient 'one-package' urethane system is also available. One such system uses atmospheric moisture that reacts with the terminal N=C=O to form an $—NH_2$, which acts as a catalyst, thereby continuing the reaction. The other one-package urethane system uses blocked isocyanate monomers; however, this system requires baking of the film, and therefore is not discussed in this article.

Vinyl Resins

Vinyl resins are encountered in architectural coatings as water-thinned emulsion or latex paints. These are usually in the form of polymers made of vinyl acetate, vinyl chloride, or a copolymer of the two. Vinyl polymers are formed by monomers that

Table 3 Examples of oils, their degree of unsaturation (as determined by their 'iodine number' – a method to determine the amount of hydrogen that is required to convert each from an unsaturated to a saturated fat), and the resulting film properties

Fat or oil	*Degree of unsaturation (iodin number)*	*Speed of drying*	*Non-yellowing on aging*	*Gloss*
Linseed oil	173–201	Excellent	Poor	Fair
Tung oil	170	Excellent	Poor	Fair
Soybean oil	137–143	Good	Good	Excellent
Sunflower oil	119–135	Excellent	Excellent	Good–excellent
Cottonseed oil	108–110	Fair	Excellent	Good–excellent

Information compiled from class notes from the University of Missouri-Rolla *Basic Compositions of Coatings* course.

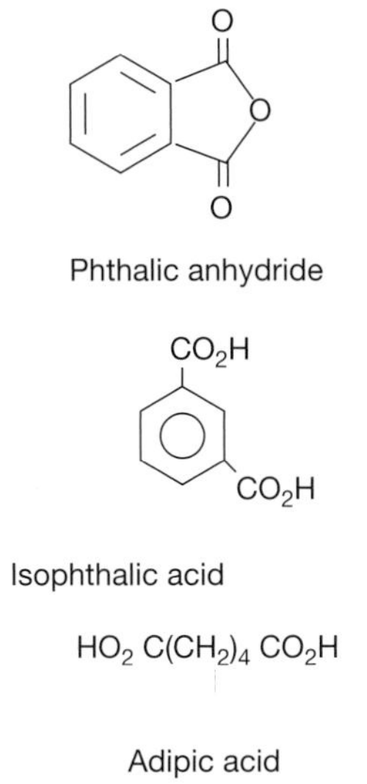

Phthalic anhydride

CO_2H

CO_2H

Isophthalic acid

$HO_2C(CH_2)_4CO_2H$

Adipic acid

Figure 4 Anhydride form of orthophthalic acid (phthalic anhydride) and other polybasic acids.

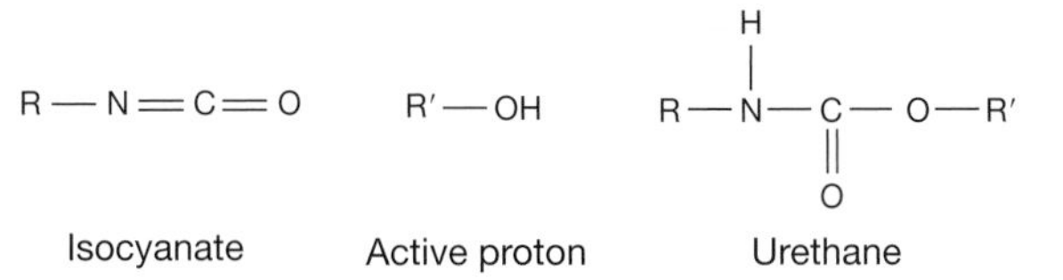

R—N=C=O R′—OH R—N(H)—C(=O)—O—R′

Isocyanate Active proton Urethane

Figure 5 The structure of isocyanate and an active proton that form the resulting urethane.

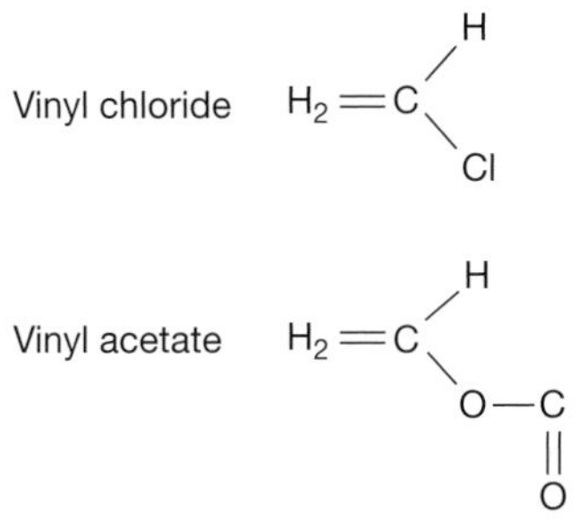

Vinyl chloride $H_2=C(H)(Cl)$

Vinyl acetate $H_2=C(H)$—O—C(=O)

Figure 6 Primary monomers used in the polymerization of vinyl resins.

contain a vinyl group (-C=C-); therefore, an acrylic polymer is technically a vinyl polymer. However, vinyl polymers are primarily defined as the polymerization product of vinyl chloride and/or vinyl acetate (**Figure 6**).

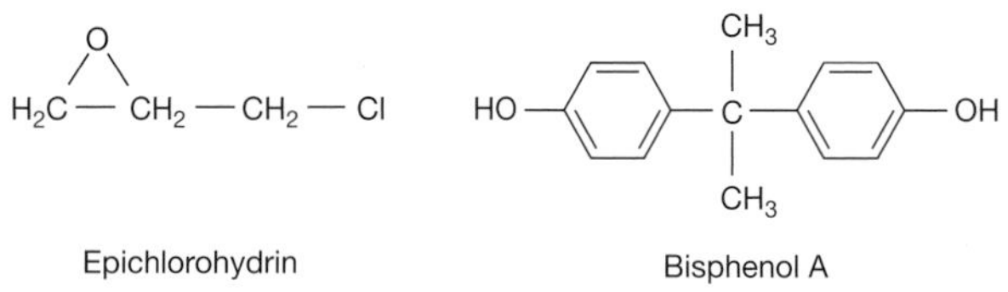

$H_2C(O)—CH_2—CH_2—Cl$ HO—C6H4—C(CH_3)(CH_3)—C6H4—OH

Epichlorohydrin Bisphenol A

Figure 7 The primary monomers used in the polymerization of epoxy resins.

Styrene–Butadiene

The copolymer of styrene–butadiene is found in latex or emulsion coatings used primarily for interior architectural paints because of its tendency toward oxidation, which causes the film to become brittle. Styrene–butadiene coatings have lost their market share in recent years, even though they are usually less expensive than vinyl or acrylic latex paints.

Epoxy

Epoxy resins have limited use in architectural paints but they are used in applications where chemical resistance is required. The two major epoxy resins are the glycidyl ether epoxide resins and the epoxidized olefins; the former is primarily used in the coatings industry. Glycidyl ether epoxides, based on bisphenol A and an oxirane ring-containing compound, usually epichlorohydrin, are the most prominent in this category and are polymerized using a condensation reaction (**Figure 7**). Epoxidized olefins have inferior chemical resistance, and therefore are not used for coatings.

Varnish, Lacquer, and Shellac

The terms 'varnish' and 'lacquer' are historically used interchangeably. To minimize confusion, each is described on the basis of its component parts and curing properties. A varnish consists of resin, oil, and solvent. Formerly called oleoresinous varnishes, varnishes are convertible and cannot be redissolved using the original solvent. The film forms by oxidation if allowed to air dry, or it can be baked into a harder, tougher, and more solvent-resistant film. The hardness of the final film depends on the resin and the oil. Oils are classified as soft oils (isolated double bonds such as linseed and safflower oils) or hard oils (containing conjugated double bonds, such as tung and oiticia oils). The resins can be natural, such as rosin, or synthetic, such as the product of the reaction of phenol and formaldehyde.

Lacquers are made of nonconvertible resins (they can be redissolved in a solvent), such as nitrocellulose and a solvent. Lacquers may also be clear or pigmented. Other resins used in lacquers are ethyl cellulose, cellulose acetate butyrate, and certain vinyl copolymers. Coatings using the term 'spirit varnish' are lacquers.

Shellac is generally a clear lacquer made by dissolving the secretions of the lac bug in alcohol. It cures through evaporation (nonconvertible coating), and therefore should not be used in a location where it would be exposed to alcohol.

Pigments

Pigments impart color, add bulk to liquid paint, or impart a desired physical quality to the final film. However, not all coatings contain pigments. Colorless coatings are used to protect the substrate and usually add some kind of reflective finish (high gloss, low gloss, matte) to the surface. Pigments consist of particles that are introduced into the paint by first incorporating them into an appropriate resin and/or solvent called 'pigment dispersion.' The pigment dispersion is necessary to separate aggregated and agglomerated particles of the pigment and disperse them into the chosen resin/solvent by the use of a mill (ball mill, three-roll mill, or Netzsch mill) or the sheering action of a specialized spinner blade. This process stabilizes the pigment in the resulting resin system, thereby preventing re-aggregation, flocculation (formation of loose reaggregations of pigments), and settling of the pigment particles. Also, this process reduces the size of the pigment particle so that it is smaller than the final film thickness. If the pigment particle size is greater than the film thickness, the pigment particles will protrude from the film. In some instances (such as in flat coatings or primers), pigment protrusion is a desired quality as it allows a matte finish and/or better adhesion of subsequent coatings. The pigment protrusion from flat films and primers is a deliberate result achieved by the formulator of the coating; it is due to the proportion of resin to pigment and not necessarily to the size of the pigment particles resulting from improper pigment dispersion.

The pigments that are used in architectural coatings include black and white pigments, absorptive color pigments, and extender pigments.

White and Black Hiding Pigments

One important aspect of colored coatings is that they conceal the previous color or they hide any visual imperfections (such as two different colors) that occur in the undercoat. Pigments used to perform this function are called 'hiding pigments.' Hiding pigments are primarily white and black; however, colored pigments are used in dark-shade coatings as discussed below.

The white hiding pigments consist of titanium dioxide and, to a much lesser degree, zinc oxide. There are three crystal types or polymorphs of titanium dioxide: anatase, brookite, and rutile. Anatase and brookite are not stable forms, and the natural supply of brookite is not abundant. Also, the anatase form has only about 75% of the hiding capacity of the rutile form and has a tendency to chalk or degrade with exposure to ultraviolet radiation. The rutile form is the primary white pigment in paints because of its cost, hiding ability, and chalk resistance. The ability of the rutile form to perform as an excellent hiding pigment is due to its high refractive index ($n_{iso}{\sim}2.7$).

The other white hiding pigment in use today, zinc oxide, has only about 15% of the hiding power of rutile titanium dioxide and comes at a higher price. However, it is used to help reduce chalking, prevent the growth of mildew, improve color retention, and add hardness to the final film.

It should be noted that, even though titanium dioxide and zinc oxide are used almost exclusively now for the white pigment, it was not always so. Older buildings may have been painted with coatings that used white pigment containing lead, such as basic lead carbonate, basic lead sulfate, and dibasic lead phosphate. Other white architectural paint pigments not in common use include antimony trioxide, zinc sulfide, and lithopone (a mixture of titanium dioxide and barium sulfate).

Black pigments are made by various techniques. The pigments that have the best hiding power and tinting strength (less pigment is needed to impart color) are furnace black and channel black. Furnace black is produced by injecting an oil with a high aromatic content into a hot (~2600 °F) refractory chamber. The minute carbon particles produced are then passed through a cooling zone and collected. Channel black is produced by burning natural gas and impinging the flame onto a metal surface. Other black pigments used for tinting or adding mechanical/chemical properties to paint are graphite, bone, vegetable, mineral, and iron oxide blacks.

Color Pigments

Colored pigments are of two types: organic and inorganic. Organic pigments are brighter, purer, and richer in color than inorganic pigments; however, they are more susceptible to ultraviolet radiation damage, chemical damage, and color bleeding. Also, organic pigments are translucent and therefore do not add to the hiding ability of the paint. Inorganic pigments are considered hiding or semihiding pigments and are low priced. However, the colors of inorganic pigments tend to be earthy and muddy.

The colorants in architectural coatings are further categorized as 'light shade' or 'dark shade.' Light-shade coatings are built upon a titanium dioxide base and use a tint paste to impart subtle color differences. Almost any pigment suitable for an architectural paint may be used to tint a light-shade coating. In dark-shade coatings, the major pigment is something other than titanium dioxide. For example, a blue dark-shade paint may have phthalocyanine blue as the major pigment. It should be noted that pigments that are suitable for interior coatings may not necessarily be suitable for exterior coatings. Discussion of these differences is outside the scope of this article. See **Table 4** for examples of pigments in architectural coatings.

Extender Pigments

Extender pigments were initially added to paints to increase their volume or bulk, and thereby to lower the cost, extender pigments being less expensive than color pigments. However,

Table 4 Examples of pigments used in architectural coatings

Color	*Pigment*
Red	Toludine red, iron oxide red, quinacridone red, lithol red
Orange	Chrome orange, molybdate orange, dinitroanaline orange
Yellow	Chrome yellow, Hansa yellow, cadmium yellow, iron oxide
Green	Chrome green, phthalocyanine green, chromium oxide green
Blue	Iron blue, phthalocyanine blue, molybdate blue
Black	See text
White	See text

Weismantle GE (ed.) (1981) *Paint Handbook*. New York: McGraw-Hill book Company.

it was found that some extender pigments impart certain desirable qualities on the final film. The following are some of the common extender pigments found in architectural paints:

Calcium carbonate (calcite) and magnesium–calcium carbonate (dolomite): These extender pigments are commonly referred to as limestone and can come in a variety of particle sizes and surface treatments. They can be used to control the degree of flow, the degree of flatting, and tint retention. As their natural pH is between 9 and 10, care must be taken if an acidic component is introduced into the coating. Calcite and dolomite also act as fire retardants.

Magnesium silicate (talc): Talc provides a beneficial suspension for other pigments, thereby preventing settling. It also increases the viscosity of latex coatings, affects the gloss of the paint, and provides excellent brightness.

Aluminum silicate (kaolinite): Kanolite will improve 'scrubability' and stain removal because of its plate-like microstructure. Kaolinite also improves flow and leveling, and contributes to dry hiding (the ability of the pigment to hide the proceeding coating in the dry film due to the difference in the refractive difference between the pigment and resin).

Potassium aluminum silicate (mica): Mica's plate-like microstructure causes it to leaf or 'lie flat' in coatings, which strengthens and reinforces the coating. The mica plates also form a moisture barrier and help to minimize cracking and checking in the final film.

Amorphous silicas: These are used for their pronounced flatting effect and their contribution to thixotropic flow.

Calcium silicate (wollastonite): Wollastonite improves flow after application, thereby ensuring a uniform dry film. It also increases dry-paint durability and wet-paint stability.

Coatings Application and Film Formation

Architectural paints and coatings are usually applied to a substrate using a brush or roller. Occasionally, the paint is sprayed on or applied with a mitt or fabric. Texturing tools, such as fabrics of various textures, sponges, whisk brooms, etc., may also be used.

The liquid coating becomes a solid film by evaporation, polymerization, or coagulation (addition polymerization). The film must form at ambient conditions because there is generally no way to bake the surface at a higher temperature.

OH, CH_2OH + OH → OH CH_2 OH + H_2O

Figure 8 An example of condensation polymerization.

Evaporation

Film formation by evaporation is simply the action of the solvent evaporating and leaving behind the resin and any pigments to form the film. The use of a particular solvent in a resin system is based not only on the rate of evaporation of the solvent but also on the ability of the resin or polymer to dissolve in it (solvency), on its odor, and on its toxicity. If a solvent has excellent solvency and flow but is highly toxic, clearly it cannot be considered. If the odor is particularly strong or lingering, its use in interior architectural coatings may be unacceptable. The rate of evaporation will determine the flow of the coating on the substrate and how fast the coating dries to form the film. For this reason, a combination of solvents may be used, including a slower evaporating solvent to slow down the drying time, thereby allowing the coating to form a smoother finish. A faster evaporating solvent will be added to prevent the coating from sagging or 'tearing' on vertical surfaces. As a rule, a polar resin will be more compatible with a polar solvent; therefore, the polarity of the resin and solvent should be consistent. Lacquers use evaporation for film formation.

Condensation and Oxidation Polymerization

Polymerization of the film occurs when the polymers in the binder or resin of the paint cross-link to form a convertible coating. This comes about in architectural coatings as condensation or oxidation polymerization. Another type of polymerization, namely, addition polymerization, occurs with acrylic and vinyl polymers during the coagulation of the emulsion coating system and is addressed in the following section. Condensation polymers form by-products such as water, carbon dioxide, or hydrogen gas when the monomers polymerize (**Figure 8**). Urethane and epoxy resins form films using condensation polymerization.

Oxidation occurs in resin systems containing oils, namely, varnishes and alkyds. The oils in such systems are classified as drying, semidrying, and nondrying. The degree of drying is related to the amount of unsaturation in the oil (**Table 3**). The conjugation of the double bonds also affects the ability of the oil to dry. However, to facilitate and accelerate the drying process, 'driers' may be added. Driers are heavy metal soaps of organic acids. It is believed that the oxidation mechanism occurs when hydroperoxides are formed on the double bonds, creating free radicals (**Figure 9**). Driers assist in catalyzing the decomposition of the hydroperoxide to a free-radical state.

Coagulation or Addition Polymerization

This type of film formation occurs in systems that involve emulsion technology. In an emulsion, particles of the monomers are dispersed in a liquid (continuous phase) in which

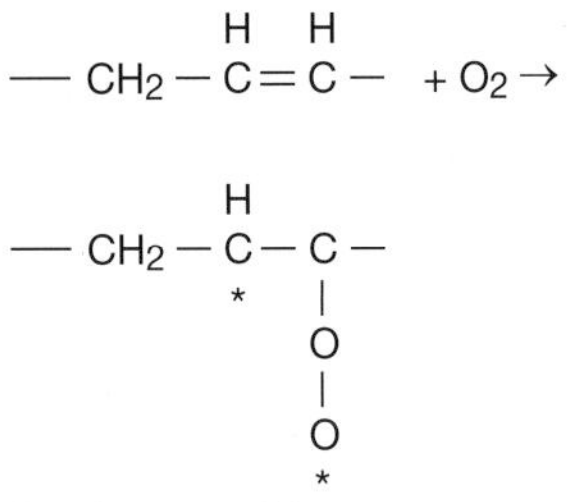

$$-CH_2-\overset{H}{C}=\overset{H}{C}- \; + O_2 \rightarrow$$

$$-CH_2-\underset{*}{\overset{H}{C}}-\underset{\underset{\underset{*}{O}}{|}}{\underset{O}{|}}{C}-$$

Hydroperoxide

Figure 9 Formulation of a hydroperoxide.

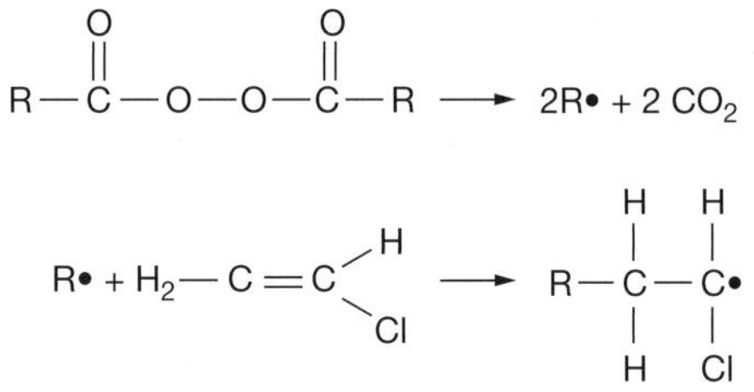

$$R-\overset{O}{\overset{\|}{C}}-O-O-\overset{O}{\overset{\|}{C}}-R \longrightarrow 2R\bullet + 2\,CO_2$$

$$R\bullet + H_2-C=C\genfrac{}{}{0pt}{}{H}{Cl} \longrightarrow R-\underset{H}{\overset{H}{C}}-\underset{Cl}{\overset{H}{C}}\bullet$$

Figure 10 An example of coagulation or addition polymerization.

they are not miscible. In regard to architectural paints, water is the continuous phase. To keep the immiscible phases from separating, emulsifiers are added. Coagulation is based on addition polymerization and occurs when a free radical is formed, initiating and propagating polymerization without the creation of by-products (Figure 10). Polymerization is initiated in the water phase. A growing radical (addition polymerization) precipitates into a micelle containing monomers and continues to polymerize, being resupplied with additional monomers by diffusion from the emulsion solution. Acrylic and vinyl latex films cure through coagulation or addition polymerization.

Additives

As mentioned previously, driers, in the form of heavy metal soaps, are added to oil-containing polymers to facilitate polymer formation. The following are some of the additives that are added to architectural coatings:

Antisettling agents: These are used to prevent the pigments from settling or separating from the vehicle in the wet coating. Magnesium silicate (also known as talc, and considered an extender pigment) is an example of an antisettling agent.

Antiskinning agents: These are used to prevent premature oxidation in the wet film, which causes a 'skin' to form on the surface. Methylethylketoxime and butyraldoxime are examples of antiskinning agents.

Mildewcides: Mildewcides are used to prevent the growth of mildew on the surface of the paint. The white pigment zinc oxide is used for this purpose.

Flatting agents: Flatting agents are used to reduce the gloss in a finished film. Extender pigments such as amorphous silica and talc are examples of a flatting agent.

Coalescing agents: These are used in latex films to soften and partially solvate the latex particles, thereby assisting in the coagulation process to form a nearly continuous film. Butyl cellosolve and butyl carbitol are examples of coalescing agents.

See also: **Chemistry/Trace/Paint and Coating:** Automotive Paint; Forensic Paint Analysis; Interpretation of Paint Evidence; **Chemistry/Trace/Trace Evidence:** Microchemistry.

Further Reading

Allen RA (1981) *Epoxy Resins in Coatings*. Philadelphia, PA: Federation of Societies for Paint Technology.
Allyn G (1971) *Acrylic Resins*. Philadelphia, PA: Federation of Societies for Paint Technology.
Blegen JR (1979) *Alkyd Resins*. Philadelphia, PA: Federation of Societies for Paint Technology.
Patton TC (ed.) (1973) *Pigment Handbook*, vols I and II. New York: Wiley.
Rheineck AE (1979) *Modern Varnish Technology*. Philadelphia, PA: Federation of Societies for Paint Technology.
Rodrigues F (1989) *Principles of Polymer Systems*, 3rd edn. New York: Hemisphere Publishing Corporation.
Thornton JI (2002) Forensic paint examination. In: Saferstein R (ed.) *Forensic Science Handbook*, 2nd edn., pp. 430–478. Upper Saddle River, NJ: Prentice Hall.
Tracton AA (ed.) (2007) *Coatings Materials and Surface Coatings*. Boca Raton, FL: CRC Press.
Weismantle GE (ed.) (1981) *Paint Handbook*. New York: McGraw-Hill book Company.

Relevant Websites

http://www.swgmat.org/ – Scientific working group for materials analysis (SWGMAT).
http://www.swgmat.org/paint.htm – SWGMAT forensic paint analysis and comparison guidelines.

Automotive Paint

L (Brun-Conti) Bender, National Laboratory Center, Ammendale, MD, USA

Published by Elsevier Ltd.

Glossary

Coating A generic term for paint, lacquer, enamel, or other liquid or liquefiable material that is converted to a solid, protective, or decorative film or a combination of these types of films after application.

Paint Commonly known as a pigmented coating.

Pigment Particles that impart color, opacity, effect (sparkle or sheen), bulk (filler and extender pigments), and/or desirable physical properties paint. Pigment particles are suspended in place in the final dry film by the resin.

Resin or binder Any polymer that is dissolved in or suspended in a solvent that can be converted into a self-sustaining film.

Solvent Low-viscosity volatile liquids used in coatings allowing the polymer, pigments, and other components to remain in solution until the paint is ready to be applied to a substrate.

Thermosetting polymer A polymer formed from resins containing reactive sites that will react with a cross-linking agent to form a durable film that cannot be reconstituted into solution. This is usually accomplished with the addition of energy, commonly in the form of heat.

Vehicle The liquid forming constituents of a coating. In general, the vehicle is comprised of the binder and any volatile solvents, driers, and other components. The nonvolatile portion is referred to as 'vehicle solids'.

Forensic chemists receive automobile paint most often in association with hit-and-run cases. In a typical case, the unknown paint is collected from the clothing of an individual, another vehicle, or a structure that has been struck by a vehicle which has left the scene. However, paint can also be used as evidence in insurance fraud cases and even in breaking and entering, where the vehicle is used as the break-in 'tool.' Automotive paint is a highly engineered coating which is applied in a very controlled environment in a specific order. Automotive body panel substrates include metal or various types of plastics such as thermoplastic olefins, polycarbonates, nylon, and polyester resins. The metal portions are always coated with an electrocoat primer in newer cars from the assembly plant and there may be additional primer(s) present. The plastic portions may or may not be primed. The plastic portions may be flexible or rigid and this will dictate the formulation of the coating. Occasionally, the plastic portions are colored to match the vehicle color.

Liquid paints or coatings consist of three basic components: the resin or binder, the particle portion (color pigments and extender pigments), and the solvents. Additionally, small amounts of additives may be included, such as those that prevent the breakdown of the film by ultraviolet (UV) radiation (UV absorbers, hindered amine light stabilizers). However, due to the minute amount added to the coating, these, most likely, will not be detected by the forensic examiner in the dried film.

The resin is the substance that will give the dried film its physical properties: hardness, flexibility, acid and alkali resistance, etc. In addition, automotive coatings may be original equipment manufacturer (OEM) or refinish coatings. OEM coatings are applied in the factory and, therefore, are usually polymerized using heat or some kind of mechanism to encourage and propagate the cross-linkage between polymers. The latter is applied to a vehicle which is already constructed, including plastic portions that cannot be exposed to excessive heat, and therefore, polymerization must be completed by other means.

The pigments are classified as either color, extender (imparting bulk and/or physical properties), or effect (metallic and nacreous pigments which result in various light-reflecting qualities). The color and extender pigments must first be processed with an appropriate resin or solvent to form a 'pigment dispersion' of particles before it can be introduced into the paint. Effect pigments consist of metal flake (aluminum being the most common for automotive paint) and nacreous pigments (usually mica between layers of a metal oxide such as titanium dioxide or iron oxide in which the finished film effects a pearl-like luster).

Solvents are used in automotive coatings to ensure that the paint does not dry too quickly (leaving a wrinkled appearance) or too slowly (causing drips and sags). Solvents may also be combined in such a way as to optimize the wet paint with regard to the specific application technique used.

The Binder or Resin

Resins or binders are the polymeric portion of the paint that binds the solids (pigments) into place and, as stated above, gives the final film physical properties such as gloss, hardness, and chemical resistance. Polymers used in automotive coatings include acrylics, alkyds and polyesters, amino resins, carbamates, polyurethanes, and epoxies.

Acrylic Resins

Acrylic resins are polymers comprised of monomers based primarily on acrylic and methacrylic acids (**Figure 1**). Polymerization occurs via additional polymerization at the ethylenic double bond and is initiated by free radicals. Monomers such as ethyl, butyl, 2-hydroxyl ethyl, and 2-propyl esters of acrylic and methacrylic acids are used, along with styrene, to impart certain qualities to the final film (see **Table 1**). Polymer chemists will construct the acrylic polymer to the desired molecular weight and then stop polymerization with a peroxide or other appropriate material. The monomers can be modified with pendant groups, such as hydroxyl or carboxylic acid, which will enable the acrylic polymer to cross-link with other monomers or polymer chains forming a thermosetting polymer. Thermosetting polymers cross-link with the addition of heat to form a polymeric 'spider's web,' which cannot be reversed or put back into solution. Acrylic resins are used in basecoats, both solvent-borne and waterborne, clearcoats, and primers.

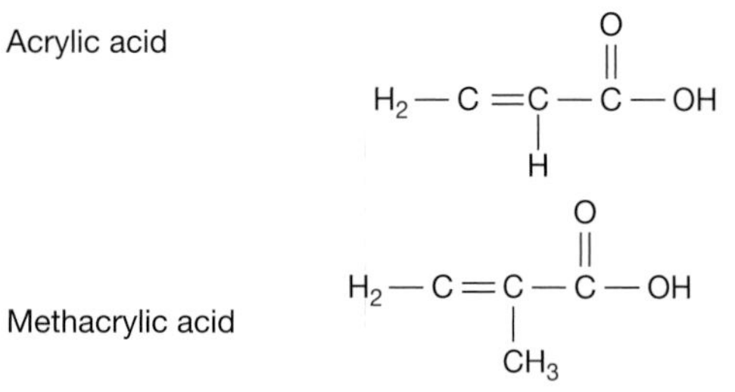

Acrylic acid

$H_2—C=C(H)—C(=O)—OH$

Methacrylic acid

$H_2—C=C(CH_3)—C(=O)—OH$

Figure 1 Acrylic acid and methacrylic acid monomers.

Table 1 Examples of monomers and the qualities that they impart onto the finished film

Qualities imparted to finished film	*Monomers*	
Hardness	Acrylic acid	$H_2C=C(H)—C(=O)—OH$
	Also styrene, methacrylic acid, and methyl methacrylate	
Gloss	Styrene	$HC=CH_2$ 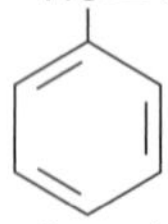 (attached to benzene ring)
	Also other aromatic-containing polymers	
Flexibility	Butyl acrylate	$H_2C=C(H)—C(=O)—O—C_4H_9$
	Also ethyl acrylate and 2-ethylhexyl acrylate	
Water resistance	Methyl methacrylate	$H_2C=C(CH_3)—C(=O)—O—CH_3$
	Also methyl methacrylate	
Exterior durability	Methyl acrylate	$H_2C=C(H)—C(=O)—O—CH_3$
	Also acrylates	

Source: Information compiled from Gerould A. *Acrylic Resins*. Philadelphia, PA: Federation of Societies for Paint Technology.

Alkyd and Polyester Resins

Any resin that is a polymer of ester-type monomers is considered a polyester. With this definition, alkyds are polyesters and can be thought of as a separate subset of a polyester polymer. A polyester resin is made of polyols and polybasic acids. In general usage, the term 'alkyd' is a polyester that is modified with a triglyceride oil or the acids of such an oil (**Figure 2**). In automotive finishes, the alkyd resin is frequently modified with acrylic for OEM finishes and phenol–formaldehyde for automotive refinishes.

Common polyols, other than glycerol (3 -OH), include ethylene glycol (2 -OH), pentaerythritol (4 -OH), and sorbitol (6 -OH). The choice of polyols will affect the degree of branching in the subsequent polymer. Also, the distance between the hydroxyl groups will have an influence on the flexibility of the resulting film. For example, if diethylene glycol is used in the polymer, it will produce a more flexible coating than one using ethylene glycol (**Figure 3**).

The fatty acids or oils used have a significant effect on the curing and physical properties of the final film. The more unsaturated the fatty acid, the faster the resulting coat will dry. Alkyds are classified according to the percentage of fatty acid in the resin. Short oil alkyds contain <30%, medium oil alkyds 45–55%, and long oil alkyds >55% fatty acid. The majority of fatty acids come from vegetable oils, with soybean oil being the most utilized. Fish oils may be used and rosin is employed occasionally to improve hardness. Some coatings containing short oil alkyd resins must be baked to form a solid film.

Orthophthalic acid is primarily used as the polybasic acid, usually in the anhydride form (phthalic anhydride). Isophthalic acid will be added to increase chemical resistance and toughness in the final film as well as to promote faster drying. Longer aliphatic dibasic acids will be added in small amounts to increase flexibility. Polyester resins are used in basecoat and primer coatings and alkyds are used in basecoats.

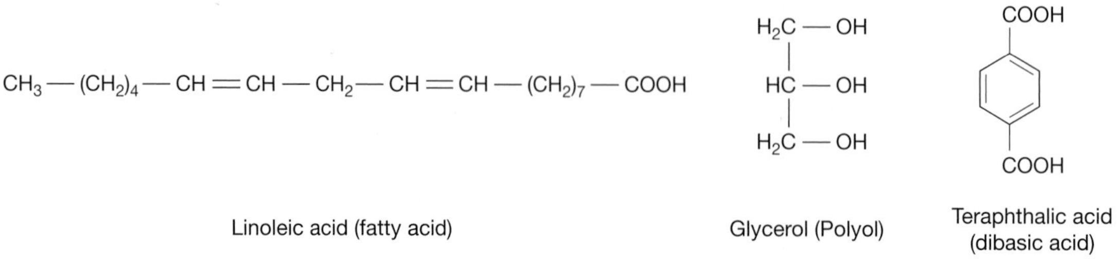

$CH_3—(CH_2)_4—CH=CH—CH_2—CH=CH—(CH_2)_7—COOH$

Linoleic acid (fatty acid)

$H_2C—OH$ / $HC—OH$ / $H_2C—OH$

Glycerol (Polyol)

COOH (benzene ring) COOH

Teraphthalic acid (dibasic acid)

Figure 2 Examples of a fatty acid from a triglyceride (linoleic acid), polyol (glycerol), and a polybasic acid (teraphthalic acid).

Amino Resins

This class of resins includes melamine and urea. Melamine is exposed to formaldehyde and either methanol or butanol to form an alkylated melamine. A useful and stable form of alkylated melamine is hexamethoxymethylmelamine (HMMM), which is formed using formaldehyde as mentioned earlier and then further reacted with methanol to be completely alkylated (methylated; **Figure 4**). The alkylated melamine will cross-link with polymers containing the functional groups of -OH, -COOH, or -CONH2, forming an ether linkage with the hydroxyl functional group, an ester linkage with the carboxyl functional group, or an amide linkage with the amide functional group (**Figure 5**). Amino resins are used as cross-linking agents with acrylic, alkyd, polyester, and epoxy resins to form thermoset coatings.

Epoxy

The two major epoxy resins are the glycidyl ether epoxide resins and the epoxidized olefins; the former is primarily used in the coatings industry. Glycidyl ether epoxides, based on bisphenol A and an oxirane ring-containing compound, usually epichlorohydrin, are the most prominent in this category and are polymerized using a condensation reaction (**Figure 6**). Epoxidized olefins have inferior chemical resistance, and therefore are not used for exterior coatings. Epoxies are used in automotive coatings as in some primers and clearcoats.

Urethane Resins

The film is formed by the reaction of isocyanates and a compound containing an active proton (**Figure 7**). The reactive proton can be (in order of reactivity) alkyl-NH_2, aromatic R-NH_2, primary -OH, secondary -OH, tertiary -OH, or aromatic -OH. The two components are kept separately and are called a 'two-package' system. When they are combined, cross-linking begins immediately; therefore, they can only be mixed immediately before application. Two more convenient 'one-package' urethane systems are also available. One such system uses atmospheric moisture that reacts with the terminal NCO to form a -NH_2, which acts as a catalyst, continuing the reaction. The other one-package urethane system uses blocked isocyanate monomer. The reactive proton-containing resin is mixed with the blocked isocyanate and only upon heating will the blocking component split, allowing the isocyanate group to be free to react with the active proton. Polyurethane coatings are used extensively for the clearcoats in automotive refinishes.

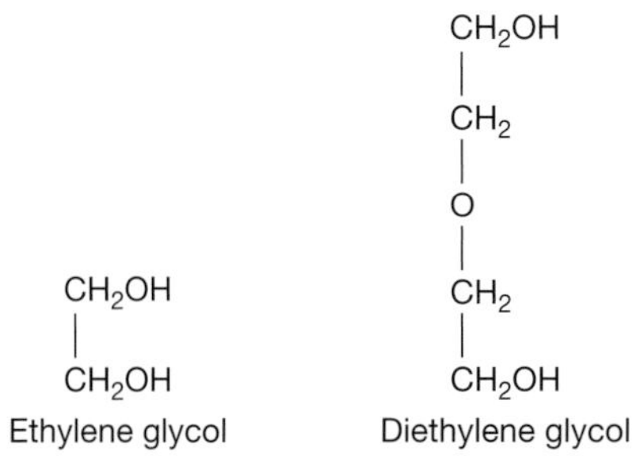

CH2OH
|
CH2OH
Ethylene glycol

CH2OH
|
CH2
|
O
|
CH2
|
CH2OH
Diethylene glycol

Figure 3 Examples of polyols with varying spatial characteristics.

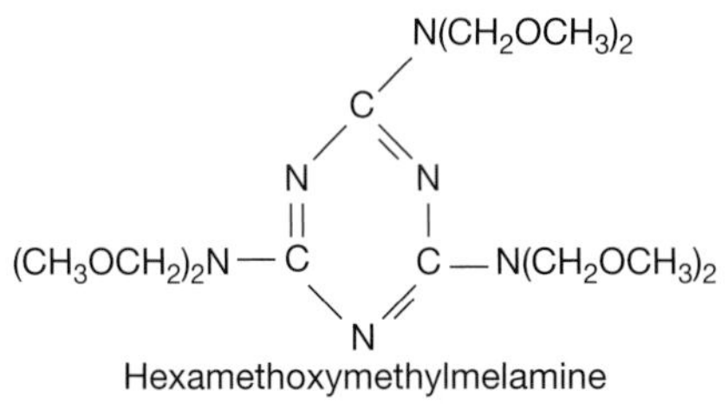

N(CH2OCH3)2 / C; N, N; (CH3OCH2)2N—C, C—N(CH2OCH3)2; N
Hexamethoxymethylmelamine

Figure 4 Alkylated melamine (hexamethoxymethylmelamine).

Carbamates

Carbamates are used in conjunction with an acrylic polymer and, therefore, will be cross-linked with resins, such as alkylated melamines, including HMMM, forming a urethane-type linkage (**Figure 8**). Unfortunately, analysis of the resulting dried film does not usually show the presence of either the carbamate monomers or the urethane-type linkages because they are so sporadically interspersed in the acrylic backbone that only the acrylic–melamine is detected. Carbamates are used in clearcoat resin systems because of their acid-resistant quality.

Pigments

Color Pigments

Color pigments are added to a coating by first making a 'pigment dispersion.' The pigment dispersion is necessary to separate aggregated and agglomerated particles of the pigment and disperse them into the chosen resin/solvent with the use of a mill (e.g., ball mill, three roll mill, or Netzsch mill) or by using the sheering action of a specialized spinner blade. This process will stabilize the pigment in the resulting resin system preventing reaggregation, flocculation (formation of loose re-aggregations of pigments), and settling of the pigment particles. Also, this process will reduce the size of the pigment particle so that it is smaller than the final film thickness. If the pigment particle size is greater than the film thickness, the pigment particles will protrude from the film. Color pigments are divided into organic and inorganic pigments. Of the inorganic pigments, white and some black pigments are considered 'hiding pigments.'

Hiding pigments

Hiding pigments are important in a coating because they obliterate or 'hide' any color variation in the previous coating or surface; therefore, all that is seen is the color of the top coating. The predominant white hiding pigment is titanium dioxide. Because of the high refractive index ($n_{iso} \sim 2.7$), it is able to conceal the previous color of the painted surface using a relatively thin film. As there are a number of layers of paint used on a vehicle, it is important to keep film thicknesses to a minimum. Also, titanium dioxide provides the base for most non-black and nonmetallic colored paints (i.e., a blue, nonmetallic coating). There are three crystalline types or polymorphs of

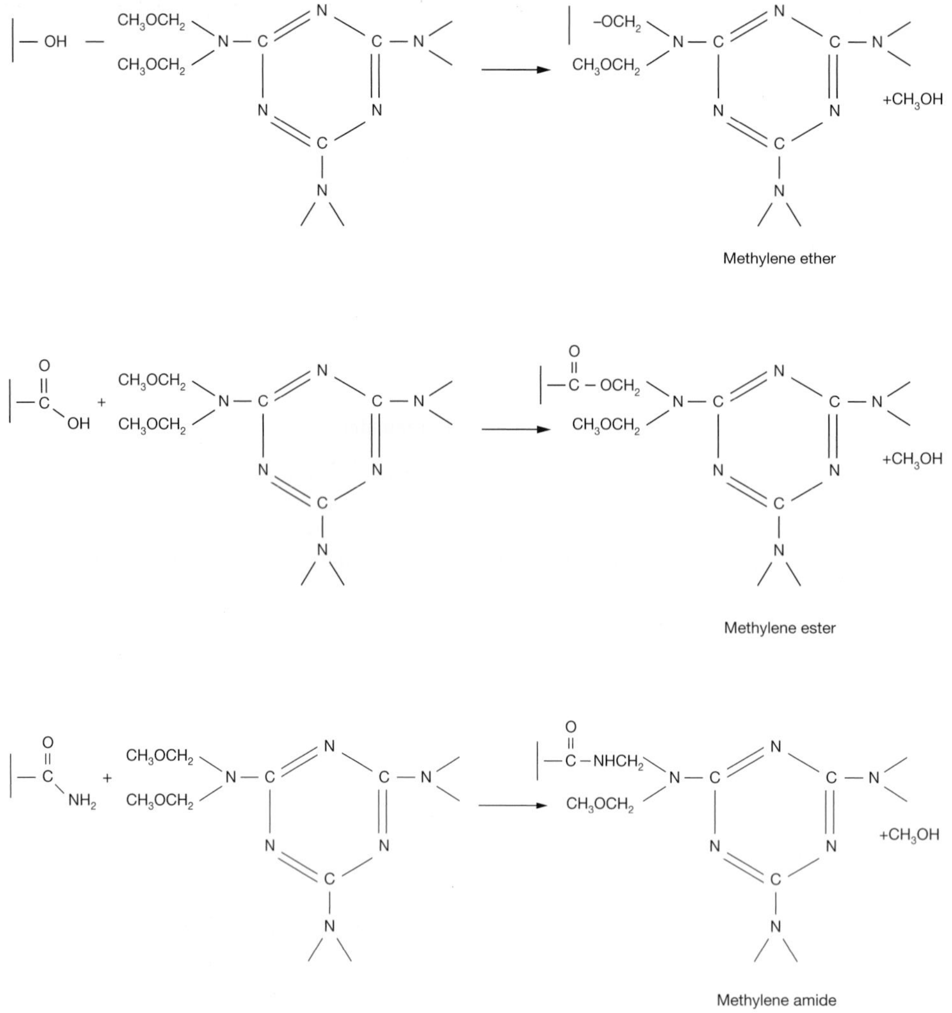

Methylene ether

Methylene ester

Methylene amide

Figure 5 Methylene ether, methylene ester, and methylene amide.

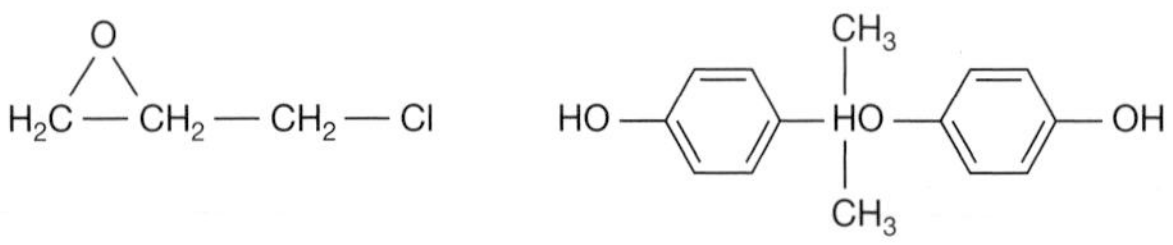

Epichlorohydrin

Bisphenol A

Figure 6 Epichlorohydrin and bisphenol A typically used to form glycidyl ether epoxies.

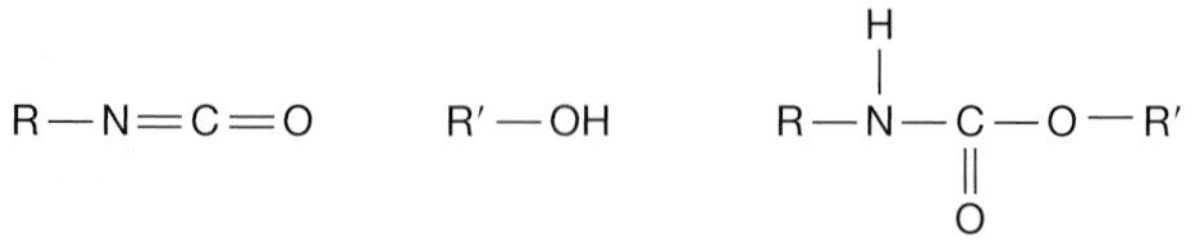

R—N=C=O

R′—OH

Isocyanate

Active proton

Urethane

Figure 7 Examples of an isocyanate and an active proton used to produce a urethane polymer.

titanium dioxide: anatase, brookite, and rutile. Anatase and brookite are not stable forms, and an abundant natural supply of brookite is not available. Also, anatase titanium dioxide has only about 75% of the hiding capacity of the rutile form and has a tendency to chalk or degrade with exposure to UV radiation. Therefore, the rutile crystalline form of titanium dioxide is used as the white pigment in automotive paint.

Black pigments are made using various techniques. The black pigments that have the best hiding power and tinting strength (less pigment is needed to impart color) are furnace black and channel black. Furnace black is produced by injecting an oil having a high aromatic content into a hot (~2600 °F) refractory chamber. The minute carbon particles produced are then passed through a cooling zone and collected. Channel black is produced by burning natural gas and impinging the flame onto a metal surface. Other black pigments, used for tinting or adding mechanical/chemical properties to paint are graphite, bone, vegetable, mineral, and iron oxide blacks.

Alkylated Melamine-formaldehyde + Secondary Carbamate

(R = alkyl hydrocarbon chain)

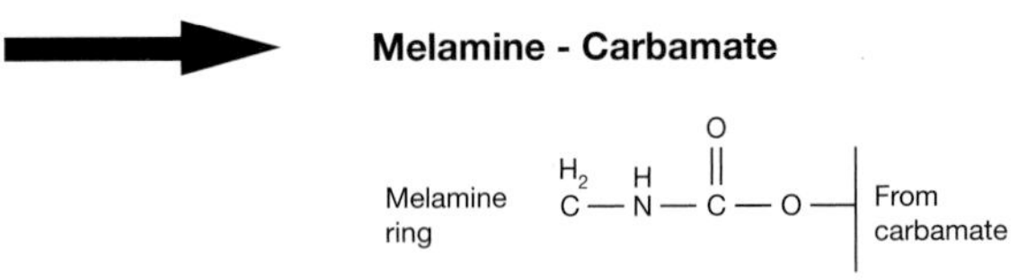

Note: isocyanate

R—N=C=O

+

HO—R′

= urethane

Figure 8 The bond between an alkylated melamine–formaldehyde molecule and a secondary carbamate. Note how the melamine–carbamate bond resembles a urethane bond.

Organic and inorganic colored pigments

Colored pigments, those other than white and black, are categorized as organic or inorganic pigments. Organic pigments are brighter, purer, and richer in color than inorganic pigments; however, they are more susceptible to destructive influences such as UV radiation, chemical damage, and color bleeding. Inorganic pigments are considered hiding or semi-hiding pigments and are low cost. However, the colors of inorganic pigments tend to be earthy and muddy. Examples of pigments used in automotive coatings are found in Table 2.

Extender Pigments

Extender pigments were first added to paint to increase volume, or bulk, and, therefore, lower the cost as extender pigments are less expensive than the hiding pigments. However, it was found that some of the extender pigments also impart certain desirable qualities to the final film. Some common extender pigments include the following.

Calcium carbonate

This can come in a variety of particle sizes and surface treatments. It can be used to control the degree of flow and tint retention. As its natural pH is between 9 and 10, care must be taken if an acidic component is introduced into the coating.

Table 2 Examples of pigments used in automotive paints

Black
Carbon black
Lamp black
White
Titanium dioxide
Red
Iron oxide
Quinacridones
Cadmium red
Thioindigo
Cadmium red
Pyranthone
Orange
Molybdate orange
Quinacridone
Anthanthrone
Benzimidazolone
Yellow
Nickel Azo
Iron oxide
Zinc chromate
Benzimidazolone
Green
Phthalocyanine green
Chrome green
Chromium oxide
Blue
Iron ferrocyanide
Phthalocyanine blue
Indanthrone
Brown
Iron oxide
Quinacridone
Benzimidazolone

Source: Information compiled from Thornton JI (2002) Forensic paint examination. In Saferstein R (ed.) *Forensic Science Handbook*, 2nd edn., pp 430–478; Patton TC (ed.) (1973) *Pigment Handbook*, vol. II. New York, NY: John Wiley and Sons.

Magnesium silicate (talc)

Talc provides a beneficial suspension for other pigments, thus preventing settling. It also increases the viscosity.

Barium sulfate

This extender is blended with hard-to-disperse inorganic colored pigments to aid in their dispersion. Moreover, as it is pH-neutral, it can be used with alkali-sensitive pigments such as iron blue and chrome green.

Potassium aluminum silicate (mica)

Mica's plate-like microstructure causes it to leaf or lie flat, which strengthens and reinforces coatings. Mica is also the base structure for a type of nacreous pigment (see 'Nacreous Pigment' section later).

Amorphous silicas

These are used for their contribution to coating flow during application.

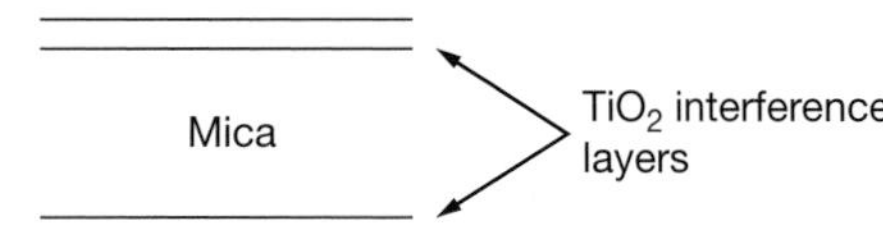

Figure 9 Cross section of a nacreous pigment.

Metallic Pigments

Aluminum flake is the most widely used metal flake in automotive paint. The aluminum metal flake used in automotive finishes is the nonleafing grade. Aluminum flakes come in leafing and nonleafing forms and the difference is only due to the nature or condition of the lubricant on the surface of the flake. Nonleafing aluminum flakes are milled (dispersed) using fatty acids, such as lauric or oleic fatty acids, and other proprietary milling aids that allow the flakes to be dispersed into the liquid paint. The aluminum flakes can be of various sizes and appearances (smooth or rough edges to the flakes) and can add a sparkle (larger flakes) or a subtle sheen (smaller flake) to the appearance of the paint surface.

Nacreous Pigments

Nacreous pigments give a product a pearl-like finish. There are many nacreous pigments used in a number of items (buttons, cosmetics, plastics) consisting of bismuth oxychloride, basic lead carbonate, and natural pearlescence obtained from shells, and fish scales and skins. However, the nacreous pigments used in automotive paints consist of a platelet of muscovite mica coated on the broad face with titanium dioxide or other metal oxide (Figure 9). The content of the titanium dioxide varies from 20% to 50%. A thinner application of titanium dioxide results in a white or pearl effect. If a thicker application is made of the titanium dioxide, then the light reflected from the pigment will emit a color which is dependent on the thickness of the titanium dioxide. These color-reflecting pigments are called interference pigments. It should be noted that the color reflected from these pigments are the complimentary color of the color seen using transmitted light (i.e., if the reflected color is green, the color seen using transmitted light is red). If the metal oxide used to coat the mica particle is iron oxide, the resulting colors range from bronze to copper-red and will have a more metallic quality.

New Effect Pigments

New effect pigments have come on the market and may be encountered more in the coming years. One of these consists of aluminum oxide coated with another metal oxide (like titanium dioxide or iron oxide) to produce an appearance which is a bit flashier than the metal oxide-coated mica particles, which produce a satiny effect. There are also hue-shifting particles produced by coating aluminum with magnesium fluoride or silicon dioxide coated with a metal oxide (titanium or iron oxide) which cause the color to shift when the coating is viewed at varying angles.

Holographic pigments are produced by embossing physical grooves on the surface of a solvent-inert material. This material is then coated with a metal, usually aluminum, using vapor deposition and sealed with a clearcoat. The resulting appearance is a prismatic effect.

Solvents

Automotive paint in solution form is generally not encountered by forensic chemists. However, solvents are important when formulating paint. The paint chemist must consider a number of factors when considering the type of solvent used, including the application technique and application location. Application techniques, which will be addressed later in the article, include spraying the paint using air or placing an electric charge on the paint allowing it to be drawn to the part being sprayed. The same paint, which is sprayed using the two different techniques, may require different solvent combinations to achieve optimum appearance and performance. Application location refers to the physical conditions in the location in which the paint is to be sprayed. Considerations include whether the facility is located in an area of the country that is particularly dry or humid, or whether the assembly plant is air-conditioned or in any way temperature controlled.

The primary function of solvents in paint is to keep the film-forming resins, pigments, and any other additives in a liquid form so that they can be applied to a surface. Solvents are evaluated for their solvency (the ability to dissolve the film-forming resin into solution), volatility (how fast it evaporates), odor, and toxicity. The rate of evaporation, flow properties, and viscosity are all considered when a coating is formulated. Examples of solvents used in automotive coatings are hydrocarbon solvents (derived from petroleum and coal tar, and consisting primarily of only carbon and hydrogen), oxygenated solvents (containing oxygen along with carbon and hydrogen), and water. All of the aforementioned solvents (except for water) are considered volatile organic compounds (VOCs) by the Environmental Protection Agency (USA), and, thus, are regulated. Therefore, paint and coating manufacturers are creating paint formulations so as to minimize the VOC content of their products.

It should be noted here that waterborne paint systems are becoming popular in automotive coatings, especially in the basecoat portion, because water has less of an environmental impact than other solvents. In essence, a water-reducible resin is used in the formulation of the coating and that resin can either be an acrylic, alkyd, or possibly even an epoxy polymer. However, in the final dry film, it will most likely be impossible to determine whether or not the original wet paint was a waterborne or solvent-borne paint. Waterborne basecoats are used in both OEM and refinish basecoats.

Order of Deposition and Identification of Paint Layers

Automotive paint has a highly engineered application sequence. The first layer, closest to the substrate, is the primer layer. Recently, all metal portions of the outer body of all OEM vehicles have been exposed to electrodeposition primer (see 'Application Techniques' section later). For the plastic portions of the vehicle body, a primer may or may not be used. A second primer may be applied on top of the electrodeposition primer.

Occasionally, this primer is of a color similar to the basecoat color so that the basecoat can be applied thinner as a cost-reducing measure. It should be noted here that the basecoat and the clearcoat decorating and protecting the outside of a vehicle body are one of the single most expensive parts of the car; therefore, reducing quantity of these costly coatings is important. The primer can also be a powder coating. Usually, the primer is baked and, therefore, cross-linked into a thermosetting film prior to the addition of the basecoat and clearcoat. However, a current trend is toward 'integrated processing' in which the primer would not be baked into a cross-linked film before spraying the basecoat and clearcoat. This process will both save on energy and decrease the processing footprint (less area used for the primer ovens).

There may be a coating to prevent stone chips near the lower portions of the vehicle panels which consists of a thin film applied over the finished paint film. In lieu of this coating, 'cladding' may be employed, which is a plastic film that is bolted over the finished film.

On top of the primer coat(s) is the basecoat, which is the layer that contains the color and any effect pigments. The basecoat is usually applied by spray application. It is then allowed to air-dry or 'flash' to allow for evaporation of some of the solvents. If the basecoat is a waterborne basecoat, it may even be dry to the touch after allowing it to flash; however, it is not a durable film and will still need to be baked.

Finally, the clearcoat is applied over the wet or uncured basecoat. The clearcoat can be the same resin system as the basecoat or a different system. This coat will be allowed to flash, and then the whole item is baked in an oven for the specified temperature and amount of time needed. If a part is damaged, it can be repainted with a basecoat and clearcoat (generally without repainting the primer). Therefore, if a layer system is encountered that consists of a series of basecoats and clearcoats with no additional primer, it can be assumed that the recoating of the item was done in the factory. If, however, there is a primer over a previous coat of basecoat and clearcoat, and if the basecoat and clearcoat layers consist of alkyd and/or polyurethane resin systems, it is likely that the item has been painted 'aftermarket,' meaning that it was repainted at a body shop after the vehicle has been completely assembled. Aftermarket or refinished coatings have to be able to cure to a durable finish without the benefit of high heat.

On some vehicles, mostly older ones, there is only one coat of colored paint without a clearcoat. Therefore, the one-color coat must be durable, glossy, and contain all the components and additives necessary to protect the underlying substrate. Less than 2% of automotive topcoats worldwide are a one-coat topcoat system.

Finally, there is a layer system that includes a second 'clearcoat,' located between the basecoat and the final clearcoat, which contains nacreous pigments. This coat is not designed to hide the coat below it; it is designed to give additional luster and depth to the appearance of the coating. This system is usually found in higher-end vehicles. The layers in this system are as follows: primer(s), basecoat (usually a light color like white, cream, or buttery yellow), nacreous-containing clearcoat, and clearcoat.

As stated, the application of automotive coatings is a highly engineered sequence and, therefore, the layer thicknesses of the resulting layers should be monitored. Here is an example of the sequence and layer thicknesses of the resulting films starting with the coating nearest to the substrate:

Electrocoat primer – 1.0–1.2 mils (1 mil = 0.001 in.)
Primer surface (if present) – 1.2 mils
Basecoat – 0.4–1.0 mils
Clearcoat – 1.4–2.0 mils

Application Techniques

Automotive coatings are applied by spray, electrodeposition, and application as a powder.

Spray

Spraying the paint onto the surface constitutes the majority of application techniques. The equipment can be an air spray gun (which propels the paint in a stream of air), airless spray gun (in which pressure propels the paint), or an electrostatic spray method. In the electrostatic spray method, the part to be coated is grounded and the paint is given a negative charge. Therefore, the paint is attracted to the intended part. This method of spray deposition limits waste. If the parts to be coated are plastic, a conductive primer is applied to them before electrostatic spray deposition of the topcoats.

Electrodeposition

Electrodeposition essentially 'electroplates' the item or part with paint. The part is dipped into a tank and a current is activated. The part, acting as either the cathode or anode, will receive a uniform coating of paint on all conductive areas. The thickness is determined by the electrical potential. This process is usually reserved for primers.

Powder Coating

Powder coats contain all the components of paint except for the solvent. A dry mix of resins, pigments, additives, and fillers are mixed, melted together (below the temperature at which it cross-links), and milled into a powder. The powder can be applied in many ways to the part but the most widely used method is electrostatic spraying, where the powder particles are charged and will adhere to the part which is grounded. In this method of coating, the powder that is not deposited onto the part is reclaimed and reused. The part is then baked to melt and cross-link the polymers. Powder coats are used in the automotive industry primarily for primers. Reclaimed powders of various colors may be mixed together and used as a primary primer. This primer will consist of many colors and, therefore, will probably be primed with a neutral or color-specific second primer before coating with the basecoat/clearcoat.

See also: **Chemistry/Trace/Paint and Coating:** Architectural Paint; Forensic Paint Analysis; Interpretation of Paint Evidence; **Chemistry/Trace/Trace Evidence:** Microchemistry; **Methods:** Microscopy (Electron).

Further Reading

Allen RA (1981) *Epoxy Resins in Coatings*. Philadelphia, PA: Federation of Societies for Paint Technology.

Allyn G (1971) *Acrylic Resins*. Philadelphia, PA: Federation of Societies for Paint Technology.

Blegen JR (1979) *Alkyd Resins*. Philadelphia, PA: Federation of Societies for Paint Technology.

Hensley WL and McGinty WE (1979) *Amino Resins in Coatings*. Philadelphia, PA: Federation of Societies for Paint Technology.

Patton TC (ed.) (1973) *Pigment Handbook*, vols. 1–3. New York, NY: Wiley.

Rodrigues F (1989) *Principles of Polymer Systems*, 3rd edn. New York, NY: Hemisphere Publishing Corporation.

Thornton JI (2002) Forensic paint examination. In: Saferstein R (ed.) *Forensic Science Handbook*, 2nd edn., pp. 430–478. Upper Saddle River, NJ: Prentice Hall.

Tracton AA (ed.) (2007) *Coatings Materials and Surface Coatings*. Boca Raton, FL: CRC Press.

Relevant Website

http://www.swgmat.org/ – Scientific Working Group for Materials Analysis (SWGMAT).

Forensic Paint Analysis

C Muehlethaler, L Gueissaz, and G Massonnet, Université de Lausanne, Lausanne, Switzerland

Forensic Considerations About Paint Evidence

Introduction

Paint evidence is often encountered in criminal cases, as many items used in our daily lives have a coating. In forensic science, paint can be grouped into two main categories.

The first one includes coatings applied to all means of transportation such as automobiles, bicycles, motorbikes, boats, and aircraft. The application of these coatings generally follows rigorous industrial processes and includes several different paint layers.

The second category includes coatings on household objects such as walls, doors, window frames, safes, and tools. Graffiti paints are also part of this group. The application of such paints is usually less standardized and they may be applied in only one layer.

Finally, the forensic laboratory can also work on art objects or paintings in order to detect forgeries, anachronisms, alterations, or underlying pictures. The requirements concerning art objects are highly diverse and case related. Working with other specialists in art or museums is often recommended. This specific area is not covered in this article.

Transfer and Persistence

When a contact occurs between a coated object and a substrate, paint transfer may occur. The quantity and the nature of the paint transferred (e.g., fragments or smears) will depend on the properties of the paint (e.g., adherence and quality), the nature of the substrate surface (e.g., rough and smooth), and the intensity of the contact (e.g., the force or pressure involved). If the substrate is also coated, a cross-transfer may occur.

Road accidents are good examples of such paint transfers. Usually, automobile paints are strongly bound to their metallic or polymeric substrates. Normally, paint fragments will transfer when the force of the contact is sufficient to cause a deformation of the car body. When only minor or frictional forces are involved, it is more probable that only a smear of the paints is transferred. As for domestic paints such as the ones found on tools, buildings, or other decorative objects, their transfer also requires intensity, to some extent. A burglar trying to force an entry into a house with a crowbar will possibly transfer paint from the door onto his crowbar or leave traces of the crowbar coating on the door.

Another possibility of transfer is by direct contact with wet paint, such as freshly painted surfaces. The use of spray cans also result in microdroplets, which are likely to be recovered from the suspect's skin, clothes, or shoes.

Wet paint or smears usually adhere rather strongly to the substrate onto which they are transferred. Their persistence is high and they will be lost mostly if an external force is applied (e.g., washing, cleaning, scraping, or other subsequent contacts). Paint fragments are more easily lost by normal activities or by environmental conditions (e.g., wind and rain). In all cases, the time elapsed between the contact and the recovery of the traces is important to limit the possible loss of evidence.

Aims of Forensic Paint Analysis

The goal of a forensic paint analysis will depend on the case itself and will be clearly delimited in accordance with the needs of the client and the capabilities of the laboratory. The presence or absence of control material is also an important element to consider (see Figure 1).

Absence of control material

In some cases, a control sample may not be (directly) available. In such a scenario, the trace sample may be characterized and/or analyzed in order to obtain intelligence information to be communicated to the police (e.g., to provide information concerning the possible source of a paint sample).

The most common example is the search for a potential vehicle based on the analysis of a paint flake found in a hit-and-run accident. In this case, the first step is the observation of the traces in order to determine the number of layers and whether the paint is an original equipment manufacturer (OEM) sample. If this is the case, the color can be compared with reference tables such as the AKZO Colormap (AKZO Nobel Coatings) or Nexa Autocolor (PPG Industries). These tables are used by automobile repair shops and provide information on possible make of vehicles based on color comparison. Infrared (IR) spectra will be recorded for each layer and compared with reference IR databases of automobile paints. In Europe, the European Paint Group (EPG) of European Network of Forensic Science Institutes has built up the European Collection of Automotive Paint, which contains several thousands of IR spectra. In the United States and Canada, the database in use is the Paint Data Query. These databases include information about the make, model, year of production, and production plant of a specific sample. The expert will combine the results obtained from the comparison of the IR spectra and those obtained from the comparison with color tables to provide the police a list of possible vehicles.

Reference collections are also available for the EPG members on some spray or tool paints. If necessary, each laboratory can undertake its own market study adapted to the case in question.

Presence of control materials

Generally, a control sample is available and the forensic scientist will compare the trace and control samples in terms of physical and chemical characteristics to reach one of the following conclusions: (1) the two samples are distinguishable or (2) the two samples are indistinguishable.

 http://dx.doi.org/10.1016/B978-0-12-382165-2.00109-4

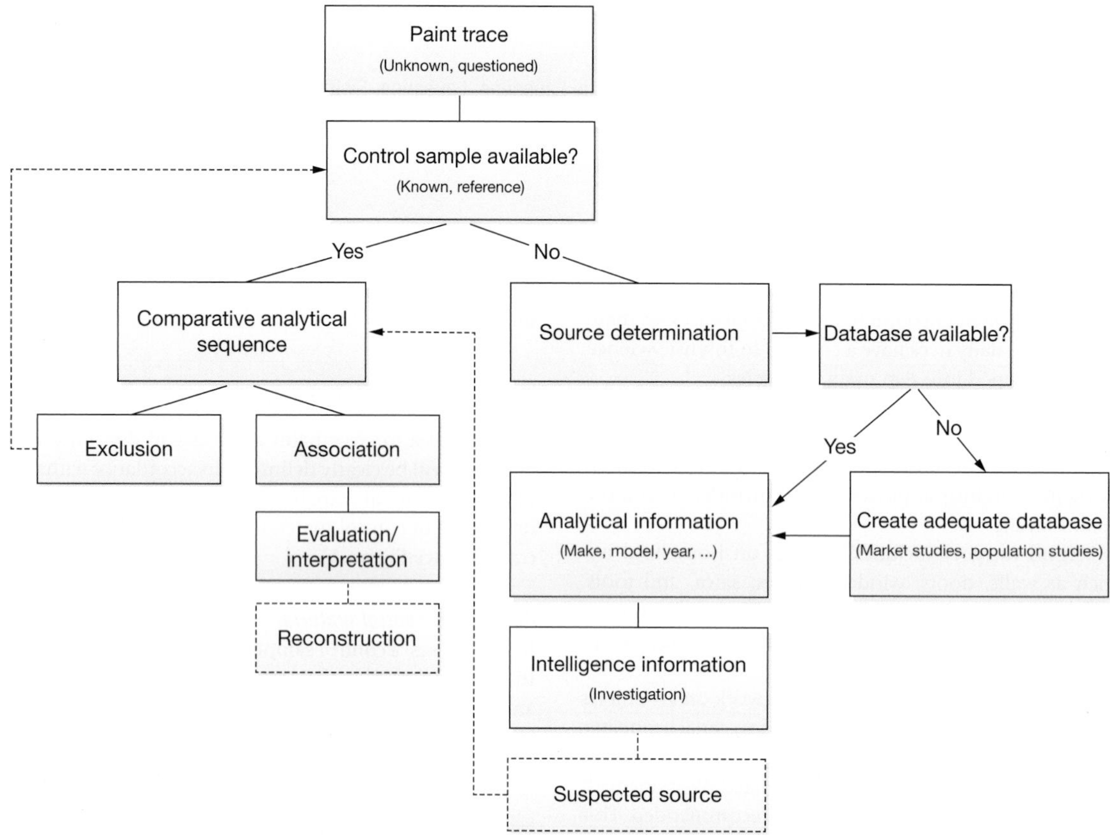

Figure 1 Flowchart of a typical forensic paint analysis.

If the samples have different optical and/or analytical characteristics, a common origin can be excluded provided the reference material is representative of all the variations encountered in the reference object. When only a portion of the reference material is available, it might be more difficult to arrive at a conclusion.

In the case of a positive association, that is, when the trace and control samples are indistinguishable in all their physical and chemical characteristics, the evidential value of these findings must be assessed by an expert.

Finally, once the contact between two objects has been demonstrated and interpreted, very good information can be had about the nature of the contact, the relative position of the objects, and the sequence of events that took place. For instance, in a road accident, the exact position and origin of the contact traces such as paints may help in the reconstruction of the course of events.

Sequence of Examination

Before starting any paint examination, a pre-evaluation of the case will enable the expert to define the potential and the limitations of his/her examinations depending on the case-specific circumstances. This step is important and may influence the wordings of the report submitted to the laboratory. The pre-evaluation step should be carried out as quickly as possible, so that all the items are still under the control of the police (e.g., if there is a need to collect more material, or to see the objects such as vehicles).

The choice of the appropriate sequence of examination (see Figure 2) will depend on the samples (e.g., quality, quantity, color, and morphology), the nature of the request, and the equipment available in the laboratory.

Optical examinations are essential and include stereomicroscopy and microscopy. These observations can provide information on the type of paint involved, its homogeneity, morphology, and layer sequence. Each layer is then analyzed separately.

A dry paint is usually mainly composed of an organic binder and some organic and/or inorganic pigments; it may also contain some inorganic extender. Additives will be present in relatively low percentages. Chemical analysis will tend to compare and identify the main paint constituents.

IR spectroscopy is usually the first analytical method used, and it mostly detects the organic composition of a paint. Complementary information concerning the inorganic composition can be obtained by methods such as elemental analysis. Pyrolysis–gas chromatography–mass spectrometry (Py–GC/MS) provides information about the organic content (major and minor components). Microspectrophotometry (MSP) and Raman spectrometry are chosen mostly to measure colored samples.

Evidence Collection

The collection of evidence, including traces and reference materials, is the most important step in any forensic case. Any

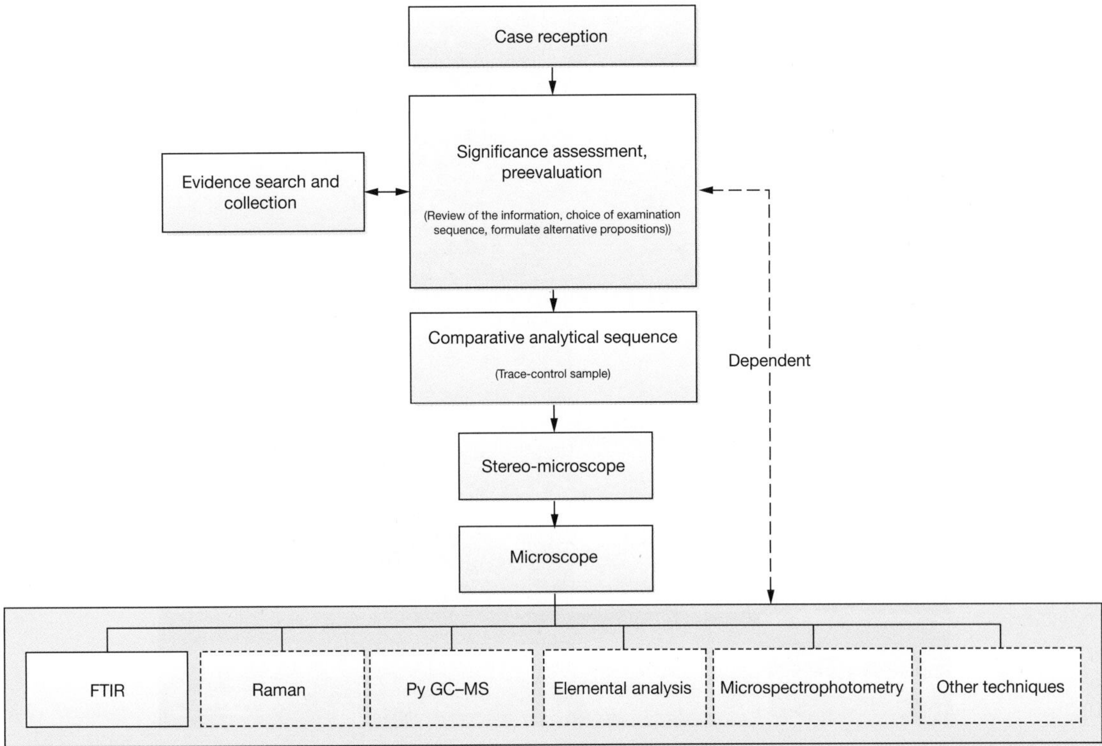

Figure 2 Flowchart of a comparative analytical sequence between a trace sample and a control sample.

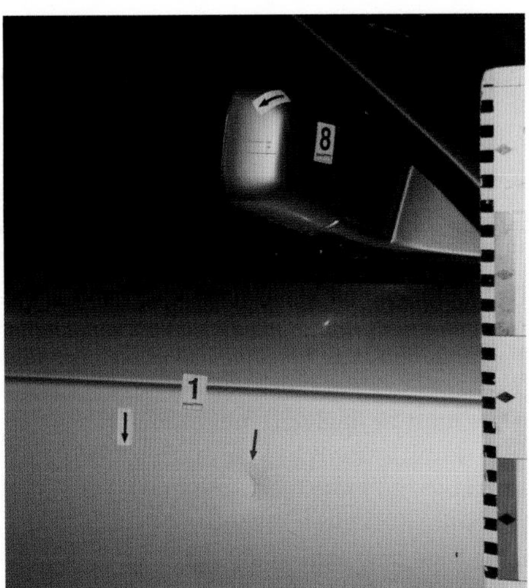

Figure 3 Detailed position of two traces on a vehicle.

subsequent analysis will depend on the samples recovered. Any omission at this stage may have disastrous consequences.

Nontransportable items such as automobiles or doorframes are examined in situ with a proper light source (torch). The position of each trace is recorded (**Figure 3**) and the traces taken, if possible, with tweezers. Another possibility is to collect the substrate and the trace together using a scalpel. The samples are conditioned in a folded paper sheet. An adhesive tape can be useful on the crime scene, but it might be problematic with small particles owing to possible glue contamination.

Control samples must be taken at several locations close to the point(s) of impact(s) and the entire layer system must be collected. The localization of known material is of critical importance, because slight differences in layer thickness and/or layer sequences can be present in large coated surfaces such as vehicles.

If a contact between two painted surfaces is plausible, the possibility of cross-transfer has to be considered. Both surfaces should be meticulously observed, and any sample, if available, should be collected.

In the laboratory, the search for paint traces is undertaken with the help of appropriate stereomicroscopic equipment (if possible with a flexible arm). The items are observed on flat, cleaned, and covered surfaces following proper anticontamination procedures. Any visible paint trace is described and recorded. Paint in the form of flakes or fragments can be collected with a pair of tweezers. Paint in the form of smears or powders can be preserved as such, and a portion of the latter taken for analysis. Latent paint traces can be systematically searched for by other means such as adhesive tapes, vacuum cleaner equipped with a special collection filter, shaking, or brushing over a clean surface.

Optical Examination

The first and foremost part of any paint analysis concerns the optical examination. Stereomicroscopy and microscopy are very powerful techniques that provide accurate information concerning the morphology of paint traces. Properties such as surface characteristics, the number of layers, colors, size, and appearance are specific to automobile OEM coatings as well as repair or household paint. Analytical techniques are then applied selectively to each layer. The global discriminating power of an optical examination is very high.

Figure 4 Microscopic examination of the cross-section (5 μm) of a repainted automobile fragment. The global layer sequence is around 1.2 mm thick and composed of 25 distinct layers. (a) Bright field. (b) Dark field. (c) Crossed polarizers. (d) UV fluorescence (excitation 340–380 nm, emission 425 nm).

First, the samples are globally observed and described under a stereomicroscope (typically from 5× to 60× magnification) with reflected light. The shape, color, surface properties, and presence of layers are reported and/or sketched. Then, using a microscope of magnification ranging from 100× to 400×, together with the use of bright field, dark field, polarization, and fluorescence illuminations, further characterization of the inner and outer surfaces can be done. The use of episcopic illumination permits the observation of effect pigments and of surface defects such as striae or scratches; it can be used while attempting to physically match two fragments. A physical match is generally based on contours, striaes, and scratches and needs to be discussed (quality and numer of concordances). Accurate examination of layers is performed by using cross-sections (a few micrometers thick, usually cut with a microtome) of the fragments embedded in resin. This technique is, however, to be considered semidestructive, as the fragment is not retrievable from the resin. Microscopic examination of the cross-sections with the above-mentioned techniques allows the determination of the number, color, sequence, and thickness of the layers, all of which are very useful information used for discrimination.

Figure 4 shows the complementarity of the different illuminations: bright field enhances the contrast of the red layers, whereas dark field enhances the color contrast between the opaque layers. Crossed polarizers allow the observation (or identification) of birefringent material (mainly extenders). Observation under ultraviolet (UV) light is the only technique that allows a good observation of the clearcoat layers based on their fluorescence.

IR Spectroscopy

IR spectroscopy deals with the IR region of the electromagnetic spectrum and exploits the fact that molecules absorb specific frequencies that are characteristic of their structure.

A Fourier transform IR (FTIR) spectrometer equipped with an IR microscope is the most commonly used instrument type. Paint samples are usually flattened (a few micrometers) and measured in the transmittance mode, either deposited on a KBr pellet or squeezed in a microdiamond anvil cell. Each layer of a paint sample must be analyzed independently.

IR spectroscopy is the technique of choice for characterizing the main organic and inorganic components of a paint system, including mainly the binder, the extenders, and some organic or inorganic pigments. Minor or trace constituents, such as additives, will generally not be detected. FTIR spectroscopy is routinely used in forensic laboratories for several reasons: it is fast, repeatable, semidestructive, and when coupled to an IR microscope, it has excellent microsampling capabilities (surfaces as small as 10 × 10 μm can be analyzed with very little sample preparation). This technique is also known to have a high discriminating power for most of the paint types encountered in forensic laboratories. Another advantage is that several commercial or forensic spectral databases exist or can easily be created. These databases can be of help in paint identification, or they could provide intelligence for police services (such as the make and model of an automobile). Laboratory spectral databases can also give the relative frequency for a given paint type based on its IR spectrum, which is relevant in the interpretation stage.

Raman Spectroscopy

Raman spectroscopy measures the inelastic (Raman) scattering of a molecule irradiated by a monochromatic light, usually from a laser. This inelastic scattering provides information about the vibrational modes of a specimen.

A dispersive Raman instrument equipped with a microscope is the most suitable for trace analysis. The choice of the laser(s) is also important, as it will affect the quality of the Raman spectrum. Paint traces can be analyzed in situ without any sample preparation. Multilayered paint fragments are usually cut into thin cross-sections and mounted on an aluminum foil so that each layer can be analyzed independently. When coupled to a microscope, Raman spectrometers have a spatial resolution of a few micrometers.

Raman spectroscopy can provide information mainly about the organic and inorganic pigments as well as some extenders present in a paint sample, provided a suitable Raman database is available.

Raman spectroscopy is actually not routinely used in all forensic laboratories, but it is quite often implemented in the analytical sequence of paint when the instrument is available. The main advantage of Raman spectroscopy is the absence of sample preparation and its very high spatial resolution. Its main disadvantage is the possible fluorescence of the sample, which will totally or partially mask the Raman spectrum. One way of avoiding fluorescence is to change the excitation wavelength (e.g., from the visible range to the near-IR).

Pyrolysis–Gas Chromatography–Mass Spectrometry

Pyrolysis is the breaking up of chemical bonds by the use of thermal energy. Macromolecules such as paint binders will decompose into smaller volatile fragments. Under controlled conditions (temperature, heating rate, and time), the same distribution of smaller molecules can be produced. The fragments are then separated by GC and identified or characterized using MS.

A minimum of 10 μg is necessary for the analysis, and the samples must be prepared under controlled conditions. Each layer of a paint flake must be isolated prior to analysis.

This technique is used to characterize the monomers used in binder systems, but it might also identify some additives or pigments if reference pyrograms and/or MS spectra are available.

An enormous advantage of Py–GC/MS is its high discriminating power and its ability to detect and compare minor constituents. Its disadvantages are its destructive nature and time-consuming analysis.

Elemental Analysis (Scanning Electron Microscopy/Energy Dispersive x-Ray Analysis, Micro x-Ray Fluorescence)

Elemental analysis consists of the measurement of the atomic emission of the elements present in a paint sample. The most commonly used methods are based on the atomic emission of characteristic x-ray lines from a material that has been excited by high-energy x-rays. In this category, scanning electron microscopy coupled with energy dispersive spectrometry (SEM/EDS) is the most commonly used method in forensic Laboratories. Micro x-ray (μXRF) fluorescence instruments might also be an option, mostly for homogeneous samples. Multilayer samples have to be prepared (by embedding, polishing, or sectioning). If a high-vacuum SEM is used, a metallic coating of the samples is required. This is not the case for low-vacuum SEM or μXRF.

Elemental analysis is mainly used for comparison purposes in qualitative or semiquantitative modes. Elemental analysis also provides an indirect identification of the inorganic content of paint through the detection of the elements present. This technique will mostly characterize the extenders and inorganic pigments as well as some organic pigments.

The analyses are rapid and rather sensitive ($\sim$0.1 wt%) and provide complementary information as against FTIR, Raman, and Py–GC/MS, which mostly characterize the organic components of a paint.

Microspectrophotometry

A microspectrophotometer measures the light intensity that is transmitted, absorbed, or reflected by a sample at each wavelength of the visible or ultraviolet region of the spectrum. It allows an objective measurement of the color.

Paints are mainly measured in situ and in the reflectance mode using dark field optics. If necessary, transmittance spectra in the UV or visible range can be recorded. It requires some sample preparation and quartz microscope slides.

MSP is mostly used to compare samples. Pigment identification is rather difficult for several reasons: most of the paints contain two or three pigments and the resulting spectrum will be a combination of all their spectra (mostly the major ones); also, the MSP spectra of pigments are often not very characteristic, especially in reflectance mode.

MSP can provide an objective measure of the color and might be able to differentiate between optically identical samples (metamers). However, this method is more problematic for effect coatings (large variation in the spectral response), and measurements must be carried out on clean and undamaged sample areas of similar size and morphology.

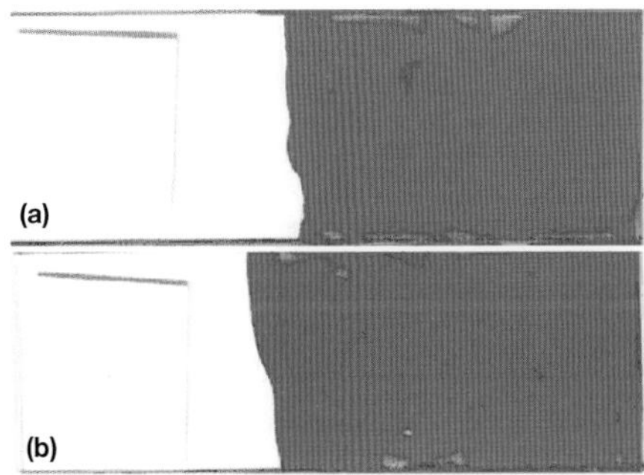

Figure 5 Domestic red paints deposited on microscopic slides. (a) (top) and (b) (bottom), very similar in color.

Other Analytical Techniques

Many additional techniques exist, but they refer to specific analytical schemes. They are not routinely used in the forensic analysis of paints but can represent novel solutions to particular problems. Of interest among them are x-ray diffraction (XRD), laser ablation inductive coupled plasma MS, thermal analysis, and cathodoluminescence.

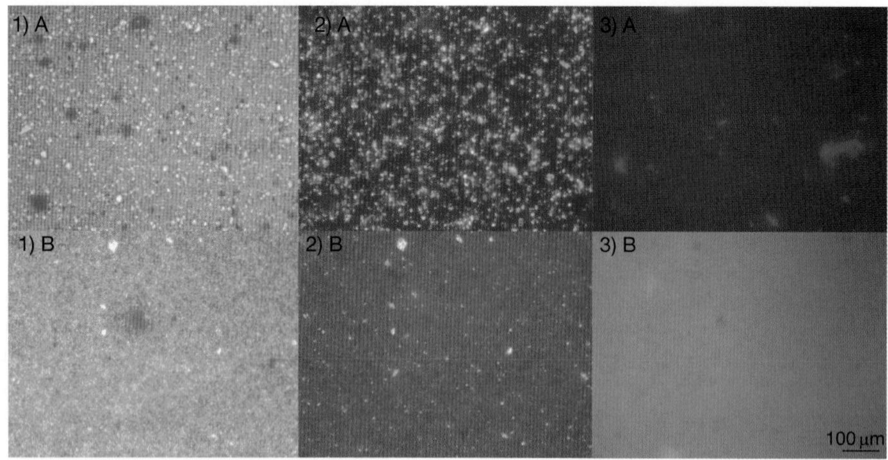

Figure 6 Microscopic examination of paint A (top) and B (bottom) using transmitted light (10× objective). (1) Bright field, (2) crossed polarizers, and (3) UV fluorescence (excitation 340–380 nm, emission 425 nm).

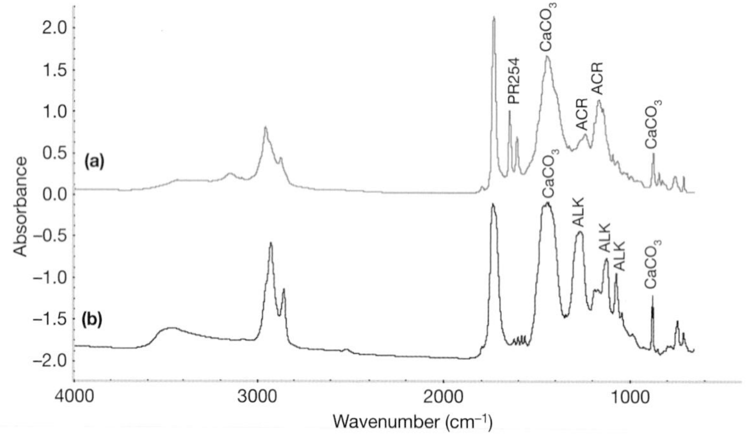

Figure 7 Fourier transform infrared spectra of two domestic red paints. The main absorption bands of the binders and extenders and the presence of the organic pigment (PR 254) are seen. Measurements were made on KBr pellets in transmittance mode. Paint A (red), acrylic–calcium carbonate, pigment red 254. Paint B (blue), alkyd (based on orthophthalic acid)–calcium carbonate.

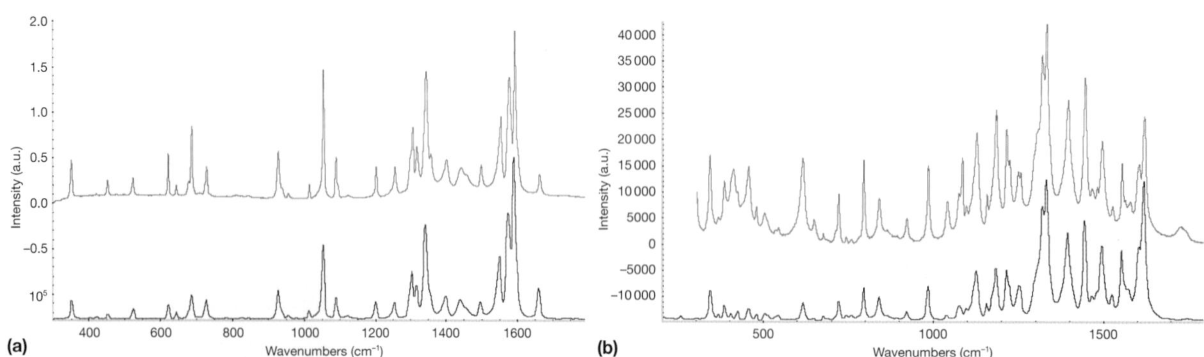

Figure 8 Raman spectra with the identification of the main organic pigments in two domestic red paints. (a) Paint A containing C.I. pigment red 254 (red) and reference spectrum of C.I. pigment red 254 (Ciba-Irgazin, 1,4-diketo-3,6-diaryl-pyrrolo(3,4-c)pyrrole) (blue). (b) Paint B containing C.I. pigment red 3 (red) and reference spectrum of C.I. pigment red 3 (Hoechst–Hansa Scharlach, 1-(4-methyl-2-nitrophenylazo)-2-naphthol) (blue).

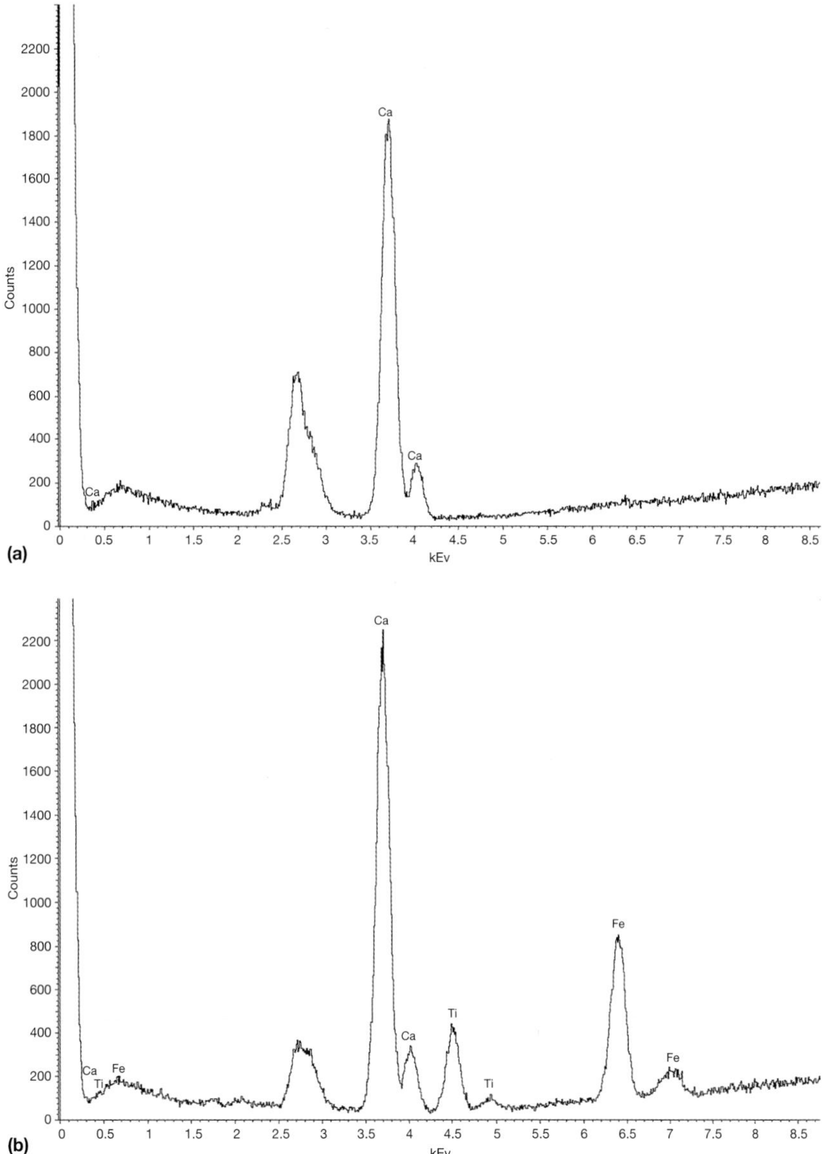

Figure 9 x-Ray fluorescence spectra illustrating the detection of elements present in two domestic red paints. (a) Paint A, presence of calcium (Ca). (b) Paint B, presence of calcium (Ca), titanium (Ti), and iron (Fe).

Illustration of Different Techniques

Two optically similar domestic red paints (**Figure 5**), samples A and B, are used to illustrate the potential and the limitations of different techniques in terms of discrimination and identification of the paint constituents. Both paints have the same color code number RAL 3000 (RAL is the color matching system used in Europe).

Microscopic examination of these paints (**Figure 6**) shows clear color differences in transmitted light: sample A is magenta and sample B is orange. These observations also show the nonhomogeneity of the paint film, with clearly visible pigment agglomerates and extenders. In cross-polarization, the density of birefringent particles is different; these particles correspond to calcium carbonate ($CaCO_3$). Sample B has a strong blue

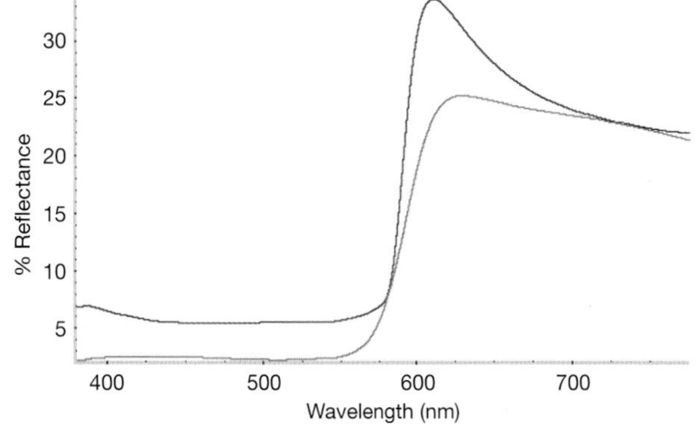

Figure 10 Color measurements of two red household paints by microspectrophotometry. Reflectance spectra of paint A (blue) and B (red).

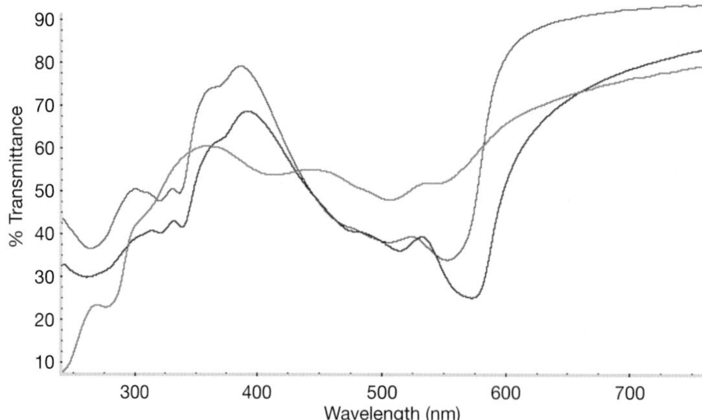

Figure 11 MSP transmission spectra in the UV–visible range of paint A (blue), B (red), and reference spectrum of C.I. pigment red 254 (purple).

fluorescence under UV light, while sample A has a less intense fluorescence.

IR spectroscopy (Figure 7) confirms the presence of $CaCO_3$ in both paint samples. These paints have different organic binder systems: acrylic for sample A and orthophthalic alkyd for sample B. The organic pigment, C.I. pigment red 254, is also present in paint A and can be identified with its characteristic doublets around 1650 cm^{-1}. Reference databases of pigments, extenders, and binder systems are necessary to identify each paint constituent.

Raman spectroscopy (Figure 8) enables the identification of one organic red pigment in each of the samples. Sample A contains the organic pigment, C.I. pigment red 254 (already detected by IR spectroscopy). Sample B contains the C.I. pigment red 3. Reference databases are required to identify these pigments.

Elemental analysis (μXRF) shows the presence of calcium (Ca) from the extender $CaCO_3$ in both samples (Figure 9). Sample B contains titanium (Ti), most probably from the white pigment titanium dioxide. This pigment is not detected by IR and Raman spectroscopy probably because of its low concentration. Iron (Fe) is also present in sample B; its source might be an inorganic iron pigment. To further identify these pigments, XRD analysis would be necessary.

MSP spectra are measured in situ in reflectance mode, and the mean spectra are displayed in Figure 10. Samples A and B can be differentiated by MSP, but their spectra are rather featureless and differ only in the area between 550 and 650 nm. Pigment identification is difficult in this case.

The same paints are mounted on quartz microscopic slides and their transmittance measured in the UV–visible range (Figure 11). Samples A and B show clear differences and more informative spectra compared to reflectance measurements. C.I. pigment red 254 was also measured: most features of this pigment are present in the spectrum of paint A.

Summary

This example illustrates the complementary nature of the methods in terms of the characterization of the main paint constituents. It also emphasizes the need for appropriate databases and/or reference material (measured under the same analytical conditions) in order to identify the paint constituents.

In this example, each method used as a stand-alone technique has enabled the discrimination of paints A and B. This also highlights the importance of microscopic examinations as the first step of the comparative analytical sequence, as it already differentiated paint samples of identical color codes.

On the other hand, the characterization of major organic and inorganic constituents is possible only when using a sequence of complementary methods. Minor constituents, such as additives, are often problematic with forensic traces because of the low amount of material available. In order to detect and identify minor constituents, more samples and more sensitive methods as well as exhaustive reference materials would be required.

See also: **Chemistry/Trace/Paint and Coating:** Architectural Paint; Automotive Paint; Interpretation of Paint Evidence; Overview.

Further Reading

Bartick E and Tungol M (1993) Infrared microscopy and its forensic applications. In: Saferstein R (ed.) *Forensic Science Handbook*, vol. III, pp. 196–252. Englewood Cliffs, NJ: Regent Prentice Hall.

Buzzini P, Massonnet G, and Monard Sermier F (2006) The micro Raman analysis of paint evidence in criminalistics: Case studies. *Journal of Raman Spectroscopy* 37(9): 922–931.

Caddy B (1999) *Forensic Examination of Glass and Paint, Analysis and Interpretation*. London and New York: Taylor and Francis Forensic Science Series.

Challinor J (2007) Examination of forensic evidence. In: Wampler T (ed.) *Applied Pyrolysis Handbook*, 2nd edn., pp. 175–199. Boca Raton, FL: CRS Press.

Petraco N and Kubic T (2004) Color atlas and manual of microscopy for criminalists, chemists, and conservators, Chapter 2: Preliminary examination, stereomicroscopy, and basic sample preparation, pp. 21–35, Chapter 10: Paint examination, pp. 123–134. Boca Raton, London, New York, Washington D.C.: CRS Press.

Scientific Working Group on Materials Analysis (SWGMAT) (2008) *Forensic Paint Analysis and Comparison Guidelines*. ASTM E1610. US Department of Justice, FBI.

Suzuki E (1993) Forensic applications of infrared spectroscopy. In: Saferstein R (ed.) *Forensic Science Handbook*, vol. III, pp. 71–195. Englewood Cliffs, NJ: Regent Prentice Hall.

Relevant Websites

http://www.enfsi.eu – ENFSI Paint and Glass Working Group.

http://www.swgmat.org – Scientific Working Group on Materials Analysis.

Interpretation of Paint Evidence

L (Brun-Conti) Bender, National Laboratory Center, Ammendale, MD, USA

Published by Elsevier Ltd.

Glossary

Coating A generic term for paint, lacquer, enamel, or other liquid or liquefiable material that is converted to a solid, protective, or decorative film or a combination of these types of films after application.
Double transfer The transfer of a substance from item 1 to item 2, and the additional transfer of a substance from item 2 to item 1.
Inter-sample variation Variation that occurs between different samples.
Intra-sample variation Variation that occurs within the same sample.
Known sample A coating sample of established origin.
Mean-value The average obtained by dividing the sum of all the quantities by the total number of quantities.
Paint Commonly known as a pigmented coating.
Pigment Particles that impart color, opacity, effect (sparkle or sheen), bulk (filler and extender pigments), and/or desirable physical properties to paint. Pigment particles are suspended in place in the final dry film by the resin.
Questioned Sample A coating sample whose original source is unknown.
Resin or binder Any polymer that is dissolved in or suspended in a solvent that can be converted into a self-sustaining film.
Significance of association What value or meaning can be drawn from the data obtained by the analysis of the questioned and known item.
Single transfer The transfer of a substance from one item to another.
Solvent Low-viscosity volatile liquids used in coatings allowing the polymer, pigments, and other components to remain in solution until the paint is ready to be applied to a substrate.
Standard deviation The measure of the variability in a frequency distribution. One standard deviation contains roughly 68% of the data in a symmetrical Gaussian curve.
Vehicle The liquid-forming constituents of a coating. In general, the vehicle coating comprises the binder and any volatile solvents, driers, and other components. The nonvolatile portion is referred to as *vehicle solids*.

The analysis of paints and coatings, as with any trace evidence, is a systematic process that begins with nondestructive methods of analysis. If no significant differences are found between the questioned and known paints, analysis continues with the more destructive analysis techniques. If, at any point in the scheme of analysis, the paint from the known source is found to be significantly different from the questioned paint, then it is concluded that the questioned paint is eliminated as having a common source with the known paint and the analysis discontinued. However, if the paint from the known source is found to be indistinguishable from the questioned paint using a particular analytical method or instrument, then the analysis continues until every aspect of the paint has been examined (physical, elemental, and chemical). If the known and the questioned paint are still indistinguishable, then it is determined that the two paints could have a mutual origin. Given the fact that paint is a material that is manufactured in large batches, a stronger conclusion is not possible unless a questioned paint chip can be physically fitted (fracture match) into the known paint. If a fracture match is made between the questioned and the known paint, then the analyst can positively conclude that the questioned paint particle originated from the known paint.

Evaluation of the Paint Samples for Analysis

Determining Whether an Investigative Lead or Paint Comparison Is Desired

One of the first questions regarding the evidence is what information the submitter needs from the paint submission. Sometimes an investigator submits only a questioned paint requesting information to develop an investigative lead regarding the source of the paint. For investigative leads for automotive paint, the analyst may use the Paint Database Query (PDQ), a database of automotive topcoats and primers or books of automotive refinish colors in an attempt to identify the make, model, and year(s) of the vehicle from which the questioned paint originated. If the submitted paint is from both a questioned source and a known source, then a comparison is desired.

Condition of the Questioned Paint-Evaluating the Questioned Paint Sample for Suitability

The condition of the paint sample to be analyzed needs to be evaluated. If a particle of paint is too comingled ('smeared') with other layers of paint from the same item, or paint from another item, or any substance from another source, it may not be prudent to analyze the sample. Caution should be used so as to not make a false inclusion or mistakenly eliminate the sample. Either type of error will be misleading or confusing to the investigation. In the case of a smeared paint that is in such poor condition that it is not possible to reliably analyze it, it may be best to conclude that it is 'unsuitable for analysis.'

Sample size may be a limiting factor in the analysis of paint if the questioned paint sample is particularly small. In order to determine if a technique will generate useful information, a known paint sample similar in size and shape to the questioned sample should be analyzed. Usually, some

 http://dx.doi.org/10.1016/B978-0-12-382165-2.00110-0

analyses can be done on very small samples, but perhaps not a complete analysis scheme. This evaluation will depend upon, among other considerations, the type of paint and the instrumentation available to the analyst. For example, very small pieces of white architectural paint, especially if the paint contains a large quantity of extender pigments, will not supply as much data when analyzed on the Py-GC as a particle of automotive topcoat of the same size due to the fact that the proportion of resin to pigment is much less in a highly filled architectural paint than in a sample of automotive paint of the same size. Both the scanning electron microscope/energy dispersive spectrometer (SEM/EDS) and the x-ray fluorescence spectrometer (XRF) provide data on the elemental composition of a substance; however, the SEM/EDS is usually able to analyze much smaller paint samples than the XRF. Therefore, if only an XRF is available, the sizes of paint samples that can be analyzed using this instrument may be limited.

When analyzing minute paint particles, thought must be given to the inherent heterogeneity of paint. Therefore, steps should be taken to insure that the particle of paint is representative of the whole by, for example, analyzing a number of samples of the known paint to obtain representative data. Once the variation of the known paint is recognized, an evaluation can be made as to whether or not the data of the questioned paint can be included or excluded.

Obtaining a Proper Known Sample

The submitter has no influence regarding the condition of the questioned paint sample but normally they do have control regarding how and where the known paint sample is obtained. The known sample should include all layers of paint down to the substrate. Care should be taken with regard to obtaining proper known sample(s) from coatings that may be from 'different parts' of a whole item. This is a consideration when taking samples of architectural paints (e.g., ensuring that the known paint sample is taken from an area as close as possible to the tool mark from a break-in tool on a doorjamb), but it is most often encountered as an issue when collecting known automotive paint samples. When damage occurs to a vehicle, it is not always limited to one body part. Two adjoining body parts (e.g., the door and the quarter panel) may have the same color and layer structure, but the binder system in one of the coatings may be different; alternatively, the color and binder systems may be consistent but the layer structure or the primers are different. It must be ascertained that paint from all damaged parts of the vehicle is submitted. Another consideration regarding the collection of automotive paints is body fillers. If body filler is used in only part of a body panel, then the remainder of the panel may have a different layer structure. It should also be noted that the questioned paint sample may not contain all of the paint layers found in the known paint sample. However, if the layers present in the questioned sample are in the same order as exhibited in a portion of the known sample, the questioned paint should not be eliminated at that point and the analysis should continue.

Variations in the Samples

Variation Within the Samples (Intra-Sample Variation)

To reiterate, paint is a heterogeneous substance for a number of reasons. Color pigments and extender pigments are solid particles and, therefore, by their nature will not be perfectly distributed throughout the dried paint film. Also, depending upon the type of paint, incomplete mixing prior to application may cause an uneven distribution of the components. Therefore, when analyzing paint using the various methods, there may be differences noted in the resulting data. One way to approach the analysis of heterogeneous material is to analyze a number of particles of paint from a known source and note if variation occurs. The paint from the questioned source, when analyzed, should then fall within any variation displayed in the known source. Some instruments have software to assist in the evaluation of whether or not the data from the questioned source lie within the variation of the data from the known source. For other instruments, the spectra can simply be overlaid and viewed to evaluate whether or not the data from the questioned source are within the range of the data from the known source to determine if analysis is to continue or if analysis can be terminated and the samples deemed different. For example, a number of different paint particles from the known sample may be analyzed using the Fourier transform infrared (FTIR) spectrophotometer and any variation noted. When the questioned sample is then analyzed, it should fall within any variation of the known sample.

Variation Between Samples (Inter-Sample Variation)

Variations between the data from questioned and known samples can mean that the samples are definitely different or that there is a contribution from another source which may give the appearance of a difference. Variations between samples that are different are quite obvious. For example, if questioned and known paint particles are visibly free of any extraneous substances, the presence of different elements in XRF data or additional peaks in an FTIR spectrum denotes that the questioned and known paints are likely from different sources. Variations may occur if one of the paint samples contains small amounts of a substance or small particles which will be detected by the instrumentation used and perceived as a true difference. Therefore, caution should be taken to ensure that each sample is clean of any extraneous substance. If extraneous material is the suspected difference between the questioned and known coatings, a scrupulously clean sample should then be analyzed. If the differences are still present in the spectra, then it must be determined that the differences are real and that the sources of the questioned and known paint are dissimilar.

Interpretation of Data from Instruments Commonly Used in Paint Analysis

In the analysis of paint, various instruments are used to examine the visual appearance as well as the organic and inorganic compositions of the coating. Some are considered destructive, Py-GC in particular, where the particle of paint is pyrolyzed and, therefore, consumed in testing and unavailable for further testing. The remaining techniques covered in this article are considered nondestructive techniques; the sample is not destroyed, per se, and will be available in the preparation for examination by another technique. If at all possible, some of the questioned and known samples should be retained for possible reexamination.

Stereomicroscopy

In general, the first instrument used in the examination of paints is a stereomicroscope. The questioned and known paint particles are evaluated for consistency in color, layer structure, texture, gloss, relative layer thickness, and any unusual characteristics that may be common to both. Any unexplained differences are cause for eliminating the questioned particle from being considered as coming from the known paint source.

Polarized Light Microscopy

Examination of paints using a polarizing light microscope (PLM) will allow for examination of color, effect, and extender pigments. Many of the color pigments, organic pigments in particular, are processed into particles so small that the individual pigment particles are difficult to discern and only the residual color is observed. However, occasionally the organic color pigments will agglomerate or form small bundles that can be seen using the PLM. Evaluation of the presence or absence of these pigment agglomerations can be a point of comparison between samples along with their actual color. Some inorganic absorptive pigments, such as titanium dioxide (white) and iron oxide (red and yellow), are seen as small black particles (due to their high refractive indices) with uncrossed polarizing filters but their color is perceived when the polarizing filters are crossed.

The presence and physical characteristics of extender pigments can also be used to evaluate whether or not two paint samples have a common source. Such extender pigments as calcium carbonate and magnesium silicate (talc) are easily observed with crossed polarizing filters.

Effect pigments include nacreous pigments and aluminum or metal flakes. Nacreous pigments are created from coating mica platelets with titanium dioxide or other metal oxides. If the titanium dioxide coating is thin, the reflected appearance of the pigment is that of a whitish sheen but the appearance with transmitted light shows interference colors, not unlike the colors and effects seen when there is a small amount of gasoline floating on water. If the titanium dioxide deposition is thicker, the nacreous pigments actually reflect a color, but the complementary color will be seen with transmitted light. For example, if the color of the reflected nacreous pigment is red, the transmitted color will be green. Finally, if aluminum pigments are used in the film, it should be examined whether the edges of the pigments are smooth or sharp, and if, when comparing two samples, the aluminum pigments are relatively the same size.

All of the aforementioned observations may be made using the PLM. After analyzing a number of mounted samples from the known and the questioned paints, if some of the microscopic pigment particles are present in one sample and not in the other, or are significantly different in appearance, it may be concluded that the two paints are from different sources.

Microspectrophotometer

Since color is an important aspect of paint, analysis of the color may be done using the microspectrophotometer (MSP). It is important when using the MSP, as with most methods of comparison, to assure that the known sample is taken from a location as close as possible to the suspected source of the questioned sample. Differences in color from various areas of an object may change due to environmental conditions such as exposure to chemicals, acids and bases, and ultraviolet radiation. For example, the color of a wall that has been protected by a painting or other object may be a different color from an area of the wall that was exposed to sunlight.

It should be noted that MSP evaluation of the spectra using the transmission mode (ultraviolet or visible) may be observed as either % transmittance or absorbance, and reflectance (visible) spectra may be observed in either % reflectance or absorbance. Only the absorbance data are linear with regard to concentration, and, therefore, may provide information on the relative concentrations of the components being examined.

When comparing two samples, the spectra as a whole should first be examined followed by a critical examination of each peak within the spectra. Comparisons should be made of the peak shape, minima, maxima, inflection points, trough, shoulders, and the curves or slopes between peaks. The questioned spectra should fall within the range established for the known material. It should be noted that peaks in the absorbance spectra should have identical shapes between questioned and known spectra; however, they might not superimpose exactly. Care should be taken to ensure that the samples are orientated perpendicular to the optical axis for samples where the data are collected in reflectance. If the instrument has the appropriate software, the mean-value spectra and $\pm$ one or more standard deviations may be used to assist in evaluating whether or not the questioned spectra fall within the variation of the known spectra; alternatively, a visual comparison can be conducted by overlaying the spectra using a light box, or plotting the spectra on the same graph may be done.

FTIR Spectrophotometer

When used in paint analysis, the FTIR spectrophotometer provides molecular structure information on a number of organic and inorganic components of the coating as well as some of the color pigments and extender pigments. The FTIR may also assist in the classification of the binder system used. In comparing the FTIR spectra from a questioned and known coating, either transmittance or absorbance spectra may be used. Therefore, the FTIR spectra acquired in transmission mode may be compared in either %transmittance or absorbance and the FTIR spectra acquired in reflectance mode may be compared in either %reflectance or absorbance. It should be noted that the absorbance spectra (regardless of sampling technique) are directly proportional to the concentration of the components of the sample. Therefore, the data from transmission spectra evaluated in %transmittance or absorbance may appear different from one another and some information may be more easily seen in one format over the other. The same applies to data from reflectance spectra evaluated in either %reflectance or absorbance. The important aspects of comparison with evaluating FTIR spectra are the location, relative intensity, and shape of the absorption bands.

Location

The positions of the absorption bands should have a reasonable agreement with one another. The rule of thumb is that they should be within $\pm 5\ cm^{-1}$ of the corresponding absorption band. The width of the band should be taken into consideration when determining the actual wavenumber of the band. For broader absorption peaks, a wider constraint may be applied. If the samples show a greater difference than $5\ cm^{-1}$, then replicate samples should be analyzed to discern whether or not variation exists at that peak location.

Relative intensity

When comparing two spectra, the relative intensities of the major absorption bands should be similar. If necessary, additional samples should be analyzed to assess any variation.

Shape

Absorption bands range from very sharp to quite wide. When comparing spectra, corresponding bands should be relatively the same in shape.

Pyrolysis-Gas Chromatograph and Pyrolysis-Gas Chromatograph-Mass Spectrometer

Pyrolysis-gas chromatograph (Py-GC) and the pyrolysis-gas chromatograph-mass spectrometry (Py-GCMS) examine the polymeric portion of the paint. The polymer is thermally degraded by the pyrolyzer, and the resulting complex mixture is separated by the gas chromatograph. The mass spectrometer (present in the Py-GCMS) then detects and aids in the identification of the individual components resulting in a signal displayed as the total ion chromatograph (TIC). The TIC is then compared between the questioned and known samples.

Sample size is an important consideration when using the Py-GC or Py-GCMS. If the questioned paint particle is small, it may be necessary to analyze a number of known paint particles of the same relative size to assess not only the viability of the Py-GC or Py-GCMS analysis on a particle of that size but also the variation within the known particles given the size limitation. Referring back to the inherent heterogeneity of paint, a small particle may not be representative of the coating as a whole. Another consideration when evaluating the sample size is the type of paint. An architectural paint which contains a large quantity of components that do not degrade with pyrolysis (usually pigments) will require a larger sample than a less 'filled' automotive paint. Variable peak height between samples may be another consideration when regarding paint heterogeneity.

When comparing the TIC between questioned and known samples, a visual comparison of the TIC from the questioned and known samples can be made by overlaying them on a light box or displaying the TICs on the same graph. There are a number of factors that should be considered when comparing pyrograms including the presence or absence of peaks, their retention time, shape, and relative intensity.

To identify the composition of the peaks in the TIC, mass spectral libraries and the analyst's knowledge of mass spectra can be employed. Additionally, some instruments offer searchable spectral library software for identification of peaks.

Scanning Electron Microscopy/Energy Dispersive Spectrometer and XRF spectrometer

The SEM/EDS and XRF spectrometer, including micro-XRF, are used to evaluate and compare the elemental components of paint. The differences between these two instruments are outside the scope of this article; however, assessment of data from the two instruments is similar. The elemental component of paint samples may also be determined by using other instruments such as inductively coupled plasma-mass spectrometer (ICPMS) or x-ray diffraction (which gives information on both the crystalline structure and elemental composition of the particle portion of the paint). However, these instruments will not be covered in this article.

It is important that the samples are meticulously examined for any foreign particles adhering to the samples before they are analyzed. Minute particles of soil or other extraneous material may cause additional peaks, resulting in an erroneous conclusion. Labeling the peaks to identify the associated elements may be accomplished by using the software integrated in the instrument or identifying the peaks evaluating the corresponding kiloelectron volts (keV). When a peak is small, it must be appraised as to whether it should be considered when comparing spectra. The section below on 'peak determination' addresses this question. A visual comparison may be affected by directly overlaying the spectra on a light box or plotting them on the same graph. Since the elemental components associated with paint are usually present in the pigment portion, consideration must be given to the inherent heterogeneity of paint and the sample size. If the sample size is particularly small, the sample may not contain a representative sample of the pigments contained in the paint as a whole. This would be seen as a difference in the ratio of the peaks, since these are proportional to the quantity detected. Sampling a number of similarly sized small particles of the known paint may allow the analyst to assess the variability caused by a limited particle size. If this analysis technique does not solve the problem, then the analyst may exclude the questioned paint from having a common source with the known paint or state that the results using these instruments are inconclusive.

Peak determination – signal-to-noise ratio

Signal-to-noise ratio (SNR) is a way to determine whether or not a peak should be considered when evaluating the data. First, the SNR is determined. One way to determine this ratio is

$$\mathrm{SNR} = \frac{\text{Signal level}}{\text{rms}}$$

where 'rms' is 'root mean squared,' a value obtained by determining the peak-to-peak amplitude of the noise and dividing this value by 5. Once SNR is determined, it is then multiplied by 3. If a peak is greater than this final value, then it should be considered. However, instead of using the cumbersome calculations stated above, the rule of thumb is that a peak is considered when it is three times the height of the noise.

Determination of the Significance of an Association

Except in cases where a physical fit/fracture match is made, further considerations are required to assess the significance of an association. This means to assess the chance to obtain the association assuming an alleged set of circumstances as opposed to other explanations. During this process, it is important to keep an open mind and seek for alternative explanations.

Disciplines such as DNA analysis use statistics to determine significance. The same type of statistics may not be used with mass-produced materials, such as paint. To determine the significance of an association, studies have been done on random sample sets and 'worst case scenario' samples using the customary analytical techniques for paint analysis. The results of these studies show that a high percentage of discrimination is achieved using these standard methods. With the assistance of these studies, the analyst may be able to word the final report to reflect the significance of the association.

Another method that reflects the significance of an association is the use of Bayesian statistics. Bayesian statistics are based on a method developed by Thomas Bayes (1702–61) that determines the 'likelihood ratio' (LR) of obtaining the results assuming an event happening versus an alternate version of the event. An explanation of Bayesian statistics is beyond the scope of this article but can be found in other relevant entries in the Encyclopedia.

Reporting the Significance of an Association

After the significance of an association has been determined, the results must be reported in a clear manner without overstating or understating the conclusion. The most common method of doing this is simply writing the report explaining the conclusion of the analysis in a concise, nonambiguous way. A grading system in which each grade or level comes with an explanation of the significance of the association may also be used. Usually referred to as 'The Levels of Association', this system is a verbal description of how much weight an association should be given. Many times these levels are given numbers to assist the investigator, attorney, and juror in understanding the significance of the association. For example, a double paint transfer (paint from the victim's vehicle on the suspect vehicle and vice versa) is more significant than a single transfer. In addition, the number of corresponding layers in the questioned and known paints may increase the evidential value of the association. The Levels of Association is one way to help explain these nuances. A list of the Levels of Association could be included with the analyst's report or as an appendix to the report so that it is clear to the reader what constitutes an association at each level.

Example of Levels of Association

The following illustrates examples of evidential association that would be described by each level and is not meant to be used for an official version of Levels of Association. Each agency will have to determine the wording and levels that suits their particular situation.

Level 1: Identification
The questioned paint positively came from the known source. This is usually determined by a physical match.

Level 2: High degree of association in which the evidence contains unusual characteristics
This level would include a paint layering system that is so unusual or complex that only intentional duplication could produce a similar product. This level could also include double paint transfers. These associations include not only conventional characteristics in common but also unusual characteristics.

Level 3: Conventional association
A single paint transfer found on a hit-and-run victim's clothing or transfer of green architectural paint onto a break-in tool. This is an association where all the measurable examination and analyses are consistent between the questioned and known paint, but there is nothing extraordinary or unusual to what is found in the standard population of that paint.

Level 4: Limited association
Due to sample size or condition, only certain aspects of the paint could be examined. A small particle of heavily filled architectural paint would be an example of this due to the size constraints and the heavy pigment load. The information obtained from such a sample would be limited.

Level 5: Inconclusive
There are similarities between the questioned and known paints; however, due to either the condition of the paint (severely comingled with another substance) or aging/exposure issues (e.g., damage due to ultraviolet radiation or chemical exposure), the paint cannot be confidently associated with the known paint from a source that was not exposed to these conditions. In this level, the paints cannot be eliminated, because the differences can be explained, but they cannot be associated because the differences cannot be duplicated.

Level 6: Elimination/exclusion
There is a fundamental difference between the questioned and known paint. Significant differences in color, appearance, polymer type, or elemental composition will result in elimination.

See also: **Chemistry/Trace/Paint and Coating:** Architectural Paint; Automotive Paint; Forensic Paint Analysis; **Chemistry/Trace/Trace Evidence:** Microchemistry.

Further Reading

ASTM E1610–02 (2005) *Standard Guide for Forensic Paint Analysis and Comparison.* West Conshohocken, PA: ASTM International.

Eyring M, Lovelace M, and Sy D (2007) A study of the discrimination of some automotive paint films having identical color codes. *Proceedings of the NIJ/FBI Trace Evidence Symposium*, Clearwater Beach, FL, USA, 13–16 August. Washington, DC: US Dept of Justice, Office of Justice Programs.

Govaert F and Bernard M (2004) Discriminating red spray paints by optical microscopy, Fourier transform infrared spectroscopy, and X-ray fluorescence. *Forensic Science International* 140(1): 61–70.

Laing DK, et al. (1982) The discrimination of small fragments of household gloss paint by microspectrophotometry. *Forensic Science International* 20: 191–200.

Plage B, Berg A-D, and Luhn S (2008) The discrimination of automotive clear coats by pyrolysis-gas chromatography/mass spectrometry and comparison of samples by a chromatogram library software. *Forensic Science International* 177: 146–152.

Roux C, Inkster J, Maynard P, and Ferguson B (2007) Intra-sample vs. inter-sample variability in architectural paint. *Proceedings of the NIJ/FBI Trace Evidence Symposium*, Clearwater Beach, FL, USA, 13–16, August. Washington, DC: US Dept of Justice, Office of Justice Programs.

Ryland S (2010) Discrimination of retail black spray paints. *Journal of the American Society of Trace Evidence Examiners* 1(2): 109–126.

Ryland SG, et al. (2001) Discrimination of 1990s original automotive paint systems: A collaborative study of black nonmetallic base coat/clear coat finishes using *infrared spectroscopy. Journal of Forensic Sciences* 46(1): 31–45.

Thornton JI (2002) Forensic paint examination. In: Saferstein R (ed.) *Forensic Science Handbook*, 2nd edn., pp. 430–478. Upper Saddle River, NJ: Prentice Hall.

Wright DM, Bradley MJ, and Mehltretter AH (2011) Discrimination of architecturalpaints. *Forensic Science International*. http://dx.doi.org/10.1016/j.forsciint.2011.01.001.

Relevant Websites

http://www.swgmat.org/Standard%20Guide%20for%20Microspectrophotometry%20and%20Color%20Measurement%20in%20Forensic%20Paint%20Analysis.pdf – Standard Guide for Microspectrophotometry and Color Measurement in Forensic Paint Analysis, Scientific Working Group for Materials Analysis (SWGMAT), Forensic Science Communications, Vol. 9, No. 4, October 2007.

http://www.swgmat.org/SWGMAT%20infrared%20spectroscopy.pdf – Standard Guide for Using Infrared Spectroscopy in Forensic Paint Examinations.

http://www.fbi.gov – Standard Guide for Using Scanning Electron Microscopy/X-ray Spectrometry in Forensic Paint Examination, Scientific Working Group for Materials Analysis (SWGMAT), Forensic Science Communications, Vol. 4, No. 4, October 2002.

CHEMISTRY/TRACE/TRACE EVIDENCE

Contents

Trace Evidence Overview

C Roux, University of Technology, Sydney, NSW, Australia
J Robertson, University of Canberra, Canberra, ACT, Australia

Introduction

The key role of a forensic scientist is to assist in determining whether a crime has been committed, and in case it is so determined, to assist in identifying the offender and help reconstruct the circumstances of the crime. Trace evidence, as material transferred during the commission of a crime, is at the core of the process, and, for this reason, it is often called the 'silent witness.' In other words, trace evidence has the ability to tell the story of what actually happened and who may have been involved. Unfortunately, the value of trace evidence is often underestimated and its collection is often neglected, due to the lack of knowledge, time, or resources.

It is also important to note that, historically, trace evidence has been at the core of forensic science, having played a crucial role in the development of the field in the twentieth century, prompted by the seminal work of pioneers such as Gross, Reiss, and Locard. In line with these early works, there has been a recent resurgence of the more general concept of 'trace' (see the following section), which itself can define forensic science as a discipline because a trace constitutes the most basic material or physical information on crime.

This article presents an overview of trace evidence, including its relevant definitions and methods of detection, recovery, and analysis, as well as its significance in the context of investigations and court proceedings.

Trace, Physical Evidence, or Trace Evidence?

The terms 'trace,' 'trace evidence,' and 'physical evidence' have been used over the years to describe entities that are closely related or overlapping with each other or sometimes even fully equivalent, depending on their usage. It may be useful to clarify the situation:

Trace

'Trace' is the most general, but also the most accurate, term. It applies to any remnant of the crime, generally the remnant of a presence or an activity. As a proxy of the crime, it can be considered as the object of study for the forensic scientist; for instance, an artifact or a newspaper excerpt would be examined by an archeologist and a historian to study an ancient civilization or a historical event, respectively. These are silent witnesses that need to be detected and understood to make reasonable inferences about criminal phenomena, investigation or demonstration for intelligence, investigation and court purposes. As remnants of the crime, traces can:

- provide leads;
- eliminate suspects;
- reconstruct the events and their sequence;
- establish charges;
- identify links in serial crime.

The absence of traces or the presence of a large quantity of traces that do not fit some allegations may have some significance and must be carefully considered in the context of the case under investigation.

It is important to realize that, in normal circumstances, traces are unwillingly transferred during the crime and that the transfer is often incomplete and unrepresentative in the statistical sense. This is particularly significant when discussing the detection, preservation, and collection of traces, as well as their significance for investigation or court purposes.

In this context, the size and even the physical nature of the trace are irrelevant because an entity is a trace as long as it is a remnant of the crime, whether we consider a truck, a computer file, or touch DNA. Obviously, what is commonly known as trace evidence is a subclass of trace.

Physical Evidence

Evidence can be defined as something legally submitted to a competent tribunal as a means of ascertaining the truth of any alleged matter under investigation before it. There are numerous ways of classifying different types of evidence. At the general level, two types of evidence exist, testimonial and physical:

- Testimonial evidence is evidence given in the form of a statement made under oath, usually in response to questioning;

 http://dx.doi.org/10.1016/B978-0-12-382165-2.00086-6

- Physical evidence is any type of evidence having an objective (real) existence.

Obviously, the latter is the type of evidence that is relevant to forensic science in general, and to the present discussion in particular. Physical evidence can take almost any form, and it can be as large as a house or as small as a fiber. It may range from material of natural origin (biological traces such as blood, hair, seminal stains, and some drugs), material of natural origin manufactured into a finished product (such as glass, paper, and natural textile fibers) to completely synthetic and manufactured products (such as plastics, paints, and synthetic textile fibers).

It should be pointed out that 'physical evidence' is often used synonymously with 'trace' (as defined earlier). However, it is not accurate to use the term 'evidence' during the early stages of a case because of the reference to the court in the definition of this term.

Trace Evidence

Trace evidence can be considered as a subclass of physical evidence (and hence trace). At the conceptual level, it is commonly defined as:

- A very small amount of substance, often too small to be measured and
- The surviving evidence of a former occurrence or action of some event or agent.

Further, at a more practical level, trace evidence is defined as the analysis of materials that, because of their size or texture, transfer from one location to another and persist there for some period of time. Microscopy, either directly, or as an adjunct to another instrument, is involved.

In this context, size matters; typical examples of trace evidence include fibers, hairs, glass fragments, paint chips, soil, botanical traces, gunshot residues, and so on.

It could be argued that 'trace evidence' is a misnomer and that using this term unnecessarily confuses the topic. It might therefore be better to use the term 'microtrace' that is generally used in German ('Mikrospur') and in French ('microtrace'). However, because of the widespread use of 'trace evidence' in the English-speaking world, especially in North America, this term is used throughout this discussion.

Locard Exchange Principle

No discussion about trace evidence would be complete without a reminder of the Locard exchange principle:

> The truth is that none can act with the intensity induced by criminal activities without leaving multiple traces of his path. [...] The clues I want to speak of here are of two kinds: Sometimes the perpetrator leaves traces at a scene by their actions; sometimes, alternatively, he/she picked up on their clothes or their body traces of their location or presence.

The Locard principle was embraced in North America in the 1930s. However, its traditional English translation, *every contact leaves a trace*, removed the activity dimension of the original principle. This is unfortunate because the value of trace evidence is especially seen in relation to the activity (in addition to the fact that this has some implications on the discussion of the scientific underpinnings of forensic science – see Foundations entries in the encyclopedia). In any case, in his texts and interviews, Locard always strongly emphasized that the discipline should consider all the traces available, depending on the activity and its information potential, and not focus only on a single type of (generally identifying) trace. This cannot be more relevant than in the present day!

The Three Rs of Trace Evidence – Recognition, Recording, and Recovery

The importance of trace evidence is that it links people to each other or to a location, or locations to each other (source) and also helps reconstruct what happened (activity). Although mostly microscopic, trace evidence can become a significant part of an investigation. Unfortunately, as described above, its value is often underestimated and its collection is often neglected.

The crime scene is the place from which most trace evidence will be obtained. It is also widely recognized that good forensic science starts at the crime scene. This mantra is especially true for trace evidence. Trace evidence is almost always very fragile, transitory in nature, and its presence will most often not be immediately visible and, hence, recognizable. As a result, trace evidence must first be recognized before it can be recorded and then recovered. We consider these as the three 'Rs' of evidence – recognition, recording, and recovery. The recovery of trace evidence relies heavily on understanding how such traces are transferred, how they persist, and how best what remains from a contact event can be collected.

Crime scene examiners and first respondents need to be aware of the value of trace evidence. Relevant trace evidence must be detected among heavy 'background noise.' Bertillon used to say *We only see what we look at, and we only look at what we already have in our mind.*

To avoid contamination, strict rules involving protective clothing recovery and examination protocols need to be in place as part of an overall quality system. It is beyond the scope of this entry to describe in detail anticontamination procedures. However, it is important to emphasize the need to avoid the potential for items from different sources to be in contact, directly or indirectly. This includes situations where garments are collected in hospital or by paramedics, or when persons of interest and victims are being transported in a police car or interviewed in the same office.

As far as is practical, potential trace evidence should be collected at the first possible opportunity following the GIFT (Get It First Time) principle. Many factors interact to influence the transfer of trace evidence and their subsequent persistence and these are discussed in more detail in the relevant entries in this Encyclopedia. The important thing to remember is the transient nature of physical traces and the need to collect it at the earliest opportunity and to protect items against further loss.

Recovery of Trace Evidence

A number of methods are available for the recovery of trace evidence, and, to some extent, they may depend on the type of trace and on the context of the case. However, in general, the recovery process should be made sequentially and in a specific order to optimize the chances to obtain relevant and probative results:

1. Any visible relevant material is selectively collected using fine tweezers and appropriately labeled and stored. This step can be aided by an appropriate light source and simple optical means (magnification lens, low power stereomicroscope, etc.).
2. The interior of the container which contained the evidential item is examined in detail. Relevant trace evidence which was on the surface of the main item may have fallen off during the transport.
3. Stains which were possibly observed under (1) are cut out or collected by swabbing according to standard operating procedures.
4. A 'blind collection' is undertaken using tape lifting. This method is very efficient, but nonselective. Not only is trace evidence coming from a particular contact recovered but also material coming from the recipient substrate as well as from previous contacts are collected. In some circumstances, the so-called 'one to one' tape lifting may be warranted; however, a zonal search pattern is more common.
5. The use of a vacuum cleaner with a special device is potentially very efficient, but suffers from important drawbacks because of its lack of selectivity and its tendency to highlight the smallest particles, often recovered in the depth of the items (i.e. particles which often have no link with the crime under investigation = evidence dilution). For this reason, this method must be used with caution and in the end of the sequence.

The use of scraping techniques is not recommended in cases involving light items (e.g., fibers and hairs), as it is not very efficient and increases the risk of contamination. However, such techniques may be applicable for heavier or bigger types of trace evidence, such as glass fragments, for example.

The whole process is summarized in **Figure 1**.

Examination of Trace Evidence

Generalities

Once recovered, trace evidence is conditioned in such a way that it can be submitted to a forensic examination, in general in a laboratory environment. The specimen preparation is obviously highly dependent on the type and size of the trace evidence. The reader is referred to relevant entries elsewhere in this Encyclopedia for further information.

The actual examination and the methods used not only depend on the type of materials recovered but also on the questions being asked. It is essential that the scientist has all relevant information as this will result in resources being channeled where they are needed with more effective case management and use of available resources. As a result, the whole process is, in general, case specific.

It would be impossible to identify an exhaustive list of possible questions that could be answered by trace evidence. However, typical questions include:

- What is the item recovered?
- Can it support or refute an alleged scenario or circumstances?
- Can it be associated with a person (usually suspect or victim) or a location relevant to the investigation?
- Can it provide information about time, season, year, etc.?

To answer these questions, there is a great need for various forms of technical and scientific analyses. This process involves the determination of the morphological features of the sample, its chemical make-up, the frequency distribution of this type of material, the permanence and the robustness of the trace over time, and the variation in the composition over the population of materials of this type.

The purpose of the examination often includes the following:

- Identification of the specimen;
- Comparison of specimens coming from different sources; and
- Interpretation of the findings obtained in the context under investigation.

It is worth pointing out that the driving principle in any comparative examination is to look for meaningful differences between recovered trace evidence and a known source or item. When one or more recovered specimens show no meaningful difference, then the scientist needs to interpret what this may mean in the context of the case circumstances.

Analysis

A methodical approach is required, not only for gathering but also for analyzing trace evidence. First, only general characteristics are considered. More detailed features are studied only when the environment is ordered and classified. In addition, a nondestructive technique is always applied before a destructive one in order to preserve the specimen integrity as far as possible. The method requires a stepwise progression from simple, general, rapid, widely applicable, and nondestructive screening techniques to the more discriminating and specific ones. The ability to choose the most appropriate analytical sequence for a particular set of circumstances is one of the specific skills required of the forensic scientist. Once again, techniques and instruments are useful only as far as they can contribute to answer the questions being asked. However, in most cases, microscopy plays a major role in this process because of the nature of trace evidence.

Techniques used for the examination of trace evidence are generally classified as nondestructive and destructive techniques. Nondestructive techniques include optical methods (simple observation, microscopy, and photography) and spectroscopic techniques (ultraviolet (UV)–visible absorption, Fourier transform infrared microspectroscopy (FTIR), x-ray fluorescence, fluorimetry, etc.). Destructive techniques include chemical reactions (screening tests for explosives, drugs, etc.), spectroscopic techniques (mass spectrometry, MS; inductively coupled plasma, ICP; ICP-MS) and analytical separation techniques (thin layer chromatography, TLC; gas chromatography, GC; GC–MS, HPLC, CE, etc.).

It is beyond the scope of this article to describe these techniques and the reader is referred to other relevant entries elsewhere in this Encyclopedia. However, it is important to emphasize the following points:

- The first methods to be applied are simple *optical examinations* with the unaided eyes (transmitted, reflected, or grazing light) under natural daylight and filtered or unfiltered artificial light. These observations may be extended from UV to infrared (IR) using light converters (usually video cameras). Features such as color, shape, design, dimensions, and surface quality allow for rapid selection and discrimination of a large majority of the products encountered in an investigation. For example, it is generally sufficient to prove the identity of broken glass, paint, and paper by physical fit.

- *Microscopy* is universally used as a first screening or sorting tool and for the examination of small samples such as hairs, fibers, and paint smears/chips. It extends the capabilities of our eyes, and its scientific applications are numerous and often underestimated. It enables the examination of the optical attributes of the item under investigation such as color, opacity, refractive index, reflectance, fluorescence, and birefringence. Many cases can be solved with only a microscope; there is a current tendency to use the most sophisticated and expensive techniques when a microscope would have been sufficient. It is also worth mentioning that modern solid-state analytical techniques often have microscope attachments or microprobes extending their application to trace evidence analysis.
- *UV–visible absorption* (including reflectance) *microspectrometry* has extensive use in examining pigments and colors in paint, inks, fibers, and other small colored items.
- FTIR is an established method of choice for the analysis of trace evidence, in particular, organic materials from fibers, paint, glue, polymers, drugs, greases, and oils to inks, papers, and toners. Many IR databases have been produced that are extensively used by forensic laboratories.

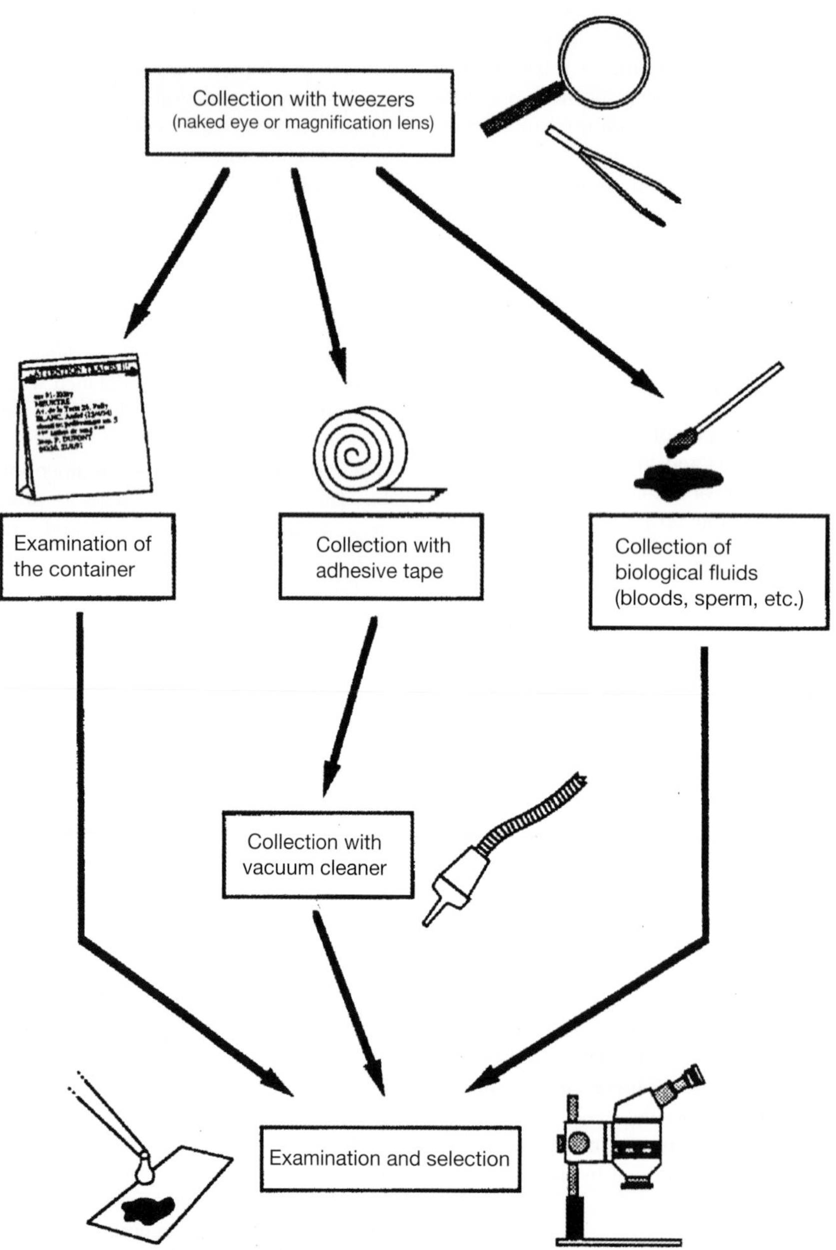

Figure 1 Recommended sequence for the recovery of trace evidence.

- *Raman microprobe* analysis has found valuable applications as a complementary method to FTIR, especially for the *in situ* analysis of fiber dyes and minute paint smears.
- *Micro-x-ray fluorescence* has found extensive applications in the analysis of inorganic materials (e.g., metal residues, paint, glass, and minor elements in various polymers).
- *Laser ablation inductively coupled plasma mass spectrometry* (LA-ICP-MS) is a powerful multielement analytical tool that is making an increasing impact on the analyses of trace evidence ranging from pollution source determination to traditional trace exploitation. Examples include the analysis of metals, paint, and glass. However, the high level of sensitivity of such a technique often raises difficult questions when interpreting the results. At this level of sensitivity, the variability within a sample may often be superior to the difference existing between samples from different sources.
- *Scanning electron microscopy with energy dispersive x-ray spectrometry* has found extensive applications in the analysis of glass, paint, fibers, and especially in the identification of gunshot residues (where it is the method of choice). This technique offers high resolution, great depth of field, and qualitative and quantitative information on small samples. However, although this technique has much to offer, its use in crime detection is often overrated.
- Although considered destructive, *separation techniques* are regularly used by forensic laboratories for the analysis of trace evidence because most types of trace evidence are made up of complex combinations of the molecules and atoms that constitute our environment. In the context of trace evidence, separation techniques include TLC (inks and fiber dyes), GC (fire residues, polymers when used with a pyrolyzer), liquid chromatography (drugs, paint, inks, and oils), and capillary electrophoresis (inks and dyes, proteins, enzymes, and DNA fragments). All these separation techniques are used in combination with other analytical processes designed to detect the analyte. Spectrometric detection gives an additional identification capability (typical examples are GC, liquid chromatography, etc. with mass spectrometric detection and liquid chromatography or capillary electrophoresis with UV–visible diode array spectrophotometric detection).

Recent Analytical Developments

Analytical sciences have seen extraordinary developments in recent years. To some extent, they also drove, or at least sped up, recent significant technology transfers into forensic science. However, there is a real risk of falling into a 'gadgetry' trap if the technology is not fit for the purpose and if the prime consideration of the forensic context (i.e., holistic forensic science approach from the detection of evidence to the interpretation of results) is not taken into account.

It is impossible to dress an exhaustive list of promising emerging technologies applicable in the area of trace evidence. However, typical examples are:

- *Hyperspectral imaging* (chemical imaging): It combines molecular spectroscopy and digital imaging, providing both spatial and spectral information about materials. Chemometric processes, such as principal components analysis, can be applied to the raw data, allowing for information to be extracted from the large data sets that are generated. This technique is applicable in various spectral ranges (visible–near IR (NIR) and mid-IR regions) and magnifications. The potential for the use of visible and NIR chemical imaging in trace evidence applications has been demonstrated in the detection and analysis of firearm propellants and the analysis of automotive paint chips, bicomponent fibers, and the detection of illicit substances (drugs and explosives) in fingermarks.
- *Stable isotope ratio mass spectrometry*: It is based on the precise and accurate measurement of variations in the natural isotopic abundance of light stable isotopes. The underlying principle is that if the isotopic compositions of two samples are indistinguishable, and isotopic fractionation can be excluded from having occurred during handling, analysis, etc., then the two samples are likely to have originated from the same source. A difference may indicate that the two samples originated from different sources. Among the large number of applications, those related to trace evidence include explosives, ignitable liquids, hairs, paper, etc.
- *Microfluidics/lab-on-a-chip (LOC)*: The miniaturization of chemical instrumentation using microfabrication technology is an emerging area of analytical research that has been developed over the past 10 years. These so-called LOC devices dramatically downscale the analytical processes and can incorporate a wide variety of separation and detection methodologies. The main advantage of LOC devices is their amenability to field detection of DNA, illicit drugs, and explosive residues. By doing so, they blur the artificial boundary between the scene and the laboratory. They also allow modern forensic science to provide a quick, if not real time, response with little tradeoff in terms of discrimination and reliability.

Interpretation of Trace Evidence

An analytical result, however accurate and precise it may be, is generally insufficient for the investigation or for the court and should be interpreted in the context of the case under investigation. During this step, the forensic scientist must provide reliable information that help answer the questions being asked. This is not an easy task because the meaning of the results must be explained in such a way that it is understood without ambiguity by investigators and actors of the judicial system (lawyers, judges, jurors, and other scientists). It is fair to say that most issues in cases involving trace evidence usually arise from problems of interpretation rather than from experimental errors. The ability to meet this challenge relies heavily on the trace evidence examiner's deep knowledge and understanding of how the relevant type of trace evidence can be generated (usually transferred), and how it can persist, change over time, and vary across the relevant population, in addition to his or her purely analytical competencies. The context is also crucial as the same analytical result may have completely different meanings depending on the accepted circumstances.

Very broadly, interpreting trace evidence means to assess the chance of obtaining the findings (e.g., three 'matching' glass fragments) assuming an alleged set of circumstances as opposed to other explanations. During this process, it is important to keep an open mind and look for alternative explanations (e.g., could we find these types of gunshot residues by pure coincidence?). In many cases, it may be necessary to perform experiments reenacting the context to clarify points of contention.

Trace evidence usually assists in answering questions related to the source (e.g., could this paint chip have come from this car – as opposed to another car?) and/or the activity (e.g., were these fibers transferred during the alleged violent assault – as opposed to a 'legitimate' contact occurring before or after the event being investigated?).

At the source level, as in most other types of forensic examinations, trace evidence comparisons are essentially a reduction process whereby the scientist aims at distinguishing between different sources of the same specimen or substance. If no meaningful differences could be found, then it can be inferred that the two samples *could come from the same source*. It must be recognized that such a conclusion is not sufficient as it does not evaluate the strength of the apparent associative link (i.e., the *could have come from* statement is seen as independent of the circumstances, which is rather misleading). There is some uncertainty attached to this link and, further, this level of uncertainty can be widely variable depending on a number of objective and subjective parameters.

Inference of identity of source along with identification versus individualization and forensic interpretation are essential concepts that are explained elsewhere in this Encyclopedia.

The application of a coherent model based on subjective probabilities (Bayesian framework) has become standard practice in a number of forensic science disciplines, especially DNA. However, such a model is less widely applied in non-DNA trace evidence, mainly because of the lack of background data that are needed for its effective application. One notable exception is glass evidence and, to a lesser extent, fibers. It is argued here that efforts in designing research to produce relevant and reliable statistical data should be significantly expanded to most, if not all, types of trace evidence. This will eventually improve the value of trace evidence.

It is, however, important to realize that, in many cases, the relevant questions do not relate to the source but rather to the activity. In other words, the source of the trace evidence examined is not challenged by the parties. The dispute rather relates to the story explaining how the relevant trace evidence was generated, how it persisted, and how it was ultimately recovered. To this end, trace evidence is a value-added source of information for the reconstruction of a case, or, more broadly, for investigative purposes. This kind of information is rarely obtained with other types of forensic evidence, especially those focusing on identification only. Ultimately, the combination of trace evidence with 'identifying evidence' can deliver the key to the famous questions 'what happened?' and 'who dun it?'

The discussion above focused on the traditional use of trace evidence in court. However, it is well known and accepted that the application of forensic science, including trace evidence, starts at the scene. In other words, the value of trace evidence resides in its ability to not only support the proposition that, say, *60 fibers come from a given jumper*, but to also give investigative leads in the absence of comparative material. This is in addition to assisting in reconstructing the scene or a series of events, identifying links between different cases or, more broadly, systematically analyzing large-scale criminal phenomena. The value of integrating traditional forensic evidence with other dimensions of the investigative process has recently been highlighted by research in an area known as forensic intelligence. Although rapidly growing, this novel application of forensic science data is still underexploited. When this potential is fully realized, the value of trace evidence will also be upgraded because it can be seen as a crucial source of information in an investigative or intelligence framework.

Conclusion

Trace evidence, as material transferred during the commission of a crime, is at the crux of forensic science. When properly detected, recovered, analyzed, and interpreted, it has the ability to tell a story about what actually happened and who may have been involved. For this reason, it is crucial that crime scene examiners and associated first respondents (e.g., paramedics) recognize the potential value of existing trace evidence and conduct appropriate investigation at the crime scene and possibly later in hospital or at the morgue.

Trace evidence examination requires proper case management and appropriate recovery and analytical schemes. The ultimate aim of the trace evidence examiner is to evaluate and interpret what meaning can be attached to recovered specimens in the context of what is alleged to have occurred. This assumes not only technical and analytical competencies but also sound knowledge and understanding of how the relevant type of trace evidence can be generated, and how it can persist, change over time, and vary across the relevant population. This information is necessary to interpret the findings in the context of the case. If required, experience, professional expertise, and available data can be complemented with data obtained through reenactment experiments and/or studies aiming at gaining information about the prevalence and variability of the trace evidence of interest in the relevant population.

Trace evidence is essential for the holistic application of forensic science as it provides leads in the early stages of an investigation and ultimately assists in answering questions related to the source and/or the activity. Further information specific to various types of trace evidence is provided elsewhere in this Encyclopedia.

See also: **Behavioral**: Interpretation; **Biology/DNA**: Microbiology and Bioterrorism; **Chemistry/Trace/Adhesive Tapes**: Adhesive Tapes; **Chemistry/Trace/Decomposition Chemistry**: Decomposition Chemistry: Overview, Analysis, and Interpretation; **Chemistry/Trace/Environmental Analysis**: Overview, Analysis, and Interpretation of Environmental Forensic Evidence; **Chemistry/Trace/Fibers**: Color Analysis; Fiber Microscopy; Fiber: Protocols for Examination; Identification and Comparison; Interpretation of Fiber Evidence; Persistence and Recovery; Transfer; **Chemistry/Trace/Fire Investigation**: Analysis of Fire Debris; **Chemistry/Trace/Firearm Discharge Residues**: Overview, Analysis, and Interpretation; **Chemistry/Trace/Forensic Geosciences**: Botany; Crime Scene Considerations; Soils; **Chemistry/Trace/Glass**: Glass Analysis; Interpretation of Glass Evidence; Overview (Glass); **Chemistry/Trace/**

Miscellaneous Unknowns: The Forensic Analysis of Chemical Unknowns; **Chemistry/Trace/Paint and Coating**: Architectural Paint; Automotive Paint; Forensic Paint Analysis; Interpretation of Paint Evidence; Overview; **Chemistry/Trace/Trace Evidence**: Microchemistry; **Foundations**: Forensic Intelligence; Overview and Meaning of Identification/Individualization; Interpretation/The Comparative Method; Principles of Forensic Science; Statistical Interpretation of Evidence: Bayesian Analysis; **Investigations**: Collection and Chain of Evidence; Contamination; Crime Scene Analysis and Reconstruction; Evidence Collection at Fire Scenes; Packaging; Preservation; Recording.

Further Reading

Bartick E and Tungol M (1993) Infrared microscopy and its forensic applications. In: Saferstein R (ed.) *Forensic Science Handbook*, vol. III, pp. 196–252. Englewood Cliffs, NJ: Regent Prentice Hall.

Bottrell MC (2009) Forensic glass comparison: Background information used in data interpretation. *Forensic Science Communications* 11(2).

Caddy B (1999) *Forensic Examination of Glass and Paint, Analysis and Interpretation*. London and New York: Taylor and Francis Forensic Science Series.

Challinor J (2007) Examination of forensic evidence. In: Wampler T (ed.) *Applied Pyrolysis Handbook*, 2nd edn., pp. 175–199. Boca Raton, FL: CRS Press.

Coulson SA and Lynch BF (2009) Glass analysis. In: Freckelton I and Selby H (eds.) *Expert Evidence*, 6th edn., ch. 89, New South Wales: Law Book Co.

Curran JM, Hicks TN, and Buckleton JS (2000) *Forensic Interpretation of Glass Evidence*. Boca Raton, FL: CRC Press.

Dalby O, Butler D, and Birkett J (2010) Analysis of gunshot residue and associated materials – A review. *Journal of Forensic Sciences* 55: 924–943.

Donnelly LJ (2003) The applications of forensic geology to help the police solve crimes. *European Geologist. Journal of the European Federation of Geologists* 16: 8–12.

Fitzpatrick RW (2008) Nature, distribution and origin of soil materials in the forensic comparison of soils. In: Tibbett M and Carter DO (eds.) *Soil Analysis in Forensic Taphonomy: Chemical and Biological Effects of Buried Human Remains*, pp. 1–28. Boca Raton, FL: CRC Press.

Gaudette BD (1988) The forensic aspects of textile fibre examination. In: Saferstein R (ed.) *The Forensic Examination of Fibres*, vol. 2. Englewood Cliffs, NJ: Prentice Hall.

Grieve MC (1990) Fibres and their examination in forensic science. In: Maehly A and Williams RL (eds.) *Forensic Science Progress*, vol. 4. New York: Springer Verlag.

Koons RD, Buscaglia J, Bottrell M, and Miller ET (2002) Forensic glass comparisons. In: Saferstein R (ed.) *Forensic Science Handbook*, 2nd edn., vol. 1, pp. 161–214. Upper Saddle River, NJ: Prentice Hall.

Meng HH and Caddy B (1997) Gunshot residue analysis – A review. *Journal of Forensic Sciences* 42(4): 553–570.

Murray RC (2011) *Evidence from the earth: Forensic geology and criminal investigation*, 2nd edn. Missoula, MT: Mountain Press.

Murray RC and Tedrow JCF (1992) *Forensic Geology*. Englewood Cliffs, NJ: Prentice Hall.

Patton TC (ed.) (1973) *Pigment Handbook*, vols. I–III. New York: Wiley.

Petraco N and Kubic T (2004) *Color Atlas and Manual of Microscopy for Criminalists, Chemists, and Conservators*. Boca Raton, FL: CRS Press.

Pirrie D, Butcher AR, Power MR, Gottlieb P, and Miller GL (2004) Rapid quantitative mineral and phase analysis using automated scanning electron microscopy (QemSCAN); potential applications in forensic geoscience. In: Pye K and Croft DJ (eds.) *Forensic Geoscience: Principles, Techniques and Applications*, pp. 103–122. London: Geological Society of London. Special Publication 232.

Pye K (2007) *Geological and Soil Evidence: Forensic Applications*. Boca Raton, FL: CRC Press.

Ritz K, Dawson L, and Miller D (eds.) (2008) *Criminal and Environmental Soil Forensics*. Amsterdam: Soil Forensics International, Edinburgh Conference Centre, Springer Science+Business Media B.V.

Robertson J and Grieve M (eds.) (1999) *Forensic Examination of Fibres*. Philadelphia, PA: Taylor & Francis.

Rodrigues F (1989) *Principles of Polymer Systems*, 3rd edn. New York: Hemisphere Publishing Corporation.

Romolo FS and Margot P (2001) Identification of gunshot residue: A critical review. *Forensic Science International* 119(2): 195–211.

Ruffell A and McKinley J (2008) *Geoforensics*. Chichester: Wiley.

Schoeneberger PJ, Wysocki DA, Benham EC, and Broderson WD (eds.) (2002) *Field Book for Describing and Sampling Soils*. Lincoln, NE: Natural Resources Conservation Service, National Soil Survey Center. Version 2.0.

Suzuki E (1993) Forensic applications of infrared spectroscopy. In: Saferstein R (ed.) *Forensic Science Handbook*, vol. III, pp. 71–195. Englewood Cliffs, NJ: Regent Prentice Hall.

Textile Institute (1975) *The Identification of Textile Materials*, 7th edn. Manchester: Textile Institute.

Thornton JI (2002) Forensic paint examination. In: Saferstein R (ed.) *Forensic Science Handbook*, 2nd edn., pp. 430–478. Upper Saddle River, NJ: Prentice Hall.

Tracton AA (ed.) (2007) *Coatings Materials and Surface Coatings*. Boca Raton, FL: CRC Press.

Trejos T, Castro W, Almirall JR (2006) Elemental analysis of glass and paint materials by laser ablation inductively coupled plasma mass spectrometry (LA-ICP-MS) for forensic applications. NIJ Technical Report 2006. Available: http://www.ncjrs.gov/pdffiles1/nij/grants/232133.pdf.

Wallace J (2008) *Chemical Analysis of Firearms, Ammunition, and Gunshot Residue*. Boca Raton, FL: CRC Press.

Weismantle GE (ed.) (1981) *Paint Handbook*. New York: McGraw-Hill book Company.

Relevant Websites

http://www.swgmat.org/ – Scientific Working Group for Materials Analysis.

Microchemistry

VM Maxwell, University of New Haven, West Haven, CT, USA

Glossary

Catalyst A substance that increases the rate of a chemical reaction and is itself unchanged upon completion of the reaction.

Confirmatory test A test used to confirm the identity of a substance. Generally used after a screening test.

Controlled substance A drug, or chemical, whose manufacture, possession, and use are regulated by government.

Definitive identification Identification of a substance with absolute certainty and to the exclusion of all other possible substances.

Enzyme Protein molecules that are produced by living cells and act as catalysts in specific biochemical reactions.

Firearms discharge residue Material, other than the bullet, expelled from a firearm during discharge. The components include burned and unburned gunpowder, primer residues, metal shavings, and hot gases.

Functional group That portion of an organic molecule responsible for the characteristic behavior of the class of compounds in which this group occurs.

Paint binder That portion of a paint that contains pigments and additives.

Screening test A test used to narrow down the possible identification of a substance.

Supersaturated solution A solution of a substance in which the concentration exceeds saturation.

Introduction

Microchemistry is considered to be the branch of chemistry that is concerned with the reactions and properties of materials on a minute scale. Historically, microchemistry has been in practice for many years. Francois-Vincent Raspail (1794–1878) is considered to be the founder of microchemistry because of his early work on the application of the iodine test to starches and the subsequent development of new reagents for other color tests.

Microchemical methods are, in general, highly sensitive and permit the use of samples that are far smaller than needed for conventional chemical identification. Microchemistry is used widely in forensic science for several different purposes, whether for screening to determine possible identity to rapid definitive identification of materials. Although many forensic laboratories have replaced routine chemical testing with instrumental analysis, there are many advantages to using microchemical reactions. They are well-established techniques, and in most cases, the chemistry behind the reaction has been characterized and is well understood. Microchemical testing is very sensitive and may be achieved using minuscule amounts of both unknown analyte and reagents. The specificity of the testing varies from identification of class of materials to highly specific, virtually definitive identification. In many cases, the use of microchemistry for identification may be achieved without the need to separate different components of a mixture before testing. Microchemical testing is ideal for tentative identification of substances at the crime scene where portable instrumentation is not available.

Although it is no longer considered to be definitive identification, in some situations, the ease with which microchemical testing may be conducted, in comparison with the absence of sample preparation, has resulted in microchemistry being the technique of choice for certain analyses. An example of this is the testing of holes in clothing using sodium rhodizonate to identify the presence of bullet wipe around the edge thus showing the holes to be the result of a shooting rather than originating from some other object.

Types of Microchemical Reactions

A comprehensive review of chemical and forensic literature since the early nineteenth century shows that microchemistry is a far-reaching and extremely versatile method of analysis. There are few types of evidence for which no microchemical analysis can be applied, whether a simple one-step test or a more complex analysis scheme. Microchemical reactions used in forensic science can be classified into three major groups of test based on the general reaction type: spot tests, crystal tests, and solubility tests. For certain types of materials, useful information can be obtained from all three classes of tests while, for others, only one class of test may be applicable.

Spot Tests

Spot tests are primarily color tests in which a reagent is added to the analyte of interest with a resulting color change indicative of the material present. Final diagnostic colors are usually achieved rapidly, in some cases, immediately but generally after no longer than 1 min. Caution needs to be exercised when interpreting color changes after greater elapsed time. Color tests range from being highly specific to indicative only of a general class of material being present; the specificity is often a product of whether the test is of an anion, a cation, or a functional group.

Spot tests are the most common of preliminary screening tests used in forensic analysis and are used to assess the presence or absence of a substance. Numerous types of evidence can be effectively screened before more definitive analysis from possible bloodstains to explosives. Spot tests can be used at the crime scene to screen evidence before collection, as well as back

 http://dx.doi.org/10.1016/B978-0-12-382165-2.00087-8

at the forensic laboratory as part of an analytical scheme. Advances in instrumental technology have limited the relative importance of spot tests; in early laboratory protocols, they were often considered to be a positive form of identification of a material, whereas modern forensic science limits them for the most part to narrowing the list of substances possibly present. Despite this limitation, there are certain instances where the rapid results of the spot test and the ability to identify with relative certainty the substance present have made spot tests the method of choice for forensic analysis. This is seen most readily in the use of sodium rhodizonate for the identification of lead in firearms-related cases.

The mechanism by which color tests work is through one of two different types of reactions resulting in a colored product. The first type of reaction is the oxidation/reduction reaction involving the transfer of electrons but without the formation of a molecular product incorporating the analyte into the reagent. These reactions generally lack a high level of specificity and are susceptible to interferents that can participate in the oxidation/reduction reaction in a similar manner; for example, the *o*-tolidine test for blood. The second class of reactions involves the incorporation of the analyte into the product of the reaction. This class of reactions is generally more specific than the first; however, it should be noted that they are testing for the presence of a particular functional group rather than a specific molecule and are subject to interference from materials having the same functional group in their structure. Many tests for drugs of abuse fall into this category.

In the early practice of microchemistry, many spot tests were developed for different materials. However, not only were the reaction mechanisms poorly understood but also there was contradiction and confusion regarding the sensitivity of the different tests. Therefore, although the existing spot tests were undoubtedly useful, with neither standardization of methods nor an understanding of the sensitivity of the different tests, their results were of limited value despite their widespread use. Fritz Feigl developed the concepts of specificity, selectivity, and sensitivity in relation to chemical spots test. Specificity refers to the degree to which a test can identify a particular analyte and therefore with a positive reaction, the certainty with which the analyte has been identified. This can be in the presence or absence of other materials. The term selectivity is used as an expression of the extent to which a test can identify a particular analyte present in a mixture under given conditions without interference from other components of the mixture. Thus, although the terms are somewhat similar, they are distinct from each other. Equally important is the issue of sensitivity, which is defined by two terms: the limit of detection, the smallest amount of an analyte that can be detected by the test reaction, and the limit of dilution, the most dilute solution in which the analyte can still be detected.

False-positive results are a concern for spot testing. However, as the primary role of these tests is as a screening test, the subsequent use of more definitive forms of identification means that a false-positive does not usually impact the final identification of the material. Nonetheless, the analyst should be aware of possible interferents for all tests that they conduct in order to assess the result of the test accurately. Similarly, they should be aware of the limit of detection for the spot tests employed when assessing negative results.

The simplest type of spot test involves mixing a drop or a few particles of an unknown substance with a drop of a reagent solution, with observation of any color change or precipitate formation. The required equipment for these tests is extremely simple; microscope slides and cover slips or well plates are usually used along with dropper bottles for reagents. The development of simple field testing kits has seen the appearance of numerous self-contained units in which an unknown material is added to a container in which the required reagent already resides. In forensic applications, the simple addition of a drop of reagent to a minute amount of the unknown material does not usually require absolute control of the volume of the drop added. Thus, the use of a reagent bottle and a well plate or microscope slide is usually adequate. In some testing, the analyte may be in a filter paper or a cotton swab, but again, although consistency is desirable, an absolute volume of reagent does not usually have to be fully controlled.

The screening of biological evidence before DNA examination is an area of forensic science that uses many simple spot tests. Here, the examiner uses a test to determine whether or not a stain is potentially a body fluid, such as blood or semen, although the tests are not specific for human body fluids, and further testing is used to determine the species of origin of a substance.

Many blood-identification techniques are contingent on the presence of hemoglobin and its enzymatic properties. Useful and relatively user-friendly tests, which exploit the catalytic activity of hemoglobin in the blood, have been developed for both in-field and laboratory application and are governed by chemical reactions that result in an observable color change. In the presence of hemoglobin, a colorless or colored reagent will be oxidized by the catalytic activity of hemoglobin resulting in a new colored product.

Kastle–Meyer/phenolphthalein and leucomalachite green are screening tests that result in a color change, pink and green, respectively, when blood is detected. The tests have a comparable sensitivity, detecting blood as dilute as 1:10 000. However, some pitfalls exist in their application and specificity. Sample consumption may become an issue when samples are very minute and preservation of the sample for DNA testing may impinge on the screening of the sample with this method. Second, these tests are not solely specific for human blood, and false-positive results are encountered with blood from higher primates and other oxidizing agents.

Benzidine, tetra-methyl benzidine (TMB), and *ortho*-tolidine are all catalytic tests that result in a blue-colored product in the presence of blood. Benzidine was originally utilized because of its high sensitivity but was replaced by the later two tests because of its carcinogenic properties. TMB and *ortho*-tolidine possess comparable sensitivities, but other oxidants such as plant materials can yield false-positive results. **Figure 1** shows positive reactions of blood to Kastle–Meyer (pink color) and *o*-tolidine (blue color).

Luminol and fluorescein are tests that result in the identification of blood though production of a fluorescent substance. Luminol has found popularity at the crime scene because of its high sensitivity to very minute levels of blood and its capability to detect aged blood samples. Luminol testing, however, must be carried out in a completely dark environment, and the duration of the luminescence is not permanent, so the sample must be photographically documented. Fluorescein is not self-illuminating and requires visualization using a 425–485-nm alternative light source. Although these fluorescent reagents are 'spot tests,' they are generally conducted at the macroscopic level by spraying large areas at a crimes scene.

Color tests for seminal fluid are based on the presence or absence of acid phosphatase, an enzyme found in high concentrations in seminal fluid and relatively low concentrations or absent in other body fluids. A number of tests exist for the identification of saliva; however, all are based on the action of salivary amylase, an enzyme responsible for the hydrolysis of starch, which is found in high concentrations in saliva, but it should be noted that it is present in detectable level in several other body fluids. The Jaffe test for creatinine is the oldest color test for identifying the presence of urine. Other tests for urine are based on the presence of urea.

Spot tests are widely used in the area of drug analysis. When confronted with a potential controlled substance, the analyst must adopt an analytical scheme that involves narrowing down the potential sources of the material. Numerous controlled substances can present in a similar appearance, such as a white powder, yet tentative identification is crucial before embarking on instrumental analysis because of analytical incompatibility of some drugs of abuse with common instrumentation. Many simple color tests are available with the reagents being either commercially available or simple to prepare. Many of these reagents are available as kits ready made for the crime scene investigator. The sensitivities of these tests are in the range of 1–50 μg on an average, but selectivities vary considerably and whole classes of controlled substances may be identified rather than one specific material, as tests identify the presence of a particular functional group. The common spot tests for drugs of abuse may also be used in thin-layer chromatography to assist in the visualization of spots on the plate.

While the use of simple spot tests in the field of toxicology requires some preparatory steps because of the nature of the samples, they can successfully be performed directly on urine or a protein-free filtrate of blood or tissues. The toxicologist can rapidly screen samples for the presence of many potential drugs and poisons. The sensitivity of the color tests used in toxicology varies, and in some cases, the sensitivity is such that only levels consistent with an overdose are sufficient to give a positive reaction. All positive results, regardless of the test, require confirmation using another form of analysis.

Color spot tests are used extensively in the detection of explosives both in the field, as a rapid means of detecting chemicals consistent with explosives, and in the laboratory, as preliminary tests in an analytical scheme. The explosives examiner relies on spot tests as a tentative means of identifying anions and cations, which may be consistent with explosive materials. In general, the most useful tests ionic species are those for ammonium, barium, calcium, chlorate, lithium, nitrate, nitrite, perchlorate, permanganate, potassium, sodium, strontium, and sulfate. **Figure 2** illustrates a positive reaction of Griess reagent with a nitrite-containing material. Color tests for organic components are available for TNT-, DNT-, tetryl-, RDX-, PETN-, TATP-, nitrocellulose-, and nitroglycerine-based explosives. Detection thresholds are in the range of 25–100 ng depending on the material of interest. Many color tests for explosives are now being used in field kits for the identification of residues on hands and other surfaces.

Firearms discharge residues are a particular interest in a discussion of microchemistry, as color tests used for lead, nitrites, and copper are used as identification without an ensuing confirmation step. This is due to the highly specific nature of the tests, as well the presence of associated evidence and circumstances of their use. Determination of shooting distance employs sodium rhodizonate to identify patterns of lead residues, and the Griess tests for nitrites. The use of sodium rhodizonate as a spot test for lead and rubeanic acid as a spot test for copper is also common, especially in the identification of bullet wipe and location of possible bullet ricochets (**Figure 3**).

Spot tests are particularly useful to the forensic examiner when confronted with unknown samples for which identification is necessary, whether these samples are fibers, paint,

Figure 2 The reaction of a nitrite with Griess reagent.

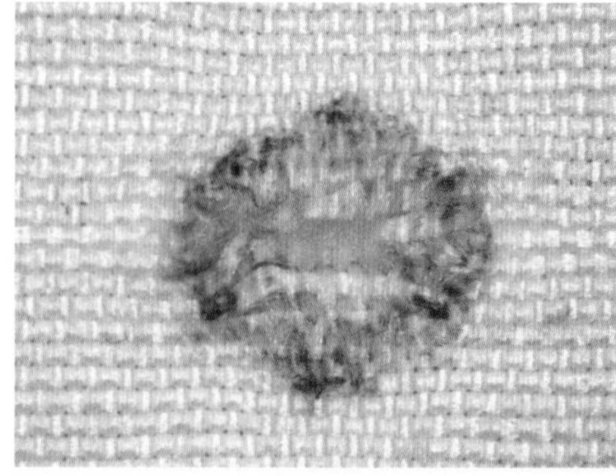

Figure 3 The reaction of the lead residues in bullet wipe with sodium rhodizonate giving a characteristic deep link color around a bullet hole.

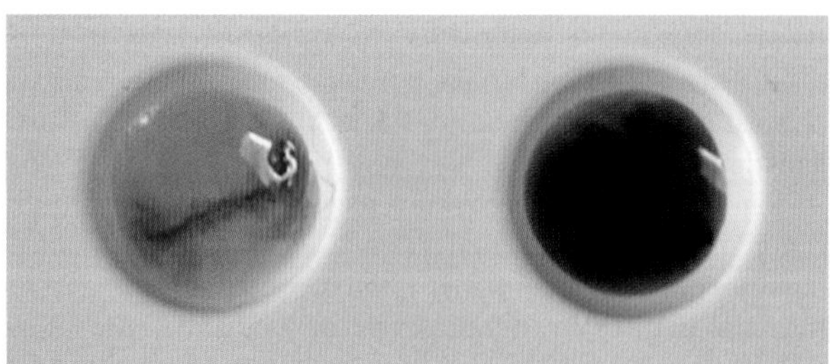

Figure 1 The reaction of Kastle–Meyer reagent (left) and *o*-tolidine (right) with blood.

and other common materials, or an unknown white powder. Careful selection of spot tests in combination with visual observation can provide at least a tentative identification that can then be confirmed via further testing with instrumentation.

Crystal Tests

Historically, microcrystal tests were considered a confirmatory test following preliminary spot tests. For example, a reddish brown stain giving a positive reaction with *o*-tolidine would then be subjected to the Takayama or Teichmann tests, crystal tests, to positively identify the presence of blood. Nowadays, many crystal tests for biological materials have been replaced by immunological tests giving not only confirmation of the body fluid type but also the identification of the species of origin. Many other microcrystal tests were developed from the early nineteenth century onward through the use of heavy metal reagents such as those based on platinum, mercury, or gold. Microcrystal tests are relatively simple to perform and do not require sophisticated equipment such as analytical instrumentation. A compound microscope is sufficient for many of the tests, although polarized light microscopy is preferable and required for some tests. It should be noted that a disadvantage of the tests lies with the skill of the analyst, as accurate determination of optical properties of crystal formations may be essential to the accuracy of the identification of the unknown material. This reservation has lead to a discontinuation of the use of microcrystal tests as definitive identification of material, especially with the widespread use of analytical instrumentation. From a technical standpoint, concentration of reagent is important in the development of well-formed crystals, and therefore in the accurate identification of a material, supersaturated solutions are required, and the analyst should take care to observe areas of higher concentration for the formation of characteristic crystals.

Microcrystal tests have been used extensively in the analysis and identification of drugs of abuse. Microcrystal tests are particularly useful for amines, such as all alkaloids, and amides, such as phenacetin and acetanilid. The method of identification using the formation of characteristic crystals under the microscope was developed and reported as early as 1885, and its value only increased by the use of additional crystallizing reagents. The widespread use of instrumentation and the ability to analyze most drugs of abuse with some form of instrumentation have supplanted the use of microcrystal testing of drugs of abuse particular as a form of definitive identification, but many laboratory systems still consider it to be a valuable form of confirmatory screening and continue to use it in their analytical schemes. A major advantage of microcrystal testing in drugs of abuse, and a reason for the continued use, is that it can be employed without any need for purification or extraction of the analyte of interest; either the crystals form or they do not. Thus the presence of cutting agents does not pose a problem, and the analyst can rapidly screen a material to determine whether extraction and instrumental analysis would be required. Microcrystal tests may also be used to identify the cutting agents themselves as seen in **Figure 4**, the formation of characteristics crystals by caffeine using mercuric chloride. Additional information that may be determined by the skilled analyst is the approximate relative concentration of the material of interest in the sample, thus allowing the analyst to make a determination as to the appropriate means of further testing. Microcrystal tests also allow the distinction of different optical isomers, another important characteristic in the accurate identification of drugs.

Figure 4 The crystals formed by the reaction of caffeine with mercuric chloride as seen with a polarized light microscope.

Following the use of screening tests for biological fluids, confirmatory tests are employed because of the limitations of screening tests and the possibility of interferents and false-positive reactions. Confirmation may be via crystal tests, precipitation tests, and commercial kits. The crystal tests depend on hemoglobin and/or its derivatives in the same manner as that of screening tests, but definitive identification of blood is indicated by the formation of specific microscopic crystals. Two common crystal tests are the Teichmann and Takayama tests. The Teichmann test is performed by heating dried blood with glacial acetic acid and a halide, usually a chloride. The main difficulties encountered are due to poor heat control and a potential lack of sensitivity. The Takayama test is based on the formation of characteristic pink crystals by heme in the presence of pyridine. The suspected blood is heated gently with pyridine under alkaline conditions in the presence of a reducing sugar such as glucose. The formation of crystals of pyridine ferric protoporphyrin indicates the presence of hemoglobin, and therefore blood. The Takayama test is extremely sensitive and has given positive reactions with bloodstains in situations where the Teichmann test reaction was negative. The crystal tests are no longer utilized for the confirmation of blood and have been replaced by immunological tests, which provide simultaneous identification of blood and species and therefore consumes less or the available sample.

Solubility Tests

Solubility testing is a technique used only occasionally in forensic science. The types of evidence that might be examined by solubility include paint, fibers, plastics, explosives, and drugs. However, as solubility tests are destructive tests, they are not routinely used, particularly if only small samples are available and nondestructive testing would provide a similar means of discrimination. There are, however, some cases in which information obtained through solubility testing cannot be achieved in any other way. The results of solubility testing depend on many different properties of the material, such as the molecular size and shape, polarity, solvent strength, viscosity, diffusion, and solvation mechanism. The destructive nature of solubility testing means that it is advisable to test the known sample before consuming any of the questioned samples in order to test the efficacy of the solubility results in an analysis scheme.

A wide range of solvents with different polarities and acidities are used in ways that extend from a simple test using only one solvent for comparison purposes to elaborate solubility schemes, leading to an almost definitive identification of the material, such as with fibers. For drugs and explosives, testing water solubility can be useful. For example, if a drug such as cocaine is diluted with flour, the flour will not dissolve in water. Solubility testing can thus be a prelude to solvent extraction and separations that are performed before instrumental techniques. While solubility testing can help establish similarities between two samples, it cannot individualize them to a common source.

In paint analysis, a solubility scheme can be used to distinguish between nonaqueous dispersion lacquers, solvent-thinned lacquers, solvent-thinned enamels, and water-based enamels. The solvents used in this scheme include xylene, glacial acetic acid, nitric acid, and hot alcoholic potassium hydroxide. In addition to the dissolution of paint binders, also of note are the color reactions of binder components and pigment with the oxidizing and reducing agents commonly found in solubility reagents. As many questioned paint samples are microscopic in size, the analyst must determine whether the value of the information obtained outweighs the destructive nature of the test. This may be the case for some automotive paints, particularly those based on acrylic binders, which may be considered to be either solution or dispersion lacquers. Instrumental techniques cannot distinguish between the two types of acrylic binder; however, xylene solubility provides a rapid answer as dispersion lacquers are soluble, whereas solution lacquers are not.

Solubility testing of fibers can provide useful supplemental information for the identification of manufactured fibers when used in conjunction with typical nondestructive methods. Although testing can be conducted on an unidentified fiber without a known sample for comparison, it is most useful to conduct solubility testing in fibers while observing both the known and questioned samples side by side. In some cases, complete solubility is not observed and other possible responses of fibers to solvents include color changes, swelling, gelling, and shrinking. The response to a particular solvent is directly related to the chemical composition of the fiber. In general, cellulosic fibers, both natural and regenerated, react to acidic solutions, as does nylon. However, nylon reacts to hydrochloric acid, and cellulosic fibers react to sulfuric acid. The use of solvents with a variety of polarities and acidities is recommended and common solvents used on a fiber solubility scheme include formic acid, glacial acetic acid, acetonitrile, chloroform, cyclohexanone, acetone, nitric acid, sulfuric acid (75%), sulfuric acid (100%), and water. As most fibers can be identified through a combination of microscopy and instrumental analysis, the use of solubility for identification is now uncommon.

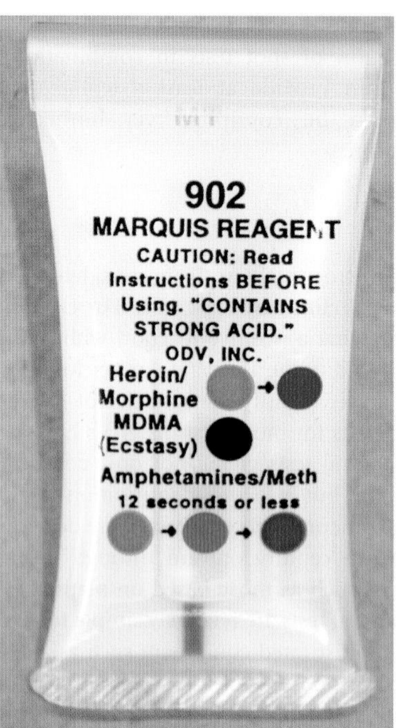

Figure 5 A commercially available field testing kit for controlled substances based on color test chemistry. Credit attributed to Alysha Hines, University of New Haven.

Microchemical Analysis

In summary, the use of microchemistry has, for the most part, seen a change from a means of definitive identification to a screening test. Nonetheless, many of the techniques are still in daily use in the forensic laboratory and continue to have great value. In some cases, specific information can be obtained only through microchemical techniques or the circumstances dictate that microchemical identification alone is sufficient. The use of microchemistry in conjunction with analytical instrumentation allows definitive identification of virtually all materials. Many of the early principles and reagents of classical microchemistry are now available as preprepared strips or simple kits for use in the field by nonscientific personnel for rapid screening of materials whether for identification of potential evidence, or the safety of personnel through the identification of hazardous materials (Figure 5). Thus, although the use of microchemistry may have been supplanted by the widespread use of analytical instrumentation in the laboratory, the tests continue to be used in a variety of formats.

See also: **Chemistry/Trace/Drugs of Abuse**: Analysis of Controlled Substances; **Chemistry/Trace/Explosives**: Explosives: Analysis; **Chemistry/Trace/Fibers**: Identification and Comparison; **Chemistry/Trace/Paint and Coating**: Forensic Paint Analysis; **Methods**: Presumptive Chemical Tests; Spectroscopic Techniques; **Toxicology**: Methods of Analysis – Confirmatory Testing; Methods of Analysis – Initial Testing.

Further Reading

Benedetti-Pichler AA (1964) *Identification of Materials via Physical Properties, Chemical Tests and Microscopy*. New York: Springer.

Chemot EM and Mason CW (1940) *Handbook of Chemical Microscopy, vol. II: Chemical Methods and Inorganic Qualitative Analysis*, 2nd edn. New York: Wiley.

Emich F (1932) *Microchemical Laboratory Manual*. New York: J. Wiley & Sons Inc.; London: Chapman & Hall Limited.

Feigl F (1966) *Spot Tests in Organic Analysis*, 7th edn. Amsterdam: Elsevier.

Feigl F (1972) *Spot Tests in Inorganic Analysis*, 6th edn. Amsterdam: Elsevier.

Fulton CC (1969) *Modern Microchemical Tests for Drugs: The Identification of Organic Compounds by Microcrystalloscopic Chemistry*. New York: Wiley.

Jungreis E (1997) *Spot Test Analysis: Clinical, Environmental, Forensic and Geochemical Applications*, 2nd edn. New York: Wiley-Interscience.

National Institute of Standards and Technology (2000) *Color Test Reagent/Kits for Preliminary Identification of Drugs of Abuse*. Washington, DC: NIJ.

Palenik SJ (1979) Microchemical reactions in particle identification. In: McCrone WC, Delly JG, and Palenik SJ (eds.) *The Particle Atlas*, 2nd edn., pp. 1174–1175. Ann Arbor: Ann Arbor Science.

Smith FP (ed.) (2004) *Handbook of Forensic Drug Analysis*. Oxford: Elsevier.

Wormley TG (1867) *Microchemistry of Poisons*. Philadelphia, PA: J.B. Lippincott.

Relevant Websites

www.abft.org – American Board of Forensic Toxicology.
www.microchem.org – American Microchemical Society.
www.swgmat.org – Scientific Working Group for the Analysis of Materials.
www.swgdrug.org – Scientific Working Group for the Analysis of Seized Drugs.
ncfs.org – Technical Working Group for Fire and Explosions.

Further Reading

Relevant Websites

DIGITAL EVIDENCE

Contents

Child Pornography

E Quayle, University of Edinburgh, Edinburgh, UK

Glossary

COPINE scale A rating system created in Ireland and used in the United Kingdom to categorize the severity of child pornography.
Digital child pornography This may refer to images that have been created by a computer program or images that are of a real child which have been altered by a computer program.
Social networking websites These have been defined as web-based services that allow individuals to create a public or semipublic profile within a system, define a list of other users with whom they share a connection, and view and access content from their list of connections and those made by others within the system.
The International Centre of Missing & Exploited Children A leading a global movement to protect children from sexual exploitation and abduction.
User-generated content The production of content by the general public rather than by paid professionals and experts in the field. Also called 'peer production' and mostly available on the Web through blogs and wikis.

Introduction

The past decade has seen a substantial increase in the number of international research publications, policy documents, and legislative changes in relation to still and moving sexualized images of children, variously called child pornography, abuse images, or child exploitation materials. This increased interest in part reflects the growing number of people in the criminal justice system convicted of crimes related to the production, distribution, and possession of child pornography. Data to support this are largely drawn from the United States, Europe, and Australia, although it is unclear whether increased availability of the Internet in Asia, Africa, and South America will change this. While child pornography is not new, it is the case that, with each technological advance, one has seen an increase in the availability of such materials, and this has been most noticeable in relation to the advent of the Internet. In this context, it is one of a number of cybercrimes, a term used to describe a wide range of offenses, including offenses against computer data and systems (such as 'hacking'), computer-related forgery and fraud (such as 'phishing'), content offenses (such as disseminating child pornography), and copyright offenses (such as the dissemination of pirated content).

There are historical accounts of child pornography and its distribution, which appeared to be facilitated by the popular use of photography. The criminalization of such material, however, made access both difficult and dangerous, although there was a period of approximately 10 years when in some European countries (Denmark and Sweden) all pornographic materials were decriminalized. It has been argued that

 http://dx.doi.org/10.1016/B978-0-12-382165-2.00122-7

recognition of child pornography as a societal problem dates to the late 1970s, and this is certainly reflected in the increase of legislation from this time in countries such as the United States. The advent of Internet technology lowered the cost of the production of these images, dramatically increased their availability, and reduced the risk of detection that was associated with the criminalization of production and possession. The move internationally to legislate against the production, dissemination, and possession of these images has meant an increasing focus on the 'Internet sex offender' and an expansion of activities that might potentially be criminalized (e.g., in relation to text or audio files).

International Law

In recent years, one has seen the development of supranational and international policy documents which set out to define 'child pornography' and four policy documents that are central to this issue. The European Union's Framework Decision on combating the sexual exploitation of children and child pornography entered into force in 2004 and required member states to take steps to ensure compliance by 20 January 2006. Here, child pornography is defined as pornographic material that visually depicts or represents: (i) a real child involved or engaged in sexually explicit conduct, including lascivious exhibition of the genitals or the pubic area of a child, or (ii) a real person appearing to be a child involved or engaged in the conduct mentioned in (i), or (iii) realistic images of a nonexistent child involved or engaged in the conduct mentioned in (i). As one can see, the definition in the EU Framework Decision talks about a 'real' child, 'real' person, and 'realistic' images, which may prove unlikely to cover virtual images or cartoons. The Council of Europe's Cybercrime Convention came into force in July 2004, and Article 9 defines child pornography as pornographic material that visually depicts a minor engaged in sexually explicit conduct, a person appearing to be a minor engaged in sexually explicit conduct, or realistic images representing a minor engaged in sexually explicit conduct. This relates to all people under the age of 18, but it is possible for a lower age limit of 16 to be set. The third document is the United Nation's Optional Protocol to the Convention on the Rights of the Child on the Sale of Children, Child Prostitution, and Child Pornography which came into force in January 2002 and defines child pornography as any representation, by whatever means, of a child engaged in real or simulated explicit sexual activities or any representation of the sexual parts of a child for primarily sexual purposes.

In all three, a child is defined as someone under the age of 18 years and includes both photographs of actual children and representations of children, which would appear to include computer-generated images. However, the issue of age is subject to several reservations and complicated by the age of sexual consent established under national law. The UN definition is broad and, as it refers to 'any representation,' would also include textual material, cartoons, and drawings. The most recent relevant instrument establishing a definition of child pornography is the Council of Europe Convention on the Protection of Children against Sexual Exploitation and Sexual Abuse. While this definition is restricted to visual materials, it does not require that a real child be used in their production (as is the case in the United States). However, member states may opt not to criminalize the production and possession of virtual child pornography.

This UN definition was used in a study of the 184 Interpol member countries. The results indicated that at the time of publication, 95 countries had no legislation at all that specifically addresses child pornography, and 41 countries do not criminalize possession of child pornography, regardless of intent to distribute. However, in law, offenses related to child pornography are not all treated as the same. This has been referred to as a chain of liability. At the top of the chain are those who produce abusive images or content, and these will be made up of, although not exclusively, those who will have sexually abused the children in the images. Many of these will produce images within a domestic setting where production is part of a spectrum of abusive practices. The second group that sexually exploits consists of those who distribute child pornography over the Internet, either commercially (for financial gain) or noncommercially, where the images themselves function as a form of currency or possibly as a means to raise their status in a group or to confirm their allegiance and sense of belonging to a group. The final group includes those who sexually exploit the child through the possession of images downloaded from the Internet. However, it is the enforceability of international law perhaps that demonstrates the biggest weakness of its applicability to child pornography. Although it is easy for countries to sign treaties and conventions and make pledges to tackle child pornography, it is also very easy for countries to simply ignore them.

Harm

One assumption underpinning the interest in abuse images is that of harm. This may be expressed as harm toward the child who was photographed, but equally harm has been argued to take place when someone views the image of the child, even without any contact having taken place. The reasoning is that there is the potential for additional harm, as looking at images may increase the likelihood of the commission of a contact offense against a child at some point in the near, or distant, future. Such arguments have become enshrined in the laws of many countries with, for example, the United States Department of Justice prosecuting possession under the rationale that (a) possession leads to contact offenses, (b) demand drives supply, and (c) the availability constitutes continued and indirect abuse of the child depicted. Some researchers have challenged assumptions of harm, arguing that the majority of images depict children not engaged in acts that are harmful in themselves.

Few studies have examined these images, which in part may be due to the difficulties in researchers gaining access without committing an offense, along with the ethical challenges posed by repeat viewing. It might seem that the seriousness of the problem has largely been measured in terms of the number of offenders in the criminal justice system and the proportion of these who have already committed a contact offense or who are deemed at risk of committing one. Where the images in their possession have been explored, this is most often in relation to what it might tell us about the offender: The nature of their sexual interests and fantasies, their sexual orientation, and the intensity of their interest or preoccupation. All of this reflects a legitimate concern with the offender and the nature of the offense, but, unlike the research on solicitation or grooming, does little to help us understand what has happened from the perspective of the child.

Typologies of Child Pornography

Challenges to a systematic analysis of child pornography stem from difficulties in describing the content in any meaningful way outside of the age or gender of the child or children. The adoption by the UK Sentencing Advisory Panel (SAP) of the COPINE scale as an objective measure of content was probably not a reflection of the integrity of the scale but rather the absence of anything else. The original COPINE scale had 10 levels ranging from indicative images (e.g., pictures of children in bathing costumes or underwear) to ones depicting extreme sexually abusive acts such as sadism or bestiality. In 2002, in England and Wales, the SAP published their advice to the Court of Appeal on offenses involving child pornography. The SAP believed that the nature of the material should be the key factor in deciding the level of sentence, and adapted the COPINE scale to five levels. They dropped levels 1–3 completely, arguing that nakedness alone was not indicative of indecency. The five levels were now described as:

- Level 1: Nudity or erotic posing with no sexual activity
- Level 2: Sexual activity between children or solo masturbation
- Level 3: Nonpenetrative sexual activity between adult(s) and child(ren)
- Level 4: Penetrative sexual activity between adult(s) and child(ren)
- Level 5: Sadism or bestiality

In spite of concern over its use and the confusion as to whether it is the original scale or the SAP guidelines that are being referred to, having some objective measure does allow us to make comparisons between samples and have some sense of both preferred materials, and also (although rarely referred to) the types of sexual activity that the depicted child has been exposed to. However, it has been argued that the kinds of images that have the capacity to be described as child pornography are increasing. In addition to photographs that depict the sexual abuse of children, images and texts in countries such as Australia and Canada risk breaking the law for any depiction of minors in a sexualized context. A revised typology of child pornography has been proposed that makes reference to content (as with the COPINE scale), biological development of the child within the image, level of purported consent given by the child, veracity of the image, and the particular genre portrayed.

While analyses of images by law enforcement agencies would suggest that the typical child depicted is a prepubescent girl, an analysis of a sample of seized images within one UK law enforcement database would suggest that the odds of the abuse images being of females versus males were about 4–1, and the odds of the images being of White children versus non-White children were about 10–1. Of those white female children, approximately 48% were pubescent. It may be that, in many instances, one can at best approximate the content of image collections, given the potential volume of images collected, and the limited forensic resources of most specialist police units, and it has been suggested that the volume, complexity, and inaccessibility of digital evidence have deterred a systematic analysis of the relationship between downloaded material and potential risk.

Internet Sex Offenders

Interest in the content of child pornography images parallels concern that what is downloaded from the Internet is a good indicator of pedophilic interest, and that the content of images may prove to relate to who might also commit contact offenses and how such offenses might find expression. In relation to this, the ongoing concern with how similar, or different, people who access online child pornography (Internet sex offenders) are from contact offenders (those who commit a sex offense against a child in the offline environment) dominates much of the current research. It is apparent that a proportion of people who commit an online offense involving child pornography share similar characteristics to those who offend in the offline environment. In a large United Kingdom sample of psychometric test results from child pornography offenders, clusters were identified which were labeled normal, inadequate, and deviant. The authors felt that their results were similar to the clusters found in contact offender groups. A Canadian meta-analysis of published studies indicated that approximately half of the online offenders admitted to committing a contact sexual offense and 12.2% had an official history of contact sexual offenses.

However, differences between Internet and contact sex offenders do exist and appear to be related to demographic characteristics such as age, level of education, and measures of intelligence as well as psychological variables such as cognitive distortions, emotional dysregulation, empathy, and impression management. A meta-analysis of 27 samples from published studies found that online offenders tended to be Caucasian males, who are younger than the general population and more likely to be unemployed. Both online and offline offenders had an increased incidence of physical and sexual abuse than the general population. In comparison with offline offenders, online offenders had greater victim empathy, greater sexual deviancy, and lower impression management. These authors concluded that youth and unemployment are risk factors for online sexual offending and that this was consistent with typical crime patterns.

Risk

Research on the offense histories of Internet offenders and the likelihood of future offending would suggest that with a longer period post-offense more offenders are detected for new offenses, with recidivism for contact sexual offenses predicted by criminal history, and in particular violent offense history and the age of the offender at the time of their first conviction. Importantly, Canadian researchers also examined failures on conditional release, in particular where offenders put themselves in 'risky' situations, such as being alone with children. The finding that one-quarter of this offender group was charged with failures was consistent with the findings from other sex offender groups. Such failures included breaches of conditions about being alone with children, accessing the Internet, and contacting children and downloading child-abuse materials, as well as other violations which were nonsexual or indicated noncompliance. This is of interest because while 34% of offenders had a charge for any type of further offense, only 4% were charged with any new contact sexual offense and 7% were charged with new child pornography-related offenses. Recidivism has also been found to be low in other recent studies in the United States and Europe.

Studies of risk that have explicitly examined the content of child pornography images have produced what looks like conflicting information, with data suggesting an inverse relationship between the severity of the victimization within the images and the likelihood of recidivism. However, these results appear different to a United Kingdom sample of contact offenders and noncontact offenders, all found in possession of child-abuse images and all of whom were arrested after 2000. Contact offenders were found to have a significantly higher percentage of Level 3 and Level 4 still images than noncontact offenders. Noncontact offenders could be distinguished by the larger number of Level 1 images downloaded. Possession of Level 1 and Level 3 images was the best predictor of noncontact and contact offending, respectively. With contact offenders, the more severe the contact offense, the higher the SAP level of the images possessed. The content of the images, including gender and age of the children, was directly associated with those of the contact offense victims. Contact offenders tended to view content with a smaller victim range and were polymorphic with regard to gender. This is the first evidence of congruence between images sought and collected and the type of offense committed against a child.

These studies raise additional concerns about how images are used to determine the sentence given to the offender, and whether the sentence should be based on principles of harm or on the likelihood of recidivism. It is apparent that, in reality, these might yield very different decisions.

Digital Child Pornography

One further challenge relates to digitally altered or pseudo-images and virtual child pornography. Important issues have been raised about how different an image has to be for it to constitute a pseudo-image, the possession of which is likely to attract a lower sentence. In the United States, the constitutionality of virtual child pornography remains a critical issue. In Ashcroft versus Free Speech Coalition in 2002, a majority of the Supreme Court struck down portions of the Child Pornography Prevention Act of 1996, stating that virtual child pornography created without real or identifiable minors was unconstitutionally overbroad. One of the primary producers of such imagery is Japan where there is a huge market in *manga*, and other forms of animation, that many believe are sexually exploitative. In countries outside of Japan, there has been a bid to criminalize the possession of nonphotographic visual depictions of child sexual abuse. Recent legislation in the United Kingdom has criminalized nonphotographic pornographic images of children; that is, fantasy visual representations of child pornography in the form of, for example, computer-generated images, cartoons, or drawings. Opponents of these measures, such as the American Civil Liberties Union, have argued that people's thoughts are their private thoughts, and that prohibition of pseudo-child pornography is a violation of free speech rights.

User-Generated Content and Sexting

One final consideration is self-generated, or user-generated, child pornography. In a United States nationally representative survey, 4% of teenagers aged 12–17 who own a mobile phone reported that they have sent sexually suggestive nude or nearly nude images of themselves to someone else via text messaging and 15% have received such images. This increases to 8% and 30%, respectively, in those who are 17 years old, with teenagers who pay their own bills more likely to send sexual images. This activity is frequently referred to as 'sexting': the practice of sending or posting sexually suggestive text messages and images, including nude or seminude photographs, via cellular telephones or over the Internet. Typically, the young person takes a picture of himself or herself with a mobile phone camera (or other digital camera), or has someone else take the picture; this is then stored as a digital image and transmitted via mobile phone as a text-message, photo-send function, or electronic mail. Additionally, the subject may use a mobile phone to post the image to a social networking website.

These materials have been referred to as 'self-produced child pornography.' Self-produced child pornography refers to images that possess the following criteria: they meet the legal definition of child pornography and were originally produced by a minor with no coercion, grooming, or adult participation whatsoever. The definition does not focus exclusively on the young person who makes the image but also on those juveniles in the distribution chain who may coerce production, or later possess, distribute, or utilize such images. It highlights that the term sexting has been used variously to describe: one minor sending one picture to a perceived significant other; a minor taking and/or distributing pictures of him/herself and others engaged in sexually explicit conduct; a minor extensively forwarding or disseminating a nude picture of another youth without his/her knowledge; a minor posting such pictures on a website; an older teen asking (or coercing) another youth for such pictures; a person impersonating a classmate to 'dupe' and/or blackmail other minors into sending pictures; and adults sending pictures or videos to minors or possessing sexually explicit pictures of juveniles, as well as adults sending sexually suggestive text or images to other adults. These are all different activities, only some of which would be deemed illegal in many jurisdictions.

There are many recent cases in the United States where young people have been prosecuted for taking photographs of themselves while engaging in lawful sexual activity, and the harms that might follow from a possible child pornography conviction. It has been concluded that one cannot ignore that there are also generational factors at work in the prosecutions of teens for sexting and 'auto-pornography,' and that the prosecutorial and judicial personnel who are acting in these prosecutions are typically two or more generations removed from the teenagers whose sexual expression is condemned and whose future outlooks are drastically affected. The argument is that such efforts might be seen to be generally futile, and that the future and its values belong to those whose lives lie mostly ahead of them. However, there does appear to be a legitimate concern to distinguish between sexting as a serious offense which poses a danger to others, and when it is simply the product of a legitimate sexual relationship.

See also: **Forensic Medicine/Clinical:** Child Abuse.

Further Reading

Akdeniz Y (2008) *Internet Child Pornography and the Law: National and International Responses*. Aldershot: Ashgate.

Babchishin KM, Hanson RK, and Hermann CA (2010) The characteristics of online sex offenders: A meta-analysis of online sex offenders. *Sexual Abuse: A Journal of Research and Treatment* 1–32.

Eke AW, Seto MC, and Williams J (2010) Examining the criminal history and future offending of child pornography offenders: An extended prospective follow-up study. *Law and Human Behavior* 1–13.

Glasgow D (2010) The potential of digital evidence to contribute to risk assessment of internet offenders. *Journal of Sexual Aggression* 16(1): 223–237.

Goode SD (2010) *Understanding and Addressing Sexual Attraction to Children: A Study of Paedophiles in Contemporary Society*. London: Routledge.

Hebenton B, Shaw D, and Pease K (2009) Offences involving indecent photographs and pseudo-photographs of children: An analysis of sentencing guidelines. *Psychology, Crime and Law* 15(5): 425–440.

Humbach JA (2009) 'Sexting' and the First Amendment. *37 Hastings Const. L.Q.* 433–486.

Leary MG (2010) Sexting or self-produced child pornography? The dialog continues – Structured prosecutorial discretion within a multidisciplinary response. *17 Va. J. Soc. Pol'y & L.* 486–566.

Quayle E and Jones T (2011) Sexualized images of children on the Internet. *Sexual Abuse: A Journal of Research and Treatment* 23(1): 7–21.

Quayle E and Ribsil K (eds.) (2012) *Understanding and Preventing Online Sexual Exploitation of Children*. London: Routledge.

Seto M (2010) Child pornography use and Internet solicitation in the diagnosis of pedophilia. *Archives of Sexual Behavior* 39: 591–593.

Stapleton A (2010) Knowing it when you (don't) see it: Mapping the pornographic child in order to diffuse the paedophilic gaze. *Global Media Journal: Australian Edition* 4(2): 1–21.

Taylor M, Holland G, and Quayle E (2001) Typology of paedophile picture collections. *The Police Journal* 74(2): 97–107.

Teens and Sexting. Pew Research Centre. Available online at http://www.pewinternet.org//media//Files/Reports/2009/PIP_Teens_and_Sexting.pdf.

UNODC (2010) *The Globalization of Crime: A Transnational Organized Crime Threat Assessment*. Vienna: United Nations Office on Drugs and Crime. http://www.unodc.org/documents/data-and-analysis/tocta/TOCTA_Report_2010_low_res.pdf.

Wolak J, Finkelhor D, Mitchell K, and Ybarra M (2008) Online 'predators' and their victims: Myths, realities, and implications for prevention and treatment. *American Psychologist* 63(2): 111–128.

Relevant Websites

http://www.ceop.police.uk/ – Child Exploitation and Online Protection Centre.

http://www.ecpat.net/WorldCongressIII/index.php – World Congress against Sexual Exploitation of Children and Adolescents.

http://www.unh.edu/ccrc/internet-crimes/ – Crimes Against Children Research Center, University of New Hampshire.

Cellular Phones

GC Kessler, Embry-Riddle Aeronautical University, Daytona Beach, FL, USA
RP Mislan, RP Mislan, DeTour, MI, USA

Glossary

Code Division Multiple Access (CDMA) A digital cellular phone technology employing spread spectrum, where users are assigned a code and hop between frequencies in a prearranged fashion.
Faraday box (or bag) Named for scientist Richard Faraday, a *Faraday cage* is an enclosed space surrounded by material that blocks electromagnetic signals, such as radio transmissions. A Faraday box or Faraday bag is merely small versions of such an enclosure and, like *flight mode*, ensures that a mobile device is isolated from the mobile carrier network. If *flight mode* is not available on a phone, a Faraday box is another option to secure the phone from receiving incoming network signals.
Flight mode Also known as *airplane mode*, an operational mode of a mobile phone where the radio is turned off, thus allowing the user to access all features of the phone except the ability to place and receive calls. This is ideal for investigations and analysis because the phone is isolated from the network.
Global System for Mobile communications (GSM) A TDMA technology used for cellular telephones. GSM is in growing use in North America and widely used throughout the rest of the world.
Integrated Digital Enhanced Network (iDEN) A Motorola-developed TDMA mobile telecommunications technology. iDEN phones allow normal two-way telephone conversations as well as a walkie–talkie capability.
Short Message Service (SMS) The protocol for cell phone text messages. SMS messages are limited to 1120 bits, or 160 7-bit (ASCII) characters, 140 8-bit (ASCII) characters, or 70 16-bit (Unicode) characters.
Subscriber Identity Module (SIM) A smart card that provides storage and other features for some types of cell phones, such as contact names and SMS messages (sometimes including deleted SMS messages). Always found in GSM and iDEN phones.
Time Division Multiple Access (TDMA) One of the digital cellular phone technologies, where multiple users share one frequency range but each only gets a preassigned fraction of the time. TDMA is the underlying technology used in GSM and iDEN phones.
Wideband Code Division Multiple Access (WCDMA) A newer, third-generation (3G) mobile device technology for voice and data. WCMDA is not compatible with CDMA.

Introduction

Cellular phones – a term that encompasses a wide array of mobile devices that include simple cellular telephones, personal digital assistants (PDAs), and smartphones (which are essentially portable Internet terminals) – represent that fastest growing specialty in the realm of digital forensics. It has often been observed that computers have been the fastest growing instrument, target, and/or record keeper of criminal activity over the last two decades. This observation is even more true for cell phones, devices that are pervasive in society worldwide and are present at nearly every arrest and crime scene. The worldwide rate of adoption of cell phones has occurred at a rate faster even than adoption of the Internet.

In some ways, cell phones provide better opportunities for finding probative evidence than traditional computers. First, cell phones are generally single-user devices, and it is often easier to place a suspect's finger on the phone than on a computer's keyboard. Second, because of their compactness and constant use for communications – everything from phone calls and photographs to text messages and electronic mail (e-mail) – there is more probative information per byte examined on a cell phone than on a typical computer.

This all said, cell phone forensics is different than traditional computer forensics in several fundamental ways. First, in most cases, forensics examiners cannot make a forensic copy (i.e., an image) of the cell phone as they would a computer hard drive. Second, many cell phone forensics tools make analysis of phones appear to be simple and, therefore, many untrained (or undertrained) examiners fail to properly and completely examine phones. Finally, the information on cell phones is fragile and is often lost due to mishandling during seizure, storage, and examination.

There is a process for acquiring and examining cell phone data, but it is very different from the procedures for handling computers. The sections below address some of the high-level issues related to forensically processing mobile phones.

Mobile Phone Network Technology

Cell phones are so called because they utilize radio technology over a small geographic area called a *cell*. Cells are defined by the presence of towers at the edge of the cell; it usually requires the antenna on three towers to cover the area of a cell. The geographic size of a cell is governed by the topology, capacity

 http://dx.doi.org/10.1016/B978-0-12-382165-2.00124-0

of the communication channels, placement of antenna, and network architecture; cells can be as small as a few square kilometers to several hundred square kilometers.

There are three basic technologies used to allow multiple users to share radio frequencies on mobile phone networks:

- *Frequency Division Multiple Access* (*FDMA*): Each call is on a different assigned frequency.
- *Time Division Multiple Access* (*TDMA*): Multiple calls are each assigned a time slot on a shared frequency band.
- *Code Division Multiple Access* (*CDMA*): Calls are assigned a code and hop through the given set of frequencies (spread spectrum).

These technologies are the basis for the primary types of cell phone networks used around the world today.

- The Advanced Mobile Phone Service (AMPS) was an analog network that employed FDMA. This technology, originally introduced in the early 1980s, is no longer deployed. FDMA was the basis of so-called first-generation (1G) cell phone networks.
- CDMA One and CDMA 2000 are the second-generation (2G) and third-generation (3G) networks, respectively, deployed in North America.
- The Global System for Mobile (GSM) communication network is widely used throughout the world but only in the late-2000s introduced in North American networks. GSM 2G uses TDMA technology and GSM 3G uses wideband CDMA (WCDMA); this is also referred to as the Universal Mobile Telecommunications System (UMTS).
- Motorola's Integrated Digital Enhanced Network (iDEN) employs TDMA technology for two-way voice calls, as well as a walkie–talkie mode.

A final classification of cell phone networks and devices is by 'generation' (Table 1):

- First-generation networks employed analog (FDMA) technology.
- Second-generation networks employed digital communication over TDMA and CDMA.
- Third-generation networks utilized technologies to offer enhanced data services, such as support for multimedia and data rate greater than 200 kbps. In most cases, 3G data networks are overlaid over the voice network. 3G standardization and development efforts are being led by the third-Generation Partnership Project (3GPP) group, while North American 3G efforts are being led by the 3GPP2 group.
- Fourth-generation networks will be Internet Protocol (IP)-based, offering Voice over IP (VoIP) services and truly integrating the voice and data infrastructures (much as what has happened to the landline networks). 4G networks will employ long-term evolution (LTE) technology, merging the efforts of the 3GPP and 3GPP2 bodies.

Although there is a merging of the technologies used by mobile phones, it should be noted that the radio frequencies used by various countries varies widely. The 800 and 1900 MHz bands are widely used in North America and some other countries, while 900, 1800, and 2100 MHz are used in most of the rest of the world.

The text message and multimedia capabilities of mobile devices are also related to the phone's technology. The original text message protocol was the short message service (SMS). SMS supports short messages of up to 1120 bits in length, which can comprise 160 seven-bit characters, 140 eight-bit characters, or 70 16-bit Unicode characters. The enhanced message service (EMS) was an extension to SMS that allowed for the exchange of ringtones and simple graphics. EMS supported limited size attachments but required no infrastructure change to the cell phone network. SMS and EMS messages are sent over the cell phone network's out-of-band signaling network.

The Multimedia Message Service (MMS) is the current protocol for sending true audio, image, and video attachments to 'text' messages. MMS was designed for GSM and CDMA networks.

Table 1 Evolution of network technologies

Generation	*3GPP family*	*3GPP2 family*	*Other*
1G			AMPS
2G	GSM	CDMA One	iDEN
2G transition	GPRS, EDGE	CDMA 2000 1xRTT	WiDEN
3G	WCDMA/ UMTS	CDMA 2000 1xEV-DO	
3G transition	HSDPA, HSPA, LTE	CDMA 2000 1xEV-DO	Mobile WiMAX (IEEE 802.16e)
4G	LTE advanced	LTE advanced	IEEE 802.16m

EDGE: Enhanced data for global evolution.
IEEE: Institute of electrical and electronics engineers.
EV-DO: Evolution – data optimized.
RTT: Radio transmission technology.
GPRS: General packet radio service.
WiDEN: Wideband iDEN.
HSDPA: High-speed downlink packet access.
WiMAX: Worldwide interoperability for microwave access.
HSPA: High-speed packet access.

Mobile Phone Hardware Components

There are three possible hardware components in a mobile phone that can contain probative data. Each component has its own method of identification, type of data content, and methods for processing. This section discusses those three components; namely the handset, subscriber identity module (SIM), and memory expansion card.

The Phone Handset

The mobile phone handset is what most people think of as *cell phone*. The handset is the physical housing that contains the radio transceiver, memory chip for the operating system and data, screen, camera (if present), a SIM card (if present), memory expansion card (if present), battery, and other hardware components. Handsets generally have a label under the battery that will list the manufacturer, handset model number, serial number, and other identifying numbers.

CDMA handsets are identified by an electronic serial number (ESN) or mobile equipment identifier (MEID). An ESN is a 32-bit number that is provided in decimal and/or hexadecimal format. (Because of the way in which the ESN and MEID are interpreted, the hexadecimal value is not a direct representation of the decimal value.) Because of the way in which the ESN and MEID are interpreted, the hexadecimal value is not a direct representation of the decimal value. Because of the exhaustion of the 32-bit ESN number space, most new CDMA handsets have an MEID, which is a 56-bit value. The ESN and MEID values contain a field that identifies the handset manufacturer.

GSM and iDEN handsets are identified by an international mobile equipment identifier (IMEI). The IMEI is a unique 15-digit value that is specific to the handset.

Phone numbers assigned to CDMA phones are called the mobile identification number (MIN) and mobile directory number (MDN). The MIN is a carrier-specific ten-digit number. The MIN is the carrier's internal reference to the handset. The MDN is the actual globally unique telephone number of the device that would be used to call this phone. The MIN and MDN are generally the same when a user first acquires a phone. Wireless number portability rules, however, allow a subscriber to change carriers yet keep their old telephone number; in that case, the MDN would stay the same but the MIN would change upon changing carriers.

Phone numbers are not assigned to GSM and iDEN phones, but are contained in the SIM card.

Subscriber Identity Module

A SIM card is a form of read-only memory with a usual capacity of 16–128 kb. A SIM card will contain a phone number and can also store contact lists, call history, last number dialled, location information, and SMS messages (including deleted SMS messages). GSM and iDEN phones have SIM cards, although they are not interchangeable. A Universal SIM (USIM) card is a SIM card for 3G phones, allowing for multiple phone numbers to be assigned to a single card. A Removable User Identity Module (R-UIM) provides GSM SIM capabilities to CDMA handsets; an extension of the GSM SIM standard, R-UIMs generally contain the same kind of user information as a GSM SIM.

A SIM card usually has an integrated circuit card identification (ICCID) printed on it, along with the logo of the network service provider. The ICCID is a 19–20-digit number that includes a country code, network code, and SIM serial number.

GSM and iDEN SIM cards contain two numeric identifiers. The first is the international mobile subscriber identity (IMSI), a 15-digit code that identifies the country, network, and SIM card. The second number is the mobile station international subscriber directory number (MSISDN), a 15-digit globally unique telephone number. SIMs in iDEN phones also contain a direct connect number (DCN) to facilitate the walkie–talkie mode.

SIM cards – and their handsets – can be protected using a personal identification number (PIN). A PIN1 code, if defined by the user, protects access to the SIM card and the handset. After some number of incorrect PIN entries – usually between 3 and 10 – will lock the SIM card. A PIN2 code, if defined, is used to protect a small number of network settings on the card and do not affect handset features protected by the PIN1 code.

A PIN-locked SIM can be unlocked a personal unlocking key (PUK), which can be obtained by the service provider issuing the SIM. The PUK1 code is used to bypass a PIN1-locked SIM; after ten incorrect entries of the PUK1 code, the SIM will be permanently locked. The PUK2 code is required to unlock a PIN2-locked SIM.

It is worth noting that some newer phones have slots for two or more SIM cards. This allows a single phone to have multiple personalities without requiring the user to swap out SIM cards. These phones are more common today in Asia than in North America or Europe.

Memory Expansion Cards

The most common form of memory expansion card in mobile phones is that of a microSD card, usually with a capacity of up to 16 GB. These cards generally formatted to use the FAT16 file system. From a digital forensics perspective, then, these can usually be processed as if they were a hard drive, using traditional computer forensics imaging and analysis methods.

In older phones, the memory expansion card usually just stores media files, such as images and video files. Newer smartphones actually use the memory expansion cards as an extension of the handset's internal memory. To that end, the memory card may contain system and user files.

Mobile Phone Software

The cell phone's radio technology will drive several aspects of the examination of a mobile device; some of these aspects are described below when seizure and identification is discussed. The other major factor in the data acquisition and analysis of cell phones, however, is the operating system of the phone. While computers today generally use one of three operating systems (Linux/Unix or a variant, MacOS, or a version of Windows), there are no fewer than six major operating systems (OS) found on cell phones:

- *Android*: Although a major initiative of Google, development is under the control of the open handset alliance (OHA), which includes Google, HTC, Intel, LG, Motorola, Qualcomm, Samsung, and many more hardware and software developers. Android is built around a lightweight Linux kernel and an open app marketplace.
- *Blackberry OS*: Developed by research in motion (RIM), the Blackberry runs a proprietary OS. Version releases of the OS are carrier specific.
- *iPhone OS* (*iOS*): Developed and distributed solely by Apple Corp., iOS is evolving into the universal operating system for Apple's mobile devices, including the iPad and iPod Touch. iOS is a Unix-like system. Apple manages and closely monitors the app store.
- *PalmOS/WebOS*: The PalmOS was developed by Palm Computing, renamed WebOS when Palm was acquired by HP, and then discontinued in 2011. PalmOS was a leader in

PDA devices and software. WebOS, in particular, is based around a Linux kernel.

- *Symbian*: Nokia's operating system was inspired by OpenVMS, which itself derived from Digital Equipment Corporation's virtual memory system (VMS) OS. Nokia accounts for ~40% of smartphones worldwide, although the OS is not widely seen in North America.
- *Windows CE*: Microsoft's mobile OS, which is also found on the PocketPC, Windows Mobile, and Smartphone products. Although similar to Windows, Windows CE is optimized for devices with a small amount of storage.

The operating system will directly affect how the examiner can access the handset; for example, the examiner can gain direct terminal access to the Linux-based operating systems above. The OS will also affect the capabilities of the device as well as what data elements are available for download. Consider that even low-end cell phones might include any or all of the following types of data: contact list, call history, text messages, multimedia (images, audio, and video) files, ringtones, calendar entries, and alarm information. Smartphones, of course, will generally contain all of that, plus global positioning system (GPS) data, e-mail, Web browser history, cache, and cookie files, music files, documents, and a variety of applications and their log files.

The Mobile Phone Forensics Hierarchy

Standard computer tools operate essentially the same on all hard drives in order to create forensics images and allow analysis of the contents. Such is not the case with cell phones. In fact, the tools for cell phone forensics will be largely dependent upon the technology of the handset and the phone's operating system.

Sam Brothers first described a hierarchy of cell phone forensic analysis. The higher up in the hierarchy that the examination takes places will yield the greatest amount of information; those steps are also the most technically challenging and time consuming:

1. *Manual extraction*: This is the easiest – and least complete – method of acquiring data from a phone. A manual extraction merely refers to accessing data on the phone via the device's interface and preserving any such information by taking notes and/or photographs of the screen. This method is prone to error, by either missing certain data due to unfamiliarity with the interface and/or inadvertently modifying handset data.
2. *Logical analysis*: This method involves a physical connection to the phone via a data cable and access to the contents of the phone that the processor allows. In many cases, data that is known to be on the phone (e.g., SMS messages) may be inaccessible to the analysis software. In addition, deleted data is almost never accessible. Some level of logical analysis can be employed on nearly all phones on the market today and nearly all computer forensics tools can perform a logical extraction on some number of phones.
3. *Hex dump*: A hex dump of memory can be achieved by using a data cable to the handset and sending commands to the phone's processor in order to download the contents of memory. This method allows the examiner to access contents of memory that would not be accessible via the phone's handset and also allows access to deleted data (as do the methods above, as well). Information is downloaded in a raw format and has to be parsed, decoded, and interpreted. This is the most superficial level of physical analysis; a number of tools are currently able to physically acquire a large range of cell phones – particularly smartphones.
4. *Memory read*: This method requires removing the memory chip from the handset and extracting all the contents by a direct connection. This method requires specialized equipment in order to make the physical connection to the memory chip. As above, the information comes out of memory in a raw format and has to be parsed, decoded, and interpreted.
5. *Micro read*: A micro read provides access to the handset's memory chip so that it can be read it with an electron microscope. With this method, the examiner can view the actual state of memory, thus being able to extract and verify all the data from the handset's memory. This method obviously requires highly specialized equipment in a specialized laboratory and would generally be reserved for very high-value items. As above, information comes out of memory in a raw format and has to be parsed, decoded, and interpreted.

Seizing and Handling Cell Phones

When a cell phone is physically obtained as part of a criminal or civil investigation, it should be treated just as any other item so as to maintain evidentiary integrity. The circumstances surrounding the seizure should be described, such as the specific location where the device was found and the physical condition of the device. A chain-of-custody form should be completed to document the transfer and photographs of the device taken. Any manipulation or use of the device after being seized should be documented. If possible, also seize any manuals, chargers, or cables associated with the device.

There are other actions that should be taken with cell phones that can help to preserve the information on the phone. It is of utmost importance that the phone be isolated from the network as soon as possible. There are any number of services and applications that can be employed to remotely wipe a cell phone under a variety of circumstances. To avoid this eventuality, the phone should be placed into *airplane mode* (which shuts telephone and 3G/4G data services) and all other network communications, such as IEEE 802.11 WiFi, Bluetooth, and infrared, turned off.

If the phone is protected with a password and/or PIN, it is a good idea to ask the owner for this information. If that information is provided, attempt to use it to access the phone; if successful, it is also a good idea to actually disable those protections. It is important to be careful with multiple attempts or guesses at a password as for many phones, especially the smartphones, there are limits to incorrect attempts or guess. Failure to get the right code results in permanent locking or deletion of all data. Under no circumstances should the device be returned to the owner once it has been seized.

Table 2 Mobile phone forensics tools

General device tools	*Specific OS tools*
BitPim	Elcomsoft Blackberry Backup Explorer
Cellebrite UFED and Physical Analyzer	Lantern for iOS
FinalMobile	WinMoFo (Windows Mobile)
MicroSystemation XRY and XACT	viaExtract (Android)
Oxygen Software Forensic Suite	
Paraben Device Seizure	
Radio Tactics Aceso	
Susteen SecureView	

In most instances, the best way to transport the phone is to power it down, keeping in mind that powering it back on may result in a handset or SIM lock code. At this point, the phone label (usually found under the battery) should be photographed and all identifying information (e.g., make, model, serial number, and ESN/MEID/IMEI) documented in the case notes.

Mobile Phone Forensic Tools

There are a variety of tools currently available that a mobile phone forensic examiner can employ. At a high level, they can be sorted into two categories, namely, those tools that cover numerous phones and other personal digital devices (such as PDAs, GPS systems, or even satellite phones), and those tools that cover a specific operating system. Table 2 lists some of the more popular tools for each category.

All the tools have their strengths and weaknesses, and it is a fundamental truth that no one tool is sufficient for all purposes. Indeed, many tools 'support' a given device but will only be able to acquire a subset of the available data from the device; it is often the case where multiple tools will have to be used in order to reliably acquire a phone. In addition, there are a variety of specialty programs that can process raw data after it is downloaded from a phone, such as software to carve images or SMS messages from raw memory dumps or editors to read the database files that many phones use to store information.

Further Reading

Ayers R, Jansen W, Cilleros N and Danielou R (2005) *Cell Phone Forensic Tools: An Overview and Analysis*. Gaithersburg, MD: National Institute of Standards and Technology (NIST) Interagency Report (IR) 7250. Retrieved from http://csrc.nist.gov/publications/nistir/nistir-7250.pdf.

Brothers S (2008) How cell phone "forensic" tools actually work (proposed leveling). In: Mislan R (ed.) *Proceedings of Mobile Forensics World*. Chicago, IL: Purdue University.

Daniels K and Wagner W (2009) *Creating a Cell Phone Investigation Toolkit: Basic Hardware and Software Specifications*. Sacramento, CA: SEARCH. Retrieved from http://www.search.org/files/pdf/celldevicetoolkit101309.pdf.

Hoog A (2011) *Android Forensics: Investigation, Analysis and Mobile Security for Google Android*. Waltham, MA: Syngress.

Hoog A and Strzempka K (2011) *iPhone and iOS Forensics: Investigation, Analysis and Mobile Security for Apple iPhone, iPad and iOS Devices*. Waltham, MA: Syngress.

Jansen W and Ayers R (2007) *Guidelines on Cell Phone Forensics*. Gaithersburg, MD: National Institute of Standards and Technology (NIST) Special Publication (SP) 800-101. Retrieved from http://csrc.nist.gov/publications/nistpubs/800-101/SP800-101.pdf.

Jansen W, Delaitre A and Moenner L (2008) Overcoming Impediments to Cell Phone Forensics. *Proceedings from the Hawaii International Conference on System Sciences (HICSS)*. Waikoloa, HI: IEEE Computer Society. Retrieved from http://csrc.nist.gov/groups/SNS/mobile_security/documents/mobile_forensics/Impediments-formatted-final-post.pdf.

Mellars B (2004) Forensics examination of mobile phones. *Digital Investigation* 1(4): 266–272.

Mislan RP, Casey E, and Kessler GC (2010) The growing need for on-scene triage of mobile devices. *Digital Investigation* 6(3–4): 112–124.

Relevant Websites

http://www.garykessler.net - GCK's Cybercrime and Cyberforensics-related URLs: Mobile Device Forensics.

http://csrc.nist.gov/groups/SNS/mobile_security/ – National Institute of Standards and Technology (NIST), Computer Security Division, Computer Security Resource Center, Mobile Security and Forensics.

http://www.ssddfj.org – Small Scale Digital Device Forensics Journal.

http://www.e-evidence.info/cellular.html – The Electronic Evidence Information Center: Cellular/Mobile Phone Forensic TRools.

http://www.e-evidence.info/cellarticles.html – The Electronic Evidence Information Center: Cellular/Mobile Phone Forensics.

Digital Imaging: Enhancement and Authentication

C Grigoras and JM Smith, University of Colorado Denver, Denver, CO, USA

This article is a revision of the previous edition article by G. Oxlee, volume 3, pp. 1264–1271, © 2000, Elsevier Ltd.

Glossary

Artifact A visual/aural aberration in an image, video, or audio recording resulting from a technical or operational limitation. For example, speckles in a scanned picture, 'blocking' in JPEG compressed images, unnatural 'birdy' noises as a result of MP3 audio compression.

Aspect ratio The width to height ratio of an image.

Authentication The process of substantiating that the data is an accurate representation of what it purports to be.

Cognitive image analysis The process used to extract visual information from an image.

Deblurring A type of image restoration used to reverse image degradation, such as motion blur or out of focus blur. It is accomplished by applying algorithms based on knowledge or an estimate of the cause of the original degradation.

Deinterlacing Separating an interlaced frame into two discrete fields.

Demonstrative comparison A method of presenting the similarities and/or differences among images and/or objects without rendering an opinion regarding identification or exclusion.

Digital image An image that is represented by discrete numerical values organized in a two-dimensional array. When viewed on a monitor or paper, it appears like a photograph.

Field An element of a video signal containing alternate horizontal lines. For interlaced video, the scanning pattern is divided into two sets of spaced lines (odd and even) that are displayed sequentially. Each set of lines is called a field, and the interlaced set of the two sets of lines is a frame.

Frame Lines of spatial information of a video signal. For interlaced video, a frame consists of two fields, one of odd lines and one of even lines, displayed in sequence. For progressive scan (noninterlaced) video, the frame is written through successive lines that start at the top left of the picture and finish at the bottom right.

Image An imitation or representation of a person or thing, drawn, painted, photographed, etc.

Image analysis A subdiscipline of Digital & Multimedia Evidence, which involves the application of image science and domain expertise to examine and interpret the content of an image and/or the image itself in legal matters.

Image averaging The process of averaging similar images, such as sequential video frames, to reduce noise in stationary scenes.

Image comparison (photographic comparison) The process of comparing images of questioned objects or persons to known objects or persons or images thereof, and making an assessment of the correspondence between features in these images for rendering an opinion regarding identification or elimination.

Image content analysis The drawing of conclusions about an image. Targets for content analysis include, but are not limited to, the subjects/objects within an image; the conditions under which, or the process by which, the image was captured or created; the physical aspects of the scene (e.g., lighting or composition); and/or the provenance of the image.

Image enhancement Any process intended to improve the visual appearance of an image or specific features within an image.

Image output The means by which an image is presented for examination or observation.

Image processing Any activity that transforms an input image into an output image.

Multiplexer/demultiplexer A device used to combine multiple video signals into a single signal or separate a combined signal. These devices are frequently used in security and law enforcement applications for recording and/or displaying multiple camera images simultaneously or in succession.

Noise Variations or disturbances in brightness or color information in an image that do not arise from the scene. Sources of noise include film grain, electronic variations in the input device sensor and circuitry, and stray electromagnetic fields in the signal pathway. It frequently refers to visible artifacts in an image.

Quantitative image analysis The process used to extract measurable data from an image.

Sharpening A process used to emphasize edge detail in an image by enhancing the high-frequency components.

Video The electronic representation of a sequence of images, depicting either stationary or moving scenes. It may include audio.

Video analysis A subdiscipline of Digital & Multimedia Evidence, which involves the scientific examination, comparison, and/or evaluation of video in legal matters.

Video enhancement Any process intended to improve the visual appearance of video sequences or specific features within video sequences.

Video stabilization The process of positioning individual frames so that a selected object or person will remain in the same location as the video is played.

Abbreviations

BMP	Bitmap or Bitmap Image File, a raster graphic image format
CFA	Color filter array, a mosaic of tiny color filters (e.g., red, green, blue) placed over the camera sensor to filter and capture color information
CLA	Compression level analysis, a numerical method to assess the lossy compression effects of a finite sequence
DCT	Discrete Cosine Transform, a numerical algorithm to decompose a finite sequence in a sum of cosine functions
DFT	Discrete Fourier Transform, a numerical algorithm to decompose a sequence of values into different frequency components
DLFC	Digital light field camera, a camera that captures the color, intensity, and direction of all the light in one exposure
ELA	Error level analysis, a numerical algorithm to assess traces of editing on JPEG files
FFT	Fast Fourier Transform, a mathematical algorithm to compute the Discrete Fourier Transform
JPEG, JPG	Joint photographic experts group, a common lossy compression algorithm for images
MAC	Modified, Accessed, Creation time stamps of a digital file
RAW	A minimally processed data from an image sensor
TIFF, TIF	Tagged image file format, a file format to store images

Introduction

Digital images (considered to be both still photographs and video) play a key role in civil and criminal cases, law enforcement investigations, and extrajudicial inquiries. Its application areas include closed-circuit television systems, surveillance operations, media, Internet, crime scene investigations, etc. Digital technology is everywhere and it can both enable criminal activity as well as be the media that captures and stores events related to a crime. When seized, analyzed, and interpreted according to best practices, this kind of digital evidence can be extremely useful for criminal investigation. Additionally, digital images created by law enforcement during a crime scene investigation or during laboratory analyses represent digital evidence as well and must be handled properly to maintain integrity.

Digital images open new frontiers for modern types of analysis and enhancement that were not available for classic photography. Still, the proper choice of a filter for instance for a specific type of noise or the chain of processes for video enhancement can be crucial to obtain optimal results to help solve a case.

Digital images also raise new challenges for forensic scientists who are asked to authenticate this kind of evidence because counterfeiting tools are freely available and easy to use.

Digital Imagery: Legal Constraints

With digital and multimedia evidence, the collection, preservation, analysis, and any other kind of evidence handling is crucial for a forensic investigation. According to the forensic science principle concerning evidence recovery, nothing should be modified during the recovery process, and digital media and evidence shall not be contaminated at all, by any digital, chemical, mechanical, or any other mean. In special cases, where there is no possibility to seize digital evidence without modifying the original data, the appropriate experts should be called in who have the training and proficiency to introduce the least possible contamination of evidence, document their activities and assume the responsibility. It is also recommended that forensic experts inform the investigators or representatives of the Court about the risks of and necessity to irreversibly modify digital evidence, clearly state the scientific limitations and the reason that there is no other nondestructive solution, assume responsibility for them, and request written permission.

For instance when labeling digital cameras or digital media, special attention shall be taken to not destroy fingerprints, DNA, or any other traces. A wire with a label indicating the evidence ID may be preferred to write or stick an ID on a camera's body, while a paper bag can be used for media cards to avoid contaminating trace evidence. For mobile phones containing digital image evidence, a special shield bag or case should be used to isolate the equipment against any network or electromagnetic source that can contaminate the evidence.

Just like other forms of digital evidence, photos and videos shall be duplicated through bit-stream image from the media unto which they were created to a working medium using write-blockers and forensic software. Analysis should be carried out on working copies while safe back-ups are kept for archival. Appropriate safety measures should also be taken when transporting and preserving digital evidence to the laboratory or archive to avoid their contamination or degradation.

Furthermore, analysis of digital images in the lab should be based on scientific methods to ensure: accuracy, repeatability by the same scientist, and reproducibility by other scientists of the entire set of functions applied on the digital image working copy.

Digital Image Enhancement

Digital imaging technology is commonly embedded in equipment for applications like video surveillance systems, high definition TV, mobile communications, Internet, social networks, commercial digital cameras, crime scene investigations, etc.

Digital image enhancement is needed in different forensic sciences, and its goal is to filter out the unwanted noises and fix the distortions or other unwanted phenomena by introducing the fewest possible artifacts on the analysis image.

Following the digital evidence collection and seizure of the original evidence, any subsequent enhancement functions shall be documented and their results should be compared with the working copy of evidence. In order to respect the requirement for repeatability and reproducibility, enhancements are commonly performed using software that can generate audit trials. Alternatively, print screens of function menus and their settings can also be an option.

Digital Image Authentication

In forensic imagery, the primary image consists of the data first recorded onto digital media from which the digital signal or file can be transferred in the native format or exported to another one. The digitally recorded information is stored as a finite set of binary values and exact duplicates or clones can be further made. Each stage of copying is exact, there is no loss of information between generations of digital copies or multiplications and it becomes impossible to assess which is a first generation or original, and the implications are that any digital image copy or clone can be thought of as being 'the original' even if it is produced from a copied set of data, unless it is tagged in some way to identify it as the first-generation made.

Special attention should be paid to the distinction between an original file containing a digital image, and the visual image represented therein. If an original image is not bit-to-bit transferred but rather copied/pasted from the original media it will leave the original Modified/Accessed/Created (MAC) time stamp irreversibly modified. In this case, we deal with a nonauthentic file that is in fact a copy of the original digital image file, containing exactly the same visual image like the original. In another scenario, the copy of the original image can be opened with an image editor, tampered with or edited using commonly known techniques in order to create an illusion or deception, and saved back on the same or different format. Ideally the forensic image analysis shall detect all the editing traces, and their interpretation shall allow the expert to assess the tampering processes applied on the image. In real cases, it is known that some tampering techniques are difficult or even impossible to be detected and their quality depends on the operator's skills. Even so, an ideal or 'perfectly counterfeited image' is also known to be difficult or even impossible taking into consideration the time and skills needed to do it.

When the forensic analysis reveals no traces of image manipulation, prudence is recommended in drawing conclusions with a general finding being stated as such: 'the evidence is consistent with an authentic image'.

Other reported techniques for establishing digital image integrity consist of watermarking, encryption, and proprietary methods (proposed by different producers of digital cameras) to check the digital image authenticity. Each of them can be useful unless a reversible solution or access to encryption key is reported by third parties and the authentic procedure is compromised.

Digital Image Enhancement Techniques

As presented previously, digital image enhancement is necessary to reveal data that would be imperceptible or distorted to the human eye. The results of any enhancement are dependent on the quality and quantity of the original imagery, and the types of noise and distortions. These limitations will further dictate the optimum type of enhancement tools used. A typical digital enhancement system has facilities such as enlarge, crop, brightness/contrast-adjustment, histogram equalization, fix out of focus or motion blur, average frames, deinterlace, etc. It is also possible to combine different systems or plug-ins to reach optimal results. It is not possible to cover all filters in this article; a representative collection is discussed below.

Enlargement

The most common enlargement filters are based on pixel expansion, near or natural neighbor, bilinear interpolation, and cubic convolution with the last two being most common in forensic applications.

The bilinear interpolation algorithm is based on a weighted average of neighboring pixels surrounding the pixel location of interest. With this system of enlargement, it may be possible to completely eliminate pixelation artifacts.

Cubic convolution is a more complex interpolation algorithm. It is also based on a special averaging of the pixels surrounding the pixel location of interest. With cubic convolution, pixel breakthrough is eliminated and the system maintains the integrity of the object with respect to its background, irrespective of the degree of enlargement. The limitations are, therefore, the same as those of lens-based optical enlargement systems, that is, the degree of enlargement is limited only by the resolution of the picture (Figure 1).

Figure 1 Original image (left), bilinear interpolation (center), and cubic convolution (right).

Sharpening

Sharpening may be required because the process of capturing digital images often produces stills lacking definition due to the optics, sensor, or settings. Sharpening high-frequency detail can enhance the edges in a digital image, while the image focus and clarity can be adjusted by increasing the contrast between adjacent pixels.

Edge detection filters produce sharp edge definition and can be used to enhance edges with both positive and negative brightness slopes. All algorithms used for edge detection work on a weighting system for the value of the pixels surrounding the pixel of interest. In a 3×3 filter, the system diagnoses the eight pixels around the main pixel. The system applies a weighting to maintain a balance where the sum of all the weights equals zero.

Edge sharpening uses a subtractive smoothing methodology by applying an average spatial filter that retains the frequency data but reduces high-frequency edges and lines. The averaged image is subtracted from the original image to leave the edges and linear features intact. Once the edges are identified in this way, the difference image is added to the original. This method provides clearer edges and linear features but has the disadvantage that any system noise is also enhanced. Examples of detail and edge enhancement are presented in **Figure 2**.

Brightness and Contrast Adjustments

Because images may be captured with nonideal settings or in nonideal conditions, it may be necessary to adjust their brightness or contrast. These are the most commonly applied enhancement tools and will help to enhance differences between image details by bringing them into the accommodation range of the human eye. A full grayscale 8 bit monochromatic image will have up to 256 grayscale steps. However, the human eye can only 'see' up to 26 of these. Furthermore, an observer's visual perception is improved when color is introduced (e.g., red, green, and blue layers). By subjectively shaping these ranges, one can make details more clearly to the human eye.

Histogram Equalization

Histogram operations modify the brightness response curve of an image and alter the distribution of contrast within the spectrum of dark to bright pixels. One of the most important operations is histogram equalization, which modifies the response curve nonlinearly by distributing the total pixel dynamic range in a balanced and uniform manner. This emphasizes contrast in bright areas where it is increased the most. Also, histogram operations allow the operator to change the material from a positive image to a negative image. In complex and difficult images, the eye can sometimes appreciate contrast better in the negative domain and vice versa (**Figure 3**).

Blur

Out of focus blur makes the image unclear, less distinct, and it is a common phenomenon in photography. The digital image is blurred the same amount in all directions and mathematical deconvolution can be applied to recover a part of the lost details. **Figure 4** shows an example using deblur.

Motion blur is another common problem in photography where the image is blurred in one direction only due to motion in either the subject or the camera. It is important to correctly differentiate this from out-of-focus blur. Usually, the length of blur in pixels is provided to the motion deblur algorithm

Figure 2 Original image (left), detail enhance (center), and edge enhance (right).

Figure 3 Original image (left), brightness/contrast adjustment (center), and histogram equalization (right).

where the more accurately the color of each pixel is defined, the better the results (Figure 5).

Color Deconvolution

Color deconvolution allows the separation of different features from an interfering background or foreground, or the extraction of a specific color within an image. This is also known as a type of color separation in various forensic science disciplines including digital images, questioned documents, and fingerprint examination. The color deconvolution algorithm uses subtle color differences that are invisible to the naked eye in a nondestructive way. There are advantages of this method against other physical/chemical methods such as thin-layer chromatography, high-performance liquid chromatography, and capillary electrophoresis. These include nondestructive, higher speed, direct visual contact with the digital image, higher resolution even then IR/UV visual spectral comparators and less color artifacts after processing. Figure 6 shows the color separation of a questioned document, whereas Figure 7 shows a fingerprint separation.

Noise Reduction

Noise is unwanted data in a digital image. Two of the most common noises are 'salt-and-pepper' and periodic noise. Salt-and-pepper can be defined as a distribution of black and white pixels over the digital image as seen in Figure 8. Periodic noise can be described as a distribution of unwanted equidistant forms, usually lines or segments, over the entire image as seen in Figure 9. It is recommended to apply the noise reduction filters at the beginning of the enhancement stage because many other enhancement techniques enhance the noise as well as the required signal. It should be noticed that most enhancement filters also affect the desired image information so caution shall be taken to remove as much noise and introduce the fewest artifacts on the desired image information.

Figure 4 Original out-of-focus blurred image (left) and deblurred image (right).

Deinterlacing

Deinterlacing is a procedure applied to analog and digital video to remove artifacts due to the interlacing of fields within a frame. Analog video (which is captured on a VHS system) is composed of a series of frames with each frame being made up of two interlaced fields. It is important to know that these fields represent two distinct images. This phenomenon is a result of the helical scan technology employed in VHS systems. If still images from this system without deinterlacing are reproduced, quickly moving objects will have jagged or stepped edges as a result of the composite image being from two fields representing two distinct moments in time.

Multiplexed video, which is commonly acquired in forensic investigations, exploits interlaced VHS technology by recording separate video channels to each field. The most common VHS recording solution in security CCTV systems has four or more video channels multiplexed to one VHS tape periodically interlacing images from the cameras to adjacent fields. Upon playback in a standard VHS player, a convoluted series of unrelated images will greet the examiner.

Therefore, when working with this medium, it is necessary to separate the fields through a deinterlacing process in order to reconstitute separate video channels from one recorded tape or to remove motion artifacts. Once digitized and deinterlaced, it is necessary to interpolate the missing fields in order to maintain the native resolution and proper aspect ratio. Alternatively, if working with nonmultiplexed video, a process called video field alignment can be applied where it is possible

Figure 5 Original motion blurred image (left) and motion deblurred image (right).

Figure 6 Scanned region of interest (left), the handwriting ink separation (second to the left), the stamp ink separation (second to the right), and the form ink separation (right).

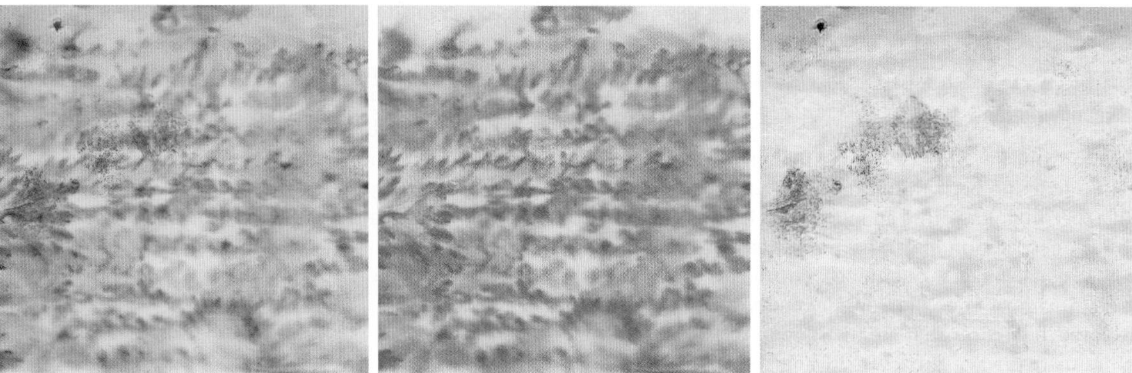

Figure 7 Scanned evidence (left), ink separation (center), and fingerprint separation (right).

Figure 8 Salt-and-pepper noisy image (left), filtered image (center), and the removed noise (right).

Figure 9 Periodic noisy image (left), filtered image (center), and the subtracted periodic noise (right).

to shift an odd field's position relative to the even (or vice versa) rather than removing a field in order to reduce the interlacing artifacts for objects in motion. This approach may be preferred in some circumstances as it maintains a higher resolution than deinterlaced images with subsequent interpolation. In Figure 10, see an example of deinterlacing applied to a still from multiplexed video.

Because modern digital technology has fewer limits especially with regard to the equipment necessary to capture it, interlaced digital video is not common but the procedure remains the same.

Frame Averaging

Frame averaging can be considered a special type of noise reduction for digital video. Not only does each frame of a video contain scene content relevant to the action being filmed but also dynamic noise that is captured by the imaging sensor with a random distribution across the entire image and between exposures. By averaging a series of frames to produce one still image, the intended details of stationary objects are enhanced while the overall noise is reduced (**Figure 11**).

Super Resolution

Super-resolution techniques produce one or a set of higher-resolution images from a sequence of lower-resolution frames. There are single-frame and multiple-frames algorithms used to improve the image fusing information from low-resolution stills producing images that contain clearer details of the scene (see Figure 12).

Image Stabilization

Image stabilization is a set of techniques applied to reduce the motion effects on depicted stills. It can be incorporated within a digital camera capturing a single image or video, or applied

Figure 10 Original image (left), deinterlaced image – odd fields (right).

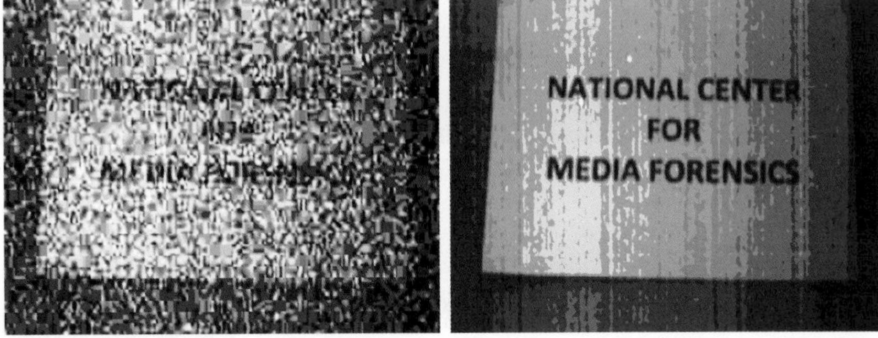

Figure 11 One original frame (left) and averaged frames (right).

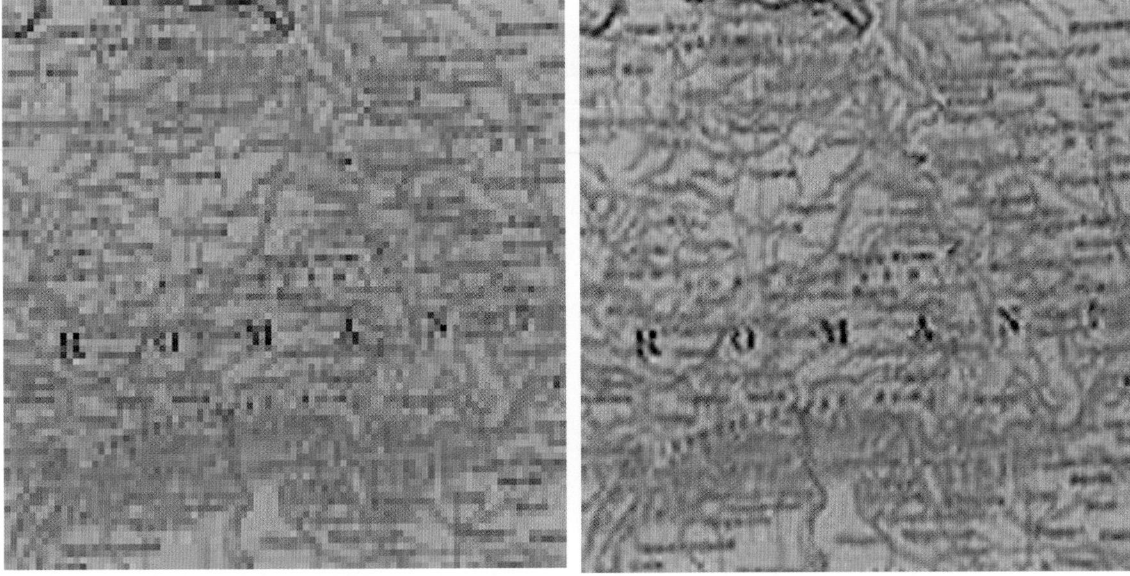

Figure 12 One original frame (left) and super resolution processed frame (right).

to video during postprocessing using specific software (see Figure 13 for frames from a stabilized video).

Lens Distortion Correction

The most common distortions for rectilinear lenses are pincushion distortion and barrel distortion. In pincushion distortion, the edges curve away from the center. For barrel distortion the edges of the image curve toward the center. Both types of distortions can be corrected by image processing, as it is exemplified in Figure 14.

Perspective Correction

Perspective correction allows user to transform an oblique image into a perspective different from that which was

Figure 13 Original shaking frames (upper row) and stabilized frames (lower row).

Figure 14 Original image with barrel distortions (left), barrel corrected image (center), and perspective corrected image (right).

originally captured. This procedure maintains the object's original scale whereby dimensions can be geometrically derived. This is usually applied to flat field surfaces and traces (see Figure 14 for a perspective correction example).

3D Modeling

In some situations, it may be useful to model an environment for courtroom demonstration usually to reconstruct a crime scene. This approach can be costly in terms of time and money and may require building plans or specific equipment that uses lasers for precise measurements. Special software will be required and operated by adequately trained personnel to model the space and animate the crime scene.

Holograms

Holograms are images created by a technique that record and reconstruct the light scattered by an object. The resulting holographic images appear in three dimensions while the position and orientation of the viewing system change in the same manner as if the objects were still in the same place. With advances in the technological development and a decrease in price for the end-user, holograms are suitable for more realistic crime scene reconstructions than 3D modeling.

Digital Light Field Cameras

Digital light field cameras (DLFCs) represent a solution to the long-standing problems related to focusing images accurately and compensating for out-of-focus objects during post-processing. While conventional analog and digital cameras do not record the amount of light traveling along individual rays that contribute to the image, DLFCs sample the total geometric distribution of light passing through the lens in a single exposure. The resulting information can be image processed to refocus on the intended details. As DLFCs capture the color, intensity, and direction of all the light, investigators can much more quickly depict the details of a crime scene, with much more information in one exposure than conventional analog or digital cameras.

Digital Image Authentication Techniques

Owing to the widespread availability of image processing software, it has become easier to produce visually convincing image forgeries. To overcome this issue, there has been considerable work in the digital image analysis field to determine forgeries when no visual indications exist. However, while certain manipulation techniques can elude one or more analyses, it may be difficult to elude them all. For the most part, a digital image is composed of a finite set of numbers, arranged by a series of mathematical algorithms to create a digital image file. Like all mathematical functions, these algorithms operate in a predefined, predictable way. If the output of one algorithm is altered, the alteration will most likely affect the output of other algorithms. In some cases, when the authenticity of this kind of evidence is questioned, it is necessary to perform forensic analysis.

Forensic image authenticity is defined by SWGIT as "the application of image science and domain expertise to discern if a questioned image or video is an accurate representation of the original data by some defined criteria". Furthermore, the authenticity of a digital image can be defined as "an image made simultaneously with the visual events it purports to have recorded, and in a manner fully and completely consistent with the method of recording claimed by the party who produced the image; an image free from unexplained artifacts, alterations, additions, deletions, or edits".

Different techniques have been developed for forensic image analysis, and this article presents some of them.

Scene Inconsistencies

Scene inconsistencies like shadows, eye reflections, object positions or sizes, event mismatches, etc., can be extremely important in a forensic image analysis. The visual analysis of image evidence can reveal these kinds of scene inconsistencies and can be extremely important especially in cases when other techniques cannot be applied or their results are not relevant.

File Structure Analysis

File structure analyses investigate the format of the digital information such as the file type, EXIF, hex data, and MAC stamps (the Modify, Access, Creation time stamp of a file and/or digital media). Digital cameras create files in a particular way, each with its own unique structure. Information is embedded into image files, which can be distinct between manufacturers and cameras. When computers, or image processing software, interact with the file, this structure could be altered in some way. While this type of alteration does not necessarily mean that image content has been altered, it can raise concern about the authenticity of the file.

The information indicated by the MAC time stamps can reveal useful information about the history of a file: if it is consistent with the claimed recording procedure, if it is the original or a copy of it, if it was modified, and it may be correlated with information in the EXIF. Structure analysis can also reveal the presence of JPEG thumbnail and preview images, which should be investigated for their properties and consistency with a camera.

The EXIF represents the metadata located in the digital photo's header, and, on authentic files, it stores information about the make, model, camera settings, image size and resolution, as well as GSP coordinates and user's ID in some cases. Figure 15 shows examples of EXIF fragments from three authentic files: one joint photographic experts group (JPEG) from a Canon PowerShot G2, one tagged image file format (TIF) from a Pentax Optio 550, and one ORF from an Olympus E-PL1.

The EXIF analysis can also reveal traces of image processing, left by image editors or conversion engines (e.g., social networks), as it is shown in Figure 16.

Image editors can also leave traces in the body of an images data. Again, the name of the software used to process the

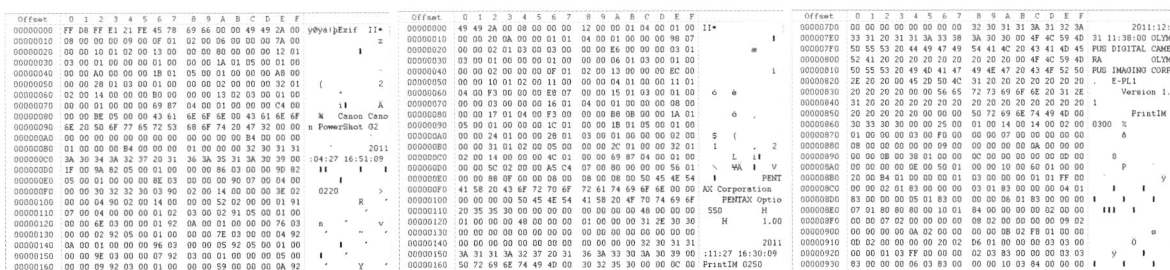

Figure 15 EXIF fragments of a JPG (left), TIF (center), and an ORF file (right).

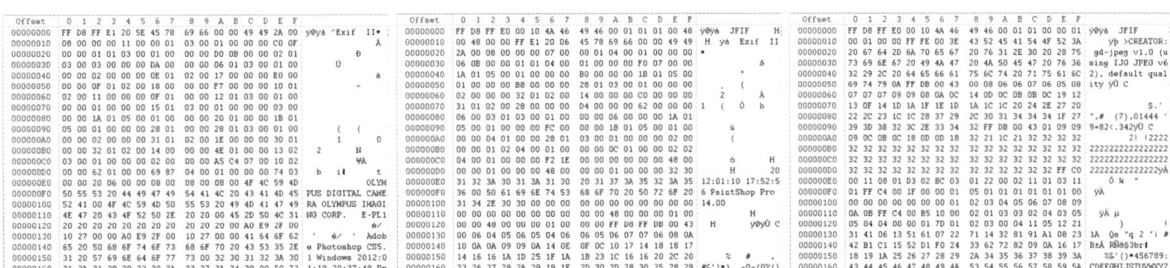

Figure 16 EXIF traces left by Adobe Photoshop (left), Corel PaintShop Pro (center), and Facebook (right).

images in **Figure 17** is seen in each image's hex data. As cameras do not introduce these kinds of traces in the original files, the detection of specific words can indicate previous edits with a specific software.

Quantization Table

The JPEG compression algorithm employs one or more quantization tables that define the amount of compression achieved. Various camera producers and their camera settings typically embed different quantization tables. Some of them can be fixed per camera and setting, while others may depend on the camera settings and image content. Software image editors also use their own quantization tables when saving JPEG files with specific quality settings. A quantization table is an 8×8 matrix, as it is exemplified in **Figure 18**.

Color Filter Array

A color filter array (CFA) consists of three color filters (red, green, and blue) placed on the camera's sensor. Each pixel records one single color sample, and the other two colors have to be estimated through a CFA interpolation algorithm, which introduces a specific statistical periodic correlation between subsets of pixels, per color channel. This can be estimated as a digital signature of a camera model and, when a JPEG image is resaved with an image editor, the original CFA correlation is changed too. The CFA analysis can reveal inconsistencies with an original JPEG and/or indicate traces of image recompression.

Resampling

One digital image manipulation technique involves copying and resampling an area from one image and pasting it into another. Resampling changes the original structure of pixels and the correlation between neighboring blocks and can therefore be detected.

DCT Coefficients

The JPEG compression algorithm involves using the Discrete Cosine Transform (DCT) that converts data from the spatial domain into the frequency domain, where it can be more efficiently encoded. The resultant values from the DCT transformation are sets of 64 signal-based amplitudes referred to as the DCT coefficients. The DCT coefficients are separated into two types of signals, DC and AC components. The DC coefficient refers to the mean value of the data and represents the average of the input samples. The DC components typically contain a significant portion of the total energy for the image. The remaining 63 coefficients are referred to as the AC coefficients. Each JPEG recompression operation involves irreversible modifications to the DCT coefficients that can be very important information in forensic image authentication. **Figure 19** shows the DCT histograms of an original compared with second-generation recompression of a JPEG image.

The DCT map technique is also based on DCT coefficients, by displaying the values per 8×8 sample blocks, for DC or AC coefficients, as shown in **Figure 20**.

Error Level Analysis

Alterations in JPEG images can be identified using the quantization and rounding errors inherent in the JPEG compression process. The error level analysis (ELA) technique consists in the conversion of an image from the spatial domain into the frequency domain using the DCT. A quantization table then quantizes the resulting DCT frequency coefficients. The main loss of information is due to the quantization error, or rounding of decimal values to the nearest integer. JPEG ELA focuses

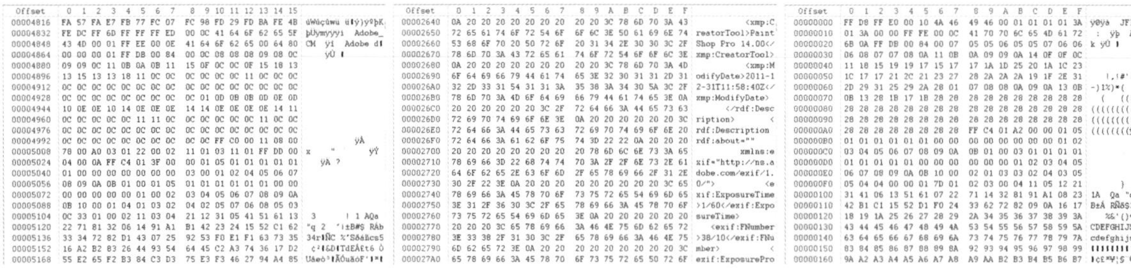

Figure 17 Traces left by Adobe Photoshop (left), Corel PaintShop Pro (center), and QuickTime PictureViewer (right).

Luminance								Chrominance							
9	6	5	9	13	22	29	35	9	9	12	20	15	26	79	79
6	6	8	11	15	33	34	30	9	10	12	10	26	26	79	79
8	7	9	13	22	33	39	31	12	12	10	10	26	79	79	79
8	9	12	16	28	49	45	34	20	10	10	26	79	79	79	79
10	12	21	32	39	61	58	42	15	26	26	79	79	79	79	79
13	19	31	36	45	58	63	51	26	26	79	79	79	79	79	79
28	36	44	49	58	68	66	55	79	79	79	79	79	79	79	79
41	52	54	55	62	56	57	54	79	79	79	79	79	79	79	79

Luminance								Chrominance							
6	4	7	11	14	17	22	17	7	9	19	34	20	20	17	17
4	5	6	10	14	19	12	12	9	12	19	14	14	12	12	12
7	6	8	14	19	12	12	12	19	19	14	14	12	12	12	12
11	10	14	19	12	12	12	12	34	14	14	12	12	12	12	12
14	14	19	12	12	12	12	12	20	14	12	12	12	12	12	12
17	19	12	12	12	12	12	12	20	12	12	12	12	12	12	12
22	12	12	12	12	12	12	12	17	12	12	12	12	12	12	12
17	12	12	12	12	12	12	12	17	12	12	12	12	12	12	12

Figure 18 Quantization tables of two JPEG files: Canon PowerShot G2 (left) and Adobe Photoshop (right).

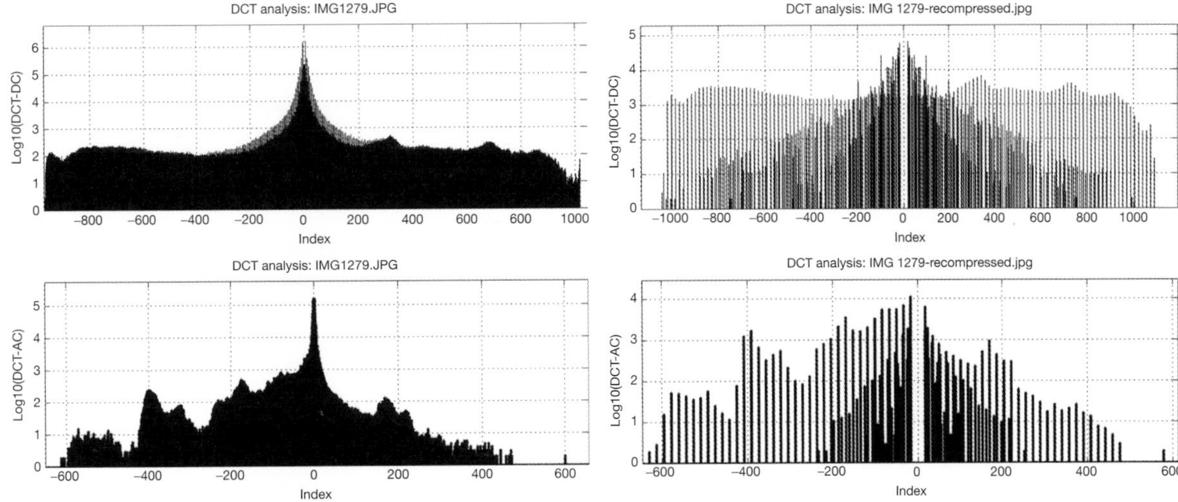

Figure 19 DCT histograms of two JPEG files: original (left) and JPEG recompressed (right).

Figure 20 Original image (left), tampered image (2nd to the left), DCT map (2nd to the right), and ELA (right).

Figure 21 Original image (left), tampered image (center), and clone detection results (right).

on the quantization and rounding error caused by the quantization and dequantization process in the DCT coefficients of a JPEG compressed file, as shown in **Figure 20**.

Photo-Response Nonuniformity

Pattern noise is a systematic distortion inherent in the operation of a particular electronic sensor. The pattern of this noise is consistent from one image to the next and consists of dark current noise and photo-response nonuniformity (PRNU). PRNU is the dominant part of the pattern noise and is caused by imperfections in the manufacturing process, sensor components, as well as the nonhomogeneity of the silicon wafer that is used in the sensor. These slight imperfections affect a pixels ability to convert photons to electrons, causing minor variations to exist between pixels, so that some pixels are more sensitive to light while others are less sensitive. This imprints a fingerprint, so to speak, onto each image produced by the sensor. PRNU is light dependent and the strength of the fingerprint amplifies as the intensity of light hitting the sensor increases. Characteristics exhibited by the PRNU make this component of the digital image a unique and helpful tool in identifying the 'fingerprint' of digital sensors. The PRNU is inherent in all imaging sensors, which makes it a universal identifier.

Clone Detection

The clone detection technique allows the detection of identical pixels or groups of pixels as a result of the copying and pasting of areas inside the image, as shown in **Figure 21**.

See also: **Digital Evidence/Audio Forensics:** Audio Enhancement and Authentication; **Digital Evidence/Photography and Digital Imaging:** Digital Imaging and Photography: An Overview; **Investigations:** Recording.

Further Reading

Bayram S, Sencar HT, Memon N, and Avcibas I (2005) Source camera identification based on CFA interpolation. *Proceedings of the 2005 IEEE International Conference on Image Processing*, pp. 69–72.

Conotter V, Boato G, and Farid H (2010) Detecting photo manipulation on signs and billboards. *Proceedings of the 2010 IEEE International Conference on Image Processing*.

Fridrich J, Soukal D, and Lukas J (2003) Detection of copy-move forgery in digital images. *Proceedings of the 2003 Digital Forensic Research Workshop*.

Gallagher AC (2005) Detection of linear and cubic interpolation in JPEG compressed images. *Proceedings of the 2nd Canadian Conference on Computer and Robot Vision*.

Geradts ZJ, Bijhold J, Kieft M, Kurosawa K, Kuroki K, and Saitoh N (2001) Methods for identification of images acquired with digital cameras. *Proceedings of the International Society for Optics and Photonics* 4232.

Kee E, Johnson MK, and Farid H (2011) Digital image authentication from JPEG headers. *IEEE Transactions on Information Forensics and Security* 6(3): 1066–1075.

Luo W, Haung J, and Qiu G (2010) JPEG error level analysis and its applications to digital image forensics. *IEEE Transactions on Information Forensics and Security* 5(3): 480–491.

Mahdian B and Saic S (2009) Detecting double compressed JPEG images. *IET Seminar Digests* 2: 12–17.

Petre A and Grigoras C (2010) *Inregistrarile Audio si Audio-Video*. Bucharest, Romania: C.H. Beck.

Popescu AC and Farid H (2005) Exposing digital forgeries by detecting traces of re-sampling. *IEEE Transactions on Signal Processing* 53(2): 758–767.

Popescu AC and Farid H (2005) Exposing digital forgeries in color filter array interpolated images. *IEEE Transactions on Signal Processing* 53(10): 3948–3959.

Relevant Websites

www.swgde.org – Documents of the Scientific Working Group on Digital Evidence.

www.swgit.org – Documents of the Scientific Working Group on Imaging Technology.

DIGITAL EVIDENCE/AUDIO FORENSICS

Audio Enhancement and Authentication

C Grigoras and JM Smith, University of Colorado Denver, Denver, CO, USA

Glossary

Artifact A visual/aural aberration in an image, video, or audio recording resulting from a technical or operational limitation. For example, speckles in a scanned picture, 'blocking' in JPEG compressed images, unnatural 'birdy' noises as a result of MP3 audio compression.
Audio enhancement Processing of recordings for the purpose of increased intelligibility, attenuation of noise, improvement of understanding the recorded material and/or improvement of quality or ease of hearing.
Dynamic range The ratio of the strongest nondistorted signal to that of the weakest discernible signal in a unit or system as expressed in decibels (dB); a way of stating the maximum signal-to-noise ratio.
Forensic audio A subdiscipline of digital and multimedia evidence, which involves the scientific examination, analysis, comparison, and/or evaluation of audio.
Media Physical objects on which data can be stored.
Media authentication The process of substantiating that the data in an image, video, or audio recording is an accurate representation of what it purports to be.
Multimedia evidence Analog or digital media, including, but not limited to, film, tape, magnetic and optical media, and/or the information contained therein.

Introduction

Audio forensics is a discipline within the digital and multimedia evidence (DME) field of forensics. DME includes digital evidence such as computers and mobile phones as well as recorded evidence in the form of audio, video, or still images. This confluence comes as a result of the ubiquity of digital technology and the commonality of media used to store digital data. For example, an external hard drive that is collected at a crime scene may contain audio recordings relevant to a case while the digital video recorder-based security system in the next room recorded audio and video to a hard disk drive during the events being investigated. Or, a cell phone found on a suspect may have been used to record voice notes and videos all related to a case under investigation. Because these items of evidence coexist in a digital realm that is not tangible as most other forensic sciences are known to be, the necessities of handling digital evidence must be respected throughout the DME discipline.

Audio evidence is commonly found during the course of investigation when circumstances such as these arise: a victim records audio for their protection, perpetrators use recordings to carry out their crimes, or phone call logging systems such as emergency assistance record a violent crime that occurred during a call. Similarly, investigators employ audio recording technology in covert operations or with a cooperative subject during an interview. The possible scenarios are too numerous to list here, but it is obvious that recorded audio evidence can be an important part of both criminal and civil proceedings where recordings of speech or other acoustic events can be very useful.

Because most forensic audio recordings are made in nonideal environments and the circumstances under which they are made are hard to control, quality, and intelligibility often suffer. The details that have been recorded are often hard to understand or not clear enough to make confident decisions. This is when it may be necessary to enhance or clarify the recorded audio by removing interfering noises and distortions or adjusting the amplitude of low-level information. Likewise, the authenticity of audio recordings must be established if they are to be given any weight in criminal prosecution or in the settlement of a civil dispute. This is necessary in order for the Trier of Fact to be assured that the recorded information accurately represents the events under investigation. A brief background on the topics of forensic audio enhancement and authenticity is provided in the sections below.

Technology

There are many elements to consider when presented with audio evidence before processing or conducting an analysis. Chiefly, is the recorded audio analog or digital? If dealing with analog recorded sound, it is imperative to understand analog media in order to choose the proper playback equipment. Once identified, all equipment used for the playback, analysis, and digitization of analog material should be properly maintained and calibrated according to the manufacturer's specifications. If working with recorded audio that is digital, it is no less imperative to understand the equipment and media used to record the audio digitally. It is also crucial to understand the variety of digital audio formats that are available and the

 http://dx.doi.org/10.1016/B978-0-12-382165-2.00128-8

difference between those that are native uncompressed and those that are compressed using either lossy or lossless compression algorithms. While an in-depth description of these principles will not be presented here, the following outline will give one a basic understanding.

Sound can be described as the compression and rarefaction of a medium (in most cases air) as a result of an acoustic impulse or vibration. In a relevant example, one can imagine the human mechanism that produces speech where air is forced through the larynx by the lungs causing the vocal folds to vibrate. The periodicity of this vibration produces sound with a perceived pitch while the modulation of this sound by the tongue and teeth establish language communication. Further modulation to the sound is caused by the acoustic space in which the sound is made by either absorbing or reflecting certain frequencies lending greater or lesser energy to the speech impulses. The acoustic space can obviously vary; it could be an office, auditorium, stairwell, or in an extreme example an anechoic chamber which absorbs all frequencies of sound resulting in reverberant energy close to zero. Acoustic impulses such as speech are fleeting and unless recorded, last no longer than a fraction of a second.

The ability to record and playback sound has been around since Thomas Edison perfected the phonograph in 1878. The principles of sound have obviously not changed since this time but methods to record sound have undergone many technical advances and every day we see innovations in sound recording technology. In the broadest and most basic sense, recording technology can be summarized as a microphone that acts as a transducer converting the acoustic energy into an electrical signal, which may be recorded on some sort of medium. Once an acoustic sound is represented in this way, it may be referred to as audio and recorded in one of two ways: as an analog or a digital signal. Although becoming more and more obsolete, the media used to record analog audio is most commonly in the form of a cassette or microcassette tape. On tape-recorded media such as this, the analog waveform is recorded as varying fluctuations of magnetic energy representing the original compression and rarefaction of sound. When played back, variation of the stored magnetic flux is converted back to an electrical signal and, in a process opposite that of a microphone transducer, the speaker driver acts as a transducer converting electricity back into a series of acoustic impulses. While digital audio may be played back in a similar fashion, it is recorded onto media as a representation of the acoustic waveform as a finite set of binary values, or samples. In this case, sound is quantized at a specific sample rate and bit depth. The sample rate refers to the number of samples per second used to quantize the waveform and the bit depth is the number of bits per sample available to represent the amplitude of the waveform. Once sampled and stored in some sort of file format, digital audio is no different than any other file on a computer and may be saved for later use and playback. Digital audio may be saved as a common file format such as .WAV or .AIFF or bit compressed in some manner to reduce the size of the recorded file. Compression algorithms used to achieve smaller file sizes or bit rates vary but will either be lossless like the Free Lossless Audio Codec or lossy such as MP3, AAC, WMA, and many more. With lossy encoding algorithms, the digital audio is typically limited in its frequency range and/or perceptually encoded resulting in the permanent degradation of the original, uncompressed digital waveform. It is crucial when working with digital audio to understand the principles behind audio sampling and encoding.

Competency and Proficiency

In order to work in the field of audio forensics, as with all forensic sciences, a level of education and training must be met. This is crucial because of the role the forensic expert plays in the courtroom and in the litigation process. It is common for an examiner to prove competency with a relevant educational background and up-to-date training and/or scientific research in order to conduct examinations. Once deemed competent and approved by either a court or by their agency, the analyst may work with evidence and provide scientific and unbiased opinion in matters related to their field.

The foundation of knowledge one should possess regarding the science of sound, audio technology, and laboratory practices is broad and may be garnered through various avenues including but not limited to training in audio production and recording or electrical engineering and signal processing. For an inclusive list of the minimum areas one should know and demonstrate competency and proficiency in, refer to documents from working groups such as the Scientific Working Group on Digital Evidence, European Network of Forensic Science Institutes – Forensic Speech and Audio Analysis Working Group, etc. A summarized list of these areas would include: audio recording technology, audio evidence collection and handling, audio laboratory configuration to include analog and digital signals, the repair and recovery of analog and digital audio media, and a working knowledge of the ethical and legal issues surrounding the processing, analysis, and interpretation of audio evidence.

Evidence Handling

As stated earlier, the handling of audio evidence is crucial. Thorough documentation at each stage of analysis is important to establish and maintain the provenance of recorded media upon seizure and throughout the term in which it is in possession. Some important considerations follow. A chain of custody or audit trail shall be initiated and maintained for all items of evidence. Digital evidence media shall be bit-stream imaged to ensure provenance and integrity of data. Digital analyses and processing shall be carried out on a working copy of recordings so that the original unprocessed files may remain unchanged. All actions taken to enhance or process evidence shall be logged so that a similarly trained examiner may reproduce results. The audio as it was originally recorded must be provided to the examiner for analysis. In cases where this is not possible, the examiner should be aware of and make others aware of limitations including those related to enhancement and authentication.

Forensic Audio Enhancement

Forensic audio recordings are typically made in nonideal environments in circumstances that are hard to control leading to poor fidelity and intelligibility. The details that have been

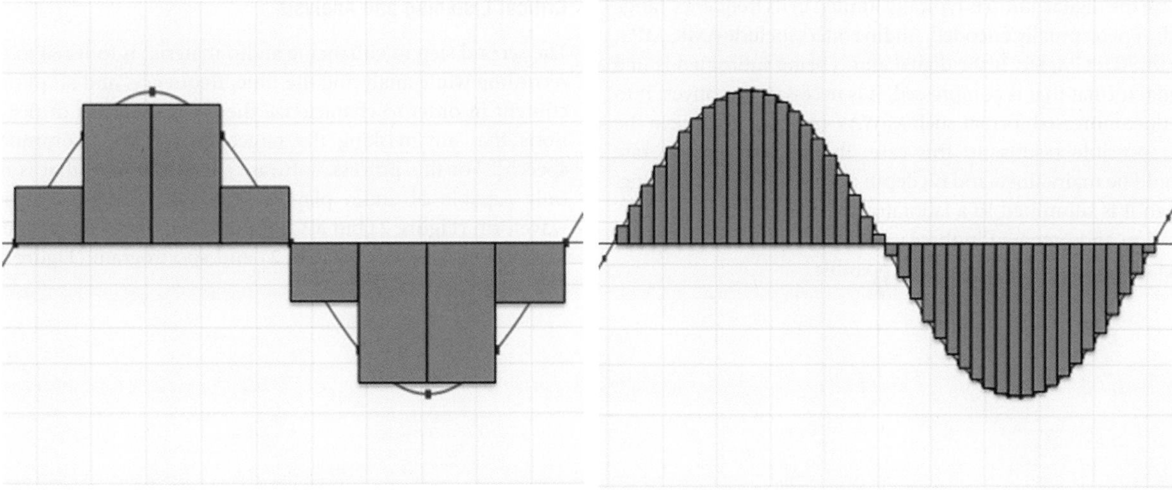

Figure 1 1 kHz sine wave sampled at 8 kHz (left) and at 44.1 kHz (right).

recorded are often hard to understand or not clear enough to make confident decisions. This is when it may be necessary to enhance or clarify the recorded audio by removing interfering noises and distortions or adjusting the amplitude of low-level information. This can either be done in real time while monitoring the audio of events or in a postprocessing phase after the recorded events have taken place. Either way, the application of signal processing in the digital domain is standard practice. There is often a trade-off where one can increase intelligibility by increasing the signal-to-noise ratio only to a certain point before the artifacts created by signal processing algorithms themselves interfere. Therefore, care should be taken to notover process material and abide by a general 'less-is-more' rule of thumb.

A simplistic approach to enhancing forensic audio can be followed as such: file preparation, critical listening and analysis, audio processing, and preparation of output file for distribution.

File Preparation

It is necessary to prepare audio for analysis and enhancement prior to examination. This means taking steps necessary to digitize, transfer, or convert recordings into an uncompressed format (most commonly WAV) and at a relevant sample rate, bit depth, and channel configuration (mono or stereo). Before describing this process, a brief introduction will be given on digital sampling with regard to sample rate and bit depth.

Digital audio is represents an acoustic sound wave as a finite set of binary values, or samples. When an analog signal is received by an analog to digital converter, the acoustic waveform is quantized at a specific sample rate and bit depth. The sample rate refers to the number of samples per second used to quantize the waveform and the bit depth is the number of bits per sample available to represent the waveform's amplitude at that moment in time. The resolution of the recording, then, is a function of the rate at which the waveform is sampled according to Nyquist's theorem that defines the upper bound of a sampling system. As two discrete sample points are required to represent the waveform of a specific frequency, the sampling rate must be twice that frequency. In other words, an 8 kHz audio recording only represents frequencies up to 4 kHz. Thus, the higher the sample rate, the more accurately the acoustic waveform is represented. See **Figure 1** below demonstrating one period of a 1 kHz sine wave sampled at two different sample rates.

For analog media like cassette and microcassette tapes, it is necessary to digitize the audio so that is may be processed, distributed, and played back more conveniently. For this process, all analog playback equipment shall be maintained and calibrated regularly according to the manufacturer's specifications and the analog to digital converter used should be external from the host computer and connected via Firewire, USB, or similar. The sample rate and bit depth used to digitize analog tape should be a minimum of 44.1 kHz, 24 bits (or 16 bits in the unlikely event that 24 are unavailable).

It is also possible to receive recordings on digital media that will require a transfer. These types of legacy media include digital audio tapes, Minidisc, and others. As the recordings that reside on these devices are native digital, it is best to digitally transfer the audio to the host computer using digital outputs on the media player. This maintains the originally quantized waveform and avoids redigitizing a quantized waveform if one were to use analog outputs on the digital media player. When performing a digital transfer, the original sample rate and bit depth should be used rather than resampling during the process in order to preserve the originality of the recordings.

The third general type of recording submitted would be one that was recorded as a digital audio file. There are many devices capable of recording digital audio files with the most common being hand-held recorders and cell phones. The digital audio files may be recorded in an uncompressed format such as WAV or AIFF. More commonly, however, recorded files are bit compressed in some manner to reduce the size of the recorded file. This process employs compression algorithms in order to achieve a smaller file size or bit rate and will either compress the audio waveform losslessly, causing no detrimental effect to the sound when played back, or in a way that causes permanent degradation of the original digital waveform. The term 'lossy' is used for these codecs (short for compression/decompression) where the digital audio is typically limited in its frequency range and/or perceptually encoded. Audio codecs include AMR, MP3, WMA, ADPCM, etc. If the digital audio being submitted is in a digital format that is compressed, it is necessary to convert it to an uncompressed format such as WAV in order to achieve the best possible results. In this case, the original sample rate should be maintained and bit depth maximized for processing. When it is submitted to a laboratory for enhancement or clarification and prepared in these ways, it can be easily processed to clarify the content as much as possible.

Critical Listening and Analysis

The second step to enhancing audio material is to listen to the recording while analyzing the time, frequency, and amplitude content in order to characterize the types of noises or distortions that are masking the target signal (most commonly speech). For this process, software should be used that is not only capable of audio playback and displaying the digital waveform (**Figure 2**) but also display of the fast Fourier transform (FFT) spectrum (**Figure 2**) and spectrogram (**Figure 2**).

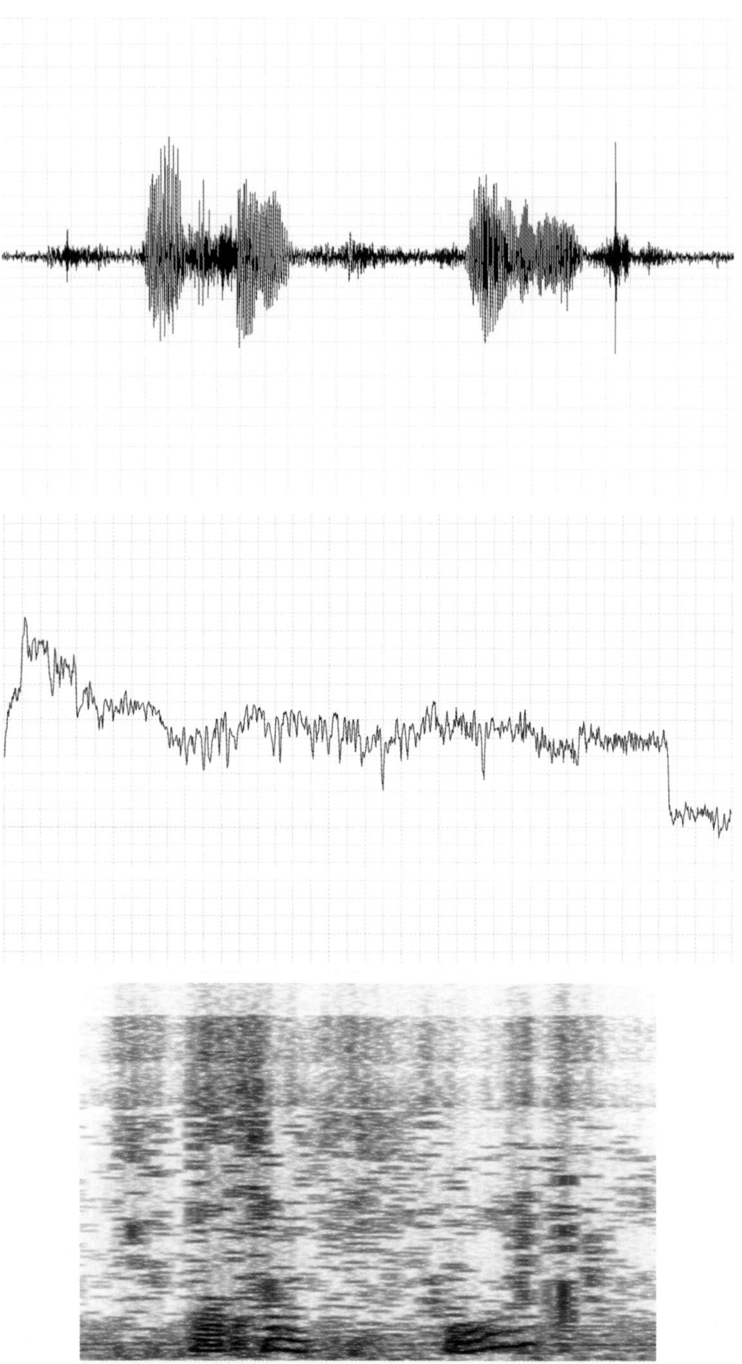

Figure 2 Waveform (top) with time on the *X*-axis and amplitude on the *Y*-axis. FFT spectrum (middle) with frequency on the *X*-axis and amplitude on the *Y*-axis. Spectrogram (bottom) with time on the *X*-axis, frequency on the *Y*-axis, and intensity of color (or gradient of grayscale) representing amplitude.

The FFT is the algorithm employed to convert the time-based audio signal to the frequency domain for frequency analysis. By listening to the material while conducting visual analyses, interfering noises and distortions masking the intended material can be observed and measured.

Generally, an interference masking the target signal can be characterized as either a noise or a distortion. These differ in that 'noises' are acoustic or electromagnetic events captured while the recording was made. 'Distortions' on the other hand are changes to the content of an audio signal during transmission or recording that disrupt the original waveform, much like a reflection on water distorted by ripples that would otherwise be accurate. In this same example, noise would be leaves floating on the surface of the water masking the reflection itself. Once noises and distortions are classified and measured, digital processing can be applied to remove them as much as it is possible.

Common types of noise in forensic audio recordings can be grouped into four categories: tonal, continuous broadband, variable broadband, and convolved. Tonal noise commonly comes from mains power hum, when an audio signal is not properly shielded, or acoustic noises from machines that oscillate at a specific frequency or set of frequencies (**Figure 3**). Continuous broadband noise (**Figure 4**) occupies a broad range of frequencies with little spectral change in time. For instance: tape hiss, machine or channel noise, or building ventilation systems. Variable broadband noise is a term used to describe interferences that occupy a broad range of frequencies with variable spectral content. For instance: wind, rain, and speech other than the target signal (**Figure 5**). Lastly, convolved noise is excessive reverberation interfering with the source signal (**Figure 6**).

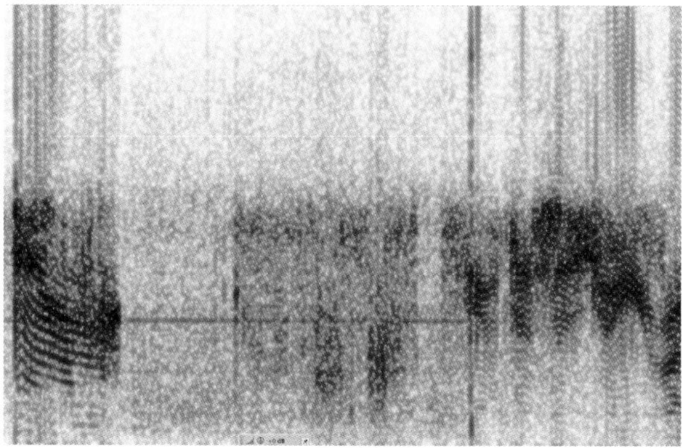

Figure 3 Spectrogram showing speech with tonal noise (the vertical line at approximately 1.6 kHz).

Distortions disrupt a signal and prevent the acoustic waveform from being accurately recorded due to interference or faulty equipment. One common example includes mobile phone interference (GSM bursts shown in **Figure 7**). In another example, **Figure 8** shows artifacts due to the application of aggressive lossy compression.

Audio Processing

Once the various interfering noises and distortions are identified, specific filters and algorithms can be applied in an attempt to remove or attenuate them. At this stage, the recorded audio may be enhanced for increased intelligibility or ease of listening. Not all noises can be removed nor all distortions fixed. In cases where the ratio of target signal amplitude to noise amplitude is too small, content in the waveform representing the target signal is not adequately represented. Therefore, it must be noted that some audio is recorded so poorly and with such compromising conditions that speech is not recoverable. In these instances, the submitter of the recording must be made aware of the limitations when working with forensic audio. Specific filters and algorithms designed to remove noises and fix distortions are provided here. While this section is not entirely exhaustive, the elements provided represent commonly employed techniques. In most cases, distortions should be fixed before attempting to remove noise.

- Clipped audio may be repaired manually or by using a *Declipping* algorithm that analyzes the distorted waveform with flattened or clipped peaks and interpolates the waveform that should otherwise be sinusoidal in nature.
- *Mobile phone interference* is induced into audio equipment electromagnetically as mobile devices transmit packets of data in very short bursts. These bursts are tonal in nature but use of notch or comb filters is not typically successful because of the interference has multiple harmonics of very high amplitude. It is possible to remove the bursts by determining the fundamental frequency of the distortion (based on the carrier network) and removing them with an adaptive filter. Modern filters built for this purpose will then interpolate the information obscured by the bursts.

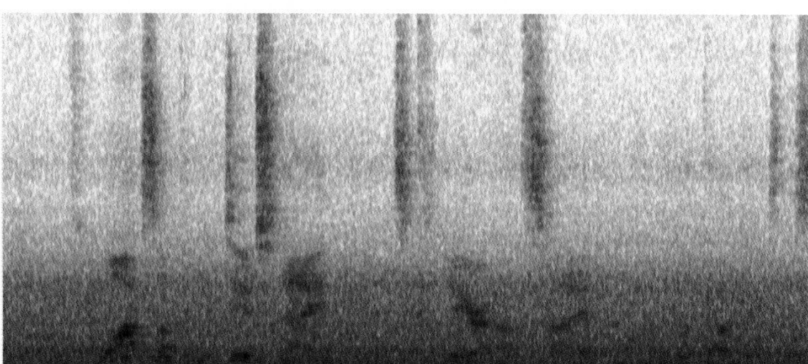

Figure 4 Spectrogram showing speech in the presence of continuous broadband noise.

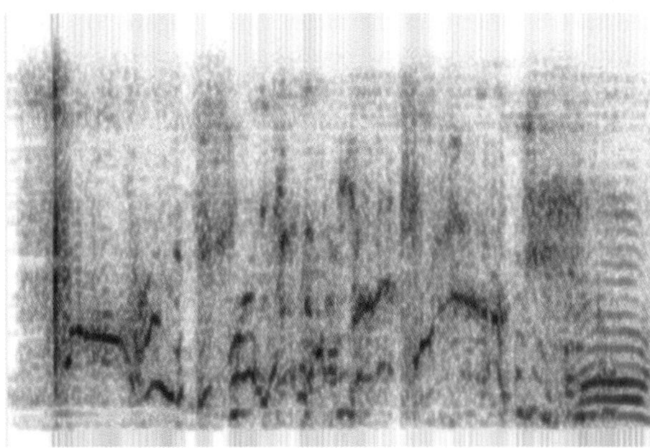

Figure 5 Spectrogram showing speech in the presence of variable broadband noise.

- *Time domain distortions,* such as tape wow and flutter, can be compensated for by applying time compression or expansion on appropriate segments of recorded audio.
- *Lossy compression artifacts* can in some cases be removed and the missing information reconstructed using algorithms designed for musical recordings. However, with forensic audio where speech is typically the target signal and other noises are present, these solutions are not very useful.
- *Notch, comb, and band-pass filters* are digital filters that are designed to attenuate or remove a specific frequency or frequencies. They are therefore useful in the removal of tonal noises. While a notch filter can be used to attenuate one specific frequency (such as 1.6 kHz in **Figure 3**) comb filters are designed to attenuate a fundamental frequency and its harmonics. This is especially useful in the case of

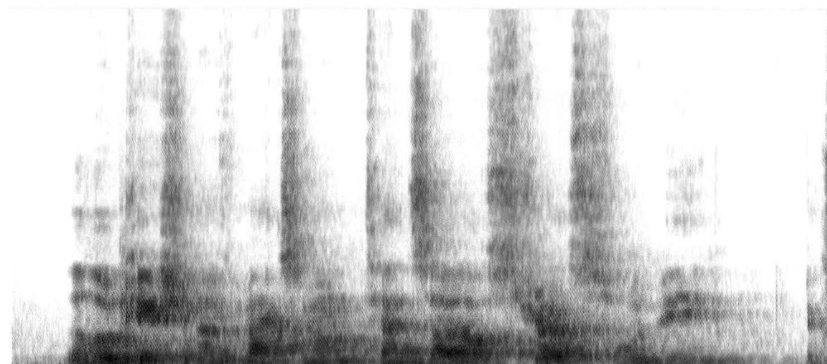

Figure 6 Spectrogram showing speech recorded in excessively reverberant conditions. The clarity of speech formants are smeared in time due to reflections from the environment.

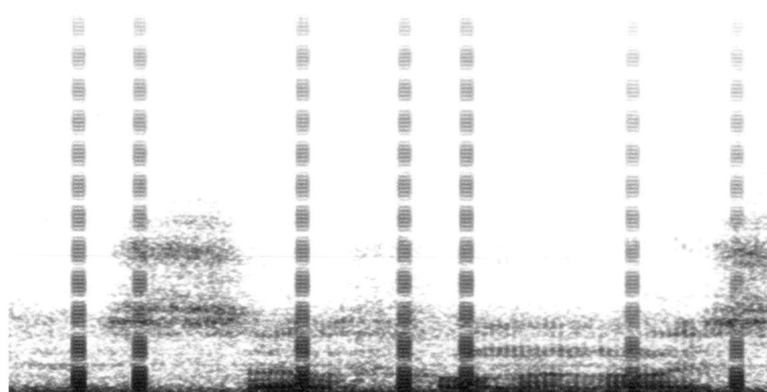

Figure 7 Spectrogram showing speech obscured by GSM burst interference.

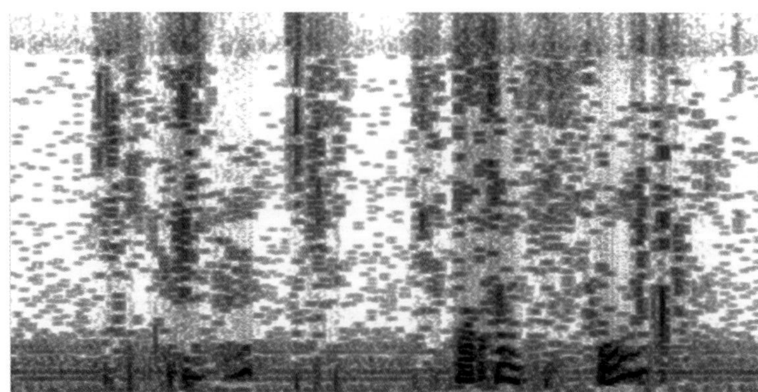

Figure 8 Spectrogram showing speech recorded with lossy WMA compression.

induced mains power hum (at 60 or 50 Hz depending on the country) where harmonics at multiples of the fundamental are present. By selecting the fundamental frequency, harmonics are automatically calculated and attenuated. Band-pass filters on the other hand will attenuate a range of frequencies. For instance, a high-pass filter can easily be applied to attenuate frequencies from 0 to 150 Hz in order to reduce low-frequency rumble and make speech more intelligible.

- *Spectral subtraction* is very useful in removing continuous broadband noise where the spectral content of noise does not vary greatly over time. In a simple arithmetic procedure, this algorithm subtracts an input noise profile from recorded audio to effectively remove noise and enhance intelligibility.
- *Adaptive filters* can work in both the time and frequency domains and achieve spectral subtraction on short time windows that change as the noises in the environment change. These filters develop predictive coefficients to continually update the input noise profile to be subtracted and can therefore be useful in dealing with variable broadband noise like outdoor environments where background conversations, rain, etc. may be present.
- *Convolved noise*, or excessive reverberation, can be removed with some success using algorithms designed for this purpose. While many methods have been proposed, typical techniques that are commercially available use adaptive de-reverberation algorithms where spectral subtraction of convolved elements is achieved based on predictive coefficients.
- *Stereo source separation* can be very powerful when available. In this situation, a stereo recording is provided that has speech in the presence of, most likely, variable broadband noise. If the target speech signal is present on only one channel, the second channel can be used to inform the algorithm of the noise profile to be removed. For example, for a stereo recording of a noisy bar where the background voices, music, and other acoustic impulses are captured in relatively equal amplitude on both channels and speech is on one. Alternatively, when dealing with mono recordings, it is possible to provide the algorithm with the second reference channel containing identical noise information as that which is present on the source. For instance, when presented with a mono recording of speech obscured by commercially released music or a media broadcast, the music or broadcast can be obtained to build the reference channel for subtraction.
- In some cases, conversations are recorded in which one person is at a higher amplitude than another. This situation is referred to as *near-party/far-party* and can easily be compensated for by either manually adjusting the volume of the digital file during quiet portions or by applying amplitude compression/limiting to bring loud and quiet material to within the same range of volume. Some systems provide an automatic gain control feature that will expand and compress portions of audio to achieve a more balanced overall level.

A forensic audio recording that requires enhancement may be processed with one or many of the above techniques. Depending on the noises and distortions present, it is up to the examiner which ones will be appropriate and in which order. This is done by comparing and contrasting the audio before and after each step of processing. It is advised to save each iteration of processing as an independent audio file to maximize efficiency if any alterations to previous steps must be taken. For any processing that is applied, it is necessary to document filters and settings used so that identical results may be achieved at a later time by the same examiner or by another adequately trained examiner. This helps to establish the provenance of the original material and can demonstrate, if necessary, that the content or meaning of the audio was not changed during the course of enhancement.

Preparation of Output File

Once noises and distortions have been compensated for satisfactorily, further processing may be needed to make the recording appropriate for playback in a courtroom: adjusting the overall amplitude of the audio, for example. Or it may be desired to further shape the frequency response of the recording by applying equalization. Once complete, it is necessary in this last stage of the forensic audio enhancement procedure to prepare the audio in a format as deemed appropriate by the analyst and the submitter of evidence. For example, due to technology limitations of the contributor or the court, it may be requested to provide an audio CD that can be played back in a CD player requiring the output audio to be at 44.1 kHz 16 bits. If the file is to be converted in any way from the resolution that it was processed at, the unconverted output file should be also provided as it represents the most original form of the enhanced evidence. Finally, the original unprocessed audio should also be provided to the contributor especially in cases where the originally supplied recording is not in a format useful for the contributor or the courts.

Forensic Audio Authentication

Commonly, a review of audio authenticity is requested to determine whether the material presented accurately represents the events recorded with requests coming either through investigation or as a request from the court or its advocates. An audio authenticity examination, as defined by the Scientific Working Group on Digital Evidence, seeks to determine if a recording is original, unaltered or continuous, and/or consistent with the manner in which it is alleged to have been produced. Many elements from a recording may be analyzed and the methodology employed will depend on whether the recording was made digitally or on analog media. In either case, the questioned original recording on its original media must be analyzed and, if available, the original recording device must be obtained. This is crucial in establishing the provenance of the recording; otherwise analyses and conclusions are compromised. If the original recorder is not available, a recorder of the same model and brand may be used to produce test recordings. Test recordings are necessary to produce known data from which comparisons to the questioned recording can be made.

Analog Tape Authentication

Analysis methods in tape authentication examinations first began with the Watergate Scandal of 1972. Since that time, the methodology employed to analyze analog tape recordings has not changed greatly nor have the tools for analysis. Once the questioned recording has been obtained, an analysis of the magnetic material on the tape is conducted along with digital analysis of the audio material. In essence, the examiner must analyze any inconsistencies in the questioned recording and make comparisons with test recordings in order to determine whether they are a result of normal operation or possible editing.

Bruce Koenig published a paper in 1990 describing a formal methodology for conducting analyses of analog recordings that

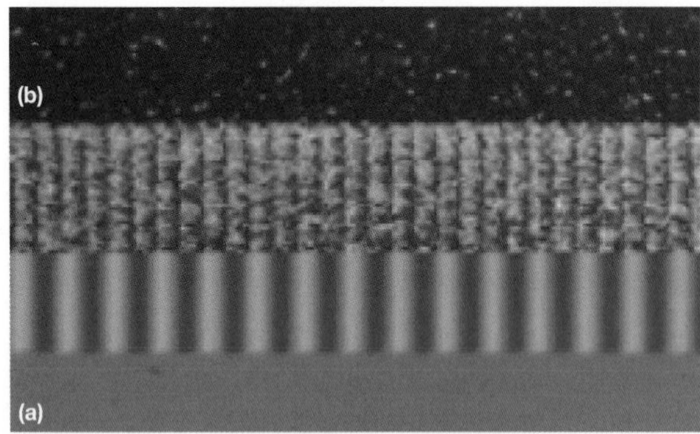

Figure 9 (a) 1 kHz sine wave imaged using a magneto-optical system. (b) 1 kHz sine wave imaged using Freon-based ferrofluid. Photo courtesy of Jonathan Broyles, www.iasforensics.com.


```
  0 52494646 2CBD1900 57415645 666D7420
 16 10000000 01000100 803E0000 007D0000
 32 02001000 64617461 08BD1900 B6FE8FFE
 48 81FECAFE F7FEB9FE 92FEF4FE BFFE56FE
 64 23FE38FE ADFEF7FE 11FF0DFF 3CFF2FFF
 80 1BFFFFFE 43FF45FF F7FE0DFF 46FF58FF
 96 36FF46FF 74FF88FF 87FFE3FF FFFF0400
112 48007D00 9B000F01 8D01BA01 DD014902
128 A6028502 96023503 A6039703 1D030303
144 1E032603 C8028B02 B102C502 A7023E02
160 DE01A901 5E016701 49013E01 3B01B300
176 14003100 1D00FBFF B4FF94FF AFFF49FF
192 26FF53FF B5FFBAFF C8FE21FE 87FE4FFE
208 13FEA0FD E3FDCAFD 00FE00FE 31FEF8FD
224 01FE00FE EBFD6EFE B3FE85FE A4FE7DFE
240 94FE6AFE 88FE96FE C9FED8FE EBFE24FF
256 18FFFAFE FDFE07FF 34FF70FF 83FFB5FF
272 93FFB5FF A6FF9CFF B5FFD3FF BAFFF3FF
288 18005200 2E006500 83004700 F0FFF4FF
304 F6FF4600 5C000600 06005500 61007E00
320 8E009E00 D300DB00 9100A900 04011701
336 62018001 9E016101 20011E01 FE001101
352 07011701 28010201 0601EA00 CA00E300
368 9000AF00 0D01EA00 AB00C400 B600DD00
384 B2008A00 A300F200 EF00E100 D3007300
400 6F001200 22001500 D6FFB7FF D4FFD7FF
416 BEFFF4FF 9DFF2EFF CBFE04FF 4EFF94FF
432 39FF25FF 7BFF88FF 52FF34FF 3EFF21FF
448 32FF6FFF B5FF6BFF 30FF12FF 15FF65FF
464 13FF3DFF 5CFF5FFF 9AFFDBFF 06000700
480 1C006C00 8F002A00 6800A600 A700AF00
```


Figure 10 Hexadecimal display of audio data.

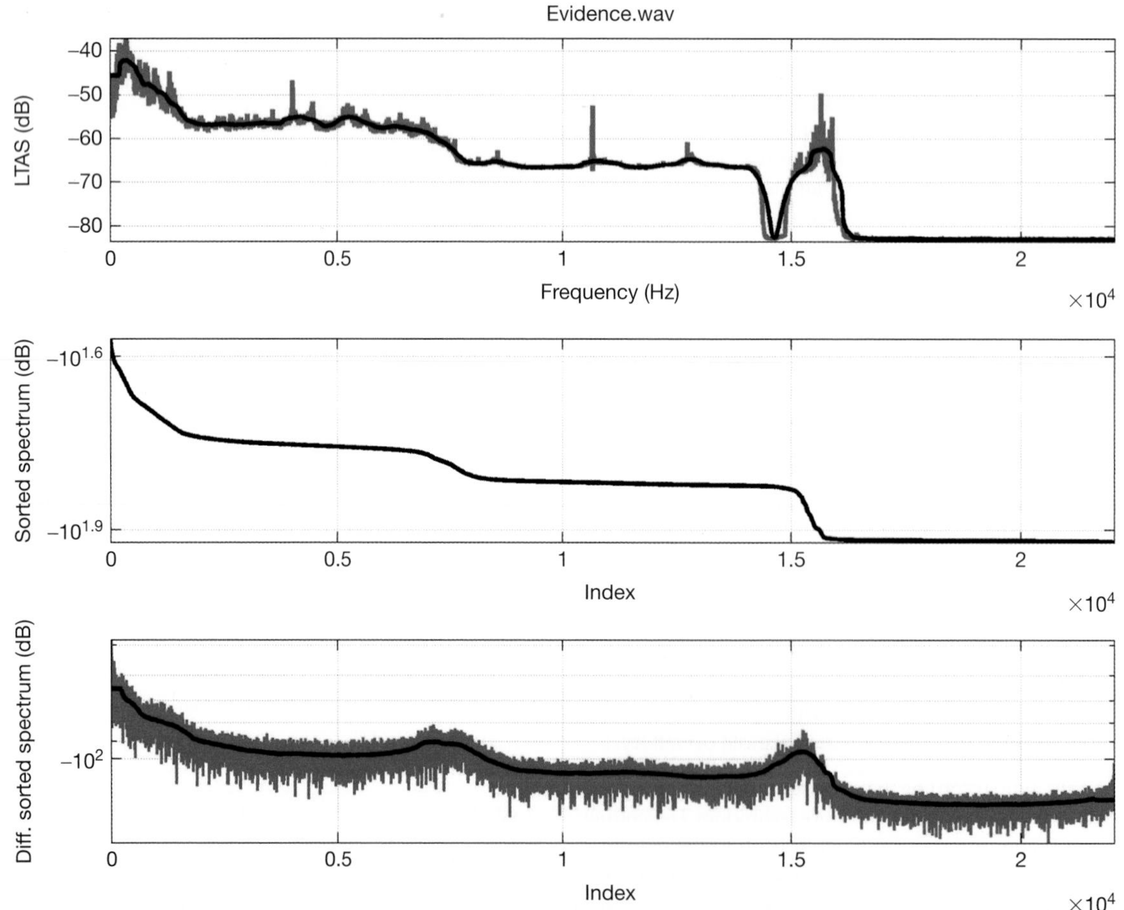

Figure 11 Long-term power spectrum, sorted spectrum, and differentiated sorted spectrum of long-term average spectrum.

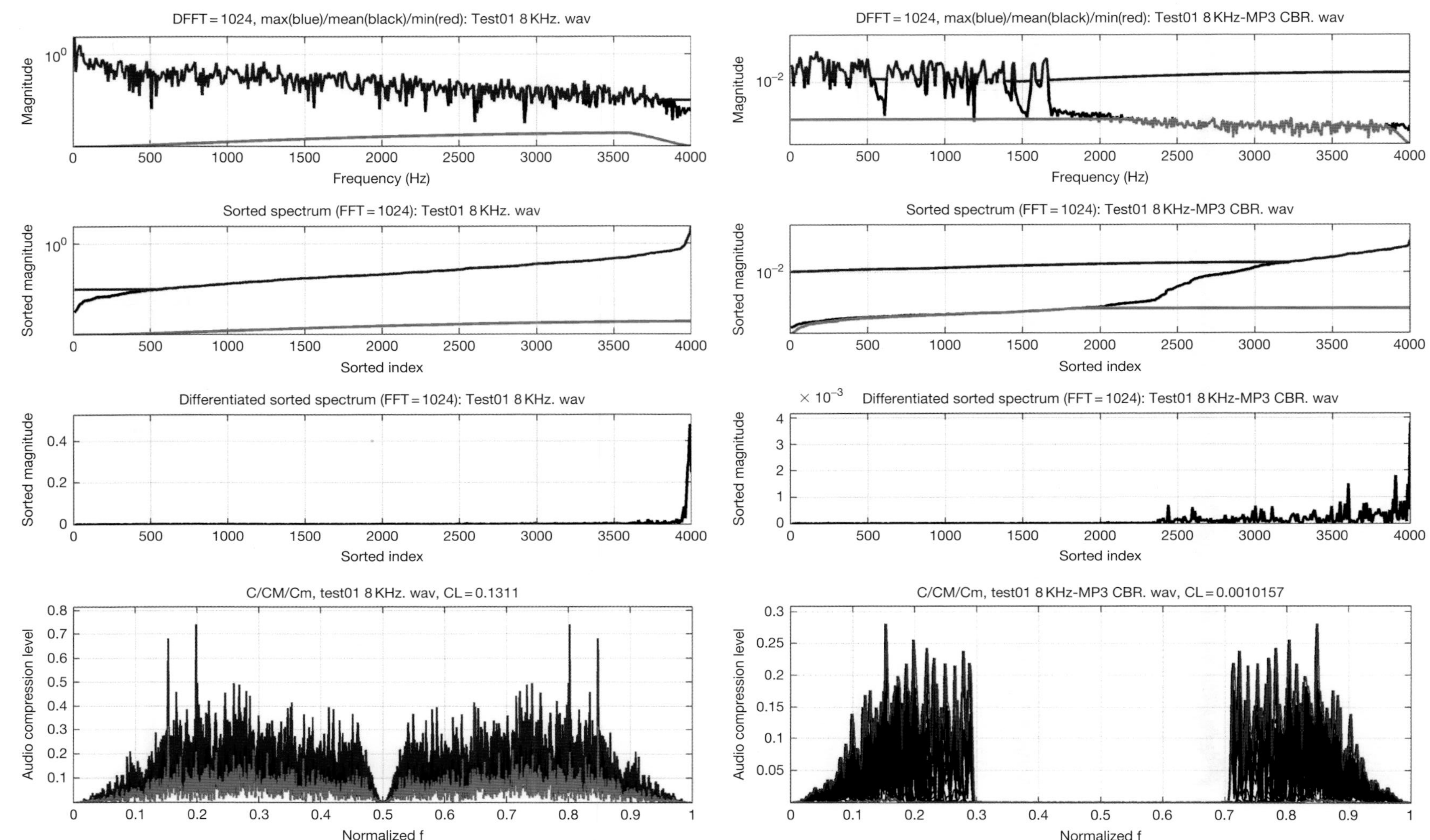

Figure 12 Compression level analysis, original WAV PCM recording (left column), MP3 CBR (right column).

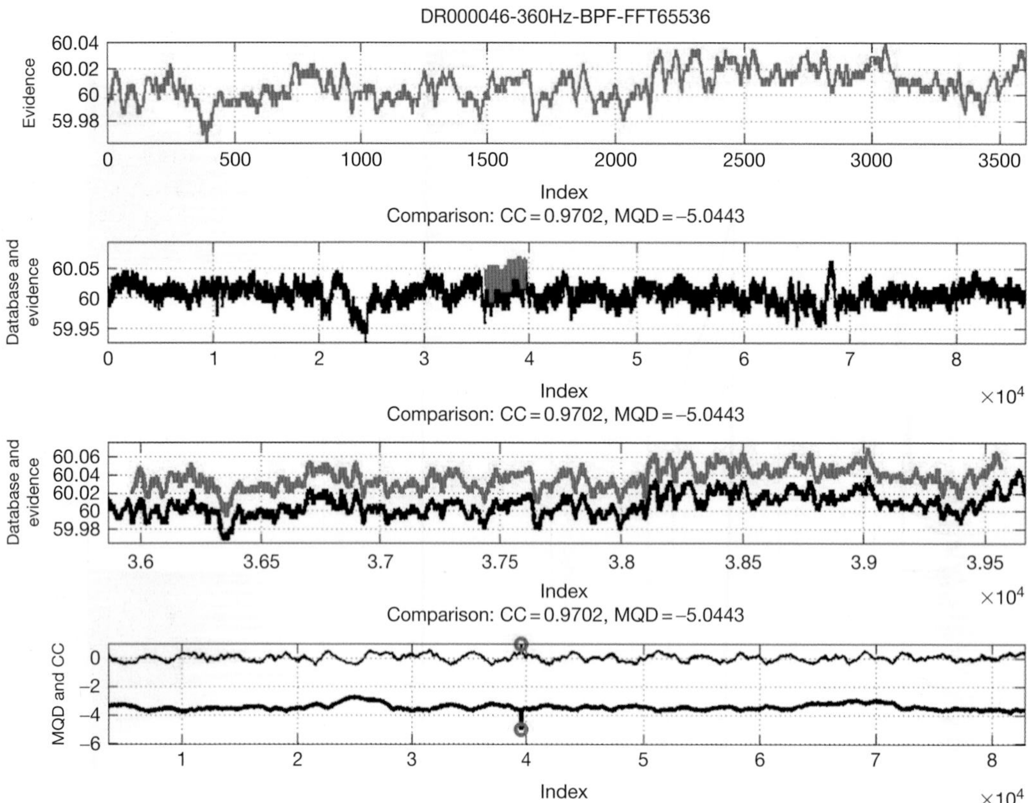

Figure 13 ENF analysis against a forensic database.

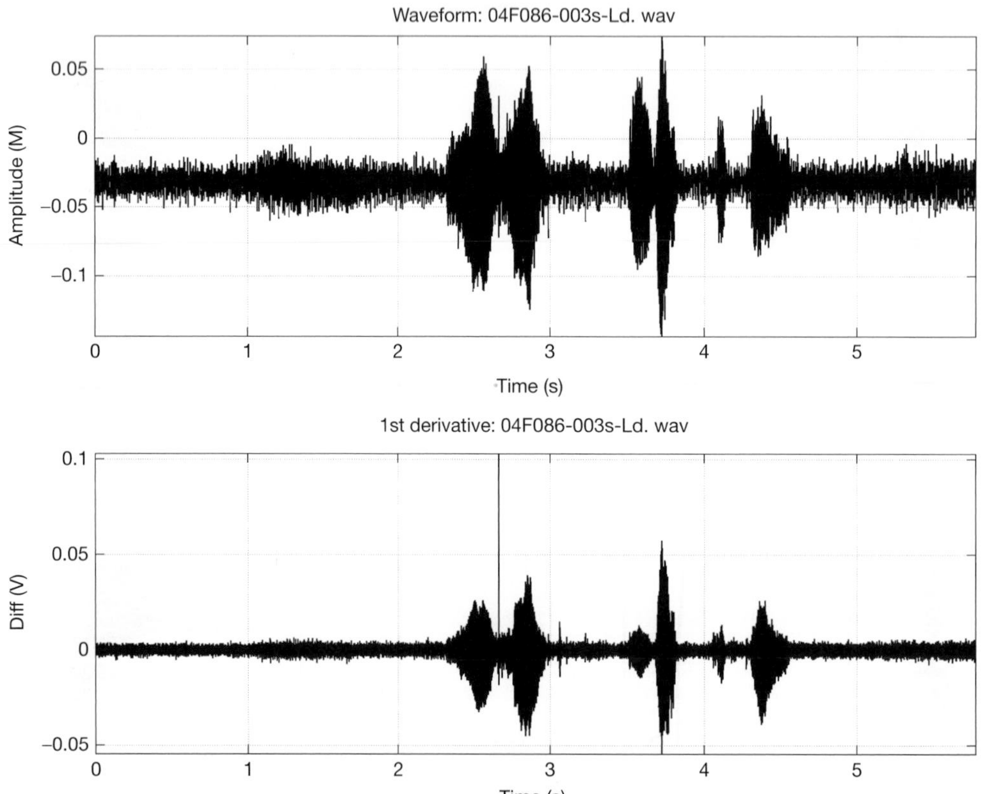

Figure 14 Butt-splice detected at 2.665 s.

employs Freon-based ferrofluid to conduct visual examinations of the magnetic waveform stored on the tape (**Figure 9**). An alternative method of visualizing magnetic flux that provides higher frequency resolution and less physical contact with the tape itself employs a magneto-optical imaging system (**Figure 9**).

Digital Audio Authentication

An analysis of digitally recorded audio does not differ in scope from an analog examination in that the examiner seeks to explain observed anomalies, through the analysis of test recordings, as a result of normal recorder operation or inconsistencies which may indicate alteration or editing. However, the techniques employed vary greatly. These should include but not be limited to analysis of: header and file structure, waveform, FFT spectrum, spectrogram, compression level, and electric network frequency (ENF). Koenig and Lacey provide a formal methodology for the authentication of digital audio recordings while information regarding analysis can be found in the references section as well. Different techniques have been developed for forensic audio authenticity analysis and this chapter presents some of them.

MAC, header, and file structure analysis can be carried out checking the MAC (Modify, Access, Creation time stamp of a file and/or digital media) and using software capable of viewing the individual bits and bytes that make up a file represented as hexadecimal, or hex, data (**Figure 10**). In viewing the hex data of a digital audio file, comparisons may be made between a questioned recording and test recordings to observe recorder and file write behavior. The internal arrangement of proprietary files can confirmed as well as the header structure. Header information may also include the date/time of the recording, recording duration, make/model/serial number of the recorder, file type, and compression scheme and rate. Any observed inconsistencies in this information may be a result of alteration or editing.

Power spectral analysis may be useful in identifying traces of file recompression or inconsistencies between the recording and the claimed recorder. If present, inconsistencies can be easily detected by comparing the long-term power spectrum, sorted spectrum, and differentiated sorted spectrum of unknown and test recordings as well as comparing histograms of their spectral power (**Figure 11**).

Compression level analysis may also be useful in identifying traces of file recompression or inconsistencies between the recording and the claimed recorder. This function, proposed by Grigoras, applies the discrete fast Fourier transform on the second derivative of consecutive frames to produce a plot of the compression level. By comparing an unknown recording's compression level with test recordings of the claimed recorder, inconsistencies may be found if present.

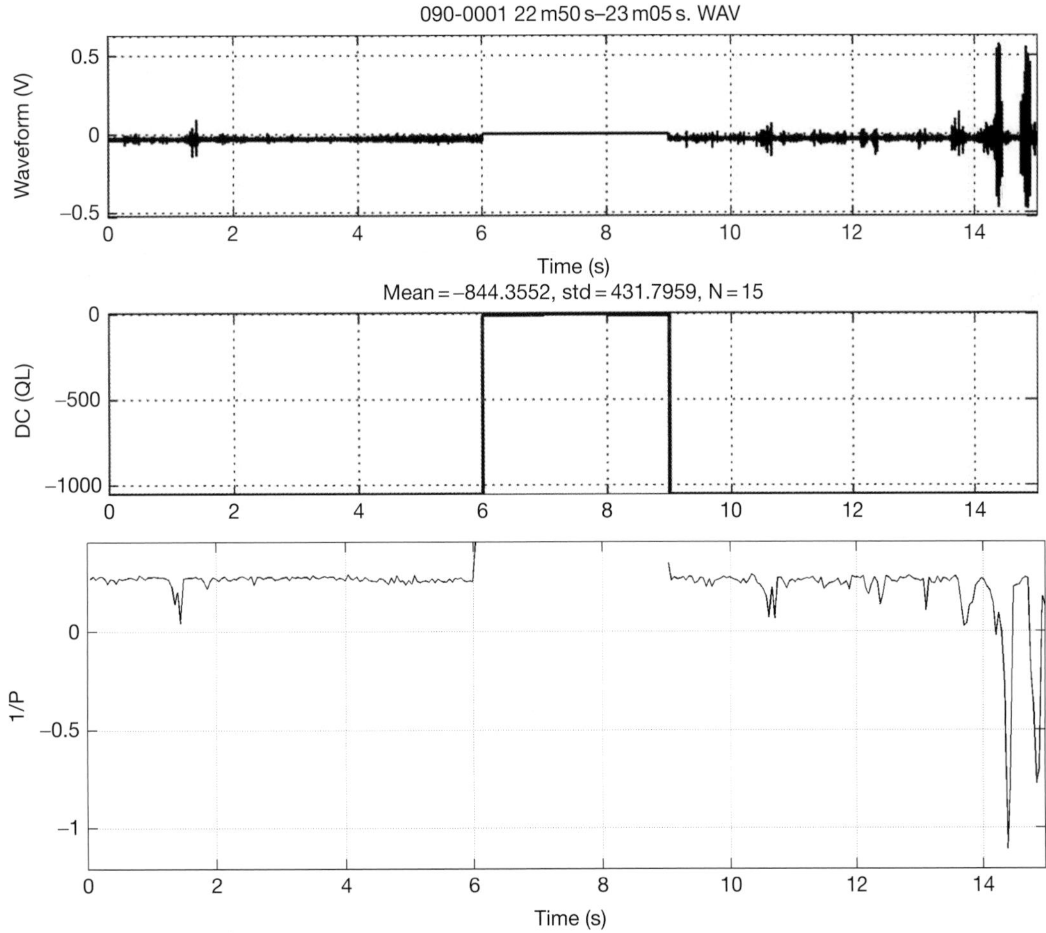

Figure 15 DC and power analysis, showing a signal's discontinuity.

ENF analysis involves the detection, extraction, and comparison of the ENF trace induced onto recording from mains power. If present, ENF may help an examiner do many things in addition to identifying the presence of edits, insertions, and deletions. With a reference database of ENF, it is possible to determine the date/time a recording was made, how the device was powered, and gross geographical location, all of which can further corroborate the authenticity of a recording (Figure 13).

Butt-splice detection can be useful in identifying the insertion or deletion of material without the application of cross-fades (Figure 14).

DC level analysis may be used to determine the insertion of material or to compare an unknown recording to the recorder claimed to have made it (Figure 15).

In the examination of digital audio for authenticity, a sound methodology should be used that is based on validated methods and principles. While the specific analyses will depend on the situation, the examiner should not rely on one specific element or tool but seek to exhaust all possible techniques because an inconsistency observed through one analysis may not be present in another. Specific determinations from analyses will also vary depending on the situation but will generally conclude that the recording is: consistent with an authentic recording, inconsistent with an authentic recording, or inconclusive.

See also: **Behavioral:** Forensic Linguistics; Forensic Phonetics; **Digital Evidence:** Digital Imaging: Enhancement and Authentication; **Digital Evidence/Photography and Digital Imaging:** Digital Imaging and Photography: An Overview; **Investigations:** Recording.

Further Reading

Bouten J, van Rijsbergen M, and Donkers S (2007) Derivation of a transfer function for imaging polarimetry used in magneto-optical investigations of audio tapes in authenticity investigations. *Journal of the Audio Engineering Society* 22: 257–265.

Brixen EB (2011) *Audio Metering: Measurements, Standards, and Practice*, 2nd edn. Burlington, MA: Focal Press.

Cooper A (2010) Detecting butt-spliced edits in forensic digital audio recordings. *Proceedings of the 39th International Conference of the Audio Engineering Society: Audio Forensics*. Denmark, 2010.

Grigoras C (2009) Applications of ENF analysis in forensic authentication of digital audio and video recordings. *Journal of the Audio Engineering Society* 57: 643–661.

Grigoras C (2010) Statistical tools for multimedia forensics. *Proceedings of the 39th International Conference of the Audio Engineering Society: Audio Forensics*. Denmark, 2010.

Harris CM (1998) *Handbook of Acoustical Measurements and Noise Control*, 3rd edn. Woodbury, NY: Acoustical Society of America.

Koenig BE (1990) Authentication of forensic audio recordings. *Journal of the Audio Engineering Society* 38: 3–33.

Koenig BE and Lacy D (2009) Forensic authentication of digital audio recordings. *Journal of the Audio Engineering Society* 57: 663–695.

Loizou PC (2007) *Speech Enhancement: Theory and Practice*. Boca Raton, FL: Taylor and Francis Group.

Pohlmann KC (2005) *Principles of Digital Audio*, 5th edn. New York, NY: McGraw-Hill.

Relevant Websites

www.enfsi.eu – Documents of the ENFSI Expert Working Group Forensic Speech and Audio Analysis.

www.swgde.org – Documents of the Scientific Working Group on Digital Evidence.

www.aes.org – The EOB Tape of June 20, 1972 by the Advisory Panel on White House Tapes.

DIGITAL EVIDENCE/BLACK BOXES AND SECURITY CAMERAS

Aircraft Flight Data Recorders

VL Grose, US National Transportation Safety Board, Washington, DC, USA

Glossary

Adversary truth Pursuit of truth in the law involving a process of confrontation between opposing parties that eliminates voluntary disclosure of uncertainties, must be certain, known firsthand, and excludes hearsay, rumors, and guesses.
Air Line Pilots Association (ALPA) Representing more than 53 000 pilots at 37 US and Canadian airlines, it is chartered by the AFL-CIO and the Canadian Labour Congress and is a member of the International Federation of Air Line Pilot Associations.
Analog information Continuous phenomena with no quantized or discrete variances whose recorded result is subject to interpretation as to meaning and significance.
Bureau d'Enquêtes et d'Analyses pour la sécurité de l'aviation civile (BEA) The French authority responsible for safety investigations into accidents or incidents in civil aviation.
Coalition of Airline Pilots Associations (CAPA) A trade association comprised of over 28 000 professional pilots in five individual member unions.
Cockpit voice recorder (CVR) An electronic device used to record conversation in the cockpit, radio communications between the cockpit crew and others (including conversation with air traffic control personnel), as well as ambient sounds.
Collision Safety Institute (CSI) An independent traffic collision research, training and crash consulting organization with a mission to provide state-of-the-art training and technology transfer to both public and private entities involved in the analysis and evaluation of motor vehicle collisions.
Digital information Discrete values of quantized time, frequency, and amplitude that are not subject to interpretation as to content.
Event data recorder (EDR) An electronic device used to record information related to vehicle (automobile, truck, locomotive) performance that can be retrieved and analyzed following an accident.
Federal Aviation Administration (FAA) The national aviation authority of the United States. An agency of the Department of Transportation, it has authority to regulate and oversee all aspects of civil aviation.
Flight data acquisition unit (FDAU) A junction box that receives various discrete, analog, and digital parameters from a number of sensors and avionic systems, then routes them to a flight data recorder (FDR).
Flight data recorder (FDR) An electronic device used to record hundreds of specific aircraft flight performance parameters, including control and actuator positions, engine information – all on a time basis.
National Transportation Safety Board (NTSB) An independent US Federal agency charged with determining the probable cause of transportation accidents, promoting transportation safety, and assisting victims of transportation accidents and their families. It has five Board Members, each nominated by the President and confirmed by the Senate to serve 5-year terms.
Probable cause Conclusions reached by an investigating body as to the factor or factors that caused an accident.
Proximate cause An event directly related to a loss and legally held to be its cause.
Technical truth Pursuit of truth in scientific work that includes not only what is known but also open admission of uncertainties, assumptions, suppositions, and hunches – all of which are probabilistic; that is, never certain and always subject to reversal should new findings disprove them.
Underwater locator beacon (ULB) A device fitted to both CVRs and flight data recorders that, when triggered by water immersion down to depths of 14 000 ft, emits an ultrasonic pulse of 37.5 kHz at once per second.

Introduction

Commercial aircraft crashes arouse wide public interest for several reasons. They generally involve massive, unexpected death and destruction. The flying public easily correlates an airliner crash with its own perceived risk beyond any possible personal control. Even though the probability of a crash per flight is one in every 19 000 years, it is one of the six most feared causes of death. So such disasters appear mysterious – but demand a raison d'etre. Aircraft flight data recorders (FDRs) help to answer that demand.

 http://dx.doi.org/10.1016/B978-0-12-382165-2.00129-X

Pursuit of Truth

Airliner crashes and criminal acts both provoke public concern for their avoidance – focused on what needs to be eliminated or corrected. Crash-free airliners and crime-free society are admirable goals but never likely to be fully achieved.

Approaches to perfection for both goals are similar but not identical. Truth in airliner technology involves traditional scientific freedom to look anywhere at any time under unrestricted rules. In contrast, truth sought under rules of criminal law is bound by restrictions as to its relevance. These two types of truth may lead to contrasting use of recorders.

Adversary Versus Technical Truth

Adversary truth pursued in the law involves a process of confrontation between opposing parties. That eliminates the voluntary disclosure of uncertainties. To be admissible in court, information must be certain and known firsthand. Hearsay, rumors, and guesses are not allowed.

Technical truth sought in scientific work includes not only what is known, but also open admission of all uncertainties. So assumptions, suppositions, and hunches have a large role in science. In contrarst to public perception, science is probabilistic – never certain and always subject to reversal and should new findings disprove it. **Figure 1** illustrates these two types of truth.

These two truths are not competitive because they have different truth objectives. However, digital recordings may play contrasting societal roles in providing information. Law enforcement's use of recorded automobile data (e.g., velocity and location) does not enjoy the same public endorsement that recorded aircraft data used in postcrash analysis does.

Immediately after an airliner catastrophe, the public expects someone to determine not only what happened but also why it happened. In the United States, the National Transportation Safety Board (hereinafter NTSB) pursues both.

That process consists of nine steps:

- On-scene fact finding
- Collection of physical evidence
- Interrogation of witnesses
- Conduct of public hearings for sworn expert testimony
- Analysis of all obtained evidence (including FDR readouts)
- Formulation of conclusions
- Determination of causation
- Creation of recommendations to preclude a similar accident
- Summary and publication of the determinative process

Two truths Vernon L. Grose, DSc	
Adversary truth Only what has been elicited as *known*	Technical truth What is *known* plus full disclosure of all *uncertainties*
Fault-finding, blame assessment	Accident-preventing
Protection of deficiencies	Openness to deficiencies
Reaction to events	Foreseeability
Post-facto review	"A priori" projection
Involuntary, screened data	Voluntary exposure
First-hand facts	Hunches, possibilities

Figure 1 Two truths.

This evidentiary pursuit can often require a year. All nine steps revolve around history – dealing with what has already been transpired but was unplanned and unforeseen. Most require human judgment that is subjective rather than objective.

Compounding that search is the likely disintegration of the aircraft and its contents because of their velocity at impact and release of onboard energy sources that frequently results in wide distribution of wreckage.

What is being sought? Accurate knowledge of something that can never be fully replicated. That airliner crash knowledge deficiency likewise exists in criminal situations that forensic sciences attempt to solve. Therefore, pursuit of what, how, and why of airliner crashes – utilizing FDR data – is explored for its application to forensic sciences.

Desired Knowledge

Knowledge about past events – regardless of nature – is always limited. Airline disasters suffer this limitation in several ways.

First, a limit exists because there are seldom any surviving on-scene witnesses. So knowledge can only be inferred by deduction.

Second, even if witnesses survive, humans are not accurate observers. They have limited sensory capacity at best. Eyewitnesses of any accident are rarely unanimous in recalling what happened.

Third, human recollection of major disasters often atrophies over time as testimonies disagree. Therefore, individual witness memory is quite unreliable.

Fourth, there can be motivational conflict in obtaining truth of what has transpired. On one hand, desire for revenge, emotional resolution, justice, future prevention, or historical accuracy stimulates intensity to pursue such knowledge. But on the other hand, witnesses of tragedies often desire to suppress or purge painful recollection of them.

Despite these limitations, postevent knowledge is essential to understanding how both airline crashes and major criminal acts occur.

Seeking Causation

A force for obtaining knowledge of past events is the belief that they were caused. This emanates from the philosophical concept of causality – where one event is believed to produce a responding subsequent event. An airliner crash thereby becomes an outcome of an initial cause or causes that enabled the disaster to occur.

Single Versus Multiple Causes

Seldom are catastrophes due to a singular cause. The NTSB, initially part of the Department of Transportation (DOT), was separated in 1974 from DOT by Congress as an independent agency and charged with determining the probable cause(s) of aircraft accidents. However, for many years thereafter, controversy and political pressure within the NTSB forced it to promote singularity of causation.

On one hand, advocates of adversary truth favored a sharp, singular focus on defining fault that would facilitate legal action following a crash. Underlying this position was blame assessment but thereby subordinating loss prevention (the prime NTSB objective).

On the other hand, proponents of technical truth insisted that causality is never singular. Being forced to discard the known causes (or list them only as contributory to a single cause in order to select only one) needlessly fragmented the causality search.

Testimony before the US Senate on 22 October 1985 resolved this controversy in favor of the scientific position that retains pursuit of causation plurality and assures focus on maximizing safety.

Approximate Versus Proximate Cause

There are two types of causation in the law: cause-in-fact and proximate or legal cause. Cause-in-fact says, 'But for this, the accident would not have occurred . . . ' while proximate cause is an event directly related to a loss and held to be its cause.

Given that aircraft crashes have several causes, the purpose of seeking causation is to (a) define, (b) isolate, and (c) remove or control all factors believed to have contributed to the crash.

The US Air Commerce Act uses 'probable cause' to define aircraft accident causation. This term stops short of 'proximate cause' to remove any stigma of blameworthiness. This distinction allows investigators to freely discuss anything related to an accident without fear of legal action.

This contrast between proximate and probable cause may likely affect digital recording in forensic science. Beyond that distinction, two contrasting – negative and positive – concepts regarding accident causation in Figure 2 may also influence forensic data recording.

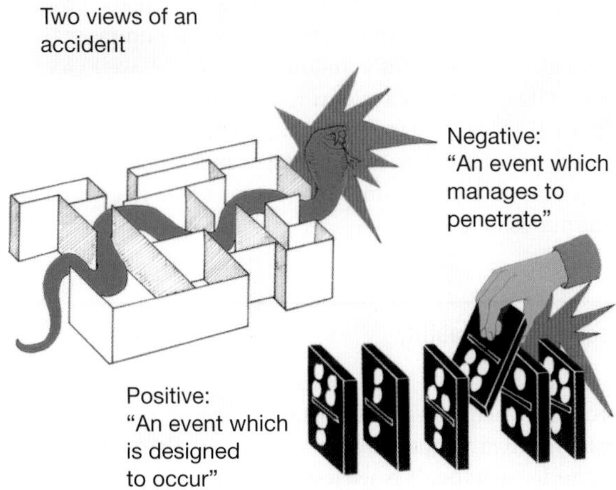

Figure 2 Contrasting views of causation.

First, the public believes that most airliner crashes somehow occur in spite of all countermeasures incorporated to prevent them – much like a snake mysteriously slithering with diabolical intent through a maze of preventive measures.

A second view – proposed by Dr. Nestor B. Kowalsky – is that an aircraft crash is a positive, successful event – inevitable when preceded by a series of committed or omitted acts. It is created by decisions. Thereby, FDRs identify some of the dominoes to be eliminated to preclude future crashes.

Role of Evidence in Establishing Truth

Knowledge of truth about the past – whether pursued by adversary or technical means – ultimately becomes classified as evidence. It has different meanings in the law (adversary truth) and in airliner crash investigation (technical truth).

Evidence produced by FDRs is generally objective (free from human manipulation) and can be interpreted by experts in science, engineering, psychology, sociology, management, and operations.

Digital Versus Analog Evidence

The FDR evidence is either digital or analog. Digital information consists of discrete values of quantized time, frequency, and amplitude. Those signals are not subject to interpretation as to content (though there may be interpretive disagreement regarding raw data conversion into engineering units). Analog information consists of continuous phenomena with no quantized or discrete variances. Its recorded output is therefore subject to interpretation as to meaning and significance.

Multiengine, turbine-powered aircraft carrying over ten passengers must have an FDR. A cockpit voice recorder (CVR) is required for multiengine aircraft with two pilots, which carry over six passengers. FDR inputs are digital while CVR inputs are analog. When both recorders are recovered and their outputs can be correlated on a common time line, unique evidence of what has transpired is available.

Validity of FDR digital data – being virtually free of interpretation – is universal, giving it objectivity over CVR analog evidence. CVRs record more than cockpit conversation. All audio data in the cockpit, including switch clicks, wind noise, control equipment operation, and ambient acoustics such as engine pitch are available. However, translating, interpreting, analyzing, and affirming recorded conversation requires excellent linguistic and cultural skills.

Aircraft Flight Data Recorder History

The genesis of flight data recorders was a series of mysterious crashes in 1953 of the world's first jet airliner – the British 'Comet.' The Comet revolutionized commercial flight in altitude, speed, quietness, and freedom from vibration – until several of them crashed inexplicably.

Cause of Comet disasters was not soon determined. Dr. David Warren (1925–2010), a Principal Research Scientist for the Aeronautical Research Laboratories in Melbourne, Australia was engaged to investigate the crashes.

Dr. Warren early proposed recording flight crew voices in the cockpit. Initially, his idea raised little interest. He built an experimental device to store four hours of speech and flight instrument readings. He then published a report 'A Device for Assisting Investigation into Aircraft Accidents.' But it took 5 years for the device to be accepted.

Warren's first recorder was produced in 1958. It was about the size of an adult hand but was rejected by Australian aviation experts who said it had 'little immediate direct use in civil aircraft.' Pilots joined opposition by calling it 'a spy flying alongside.' Warren then took it to England where their aviation experts endorsed it – urging its installation in all British civil aircraft.

Before long, aircraft flight recorders were adopted – for both cockpit sounds and aircraft performance – by 1964, the US Federal Aviation Administration (hereinafter FAA) mandated them in commercial aircraft.

'Black Boxes'

News media early began to call flight data recorders 'black boxes.' This designator may be traced to its use in technology as 'a device, system, or object viewed solely for its input, output, and transfer characteristics without concern about its internal workings.' In that sense, how black boxes function may be unknown – even unnecessary to be understood but only to be useful – and thereby opaque or black.

However, flight data recorders are never black in color. In stark contrast, they are painted International Orange or Yellow (per US Federal Standard 595) to increase their visibility for recovery from amidst wreckage.

Cockpit Voice Recorder Hostility

From the beginning, pilots opposed recorders in a cockpit based on their reduction of the pilot's personal privacy.

No other profession endures the surveillance, oversight, and potential for second guessing – particularly after death – that CVRs represent. Voice recordings cannot fully provide rationale for past human behavior, especially under stressful circumstances. CVRs personify George Orwell's '1984' Big Brother syndrome to pilots.

On the other hand, airline passengers totally surrender their lives to pilots when the door closes, and the aircraft departs the terminal. This unusual transfer of life-and-death responsibility to someone unknown seems to justify unusual accountability and oversight.

Beyond this pilot–passenger trust relationship is the larger issue of maintaining airline safety. Obtaining recorded cockpit audio following a fatal crash enhances prevention of future disasters – invaluable in advancing flight safety.

Thus, tension between pilot freedom and airline passenger dependence on the pilot is likely to continue.

Evolution of Recording Processes

Flight recording technology has progressed in parallel with commercial aircraft development. The first generation of recorders – installed in early jet airliners such as B-707, DC-8, and Caravelle – recorded five analog aircraft parameters (heading, altitude, airspeed, vertical accelerations, and time).

To survive high impact velocity and sustained postimpact fire, the readouts of five parameters were embossed onto a metal foil (Incanol Steel) used only once (i.e., not recorded on a repeatable loop). Although the recording foil was nearly indestructible, crash survival of these recorders was a serious problem. By 1965, the original 100 g (100 times the accelerative force of impact by simply being dropped) requirement was upgraded to 1000 g.

A second FDR generation emerged after aircraft performance data proved insufficient for determining accident causation. Magnetic tape technology (recording data in digital format) was adopted for FDRs, replacing metal foil. These upgraded FDRs covered additional parameters such as engines, flight controls, and flaps. Use of magnetic tape, however, required even more complex fire and crash protection. This second class of FDRs was installed in B-747, DC-10, L-1011, and A300 wide-body aircraft during the late 1960s and early 1970s.

Based on Dr. David Warren's earlier work, advanced audio recording technology enabled capture of a wider range of cockpit sounds, including crew conversation, air traffic control communications, and aircraft noises. By 1965, all US commercial airlines carrying over 20 passengers had a CVR retaining the latest 30 min of cockpit sounds.

A third generation of solid-state recorders was available by 1990. These recorders store data in semiconductor memories or integrated circuits – replacing electromechanical techniques. One of its advantages is that such memory does not require scheduled maintenance or overhaul. At present, solid-state recorders provide vastly expanded data while also saving airline operational costs when the aircraft is in service. Stored flight data in these recorders can be readily evaluated for aircraft flight performance or whether a device requires maintenance.

Adaptation of solid-state recorders for the CVR occurred later than for the FDR – primarily because more memory capacity was required for audio data. In 1992, a 30-min CVR became available. By 1995, a 2-h CVR was introduced.

Most current FDRs receive inputs via specific data frames from a flight data acquisition unit (FDAU) that records many flight parameters – including control and actuator positions, engine information, and time of day. A minimum of 88 parameters are currently required (only 29 were required until 2002), but some systems today monitor even thousands of variables. Most parameters are recorded a few times per second, but some data are stored at a much higher frequency. FDRs record a minimum time frame of 25 h of data in a continuous loop.

Recorder Survivability

Two simultaneous and violent forces are unleashed on recorders when an aircraft crashes – high impact velocity and sustained high-temperature fire. As technically sophisticated as a recorder may be, it is useless unless it survives those forces generated by the very event it is designed to record. Therefore, recorder survival is fundamental.

Figure 3 Flight data recording and storage.

First, if the aircraft is integral when impacting the ground, recorders must survive not only that initial blow but also a possible secondary impact if they are launched by explosion of jet fuel. Early recorders were installed in the forward avionics bay of the aircraft and required to survive a 100 g impact. After several crashes, recorders failed to survive. At present, the acceleration requirement has been raised from 100 g to the current 3400 g for 6.5 ms.

The second survival factor for recorders is fire generated by Jet A or Jet A-1 fuel with open air burning temperatures of 1000 °C. This fuel can ignite other aircraft materials surrounding the recorders, resulting in even higher ambient temperatures. Damage by fire is dependent on not only temperature but also time at temperature. So, at present, recorders must survive 1100 °C for 1 h.

Additional recorder requirements exist for penetration resistance, static crush, deep-sea pressure, sea water immersion, and fluid immersion.

Installed Location of Flight Data Recorders

After increasing recorder impact requirement to 1000 g, the FAA also required relocation of both CVR and FDR recorders to the rear of the aircraft where survival was believed to be higher. **Figure** 3 shows the position of both recorders and their recording pickup instrumentation.

Relocation rationale was that most crashes occur while the aircraft is moving forward and considerable energy is absorbed before the tail impacts the ground. Further, as the aircraft breaks apart, the tail is often separated from remaining wreckage and fuel sources in the wings. Of course, this reasoning does not apply when the aircraft disintegrates in the air before hitting ground or water, for example, following an airborne explosion.

Underwater Locator Beacons

Both CVR and FDR have an underwater locator beacon (ULB) to assist in locating them following an overwater airliner crash. The ULB – called a 'pinger' – is activated once it is immersed in water. Therefore, it never emits a signal following crashes on land. The pinger transmits a 37.5-kHz acoustical signal detected only with a special receiver. It can transmit from depths down to 14 000 ft.

Recorder manufacturers install pingers as part of their individual recorder models. The airline owning and installing a recorder is required to replace its pinger batteries to keep them operational. Required pinger life is 6 years.

Government Regulation

The Air Line Pilots Association International (ALPA), founded in 1931, currently represents 59 000 pilots of 39 US and Canadian airlines. The ALPA was an early and vocal opponent of the CVR.

An initial ALPA-NTSB compromise stipulated (a) 30-min duration of retained recorded information, (b) flight crew erasure of recording once on the ground, and (c) disclosure of recorded information only for accident investigation. CVR acceptance by airline pilots is thereby viewed as a reasonable, needed component of aircraft crash investigation.

However, political pressure occasionally arises to expand CVR use beyond accident investigation to disciplinary enforcement of pilot behavior that violates the 'sterile cockpit' rule. That rule prohibits, below 10 000 ft, any cockpit conversation not directly related to flight operation.

The source of such pressure is generally public reaction – stimulated by dramatic news media coverage – to obtained

CVR recordings that reveal bizarre or irrelevant chatter or behavior in the cockpit.

In February 2010, the US Senate Pilot Professionalism Act (S.3048) was introduced 'to improve air safety by authorizing the limited use by air carriers of information collected through CVRs and flight data recorders, to prohibit tampering with such devices, and for other purposes.'

Both the ALPA and the Coalition of Airline Pilots Associations (CAPA) representing over 28 000 pilots objected seriously to this bill because it could allow airlines to administer discipline – even terminate or require a pilot to pass a proficiency check in a simulator – based on CVR and FDR findings.

Ultimately, S.3048 was not adopted.

Public Access to Voice Recordings

Interest in listening to final minutes of a fatal aircraft crash occasionally arises. On some occasions, families of deceased pilots have demanded to listen to those final moments of life. News media also seek recordings to satisfy public interest after crashes. Increasing electronic capability and exposure via the Internet have made recordings available – although a large percentage of alleged recordings are created artificially.

Historically, the NTSB has exercised tight discipline in permitting cockpit voice recordings to be heard only by parties engaged in translating and converting conversation to written format. The recorders are the property of the involved airline. Once a transcription of the CVR has been officially documented, the recorder is released back to its airline owner who is responsible for whatever public access is subsequently obtained.

The US Congress has imposed reasonable restrictions on the use of CVR materials. It exempts CVR data from Freedom of Information Act requests. In the Transportation Safety Act, Congress limited public disclosure of CVR data involving aircraft crash investigations. However, that Act allows the NTSB to publicize any transcript segment believed relevant to a crash – provided it holds a public hearing or if it is discussed along with other factual reports at the same time. The Board is also allowed to refer to CVR recordings in its safety recommendations.

A court may allow discovery of a CVR recording or transcript without prior public release of the information. If the CVR transcript is publicly released, the transcript becomes discoverable. Each CVR audio transcription released to the public by the NTSB carries the warning shown in Figure 4.

The Bureau d'Enquetes et d'Analyses (hereinafter BEA) is the French equivalent to NTSB. Citing Article 14 of the European Regulation of 20 October 2010 as its policy standard governing public release of CVR transcripts, it came into effect on 2 December 2010 following the crash of Air France Flight 447.

NTSB warning on cockpit recording transcription

- The reader of this report is cautioned that the transcription of a CVR tape is not a precise science but is the best product possible from an NTSB group investigative effort.
- The transcript, or parts thereof, if taken out of context, could be misleading.
- The attached CVR transcript should be viewed as an accident investigation tool to be used in conjunction with other evidence gathered during the investigation.
- Conclusions or interpretations should not be made using the transcript as the sole source of information

Figure 4 CVR transcript protection.

Current Recorder State-of-the-Art

Recorder technology continues to expand. At periodic intervals, the FAA upgrades performance requirements as shown in Figure 5. These revisions result from technological, operational, and financial forces that demand increasing knowledge of truth about the past to advance airline safety.

Image Recorders

Superiority of visual-and-aural images over oral recordings to obtain knowledge of the past is undeniable. Therefore, video technology increases to be considered to augment CVR output. Cockpit video recorders are not yet required in commercial airliners, but they are installed in smaller aircraft and helicopters.

Cultural Repercussion of Recorders

Two airliner crashes are summarized to illustrate the significant role recorders have played in international, political, cultural, and business controversies, thereby highlighting the influence that recorders can contribute to ascertaining truth.

EgyptAir Flight 990

On 31 October 1999, the Boeing 767 en route from JFK airport in New York to Cairo crashed into the Atlantic Ocean about 60 miles south of Nantucket Island, Massachusetts, killing all 217 people on board. As the crash occurred in international waters, the Egyptian Civil Aviation Authority (ECAA) had investigation responsibility. But since ECAA lacked adequate technical resources, the Egyptian government asked the NTSB to conduct the investigation.

Within two weeks, NTSB proposed transferring the investigation to the US Federal Bureau of Investigation (FBI) since evidence suggested that (a) a criminal act had taken place and (b) the crash was intentional rather than accidental. The Egyptians rejected this proposal. So the NTSB continued to lead the investigation.

As evidence of the deliberate crash increased, the Egyptian government reversed itself, and the ECAA began its own investigation. The two investigations reached conflicting conclusions. NTSB concluded that the cause was a deliberate action of the EgyptAir Relief First Officer (RFO). ECAA found the cause to be the mechanical failure of the airplane's elevator control system.

FAA proposed revisions of aircraft recorders 24 February 2005	
Cockpit voice recorders (CVRs)	
Proposed	Current
Two hours recording time	15–30 min recording time; valuable communications can be taped over
No magnetic tape recorders	Magnetic tape OK; can sustain damage in crash
10-minute independent backup power supply	Recorder stops if aircraft electrical power fails
Standardized recording start: Begins when pilots start checklist	Variable requirements for recording start
Mounted in box separate from FDR (except helicopters)	Separate box is FAA policy but not a regulation
No single electrical failure can disable both CVR and FDR	Both CVR and FDR can stop working if aircraft electrical power fails
Flight data recorders (FDRs)	
Proposed	Current
Measurement of control surface (rudder, ailerons, elevators, etc.) movements every 0.0625 s	Measurements every 0.25 or 0.5 s; may not permit accurate reconstruction of movements in all circumstances
Measurement of pilot inputs on control wheel, control column, rudder pedals (airplanes aircraft) every 0.0625 s	Measurements every 1 s; may not permit accurate reconstruction of forces in all circumstances
Measurement of cockpit controls and flight control surfaces (helicopters) 4X per second	Measurements 2X per second; may not permit accurate reconstruction of movements in all circumstances
Mounted in box separate from CVR (except helicopters)	Separate box is FAA policy but not a regulation
No single electrical failure can disable both CVR and FDR	Both CVR and FDR can stop working if aircraft electrical power fails

Figure 5 Aircraft recorder updating.

Both CVR and FDR provided determinative evidence that (a) the RFO had committed suicide by deliberately diving the aircraft into the ocean and (b) no mechanical failure scenario could have produced the aircraft movements recorded by the FDR.

An international firestorm erupted. Egypt's state-owned *Al Ahram Al Misai* called RFO Al-Batouti a 'martyr.' The Islamist *Al Shaab* newspaper even accused US officials of secretly recovering the FDR, reprogramming it, and throwing it back into the water to be publicly recovered.

Given strong Egyptian cultural aversion to suicide, the possibility of a common NTSB–ECAA agreement on probable cause evaporated. The NTSB probable cause, however, avoided discussing suicide.

> The airplane's departure from normal cruise flight and subsequent impact with the Atlantic Ocean was a result of the relief first officer's flight control inputs. The reason for the relief first officer's actions was not determined.

Air France Flight 447

On 1 June 2009, the Airbus A330-200 aircraft crashed in the Atlantic Ocean en route from Rio de Janeiro to Paris, killing 228 persons. After 30 months of investigation, BEA had not determined probable cause – as CVR and FDR were not recovered for 23 months. CVR and FDR unavailability allowed widespread and conflicting speculation – overshadowed by several factors seldom acknowledged publicly.

First, intensive worldwide competition in the commercial aircraft market between Airbus and Boeing meant that US markets were pitted against those in Europe – even free enterprise (Boeing) challenging government enterprise (Airbus).

Second, these two aircraft giants employ contrasting approaches to the pilot–aircraft interface. To summarize: Boeing designs aircraft control around the pilot as primary, augmented by automation while Airbus reverses those roles – automation prime, pilot as secondary. While the Airbus approach eases the piloting load, its automation is more complex and less intuitive.

Third, where Boeing has continued to use the traditional control yoke in front of the pilot, Airbus employs a control sidestick beside the pilot. Advocates for both approaches abound but controversy remains – primarily because the 'feel' or feedback to pilot varies considerably.

Air France announced 3 days after the crash that an onboard monitoring system had transmitted – before crashing – a 4-min series of electronic messages concerning failures and warnings in navigation, autoflight, flight controls, and cabin air-conditioning. These sketchy data – while insufficient for cause determination – ignited extensive but unresolved prognosis about both crew and aircraft performance that persisted for over two years.

On 7 June 2009, the AF447 vertical stabilizer was recovered (confirming crash location), so initial search for the recorders ensued. Three more independent recovery attempts occurred before 2 May 2011, when both CVR and FDR were found in about 13 000 ft of water. Amazingly, data on both recorders were recovered.

During the years since the crash, recorders have remained the prime focal point. Their recovery, however, failed to resolve its probable cause even after nearly three years likely because of two unique factors – the responsibility for investigation and anticipated legal culpability. In contrast to NTSB investigations in the United States, the French government opened two independent and simultaneous investigations of AF447.

Technical Investigation

BEA was charged with the investigation since the aircraft was of French registration and crashed over international waters. Representatives from Brazil, Germany, UK, and United States were directly involved. In addition, observers were appointed from China, Croatia, Hungary, Ireland, Italy, Lebanon, Morocco, Norway, South Korea, Russia, South Africa, and Switzerland because their citizens were onboard.

Criminal Investigation

French law requires – for any accident involving loss of life (but implying no presumption of foul play) – that manslaughter be charged against Air France and Airbus. This investigation has been overseen by the Gendarmerie nationale, which conducted it through its aerial transportation division (Gendarmerie des transports aériens or GTA) and its forensic research institute (Institut de Recherche Criminelle de la Gendarmerie Nationale or FR).

Expanded Employment of Recorders

As data recorders gain acceptance, aviation is not the only transportation mode utilizing them. In 1993, the Federal Railroad Administration (FRA) required event data recorder (EDRs) in locomotives.

An EDR is also being installed in automobiles to record vehicle information immediately before and/or during a serious crash. Police and crash investigators download EDR data to learn what happened to the vehicle and how its safety features are performed. In some cases, those data help establish culpability.

Most EDRs are built into a vehicle's airbag control module and record data on airbag deployment. Some vehicles also record precrash data, such as engine throttle and vehicle speed from the engine control module. Certain airbag and engine control modules store only diagnostic trouble codes and whether there was a signal to deploy supplemental restraint systems (i.e., airbags and belt tensioners).

Built-in vehicle modules are not considered to be an EDR. Therefore, they are not governed by Federal regulations, as are EDRs that record vehicle speed before a crash or speed change during impact.

In summary, there is no way that David Warren could have foreseen how aircraft flight recorders would impact both civil and criminal litigation. They also affected economics of the expert witness field. The Collision Safety Institute reports that expert testimony based on EDR data has increased both criminal convictions and death-penalty sentences, as well as high-dollar verdicts in civil cases.

See also: **Engineering:** Analysis of Digital Evidence; Human Factors Investigation and Analysis of Accidents and Incidents; **Forensic Medicine/Clinical:** Airplane Crashes and Other Mass Disasters; **Investigations:** Explosions; Major Incident Scene Management; Recording; **Legal:** History of the Law's Reception of Forensic Science.

Further Reading

Craig MW (2008) *Thinking outside the black box: how an electronic security device became a police informant.* http://works.bepress.com/mary_craig/1.

Grose VL (1987a) *Managing Risk.* Englewood Cliffs, NJ: Prentice Hall.

Grose VL (1987b) *Commercial Airline 'Margin of Safety'.* Presidential Aviation Safety Commission. Aviation Safety Commission report ISBN-13: 9780160032875.

Grose VL (1987c) *Coping with Boredom in the Cockpit Before It's too Late.* Presidential Aviation Safety Commission. Aviation Safety Commission report ISBN-13: 9780160032875.

Grose VL (1995a) Your Next Airline Flight: Worth the Risk? *Risk Management* 42(4): 47–56.

Grose VL (1995b) Technology's Impact on Human Risk. *Proceedings of the Marine Safety Council* 52: 57–63.

DIGITAL EVIDENCE/PHOTOGRAPHY AND DIGITAL IMAGING

Digital Imaging and Photography: An Overview

P Jones, Purdue University, West Lafayette, IN, USA

Glossary

Charged coupled device The sensor that acts 'sees' the image and records it to magnetic media.
IR Infrared light.
Jpg or jpeg Joint Photographic Experts Group. A lossy compression format.
Lossless A compression format that allows the exact original data to be reconstructed from the compressed file.
Lossy A compression encoding format that compresses data by losing some of it.
Meter A meter equals 39.37 inch. The meter is the length of the path traveled by light in vacuum during a time interval of 1/299 792 458 of a second.
Nanometer 1/1 000 000 000 of a meter.
Single-lens reflex (SLR) SLR camera. A camera that has a moving mirror system that allows the photographer to see exactly what the lens 'sees.'
tif or tiff Tagged image format. A lossless compression format.
UV Ultraviolet light.
Visible spectrum 400–750 nm.

History of Images in Forensic Science

The use of images to reconstruct a crime scene goes back to the early days of photography. In the 1880s, Jack the Ripper was active in London, England. In 1888, photography was used to document and record both victims and crime scenes (Figures 1 and 2). There were no 'rules' or 'best practices'; in fact, there were no 'forensic photographers.' The local newspaper photographers were summoned by the police to take the picture. There was no complete coverage taken, in most cases, just one or two images were taken. It is only possible to image the level of reconstruction of the Whitechapel murders that could be done today if a complete set of images were taken.

What is photography and digital photo imaging? Reducing it to its most basic definition, it is the capturing of an image of a person, place, or thing at a specific time and place. Photography and digital photo imaging are synonymous. Photography has been identified with film cameras while digital photo imaging has been associated with using digital media as an image storage device. Both record an image of a person, place, or thing, and they differ only as far as to the media on which the image is stored. This is similar to moonshiners' still and a professional brand maker's still. They both end up with whiskey; each uses a different method to get to the end product.

When the image of a person, place, or thing is 'captured,' the object is not actually captured, but rather the reflected light from that object. Photons from a light source are projected toward an object of interest or are in the path of an existing photon producing light source such as the sun. The object of interest, the moon, does not generate energy or photons; therefore, only the reflected light (from the sun) is seen when one looks at the moon.

Human eyes work the same way as the camera. The eyes see the reflected light from objects. The human eye is much more complicated than any camera, allowing us to see in low, normal, and intense light. Human eyes and brain make adjustments so that one sees effectively color balanced, proper contrast, and brightness – all, automatically.

Forensic

The term 'forensic' is often misunderstood. As a result of the many 'CSI' shows on television and the movies, it has come to mean anything from murder investigations, crime scene work, to laboratory analysis. Breaking it down to the most basic, it means 'as pertains to a court of law.' For example, if an individual is a plumber, and he testifies in a court concerning plumbing, be it a criminal or a civil court, he has acted as a 'forensic plumber.' Forensic science is applying a specific discipline of science to a court or legal proceeding. Forensic imaging or forensic digital imaging is applying photography to a court or legal action.

Technical Photography Versus Creative Photography

Technical photography reconstructs a person, place, or thing with exacting accuracy without distortion. It has to show, in many cases to a juror, exactly what a scene, a victim, or perhaps

 http://dx.doi.org/10.1016/B978-0-12-382165-2.00126-4

Figure 1 The mortuary photo of Elizabeth Stride, one of two prostitutes who was murdered in the Whitechapel district of London on 30 September 1888 by Jack the Ripper.

Figure 2 Mary Jane Kelly was found lying on a bed in a single room at 13 Miller's Court on Friday, 9 November 1888.

Figure 3 Kodacolor 35 mm film.

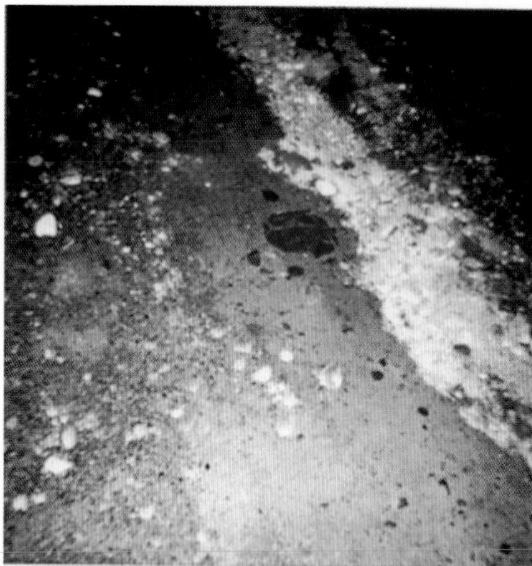

Figure 4 Polaroid picture shot at a crime scene. A positive image only, no negative is produced. It can only be duplicated by rephotography or scanning.

a weapon looked like without distorting distance, perspective, and, in some cases, lighting. Forensic photographers have to be able to answer in the affirmative when asked, 'Does this picture, taken by you, truly and accurately depict the scene on the date and time in question?'

Forensic photographers are not creative photographers who will photograph a person on his or her 'best side,' but rather on all sides so that the scene is accurate and not misleading. Photographs are taken to assist in reconstruction of the scene, not for beauty. It is necessary when a forensic photographer photographs an item for record that the object be photographed with the camera at 90° to the object so that the object is not distorted. This is important. Perception can be skewed. Draw a circle on a sheet of paper. Look at it at 90°. One sees a circle. View the same circle at 10°. The circle appears to be an oval. If the picture is taken at this angle, what is the answer to the question: 'Does this picture, taken by you, truly and accurately depict the scene on the date and time in question?'

The Film Camera

The film camera records images on film. There are many different types of films. Black and white negative, color negative (both of these used to make positives or photographic pictures), color reversal (slides), and many special-purpose films, as well as infrared (IR), ortho, and the like. The film is currently made of cellulose acetate originally introduced by Kodak, 1908. Black and white film has a single emulsion of silver halides which is sensitive to light. Once 'exposed' to light, it must be developed in chemicals to produce a negative which can then be 'printed' to photographic paper. Color film has a minimum of three emulsion layers and films such as Kodacolor II (**Figure 3**), a color negative film, has as many as 12 emulsion layers.

The Polaroid camera, while not a film camera, is also not a digital camera either. It was used in years past in forensic photography, when a positive image was needed immediately (**Figure 4**) – immediately was a minimum of 60 s. It produced a developed positive photo image. While the camera did produce a good picture, usually measuring 3″ × 3″, it did not have a negative. If additional copies were needed, one would have to rephotograph the positive Polaroid image with a 35-mm or other camera which produced a negative, then have that negative printed. This resulted in degradation of the copy. A 'generation' was lost when the copy was made. Since the advent of digital imaging, obtaining an 'instant image' is truly instant. Not only can the images be seen and checked for quality in less than a second, but also an exact duplicate of the original can be copied, enlarged, and sent to the other side of the world instantaneously with no loss of resolution from the original. The other issue has always been cost. Each 3″ × 3″ image costs over a dollar each.

The 'speed' of the film or, more properly, the sensitivity of the film to light measured in a scale 'ISO' (former scales such as ASA – American Standards Association, now ANSI and DIN – Deutsches Institut fur Normung) must be part of the calculation to determine a properly exposed picture. Other parts of the calculation are shutter speed and aperture. The higher the film's ISO rating, the more sensitive the film is to light.

The Digital Camera

The 'Point and Shoot' Digital Camera

The digital 'point and shoot' camera has significantly improved over the past several years. Modeled after the 'instamatic' 126 and the 'disposable' 35-mm cameras, these cameras have sufficient quality to be used in forensic photography (**Figure** 5). They have many features of the digital single-lens reflex (SLR), yet are somewhat inexpensive. Many of their features are equal to that of the digital SLR. The Nikon Coolpix, for example, is 14 MP (megapixel) and can take 720p videos. Their limitations are the fixed lens and limited controls on the camera. Composing the image is done through the camera's image sensor seen on the LCD view screen on the back of the camera.

Digital Imaging

The term 'digital imaging' is very often confused with photo digital imaging. Digital imaging refers to the material stored on a computers' hard drive, data stored on memory cards and other types of storage media, and on other various computer-like devices such as iPhones, iPads, cell phones, and pagers. SWGDE, the Scientific Working Group on Digital Evidence, is the working group tasked with the creation of 'best practices' associated with digital evidence stored on magnetic media. This includes memory cards, CDs, DVD, and hard drives. The entire SWGDE document is available on the web at http://www.swgde.org/.

Digital SLR

The digital SLR is similar in concept to the film camera. It is focused on an object and light is allowed to flow through the lens when its shutter is opened and it is then recorded on the film (**Figures** 6 and 7). The digital SLR's adjustment knobs are 'read' on an LED screen instead of increments marked on the dials. One of the major differences is in how the image is recorded. In the film camera, the shutter is opened and reflected light from the object of interest is allowed to show on the sensor. In most digital cameras, this sensor is a CCD or charged coupled device. In more expensive digital SLRs. the sensor is a c-mos.

The digital SLR differs from the point and shoot camera in that one looks through the lens which is used to record the image on to the magnetic media (**Figure** 8). This is

Figure 5 Nikon Coolpix 3100 point and shoot camera.

Figure 6 Nikon digital SLR camera front view.

Figure 7 Nikon digital SLR camera rear view.

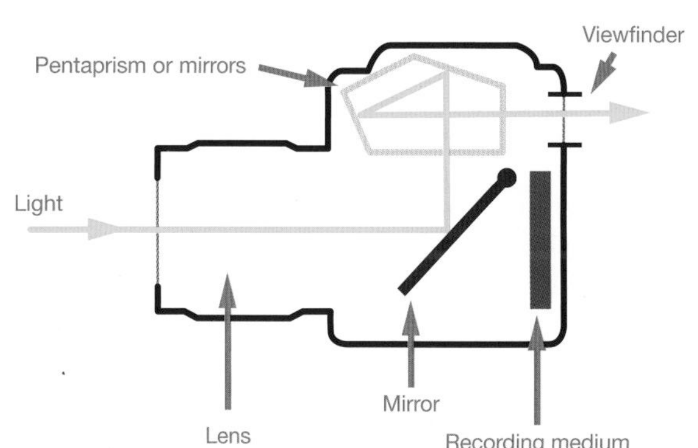

Figure 8 Diagram of an single-lens reflex (SLR) camera.

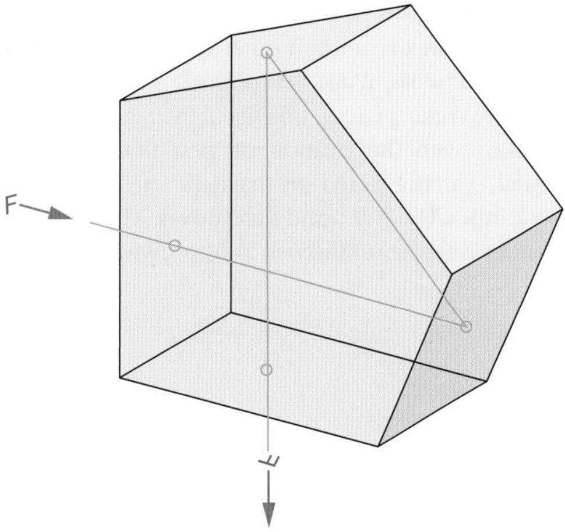

Figure 9 This is a pentaprism. Used inside SLR cameras so the photographer can see exactly what the lens sees.

Figure 10 Logo of SWGIT – Scientific Working Group on Imaging Technology.

accomplished by the use of a mechanical mirror system and a pentaprism to direct light from the lens to the sensor in the camera (**Figure 9**).

Scientific Working Group on Imaging Technology

SWGIT is the Scientific Working Group on Imaging Technology. The Technical Working Group on Imaging Technology was formed by the Federal Bureau of Investigation in December 1997. In 1999, the name of the group was changed to the SWGIT. The group has been comprised of individuals from federal, state, and local law enforcement agencies, the American military, academia, foreign law enforcement agencies, and other researchers. Those selected for membership in the group are experienced professionals working in the field of imaging technology or a related field and demonstrate the willingness to participate by consulting on the release of best practices and guidelines for the use of imaging technology in the Criminal Justice System (**Figure 10**). Because SWGIT is so interwoven with forensic digital photo imaging, individual sections have been listed:

Section	*Title*
Section 1	Overview of SWGIT and the use of imaging technology in the criminal justice system
Section 2	Considerations for managers migrating to digital imaging technology
Section 3	Field photography equipment and supporting infrastructure
Section 4	Recommendations and guidelines for using closed-circuit television security systems in commercial institutions
Section 5	Guidelines for image processing
Section 6	Guidelines and recommendations for training in imaging technologies in the criminal justice system
Section 7	Best practices for forensic video analysis
Section 8	General guidelines for capturing latent impressions using a digital camera
Section 9	General guidelines for photographing tire impressions
Section 10	General guidelines for photographing footwear impressions
Section 11	Best practices for documenting image enhancement
Section 12	Best practices for forensic image analysis
Section 13	Best practices for maintaining the integrity of digital images and digital video
Section 14	Best practices for image authentication
Section 15	Best practices for archiving digital and multimedia evidence (DME) in the criminal justice system
Section 16	Best practices for forensic photographic comparison
Section 17	Digital imaging technology issues for the courts
Section 18	Best practices for automated image processing
Section 19	Issues relating to digital image compression and file formats
Section 20	Recommendations and guidelines for crime scene/critical incident videography – DRAFT; open for public comment until 23 September 2011
Section 21	Procedure for testing scanner resolution for latent print imaging – DRAFT; open for public comment until 23 September 2011
Section 22	Procedure for testing digital camera system resolution for latent print photography – DRAFT; open for public comment until 23 September 2011

Admissibility in Court of Digital Photo Images

Since the word 'forensic' is defined as 'as relates to a court of law,' there has been much discussion concerning the admissibility of digital photo images in court proceedings. Several of these untruths are discussed here.

- Digital images can be manipulated, film images cannot. This is false. Film images can also be altered. It is just more difficult. Both altered film and digital images can be examined and discovered to be altered or not altered.
- Film has a higher resolution than digital images. This is false. As technology progresses (it seems on a daily basis), digital cameras are available that produce 25-MP images. This surpasses the much-used 100-speed (ISO) film used in crime scene photography.
- Digital cameras do not accurately depict color. No again. The sensor in the digital camera is no more or no less accurate in recording color.
- All digital images must be electronically authenticated in order to be admissible in court. Digital images, film images, and other evidence as well as authenticated by TESTIMONY. The courtroom authentication of images must be able to pass the scrutiny of the question 'Does the image in front of you truly and accurately represent the scene on the date and time in question?'

In the past, when color was an issue as to whether it should be shown to a jury, our question, 'Does the image in front of you truly and accurately represent the scene on the date and time in question' must be answered 'No.' This is because the scene was in color and the black and white photo is not. Eventually, color is now a commonly accepted media to use in court.

Additional and more detailed 'myth and facts' can be reviewed in the SWGIT Document, Section 17, on the website http://www.theiai.org/guidelines/swgit/.

Official Images

The official images of a crime scene are the first one's take. This statement is actually very logical. If an image is taken 5 min after a murder, another taken 30 min after the murder, and a third is taken 60 min after the murder, which is most accurate? It again comes down to the question, 'Does the image in front of you truly and accurately represent the scene on the date and time in question?' The image taken 30 min after the murder could be significantly different from the one taken 5 min after the murder. Likewise, the image taken 60 min after the murder could be significantly different from both the 5- and 30-min pictures. Other than having images of a crime scene appear on the evening TV news, this is another good reason to insure the media do not get photo images before the police photographer takes his forensic images.

Photographic Filters

A filter is an optical device placed between the camera lens and the reflected light from the object of the photo. They modify the reflected light from the images in question. A very helpful filter is the polarizing filter. This is an accessory that is placed between the camera lens and the reflected light from the object of interest. Light reflected from, for example, a body of water can be minimized with the use of a polarizing filter. When the filter is rotated, only light polarized in the direction perpendicular to the reflected light is reflected. The filter absorbs much of the reflection. This effect is similar to that seen in Polaroid sunglasses.

There are band-block, band-pass, and special effects filters. Special effects filters are soft focus, star or cross screen (they make all light points into stars), kaleidoscope, and many others.

These special effects filters have little or no use in forensic photo imaging.

Visible light (to the human eye) covers the spectral region of approximately 400–750 nm (**Figures 11–13**).

The band-pass filter allows a specific bandwidth to pass through to the camera's sensor and rejects others outside this bandwidth. This is important when doing IR and UV (ultraviolet) photography.

UV light technologies are used for multiple purposes in forensic investigations, including authenticating paintings and other fine art, authenticating signatures, analyzing

Figure 11 This image is to be hidden in an e-mail or word processing document.

Figure 12 This shows the same image as **Figure 11** but with a white rectangle placed over the picture image. This rectangle can be enlarged to cover the entire picture rendering it virtually invisible.

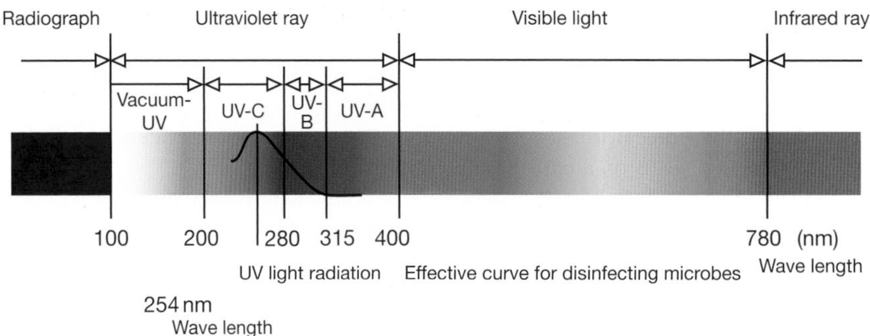

Figure 13 The electromagnetic spectrum.

Figure 14 Fuji IS Pro camera is designed to see light from the IR, UV, and visible light spectrum. It has features that are used in law enforcement, forensic lab, and research applications.

questioned documents, illuminating latent fingerprints at crime scenes and trace evidence on clothing, analyzing ink stains, and revealing residual stains of body fluids.

Fuji IS Pro

The Fuji IS Pro is a digital SLR camera designed for specialty work using IR and UV light.

The camera is designed by Fuji and built around a Nikon frame and using Nikon lenses. It has unique software and modifications developed and designed by Fuji. It does not have a 'hot filter.' The 'hot filter' is a UV/IR band-block filter present in almost all digital cameras (**Figure 14**). The Fuji IS Pro can have a UV/IR band-block filter attached on the front of the lens to allow it to operate as a regular digital SLR, blocking much of the UV and IR wavelengths.

It has some very unique features. One of the best is the 'live image preview.' In the past with film cameras, when using IR film, one would focus on the subject matter, then 'adjust' the focus using the 'little red dot' on the lens. This is because the IR spectrum is slightly out of focus as one looks at it in the visible spectrum. The live preview gives a 20-s window in which you can actually focus the camera, while viewing in the IR spectrum.

Conclusion

This article is an overview of digital forensic photo imaging. It is definitely not all-inclusive and is meant to address only some of its characteristics. Being in an era of technology one should expect to see extreme leaps in technology relating to the photo imaging process. Film photo imaging had come a long way since the 1990s. As the world migrates to digital photo imaging from film photo imaging, one cannot even imagine what is on the horizon. From the author's first digital camera, 1/2 MP, to his current Nikon D300 and its 12.3 MP is a long way to come in just 10 years. Applying this and other digital photo imaging technology to forensic work is a great pleasure. The courts do and will accept new technology as long as one uses good science and operates under rules and standards.

See also: **Digital Evidence:** Cellular Phones; Child Pornography; Digital Imaging: Enhancement and Authentication; **Documents:** Handwriting; Ink Analysis; Paper Analysis; **Engineering:** Accident Investigation – Determination of Cause; Forensic Engineering/Accident Reconstruction/Biomechanics of Injury/Philosophy, Basic Theory, and Fundamentals; **Forensic Medicine/Clinical:** Airplane Crashes and Other Mass Disasters; Suicide; Traffic Injuries and Deaths; **Forensic Medicine/Pathology:** Autopsy; External Postmortem Examination; Postmortem Imaging.

Further Reading

Geberth V (2011a) *Practical Homicide Investigation*, 4th edn. Boca Raton, FL: CRC Press.

Geberth V (2011b) *Sex Related Homicide and Death Investigation*, 2nd edn. Boca Raton, FL: CRC Press.

Jones P (2009) Forensic Digital Photo Imaging. In: James S and Nordby J (eds.) *Forensic Science*, 3rd edn., pp. 185–202. Boca Raton, FL: CRC Press, Taylor and Francis Group.

Jones P (2010) *Practical Forensic Digital Imaging: Applications and Techniques*. Boca Raton, FL: CRC Press, Taylor and Francis Group.
Jones P and Williams RE (2009) *Crime Scene Processing and Laboratory Workbook*. Boca Raton, FL: CRC Press.
Redsicker D (2001) *The Practical Methodology of Forensic Photography*. Boca Raton, FL: CRC Press.
Robinson E (2007) *Crime Scene Photography*. San Diego, CA: Academic Press.
Weiss S (2008) *Forensic Photography: The Importance of Accuracy*. Englewood Cliffs, NJ: Prentice Hall.

Relevant Websites

http://www.swgde.org/ – Scientific Working Group on Digital Evidence.
http://www.theiai.org/guidelines/swgit/ – Scientific Working Group on Imaging Technology.

DOCUMENTS

Contents

Analytical Methods

J de Koeijer, Netherlands Forensic Institute, The Hague, The Netherlands

Glossary

Multispectral analysis Optical analysis of reflection and fluorescence characteristics at various wavelengths in the ultraviolet, visible, and near-infrared region of the electromagnetic spectrum.

Questioned documents analysis The forensic analysis of documents to determine authenticity, date of production, latent contents, or (common) origin.

Introduction

In the past decade, research in document examination has been largely technology driven. The introduction of new analytical techniques has opened the door to new and improved methods for the analysis of inks, toner, and paper. A second driving force has been changes in the materials and technologies used to produce documents, which have fueled the need for new methods of analysis. The move from soluble dye-based inks to insoluble pigment-based inks is a good example of such a change necessitating a new analysis strategy. Document examiners in the past relied heavily on chromatographic techniques such as thin-layer chromatography (TLC) to analyze inks, but these techniques have become increasingly less applicable as modern pigment-based inks such as gel pen ink and black inkjet inks cannot be extracted from the paper anymore. The newer so-called 'hyphenated' techniques with a mass spectrometer as a detector show much potential in this area of analysis, combining high discrimination power with low detection limits. Techniques such as laser ablation inductively coupled plasma mass spectrometry (LA–ICPMS), laser desorption. mass spectrometry, and secondary ion mass spectrometry (SIMS) are now being discovered by document examiners. Also, chromatographic techniques such as thermal desorption gas chromatography–mass spectrometry (TD–GC/MS) and high-performance liquid chromatography–MS (HPLC–MS) have become more and more mainstream and are slowly replacing the traditional analytical methods. Many document examiners, however, often still rely on trusted, nondestructive, relatively inexpensive, and often highly effective techniques such as ultraviolet fluorescence, infrared fluorescence, TLC, Raman spectroscopy (RS), and Fourier transform infrared (FTIR) spectrometry. This article discusses both the traditional and the newer trends of analysis and their application to document examination.

The Traditional Methods

The traditional document analysis methods fall into three main categories: optical, spectroscopic, or chromatographic. Whereas the methods in the first two are essentially nondestructive, often needing little sample preparation, chromatography generally needs a destructive form of sampling.

 http://dx.doi.org/10.1016/B978-0-12-382165-2.00131-8

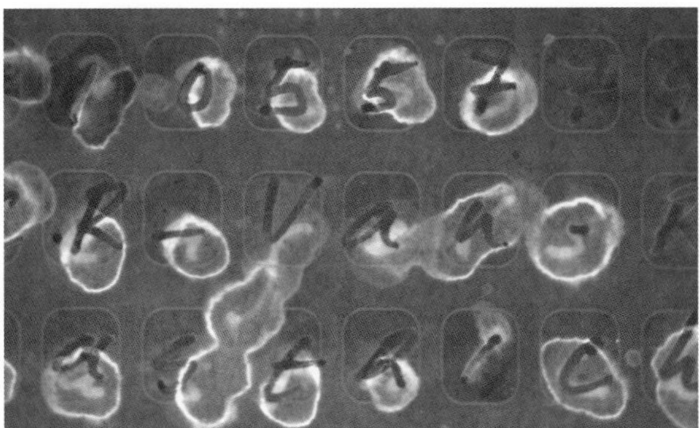

Figure 1 Infrared fluorescent image of the chemical erasure of a bank draft.

Optical Methods

For decades now, document examiners have relied on optical methods exploiting both luminescent and reflective properties of inks and paper for the examination of questioned documents. While the stereomicroscope may still be considered one of the most important tools for an examiner of questioned documents, multispectral examination of documents in the ultraviolet (UV), visible (Vis), and near-infrared (NIR) region of the electromagnetic spectrum has also become one of the first methods a document examiner will turn to in daily casework. In dealing with the authentication of documents or the examination of added, concealed, erased, or faded entries, the luminescent and reflective properties of inks and paper provide document examiners with the possibility of quick discrimination and enhancement of weak or latent features. Manufacturers of security documents have also picked up on this by adding fibers and inks with special luminescent or reflective properties as security features. These may be checked using the standard multispectral equipment a document examiner will normally have access to (Figure 1).

Microscopy, as mentioned earlier, is still an essential part of the examination of a questioned document and is mainly used to study the morphology of the surface of the paper or ink to determine, for example, the writing instrument or printing method used to produce a document, unusual paper fiber disturbance, faint remnants of previous entries, or the sequence in which entries have been placed on the document. Besides the traditional microscopic examinations, miniaturization of security features is also demanding more and more from a microscope in terms of magnification and depth of field. This often forces the document examiner to opt for a digital video microscope, which can deal with these new specifications.

Spectroscopic Methods

Spectroscopy has always been a firm basis for a document examiner to rely on when dealing with the comparison of paper, inks, toners, tapes, etc. The spectroscopic techniques applied to documents may be roughly divided into two main categories: those dealing with elemental analysis and those based more on molecular phenomena.

Elemental spectroscopy

The most commonly used method for elemental spectroscopy is x-ray fluorescence (XRF) spectroscopy or micro XRF (μ-XRF) if smaller areas are to be analyzed. While XRF is often used for comparison of paper, μ-XRF can also be applied to toner and other pigmented inks. Similar applications are also dealt with at a much higher magnification using a scanning electron microscope with an energy dispersive x-ray detector (SEM–EDX or SEM–EDXRF). In the above methods, bombardment of a sample with highly energetic x-rays, gamma rays, or electrons results in the emission of secondary (or fluorescent) x-rays that are characteristic of the elemental content of the sample.

Molecular spectroscopy

Some of the more traditional molecular spectroscopic methods such as FTIR spectroscopy and microspectrophotometry (MSP) are still being used for the analysis and comparison of documents. MSP, now often found on most routinely used multispectral analysis equipment, is mainly used for the comparison of inks based on their UV/Vis/NIR reflection or fluorescence spectrum.

FTIR may, depending on the substrate and the accessories at hand, be used in different operation modes, for example, diffuse reflection (DRIFTS) for powders, (micro)-attenuated total reflection for surface analysis, and diamond cells and FTIR microscopes for micro-analysis of solids.

FTIR is a form of vibrational spectroscopy in which molecules absorb specific wavelengths of radiation related to the vibrational energy of the molecular bonds present. FTIR therefore delivers a compound spectrum of all excitable molecular bonds in a sample within the applied wavelength range. Their identification can be very difficult due to matrix effects. Large libraries containing FTIR spectra can, however, assist the analyst greatly in this task.

Applications of FTIR spectroscopy in questioned documents are mainly in the analysis, classification, and comparison of organic compounds in toners, tapes, and coatings.

Closely related to infrared spectroscopy but often delivering complementary information is RS where the inelastic scattering of laser radiation produces information on the molecular composition of a sample. Its main application in the analysis of documents is the comparison of inks and toners. Spectra of inks will sometimes improve dramatically when a silver or gold colloid is applied, resulting in surface-enhanced Raman scattering or an even stronger surface-enhanced resonance Raman scattering if the excitation wavelength also matches the maximum absorption of the molecule being analyzed (Figure 2).

Chromatographic Methods

Document examiners have in the past relied heavily on chromatographic methods for the discrimination and characterization of writing, stamp, and printing inks. As the use of optical methods is most often limited to the comparison of inks on the same paper, chromatographic methods such as TLC and HPLC are needed for comparing inks between documents. These

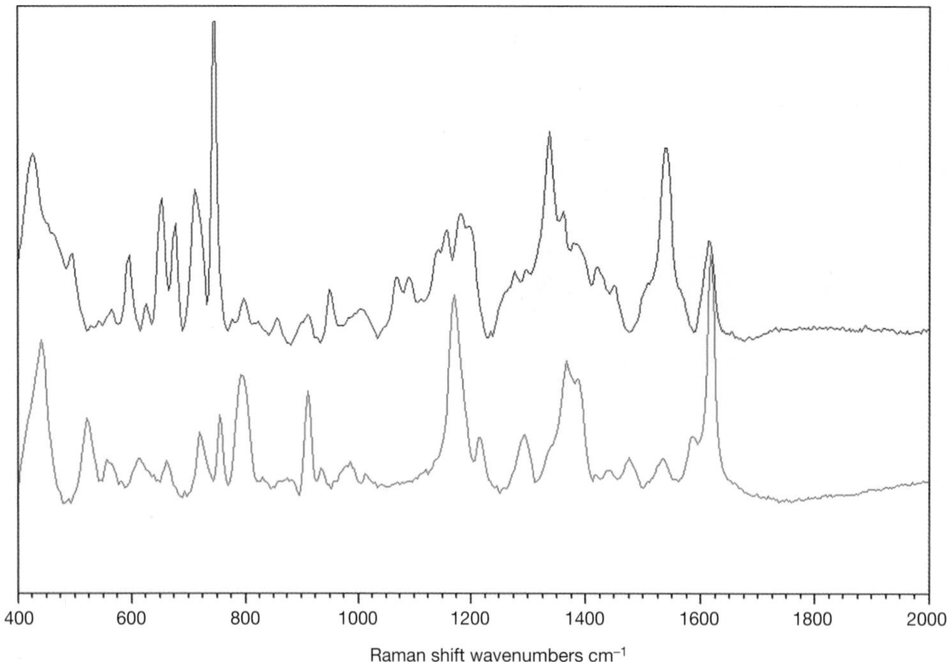

Figure 2 Raman spectra of two black ballpoint pen inks.

methods often offer a higher degree of discrimination than the optical methods.

Gas chromatography

Gas chromatography with mass spectrometric detection (GC/MS) is one of the workhorses of a forensic laboratory with applications in illicit drugs, fire accelerants, explosives, toxicology, environmental crime, materials science, and questioned documents. GC/MS is used for the analysis of organic volatile compounds. Separation of the different components is obtained from a partitioning between a gas and a solid phase in combination with a temperature programming of the oven containing the column. A further separation based on the mass-to-charge ratio and detection of the eluting compounds is achieved with a mass spectrometer. The resulting fragmentation patterns provide structural information that can be used for identification and quantification purposes. Specific fragmentation patterns can also help to identify different species with similar chromatographic behavior. The mass spectrometer can be run in the total ion current (TIC) or selected ion monitoring (SIM) mode. In the TIC mode, the sum of the intensities of all detected masses within a specific time interval is used, while in the SIM mode, one specific mass-to-charge ratio is monitored, resulting in high selectivity and high sensitivity for one specific compound.

While standard GC/MS is aimed at the analysis of volatiles, pyrolysis GC/MS (Py–GC/MS) can deal with nonvolatiles or solids. In Py–GC/MS, a sample is thermally decomposed at high temperatures, after which the resulting volatile fragments are analyzed with GC/MS. Substances such as ink resins, polymers, and paper sizing materials may be analyzed in this manner. Within questioned documents, Py–GC/MS has mainly been used for the analysis of toners and pigment-based inks such as black inkjet inks and gel pen inks. The resulting pyrogram has a high discrimination power, giving a detailed chemical fingerprint of the analyzed substance.

Liquid chromatography

TLC or, more importantly, high-performance TLC has been the chromatographic method of choice for the past generations of examiners of questioned documents if it came to a chemical comparison and/or identification of inks. An extract from an ink line of 5–10 mm is manually or automatically spotted onto an (HP)TLC plate and allowed to develop in a suitable solvent mixture. Separation is based on the partitioning behavior of the different dyes between the solid stationary phase of the TLC plate (usually a silica gel) and the liquid mobile phase, which travels up the plate due to capillary action. Comparison of inks is done after side-by-side analysis followed by an evaluation of the resulting separation profile by naked eye, multispectral methods, or with a dedicated TLC scanner with UV/Vis spectral capabilities. Identification of the inks is done by comparison of the separation profile or chromatogram to an ink library of similar analyses, followed by a side-by-side analysis of the main remaining candidates (Figure 3).

TLC is also still in use for ink dating applications. Different approaches may be identified:

- The 'static' approach, where an ink manufacturer is identified from the combination of dyes used in the ink or from specific tagging compounds which have been added by the manufacturer. This approach may sometimes lead to information concerning the date of introduction of the ink, which may then be used for dating purposes.
- The 'dynamic' approach, where chemical changes in the dyes or their extraction efficiency is used to determine the (relative) age of the inks. This approach to ink dating, however, has always been quite controversial in the questioned documents community.

In HPLC, the stationary phase is not located on a glass or aluminum plate (as in TLC) but in a glass or stainless steel column. The ink extract is injected into the mobile phase, which is pumped through the column under high pressure. After separation, the dyes may be detected with a UV/Vis detector at a fixed wavelength, resulting in a two-dimensional chromatogram (time vs. absorbance). If a photodiode array (PDA) detector is used, the absorbance of every eluting component is monitored over a specific wavelength range, resulting in a three-dimensional chromatogram (time vs. wavelength vs. absorbance). This gives greater capabilities for a more reliable comparison and identification of the separated compounds. Applications of HPLC range from writing, stamp pad, and printing inks to toners and paper additives such as optical brighteners (Figure 4).

The Newer Trends

Optical Methods

The two major developments in optical methods are the move from multispectral to hyperspectral or chemical imaging and the gradual increase in the use of digital image analysis.

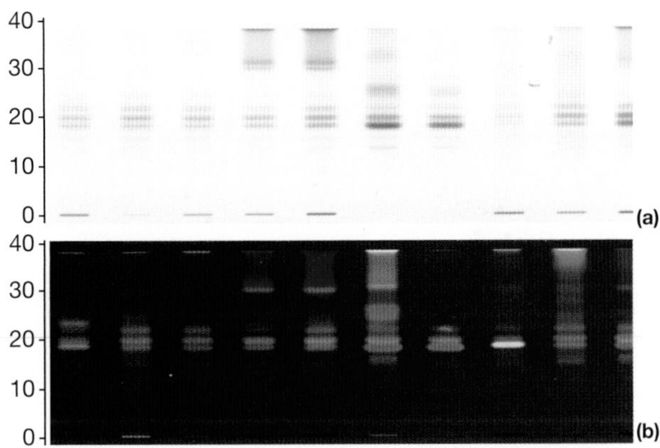

Figure 3 TLC separation of five blue and five black ballpoint pen inks on a LiChrospher Si 60 F254 TLC plate. (a) Real-color image. (b) Artificial-color image composed from the three luminescence channels R: 550/650 nm; G: 500/600 nm; B: 400/500 nm produced on a Sentinel® Quantitative Hyperspectral Imager by DEMCON Advanced Products, Oldenzaal, The Netherlands. Klein ME, Aalderink BJ, Berger CEH, Herlaar K, and de Koeijer JA (2010) Quantitative hyperspectral imaging technique for measuring material degradation effects and analyzing TLC plate traces. *Journal of the American Society of Questioned Document Examiners* 13(2): 71–81.

Hyperspectral imaging

A hyperspectral imager differs from a conventional multispectral imaging device in two important ways. First, the new instrument features a considerable increase in the number of independent spectral bands realized by using either liquid crystal tunable filters or a large number (up to several hundred) of optical filters. This increases the chances of finding differences between compared features.

Second, postprocessing in hyperspectral imaging makes it possible to calibrate the spectral curve for every pixel of the recorded image. This has several important advantages for the way in which the data can be analyzed:

- Spectral curves can be easily extracted from all desired locations in the image, plotted together in diagrams and processed numerically so that any differences between the curves can be established in a quantitative way.
- Optimization of the workflow of a case investigation can be achieved. The tasks of measuring a document sample and of analyzing the results with respect to particular forensic questions have become quite independent of each other. After having measured all available spectral bands of a document in a single, relatively short session, the forensic analysis on the collected data can be performed offline.
- Image analysis algorithms aimed at retrieving the best information possible from the total image data cube are introduced. Examples of such algorithms are principal component analysis, color deconvolution, and image subtraction and multiplication (Figure 5).

Digital image analysis techniques

Since the introduction of flatbed scanners, digital cameras, and software packages such as Adobe Photoshop, digital image analysis has been made available to the general public, and hence it has become an important new tool for forensic document examiners. Tasks that were quite complicated for an analog forensic photographer have now become as simple as a mouse click for the modern document examiner. Specialized forensic filters or plug-ins have been designed to assist the document examiner in performing tasks such as:

- Contrast stretching or optimization, which can be applied to enhance weak (barely legible) images of, for example, erased or faded writing/printing, writing on charred documents, etc.;
- Color filtering or deconvolution, which can be used to discriminate between two closely related colors, remove background color, or just enhance a specific color;

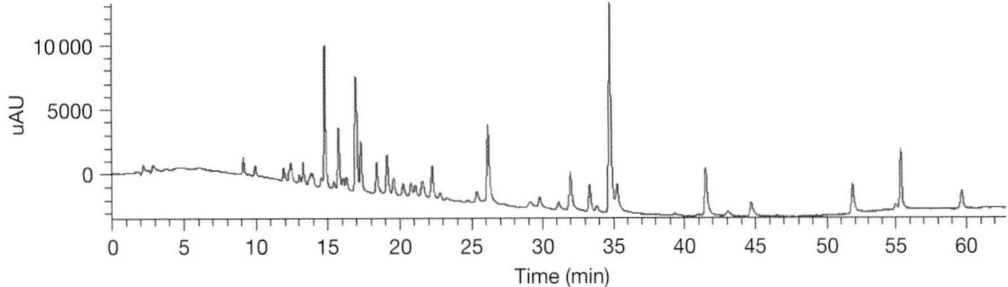

Figure 4 HPLC chromatogram of a blue ballpoint pen ink.

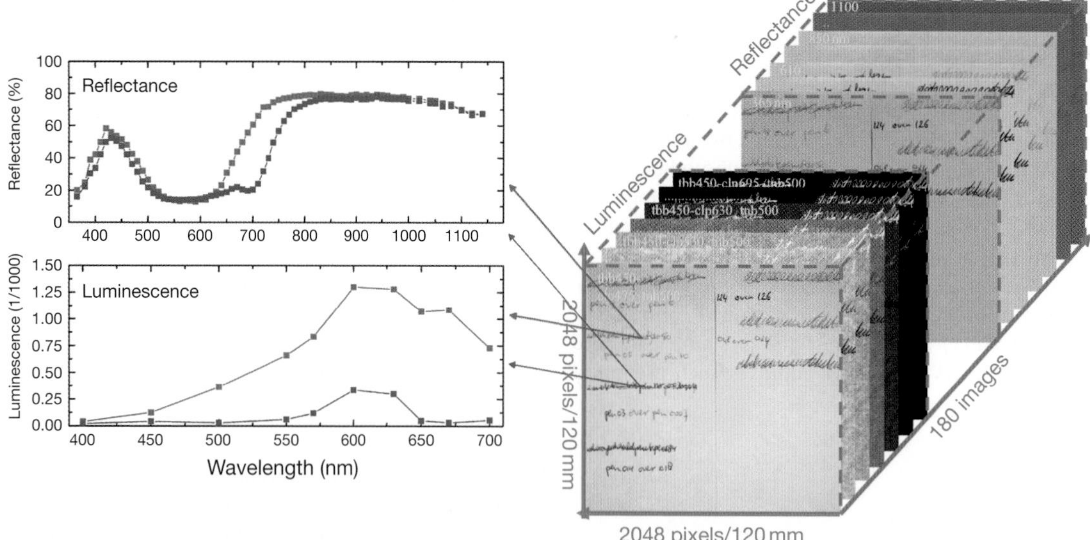

Figure 5 The hyperspectral data cube consisting of the calibrated spectral reflectance and luminescence images of the recorded document area. For each point on the document, the entire reflectance and luminescence curves can be extracted. The illustration indicates the spectral reflectance and luminescence curves for two ink areas as blue and red curves. Generated on a Sentinel® Quantitative Hyperspectral Imager by DEMCON Advanced Products, Oldenzaal, The Netherlands. Klein ME, Aalderink BJ, Berger CEH, Herlaar K, and de Koeijer JA (2010) Quantitative hyperspectral imaging technique for measuring material degradation effects and analyzing TLC plate traces. *Journal of the American Society of Questioned Document Examiners* 13(2): 71–81.

- Making digital overlays, which can assist the document examiner with the comparison of traced or copied signatures, stamp impressions, etc.;
- Sharpening, which may be applied to increase image detail;
- Morphing, used to remove warping or skew in an image;
- Fast Fourier transform (FFT) analysis, which is a mathematical transformation of an image used to remove or visualize/enhance regular patterns. Removal of specific frequencies is accomplished by transforming the image to the frequency domain where specific frequencies may be selected and erased, resulting in removal of the pattern with that frequency in the original image after performing a reversed FFT. Another useful application is the comparison of paper. FFT spectra of a paper scanned in the transparency mode will contain specific frequencies from machine components with which the wet paper (pulp) has been in contact during the papermaking process. Such an FFT image can show whether two different sheets of paper were produced on the same machine (Figure 6).

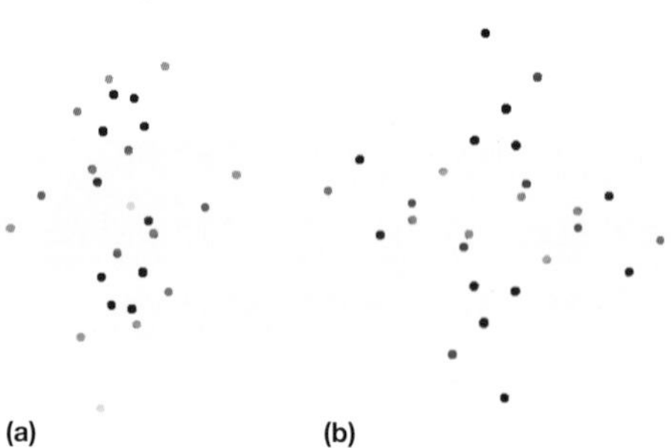

Figure 6 Digitally enhanced FFT spectra of two different sheets of paper.

Spectroscopic Methods

New developments in spectroscopic techniques have boosted the capability of not only questioned document examination but also forensic science in general. The many new MS-related methods have been a driving force for developments in chemical analysis in the forensic domain. Methods such as LA–ICPMS, laser desorption ionization MS (LDI–MS), and isotope ratio MS (IRMS) have become more and more mainstream methods of analysis for the larger forensic labs.

Elemental spectroscopy

A relatively new addition to the elemental analysis used in document examination is laser-induced breakdown spectroscopy (LIBS). This is a form of atomic emission spectroscopy using a highly energetic pulsed laser source to form a plasma of excited atoms emitting light of characteristic wavelengths. This type of elemental spectroscopy has recently been applied to the analysis of paper and pigmented inks. LIBS is extremely rapid, needing little to no sample preparation and with only very minor microscopic destruction of the sample.

Molecular spectroscopy

The surface mapping possibilities of new FTIR and Raman microscopes have introduced a new type of spectroscopy called 'chemical imaging.' The technique has a strong resemblance to hyperspectral imaging mentioned in the section 'Optical Methods.' Here, a surface is scanned and at every coordinate,

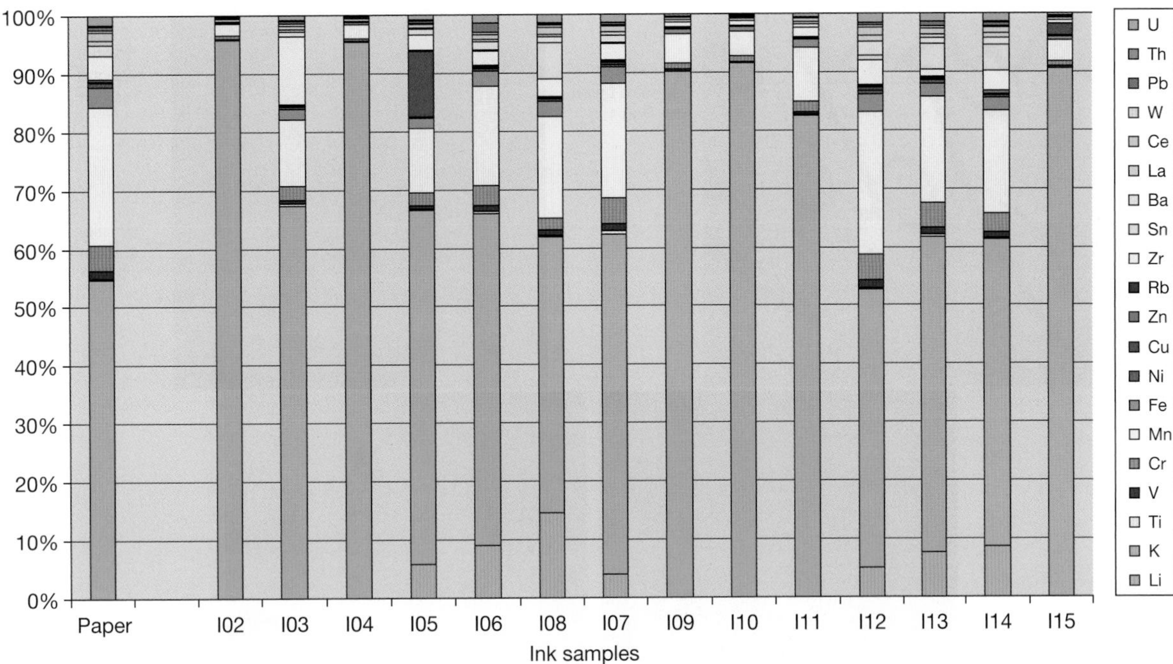

Figure 7 Graphical representation of elemental profiles of black inkjet inks on the same paper by LA–ICPMS.

a full spectrum is generated. By selecting specific frequencies, an image of the surface details absorbing these frequencies is generated. Applications, although still in their infancy, have been published in the area of fingerprints, paints, and documents. Work has been done on the sequencing of crossing ink lines and the suppression of background printing.

Mass spectrometry

Mass spectrometric methods have developed explosively in the past decade, showing large potential in forensic science in general and document examination in particular. Methods such as LA–ICPMS and LDI–MS are currently leading the way to smaller samples, less sample preparation, increased sensitivity, and almost unlimited discrimination possibilities.

In LA–ICPMS, a minute sample is taken by ablating the surface with a pulsed laser beam. The aerosol formed is transported into an inductively coupled argon plasma, which generates temperature of ~8000 °C. The ions generated here are then introduced into a mass spectrometer where they are separated according to their mass-to-charge ratio. The strength of sampling by laser ablation is that all types of solid samples can be analyzed regardless of sample size and often without preparation. Up to 70 different elements can be detected and quantified down to the ppb (parts per billion) level with only microgram quantities of sample. Analysis of paper by LA–ICPMS has shown discrimination possibilities at batch level. LA–ICPMS is also suited for the analysis of writing and printing inks, especially pigment-based inks, which do not readily dissolve from the substrate (**Figure 7**).

LDI–MS and matrix-assisted laser desorption ionization MS (MALDI–MS) are two closely related methods that also use a laser to vaporize and ionize a solid sample. LDI–MS can analyze inks directly on the paper or from an extract deposited on a metal surface. Extreme sensitivity has been shown with LDI–TOFMS (TOF, 'time of flight'), where a single ink-containing fiber is enough to analyze its dye composition. MALDI–MS, however, needs more sample preparation as a matrix that protects the sample molecules from destruction (too much fragmentation) needs to be introduced. To accomplish this, a matrix solution is added to an extract of the ink, which is then allowed to dry on a metal surface before analysis.

By scanning the surface with a scanning microprobe (MA) LDI–MS for specific ions from two inks of different composition, this technique can be used to determine the sequence of intersecting ink lines. Similar results may also be obtained by TOF–SIMS analysis of the surface of such an intersection (see below; **Figure 8**).

In TOF–SIMS, a pulsed beam of focused ions hits a surface, resulting in secondary ions being emitted from the surface to be detected in the mass spectrometer. TOF–SIMS is a surface scanning technique with the possibility of analyzing ultrathin molecular layers. Detection possibilities include all elements from the periodic table as well as molecular species. Depth profiling is also an option.

New additions to the field of mass spectrometric techniques are the so-called ambient ionization methods where ions are generated under ordinary ambient conditions in their native environment, without any sample preparation or pre-separation. Methods belonging to this category are, for example, desorption electrospray ionization MS (DESI–MS) and direct analysis in real-time MS (DART–MS). In DESI, a solvent is electrosprayed to generate charged droplets, which are directed at the analyte surface. The secondary scattered droplets containing dissolved surface ions are then mass analyzed. DART, on the other hand, uses a heated stream of excited and ionized helium or nitrogen gas to ablate and ionize

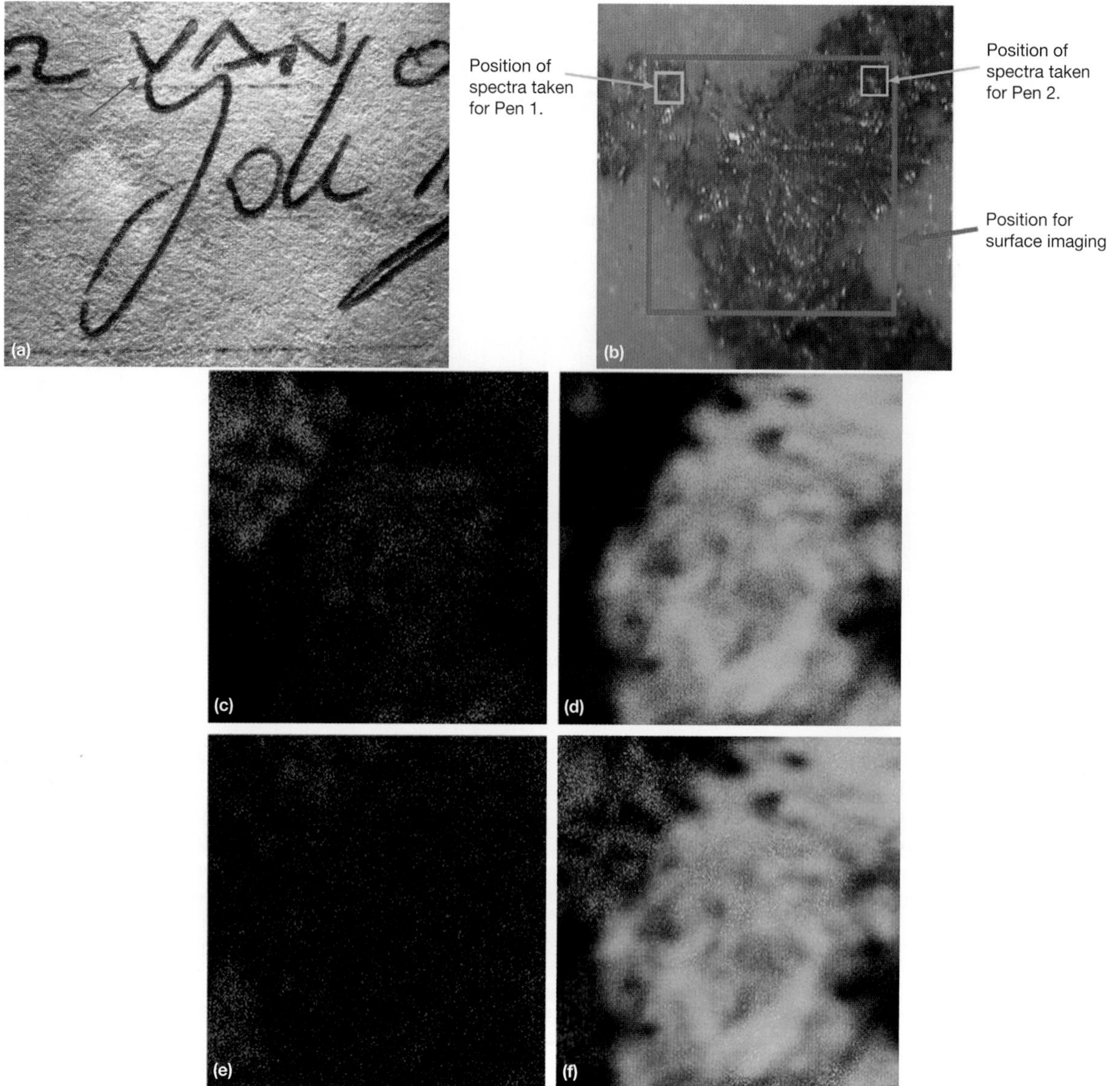

Figure 8 TOF–SIMS analysis of crossing ballpoint pen inks showing (a) the original image of the crossing between text and signature, (b) the areas where the separate inks were sampled and the intersection was imaged, (c) TOF–SIMS imaging of Pen 1 at the intersection, (d) TOF–SIMS imaging of Pen 2 at the intersection, (e) TOF–SIMS imaging of the paper at the intersection, (f) a composite image of the TOF–SIMS analysis of the Pen 1–Pen 2 intersection showing that the ink of Pen 2 is situated on top of that from Pen 1.

material from a sample so that it may be analyzed by the mass spectrometer. DART produces relatively simple mass spectra characterized in the positive-ion mode by $M^{+}/[M+H]^{+}$ and $M^{-}/[M-H]^{-}$ in the negative-ion mode. Both DESI and DART have been used in document examination for real-time analysis of inks. Besides direct analysis, DESI also allows chemical imaging of a surface, making it possible to detect any changes to a questioned handwritten entry.

Last, but certainly not least, IRMS has claimed its position in forensic science with applications in the areas of explosives, illicit drugs, materials, and the identification of human remains based on their geographical history. In document examination, IRMS has shown potential for the analysis of isotopic ratios in paper, differentiating paper based on its $\delta^{2}H$, $\delta^{13}C$, and $\delta^{18}O$ isotopes (Figure 9).

Chromatographic Methods

In the challenges of dealing with the frequently asked question to date documents, chromatography has played a major role. After the first attempts using TLC to determine the age of an ink by differences in the extraction rate of the dyes, the focus shifted to the volatiles using solvent extraction and GC/MS. Further developments in this area have led to methods combining solid-phase microextraction (SPME) with GC/MS, TD with GC/MS and finally HPLC with fluorescence detection.

Also in the area of ink comparison, progress has been made with methods such as HPLC–MS(/MS) and capillary electrophoresis (CE).

Gas chromatographic techniques

GC in the examination of questioned documents has mainly been used for ink dating purposes. Recent developments in this area are the use of SPME with TD–GC/MS. SPME uses a fused silica fiber coated with a polymeric phase tailored to absorb certain classes of compounds. The fiber is placed in a closed environment in close proximity to the (heated) sample. After equilibrium is reached between the absorbed analytes on the fiber and the sample matrix, the fiber is placed in the injector of the GC/MS where desorption takes place followed by further analysis.

In TD–GC/MS, the ink sample is placed in a desorption tube, which is then heated. A steady gas flow through the tube transfers the evaporated analytes to a cold trap area where they are collected. Once this process is complete, the cold trap is heated and the gas flow takes the analytes to the GC column for further separation.

Both SPME–GC/MS and TD–GC/MS use mass-independent sampling strategies where the same ink sample is extracted/ desorbed at two different temperatures and the ratio of solvent from both analyses is used as an age indicator. Almost all ink dating work has been aimed at the analysis of 2-phenoxyethanol (PE), which is the most common solvent used in ballpoint pens. The analysis strategy is aimed at determining the relative freshness of the ink (<6–12 months old) in contrast to the date mentioned on the document, which may suggest a much earlier date of production.

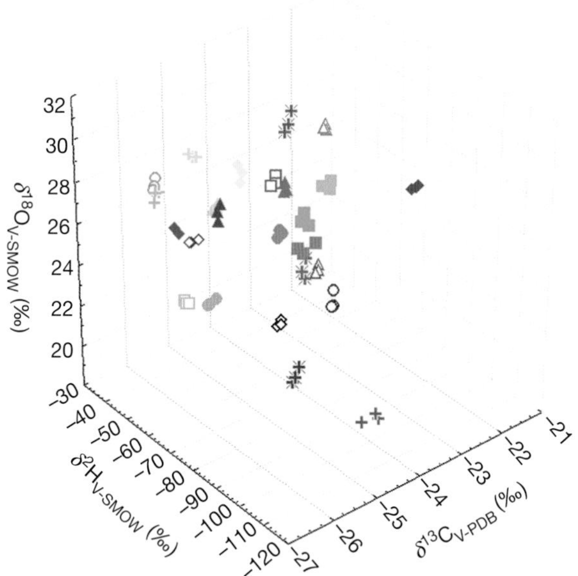

Figure 9 IRMS analysis of 25 different brands of multifunctional printing paper.

Liquid chromatographic techniques

A promising method for the analysis of soluble inks is HPLC–MS(/MS). As HPLC–MS interfaces have improved, the range of applications for this powerful separation method has increased dramatically. The combination of HPLC-MS with a PDA detector promises the best of both worlds, with both UV/Vis detection of the dyes and the enhanced MS functionality of detection of noncolored species and their identification.

A new approach to the determination of the age of an ink is the use of HPLC with a fluorescence and a PDA detector. The fluorescence detector is used to quantify PE, while the PDA detector detects the methyl violet dyes. The dyes can now be used as internal standards for the quantification of PE from

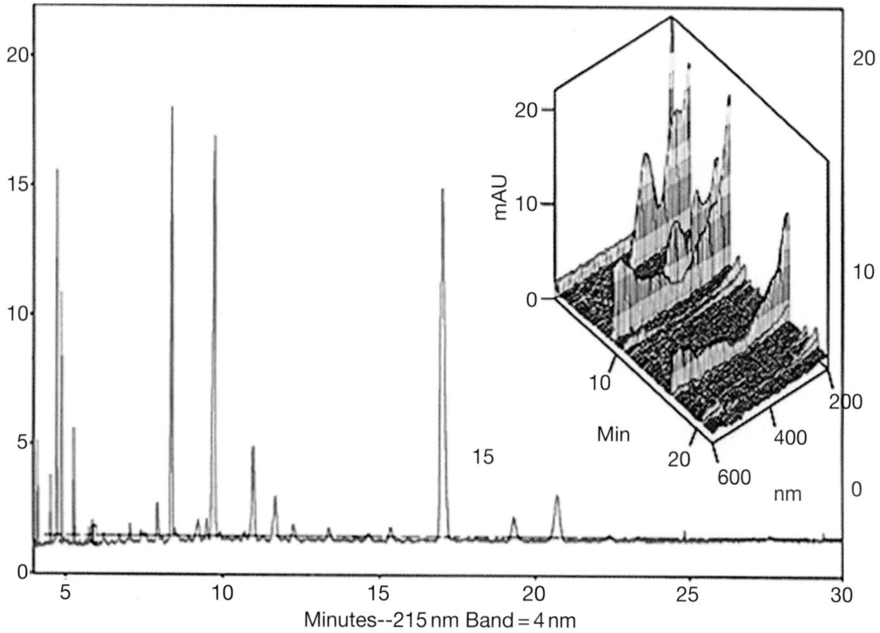

Figure 10 MECC analysis of a black inkjet printer ink.

two ink samples, one sample taken directly and one after a period of (artificial) aging in the laboratory.

Another promising development in this area is the use of ultra performance liquid chromatography (UPLC) instead of HPLC. In UPLC, smaller stationary-phase particles are used. The main advantages of UPLC are higher separation efficiency, faster chromatographic process, and increased sensitivity. The main disadvantage is that specialized equipment is needed to deal with the increased pressure needed to force the mobile phase through the column.

A technique that is used extensively in forensics but has been used only to a limited extent in document examination is CE. This is a separation technique based on the transport of ionic species in an electric field. CE is characterized by its extremely low solvent and sample consumption, its high separation power, and its broad range of applications. Separation in CE depends on the size and charge of the analyte molecules. Ions migrate in an electric field applied over the capillary in the direction of the electrode of the opposite charge. The migration rate is related to the following sequence: multiply charged small ions, singly charged small ions and/or multiply charged large ions, and, finally, singly charged large ions. One of the main driving forces of CE is electroosmosis causing an electroosmotic flow (EOF). CE has different operation modes, of which capillary zone electrophoresis (CZE) and micellar electrokinetic capillary chromatography (MECC) have been used for the analysis of ink and paper. CZE can be used for the separation of water-soluble ionic species, while MECC can also deal with neutral and even hydrophobic molecules.

MECC is a mode of CE in which surfactants are added to the buffer solution, which then form micelles (cluster of molecules with the polar groups toward the solution). The MECC separation is based on the differential partitioning of an analyte between two phases, that is, a mobile (aqueous) phase and a stationary (micellar) phase. The charge of the micelle is chosen so that the migration force of the micelle is opposite to the direction of the EOF. However, due to the fact that the mobility of the EOF is greater than that of the micelle, the micelle will slowly migrate in the direction of the EOF. Analytes partitioning between the micelle and the buffer solution will therefore elute between the EOF and the micelle. Excellent separation of closely related dye compounds including isomers has been achieved for the analysis of different kinds of writing and inkjet printing inks (**Figure 10**).

See also: **Documents:** Document Dating; Forgery/Counterfeits; Ink Analysis; Paper Analysis; **Methods:** Capillary Electrophoresis: Basic Principles; Capillary Electrophoresis in Forensic Chemistry; Chromatography: Basic Principles; Gas Chromatography; Gas Chromatography–Mass Spectrometry; Liquid and Thin-Layer Chromatography; Liquid Chromatography–Mass Spectrometry; Mass Spectrometry; Spectroscopic Techniques; Spectroscopy: Basic Principles.

Further Reading

Berger CEH (2009) Objective paper structure comparison through processing of transmitted light images. *Forensic Science International* 192: 1–6.

Berger CEH, de Koeijer JA, Glas W, and Madhuizen HT (2006) Color separation in forensic image processing. *Journal of Forensic Sciences* 51(1): 100–102.

Bojko K, Roux C, and Reedy BJ (2008) An examination of the sequence of intersecting lines using attenuated total reflectance – Fourier transform infrared spectral imaging. *Journal of Forensic Sciences* 53: 1458–1467.

Brazeau L, Chem C, and Gaudreau M (2007) Ballpoint pen inks: The quantitative analysis of ink solvents on paper by solid-phase microextraction. *Journal of Forensic Sciences* 52(1): 209–215.

Bügler JH, Buchner H, and Dallmayer A (2008) Age determination of ballpoint pen ink by thermal desorption and gas chromatography–mass spectrometry. *Journal of Forensic Sciences* 53(4): 982–988.

Coumbaros J, Kirkbride KP, Klass G, and Skinner W (2009) Application of time of flight secondary ion mass spectrometry to the in situ analysis of ballpoint pen inks on paper. *Forensic Science International* 193: 42–46.

Dunn JD and Allison J (2007) The detection of multiply charged dyes using matrix-assisted laser desorption/ionization mass spectrometry for the forensic examination of pen ink dyes directly from paper. *Journal of Forensic Sciences* 52(5): 1205–1211.

Ifa DR, Gumaelius LM, Eberlin LS, Manickea NE, and Cooks RG (2007) Forensic analysis of inks by imaging desorption electrospray ionization (DESI) mass spectrometry. *Analyst* 132: 461–467.

Jones RW, Cody RB, and McClelland JF (2006) Differentiating writing inks using direct analysis in real time mass spectrometry. *Journal of Forensic Sciences* 51(4): 915–918.

Klein ME, Aalderink BJ, Berger CEH, Herlaar K, and de Koeijer JA (2010) Quantitative hyperspectral imaging technique for measuring material degradation effects and analyzing TLC plate traces. *Journal of the American Society of Questioned Document Examiners* 13(2): 71–81.

Ostrum RB (2006) Application of hyperspectral imaging to forensic document examination problems. *Journal of the American Society of Questioned Document Examiners* 9(2): 85–93.

Sarkar A, Aggarwal SK, and Alamelu D (2010) Laser induced breakdown spectroscopy for rapid identification of different types of paper for forensic application. *Analytical Methods* 2(1): 1–100.

Van Es A, de Koeijer J, and van der Peijl G (2009) Discrimination of document paper by XRF, LA–ICPMS and IRMS using multivariate statistical techniques. *Science and Justice* 49(2): 120–126.

Weyermann C, Marquis R, Mazzella W, and Spengler B (2007) Differentiation of blue ballpoint pen Inks by laser desorption ionization mass spectrometry and high-performance thin-layer chromatography. *Journal of Forensic Sciences* 52(1): 216–220.

Xu X, de Koeijer JA, de Moel JJM, and Logtenberg H (1997) Ink analysis for forensic science applications by micellar electrokinetic capillary chromatography with photo-diode array detection. *International Journal of Forensic Document Examiners* 3(3): 240–260.

Relevant Websites

http://www.aafs.org – American Academy of Forensic Sciences.
http://www.asqde.org – American Society of Questioned Document Examiners.
http://www.enfsi.eu – European Network of Forensic Institutes.
http://dl.dropbox.com – Forensic Science Resources.
http://english.forensischinstituut.nl – Netherlands Forensic Institute.
http://forensic.to/index.php – Zeno's Forensic Site.

Document Dating

WD Mazzella and DC Purdy, University of Lausanne, Lausanne, Switzerland; Forensic Document Examination Services Inc., Vancouver, BC, Canada

This article is a revision of the previous edition article by D.C. Purdy, volume 2, pp. 570–580, © 2000, Elsevier Ltd.

The misrepresentation of dates on documents is not a recent challenge faced by forensic document examiners. In his book, *Questioned Documents*, Albert S. Osborn provided several examples of documents, which were altered or backdated to make it appear as though they were written much earlier. Many frauds still involve document dating problems and forensic document examiners should diligently search for any clues that suggest a document was prepared some time other than indicated.

Various methods can be employed to backdate or fabricate documents. Such incidents can involve the relatively simple process of overwriting the date on a receipt to far more complex undertakings such as falsifying an entire document. Regardless of the method used, dating suspect documents is a very challenging problem for the document examiner and should be approached cautiously.

The most straightforward method for solving a dating problem considers the type of office equipment and the technologies that were used to produce the questioned document. This method, often called the 'static' approach, can prove a document is false if the instruments and materials used to produce it were unavailable when it was supposedly prepared. A subgroup of the static approach involves the analysis of materials that make up a suspect document. For example, specialty papers or writing inks may contain materials that have been added to improve their quality. If it can be established that these materials were introduced on a specific date, any document in which they are found must have been prepared at a later time.

The second method, described as the 'dynamic' approach, takes into account certain features in a contested document that vary over time. Defective letters produced by a worn typewriter or photocopier 'trash marks' that originate from dirt on a copier's platen glass are two examples of this type of evidence that have dating significance. An important related issue concerns the natural aging of components that are present in the ink and paper. The aging of writing media will not be discussed here as the topic is covered in another chapter of this encyclopedia.

The third method of solving dating problems involves determining the chronology or sequence of events responsible for the production of a document. The sequence of intersecting lines, page substitutions, and adding information to the body of a document can all challenge the alleged history of a contested document.

The following sections describe different areas that can be examined to determine when a document was drawn up or whether its date is false. The results of these tests do not always provide conclusive evidence of fraud. They can, however, draw attention to irregularities that must be reconciled before a suspect document can be relied on as genuine.

Paper Products

Watermarks

Conventional paper watermarks are produced during the manufacturing process by a 'dandy roll' cylinder located at the beginning of the papermaking machine where paper is formed into a web. The dandy roll cylinder consists of a woven wire gauze onto which raised designs are soldered or otherwise attached. A watermark is created when the relief areas of the dandy roll press into and displace paper fibers. These unique designs permit sheets of watermarked paper to be traced to their manufacturer.

Paper mills usually maintain accurate records concerning their watermarks. Once the paper manufacturer of a questioned document is known, the company can be contacted to determine the earliest date that a watermark design was used. Any document dated earlier than this time must have been backdated.

The design of a watermark can also change over time as relief areas of the dandy roll suffer damage through normal wear and tear. Detached or broken wires produce slight but visible changes in the design that are transferred to the paper. Paper mills usually keep records when dandy roll damage occurred and when repairs were made. This information can be very helpful in narrowing the period during which a watermarked paper was manufactured.

A few paper companies have intentionally changed the design of their watermarks from time to time. Such watermarks are said to contain a 'date tag,' which will often indicate the year that a sheet of paper was produced. For example, Southworth Paper Company placed a short bar under or over the letters in their watermark to indicate the last digit of the year in which the paper was manufactured (**Figure 1**). If a document bears a watermark that was not in existence when it was allegedly dated, the genuineness of its date must surely be challenged.

When using watermarks to date paper, it is strongly recommended that the paper manufacturer be contacted to verify the time period when the noted features were present.

Paper Composition

Over the years, different fillers, surface coatings, or chemical additives have been added during the paper-making process to improve the quality of the product. Other changes in the manufacturing processes have occurred for economic or environmental reasons. These innovations and modifications can establish the earliest date or period a particular sheet of paper was manufactured.

Many North American paper manufacturers stopped producing acidic paper in favor of alkaline or neutral process papers during the late 1980s and early 1990s. A simple pH test can indicate if a questioned document was produced before

 http://dx.doi.org/10.1016/B978-0-12-382165-2.00132-X

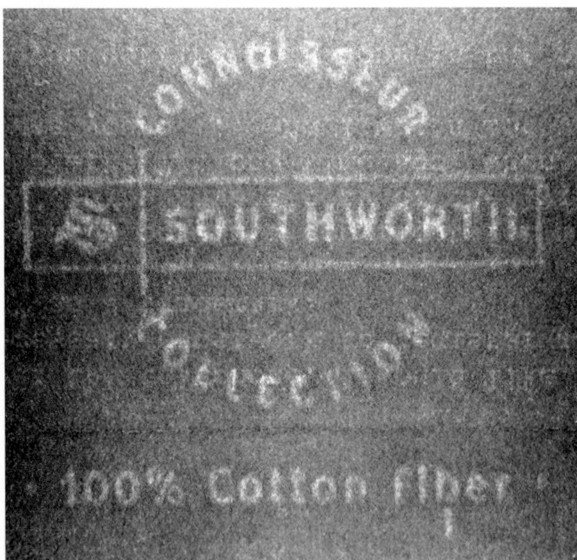

Figure 1 The short vertical bar under the letter b of 'Fiber' in this watermark confirms the sheet of paper was manufactured during 2004.

its purported date. This finding can be corroborated if certain chemicals that were introduced after the date on the document are present in the paper. For example, when mills converted their operations to an alkaline process, many also began using calcium carbonate ($CaCO_3$) as a substitute for titanium dioxide (TiO_2) in order to improve the brightness and opacity of papers. Paper production based on acidic processes is still carried out in other areas of the globe. Consequently, caution should be exercised when interpreting such evidence and the paper manufacturer should be consulted to confirm when the observed processes and materials were introduced.

Specialty papers can also contain information of dating significance. For example, NCR (no carbon required) paper first appeared in the United States during 1954. The formula for manufacturing this product was changed several times during the 1960s and 1970s. In 1972, NCR developed a coding scheme to identify the source and date of its papers. Trace amounts of various high-atomic weight elements have been added by other manufacturers as a means of tagging their products. The dates of documents produced on specialty papers that contain tags can be verified by taking such information into account.

A more sophisticated technique can occasionally be used to date the paper, which takes into account strong increases in atmospheric radiocarbon concentration caused by nuclear weapons tests conducted during the last 50 years. Such tests reportedly allow papers, less than 50 years old, to be dated within a few months of their dates of production independent of storage conditions.

Envelopes

Envelopes are often discarded once their contents are removed. This is unfortunate because an envelope may contain important information about when it was mailed and possibly when its contents were prepared. The following envelope areas can have dating significance: postage stamps, postage cancellation marks, envelope shape, and printed information.

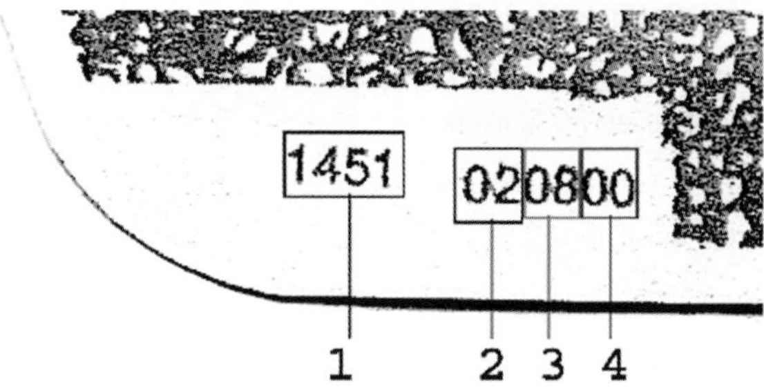

Figure 2 A notation '1451 020800' on the inside of an 'Elco' envelope represents (1) personnel number, (2) machine code, (3) month of manufacturing, and (4) year of manufacturing.

Postage stamps affixed to envelopes can be examined to determine if they were available when the envelope's contents were prepared. A new postage stamp is released for sale as a 'first day cover' on a particular date. Postal officials or a knowledgeable stamp collector should be able to provide the precise date a stamp was issued. Once this date is known, the envelope and its contents must have been mailed some time after this period.

Stamps on many envelopes bear cancellation marks that are applied by the post office. Even if a cancellation mark is not legible, the format of the mark, the way it was struck, and the chemical composition of ink can serve to establish the period when it was applied.

Occasionally, logos or product codes are applied to envelopes while they are being manufactured, which can have dating significance. The impression shown in **Figure 2** was found on the inside of an envelope manufactured by Elco. This notation represents the personnel number (1451), the printing machine code (02), as well as the month and last two digits of the year (0800) the envelope was printed. Numbers (0800) corresponding to the month (August) and the last two digits in the year (2000) it was manufactured. The envelope manufacturer should always be contacted to confirm the accuracy of any dating information.

The design and appearance of some envelopes are unique to their manufacturers and may well indicate when they were produced. These include, but are not limited to, the following:

- small irregularities along the edges of the paper related to a damaged die stamp;
- types of adhesives applied to the side-seams and the flap areas of the envelope; and
- striation patterns in adhesive layers associated with the method of application.

Other areas sometimes overlooked are addresses, which appear on an envelope. A particular mailing or return address may not have existed when the document was supposed to have been sent. Postal or zip codes change from time to time and these should always be checked to ensure that they existed during the period in question.

Inks and Writing Instruments

One of the most challenging dating problems facing the document examiner is estimating when a particular document was signed or written. If a document was supposed to have been written many years ago, it may be possible to prove it was backdated if the type of pen and writing materials used were not available at that time. Important milestone events concerning the development of modern writing materials are shown in **Table 1** along with their dates of introduction.

Clues as to when a document was signed can also be found by analyzing the questioned writing ink. A small sample of ink removed from a document can be separated into its solid components by thin-layer chromatography (TLC). The result of this analysis is a chromatogram that isolates the different dyes present in the ink formulation on a coated glass or plastic plate. Success of this method relies on the different physical and chemical properties of the ink and the existence of a sufficiently complete set of ink reference standards.

TLC can also detect the presence of tags, which have been added to some writing inks by their manufacturers. During the 1970s, several US ink producers participated in an ink tagging program organized by the Alcohol, Tobacco and Firearms (ATF) Laboratory in the United States. This scheme urged ink manufacturers to add trace amounts of different materials with distinct properties to their inks. These materials would be changed annually and thereby indicate the year an ink was manufactured. By 1978, approximately 40% of writing inks produced in the United States contained such dating tags. Although this initiative greatly increased the ability of forensic scientists to date domestic writing inks, the continued growth of imported products threatened the success of the program. Although most ink manufacturers withdrew from the tagging program by the early 1980s, documents purportedly written before this period may contain chemical taggants that suggest they were manufactured at a much later date. A US company commenced tagging their products in 2002 but this program ended in January of 2010 when the ink company was purchased by a competitor.

Ink chemists have observed that many writing inks begin to change or age the instant they are applied to paper. Most people have noticed writing inks fade or become lighter with the passage of time. In addition to this obvious physical transition, investigations have shown that the chemical composition of an ink also changes over several months or years.

Table 1 Significant dates of introduction in the history of writing instruments

Year	*Historical development*
624	Earliest reference to the quill pen
1662	Pencils made in Nuremberg, Germany
1700	Early reference to steel pens
1780	Steel pens made in England by Samuel Harrison
1857	First appearance of 'copying pencils'
1945	Ballpoint pen first marketed in New York City
1951	Felt-tip markers introduced
1955	Liquid lead pencil introduced
1963	Fiber-tip pen first produced
1967	Roller ball pen first produced
1979	Eraser Mate erasable pen introduced by Paper Mate
1984	Gel pens introduced by Sakura in Japan
1993	Gel pens introduced in USA
2006	Frixion ball, based on thermochromic ink, introduced by Pilot

These effects are especially true with respect to the color, solubility, and solvent volatility of the writing inks.

Other testing methods rely on sophisticated analytical techniques such as gas chromatography/mass spectrometry (GC/MS) to measure the concentration of volatile components, such as phenoxyethanol, in an ink sample. This technique also requires two samples be taken from the suspect ink entry. After exposing one to heat, both samples are tested and the extent to which their solvent components differ provides an estimate of when the ink entry was written. This method is better suited for entries made within 4–6 months of testing and do apply to some ball point ink formulations.

The described methods are beyond all but a few specialists who possess the equipment, knowledge, and experience needed to analyze and date writing inks. Some controversy still surrounds certain ink testing methods and further validation studies could resolve these debates. The aforementioned ink dating methods have not been validated by an international intralaboratory double blind test and, therefore, should be applied with extreme caution.

Commercially Printed Documents

Many documents subjected to forensic examinations take the form of documents with letterheads, contracts, envelopes, notary records, receipts, and other types of printed stationery. Apart from typewriting, handwriting, and other information they may contain, commercial printing on documents can be used to establish whether they were produced during or after a certain period.

Minuscule printing defects such as irregular letter outlines, uneven inking, or small breaks in line work can associate a questioned document with a particular stationery order produced by a commercial printer. Once the company that produced a printed document is identified, more precise information about when the order was delivered and the earliest time the stock was put into circulation can be determined. Access to samples from the order retained by the print shop can also be of value when attempting to date commercially printed documents.

A coded mark within the body of a printed document can also provide important information about a print job. For example, the bottom corner of the form shown in **Figure 3** bears the notation 'A-5(80-08) 7530-21-029-4767' that describes the form number (A-5) and digits corresponding to the year and month (80-08) the form was created. The remaining 13 numbers are internal codes that refer to the work order, the location where the form was printed and other internal information. It is always advisable to contact the printer to confirm the interpretation of coded information and to determine if the document contains other characteristics (e.g., dimensions, color/type of paper, and applied adhesives) that might have dating significance.

Typewriting

The typewriting technology used to produce a questioned document is one of the first factors that should be considered when its date is at issue. During the last century, many

Figure 3 The alphanumeric code 'A-5(80-08) 7530-21-029-4767' within this advertisement on a patient's medical form was used to establish the date the stationery was printed. The date (year/month 80-08) the form was created is embedded in the notation, which appears along the left margin near the bottom of the sheet.

Table 2 Significant dates of introduction in the development of the typewriter

Year	*Technological development*
1909	First use of bicolored ribbon (Underwood)
1927	First use of carbon ribbon (Hammond-Varityper)
1944	IBM executive proportional spaced typewriter
1956	Remington Statesman the first proportional typewriter by Remington
1960	First Underwood proportional spaced typewriter
1960	Underwood electric standard typewriter with duplex carbon and fabric ribbons
1961	IBM Selectric I dual pitch single element typewriter
1963	First use of IBM Selectric polyethylene film ribbon
1971	IBM Selectric II dual escapement, half backspace machine
1971	Tech III ribbon cartridge for IBM Selectric
1972	First daisywheel produced by Diablo Systems
1973	IBM Correcting Selectric II with special lift-off ribbon
1975	Thermal transfer ribbon developed by IBM
1977	First use of polyurethane ribbons (Olivetti)
1978	First dot-matrix printer for personal computer (Epson TX 80)
1962	IBM Electronic 65 and 85 typewriters with triple pitch and right justification
1982	Brother EP-20 seven-pin thermal typewriter
1984	Diablo releases EPM 1 – first thermal ribbon transfer printer
1984	IBM Quietwriter with nonimpact thermal print head
1984	Quietwriter ribbon by IBM
1999	IBM Courier typestyle introduce a special character to represent Euro currency

advances have occurred in the development of the modern typewriter. Some important events and when they occurred are listed in Table 2.

The date a typewritten document was prepared can be determined in other ways. One method considers the typestyle that appears on a questioned document. The shape and size of typed letters can indicate the make(s) and model(s) of typewriter(s) that might have been used to produce the typewriting. The results of searching a large collection of typewriter specimens can indicate that the questioned typestyle was introduced to the market on a particular date. Should the typestyle's date of introduction be later than the date on the suspect document, the questioned document must certainly be regarded with suspicion.

The second method of dating typescript takes into account any typeface defects present in the questioned typewritten text. Typewriters contain many moving parts, which gradually become worn or defective with use. These defective components produce misaligned or damaged letters that become quite apparent when examined with a microscope. Subsequent adjustments or repairs by a service technician can create further changes to the appearance of typewriting produced by a machine. The dates when typewriter damage occurred or disappeared are very significant for dating purposes.

If a typewriter is not cleaned regularly, oil, ribbon particles, dirt, and paper fibers can accumulate within the crevices of certain letters. When dirty typefaces strike the paper through the ribbon, the letters appear filled-in rather than clear letters and numbers. These imperfections will remain until the dirt is removed by cleaning the typefaces. Access to uncontested document produced on the same typewriter over a period of time will reveal when changes to the appearance of the typescript occurred. Figure 4 shows how the appearance of typeface dirt and damage can expose a fraudulent document.

Typewriter single-strike and correcting ribbons can also indicate the date when documents were produced on a particular typewriter. A used single-stroke ribbon will contain impressions of all the characters struck by the machine in chronological order as the ribbon was last changed. If the typewriter ribbon used to produce a questioned document is available for inspection, it can be examined to ensure the date of a questioned typewritten document is contemporaneous with the dates of typed documents, which precede and follow it. If it is not, dated correspondence appearing immediately before and after the location of the question passage can serve to determine the approximate period when the contested document was typed.

Correction fluids applied to conceal typing errors can also help date a typewritten document. Wite-Out Company first introduced this product to the market in 1965. In 1984, Liquid Paper introduced colored correcting fluid to mask corrections on different colored paper stock. The presence of these materials on a typewritten document before their respective introductory dates will strongly suggest a document has been backdated.

Correcting fluids are complex substances composed of different resins, plasticizers, pigments, solvents, and binders. The manufacturer of a correcting fluid can be identified by extracting a sample from the document, analyzing it by infrared spectroscopy, and comparing the result to a database of correcting fluid spectra. Once known, the manufacturer can be contacted to determine when a particular correcting fluid formulation was first produced. Of course, a correcting fluid could not have been applied to a questioned document before its date of introduction.

Photocopiers

Photocopied documents that suddenly surface during a litigation are often regarded with suspicion. In some cases, these documents are genuine, but in other instances, they are produced at the last moment with an astonishing story that they

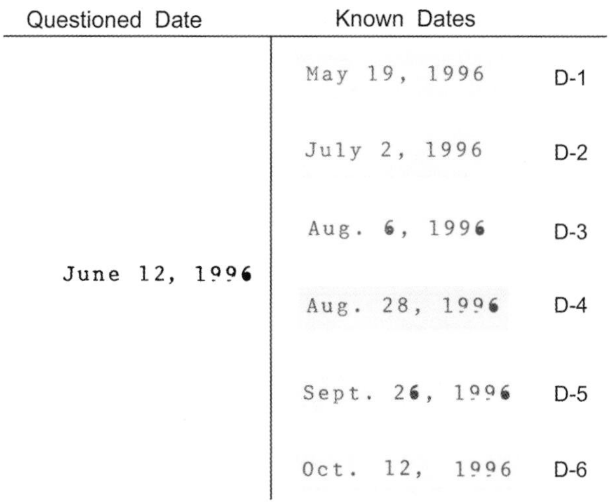

Questioned Date	Known Dates	
	May 19, 1996	D-1
	July 2, 1996	D-2
	Aug. 6, 1996	D-3
June 12, 1996	Aug. 28, 1996	D-4
	Sept. 26, 1996	D-5
	Oct. 12, 1996	D-6

Figure 4 The questioned document could not have been typed on 12 June 1996. Damage to the digit '9' and the filled-in-body of the '6' occurred after 6 August 1996 and before 12 October 1996.

were just discovered recently by some strange coincidence. The subject of interest in these cases is not when the original document was produced but rather the date or period it was photocopied. Three facets of photocopied documents that have dating significance include the copier technology used, the presence of copier defects, the properties of the toner and/or paper and, since about 1993, the introduction of security codes into color photocopiers. These codes contain the machine's serial number and indirectly the manufacture date. Some manufacturers also include the time, date, month, and year a document was produced into the security code on each color copy produced by their machines. Please note that the security codes may also be present into digital color laser printers.

Copier Technologies

Just as milestone events in the development of the typewriter are useful for dating purposes, the date of a copied document can be checked against the release date of a particular office technology to ensure that it was available when the document was allegedly produced. Different copier technologies include (1) dual spectrum, (2) stabilization, (3) diffusion transfer, (4) indirect electrostatic, (5) diazo, (6) dye transfer, (7) direct electrostatic, (8) thermographic, and (9) laser. A questioned copied document should be checked to ensure its date follows the introductory date of the technology used to produce it, keeping in mind that introductory dates may vary from region to region.

Examination of Defects

The most straightforward means of dating photocopied documents relies on defects, 'trash marks,' or small flecks of toner that appear in 'white' areas of a copied document. These marks can originate from dirt, foreign material, or defects on the glass, platen cover, or photosensitive drum of the photocopier (**Figure 5**). Scratches to the glass or drum, tend to be more permanent and will generate marks on copies produced by a machine until such time as the defective component is removed and replaced. The nature of other defects, such as those originating from dirt or foreign material on the glass, lid, or internal components, is temporary in that they can be removed by cleaning the copier surfaces. Genuine photocopied documents made by the same copier that produced the questioned document provide an excellent means of confirming its date. Logs and service records maintained by repair technicians are also helpful in that they often contain photocopies produced before and after copier repairs were made.

Toner Analysis

Most photocopier toners consist of a pigment (usually carbon black), a binder, which fixes the pigment to the paper (usually an organic resin such as polystyrene), and additives used to improve the properties of the toner. When any of these components are changed, the event can provide a useful means of dating photocopied documents. Analysis of photocopier toners by infrared spectroscopy and scanning electron microscope equipment with energy dispersive spectrometry can yield information about the chemical and physical properties of toner. A comprehensive library of toners can be used to establish initial production dates. In some cases, the manufacturer will confirm that a particular ingredient was first used several years after the date the photocopy was supposed to be prepared. This would constitute conclusive evidence that the alleged date of the photocopy was false.

The process used to fuse toner to the paper can vary from one photocopier to another. Older photocopiers use cold pressure fusing wherein toner is pressed into the paper surface. Newer generations use either heat alone or both heat and pressure to fuse toner to the surface of the paper. The date a given fusing process first appeared is the earliest that a photocopy bearing this technology could have been produced.

In 1992, it was reported that indentations are imparted to the surface of toner by damage to the surface of a copier's fusing rollers. Fusing roller defects occur through normal wear and tear. They vary with time and consequently, the indentations they produce in the surface of toner can be used to estimate when a given photocopied document was produced.

Handwriting and Signatures

The writing of many individuals does not change significantly for most of their adult life. However, despite the constant and repetitive nature of developed handwriting, practically everyone has noticed that their signatures and handwriting do change – especially over long periods of time. The development, progression, and eventual disappearance of handwriting features can be very helpful in solving dating problems. Access to a quantity of specimen material produced during a period of time can show that writers change the shape of certain letters or the form of their signatures (**Figure 6**). The quantity of specimens required for this purpose will depend on many factors including (1) how rapidly the writing changes; (2) what factor(s) influenced the changes; and (3) the number of specimen writings prepared near the period in question and

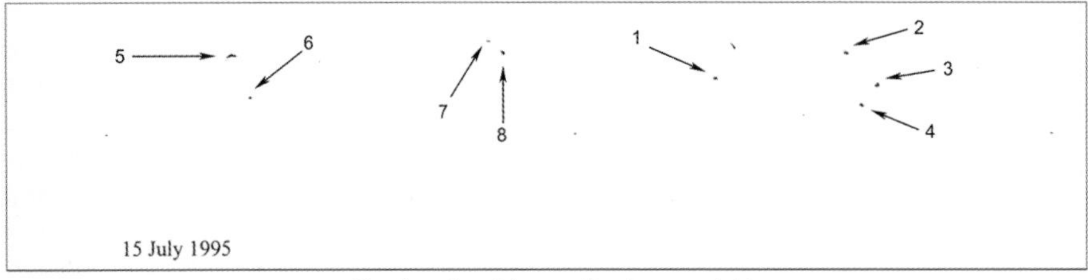

Top of questioned document bearing suspect date

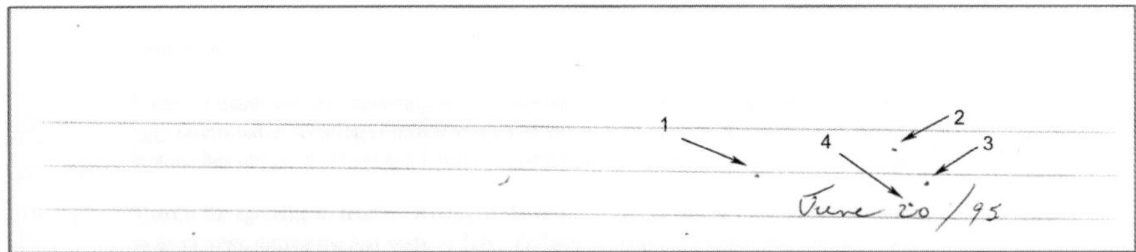

Top of document photocopied on 20 June 1995

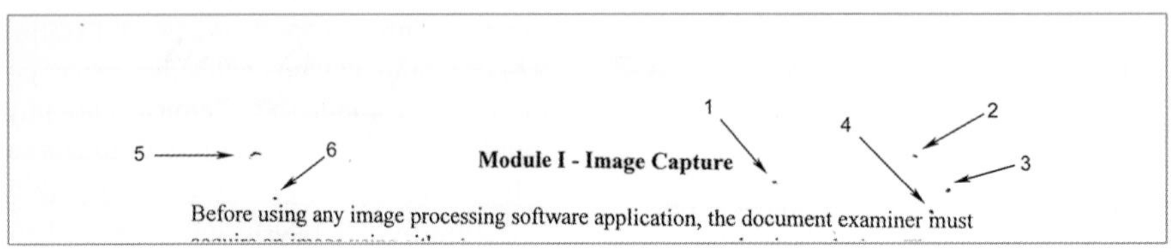

Top of document photocopied on 3 August 1995

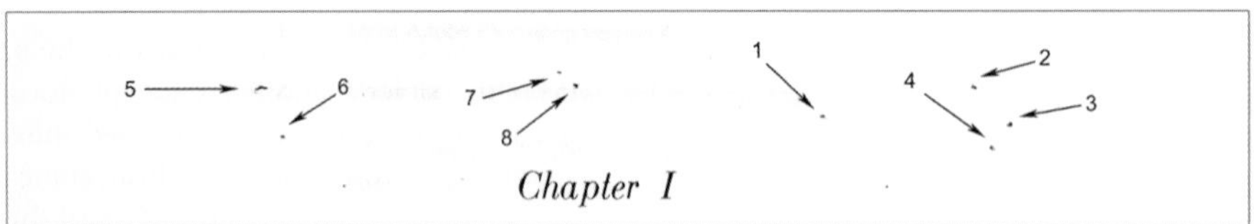

Top of document photocopied on 8 September 1995

Figure 5 The combination of photocopier 'trash' marks on the questioned document (top) emerged during the period 3 August 1995 to 8 September 1995 and could not have occurred on 15 July 1995 when copies of the questioned documents were allegedly prepared.

their homogeneity during a fixed period of time. Once the specimens are arranged in chronological order, it is often possible to date a disputed writing within a particular time period.

Rapid changes in a person's writing can result from the sudden onset of a serious illness, the administration of therapeutic drugs, or the consequence of a debilitating accident. Although such sudden transitions can create problems for the document examiner, they also provide a means of determining when a questioned signature or handwriting might have been produced.

Contents of a Document

Proof that a document was backdated or postdated can occasionally be found within its contents. These details are often overlooked by the perpetrator as his attention is focused on producing a document that contains the right information. Names, addresses, postal codes, phone numbers, trade names, and job titles mentioned in a document might provide evidence that it was produced at a different time.

Events are occasionally mentioned in correspondence that did not occur until months or years after the date appearing on the document. Verb tenses in relation to events mentioned can also indicate a document was prepared after its purported date. When preparing a postdated or backdated document, the writer may not remember what verb tense to use. Such inconsistencies, especially when repeated, provide a good indication that something is amiss.

When preparing business correspondence, the typist's initials are often placed at the bottom of the document. In fraudulent documents, the initials of a typist who is currently employed by a company may be used instead of the person who held the position on the date that appears on the document.

Computer-Printed Documents

Dating computer-printed documents is approached in much the same manner as dating typewritten documents. The debut of computer printer technologies are all associated with a date of introduction. Consequently, any document produced by a daisy-wheel, dot-matrix, inkjet, or laser printer cannot bear a date that precedes the respective periods when these printers first appeared on the market.

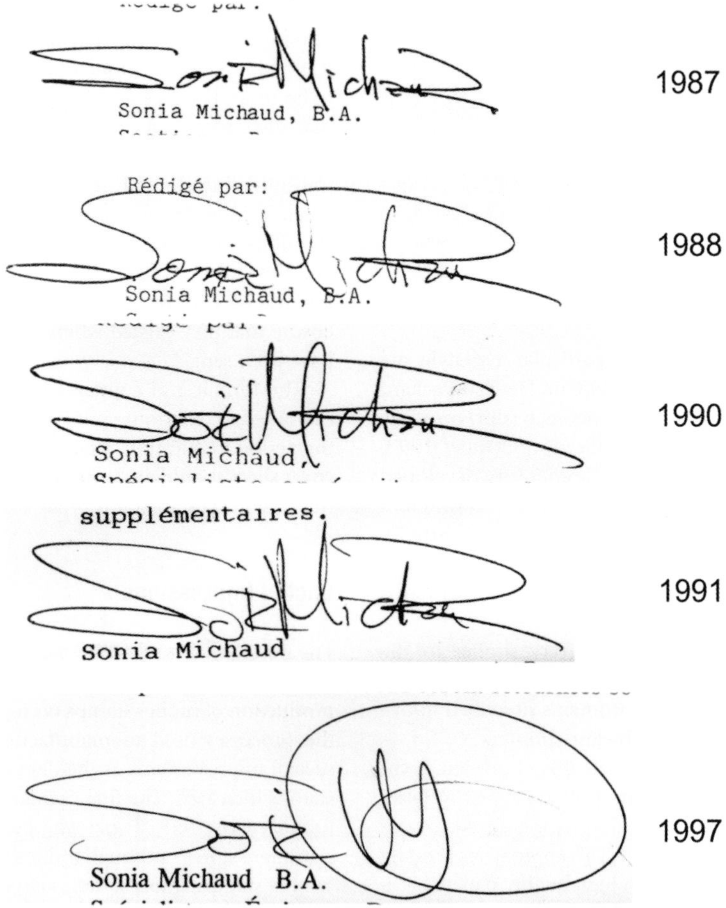

Figure 6 Six signatures produced by a writer during a 10-year period show some features that have a temporal significance.

Daisy-Wheel Printers

The daisy-wheel printer, using a similar impact technology to the typewriter, bridged the gap between typewriters and later generations of computer printers. Although very popular during the 1970s, a few daisy-wheel printers are still in use. The print elements of these machines contain a full set of characters positioned on the end of long spokes attached to a central hub. As the elements spin on a central shaft, the characters are struck at the appropriate time from behind with a plunger. The action of the character striking the paper through an inked ribbon produces a letter on a document.

Like their typewritten counterparts, documents produced by daisy-wheel printers can be dated by considering irregularities in the alignment of letters or damage to their outlines through wear and tear. The source of other temporal defects can be traced to faulty moving components of the printer. These changes provide a means for dating the work of a particular printer. It should be kept in mind, however, that daisy wheels can be easily removed, discarded, and replaced by a new element. All defects associated with the old daisy wheel will disappear and only those that relate to the printer will remain.

Dot-Matrix Printers

Dot-matrix printers gained popularity during the early 1980s. Early models had nine metal pins arranged along a vertical axis that struck the paper through an inked ribbon, whereas the printhead moved across the page. At the end of a single pass, the paper would advance slightly and the printhead would return across the page in the opposite direction. This process would be repeated until the entire page was printed. Printing produced by dot-matrix printers improved as 12-, 18-, and 24-pin models became available. These produced sharper printing which was referred to as 'near letter quality' or NLQ printing. The dates when these progressive improvements occurred provide a further means of limiting computer printed document to a particular period.

Documents printed by dot-matrix printers can also be dated by the sudden appearance of printing defects, which are due to broken or bent pins, worn printhead housings, or other manifestations caused by defective printer components.

Ink-Jet and Laser Printers

Documents produced by ink-jet or laser printers could only be produced after these technologies were introduced. A computer-generated document can often be associated to a particular printer manufacturer based on the presence of class characteristics. The chemical composition of ink-jet ink or toner can also be useful for determining if a document has been backdated.

All nonimpact computer printers use computer software to generate printed characters. Printer control language (PCL)

Figure 7 Letters 'r' produced by HP laserJet III printer (left) and by an HP Laserjet 4 (right) introduced to the market in October 1993 show several conspicuous differences between the internal Courier fonts installed on these printers.

defines how letters belonging to a particular typestyle are shaped. For example, until October 1993, no Hewlett Packard PCL was capable of handling 600 dots per inch (dpi) printing. The Hewlett Packard LaserJet 4, introduced in October 1993, was distributed with a special internal Courier font developed specifically for 600 dpi printing. This typestyle was different from any prior Courier font used in LaserJet printers (**Figure 7**). Since the LaserJet 4 was introduced in October 1993, any document which contains this special Courier font but dated earlier than this must be backdated.

The mechanics of laser printers are very similar to the processes used by modern photocopier machines. Hence, methods for dating photocopied documents described above also apply to documents produced by laser printers.

An interesting approach to try to date ink-jet printed documents is to measure the area of the dots because the latter diminish within the time, that is, the dot size is reduced according to the technological development. This approach is actually limited to the documents printed on high-quality papers.

Facsimile Documents

Recently, facsimile machines have become a common form of business communication. Although the first fax was designed by Alexander Bain and patented during 1843, the machine has only really gained popularity since the early 1980s. Facsimile documents are often presented as proof that business transactions or agreements took place on a particular date. Not all of these documents, however, are genuine. Fast and convenient for their users, facsimile machines also provide fraud artists with an opportunity to fabricate documents and defraud unsuspecting victims.

The transmitting terminal identifier (TTI) header usually appears at the top of most facsimile documents. This header may contain the page number, the date, the time the message was sent, and other information supplied by the sending machine. Although dispatched by the sending machine, this information is printed by the fax that receives the message. A receiving terminal identifier (RTI) printed by the receiving fax machine can also appear at the bottom of transmitted documents. The TTI and RTI of every suspected faxed document warrant close inspection.

In many cases, the date and time appearing in the TTI of faxed message are correct. It should be noted, however, that these settings can be quickly changed by anyone who has access to the machine and who possesses the knowledge to make the adjustments.

It is possible to identify the make and model of both sending and receiving machines by comparing the TTI and RTI of a received facsimile document to a library or collection of fax fonts. If such a search indicates that one or both facsimile machines were not available when the questioned fax was received, then it casts suspicion on the authenticity of the transmitted document. If long-distance charges were incurred when sending the facsimile transmissions, telephone records should be examined for evidence that a fax was sent on the date and time alleged. Telephone numbers and area codes appearing in the TTI or on the cover sheet should also be checked to ensure that they existed when the document was supposed to have been sent.

The format and content of the fax cover sheet should be examined to determine if it is consistent with that used during the period in question. Details of the transmitted message and cover sheet should also be examined to ensure people's names, titles, or initials are appropriate for the period in question.

Cachet Impressions

The development of rubber stamps followed the discovery of vulcanizing rubber by Charles Goodyear. The first commercial production of rubber stamps occurred in 1864. Since that time, the processes used to manufacture stamps have undergone several improvements as the demand for better quality rubber stamps increased. The first preinked stamp, Perma Stamp, was produced in 1958. These stamps are still a popular item in stationery stores. Although today's stamps are still referred to as 'rubber stamps,' most stamps are now produced from a plastic-based photopolymer material.

Both rubber and plastic deteriorate over time. The relief edges of a stamp can crack- or break-off, an ink/dirt mixture can clog deep crevices, and the relief areas of a stamp can become worn through constant use. These events introduce flaws that are reproduced in the impressions produced by a worn stamp. The approximate period when a stamp impression was made can be determined by comparing its defects with standards from the same stamp arranged in chronological order.

Another method by which stamp impressions can be dated involves changes to the size of some stamps with time. It has been found that stamps can shrink as much as 1.5 mm during a 4-year period. Although this phenomenon is relatively rare, it does provide yet another means of dating stamp impressions.

Glues, Tapes, and Paper Fasteners

Adhesives used to manufacture envelopes, stationery pads, and tapes occasionally undergo changes or modifications to improve their properties. Such changes can be used to establish the earliest date that a document manufactured with a given adhesive was produced. The stationery manufacturer or adhesive company should always be contacted to verify the date when a particular adhesive was first used.

Lift-off tape was introduced by IBM to facilitate the correction of typewriting errors. This innovation, first introduced to the market by IBM on the 1 April 1973, removed unwanted typed characters by overstriking letters through the lift-off tape. This action would lift the letter from the document and allow the typist to correct errors with little disturbance to the paper surface.

Indented Writing

Indented handwritten impressions made in the surface of a document can reveal important information about whether written entries on a piece of paper were made before or after the indented writing occurred. Such sequence determinations are confirmed by subjecting the document to an electrostatic detection apparatus (ESDA) examination.

It is often possible to establish the exact date when indented handwritten impressions on a document were produced. An ESDA examination that establishes the visible writing on a questioned document was made after dated indented impressions can provide an unusual but effective method for confirming the document was backdated.

Handwritten entries in a journal, ledger, notepad, or receipt book usually produce indented impressions on underlying sheets of paper. If it is necessary to date one of the sheets which was removed, its original location can be confirmed by matching writing on the document with corresponding impressions on the other bound papers. If the dates on adjacent pages are reliable, this simple method enables the document examiner to place the questioned document within a particular time frame.

Guillotine Marks

The exposed edges of receipt books, reams of paper, and stationery pads may contain marks produced by cutters or guillotine blades used to trim these products to size. These stria, often referred to as 'guillotine marks,' do not run perpendicular to the surface of the paper but run at an angle across the trimmed surfaces. Their locations along the four edges of a document can indicate where a sheet was positioned in the original stack of paper.

Access to several documents from the same stack of paper is needed to establish a cutting pattern against which the contested document is compared. Once the location of guillotine marks on the four edges of the questioned sheet match the position of sheets from the same lot, any dating information on adjacent sheets can be used to determine when the questioned document was written. If the questioned document is not contemporaneous with information on adjacent sheets of stationery, some plausible explanation should be sought.

See also: **Digital Evidence:** Digital Imaging: Enhancement and Authentication; **Documents:** Analytical Methods; Forgery/Counterfeits; Handwriting; History of the Forensic Examination of Documents; Ink Analysis; Paper Analysis.

Further Reading

Brunelle RL and Reed RW (1984) *Forensic Examination of Ink and Paper*. Springfield: Charles C Thomas.

Cantu AA (1995) A sketch of analytical methods for document dating. Part I. The static approach: Determining age independent analytical profiles. *International Journal of Forensic Document Examiners* 1: 40–51.

Cantu AA (1995) A sketch of analytical methods for document dating. Part II. The dynamic approach: Determining age independent analytical profiles. *International Journal of Forensic Document Examiners* 2: 192–208.

Dietz G (2010) Research in paper structures and its opportunities for forensic tasks. *6th EDEWG Conference*, Dubrovnik.

Ezcurra M, Gongora J, Maguregui I, and Alonso R (2010) Analytical methods for dating modern writing instrument inks on paper. *Forensic Science International* 197: 1–20.

Gerhart J (1992) Identification of photocopiers from fusing roller defects. *Journal of Forensic Sciences* 37: 130–139.

Godown L (1969) Forgeries over genuine signatures. *Journal of Forensic Sciences* 14: 463–468.

Kelly JS (1983) *Classification and Identification of Modern Office Copiers*. Houston: American Board of Forensic Document Examiners, Inc.

Kelly JS and Lindblom BS (2006) *Scientific Examination of Questioned Documents*. Boca Raton, FL: CRC Taylor Francis.

LaPorte GM, Stephens JC, and Beuchel AK (2010) The examination of commercial printing defects to assess common origin, batch variation and error rate. *Journal of Forensic Sciences* 55: 136–140.

Mazzella WD and Taroni F (2005) A simple logical approach to questioned envelopes examination. *Science and Justice* 45: 35–38.

Osborn AS (1929) *Questioned Documents*, 2nd edn. Albany: Boyd Printing Co.

Purtell DJ (1980) Dating a signature. *Forensic Science International* 15: 243–248.

Starrs J (1991) The case of the doctor who doctored the documents. *Scientific Sleuthing Review* 15: 1.

Totty RN (1990) The examination of photocopy documents. *Forensic Science International* 46: 121–126.

Tweedy J (2001) Class characteristics of counterfeit protection system codes of color laser copiers. *Journal of the American Society of Questioned Document Examiners* 4: 53–66.

Welch J (2008) Erasable ink; something old, something new. *Science and Justice* 48: 187–191.

Weyermann C, Almog J, Bügler J, and Cantu A (2011) Minimum requirements for application of ink dating methods based on solvent analysis in casework. *Forensic Science International* 210: 52–62.

Zavattaro D, Quarta G, D'Elia M, and Calcagnile L (2007) Recent documents dating: An approach using radiocarbon techniques. *Forensic Science International* 167: 160–162.

Forgery/Counterfeits

T Trubshoe and J McGinn, Department of Immigration and Citizenship, Perth, WA, Australia; Document Examination Solutions, Perth, WA, Australia

Glossary

Biographical data page The page or pages in a passport that contain personal information belonging to the bearer of the document. This information commonly contains full names, date of birth, place of issue, and dates of issue and expiry, as well as a photograph of the bearer.

Covert security features Security features that are included in a document and require a complex understanding of document security and access to sophisticated equipment to enhance. Generally information of a restricted nature with limited disclosure, these features are the final line of security that can be used to confirm or discredit the authenticity of a document.

Optically variable devices Features that show multiple optical effects by changing the angle with which light strikes it, and with which it is viewed. These effects can show movement and/or changes in color, and cannot be photocopied or scanned.

Overt security features Security features that are included in a document and require a minimal understanding of document security and no equipment to visualize. These features are designed to be difficult to effectively counterfeit and to be easily detected by those persons to whom they are presented.

Planchettes Small colored discs of $\sim$2 mm diameter that can be incorporated into the manufacture of security paper. The discs can be designed to be viewed under visible and/or ultraviolet light sources, and may include additional security features such as microprinting.

Radio frequency identification devices (RFIDs) They are contactless microchips embedded into a document such as a passport or identity card, which allow for the storage and processing of data. Communication with chip readers is via electronic waves, which are able to be read when within a defined proximity to the reader and when authenticated by public key infrastructure (PKI).

Semicovert security features Security features that are included in a document and require a basic understanding of document security and access to basic handheld equipment. These features are designed to be viewed with magnification of $\sim$10 $\times$ or simple white and ultraviolet light sources, while still being recognizable by the person to whom they are presented in a minimal time period.

Introduction

History is riddled with attempts to deceive through the forgery of documents, such as by Frank Abagnale Jr throughout the 1960s, made famous through the 2002 movie *Catch Me if You Can*, and by Mark Hoffmann throughout the 1980s with the various Mormon documents.

Although there has been a shift toward transactions occurring electronically, the fact remains that documents continue to be a pivotal requirement in a range of financial and other activities. In any given circumstance, a document can contribute to the facilitation of a transaction, whether for financial gain or some other purpose. Given the resultant value of many documents, it is an attractive proposition for forgers to explore methods of simulating or altering some or all of the information to gain an advantage or benefit.

As a result, there has been significant technological development in the nature and appearance of documents used for a variety of transactions. Governments worldwide have a vested interest in the development of documents to withstand attempts at simulation or alteration, which is undertaken in partnership with a range of organizations and businesses including security document manufacturers, research scientists, and document examination specialists. Documents produced with a high level of security and therefore integrity pose a challenge to forgers; however, it is also recognized that any document is capable, in a given circumstance, of being attractive as a 'tool' to facilitate a greater deceit. Documents classified in any quadrant of **Figure 1** may contribute to fraudulent activities.

Although they are devoid of financial value and have limited or no security characteristics, there are documents that enable or support transactions. These are often referred to as 'breeder documents,' which can enable a forger to gain credibility or potentially provide a mechanism to obtain high-value documents with a high level of integrity. This is particularly relevant with respect to identity documents. For this reason, it should be stated that forgery is not limited to high-quality documents displaying a high level of security and therefore integrity, but can also include any document that may provide a mechanism to gain this high-value document.

The Nature of Documents Used for Deceit

The distinction between different types of documents used to deceive is important. Counterfeit documents are produced with the appearance of a genuine document and, where appropriate, will display features that attempt to replicate the security characteristics of the said document.

Counterfeit documents are based on a genuine model and are manufactured completely without authority. It is a generalization with some merit that counterfeit documents are a

 http://dx.doi.org/10.1016/B978-0-12-382165-2.00133-1

Low value Low integrity	High value Low integrity
Low value High integrity	High value High integrity

Figure 1 The nature of documents in terms of their value and integrity.

reproduction of a document of some value, either in terms of integrity or financial value.

Fantasy documents differ; these may have the appearance of a document of value or integrity, but they are not based on a genuine and credible base document model. They are fabricated documents commonly marketed as novelty items, although they can be and are used for illicit purposes.

Forged documents are original, genuine documents that have been altered in some way. The alterations may be complex and may relate to the document itself, such as the replacement of pages within a passport, or they may be the inclusion of additional information, such as the inflation of the dollar value of a check.

In considering these basic definitions, experience with fraudulent documents can be generally categorized. Certain documents such as currency are more likely to be counterfeited; documents such as checks are more likely to be forged; and experience has shown that documents such as passports are not confined to either method.

The use of counterfeit or forged documents can be considered broadly under the following sections.

Organized Crime

Given that documents are used to facilitate a range of activities including, but not limited to, the transfer of funds or title, the verification of identity or cross-border movements, and the smuggling and trading of drugs and firearms, it is not unexpected that the production and use of a range of documents is organized. Whether it contributes to a direct fraudulent activity, such as financial fraud, or enables alternative activities such as drug smuggling, people-trafficking (or smuggling), or terrorism, there is a high prevalence of organized crime elements involved. These elements are involved in both the production and the distribution of counterfeit and forged documents associated with these illicit activities.

Opportune Crime

Opportune crimes involving counterfeit or forged documents are events that generally occur in isolation, involving limited perpetrators. It is not uncommon for the quality of documents created under these circumstances to be inferior. Perpetrators are reliant on the ability to obtain a successful outcome with little effort. Many opportune crimes are possible through a lack of vigilance on the part of the receiving person, or a lack of understanding regarding the nature, appearance, and security value of documents that are presented.

Combating Counterfeit and Forged Documents

There are a number of elements that combine as combative measures to activities involving fraudulent documents.

First and foremost, there is recognition that documents with a high value or purpose are produced with a range of features that allow the receiver, and therefore the person assessing the documents, to judge the genuineness or otherwise of the documents presented. Both organized and opportune crime perpetrators are reliant on various factors such as limited time, minimal training, and various distractions to impact on this person's ability to detect the fraudulent documents.

It can therefore be said that the ability to determine counterfeit or fraudulent documents and activities relies on an understanding of the process of production of genuine documents, together with appropriate training and organizational processes to allow their examination. This includes an understanding of fundamental document security features and characteristics, as well as the limitations associated with their examination.

To enable consideration of whether a document is forged or counterfeited, an understanding of the production of genuine documents must first be gained within the following broad categories:

1. Document security features
2. Quality of manufacture
3. Credible issuing protocols and data registration
4. Verification mechanisms

Some of these aspects are discussed in detail in the following sections.

Document Security Features

The high-quality production of important documents in itself adds a level of integrity. In addition, security features with varying degrees of complexity are introduced into such documents. The purpose of these features can generally be considered as twofold:

- To verify the genuineness of the document and/or,
- To allow for identification of intentional alteration, manipulation, or addition.

It could be expected that the complexity of features would bear a direct relationship to the value of the document. However, this is not always the case. There are many valuable documents bearing limited features or features that are easily compromised. In documents used for travel and identity purposes, a range of initiatives over many years have seen quality standards increase to a level that can and does influence the ability of forgers to easily create counterfeit or forged documents. This has, in part, increased the requirement of organized syndicates to produce high-quality fraudulent documents and has generated alternative methodologies for illegal activities, some of which include the use of genuine but fraudulently obtained documents.

Owing to the different situations in which documents are used and the ways in which they are examined, various overt, semicovert, and covert security features are incorporated into their design. By including security features at these different levels, the documents are designed to enable examination with minimal or no equipment at a bank, airport, or retail outlet as well as with sophisticated equipment within laboratories.

Security features and characteristics are introduced into a document during the manufacturing process, and where they are used for identity through the issuing process as well. The document's components can roughly be divided into the substrate, printing, personalization, and issuance security, with it being possible to incorporate as many or as few security features in each component as desired.

Substrate

Although secure documents were traditionally manufactured using only paper-based substrates, recent technological developments in synthetic polymers have allowed for a wider range of substrates to be manufactured and a larger number of features to be incorporated.

With paper being the substrate on which the majority of secure documents are still manufactured, various security features are available for incorporation into paper manufacture and therefore available to be evaluated in an examination. Secure documents generally incorporate one or more of the following security features: watermark, security thread, security fibers, and planchettes, and omit the optical brighteners traditionally included in plain or copy paper. With the security features being incorporated into the physical manufacture of paper, postproduction inclusion of genuine security features into commercially available paper is not possible.

Whether as a generic laid pattern or as an intricate image, the watermark is incorporated into paper during the forming stage, where paper fibers are clumped together or pushed apart, to change the density of the paper to create the required design. Using a transmitted light source (light shining through the document from behind), the pattern or image can be viewed as tonal changes in the paper. **Figure 2(a)** and **2(b)** show the watermark under reflected and transmitted light, respectively. Simulated watermarks, on counterfeit documents, are often the result of printing or embossing and as such are regularly viewed using oblique (light grazing a document from the side) or ultraviolet light.

Security threads, traditionally associated with high-security documents such as currency and passports, are now being seen in the packaging of computer software and the like because of the increasing counterfeit market that has emerged for these products. Either fully embedded into the paper, or being woven into and out of the paper in a uniform manner (often referred to as a windowed security thread), the security thread, as with the watermark, is incorporated into the paper during the forming stage and is examined using a transmitted light source. **Figure 2(a)** and **2(b)** show the two types of security threads under reflected and transmitted light, respectively. Printing of these threads, either as a solid line or text, is the most frequently encountered simulation of this feature in the production of counterfeit documents.

Although they are different paper security components, security fibers and planchettes are incorporated into paper and examined in the same way. End product requirements determine the color of the fibers and planchettes used and whether they are to be visible under white light, ultraviolet light, or both. Included in the pulp stage of the paper's manufacture, the resulting fibers and planchettes will be randomly placed throughout and sit within the structure of the paper. Should a counterfeiter attempt to simulate either of these components, it is most often through printing and can result in the appearance of fibers or planchettes occurring in the same position on multiple pages.

(a)

(b)

Figure 2 (a) A 100 Peso note displaying a windowed security thread under reflected light. (b) A 100 Peso note displaying a watermark, security thread, and windowed security thread under transmitted light.

Ordinary white copy paper incorporates optical brightening agents in its manufacture to give the paper a brighter white appearance. Under an ultraviolet light source, these agents give off a bright blue/purple fluorescence. It is generally accepted that security paper does not incorporate optical brightening agents in its manufacture and, as such, under an ultraviolet light source the paper remains relatively dull. When counterfeiters use optically bright paper in the manufacture of their documents, it is not uncommon for them to attempt to mask the ultraviolet fluorescence by using ultraviolet-absorbing substances such as lacquer.

Synthetic polymer substrates have become a part of everyday life because of technological advances in financial and identity systems and requirements. From relatively simple store gift cards and telephone cards, to various types of credit cards and currency, synthetic polymer documents have become a popular option in the creation of a low-cost item with a financial value. Identity documents manufactured with these substrates have also increased in popularity, whether as a document in its entirety, such as a drivers license or identity card, or in part, such as a biographical data page within a passport. Various synthetic polymers are used in the manufacture of such documents, with specific polymers chosen because of the particular properties appropriate for the intended use. For example, polyvinyl chloride is most commonly used for credit cards and loyalty cards because of its low cost and ease of mass production; polycarbonate offers an extended lifespan and embedded layers for security printing methods and features to be included; and polypropylene is used in the manufacture of synthetic polymer currency.

As with secure paper, numerous security features can be incorporated into the synthetic polymers during their manufacture. These include, but are not restricted to, Multiple Laser Images™, optically variable devices, security threads, and contact chips, or radio frequency identification devices. In addition to the specific polymers mentioned above, composite substrates are also used, allowing security features available to different substrates to be incorporated into the one substrate structure.

The introduction of substrate security features is designed to impact on the ability of forgers to counterfeit the document.

Printing

Depending on the type of document, portions of, or all of, the printing can be created using commercial processes. Currency as an example is a document that is printed consistently and repetitively throughout the course of the series of note with no variable printing required except for the serial number. Identity documents differ in that they too have the consistent repetitive printing throughout the series of the document, but in addition to the commercial printing, desktop printing processes are required to allow for the printing of variable data.

Although not a secure printing process in its own right, the most common commercial printing process used in secure documents is offset lithography. Having a flat and sharp image, this process contributes the majority of the background printing and a great portion of the overprinting on any secure document, and is often utilized in the printing of security features. Other commercial printing processes such as letterpress, flexography, gravure, and screen printing are again not specific to secure documents, but are often used in areas such as document numbering, laminate printing, and security feature inclusion.

Some key security features can be printed using only the secure commercial printing process of intaglio. This process is available only to secure printers and is used to manufacture a raised print with fine detail and high-quality security capabilities. The latent image is an example of a security feature that will operate correctly only if intaglio is used. Using side light, and relying on the height of the ink to create a shadow and reveal a word or image, the latent image will not be revealed if a flat printing process is utilized. **Figure 3(a)** and **3(b)** show the intaglio printing of a latent image under reflected and side lights, respectively. The background is printed with a lithographic process.

The printing processes used and the associated security features printed are intended to allow for the detection of counterfeits and to provide the capacity to reveal alterations in forgeries.

(a)

(b)

Figure 3 (a) A 100 Baht note displaying intaglio printing over a lithographic printed background under reflected light. (b) A 100 Baht note displaying an intaglio printed latent image using side light.

Personalization

A number of documents, especially identity documents, require additional printing to allow personalization, thereby individualizing the document. This inclusion of unique information on each document requires printing methods that are readily available, versatile, and cost effective. These types of printing are commonly referred to as 'desktop printing' processes and are readily accessible to the ordinary person. Although a desktop process, the hardware for high-volume requirement can be of a commercial standard. Depending on the type of substrate used to create the base document, various desktop printing processes may be employed.

Traditional processes such as typewriters and dot matrix machines are no longer expected to be used in modern, high-level identity documents, but they can be regularly seen in older identity documents. Most documents have moved toward using one of four processes, namely, inkjet, laser, thermal transfer, or dye diffusion thermal transfer (often referred to as D2T2), and in the case of synthetic polymer documents, laser engraving.

Typewriters and dot matrix printers, together with the more commonly used processes inkjet and toner, are confined to

Figure 4 A magnified image of the characteristics of thermal transfer printing on a synthetic polymer document.

printing directly on paper-based documents. The exception is where the information is printed onto the reverse of a laminate and the laminate material is adhered to the substrate. Should a photo have to be included in the personalization, a physical patch photograph needs to be attached alongside the traditional processes, while inkjet and toner can print text and images directly onto the document.

The more modern thermal transfer printing is able to be used on both paper and polymer documents, whereas the D2T2 combination requires a polymer substrate to print correctly. As with inkjet and toner, both of these processes allow for the printing of black and white or colored photos directly onto the substrate. The characteristics specific to thermal transfer printing can be seen in **Figure 4**.

Laser engraving, the most recent of the common personalization processes, can be used only on synthetic polymer documents. Activating a carbon sensitized layer within the polymer substrate, the resulting personal information becomes a component within the document. Because the printing is carbon, it can create only black and white images. This laser-based process is somewhat unique in that it is able to create flat and/or raised printing, adding further security to a document.

Issuance security

Added to protect personal information from being altered or added, additional security covering a portion of, or the entire, document is applied. This will be an action on the part of the issuing authority or organization, with the fundamental purpose of protecting the personal data. As with other components utilized in the document manufacture, issuing security may include quite simple and/or dated features, or modern features developed through technological advances and research.

A traditional patch photograph on a paper substrate, for example, may be sufficiently protected by the application of a dry or wet seal stamped partially over both substrates, or through attachment by a metal grommet or eyelet. A polymer identity card, on the other hand, may include security features that not only cover the substrate surface but are bonded in such a way as to make a separation attempt on the layers impossible.

Commonly synthetic polymers, laminate security products protect a document from forgery or counterfeit by ensuring that there is a layer that requires removal to alter information or needs simulation when an original is not available. Numerous types of laminates are manufactured, each encompassing various security features and designs. Laminates can include simple security features such as embossed patterns, ultraviolet reactive ink, and visible printed geometric images in strategically placed sections. More sophisticated laminates can be formed using glass beads to mask a covert image that becomes visible only through correct use of coaxial light, or can include holography across the entire surface creating various diffracting images and patterns when viewed from different angles.

The purpose of including issuing security is to render a forgery to the document or a counterfeit of the document detectable.

Issuing Protocols

The role of issuing authorities is important to the overall integrity of a document and the document security continuum. A document can be designed and manufactured to have the highest level of security imaginable, but without appropriate issuing protocols in place it cannot be assumed that the bearer of the document is the owner of the presented identity.

For high-level documents to be obtained, breeder documents comprising birth, death, and marriage certificates, land title certificates, credit cards, and other documents of this nature are required to be shown as proof of identity. Often, the methods available to verify the authenticity of the breeder documents are limited, and the security features incorporated within them poor, making it difficult for issuing authorities to place a high level of integrity on either the document or the information contained within. As document security features become more sophisticated and systems related to their use more developed, there is a visible increase in the number of fraudulently obtained genuine base documents being used; forged or counterfeit breeder documents are used in their acquisition. An examination of these fraudulently obtained documents would result in the determination of genuineness as to their manufacture, with no way of fraud detection being possible.

International standards, through organizations such as the International Civil Aviation Organization, are widely acknowledged and implemented in the manufacture of high-security documents such as passports and identity cards. With standardization of these documents being in place, capacity building and assistance to aid countries, through international organizations, has turned toward the manufacture and issuing protocols of breeder documents to assist in raising the integrity of the complete security continuum.

The Examination Role

The nature of counterfeits and forgeries is such that the initial encounter with a document requiring examination is rarely within a specialized document examination laboratory. A passport may first be viewed by immigration or customs officers, a credit card by a shop assistant in a department store, currency by a bank clerk, identity documents by a transport authority officer, etc.

The examination of documents to determine their genuineness or otherwise is separated into three levels. Depending on the country or organization, these three levels of examination are described under the following headings: detection, assessment, and specialist.

Depending on the level of examination undertaken, a decision is then made to refer the document for further examination or to determine the outcome as required.

The distinction between counterfeit and forged documents is important. On commencement of any examination, the base document is examined to determine whether it was manufactured through genuine means and contains security features expected in a secure document or a document of that nature. This first level can enable counterfeit documents to be identified on the basis of an evaluation of key but generic document security components, which should be consistent from one document to another in a particular series.

Following the determination of the authenticity of the base document, evidence of forgery to the original document can be identified. At this stage of examination, methods used to alter documents are considered, security features of documents are examined to determine their genuineness or otherwise, and any areas where tampering might have occurred are examined in detail.

To assist in formulating opinions, sample documents, reference databases, and experienced examiners or document examination networks are often engaged.

Detection

For a forged or counterfeited document to be identified, it must first be detected. The detection level of examination is arguably the most important level which is why so much of a document's design focuses on incorporating simple but effective security features that can be examined with minimal training and no equipment.

With timeframes as short as 30 seconds allocated for the examination of each document, the overt features must be easily examinable to ensure correct operation and to recognize signs of tampering. The detection process may include evaluation of substrate security features such as a watermark, the changing of color and/or image of optically variable devices, the consistency of manufactured components such as number perforations, commercial printing, etc., and the overall quality of the document.

If a document does not raise concern within the short examination period available, it is assumed to be genuine and the processing or transaction proceeds. It is because of the minimal scrutiny that is possible at this point that a forged or counterfeit document, even though crude in appearance, is accepted as being genuine.

Assessment

The assessment level of examination occurs once a document has been detected as being of concern. It is here that a more detailed understanding of document manufacture and security is required, together with equipment capable of examining semicovert levels of security within the document. Depending on the examination environment, the resources utilized may range from being quite simple and consisting only of handheld equipment such as a magnifier, an ultraviolet light, and a white light source, to quite sophisticated technical equipment such as a stereomicroscope and a multispectral imaging system.

With more time available for examination, often ranging from hours to days, the document is usually examined in depth by a document examiner or someone whose function includes the examination of documents. With the information that is obtained through the examination, additional avenues of questioning or investigation may be determined.

Documents assessed as being a forgery or counterfeit at this stage may or may not require further examination for judicial or organizational needs.

Specialist

The traditional forensic document examiner, or a specialist in a particular field of document manufacture, undertakes the most in-depth examination of a document to determine its authenticity, which may include a detailed assessment of the covert security features. With many years of specialist training and access to sophisticated technical equipment, systems, and databases, the examiner can undertake an examination that is often limited only by the requirements of the organization. The examination timeframes are not as stringent, so the specialist can undertake complex examinations if deemed necessary.

Technical equipment such as a stereomicroscope and a multispectral imaging system allow the examination of a document in fine detail, under various lighting and filtering conditions. In addition to these core pieces of equipment, electrostatic detection systems, photography accessories, and a selection of other microscopy and spectroscopy equipment are often employed for their respective examinations of impressions on the paper, for the capture of images for evidence, and for the detailed analysis of various components of a document.

Throughout the examination process, observations are made of areas within the document, allowing propositions for the document's condition to be formulated and, where possible, opinions to be expressed.

Conclusion

The production of counterfeit and forged documents is a significant international issue. The use of documents to facilitate illicit acts cannot be understated, nor can the fact that documents remain cornerstones of identity verification be negated.

The development of advanced document security features, in combination with sound issuing protocols and verification methodologies, ongoing emergence of biometric capabilities associated with documents, and an increase in community awareness, are all strategies to be designed to enhance a receiver's ability to accept documents as genuine, or positively identify the effects of counterfeit and forged documents.

When a document is determined to be a counterfeit or a forgery, it is possible that, through additional analysis of the document, linkages to other documents, their components, or manufacturers may be made. This type of forensic intelligence can assist in the disruption of document manufacturing syndicates and of organized criminal activities such as people smuggling, drug trafficking, and terrorism.

See also: **Documents:** Analytical Methods; Document Dating; Handwriting; Ink Analysis; Paper Analysis; **Investigations:** Counterfeit Currency; Identity Theft.

Further Reading

Ellen D (2006) *Scientific Examination of Documents – Methods and Techniques*, 3rd edn. Boca Raton, FL: Taylor and Francis Group.

Harrison WR (1981) *Suspect Documents: Their Scientific Examination*. Chicago, IL: Nelson-Hall.

Kelly JS and Lindblom BS (2006) *Scientific Examination of Questioned Documents*, 2nd edn. New York, NY: CRC Taylor & Francis.

Ng PK, Hui WS, Chim JLC, Li C-K, and Poon NL (2004) Methods of forgery in counterfeit travel documents. *Journal of the American Society of Questioned Document Examiners* 7(2): 83–90.

Nugent N (2008) How to personalize a passport – Part 1. *Keesing Journal of Documents and Identity* 27: 3–8.

Nugent N (2009) How to personalize a passport – Part 2. *Keesing Journal of Documents and Identity* 28: 11–15.

Ombelli D and Knopjes F (2008) *Documents: The Developer's Toolkit*. European Union: Occidentalis Editora Lda.

Rettig R (2011) Security features in composite material documents. *Keesing Journal of Documents and Identity* 34: 13–17.

United Nations Office on Drugs and Crime (2010) *Guide for the Development of Forensic Document Examination Capacity*. New York: United Nations.

Van Renesse RL (2005) *Optical Document Security*, 3rd edn. Boston: Artech House.

Relevant Websites

www.icao.int – International Civil Aviation Organization.
www.iso.org – International Organisation for Standardization.

Handwriting

CL Bird, Forensic Science SA, Adelaide, SA, Australia

This article is a revision of the previous edition article by M. Vos, S. Strach & P. Westwood, volume 2, pp 584–590, © 2000, Elsevier Ltd.

Glossary

Copybook A manual of handwriting instruction that contains models of penmanship to be copied.
Diacritic A mark added to a letter to indicate a particular pronunciation. Also used to refer to the dots over the 'i' and 'j'.
Disguised writing The writing of a person who has deliberately attempted to alter their usual writing habits in order to conceal their identity.
Fluency Quality of smoothness and flow of movement.
Line quality A measure of fluency of handwriting, the degree of regularity.
Natural variation Normal or usual deviations found between repeated instances of any individual's writing.
Retouching Touching up to correct or perfect a written character.
Simulated writing Writing that is produced by attempting to copy the pictorial characteristics of a target writing. It may be created freehand with the use of a physical or mental model, or by a tracing process.
Tremor A lack of smoothness in the writing trace, due to lack of skill, deliberate control of the writing implement, or involuntary movement (illness affecting motor control).

Introduction

Handwriting is the process, and outcome, of creating letters, numbers, or symbols using a writing implement, usually following a set of guidelines such that the content may be communicated to another person. Opinions on the authorship of handwriting and signatures have been accepted as expert evidence in courts of law around the world for over 100 years. These opinions may be on writings related to criminal investigations or civil litigation. In the majority of cases, the markings being examined are present on conventional paper documents; however, examinations are not limited to these and may also encompass writings appearing on such surfaces as doors, walls, vehicles, furniture, and skin. Examples of commonly encountered documents on which questioned handwriting may appear are wills, contracts, mortgages, and other legal documents, checks, credit or withdrawal vouchers, anonymous or threatening letters, and diaries.

While there are slight differences in the way handwriting and signatures are produced and examined (discussed in more detail below), throughout this article when the term handwriting is used, it will usually imply both handwritten text and signatures.

Theoretical Basis for Handwriting Comparison

In relation to other 'identification sciences' such as DNA profiling, fingerprints, or tool mark comparisons, handwriting opinion evidence stands alone as the examinations and evidence evaluations are based solely on movement outcomes. The basis for this is that handwriting features embedded within the writing trace are believed to be somewhat characteristic of an individual. Since handwriting is a learnt behavior, it is found that the features of the writing can vary normally, can be purposefully distorted, or can be copied by others. The effectiveness of forensic handwriting comparisons is reliant upon the relationship between the features observed in the movement outcome and the extent to which those features characterize an individual.

Why Does One Believe Handwriting Can Be Used as an Individuating Feature?

Handwriting is a complex learned behavior that is the product of cognitive, psychomotor, and biomechanical processes directing the movement of the arm, hand, and fingers in order to manipulate the writing implement in three-dimensional space to produce a visual trace on the writing surface. Like any type of complex movement, the handwriting learning process is comprised of three relatively distinct phases of movement acquisition. During the *cognitive phase*, the learner writer is concerned with how to construct letters and symbols. This usually requires a high degree of cognition as different motor strategies are trialed and successful strategies preserved. As each step in the movement progression is considered and controlled, writing produced during this phase usually displays poor fluency. The *associative phase* occurs when the writer has determined an effective way of constructing characters and is employing subtle adjustments in order to improve their output. The movement, and therefore the handwriting, becomes more consistent in this period. The associative phase for handwriting movement acquisition extends over months or years. When the writer reaches a stage where movement production becomes 'automatic,' they have reached the *autonomous stage*. Now, their handwriting can be carried out seemingly without attention to the process.

People carry out this skilled movement in different ways to achieve similar goals, and their movement style may be characteristic to some extent. Although the formation of letters is initially dependent on the copybook style learnt by the writer, as the skill develops over many years variations may be introduced due to differences in teaching methods, muscular control, sequence of movements employed, esthetic

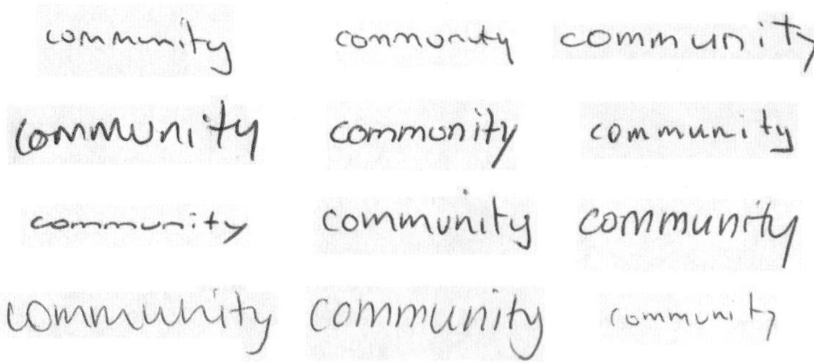

Figure 1 The word 'community' written by 12 different people, illustrating inter-writer variation.

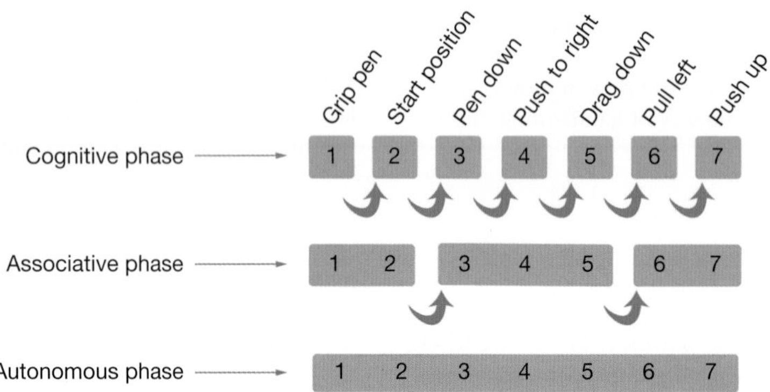

Figure 2 Phases of handwriting movement acquisition. Adapted from Keele SW and Summers JJ (1976) The structure of motor programs. In: Stelmach GE (ed.) *Motor Control: Issues and Trends*, pp. 109–142. New York: Academic Press.

preferences, exposure to writings of others, and frequency of writing. This results in inter-writer variation in form (**Figure 1**).

An analogous progression is made through these phases as a person's signature is developed. Initially, the writer will consider how they want their signature to look and how to achieve that look. With practice and over time the output may change, perhaps under the influence of the factors mentioned above, until the production of the signature becomes automatic and, to some extent, individual to them.

At the autonomous stage of handwriting movement acquisition, the abstract motor programs controlling the muscles responsible for the movement are generated by stringing together smaller programmed units of behavior, which are eventually controlled as a single unit (**Figure 2**). These motor programs are not muscle specific, that is, the movements required to produce a character, word, or signature are differentially transferable between muscle sets not normally associated with writing tasks. There are numerous spatial and temporal features that are preserved in the movement patterns, resulting in a constancy of form production within a writer, in spite of influences such as body, arm and hand position, writing speed, writing surface, or even limb used for writing.

However, no person writes so consistently that every character is exactly the same each time it is written. There will be a small range of variation in features such as proportions, size, slope, and spacing. This intra-writer variation arises from a combination of the writer's motor output varying to different extents due to the nature of the movement's representation in the brain as well as features associated with particular letter combinations, position in a word, style, format of the document, or the writer's mood. External factors and deliberate changes to the movement process can also affect the appearance of a person's writing, and will be discussed later in the article.

The general propositions of handwriting examinations, which enable handwriting to be a useful form of 'opinion identification evidence' in the forensic sciences, are:

- Given a sufficient amount of handwriting, no two skilled writers exhibit identical handwriting features (inter-writer variation).
- The natural handwriting of individual writers varies (intra-writer variation).
- Due to the ingrained nature of handwriting production, individuals find it difficult to disguise extended bodies of their writing, and to accurately simulate the writing characteristics of others.

Handwriting Comparison Method

Historically, forensic handwriting examination has been based on the underlying belief that training and experience enable the handwriting examiner to distinguish between 'class' (or 'style') and 'individual' characteristics. 'Style' characteristics are those that are derived from the general model or copybook system taught, and 'individual' characteristics are deviations from the copybook form, introduced into the writing or developed over time either consciously or unconsciously. Class characteristics may be shared with many other people taught the same system of handwriting, while individual characteristics are the primary features that a forensic document examiner (FDE) relies upon to differentiate the writings of different people. However, while this theory seems logical, there is no clear evidence that experience increases the validity of findings, FDEs do not claim that they can reliably identify the class and individual characteristics of samples that they examine, and FDEs can subscribe to the theory yet express opinions as to the authorship of foreign writings where the class system is unknown to them. Furthermore, signatures may exhibit no class characteristics, being partially or entirely stylized, but are still examined.

More recently, complexity and feature detection theory has been put forward as an explanation for identification expertise. Complexity theory, while embracing class and class-divergent properties of writings, proposes an inverse relationship between the complexity and amount of handwriting examined, and the ease of successful simulation of that handwriting. In addition, as the amount of skilled writing increases, the likelihood of a chance match also decreases (**Figure 3**). This theory explains the common ground between text based and signature examinations and informs the assessment of whether sufficient material is available on which to express a valid opinion.

Feature detection theory is based on the rationale that under normal conditions, given a sufficient amount of writing, skilled writers are unlikely to produce handwritten images that are exactly the same in terms of the combination of construction, line quality, form variation, and layout. These features are compared between questioned and comparison writings and used as a basis for a primary opinion on the similarity or dissimilarity of the writings.

Examination of Questioned Writing

When a questioned document is received for handwriting examination, the FDE will examine the writing visually using a hand-held magnifier and a microscope. Pictorial and spatial features are noted, including line quality, construction of each character, connectivity, size relationships within and between letters, slope, apparent pen pressure, spacing within and between words, line spacing, margin and baseline habits, diacritics, and punctuation. Pen direction and stroke order can often be assessed from microscopic features, particularly at the commencing or terminating strokes of a character or element. These spurs, ticks, or faint drag lines show the direction of the writing implement just prior to or following its contact with the writing surface. Striations, evident in ballpoint pen writings, can also be used to determine pen direction as these lines run from the inside to the outside of a curve in the direction of motion (**Figure 4**). The striation pattern present when the pen is lifted from the paper at the conclusion of a stroke may be preserved on the ball of the pen and transferred to the beginning of the next stroke ('memory effect'). At other times, all of the ink on the ball tip at the terminus of a stroke is deposited on the page, so that the next stroke displays a deficiency of ink at the commencement ('inkless start'). These features may be used to help determine the sequence of strokes in ballpoint pen writings, and thus a writer's habits.

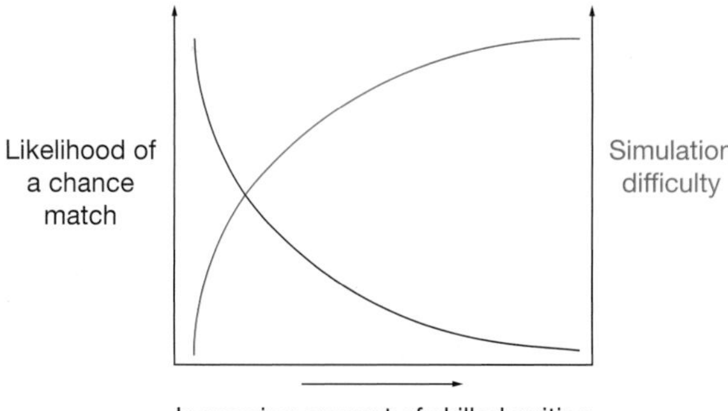

Figure 3 Generalized complexity relationships between the amount of skilled writing available in a sample, the difficulty with which the sample may be simulated, and the likelihood of a chance match with more than one writer.

Examination of Known Writing

Known (also referred to as comparison, specimen, or exemplar) writing may be either *collected* from documents written during normal course of business or social activity, or *requested* to be written specifically for the purposes of comparison. Features of known handwriting are examined in the same way as questioned writings. These writings must be in a comparable style, for example, if the questioned writing is in a cursive style, the comparison writing also needs to be in a cursive style. There will be few, if any, comparison points if the known writing was in an uppercase print style. Furthermore, the format of a document may impact on the way handwriting appears. If there is a limited amount of space available for writing, the writer may cramp their writing to a greater extent than usual, or if there are printed boxes within which to write individual letters or words (e.g., on an application form), the normal spacing and connectivity may be affected. Wherever possible, comparison writing appearing in a similar format to the questioned writings should be examined. Another important aspect of the examination of known writings is assessing whether the writings are consistent when compared among themselves. Any inconsistencies observed are referred to as contamination, and may be due to having been written by more than one writer, the specimen writer having more than one writing style (aside from the expected dissimilarities associated with writings in uppercase, lowercase, and cursive), or the writings having been created by the specimen writer at significantly different times. Contamination appearing in small amounts is excluded from the specimen pool of writing, but if a significant amount of potential contamination is identified, the FDE

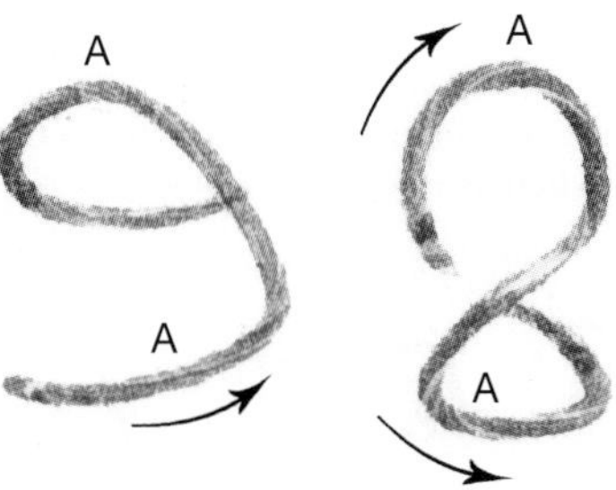

Figure 4 Ballpoint pen writings with (A) striations, which show the direction of pen movement (indicated by the arrows).

should contact the investigator for clarification of proof of authorship. FDEs should be aware that contamination may also be an issue in questioned writings. Inconsistencies due to multiple writers must be carefully considered, while those due to one writer having different writing styles or writing at different times may be addressed with sufficient comparison material.

It should be noted that some examinations will not include known writings, but involve the comparison of a number of different questioned documents in order to determine whether common authorship exists. In these cases, feature comparison can proceed as outlined below.

Feature Comparison

Once the specimen material is established as suitable for comparison, and the features of the questioned and known writings have been examined separately, these are compared with each other with the aim to express an opinion as to whether the questioned writing is similar or dissimilar to the specimen writing. That is, whether the questioned writing is consistent or inconsistent with having been produced by the same motor memories as the specimen writing.

Similarities can be defined as pictorial or structural features that appear consistent between the populations of questioned and known writings. Put another way, a character in the questioned writing would be considered similar if it fell within the range of variation exhibited for that character in the known writings. Differences are pictorial or structural features that appear dissimilar between the populations of questioned and known writings. These may be observed in terms of one or a combination of fluency, stroke direction, stroke order, and connectivity. For these features to be described as different, they need to be fundamental to the pictorial or structural character of the writing, and not shared between the bodies of questioned and known writings (**Figure 5**).

Evaluation and Opinion

If either similarities or differences are observed between the questioned and known writings, these may each be explained by a number of different propositions.

Similarities

1. The questioned writings were written by the writer of the comparison writings.
2. The questioned writing is a simulation or disguised form of the genuine writing and no evidence of the process remains.
3. A different writer's handwriting resembles the comparison writing by chance.

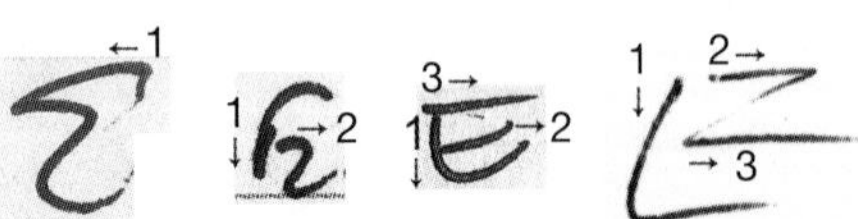

Figure 5 Four forms of the letter E showing different construction and stroke order as indicated by numbers.

Differences

1. The questioned writings were not written by the writer of the comparison writings.
2. The questioned writing is either simulated or disguised and there is evidence of this process.
3. The writer of the comparison samples wrote the questioned writings; however:
   (a) They have more than one writing style and these are not all represented in the comparison material, or the comparison writings are not a complete representation of the individual's handwriting, or
   (b) Their writing has been affected by unknown internal or environmental factors such as age, illness, intoxication, and so on.

In some instances, the examiner may observe a combination of marked similarities and differences within the questioned writing, such that it will not be clear which of the two proposition sets to consider.

FDEs may find it difficult to support any one of these propositions over one or more of the others. The relationship between complexity, amount of handwriting, and ease of simulation can be used to aid in the process of forming an opinion. For example, if the questioned writing is similar to the specimen writing, but the writing is not complex and restricted to a few words (or elements in a signature), the possibility that the writing has been simulated or that a chance match has occurred cannot be practically excluded (**Figure 6**) and an inconclusive or qualified opinion may be expressed. However, if the questioned writing is similar to the specimen writing and the writing is complex and comprises a paragraph or more, the possibility that the writing has been simulated or that a chance match has occurred can be practically excluded (**Figure 7**) and an unqualified opinion that the writer of the specimen material wrote the questioned writing may be expressed.

If significant differences are found in structural features, this usually results in an opinion that the two writings are unlikely to have been written by the same writer, or that there is nothing to link the questioned and specimen writings as having been written by one writer. Although unqualified exclusionary opinions are sometimes justified (e.g., in cases where the questioned writing displays far greater skill than the comparison writer is capable of), they should be used with caution, taking into consideration the possibility that the specimen writer has more than one distinct handwriting style.

Dissimilarities in line quality may be generally attributable to one of two groups:

1. Those deemed the result of simulation behavior, where the questioned material is written slowly but shares features with the specimen material that are unlikely to be the result of chance match. In these cases, the likelihood of being able to identify or exclude specific writers (including the person whose writing is 'simulated') as a potential author is limited.
2. All other types of line quality dissimilarities, including uneven writing surface, poor pen function, the effect of illness or drugs or disturbances due to disguise behavior. In these cases too, the ability to express an opinion as to authorship may be limited.

Figure 6 Questioned signature that is similar to the specimen material, but not complex, therefore the possibility that the signature has been simulated or that a chance match has occurred cannot be practically excluded.

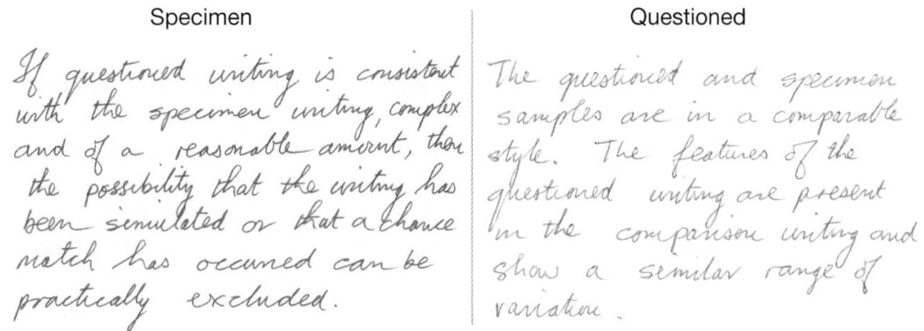

Figure 7 Questioned writing that is similar to the specimen writing, complex and of a reasonable amount, therefore the possibility that the writing has been simulated or that a chance match has occurred can be practically excluded.

Generally, the examination process and therefore the opinion able to be expressed are affected by the quality and quantity of both the questioned and comparison material. The quantity of the questioned writing cannot usually be controlled. The amount of comparison material should be sufficient so as to represent the writer's normal range of natural variation, and is often easier achieved through collected than requested writings. The quality of writings includes the following considerations, which may each impose limitations on the examination:

- The comparability of the writings. The comparison material should be written in the same style as the questioned writing.
- The complexity of the handwriting.
- The relative timing of the writings. Ideally the comparison material should have been written at around the same time as the questioned writing. This is particularly important if the known writer suffers from an illness affecting motor control, or is elderly.
- The evidence of an un-natural writing process (see below). This may be due to disguise, simulation, or some other factor.
- The original or nonoriginal nature of the documents.

If the limitations associated with an examination are deemed to be too great, for example in cases with entries restricted to a few words, severe distortion of the questioned or comparison writing due to simulation or disguise, or a poor reproduction quality non-original document, the FDE will be unable to support any of the possible propositions over the others and will express an inconclusive opinion. This is also the case when both similarities and dissimilarities are observed between questioned and known writings. Qualified and inconclusive opinions noting the possible propositions to explain the observations may still be of assistance to investigators, lawyers, and the courts as they may have access to other evidence that may lend support to one of the propositions over the others.

Signature Comparison Method

Signature comparisons are approached in much the same way as handwriting comparisons, with the same general process followed. However, as signatures are usually the result of a single, over learnt abstract motor program and may be highly stylized, it is often possible to express an unqualified opinion on the authorship of a questioned signature where a handwriting examination of a similar amount would be limited. Again, complexity and feature detection theory can be applied, so that the more complex the signature, the lower the likelihood of a chance match, and the more difficult it would be to successfully simulate.

The general limitations associated with handwriting examinations also apply here. It can sometimes be difficult to assess whether the comparison material available is sufficient to represent the writer's full range of natural variation, and ensuring the comparison signatures are contemporaneous with the questioned signature(s) is particularly important.

Un-Natural Handwriting Behaviors

The features of un-natural writing habits can be quite different from normal writing due to their physiological and psychological characteristics. Un-natural handwriting may be considered that which is simulated, disguised, or modified by internal or external factors such as the writing environment (e.g., paper surface, writing implement, and writing surface), illness, and medication or intoxication by drugs or alcohol. Each of these may result in writing displaying poor line quality, tremor, or other distortions; however, medication may lead to an improvement in the writing movement which the examiner should consider.

Simulations may be freehand, traced, or machine generated. Signatures are more commonly simulated than handwritten text. Freehand simulations are 'drawn' either based on a physical model or a mental image. In this case, the writer is required to imitate another person's complex mechanisms for controlling muscle contractions while suppressing the characteristics of their own system. The same areas of the brain will be used, but differently configured, with more input from the sensory areas (feedback) and an increased cognitive load. The movement will generally be slower and less fluent than natural handwriting movements, as the writer stops frequently to check letter construction and progress against the model. This writing behavior is likely to be reflected in the static handwriting trace in terms of features that can be readily observed: a lack of fluency, unusual pen lifts, pauses, retouches and internal inconsistencies in pen direction, and letter construction or connectivity.

Tracings may result in writings that are more pictorially similar to the specimen writing, but fluency of the line trace will almost invariably be lacking. There may be evidence of the process on the questioned document if traced guide lines in the form of indented impressions or pencil transfers have been used. Similar marks may be present on the document used as the template, should this be available.

Generally, simulations may capture one or the other of the pictorial or line quality features of the genuine writing, but very rarely both. However, the possibility of a well-practiced simulator or expert penman may need to be considered. Machine-generated simulations are created from source writing using a scanner, photocopier or other machine. The simulation may be a direct reproduction or be electronically manipulated to alter some aspects, e.g., size or slant.

Like freehand simulation, disguise behavior imposes taxes on the movement system, resulting in a similar disturbance to fluency. When attempting disguise, a writer will again have to suppress their normal writing behavior and introduce new features that they consider significantly different. Typically, changes are made to obvious features such as slope, size, or letter design, while inconspicuous features are left unchanged. Some writers may not realize what characteristics are significant, or find the task of disguise so difficult, that their attempts are unsuccessful and an examination may lead the examiner to express an opinion that the writing is genuine.

Signatures may be disguised in such a way as to be initially accepted by a third party, with the writer later denying that they wrote it. These will often closely resemble the specimen signatures in all but one or two features and may be able to be associated with the specimen writer. Auto-simulation (or self-simulation) may also be employed as a means of disguise, where a writer attempts to simulate their own handwriting or signature. Because of this, the term simulation does not exclude the writer of the target writing as an author. Auto-simulated writings may be impossible to differentiate from writings simulated by a different writer.

It is difficult for writers to maintain either type of un-natural writing behavior, so with extended writing some of the writer's normal characteristics are likely to appear. This results in the presence of both similarities and dissimilarities with the comparison writing. Recent research provides empirical data for the difficulty that FDEs have in distinguishing between disguised and simulated writing behaviors. Therefore, it should be noted that where there is evidence of a simulation or disguise process in questioned writing, it is not generally possible to express an opinion as to authorship.

Examination of Nonoriginal Writing

The examination of nonoriginal writing gives rise to a number of issues for FDEs. Examples of nonoriginal documents include photocopies, facsimiles, carbon or carbonless duplicates, photographs, and scans. Most of these reproduction processes will result in a loss of microscopic detail, making features such as pen lifts, retouching, striations, and line quality difficult or impossible to determine. Features associated with disturbances to the substrate, such as traced guidelines to assist copying, or erased pencil marks will also be undetectable. Nevertheless, useful handwriting comparisons of nonoriginal documents can be undertaken. However, the limitations should be taken into account when expressing opinions, so that suitably qualified opinions will usually be expressed along with a statement that the opinions are expressed on the assumption that the questioned document examined is a true and accurate representation of the original document, and that if this assumption is proven, by whatever means, not to be true, then the opinion should be reviewed.

Recent Research in Handwriting Comparisons

While other forensic science disciplines such as DNA and drug analysis have solid theoretical and empirical footings, forensic handwriting examination has evolved outside of any mainstream scientific culture. The past two decades have seen the emergence of academic critics of forensic handwriting examination. Their published works have principally focused on the lack of empirical testing of the theoretical basis underlying authorship opinions and perceived shortfalls in data dealing with the accuracy, reliability, and validity of these opinions. In order to strengthen the scientific basis for handwriting comparisons, a number of studies addressing these issues have been undertaken. Tests of FDEs' proficiency compared to that of a control group of lay people have found that handwriting identification expertise does exist, with the expertise characterized by what may be described as the 'conservatism' of the professional group compared to the control group. Using blinded studies where participants compare questioned samples to known samples, it has been found that both FDE and lay groups report a similar number of correct associations of questioned writings with known writings. The difference between the FDE and lay groups is in the significantly lower error rate for FDEs. This has been attributed to FDEs expressing more inconclusive opinions, where the control group express erroneous false matches.

Statistical studies on the individuality of handwriting have shown that based on the sample sets examined, handwriting is unique and identifiable. A number of software programs have also been developed for automated, computer-based writer identification and verification based on feature extraction algorithms, designed to assist in the examination process. Results from these automated searches require verification by an FDE.

Reporting Opinions

Along with the move toward investigating the scientific validity of the principles underpinning forensic handwriting examination and obtaining empirical data on the skill of examiners, pressure is also on for forensic document examination and other identification sciences to apply a more scientifically correct reporting terminology. Different professional groups of FDEs around the world approach reporting in different ways. The ASTM standards, in use in the United States of America, recommend a nine-point reporting scale ranging from 'identification' to 'elimination,' with varying levels of probability (or degrees of confidence) between them. However, categorical opinions of identity of source are not intrinsically scientific, and recent publications have supported logical, scientific methods for expressing evaluative opinions. This approach (known as the Bayesian approach) requires the forensic scientist to consider their observations in the light of propositions that represent the prosecution and defence, respectively. Opinions ought to be presented in terms of the ratio of the probability of the observations given the prosecution hypothesis to the probability of the observations given the defence hypothesis, which is known as the *likelihood ratio*. This may be expressed along the lines of 'the observations are much more probable if the questioned note was written by the writer of the comparison sample than if it was written by someone else.' The Board of the European Network of Forensic Science Institutes (ENFSI) has engaged itself to work toward full implementation of this approach within the ENFSI laboratories.

Other Examinations

Although this article focuses on handwriting and signature comparisons undertaken by FDEs, there are many other types of examinations that may be carried out in a forensic document examination laboratory. These include analysis of inks (writing and printing), printing processes and paper, stamp and seal impressions, impressions of writing or other marks on the document, and reconstruction and restoration of damaged documents. In some laboratories, an FDE performs all of these examinations along with handwriting comparisons; in others, handwriting comparisons and the other document examinations are completed by different people.

FDEs should not be confused with graphologists. Graphology, also known as graphoanalysis or handwriting analysis, is concerned with the examination of handwriting to reveal psychological or personality traits of the writer. No aspects of this field qualify a graphologist as an FDE.

See also: **Documents:** Analytical Methods; Document Dating; Forgery/Counterfeits; History of the Forensic Examination of Documents; Ink Analysis; Paper Analysis; **Foundations:** Evidence/Classification; Overview and Meaning of Identification/Individualization; Interpretation/The Comparative Method; Statistical Interpretation of Evidence: Bayesian Analysis; The Frequentist Approach to Forensic Evidence Interpretation.

Further Reading

Association of Forensic Science Providers (2009) Standards for the formulation of evaluative forensic science expert opinion. *Science and Justice* 49(3): 161–164.
ASTM Standard E1658 (2008) Standard terminology for expressing conclusions of forensic document examiners, ASTM International, West Conshohocken, PA, http://dx.doi.org/10.1520/E1658-08.
Bird C, Found B, Ballantyne K, and Rogers D (2010) Forensic handwriting examiners' opinions on the process of production of disguised and simulated signatures. *Forensic Science International* 195: 103–107.
Bird C, Found B, and Rogers D (2010) Forensic document examiners' skill in distinguishing between natural and disguised handwriting behaviors. *Journal of Forensic Sciences* 55(5): 1291–1295.
Conway JVP (1959) *Evidential Documents*. Springfield: Charles C Thomas.
Ellen D (1997) *The Scientific Examination of Documents: Methods and Techniques*, 2nd edn. London: Taylor and Francis Ltd.
Evett IW (1998) Towards a uniform framework for reporting opinions in forensic science casework. *Science and Justice* 38(3): 198–202.
Evett IW, et al. (2011) Expressing evaluative opinions: A position statement. *Science and Justice* 51(1): 1–2.
Found B and Rogers D (1995) Contemporary issues in forensic handwriting examination. A discussion of key issues in the wake of the Starzecpyzel decision. *Journal of Forensic Document Examination* 8: 1–33.
Found B and Rogers D (1998) A consideration of the theoretical basis of forensic handwriting examination. *International Journal of Forensic Document Examiners* 4(2): 109–118.
Found B and Rogers D (1999) Documentation of forensic handwriting comparison and identification method: A modular approach. *Journal of Forensic Document Examination* 12: 1–68.
Found B and Rogers D (2008) The probative character of forensic handwriting examiners' identification and elimination opinions on questioned signatures. *Forensic Science International* 178: 54–60.
Found B, Sita J, and Rogers D (1999) The development of a program for characterising forensic handwriting examiners' expertise: Signature examination pilot study. *Journal of Forensic Document Examination* 12: 69–80.
Harrison WR (1958) *Suspect Documents*. London: Sweet and Maxwell Limited.
Hilton O (1982) *Scientific Examination of Questioned Documents*, revised edn. New York: Elsevier North Holland, Inc.
Huber RA and Headrick AM (1999) *Handwriting Identification: Facts and Fundamentals*. New York: CRC Press LLC.
Kam M (2010) Proficiency testing and procedure validation for forensic document examination. Technical Support Working Group, Requirement Number: 000/IS-001-DREXEL-03-FP.
Kam M, Fielding G, and Conn R (1997) Writer identification by professional document examiners. *Journal of Forensic Sciences* 42(5): 778–786.
Kam M, Wetstein J, and Conn R (1994) Proficiency of professional document examiners in writer identification. *Journal of Forensic Sciences* 39(1): 5–14.
Keele SW and Summers JJ (1976) The structure of motor programs. In: Stelmach GE (ed.) *Motor Control: Issues and Trends*, pp. 109–142. New York: Academic Press.
Levinson J (2001) *Questioned Documents: A Lawyers Handbook*. Avon: Academic Press.
Marcelli A, Rendina M, and De Stefano C (2011) Disguising writiers identification: An experimental study. *Journal of Forensic Document Examination* 21: 23–35.
Morris RN (2000) *Forensic Handwriting Identification*. Avon: Academic Press.
National Research Council of the National Academies (2009) *Strengthening Forensic Science in the United States: A Path Forward*. Washington, DC: The National Academies Press.
Osborn AS (1929) *Questioned Documents*, 2nd edn. Chicago: Nelson-Hall Co.
Risinger D, Denbeaux MP, and Saks MJ (1989) Exorcism of ignorance as a proxy for rational knowledge: The lessons of handwriting identification "expertise". *University of Pennsylvania Law Review* 137: 731–792.

Risinger D, Denbeaux MP, and Saks MJ (1998) Brave new "post-*Daubert* world" – A reply to Professor Moenssens. *Seton Law Review* 29: 405–485.
Risinger D and Saks MJ (1996) Science and nonscience in the courts: *Daubert* meets handwriting identification expertise. *Iowa Law Review* 82: 21–74.
Saks MJ and Koehler JJ (2005) The coming paradigm shift in forensic identification science. *Science* 309: 892–895.
Saks MJ and VanderHaar H (2005) On the "general acceptance" of handwriting identification principles. *Journal of Forensic Sciences* 50(1): 1–8.
Sita J, Found B, and Rogers DK (2002) Forensic handwriting examiners' expertise for signature comparison. *Journal of Forensic Sciences* 47(5): 1117–1123.
Slyter SA (1995) *Forensic Signature Examination*. Springfield: Charles C Thomas.
Srihari SN, Cha S, Arora H, and Lee S (2002) Individuality of handwriting. *Journal of Forensic Sciences* 47(4): 856–872.
Srihari S, Huang C, and Srinivasan H (2008) On the discriminability of the handwriting of twins. *Journal of Forensic Sciences* 53(2): 430–446.
Srihari SN, Srinivasan H, and Desai K (2007) The relationship between quantitatively modelled signature complexity levels and forensic document examiners' qualitative opinions on casework. *Journal of Forensic Document Examination* 18: 1–19.

Relevant Websites

http://www.abfde.org/ – American Board of Forensic Document Examiners, Inc.
http://www.asqde.org/ – American Society of Questioned Document Examiners.
http://www.afde.org/ – Association of Forensic Document Examiners.
http://www.asfdeinc.org/ – Australasian Society of Forensic Document Examination, Inc.
http://www.enfsi.eu – European Network of Forensic Science Institutes' European Network of Forensic Handwriting Experts.
http://www.graphonomics.org/ – International Graphonomics Society.
http://www.safde.org/ – Southeastern Association of Forensic Document Examiners.
http://www.swafde.org/ – Southwestern Association of Forensic Document Examiners.

Ink Analysis

JA Siegel, Indiana University Purdue University Indianapolis, Indianapolis, IN, USA

This article is a revision of the previous edition article by R.L. Brunelle, volume 2, pp. 591–597, © 2000, Elsevier Ltd.

Glossary

Densitometry A technique whereby a light-sensitive element measures the depth and concentration of color associated with a solid material.

Scanning Auger microscopy An analytical method whereby the elemental composition of a solid surface such as paper can be determined by the Auger effect, which measures the release of electrons from various elements.

Thin-layer chromatography An analytical chemical method whereby a mixture of substances may be separated by their differential adherence to a solid stationary phase that is coated onto a solid platform such as a microscope slide. The mixture is dissolved in a solvent and spotted at the bottom of the platform and then the platform is introduced into a mobile liquid phase which carries the spots up the platform, separating the components of the mixture.

Introduction

Most people identify questioned document analysis with handwriting and that remains one of the principal areas of analysis in this type of forensic science. Even though computers and computer printing seem to have taken over the world of documents, handwritten documents and especially signatures are still very important in society. Although some documents are written using a pencil, the vast majority employs some type of ink pen. Analyzing only the characteristics of the handwriting leaves out an important piece of evidence, that is, the ink. Chemical and physical analyses of inks on questioned documents provide valuable information regarding their authenticity. Comparison of the chemical and physical properties of two or more inks can determine (1) if the inks were made by the same manufacturer, (2) in some cases, whether the inks were products of the same production batch, and (3) the first production date of the specific ink formulation involved. When dating tags are detected, it is possible to determine the actual year or years when the ink was manufactured. Dating tags are unique chemicals that have been added to ballpoint inks by some ink companies as a way to determine the year the ink was made.

Relative age comparison tests performed on inks of the same formula, stored under the same conditions and used on the same type of paper (performed by measuring changing solubility properties of inks) can help to estimate the age of ink on questioned documents. This is done by (1) comparing the rates and extent of extraction of questioned and known dated inks in organic solvents by thin-layer chromatography (TLC) densitometry, (2) comparing changes in dye concentrations by TLC and TLC densitometry, (3) comparing the volatile ink components by gas chromatography-mass spectrometry (GC-MS), and (4) using mass spectrometric methods for following the degradation of ink components, mainly dyes or pigments, with time. In cases where known dated writings are not available for comparison with questioned inks, accelerated aging (heating the ink to induce aging of the ink) can sometimes be used to estimate the age of ink using any or all of the above-described techniques. Iron-based inks can be dated by measuring the migration of iron along the fibers of the paper by scanning auger microscopy.

This article describes state-of-the-art procedures for the chemical and physical comparison, identification, and dating of inks on questioned documents.

Composition of Major Types of Writing Inks

Knowledge of the composition of inks is necessary to understand the reasons for the various methods used to analyze inks. In addition, knowledge of the first production date for each type of ink or certain ingredients in the inks is useful for dating inks.

Carbon (India) Ink

In its simplest form, carbon ink consists of amorphous carbon shaped into a solid cake with glue. It is made into a liquid for writing by grinding the cake and suspending the particles in a water-glue medium. A pigmented dye may be used to improve the color. Liquid carbon inks are also commercially available. In the liquid carbon inks, shellac and borax are used in place of animal glue and a wetting agent is added to aid in the mixing of the shellac and carbon. Carbon inks are insoluble in water, very stable, and are not decomposed by air, light, heat, moisture, or microbiological organisms. This class of ink has been available for more than 2000 years.

Fountain Pen Inks

There are two types of fountain pen inks: (1) the iron gallotannate type of inks and (2) aqueous solutions of synthetic dyes. Modern inks of type (2) contain synthetic blue dyes to provide an immediate blue color to the ink which gradually turns black after oxidation on paper. This explains the origin of the name blue–black fountain pen ink. This class of ink is also very stable. This ink is insoluble in water and cannot be effectively erased by abrasion. The most popular fountain pen ink (developed in the 1950s) consists of an aqueous solution of synthetic dyes. These inks are bright and attractive in color, but they are not nearly as stable as the carbon or blue–black inks. Some of the synthetic dyes used fade and are soluble in water. The most modern inks of this type contain pigmented dyes, such as copper phthalocyanine (introduced in about 1953), which makes these inks much more permanent.

Ballpoint Inks

The ballpoint pen was developed in Europe about 1939 and was initially distributed in Argentina about 1943. In 1946, several million Reynolds ballpoint pens reached the market in the United States.

Ballpoint inks consist of synthetic dyes (sometimes carbon or graphite is also added for permanence) in various glycol solvents or benzyl alcohol. The dyes in ballpoint inks can make up nearly 50% of the total formulation. Several other ingredients are usually added to the ink to impart specific characteristics. These ingredients consist of fatty acids, resins, surface active agents, corrosion control ingredients, and viscosity adjustors. The fatty acids (oleic is the most common) act as lubricants for the ball of the pen and they also help the starting characteristics of the ballpoint.

Ballpoint inks made before 1950 used oil-based solvents such as mineral oil, linseed oil, recinoleic acid, methyl and ethyl esters of recinoleic acid, glycerin monoricinoleate, coconut fatty acids, sorbital derivatives, and plasticizers such as tricresylphosphate. Modern ballpoint inks (post-1950) are referred to as glycol-based inks, because of the common use of ethylene glycol or glycol derivatives as a solvent for the dyes. Benzyl alcohol is also commonly used as the vehicle (solvent) by some ink manufacturers. Chelated dyes (introduced commercially in about 1953) are stable to light. Red, green, yellow, and other colored chelated dyes are now used for various colored ballpoint inks.

Pressurized ballpoint inks were developed about 1968. These pens contain a pressurized feed system instead of gravity flow. The physical characteristics of these inks are quite different from the standard glycol-based ballpoint inks. The composition is basically the same, but this ink does not become fluid until disturbed by the rotation of the ballpoint in the socket. Cartridges containing this ink are under the pressure of nitrogen or some other inert gas. The positive pressure on the ink allows the pen to write in all positions and in a vacuum. These pens are used by astronauts during space travel.

Rolling Ball Marker Inks

Rolling ball marker inks were introduced in Japan in about 1968 and shortly thereafter in the United States. These inks are water based and usually contain organic liquids such as glycols and formamide to retard the drying of the ballpoint. The dyes in these inks are water soluble or acidic dye salts. The light fastness of these dyes ranges from good for the metalized acid dyes to poor for some of the basic dye salts. Water fastness is usually poor, except that some of these dyes have an affinity for cellulose fibers in paper, which produces a degree of water fastness. Water-resistant rolling ball marker inks are also available. These inks are totally insoluble in water and can only be dissolved in strong organic solvents, such as pyridine or dimethylsulfoxide.

Fiber- or Porous-Tip Pen Inks

This class of inks was developed in Japan in about 1962 and in the United States in about 1965. Fiber-tip inks are usually water or xylene based and contain dyes and additives similar to those in rolling ball marker inks and fountain pen inks. The water-based inks are obviously water soluble, whereas the xylene-based inks are water resistant and can only be dissolved with strong organic solvents. Formamide or glycol solvents are essential ingredients in fiber-tip inks to keep the fiber tip from drying out. Fiber-tip inks that contain metalized dyes are light fast.

Gel-Pen Inks

The most recent development in the writing instrument industry is the introduction of the gel pen by the Japanese. Four brands of gel-pen inks have been introduced: (1) the Uniball Signo by Mitsubishi, (2) the Zebra J5, (3) the Pentel Hybrid, and (4) the Sakura Gelly Roll pen. These pens have been marketed by the Japanese since the mid-1980s and a limited supply of the pens was sold in the United States in about 1993. Two US manufacturers are now producing these pens.

Gel inks contain completely insoluble colored pigments rather than organic dyes. Writing with this ink is very similar to the appearance of the writing with a ballpoint pen. This ink, which is water based, is a gel and not a liquid. It is insoluble in both water and strong organic solvents. This physical property makes it impossible to analyze (by traditional methods) for the purpose of comparing two or more inks of this type.

Ink Comparisons and Identifications

Inks are usually examined for three reasons:

1. To compare two or more ink entries to determine similarities or differences in inks which can provide information concerning whether entries have been added or altered.
2. To determine if two or more entries were written with the same formula and batch of ink, thus providing a lead as to whether certain entries could have been written with the same pen.
3. To date ink entries to determine whether documents have been backdated. This section deals with the first two reasons for analyzing inks.

Nondestructive methods of comparison should be carried out first, because chemical analysis causes minor damage to the document by removing ink samples for analysis. Typically, the nondestructive methods include (1) a visual and microscopic examination of the writing to assess its color and the type of pen used, (2) infrared reflectance and luminescence examinations to determine whether the inks reflect or absorb infrared light and whether the inks luminesce, and (3) viewing the inks under long- and shortwave ultraviolet light to determine if the inks are fluorescent under these wavelengths of light. Often, these techniques are sufficient to determine if two or more inks are different. However, if these techniques fail to detect any differences in the inks, then further chemical analysis is necessary to determine if the inks being compared really have the same formula.

The most widely used technique for comparing and identifying inks is TLC. This technique separates the dyes in the ink and the invisible organic components in the ink. This allows a direct comparison of the composition of inks being examined on the same TLC plate. To determine the relative concentrations of dyes present in the ink, the dyes separated on the TLC plate are scanned in a TLC scanning densitometer. The method is fast, reliable, and inexpensive. High-performance liquid chromatography has also been used for comparing inks with some success. GC-MS is a very useful technique but the equipment is expensive.

Dating of Inks

As mentioned earlier in this article, there is a huge demand for the dating of inks on questioned documents. Any time during an investigation when there is a question about the date of preparation of a document, an ink-dating chemist is needed. Over the past 30 years, the ability to perform these examinations has become widely known among forensic scientists, document examiners, and attorneys throughout the world. The ink-dating procedures that are described have passed the Frye and Daubert tests on numerous occasions and are routinely accepted in US courts. Testimony has also been admitted using these techniques in Israel and Australia.

First Date of Production Method

After the ink is uniquely/positively identified, the first date of production of that ink or certain ingredients in the ink is determined from the manufacturer of that specific ink formulation. If the ink was not made until after the date of the document, then it can be concluded that the document was backdated. If the ink was available on the date of the document, then the document could have been written on that date.

Ink Tag Method

If an ink tag is identified in an ink, it is possible to determine the actual year or years when an ink was made. Tags were added to some ballpoint inks by the Formulab Company before 1970; however, the use of tags in their inks was discontinued in June 1994. Since the tags are considered proprietary information by Formulab, no further information about the tags can be reported here. Formulab should be contacted directly, if this information is needed.

Ink-dating tags are detected and identified by TLC using a solvent system of chlorobenzene and ethyl acetate (5:1, v/v). Standard samples of the tags should be run simultaneously on the same TLC plate as the questioned inks. The tags, if present, are viewed under longwave ultraviolet light and the RF values of the tags present in questioned inks are compared with the RF values of the standard tags. The dates the various tags were used must be obtained from Formulab.

Relative Age Comparison Methods

Dating inks by this procedure is based on the scientifically supported premise that, as ink ages on paper, there are corresponding changes in the solubility properties of the inks. Therefore, by comparing the solubility or extraction properties of questioned inks with known dated inks of the same formula on the same type of paper and stored under the same conditions, it becomes possible to estimate how long the ink has been written on the document. Two or more inks of the same formulation can be compared without known dated writings to determine whether the writings were made at the same or different times. This is only true if the inks being compared are still aging (drying), because after the ink has aged out (completely dry), no differences in solubility properties are expected, even if the inks were written at different times. Typically, inks will become totally dry (as measured by these procedures) within 6 years; some inks become dry in less than 6 years.

When two or more matching inks are compared without known dated writings, it is still possible to determine the sequence in which the inks were written. This again requires knowing that the inks are still aging and also knowing how the inks age. For example, some inks extract faster and more completely in organic solvents as the ink ages, whereas others extract more slowly and less completely as they age. To determine which way the ink ages, a sample of the ink is heated at 100 °C for 30 min. The rate and extent of extraction of this heated sample into an organic solvent are compared with an unheated sample of the same ink to determine if the heated (totally aged) sample extracted faster and more completely than the unheated sample, or vice versa.

Accelerated Aging

In situations where known dated inks are not available for comparison with questioned inks, accelerated aging of a questioned ink can be performed to estimate its age. The measurement procedures are identical to those described for R-ratios, percent extraction, and dye ratios. This test involves just one additional step, which is to heat a sample of the questioned ink

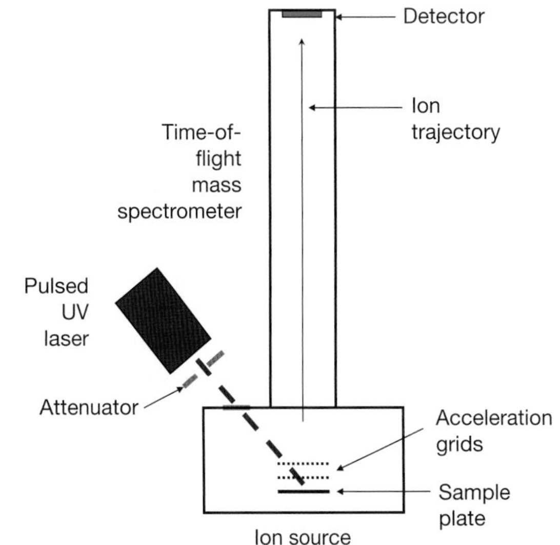

Figure 1 A diagram of an LDMS time-of-flight mass spectrometer.

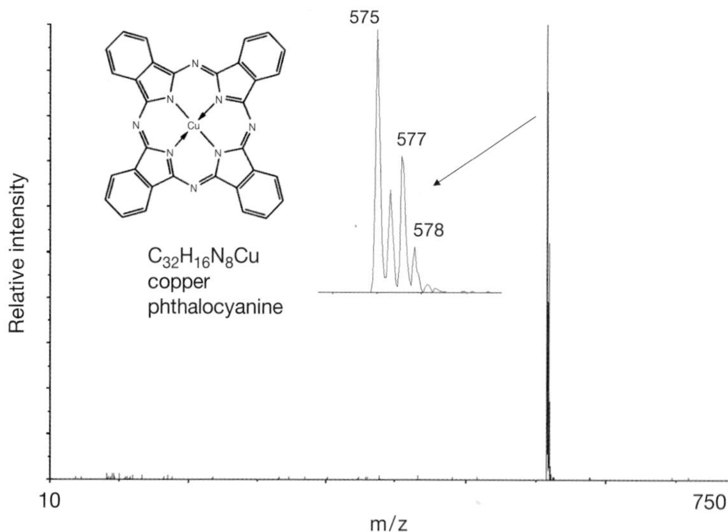

Figure 2 The LDMS spectrum from a penstroke of a blue-pigmented ink. The mass and isotopic compositions are consistent with the very popular blue pigment, copper phthalocyanine (structure shown).

for 30 min at 100 °C, allow it to cool and equilibrate with the temperature and humidity in the room for 1 h, and then compare the results of the various measurements (using any or all of the R-ratio, percent extraction, and dye ratio methods) with the results obtained from an unheated sample of the same ink.

Significant differences obtained by any one of the methods indicate that the ink is still drying and is therefore less than 6 years old, as no inks have been found to take longer than 6 years to become completely dry using these methods. If it is known that the specific ink in question takes only 3 years to dry, then it can be concluded that the questioned ink is less than 3 years old. This method can also be used to determine which of two or more inks is newer than the other. This is done by observing which ink changes more with heat; the larger the change caused by heat, the newer the ink. This can only be done when all inks compared consist of the same ink formulation on the same type of paper and stored under the same conditions. This statement applies to all of the relative age comparison techniques described here.

Time-Dependent Degradation of Ink Dyes

Research over the past two decades indicates that many dyes and pigments in inks degrade over time in a linear, time-dependent, predictable fashion. This is due to both light and oxygen and thus it is sensitive to the environmental conditions under which the ink is stored. The major recent method for tracking the chemical degradation of inks is by means of laser desorption mass spectrometry (LDMS). This is a variant of matrix-assisted laser desorption ionization mass spectrometry, the chief difference being that no matrix is used.

In 2001, Grim et al. reported the first application of LDMS for the analysis of ink on paper. The technique proved to be an excellent analytical tool for such analytes. The technique uses a pulsed ultraviolet laser that can directly desorb colorant molecules from a penstroke off of paper, carrying a charge, such that they can be analyzed using time-of-flight mass spectrometry. A schematic of a simple LDMS instrument is shown in **Figure 1**. The laser generates 2-ns pulses of 337 nm (UV) light, which impinges on a sample inside the vacuum system of the mass spectrometer. If compounds are present that absorb at this wavelength, they may be desorbed and ionized. Ions formed are accelerated to a constant kinetic energy such that ions of different masses will have differing velocities; thus, the time it will take for them to travel approximately 1 m to the ion detector will be proportional to their mass. No sample preparation is needed. Initial work involved the detection and identification of crystal violet, the dye commonly used in ballpoint pen inks. Like many dyes, this is a cationic dye which, when desorbed, already has a charge associated with it. While unexpected, several related compounds were detected as well. These were shown to be degradation products that form slowly over time, through a process known as oxidative dealkylation, and thus they can provide a 'chemical clock' for estimating the time that the ink has been on the paper. A similar process was observed for the red pen ink dyes Rhodamine 6G and Rhodamine B. Since 2000, the pen and inkjet printer industries have been replacing dye-based inks with pigment-based inks. In the case of printers, color photos printed with dyes fade quickly while pigmented inks with a well-chosen paper can yield an archival copy that will remain unfaded and vibrant for hundreds of years. The conversion from dyes to pigments was of particular concern to those who used TLC for pen ink analysis, as pigments are insoluble compounds. However, LDMS efficiently analyzes small amounts of pigments in such samples. An example is shown in **Figure 2**. A penstroke was made on paper from a blue-pigmented pen ink. A small piece of the page was introduced into the ion source of the LDMS. While the ink has many components, only the pigment absorbed the UV laser light, leading to desorption/ionization of just these pigment molecules. The spectrum shown in **Figure 2** is exceedingly simple. No fragmentation is observed, just the intact cation of the pigment. At this point, it is known that the pigment is blue and has a molecular weight (monoisotopic mass) of 575. There are smaller peaks following the major peak, which represent the same molecule with different isotopes present. The isotopic distribution, unique to the elemental composition of the species, is very useful in identifying the pigment. For example, if one carbon atom is C(13) instead of the most abundant form C(12), the mass will increase by one atomic mass unit. If the molecule is a simple organic molecule, isotopic peaks usually decrease in relative intensity as their mass increases. Here, we see an enhanced peak at m/z 577. This is due to the fact that the pigment contains copper, which has two prominent isotopes with masses of 63 and 65 atomic mass units. The distribution of isotopes is consistent with the formula for copper phthalocyanine, as shown in the figure.

LDMS has been used to characterize artist's colorants and was demonstrated to be useful in an investigation of the authenticity of a page of the Qur'an, purportedly from the 1600s. LDMS showed that the handwritten black, gold, and red inks used in this document contained inorganic pigments such as arsenic sulfide and mercury sulfide, which were used at the time.

See also: **Documents:** Analytical Methods; Document Dating; Forgery/Counterfeits; Handwriting; **Forensic Medicine/Clinical:** Clinical Forensic Medicine – Overview; Domestic Violence.

Further Reading

Aginsky VN (1996) Dating and characterizing writing, stamp pad and jet printer inks by gas chromatography/mass spectrometry. *International Journal of Forensic Document Examiners* 2: 103–115.

Brunell RL and Speckin EJ (1988) Technical report with case studies on the accelerated aging of ballpoint inks. *International Journal of Forensic Document Examiners* 4: 240–254.

Brunelle RL (1992) Ink dating - the state of the art. *Journal of Forensic Sciences* 37: 113–124.

Brunelle RL (1995) A sequential multiple approach to determining the relative age of writing inks. *International Journal of Forensic Document Examiners* 1: 94–98.

Brunelle RL and Cantu AA (1987) A critical evaluation of current ink dating techniques. *Journal of Forensic Sciences* 32: 1511–1521.

Brunelle RL and Lee H (1989) Determining the relative age of ballpoint ink using a single solvent extraction mass independent approach. *Journal of Forensic Sciences* 34: 1166–1182.

Brunelle RL and Reed RW (1984) *Forensic Examination of Ink and Paper*. Springfield, IL: Charles C Thomas.

Cantu AA (1988) Comments on the accelerated aging of inks. *Journal of Forensic Sciences* 33: 744–750.

Cantu AA (1996) A sketch of analytical methods for document dating, Part II. The dynamic approach: Determining age dependent analytical profiles. *International Journal of Forensic Document Examiners* 2: 192–208.

Cantu AA and Prough RS (1987) On the relative aging of ink – the solvent extraction technique. *Journal of Forensic Sciences* 32: 1151–1174.

McNeil RJ (1984) Scanning auger microscopy for dating of manuscript inks. In: Lamber JB (ed.) *Archeology Chemistry III*, pp. 255–269. Washington, DC: American Chemical Society Advances in Chemistry Series No. 205.

Paper Analysis

T Fritz and S Nekkache, IRCGN, Rosny Sous Bois, France

Glossary

Basis weight or grammage The weight of paper in grams per square meter.
Flocks Fiber aggregates.
Forming fabric Element of endless wire screen dedicated to drain off the water present in the paper pulp.
Headbox Element of the paper machine where the pulp is homogeneously distributed on the forming fabric.
Hygrometry rate (relative humidity) The amount of water vapor in the air.
Infrared (IR) Part of the electromagnetic spectrum between about 780 nm and 1 mm.
Look-through appearance The aspect of paper when viewed using transmitted light.
Luminescence The emission of radiant energy that takes place during the transition from an excited electronic state of an atom, molecule, or ion to a lower electronic state (which includes fluorescence and phosphorescence).
Metamerism Phenomenon where two surfaces show the same color under one illumination but different colors under a different illumination.
Ultraviolet (UV) Part of the electromagnetic spectrum between about 10 and 380 nm. In questioned documents, three different wavelengths are often used: 254, 312, and 365 nm.
Watermark A design or text created in the paper during the manufacturing stage by locally modifying the amount of fibers.
Whiteners Bleaching agents used to bleach paper.
Wire marks Repetitive marks left by the forming fabric(s) on the paper side that is in contact with it.

Paper analysis is often seen as a secondary issue by questioned documents examiners (QDEs), although, as a corroborative proof, it can provide complementary evidence that may be useful to investigators and the courts. Paper analysis can be a valuable complementary tool for enriching traditional questioned document examination techniques. One has always to keep in mind that expertise in analyzing questioned documents requires a multidisciplinary approach, and experience has taught us that downplaying or bypassing paper analysis can lead to irreversible mistakes as occurred in the case of the fake Hitler diaries (see section 'Dating'). With the exception of security paper, examinations of paper are a challenge, first, because paper is a product of mass consumption and, second, because manufacturers may use processes that are similar to those of their competitors. However, in many instances, it is possible to provide useful answers to the judicial authority, even in the case of ordinary papers. This article aims at presenting the major physical, optical, and chemical techniques used to analyze paper substrates in the forensic environment.

Paper Manufacturing Process

In order to better understand the methods used in the forensic analysis of printing and writing paper, and to provide a better appreciation of the difficulties met by QDEs when interpreting the result of their examinations and comparisons on paper substrates, the common manufacturing process (Fourdrinier machine) is briefly overviewed. Speciality papers (e.g., thermal paper, adhesive sticker paper, and semiconducting paper) are not considered in this article.

Paper is essentially made of hardwood and softwood fibers, which originate from thermomechanical (TMP), chemical, or chemithermomechanical (CTMP) pulp. In some cases, plants (e.g., linter, cotton, and alfa) or synthetic fibers are used. These different families of fibers are mixed in the paper pulp in various proportions depending on the required characteristics of the paper (good resistance or good opacity, for example).

To improve paper characteristics, other nonfibrous raw materials are introduced into the pulp or into the paper itself during the manufacturing process. Thus, we find such additives as starch (to increase the resistance of the paper sheet), whiteners (to bleach the paper), and fillers such as china clay, talc, or calcium carbonate (to improve opacity).

The paper machine consists of two main parts: the wet part and the dry part. The refined and purified pulp is thrown by the headbox onto the wire part. The continuous movement of the forming fabric will orient the fibers in a preferential way called 'machine direction.' The perpendicular direction is called 'cross direction' (**Figure 1**). The degree of orientation is directly linked to the difference in speed between the pulp jet and the wire.

Water trapped in the just-formed sheet of paper, which may create asymmetry between the two sides of the sheet, the 'wire side' and the 'felt side,' is drained through the forming fabric. The wire side is the side that presses against the forming fabric, whereas the felt side is the opposite side, which will be in contact with dryer felts in the next sector of the wet part, that is, the press section. In this section, some more water is removed under reduced pressure. In some particular cases, forming fabrics are used on both sides of the paper sheet as in the case of the Fourdrinier machine, completed by a top former at the end of the wet part, and of the twin-wire machine. Although asymmetry remains generally true, the classical distinction of wire side and felt side becomes optically irrelevant.

The sheet of paper then enters the dry part of the paper machine, where the remaining water is evaporated by heat and

 http://dx.doi.org/10.1016/B978-0-12-382165-2.00136-7

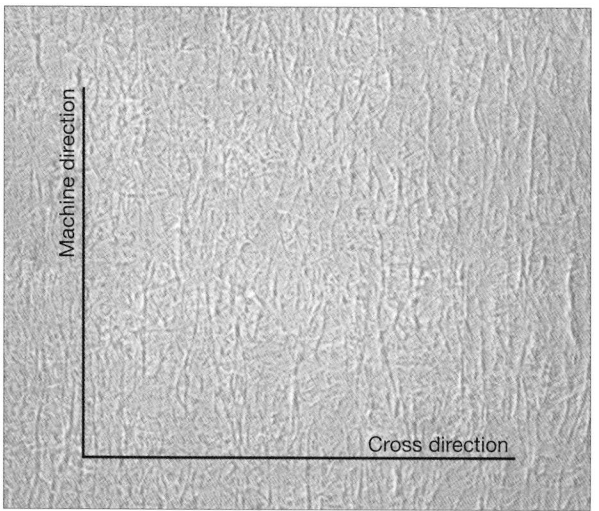

Figure 1 Fiber orientation observation.

air. Surface treatment (sizing or coating, for instance) can be used to improve printability or the optical aspect of the sheet. At the end of the process, the sheet is wound onto a jumbo roll. Finally, the finishing consists of the conversion of the jumbo roll into commercial products such as rolls or paper reams. Paper reams are obtained by guillotining several rolls which may or may not come from the same master roll, and, therefore, may or may not belong to the same production run. Thus, it is possible to get some paper products with minor physical, optical, and chemical differences between them in spite of their originating from the same ream (see **Figures 2** and **3**, where the florescent fibers have a different repartition rate although the two samples come from the same paper ream). When comparing papers to determine whether they may have come from an identified ream, it is therefore important to take a large sample of the ream. Also, the guillotining can provide unique traces that might be useful in identifying the source.

Indeed, during the finishing process, which is aimed at transforming rolls into reams, cutters and guillotine blades are used. Because of their use and their sharpening process, the blades may develop faults. The observation of these faults can assist the QDEs in identifying a common source or even locating a sheet inside its original ream.

Forensic Examination of Paper

Because paper is a complex product that can be used in so many ways, the industry applies numerous techniques to evaluate a range of parameters, such as basis weight, brightness, opacity, and so on. However, industry standards are far from compliant with the forensic environment, which is often required to preserve samples for further investigations (fingerprint identification, for instance). This may limit the extent to which any potentially destructive analysis can be performed, particularly when the item of evidence is small. Moreover, the industry standards only deal with newly manufactured paper, whereas in forensic sciences, the life conditions of the substrate may be unknown and environmental elements may alter the substrate characteristics. Indeed, paper is a heterogeneous material very sensitive to variations under ambient conditions (e.g., temperature, humidity, and sun exposure). Thus, only a subset of applicable industry standards are used or partially used in questioned document examination methods.

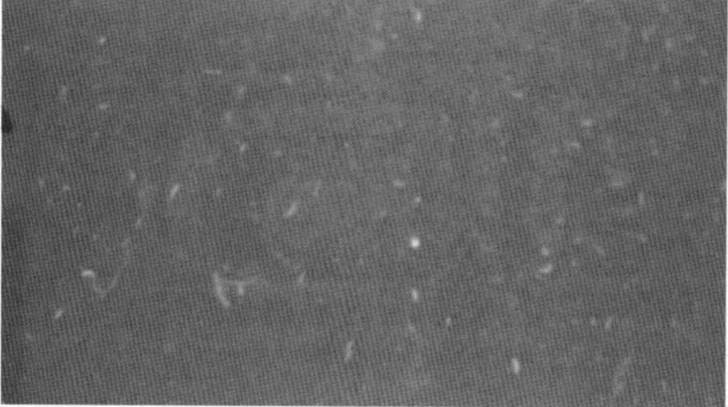

Figure 2 Different repartition rate of fluorescent fibers in two paper sheets coming from the same ream.

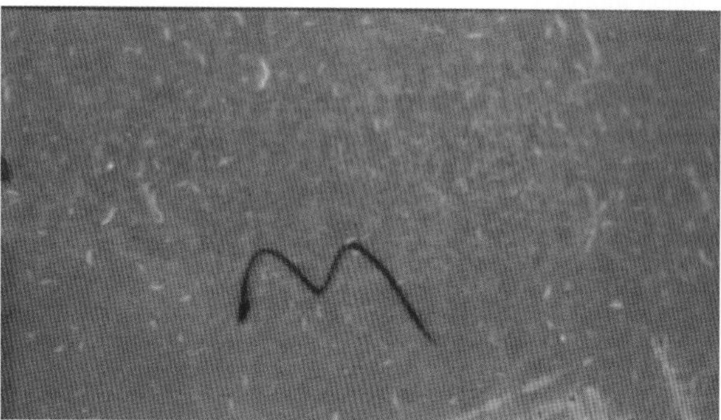

Figure 3 Different repartition rate of fluorescent fibers in two paper sheets coming from the same ream.

Physical Analysis

Physical examinations are used to assess the dimensions of the paper sample (length, width, and thickness) including its basis weight or grammage. Because of the heterogeneous structure of paper, QDEs need to be aware of some singularities before any results can be interpreted:

- The thickness has to be the average value of at least ten measurements per A4 sheet of paper taken with a calibrated micrometer.
- In the same paper production run, the basis weight can vary from one sheet to another. The classically accepted variations by the manufacturer are given in **Table 1**.
- Paper basis weight can vary because of the relative humidity. Thus, comparisons have to be made preferably under the same ambient conditions.

The samples studied by QDEs are often irregular, because the document may be torn. Thus the measurement of area, which is necessary to determine the basis weight, can be difficult. In such case, it may be advantageous to use a calibrated

Table 1 Classically accepted variations by manufacturers in a same paper production run

Basis weight ordered	*Variations acceptance (%)*
Till 32 g m^{-2} included	±2.5
From 30 to 39 g m^{-2} included	±8
From 40 to 59 g m^{-2} included	±6
From 60 to 179 g m^{-2} included	±5
From 180 to 224 g m^{-2} included	±6
From 225 g m^{-2} and more	±7

automated process of surface measurement based on an image analysis software (for instance, AutoCAD, Visilog, ImageJ, etc.).

Optical Analysis

Optical analysis relies on the study of color, fluorescence under ultraviolet (UV) light, and look-through appearance, and also on the determination of the wire and the felt sides. It is complemented by infrared (IR) and IR luminescence examinations. However, the classical recommendations in the field of questioned document examination are often limited when it comes to the means of observation and measurement. For instance, it is recommended to judge the color of the substrate only in daylight or to measure it using a microspectrophotometer. Further, 'the fluorescence may be compared with a fluorescent scale' (e.g., Ciba Geigy). Fluorescence is essentially linked to the presence of a whitener in the paper composition.

Human perception of color can be tricky, as it is influenced by several parameters such as the size of the sample, the light source (type and intensity), the background and environment, and the length of observation. These methods can be usefully complemented or totally replaced by the use of a specific paper spectrophotometer that is capable of measuring brightness, fluorescence, whiteness, opacity, metamerism, and color difference in compliance with most industry standards. The advantage here is that all the measurements are objective, made with known repeatability and reproducibility. Moreover, the results can be implemented in internal databases for possible further comparisons or for a second opinion. The limits are the presence on the substrate of printed or written entries, because the standard aperture size for measurement is 30 mm. However, professional paper spectrophotometers provide optional measurement aperture sizes with a smaller radius (down to 2.5 mm depending on the brand).

Regarding the look-through appearance, it is accepted by paper manufacturers and QDEs that this parameter may differ between different paper machines (see **Figures 4** and **5** illustrating differences in look-through appearance of papers manufactured by two different paper machines). Thus, instruments exist that are dedicated to measure look-through visuals (illustrating similarities or differences in flock size and orientation of the flocks). However, these types of apparatus are widely influenced by the presence of printed or written material on the substrate or even the surface aspect. It is then easy to understand why they are of little help in forensic applications. In this case, the visual observation remains the best method, although automated analysis could be a useful future tool for the QDE.

Figure 4 Differences in look-through appearance of papers manufactured by two different paper machines.

Figure 5 Differences in look-through appearance of papers manufactured by two different paper machines.

The look-through examination can lead to the observation of a strong security feature, namely, the 'watermark.' Watermarks are either symbols or drawings formed into the paper substrate during the papermaking process. Watermarks were first introduced in the thirteenth century, when they were integrated in quality paper, allowing the identification of its source. Its dark areas are created by increasing the quantity of fibers, whereas the light areas are made by decreasing their quantity. Two main processes exist (Fourdrinier machine for single-tone or dual-tone watermarks and cylinder mold processes for multitone watermarks). Because a watermark is the result of a controlled variation of fiber distribution, it is observable by looking through the paper and/or with oblique lighting. For faded watermarks, the observation can be improved by using a radioactive source and photographic paper. This kind of image enhancement is, however, rare in the questioned document examination field. Today, watermarks are essentially used for security papers (**Figure 6**). It is the easiest and most reliable way to identify the paper source accurately.

Concerning the discrimination of the wire side and the felt side, simple visual observations of a sample may be ineffective as paper makers tend to avoid pronounced wire marks in their

Figure 6 Watermark of a security paper.

products so as to improve printability. Also, in some cases, top-former or twin-wire machines can produce paper with wire marks on both sides. Because wire marks are a repetitive phenomenon occurring at the millimeter scale on the paper, an appropriate technique to observe and compare them objectively is to apply 'two-dimensional fast Fourier transform' to a scanned image. This technique allows the transformation of a spatial image into a frequency image where wire mark angles and periods are easily observable. Spectra can be compared directly or by using cross-correlation. The advantages of this method are that it is nondestructive; it is independent of the other paper parameters; and it has good discriminating power. This technique provides exploitable results even for paper with invisible wire marks and/or paper where written and printed entries are present (see **Figures 7–10** where fast Fourier transform is applied to a scan of virgin paper and then to a paper of the same brand bearing written entries. In both cases, the spectra show the same peaks, which correspond to the characteristics of the wire marks).

Additional evidence associated with the paper substrate can also be obtained by observation of the sample under various lighting conditions (UV, IR, and luminescence). Indeed, these techniques can reveal evidence that cannot be obtained visually from a paper document that was accidentally or purposely erased. These observations are essentially based on the principle of difference of wavelength absorption and luminescence. In the latter case, the emission of radiant energy can display invisible writings. It is obviously possible, when a printed grid is present, to measure line length and spacing. The appearance of these lines under UV, IR, and luminescence is also useful for comparison.

Chemical Analysis

To this day, no unique forensic standard dealing with chemical analysis of paper has been published. The reason lies in the destructive aspect of most of the existing standards pertaining to the industry. Moreover, the precision and accuracy of the results obtained are often considered to be too unreliable to help the QDE answer questions posed by investigators or courts. Paper is indeed a material with significant intrasample variability, and logically, to get reliable results, the number of samples available for examination must be high. In the forensic field, where the questioned document is often a single sheet of paper, one can easily understand that the quantity of the required material is extremely small. However, a technique like paper micrography can help. This technique allows the identification of the pulp (TMP, CTMP) and the fibers' origin (hardwood, softwood, plants or synthetic, thanks to the length and width of the fibers), as well as the possible presence of vessels, with only a very small sample. This method can even help to identify the types of trees or plants used (e.g., pine, oak, aspen, cotton) thanks to the shape characteristics of fibers and vessels (see **Figure 11** showing birch vessels and pine fibers from a chemical pulp).

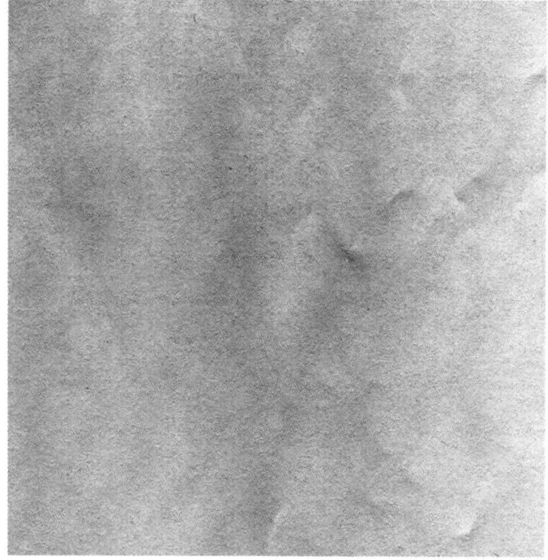

Figure 7 Scan of a virgin paper.

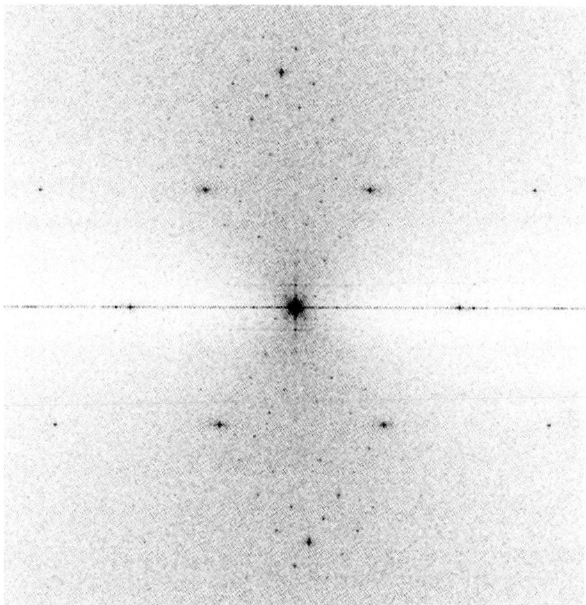

Figure 8 Observation of wire marks by fast Fourier transform applied to the scan of a virgin paper.

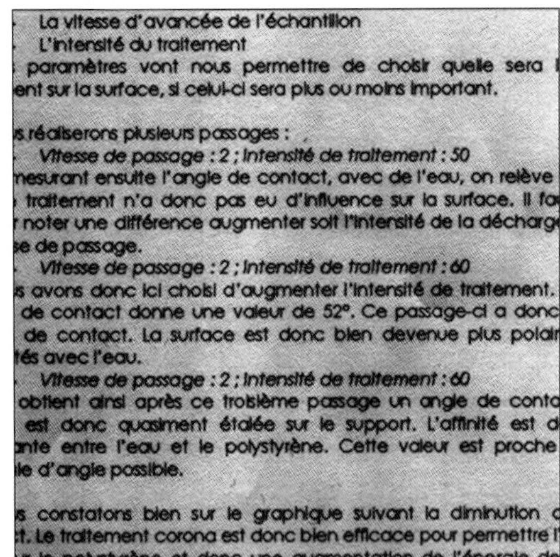

La vitesse d'avancée de l'échantillon
L'intensité du traitement
paramètres vont nous permettre de choisir quelle sera
ent sur la surface, si celui-ci sera plus ou moins important.

s réaliserons plusieurs passages :
Vitesse de passage : 2 ; Intensité de traitement : 50
nesurant ensuite l'angle de contact, avec de l'eau, on relève
traitement n'a donc pas eu d'influence sur la surface. Il fa
r noter une différence augmenter soit l'intensité de la décharg
se de passage.
Vitesse de passage : 2 ; Intensité de traitement : 60
s avons donc ici choisi d'augmenter l'intensité de traitement.
de contact donne une valeur de 52°. Ce passage-ci a donc
de contact. La surface est donc bien devenue plus polair
tés avec l'eau.
Vitesse de passage : 2 ; Intensité de traitement : 60
obtient ainsi après ce troisième passage un angle de conta
est donc quasiment étalée sur le support. L'affinité est d
ante entre l'eau et le polystyrène. Cette valeur est proche
le d'angle possible.

s constatons bien sur le graphique suivant la diminution d
t. Le traitement corona est donc bien efficace pour permettre l'
ur le polystyrène et donc une augmentation de l'énergie de

Figure 9 Scan of a paper bearing written entries.

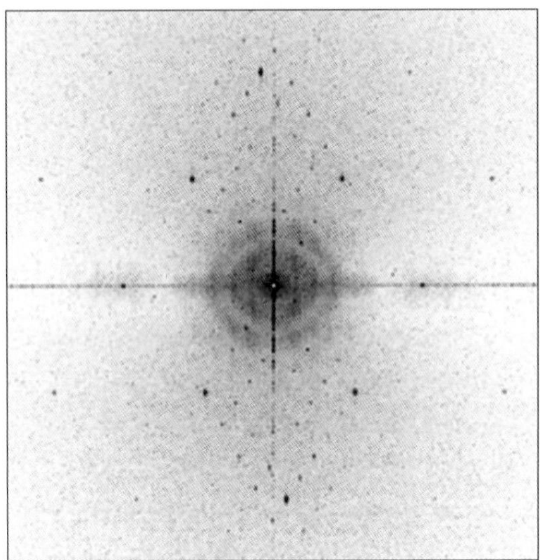

Figure 10 Observation of wire marks by fast Fourier transform applied to the scan of a paper bearing written entries.

In some cases, a quantitative analysis can be carried out to evaluate the proportion of each type of fiber. However, the results have to be taken with caution because of the possibility that manufacturers might have integrated different pulps in the same paper production batch. Sometimes, broken pulp (waste pulp from a previous production) can be integrated during the papermaking process, which can result in differences among the sheets of paper coming from the same run.

X-ray fluorescence is often quoted in the literature as an efficient method for identification of the elemental composition of paper. In some cases, the technique does produce results that are useful in discriminating between different papers. Recently, it was shown that the combination of XRF, laser ablation inductively coupled mass spectrometry, and isotope ratio mass spetrometry analysis gives a better discriminating power than the use of only one of these techniques.

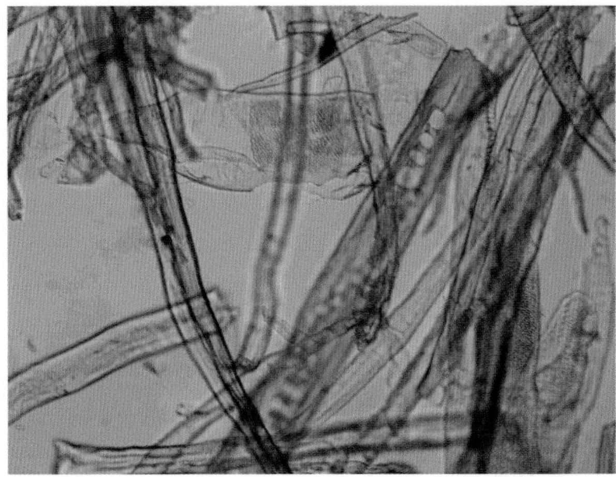

Figure 11 Paper micrography: birch vessels and pine fibers from a chemical pulp.

Finally, it can be said that the chemical analysis of the printed grid, following forensic methods for ink analysis, can usefully complement the measurement and observation of this grid under different light sources.

Dating

'Can you tell the date of this document?' is a question often asked of the QDE. To better understand the problem, one must comprehend that it is well nigh impossible to give a precise date to a paper sample unless it contains typical and referenced watermarks, allowing for an identification of both the manufacturer and the period of production. This particular case is becoming rarer and rarer, as watermarks are essentially reserved today for use in the manufacture of security and quality papers. In spite of this, anachronisms can still be detected and backdating of documents can be proved by closely inspecting the type of paper, ink, typewriting, or printed information that is present on the questioned document.

Paper composition has evolved through time, thanks to the progress of the industry and the evolution of public demand. The presence of a single specific component in the substrate can be sufficient evidence to prove that a document does not belong to its alleged timeframe. For instance, optical whiteners were discovered by Krais in 1929, but were first introduced in the paper industry only in the 1950s.

One of the most famous and published examples of anachronism ever brought to light is the fake Hitler diaries case. In 1983, the German magazine 'Stern' published excerpts from what it claimed to be the authentic diaries of Hitler, allegedly written between 1932 and 1945. While some historians and handwriting experts disagreed about the origin of these diaries, the hoax was clearly revealed by technical analysis of the ink, paper, and binding. For instance, it was demonstrated that the whitener and fibers used in the paper were of post-World War II manufacture.

In fact, for the specific case of dating, it is useful to first understand the real need of the investigators or the courts.

Figure 12 Printer-specific marks revealed by an electrostatic detection apparatus.

Indeed, a document is often asked to be dated just to determine the authenticity of the sample. Hence, it is often possible to demonstrate it by other more straightforward approaches: display of a paper substitution for instance; or combination of questioned document analysis, handwriting comparison, ink analysis, etc. Indeed, in the questioned documents field, paper analysis remains a corroborative proof.

Miscellaneous

Paper is as much a vector of information as is writing or printing. Some information may be hidden, as is the case with indented writings or indented printer-specific marks (see **Figure 12** where printer-specific marks are revealed by the electrostatic detection apparatus). The detection method to reveal these indented printings depends on their depth. Indeed, deep indented printings are usually well revealed by using an oblique light source. The best method is to use an electrostatic detection apparatus, which is very sensitive to weak marks. In fact, the two techniques complement each other. Owing to the nondestructive nature of this kind of analysis and the evidential importance of the results that can be revealed, it is recommended to begin each questioned document analysis by looking for indented writings or printings.

Moreover, the QDE is often asked whether a single sheet of paper came from a specific pad. In this kind of analysis, the QDE has at his/her disposal many methodologies. Of course, all of the aforementioned methods are necessary (physical, optical, chemical, and indented printings analysis), but they can usefully be complemented by the evaluation of physical match of paper cuts, tears, and perforations. For instance, the examination of the edges under magnification can reveal remnants of binding, adhesives, or padding materials.

Paper is a complex and heterogeneous material, often used for criminal purposes such as anonymous letters, forgery, and counterfeiting. The knowledge of the paper manufacturing process and its consequences on the final product is a prerequisite for the discrimination or identification of the paper source. Thus, paper examination techniques need to be considered, as the results may provide corroborative proofs, along with all the other possible techniques utilized in the field of questioned document analysis.

See also: **Documents**: Document Dating; Handwriting; Ink Analysis; Overview of Forensic Document Examination.

Further Reading

Aitken Y, Kaden F, and Voillot C (1988) *Constituants fibreux des pâtes, papiers et cartons, pratique de l'analyse.* Saint Martin d'Hères: EFPG Ecole Française de Papeterie et des Industries Graphiques.

ASTM International. ASTM E 2325-05 STANDARD (2005) *Guide for Nondestructive Examination of Paper.* ASTM International, West conshohocken, Pennsylvania.

Bodziak WJ (1998) EDGE characteristics of commercially produced paper stock. *Journal of the American Society of Questioned Document Examiners* 1(1): 57–66.

Browning BL (1977) *Analysis of Paper*, 2nd edn. New York: Marcel Dekker.

Brunelle RI and Reed RR (1984) *FORENSIC Examinations of Ink and Paper.* Springfield, IL: Charles C. Thomas.

Burton M and Delefosse M (1994) *GUIDE du papier édition 1992/1993.* Paracel – Caractère.

Caywood D (1995) WATERMARKS and the questioned document examiner. *International Journal of Forensic Document Examiners* 1: 299.

Grant J (1985) The diaries of Adolf Hitler. *Journal of the Forensic Science Society* 25: 179.

Krais P (1929) ÜBER ein Neues Schwartz und ein neues Weiß. *Melliand Textilberichte* 10: 468–469.

Lafait J and Elias M (2006) *LA couleur: Lumière, vison et matériaux.* Paris: Belin.

Miyata H, Shinozaki M, Nakayama T, and Enomae T (2002) A discrimination method for paper by Fourier transform and cross correlation. *Journal of Forensic Sciences* 47: 1125–1132.

Pauler N (1995–2000) *Propriétés optiques du papier.* Kista: AB Lorentzen et Wettre.

Popson T, Crawford T, and Popson SJ (2010) *Measurement and Control of the Optical Properties of Paper.* Technidyne Corporation.

Sabatier J, Kerneis JC, and Bauduin S (1985) CONTINUOUS look through assessment: An industrial reality. *ATIP* 39(1): 9–14.

Steering Committee European Documents Experts Working Group (2004) *Nondestructive Paper Examination.* ENFSI, EDEWG.

Vallette P and De Choudens C (1992) *LE bois, la pâte, le papier.* Grenoble: Centre Technique de l'Industrie des Papiers, Carton et Cellulose.

Van Es A, de Koeijer J, and van der Peijl G (2009) DISCRIMINATION of document paper by XRF, LA–ICP–MS and IRMS using multivariate statistical techniques. *Science and Justice* 49(2): 120–126.

Relevant Websites

http://www.memoryofpaper.eu:8080/BernsteinPortal/appl_start.disp – Bernstein Portal – The memory of paper.

http://cerig.efpg.inpg.fr/ – Cellule de veille technologique de Grenoble INP Pagora.

http://www.enfsi.eu/ – ENFSI Website.

History of the Forensic Examination of Documents

LA Mohammed, Cherry Avenue, San Bruno, CA, USA

Introduction

Contentions in documents can relate to a whole range of factors including their authenticity, age, source, or content. Factors that must be considered are the substrate of the documents and the manner of their production. The content of the document may comprise the handwriting, typewriting, printing, or a combination of these or other forms of information.

Disputed documents can find their way into the legal system in both the criminal and civil arenas where the outcome of a case may depend on the evidential value of the document. In many cases, documents contribute to the overall evidence. However, in the cases described in this section, the documents involved were pivotal to the resolution.

The Letters of Junius

In the eighteenth century, letters critical of the ruling establishment in England were published in a newspaper. These handwritten letters were anonymous and there was great debate as to who the author was. In the days when punishment for criticism of the King would be imprisonment or death, it was no wonder that the author wished to remain anonymous. Handwriting comparison by Charles Chabot pointed the finger at Sir Phillip Francis. While little is known of Chabot, his methodology reflected a thorough understanding of the principles of handwriting examination.

The Dreyfus Case

The case of Captain Alfred Dreyfus caused a scandal in France at the end of the nineteenth century. This case involved several forged documents, one of which was the infamous 'bordereau.' Capt. Dreyfus was accused of being a spy and of passing French military secrets to Germany. Despite the evidence of several handwriting experts that Dreyfus was not the author of the suspect documents, he was convicted twice in separate trials. A letter entitled 'J'accuse' by novelist Emile Zola to a French newspaper whipped up world opinion and Dreyfus was later pardoned with all his rights restored. The true forger, a Col. Henry, confessed to the forgeries and he later committed suicide.

In the United States, expert testimony on handwriting was accepted in courts in the early nineteenth century. The experts were mainly bank tellers and penmanship teachers. Names such as Daniel T. Ames, William Hagan, and Albert S. Osborn were well known in the field. Ames and Hagan had both written books on document examination, but in 1910, Albert S. Osborn published *'Questioned Documents,'* which became the standard treatise in the field. Osborn was a penman of great note and his book was a comprehensive treatise on all aspects of document examination. The preface was written by Dean John Wigmore who was considered an authority in the law of evidence in the United States. Osborn wrote three more books *'The Mind of the Juror,' 'The Problem of Proof,'* and *'Questioned Document Problems.'* He was responsible for forming and establishing the American Society of Questioned Document Examiners. He emphasized the value of proper training for a document examiner and described the equipment needed for a fully equipped laboratory.

The Lindbergh Case

The kidnapping of the infant son of famed aviator Charles Lindbergh and the subsequent prosecution of Richard Bruno Hauptmann captivated the United States. Lindbergh's son, Charles Jr, was kidnapped from his room during the night. Fourteen ransom letters were eventually sent to the family. Eight document examiners, including Albert S. Osborn, were retained by the prosecution in this case to compare the handwriting on the ransom notes with the handwriting of the main suspect, Hauptmann. All eight examiners identified Hauptmann as the writer of the ransom notes. The examiners testified with the aid of demonstration charts. Their evidence was so convincing that even Hauptmann said, 'Dot handwriting is the worstest thing against me.' On 9 April 1936, Hauptmann was executed (**Figures 1–3**).

Hauptmann's widow, Anna, maintained that her husband was innocent and her case was supported by British author, Ludovich Kennedy. The Lindbergh case was reexamined in 2005 at the request of a television show Forensic Files by three contemporary document examiners: Peter Baier, Grant Sperry, and Gideon Epstein. Each conducted his examination independently and concluded with a varying degree of certainty that Hauptmann was indeed the writer of the ransom notes.

The Peter Weinberger Case

In another horrific case, Peter Weinberger was kidnapped from the front porch of his home on 4 July 1956 in what turned out to be a random crime. After the receipt of a ransom note for \$200 000, the FBI conducted an examination of the handwriting of over 2 million people (**Figure 4**).

The ransom note contained what were considered to be characteristic letter formations. The FBI trained investigators to look for these specific features. Eventually, the handwriting of one person, Angelo De Marca, was identified from the Department of Motor Vehicle records. The body of Peter Weinberger, however, had already been found under some bushes near a road not far from the Weinberger home.

Angelo de Marca confessed to the kidnapping and murder and was executed at Sing Sing prison on 7 August 1958. This

 http://dx.doi.org/10.1016/B978-0-12-382165-2.00137-9

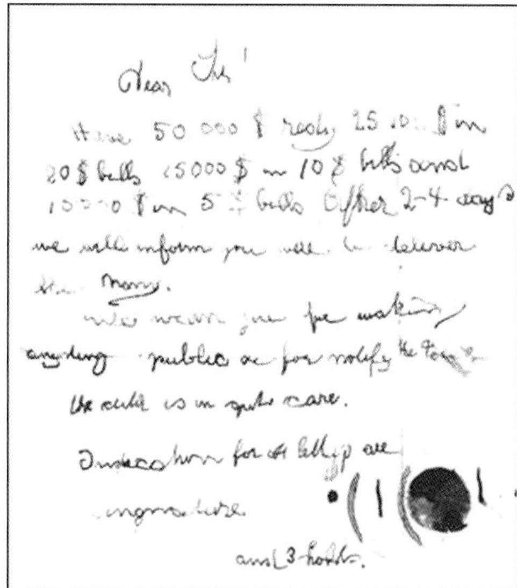

Dear Sir!

Have 50.000 $ redy 25 000 $ in 20 $ bills 15000 $ in 10 $ bills and 10000 $ in 5 $ bills After 2-4 days we will inform you were to deliver the mony.

We warn you for making anyding public or for notify the Police the child is in gut care.

Indication for all letters are singnature and 3 holds.

Figure 1 Copy of one of the ransom notes. Source: www.fbi.gov

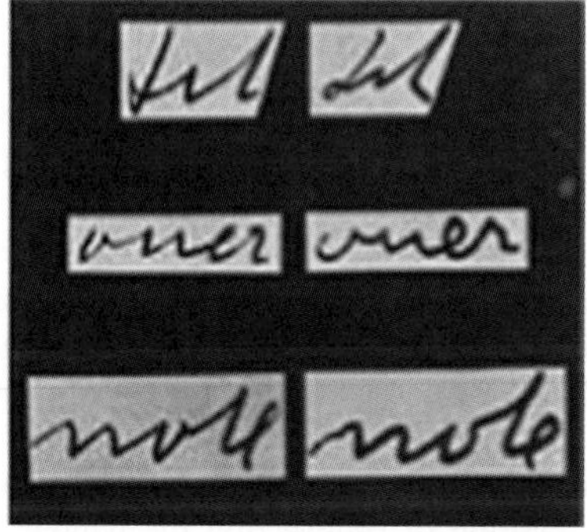

Figure 2 Comparison chart used to demonstrate the similarity between Hauptmann's handwriting (left) and the writing on a ransom note (right). The words from top to bottom are 'Did,' 'our,' and 'note.' Source: www.fbi.gov

case had an impact on the timelines for kidnapping investigations. Instead of a waiting period of 3 weeks, the FBI could now be brought into a case within 24 h.

The Hitler Diaries

The investigation of the Hitler Diaries was a remarkable one given the number of documents that were forged and the simple way they were ultimately exposed as fakes. The German magazine '*Stern*' paid 2 million marks for 63 volumes of diaries purported to be of Adolf Hitler. In 1982, three document examiners (one Swiss, one German, and one American) also compared the handwriting from the diaries with handwriting purportedly of Adolf Hitler. They each declared the handwriting in the diary to be authentic. However, the specimen

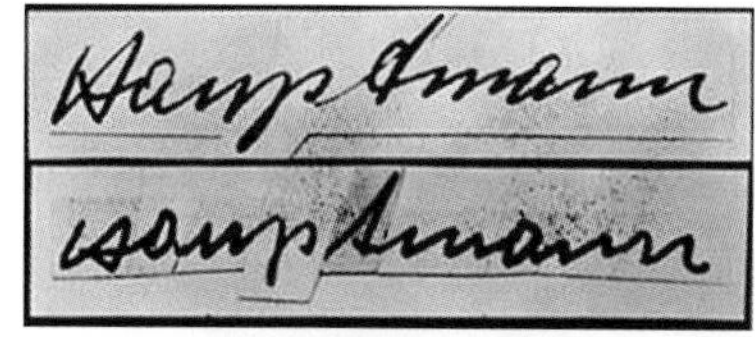

Figure 3 A chart showing Hauptmann's signature (top) and a composite of individual letters from a ransom note (bottom). Source: www.fbi.gov

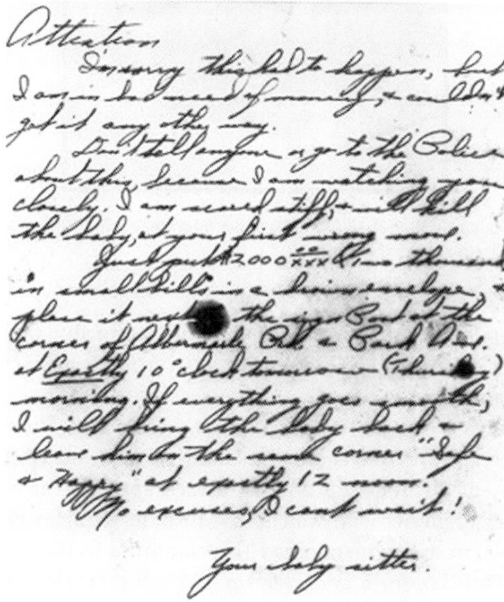

Attention

I'm sorry this had to happen, but I am in bad need of money, & couldn't get it any other way.

Don't tell anyone or go to the Police about this because I am watching you closely. I am scared stiff, & will kill the baby at your first wrong move.

Just put $2000 — in (two thousand) in small bills in a brown envelope & place it next to the sign post at the corner of Albermarle Rd & Park Ave. at exactly 10 o'clock tomorrow (Thursday) morning. If everything goes smooth, I will bring the baby back & leave him at the same corner "Safe & Happy" at exactly 12 noon. No excuses, I can't wait!

Your baby sitter.

Figure 4 The first of the Weinberger ransom notes. Source: www.fbi.gov

handwriting that was provided to the examiners for comparison as the known handwriting of Adolph Hitler also included samples that had been written by the forger of the diaries. Therefore, while the examiner's handwriting examination was correct, his conclusion that the handwriting in the diaries was Hitler's was wrong. The voluminous material was examined by historians in 1983 and declared to be genuine.

Eventually, in 1983, Dr. Julius Grant exposed the diaries as a fraud by the simple fact that the pages in the diaries contained optical brighteners. The optical brighteners, which were apparent when exposed to ultraviolet (UV) radiation, were not used in paper that was manufactured during the dates when the diaries were purportedly written. Also in 1983, the Federal Bureau of Criminal Investigation examined three of the diaries (1934, 1943, and 1944) and found evidence from the inks, bookbinding, paper, and typewriting that confirmed the hoax.

The Mormon Forgeries and Murders

The Mark Hoffman case was a crime that ballooned from forgery to mayhem and murder. Mark Hoffman was a dealer in old books and papers. He was a Mormon and soon realized that he could make a lot of money selling documents pertaining to the Mormon Church. The first document that Hoffman found was 'The Salamander Letter.' After several years of selling and trading documents, Hofmann began to be suspected of

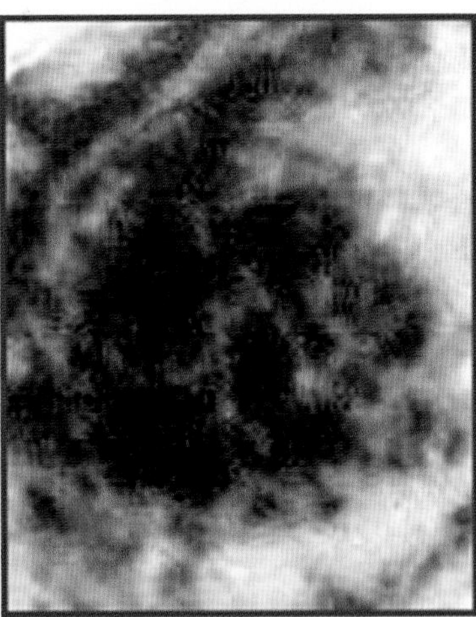

Figure 5 Example of alligatoring in ink seen under the microscope. Source: http://www.trutv.com

peddling forged documents. To throw off suspicion, he started a series of bombings in the 1980s in which he was the first to get injured.

In 1985, George Throckmorton, an forensic document examiner (FDE) from Utah, was hired to examine Hoffman's documents. Throckmorton was a Mormon and he wanted another examiner who was not a Mormon. William Flynn, a Catholic from Arizona, joined Throckmorton in the examination. Throckmorton and Flynn noted a peculiar feature that was common to Hoffman's documents. The ink on the documents displayed a cracked or alligator pattern (**Figure 5**).

They researched old ink formulas with which they knew Hoffman was familiar and hit upon one that had the same alligatoring effect when combined with sodium hydroxide. They could now unerringly pick Hoffman-produced documents.

Throckmorton and Flynn devised a combination of tests that could detect Hoffman forgeries. UV radiation was used to disclose a discoloration caused by the treatment of documents with chemicals such as sodium hydroxide. They described the effect as blue haze. UV radiation also disclosed a unidirectional running of iron-gall ink caused by the chemicals, which Hoffman used to mimic artificial aging. Chemical treatment also caused 'bleed thru' which depended to some extent on the paper type.

Microscopic examination revealed the 'alligatoring' effect caused by the iron-gall ink cracking when treated with hydrogen peroxide and ammonium hydroxide. Solubility tests, the presence of printing flaws from photographic negatives, observation of the lack of stains from old iron-gall ink, and scanning auger microscopy dating were other techniques used to reveal the Hoffman forgeries. These techniques were used in combination and it is this use of multiple tests that provided conclusive proof of the forgeries.

During their 18-month investigation, Flynn and Throckmorton examined over 6000 documents dated between 1792 and 1929. Four hundred and forty-eight of these were Hoffman documents of which 268 (60%) were found to be authentic, 68 (15%) not proven as genuine or forged, and 107 (27%) proven as forged.

Hoffman eventually pled guilty to two counts of second-degree murder, forgery of the Salamander Letter, and other associated crimes. He was sentenced to four concurrent terms of 5 years to life in the state penitentiary.

The Howard Hughes 'Mormon Will' Case

On 5 April 1976, billionaire and recluse Howard Hughes died. No official will of Hughes could be found despite the fact that he owned a vast business empire. Once word of this spread, over 30 wills were submitted to the County Clerk in Nevada. One of these wills became known as 'The Mormon Will' as it was delivered by an official of the Mormon Church. The will had been left at the Church addressed to the President of the Church. The handwritten will gave one-sixteenth of Hughes estate to the Mormon Church and another one-sixteenth to an individual named Melvin Du Mar [sic]. Melvin Dummar's story was that he had picked up Hughes hitchhiking in the desert several years before. Dummar initially denied knowing anything about the will. However, his fingerprint was found on one of the envelopes left at the Mormon Church. He later admitted to writing the note to the Church and that he delivered the will to the Church.

The will was examined in court in Las Vegas by FDE John 'Jack' Harris. Harris knew almost immediately that the will was as he described 'a rank forgery.' Harris had access to numerous samples of Hughes' handwriting and signatures and he found many features in the will that did not correspond with Hughes' handwriting. Harris described the writing on the will as slow and laborious and several letter forms did not match. He also pointed out differences in features such as i-dots, t-crossings, and commas. The natural variation seen in the specimen Hughes handwriting was absent in the handwriting on the will.

There were four signatures in the name of H.R. Hughes on the will and another on the envelope. These were also shown to be palpable forgeries. The forgeries appeared to be copied from signatures of Hughes that were illustrated in the book *Hoax* which was written about the forgery of a biography of Hughes.

There were numerous other discrepancies between the known handwriting of Hughes and the handwriting on the will. Nevertheless, there was a trail that commenced on 7 November 1977 and finished on 8 May 1978. The jury took a day and a half to return a verdict that the 'Mormon Will' was a forgery.

The Alger Hiss Case

A Woodstock typewriter, bearing the serial number 230099, played a central role in the Alger Hiss case. The case for the US Government was that Hiss, alleged to be a Soviet spy, used the typewriter to copy secret documents. The case for Hiss' defense was that the US Government forged Hiss' typewriter by building an exact replica. During Hiss' trial in 1948, the prosecutor Thomas Murphy described the typewriter as the main witness against Hiss. Hiss' defense engaged the services of Martin Tytell of New York to build a typewriter to show that forgery of a typewriter was possible. Tytell only had to work from specimens of the Woodstock's typing which made it a very difficult job as he had to get the defects in the typefaces and alignment in the typing correct. However, he owned a typewriter repair shop that contained thousands of typefaces and he had extensive experiences in typewriter repair. Tytell constructed the 'Woodstock' at a cost of $7500.00. Prominent FDEs such as Donald Doud and Ordway Hilton considered that Tytell could not have built a perfect replica that would be good enough to get past a trained FDE. Hiss was tried for perjury twice with the first trial ending in a hung jury. He was found guilty in the second trial on two counts of perjury. Tytell's typewriter was built for an appeal by Hiss for a new trial. However, it was denied as the trial judge ruled that there was no evidence that the prosecution had access to a typewriter fabricator with Tytell's skill.

Hiss could not have been tried for espionage as the statute of limitations had run out. He was sentenced to 5 years and eventually served 44 months. At his sentencing on 25 January 1950, Hiss remarked that "I am confident that in the future the full facts of how Whittaker Chambers was able to carry out forgery by typewriter will be disclosed." Despite the length of time that has passed, the Hiss case remains controversial in the United States. Former President Richard. M. Nixon had been involved early on in the investigation of Hiss when Nixon was a member of the House of Representatives. Hiss' family still actively defends his innocence.

The Unabomber

Between 25 May 1978 and 24 April 1995, Theodore Kaczynski was responsible for sending a series of bombs through the mail to universities and airlines. Because of this, he was dubbed the unabomber – 'una' for 'university' and 'a' for 'airlines.' Kaczynski, who held a doctoral degree in mathematics, was anti-technology and produced a typewritten manifesto in which he detailed his demands in order to have the bombings stopped. After he was arrested based on a tip from his brother, investigators found three manual typewriters in Kaczynski's rustic home in Montana. One of the typewriters, a Smith-Corona, was identified as the machine that was used to type the manifesto. Kaczynski eventually pled guilty in 1998 to 13 counts of attacks in three states that killed three and injured two. He was sentenced to life and is confined in isolation at a 'Supermax' prison in Colorado without any possibility of parole.

The Killian Memos

During the 2004 General Election in the United States, a document was produced that indicated that incumbent President George W. Bush had attempted to evade National Guard duty. The document was a copy, and CBS News hired several FDEs to determine whether or not the document was authentic. The FDEs' opinions ranged from inconclusive to authentic. Peter Tytell, an FDE from New York and a noted typewriter expert, quickly showed that the document was very likely not to be authentic as the typewritten date had a superscript for the 'th.' In the early 1970s, there were very few typewriters that could type a superscript and the possibility of one being on a far-flung military base was remote. There were also differences in typestyle and spacing which caused Tytell to conclude that the memos were prepared by a word processing program rather than on an Olympia manual typewriter. A panel appointed by CBS News concluded that there were serious problems about the authenticity of the memos. The panel strongly criticized CBS News. The producer was fired and several top executives resigned.

The Jon Benet Ramsey Case

On the night of Christmas in 1996, six-year-old Jon Benet Ramsey was put to bed at 9.30 p.m. The next morning her mother, Patricia, went down to breakfast at 5.00 a.m. and in the kitchen found a two-page ransom note demanding $118 000 for the return of Jon Benet. Eight hours later, during a search of the house, John Ramsey found his daughter's body in a basement room. The young girl, according to the autopsy report, had been strangled, suffered severe head injuries, and may have been sexually assaulted. During the search of the home, police officers allowed the family and friends throughout the house, thereby compromising possible forensic evidence.

Attention was immediately focused on the handwritten ransom letter. The amount of $118 000 curiously matched John Ramsey's bonus for that year. The family became the main suspects. Document examiners compared the writing on the note with samples taken from Patricia, John, and Jon Benet's brother, Burke, who was nine at the time. John and Burke as well as John's two adult children from a previous marriage were quickly cleared as possible authors of the note. Patricia became the prime suspect. Several FDEs were asked to conduct examinations and the majority opined that Patricia was probably not the writer, though a minority of FDEs opined that she had indeed written the note.

The handwriting on the note may have been disguised, which led to some of the problems in identifying the writer. However, the general consensus was that none of the Ramsey family members were involved in writing the note. In June 2006, Patricia Ramsey died from ovarian cancer. Two months later, John Mark Kerr who was in prison in Thailand confessed to killing Jon Benet. He was extradited to the United States where DNA evidence quickly showed that he was not the guilty party in this case.

The Jon Benet Ramsey case remains unsolved at the time of writing. Most investigators now believe that an unknown intruder was involved. The evolution of forensic DNA and handwriting examination techniques may be the key to solving the murder of a six-year-old child on Christmas night in 1996.

The Zodiac Killer

In July 1969, letters were mailed to three newspapers in San Francisco. The writer claimed to be responsible for two attacks on courting couples. In the first attack, the couple was killed and, in the second, the male survived but the woman died. The letters were handwritten in blue felt-tip ink and described facts that only the investigators would know. In each letter, the writer enclosed a coded cipher and demanded that the newspapers publish his letters on their front pages warning that he would go on a murderous rampage if they did not comply. The newspapers complied and sent the San Franciscans into a state of panic (**Figure 6**).

Figure 6 Cipher sent to the Vallejo Times-Herald. Source: http://www.trutv.com

The killings continued with the stabbing of a couple in which the woman died. After shooting to death a cabdriver on 13 October 1969, the killer mailed a letter to the San Francisco Chronicle, which included a bloodstained piece of the cabdriver's shirt. He called himself 'The Zodiac.' He then threatened to kill schoolchildren either by shooting or with a bomb. However, despite sending several more letters, no more killings were reported.

The handwriting on the letters (14 of them) was compared to many suspects but no one was identified as the Zodiac. Three main suspects were developed by amateur investigators. Development of partial DNA evidence from the back of a stamp on an envelope excluded all three suspects. The DNA from saliva on the back of the stamp was assumed to be that of the Zodiac. The case remains unsolved.

Admissibility

Questioned document evidence was readily accepted in US courts where the standard of admissibility was the Frye rule of general acceptance. In 1993, the US Supreme Court established what came to be known as the Daubert guidelines in the case of Daubert v. Merrell-Dow Pharmaceuticals. The intent of these guidelines was to make the trial judge the 'gatekeeper' of scientific evidence in an effort to keep junk science out of the courts. In 1998, a Daubert hearing to exclude handwriting evidence was held in the case of United States v. Starzecpyzel. The trial judge ruled that while handwriting evidence was not scientific, it was admissible under the Daubert guidelines as technical evidence.

Two trials, General Electric v. Joiner (1997) and Kumho Tire Company v. Carmichael (1999), became the second and third parts of the Daubert trilogy. The Kumho decision ruled that technical evidence was also subject to Daubert guidelines. Daubert hearings were held to exclude the testimony of FDEs in several cases. In some cases, the FDE was limited to testifying to findings but not being able to express an opinion. In other cases, the FDE was excluded altogether.

However, the FDE community was hard at work responding to the criticisms aimed at it in the Daubert hearings. Empirical research in conjunction with the academic community was conducted and the results published. Additional Daubert requirements were addressed and met. In 2002, in the case of United States v. Prime, a Daubert hearing was conducted and the judge ruled that the FDE had met all the Daubert guidelines.

FDEs have met the challenges posed by the development of the ballpoint pen, the typewriter, photocopiers, fax machines, imaging software, and laser and inkjet printers. Research by FDEs, neuroscientists, motor control scientists, and computer scientists is ongoing to investigate and strengthen the foundations of forensic document examination, in particular, handwriting examination.

See also: **Documents**: Analytical Methods; Document Dating; Forgery/Counterfeits; Handwriting; Ink Analysis; Overview of Forensic Document Examination; Paper Analysis.

Further Reading

Ames DT (1992) *Ames on forgery*. Littleton, CO: Fred B. Rothman & Co.

Baier PE and Michel L (1985) The diaries of Adolf Hitler implication for document examination. *Journal of the Forensic Science Society* 25: 67–178.

Cantu AA (1986) The Paper Mate® ink on the Howard Hughes 'Mormon Will'. *Journal of Forensic Sciences* 31(1): 360–364.

Chabot C (1871) *The Handwriting of Junius 1769*. London: John Murray.

Chapman G (1972) *The Dreyfus Trials*. New York, NY: Stein and Day.

Cook FJ (1958) *The Unfinished Story of Alger Hiss*. New York, NY: William Morrow & Company.

Fisher J (1987) *The Lindbergh Case*. New Brunswick and London: Rutgers University Press.

Fisher J (1999) *The Ghosts of Hopewell. Setting the Record Straight in the Lindbergh Case*. Carbondale and Edwardsville: Southern Illinois University Press.

Freese PL (1986) Howard Hughes and Melvin Dummar: Forensic science versus film fiction. *Journal of Forensic Sciences* 31(1): 342–359.

Grant J (1985) The diaries of Adolf Hitler. *Journal of the Forensic Science Society* 25: 189.

Graysmith R (2007) Zodiac Unmasked. New York, NY: Penguin Group.

Hagan WE (1974) *Treatise on Disputed Handwriting*. New York, NY: Ames Press Inc.

Haring JV (1937) *The Hand of Hauptmann*. Plainfield, NJ: The Hamer Publishing Company.

Harris JJ (1986) The document evidence and some other observations about the Howard R. Hughes 'Mormon Will contest'. *Journal of Forensic Sciences* 31(1): 365–375.

Hicks FA (2003) The greatest handwriting mystery of the eighteenth century: The Junius Letters. *Journal of the American Society of Questioned Document Examiners* 5(2): 67–77.

Hilton O (1979) History of questioned document examination in the United States. *Journal of Forensic Sciences* 24(4): 890–897.

Kennedy L (1985) *The Airman and the Carpenter. The Lindbergh Case and the Framing of Richard Hauptmann*. London, UK: Collins.

Osborn AS (1929) *Questioned Documents*, 2nd edn. New Montclair, NJ: Patterson Smith.

Rhoden H (1980) *High Stakes. The Gamble for the Howard Hughes Will*. New York, NY: Crown Publishers, Inc.

Sillitoe L and Roberts A (1988) *Salamander. The Story of the Mormon Forgery Murders*. Salt Lake City, Utah: Signature Books.

Wood JF (1930) The Leopold-Loeb case (From the standpoint of the handwriting, pen printing, and typewriting expert). *American Journal of Police Science* 1: 339–352.

Relevant Websites

http://abcnews.go.com – ABC News.

www.cedartech.com – CedarTech, Pattern Recognition Technology.

www.trutv.com/librar – crime library, Criminal Minds and Methods.

http://www.washingtonpost.com – Expert Cited by CBS Says He Didn't Authenticate Papers.

http://www.fbi.gov – The FBI, Federal Bureau of Investigation: Famous Cases and Criminals.

http://www.usatoday.com – USA Today. News.

Overview of Forensic Document Examination

DL Hammond, U.S. Army Criminal Investigation Laboratory, Forest Park, GA, USA

Glossary

Black box testing – A research/testing strategy used to assess the reliability and validity of forensic methods and/or techniques which rely primarily on subjective and experience-based decision making.

What is a Forensic Document Examiner?

When was a document created? How was it created? Who prepared the document? What device was used to create the document? Is the document genuine? Has the document been altered? Experts in the field of forensic document examination are confronted with these, and other, questions on a daily basis. The field of forensic document examination has developed over time because of the courts' needs to correctly interpret and resolve these types of questions. These issues typically arise in legal matters, both civil and criminal, and often require the unique talents of highly skilled and reliable experts referred to as forensic document examiners (FDEs).

What are the Duties of a FDE?

An FDE's primary duties include the examination, comparison, and analysis of documents in order to (1) determine genuineness or nongenuineness, to expose forgery, or to reveal alterations, additions, or deletions, (2) provide evidence as to the authorship or nonauthorship of handwritten entries (i.e., cursive handwriting, hand printing, and signatures), (3) provide evidence as to the source of typewriting or other mechanical impressions, marks, or relative evidence, and (4) prepare written reports and provide expert testimony as needed.

For many examiners, the examination and comparison of questioned (i.e., disputed) and known writing specimens for the purpose of determining authorship dominate their daily casework. As a result, FDEs are commonly referred to as handwriting experts. As a general rule, this title is appropriate; however, it does not do justice to the variety of examinations and comparisons that fall within the discipline of forensic document examination.

Exploring FDE Casework

In spite of the continued push for a paperless society, FDEs remain actively employed in local, state/province, federal, and private forensic laboratories worldwide and are routinely called upon to provide forensic support in all types of civil and criminal cases. Homicides, sexual assault, drugs, identity theft, bank robberies, hate crimes, terrorism, financial fraud, child abuse, theft, counterfeiting, medical malpractice, and a plethora of almost any other civil and criminal issues can arise that may require the assistance of an FDE.

Types of Examinations

There are a broad range of examinations and comparisons conducted in traditional forensic document laboratories and may involve almost anything relating to the production of a document. One case may focus on a single examination type (e.g., handwriting comparison), while another case may present the need to take a multifaceted approach (e.g., ink analysis, detection and development of indented writing, and handwriting comparison) and require various examination methods in order to develop the full evidentiary value of the item(s).

Handwriting

Handwriting comparisons (the examination and comparison of questioned and known handwriting, hand printing, and signatures) are the most prevalent examination type encountered and often constitutes 80% or more of the day-to-day case load in many modern forensic document laboratories.

Handwriting examinations can either consist of the examination of questioned writing and known specimen writing or be based solely on a comparison of one questioned document to one or more additional questioned documents (e.g., determination of common authorship among a series of threatening anonymous letters). However, the typical handwriting comparison will involve the comparison of a questioned handwritten item(s) to a set of known writings from one or more individuals. In this instance, the analyst will attempt to determine whether there is evidence to support which, if any, of the writers of the known specimens wrote, or did not write, the disputed writing.

Other examinations

Aside from handwritten text and signature examinations, FDEs may use their expertise in a large number of areas including the following:

- The detection and decipherment of indented writing in paper
- Physical matching, reconstruction, and dating of paper, tape, and adhesives
- Differentiating different types of inks
- The detection and decipherment of alterations, obliterations, and erasures
- The examination of type and typewriters (e.g., typestyle classification to establish make/model of typewriter; ribbon and correction ribbon examination; the identification of the source of a typewritten document and the establishment of the date of manufacture of a typewritten document)

- The examination of printers (laser, inkjet, etc.) and printed documents, fax machine, and facsimile documents
- The determination of the sequence of two or more intersecting strokes
- The determination of printing processes associated with counterfeit documents

Types of Documents Examined

Documents exist in our day-to-day lives and can provide a 'paper trail' of our activities. Documents can play an important role in linking an individual to a crime by placing them at a location and perhaps during a specific time period. A document may provide evidence that one person knows or has had contact with another person. The information on a document can also form the basis to determine where or how a document was prepared, who prepared it, and when the document was prepared. Information altered on a document can be detected to verify that the content of a document has been changed or modified to appear to be something else.

Some examples of the types of documents examined include the following:

- Anonymous letters (threatening notes, bomb threats, and robbery notes)
- Financial documents (checks, credit card/debit cards receipts, promissory notes, tax returns, purchase receipts, and bill-of-sale)
- Deeds, wills, contracts and agreements, and applications
- Log books
- Suicide notes
- Prescriptions
- Time sheets
- Work orders
- Certificates
- Performance evaluations
- Diaries and journals
- School papers
- Post-it-notes
- Envelopes and letters
- Address books
- Graffiti
- Lottery tickets
- Counterfeiting (currency, credit cards, I.D. cards, driver's license, passports, immigration documents, etc.)

Instrumentation

The most common method of analysis in the examination of documents is a side-by-side comparison of items. As a result, the examiner's cognitive machinery serve as the most used 'instrument' in the analysis, comparison, and evaluation process. A stereomicroscope is often used to aid and enhance the examiner's ability to distinguish fine detail through the use of low-power magnification (i.e., up to ×40).

Some of the other instruments and tools commonly used may include, but are not limited to the following:

- Video spectral analysis devices (ink and paper differentiation)
- Hyperspectral analysis devices (ink and paper differentiation)
- Ultraviolet light boxes and handheld wands (ink and paper differentiation)
- Micrometers (paper thickness)
- Electrostatic detection devices (development of indented writings)
- Digital imaging processing software (ink and paper differentiation)

The Origins of Modern Forensic Document Examination

Before the establishment of law enforcement crime laboratories, forensic document examination was dominated by individual practitioners primarily working in private practices. These practitioners, often expert penmen, calligraphers, and others interested in handwriting, were self-taught experts who turned their expertise into one of the first forensic science disciplines.

Arguably, the most influential individual in the development of modern forensic document examination was Albert S. Osborn. Osborn worked tirelessly to promote the field and to extend its acceptance in the legal system of the United States. Considered by many to be the founding father of document examination, Osborn was a prolific writer, who in 1910 published *Questioned Documents*. Later republished in 1929, this book provided many of the theories and principles that are still relevant and used in practice more than a century later.

The development of the discipline

Before about the middle of the twentieth century, self-education was about the only manner in which one could become an FDE. Albert S. Osborn believed strongly in the development of the profession through the sharing of information among colleagues. Osborn often invited small groups of well-respected colleagues to his home to foster the sharing of information and ideas. These meetings eventually led to the creation of the American Society of Questioned Document Examiners in 1942.

Establishing formal training programs

The American Academy of Forensic Sciences was established in the late 1940s; and by the 1960s, forensic document examination, known at the time as 'questioned document examination' or 'document examination,' was starting to mature and grow. Up until this point, self-education and informal apprenticeships were the only methods for training in forensic document examination. As the need for crime laboratories increased, it became apparent that formal training programs needed to be developed and qualifications for forensic experts established and defined. By the late 1960s, formalized, structured written training programs began to appear. Although still centered on an apprenticeship-based model, the 2-year training programs provided detailed required reading lists, lectures, practical exercises and knowledge- and competency-based written, practical, and/or oral examinations. In the years since, the model for training in forensic document examination has essentially remained unchanged. In 2005, a modified version of this training model was established and published as a voluntary consensus standard within the international community.

Qualifications of a Modern FDEs

Regrettably, a wide variance exists in the qualifications of those currently practicing as FDEs. In spite of the fact that many of the organizations within the profession have set high standards of qualification, courts have established thresholds for the admission of expert witnesses, which fall well short of the modern standards held in the FDE community.

As a general rule, courts will admit someone as an expert witness in a scientific or other field provided that the witness' knowledge in that subject matter (by way of their education, training, experience, or skill) is perceived to be beyond that of the average person. If the 'expertise' of a potential expert witness is not thoroughly vetted, the door may be left open to a number of pseudoexperts and charlatans.

Education

Most forensic laboratories and document-related professional organizations require examiners to have a baccalaureate degree from an accredited academic institution. As the interest in forensic science has increased dramatically in recent years, the number of academic institutions offering undergraduate- and graduate-level degrees in forensic science has greatly expanded. Forensic laboratories have been the immediate benefactor, as incoming trainees are entering into careers in forensic document examination with graduate-level degrees in forensic science or with degrees that have a strong background in science. With an ever-growing interest in strengthening the 'science' in the forensic sciences, the influx of more traditionally trained scientists should continue to push the field of forensic document examination forward.

Visual Acuity

As most of the tasks conducted by FDEs involve visual examinations and comparisons, a key prerequisite is the ability of the examiner to distinguish fine detail. To assess this ability, applicants must be able to successfully complete several preliminary tests to evaluate their suitability for training. Typical prehire evaluations may therefore include the following:

- Form blindness/form discrimination tests
- Color perception/color blindness tests
- Visual Acuity tests

The absence of even one of these abilities is likely to serve as a basis of exclusion from a forensic document training program.

Training

The modern standard for training in forensic document examination is the successful completion of a broad-based formal 2-year apprenticeship style training program under the tutelage of a qualified principal trainer. The FDE training programs typically cover all aspects of modern forensic document examination methods and procedures. Teaching methods include:

- Required reading
- Lectures
- Demonstration (i.e., practical exercises)
- Knowledge and competency assessments (e.g., written, practical, and oral examinations)
- Mock trials
- Supervised case work
- Research projects
- Tours of manufacturing plants

Specialists

Owing to the limited nature of their casework, some laboratories limit the examiner's training to a specific element(s) of forensic document examination. Examples of some forensic document-related specialties include the following:

- Forensic ink chemists
- Handwriting experts/specialists
- Counterfeit specialists

To account for this diversity, one forensic document organization (the American Society of Questioned Document Examiners) recently created a 'specialist' membership category.

Posttraining Qualifications

The continuing education and professional development of FDEs do not end at the completion of training but should continue throughout the career of the individual. Skill sets need to be continually assessed and the examiners should make every effort to keep up with emerging technologies and changes in examination methodologies and procedures.

Certification

Certification provides a mechanism whereby members of the judicial system and other interested parties can easily identify those individuals engaged in forensic document examination that have demonstrated adequate levels of qualification and competence. While there are several certification boards worldwide that certify FDEs, there are only a few that have been externally accredited.

Some of the key elements of any certification program include the following:

- Credentials review
- Testing
- Requirements for recertification
- Verification of training
- Code of ethics

Unfortunately, individual certification is generally neither a requirement to work in most forensic laboratories nor a requirement that must be met in order to provide expert testimony in most courts. This may soon change, at least in the United States, as there has been a renewed interest in the last few years toward requiring all forensic scientists to obtain individual certification.

Proficiency testing

Proficiency testing can be used as a means to assess the skills and expertise of the examiner for the various tasks associated with forensic document examination. However, proficiency testing is similar to certification in that it is another element of continuing education and ongoing professional development that is often underappreciated, and depending on where one is employed, it may not even be required.

Proficiency tests that are not based on actual casework are preferred. Feedback that is based on tests, where there are true known answers, provides a mechanism for learning. In the absence of true known answers, there will always exist the possibility that bad habits or bad methodology or procedures will not be revealed.

Proficiency tests should be challenging. Being able to successfully complete easy tasks does nothing to develop expert performers and may serve only to further the examiner's belief of expertise when s/he may not have any. This false belief can be extended especially if the examiner's exposure to testing is limited. Anytime that a human element is involved, errors are sure to happen. If an examiner, whether an FDE or an examiner in any other forensic discipline, claims to have a 'zero error rate,' it is probably safe to say that they have not been exposed to enough testing.

Error rates and skill-task assessments

In the past decade, there has been a large increase in the number of studies and tests aimed at assessing the potential error rates associated with the various tasks conducted by FDEs. Slowly, these studies are helping to define the limits of forensic document examination and have helped identify areas where additional research should be targeted.

It is unlikely that these tests will ever be able to provide a definite error rate for a given task. However, over time and through exposure to multiple tests covering a range of problems with varying difficulties, a clearer picture of the nature of the skill and expertise of FDEs will emerge. In time, perhaps, courts will begin to require some form of documentation from all forensic scientists, which illustrates their individual skills based on some form of 'black box' testing.

Other mechanisms for professional development and continuing education

An excellent means to further one's knowledge and education within forensic document examination is by being active in professional organizations. There are numerous professional organizations and societies around the world where an FDE can seek membership. Many of these organizations host annual conferences, seminars, and workshops, where emerging techniques and methods of analysis are presented and discussed. Attendees are also exposed to new technologies that may redefine the boundaries of a technique or allow an analysis to be completed faster and/or cheaper. The ability to network within the community is also an important element of being involved in the larger community. Sooner or later, every expert is bound to come across something that is unfamiliar and that requires consultation within the peer group before taking a step forward.

Issues for the Future

Forensic science continues to grow and evolve, as new techniques and capabilities are rapidly emerging. With this growth, more and more emphasis is being placed on the need to conduct research. Fortunately, after years of neglect, funding for research related to forensic document examination is starting to appear. Given the legal challenges over the past 15 years to all of the comparative sciences (e.g., document examination, latent prints, firearms and tool marks, etc.), the renewed emphasis on research will only aid in placing each of these fields on a stronger scientific footing.

Acknowledgment

The opinions or assertions contained herein are the private views of the author and are not to be construed as official or as reflecting the views of the Department of the Army or the Department of Defense.

See also: **Documents**: Analytical Methods; Document Dating; Forgery/Counterfeits; Handwriting; History of the Forensic Examination of Documents; Ink Analysis; Paper Analysis.

Further Reading

ASTM Standard E2388-11 (2008) *Standard Guide for Minimum Training Requirements for Forensic Document Examiners*. West Conshohocken, PA: ASTM International. http://dx.doi.org/10.1520/E2388-11.

ASTM Standard E444-09 (2008) *Standard Guide for Scope of Work of Forensic Document Examiners*. West Conshohocken, PA: ASTM International. http://dx.doi.org/10.1520/E0444-09.

Dyer AG, Found B, and Rogers D (2006) Visual attention and expertise for forensic signature analysis. *Journal of Forensic Sciences* 51(6): 1397–1404.

Fisher J (1994) *The Lindbergh case*. Piscataway, NJ: Rutgers University Press.

Found B and Rogers D (2003) The initial profiling trial of a program to characterize forensic handwriting examiners' skill. *Journal of the American Society of Questioned Document Examiners* 6(2): 72–81.

Huber RA and Headrick AM (1999) *Handwriting Identification: Facts and Fundamentals*. Boca Raton: CRC Press.

Kam M, Gummadidala K, Fielding G, and Conn R (2001) Signature authentication by forensic document examiners. *Journal of Forensic Sciences* 46(4): 884–888.

Kam M and Lin E (2003) Writer identification using hand-printed and non-hand-printed questioned documents. *Journal of Forensic Sciences* 48(6): 1391–1395.

Kelly JS and Lindblom BS (2006) *Scientific Examination of Questioned Documents*. Boca Raton: CRC Press.

Merlino ML, Sprinter V, Kelly JS, Hammond D, Sahota E, and Haines L (2007) Meeting the challenges of the Daubert trilogy: Redefining the reliability of forensic evidence. *Tulsa Law Review* 43(2): 417–445.

Mnookin JL (2008) Of black boxes, instruments, and experts: Testing the validity of forensic science. *Episteme* 5: 343–358.

Osborn AS (1929) *Questioned Documents*, 2nd edn. Chicago: Nelson-Hall Co.

Risinger DM (2009) Handwriting identification. In: Faigman DL, Saks MJ, Sanders J, and Cheng EK (eds.) *Modern Scientific Evidence: The Law and Science of Expert Testimony*, vol. 4, pp. 451–643. Eagan, MN: Thomson Reuters/West.

Sita J, Found B, and Rogers D (2002) Forensic handwriting examiners' expertise for signature comparison. *Journal of Forensic Sciences* 47: 1117–1124.

Srihari SN, Cha S, Arora H, and Lee S (2002) Individuality of handwriting. *Journal of Forensic Sciences* 47(4): 856–872.

Relevant Websites

http://www.aafs.org – American Academy of Forensic Sciences.
http://www.asqde.org – American Society of Questioned Document Examiners.
http://www.astm.org – ASTM International.
http://www.collaborativetesting.com – Collaborative Testing Service, Inc.
http://www.st2ar.org – Skill-Task Training, Assessment and Research, Inc.
http://www.thefsab.org – Forensic Specialties Accreditation Board.

ENGINEERING

Contents

Forensic Engineering/Accident Reconstruction/Biomechanics of Injury/Philosophy, Basic Theory, and Fundamentals

SC Batterman and SD Batterman, Batterman Engineering, LLC, Cherry Hill, NJ, USA

Introduction

Forensic engineering may be defined as the application of engineering principles toward the purposes of the law. It is important to remember that although the analysis and results are to be applied to the understanding and resolution of legal matters, they must follow from a rigorous application of the governing natural laws and application of scientific principles, consistent with the available information and data. As in all areas of scientific inquiry and endeavor, the quality and reliability of an analysis and the resulting solution are directly related to the quality and detail of the input data. At times, there may be considerable uncertainty associated with the results, or insufficient information and data available with which to reach objective conclusions to a reasonable degree of engineering and scientific certainty. In such cases, this in and of itself may be an important conclusion for the finders of fact (i.e., the judge and jury).

It is important to note at the outset that although individuals may refer to themselves as forensic engineers, such individuals are typically formally educated and rigorously trained engineers applying their scientific and engineering backgrounds, education, and knowledge in one (or more) of the traditional engineering disciplines to the solution of engineering problems that arise in forensic settings. Although colleges, universities, and institutions of higher learning may offer select courses in forensic engineering, in the United States, currently, there are no degree granting programs in forensic engineering, per se. Qualified practitioners of forensic engineering are rigorously trained and formally educated in the traditional engineering disciplines and/or closely related sciences.

 http://dx.doi.org/10.1016/B978-0-12-382165-2.00139-2

In performing a scientific accident reconstruction, the available physical evidence is utilized in conjunction with the governing laws of nature and physical principles to work backward from the aftermath of an event in order to determine the conditions at the commencement of, or immediately before, the subject incident sequence. With the final state, or condition known, the objective of any forensic investigation in general, or accident reconstruction specifically, is to determine the initial conditions, or state of the system at the commencement of the event sequence. It is this knowledge of the final state of the system, with the objective being to solve for the initial conditions that distinguishes investigations and analyses in forensic science from more typical, or mainstream scientific, investigations where the state of the system at some initial time (t_0) is known and the objective is to solve for the final state of the system at some later time (t_f).

In cases involving accidental injury and/or death allegedly caused by defectively designed and/or manufactured products (i.e., products liability), forensic engineers are often called upon to either help support or defend against allegations of a product defect being causally related to the subject accident and/or injuries. Suffice it to say that in order to be legally significant in matters of personal injury litigation, it is typically not sufficient to simply demonstrate, or prove, that a particular product is defective. It must also be demonstrated through the appropriate analyses that the defective condition was causally related to the resulting injuries and/or death(s). The goal of an automotive accident reconstruction is often the determination of impact velocities (speeds, i.e., the magnitudes of the velocities) and/or changes in vehicle velocities (delta-v's), which are important considerations in determining responsibility for an accident and also in assessing the severity of an accident in terms of its injury-producing potential. However, oftentimes there are also allegations of defective vehicle design and/or manufacturing being causally related to the happening of an accident and/or the failure of safety features to function properly and/or to protect an occupant as intended or designed. For example, in automobile crashes involving occupant injury and/or death, the issue often arises as to whether or not the air bag(s) should have deployed by design, and/or whether or not the proper use of seat belts and/or an air bag deployment would have mitigated and/or prevented the resulting injuries. Before these questions can be answered to a reasonable degree of engineering and scientific certainty, an engineering accident reconstruction must be performed along with the appropriate biomechanical analyses.

Basic Principles

Classical mechanics may be defined as the science that treats the response of material bodies to the forces, motions, and displacements imposed upon them. Basic concepts are *space, time, mass,* and *force*.

Biomechanics, a specialty within the more general field of classical mechanics, is then defined to be the science that treats the response of living systems to the forces, motions, and displacements imposed upon them. Typically, as is the case in most accident reconstruction analyses, biomechanicians (or biomechanists as some refer to them) are concerned with the response of the human body to the forces, motions, and displacements experienced during a crash. However, as the biomechanical response of an occupant is highly dependent upon the crash response of the vehicle (or system) that he/she occupies, a rigorous engineering accident reconstruction must be performed before a biomechanical analysis of the occupant response to a crash can be performed, and the injury-producing potential of the accident evaluated. This article begins with a review of the relevant physical principles.

In 1687, Sir Isaac Newton published his, now famous, three (3) natural laws of classical mechanics. These laws govern the motion of all bodies in the universe omitting relativistic effects, that is, they are the operative laws for all problems when speeds do not approach the speed of light (299 million ms^{-1} or approximately 186,000 miles s^{-1}). These laws, originally stated for a particle of mass, *m*, are summarized below.

First law: Every material body continues in its state of rest, or of constant velocity motion in a straight line, unless acted upon by external forces, which cause it to change its state of rest or motion.

Second law: The time rate of change of linear momentum of a particle (product of mass and velocity) is proportional to the external force acting on it and occurs in the direction of the force. An alternate form of this law, and the one that is most familiar, is that the resultant force ($\bar{F}$) acting on a particle is equal to the product of its mass (m) and acceleration ($\bar{a}$) or $\bar{F} = m\bar{a}$ (where vector quantities are indicated with a bar above the symbol).

Third law: To every action there is an equal and opposite reaction; or, equivalently, the mutual forces of two bodies acting upon each other are equal in magnitude and opposite in direction.

It is important to realize that there is a considerable amount of sophisticated philosophy embodied in Newton's laws, which must be understood by the forensic engineer/accident reconstructionist and is critical to mention here. The following are noted.

First, the laws are not scalar statements (which consider magnitude only) but are vector statements. This means that both the magnitudes and directions of forces, velocities, and accelerations must be considered. For example, speed and velocity are not interchangeable and constant speed is not the same as constant velocity. A vehicle traveling at constant speed in a circular path has a different velocity at each instant of time because the travel direction of the vehicle is constantly changing. In fact, the vehicle is indeed accelerating toward the center of curvature. However, a vehicle traveling in a straight line at a constant speed is also traveling at a constant velocity and is not accelerating.

Second, 'motion' and 'rest' are relative terms when compared to a frame of reference. For accident reconstruction applications, the earth is typically a suitable, 'fixed' frame of reference. However, for other applications such as rocket launchings, space flights, and general astronomical considerations, the earth would not be a suitable fixed reference frame and distant stars would then be used.

Third, Newton's laws mention forces without ever defining them. Force is an abstract concept and nobody has ever seen a force, that is, only the effects of forces are felt. Forces may be defined as the actions of one body on another, and are classified as either contact forces (surface forces) or forces at a distance, such as those due to gravity (weight) or electrical and/or magnetic effects. Again, it is noted that force is a vector quantity, which has both an associated magnitude and direction. It is further worth noting that in automobile accidents, or other vehicular crash scenarios, forces on occupants only arise when the occupant contacts, or is restrained by, another surface such as a seat, seat belt, air bag, door, another person, or other vehicle structure. When this occurs, the occupant is accelerated (decelerated) and Newton's second law must be used to determine the forces acting on the occupant.

Fourth, Newton's laws are stated only for a particle, which is a mathematical idealization of a point with constant mass. It requires further rigorous treatment to extend Newton's laws to the motion of rigid or deformable bodies of finite dimension, the motion of the mass center of a body, or the motion of variable mass systems such as rockets, for example.

Fifth, the concept of units is embedded in Newton's second law. In the International System (SI), mass is given in kilograms (kg), acceleration is given in meters per second squared (m s^{-2}), and force is the derived unit given in Newtons (N). One Newton is the force required to impart an acceleration of 1 m s^{-2} to a mass of 1 kg and has units of kg m s^{-2}. In the US–British system of units, force is given in pounds (lb), acceleration in feet per second squared (ft s^{-2}), and mass is the derived unit given in slugs. One slug is equal to 1 lb s^2 ft^{-1}.

It is also worth noting that the second law introduces the concept of acceleration. Mathematically, the acceleration of a particle, $\bar{a}$, is the time rate of change of its velocity, $\bar{v}$, or in the language of calculus, the first derivative of velocity with respect to time. For the purposes herein, it is noted that acceleration can be considered the change in velocity ($\Delta\bar{V}$) divided by the short time interval (Δt) of a crash over which the change in velocity occurs. Defined in this manner, the ratio $\Delta\bar{V}/\Delta t$ rigorously defines the average acceleration over the time increment considered. As the actual crash is typically a very rapid event occurring over milliseconds, the change in velocity ($\Delta\bar{V}$) of the center of mass of a vehicle, which is often more easily calculated than the acceleration, provides useful information concerning the severity of a crash and is discussed further in the following sections.

This section is ended by noting that Newton's laws can be utilized to further derive three (3) principles, which are often convenient for solving dynamics problems. These principles are *the principle of work and energy*, *the principle of linear impulse and momentum*, and *the principle of angular impulse and angular momentum*. The reader is referred to a text or reference in physics or engineering mechanics (such as appear in the reference list at the end of the article) for the derivations and detailed discussions of these fundamental principles.

Methodology

As mentioned above, accident reconstructions are *a posteriori* investigations and analyses of accidents or events for the purpose of trying to determine how and what occurred during the event consistent with the available data and governing natural laws. In this sense, accident reconstructions are similar to human postmortem examinations or autopsies. Accident reconstruction is defined as the scientific process of analyzing an accident utilizing the available data and the appropriate natural or physical laws. The availability of data and physical evidence in combination with the reconstructionist's knowledge and understanding of scientific/engineering principles are critical factors in determining the quality, accuracy, and reliability of the reconstruction.

The basic philosophy of accident reconstruction is the one in which the analyst/reconstructionist generally works backward in time and space. Detailed documentation of the accident scene, to the extent possible, is critical for a rigorous, quantitative accident reconstruction. The starting point for the analysis is the final rest position(s) of the vehicle(s), accident debris, and sometimes victims/bodies in the cases of pedestrian impacts and occupant ejections from vehicles. From this known information/data, the reconstruction proceeds backward in time and space to the point(s) of impact, and if sufficient physical evidence exists, to points in time and space prior to the impact(s). The natural laws utilized will be Newton's laws of motion. In addition, the reconstructionist must use physical evidence left at the scene as a result of the accident, as well as relevant vehicle data and scene geometry. Typically, this information includes vehicle weights (masses) inclusive of the vehicle occupants, miscellaneous items and cargo, location(s) of the point(s) of impact on the roadway and on the vehicle(s), distances and trajectories moved post-impact, tire marks, gouge and scratch marks on the roadway, vehicle crush damage and damage locations, paint transfer, debris locations, body contact marks, location of blood and other body tissue, etc. The evidence left at the scene, or within (or on) a vehicle, or on a body are sometimes referred to as witness marks. Typically, it is the police or presiding law enforcement agency, who are the first responders to an accident scene and they are in responsible charge of documenting, photographing, and measuring/mapping the accident scene and preserving the available evidence. Obviously, the quantity and quality of the available data will affect the accuracy and reliability of the reconstruction, and proper documentation of the scene is critical to ensuring a high quality, scientifically reliable accident reconstruction. It is better if the scene and vehicles are inspected as soon as possible after an accident. Not only do witness marks and transfer evidence tend to degrade/disappear with time, but also vehicles can be repaired, or disposed of, and the scene may change. Often, the reconstructionist becomes involved in an investigation long after the accident occurred and may not have the opportunity to examine the scene and vehicles. He/she will then have to rely upon the previously documented evidence including, but not necessarily limited to, measurements and photographs. High-quality photographs contain a large amount of useful information, some of which can be quantitatively extracted utilizing photogrammetric techniques, that is, the science of making measurements from photographs. Examples of information obtained from photographs include the character(s) and relevant length (s) and geometric characteristic(s) of tire marks, pothole depths, as well as vehicle crush patterns and dimensions. It is noted that not all tire marks are skid marks, and a proper identification of the type of tire mark is necessary to properly characterize the motion and/or acceleration/deceleration of the vehicle that left the tire mark in question. In addition to dimensional information and data being obtained from photographs, photographs can often be digitally enhanced – not merely enlarged – to reveal significant details such as sharp edges of potholes, tire defects, paint transfer evidence, tire tracks, and so on. Although actual physical inspections are always best, good-quality photographs may also play a key role in formulating reliable and supportable scientific opinions concerning the happening of an accident, or catastrophic event/failure.

The main objective of an engineering accident reconstruction is to obtain quantitative answers and this requires making calculations based upon Newton's laws and the available data. This often involves the calculation of vehicle impact speeds and/or the change in velocity ($\Delta\bar{V}$) of a vehicle for the purpose of assessing the severity and injury-producing potential of an impact and/or accident sequence. The correlation between $\Delta\bar{V}$ and the injury-producing potential of an accident is discussed in greater detail below when considering the biomechanical and occupant kinematic responses to an impact. Calculations can be performed by hand, computer, or both. Numerous accident reconstruction computer programs are commercially available, and it is not the purpose of this article to discuss these programs. For a more detailed discussion, the interested reader is directed to the article appearing herein on Computer Methods in Accident Reconstruction. Suffice it to say that computer programs are based on Newton's laws, as they must be, and many also contain special algorithms and techniques particular to automobile accident reconstruction. As a word of caution, it is noted that some programs are so user-friendly that they can be used by individuals lacking in an adequate educational background and/or sufficient experience to obtain results that may not be valid for a particular accident. It is also noted for completeness that accident reconstruction programs should not be confused with *simulation* programs. As opposed to reconstruction programs, which utilize the governing laws of physics and available scene data to work backward from the final rest positions of the vehicles to the conditions at impact, and then before impact if sufficient data is available, simulation programs, which contain many assumptions and limitations, proceed forward in time and space commencing before, or at, impact, and then continue proceeding to the post-impact and rest positions of the vehicles. Solutions obtained utilizing these (simulation) programs are very sensitive to the initial conditions and assumptions made by the reconstructionist, and are not unique, that is, several answers can be obtained for the same problem.

Accident Reconstruction

Often, Newton's laws are cast in other forms for ease in performing calculations and solving a problem. As discussed above, alternate forms of the Newton's laws are the work–energy principle and impulse–momentum principle. It is emphasized that these principles are not separate laws of physics but are derived from the Newton's second law and are mathematically integrated statements of the second law. Ignoring ground reaction forces at the tires, which are typically small compared to the equal and oppositely directed collision forces acting on the vehicles (Newton's third law) at the moment of impact, the linear impulse–momentum principle is very useful in analyzing collision problems because the total (impulsive) external force acting on the system of colliding vehicles is zero at impact. This is equivalent to stating that the linear momentum of the vehicle system immediately before (or at) impact is conserved, and leads to the well-known principle of conservation of linear momentum. It is emphasized that the principle of conservation of linear momentum is a vector statement and directions, therefore, must be properly accounted for. It is also worth noting that although linear momentum is conserved at impact, the kinetic energy of the system of vehicles, in general, is not (for inelastic collisions). That is, energy is permanently dissipated in crushing/deforming the vehicles. However, as illustrated below, if sufficient scene information is available, it is not necessary to use energy methods to solve a problem.

To illustrate the methodology and calculation procedures discussed above, consider the common case of a right angle (90°) intersection collision between two vehicles (**Figure 1**). As shown, vehicle 1 proceeds into an intersection from left to right (in the positive x-direction), whereas vehicle 2 proceeds into the intersection traveling in the positive y-direction. Subscripts 1 and 2 are used to denote quantities for vehicles 1 and 2, respectively. A collision occurred, and the vehicles came to rest in the positions shown. In this illustration, each vehicle skidded before impact (shown in bold by the lines behind and leading up to the vehicles at impact and denoted by the lengths d_1 and d_2). Skidding means that the wheels locked up due to driver braking and the vehicles then slid, not rolled, to the point of impact (POI). It is parenthetically noted that most modern motor vehicles are equipped with antilock braking

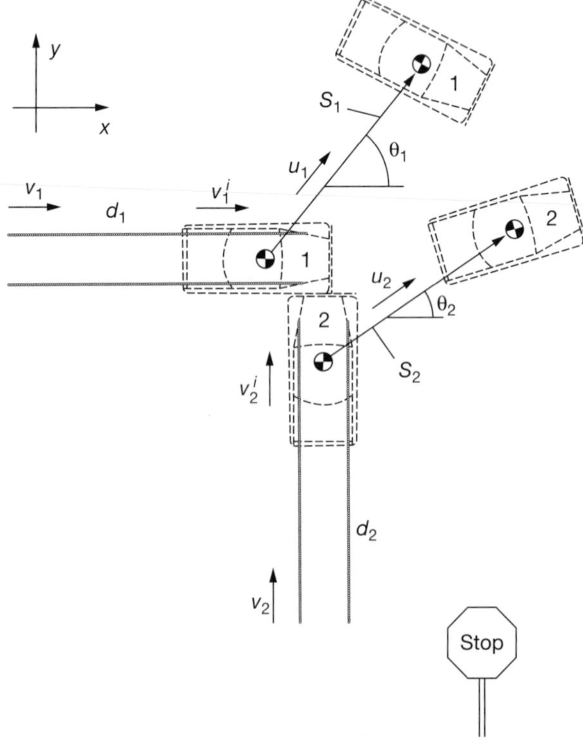

Figure 1 Intersection collision.

systems (ABS), which prevent full wheel lockup during a hard brake application, and often times do not leave discernable physical evidence of braking even during a hard brake application. However, in this illustration, it is assumed that both vehicles did skid/slide before impact. Investigation at the scene determined the POI to be as shown. Location of the POI on the roadway is typically determined by abrupt changes in the direction of the skid marks, collision scrub marks from the tires, and/or gouges in the roadway surface made by vehicle components and/or portions of the vehicle being displaced downward into forceful contact with the roadway surface. The location of solid vehicle debris on the roadway is, in general, not a good indicator of the POI because it travels when it is dislodged from the vehicle and does not fall straight down to the roadway surface and stop. However, fluid spatter, resulting from the sudden release of high-pressure fluid as oftentimes occurs when a radiator bursts at impact, indeed may be a good indicator of the point/area of impact as the explosive release of radiator fluid occurs very quickly. However, the reader is cautioned when identifying a POI through the use of fluid evidence that high-pressure fluid spatter patterns not be confused with fluid debris left at an accident scene by slowly draining/discharging fluids that take time to deposit on the roadway surface, as such evidence will, in general, not be a good indicator of the POI. Impact speeds are designated with the superscript *i*, and postimpact speeds upon vehicle departure from the POI are designated by u_1 and u_2. The distances moved by the centers of gravity (or mass) of the vehicles from impact to their final rest positions are denoted by the distances s_1 and s_2, while the angles measured from the centers of gravity are also shown in the figure. The data shown in **Figure 1** are very complete and representative of an excellent on-scene investigation. In this case, the goal of reconstruction is to determine the speeds of the vehicles at impact ($v_1{}^{\mathrm{i}}$ and $v_2{}^{\mathrm{i}}$) and at commencement of preimpact skidding (v_1 and v_2). Although this example is relatively simple, it does illustrate many of the principles used in accident reconstruction.

All of the basic equations utilized to solve this problem are derived from Newton's second law. As the philosophy is to work backward from the points of rest to the POI, the postimpact speeds u_1 and u_2 of the centers of gravity of the vehicles immediately after impact, that is, at the point of vehicle separation, are determined. The reasonable assumption is made that the vehicles did not simply roll to their rest positions, but that the vehicles were displaced laterally and may have also rotated. This means that the tires were also moving laterally and essentially sliding over the road surface. For simplicity, the vehicles are considered point masses, and their rotations from impact to their final rest positions are not explicitly considered in this example. Noting that the centers of gravity of the vehicles moved for distances s_1 and s_2 from impact to final rest, using Newton's second law, it can be shown that the postimpact speeds are given by

$$u_1 = \sqrt{2\mu g s_1}$$

$$u_2 = \sqrt{2\mu g s_2}$$

where μ is the coefficient of friction (or drag factor) between the tires and roadway surface and g is the acceleration due to gravity. At the earth's surface, g is approximately equal to $9.8\ \mathrm{m\,s^{-2}}$ ($32.2\ \mathrm{ft\,s^{-2}}$). The coefficient of friction μ is a nondimensional parameter, which is a measure of the relative slip resistance of the two surfaces in contact. It can be measured at the scene immediately following the accident before conditions change, which is preferred as long as it is done correctly, or ranges can be obtained from published references for tires on various roadway surface materials under a variety of conditions in the absence of measurements. For the example under consideration, it is assumed that μ was determined to be 0.65, which represents a typical value for a road surface in an average condition.

The principle of conservation of linear momentum (which derives from Newton's second law) states

$$m_1\bar{v}_1{}^{\mathrm{i}} + m_2\bar{v}_2{}^{\mathrm{i}} = m_1\bar{u}_1 + m_2\bar{u}_2$$

where m_1 and m_2 are the respective vehicle masses and bars over the velocities are used to denote vectors.

Considering the components of linear momentum in mutually perpendicular *x*- and *y*-directions, the following are obtained.

$$x:\quad m_1 v_1{}^{\mathrm{i}} = m_1 u_1 \cos\theta_1 + m_2 u_2 \cos\theta_2$$

or

$$v_1{}^{\mathrm{i}} = u_1 \cos\theta_1 + \frac{m_2}{m_1} u_2 \cos\theta_2$$

$$y:\quad m_2 v_2{}^{\mathrm{i}} = m_1 u_1 \sin\theta_1 + m_2 u_2 \sin\theta_2$$

or

$$v_2{}^{\mathrm{i}} = \frac{m_1 u_1}{m_2} \sin\theta_1 + u_2 \sin\theta_2$$

Note that in this example, since the collision occurred at a right angle, application of the principle of conservation of linear momentum in the *x*- and *y*-directions gives rise to two decoupled (independent) equations for the impact speeds, without the necessity of solving two simultaneous equations.

Since the vehicles skidded to impact, again using kinematic relations derived from Newton's second law, it can be shown that the vehicle speeds at the commencement of their respective preimpact skidding are given by

$$v_1 = \sqrt{2\mu g d_1 + (v_1{}^{\mathrm{i}})^2}$$

$$v_2 = \sqrt{2\mu g d_2 + (v_2{}^{\mathrm{i}})^2}$$

To obtain a numerical solution, consider the following set of input data. Vehicle 1: $m_1 = 1750$ kg (weight = 3860 lb), $s_1 = 6.0$ m (19.7 ft), $d_1 = 26.0$ m (85.3 ft), $\theta_1 = 48^{\circ}$; Vehicle 2: $m_2 = 2100$ kg (weight = 4630 lb), $s_2 = 4.6$ m (15.1 ft), $d_2 = 7.6$ m (24.9 ft), $\theta_2 = 36^{\circ}$. Substituting these data into the above equations yields

$$\begin{aligned}
u_1 &= 8.7\ \mathrm{m\,s^{-1}}(31.3\ \mathrm{km\,h^{-1}})(19.5\ \mathrm{mph})\\
u_2 &= 7.6\ \mathrm{m\,s^{-1}}(27.4\ \mathrm{km\,h^{-1}})(17.0\ \mathrm{mph})\\
v_1{}^{\mathrm{i}} &= 13.2\ \mathrm{m\,s^{-1}}(47.5\ \mathrm{km\,h^{-1}})(29.5\ \mathrm{mph})\\
v_2{}^{\mathrm{i}} &= 9.9\ \mathrm{m\,s^{-1}}(35.6\ \mathrm{km\,h^{-1}})(22.1\ \mathrm{mph})\\
v_1 &= 22.5\ \mathrm{m\,s^{-1}}(81.0\ \mathrm{km\,h^{-1}})(50.3\ \mathrm{mph})\\
v_2 &= 14.0\ \mathrm{m\,s^{-1}}(50.4\ \mathrm{km\,h^{-1}})(31.3\ \mathrm{mph})
\end{aligned}$$

where the answers were first calculated in $\mathrm{m\,s^{-1}}$ and then converted to $\mathrm{km\,h^{-1}}$ and mph.

Hypothetically, the results of the above analysis can be used as follows. Suppose driver 2 claimed that he stopped at the stop sign, located 10 m (32.8 ft) from the POI in the negative y-direction, as shown in **Figure 1**, and further claimed that the reason for the accident is driver 1, who had the right of way, was speeding through the intersection. The speed limit was posted at 80 $\mathrm{km\,h^{-1}}$ (50 mph). Examination of the numbers obtained from this analysis indicates that vehicle 1 was sensibly traveling at the speed limit when the brakes were locked up. Furthermore, vehicle 2 could not have obtained a speed of 50.4 $\mathrm{km\,h^{-1}}$ (31.3 mph) at the start of preimpact skidding if that driver had started from rest at the stop sign. In fact, for a two-wheel drive vehicle, driver 2 likely could not have reached an impact speed of 35.6 $\mathrm{km\,h^{-1}}$ (22.1 mph) if he/she accelerated at a constant rate from rest at the stop sign to the POI even if no preimpact skidding (deceleration) occurred. This has been noted for two reasons. First, driver 2 may claim that the skid marks are not from his vehicle. Second, often there are no preimpact skid marks left by the vehicles, as may be the case for vehicles that do not experience brake lockup, that is, those equipped with ABS, or there may be only partial (or no) brake application at all before impact. In this case, the linear momentum analysis would then be able to reliably determine the impact speeds only. However, based on the results of the analysis just presented, an accident reconstructionist would then opine to a reasonable degree of engineering and scientific certainty that vehicle 2 did not stop at the stop sign before proceeding into the intersection. It is noted for completeness, however, that as more vehicles are equipped with electronic data recorders (EDRs), or 'black boxes,' accident reconstruction calculations can be checked and supplemented with data obtained from the EDRs. For further discussion on EDRs, the interested reader is referred to the article on EDRs appearing herein.

Another quantifiable parameter used in accident reconstruction and biomechanical injury analysis is the change in velocity ($\Delta\bar{V}$) of a vehicle due to an impact. Noting that $\Delta\bar{V}$ is a vector quantity that must account for direction in its computation, it is not simply the change in speed of a vehicle. $\Delta\bar{V}$ is defined as the change in velocity of a vehicle from its impact velocity to its immediate post-impact (separation) velocity and is a quantifiable measure of crash severity and injury-producing potential. As acceleration is defined as the time rate of change of velocity, $\Delta\bar{V}$ is strongly related to, and can be correlated with, the average acceleration of the vehicle during the impact, which typically occurs over a time duration typically expressed in milliseconds. The magnitude and direction of the $\Delta\bar{V}$ vector are significant in determining occupant motion.

To illustrate the proper computation of vehicle $\Delta\bar{V}$'s, the numbers obtained in the previously discussed intersection collision example are used to demonstrate the calculation of $\Delta\bar{V}$. Again, noting and emphasizing that $\Delta\bar{V}$ is a vector quantity, it is generally incorrect (except for the special case of a one-dimensional analysis) to simply algebraically subtract the speeds (magnitudes of the velocities) before and after impact to obtain $\Delta\bar{V}$. Hence, it is incorrect to calculate $\Delta\bar{V}$ of vehicle 1 as $31.3-47.5=-16.2\ \mathrm{km\,h^{-1}}$ (-10.1 mph) decrease. The correct calculation requires using the components of the velocity vector in the x- and y-directions as follows.

$$\begin{aligned}\Delta v_x &= u_1\cos\theta_1 - v_1{}^{\mathrm{i}} = 31.3\cos 48^{\circ} - 47.5\\ &= -26.6\ \mathrm{km\,h^{-1}}(-16.5\ \mathrm{mph})\ \text{decrease}\\ &\qquad(\text{points in negative } x\text{-direction})\end{aligned}$$

$$\begin{aligned}\Delta v_y &= u_1\sin\theta_1 - 0 = 31.3\sin 48^{\circ}\\ &= 23.3\ \mathrm{km\,h^{-1}}(14.5\ \mathrm{mph})\ \text{increase}\\ &\qquad(\text{points in positive } y\text{-direction})\end{aligned}$$

Hence, the magnitude of the $\Delta\bar{V}$ vector for vehicle 1 is:

$$\begin{aligned}\Delta V_1 &= \sqrt{(\Delta V_x)^2 + (\Delta V_y)^2}\\ &= \sqrt{(-26.6)^2 + (23.3)^2}\\ &= 35.4\ \mathrm{km\,h^{-1}}(22.0\ \mathrm{mph})\end{aligned}$$

Similarly, for vehicle 2, it would be incorrect to calculate $\Delta\bar{V}$ as $27.4-35.6=-8.2\ \mathrm{km\,h^{-1}}$ (-5.1 mph) decrease. The proper calculation for vehicle 2 follows using the velocity components.

$$\begin{aligned}\Delta V_x &= u_2\cos\theta_2 - 0 = 27.4\cos 36^{\circ}\\ &= 22.2\ \mathrm{km\,h^{-1}}(13.8\ \mathrm{mph})\ \text{increase}\\ &\quad(\text{points in positive } x\text{-direction})\end{aligned}$$

$$\begin{aligned}\Delta V_y &= u_2\sin\theta_2 - v_2{}^{\mathrm{i}} = 27.4\sin 36^{\circ} - 35.6\\ &= -19.5\ \mathrm{km\,h^{-1}}(-12.1\ \mathrm{mph})\ \text{decrease}\\ &\quad(\text{points in negative } y\text{-direction})\end{aligned}$$

with the magnitude of the $\Delta\bar{V}$ vector for vehicle 2 being

$$\begin{aligned}\Delta V_2 &= \sqrt{(22.2)^2 + (-19.5)^2}\\ &= 29.5\ \mathrm{km\,h^{-1}}(18.4\ \mathrm{mph})\end{aligned}$$

Note that in this case, the incorrect calculations seriously underestimate the magnitudes of the $\Delta\bar{V}$ vectors and say nothing about their directions. $\Delta\bar{V}$ (and it's vector components) for each vehicle is shown in **Figure 2**. As shown, the $\Delta\bar{V}$ values are those for the centers of gravity of the vehicles, which are not the same as those for the occupants, particularly when vehicle

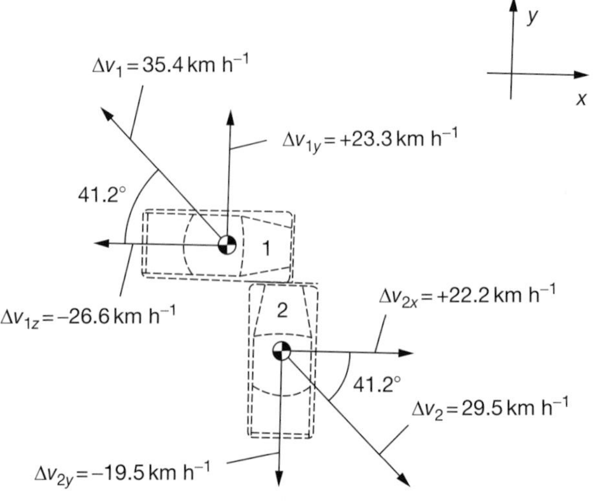

Figure 2 Δv.

rotations are considered and there is relative motion between the occupants and the vehicles. Furthermore, by Newton's third law, the impact forces acting on the vehicles must be equal and opposite and it is these impact forces, which determine the vehicle accelerations by Newton's second law. Hence, the vehicles' $\Delta\bar{V}$s have to be oppositely directed, as shown, although their magnitudes will generally be unequal since the vehicles have different masses. It is also noted for completeness that in the calculations above, the $\Delta\bar{V}$s were computed and expressed in terms of the global, or scene fixed, coordinate system. Additionally, it is noted that since vehicles' $\Delta\bar{V}$s are often calculated to study occupant kinematic motion and to evaluate the injury-producing potential of an accident, it is often convenient to express $\Delta\bar{V}$ vectors in terms of vehicle fixed coordinate systems. Once properly calculated in any well-defined coordinate system, a straightforward application of coordinate transformation rules can be used to express the $\Delta\bar{V}$ vector (and its components) in any other well-defined coordinate system.

Before closing the calculation section, it is important to mention another concept often utilized in accident reconstruction analyses. This is the concept of obtaining vehicle speeds from crush damage. It is noted immediately that only estimates to the $\Delta\bar{V}$ can be obtained from an idealized crush analysis and not individual vehicle speeds, in general. Although, there are special cases where vehicle speeds can be obtained, if the investigator fully understands how the $\Delta\bar{V}$'s were calculated and how they should be combined or utilized, such as a collinear collision with one vehicle known to be stopped at the time it was impacted. Another fairly common special case is that where a vehicle is essentially stopped at the POI by the impact, as may occur when a vehicle collides with a wall at a moderate-to-high speed, where the elastic rebound can be ignored. In such a case, the damage-based vehicle $\Delta\bar{V}$ calculation for the subject vehicle will also yield the approximate magnitude of the impact speed of the vehicle as (neglecting the relatively low rebound velocity) the immediate postimpact speed can be approximated to be zero.

Crush damage calculations are based on an idealized energy dissipation algorithm, which is utilized in many computer programs. This algorithm contains assumptions on vehicle structural behavior, is based on an idealized crush pattern, and also depends on certain measured properties of the vehicles known as stiffness coefficients, which are obtained from crash testing of vehicles. However, the damage algorithm is not a law of physics and its limitations and assumptions must be understood by accident reconstructionists before making damage-based calculations and drawing conclusions from them.

It is well known that significant discrepancies can arise when the results of actual crash tests of vehicles are compared to the idealized energy dissipation crush analyses. If the data permits, a momentum calculation, which does not require any assumptions on vehicle damage or crush, is preferable to a damage-only calculation. Note that in the example previously given, it was not necessary to use any aspect of vehicle crush or energy considerations in order to reconstruct the vehicle speeds. However, this should not be interpreted to mean that crush calculations are unimportant and should never be made. Sometimes, there is insufficient scene data available with which to perform a momentum analysis in order to determine speeds. In this situation, a crush analysis based on actual field measurements or on photogrammetric determinations of crush can provide useful information. In addition, a skilled and knowledgeable reconstructionist can often obtain bounds on $\Delta\bar{V}$s, which may be significant in reconstructing an accident. Care and caution must always be used when interpreting the results of crush calculations.

Occupant Kinematics and Related Concepts

The previous section dealt only with the reconstruction of vehicle speeds (velocities) and no attention was paid to the occupants. Occupant kinematics is the term used to describe the motion of occupants relative to the vehicle in which they are riding, and not the absolute motion of the occupant with respect to a fixed frame of reference. An occupant kinematics analysis may be a significant part of an accident reconstruction if an injury analysis is necessary. The complete determination of an occupant's motion in a crashing vehicle can be the most difficult part of an accident reconstruction and analysis.

The design purpose of vehicle seat belts is to restrain occupant motion in order to minimize or prevent occupant contact with interior vehicle structure. However, depending on both the magnitude and direction of $\Delta\bar{V}$, that is, the crash severity, occupants can still impact vehicle structures, which will affect their occupant kinematics. In addition, it is the contact between the occupant and the vehicle structure, the so-called 'second collision,' that can cause serious injury or death in an accident. The second collision causes an occupant to rapidly decelerate, and by Newton's second law, thus have high direct contact forces imposed upon his/her body. Even properly worn and designed seat belts cannot prevent an occupant from impacting interior structure in all types of crashes. However, there is a dramatic difference in the protection afforded by different types of seat belt systems. For example, combination lap–shoulder belts are superior to lap-only belts. Lap (only) belts do not prevent upper torso jackknifing, which can lead to serious injuries, even death, in relatively minor crashes. 'Lap-belt syndrome' injuries, such as abdominal injuries and tension fractures (Chance fractures) of the lumbar spine, can occur in frontal crashes with lap-belted (only) occupants, typically seated in the rear of the vehicle. In a given accident, these same injuries would likely not have occurred if the vehicle manufacturer had provided lap–shoulder belts in the rear. Fortunately, rear-seat lap-only belts are rapidly vanishing from properly designed and manufactured vehicles, and now all new vehicles to be sold in the United States must be manufactured with lap–shoulder seat belts at all rear seat and front outboard occupant seating positions. It is also worthwhile to review a few occupant kinematics scenarios for restrained and unrestrained occupants. In general, an occupant will tend to initially move toward the impact, that is, toward the direction which is opposite of the vehicle $\Delta\bar{V}$ and the resultant vehicle acceleration. This is why care and caution was used in the illustrative example where $\Delta\bar{V}$ was properly calculated for both vehicles. Because of the directions of the vehicle $\Delta\bar{V}$s (**Figure 2**), occupants in vehicle 1 will tend to move forward and to their right (relative to vehicle 1), whereas occupants in vehicle 2 will tend to move forward and to their left (relative to vehicle 2). In a purely frontal vehicle crash, occupants will tend to move forward relative to the vehicle. If unrestrained, front-seat occupants can impact the steering wheel, dashboard, and windshield, whereas rear-seat occupants can impact the backs of the front seats. After the initial motion into, or toward, interior vehicle structure, the occupants will rebound or be deflected and/or impact each other, and otherwise undergo complex motions. Seat belts can limit the occupant excursions in the vehicle but, depending on $\Delta\bar{V}$ of the vehicle, may not prevent interior vehicle contacts. In a vehicle, which is impacted in the rear, occupants will first tend to move backward into their seats (relative to their vehicle), and potentially ramp up the seat backs, followed by a rebound phase toward interior vehicle front structure. Unrestrained occupants can move forward into interior structure, whereas restrained occupants will not rebound as far. However, before rebounding, an occupant's head and neck may extend or hyperextend over the seat back and/or head restraint leading to vertebral column injuries typically located in the cervical or high thoracic spine, although depending on the severity of the impact and the physical condition of the occupant, lumbar injuries cannot be ruled out. Occupant anthropometry is significant and tall people, greater than the 95th percentile in height, *may* be at high risk in vehicles where the head restraint cannot be adjusted high enough or may not even be adjustable at all. Although it is not discussed in detail here, low $\Delta\bar{V}$ rear-end accidents also have the potential for causing cervical and lumbar spine injuries (such as bulging or herniated intervertebral discs), but these typically have a delayed onset. Another occurrence in rear impacts is the failure of seat backs, even in relatively minor crashes. When this occurs, occupants can tumble into the rear of a vehicle (back seat or cargo area) resulting in serious injuries. It is not commonly appreciated that the seat is an integral part of proper occupant packaging and failure of the seat back, or the entire seat not remaining in place, can lead to serious injury or death for both restrained and unrestrained occupants. Lateral crashes can be particularly devastating because the nearside occupant immediately adjacent to the impact site on the vehicle may be at high risk of serious or fatal injury independent of the design of the vehicle. Initial occupant movement is toward the impact and it is not uncommon for the nearside occupant to physically contact the impacting vehicle or roadside object, such as a pole or a tree. Lap–shoulder belts would generally not be effective in preventing lateral movement in this type of crash. Padding may be effective in minimizing the effect of interior vehicle contacts and lateral (side) air bags, which are now readily available, will also offer some protection. A restrained far-side occupant in a lateral crash will, in general, derive benefit from a lap–shoulder belt, which will limit occupant excursions toward the far-side lateral impact site. However, an unrestrained far-side occupant can move across the vehicle into interior structures as well as into other occupants, which can cause injuries or death.

Detailed descriptions of occupant kinematics generally require the use of very complex computer programs. These programs are fundamentally based on Newton's laws but also require the human body to be modeled as an engineering structure. In addition, a large amount of vehicle information is required such as physical properties of restraint systems and those interior vehicle occupant compartment (and other) structures that can be contacted by occupants. These include, but are not limited to, padding, door structures, steering wheel, air bags, seat belts, dashboard, and so on. It is also generally necessary to specify a large amount of input information (data) in order to achieve an accurate solution. Even slight changes in the input data can result in significant changes in the output and, hence, care must be exercised when interpreting the results of a complicated occupant kinematics computer-generated solution.

Biomechanics of Injuries

Biomechanics is a compound word which means the application of Newtonian mechanics to biological systems, including but not limited to the human body. The field of biomechanics is vast, with applications beyond those considered herein in an automotive context. For example, to name a few areas, biomechanicians are involved in the design of prostheses, artificial organs, anthropomorphic test devices, bioinstrumentation as well as with the analysis of biological systems on the macroscale and the microscale, such as cellular mechanics. Biomechanics of injuries has already been mentioned several times herein. The remaining discussion provides a few additional concepts, but a complete discussion of injury biomechanics is beyond the scope of this article.

Injuries are often correlated with the vehicle $\Delta\bar{V}$ for both restrained and unrestrained occupants. Apart from what has already been mentioned, it should be noted that for unrestrained occupants, $\Delta\bar{V}$ physically corresponds to the velocity of the occupant relative to the vehicle. For example, if a vehicle is traveling at 50 km h^{-1} and crashes into a brick wall, unrestrained occupants will move forward at 50 km h^{-1} relative to the vehicle as the vehicle is rapidly decelerated and brought to a stop by the frontal crash.

Since $\Delta\bar{V}$ is a vector quantity, injury correlations appear in the biomechanics literature as a function of $\Delta\bar{V}$, seating position, and the type of crash (frontal, lateral, rear, etc.). It must be emphasized that the injury correlations are statistical in nature, not absolute, and only attempt to quantify the probability of injury.

Sometimes people walk away from a high-$\Delta\bar{V}$ accident without permanent injuries, whereas others are seriously injured or killed in a low-$\Delta\bar{V}$ accident. Furthermore, the severity of the injury is usually given in terms of the abbreviated injury scale (AIS) published by the Association for the Advancement of Automotive Medicine (AAAM). The AIS is based on anatomical injury at the time of the accident and does not score impairments or disabilities that may result from the injuries. Table 1 gives the injury severity code as used in the AIS.

Table 1 Injury severity scale

AIS	*Injury severity*
0	None
1	Minor
2	Moderate
3	Serious
4	Severe
5	Critical
6	Maximum (currently untreatable, fatal)

The concept of threshold injury criteria is also important to the understanding of injury biomechanics. Threshold injury criteria, along with human tolerance conditions, refer to those combinations of forces, moments, impact durations, stresses, strains, and so on, which will result in traumatic injury. Caution is in order here since it is not reasonable to expect that a given injury criterion, if it exists at all, will apply across the entire spectrum of the human population. This is because biomaterials (human tissues) have a normal variability range in response to loading, and all people are not equal in their biomechanical response to impact. Human impact response can be, and is, a function of many factors including but not limited to age, gender, preexisting conditions which may or may not be symptomatic, anthropometry (body size and measurements), and so on.

Currently there are essentially three threshold injury criteria in common use. These are written into the Federal Motor Vehicle Safety Standards (FMVSS), which vehicle manufacturers must comply with by law. The FMVSS is an attempt to require a minimum level of safety and crashworthiness for all automobiles sold in the United States. The injury criteria refer to the head, femur, and chest and are as follows for a front-seat lap–shoulder seat-belted occupant in a vehicle during a 30 mph frontal barrier crash test.

The first, known as the head injury criterion (HIC), requires that a certain mathematical integral expression explicitly dependent on the resultant acceleration at the center of gravity of a test dummy's head in a frontal crash cannot exceed the numerical value of 1000 or else, the standard has not been met and the vehicle fails to comply. There are many limitations to the HIC, which are worth noting. The HIC does not even define or discriminate between types of head injuries, which can range from subdural hematomas to diffuse axonal injuries to skull fractures. In addition, the use of a test dummy may be open to question when attempting to assess the effects of injury on live human beings; a live person may survive a HIC significantly greater than 1000 but may be killed in a crash when the HIC is significantly less than 1000.

The second criterion refers to the force measurement made in the femur of a test dummy during a frontal crash. The compressive force in the femur cannot exceed 10.0 kN (2250 lb) or else the standard has not been met and the vehicle fails to comply. This injury criterion, similar to all injury criteria, does not account for the wide and normal range of biomaterial variability among individuals. Compressive fracture loads can be considerably less than 10.0 kN for a significant portion of the population.

The third criterion refers to the resultant acceleration measured at the center of gravity of the thorax (chest) of a human surrogate test dummy. This criterion requires that the acceleration cannot exceed 60 times the acceleration due to gravity (60 g) except for time intervals whose cumulative duration is not more than 3 ms in a test crash. Depending upon the test dummy used, another chest injury criterion, which relates to chest deflection, may also be required. As above, shortcomings in these criteria are that they do not distinguish between types of chest trauma (rib or sternum fractures, transected aorta, etc.) and do not account for normal population variability.

For completeness it is noted that other injury criteria have also been proposed and/or are undergoing intense research investigation. Biomechanics injury research is a vast and complex field which requires the collaborative efforts of engineers, physicians, and other researchers in order to understand the response of the human body to impact. The brief discussion presented herein has only been intended as an introductory exposure to the field. Major advances in understanding the biomechanics of injury can be expected as forensic applications to automobile accident reconstruction become more commonplace.

See also: **Engineering**: Accident Investigation – Determination of Cause; Airbag Related Injuries and Deaths; Electronic Data Recorders (EDRs, Black Boxes).

Further Reading

Accident Reconstruction Technology Collection (2012) CD-ROM, Society of Automotive Engineers.
Association for the Advancement of Automotive Medicine (1990) *The Abbreviated Injury Scale*. Des Plaines, IL: Association for the Advancement of Automotive Medicine.
Batterman SC (1990) Education of forensic engineers. *American Academy of Forensic Sciences (Newsletter)* 20(6).
Batterman SC and Batterman SD (1999) Forensic engineering. In: Caplan YH and Frank RS (eds.) *Medicolegal Death Investigation, Treatises in the Forensic Sciences*, 2nd edn. Colorado Springs: The Forensic Sciences Foundation Press.
Batterman SC and Batterman SD (2002) Forensic engineering. *McGraw-Hill Yearbook of Science and Technology*. New York: McGraw-Hill.
Batterman SC and Batterman SD (2004) Forensic engineering. *Legal Medicine, American College of Legal Medicine*, 6th edn. Philadelphia, PA: Mosby, Inc.
Batterman SD and Batterman SC (2002) Delta-V, spinal trauma, and the myth of the minimal damage accident. *Journal of Whiplash and Related Disorders* 1(1): 41–52 The Howarth Medical Press.
Batterman SD and Batterman SC (2011) Introduction to forensic engineering and accident reconstruction. In: Mozayani A and Noziglia A (eds.) *The Forensic Laboratory Handbook Procedures and Practice*, 2nd edn. New York, NY: Humana Press.
Beer FP and Johnston ER (1977) *Vector Mechanics for Engineers: Statics and Dynamics*. New York, NY: McGraw-Hill.
Bohan TL and Damask AC (eds.) (1995) *Forensic Accident Investigation: Motor Vehicles*. Charlottesville: Michie Butterworth.
Brach RM (1991) *Mechanical Impact Dynamics; Rigid Body Collisions*. New York: Wiley.
Campbell KL (1974) Energy basis of collision severity. *Proceedings of the 3rd International Conference on Occupant Protection*, paper 740565. Troy, MI: Society of Automotive Engineers.
Carper KL (1989) *Forensic Engineering*. Amsterdam: Elsevier.
Damask AC and Damask JN (1990) *Injury Causation Analyses: Case Studies and Data Sources*. Warrendale, PA: Michie.
Evans FG (1973) *Mechanical Properties of Bone*. Springfield, IL: Charles C Thomas.
Greenwood DT (1977) *Classical Dynamics*. Englewood Cliffs, NJ: Prentice-Hall, Inc.
Hyzer WG (1989) Forensic photogrammetry. In: Carper KL (ed.) *Forensic Engineering*. Amsterdam: Elsevier.
Limpert R (1984) *Motor Vehicle Accident Reconstruction and Cause Analysis*, 2nd edn. Tokyo: Michie.
McElhaney JH, Roberts VL, and Hilyard JF (1976) *Handbook of Human Tolerance*. Tokyo: Japan Auto Research Institute.
Mills PJ and Hobbs CA (1984) The probability of injury to car occupants in frontal and side impacts. *Proceedings of 28th Stapp Car Crash Conference*, pp. 223–235. Warrendale, PA: Society of Automotive Engineers.
Nahum AN and Melvin J (1985) *The Biomechanics of Trauma*. New York: Appleton-Century-Crofts.
Newman JA (1980) Head injury criteria in automotive crash testing. *Proceedings of the 24th Stapp Car Crash Conference*, pp. 703–747. Warrendale, PA: Society of Automotive Engineers.
Pike JA (1990) *Automotive Safety; Anatomy, Injury, Testing and Regulation*. Warrendale, PA: Society of Automotive Engineers.

Smith RA and Noga JT (1982) *Accuracy and Sensitivity of CRASH, paper 821169*. Warrendale, PA: Society of Automotive Engineers.

Society of Automotive Engineers (1993) *Biomechanics of Impact Injury and Injury Tolerances of the Head–Neck Complex, SAE PT-43*. Warrendale, PA: Society of Automotive Engineers.

Society of Automotive Engineers (1994) *Biomechanics of Impact Injury and Injury Tolerances of the Thorax-Shoulder Complex, SAE PT-45*. Warrendale, PA: Society of Automotive Engineers.

Society of Auto Engineers (1986) *Human Tolerance to Impact Conditions as Related to Motor Vehicle Design, SAE J885*. Warrendale, PA: Society of Automotive Engineers.

Stapp Car Crash Conference Proceedings (1998) CD-ROM. Society of Automotive Engineers.

Thorpe JF and Middendorf WH (1979) *What Every Engineer Should Know About Product Liability*. New York: Marcel Dekker.

US Dept of Transportation (1986) CRASH 3 Technical manual. Cambridge, MA: NHTSA.

Weinstein AS, Twerski AD, Pichler HR, and Donaher WA (1978) *Products Liability and the Reasonably Safe Product: A Guide for Management, Design and Marketing*. New York: Wiley.

Yamada H (1973) *Strength of Biological Materials*. Huntington, NY: Krieger.

Yeh H and Abrams JI (1960) *Principles of Mechanics of Solids and Fluids; Particle and Rigid Body Mechanics*. New York: McGraw-Hill.

Accident Investigation – Determination of Cause

H Steffan, Graz University of Technology, Graz, Austria

Introduction

Car traffic has increased dramatically. Although additional traffic regulations such as speed limits or other restrictions were imposed to reduce accidents, crashes can be seen every day. Many result in vehicle damages or injuries of occupants or other people involved. Claims, resulting from these accidents, often have to be settled in court.

In most countries, special 'accident reconstruction experts' assist the judges by reconstructing the accident situations based on information such as eyewitnesses, car deformations, or tire marks. In many countries, these experts are either specially trained police officers or members of the road authorities. In other places, the reconstructions are performed by independent specialists. The necessity to understand the accident for court decisions initiated specific accident research.

Meanwhile, accidents are also reconstructed for many other reasons. Car manufacturers perform in-depth studies of real accidents to both learn more about accident mechanisms and study the potential and the effectiveness of new safety devices in cars. Also for improved road planning, accidents are often reconstructed and analyzed.

There are several questions which must be answered, when reconstructing a car accident. Today's accident reconstruction tries to provide full information about the movement of all involved vehicles or other involved persons or objects from the point of first visual contact to their rest positions. Time history of velocities, positions, as well as crash-related data such as velocity changes, deformation energies, or passenger loads must be analyzed. In addition, prevention analyses are often included. These analyses allow one to determine the conditions necessary to prevent the accident.

There is one general rule in any accident reconstruction: A detailed collection of scene data forms the basis for a good accident reconstruction. Some of the most important scene data can be summarized as follows:

- Vehicle or human rest positions
- Road marks
- Vehicle damages and marks
- Personal injuries

Due to the increased number of cars with antilocking brakes, fewer tire marks, which formed the most objective basis, can be seen and thus one major basis for the reconstruction is lost. On the other hand, the increased performance of personal computers made it possible to use highly sophisticated reconstruction or simulation algorithms to study the accidents.

In recent years, several software products have been developed for the reconstruction of vehicle accidents. Some of them are designed to just calculate vehicle velocities from kinematic relations for specific accident types. Others, containing full vehicle simulators, allow one to simulate the car motion during the accident starting from the point of reaction to the end position for any kind of accident. Due to the availability of powerful PCs, it is now even possible to visualize the three-dimensional (3D) car motion on the screen during the calculation in real time. 3D geometrical information regarding road marks can be imported from drawing programs through defined interfaces such as DXF, or from photographs as scanned Bitmaps, and all-important road, car, and tire characteristics can be taken into account as well as the reactions of the driver.

Targets

It is important, when formulating the physical and mathematical model of the car, to take into account the fact that many parameters are not well known when reconstructing the accident. Especially, certain conditions of the tires such as their age or air pressure, the condition of the shock absorbers or the steering system are often not well documented. The stiffness of the car body is only known for well-defined crash conditions and not for the specific accident situation. Therefore, it is important to find a compromise between accuracy and the amount of input data necessary to perform the calculation. On the other hand, the user should be able to take into account all parameters which are documented and known to influence the driving and crash behavior. Based on this knowledge, simplified models have to be used, which guarantee that the basic driving behavior is predicted correctly. All necessary input parameters must be defined on the bases of physical parameters, and a simple possibility to vary the parameters guarantees that the expert can crosscheck their influence on the simulation result.

The automotive industry uses several simulation models to learn about the driving behavior of their vehicles. These industrial vehicle dynamics simulation programs are optimized to predict the driving behavior under well-defined initial and boundary conditions. As a result, these models require many input parameters. For the reconstruction of a vehicle accident, such detailed knowledge, especially regarding the suspension, the tires, and the road conditions, is normally not available. In addition, the steering as well as the degree of braking is often not known. It is thus difficult to use these simulation models for the reconstruction of vehicle accidents.

Regarding collision models, a similar problem exists. Several programs (mainly Finite Element based) exist, which allow the calculation of the deformations for well-defined collision conditions. To get a good agreement with real impacts, they require a very detailed knowledge of the vehicle structure and a very powerful computer. Some 10 000 000 degrees of freedom are required to model one vehicle properly. In addition, every simulation has to be calibrated with similar crash tests. This is the major reason why Finite Element programs are only used in a few specific cases for accident reconstruction.

 http://dx.doi.org/10.1016/B978-0-12-382165-2.00141-0

Several computer programs have been developed especially for the reconstruction of vehicle accidents. They allow the calculation of the vehicle motion and collisions based on various physical models. PC-CRASH is one of these programs with a worldwide distribution. It uses a kinetic time forward simulation of 3D vehicle dynamics and combines it with several collision models. So, the accidents can be reconstructed starting from the conflict point to the end position for all involved cars simultaneously. The reconstruction is performed in an interactive graphical environment, which allows a sketch or photograph of the accident scene to underlay the reconstruction. For an effective presentation of the results, 3D animations can be created directly from the calculated results.

Accident Analysis

Postcrash Movement

In the case of a conventional accident analysis, the reconstruction is normally started from the rest positions of the involved vehicles backwards to the collision position. To determine the postcrash velocity of the vehicles, an average deceleration has to be estimated. In many cases, where no tire marks are available, a straight movement of the vehicle is assumed to determine the distance of postcrash travel. Depending on road situation and involved vehicle, an average deceleration level is assumed which typically lies in the range of 0.1–10 m s^{-2}. The postcrash velocity can then be calculated according to the formula

$$v = \sqrt{2as + v_0^2} \qquad [1]$$

where v represents the postcash velocity (m s^{-1}), a the average deceleration (m s^{-2}), and s the postcrash travel of the vehicles center of gravity (m).

This is the way to determine the postcrash velocity in a conventional method. The major problem within this method is to estimate the vehicles' average deceleration during a complicated postcrash movement. In this phase, the vehicle may have been rolling or sliding and this makes a huge influence on the amount of energy dissipated. To overcome this problem, vehicle simulators are often used, to compare the vehicles' movement with marks found on the road or on the vehicles. Thus, the postcrash velocity can be determined more accurately.

Collision Model

During the collision, the contact forces between the two involved vehicles vary over time. These forces depend on the local vehicle structures, the deformation velocity, the contact situation, and several other parameters. As these dependencies are highly nonlinear and very difficult to formulate, the treatment of these parameters through their integral values has proven to be more efficient (Impuls-based).

Modern Finite Element programs allow one to investigate the time variation of the contact forces. However, these programs require enormous calculation times and a huge amount of modeling. Simplified models such as the 'CRASH algorithm' have proven to produce large errors under several conditions. In many cases, insufficient knowledge regarding the structural deformation behavior is available to estimate the proper parameters.

Therefore, 'crash hypotheses,' which only compare the velocity conditions of both vehicles before and after the impact, have been used with great success for the reconstruction of accidents. As modern programs provide both, impuls-based and force-based models, they will both be discussed.

Material Properties in the Contact Area

During the contact phase, large forces may occur, which cause deformations to one or both collision partners. These deformations may remain fully or partially after the impact (plastic deformations) or they may fully recover (elastic deformations). Through the definition of the parameter k, the amount of elasticity for a crash can be defined. This parameter k is only valid for a whole crash situation and not for one of the partners. Therefore, one crash partner may include a high degree of elasticity when impacting with partner A and may include a high degree of plasticity when impacting with partner B (Figure 1).

Through a sample of a straight central impact, the parameter k can be explained easily:

To ensure that the two partners may collide, the velocity of partner 1 must be higher than that of partner 2. In phase 1 contact forces act, which reduce the velocity of mass 1 and increase the speed of mass 2. They are equivalent in size, but with opposite direction. The relation between acceleration and contact force is calculated from

$$ma = F \qquad [2]$$

where m defines the mass, a the acceleration, and F the contact force.

The end of phase 1 is defined when both partners do have equal velocities. It is called 'compression' phase. In phase 2, the forces reduce again until the two masses separate. This phase 2 is also called 'restitution.'

In this case, the coefficient of restitution is defined as

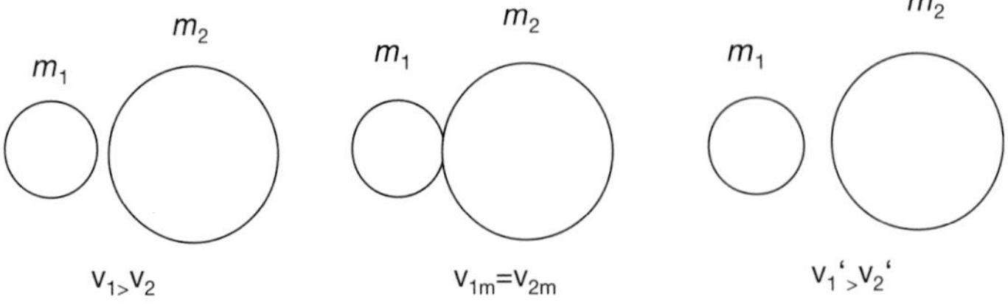

Figure 1

$$k = -\frac{\Delta v'}{\Delta v} = -\frac{v_2' - v_1'}{v_2 - v_1} \quad 0 < k < 1$$

where $k=0$ represents a fully plastic impact and $k=1$ a fully elastic impact.

The term in the numerator $\Delta v'$ is referred to as the relative separating velocity of the two vehicles after impact, and the term in the denominator Δv their relative closing velocity before impact.

Eccentric Impacts

Figure 2 shows a sample of a measurement of the two acceleration components for an eccentric impact. The compression impulse S_C and restitution impulse S_R are now defined as

$$S_C = \int_{t_0}^{t_m} F\mathrm{d}t \quad [3]$$

$$S_R = \int_{t_m}^{t_1} F\mathrm{d}t \quad [4]$$

where t_0 is the time of first contact, t_m defines the time of identical velocity for both vehicles at the point of impact, and t_1 describes the time of separation.

In the case of a generic eccentric impact, the 'coefficient of restitution' is now defined as a ratio between restitution impulse and compression impulse:

$$\varepsilon = \frac{S_R}{S_C} \quad [5]$$

The total exchanged impulse is calculated from

$$S = S_C + S_R = S_C{}^*(1 + \varepsilon) \quad [6]$$

In a full impact, the velocities of both vehicles at the impulse point must be identical at the end of the compression phase.

For simplicity, the impact model is only derived here in 2D. In some programs such as PC-CRASH, the models are also extended to 3D. They are identical except that all velocities, the momentum, and angular momentum are defined in 3D coordinates and all three components of the velocity and rotational velocity are taken into account.

As can be seen in Figure 3, a local coordinate system is defined which originates at the 'impulse point' P. The components of the relative velocity for both vehicles at the impulse point can be calculated from

$$V_{1t} = v_{s1t} + \omega_{1z} n_1 \quad [7]$$

$$V_{1n} = v_{s1n} + \omega_{1z} t_1 \quad [8]$$

where V_{1t} defines the velocity component of the impulse point for vehicle 1 in direction t and V_{1n} in direction n.

So, the components of the relative velocity for both vehicles at the impulse point can be calculated from

$$V_t = V_{1t} - V_{2t} \quad [9]$$

$$V_n = V_{1n} - V_{2n} \quad [10]$$

In addition, the balance of momentum can be formulated for both vehicles:

$$m_1\left(v'_{s1t} - v_{s1t}\right) = T \quad [11]$$

$$m_1\left(v'_{s1n} - v_{s1n}\right) = N \quad [12]$$

$$m_2\left(v'_{s2t} - v_{s2t}\right) = -T \quad [13]$$

$$m_2\left(v'_{s2n} - v_{s2n}\right) = -N \quad [14]$$

The balance of angular momentum can be formulated as follows:

$$I_{1z}\left(\omega'_{1z} - \omega_{1z}\right) = Tn_1 - Nt_1 \quad [15]$$

$$I_{2z}\left(\omega'_{2z} - \omega_{2z}\right) = -Tn_2 + Nt_2 \quad [16]$$

When combining these equations, the change of the relative velocity for both vehicles at the impulse point can be calculated from

$$V'_t = V_t + c_1 T - c_3 N \quad [17]$$

$$V'_n = V_n - c_3 T + c_2 N \quad [18]$$

with

$$c_1 = \frac{1}{m_1} + \frac{1}{m_2} + \frac{n_1^2}{I_{1z}} + \frac{n_2^2}{I_{2z}} \quad [19]$$

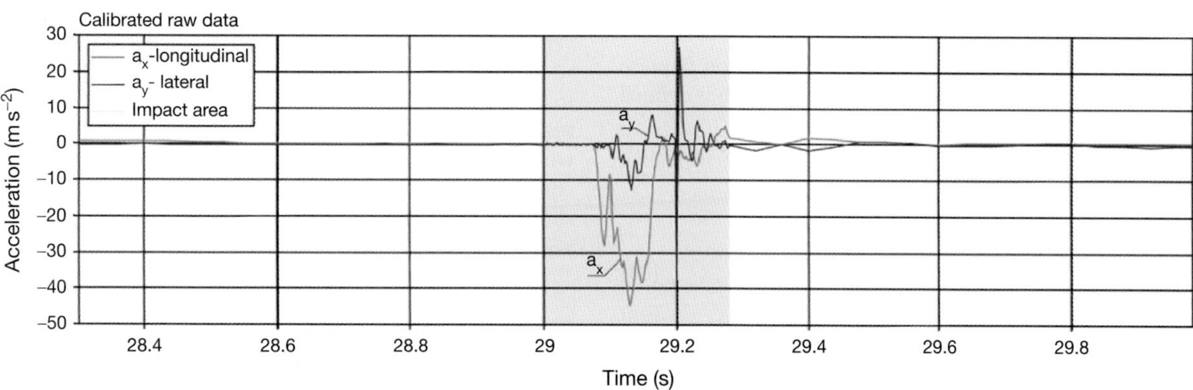

Figure 2 Measured accelerations.

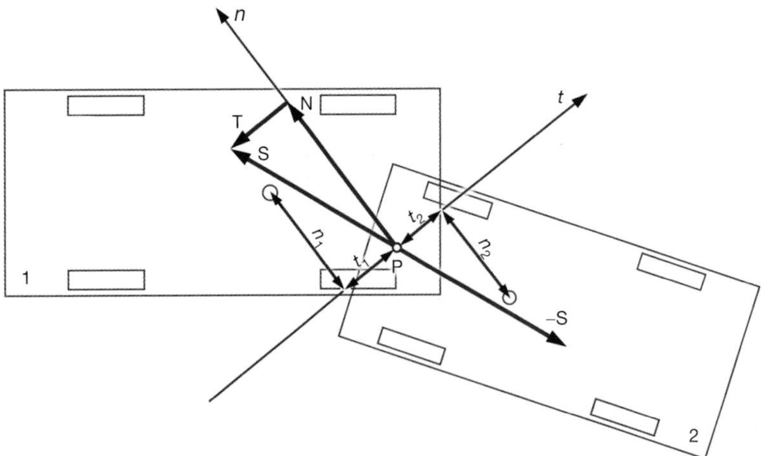

Figure 3 Impact configuration.

$$c_2 = \frac{1}{m_1} + \frac{1}{m_2} + \frac{t_1^2}{I_{1z}} + \frac{t_2^2}{I_{2z}} \quad [20]$$

$$c_3 = \frac{t_1 n_1}{I_{1z}} + \frac{t_2 n_2}{I_{2z}} \quad [21]$$

To be able to solve these equations and to calculate the post-impact velocities and rotations, two additional assumptions have to be made.

According to Kudlich and Slibar, two different kinds of impacts are treated.

The Full Impact

In the case of a full impact, two additional assumptions are made:

1. No relative movement between both vehicles can be found in the impulse point at the end of the compression phase:

$$T_c = \frac{V_n c_3 + V_t c_2}{c_3^2 - c_1 c_2} \quad [22]$$

$$N_c = \frac{V_n c_1 + V_t c_3}{c_3^2 - c_1 c_2} \quad [23]$$

2. The average between compression and restitution impulse is defined by the coefficient of restitution, which is defined according to eqn [6].
3. So, the components of the total impulse can be calculated from

$$T = T_c(1 + \varepsilon) \quad [24]$$

$$N = N_c(1 + \varepsilon) \quad [25]$$

These equations are sufficient to calculate all postimpact velocity conditions for both involved vehicles in the case of a full impact.

The Sliding Impact

In certain collisions, the two vehicles will never reach identical velocities in the impulse point during the impact. In such a case, a contact plane has to be defined, along which the two vehicles slide. The impulse point must coincide with this plane. For such a situation, the following two assumptions are made:

1. No relative movement between both vehicles can be found in the impulse point at the end of the compression phase in direction normal to the contact plane. So, N_c can be calculated from eqn [24].
2. The direction of the impulse is limited by a friction (μ). This value defines the friction between the two impacting vehicles:

$$T = \mu N \quad [26]$$

3. The average between compression and restitution impulse is again defined by the 'coefficient of restitution' according to eqn [6] and T and N can again be calculated from eqns [25] and [26].

The coefficient of restitution, which can be handled as input or output parameter, is easy to define. It generally lies in the range between 0 and 0.3. The higher the deformations of the vehicles, the lower the coefficient of restitution. Only for very small deformations values higher than 0.3 are possible.

In principle, coefficient of restitution k can range from -1 to 1, with negative values being characteristic of the so-called penetrating impact, in which the point of common velocity will not be reached. From a numerical viewpoint, this can be considered by adding a negative $\Delta v'$. It is typical of a bullet shooting through a plank but extremely rare in the case of vehicle accidents.

Energy Equivalent Speed

As modern cars are mostly designed to absorb energy during the collision, the amount of damage found on the vehicles can also be used to determine the precrash velocity. For most vehicles, crash tests are performed, which are also published. They show the vehicle's deformation after an impact with a well-defined barrier. Figure 4 shows the deformations of a certain car type in the frontal area once when impacting a rigid barrier with a speed of 15 km h^{-1} and once with a speed of 48 km h^{-1}. Significant differences can so be found in the amount of damage imposed on the vehicle.

This knowledge can also be used for the accident reconstruction.

When comparing the deformations found on the vehicle to those of the reference tests, the amount of energy absorbed by the vehicle due to the impact can be estimated. As deformation energies are not a very handsome quantity, they are recalculated into velocities and called 'energy equivalent speed' (EES). EES is so defined according to eqn [28]:

$$\mathrm{EES} = \sqrt{\frac{2E_{\mathrm{Def}}}{m}} \qquad [27]$$

where E_{Def} defines the energy of vehicle residual deformation and m the vehicles mass.

Thus, the conservation of energy can be used in addition:

$$E'_{\mathrm{kin1}} + E'_{\mathrm{kin2}} = E_{\mathrm{kin1}} + E_{\mathrm{kin2}} - E_{\mathrm{Def1}} - E_{\mathrm{Def2}} \qquad [28]$$

where $E_{\mathrm{kin}i}$ represents the kinetic energy of vehicle i before and $E'_{\mathrm{kin}i}$ after the impact.

In the United States, the concept of EBS (equivalent barrier speed) is often used. Considering a vehicle deformed in an accident, EBS is the velocity at which an identical vehicle would have to collide with a stiff and nondeformable barrier, to obtain identical permanent deformation. On the other hand, EES covers only the part of velocity that is necessary to get plastic deformation, neglecting the energy of elasticity E_{E}, absorbed without leaving any residual:

$$\frac{m \times \mathrm{EBS}^2}{2} = \frac{m \times \mathrm{EES}^2}{2} + E_{\mathrm{E}} \qquad [29]$$

The dependence combining the two parameters can be easily derived using the coefficient of restitution k:

$$\mathrm{EES} = \mathrm{EBS}\sqrt{1 - k^2} \qquad [30]$$

Both EES and EBS values of a deformed vehicle can be obtained using crash test data collected in EES catalogs or databases meeting the CRASH3 standards.

Stiffness-based and mesh-based impact models

The impact can be also simulated by means of two other models: stiffness based or mesh based. In the former, one vehicle uniform solid is converted into several hyper ellipsoids (shown in Figure 5(a)), whereas in the latter one the mesh structure of vehicle external shell is applied (Figure 5(b)). The shell is described by means of a 3D mesh of a structure analogous to the finite elements method. The idea was used to detect constraints' interpenetration during impact, determination of forces' operation, and constraints' displacements into new positions, according to the superimposed constraints. Some simplifications in relation to the FEM make it possible to increase the efficiency of calculations, with satisfactory accuracy preserved.

What is characteristic to both models is that during simulation of vehicle deformation phase impact force is calculated as a function of time.

The difference between the Kudlich–Slibar model and the stiffness-based (also mesh-based) model is illustrated in Figure 6 which shows an impact of a car against a solid wall at 55 km h^{-1}. The following denotation has been adopted: a_{KS}, v_{KS} (acceleration and velocity, respectively, in the Kudlich–Slibar model) and a_{F}, v_{F} (acceleration and velocity, respectively, in stiffness-based model). During impact simulation

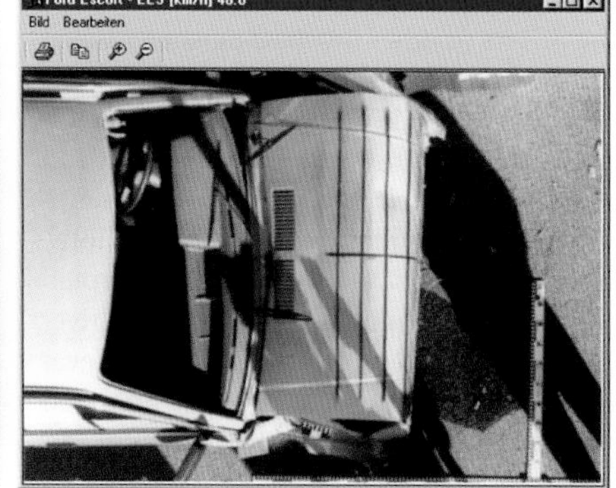

Figure 4 Vehicle damage after frontal impact with 15 and 48 km h^{-1}.

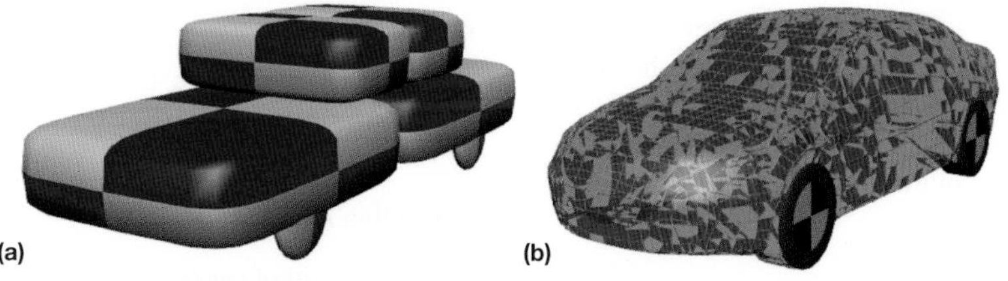

Figure 5 Vehicle structures used in: (a) stiffness-based impact model and (b) mesh-based impact model.

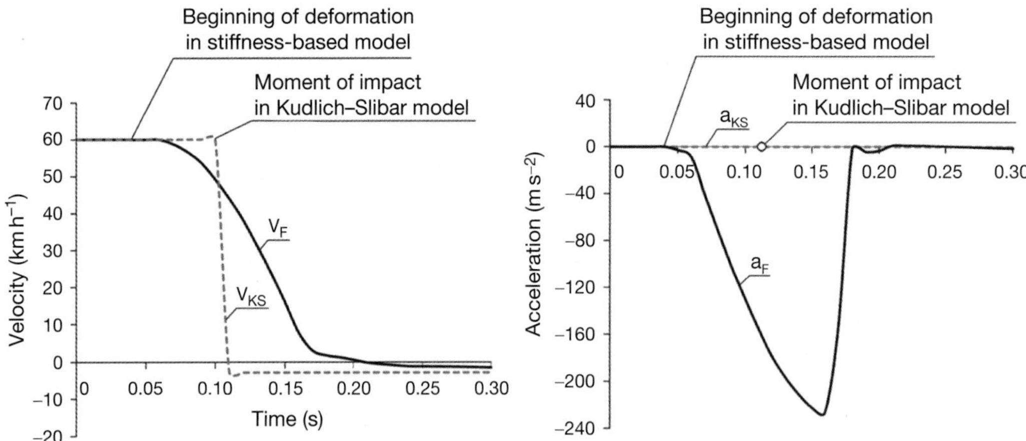

Figure 6 Accelerations and velocities during a car impact against a stiff wall: a_{KS}, v_{KS}–acceleration and velocity, respectively, in the Kudlich–Slibar model – and a_F, v_F–acceleration and velocity, respectively, in the stiffness-based model.

with the Kudlich–Slibar model, velocity change $v-v'$ occurs as a single step within an infinite short time step $\Delta t=0$. Deceleration diagram a_{KS} in Figure 6 refers to vehicle motion state immediately before and immediately after the impact, neglecting the infinitely small instant of the impact itself. Since in the sample case the car was neither braked nor accelerated, $a_{KS}=0$.

In the Kudlich–Slibar model, the time history for deceleration is not necessary to calculate the postimpact velocity. As a result, neither curve for impact force is determined. In the stiffness-based model, on the other hand, velocity v_F and acceleration a_F during deformation are calculated as functions of time, which means determination of time history of impact force.

Precrash Movement

As the impact speed in many cases is not the relevant speed, precrash analysis is also of great importance. They allow one to determine where the drivers or other involved persons reacted and when conflicts were created. In the reaction point, the velocities, relative positions, and visibilities can then be investigated. Through this calculation, the cause of the accident and the failures of the involved persons or vehicles can be identified. There are several types of failures or their combinations, which cause accidents: The vehicle velocity not being adapted to traffic situation and insufficient attention of the driver are only some of the situations causing accidents. Whenever accidents are investigated, the situation has to be analyzed from the reaction point. Only, in this way, the real cause can be found.

The Driver's Reaction

The point of reaction can be determined through various methods, depending on the accident situation.

In principle, the time from the reaction to the collision position normally consists of three major phases:

1. reaction time
2. lag
3. action time

Reaction Time

The reaction time defines the necessary time to identify the situation, decide the kind of reaction, and start the action through activation of certain muscles. The reaction time depends on many parameters, such as age, tiredness, and also on parameters which are difficult to estimate, for example, an eye blink may enlarge the reaction time by approximately 0.2 s. One aspect, which is also of greatest importance, is the visibility of the object. In the case of low contrasts or small light differences, reaction time may increase dramatically. This is the reason why so many pedestrian accidents occur during nighttime. In addition, there is a significant difference if the resulting action has to be done by the arms or by the legs. Due to the longer distance between brain and leg, an action being performed with the leg will require a significantly longer reaction time.

Typical reaction times are between 0.5 and 1.5 s. Racing drivers are known to react during the race within a time of 0.3 s.

Lag

The lag is defined through the amount of time required by the technical system to an act. For the steering system, a lag does not exist. However, for the brake system, a lag between 0.1 and 0.3 can be found. This lag is mainly caused by the amount of time necessary, to push the brake pedal to such a level, that the full brake force is applied to the wheels. One technical solution to reduce this time is the so-called brake assistant, which automatically applies the full brake force, when the brake pedal is pushed very fast.

Action Time

The action time defines the time, when the action (mainly braking or steering) is active.

Prevention Analysis

When the point of reaction was found, the so-called prevention analysis must be performed. These calculations are used to determine a fictive scenario where the accident would not have occurred. In this case, parameters such as initial velocity, shorter reaction time, better visibility, or higher friction on the road are varied. These analyses are used not only to determine the influence of the driver's failure, but often also to change the road design to prevent similar accidents.

Sample Case

The following sample case demonstrates the analysis of a vehicle–vehicle accident, mainly caused by one driver overrunning a 'Stop' sign.

The first step when simulating a new accident is the identification of all involved vehicles. Modern simulation programs allow one to access various databases containing all necessary geometrical and mass data.

In a second step, the involved cars can be moved to the 'average' collision position. Here, their correct overlapping must be taken into account.

To define the friction conditions and driver's actions, the so-called sequences can be given. They can be defined in a very simple and flexible way. The different steering, brake, and acceleration actions can be defined by listing the actions. The values for the individual actions can then be given. The validity of one sequence can be limited by definition of a time interval or a travel distance of the vehicle's center of gravity. The brake or acceleration forces can be given for every wheel independently. This is important to simulate wheels locked up through the accident.

Changes within the friction due to oil or wet areas can be defined by identifying the individual areas. The corresponding friction coefficient must then be specified (Figure 7).

After these definitions have been given, the impact can be calculated and the postcrash movement will be simulated automatically. As a result, the movement of the involved vehicles including their wheel traces can be seen on the screen. It can then be compared to a previously created DXF-drawing of the scenario. As an alternative, a scanned Bitmap can be underlayed. So, the preimpact velocities can be varied as well as all other impact parameters. PC-CRASH as one of the mayor software tools also provides an optimization tool, which allows one to vary the parameters automatically. Through the definition of target functions, the most plausible solution will be found immediately.

The following figures show the movement of two vehicles after a 90° impact in steps of 200 ms.

A dry asphalt surfaced road was assumed.

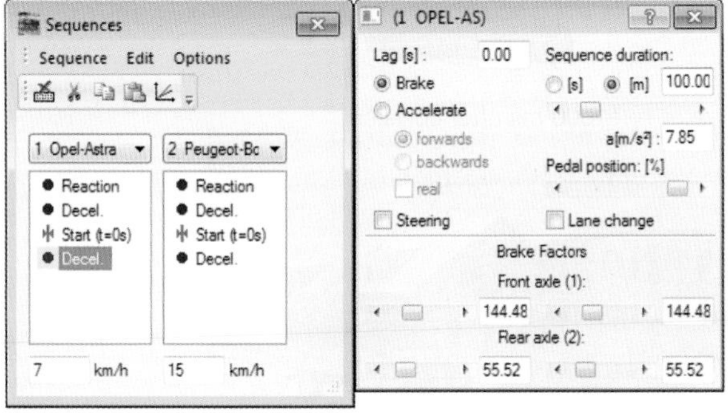

Figure 7 Definition of driver actions.

Results

The major fault, in this case, was on the side of the driver of the personal car, as he should have stopped before the crossing (Figures 8 and 9).

However, due to the fact that there were brake traces drawn from the blue truck before the impact, which had a length of 7 m, the initial speed of the truck could be determined to be 60 km h^{-1}. The truck driver reacted 1.7 s before the collision. In the case of driving at a speed of 48 km h^{-1} or lower, the accident would have been prevented, as the truck would have stopped before the impact. For these calculations, a reaction time of 1 s and a brake lag of 0.2 s was assumed.

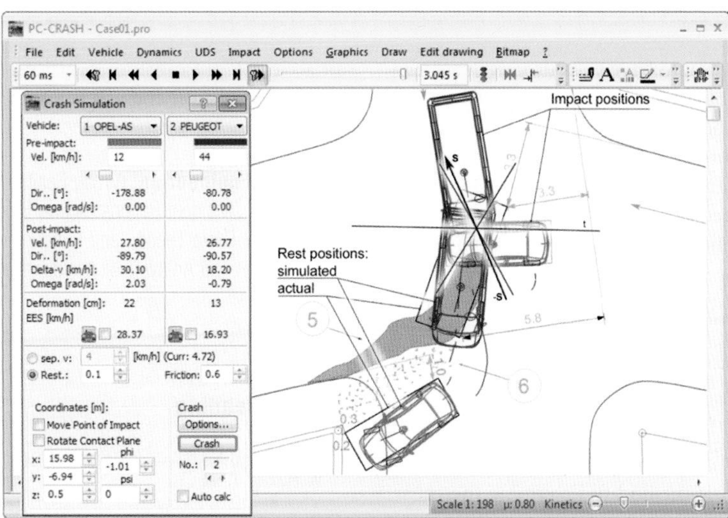

Figure 8 Definition of impact values including results.

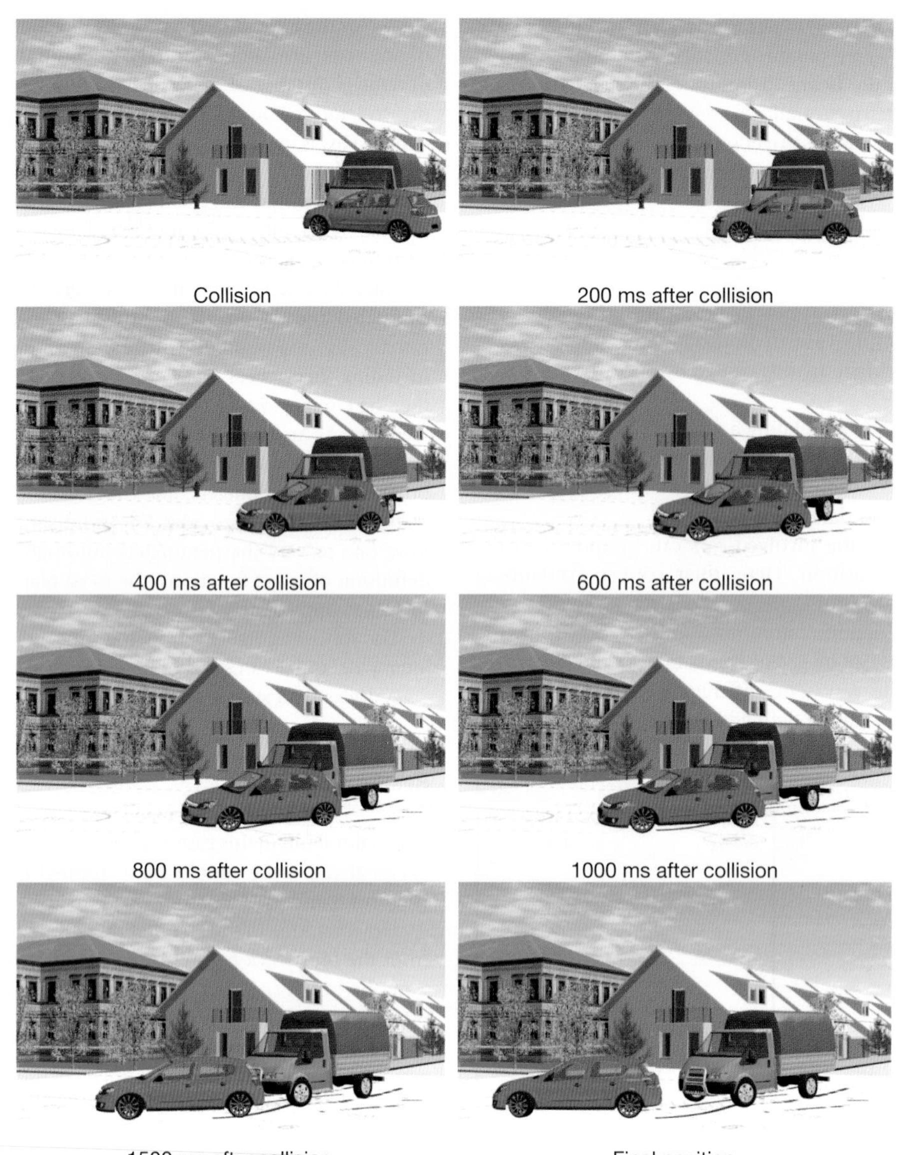

Figure 9 Vehicle movement after impact.

If the driver of the truck would have been driving at a speed of 50 km h^{-1}, the truck would have reached the collision position 2.4 s after he had reacted. This means the crossing personal car would have continued to drive for 0.7 s and thus had passed an additional distance of approximately 2.3 m. This distance would not have been satisfactory to prevent the accident. So, the accident would have also occurred at an initial speed of 50 km h^{-1} in the reaction point, but impact speed would have been reduced from 44 km h^{-1} to approximately 15 km h^{-1}.

Summary

This article outlines the basic method to determine the cause of an accident. In addition to conventional reconstruction, modern numerical methods are outlined. All three phases of an accident, precollision, collision, and postcollision, are discussed. Prevention analysis is performed within a sample case.

See also: **Engineering:** Airbag Related Injuries and Deaths; Forensic Engineering/Accident Reconstruction/Biomechanics of Injury/Philosophy, Basic Theory, and Fundamentals; Human Factors Investigation and Analysis of Accidents and Incidents.

Further Reading

Brach RM (1991) *Mechanical Impact Dynamics – Rigid Body Collisions*. New York: Wiley.
Campbell KL (1965) Energy basis for collision severity. SAE 740565.
CRASH3 Technical Manual (1986) Accident Investigation Division, NCSA, NHTSA.
Day TD (1995) An overview of the HVE vehicle model. SAE 950308.

Day TD and Hargens RL (1982) An overview of the way EDCRASH computes delta-V. Paper No. 820045, SAE, Warrendale.

Gnadler R (1971) *Das Fahrverhalten von Kraftfahrzeugen bei instationärer Kurvenfahrt mit verschiedener Anordnung der Hauptträgheitsachsen und der Rollachse.* Karlsruhe: University of Karlsruhe Dissertation.

Kudlich H (1966) Beitrag zur Mechanik des Kraftfahreug-Verkehrsunfalls. Dissertation, TU-Wien.

Lugner P, Lorenz R, and Schindler E (1984) The connexion of theoretical simulation and experiments in passenger car dynamic. Hedrick HJ (ed.) *The Dynamics of Vehicles on Roads and on Tracks*, pp. 317–330. Lisse: Swets & Zeitlinger.

McHenry RR (1976) *Extensions and Refinements of the CRASH Computer Program. Part I. Analytical Reconstruction of Highway Accidents*. DOT-HS-5-01124, February.

McHenry RR, Segal DJ, and DeLeys NJ (1967) Computer simulation of single vehicle accidents. *Stapp Car Crash Conference, Anaheim, CA (October).*

Rill G (1994) *Simulation von Kraftfahrzeugen*. Braunschweig/Wiesbaden: Vieweg & Sohn Verlagsgesellschaft mbH.

Slibar A (1966) Die mechanischen Grundsätze des Stoßvorganges freier und geführter Körper und ihre Anwendung auf den Stoßvorgang von Fahrzeugen. *Archiv für Unfallforschung* 2(1): 31.

Steffan H (1993) PC-CRASH, A Simulation Program for Car Accidents. *ISATA; 26th International Symposium on Automotive Technology and Automation, Aachen.*

Steffan H (1999) PC-CRASH 6.0: A simulation program for car accidents. Users and Technical Manual, DSD, Linz, Austria.

Steffan H and Moser A (1996) The collision and trajectory models of PC-CRASH. SAE 960886.

Steffan H and Moser A (1998) The trailer simulation model of PC-CRASH. SAE 980372.

Airbag Related Injuries and Deaths

WS Smock, University of Louisville, Louisville, KY, USA

This article is reproduced from the previous edition, volume 1, pp. 1–9, © 2000, Elsevier Ltd.

Introduction

During the past decade the motoring public had been shocked to learn that air bags, a life-saving device promoted by the automotive industry, can also induce severe and fatal injuries. Over the last 10 years in the United States, nearly 200 men, women and children have been fatally injured by deploying air bags. Thousands more have sustained serious nonfatal injuries, including cervical spine fractures, closed head injuries, and multiple fractures and amputations of digits and hands. Ironically, the vast majority of these serious and fatal injuries occurred in low and moderate speed collisions in which little or no injury would have been otherwise expected.

Historical Context

The first air bag patents were filed in 1952. Ford and General Motors began experimenting with these early prototypes in the late 1950s. Based on documents from the automotive industry, it was apparent, even as early as 1962, that deploying air bags had the potential to induce serious and fatal injuries, particularly to children. These early documents include analyses of tests conducted by Ford at their automotive safety research office in the late 1960s. The tests demonstrated that there was sufficient force associated with air bag deployment to traumatically eject a child from a vehicle. Ford also noted the amputation of a steel-hinged arm from a dummy, secondary to the explosive force of deployment. When testing involved the use of animal models, the list of severe and fatal injuries grew. Cardiac rupture, hepatic rupture, splenic rupture, aortic and vena cava transection, atlanto-occipital dislocation, cervical spine fractures, severe closed head injury and decapitation were observed.

Testing in the 1980s by the automotive manufacturers continued to demonstrate the risk of injury induction. One study conducted and reported by General Motors indicated 'many of the exposures were at loading severities beyond the level representing an estimate of nearly 100% risk of severe injury'. These laboratory tests were completed and the knowledge available to the entire automotive industry well *before* air bags were placed in American-made vehicles.

With 40 years of research behind us and all of the resultant data before us, it is apparent that steering wheel and dash-mounted air bags, devices designed to protect occupants in high-speed frontal collisions, can also maim and kill.

Automotive Industry

During the period of 1960 to 1990, the automobile industry embraced an extensive research and development program regarding air bags. This testing involved anthropomorphic dummies, anesthetized swine and baboons, and even human volunteers. It was recognized early on that occupants in the path of the deploying air bag, or who were positioned close to the air bag at the moment of deployment, were at a very significant risk of receiving a severe or fatal injury. In January 1970, at a meeting of engineers from General Motors, Ford and Chrysler, this information was discussed. As a result, a Chrysler engineer wrote: 'This is a very serious problem that must be resolved for the inflatable restraint. Having a child directly in front of the bag when it inflates could prove fatal.'

General Motors tested air bags on baboons at Wayne State University during the early 1970s. The research indicated that 'if the head is in the path of the deploying air bag, it is concluded that injury is likely to occur in the form of brain or neck injury to a child'.

Testing by Ford in the 1970s revealed that individuals involved in collisions at less than 32 kph (20 mph) experienced more severe injuries and loading forces in vehicles equipped *with* an air bag than those without one. Ford also noted that there was 'overwhelming evidence that air bags may be dangerous for small children'. In 1972, a Ford engineer wrote the following warning, which was never placed in a vehicle: 'The right front seat should be used only by persons who are more than five feet [1.52 m] tall and are in sound health. Smaller persons and those who are aged or infirm, should be seated and belted in the rear seat.'

In a series of tests conducted by General Motors in the 1980s, anesthetized swine were placed with their chests in close proximity to the air bag module. The tests revealed that when the swine's thorax was impacted by the force of the deploying air bag and the air bag module, significant thoracic and abdominal injuries were sustained. These injuries in one case included: 17 rib fractures; two cardiac perforations; a splenic laceration; a liver hematoma and death within 30 min. The proximity of the occupant to the deploying bag and module cover were the pivotal contributory factors.

Human Injuries

The serious and life-threatening injuries that were originally observed in the industry's laboratories using animal models began to be observed in humans on US roadways in the 1990s. The first six driver air bag-related deaths which were investigated by the government and the automotive industry revealed that the majority of these victims were women of short stature. It was also noted that the fatal injuries could be incurred even if the occupant was restrained by a lap and chest belt. The injuries initially seen included massive head injuries with diffuse axonal injury, subdural hematomas, and skull fractures. Additional injuries evaluated included cervical spine fracture, cardiac perforation, pulmonary contusions, and multiple rib fractures.

 http://dx.doi.org/10.1016/B978-0-12-382165-2.00143-4

Sodium azide is the explosive propellant used to initiate the deployment cycle in most air bag designs in use today (**Figure 1**). When sodium azide is ignited, the deploying air bag explodes toward the occupant at speeds of up to 336 kph (210 mph). An air bag system has two components, either of which may induce injuries: the canvas-covered air bag itself and the air bag module cover (**Figure 2**). Injuries incurred during deployment are relevant to the component inflicting them.

Obviously, the types of injuries which result from impact with the canvas air bag are different from those which result from impact with its module cover. There are three phases to air bag deployment: 'punch out', 'catapult' and 'bag slap'. Injuries can be inflicted at any point during the deployment process:

- *Punch out* This is the initial stage of deployment. If the bag makes contact at this stage, the following injuries can result: atlanto-occipital dislocation, cervical spine fracture with brainstem transection, cardiac, liver and splenic lacerations, diffuse axonal injuries, subdural and epidural hematomas, and decapitation.
- *Catapult* This is the midstage of deployment when rapidly inflating bag 'catapults' or drives the head and neck rearward. This occurs with sufficient energy to rupture blood vessels, ligaments and fracture cervical vertebrae. The neck injuries occur as the result of cervical spine hyperextension.
- *Bag slap* This is the final stage of deployment which occurs at the bag's peak excursion. Appropriately named, this happens when the canvas bag's fabric may 'slap' the occupant's face, resulting in injuries to the eye and epithelium.

The air bag module covers are located in the steering wheel on the driver's side and in the dashboard panel on the passenger side. As the bag deploys, the module cover is also propelled outward at speeds of up to 336 kph (210 mph). Most steering wheel designs house the horn within the air bag module compartment. Hand and arm injuries observed in individuals whose extremities were in contact with the module at the moment of its rupture include: degloving, fracture dislocation, fracture dislocation and amputations (partial and complete of digits and forearms). If the module cover makes contact with an occupant's face, head or neck, skull fractures and severe or fatal head injuries, and decapitations have also been observed. The driver's side cover is generally made with a rubberized plastic type of material, while the passenger side may have a metal housing. Contact with either type can prove fatal.

Figure 1 The air bag is transported as an explosive material. Sodium azide is the explosive propellant used in the majority of air bag modules.

Figure 2 The injury-producing components of the air bag system are the air bag and the module cover which overlies it.

Specific Injury Patterns

Ocular

The eye is extremely vulnerable to air bag-induced injury. These injuries range from corneal abrasions from contact with the air bag, chemical burns from contact with unburned sodium azide, to retinal detachment and globe rupture from the blunt force trauma of the expanding bag (**Figure 3**). The wearing of eyeglasses in some cases has proven to be of benefit, as it offers a degree of barrier protection between the eye and the deploying bag.

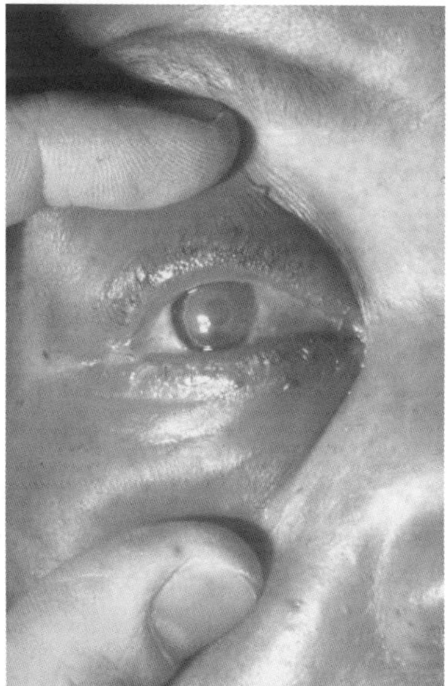

Figure 3 This patient sustained a severe corneal abrasion secondary to the membrane forces associated with air bag deployment.

Face and Head

The most common injury associated with air bag deployment is that of facial abrasion. The abrasions result from a sliding contact between the bag and the face (**Figure 4**). The injuries are not chemical 'burns' but deep abrasions.

Cranial and Intracranial

When acceleration forces are applied to the cranial vault, a variety of traumatic injuries to the brain and surrounding structures will result. These include subdural hematomas, cortical contusions, atlanto-occipital dislocations, skull fractures, and brainstem transections. Cranial injuries may result from contact with either the deploying of bag or module cover (**Figure 5**).

Cervical Spine

The blow from an air bag or module cover which produces a rapid and violent hyperextension of the cervical spine of the driver or passenger will have significant consequences for the cervical vertebrae. Injuries commonly seen as a result of hyperextension include atlanto-occipital dislocation, comminuted fractures of one or more upper cervical vertebrae, rupture of the anterior and posterior longitudinal spinal ligaments, and cervical spine disarticulation with transection of the cervical cord. The majority of these injuries are associated with the upper cervical vertebrae, although lower cervical vertebrae injuries have been observed.

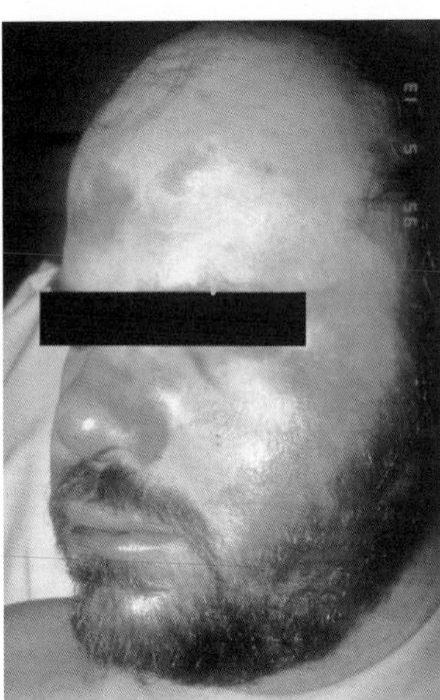

Figure 4 Abrasions to the cheeks, forehead and nose are the most common injury associated with air bag deployment.

Figure 5 Cranial or facial contact with the deploying bag.

Extremities

The upper extremities are very vulnerable to traumatic injury from the deploying bag and its module cover. When an individual's hand or forearm is on or near the module cover at the moment of deployment, the occupant can expect to sustain multiple fractures, and/or tissue degloving or amputation of fingers, hand or forearm (**Figure 6**). The horn-button-within-the-module cover design significantly increases the risk of injury to the occupant's upper extremities at the moment of deployment. Many of these upper extremity injuries are associated with an occupant's attempt to blow the horn, the button of which is located within the module cover. Forces from air bag deployment may be transmitted to the hand, wrist, or forearm and may even involve the humerus. It is not unusual to see significantly comminuted fractures involving the wrist, forearm, elbow, and distal humerus (**Figures 7** and **8**). The vehicles whose module covers are of a higher mass have the propensity to inflict more severe injuries. Some of the worst offenders are module covers located on the passenger side, which may have a soft coating of plastic on the exterior but have an underlying piece of rigid metal (**Figure 9b**). The placement of hands on the passengerside dashboard, in a bracing maneuver, has resulted in the traumatic amputation of hands and forearms (**Figure 9a**).

Respiratory

The byproducts of combustion as well as other inert materials within the air bag may produce a white cloud within the vehicle. Many occupants have thought that this indicated a vehicle fire. This whitish material is principally cornstarch, talc, and the byproducts of sodium azide combustion. There may be a small percentage of unburnt sodium azide present within this powder as well. Inhalation of these materials can result in a chemical pneumonitis and the induction of asthma-type symptoms. These byproducts may also cause a chemical irritation of open wounds and a basic (high pH) burn to the eyes.

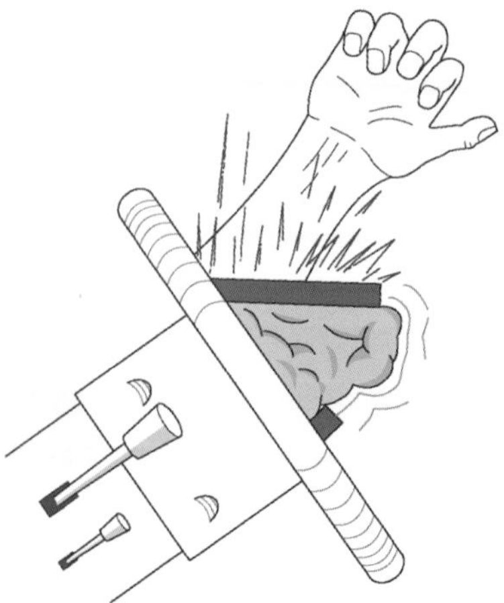

Figure 6 When the forearm is located in a horizontal fashion.

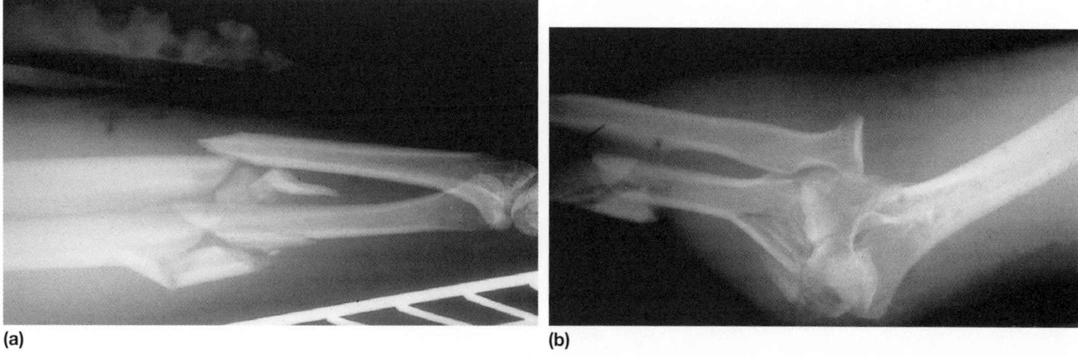

(a) (b)

Figure 7 When the hand, wrist, or forearm is on or near the module cover at the moment of deployment, for example when blowing the horn, significant fractures, degloving injuries, and amputations will result. (a) This open-comminuted bending fracture of the radius and ulna was the result of contact with the module cover. (b) This patient sustained a comminuted fracture of the proximal and midshaft ulna as well as a radial head dislocation from impact with the module cover.

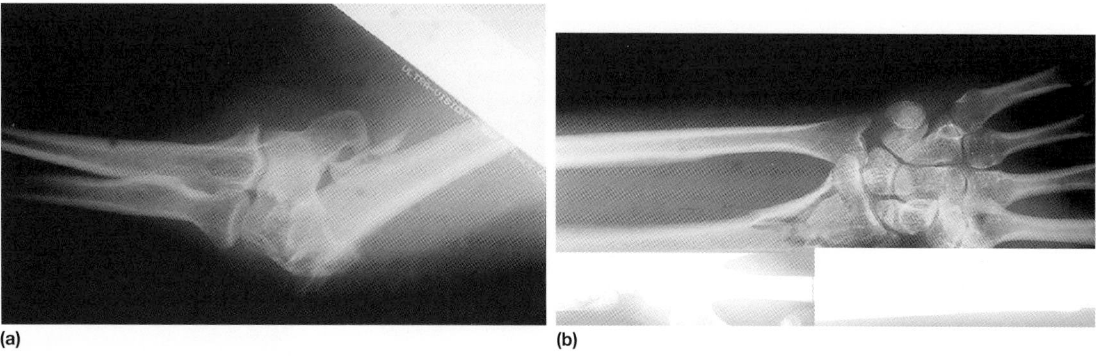

(a) (b)

Figure 8(a) and **(b)** These severely comminuted fractures resulted when this individual was blowing her horn. She sustained a frontal impact of approximately 15 kph, which resulted in air bag activation. The horn activation button was located within the module cover, which explains why the patient had her forearms over the module cover at the moment of deployment.

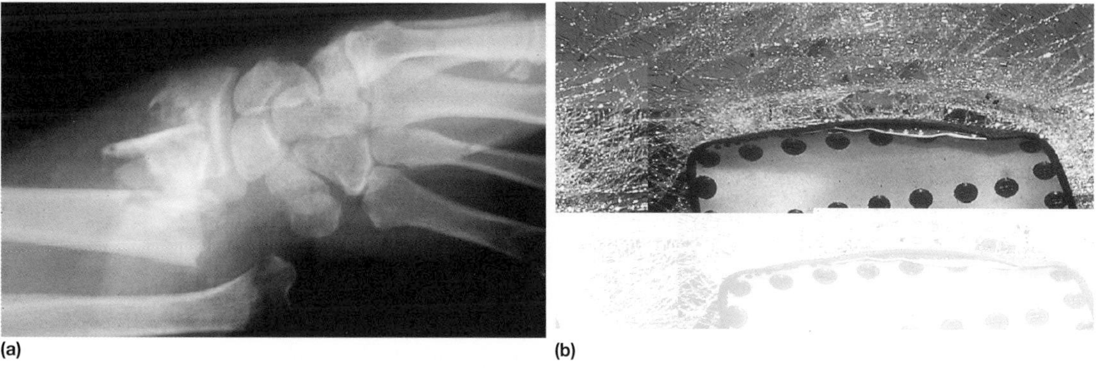

(a) (b)

Figure 9 (a) This partially-amputated wrist was the result of placement of the front seat passenger's hand on the dashboard at the moment of deployment. (b) The underlying structure of the module cover was metal.

Sample Cases

Case 1

A 35-year-old female, 1.57 m (5′ 2″) and 50 kg (110 lb.), was the restrained driver in a 1991 Ford Taurus (**Figure 10**). The vehicle's front bumper grazed a guard rail, which resulted in deployment of the driver's air bag. The patient sustained an immediate respiratory arrest, with subsequent declaration of brain death 12 h later.

A postmortem examination was conducted and revealed the following injuries: significant midface trauma with bilateral epistaxis; corneal abrasions; contusions of the chest; left subdural hematoma (overlying the frontal and parietal regions); subarachnoid hemorrhage and severe cerebral edema.

Examination of the exterior of the vehicle revealed very minor damage which was limited to the front bumper. The examination of the interior revealed a tear on the left lower portion of the module cover (**Figure 11**). This tear was the

Figure 10(a) and **(b)** A 1991 Ford Taurus was involved in a very minor glancing collision between the front bumper and a guardrail. There was no underlying frame, fender, or structural damage.

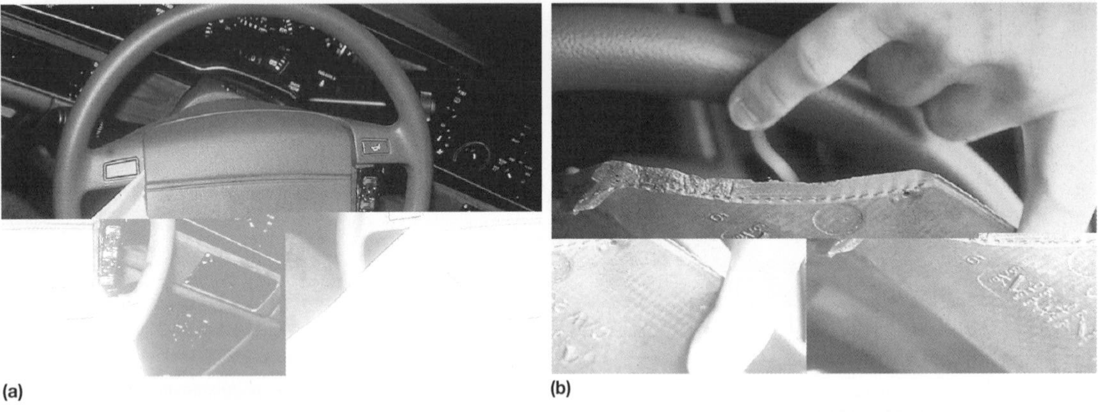

Figure 11 (a) The left lower corner of the module cover exhibited tearing from contact with the left side of the driver's face. (b) Close-up of the module cover reveals the presence of a torn area. There is also an area which indicates this piece was removed by a sharp implement.

result of contact between the left side of the victim's face and the deploying module (**Figures** 5 and 11).

Case 2

A 4-year-old male was the lap belt-restrained occupant of the front right seat of a 1995 GEO Metro (**Figure** 12). The shoulder portion of the harness was placed underneath the right arm. The patient was catapulted from the front passenger seat to the rear of the vehicle. The patient was found pulseless and apneic on arrival of emergency medical services.

A postmortem examination was conducted and revealed the following injuries: an atlanto-occipital dislocation with brainstem transection; large sub-dural hemorrhages; multiple rib fractures with underlying pulmonary contusions; liver and splenic lacerations; clavicular fracture, and significant facial abrasions underlying the mandible bilaterally and on the right cheek (**Figure** 13a). Examination of the abdomen also revealed a lap belt contusion below the umbilicus (**Figure** 13b).

Examination of the vehicle revealed front end damage consistent with a change of velocity of less than 15 kph (9 mph). There was no damage to the driver or passenger compartments. Examination of the passenger bag revealed the presence of blood and tissue transfer. The patient's injuries resulted from blunt force trauma to the chest and abdomen as well as a hyperextension injury of the neck with a rapid rearward acceleration.

Case 3

A 35-year-old female was the front seat passenger in a 1995 Nissan Altima. The patient was in a lap-shoulder belt, with the passenger seat in the most rearward position. The vehicle was stopped in a line of traffic, waiting for a traffic signal to turn, when it was hit from behind by a vehicle travelling at the speed of approximately 5 kph (3 mph). The rear impact pushed the Nissan forward into the trailer hitch of the truck in front. This resulted in air bag deployment. The air bag impacted the patient's left eye. Examination of the face revealed significant periorbital trauma. There were abrasions on the forehead as well as on the cheek and chin. Examination of the eye revealed the presence of chemosis, a hyphema, and a retinal detachment (**Figure** 14).

Examination of the vehicle revealed a 5×5 cm dent in the right front bumper (**Figure** 15). There was no significant rear end damage. Examination of the bag revealed transfer of make-up and blood to the bag.

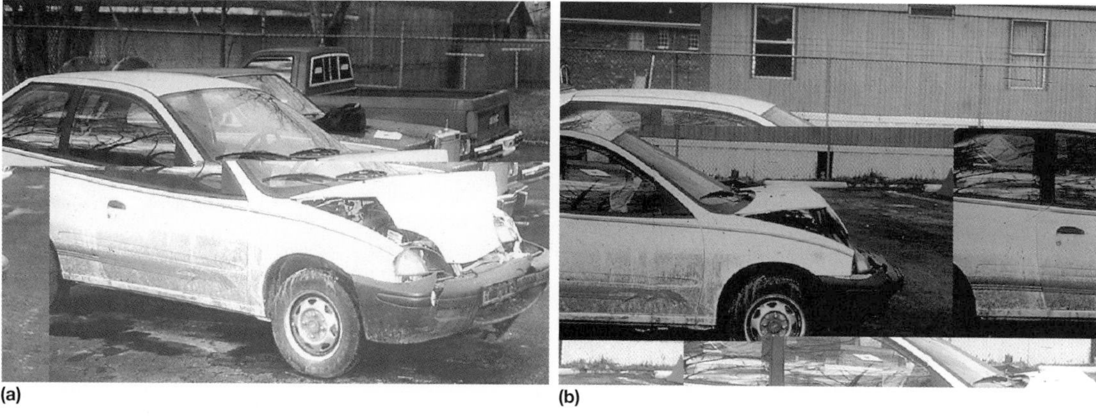

Figure 12(a) and **(b)** A 1995 GEO Metro with minor front-end damage consistent with an impact speed of less than 15 kph (9 mph).

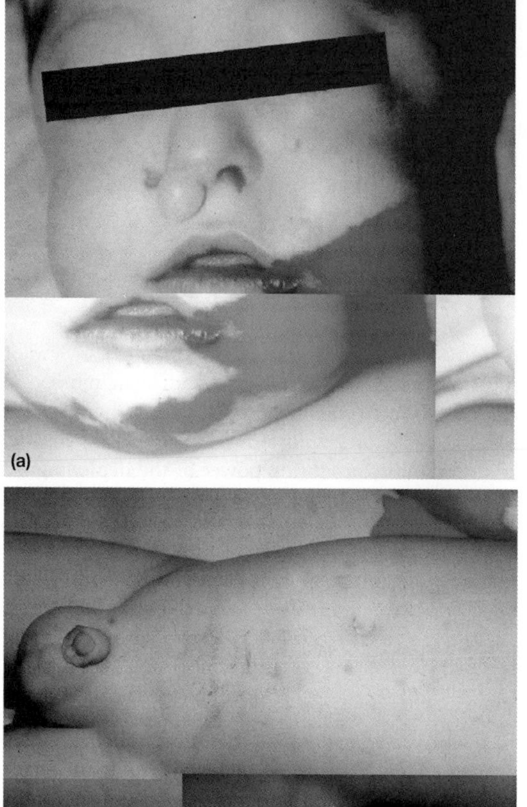

Figure 13 (a) This fatally injured 4-year-old male exhibits significant facial abrasion, overlying the mandible as well as abrasion on the left cheek. This was the result from contacts with the upwardly-deploying air bag. (b) Examination of the patient's abdomen reveals a horizontally-oriented contusion consistent with a lap belt.

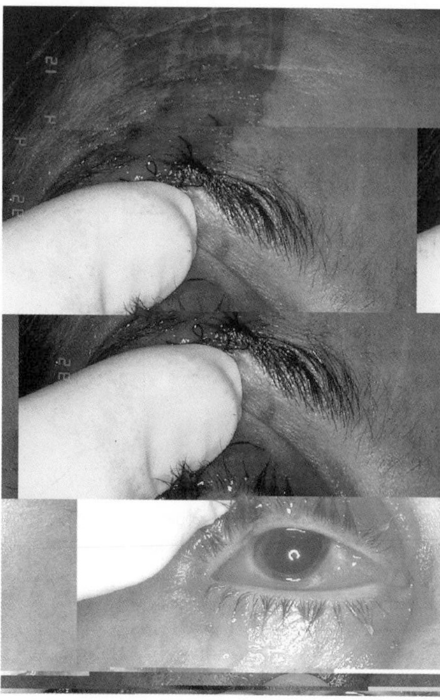

Figure 14 This 1.72 m (5′ 8″) restrained patient suffered permanent retinal detachment secondary to air bag contact.

Forensics of Air Bag Injuries

Locard's principle regarding the transfer of physical evidence between two impacting objects is dramatically evidenced in the case of air bags and air bag-induced injuries. The transfer of evidence to the air bag itself may take various forms. Blood and epithelial tissue transfer is, of course, common but transfer of make-up, including lipstick, rouge and mascara, to the air bag is also seen (**Figure 16**). Analysis of the blood spatter pattern on the bag may assist the investigator in determining the position of the occupant and the configuration of the steering wheel at the moment of air bag deployment.

Examination of the air bag module cover may reveal the presence of trace evidence. Depending on the design of the module cover, there may actually be tearing or bending of the module cover, indicative of contact with an occupant's more rigid (bony) surface: face or forearm. Scuff-type marks on the module cover indicate contact with an object, frequently the forearm (**Figure 17**). Fabric imprints may also be seen on close inspection (**Table 1**).

(a) (b)

Figure 15(a) and **(b)** A 1995 Nissan Altima. The only damage to the vehicle is a 5×5 cm indentation in the front bumper from impact with the ball of a trailer hitch.

Figure 16 Close examination of an air bag may reveal a multitude of transferred evidence. This evidence will include: hair, blood, epithelial tissue, and facial makeup.

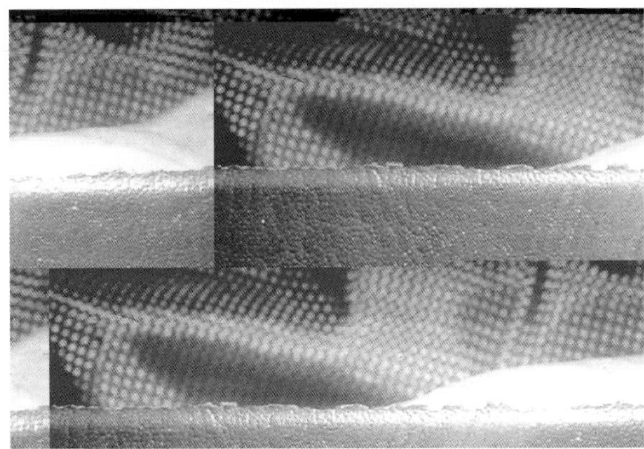

Figure 17 Close inspection of a module cover may reveal the presence of scuffing, and facbric imprints.

Summary

In the United States, the deployment of air bag has been responsible for nearly 200 deaths and thousands of severe injuries. It is clear that the forces of deployment are not insignificant and must be respected by the vehicle occupant. A review of the literature indicates that the serious and fatal injuries, which were once produced in the laboratory setting, are now being observed in 'real-world' collisions. Many clinicians may not be aware of the injury-producing power of the deploying air bag and must be informed of the patterns associated with air bag-induced injuries. The motoring public must also be informed and warned of the dangers of air bag deployment, just as the automotive industry was over 30 years ago.

Table 1 Trace evidence

Air bag
Blood
Make-up
Hair
Tissue
Module cover
Tearing of cover material
Scuff marking
Fabric imprint
Tissue
Hair

See also: **Engineering:** Accident Investigation – Determination of Cause; Forensic Engineering/Accident Reconstruction/Biomechanics of Injury/Philosophy, Basic Theory, and Fundamentals.

Further Reading

Horsch J, Lau I, Andrzegkad, et al. (1990) *Assessment of Air Bag Deployment Loads*. SAE 902324. Detroit: Society of Automotive Engineers.

Huelke DF, Moore JL, Compton TW, et al. (1994) *Upper Extremity Injuries Related to Air Bag Deployments*. SAE 940716. Detroit: Society of Automotive Engineers.

Huelke DF, Moore JL, and Ostrom M (1992) Air bag injuries and accident protection. *Journal of Trauma* 33: 894–897.

Landcaster GI, Defrance JH, and Borrusso J (1993) Air bag associated rupture of the right atrium. *New England Journal of Medicine* 328: 358.

Lau I, Horsch JD, Viano DC, et al. (1993) Mechanism of injury from air bag deployment loads. *Accident Analysis and Prevention* 25: 29.

Mertz HJ and Weber DA (1982) *Interpretations of Impact Response to a Three Year Old Child Dummy Relative to Child Injury Potential*. SAE 826048. Detroit: Society of Automotive Engineers.

Mertz HJ, Driscoll GP, Lennox JB, et al. (1982) Response of animals exposed to deployment of various passenger and portable restraint system concepts for a variety of collision severities and animal positions. In: *National Highway and Transportation Safety Administration. 9th International Technical Conference on Experimental Safety Vehicles*, pp. 352–368 Kyoto, Japan, November 1982.

Parents for Safer Air Bags (1997) *The Air Bag Crisis: Causes and Solutions*. .

Prasad P and Daniel RP (1984) *A Biomechanical Analysis of Head, Neck and Torso Injuries to Child Surrogates Due to Sudden Torso Acceleration*. SAE 841656. Detroit: Society of Automotive Engineers.

Smock WS (1992) Traumatic avulsion of the first digit, secondary to air bag deployment. In: *Proceedings 36. Association for the Advancement of Automotive Medicine*, p. 444. Des Plains, IL.

Smock WS and Nichols GN (1995) Air bag module cover injures. *Journal of Trauma, Injury, Infection and Critical Care* 38: 489–493.

Viano DC and Warner CV (1976) *Thoracic Impact Response of Live Porcine Subjects*. CvSAE 760823, 733–765. Detroit: Society for Automotive Engineers.

Electronic Data Recorders (EDRs, Black Boxes)

W Rosenbluth, Reston, VA, USA

Glossary

A/D Analog/digital (converter used in D/A processes).
ABS Antilock braking system, which prevents wheel lockup on mixed-friction road surfaces, thereby enhancing vehicle stability during braking.
AE Algorithm enable, also called algorithm wakeup, the acceleration threshold value (x time) which triggers the ECU software to start considering whether the cumulative crash pulse can be predicted to reach a value for which one or more passive restraints should be deployed.
ALDL Assembly Line Diagnostic Link, a historic term created by G.M., referring to a common diagnostic connector on a vehicle in the era before the common SAE J1962 (OBD-II) connector was in use. However, this term is now common in automotive jargon.
Algorithm wakeup Also called algorithm enable, the acceleration threshold value (x time) which triggers the ECU software to start considering whether the cumulative crash pulse can be predicted to reach a value for which one or more passive restraints should be deployed.
APS Accelerator position sensor, a sensor of the accelerator pedal which presents a position-analog voltage to an engine electronic control computer (engine control ECU).
CAN Controller area network (data bus), an advanced and robust intra-vehicle communications media for data transfer between varions on-vehicle system control ECUs.
D/A Data acquisition, a system whereby various vehicle parameters can be recorded on a common timeline for use in later analyzing vehicle performance.
DAWN Data acquisition with vehicle networks (HEM Data Corp).
Delta-V The (abrupt) change in velocity during a particular event (such as would be caused by an impact event). This distinguished from the approach velocity (vehicle velocity just before an impact event).
DLC Diagnostic Link Connector, see ALDL.
DPID Data packet identification number, usually for multiple data values (per SAE J 2190, p 4).
DUT Device under test, refers to a specific component which is the subject of a particular test step.
ECU Electronic control unit. A typical on board automotive computer assembly with a dedicated functional purpose.
EDR Event data recorder. Typically, a control ECU which incorporates non-volatile memory (EEPROM) which records vehicle and system parameters in the event of a significant event (such as a crash which causes airbag deployment).
EEPROM Electrically erasable read-only memory (typical NVRAM implementation). Memory which saves its contents via a physical charge-storage property so that it retains its data even if removed from system power. Thus when system power is removed (as in a crash event), the EEPROM memory contents are saved.
ESC Electronic stability control, a system which can modulate engine output and/or apply individual wheel braking when it senses vehicle acceleration anomalies. Usually implemented in conjunction with ABS functions.
J1962 SAE J1962 connector. Refers to SAE J1962. The standard diagnostic port on all US domestic sold vehicles since 1996. Also referred to as the OBD-II connector (on board diagnostics, version II) and the ALDL (Assembly Line Diagnostic Link).
KAM Keep alive memory, random access memory (or a subportion thereof) which is forced to retain its data while energized with system power. When system power is removed, the KAM memory contents are lost.
ms Millisecond, 1/1000 s.
NVRAM Non -volatile random access memory (see EEPROM).
OBD-II On board diagnostics connector, version II, a now Federally mandated common diagnostic connector for use in diagnosing on-board-systems DTCs (originally purposed for emissions-related DTCs).
PCB Printed circuit board, insulating substrate with plated wires that form interconnects between various Integrated Circuit components and discrete components (resistors, capacitors, diodes, etc.).
PCM Powertrain control module. The engine electronic control computer (engine control ECU).
PID Parameter identification number, usually for a single data value (per SAE J 2190, p4).
RAM Random access memory, memory in an ECU which is writable to save in-process values during the ongoing function of a control ECU. Such memory typically operates only when system power is applied, and thus loses its contents when the vehicle key is turned off, or in a significant crash event.
ROM Read-only memory, memory in an ECU which has fixed contents (such as a control program and/or default calibration constants). Such memory is fixed and not writable by the normal production ECU.
SLOT SLOT factors are defined by SAE J2178-2 to be scaling, limit, offset and transfer function specifications that allow hexadecimal encoded engineering data to be interpreted or mapped into engineering units such as DTCs, RPM, mph, lbf, psi, seconds, volts, amps, Gs, etc.
SRS Supplemental restraints system. The passive restraints system in a vehicle, which operates without operator intervention, typically controlling frontal airbags, side airbags, curtain airbags, and seatbelt pretensioners.
Thrott Throttle. Typically in EFI (electronic fuel injection) vehicles, an air valve. Fuel is adjusted by the PCM (engine computer, engine control module, ECM) to achieve an optimum mixture for the air input.

 http://dx.doi.org/10.1016/B978-0-12-382165-2.00144-6

TPS Throttle position sensor, a sensor on the throttle body of an engine which presents a position-analog voltage to an engine electronic control computer.
VSS Vehicle speed sensor (usually on the transmission output shaft). Usually a reluctance or Hall Effect device which presents a voltage pulse train whose frequency is directly proportional to the rotational speed of the transmission output shaft (and thus directly related to the speed of the vehicle). A reluctance device is a wire coil in a magnetic circuit which produces a voltage output as the magnetic field changes. A Hall effect device is a semiconductor element which produces a resistive change in its properties in response to a transverse magnetic field, thus producing a voltage difference when a constant current is flowing in that device.
WSS Wheel speed sensor (associated with each wheel, used for ABS/ESC functions). Usually a reluctance or Hall Effect device which presents a voltage pulse train whose frequency is directly proportional to the rotational speed of the wheel on which it is mounted and thus can be used for comparison to other wheels having similar sensors, thereby allowing an ABS ECU to determine if there is excessive braking slip on any particular wheel.

Abbreviations

Accel Accelerator
ECU Electronic control unit
EDR Event data recorder
VUT Vehicle under test

Background of Electronic Data in Ground Vehicles

Superceding a long tradition of analog and mechanical technology for control of vehicle functional systems, current ground vehicle control technology is dominated by pervasive use of electronic controllers. Electronic control is achieved by using small-package in-vehicle-mounted dedicated real-time computers (electronic control units, ECUs) to accomplish the logic and magnitude control of vehicle system parameters. Such controllers allow for increased calibration accuracy and enhanced diagnostics and serviceability when compared to their traditional analog forebears. Typical ECUs consist of a controller (computing) device, memory, sensor input circuits, and actuator power driver circuits. ECU memory is used to save diagnostic information which often includes diagnostic trouble codes (DTCs) and information about the status of inputs (representing vehicle parameters) to that ECU at historical moments in the operating life of that ECU. When the ECU memory is used to save data triggered by a crash event, and that data can be later accessed for investigation purposes, that ECU is often referred to as an event data recorder (EDR).

Typical ECUs incorporate a controller (computing) device, memory, sensor input circuits, and actuator power driver circuits. (Often computational, memory and analog/digital-conversion functions are integrated onto a single integrated circuit device. Such devices are identified as a microcontroller unit (MCU) device.) ECU (MCU) memory can be broadly characterized in three categories.

1. ROM (read-only memory) – a fast read-only technology which has fixed contents and is typically used to store application program code and base (default) calibration data.
2. RAM (random access memory) – a fast read–write technology which is used as a calculation scratchpad for the algorithms in the computing element.
3. NVRAM (non-volatile random access memory) – a usually slower read–write technology which is used to save update or adaptive calibration data and diagnostic information. NVRAM can be battery dependent (KAM, keep alive memory, usually a part of RAM), or it can be a different technology which retains data even when the ECU is disconnected from a vehicle electrical system (EEPROM, electrically erasable programmable read-only memory). (EEPROM data retention times are often specified for periods of 10–20 years.)

Diagnostic information almost always includes diagnostic trouble codes (DTCs) and often includes information about the status of inputs (representing vehicle parameters) to that ECU at historical moments in the operating life of that ECU. (A common use of KAM is the storage of freeze frame data in PCM ECUs to assist in the diagnosis of emissions-related PCM DTCs.)

Current vehicle systems now typically relying on electronic control mechanisms, with the inherent ability to save selected data in NVRAM, include electronic fuel injection, engine emissions feedback, antilock braking, traction control, stability control, anti-theft, occupant safety protection, and rollover protection. These various ECUs are invariably communicating with each other on one or more internal vehicle data bus(es). To give the reader an immediate reference, a series of stepped-complexity symbolic representations of distributed control ECUs and vehicle diagnostic data bus(es) are shown in **Figures** 1. through 4 Since some, or all, of the ECUs may contain NVRAM data, there can be crash-related event data in more than one ECU and this is clearly shown in **Figure** 4.

Retrieving ECU NVRAM Data for Use in Crash Investigations

A Word About the Data

EDR data exist as binary bits stored in the non-volatile memory of a particular ECU. Such data must be accessed via electronic data retrieval methods. Additionally, since binary bit

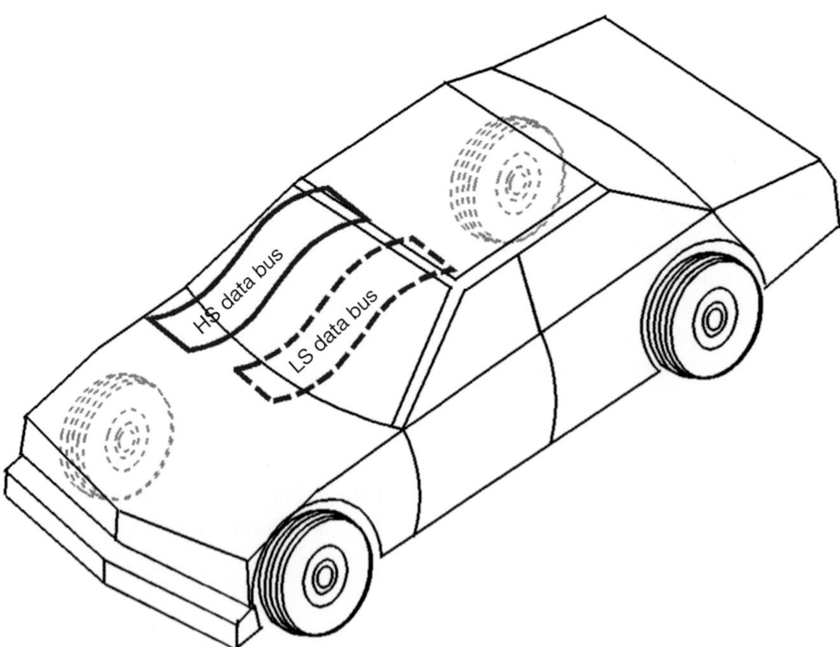

Figure 1 A generic wireframe vehicle with a dual data bus implementation, a high speed bus (HS data bus) and a low speed data bus (LS data bus).

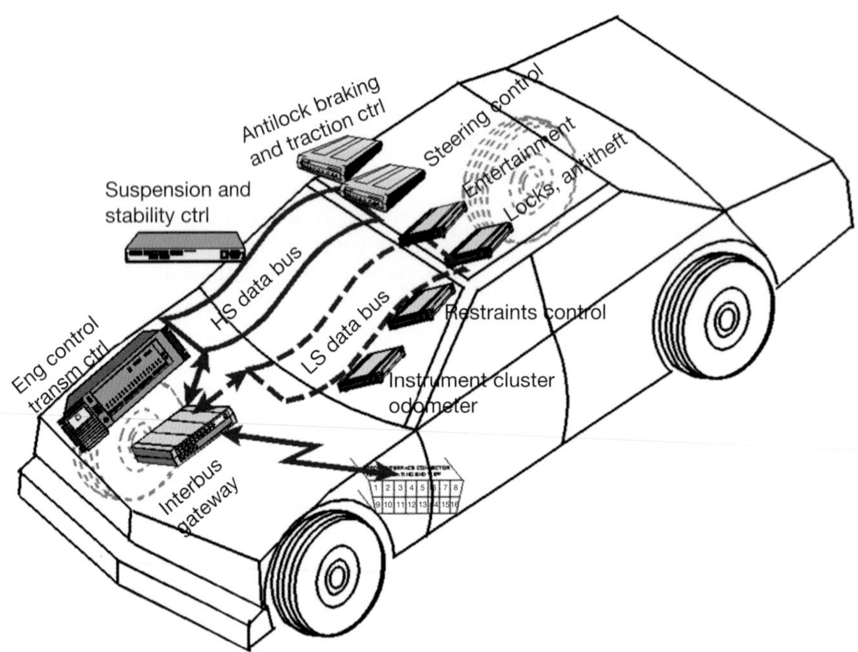

Figure 2 Vehicle operating systems controllers requiring real-time intercommunication are grouped on the HS data bus and how other systems controllers, not requiring real-time intercommunication are grouped on the LS data bus. (Although individual LS data bus controllers certainly act independently in real time. For instance, the restraints controller must autonomously act within 50 ms of the inception of a crash even to calculate the potential magnitude of such a crash event, and then deploy passive restraints if appropriate. However, once it has acted with respect to restraints deployment, the need to communicate with other controllers can take 1000 ms or more.) This figure also shows how inter-bus communications are typically accomplished by using an inter-bus communications controller, often called gateway.

representations can be long and are nearly impossible to assimilate, such data are normally represented in its most economical human readable form, hexadecimal notation. Hexadecimal notation is a base 16 arithmetic notation, with characters (0–9, A–F) corresponding to decimal values of 0–15 of the original binary value. Hexadecimal notation is most often represented with a leading dollar sign, '$.' Hexadecimal notation typically considers 'byte' quantities which consist of 8 bits of data. Each byte consists of two ½ bytes, each containing a hexadecimal character representing 4 bits (a 'nibble'). For

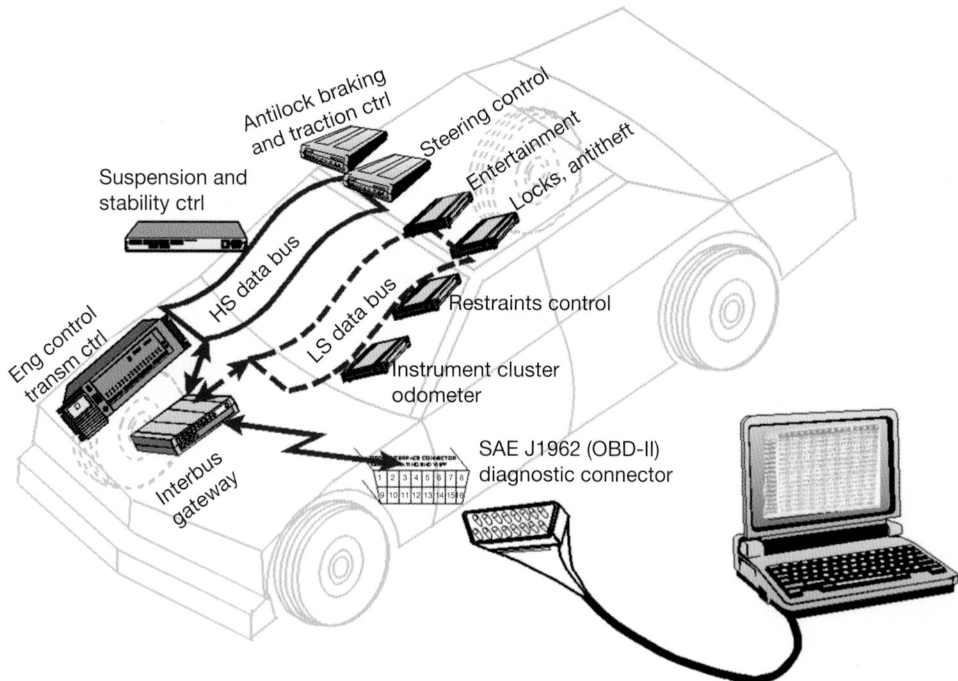

Figure 3 Vehicle diagnostics may be accomplished using a standard diagnostic data port directly accessing the gateway, which then allows indirect access to both data buses. Laptop-based diagnostics are shown In the illustration, but other small specialized computer terminals called scanners or code-scanners can also be used in this manner. The standard diagnostic port is defined by SAE J1962 and has been mandated on US-sale vehicles since 1996.

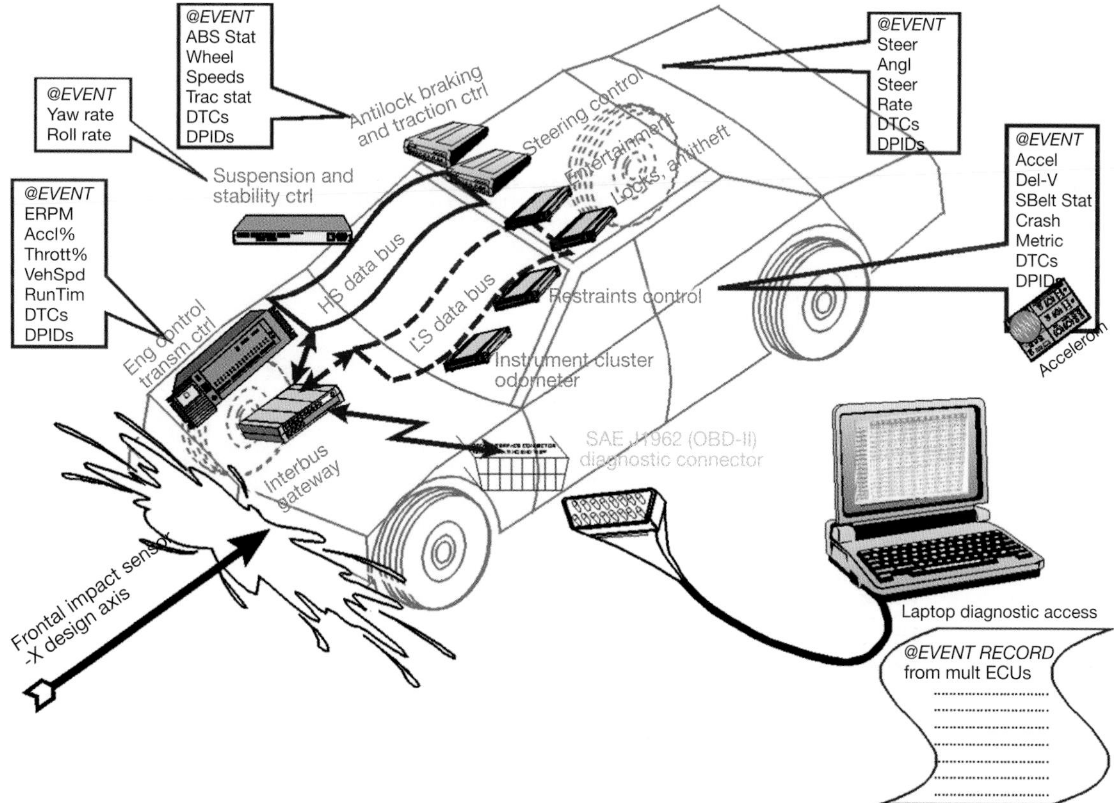

Figure 4 Vehicle operating parameters may be stored in different ECU system controllers and how these parameters, if captured at an event, may be accumulated to form an EVENT RECORD which may be retrieved via a specialized laptop access. If one ECU is designated as a central point to save the various parameter data in its non-volatile memory, that ECU is typically designated as the event data recorder (EDR).

Figure 5 A typical CDR connection to the vehicle J1962 Data Port (aka the OBD-II port or the ALDL port).

example, a binary value of '1001' = \$9 = 9decimal, and a binary value of '1110' = \$E = 14decimal. Just as in decimal arithmetic, when the maximum digit count is achieved [\$F = 15dec for hexadecimal], the next count is a carry to the left column. The first carry in decimal arithmetic (the next count after 9) gives a representation of 10; the decimal quantity, ten. The first carry in hexadecimal arithmetic (the next count after \$F) gives a hexadecimal representation of \$10; the decimal quantity, 16. As a last example, the binary value '0011 0101,' represented as hexadecimal byte = \$35, stands for a decimal quantity of 53 $(3 \times 16 + 5)$.

Post-crash-event crash investigations involving those vehicles now typically utilize such data, as translated into standard engineering units, and such investigations now commonly reference data stored in various EDRs in both bullet and target involved vehicles.

Retrieving the Data

The most common method to access EDR data on passenger vehicles and light trucks is via a standard vehicle network interface, the SAE J1962 port (a/k/a the OBD-II port, the DLC or the ALDL) as shown in **Figure 3**.

However, other, equally valid, methods can include direct umbilical-to-ECU interrogation and direct umbilical-to-EEPROM interrogation. If the objective of EDR data retrieval is its use in a litigation process, with either method, a key

Hexadecimal Data

Data that the vehicle manufacturer has specified for data retrieval is shown in the hexadecimal data section of the CDR report. The hexadecimal data section of the CDR report may contain data that is not translated by the CDR program. The control module contains additional data that is not retrievable by the CDR system.

```
$01  B2 3C 00 E6 64 69
$02  00 00 00 E0 18 00
$03  00 00 00 00 00 00
$04  70 88 40 00 00 00
$05  3F 00 00 06 C0 E2
$06  3F 00 00 06 C0 E2
$07  00 00 C0 00 22 00
$08  00 08 08 50 50 00
$09  04 64 04 64 7F 00
$0A  00 00 00 00 00 00
$0B  08 F6 00 00 FE 00
$12  FF 7F 00 84 40 00
$17  03 03 03 02 00 00
$18  03 03 00 00 00 00
$19  00 00 00 00 00 00
$1A  00 00 00 00 00 00
$1B  00 00 00 00 00 00
$1C  4F 4F 00 4F 00 01
$1D  32 C1 00 00 00 00
$1E  00 00 00 00 00 00
$1F  0C 0D 31 32 5C 5C
$20  20 93 03 00 00 00
$21  7F 7F 7E 7F 7F 7E
$22  01 00 00 00 00 00
$23  00 FF FF 1E 59 00
$24  00 FF 1E 59 F9 00
$25  82 C0 00 00 00 00
$26  41 4F 4F 4F 4F 00
$27  00 01 01 01 01 01
$29  26 26 26 26 26 00
$2A  46 46 46 46 46 00
$2B  00 00 00 00 00 80
$2C  01 01 00 01 00 40
$2F  00 00 00 00 00 80
$30  00 00 00 00 00 80
$36  8C 00 00 00 00 00
$37  00 A5 00 00 00 00
$38  00 00 00 00 00 00
$39  00 FF FF 1E 58 00
$3A  FF 1E 58 00 00 00
$3B  FF FF FF FF FF FF
$3C  FF FF FF FF FF FF
```

Figure 6 Virtual hexadecimal data (i.e., DPID data) as retrieved by the CDR.

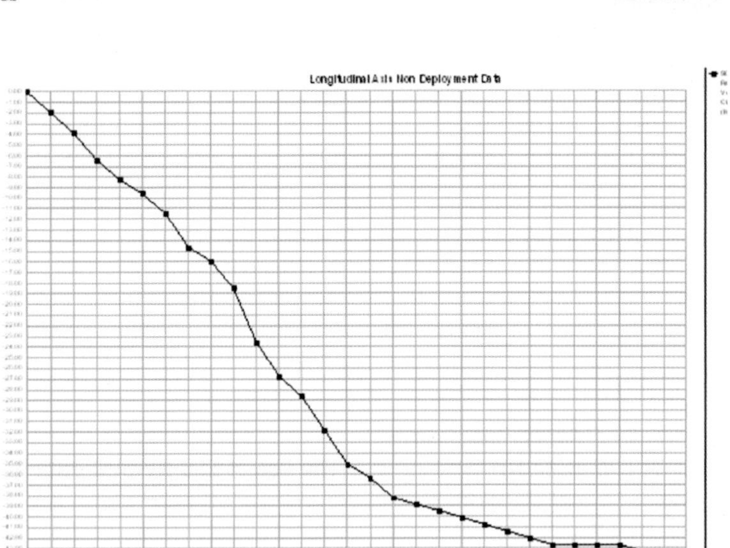

Figure 7 Typical integrated longitudinal Delta-V data as produced by the CDR post-processing software which translates the retrieved DPID data.

Figure 8 A data retrieval using a CDR direct connection to an SRS ECU.

consideration is the reliability and consistency of output data and the preservation of the source data for other investigators.

With respect to passenger vehicles and light trucks, there are public and proprietary retrieval tools which can retrieve EDR data and present that data both as hexadecimal bytes and as translated engineering values. The most common data-retrieval tool specifically designed for impact-data retrieval from select SRS ECUs and from select Engine ECUs is the Bosch/Vetronix CDR ® (crash data retrieval tool) and this tool is employed by most vehicle crash investigators. The CDR operates using a serial data interface to the vehicle diagnostic network (see **Figure 2**), and the CDR capabilities are available for specific vehicle application sets. There are CDR options for data retrieval from the J1962 port (OBD-II connector) or from an ECU directly, both employing a serial data interface.

While the CDR presents an orderly and tested means of EDR data retrieval, there are many vehicle models with NVRAM-incorporated ECUs (EDRs) not covered in the CDR application set. Many investigators, when confronted with non-CDR-covered vehicle do not pursue EDR data retrieval. Many manufacturers and EDR suppliers can access such non-CDR-coverage data with proprietary data retrieval tools; however, there is little if any public access to such proprietary tools. Additionally, when manufacturers and EDR suppliers provide data to other parties, that data can be seriously incomplete (or incompletely translated). For succeeding discussions, vehicles contained within the CDR application set are referred to as CDR-vehicles, and vehicles outside of the CDR application set are hereafter referred to as non-CDR-vehicles.

There are three options to retrieve EDR/ECU data.

Method 1. Via a vehicle serial data link communication path to the vehicle diagnostic communication port

Method 1 serial communications operate through the vehicle diagnostic connector (SAE J1962, OBD-II, connector) as described above. Often, the data retrieved via this method are DPID data, which is a representation of the actual raw NVRAM data, but not the actual NVRAM data itself. For direct access of the actual NVRAM data, there is usually a special mode and security feature incorporated into the serial access protocol – and this prevents general public access to the actual raw stored event-data (**Figures 5–7**).

Method 2. Via a serial data link communication path connected via a direct umbilical cable to the target ECU

Alternative serial communications operate via a direct umbilical cable to the EDR/ECU itself (also incorporating the security access feature). The direct-ECU umbilical method is invariably non-forensically neutral and can be non-conforming with ASTM E2493-07. That is because direct connections to the EDR/ECU generally present an incomplete system environment to the EDR/ECU and will often lead to test-induced data changes (e.g., generating DTCs for nonexisting sensors, squibs, etc.). Such violations of ASTM E2493-07 practices, when the investigation involves a litigation context, can lead to conditions considered as 'data spoliation' in that context (Figure 8).

Method 3. Via a direct umbilical to the EEPROM component on the printed circuit board within the EDR assembly

This method requires disassembly of the ECU to access the printed circuit board (PCB), cleaning the EEPROM component contacts with a solvent, and operates by using a direct electrical connection of the EEPROM device and an EEPROM reader. This process retrieves the raw binary data in Hexadecimal notation format. This process, while far more tedious and time-consuming than methods 1 and 2, overcomes the serial security access controls (by avoiding it entirely), retrieves the actual raw NVRAM binary data (in hexadecimal representation) and, also avoids the problem of test-induced data changes. Thus this process (as is method 1) is forensically neutral and in conformity with ASTM E2493-07. As this methodology works independently of serial data communications, it is especially valuable for non-CDR-vehicles. It has been demonstrated for retrieval of crash event data in EDRs on vehicles from domestic, European, and Asian manufacturers (Figures 9 and 10).

The Use of ECU NVRAM Data in Crash Investigations

Post-crash-event crash investigations involving those vehicles now typically utilize such EDR engineering data, and such

Figure 9 ECU disassembly and the direct EEPROM data retrieval process.

Figure 10 A portion of the raw hexadecimal data retrieved through a typical direct EEPROM data retrieval process. Note that in this case, the immediate ASCII translation shows the vehicle VIN as written to the EEPROM (The VIN was correct for the donor vehicle).

investigations now commonly reference data stored in various EDRs in both bullet and target involved vehicles. It is incumbent upon the investigator wishing to introduce such data as 'evidence' in the litigation process to be able to confirm to the Court that such 'evidence' is stated with reasonable engineering certainty, and that it meets certain clear tests for such admission. These tests are typically lumped under the umbrella terms, 'Frye Criteria' or 'Daubert Criteria.' These tests require that the retrieval, resultant translation, and interpretation of EDR data must:

1. Be founded on an underlying methodology of scientific tests, documentation of test results (charts, graphs, etc.), which have been reviewed by peers who have confirmed the reliability and acceptance of test methods. This can include refereed publication of tests and methods.
2. Be repeatable by any peer scientist/engineer using the conditions and/or data recorded in the subject tests. This means that other investigators must be able to repeat the subject tests and derive the same test results from the EDR at issue.
3. Have a reasonable error rate. This means that the error rate for the method employed is consistent and that is accepted by other practitioners in the field.
4. Be consistent with industry or commonly accepted standards that define or direct the tests and results postulated. This means that the procedures (methodology) must be compatible with applicable sections of ASTM E860, ASTM E1188, and ASTM E2493.
5. Pass a test of relevance and linkage to the facts at issue in the subject litigation. Obviously, the essence of the tests used must be consistent with the conditions of the accident under investigation, and the results presented must be relevant to the issues under consideration by the trier of fact (the Jury).

Acknowledgments

The author wishes to acknowledge Mr. Fred Chandler, Chandler & Sons Automotive, Herndon, VA, who contributed to many aspects of the testing and raw data retrieval work described herein.

See also: **Engineering:** Analysis of Digital Evidence; Forensic Engineering/Accident Reconstruction/Biomechanics of Injury/Philosophy, Basic Theory, and Fundamentals; Human Factors Investigation and Analysis of Accidents and Incidents; Investigation and Analysis of Structural Collapses.

Further Reading

Note: It is hoped that this introduction to EDRs encourages the reader to continue his or her research on the subject. To assist with that, several references for further reading are presented below.

American Society for Testing and Materials E1188–95 (1995) *Standard Practice for Collection and Preservation of Information and Physical Items by a Technical Investigator*. West Conshocken, PA: ASTM International 19428-2959.

American Society for Testing and Materials E860–97 (1997) *Standard Practice for Examining and Testing Items that Are or May Become Involved in Litigation*. West Conshocken, PA: ASTM International 19428-2959.

American Society for Testing and Materials E2493–07 (2007) *Standard Guide for the Collection of Non-Volatile Memory Data in Evidentiary Vehicle Electronic Control Units*. West Conshocken, PA: ASTM International 19428-2959.

Bosch/Vetronix, CDR® data retrieval tool Vehicle Coverage Information, can be found at Vetronix Corporation, 2030 Alameda Padre Serra, Santa Barbara, CA 93103-1716, USA, 1 800 321-4889, http://www.boschdiagnostics.com/testequipment/diagnostics/cdr/Pages/CDRHome.aspx.

Chidester A, Hinch J, and Roston T (2001) Real world experiences with event data recorders. In: *Proceedings of the 17th International Technical Conference on the Enhanced Safety of Vehicles (ESV) Conference*. Amsterdam, The Netherlands, 4–7 June 2001. Washington, DC: National Highway Traffic Safety Administration, DOT HS 809 220. Paper Number 247, 11 pgs.

Chidester A, Hinch J, Mercer T, and Schultz, K (1999) Recording automotive crash event data. National Highway Traffic Safety Administration Paper, *International Symposium on Transportation Recorders*, Arlington, VA, USA, May 3–5, 1999.

Gabler HC, Hampton CE, and Hinch J (2004) *Crash Severity: A Comparison of Event Data Recorder Measurements with Accident Reconstruction Estimates*. Glassboro, NJ: Rowan University; National Highway Traffic Safety Administration, Washington, DC. 8 p. Accident reconstruction 2004. Warrendale, SAE, 2004, p. 81–88. Report No. SAE 2004–01–1194. UMTRI-98091.

Gabler H, Hinch J, and Steiner J (2008) *Event Data Recorders – A Decade of Innovation*. Warrendale, PA: SAE International ISBN: 978-0-7680-2066-3, Product Code: PT-139.

Ishikawa H, Takubo N, Oga R, et al. *Study on Pre-Crash and Post-Crash Information Recorded in Electronic Control Units(ECUs) Including Event Datra Recorders*, National Research Institute of Police Science Japan, Paper Number 09-0375.

Kowalick Thomas (2004) *Fatal Exit: The Automotive Black Box Debate*. Wiley.

Murthy SK and Satish DA (n.d.) *Diagnostics for Automobiles – A Snapshot*. Bengaluru: Dearborn Electronics. http://www.deindia.com/images/downloads/whitepapers/Diganostcs_for_Automobiles-A_Snapshot.pdf.

Niehoff P, Gabler H, Brophy J, Chidester A, Hinch J, and Ragland C (2005) Evaluation of Event Data Recorders in FullSystems Crash Tests, National Highway Traffic Safety Administration, United States, Paper No: 05–0271.

Reust TJ (2004) The accuracy of speed captured by commercial vehicle event data recorders. Accident Science, Newhall, CA. 8 p. Accident reconstruction 2004. Warrendale, SAE, 2004, p. 115–122. Report No. SAE 2004–01–1199. UMTRI-98091.

Riling J (1995) Sensing and Diagnostic Module for Airbags, SAE Technical Paper, 952682, http://dx.doi.org/10.4271/952682.

Rosenbluth W (2001) *Investigation and Interpretation of Black Box Data in Automobiles: A Guide to the Concepts and Formats of Computer Data in Vehicle Safety and Control Systems*. The American Society for Testing and Materials (ASTM) and the Society of Automotive Engineers (SAE).

Rosenbluth W (2009) *Black Box Data from Accident Vehicles, Methods for Retrieval, Translation and Interpretation, ASTM Monograph 5*. West Conshocken, PA: ASTM International.

Rosenbluth W (2010) *Collecting EDR Data for Crash Investigations, Forensic Magazine*. Amherst, NH: Vicon Publishing.

Ruth R and Daily J (2011) *Accuracy of Event Data Recorder in 2010 Ford Flex During Steady State and Braking Conditions*. Detroit, MI: SAE 2011–01–0812.

Ruth R, West O, and Nasrallah H (2009) *Accuracy of Selected 2008 Ford Restraint Control Module Event Data Recorders*. Detroit, MI: SAE_2009–01–884.

Takubo N, Ishikawa H, Kato K, et al. (2009) *Study on Characteristics of Event Data Recorders in Japan; Analysis of J-NCAP and Thirteen Crash Tests*, SAE Technical Paper 2009-01-0883, http://dx.doi.org/10.4271/2009-01-0883.

Van Gaasbeck, Stephen (2007) *How to Challenge Black Box Data*, Trial Magazine, 01-FEB-07.

Relevant Websites

http://www.cdr-system.com – Crash Data Group: Crash Data Retrieval Tool.

Analog Tachograph Chart Analysis

RF Lambourn, Transport Research Laboratory, Wokingham, UK

Glossary

Odometer A device that displays the total distance traveled by a vehicle since its manufacture, usually incorporated in its speedometer.

Rolling road A set of rollers on which the wheels of a vehicle may be placed in order to test its speedometer.

Tachograph Device that records speed and distance traveled by a vehicle, primarily for the purpose of regulating a driver's hours of work and also of use in determining speeds, etc. in incidents.

Tachograph chart A stiff paper chart, usually circular, on which traces recording speeds, distances, and modes of work are scribed.

Introduction

The tachograph is a device fitted to motor vehicles, which makes a recording of the speed traveled and distance driven, together with details of the driver's periods of work and rest. Although found in vehicles worldwide, it is particularly used in the countries of the European Union (EU), where it is a requirement in most larger goods and passenger-carrying vehicles. Analog tachographs make this recording on a paper chart. However, in the EU, these devices are obsolescent, with vehicles registered from 2006 having to be fitted with digital tachographs that store the data electronically.

A note on digital tachographs will be found at the end of this article, but otherwise it is concerned only with analog tachographs and lays particular emphasis on the instrument as it is specified in EEC Regulations. However, the principles of chart analysis and the use of tachograph data described here are applicable to all types of analog device. In any case, the user of tachograph data must be aware of the characteristics of the particular make and model from which it comes, in order to appreciate the amount of information available and its limitations. The range of models is large, and this article cannot therefore cover every detail of every instrument that may be encountered.

The Forensic Use of Tachograph Data

Tachograph data have two main forensic applications:

1. in road accident investigation, to determine the speed at and immediately before an incident, the rate of braking, and the manner of driving;
2. in general criminal investigation, to find the route traveled and the time when a vehicle was at a particular location.

The Tachograph Chart

Figure 1(a) and **1(b)** shows typical paper tachograph charts, and illustrate the information provided by the instrument. The shape and design are not specified by the EEC Regulations, but the chart pattern shown here has become the standard for the industry. Other designs do exist, but the instruments that require them are obsolete.

The chart is a disk (123 mm in diameter) coated with a material that blackens under pressure. In the center is an area where the driver writes his name, the starting and finishing places for his day's driving, the date, vehicle number, and odometer readings.

Printed around the edge of the chart, and repeated further in, is the time scale of 24 h. Between these is the field where the speed is recorded, usually with a maximum of 125 km h^{-1}. Further in is the work-mode field, where the driver indicates whether he is driving, engaged on other work, or resting. The indication is made by either the track in which the recording line runs (**Figure 1(a)**) or the thickness of the line (**Figure 1(b)**). It is sometimes possible to extract useful information from the mode of work line when the vehicle has been moving very slowly.

The innermost recording is of distance, shown by a zigzag line. One stroke of this line is made during 5 km of travel; a complete V indicates 10 km of movement, whereas other distances will create partial strokes.

The Tachograph Instrument

Older models of tachograph combine their function with that of a speedometer in a single unit and are therefore designed to be mounted on a vehicle's dashboard in front of the driver. **Figure 2** shows such an instrument. More recent models, which are called 'modular,' have an appearance akin to a car radio or CD player and are located elsewhere in the cab, while being linked to a conventional speedometer. **Figure 3** shows an example of a modular tachograph.

Externally the older instruments (as in **Figure 2**) have the usual speedometer features – a speed dial and an odometer display – together with a clock and knobs with which the driver and a colleague can indicate their modes of work. (Most instruments hold two charts to cater for there being two drivers crewing the vehicle.)

In these instruments, the chart usually lies behind the face, which is hinged to open downward to allow insertion and removal. **Figure 4** shows an open instrument with a chart about to be inserted. The spindle on which it is mounted rotates once in 24 h. When the instrument is closed, the chart bears against three styluses that move up and down to make

 http://dx.doi.org/10.1016/B978-0-12-382165-2.00145-8

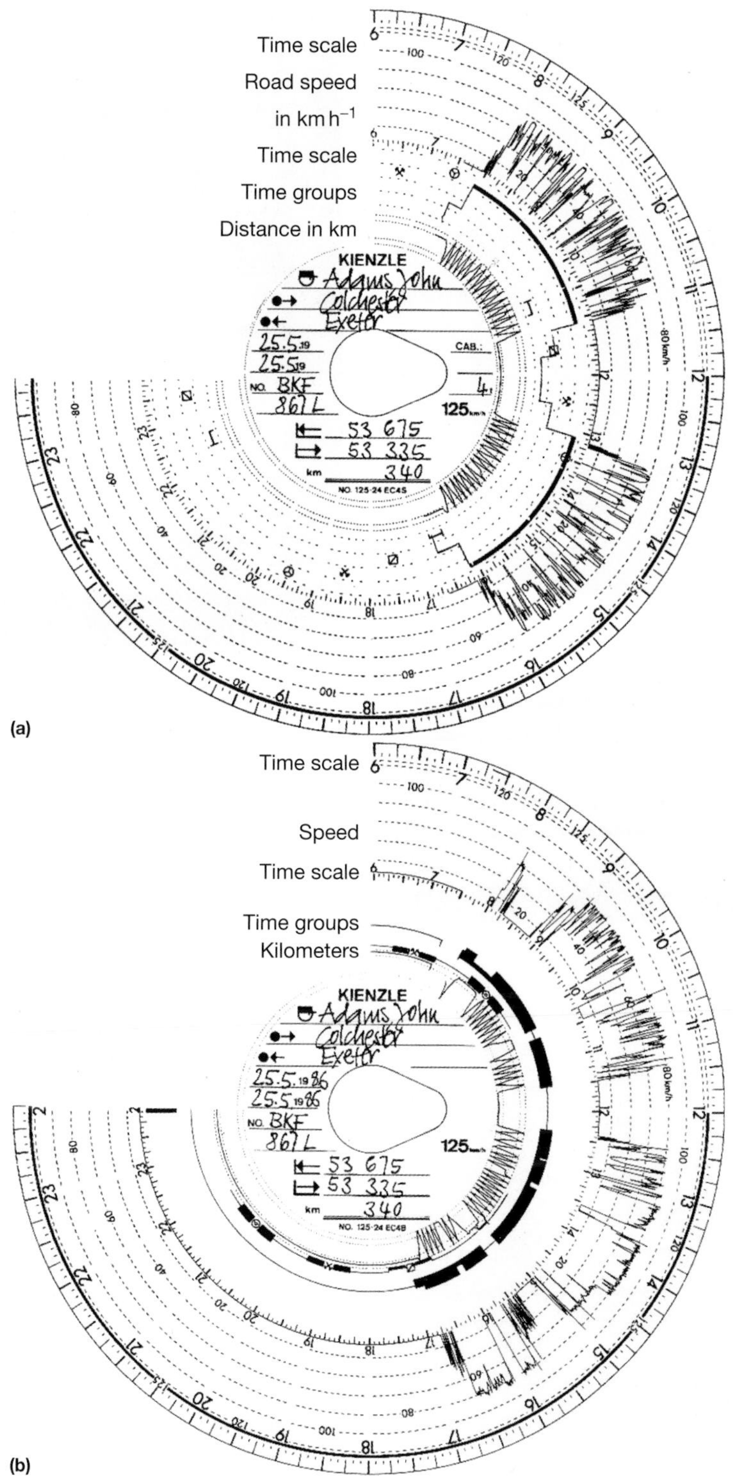

Figure 1 Tachograph chart showing recordings with (a) 'manual' time group recordings and (b) 'automatic' time group recordings (Continental Automotive Trading UK Ltd.).

the recordings. The spindle and the hole in the center of the chart are oval to ensure the correct orientation of the chart with respect to time.

With the modular instrument in **Figure 3**, the charts are placed on a tray where, when it is pushed into the body of the instrument, they are brought into contact with the recording styluses. **Figure 5** shows a modular instrument with the tray open and a chart in place.

Tachographs may operate either mechanically or electronically. Mechanical types, in which a rotating cable from the

Figure 2 The face of a Veeder Root model 8400 tachograph.

Figure 3 The Kienzle MTCO 1324 modular tachograph. The lower part is the drawer onto which the chart is placed.

Figure 4 An opened Kienzle model 1318 tachograph showing the insertion of a chart.

Figure 5 An opened Kienzle MTCO1324 tachograph with a chart placed on the drawer.

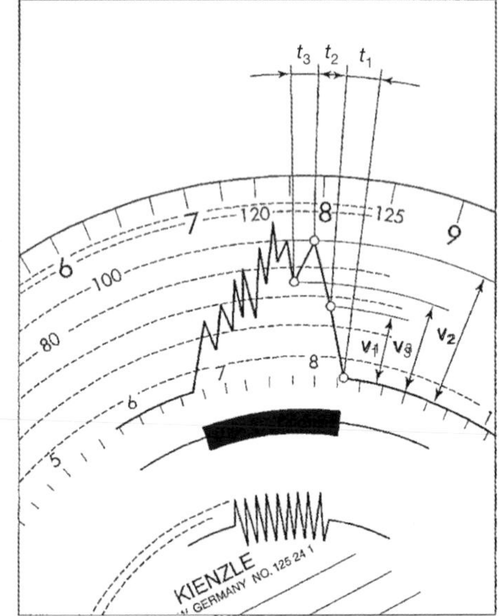

Figure 6 Schematic speed trace showing time intervals and speeds.

vehicle gearbox drives a cup-and-magnet system, are now rarely seen. Typical models are the VDO Kienzle TCO1311 and the Veeder Root 1111. Electronic types receive a train of pulses from a transducer at the gearbox, the frequency of which is translated as speed. There are many models: examples of the unitary type being Motometer EGK100, Jaeger G.50, VDO Kienzle TCO1314 and TCO1318, and Veeder Root 8300 and 8400; and of the modular type being Kienzle MTCO1324 and Stoneridge (Veeder Root) 2400.

The Principles of Chart Analysis

Figure 6 shows a schematic tachograph trace and the quantities to be measured in an analysis. The speed trace is thought of as a series of points connected by straight lines. The speed at each point (v_1, v_2, v_3) is measured, as are the time intervals between them (t_1, t_2, t_3). This provides a plot of speed against time, which can then be integrated to yield a plot of speed against

Table 1 Data from tachograph chart shown in **Figure 7**: the analysis points *a*, . . ., *i* run backward from the end of the driving

Point	*Speed (km h^{-1})*	*Time (s)*	*Distance (m)*
a	–	0	0
b	81	0	0
c	61	32	630
d	38	67	1110
e	71	83	1355
f	71	87	1435
g	40	111	1805
h	39	116	1860
i	19	122	1905

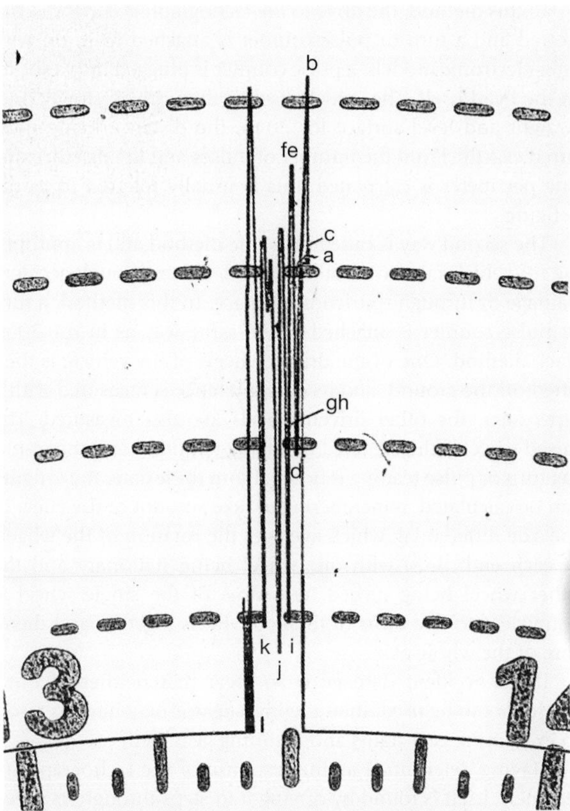

Figure 7 A real tachograph speed trace with analysis points.

distance. **Figure 7** shows a real tachograph trace, **Table 1** shows the tabulated analysis, and **Figure 8** shows the resulting plot. (This trace and analysis is used for the case example at the end of this article.)

There are various approaches to making these measurements. Taking the speed from the chart is relatively straightforward and can be done from a photographic enlargement or with a traveling microscope. Allowance has to be made for the accuracy of the speed recordings. Measurement of the time intervals is, however, not at all easy. Because the chart rotates just once in 24 h, 1 min occupies only 0.25°, and in 1 s it turns through only 15 s of arc. It is usual to mount the chart beneath a microscope on a rotating table that is turned by a micrometer.

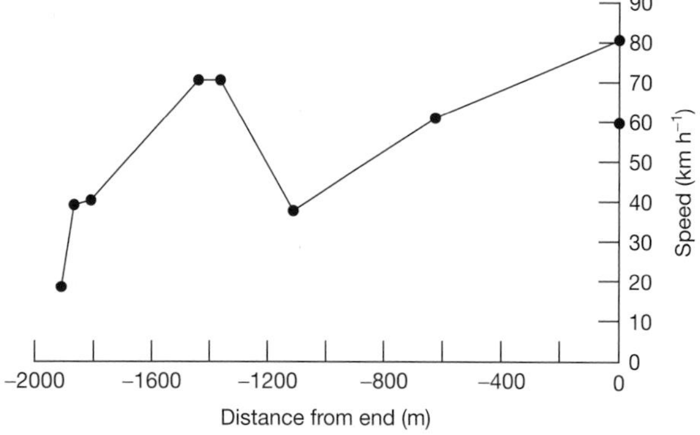

Figure 8 Plot of speed data from **Figure 7** against distance.

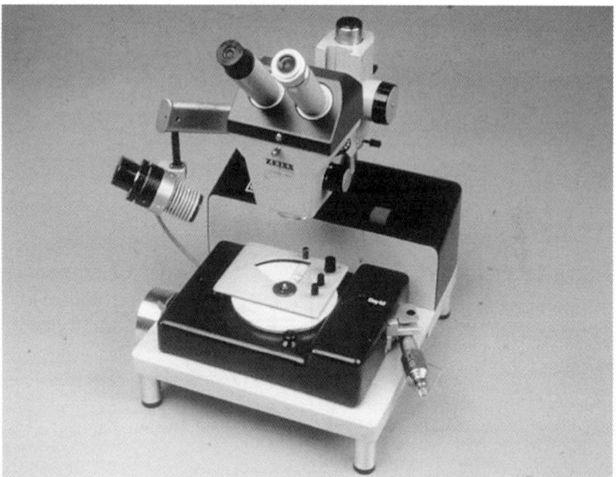

Figure 9 The Kienzle microscope with computer-linking modifications.

Figure 9 shows one such microscope, as produced by VDO Kienzle. A glass plate etched with a vertical cursor line, 3 μm wide, lies over the chart, and this combines with a horizontal line in one eyepiece to form a 'crosswire' in the field of view. Points for measurement are brought successively under the crosswire by rotating the chart table and moving it backward and forward, and transducers are attached to these two movements. Signals from the transducers, which are interpreted as time and speed, are fed to a microcomputer, where listings of these quantities and graphs of speed versus time and distance are produced.

It is very important to recognize, when measuring time intervals, that the line along which the recording stylus moved was unlikely to have passed exactly either through the center of rotation of the chart when mounted on the microscope or when mounted in the tachograph instrument, or through the geometric center of the chart itself. This is illustrated in an exaggerated form in **Figure 10**. If the vertical cursor is not arranged such that it lies along the line on which the stylus moved, any time intervals measured between points at different speeds will be in error. In the VDO Kienzle microscope, the glass plate carrying the cursor line can be swiveled about a point at the outer edge of the chart, and this adjustment is used to set the line in what the analyst judges to be the correct position.

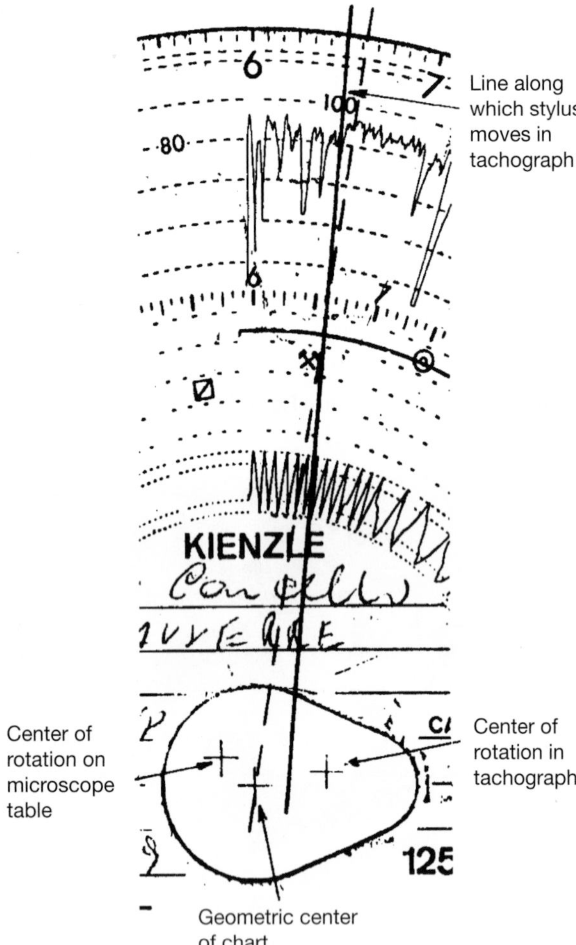

Figure 10 The need for an adjustable cursor when analyzing a chart.

The Accuracy of the Speed Record

The EEC Regulations require that having been installed and calibrated, the analog tachograph record may not have an error in its speed figures greater than ± 6 km h^{-1}. The analyst may be content to use this as a probable error figure, but the author's experience is that although the error is generally not greater than ± 3 km h^{-1}, there are occasional cases where it is substantially more than ± 6 km h^{-1}. It is therefore desirable that the calibration in each case be checked, and various methods have been devised for this.

Calibration Checks on the Tachograph Installation

The most straightforward method of checking the accuracy of a tachograph system is to employ a 'rolling road' of the sort used when tachographs are installed in vehicles. A chart is placed on the instrument, and the vehicle is then effectively driven through a range of known speeds. The chart will then show how each speed is recorded, from which the amount of error is found.

Some agencies find the rolling road method quite inconvenient, and instead use a method that requires no special facilities and that can be employed in any open space. The procedure is in two stages: first, the signal sent from the vehicle's gearbox is measured (either as pulses per kilometer in electronic systems or turns per kilometer in mechanical ones) in one of two ways, and the second, the way the tachograph instrument responds to a known set of input signals is found.

The first of the two ways of measuring the signal is called the 20-m track and is one that may actually be used by some installers. It is fully described in manuals produced by tachograph manufacturers for the guidance of their agents. It is appropriate for vehicles that can be moved slowly in a straight line; thus, they need not be fully mobile, and may have, for example, accident damage to the steering gear or the engine coolant system. The test can even be performed by towing the vehicle.

In this method, the drive to the tachograph is either disconnected and a turn or pulse counter is attached to it, or, with later electronic models, a pulse counter is plugged into a socket in the head itself. The vehicle itself is then driven slowly on a straight and level surface for 20 m, the distance being measured exactly. From the number of pulses and the distance, the rate per meter is calculated: this is usually referred to as the w figure.

The second way is called the static method and is appropriate for vehicles that cannot be moved, either through accident damage or through restriction of space. In this method, a turn or pulse counter is attached in the same way as in the 20-m track method. One of the driven wheels of the vehicle is then lifted off the ground, and its circumference is measured with a tape; later, the other driven wheels are also measured. The raised wheel is then rotated manually ten times and the resulting turn or pulse reading is noted. From these data, the w figure can be calculated, remembering to take account of the effect of the axle differential, which averages the rotation of the wheels at each end: thus, with one wheel being stationary and the other wheel being turned, ten turns of the single wheel is equivalent to five turns of the two wheels together and therefore of the whole axle.

If the accident damage is so great that neither of these methods can be used, then the investigator may have to resort to examining gear trains and counting gear teeth.

Having determined w, the response of the tachograph instrument itself is found by driving it in steps through its speed range with a sequence of signals generated by a specially constructed test unit. These units are produced by the tachograph manufacturers for the use of their installation agents, and display either the mechanical rotation rate or the electronic pulse rate (in units of min^{-1}). A new tachograph chart is put in the instrument, and a test chart similar to that in **Figure 11** is produced.

The sequence of tests in **Figure 11** is given as follows:

1. The instrument is taken up to its maximum speed (140 km h^{-1} in this example) and then very quickly back to zero to check the straightness of the recording stylus movement.
2. This is repeated three times.
3. Next, the instrument is taken to an indicated speed of 60 km h^{-1}: at this speed the input figure (in min^{-1}) is known as the characteristic coefficient or k figure, and

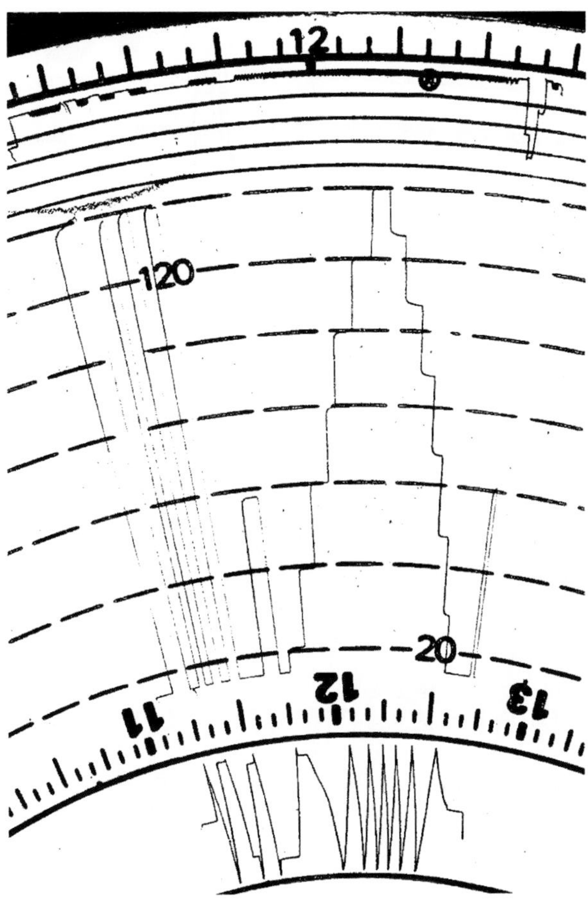

Figure 11 A typical head test chart.

should be, in a correctly calibrated system, approximately equal to the w figure of the vehicle.

4. The speed is taken from zero up to the maximum in 20 km h^{-1} steps, holding each step for 2 min, and then back down to zero at the same speed between the steps (130 km h^{-1}, 110 km h^{-1}, etc.).
5. Finally, the instrument is run at 60 km h^{-1} for as long as it takes 1 km to be recorded on its odometer, and the actual number of turns or pulses delivered is noted: this should equal the κ figure. During the last test, the activity mode switch is also changed through its four settings.

The information from part (4) of the test can now be used, together with the w figure, to construct a graph of how the recording on the chart at any point relates to the true speed. This can be done manually or by using the software associated with the Kienzle computer-linked microscope.

The 'Route-Trace' Method of Calibration

An alternative to the direct methods of calibration is the so-called route-trace method. This can only be used when the route the vehicle has taken is known and is particularly appropriate when the vehicle is unavailable for testing or has been so seriously damaged as to make the other methods impossible. The tachograph record can also be used to find the route that a vehicle has taken (see Route Tracing below). The calibration method is an inversion of this procedure and briefly involves attempting to match the recorded pattern of driving to the known route. A system that is in calibration will give an immediate match, whereas one that is out of calibration will require an adjustment of its speed by some factor before the match is found. Thus, the calibration method is one of finding what this adjustment factor is.

Problems of Interpretation

Once the cursor on the analyzing microscope has been correctly aligned and the errors, if any, in the speed record have been determined, the chart can be analyzed. However, the limitations of the recording and the individual instruments must be recognized.

Time Intervals

The clock in most tachograph instruments advances the chart in 1-s step, and it is, therefore, not possible in principle to measure the time at a particular point on the chart with a precision greater than ± 1 s. When measuring the interval between two points, the precision can therefore never be greater than ± 2 s. In any case, the edge of the speed recording trace is insufficiently smooth for these steps to be resolved. With a good trace, a confidence of ± 2 s can probably be assumed, but in some instruments an unsteadiness will be evident, which means that wider uncertainty must be accepted. It is found that although some manufacturers' instruments yield consistently good traces, other manufacturers produce tachographs that are invariably poor.

Figure 12 shows an example of a poor trace. The drive train from the clock to the chart is somewhat loose, and allowing a generally unsteady speed trace as the stylus moves up and down, it permits the stylus, as it falls after rising to a maximum, to track back along the groove it has made on the chart instead of drawing a new line. This effectively drives the clock backward for a few seconds (20 s being typical) until the slack is taken up, and only then the stylus will start to follow a new track.

In some tachographs, severe steering or swerving may cause the recording trace to deviate, and a likely example appears in **Figure 13**, where the period of perfectly constant speed, which can be seen just before the final descent of the trace to zero speed, was probably caused by a swerving action that made to chart shift slightly within the instrument.

Impacts to the Vehicle

A severe impact to the vehicle will generally produce a disturbance of the tachograph recording traces (**Figures 7** and **13**). When such a disturbance is apparent on the speed trace, it is obviously an indication of the speed of the vehicle at the moment of impact and is an item of the information easily read from the chart. However, some caution is needed before interpreting it. The disturbance was properly caused by a shock to the tachograph itself, and its magnitude therefore depends on the proximity of the impact to the instrument. A collision with a pedestrian, where the pedestrian meets the vehicle very close to the instrument panel, can cause a clear disturbance,

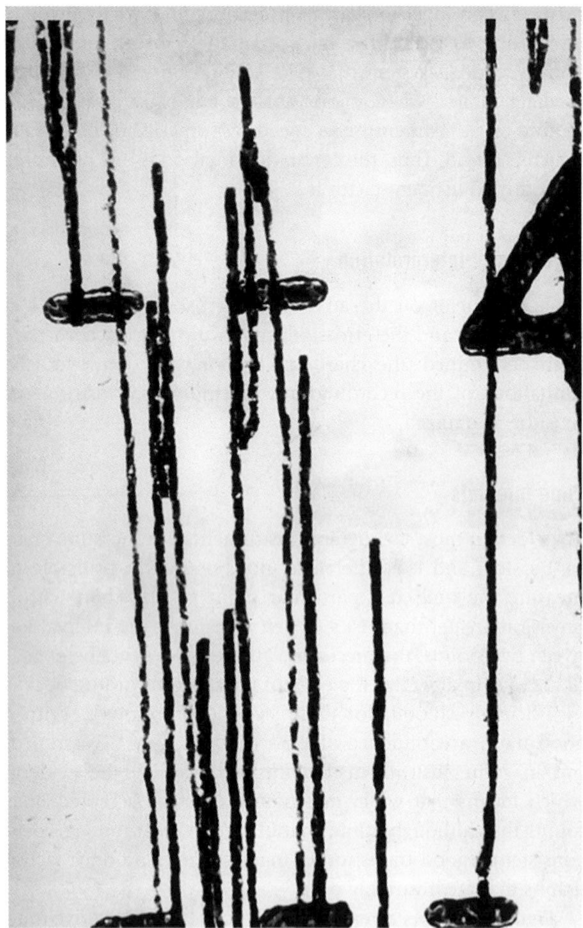

Figure 12 An unsteady trace from a Jaeger mechanical instrument.

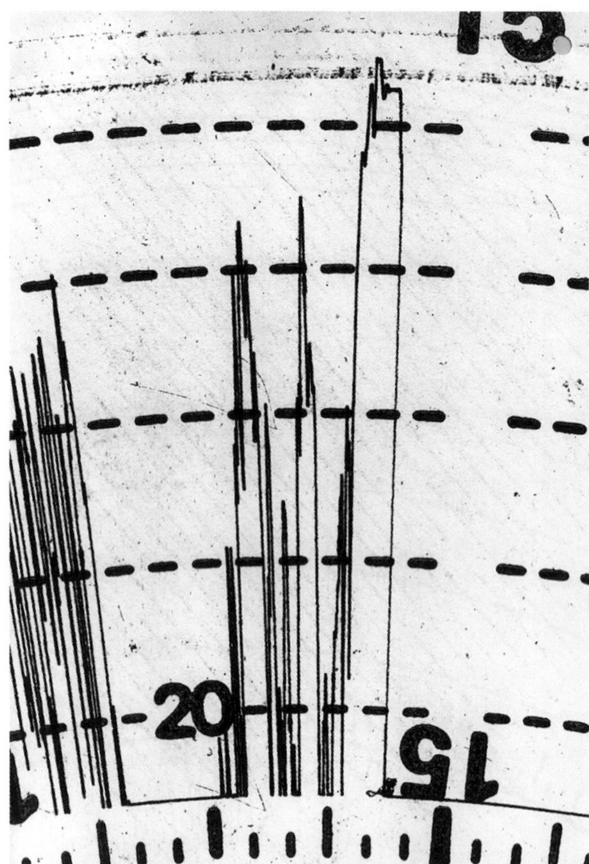

Figure 13 Chart showing lock-up followed by impact at zero speed.

whereas a severe impact from another vehicle to the rear of an articulated lorry may have little or no effect on the recording.

If heavy braking is taking place at the time of the impact, the speed at which the disturbance appears may be affected by other factors.

Finally, a severe impact will often derange the instrument for at least a few seconds, such that little or no reliance can be placed on any features that may immediately follow it.

Response of the Instrument

The EEC Regulations require tachograph instruments to be able to follow 'acceleration changes' of 2 m s^{-2}. Since during braking the deceleration of a vehicle may well be as much as 7 m s^{-2}, there is the possibility that the speed-recording stylus may not be able to keep up with the changing speed. This does not, in fact, appear to be a problem in Kienzle, Motometer, Jaeger, and mechanical Veeder Root tachographs, but there is a difficulty with older electronic Veeder Root instruments.

Earlier Veeder Root 1200 and 1400 series tachographs only just met the 2 m s^{-2} requirement; early 8300 series models had a response of 2.5 m s^{-2}, whereas later 8300 series and all 8400 series models have a response of 5.7 m s^{-2}. The consequence of a response of 2 or 2.5 m s^{-2} is that during heavy braking, the speed being recorded at any moment will be greater than the true speed, and any event recorded during the braking, for example an impact, will be shown at too high a speed. It also means that it is not possible for an analyst to give an opinion as to whether a particular piece of braking was at a normal or an emergency rate.

A response of 5.7 m s^{-2}, however, is much closer to the braking rate, which can be expected of a lorry in an emergency, and will generally allow a reasonable speed for an impact to be recorded.

An even higher response rate leads to a difficulty where there has been a wheel slip during braking.

Tire Slip Effects

The tachograph records the speed of rotation of the wheels to which it is connected, almost always the driven wheels of the vehicle. Therefore, if for some reason those wheels slip, that is, rotate at a speed that does not correspond to the speed of the vehicle over the ground, then the recording will be in error.

Wheel slip particularly occurs during heavy braking, notably when the driven wheels lock. An instrument with a fast response will react to wheel locking as though the vehicle had instantaneously come to a halt: the stylus will fall very quickly to its base position even though the vehicle is still traveling forward, and an impact may even appear to have been at zero speed. An example is shown in Figure 13, where, because the vehicle has skidded, the prominent impact feature will certainly be at a level much lower than the true speed. The operation of an antilock braking system will also cause the speed of the wheels to be less than the road speed of the vehicle.

The opposite can occur if one of the driven wheels lifts off the road, allowing it to spin. This typically occurs as a vehicle starts to roll onto its side. In **Figure 14**, the speed at C would appear to be that at which the accident has occurred. In fact, the correct speed is at B, from which the trace has jumped to C, as the wheels on one side of the lorry lifted from the road.

Low-Speed Behavior

Incidents at low speed cause particular problems in the interpretation of tachograph data because all instruments have a level below which they do not record speed. In all current models, this is about 5 km h^{-1}, although in some older instruments it is somewhat higher, up to 16 km h^{-1}. Therefore, it can neither be said, for example, whether a vehicle that has slowed before entering a main road actually stopped or merely reduced its speed to, say, 5 km h^{-1} before proceeding nor may it be possible to say whether or not during an apparent stationary period the vehicle was moved a small distance.

Some information can, however, be gained from the mode-of-work trace. Movement of the vehicle generates a thicker line, made by an oscillation, or an increased oscillation, of the recording stylus (see the examples in **Figure 1**). A small gap in the thick line can be taken as a brief stationary period. The threshold for this thick line depends on the model. Mechanical instruments will produce a noticeable movement in the stylus only when the vehicle has moved for about 20 m or more. Electronic instruments have a critical speed at which the line is made. The mode trace in Kienzle 1318 and 1319 instruments, however, operates during driving in the same way as the zigzag distance trace, making one stroke over a distance of 50 m.

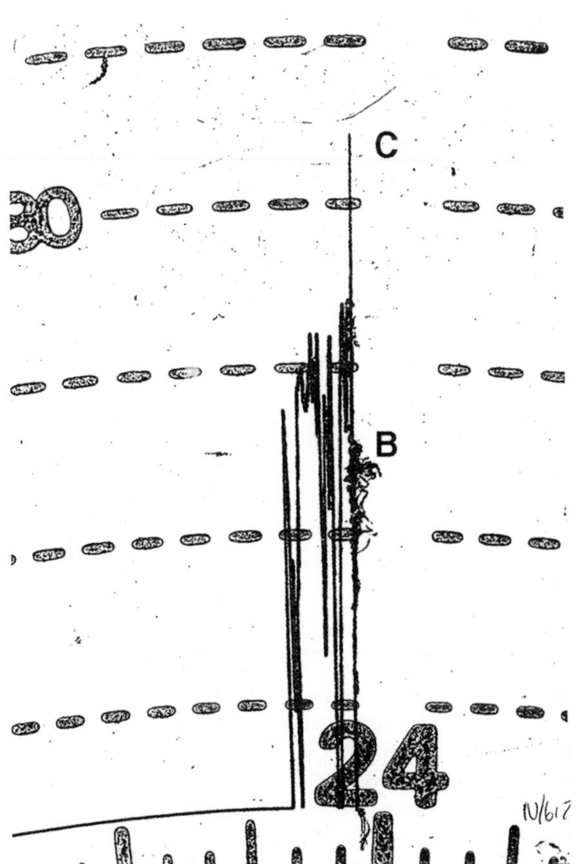

Figure 14 Spin up in roll-over.

Falsifications and Diagnostic Signals

Tachographs have always been prone to attempts by drivers to falsify the recordings, to show either lower speeds or shorter hours of work. Most falsifications are readily apparent on careful examination, for example, by comparing the apparent average speed during a journey with the recorded distance and the time taken, or by comparing the total recorded distance for the day's driving with the difference in the hand-written odometer figures. **Figure 15** shows a commonly attempted falsification, where driving has stopped at 1736, the clock has been rewound, and driving has resumed, apparently earlier, at 1623.

The scope for such tampering is greatly increased with electronic instruments, and therefore, various 'diagnostic' features are incorporated in them to show when certain irregularities occur. These depend on the individual models of instrument, and a full account of them is beyond the scope of this article. However, two examples are as follows.

If the pulse sender is disconnected in an attempt to make it appear that the vehicle is not being driven, the speed stylus will oscillate between zero and, typically, 30 km h^{-1} to make a broad band (**Figure 16**).

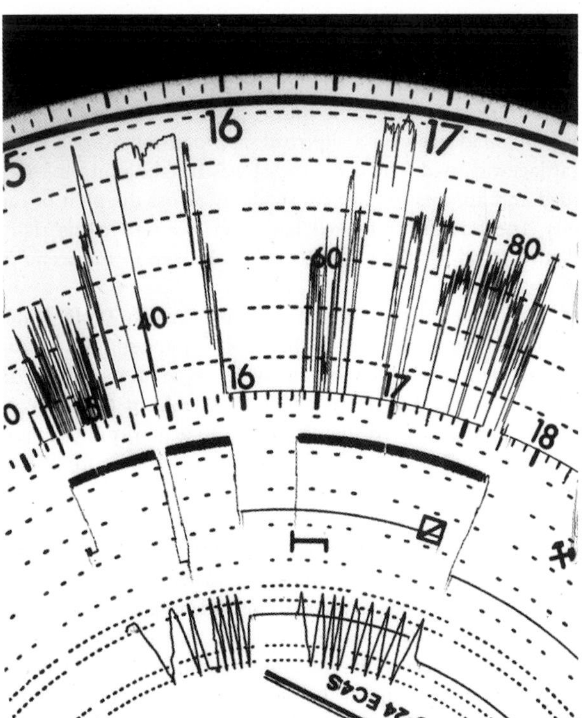

Figure 15 Fraudulent rewinding of tachograph clock. The overlapping traces show that the time was turned back from 1736 to 1623 h.

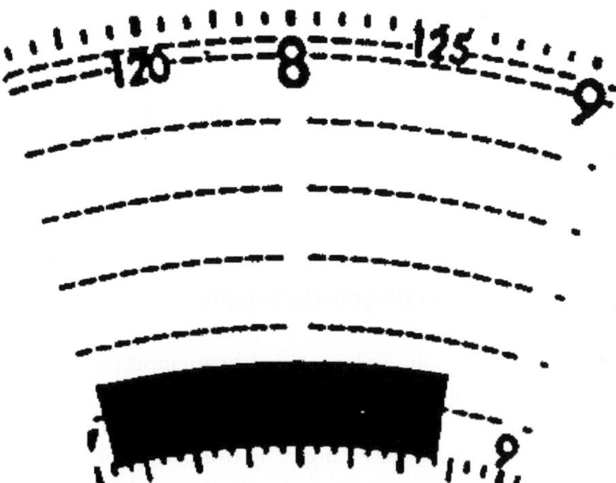

Figure 16 Broad trace generated when speed transducer is disconnected.

If the electrical supply to the instrument is interrupted, in an attempt to halt recording for a period, then, on reconnection, the speed stylus will execute a characteristic movement, for example, a full-scale deflection or a dip to zero speed.

Other attempts at falsification, that can be more difficult to detect, include connecting the wires from the pulse sender to earth; reducing the voltage to the tachograph, such that the clock continues to operate but the other electronic systems fail; and connecting certain spare terminals on the back of the instrument together, again to cause some of the electronic functions to fail.

Case Example

Figure 7 is an enlarged section of a tachograph recording made by a tourist bus that came into collision with a pedal cycle. The bus had been on a slip road, approaching a main dual-carriageway road. The pedal cyclist was traveling on the main road and appears to have cut suddenly across the path of the bus. The bus driver braked hard and swerved to his right. **Figure 17** shows the route the bus had taken to the scene of the accident.

The results of the detailed analysis, given in **Table 1** and plotted in **Figure 8**, indicate that (point *i*) about 120 s before the accident the speed of the bus was at a minimum of 19 km h^{-1} and that it was about 1900 m from the scene of the accident. Its speed then increased to a maximum (points *f* and *e*) of 71 km h^{-1} before falling to another minimum (point *d*) of 38 km h^{-1}. It was then about 67 s and 1110 m from the end.

Again the speed increased, reaching its final maximum (point *b*) of 81 km h^{-1} immediately before the collision. There was then heavy braking to a sudden disturbance of the trace (point *a*), which on the chart is at an indicated speed of 60 km h^{-1}. However, the time interval between *a* and *b* is too small to measure, and at the scene, locked wheel skid marks were found from the rear wheels on one side of the vehicle. The rapid fall of the recording trace between the last two points has clearly occurred as a result of the locking of these driven wheels, which accounts for the immeasurably small time interval and also means that the figure of 60 km h^{-1} (because of the characteristics of the particular instrument) is probably significantly less than the speed at which the disturbance occurred.

The disturbance itself consists of a thickening of the trace, caused by a small shock to the stylus, followed by a step to the left (i.e., 'backward' in time). The shock would have been caused by the impact at the front of the bus with the pedal cycle, whereas the sudden swerve would have brought about some sideways movement of the components of the tachograph instrument, to create the step to the left.

Route Tracing

The two minima of speed in **Table 1** lie at distances from the end, which, on an accurate map, can be readily identified with a roundabout (point *d*) and an intersection (point *i*). When the analysis is extended back to the start of the driving, two further minima and the start of the journey itself can be matched to a complex road junction and two more roundabouts (points *j*, *k*, and *l* in **Figure 7**). Some very slow driving before point *i* indicates that the bus started its driving from a place just before the roundabout.

In the context of a road accident, the matching of the trace to a known route serves to confirm the accuracy of the analysis process and of the calibration of the tachograph installation. If it had not been possible to check the calibration independently, this matching, with any necessary adjustment of the speed figures, could have been used as a calibration procedure in itself.

However, if it is imagined that, in different circumstances, the route of the vehicle was unknown, and there was a need for it to be found, it can be seen that working back from the known end point (*a*), it would be possible to do so by comparing distances between speed minima with distances on a map between road junctions. A typical case where this method is applied would be where a vehicle carrying a valuable load is stolen from a known location *X*, driven to an unknown place *Y* and unloaded, and then driven to a third place *Z* and abandoned. From its tachograph record, it may be possible to locate *Y* by tracing back from *Z* or forward from *X*. The success of this method depends on traffic conditions; in heavy traffic, the vehicle may have had to stop so many times at places other than road junctions, where following its route becomes impossible.

Digital Tachographs

EEC Regulations now require that from May 2006, all tachographs fitted to vehicles that fall within their scope be of the digital rather than analog type. Digital tachographs make their recording on a removable 'smart card' rather than a paper chart, although a printer within the instrument also provides a summary of some of the data on a paper strip. Digital tachographs have similarities with the event data recorders (EDRs) fitted to some vehicles. Current models of digital tachograph include Siemens VDO DTCO1381, Stoneridge SE5000, and Actia SmarTach L2000.

Figure 17 Section of Ordnance Survey map showing route of vehicle as determined from the tachograph recording in **Figure 7** (Crown copyright reserved).

The specifications to which they all conform require, among other things, that speed is recorded with a resolution of 1 Hz and that the smart card holds the record for the last 24 h of driving (not simply the last 24 h of time). The 1 Hz record of earlier driving is deleted, although simplified data are still held on times and distances traveled and maximum speeds. But manufacturers may choose to exceed the specifications, and, for example, the Siemens VDO DTCO1381 holds a record of the speed at 4 Hz for the *xx* seconds preceding the last stop made by the vehicle.

The reader is referred to EEC Regulation 1360/02, manufacturers' literature and the article on EDRs for further information.

See also: **Engineering:** Accident Investigation – Determination of Cause; Electronic Data Recorders (EDRs, Black Boxes).

Further Reading

EEC (1985) Council Regulation (EEC) no. 3821/85. *Official Journal of the European Communities* L370: 8–21.

EEC (2002) Council Regulation (EEC) no. 1360/02. *Official Journal of the European Communities* L207: 1–252.

Lambourn RF (1985) The analysis of tachograph charts for road accident investigation. *Forensic Science International* 28: 181–199.

Lehmann H (1992) Die mikroskopische Diagrammscheibenauswertung für die Unfallrekonstruktion (Microscopic analysis of tachograph charts for accident reconstruction). *Verkehrsunfall und Fahrzeugtechnik* 1: 2–4.

Lowe D (1989) *The Tachograph*, 2nd edn. London: Kogan Page.

Needham P (1988) Tachograph chart computer-linked microscopic analysis. *Forensic Science International* 36: 211–218.

Wach W, Unarski J, and Duś A (2005) Tachograph chart – Analysis of intensive braking recording. *Technical Paper 2005-01-1185*. Warrendale, PA: Society of Automotive Engineers.

Human Factors Investigation and Analysis of Accidents and Incidents

SA Shappell, Embry-Riddle Aeronautical University, Daytona Beach, FL, USA
DA Wiegmann, University of Wisconsin, Madison, WI, USA

Glossary

Decision errors These errors represent intentional actions that proceed as intended, but the plan proves inadequate or unsuitable for the situation. Usually, they are related to knowledge, problem solving, and procedural errors, such as improper procedure, exceeded ability, and poor decision.
Error Normal accepted behavior that fails to meet the desired outcome.
Human Factors In 2000, the International Ergonomics Association defined ergonomics (human factors) as "the scientific discipline concerned with the understanding of interactions among humans and other elements of a system, and the profession that applies theory, principles, data, and other methods to design in order to optimize human well-being and overall system performance."
Perceptual errors These errors can occur when the operator has perceived features of the environment inaccurately (sensory degradation); the misperception could be visual, auditory, olfactory, etc. Mostly they are related to detection, awareness, and understanding errors, such as distance misjudgments and visual illusion.
Skill-based errors These errors represent unintended/ unconscious behaviors of operators, which usually occur in the operator's execution of a highly practiced task relating to procedure or a routine. In general, they are related to attention failures, memory lapses, and inadequate techniques, such as an omitted step in procedure, an omitted checklist item, and poor technique.
Violation Refers to the willful disregard of accepted practices and norms within a field of endeavor. The keyword is willful; that is, the individual knew what the accepted practice was but chose to ignore it.

The need to manage human error comes as no great revelation to anyone involved in operations where the consequences of failure are dire. Truth be told, however, the 'battle cry' that human error is associated with some 60–80% of all accidents/ incidents in complex, high-risk systems has become passé in many organizations. The reason behind this attitude is that human error statistics have not changed appreciably in more than half a century. While safety professionals can all agree that something 'must' be done to reduce errors, a growing number of executives in the boardroom are becoming skeptical of the idea that something actually 'can' be done.

So where does one start when managing human error? Most quality and safety professionals are very familiar with the traditional system safety approach illustrated in Figure 1. While there are many variants to the approach, most involve the following components: collecting relevant data, identifying and assessing hazards, identifying/developing interventions, assessing intervention feasibility, implementing intervention, and system monitoring/program evaluation. Ideally, this is a dynamic process involving the real-time identification of threats, deployment of interventions, and, hopefully, improvements in the process.

Historically, this traditional approach to system safety has been effective in addressing mechanical and engineering problems within a variety of operational contexts; however, it has been facilitated by the development of a set of engineering tools and techniques for implementing each step. Not surprisingly, given the success of system safety in the engineering world, many quality/safety professionals have been quick to adopt this same approach when attempting to manage complex human factors issues.

Unfortunately, the requisite tools and techniques for employing system safety concepts within human factors have been largely ineffectual or nonexistent. As a result, it has been virtually impossible to get beyond the first step in the process – data collection. In fact, when an accident or incident does happen, the most common response is to simply collect more data. However, merely gathering more data about the occurrence of errors is 'not' the solution. In fact, most quality and safety departments are already swimming in data, particularly given the recent advances in technology that have increased the amount of information available.

As a result, those tasked with solving the human error dilemma have become frustrated with just watching the 'data bucket' fill up while having no means to interpret the information contained within the bucket. After all, implementing intervention programs that improve safety is the ultimate goal, and one should not confuse data collection with interventions.

Rather than systematically analyzing the aggregate data for significant trends, the modus operandi of many organizations has been to simply 'cherry pick' the hazards identified in the most recent incident or focus on select 'high profile' events that have captured everyone's attention, thereby bypassing the next two critical steps in the system safety process and jumping right on to identifying interventions (see Figure 2). However, these may have no real bearing on the more significant systemic hazards.

To make matters worse, there are few tools for systematically generating effective intervention programs that target specific forms of human error. Consequently, quality/safety professionals have been forced to bypass two more crucial steps in the safety management process – generating and

 http://dx.doi.org/10.1016/B978-0-12-382165-2.00146-X

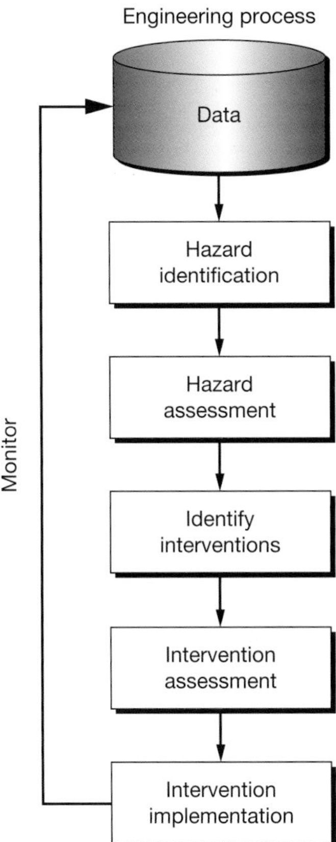

Figure 1 The safety management process.

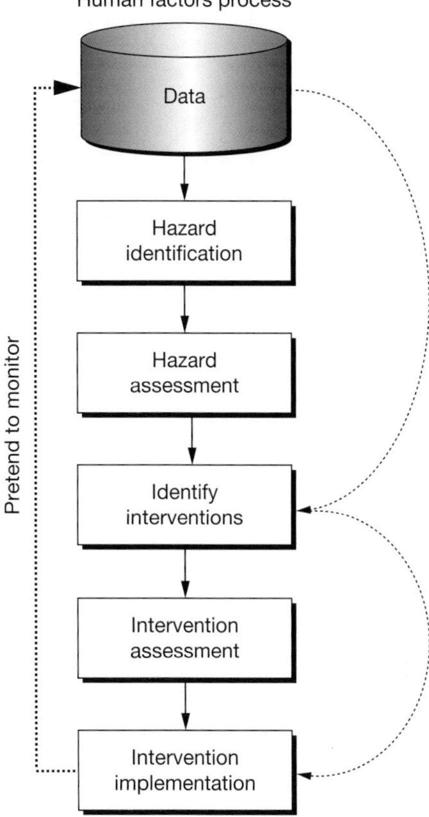

Figure 2 Lack of effective human factors tools results in key steps in the safety process being skipped.

evaluating intervention strategies (see Figure 2). Indeed, the typical process for ginning up error prevention programs is to use simple intuition, expert opinion, or 'pop psychology.' Unfortunately, such an approach often results in people pushing their pet projects, or the person with the highest authority having the last say on what gets done. Hence, this entire system engineering approach to human error management, although conceivably a good idea, has met with little success.

Over the last decade, human factors psychologists and engineers have been working on ways to improve the human factors system safety process by developing human factors tools and techniques. The remainder of this article describes one of the tools born out of aviation accident investigation to facilitate error identification and intervention development within the context of forensic science.

HFACS – A Human Factors Investigative Tool

It is generally accepted that human error is not the isolated act of a particularly unlucky individual. Rather, it is the result of a chain of events that often culminate in a less than desired outcome. This is not particularly new, as industry has embraced a sequential theory of human error for nearly a century. However, some would argue that it was not until James Reason published his 'Swiss cheese' model of human error in 1990 that industry truly began to examine human error in a systematic manner.

Reason's approach to error causation is based on the assumption that there are fundamental elements of all organizations that must work together if safe and efficient operations are to occur. Taken together, these elements comprise a 'productive system' as depicted in Figure 3. For example, forensic analysis can be viewed as a complex productive system whose 'product' is the identification and classification of forensic evidence. These so-called 'productive activities,' in turn, require the effective integration of human and mechanical elements within the system, including, among other things, an effective scientist–laboratory interface to ensure optimal performance.

Even before productive activities can occur, certain 'preconditions,' such as reliable and well-maintained equipment and a well-trained and professional workforce, need to exist. After all, most analysts work within a highly structured organization that requires effective middle management and careful supervision. Furthermore, such management and supervision is needed across numerous departments within the larger organization. But even the best managers need guidance, personnel, and money to perform their duties effectively. This support comes from decision makers who work even further up the chain of command, charged with the responsibility of setting goals and managing the available resources of the organization.

In most organizations, this highly structured and orchestrated system functions well. However, what about those rare occasions when the wheels do come off? According to Reason, accidents occur when there are 'breakdowns' in the interactions

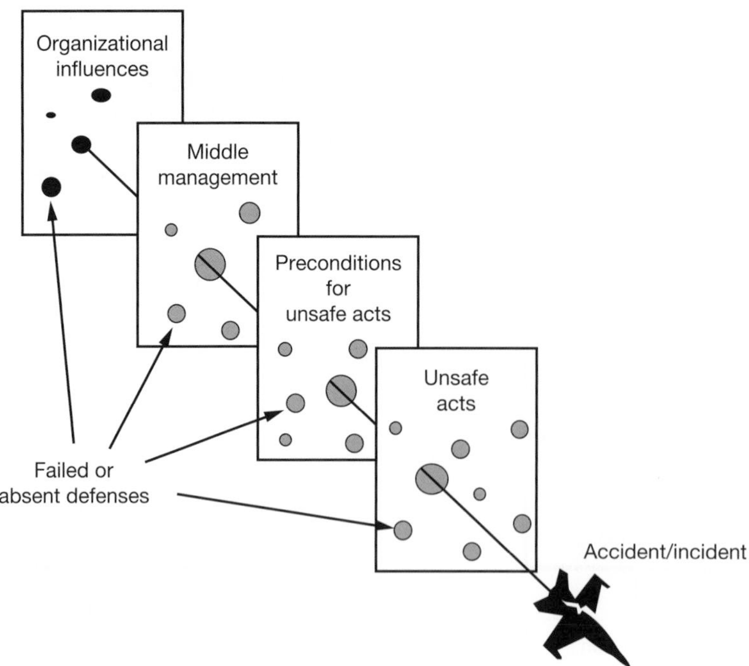

Figure 3 Components of a productive system.

among the components involved in the production process. These failures degrade the quality of the system making it more vulnerable, and hence more susceptible, to erroneous conclusions. As illustrated in **Figure 3**, these errors can be depicted as 'holes' within the different layers of the system, which transform what was once a productive system into a failed or broken-down process. Given the image of Swiss cheese that this illustration generates, the theory is often referred to as the 'Swiss cheese' model of error causation.

So, what are those 'holes in the cheese' or failure points in the system? Drawing upon Reason's concept of latent and active failures, the Human Factors Analysis and Classification System (HFACS) describes human error at each of four levels: (1) the actions of the operators (e.g., bench-level scientists and field investigators in forensics), (2) the preconditions for those actions (i.e., the conditions that influence human behavior), (3) the middle management (i.e., the individuals whose role it is to assign work), and (4) the organization itself.

In other words, the HFACS framework goes beyond the simple identification of 'who did what wrong' to provide a clear understanding of the reasons 'why' the error occurred in the first place. In this way, errors are viewed as consequences of system failures and/or symptoms of deeper systemic problems, and not simply as the fault of the examiner whose fate was tied to being at the 'pointy end of the spear.'

HFACS was originally developed and used as an aviation accident investigation and analysis tool for the U.S. Navy and Marine Corps. Since then, the framework has been adopted by a number of other aviation, transportation, and high-risk industries. More recently, HFACS has been modified by the Expert Working Group on Human Factors in Latent Print Analysis chartered by the National Institute of Standards and Technology for use in forensic science. The brief discussion that follows is a product of that effort.

Analyst Actions

The actions of the forensic analyst can be loosely classified as either errors or violations (see **Figure** 4). While both can occur within most settings, they differ markedly when the rules and regulations of the scientific field are considered; that is, while errors represent normal accepted behavior that fails to meet the desired outcome, violations refer to the 'willful' disregard of accepted practices within the field. It is within these two overarching categories that HFACS describes three types of errors (decision, skill-based, and perceptual) and types of violations.

Decision errors

Successful decision making depends upon three fundamental ingredients: (1) information – that is, information (e.g., fingerprints, DNA) must be of high quality and other variables such as the surface from which the evidence was obtained must be known; (2) knowledge – analysts must have the necessary knowledge, training, and background to reliably assess the information provided; and (3) experience – there is ample evidence in the literature that suggests that experience also contributes to decision making. Ultimately, when information, knowledge, or experience is lacking or degraded, errors can occur. Often referred to as honest mistakes, errors typically manifest as poorly executed procedures, improper choices, or simply the misinterpretation and/or misuse of relevant information (see **Table 1**).

Skill-based errors

In contrast to decision making, skill-based behavior occurs with little or no conscious thought. For instance, little thought goes into turning one's steering wheel in an automobile or

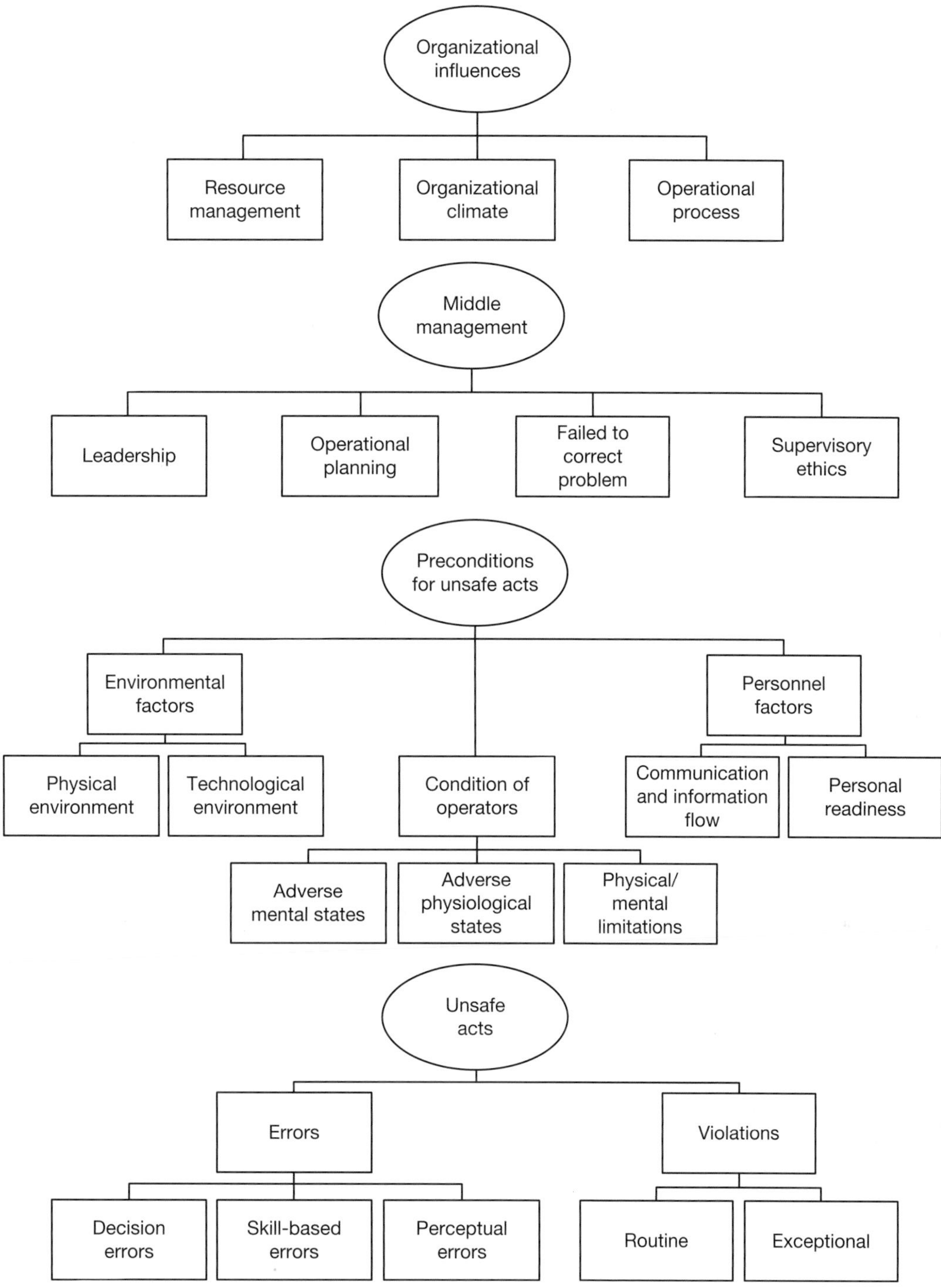

Figure 4 The Human Factors Analysis and Classification System (HFACS).

typing on a keyboard. Likewise, in latent fingerprint examination, most analysts orient latent prints for examination with little or no conscious thought. In other words, they do not have to think about it – they just do it. The difficulty with these highly practiced and seemingly automatic behaviors is that they are particularly susceptible to attention and/or memory failures. Unfortunately, even the technique or 'skill' with which we do a task can lead to erroneous conclusions (see **Table 1**).

Perceptual errors

While decision and skill-based errors are the most common error forms seen in occupational settings, perceptual errors may also impact the forensic laboratory. No less important, these 'perceiving' errors arise when sensory input is degraded, or 'unusual.' For example, latent fingerprint analysis is a decidedly visual comparison task that requires optimal visual conditions to insure accuracy and reliability. Consequently, laboratory environmental factors such as the intensity, type, and

Table 1 Selected examples of analyst actions

Errors	*Violations*
Decision errors	
• Improper orientation of data	• Intentionally issue an unsupportable conclusion
• Print improperly deemed unsuitable	• Failure to follow SOPs
• Printer improperly deemed suitable	• Refusal to use available technology
• Improper anatomical source of data	• Consistently failed to mark a difficult print
• Poor target group selection	• Consistently conduct an incomplete search
• Hurried examination	• Failed to maintain objectivity
• Thorough analysis not conducted	
• Incomplete search	
• Failure to search all exemplars	
• Misprioritized level of effort	
• Failure to use available technology	
• Conclusion exceeded ability of examiner	
• Insufficient data to support conclusion	
• Failure to recognize exemplars are insufficient/inadequate	
Skill-based errors	
• Poor search technique	
• Incomplete comparison due to failure of memory	
• Incomplete comparison due to attention failure	
• Failure to recognize distortion (i.e., variation in appearance)	
• Failure to properly weigh the significance of the data	
• Failure to find target	
• Inability to reach a conclusion	
• Misinterpreted the data	
• Distraction	
Perceptual errors	
• Failure to perceive due to poor contrast	
• Visual illusion in print	

Note: This is not a complete listing.

direction of lighting can influence what an analyst perceives as key features of a print. When confronted with less than ideal conditions, an analyst may perceive that there is more or less information in a given print than there actually is (see **Table 1**).

Violations

Although there are many ways to distinguish between types of violations, two forms have been identified based on their etiology. The first, routine violations tend to be habitual by nature and are often enabled by a system of supervision and/or management that tolerates such departures from the rules. Often referred to as 'bending the rules,' the classic example is that of the individual who drives his/her automobile consistently 5–10 mph faster than allowed by law. While clearly against the law, the behavior is, in effect, sanctioned by local authorities (police) who often will not enforce the law until more excessive speeds are observed. What's more, speeding on the interstate is something that most people do, and often it becomes a 'routine' part of the individual's behavior.

In contrast, driving at 120 mph in a 55-mph zone would be considered an exceptional violation. It is important to note, that while most exceptional violations tend to be particularly dangerous, they are not considered 'exceptional' because of their extreme nature. Rather, they are regarded as exceptional because they are neither typical of the individual(s) nor condoned by management. In essence, they are 'exceptions' to normal behavior.

Unfortunately, depending on the setting and conditions an individual is faced with, what may be a routine violation in one organization or situation may be an exceptional violation in another. For instance, driving 5–10 mph over the speed limit on a US interstate may be condoned by local authorities and is done by most people, while driving that same 5–10 mph over the posted speed limit in a school zone certainly would not be condoned nor does everyone do it. Likewise, depending on the given laboratory procedure, a violation may be perceived as routine (everyone does it) or exceptional (rarely occurs). Often, the actual causal factor (e.g., failure to follow standard operating procedures (SOPs)) is the same in both categories, only the circumstances surrounding the violation are different. Consequently, all violations are simply included within one category as shown in **Table 1**.

Preconditions Analyst Actions

Simply focusing on errors, however, is like focusing on a medical patient's symptoms without understanding the underlying disease state that caused it. As such, investigators must dig deeper into the preconditions for why errors occurred. Within HFACS, seven causal categories within three major subdivisions are described (see **Figure 4** for an illustration and **Table 1** for examples within the forensic sciences) (**Table 2**).

Adverse mental states

It is well known that human performance is affected by the mental state of the individual. Attitudes such as frustration, anger, and even misplaced motivation have all led to decision

Table 2 Selected examples of preconditions of unsafe acts

Condition of analyst	*Personnel factors*	*Environmental factors*
Adverse mental states	*Communication and information flow*	*Physical environment*
• Overconfidence	• Failure to convey adequate information	• Workspace design
• Lack of confidence	• Failure to use all available resources	• Inadequate lighting
• Distraction	• Lack of teamwork	• Inadequate ventilation
• Mental fatigue	• Confusing/conflicting directions/demands	• Noise interference
• Apprehension with reaching a conclusion	• Inadequate communication with management	• Excessive heat or cold
• Preoccupation with personal problems	• Inadequate communication between shifts	• Clutter
• Task overload	• Lack of communication	*Technological environment*
• Frustration	• Standard terminology not used	• Inadequate/outdated
• Channelized attention	• Lack of report writing skills/poor documentation	• Software or equipment
• Complacency	*Fitness for duty*	• Defective equipment
• Misplaced motivation	• Lack of sleep	• Defective tools
• Stress	• Self-medicating with prescription or over-the-counter medications	• Inadequate information technology
• Expectancy	• Use of illicit drugs and alcohol	• Confusing manuals
• Boredom	• Suffering from hangover	
• Anger	Inadequate nutrition	
• Peer pressure	• Reporting for work in ill-health	
• Haste		
• Bias		
• Compromised integrity/ethics		
Adverse physiological states		
• Medical illness		
• Impairment due to drugs or alcohol		
• Physical fatigue		
• Eye strain		
Physical/mental limitations		
• Performance limiting physical condition		
• Visual limitations		
• Dyslexia		
• Color vision deficiency		
• Chronic psychological disorder		
• Incompatible intelligence/aptitude		
• Limited experience/proficiency		

Note: This is not a complete listing.

and skill-based errors when not recognized and addressed by individuals. Likewise, cognitive states such as inattention, distraction, and task overload have all resulted in a variety of errors. Indeed, one of the more insidious adverse mental states is fatigue and stress associated with many occupations. Consider, for example, a forensic analyst who is called to a crime scene in the middle of the night and is then expected to show up the next day to attend to his or her normal caseload. Can management reasonably expect performance to remain at optimal levels? Likewise, the stress associated with working through large backlogs with limited resources or unrealistic quotas and turn-around times set by well-meaning, but uninformed, managers can lead to errors.

Adverse physiological states

Equally important, however, are those adverse physiological states that affect performance. The traditional work environment for many forensic scientists includes a standard desk, a magnifier or two, general lighting, and a variety of specialized tools with the analyst bent over a desk sifting through evidence to draw their conclusions. The strain on the neck and back can be considerable and may impact their performance. Likewise, many comparisons today are performed utilizing computer monitors, which may expose the analyst to monitor glare, resulting in headache or eyestrain. Medical illness is also known to have an impact on performance; yet, people sometimes go to work with illnesses, such as a cold, migraines, or the flu, or worse, they are self-medicating with remedies that can adversely influence their decision-making ability.

Physical and/or mental limitations

Physical/mental limitations include those instances when an individual simply may not possess the necessary aptitude, physical ability, or skill to conduct an examination adequately. After all, just as everyone cannot play linebacker for his or her favorite professional football team or be a concert pianist, not everyone has the aptitude or physical attributes necessary to be a forensic examiner. Moreover, physical and mental aptitudes change as we age. Left unabated, normal aging processes can adversely influence performance.

Communication and information flow

Communication and information are essential to case management. The analyst must effectively work with a variety of analysts, managements, investigators, and attorneys. Indeed, coordination among multiple 'players' (i.e., analysts, detectives, and the district attorney) is essential in case management. Poor communication will drastically reduce gathering of the necessary information that may affect casework. Case documentation is another mode of communication critical during technical review and for archival purposes.

Fitness for duty

Individuals, must, by necessity, ensure that they are adequately prepared for work. Consequently, this category was created to account for those instances when examiners do not get enough rest, report to work when ill, or take medications that may impair their ability to perform their duties.

Physical environment

The term physical environment refers to things such as heat and lighting toxins in the workplace, all of which are well known to impact human performance.

Technological environment

The technological environment that individuals often find themselves in can also have a tremendous impact on their performance. The term technological environment encompasses a variety of issues including the design of equipment and controls, display/interface characteristics, checklist design, and automation, to name a few. One needs to look no further than the design of automobiles to see poor design influencing performance. After all, who has not tried to turn on the lights in a rental car only to see the wipers engage instead? Similar design flaws in the laboratory can be catastrophic. Whether one is having difficulty operating a DNA sequencer or dealing with flawed software, how one designs equipment can have a dramatic influence on analyses and interpretation of complex results.

Middle Management

Ultimately, analysts and those at the front lines of forensic science are responsible for their actions. However, in some instances, they are the unwitting recipients of a variety of latent failures attributable to those who manage them. To account for these threats to quality, the overarching category of 'supervision' was created within which four categories (leadership, operational planning, failure to correct known problems, and supervisory ethics) are included (**Table 3**).

Leadership

At a minimum, supervisors must provide the analysts in their charge the opportunity to succeed. Toward these ends, it is expected that effective leaders will provide analysts with adequate training, professional guidance, oversight, and operational leadership, and that all will be managed appropriately. When this is not the case, examiners can become isolated, thereby increasing the likelihood that errors will occur. For example, it is not difficult to imagine a situation where a manager becomes so overwhelmed with answering e-mail, attending telecons, preparing countless presentations, etc. that they fail to provide sufficient oversight of their analysts.

Table 3 Selected examples of middle management

Inadequate supervision
- Lack of appropriate incentives
- Inadequate performance measurement evaluation
- Unrealistic expectations
- Insufficient initial or ongoing training
- Inadequate assessment of required skills
- Failure to track job qualifications/skills
- Lack of coaching/training on skills
- Change introduced without training
- No measurement of training effectiveness
- Inadequate leadership job knowledge
- Inadequate monitoring of work
- Personality conflicts between manager and employee
- Failed to provide professional guidance/oversight
- Failed to set a proper example

Operational planning
- Unclear/conflicting assignment of responsibility
- Inadequate communication of policy, procedure, practices, and/or guidelines
- Improper/insufficient delegation of work
- Setting objectives, goals, or standards that conflict
- Improper/insufficient delegation of work
- Setting objectives, goals, or standards that conflict
- Failure to provide adequate rest breaks
- Inadequate matching of individual qualifications and job/team requirements
- Unrealistic deadlines or quotas
- Inadequate documentation

Failed to correct a known problem
- Failure to correct known workplace hazard
- Improper performance is rewarded or tolerated
- Failure to correct inappropriate behavior (hostile work environment)
- Failure to initiate corrective actions
- Failure to correct known reportable problem
- Failure to update/revise operator guidelines, policies, and procedures

Supervisory ethics
- Management implied haste
- Undue influence toward a desired outcome
- Violation of operating guidelines, policies, and procedures by a manager
- Manager encourages bending of the rules
- Enabling excessive risk taking
- Failure to enforce rules and regulations
- Fraudulent documentation

Note: This is not a complete listing.

In the end, the employees are left with little guidance and oversight, as the 'phantom manager' is lost in an electronic world of corporate demands. In contrast, some supervisors take oversight to extremes, becoming overcontrolling and more concerned with minute details rather than the accuracy of the work. In effect, by micromanaging their analysts, decision making is often delayed, information flow between employees is often restricted, and overall confidence and efficiency can be diminished.

Operational planning

The risks associated with failures of management and supervisors come in many forms. For example, occasionally the operational tempo and/or schedule are planned such that individuals are put at unacceptable risk and, ultimately, performance is adversely affected. As such, the category of operational planning was created to account for all aspects of improper or inappropriate scheduling practices, which may involve such issues as, rest breaks, workload, deadlines, etc. Consider, for example, the supervisor who assigns a complex case to a junior or less-experienced analyst rather than someone with more experience who may be more capable. In some ways, the supervisor may 'set up' the analyst for failure. Likewise, it is not uncommon for supervisors and management to continue to 'go to the well' and overload the high performer while ignoring those who are less capable or difficult to work with. In either event, the top performers are often burdened with additional work and in some circumstances may be prone to error when they would otherwise perform optimally.

Failure to correct known problems

The remaining two categories of unsafe supervision, the failure to correct known problems and supervisory ethics, are similar, yet considered separately within HFACS. The failure to correct known problems refers to those instances when deficiencies among analysts, equipment, training, or other related safety areas are 'known' to the supervisor, yet are allowed to continue uncorrected. For example, the failure to consistently correct or discipline inappropriate behavior fosters an unsafe atmosphere but is not considered a violation if no specific rules or regulations were broken. Similarly, there are times when optimal equipment is not purchased or necessary repairs are not done on existing equipment, yet the mission can still be carried out – just not as efficiently or without undue burden on analysts.

Supervisory ethics

This category is reserved for those instances when supervisors willfully disregard existing rules and regulations. While everyone would agree that putting undue influence on forensic analysts toward a desired outcome is clearly an example of poor supervisory ethics, more subtle ethical violations can result in adverse outcomes in the forensic laboratory. For instance, permitting unqualified forensic analysts to do casework can lead to errors that may go unnoticed. Likewise, encouraging the bending of rules and procedures in the interest of reducing backlogs is a classic failure of supervisory ethics.

Organizational Influences

Where decisions and practices by laboratory supervisors and managers can adversely impact forensic analyst performance, fallible decisions of upper-level management may directly affect the supervisors and the personnel they manage. Unfortunately, these organizational influences often go unnoticed or unreported by even the best-intentioned quality assurance personnel. Within this tier, the HFACS framework describes three organizational failures: (1) resource management, (2) organizational climate, and (3) operational processes (**Table 4**).

Resource management

This category refers to the management, allocation, and maintenance of organizational resources, including human resource management (selection, training, and staffing), monetary budgets, and equipment design (ergonomic specifications). In general, corporate decisions about how such resources should

Table 4 Selected examples of organizational influences

Resource management
- Selection of personnel
- Inadequate evaluation, promotion, upgrade policies
- Inadequate hiring, firing, and promotion policies
- Staffing/manning issues
- Inadequate matching of qualifications for job
- Use of inadequate contractor/vendor
- Ineffective cost cutting
- Unfunded directives
- Lack of logistical support
- Failure to correct known design flaws
- Purchasing unsuitable equipment/parts

Organizational climate
- Inaccessibility/visibility of upper management
- Inadequate formal accountability for actions
- Unclear/conflicting assignment of responsibility
- Dysfunctional organizational culture
- Organizational values not clearly defined or articulated

Organizational process
- Work/production schedules that produce bad decisions
- Overextending resources
- Unrealistic quotas
- Organizational induced time pressure
- Lack of appropriate standards, policies, or guidelines
- Procedures not integrated into training process
- Quality process not adequately implemented/maintained
- Inadequate/inappropriate performance measures
- Failure to maintain accreditation

Note: This is not a complete listing.

be managed center around two distinct objectives – the quality of the analyses and on-time, cost-effective operations. In times of prosperity, both objectives can be easily balanced and satisfied. However, there may also be times of fiscal austerity that demand some give and take between the two. Unfortunately, history tells us that quality is often the loser in such battles, as quality improvements and training are often the first to be cut in organizations experiencing financial difficulties.

Organizational climate

The concept of an organization's climate has been described in many ways; however, here it refers to a broad class of organizational variables that influence worker performance. For example, one telltale sign of an organization's climate is its structure, as reflected in the chain of command, delegation of authority and responsibility, communication channels, and formal accountability for actions. Likewise, an organization's policies and culture are also good indicators of its climate. Consequently, when policies are ill-defined, adversarial, or conflicting, or when they are supplanted by unofficial rules and values, confusion abounds, and safety suffers within an organization.

Operational process

Finally, operational process refers to formal processes (operational tempo, time pressures, production quotas, etc.), procedures (performance standards, objectives, etc.), and oversight within the organization. Poor upper-level management and decisions concerning each of these organizational factors can also have a negative, albeit indirect, effect on operator performance and system safety.

Using HFACS to Identify and Address Threats to Quality and Safety

As described earlier, identifying what went wrong without fully understanding why it happened can lead to ineffective interventions/mitigation strategies. Consider, for example, a forensic analyst who inadvertently forgets to document a key step in the analysis, leading to an erroneous conclusion. On the surface, management might view such an error as unforgivable and resort to some form of admonishment or worse. However, without knowing 'why' the analyst forgot to document the key step, one cannot recommend a practical intervention apart from one that may appease those looking for some degree of accountability.

On the other hand, had a full human factors analysis been conducted, management might have uncovered the following:

1. *The analyst had been working overtime for several consecutive days (operational planning) in an attempt to relieve an extensive backlog of cases that had accumulated leading to fatigue (adverse mental state) and stress (adverse mental state).*
2. *The analyst had recently welcomed their first baby into the family and was still not sleeping through the night while off-duty (fitness for duty).*
3. *With the holidays fast approaching, the analyst was busy making holiday travel plans including airline reservations, with a newborn and conflicting work schedules, thereby compounding the stress he was undergoing (adverse mental states).*
4. *Due to budget cuts (resource management), the staff was reduced by 20% resulting in an increase in workload (adverse mental state) without necessary support.*
5. *In an effort to reduce the workforce, management chose to offer the employees early retirement as an incentive to retire, resulting in the more experienced analysts retiring early (resource management).*
6. *The analyst who forgot to document the key step in the analysis was relatively new, with little experience in the field (physical/mental limitation) and would not ordinarily be tasked with such a complex and high-profile case (operational planning).*
7. *Because of the reduced staffing and increased workload (resource management), the analyst was not provided necessary training (leadership) and was given minimal oversight (leadership) during the investigative process.*

Arguably, such a scenario would likely change management's view of the necessary steps to prevent this sort of event from happening again. Moreover, punishment for such a transgression clearly would not have prevented the error from occurring in the future. Indeed, it is well known that one cannot punish one's way out of an error. If anything, punishment drives reporting underground and hampers safety and quality.

What makes frameworks such as HFACS effective is that each of the causal categories is based upon years of human factors research and has very specific interventions associated with it. For example, if one is trying to address decision errors, effort should be aimed at ensuring that useful and complete information is available, and that the analyst has acquired the knowledge to deal with the information through training and the requisite experience to know when he or she may need additional training or assistance. Likewise, if one were trying to address skill-based errors, efforts should be aimed at reducing distractions, ensuring that critical items are addressed through either checklists or other memory aids and that the initial and recurrent training is sufficient to ensure the skill and proficiency of the analyst.

Closing Thoughts

The field of human factors accident investigation and quality management is a rich and growing discipline with a history dating back decades. Recently, with the integration of tools such as HFACS into traditional system safety models, management in general and forensic management in particular are better able to identify and address heretofore unknown human causal factors. Of note, however, while special emphasis was placed on HFACS in this short article, there are many other tools and techniques available to those interested in human factors accident investigation.

The interested reader is encouraged to reach out to organizations such as the Human Factors and Ergonomics Society at www.hfes.org for more information.

See also: **Engineering:** Railroad Accident Investigation and Reconstruction.

Further Reading

Australian Transport Safety Bureau (2007) Human factors analysis of Australian aviation accidents and comparison with the United States. *ATSB Transport Safety Investigation Report*, B2004/0321.

Baysari MT, McIntosh AS, et al. (2008) Understanding the human factors contribution to railway accidents and incidents in Australia. *Accident; Analysis and Prevention* 40: 1750–1757.

Beaubien JM and Baker DP (2002) A review of selected aviation human factors taxonomies, accident/incident reporting systems and data collection tools. *The International Journal of Applied Aviation Studies* 2: 11–36.

Celik M and Cebi S (2009) Analytical HFACS for investigating human errors in shipping accidents. *Accident; Analysis and Prevention* 41: 66–75.

Dambieer M and Hinkelbein J (2006) Analysis of 2004 German general aviation aircraft accidents according to the HFACS model. *Air Medical Journal* 25(6): 265–269.

Dekker S (2006) *The Field Guide to Understanding Human Error*. Aldershot, Great Britain: Ashgate Publishing Company.

Dismukes K (2009) *Human Error in Aviation*. Aldershot, Great Britain: Ashgate Publishing Company.

ElBardissi AW, Wiegmann DA, et al. (2007) Application of the human factors analysis and classification system methodology to the cardiovascular surgery operating room. *The Annals of Thoracic Surgery* 83: 1412–1419.

Gaur D (2005) Human factors analysis and classification system applied to civil aircraft accidents in India. *Aviation, Space, and Environmental Medicine* 76(5): 501–505.

Heinrich HW, Petersen D, and Roos N (1980) *Industrial Accident Prevention: A Safety Management Approach*, 5th edn. New York: McGraw-Hill.

Iden R and Shappell S (2006) A human error analysis of U.S. fatal highway crashes 1990–2004. *Proceedings of the 50th Annual Meeting of the Human Factors and Ergonomics Society*, San Francisco, CA.

Jennings J (2008) Human factors analysis and classification: Applying the Department of Defense system during combat operations in Iraq. *Professional Safety* 44–51.

Krulak DC (2004) Human factors in maintenance: Impact on aircraft mishap frequency and severity. *Aviation, Space, and Environmental Medicine* 75(5): 429–432.

Li W-C and Harris D (2005) HFACS analysis of ROC Air Force aviation accidents: Reliability analysis and cross-cultural comparison. *The International Journal of Applied Aviation Studies* 5(1): 65–72.

Li W-C and Harris D (2006) Pilot error and its relationship with higher organizational levels: HFACS analysis of 523 accidents. *Aviation, Space, and Environmental Medicine* 77(10): 1056–1061.

Li W-C, Harris D, et al. (2008) Routes to failure: Analysis of 41 civil aviation accidents from the Republic of China using the human factors analysis and classification system. *Accident; Analysis and Prevention* 40(2): 426–434.

Paletz S, Bearman C, Orasanu J, and Holbrook J (2009) Socializing the human factors analysis and classification system: Incorporating social psychological phenomena into a human factors error classification system. *Human Factors* 51(4): 435–445.

Pape AM, Wiegmann DA, et al. (2001) *Air Traffic Control (ATC) Related Accidents and Incidents: A Human Factors Analysis*. 11th International Symposium on Aviation Psychology, Columbus, OH, The Ohio State University.

Reason J (1990) *Human Error*. New York: Cambridge University Press.

Reason J (1997) *Managing the Risks of Organizational Accidents*. Aldershot, Great Britain: Ashgate Publishing Company.

Reinach S and Viale A (2006) Application of a human error framework to conduct train accident/incident investigations. *Accident; Analysis and Prevention* 38: 396–406.

Shappell S and Wiegmann D (2009) Developing a methodology for assessing safety programs targeting human error in aviation. *The International Journal of Aviation Psychology* 19: 252–269.

Tvaryanas AP, Thompson WT, et al. (2006) Human factors in remotely piloted aircraft operations: HFACS analysis of 221 mishaps over 10 years. *Aviation, Space, and Environmental Medicine* 77(7): 724–732.

Wiegmann D and Shappell S (2003) *A Human Error Approach to Aviation Accident Analysis: The Human Factors Analysis and Classification System*. Aldershot, Great Britain: Ashgate Publishing Company.

Woods D, Dekker S, Cook R, Johannesen L, and Sarter N (2010) *Behind Human Error*. Aldershot, Great Britain: Ashgate Publishing Company.

Railroad Accident Investigation and Reconstruction

RW Halstead, IronWood Technologies, Inc., Syracuse, NY, USA

Introduction

This article provides a broad introduction to the field of railroad accident investigation and reconstruction. The above term 'investigation' denotes the manner in which the scene of a railroad-related accident is secured and relevant forensic data collected and preserved, whereas 'reconstruction' denotes the application of scientific principles and analysis to the data collected so as to determine with the greatest degree of precision possible:

1. The sequence of factors that led up to the accident.
2. Whether the accident could have been prevented or its severity reduced through improvements in operating procedures, engineering design, or maintenance practices.

The 'investigator' and 'reconstructionist' may be, and often are, the same person. The final railroad accident reconstruction product may be used by governmental agencies contemplating additional regulatory activity or evaluating the effectiveness of existing regulations. It may be used by railroad companies to improve their internal engineering and operating procedures, and may be used to prosecute or defend criminal or civil legal proceedings.

Railroad accidents, as many other kinds of accidents, are rarely the product of a single factor or event, but most often result from a sequence of events, the removal of any one of which precludes the accident from occurring. Thus, it is incumbent on the railroad accident investigator and reconstructionist to cast a wide net for potential causal events; for any one of which might prove crucial to an understanding of an accident event, and its future prevention.

While this article is modeled on North American (primarily United States) operating and engineering practice, the investigative and reconstruction techniques set forth herein have broad application to the science of railroad accident reconstruction worldwide. As it is not possible to cover the entire breadth of the field of railroad accident investigation and reconstruction in any depth in this article alone, this article instead offers detailed information on a number of specific areas of interest in the field, while inviting the reader to pursue related information via supplemental sources.

Types of Railroad Accidents

Railroad accident investigators and reconstructionists may be called upon to examine a variety of railroad-related accidents, including but not limited to

- collisions between two or more trains (head-on, rear-end, sideswipe),
- derailments,
- collisions between trains and vehicles or pedestrians,
- platform gap injuries,
- electrocution (railroad employee or civilian), and
- railroad employee injuries (United States: Federal Employer's Liability Act).

Factors that may have contributed, in whole or in part, to the accident may include

- excessive speed by train crew or motorist;
- inadequate sight distance for train crews and/or motorists at level crossings around vegetation or standing equipment on adjacent tracks;
- operating rules noncompliance by train crews;
- train crew unfamiliarity with the section of track over which they were operating leading up to the accident;
- inadequate design and/or maintenance of track, level crossing surface, signaling systems for trains or motorists, or safety appliances on locomotive or cars;
- failure to thoroughly test signal system revisions or upgrades before placing in service;
- fatigue – train crew and/or motorist;
- impairment by drugs and/or alcohol;
- inability of motorist to accurately judge closing speed of train;
- motorist impatience at level crossings;
- improper operation of traffic signals at traffic intersections interconnected with active warning devices at level crossings; and
- failure to conduct safety briefing before performing task and/or failure to adequately supervise the performance of a potentially hazardous task.

Event Recorders

As time goes on and railroad signal and train control systems become more sophisticated, more and more systems are incorporating event-recording capability, many of which are useful to the accident reconstructionist.

Among the first sources of data typically pursued for preservation and analysis in a railroad accident, investigation is from the locomotives involved in the accident. In the United States, every leading locomotive (or cab car, if the train is being shoved by a locomotive at the rear) that exceeds 48.3 km h^{-1} (30 min h^{-1}) must be equipped with a functioning event recorder that must record at least the most recent 48 h of operation (49 CFR § 229.135a). Other countries may have their own event recorder installation and data retention requirements. The recorder may record data on a tape-based medium or in digital memory. Data extraction is usually performed through removal of a tape, memory module, or download of data to a laptop computer. Nonradar-based event recorders require the accurate measurement of the diameter of the wheelset from which the recorder is receiving data in order to facilitate data analysis.

 http://dx.doi.org/10.1016/B978-0-12-382165-2.00147-1

Data from the locomotive event recorder are often encrypted, and must be processed by the event recorder manufacturer's proprietary software for analysis. The date, time, and exact location of the locomotive at the time of data extraction should be noted, and a chain of custody document should be established and maintained as the data are handed off from person to person to the point of final analysis.

Locomotive event recorders typically sample their input channels and record data records in either a second-by-second manner or 'on demand' (only when one or more data input channels change state). Data input channels typically include time, speed, distance, throttle and braking status, and wayside signal aspects. Newer digital recorders accept more input channels than do the older tape-based units, and may include horn and headlight status and safety-critical messages from the train control system.

It is important to note that as the locomotive travels down the track, the (nonradar-based) event recorder samples its inputs and records data at its designed interval, but the recorder itself has no idea of where it is located along the track at the time at which each specific data sample is taken. In order to determine the train's location at specific times in the event recorder data, at least one specific event recorder data record must be correlated with a specific location along the track. This is commonly done by associating the point on the track at which the locomotive came to rest with the first event recorder data record that shows a speed of zero. Once correlated in this manner, the location along the track corresponding to any event in the event recorder data (brakes first applied, horn first sounded, etc.) can be quickly determined by adding or subtracting their corresponding distance values in the data.

Authentication of locomotive event recorder data can be accomplished by comparing the progression of the data over several kilometers or several tens of kilometers of territory before the collision point. Recorded speeds are compared to areas of known speed restrictions, horn soundings are compared to known level crossing locations, and stops (event records displaying a speed of zero) are compared with locations of known station stops to verify that the offered data most likely pertains to the subject accident, and that the recorded measurement of wheel size is reasonably accurate.

Increasingly, locomotive event recorders are being equipped with the ability to record GPS (Global Positioning System) coordinates corresponding to each individual data record. When present, GPS data offer a means of independent verification of the analysis detailed above.

If more than one locomotive or leading cab control car is involved in the accident, data from all available event recorders should be obtained. The resulting data sets can be cross-compared to ensure data integrity and verify the accuracy of the wheel diameter measurements used for data interpretation.

Additional data useful in a railroad accident investigation may be extracted from the following:

- Train dispatcher's computer logs – recording all dispatcher control inputs and resulting status indications from field signaling equipment, typically located in the main dispatching center.
- Telephone and radio audio recordings of voice transmissions from dispatcher to train, train to dispatcher, and train to train.
- Signal system computer logs – typically stored in the field by solid-state interlocking controllers or equivalent, and/or by computer-controlled level crossing control equipment.
- Nearby defect detectors – 'hot box' (overheated wheel bearings), flat wheel, dragging equipment, or excessive dimension (high/wide). Detectors often record not only the existence of a defect, but also the speed of the train at that instant for comparison with corresponding locomotive event recorder data.
- Automatic Equipment Identifier locations – scanners read magnetic tags on the side of cars as the train passes – gives a listing of each of the cars in the train (and their order) and the speed of the train as it passed through the scanner.
- Cellular telephone tower records – when obtained from the telephone company (in the United States, commonly referred to as 'Call Detail Records' and 'Cell Tower' and 'Switch' Records), they can be used to determine whether or not the train operator's cell phone was in use at a critical portion of the approach to the accident location. 'Smart phones' that internally record GPS positioning data can also be used to position the train and/or motorist at critical points in the approach to the accident, particularly in cases in which locomotive event recorder data do not exist or are unusable.
- Locomotive video – though not required in the United States (yet), more and more major railroads are equipping their locomotives with onboard video cameras. The cameras record to a computer hard drive, and are usually interfaced with the locomotive's existing event recorder.
- Surveillance video from surrounding cameras mounted on residential, commercial, or governmental structures that may have captured part or all of the accident scenes on video. Retention periods are typically short, and timely data recovery is essential.
- Motor vehicles – most modern airbag systems record pre-crash data related to the driver's speed, use of brakes and seatbelts, etc., in modules commonly referred to as an EDR (Event Data Recorder) or SDM (Sensing Diagnostic Module), that can be downloaded from the vehicle to a laptop computer through the use of specialized hardware and software.
- Motor vehicles – General Motors Corp. OnStar system or equivalent, if equipped, offers an independent record of the vehicle's GPS position as a function of time.

Once data are secured from all possible sources, it must be synchronized in order to assemble a comprehensive picture of the events leading up to the accident. To do this, a data source that uses the GPS time base is selected (if available), and all other data sources are synchronized to it by identifying one or more common events that appear across multiple event data sources, taking into account network delay and update frequency for each data source.

After all available event data have been accurately synchronized, a more complete picture of the events that led up to the accident begins to emerge. Movement of the respective vehicles can be plotted with respect to time, recorded precollision use of horn and braking can be evaluated, and the operation of the signal system can be recreated with a reasonable degree of accuracy. The synchronized event data can then be combined with physical evidence collected at the scene in a final analysis of the accident event.

Procedural Steps to Follow in Railroad Accident Investigation and Reconstruction

While there are many different kinds of railroad accidents, certain investigative procedures tend to be applicable to almost all. The generalized list below represents typical investigative activities, and is not intended to supersede more specific procedures that may already be in force in the locale in which the accident has occurred.

Collision with Motor Vehicle or Pedestrian

1. If the train is still at the scene, observe a demonstration of the leading locomotive or cab car's horn, headlight, ditchlights (if equipped), and bell.
2. Download the event recorder on every locomotive and cab car on the train. Note the exact time that the data were downloaded.
3. Download the video recorder on all equipped locomotives and cab cars.
4. Measure the distance from the point of impact to the front of the leading locomotive or cab car at rest. This distance value will be required to analyze the locomotive event recorder data. Mark the location of the front of the leading locomotive at rest on the side of the rail with a paint stick or equivalent, ensuring that that point will be preserved even after the train is moved.
5. Perform or observe testing of the active warning devices (flashers, gates, etc.) at the level crossing, if so equipped. Ensure that all governmentally required tests that apply to level crossing warning devices are performed, along with all additional tests required and customarily performed by the railroad entity that has primary maintenance and testing responsibility for the warning devices. Ensure that the results of all such testing comport with those expected for a nondefective, properly functioning system.
6. Download and preserve data from all computer-controlled warning device control equipment or auxiliary event recorders connected thereto.
7. Examine the pavement surface in the vicinity of the crossing – photograph, measure, and diagram all pavement gouges and tire skid marks attributable to the accident vehicle. Observe the condition of the pavement surface at the track for roughness, potholes, and so on.
8. If the level crossing is humped, take measurements sufficient to create a cross-sectional view of the crossing's profile, then compare its shape to generally accepted standards (United States: AASHTO standards).
9. Examine signage that governed the accident vehicle's approach to the collision for completeness, placement and visibility, and reflectivity (if at night).
10. Inspect the scene for the presence of vegetation or other fixed obstruction that may have impaired the motorist's ability to see down the track for approaching trains. If any is found, measure and diagram its relationship to the level crossing.
11. If the level crossing has active warning devices and they are interconnected with traffic signals at an adjacent intersection, perform or observe testing of the combined system to ensure that the traffic signals displayed the proper phases as required by the approach of the train.
12. Map the overall accident scene and debris field. Collect and analyze any debris that may have bearing on the accident, including all crossing signal equipment replaced immediately after the accident.
13. Collect statements from all eyewitnesses and others with potentially useful information.
14. Scan the area for security cameras oriented in the general direction of the level crossing. If any are identified, arrange to obtain the video footage from the time of the accident.
15. Collect the remains of any shattered light bulbs from the vehicle, locomotive, or crossing signals. It may be possible to perform a 'stretched filament' analysis on them to determine if they were lit at the instant of impact.
16. If the level crossing is equipped with gates, collect video footage depicting the gates going up and down repeatedly. Back in the office later, the video tape can be run in slow motion and very precise gate operating times can be determined.
17. Take lots of photographs and video footage from a variety of angles and distances from the crossing. Use a 50 mm lens for all photography – it most closely replicates the perspective of the human eye.
18. Secure audio file copies of all radio and telephone footage between the train crew and train dispatcher (if applicable) for the 5–10 min leading up to the collision.
19. Note the weather at the time of the accident, as well as sun angle.
20. If the level crossing was equipped with active warning devices, examine the incoming commercial power feed – determine if commercial power was on or off at the time of the accident.
21. Determine if the motorist/pedestrian/train crew employees were tested for the presence of alcohol or drugs.
22. Determine if cell phones were in the possession of and/or were in use at the time of the accident.

Collisions Between Trains

Though their frequency has greatly decreased over the years through the increased use of advanced technology and operating practice refinement, train collisions still occur in the United States and around the world. Potential collision causes include

1. Train dispatcher mistakenly authorized two trains to occupy the same block of track simultaneously.
2. One or both train crews incorrectly interpreted track block authority, leading them to enter a section of track for which they had no authorization to occupy.;
3. Signal system failed by displaying a 'false clear' signal to one or both trains, a signal conveying information that was more favorable than intended. Alternatively, the proper signal was displayed but was misinterpreted by the crew due to sun glare or other missed vision cue.
4. Signal system functioned properly, but train crew failed to observe and/or act on restrictive signal information due to inattention, fatigue, or drug or alcohol impairment.
5. Braking system failure occurred on one or both trains.
6. Excessive speed by one or both trains, leading to an inability to stop short of a restrictive signal as required.

When the collision occurs in territory that is equipped with a signal system, all available signal system event recorders must be downloaded, and their data content synchronized and carefully interpreted to determine if any 'false clear' signals were displayed to the accident crews. In addition, complete post-accident 'service testing' must be performed on the signal system, in which all possible combinations of train routings, including those being conducted at the time of the accident, are simulated and the signal system outputs are compared to those intended.

Derailments

Derailments may be caused by track defects, equipment defects, signaling defects, poor train handling or other human factors, improperly loaded freight, improper train makeup (heaviest cars at rear of train), or any combination of these factors.

Upon arrival at the accident scene, an investigator will typically begin at the location of the wreckage and walk down the track opposite the train's direction of travel, looking along the rails and track structure for the point of derailment (POD). This is the first evidence of a wheel climbing the rail, commonly seen as a prolonged scuff or scrape mark along the top of the rail, followed by spike and tie damage as the wheel flange contacts and begins to ride along the top of the tie plates or ties. While the initial POD is commonly found within 100 m or so of the general wreckage, it may also appear up to several kilometers from the main wreck scene, indicating that derailed equipment was pulled for some distance in a derailed state before it finally 'went off exploring.'

Once the initial POD is located, the track structure for at least 50–100 m before the POD should be examined in detail for conformance with governmentally required and generally accepted industry standards for track construction and maintenance. In the United States, these minimum requirements can be found in 49 CFR (Code of Federal Regulations) Part 213. Track defects that, depending on their severity, may lead to derailment include

1. broken joint bar between two rails (especially in older rail and at cold temperatures);
2. broken rail (internal defect in steel, especially in older rail and at cold temperatures);
3. excessive cross-level between rails – one rail higher or lower than its adjacent rail can cause car body roll and resulting wheel lift and may also cause harmonic rocking at specific speeds. Commonly caused by poorly tamped rail joints;
4. poor track alignment – 'wavy' track;
5. track gauge (distance between rails) too wide (causes wheelset 'drop-ins') or too narrow (causes wheelset/rail climbovers, rail rollovers);
6. ties deteriorated to the point that they are unable to hold spikes or other fasteners – leading to rail rollovers, particularly the high rail on curves;
7. track switch or turnout to adjacent track not properly adjusted or maintained – 'point gap' between switch point and stock rail – allows incoming wheel flanges to 'pick the point' and derail;
8. insufficient ballast or rail anchoring to support track or to restrain longitudinal movement under load (often resulting in 'heat kinks');
9. insufficient spikes or fasteners to hold the rail in place, allowing rail rollover under load, particularly the high rail on curves; and
10. insufficient rail superelevation on curves for the authorized track speed.

To be considered potentially causal in nature, track defects identified during the postaccident inspection must have existed prederailment, and not have been caused by the derailment.

Another potential cause of a derailment is equipment (rolling stock) failure. Common causes of equipment failure that can lead to derailment include

1. broken wheel – may be caused by defective steel or thermal cracking from brake shoe heating;
2. broken axle – defective steel;
3. roller bearing burn off – lack of lubrication, internal flaws, manufacturing defects. Check data from nearest hot bearing detector for confirmation;
4. rail car truck (or 'bogie') hunting – oscillating back and forth between the two rails as the train progresses, exerting high lateral forces on the rails, most common on straight track with worn rail at 70 kph or higher; and
5. truck (or 'bogie') warp – causes wheelsets to move in a canted fashion relative to the track. This accelerates wear on the track and railcar components, and may cause a wheel-lift derailment if sufficiently pronounced. Present when bogie components are worn and 'out of square' relative to the direction of travel.

The search for an equipment-caused derailment begins at the leading car in the line of derailed cars. Any equipment-related derailment cause will likely be found in this car, but in certain conditions, may be found in the first or second car to the rear of the leading derailed car, but rarely further back than this in the line of derailed cars. Bogies and wheelsets (which are often separated from their respective cars and sometimes partially buried in the ground) should be matched with their corresponding cars, if possible, and examined in detail for any of the above defects. As with track, in order to be considered potentially causal, the defect must have existed prederailment and not have been caused by the derailment. This can often be determined by the presence or absence of corrosion in cracks and fractured steel surfaces of wheels, axles, and bogie components. Freshly cracked or fractured surfaces will not exhibit corrosion on the fractured surfaces. Partial corrosion (corrosion up to a point on the fractured surface) often indicates that the crack existed for some time before it finally sheared completely. The services of a metallurgist should be secured to complete the analysis whenever such evidence is present.

Another potential derailment cause, though much rarer than any we have discussed thus far, may come into play when a train is passing over a turnout (switches trains from one track to another) that is power-operated (as opposed to hand-operated), and controlled remotely by a train dispatcher. Signal track circuitry at the location detects the presence of a train and electrically locks the switch, preventing it from changing position, for the duration of time that the train is passing over it. If this signal track circuitry fails in some fashion, it may be possible for the power-operated turnout to change position as the train is passing over it, causing a derailment.

Derailments sometimes result from improper train makeup and/or train handling. The placement of a block of heavier cars near or at the rear of a string of empty or lighter cars can produce 'slack run-ins' if the train brakes are not applied with the necessary finesse. The heavier cars will tend to bunch toward the leading end of the train, derailing lighter cars between them and the locomotives. This effect is especially pronounced on curves. A locomotive engineer's failure to control slack action in a long train, particularly in an area of undulating grades, can produce the same effect.

Human Factors Considerations – Level Crossing Accidents

No analysis of level crossing accidents would be complete without consideration of the human factors performance of motorists as they approach crossings. This subset of human factors research has been studied extensively over the past 40 years, culminating in hundreds of research reports, many of which are available on the Internet. As such, the field, as it relates to level crossings, is far too voluminous to cover here in the level of detail that it merits. We can, however, explore some of the high points and whet the reader's appetite for further investigation on the subject.

In general, motorists are imperfect decision-makers, and often underestimate the speed at which trains approach crossings, leading them to attempt movements over the track, which they have insufficient time to complete safely. The perception/reaction time (PRT) required for a motorist to perceive a hazard and begin to take corrective action varies with expectancy. The less expected a hazard is or the more complex the environment from which hazard clues must be drawn, the longer the PRT. In most cases, an assumed PRT of between 1.5 and 2.5 s is typical for level crossing accident reconstruction, unless a more detailed value derived from actual study or reenactment at the subject crossing is available.

The motorist's prior observations of one or more 'false activations' of active warning devices at level crossings (instances in which the active warning devices falsely indicate the approach of a train, indicating that it is not safe to proceed over the crossing when in fact it is) tend to reduce the credibility of crossing warning devices in general, prompting them to attempt passages over crossings in violation of activated flashers and gates. Studies have shown that motorists tend to assign a decreased credibility to activated warning devices at a particular crossing even if their observations of 'false activations' occurred at other crossings.

Frequent false activations of level crossing active warning devices have many potential causes, principal among them being poor maintenance on the part of the railroad company. Failure to maintain clean, mud-free track ballast (the crushed stone that the track rests on) within the approach to the crossing is the most common cause of false activations. This condition worsens over time, as repeated rail traffic grinds portions of the crushed stone into dust that then combines with water (rain, melted snow and ice, road salt applied over level crossings in winter for the benefit of highway traffic) to form an electrically conductive slurry bridging the two rails. This electrically conductive slurry interferes with the crossing signal equipment's ability to reliably detect approaching trains. The equipment is designed to recognize the onset of this unsafe condition and activate the warning devices continuously until ballast conditions improve (rain stops and ballast dries out) or the equipment is repaired or readjusted by signal maintenance personnel. This unsafe condition is easily preventable by careful and proactive attention to track and crossing signal maintenance.

Motorists often exhibit impatience with activated level crossing warning devices, particularly if they have been held for long periods of time, with or without the passage of a train, by such warning devices in the past. This impatience may prompt them to attempt unsafe maneuvers around activated flashers and lowered gates. The higher the degree of reliability with which the active warning devices at crossings operate, the greater their credibility is and the fewer violations of activated warning devices by motorists that are likely to occur.

See also: **Engineering:** Accident Investigation – Determination of Cause; Human Factors Investigation and Analysis of Accidents and Incidents.

Further Reading

British Columbia Institute of Technology, School of Transportation (2006) *Course RAIL-0107: Rail Accident Scene Investigation, Course Notes.*

Halstead RW (2006) *Railroad Collision Investigation, presentation to the Pennsylvania State Police Reconstruction Seminar – Course Notes* (available on request).

Halstead RW (2011) *Railroad Accident Investigation and Reconstruction, presentations to the California Accident Reconstruction Society – Course Notes* (available on request).

Loumiet JR and Jungbauer W (2005) *Train Accident Reconstruction and FELA and Railroad Litigation*, 4th edn. Lawyers & Judges Publishing Co.

Relevant Websites

www.apta.com – U.S. American Public Transit Association.

www.arema.org – U.S. American Railway Engineering and Maintenance-of-Way Association.

www.fra.dot.gov – U.S. Federal Railroad Administration.

www.fta.dot.gov – U.S. Federal Transit Administration.

http://www.ite.org/bookstore – U.S. Federal Highway Administration Railroad-Highway Grade Crossing Handbook – Revised 2nd Edition (2007).

http://mutcd.fhwa.dot.gov – U.S. Federal Manual on Uniform Traffic Control Devices.

www.ntsb.gov – U.S. National Transportation Safety Board.

Analysis of Digital Evidence

MK Rogers, Purdue University, West Lafayette, IN, USA

Glossary (SWGDE, 2011)

Bit Short for binary digit. Fundamental unit in computing. It has two possible values: 1 or 0.
Bitstream image A bit-stream image is a sector-by-sector/bit-by-bit exact copy of a hard drive or other storage device.
Data Information in analog or digital form that can be transmitted or processed.
Hash or hash value Numerical values, generated by hashing functions, used to substantiate the integrity of digital evidence and/or for inclusion/exclusion comparisons against known value sets.
Hashing function An established mathematical calculation that generates a numerical value based on input data. This numerical value is referred to as the hash or hash value.
Integrity verification The process of confirming that the data presented are complete and unaltered since time of acquisition.
Metadata Data, frequently embedded within a file, that describe a file or directory, which can include the locations where the content is stored, dates and times, application-specific information, and permissions.
Partition User-defined section of electronic media.
Storage media Any object on which data are preserved.
Work copy A copy or duplicate of a recording or data that can be used for subsequent processing and/or analysis.

History/Background

Digital evidence is an emerging area in the field of forensic science. As society becomes more dependent on technology, more of daily lives are reflected in the world of cyberspace. The notion of a carbon footprint has become popular in the media, what is equally as important is the digital footprint. Technologies such as Facebook, Twitter, Google+, and text messaging allow one to record and share almost all facets of daily lives. One has friend-finding applications on GPS-enabled cell phones, security cameras that monitor daily travels, and Internet companies record one's web-browsing activities and predilections. One's health records, phone conversations, and even book- or magazine-reading habits are monitored and recorded. These days most people conduct their banking online, with little or no interaction with the physical bank. The end result of all this is that digital evidence is poised to surpass the volume of physical evidence, such as paper documents or paper receipts.

The term digital evidence is bandied about in the vernacular and often highlighted in movies and the popular media. But what exactly does this term mean? While there are several definitions available, the more common definition of the term is

> Digital data that establish that a crime has been committed can provide a link between a crime and its victim, or can provide a link between a crime and the perpetrator.

Like physical evidence, digital evidence exists in a crime scene. To be more accurate, digital evidence exists in two crime scenes, the physical and the cyber or digital realm. An example would be e-mail evidence. This evidence could be stored on a laptop that exists in the physical world, but the actual content of the e-mail is in the digital world. Thus, one needs to define this second type of crime scene, the digital crime scene. A digital crime scene is defined as

> The electronic environment where digital evidence can potentially exist.

Digital evidence falls within the larger category of digital forensic science. Digital forensic science is defined as

> The use of scientifically derived and proven methods toward the preservation, collection, validation, identification, analysis, interpretation, documentation, and presentation of digital evidence derived from digital sources for the purpose of facilitating or furthering the reconstruction of events found to be criminal or helping to anticipate unauthorized actions shown to be disruptive to planned operations.

As a field, digital forensics is relatively new to the forensic sciences. The American Academy of Forensic Sciences (AAFS) added a Digital and Multimedia Sciences section in February 2008. Prior to this time, practitioners and scientists engaged in digital forensics belonged to other sections such as the General Section or Engineering Sciences Section.

Apart from the establishment of its own section within the AAFS, digital forensics as a concept first appeared in the 1970s as a result of the efforts of law enforcement in the United States, Canada, and Europe to have laws passed to deal with technology-related crimes. In the 1980s, police agencies in North America and Europe started to create dedicated computer crime units such as the FBI's Computer Analysis Response Team (CART), which lead to international conferences in the 1990s designed to begin the work of harmonizing efforts at the international level.

In the late 1990s, the International Organization for Computer Evidence (IOCE, European) and the Scientific Working Group for Digital Evidence (SWGDE, USA) began formal

 http://dx.doi.org/10.1016/B978-0-12-382165-2.00325-1

discussions on standardizing investigative approaches for dealing with digital evidence.

In 2000, the FBI opened their first Regional Cyber Forensics Laboratory (RCFL). The goal of the RCFL program was to provide computer forensic resources to state and local law enforcement. The program has expanded to 16 RCFL's covering the majority of the United States.

In 2003, the American Academy of Crime Laboratory Directors/Laboratory Accreditation Board (ASCLD/LAB) included specific certification criteria for laboratories handling digital evidence. The inclusion of these criteria mirrored the European efforts related to ISO 17025 requirements for international laboratories.

As was previously mentioned, the AAFS in 2008 recognized its first new subsection in over 25 years. The Digital and Multimedia Sciences section is the current home for digital forensics and digital analysis in the context of a forensic science.

Current Context

Evidence that is digital in nature is an integral part of most modern-day investigations (**Figure 1**). Digital evidence has been used as corroborative evidence in cases that range from homicides to cyber stalking, extortion, and child custody cases. Dennis Rader, the BTK killer, was eventually caught as a result of digital evidence found on a diskette. Investigations relating to intellectual property (IP) or fraud and embezzlement rely more heavily on digital evidence than on document-based evidence. In the business setting, the volume of digital documents has surpassed paper-based documents. The paper documents that exist are commonly printouts of digital or electronic documents.

E-mail-based evidence has been the proverbial 'smoking gun' in numerous high-profile cases such as Enron and the antitrust investigation involving Microsoft. The sheer volume of e-mails produced daily (estimated to be in the billions worldwide) make this kind of evidence common to any investigation. Some federal law enforcement agencies estimate that at least 80% of their current and future investigations involve or will involve digital evidence.

Standards

Given the recent emergence of digital analysis, there are no standards that are recognized as being definitive. Several organizations such as the SWGDE, American Society for Testing and Materials (ASTM), the IOCE, the National Institute of Justice (NIJ), and the Association of Chief Police Officers (ACPO) are developing guidelines and best practices. However, most of these are works are in progress and are not intended to be checklists or formal standards at this time.

The development of standards and certifications is further complicated due to the diverse communities that are enveloped by the field of digital forensics and digital evidence analysis. These communities include (1) law enforcement, (2) private sector, (3) government/military, and (4) academia. These communities have subtly different objectives and thus different requirements for practitioners in their area.

Digital Evidence Life Cycle

Similar to other forms of evidence, digital evidence has a life cycle. The digital evidence life cycle parallels the flow from data to information to knowledge. Digital evidence begins its life cycle in the domain of data. Once the data have been located, the context of the investigation as well as the content of the data moves it into the domain of information. This information is then used to make decisions, test hypotheses, or legal theories and to provide opinions – the knowledge realm.

The National Institute for Standards and Technology (NIST) in the United States has developed a diagram that illustrates the progression of the digital evidence life cycle in the context of the Digital Evidence Process Model (**Figure 2**).

DE Process Model

The digital forensics process model consists of five phases: identification, collection/acquisition, transportation, analysis/examination, and report.

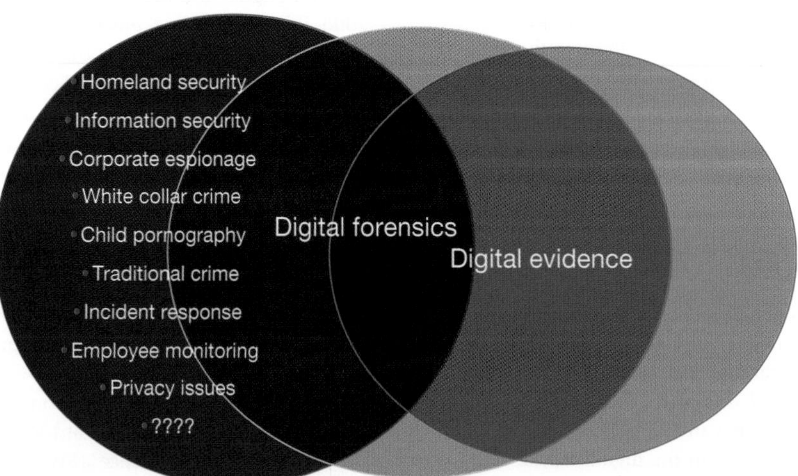

Figure 1 Context of digital evidence.

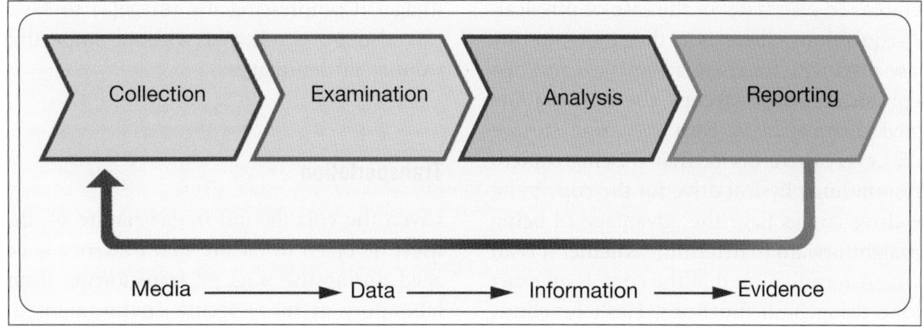

Figure 2 NIST model.

Identification

Prior to any collection, the evidence or potential evidence must first be identified. Unlike with physical evidence, digital evidence is latent. One cannot see bits and bytes or data flowing through the airways via wireless transmissions. Humans are dependent on technology to assist in abstracting and representing the data in a way that is human readable (e.g., computer monitor displaying the data, directory trees listing files on a hard drive). This latent characteristic of digital evidence makes it difficult to identify and requires that investigators take a very methodical approach.

Investigators commonly look for well-established 'containers' of data. These include hard drives, thumb drives, digital versatile discs (DVDs), mobile phones, external USB drives, laptops, etc. Unfortunately, due to the rapid changes in technology, unconventional containers must also be searched for. These can include digital video recorders, MP3 players, and even Internet-connected televisions.

Another factor that complicates the identification phase is that containers of data can have very small form factors such as USB thumb drives or SD memory cards. These devices can be as small as a quarter or a person's thumbnail and still hold Gigabytes of data. These small devices are easily hidden by someone and are easily destroyed by breaking the connector or the device in half.

Similar to the steps for collecting physical evidence, the entire identification process must be well documented and recorded. The basic foundation for a chain of custody must be established at this phase and maintained throughout the entire process. It is preferable to use a digital video camera and record the crime scene.

Collection/Acquisition

Once digital evidence and/or the containers that contain the data are identified, the data must be acquired in a manner that is consistent with the precepts of the chain of custody and ensures that the evidence will be admissible in a legal proceeding. This usually entails taking steps to ensure that the data are not modified or altered and if changes must be made, to thoroughly document what has been changed. In this phase, there are actually two major considerations: is the device/system still powered on and will remain so – live system or is the device/system powered off and/or could be powered off – dead system or autopsy approach. Devices/systems that are powered off or can be powered off without disrupting the integrity of the evidence are the easiest to deal with. An example would be a computer system such as laptop or workstation that is powered off.

The standard procedure for powered off systems is to remove the storage device and using a write blocker (preferably a physical or hardware write blocker), create an electronic copy of the drive or device. This electronic copy is referred to as a forensic copy or forensic bitstream image. There are two types of images that can be made, physical copy or a logical copy. A physical copy contains all the data on the storage device, from the very first sector to the last sector. A logical copy only captures the data in the defined volume or partition on the device/hard drive (e.g., the 'C' drive on a windows system). If possible, a physical copy is preferable, as it captures all the data and helps to place evidence in the correct context.

The approach for collecting evidence from a live system is more complicated than the autopsy approach. One of the fundamental concepts in forensics is to avoid altering the crime scene or at least keeping any disturbances or changes to a minimum. With live systems, it is necessary to execute some tool on the suspect system in order to make a copy of all the volatile data. Volatile data or evidence here refers to information that is lost when the electrical power is cut to the system. These volatile data can include contents in random access memory (RAM), process tables, connection logs, and network connections. In this situation, an investigator would use a piece of forensic software that is stored on an external device such as USB thumb drive, DVD, or some other externally connected disk. The external device contains all the necessary code to run the application without having to use any of the software resources on the suspect device other than the RAM. Here is where potential problems can occur. When the forensic software is executed, it will use a portion of the RAM on the suspect system, and this will push out or replace whatever data were in the area of the RAM that is now being used by the forensic software. The digital crime scene has now been altered, albeit in a minimal manner. However, despite altering the evidence, the courts have allowed this procedure, as it is the only viable method available at this time. Of course extensive documentation of the process and how it may have impacted the suspect system is required. The forensic software run on the suspect system will collect an image of the RAM, running processes, and other such volatile data.

While the current trend is to have investigators to create an image (block device image) of a physical device, there are certain circumstances where a physical-to-physical-device acquisition is preferable. To elaborate, in the case of physical-to-physical device acquisitions, there is a direct one-to-one relationship. In these instances, there are advantages and disadvantages. With a physical-to-physical copy, the drive that the image will be copied to must be at least the same storage capacity or larger. For every drive/device that is being copied, there will be a corresponding physical drive for the copy to be stored on. Drive-to-drive copies have the advantage of being very fast, and it is straightforward to determine whether it is an exact copy or not. The determination that the copy is an exact or valid copy is done using hash functions. Hash functions allow one to take an arbitrary-sized data input and produced a fixed sized output, a hash total of the data in our case. In the case of MD5, the output is a hash function represented by 128 bits (**Figure 3**). The hash function is very sensitive to bit wise changes. This means that if any bit of the data is changed, the resultant 128-bit hash total is completely different.

The use of hash functions to ensure integrity and validity of the forensic copies is not practical with live systems. Since the system is powered on and running, numerous changes and updates are occurring during the imaging process. If the desired image is a physical copy then using hash functions is useless, as the state of system when the original hash total is calculated will be different by the time the forensic copy is made. If a logical image is being acquired on a nonactive volume (not the partition or volume that system was booted from) then using a hash total to compare the image to original is fine, nothing will have changed on the nonactive partition during the time span of the imaging process. If an image is being acquired that included the boot volume on a live system then it is the same situation as with the physical, the state of the system will be changing during the process, making a hash total comparison meaningless.

The common practice is to compute the hashes before the drive is imaged and then calculate the hash of the image and compare the outputs. If the hash totals match, this is sufficient for the copy to be considered an exact duplicate of the original drive. In some jurisdictions, the forensic image or copy qualifies as 'best evidence,' and it can be stipulated that the original is no longer required. This is more common in large organizations that may wish to wipe the drive and repurpose it back into operations.

A second copy of the original can be made. The forensic image is copied, and the subsequent computed hash total of this copy is calculated and compared to the total of the forensic image. If they match then the second copy is considered an exact copy of the original as well. This process can be used to prepare numerous copies of the original if required, without touching the original again.

The original drive or device can be placed in secure storage or as mentioned, wiped, and repurposed. The first copy is deemed the library copy and is used to make further copies if required. The second copy is the working copy and is used in the subsequent stages of the process model.

It should be noted that the acquisition process as described could also include encrypting all the forensic images. Compressing the image(s) to save on storage space can also be conducted without impacting the integrity or validity of the images.

MD5 (Evidence.rtf) = d0221be1afb9af6dc1bd6e41243ce658

Figure 3 MD5 hash.

Transportation

Given the volatile and fragile nature of digital evidence, care must be taken to ensure that evidence is not altered or damaged during the stage of transporting from the scene to the laboratory or more secure environment. Digital evidence is very sensitive to changes in temperature, humidity, and any type of magnetic field, radiofrequency field, or static charge. The common practice is to place devices such as hard drives, thumb drives, and so on into antistatic bags and then place these into shock-resistant and water-resistant containers.

The storage of digital evidence can also be problematic as evidence (e.g., last numbers dialed) on some devices such as mobile phones can be lost if the battery is depleted. Other storage devices such as DVDs must be protected from sunlight or other natural lighting, as this will degrade the compounds used to store the data. Magnetic-based storage hard drives start to decay the minute they are manufactured, so any long-term storage (>5 years) can result in areas of the drive demagnetizing, and the data stored in these areas becomes inaccessible.

Analysis and Examination

The next step in the process is to begin examining the data in order to determine what if anything is of evidentiary value. An analogy for this phase in the process is that of a funnel (**Figure 4**). Raw data are entered into the large end of the funnel. These data are filtered based on the context of the investigation. Data that are determined to be important (in order to either confirm a legal theory or negate another) become evidence. This evidence is further filtered and interpreted by the analyst until a decision or decisions are made, which are directly supported by the derived evidence.

The extremely large capacity of storage devices (e.g., hard drives) makes it impractical to examine all the data that are contained on the device. Therefore, an examination plan is required. The plan weighs the context and goals of the investigation. Context can refer to the type of the investigation (e.g., threatening e-mails, theft of IP, possession of contraband images).

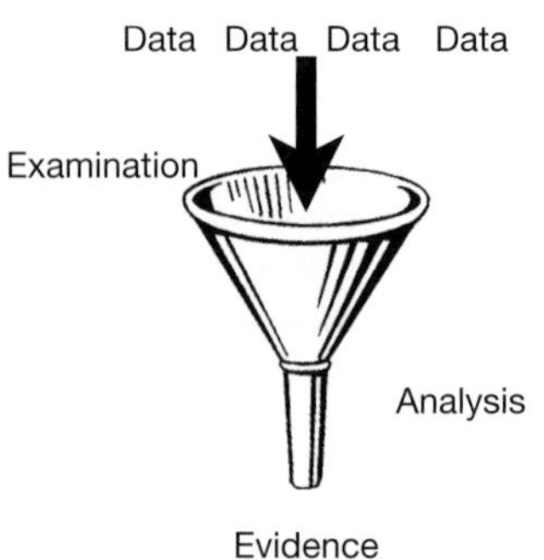

Figure 4 Examination and analysis.

Understanding this context allows the investigator to develop a decision tree to guide the exploration of the data.

Digital Evidence Artifacts

Since the analysis of the data must be somewhat focused, certain artifacts are routinely examined during the course of the analysis phase. These artifacts include e-mails, web browsing histories, chat and texting logs, deleted files, and timelines. Other secondary artifacts consist of documents, pictures, and spreadsheets.

The sheer volume of e-mails that are sent and received in any given day makes e-mail a target-rich item for investigators. E-mails contain various metadata items such as the IP address of the system sending the e-mail, the IP addresses of all the mail systems it passed through (as well as time stamps), and in some cases, the type of e-mail client used to create the message. These metadata are contained in the header portion of the e-mail that is human readable. However, e-mails can have the source address tampered with to make it look like it came from somewhere or someone else (this is referred to as 'spoofing'), and the header information can be stripped out by anonymous remailers.

The use of graphical web browsers such as Safari, Internet Explorer, and Mozilla has lead to the popularity of the Internet. Since web browsing is such a common activity, a detailed history of what sites were visited and when what was downloaded from these sites and what terms were searched for in the common search engines are important sources of evidence. In many cases, the history of search terms (e.g., buying guns, cleaning a crime scene, chloroform) have been vital in the successful prosecution or exoneration of an accused person.

The explosion of social networking and the need to be in constant communication with one's friends and family have resulted in there being an increase in evidence related to texting, chatting, and other social media technologies. Most texting and chat programs have the ability to record a log of the conversation, and many providers for this media store the conversations on their servers. Depending on the case, these records of the communications can provide a link between the suspect and the victim, the suspect and the activity, or in the case of civil disputes and IP cases, the intent of the party in question. In several criminal cases, individuals have bragged about their crimes on their social network pages or texted their accomplices or friends to discuss the criminal activity.

Files and data that have been deleted or placed in the recycle or trash bin on the system are of special interest since these are items that in some cases, a person wants to hide or get rid of (i.e., delete). Modern operating systems (e.g., Windows 7, OS X Lion) and file systems (e.g., NTFS, HFS+) allow for files to be deleted or placed in the trash without actually removing the data from the system. These files still exist but the location in the file system that they occupy is flagged as being available to store new data. Unless and until new data are written to these areas, the deleted files are recoverable.

As with physical investigations, reliable time lines are important in digital evidence analysis. A reliable reconstruction of events and cause–effect relationships can be the difference between a determination of guilt or innocence. Time lines allow for the examination of alibis and can place an individual at certain critical locations at a particular time (mobile phone evidence is often used for this purpose as most phones log their positions relative to cell towers and wireless telecommunication companies store tower records). Unfortunately, developing a reliable and accurate chronology of events can be difficult with digital evidence. While most modern operating systems and file systems record the time a file was modified, accessed, or created/copied, these timestamps depend on the system's clock and the operating system clock. Users usually have access to their clock/time applications, which they can use to modify their system's time. This modification would alter the time stamps on files and impact their reliability. Even if the system's clock is not tampered with, computer systems do not have accurate clocks. Research has shown that over the course of a day, the system clock can drift anywhere from minutes to hours out of sync with the actual time.

Electronic documents, spreadsheets, and pictures in relation to digital evidence are for the most part identical to their physical counter parts. Most individuals store their documents, spreadsheets, and pictures within default locations as determined by their operating system and file system. Unlike physical copies of documents and spreadsheets, digital versions contain metadata such as version changes, comments, and authorship and time stamps such as creation and modification. An investigator could readily determine when the document in question was created or deleted and who created the original document and could see all the different versions of the document from when it was first created to when it was last modified.

With pictures, digital images can contain information about the type of camera that was used to take the picture and if the camera or device (e.g., mobile phone) has a GPS function, the exact geographical location where the picture was taken at (i.e., geopositioning).

Conclusion

Digital evidence investigation and analysis are a relatively new field/activity within the forensic sciences. As the field matures, it will develop a standardization of methods, tools, processes, and certifications as well as a common corpus of knowledge. In its present state, the most that can be said is that the five-step process of identification, collection, analysis, and examination and reporting mirrors the phases used in the other physics-based forensic sciences and are compliant with basic crime scene investigation procedures.

Society's ongoing dependence on technology increases the importance of analyzing digital evidence. Today and into the foreseeable future, individuals live in two realities, the physical and the virtual or cyber. Hence, the need to effectively deal with evidence that is digital in nature is paramount, as this category of evidence surpasses the physical in terms of volume. This field is somewhat unique, as it deals with a man-made science (computers and technology) and not a natural science (e.g., biology and chemistry) as the other forensic sciences do. Technology is constantly changing; therefore, tools, techniques, and processes that worked yesterday may not work tomorrow.

The legal justice system is also less comfortable in dealing with digital evidence than it is in dealing with more traditional scientific evidence (e.g., physical, biological, and chemical). To some, the Internet and technology are still rather magical and therefore, evidence derived from this media is either believed at face value or classified as being suspect and incomprehensible. As the current judiciary ages out and is replaced with a newer generation, this uncertainty and fear will naturally be reduced.

Digital evidence analysis, while representing a different mode of evidence than the physical, still must be held to the same scientific and legal standards as the other forensic sciences.

See also: **Digital Evidence:** Child Pornography; **Digital Evidence/Photography and Digital Imaging:** Digital Imaging and Photography: An Overview; **Foundations:** Principles of Forensic Science; **Investigations:** Collection and Chain of Evidence.

Further Reading

ASCLD/LAB (2005) Laboratory accreditation manual.

Carrier B and Spafford EH (2003) Getting physical with the digital forensic process. *International Journal of Digital Evidence* 2(2): 1–19.

Casey E (2000) *Digital Evidence and Computer Crime*. New York: Academic Press.

Ciardhuáin SÓ (2004) An extended model of cybercrime investigations. *International Journal* 3: 1–22.

Digital Evidence: Its True Value (2009) *Tech Beat* (Vol. Winter 2009): National Law Enforcement and Corrections Technology Center.

Garfinkel SL (2010) Digital forensics research: The next 10 years. *Digital Investigation* 7: S64–S73. http://dx.doi.org/10.1016/j.diin.2010.05.009.

ISO/IEC (2005) General requirements for the competence of testing and calibration laboratories. Switzerland.

Jones K, Bejtlich R, and Rose C (2005) *Real Digital Forensics: Computer Security and Incident Response*. New York: Addison Wesley.

Kanellis P, Kiountouzis E, Kolokotrinics N, and Martakos D (2006) *Digital Crime and Forensic Science in Cyberspace*. London: Idea Group Publishing.

Kent K, Chevalier S, Grance T, and Dang H (2006) *Guide to Integrating Forensic Techniques into Incident Response*. Gaithersburg, MD: NIST NIST Special Publications.

Meyers M and Rogers M (2004) Computer forensics: The need for standardization and certification. *International Journal of Digital Evidence* 3: 1–11.

Palmer G (2001) A road map for digital forensic research. In: Report DT (ed.) Utica, New York: Digital Forensic Research Workshop.

Rogers M (2004) The future of computer forensics: A needs analysis survey. *Computers and Security* 23: 12–16. http://dx.doi.org/10.1016/j.cose.2004.01.003.

Rogers M, Mislan R, Goldman J, Wedge T, and Debrota S (2006) Computer forensics field triage process model. *Journal of Digital Forensics, Security, and Law* 1(2): 27–40.

SWGDE (2011) SWGDE and SWGIT Glossary of Terms. Retrieved from http://www.swgde.org/documents/current-documents/SWGDE-SWGIT%20Glossary%20v2%204.pdf.

Relevant Websites

http://www.cybercrime.gov/ – Computer Crime and Intellectual Property Section.
http://www.DCFB.org – Digital Forensics Certification Board.
http://www.forensicswiki.org – Digital Forensics Wiki.
http://www.ioce.org/ – International Organization on Digital Evidence.
http://www.cftt.nist.gov/ – NIST Cyber Forensics Tool Testing Project.
http://www.swgde.org – Scientific Working Group for Digital Evidence.

Investigation and Analysis of Structural Collapses

RT Ratay, Columbia University, New York, NY, USA
DB Peraza, Exponent, Inc., New York, NY, USA

Glossary

Beam A relatively long structural member, usually in a horizontal position spanning between supports, carrying loads transverse to its longitudinal axis.
Bracing Providing support against lateral movement.
Buckling Sudden lateral displacement of a slender structural member under axial compressive loading.
Collapse Total failure, falling down.
Column A structural member, usually vertical and in compression, such as a post or pillar.
Formwork A temporary construction to contain the wet concrete in the desired shape while it is hardening.
Fracture surface The surface along which a material breaks.
Lateral-torsional stability Ability to resist buckling which involves lateral deflection and twisting.
Reasonable engineering certainty The term arises from courtroom rules of evidence and, as such, is a legal term. Attained when the investigator satisfies himself/herself of the legitimacy of his/her conclusions, and supports his/her opinion with sound technical foundation.
Serviceability The capability of the structure to perform the function for which it was designed.
Space frame A three-dimensional structural framework, such as a roof structure with structural members in more than one plane.
Stress Internal force per unit area, usually given in pounds per square inch, or kilogram per square centimeter.
Understrength Having strength less than required to resist the loads.

Overview

Structural failures may be defined as the unacceptable difference between intended and actual performance. At one extreme, it may be a 'catastrophic collapse' with fatalities, and at the other extreme, it may be a serviceability issue, such as excessive deflection/displacement or premature cracking.

Most structural failures are the result of human activities. Errors that can result in failure can occur anywhere along the planning–design–construction–service lives of a constructed facility:

In planning – design concept
In design – detailed design, calculations, drafting
In the design–construction interface – shop drawing detailing, drafting, review, and approval
During construction – erection, inspection, accident
In service – misuse, overload, alteration, adjacent construction, lack of maintenance
During demolition – improper methods

Structural failures, whether they occur during construction or during the service lives of structures, are usually followed by forensic investigations. They often create claims of loss that result in legal proceedings toward the resolution of those claims. The determination of the cause of the failure and the parties responsible for it, as well as the technical presentation of the claim on the one hand, and the presentation of the technical defense on the other hand, require the engagement of structural engineering experts.

The investigator of a failure needs to have an understanding not only of structural behavior but also of codes and standards and of the design–construction process in order to recognize where along the process errors were likely to occur that could have precipitated the failure.

The purpose of a collapse investigation is threefold: (1) to determine the cause(s) of the failure, (2) to identify the party (ies) responsible, and (3) to learn from the mistakes.

The typical process of forensic investigation of a failure, hence the activities of the expert consultant investigating the case, may be coarsely outlined as follows:

- First-response and preliminary assessment
- Development of investigation strategy
- Fact-gathering and document review
- Engineering analyses to determine cause(s) and responsibilities
- Reporting

If the failure results in legal action, further investigation may be done as part of overall litigation support, or just in response to the findings of opposing experts.

Except for litigation support, the process is not country dependent. It depends rather on the nature and magnitude of the failure; fatalities, if any; the monetary value of damages and claims; and the time and money available.

Following the 10 October 2002 collapse of a footbridge during construction, shown in **Figure 1**, it was obvious that the omission of internal lateral-torsional stability in the design, absence of external bracing during construction, and lack of communication between the designer and contractor contributed to the failure. Very little investigation was required to confirm the initial findings. Following the 18 January 1978 collapse of the large space-frame roof structure, shown in **Figure 2**, under snow load years after its completion, it was clear from preliminary analyses that the primary cause of the failure was an error in the design of the compression members of the space frame, but the engineering investigation of the case continued on for years.

When a collapse occurs, the full scope of work of the investigation can include the following activities:

 http://dx.doi.org/10.1016/B978-0-12-382165-2.00150-1

Figure 1 Marcy Bridge, Utica, NY, USA, collapsed during construction (Courtesy of Robert T. Ratay).

Figure 2 Hartford Civic Center, Hartford, CT, USA, space frame roof collapsed years after construction (from Carper KL (ed.) (1989) *Forensic Engineering*. New York: Elsevier Science).

- First steps
  - Initial field observations
    - Engineering assistance in rescue operations, if any
    - Assurance of public safety
    - Documentation of field conditions
    - Preservation of physical evidence
    - Interviews of eye witnesses
    - Initial engineering assessment
    - Initial stabilization, repair, and restoration
- Main investigation
  - Familiarization with the project
  - Planning the investigation (document reviews, analyses, tests)
  - Identifying additional expertise required
  - Site inspection and collection of physical evidence
  - Review of design and construction documents

Establishing the design, construction, and service history
Formulating possible failure scenarios
Performing analytical studies and tests
Evaluating probability of possible failure scenarios
Selecting most probable failure scenario
Scrutinizing convergence of evidence
Demonstrating validity of opinion
Reporting
Interim communications
Oral presentations
Written reports
Presentation materials and exhibits
Litigation support – if required
Depositions
Preparation of demonstrative materials
Testimony

First Steps

As with any forensic investigation, the first steps in the investigation of a structural collapse must focus on the preservation of highly perishable physical evidence. There are, however, several aspects that are unique to structural investigations.

First of all, structural collapses usually involve large components. These components often can only be handled using construction equipment. In many cases, not only are the components large but they may also be numerous. A large area will often be needed in order to lay out and securely store these components for further inspection and/or testing. This area, due to its size and the need for the use of heavy equipment to handle the components, often is located outdoors. Items that cannot tolerate exposure to the environment may be placed within a secure trailer or protected in some other manner.

And of course, the nature of the perishable evidence is different than it is in other forensic sciences. Following are examples of highly perishable evidence that are associated with structural collapses.

Collapse Configuration

The collapse configuration is a highly perishable evidence. The postcollapse position of the components provides valuable information regarding the sequence of the collapse, which can help identify the area where the collapse originated. It can also provide information regarding the mechanism of collapse.

There are many valid reasons why the physical evidence will need to be moved, modified, or even destroyed. Chief among these is the need to rescue or recover victims who are trapped in the debris. Rescue workers may have to cut structural members and remove debris in order to reach victims. Another reason is the need to prevent further collapse, which could result in additional injuries or property damage. This may require the demolition of certain portions of the structure and/or the installation of shoring or bracing. Finally, there are cost-related reasons, such as minimizing business interruption or the need to complete a construction project by a given date.

It is therefore important to quickly capture the collapse configuration. There are a number of useful techniques for doing this, such as aerial photography, photogrammetry, three-dimensional (3D) laser scanning, and personal observation.

Aerial photographs help provide an overall view of the postcollapse location of components, which can be invaluable. Likewise, overall photographs from various angles and vantage points can provide valuable perspectives.

Software is available to help convert photographs into 3D digital models using the principles of photogrammetry. Digital models created using this technique can be very useful for visualization. Although the dimensional accuracy is variable, it is sufficient for many purposes. The main advantage of this technique is that no special field equipment or personnel is needed, since photographs can be taken with an ordinary camera. In many instances, the technique can be applied 'retroactively' to photographs that were not taken with this technique in mind.

A technique for quickly capturing accurate dimensional information of a large site is the use of 3D laser scanning. This is a powerful technology that is capable of capturing the coordinates of thousands of points per second, over a 360° field of view. Scanners typically have a range of nearly 1000 ft and an accuracy of approximately ¼ in. The technique involves the use of a tripod-mounted laser scanner and is often performed by firms with expertise in land surveying. The data are postprocessed with specialized software to create a 3D digital model that can be viewed from any angle.

It is important that the engineer investigating a collapse be present while the structure is dismantled. High-quality field notes, photographs, and possibly video are invaluable tools for documenting the collapse configuration and the removal process. In case of large collapses, it will be important to use a nomenclature system for uniquely identifying the various components as they are removed. If drawings for the structure are available, they will provide an obvious starting point for a nomenclature system.

Fracture Surfaces

The fracture surfaces of steel components can contain features that provide clues as to the type of load that caused the failure. These features can be obscured, or altogether destroyed, if the surface is not protected from the elements and is allowed to corrode. A common technique to protect these fracture surfaces from corrosion is to spray-paint them with a pigmented coating. The color provides visual confirmation of which surfaces have been protected. The coating can be readily removed once the item has reached the laboratory to allow study of the surface.

Curing Concrete

If a concrete building collapses during construction, one potential cause that must be investigated is whether the formwork was removed prematurely, before the curing concrete had reached the required compressive strength. It is therefore important to determine, as closely as possible, the strength of the curing concrete at the time of failure. The strength of recently placed concrete can change dramatically in the first few days and weeks of its life, so it is important that this be done as quickly as possible. The most reliable technique for doing so is to locate the standard test cylinders that were cast from the batch of concrete of interest when it was placed and to have these tested immediately, as opposed to waiting 7 or 28 days as is customary.

Snow and Other Loads

When roofs collapse under snow load, it is important to try to quantify the weight of the snow that was on the roof at the moment of collapse. The weight and distribution of the snow will change as it melts, it slides, and/or it is blown by the wind. The most direct and reliable method is to take measurements on the roof itself, using containers of known size and scales. Measurements of the snow weight on nearby roofs and on the ground next to the collapsed roof are also valuable.

If there are other loads that may have played a role, such as heavy construction materials that were stockpiled on a floor that was under construction or items stored in a warehouse, it will be important to estimate their weights and location before they are removed.

The Investigation

Once the perishable evidence has been secured, the focus of the forensic evidence turns to the actual investigation.

Investigations of collapses are usually led by structural engineers. However, depending on the nature of the collapse, additional expertise may be needed to perform a comprehensive investigation. The investigative team may need other types of engineers, scientists, and specialists, such as geotechnical engineers, metallurgical engineers, petrographers, chemists, fire engineers, wood scientists, polymer scientists, and crane engineers. It is important to identify the needed expertise early and to engage the appropriate people.

There are a number of fundamental questions that a structural investigation must address.

What was the trigger of the collapse? Every collapse has a trigger. The trigger is the event that caused the collapse to occur at that particular moment. In many cases, but not all, the trigger is obvious. Triggers fall into one of two broad categories: (1) added load applied to the structure or (2) a reduction in the strength of the structure. Examples of added load may be wind load, weight of freshly fallen snow, placement of heavy construction materials on a floor, and impact from a vehicle. Examples of reduction in strength include the removal of a structural member during renovation, corrosion of steel members, and deterioration of wood members.

What was the status of the construction at the moment of collapse? This is an important question if the structure was being constructed or renovated. In some cases, it takes considerable effort to determine this, since documentation of the progress of construction is often incomplete. A related question is what activities were being performed at that moment? These questions often require the input from eyewitnesses, who may be reluctant to share what they know. Whenever possible, eyewitness statements should be collaborated by physical evidence.

What external loads were acting at the time of the collapse? External loads include environmental loads, such as wind load, snow load, and seismic load. Other external loads include live load and loads such as people, furniture, materials, or vehicles. The self-weight, or dead load, of a structure is also usually considered an external load. Some of these loads, such as dead load, are well defined for a given structure and can be determined relatively accurately. Others, such as the load from an impacting vehicle, cannot be determined as accurately.

What were the internal stresses or forces that were acting? Once the external loads have been estimated, they are converted into internal stresses or forces using the principles of mechanics of materials and of structural analysis. For simple structures, hand calculations may be sufficient. For more complex structures, specialized software is often used to create a digital structural model and to perform the analysis. The structural model includes the geometry of the structure, the mechanical properties of each component, the restraint conditions, and the external loads. The structure can be modeled as a wireframe using 1D elements, as surfaces using 2D finite elements, or as a solid with 3D finite elements. The model may be of an entire building, including columns, beams, and floor slabs, or it may be of a single connection. The geometry may be based on design drawings for the structure, if observations of the as-built structure indicate it was built in substantial accordance with the design. Otherwise, the as-built configuration must be used.

What was the resistance of the structure? The resistance of the structure is determined using principles of structural engineering and mechanics of materials. For example, the buckling strength of a compression member depends on the material strength, the member length, the cross-sectional geometric properties of the member, end restraints, and other factors. Laboratory testing may be needed to determine the actual material strength or the strength of an assembly.

Where did the collapse originate? Most collapse initiate at a singular point, and knowing the origin of the collapse is helpful for determining the sequence and progression of the collapse. The collapse configuration, which was discussed under 'First Steps,' can often provide valuable clues regarding the origin and the sequence. The results of the structural analysis, discussed above, will also help identify the 'weakest links.' There are some cases where the precise origin is immaterial. For example, if a series of roof girders were all constructed with the same defect, and they all collapsed, it may not be important to determine which of the girders failed first.

What was the 'primary cause' of the collapse? This is the deficiency that, by itself, is sufficient to cause the collapse. Another term commonly used, primarily for failures in industrial facilities, is 'root cause.' Examples of primary causes include understrength material, an omission by the design engineer, failure to construct in accordance with the design, and inadequate inspection. The primary cause is typically determined by synthesizing all the available information: eyewitness accounts, physical evidence, laboratory testing, and results of structural analyses. As with other forensic investigations, the 'process of elimination' plays an important role in determining the primary cause(s). This involves the following:

1. Identify all possible causes.
2. Eliminate those causes that are not probable.
3. Investigate the remaining causes to determine which one(s) best satisfies the physical and engineering evidence.
4. Determine, if possible, the most probable cause to a level of reasonable engineering certainty. In some cases, there may be multiple causes that are highly probable.

What were the contributing factors to the collapse? A contributing factor is one that, by itself, is not sufficient to cause the collapse, but in combination with other factors can cause the collapse to occur at a particular moment. Or, once the collapse is initiated, a contributing factor can allow the collapse to progress further or more completely than it would have otherwise. Determining these factors also requires evaluating all the available information. It also often requires determining the relative contribution of each of these factors to the collapse, which may require performing multiple hypothetical analyses.

Who was responsible? If there is litigation involved, it may be necessary to go to the next level, which is to assist the attorneys in determining liability. In order to do this, it is necessary to understand the roles and responsibilities of the various parties, to be familiar with the applicable building codes, to be aware of industry practices, and to obtain and meticulously review all the project documents. When opining about responsibility, the investigators have to compare the activities of the various parties to some accepted standards of performance. The performance of engineers is compared to the 'standard of care,' which is defined as 'That level or quality of service ordinarily provided by other normally competent practitioners of good standing in that field, when providing similar services with reasonable diligence and best judgment in the same locality at the same time and under similar circumstances.' The performance of contractors is usually defined by the 'duty to perform,' that is, strict adherence to plans and specifications.

Several reports of seminal collapse investigations are suggested for further reading at the end of this article. They illustrate the variety of approaches that are used to answer these crucial questions.

The Investigator/Expert

There are several published definitions of the expert investigator/witness. What they all include are that the expert has the knowledge and skill necessary to evaluate the technical aspects of the case, can use that knowledge and skill to conduct the evaluation, can form an opinion with 'reasonable engineering certainty,' should be unbiased and free from conflicts of interest, should be truthful, and, if the case winds up in a court of law, should assist the trier of fact (the judge and the jury) in understanding the technical aspects of the case.

Professional opinion cannot always be with 100% certainty. The courts in the United States, for example, require that the opinion be only 'with reasonable degree of engineering certainty.' The phrase arises from courtroom rules of evidence and, as such, is a legal term. This suggests, among other things, that all mutually exclusive modes of failures need not be investigated if evaluation of the most reasonable causes leads to a definitive conclusion. This may pass the legal test, but might fall short of the definition of a thorough investigation.

Engineers should be thorough in their investigations and careful with the statements of their opinions. A credible, honest, ethical investigator satisfies himself/herself of the legitimacy of his/her conclusions and supports his/her opinion with sound technical foundation.

Often, different investigators arrive at different conclusions. This may be because two engineers working independent of each other may have access to different data, approach the problem from different directions, put unequal emphases on the same evidence, and/or be influenced by their past experiences, preexisting opinions, and biases.

Experts should be aware that their services can be subject to claims of negligence, and the liability may extend far beyond the fee for services. A client who used an expert may find the basis to sue that expert, if he/she lost the case or believes that the expert did not perform adequately. Simply being an expert on the losing side of a case is not sufficient cause for a client to bring suit against an expert; however, if the expert's performance was below the applicable standard of care, he/she may be held liable for the loss of the case.

Postinvestigation

To the credit of the structural engineering profession, failures have been and continue to be used to improve design and construction practices.

A valuable peripheral benefit of a laborious investigation is a clearer understanding of structural behavior and a better appreciation of pitfalls in the current practices. These can provide information and material to bring about changes in design and/or construction practices, codes, standards, oversight, and regulatory procedures that can prevent reoccurrence of similar collapses.

See also: **Engineering**: Materials Analysis and Failure Analysis.

Further Reading

ASCE, Technical Council on Forensic Engineering (2012) *Guidelines for Forensic Engineering Practice*, 2nd edn. Reston, VA: ASCE.

Carper KL and Feld J (1997) *Construction Failure*, 2nd edn. New York, NY: Wiley.

Cuoco DA and Panariello GF (2010) The engineering investigation process. In: Ratay RT (ed.) *Forensic Structural Engineering Handbook*, ch. 6, 2nd edn. New York, NY: McGraw-Hill.

Delatte NJ (2008) *Beyond Failure: Forensic Case Studies for Civil Engineers*. Reston, VA: ASCE.

National Transportation Safety Board (2008) *Collapse of I-35W Highway Bridge, Minneapolis, Minnesota, August 1, 2007*. National Transportation Safety Board, Washington, DC, November 2008. http://www.dot.state.mn.us/i35wbridge/ntsb/finalreport.pdf.

Peraza DB (2007) The first steps after a failure. In: *Proceedings of ASCE Structures Congress*, Long Beach, CA, USA, May 2007.

Peraza DB (2010) The first steps after a failure. In: Ratay RT (ed.) *Forensic Structural Engineering Handbook*, ch. 5, 2nd edn. New York, NY: McGraw-Hill.

Ratay RT (2009) Forensic structural engineering in the USA. In: *Proceedings of the Institution of Civil Engineers*, London, UK, Special Issue, May 2009.

Ratay RT (ed.) (2010) *Forensic Structural Engineering Handbook*, 2nd edn. New York, NY: McGraw-Hill.

US Department of Commerce (1982) *Investigation of the Kansas City Hyatt Regency Walkways Collapse*. National Bureau of Standards, US Department of Commerce, Washington, DC, May 1982. http://www.fire.nist.gov/bfrlpubs/build82/PDF/b82002.pdf.

US Department of Commerce (2010) *Final Report on the Collapse of the Dallas Cowboys Indoor Practice Facility, May 2, 2009*. Building and Fire Research Laboratory, National Institute of Standards and Technology, US Department of Commerce, Washington, DC, January 2010. http://www.bfrl.nist.gov/investigations/pubs/NISTIR7661_January%202010.pdf.

Biomechanics of Human Gait – Slip and Fall Analysis

TE Lockhart, Virginia Tech, Blacksburg, VA, USA

Glossary

Friction demand (μ_d) Friction demand (μ_d) is a ratio between horizontal and vertical ground reaction forces during the heel contact phase of the gait cycle. It represents the overall requirement for the foot to not slip significantly.

In order to analyze the principles of body stability and the mechanism of slips and falls, it is necessary to understand the dynamic principles of human locomotion. In this article, the biomechanics of human gait is presented to elaborate on the 'human' aspects of slip and fall accidents. This information may provide a comprehensive tool for forensic scientists to better understand the relationship between the 'biomechanics of human gait' and 'slip and fall accidents' and may assist in formulating cogent expert opinions.

Biomechanics of Human Gait

The purpose of this section is to assist in the understanding of the gait mechanisms involved in walking, which reflect the dynamic principles of each body segment in locomotion that are relevant for investigating slip and fall accidents. The purpose is also to describe the motor control strategies associated with walking to reveal the complex aspects of initiating events leading to fall accidents and its relationship to posture and balance in human gait. Understanding the motor control strategies associated with walking may provide us with information relevant to decouple the system into identifiable pieces for the scientific reconstruction of accidents. Here, we begin with some basic concepts in human gait.

Locomotion, an inclusive characteristic of all animals, is defined as the process by which an animal moves itself from one location to another. Walking is characterized as a method of locomotion involving the alternate use of the two legs to provide both support and propulsion. Finally, 'gait' can be described as the mannerism or style of an individual's walking pattern. Human locomotion falls into a general category known as 'striding bipedalism,' a locomotion activity in which the center of gravity is carried alternately over the right and left foot. Normal walking depends on a series of reciprocal movements involving the alternation of the function of each leg between supporting the body and advancing into the next position. These complex tasks are governed by open- and closed-loop motor control systems.

The mechanical definition of human walking and especially the function of gait may help us to better understand human locomotor control. In essence, the main purpose of walking is to transport the body safely and efficiently across the terrain. In order to do so, five major functions of gait must be performed during each step: (1) maintaining upper and lower limb support (such as preventing collapse of the leg during stance phase of the gait cycle), (2) maintaining upright posture and balance of the body, (3) foot trajectory control (such as acquiring safe ground clearance and heel contact), (4) mechanical energy generation to maintain or increase forward body speed, and (5) mechanical energy absorption to decrease forward speed of the body. All of these major functions must be performed within the biomechanical constraints of the body and the physical constraints of the environment. Additionally, the central nervous system (CNS) must also integrate efferent feedback from sensory organs to generate the correct patterns of moments of force at each joint to compare and represent the internal model against the real-world interactions.

Body Segments in Locomotion

Apart from the multiple variations that may occur between different individuals or within the same individual (for instance, as a result of changes in the speed of walking), there are certain observable events that are shared by all. This is because the mastering of the erect bipedal type of locomotion is a learned process and associated with certain personal peculiarities superimposed on the basic pattern of erect bipedal locomotion. In the following subsections, the process of walking in terms of body segments (i.e., lower and upper extremities) in locomotion is further reviewed.

Lower Extremities: Gait has been studied using the 'walking cycle,' which is the time interval between successive floor contacts of each foot. The activity of one leg can be divided into a short swing phase and a longer stance phase.

The stance phase occurs when the foot is in contact with the floor (starting at heel contact (passive) and ending at toe-off (propulsive)) and the swing phase occurs when the foot is advancing forward to take the next step (**Figure 1**). During each walking cycle, there are two periods of single-limb support and two brief periods of double-limb support (while one limb is about to begin the swing phase and while the other has just ended the swing phase).

Forward walking is achieved by pushing off the stance leg while swinging the other leg forward. At the time of the heel contact phase of the gait cycle, the forward-moving heel contacts the ground and as the limb is kept relatively straight, deceleration of the foot converts to acceleration of the hip. During this phase, the hip and knee extend. Continued forward motion of the body results in the forefoot coming to the ground, and the propulsive part of the support phase begins. At this phase (the muscles plantar flex the foot, flex the knee, and extend the hip), the heel is raised and pushes the foot

 http://dx.doi.org/10.1016/B978-0-12-382165-2.00151-3

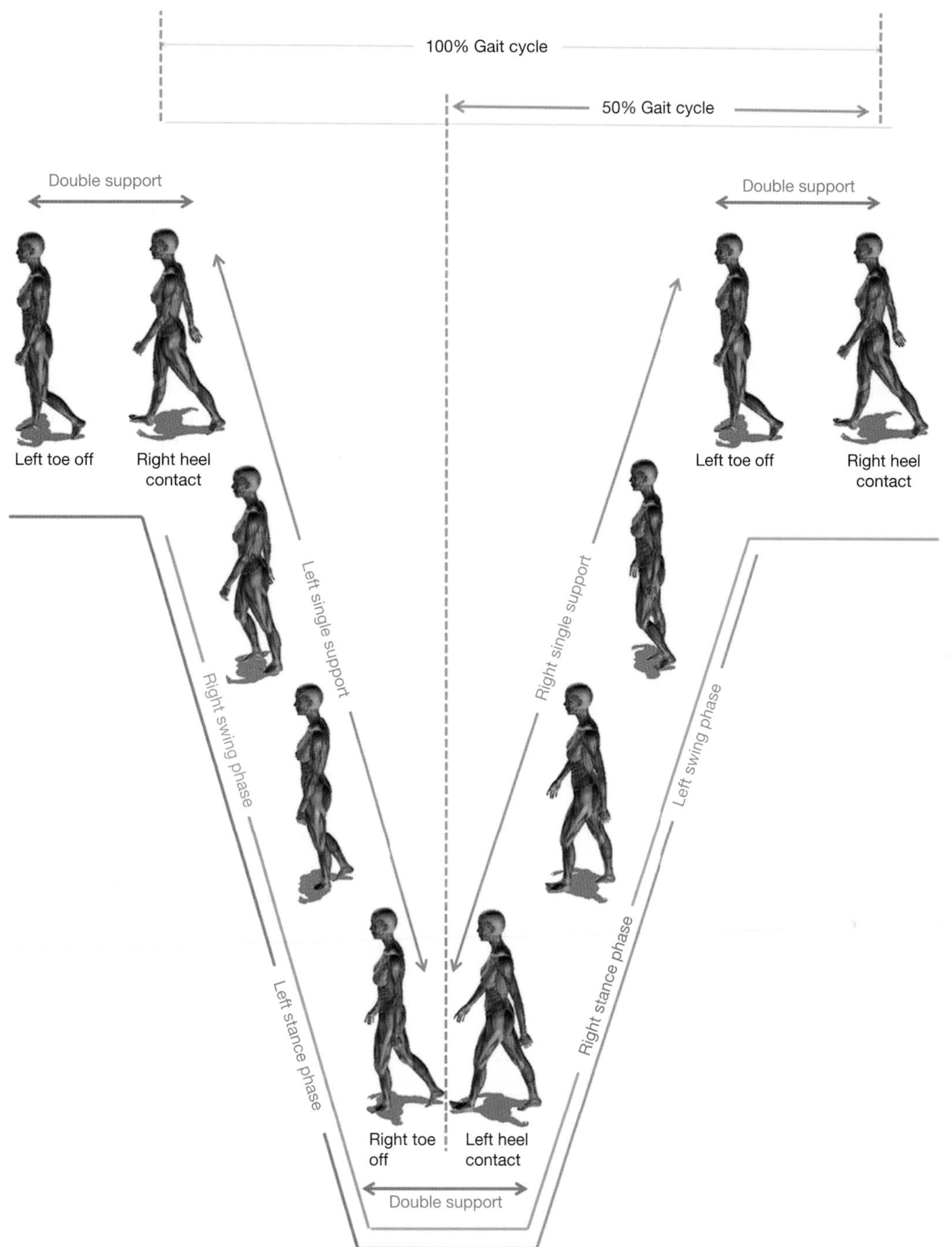

Figure 1 The time dimensions of walking cycle.

backward. This is associated with fixation and elevation of the pelvis by the abductors as well as tilting of the body toward the swing leg that allows it to land in a line anterior to the stance leg. The backward (propulsion) force is resisted by friction under the sole.

During the swing phase, the leg is flexed and slightly rotated externally at the hip, flexed at the knee, and dorsiflexed at the foot. Throughout the remainder of the swing phase, the limbs move under the influence of gravity alone, and finish in a position which allows direct entry into the next step.

Heel Velocity: An important lower extremity variable such as heel velocity during walking provides a linkage between motor control and slip severity as the control of the foot during swing is essentially a ballistic and positional task. Horizontal velocity builds up gradually after heel-off and reaches a maximum velocity late in the swing phase and drops rapidly to near zero just prior to heel contact.

The vertical trajectory during the mid- and late swing phases drops rapidly, but, just before the heel contact event (based upon the stride period), the vertical drop is arrested about 1 cm above the ground level. During the last 10% of swing, the heel is lowered very gently to the ground as horizontal velocity decreases rapidly to near zero. **Figure 2** shows the body kinematics at HC for a typical trial. It can be seen that the forward velocity of the body's center of gravity was 1.6 m s^{-1} and the heel velocity was reduced to 0.4 m s^{-1} horizontally and a mere 0.05 m s^{-1} vertically.

The significance of the heel velocity before the HC is that at the end of the swing phase, the heel velocity must be reduced sufficiently so that a dangerous slip will not occur. Walking speed influences heel contact velocity, that is, faster walking speed will increase the contact velocity. In order to reduce the forward velocity of the foot prior to heel contact, the foot is slowed through earlier and/or increased activation of the hamstring muscles. These muscles become active at the termination of swing phase by elongating as they act to decelerate the swinging leg (this is a very effective use of muscle). Decelerating the swinging leg at an appropriate time requires attentional resources via sensory modality.

Upper Extremities: Corrective postural movements are made by the upper body, arms, and shoulder. In walking, arm swing is used to offset some of the rhythmical acceleration and deceleration of the trunk by the leg movements, and also to damp out the rotational forces on the trunk. The arm swing varies considerably with variation in the speed of the walk. In the unladen state, the arm swings forward from the shoulder with the arms hanging more or less relaxed in a sagittal plane, but may move slightly toward medial plane. In the laden state, however, these dampening effects are not available. Load carrying (in front) also displaces the body center of mass (COM) anteriorly, placing it closer to the forward edge of the supporting base, thus requiring additional rotational torque at the foot–ground contact. Increasing the rotational torque during heel contact phase of the gait may increase the friction demand and increase slip severity. Additionally, blocking the visual path with a load may further influence the awareness of an impending slip perturbation.

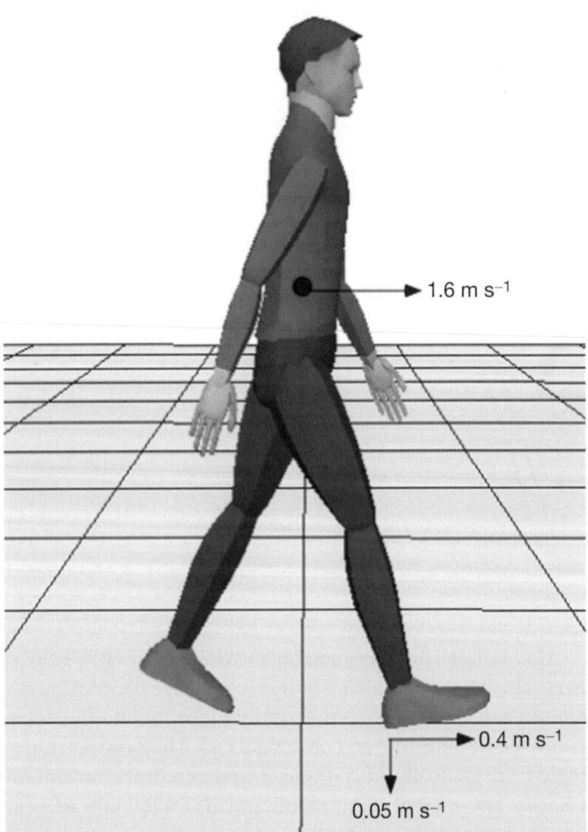

Figure 2 Body kinematics at HC for a typical walking trial. Adapted from Winter DA (1991) *Biomechanics and Motor Control of Human Movement*. New York, NY: John Wiley & Sons Inc.

Ground Reaction Force

The mechanics and the forces involved in slipping are important in understanding fall accidents. The forces applied by the foot to the floor at the point of foot–floor contact act in three directions: vertical (F_v), horizontal (F_H) in the direction of body motion, and horizontal transverse (F_T) to the direction of body motion. Note that by Newton's third law, the ground reaction forces exerted by the floor on the foot are equal and opposite to the forces exerted by the foot on the floor. During heel contact, there is a resultant forward thrust component of force on the swing foot against the floor. This results in anterior/posterior shearing forces (F_H) acting at the foot–floor interface. Walking speed, which is the product of cadence and step length, affects the magnitude of forward horizontal force (F_H). Forward horizontal force (F_H) increases with increasing step length and cadence; however, the effects of cadence are more pronounced than those of the step length.

Lateral-transverse force (F_T) is the result of the lateral momentum during the gait. This lateral momentum exists due to an out-toeing walking pattern. However, the force component F_T can be ignored in normal level walking due to the relatively small transverse forces compared to the other ground reaction force components observed in locomotion experiments.

Vertical force (F_v) is the result of the body weight and the downward momentum of the swing leg against the ground during heel contact. Vertical force (F_v) is affected by walking speed and cadence, which, as previously stated, has a more pronounced effect than step length.

Required coefficient of friction (*RCOF*): The required dynamic coefficient of friction (DCOF) represents the minimum (dynamic) coefficient of friction (COF) that must be available at the shoe–floor interface to prevent forward slipping at heel contact. Perkins used a force platform to measure the horizontal (F_H) and vertical (F_v) components of the force exerted between the shoe and the ground during normal walking. An analog divider calculated the ratio of horizontal to vertical forces (F_H/F_v) and displayed this on an oscillograph as a function of time (**Figure 3**).

Perkins found six peak forces in the normal gait cycle. The first four peaks occurred during the landing phase and the remaining two peaks occurred during the takeoff phase. Peaks 1, 3, and 4 are caused by a forward force, whereas peaks 2, 5, and 6 are caused by a backward force on the force platform.

Peak 1 is caused by the force of impact of the heel tip against the force platform and has a forward direction as a result of the approach angle of the heel to the ground.

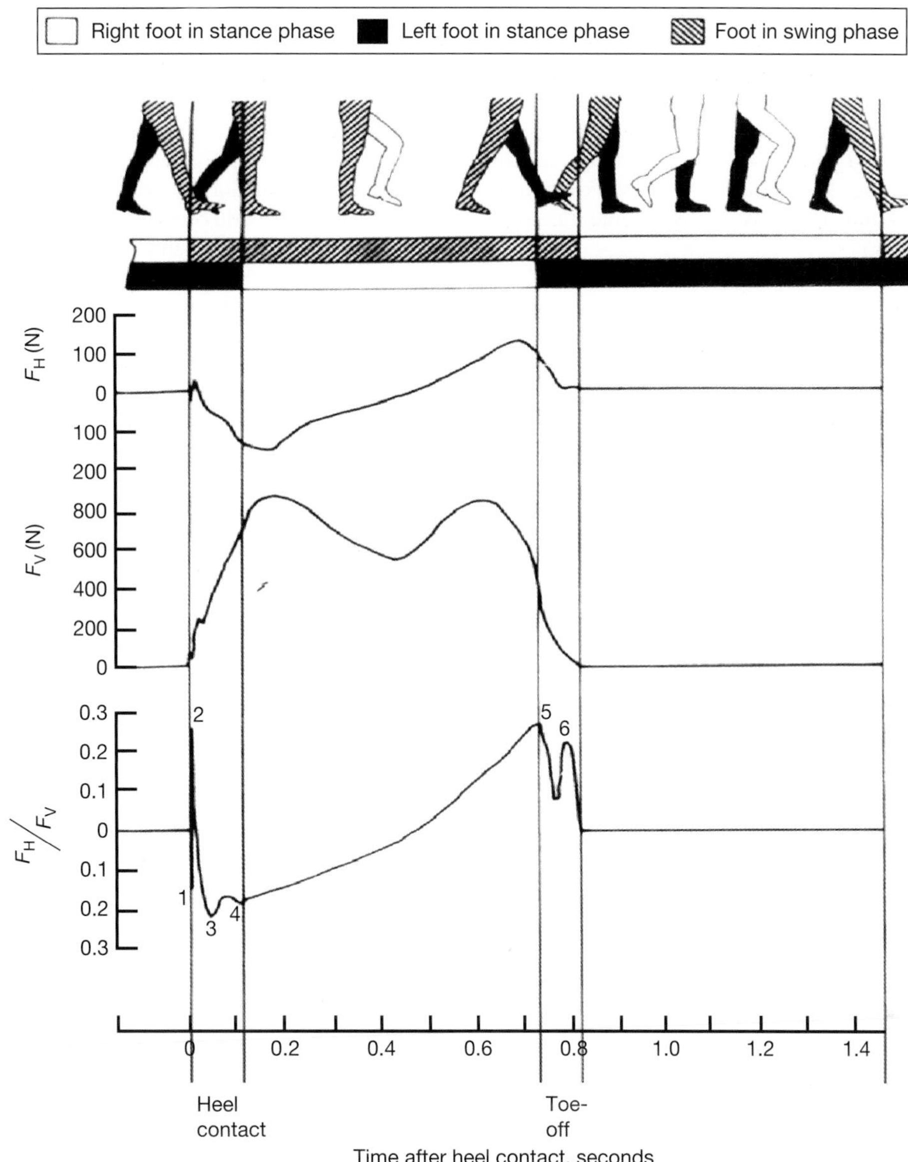

Figure 3 Gait phases in normal level walking with typical horizontal, vertical, and their ratio for one step. Reproduced from Gronqvist R, Roine J, Jarvinen E, and Korhonen E (1989) An apparatus and a method for determining the slip resistance of shoes and floors by simulation of human foot motions. *Ergonomics* 32(8): 979–995.

However, this peak has been found to be inconsistent due to low vertical force during this phase (peak 1).

Peak 2 is caused by a backward force exerted on the heel of the shoe shortly after contact. This force has been noted by several investigators but no reason for its existence has been suggested.

Peaks 3 and 4 are caused by the main forward force which retards the motion of the body and leg. During peaks 3 and 4, the vertical force has risen and a significant proportion of the body weight is being applied through the heel tip (less than 0.1 s after heel contact). Therefore, the error in F_H/F_v ratio is relatively small. As more of the body weight is progressively transferred to the contacting foot, the center of gravity of the body moves over the now stationary foot and the forward force causing peak 4 decreases. During the takeoff phase, the F_H/F_v (again) increases due to the force (peaks 5 and 6) exerted by the foot propelling the body forward. The significance of the ratio (F_H/F_v) is that it indicates where in the walking step a slip is most likely to occur. If the magnitude of F_H/F_v exceeds the COF between the two surfaces at a particular moment in time, a slip will occur. In this view, there are two critical gait phases in normal level walking from the viewpoint of slipping: (1) shortly after the heel contact, when only the back edge of the heel is in contact with the ground (peaks 3 and 4 in **Figure 3**). Peaks 1 and 2 are not considered hazardous because F_v is quite small at peak 1 and because F_H is directed backward at peak 2. (2) At the moment of toe-off, when only the forepart of the shoe is in contact with the ground (peaks 5 and 6 in **Figure 3**) – here, the required static COF demand is important to thrust the body forward. Theoretically, forward slip at peaks

3 and 4 during landing is more hazardous since the forward momentum of the body will continue to apply the body weight on the slipping foot. Conversely, backward slip at peaks 5 and 6 is less likely to be hazardous, as most of the body weight has been transferred forward from the slipping foot to the opposite leading foot. Backward slip at peak 2 shortly after landing appears to be hazardous, but the likelihood of slip continuing in a backward direction is less as the force rapidly changes direction.

Static Versus Dynamic COF (Tactile)

Tisserand found that rank-order correlation with subjective judgments of slip resistance was negligible for static COF measurements and very high for dynamic COF measurements. Additionally, Harris and Shaw found a high correlation between (walker's) opinions of slipperiness and the kinetic friction of wet floors. Their results are in close agreement with Strandberg and Lanshammar's walking experiments demonstrating that kinetic friction values, measured with sufficient sliding velocity, correlated better with the actual risk of falling than low-speed kinetic friction values or static friction values. Another study by Swensen et al. compared the perceived slipperiness of steel beams by both professional ironworkers and students. They were asked to rate and rank the slipperiness of each beam that was either uncoated or coated with contaminants (water, clay, and oil) after walking across the beams. The results of this study indicated that there is a strong correlation between dynamic COF values and subjective ratings of floor slipperiness. Figure 4 shows the result of a series of experiments using ten subjects and five different shoes. The mean subjective ranking and the ranking using the dynamic COF are very similar.

Visual Versus Tactile Sensation

Cohen and Cohen further explored the perceptual and cognitive factors involved in the perception of floor tile surface slipperiness. The results of this study also demonstrated that tactile cues are most sensitive to physical measurement of dynamic COF. A follow-up field study of the psychophysical assessment of the perceived slipperiness of floor tile surfaces concluded that people tended to make predictions about the slipperiness of walking surfaces and verified these expectations as they crossed them. The results suggest that visual cues to slipperiness are inferior to tactile sensation. They also suggested that in real-world conditions, the perception of walking surface slipperiness is probably the result of tactile cues, with visual impressions being confirmatory. Thus, in unfamiliar conditions, people may rely on the primary but inferior visual information about a surface's traction until they actually walk on it. The potential for an accident can be created due to misjudgment of slipperiness based on initial visual sensing and the limited time available to make immediate adjustments in gait to accommodate for the hazardous condition.

Slip Resistance Measuring Devices

Many devices have been developed by individuals, organizations, and federal agencies (e.g., OSHA, NIOSH, and NBS) to quantify the slip resistance of floor surfaces (i.e., COF). At least 70 different meters have been cited in the literature; however, none of these devices are universally accepted. In general, most devices fall into three categories: drag/towed-sled, pendulum, and articulated strut types.

There are two approaches to measuring friction. In the direct approach, the test device measures or indicates the horizontal and vertical forces. These include drag-type meters and articulated strut devices. The indirect approach calculates the frictional force by observing an energy loss in the test device. The most common example of the indirect approach is a pendulum-type device. These devices are limited in their ability to simulate biomechanical factors for an accurate DCOF measurement.

Strandberg and Lanshammar stated that on the basis of tribology and biomechanical analysis of slips and falls, the slip-resistance meter should reproduce the following operating variables from crucial gait phases: (a) contact time and normal

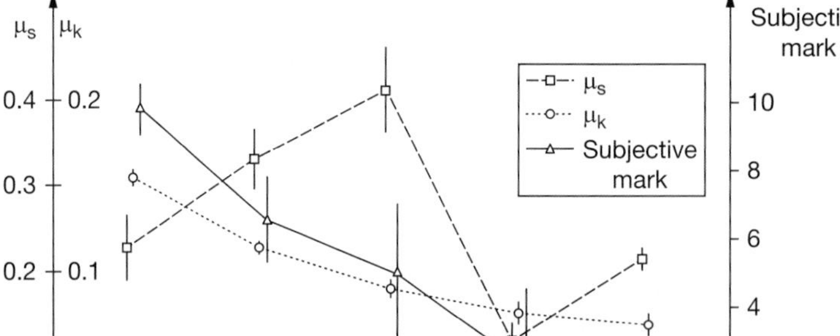

Figure 4 Comparison of mean subjective ranking by ten subjects and ranking using static and dynamic COF for five shoes. Subjective binary choice test. Reproduced from Tisserand M (1985) Progress in the prevention of falls caused by slipping. *Ergonomics* 28(7): 1027–1042.

force time derivative, for the influence of surface patterning and its drainage capability; (b) foot angle, for testing the most critical part of the shoe; (c) contact force application point at the shoe; (d) vertical force, for correct pressure in the contact area; and (e) sliding velocity, for correct dynamic friction forces.

The versatility of different meters has been compared and commented on by many investigators. Due to its heavy weight and bulkiness, the James Machine can be used only in a controlled laboratory situation for testing sample floor material, not the actual floor. The NBS-Brungraber Tester, on the other hand, is easier to handle and can be considered as a portable James Machine. The Tortus provides a permanent trace record when connected to a chart recorder, whereas most devices provide only a visual reading of the peak COF (analogy meter or gauge). However, drag-type devices have overcome most limitations and generally met with the greatest acceptance among both researchers and practitioners. The BOT 3000 digital tribometer can also provide both static and dynamic COF measures.

Trajectory of the Total Body Center of Gravity

The body's center of gravity is a key factor in human gait analysis as it reflects the motion of the whole body. The center of gravity is the theoretical point about which the mass of that body is evenly distributed. Reduction of the partial body masses into a common center of gravity or mass simplifies the movement dynamics to a point where the effect of the moving forces upon the mechanism of gait as a whole can be deduced. In the human body, the location of this theoretical point will depend upon several factors including the distribution of segmental masses and the location of those segments.

In the standing position, the center of gravity is situated centrally in the pelvis, approximately at the level of the second sacral vertebra. However, during forward walking, the equilibrium is lost with the takeoff of the propelling foot when the body's center of gravity momentarily lies beyond the anterior border of the supporting surface, and regained as soon as the swinging leg is extended forward and the heel touches the ground. Additionally, the legs move forward and backward relative to the trunk (torso), the arms swing, and the trunk moves up and down and from side to side during locomotion. Consequently, the center of gravity progresses forward and at the same time moves up and down and from side to side.

In normal level walking, the center of gravity describes a smooth sinusoidal curve when projected on the plane of progression (**Figure 4**). The path curve of the common center of gravity in the sagittal plane moves up and down. This motion is sinusoidal, with a period of approximately 50 mm in extent for adult males at normal walking speed. The summits occur at the middle of the stance phase of each side and the lowest points occur during double support when both feet are on the ground (**Figure 5**). At the peak of vertical movement, the horizontal velocity reaches a minimum (maximum acceleration). Conversely, the reverse is true at the time of lowest trajectory. The magnitude of the vertical excursion during free-cadence walking correlated significantly with the length of the stride and the peak-to-peak vertical oscillation increased as cadence increased.

In the frontal plane, the common center of gravity moves from left to right as each leg alternately becomes weight bearing. It follows a smooth sinusoidal curve, but with only one oscillation per stride as opposed to the two vertical oscillations in the sagittal plane (**Figure 6**). The center of gravity attains its greatest distance from the midline shortly after the support of the standing leg is shifted to the whole sole. At this point, there is an inversion of motion (the velocity is zero and the acceleration is maximal). Afterward, the center of gravity follows the period of double support and the velocity increases as the center of gravity again approaches the midline.

Shimba and MacKinnon reported that the lateral path of the center of gravity passes forward along the medial border of the foot (sometimes slightly outside that border: ± 2 cm; Figure 7). The lateral movements represent automatic postural adjustments, shifting the line of gravity alternately toward the eccentrically placed bases of support in keeping with the demands of stability.

In the transverse plane, the center of gravity carries out forward and backward movements (U shape). In this plane,

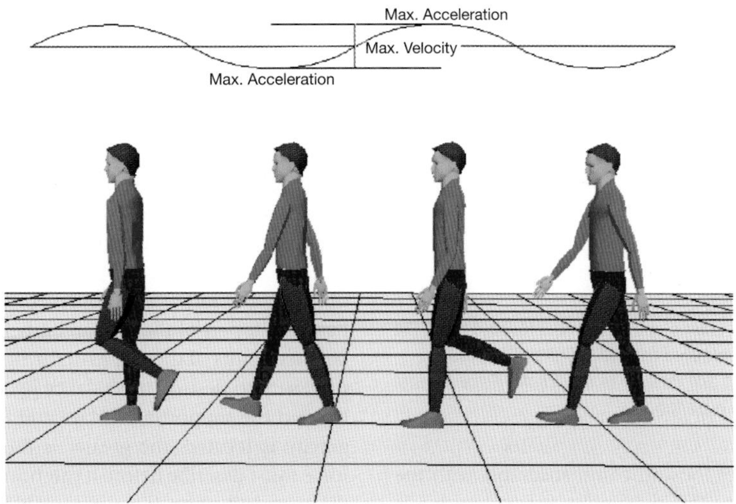

Figure 5 The path curve of the common center of gravity in the sagittal plane.

Figure 6 The path of the common center of gravity in the frontal plane.

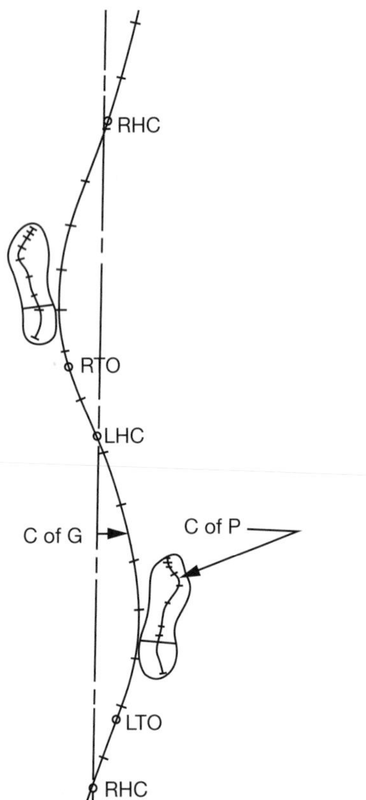

Figure 7 Lateral pathway of center of gravity passing forward along the medial border of the foot. Reproduced from MacKinnon CM (1990) *Control of Whole Body Balance and Posture in the Frontal Plane During Human Walking*. University of Waterloo.

the center of gravity moves forward commensurably with the movements of the pelvis. The maximum forward point is reached as the heel is set to the ground and the maximum backward movement occurs at the takeoff phase of the gait. The amplitude of these backward and forward oscillations is about 12 mm.

Balancing the Center of Gravity of the Human Body

Achievement of even sinusoidal displacements depends on smoothly coordinated angular displacements of the various segments of the lower limb. Various investigators used a series of simple models to illustrate how this smooth sinusoidal displacement pathway is achieved in bipedal locomotion. They show that this type of locomotion requires that the center of gravity be elevated to a height equal to the center of gravity in the standing position. Thus, it will result in a severe jolt at the point of interaction of each two arcs where there is an abrupt change in the direction of movement of the center of gravity. As such, decreasing the total elevation, depressing the center of gravity, and smoothing the series of interrupted arcs require coordinated movements involving all the joints of the lower extremities.

The balance of the human body or its parts requires that all gravitational forces be completely neutralized by counterforces. These counter-forces are supplied by the resistance of the supporting surface of the body. However, when gravitational forces fall outside of the supporting surfaces, the translatory force of gravity is not neutralized. In order to neutralize the rotatory forces, the line of COG must also fall in the supporting surface. In general, two factors influence stability: (1) the broader the supporting area (area over which one object is supported by another; in the standing position, the base of support of the human body is the area bounded by the contact points of the feet with the floor) the greater is the force necessary to destroy the balance by throwing the line of COG beyond the supporting surface and (2) the lower the center of gravity is located, the greater is the arc that an unbalancing force must describe before it can bring the center to fall outside the supporting area (i.e., more stable). In the human body, the constant mass is supported in standing on a small base.

Additionally, the area of the base and the position of the center of gravity are subject to constant and rapid changes and, therefore, require a complex reflex system involving the integration of sensory nerves and the motor nerves controlling the muscles to maintain balance in any given posture of the body. The deviation of the center of gravity is constantly monitored by

1. Sensory mechanoreceptors in the capsules and ligaments of joints, which provide information about their position and rate of movement.
2. Stretch receptors in muscles (muscle spindles), which give information on the amount and rate of muscle stretching.
3. Pressure receptors (exteroceptors) in the skin, which provide information about the amount of pressure on the skin of the soles of the feet.
4. The vestibular apparatus, including the semicircular canals found in the inner ear within the temporal bone of the skull, gives information of the motion of the head in all planes.
5. The visual system giving information about the position of the body in relation to objects and surfaces that can be seen.

All this information is processed in the CNS (principally in the cerebellum and the brainstem) and signals are sent to skeletal muscles to contract appropriately to adjust the position of the body to maintain the center of gravity over the base. This process involves unconscious prediction of body motion so that the adjustments are not merely responding to the existing body position, but arranging that the center of gravity to base relationship is appropriate for subsequent movements (i.e., the next step in walking).

Balance Task of Walking versus *Standing*: Human bipedal locomotion (walking) provides a challenging balance task to the CNS and appears to be completely different from the balance task during standing. During standing, the CNS is challenged to keep the body's center of gravity safely within the borders of the two feet (or one foot if balancing on one foot). Studies of balance and posture during quiet or perturbed standing have identified the ankle muscles (plantarflexors/dorsiflexors and invertors/evertors) as dominant. However, during locomotion, ankle muscles are no longer important because the balance task has changed. As explained in the last section (Lateral Oscillations of the COG), the lateral path of the center of gravity passes forward along the medial border of the foot (even slightly outside that border). Thus, during single support, the body is in a continuous state of falling down because the its center of gravity is outside the foot. The only way that recovery is achieved is to position the swing limb so that during double support the CNS can make any rebalancing adjustments.

Gait Model: This recovery is a challenging balance task that requires a complex interplay of neural and motor control mechanisms. Motor control is directly linked to the CNS's processing of sensory inputs (vision, vestibular, and proprioceptive systems). The brain constructs internal representations of the world by integrating information from the different sensory systems. In other words, the transformation from sensory signals to motor commands is processed within the CNS. The motor system transforms neural information into physical energy by transmitted commands from the brain stem and spinal cord to skeletal muscles. A system model that mimics the behavior of a natural process is known as an internal model, an important theoretical concept in motor control. The internal models include two main components: inverse model and forward model. An inverse model functions as a motor command computation to calculate the desired states. A forward model acts as a predictor to estimate the next state (e.g., future position and velocity). The sensory systems send inputs to an online controller to make an adjustment in real time. In essence, we use the inverse model to modify our walking behavior; that is, walking off the sidewalk to cross the street and stepping back onto the curb requires online controller. Additionally, the internal model is used to predict, and adapt to, the next step (i.e., forward model); thus, we are able feel momentum changes, for example, when walking onto a broken escalator. The importance of understanding the gait model above is to provide a better understanding of the processes associated with slips and falls. Here, it is clear that 'EXPECTANCY' is required to walk – that is, during walking, we expect the ground to be stable and, as such, we modify our gait to traverse the terrain with appropriate force and speed to safely ambulate; however, if the ground is not stable, there will be a motion perturbation (i.e., expectancy and reality did not match). This perturbation, if not controlled, could lead to slips and falls.

Gait Characteristics Influencing Slip Initiation, Detection, and Recovery

The process of slips and falls can be categorized into four levels as shown in Figure 8. The environmental phase considers the effects of contamination. As noted by Chaffin et al., 'any fluid

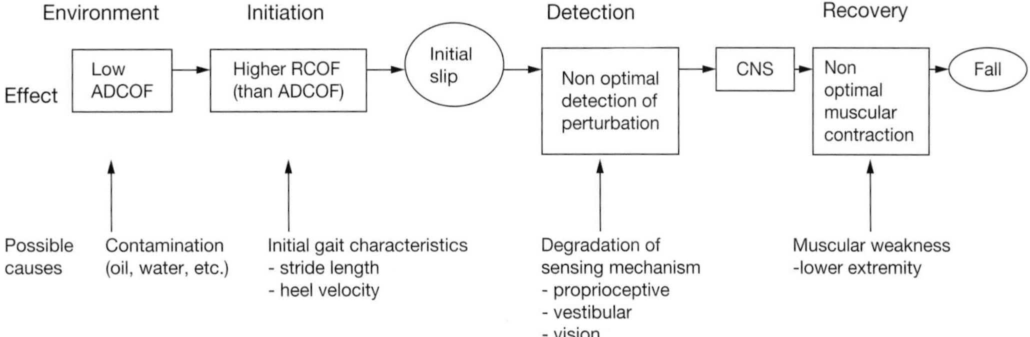

Figure 8 The process of initiation, detection, and recovery of inadvertent slips and falls with possible causes and effects. Reproduced from Lockhart TE, Woldstad J, and Smith J (2003) Effects of age-related gait changes on the biomechanics of slips and falls. *Ergonomics* 46(12): 1136–1160.

contaminant between two sliding surfaces will provide lubrication and thereby lower the DCOF values.' Therefore, the presence of contamination (oil, water, etc.) will reduce the available DCOF of the floor surfaces. In terms of slip-induced falls, friction demand characteristics between the shoe sole surface and the floor surface has been implicated as an important predictor variable related to severity of falls. It was stated that most of slip-induced falls occurred when the frictional force (F_{μ}) opposing the direction of foot movement is less than the horizontal shear force (F_h) of the foot immediately after the heel contact on the floor. The RCOF is defined as the ratio of horizontal ground reaction force to vertical ground reaction force. It represents the minimum RCOF between the shoe and floor interface to prevent slipping. Consequently, slip is initiated by the combination of lower DCOF and higher RCOF. A static COF of 0.5 on a level walking surface has been commonly recommended by standard organizations and by individual authors. Dangerous forward slips that lead to falls are most likely to occur 70–120 ms after the heel contacts the ground.

The sensorimotor degradation in older adults often leads to altered gait characteristics affecting the slip-initiation process. Lockhart et al. reported that older adults' heel velocity was faster than their younger counterparts at the heel contact phase of gait cycle. Increases in heel velocity during critical weight transfer may increase the potential of a slip-induced fall if the floor is slippery. In addition, the friction demand of older adults was found to be higher than their younger counterparts. It has also been suggested that whole body COM velocity relative to the base of support may be a factor related to RCOF. Slower whole body COM velocity and COM transitional acceleration (velocity changes from heel contact to shortly after heel contact) were reported in older adults. Alterations in these factors can increase the risk of slip initiation.

During the detection and recovery phases of the slip and fall process, the CNS control plays an important role. The CNS must undertake certain processing stages (detection phase) if a fall is to be avoided or compensated for (recovery phase). During the detection phase, a trigger must be sent through the sensory feedback to the motor control regions of the CNS. This process may be initiated by one or more of the following sensory inputs: somatosensors, vision, and vestibular function. At the input stage, any disruption in the quality of the input signal may increase the likelihood of slips and falls. The somatosensors are responsible for proprioception, the sensing of joint and limb motion. The vestibular organs located at the inner ear (semicircular canals and otoliths) detect angular velocity of the head and act as linear accelerometers. Visual cues provide information about the position and motion of the head with respect to surroundings. In the case of posture control, the relevant signals are processed by motion detection circuitry not only in the retina but also in the visual cortex. These sensory signals are fed back to a series of hierarchical feedback loops to generate motor commands.

The reactive recovery phase involves bringing the body COM within stability limits quickly after a slip is initiated. This is achieved through changes in various kinematic, kinetic, and muscle coactivity mechanisms. One of the important mechanisms during reactive recovery is to reduce the displacement of the slipping foot through increased coactivity of the muscles of the lower extremity. Electromyography (EMG) recorded from the lower extremity showed an increased co-activation of the rectus femoris and hamstrings, along with the tibialis anterior and gastrocnemius muscles, while recovering from a slip. The postural responses generated by distal perturbed leg muscles are of short latencies (65–110 ms), significant magnitude (2–3 times higher than normal walking), and long duration ($\approx$150 ms). Numerous studies have linked slower muscle activation rates in older adults as an indicator of increased risk to slip-induced falls. Kim et al. found a decreased hamstring activation rate in older adults and related it to higher risks of slip-induced falls. The postural activity of bilateral leg and thigh muscles and the coordination between the two lower extremities were found to be key to reactive recovery balance control.

An Example of an Expert Witness Report

In this section, opinions and basis for expert opinions will be further described using an example of a case involving a slip and fall accident. First, a general description of the accident is presented – usually, gathered information at this time is in the form of 'depositions' from various individuals involved either directly or indirectly in the accident. In addition to witness statements and/or discussions with the potential client, experts also inspect the area (either via photograph, video, or a visit to the accident site) in question and make measurements (e.g., COF, slope, and illumination).

Afterward, the opinion of the expert is presented using a variety of supporting materials linking human locomotor control and fall accidents. Here, we start with a general understanding of the accident at the time of a group's arrival at a restaurant.

General understanding of the accident

On the afternoon of 26 October 2012, Mrs. AC visited the C's restaurant in Parkins, Texas, for a lunch after a salon visit with a church group. Mrs. AC and the church group members arrived at the restaurant in a van. It was raining steadily and heavily at the time of their arrival (to the restaurant). As such, the van was parked close to the entrance to accommodate for the rain. Mr. Priggs (Assistant Manager of the C's at that time) held the front door open as they were entering the restaurant. The first group of ladies entered the restaurant. When Cynthia (a member of the group who witnessed Mrs. AC's fall from the posterior view) and Mrs. AC entered the restaurant, they were among the last of the group to enter the restaurant.

Mrs. AC entered the restaurant and walked toward the end of the mat to look for the group. She located the group by identifying the 'backs of their heads.' She walked from the end of the last mat onto the exposed tile floor, where she slipped and fell to the left side of her body fracturing her pelvis. Mrs. AC was assisted by the restaurant employees until the ambulance transported her to the hospital.

Opinion

The exposed tile floor surface between the 'mat' and the carpeted surface of the dining area at the C's restaurant at Parkins, TX, created an unreasonable hazard and risk of harm to pedestrians.

In order to maintain dynamic balance during locomotor activities and to help avoid slip-induced falls, gait parameters are adjusted to correct for contaminated or slippery conditions. In other words, when confronted with impending slip and fall situations, our walking style (i.e., the gait parameters) is adjusted accordingly to avoid slipping (note: online controller at work). Persons who have a prior knowledge of a contaminated walkway adjust their gait by reducing friction demand characteristics – for example, reducing heel contact velocity and step length by modifying the support leg's muscle stiffness. For younger individuals, this adaptation is quicker (within one step) than for older adults (at least two steps) – that is, it will take them at least one to two steps to adjust their gait to traverse even readily recognizable slippery floor surfaces. Mrs. AC is an older adult.

As indicated, the support leg is modified in muscle stiffness according to the walking conditions to progress the whole body smoothly without abrupt transition of friction demand. The ability to modify the muscle stiffness characteristic of our supporting leg (i.e., make rapid and adaptive adjustment of gait from walking on a nonslippery floor surface to a slippery floor surface) depends upon the quality of the user's perception of the surrounding environment. Hale and Glendon and Tisserand supported that a cognitive process occurs prior to action (locomotor activities) in order to safely traverse over slippery floor surfaces (i.e., online controller). The process starts with expectation – expecting the contaminant (i.e., water, grease, etc.) on the walkway, the area is surveyed (scanned) visually with appropriate thoroughness related to one's expectations. As such, the lack of obvious visual cues to elicit expectation can influence detection of slippery floor surfaces and modification of adaptive locomotor responses.

Furthermore, tactile cues to elicit expectation can also be important. Tisserand suggested that frictional values are estimated and memorized unconsciously from preceding steps (one's own model of slipperiness) and this information is updated whenever the subject feels the floor conditions are different from expected (reality) (note: adaptive controller). In the author's opinion, the cues necessary to correctly detect the prevailing slippery condition were neither obvious nor effective and resulted in a slip and fall accident. In other words, there were no obvious and effective cues to inform Mrs. AC that the exposed tile floor surface between the 'mat' and the carpeted surface was dangerously slippery and as a result Mrs. AC did not adjust her gait to compensate for the slippery floor surface.

Mrs. AC's expectation was influenced by several factors. Any visual cue that may distract a pedestrian's attention away from the slippery floor surface could be potentially dangerous. In this case, visual cues to distinguish the slippery floor surface were not available.

Furthermore, the assumption that the floor will be dry in the area where the fall occurred is lacking support. For example, in the case of heavy pedestrian traffic and heavy rain, water will accumulate on the mat and proceeding steps can track moisture onto the exposed tile floor surface making the floor surface very slippery. (Using a slip meter, the available (relevant) COF can be measured.) This statement is further supported by one of the witnesses to the accident – "The way I looked at it, the way that it even looked like this, I could see the skid [moisture trail] on the floor like her heel had hit instead of like the flatness of her foot." This statement further corroborates that not only was the tile floor surface wet, but Mrs. AC's gait was also not adjusted accordingly to walk on the slippery floor surface – that is, the usual gait characteristic associated with walking on a slippery floor surface is toe–heel gait to modify friction demand (more vertical ground reaction force than horizontal ground reaction force – as in walking on icy surfaces). In the author's opinion, effective tactile cues necessary for gait adjustment were also lacking.

As indicated above, tactile cues are import in eliciting protective response (i.e., gait adjustments) to walk on slippery floor surfaces. Frictional values are estimated, evaluated unconsciously from preceding steps, and updated readily to traverse the area safely. Walking on a slip-resistant mat first and then stepping onto a slippery surface may create a misperception leading to fall accidents. In other words, the slip-resistant mats provided a secure surface condition for normal walking with no need to modify gait (i.e., heel–toe gait) to traverse safely for Mrs. AC; however, when walking on a slippery surface with secure gait, her heel slipped, and she fell.

In summary, visual and tactile cues necessary to correctly detect the prevailing slippery condition (at the exposed tile floor surface between the 'mat' and the carpeted dining area) were not obvious and created an unreasonable hazard and risk of harm to Mrs. AC. In the author's opinion, the cues necessary to correctly detect the prevailing slippery condition were neither obvious nor effective and resulted in a slip and fall accident.

There are a number of measures that the C's restaurant could have taken to increase pedestrian expectation of slippery floor surfaces and/or reduce the likelihood of falls. One solution would have been to extend the mats covering the tile floor surface all the way to the carpeted area. This would have permitted Mrs. AC to get to the dining area without walking on the slippery tile floor surface. Warning signs such as 'Watch Your Step' and 'Caution – Wet Floor,' which are industry standards for hazardous floors, could have been posted (although warnings can be important, proper mats are the preferred safety measure). More probably than not, these measures would have prevented Mrs. AC's fall and injuries.

C's restaurant failed to institute reasonable measures to reduce the likelihood of falls and breached its duty to maintain its premises in a reasonably safe condition for patrons such as Mrs. AC.

In summary, although biomechanical aspects of gait and posture have been discussed in detail in this chapter, applicable codes and standards should also be referenced. As in all forensic investigations, careful and thorough investigations and analyses must be performed before scientifically credible expert opinions can be rendered.

See also: **Engineering:** Forensic Engineering/Accident Reconstruction/Biomechanics of Injury/Philosophy, Basic Theory, and Fundamentals; Human Factors Investigation and Analysis of Accidents and Incidents.

Further Reading

Brady R, Pavol MJ, Owings T, and Grabiner M (2000) Foot displacement but not velocity predicts the outcome of a slip induced in young subjects while walking. *Journal of Biomechanics* 33(7): 803–808.

Chaffin D, Woldstad J, and Trujillo A (1992) Floor/shoe slip resistance measurement. *American Industrial Hygiene Association Journal* 53(5): 283–289.

Cham R and Redfern MS (2001) Lower extremity corrective reactions to slip events. *Journal of Biomechanics* 34: 1439–1445.

Cohen HH and Cohen DM (1994a) Psychophysical assessment of the perceived slipperiness of floor tile surfaces in a laboratory setting. *Journal of Safety Research* 25(1): 19–26.

Cohen HH and Cohen DM (1994b) Perceptions of walking slipperiness under realistic conditions utilizing a slipperiness rating scale. *Journal of Safety Research* 25(1): 27–31.

Cohen HH and LaRue CA (2000) Forensic human factors/ergonomics. *International Encyclopedia of Ergonomics and Human Factors*. London: Talyor & Fracisis.

Gronqvist R, Roine J, Jarvinen E, and Korhonen E (1989) An apparatus and a method for determining the slip resistance of shoes and floors by simulation of human foot motions. *Ergonomics* 32(8): 979–995.

Hale AR and Glendon AI (1987) *Individual Behaviour in the Control of Danger*. Amsterdam: Elsevier Science.

Hanson JP, Redfern MS, and Mazumdar M (1999) Predicting slips and falls considering required and available friction. *Ergonomics* 42: 1619–1633.

Harris GW and Shaw SR (1988) Slip resistance of floors: Users' opinions, Tortus instrument readings and roughness measurement. *Journal of Occupational Accident* 9: 287–298.

Horak F and Macpherson J (1996) Postural orientation and equilibrium. *Handbook of physiology*, vol. 1, pp. 255–292.

Inman VT, Ralston HJ, and Todd F (1981) *Human Walking: Application to Lower Limb Prosthetics*. Baltimore, MD: Williams and Wilkins.

Kawato M (1999) Internal models for motor control and trajectory planning. *Current Opinion in Neurobiology* 9(6): 718–727.

Lin L, Chiou F, and Cohen H (1995) Slip and fall accident prevention: A review of research, practice, and regulations. *Journal of Safety Research* 26(4): 203–212.

Lockhart TE and Kim S (2006) Relationship between hamstring activation rate and heel contact velocity: Factors influencing age-related slip-induced falls. *Gait & Posture* 24(1): 23–34.

Lockhart TE, Smith J, and Woldstad J (2005) Effects of aging on the biomechanics of slips and falls. *Human Factors* 47(4): 708.

Lockhart TE, Woldstad J, and Smith J (2003) Effects of age-related gait changes on the biomechanics of slips and falls. *Ergonomics* 46(12): 1136–1160.

MacKinnon CM (1990) *Control of Whole Body Balance and Posture in the Frontal Plane During Human Walking*. University of Waterloo.

Nashner L (1980) Balance adjustments of humans perturbed while walking. *Journal of Neurophysiology* 44(4): 650.

Nashner L, Black F, and Wall C (1982) Adaptation to altered support and visual conditions during stance: Patients with vestibular deficits. *Journal of Neuroscience* 2(5): 536.

Noy IY and Karwowski W (2005) Perceptual-cognitive and biomechanical factors in pedestrian falls. In: Cohen HH and LaRue CA (eds.) *Handbook of Human Factors in Litigation*, ch. 19. Boca Raton, FL: CRC Press.

Pai Y and Patton J (1997) Center of mass velocity-position predictions for balance control. *Journal of Biomechanics* 30(4): 347–354.

Perkins P (1978) Measurement of slip between the shoe and ground during walking. In: Anderson C and Senne J (eds.) *Walkway Surfaces: Measurement of Slip Resistance, ASTMSTP 649*, pp. 71–87. West Conshohocken, PA: American Society for Testing and Materials.

Perkins P and Wilson M (1983) Slip resistance testing of shoes – New developments. *Ergonomics* 26: 73–82.

Redfern MS and Andres RO (1984) The analysis of dynamic pushing and pulling: Required coefficients of friction. *Proceedings of the 1984 International Conference on Occupational Ergonomics, Ontario*, pp. 569–571. Mississauga, Canada: Human Factors Association of Canada.

Shimba T (1984) An estimation of center of gravity from force platform data. *Journal of Biomechanics* 17(1): 53–57, 59–60.

Stelmach G and Worringham C (1985) Sensorimotor deficits related to postural stability. Implications for falling in the elderly. *Clinics in Geriatric Medicine* 1(3): 679.

Strandberg L and Lanshammar H (1981) The dynamics of slipping accidents. *Journal of Occupational Accidents* 3(3): 153–162.

Swensen E, Purswell J, Schlegel R, and Stanevich R (1992) Coefficient of friction and subjective assessment of slippery work surfaces. *Human Factors* 34: 67–77.

Tang P, Woollacott M, and Chong R (1998) Control of reactive balance adjustments in perturbed human walking: Roles of proximal and distal postural muscle activity. *Experimental Brain Research* 119(2): 141–152.

Tisserand M (1969) *Criteres d'adherences des semelles de securite*. Disseratation, Institute de Recherche et de Securite, Nancy.

Tisserand M (1972) Adherence statique et dynamique des chaussures de securite. *Rapport d'etude No. 11/Re*. Nancy: Institute de Recherche et de Securite.

Tisserand M (1985) Progress in the prevention of falls caused by slipping. *Ergonomics* 28(7): 1027–1042.

Winter DA (1991) *Biomechanics and Motor Control of Human Movement*. New York, NY: John Wiley & Sons Inc.

Wolpert D, Ghahramani Z, and Jordan M (1995) An internal model for sensorimotor integration. *Science* 269(5232): 1880.

Forensic Chemical Engineering Investigation and Analysis

DD Perlmutter, University of Pennsylvania, Philadelphia, PA, USA

Introduction

Chemists and chemical engineers are often asked by attorneys to offer scientific and/or technical assistance on matters in controversy when the details involve damage to persons or property from chemicals, fires, or explosions. In addition, if the subjects under examination reach into the court systems, plaintiff or defense arguments may call for expert opinions to support or to refute some position.

Because it is recognized that chemical engineers play an essential role in the design and operation of every chemical and petroleum process, they are often called upon in the aftermath of an industrial accident to evaluate the equipment and practices that were used before and during the event. Their expertise is also sought when fires or chemical events occur in homes or other residential settings. The procedures of evaluation have much in common, but of course, they must be tailored to the details of the equipment being used. In the factory or chemical plant, it will be necessary to examine any mixers, reactor vessels, distillation columns, or separators of various kinds, whereas in a residence, the focus will be on rooms, appliances, and any chemicals in use. In the best modern installations, safety considerations will already have been put in place, but sources of ignition or sources of contamination will still need to be identified.

Huge quantities of natural gas and petroleum liquids are moved every day between refineries and residences through pipelines that crisscross every state and most of the big cities in the United States. Usually the pipelines are buried, emerging only when it is necessary to cross some barrier or for servicing or pumping to the next station en route. Some of the piping is quite old and, occasionally, the welds or seals are inadequate to hold pressure. If leaks are not identified and corrected early, there is a high risk of fire and/or explosion of flammable material. Some very dramatic fires occurred as recently as 2010 in Philadelphia and Texas; the latter event caused one death and eight reported injuries. Chemical engineers are appropriate experts for any investigation of the causes of such events. The 2010 gas release and explosion from the BP Deepwater Horizon rig offshore in the Gulf of Mexico was in the news for months because it was very costly in terms of lives and property, and potentially more damaging to marine life. Eleven men died and many were injured in that event.

There are tens of thousands of chemicals in commerce around the world, and each case is potentially unique in some respect; however, there are some classes of substances and some features of accidents that occur often enough to provide recognizable patterns. With the objective of providing an overview of the wide range of approaches to presenting cases, this article identifies some of the important subclasses and their characteristics and offers examples typical of each one.

In each case being considered, it is essential not only to identify a potentially offending substance but also to consider the pathways and combinations that produce the hazard by the nature of their interactions. This means, in effect, that all the pertinent science and technology must be factored into the responses. Depending on the specifics, this may call for basic science such as chemistry, physics, or biology; transport properties for heat, mass, or momentum; or design and operations such as are central to any manufacturing process.

Many times an expert will need to find an acceptable and respected standard of practice by which to judge whether a particular device or decision is appropriate for a given circumstance. For such cases, the American Society for Testing Materials (ASTM) has published a series of indexed volumes that may easily be found in libraries or over the Internet. When fires and/or explosions are under examination, the references of The National Fire Protection Association (NFPA) provide standards and codes of behavior to be followed by experts. The Environmental Protection Agency (EPA) provides information on what is allowed in air and water and the Consumer Product Safety Commission is a source of listed hazards in their area of responsibility. Data on chemicals and their properties as well as on thermal and transport properties, heats of reaction, and chemical equilibria are listed in reference handbooks. The forensic expert will find all these useful to evaluate the crucial events in various circumstances.

More detailed discussions of these different matters are divided in this article under the general headings of Fires and Explosions; Pollution and Toxic Substances; and Unexpected Hazards and Unexpected Consequences. Specific examples may also be found in the author's website (www.chemexpertwitness.com.)

Fires and Explosions

In examining the causal chain that might lead to a fire, one must seek not only the flammable substance but also the source of oxygen (or other oxidizing agent) and the source of ignition, be it a spark, a torch, a pilot light, or a cigarette. The flammable material can be in solid, liquid, or gaseous form. Under extraordinary circumstances, it is also possible to get a flame without an external ignition source, but only at an elevated temperature. This *autoignition* temperature is different for each substance. Some examples are shown in **Table 1**.

If an explosion is under study, it may have been caused by some well-known agents such as nitroglycerine or trinitrotoluene, but it may also have occurred as the result of oxidation of a more common flammable material, if there was some barrier that contained the chemically reacting substances long enough for a pressure wave to violently rupture the barrier. Moreover, not every explosion is the immediate effect of a chemical reaction; it may be caused, for example, by a pressure buildup attributable to gas accumulation in a weak or weakened containment vessel. It is the bursting of the container

 http://dx.doi.org/10.1016/B978-0-12-382165-2.00152-5

Table 1 Selected autoignition temperatures (in °C)

Substance	*Autoignition temperature (°C)*
Acetaldehyde	175
Acetonitrile	524
Acetylene	305
Ammonia	651
Benzene	560
Carbon disulfide	90
Cyclohexanol	300
Decane	210
Diesel fuel	210
Dimethyl sulfoxide	215
Ethanol	365
Ethylene	490
Methane	580
Nitromethane	379
Pentane	260
Propane	480
Propylene	458

that qualifies as an *explosion*. If the movement within the combustion zone propagates at a velocity greater than the speed of sound in the vapor mixture, it is referred to as a *detonation*.

Flammability Limits

Typically, combustion occurs after a volatile gas or liquid has evaporated sufficiently to produce a flammable mixture in the air. In evaluating such a process, it is most important to take account of the *lower and upper flammability limits* (abbreviated as LFL and UFL). At concentrations below the LFL, there is not enough fuel in the mix to sustain a flame, and at concentrations in the air that are above the UFL, the supply of oxygen in the air is insufficient.

Because the mix is not flammable if either the LFL or the UFL limits are exceeded, fuel concentrations too low or too high as the case may be, it is possible to take advantage of this characteristic by controlled cleaning or by dilution. Before releasing a flammable mixture to the air or to contact with an ignition source, it can be cleaned by passing it through a scrubber, or it can be diluted with nitrogen or some other nonflammable gas.

An alternative description of the hazardous concentration range is sometimes expressed in terms of a *lower explosive limit* (LEL) and an *upper explosive limit* (UEL). This terminology is more precise if the mixture being considered is especially close in composition to the stoichiometric ratio of the fuel to the oxidizer, but as a practical matter, the two definitions are ordinarily treated as identical. It should be noted that organic dust clouds can also have the LEL and UEL characteristics, but the range of sensitivity depends more on particle size than on particular chemical composition.

As shown in Table 2, the LFL and UFL values vary over a very wide range, depending on the specific components involved; however, it should be noted that many common hydrocarbons can burn in air only if they are present to an extent between approximately 1 and 7 vol%. The tabulated values are for room temperature and atmospheric pressure, but the limits also depend on temperature and pressure. The flammability

Table 2 Selected values of flammability limits

Substances	*LFL Vol% in air*	*UFL Vol% in air*
Acetaldehyde	4	57
Acetyl chloride	7	19
Acetylene	3	82
Ammonia	15	28
Benzene	1	8
Carbon disulfide	1	50
Cyclohexanol	1	9
Decane	1	5
Diesel fuel	1	8
Dioxane	2	22
Ethanol	3	19
Ethylene glycol	3	22
Methyl acetate	3	16
Nitromethane	7	22
Octane	1	7
Propyl acetate	2	8
Propylene	2	11
Toluene	1	7
p-Xylene	1	6

Table 3 Selected values of flash points (°C)

Substance	*Flash point (°C)*
Acetaldehyde	−39
Acetonitrile	2
Acetylene	−18
Ammonia	11
Benzene	−11
Carbon disulfide	−30
Cyclohexanol	68
Decane	46.1
Diesel fuel	>62
Dimethyl sulfide	−49
Ethanol	12.8
Ethylene glycol	111
Methyl acetate	−10
Nitromethane	35
Octane	13
Propyl acetate	13
Propylene	−108

range widens with increasing temperature, but both the lower and higher values increase with pressure.

Flash Points

Another measure of the degree of flammability of a substance is its *flash point*, a temperature defined by a standardized empirical test. By following a procedure set down by the ASTM, a liquid is heated in a specified manner from below in either a closed or an open cup with an ignition source above. As the liquid heats, it volatilizes, and when the vapor mix with the air is sufficient to ignite, the temperature of the liquid is said to be at its flash point. As with other measures of flammability, the flash point is different for each substance tested. Some typical values are given in Table 3. The NFPA Standard 704 has assigned flammability ratings to liquids, depending on their flash points, as follows:

Rating 0: Substance will not burn.
Rating 1: Flash point equal to or greater than 200 °F.
Rating 2: Flash point between 100 and 200 °F.
Rating 3: Flash point between 73 and 100 °F.
Rating 4: Flash point less than 73 °F.

Pollution and Toxic Substances

If the subject of investigation is the release of a toxic material, it must be asked how the chemical entity was released. Did a vessel leak? Did some container crack, break, or explode? Was the release accidental or intentional for some reason? Where did the substance go and by what path? Some leaks are to the air, some to the ground, some into water tables, or to other above-ground water courses. Finally, what injury resulted from the events and their consequences?

Air Pollution

Toxic ingredients can enter the air from a variety of possible sources. Some are intentionally released if it is believed that the emission is harmless when it is diluted in the air to a low enough concentration. The Clean Air Act, which empowers the EPA, was last amended in 1990, but standards of acceptability change over time, almost always in the direction of more restrictive expectations. This is easily seen when one reviews the limitations summarized in Table 4. The allowable ozone level in city air, for example, has been reduced in the decade between 1997 and 2008 from 0.080 to 0.075 ppm. A new rule proposed in 2011 would require power plants to reduce emissions of mercury by 91% within the next 5 years. More recently, controversy has arisen also on whether the EPA can and should restrict greenhouse gas emissions, especially carbon dioxide.

Some changes in standards can also come about by responses from industry or consents unforced by governmental regulation. By international agreement, for example, the venting of chlorofluorocarbons was phased out to protect the

Table 4 National ambient air quality standards

Pollutant	*Primary standards*		*Notes on*
	Level	*Averaging time*	*Averaging time*
Carbon monoxide	9 ppm (10 mg m^{-3})	8-h	Not to be exceeded once per year
	35 ppm (40 mg m^{-3})	1-h	
Lead	0.15 $\mu g\ m^{-3}$	Rolling 3-month average	Final rule signed 15 October 2008
	1.5 $\mu g\ m^{-3}$	Quarterly average	
Nitrogen dioxide	53 ppb	Annual (arithmetic average)	
	100 ppb	1-h	To attain this standard, the 3-year average of the 98th percentile of the daily maximum 1-h average at each monitor within an area must not exceed 100 ppb (effective 22 January 2010)
Particulate matter (PM_{10})	150 $\mu g\ m^{-3}$	24-h	Not to be exceeded more than once per year on average over 3 years
Particulate matter ($PM_{2.5}$)	15.0 $\mu g\ m^{-3}$	Annual (arithmetic average)	To attain this standard, the 3-year average of the weighted annual mean PM2.5 concentrations from single or multiple community-oriented monitors must not exceed 15.0 $\mu g\ m^{-3}$
	35 $\mu g\ m^{-3}$	24-h	To attain this standard, the 3-year average of the 98th percentile of 24-h concentrations at each population-oriented monitor within an area must not exceed 35 $\mu g\ m^{-3}$ (effective 17 December 2006)
Ozone	0.075 ppm (2008 std)	8-h	To attain these standards, the 3-year average of the fourth-highest daily maximum 8-h average ozone concentrations measured at each monitor within an area over each year must not exceed the given limit (effective 27 May 2008)
	0.08 ppm (1997 std)	8-h	To attain these standards, the 3-year average of the fourth-highest daily maximum 8-h average ozone concentrations measured at each monitor within an area over each year must not exceed the given limit (effective 27 May 2008)
	0.12 ppm	1-h	The standard is attained when the expected number of days per calendar year with maximum hourly average concentrations above 0.12 ppm is ≤ 1
Sulfur dioxide	0.03 ppm	Annual (arithmetic average)	24-h not to be exceeded once per year
	0.14 ppm	24-h	
	75 ppb	1-h	Final rule signed 2 June 2010. To attain this standard, the 3-year average of the 99th percentile of the daily maximum 1-h average at each monitor within an area must not exceed 75 ppb

The EPA Office of Air Quality Planning and Standards has set national standards for six 'criteria' pollutants. The units of measure are parts per million (ppm) by volume, parts per billion (ppb) by volume, milligrams per cubic meter of air (mg m^{-3}), and micrograms per cubic meter of air ($\mu g\ m^{-3}$).

stratospheric ozone layer. This transition required substitution for the chemicals used in refrigerants and foaming agents, among other applications.

Sometimes obnoxious material is released from a chemical operation not because it is thought safe, but rather because the hazard is even greater if the toxic material is not released. This is the case, for example, if the buildup of pressure within a vessel would lead to a catastrophic explosion. A safety blow-off valve could then relieve the internal pressure by venting gas to the atmosphere. Most recently, after the huge earthquake and tsunami that damaged so much of the construction in Japan, the operators of a threatened nuclear power plant attempted to flood the reactor with sea water and vented radioactive steam in order to prevent an even worse meltdown within the reactor.

In any of the aforementioned cases, the wind in the region and the natural diffusion from higher concentrations to lower levels spread the toxins and the associated risks. Given information on the amount dispersed and the local conditions, an expert will be able to estimate the potential damage at various distances from the place of the release, allowing parties in controversy to better assess their positions.

Another class of air standards that applies in the workplace is set forth by the Occupational Safety and Health Administration (OSHA). In order to protect workers from lead poisoning, for example, OSHA has set a *Permissible Exposure Limit* of lead in workplace air at 50 $\mu g\ m^{-3}$ averaged over an 8-h workday for workers in general industry. In addition, the standard specifies the frequency and extent of medical monitoring, and other responsibilities of the employer. If controversy arises, a Chemical Engineering expert could provide information on fumes produced in the process as well as on air monitoring and possible engineering controls.

Ground and/or Water Pollution

When offending chemicals are freed from containment, they can also pass directly into the ground. This is especially noticeable if buried tanks are corroded by long exposure, whatever the setting. Fuel tanks in gas stations are frequently seen being replaced or removed entirely, and the same is sometimes also part of an agreement governing the sale of a home that has buried oil storage. Some industrial operations that need the disposal of unwanted by-products store the waste in an artificial lagoon, that is, in a lake created for the purpose by building confining dams of earth or concrete. With time, these dams can also leak. If they do, the hazardous stored material enters the ground or stream or river in the vicinity. An expert in chemical hydrology can be called upon to estimate effects on the underground water table or on the moving stream above ground.

Storage of Hazardous Materials

Many chemicals are held in storage in anticipation of later use, either as intermediates for further chemical reaction or simply as inventory for later sale. Often, the materials being stored are toxic to humans and animals and, sometimes, they are solvents or diluents that are flammable. When this is the case, special care is needed in providing vessels that will not leak or be corroded by the materials being held in them, but when these precautions prove to be inadequate, the results are catastrophic.

One of the best known serious examples of leaked material occurred in 1984 at a Union Carbide facility in Bhopal, India, when a storage vessel holding methyl isocyanate released its contents. The chemical was being stored as an intermediate in pesticide manufacture. It is a highly toxic gas and its release killed and seriously injured thousands of nearby residents. Accusations of negligence led to both civil and criminal cases in India, ending in fines and sentences of imprisonment. Improved design and practice now call for smaller inventories of toxins, backup safety procedures, and greater removal from population centers.

Unrecognized Hazards and Unexpected Consequences

A trained eye will sometimes recognize a hazard that is not recognized by an untrained user. Consider, for example, the following instances.

Fire in a Closed Room

It is common practice in construction and renovation to finish a new floor or other wooden surface by coating it with a protective finish such as polyurethane. These finishes are typically applied as a solution or suspension in a flammable hydrocarbon solvent. Upon completion of all or part of the task, the work is allowed to 'dry,' that is, the diluent solvent is allowed to evaporate in order to leave behind the finished protective surface. When the task is completed at the end of a working day, it is commonly convenient to leave the working surface unattended in order that the drying will occur overnight.

If, as is often the case, the room or house being worked on is closed and locked for the night, there is ample time for the evaporating solvent to fill the air in the room to a level that is above the lower flammable limit, creating an accident that is waiting to happen. All that is missing in such a case is a source of ignition, perhaps a pilot light left burning, or a sparking thermostat.

Fire in an Empty Container

When a container holding a flammable liquid is emptied of its contents, it is not truly empty. In fact, it is filled with the air that replaced the withdrawn liquid and with any vapors that evaporated from the liquid. When the liquid is especially volatile, the vapor concentration in the trapped air can exceed the LEL. The mixture will be harmless unless an ignition source is introduced, but this final element would be present if a torch is used to disassemble or clean the vessel.

Spontaneous Combustion

Many chemical substances liberate heat if they are allowed to oxidize in air. Usually this process occurs slowly enough that the heat escapes to the surrounding air, no visible flames are seen, and the process is harmless. Sometimes, however, the heat is trapped before it can escape. This can happen, for example, if the layer of labile substance is deep in comparison to the path of heat escape, or if the oxidizing chemical is held in a closed container.

In such circumstances, when the heat cannot escape quickly enough, the internal temperature rises. At the higher temperature, the oxidation reaction speeds up, liberating more heat even faster than before. The temperature rises still higher and this feedback snow-balling effect can run away and out of control. Eventually, this process leads to a fire, so-called spontaneous combustion, as the autoignition temperature is reached.

Charcoals and supermarket chars are commonly found to be vulnerable to such fires, especially if they are in closed or insulated containers or closets. Such materials are quite porous and can oxidize in air even when left uncovered in garden centers. Oily rags used to clean up paint spills or to wipe down greasy griddles are similarly in danger of what appears as a spontaneous fire. The recent emphasis on low trans-fat oils in restaurant and fast food cooking has exacerbated this hazard, because chemically unsaturated oils are especially easy to oxidize. Even commercial quick laundering may not sufficiently remove the offending substances from the flammable rags. In such a case, the detergents being used may be supplemented by added enzymatic agents.

Flammable or Toxic Solids

It was noted earlier that volatile materials, those that exhibit large vapor pressures under room conditions, are especially higher risks for fires because their evaporation makes them more likely to create concentrations in the air that exceed the LFL. Most often, these materials are liquids, but it should be noted that some solids, such as naphthalene or mothballs (para-dichlorobenzene), also show elevated vapor pressures at moderate temperatures and are correspondingly hazardous. An expert is able to make a quantitative estimate of the vapor composition.

An Explosive Pharmaceutical

Because chemical agents are used in such a wide variety of applications, the intended use in a particular application may obscure some secondary hazard. In some medical treatments, for example, nitroglycerine in small doses is a pharmaceutical taken by mouth or applied to the skin in the form of a patch. If it is stored in larger quantities, however, it is an unstable hazardous explosive. It was only after Nobel found that nitroglycerine could be stabilized by diluting it in a solid mixture that it could be used commercially as dynamite.

Contamination of Food in Shipment

Much of the world's food is shipped to market over great distances in the holds of freighters. To prevent spoilage, the storage spaces are usually temperature and humidity controlled by the circulation of conditioned air. A unique hazard arises when the ship is fueled, because the vapors of a volatile liquid fuel can enter the circulating air stream and contaminate the food being carried. Careful assessment of both risks and prevention techniques are called for.

Corrosive and Reactive Chemicals

Among the myriad substances that circulate in modern commerce, there are some that are immediately recognized as being corrosive to common metals as well as to people. These include all the concentrated acids (such as sulfuric, nitric, hydrochloric, and acetic), alkalis (such as lye – caustic soda and ammonium hydroxide), and gases (such as chlorine). These are all corrosives that can attack and chemically destroy exposed body tissues. They begin to cause damage as soon as they touch the skin, eyes, respiratory tract, or digestive tract. The more concentrated the corrosive material is and the longer it touches the body, the worse the injuries will be. When these materials are present in a workplace, everyone who works with them or near them must be made aware of their hazards and how to deal safely with them. A fully prepared Material Safety Data Sheet is essential information and will be asked for by an expert.

In fact, the list of reactive materials is much longer if one recognizes that significant chemical reactions can occur between many pairs of substances, including some materials that are commonly thought of as inert. Plastics can be changed in their properties by exposure to some solvents or alcohols, causing crazing, cracking, or softening, for example. Even some so-called noble metals (gold, silver, and copper) will react with thiocyanides to form soluble compounds. In each case, the result depends on the pair in question, as well as the conditions of temperature, pressure, and concentration, and an expert may be needed to make the essential distinctions.

Epilog

As a conclusion to this article, it is essential to add a caveat, because no single individual can be equally expert in all areas of any field. The forensic chemical engineer must assess any given assignment in the light of his personal skills and specialized knowledge, and be prepared to recuse himself if the matters at hand are not part of his repertoire.

The chemical engineer's skill is most effective when it is applied in direct conjunction with an attorney's view of legal constraints. An example may serve to illustrate the point. Most forensic matters that come to chemical engineers are related to civil suits, focusing on property damage or personal injury. Such cases are either settled out of court or adjudicated with monetary results. On occasion, however, a question arises that has implications for a criminal case. One such matter was raised when instructions posted on the Internet were followed by a teenager who constructed and set off a homemade 'bomb' via the chemical reaction of aluminum foil with an acidic toilet cleaner.

The punishment for this teen's behavior depended on whether or not the device he put together should properly be classified as 'an explosive device' and an expert was called on to testify on this issue. The resolution was based on the detailed understanding of the chemistry and physics involved, but it was the collaboration with the attorney in the case that brought out the distinctions on which the chemical engineering expert based his responses. In forensic matters, it should always be remembered that each profession enhances the contribution of the other.

See also: **Chemistry/Trace/Environmental Analysis:** Overview, Analysis, and Interpretation of Environmental Forensic Evidence; **Chemistry/Trace/Explosives:** Commercial; Explosions; Explosives: Analysis; **Chemistry/Trace/Fire Investigation:** Analysis of Fire Debris; Chemistry of Fire; Interpretation of Fire Debris Analysis; Physics/Thermodynamics; Thermal Degradation; **Chemistry/Trace/ Forensic Geosciences:** Soils; **Investigations:** Contamination; Explosions; Fire Scene Inspection Methodology; Types of Fires; **Legal:** Expert Witness Qualifications and Testimony; **Management/ Quality in Forensic Science:** Standard Methods; **Methods:** Analytical Light Microscopy; Chromatography: Basic Principles; Gas Chromatography; Gas Chromatography–Mass Spectrometry; Mass Spectrometry; Microscopy (Electron); **Pattern Evidence:** Tools; **Toxicology:** Interpretation of Results; Toxicology: History.

Further Reading

Carslaw HS and Jaeger JC (2000) *Conduction of Heat in Solids*, 2nd edn. Oxford: Oxford University Press.

Crank J (1975) *The Mathematics of Diffusion*, 2nd edn. Oxford: Oxford University Press.

Crowl DA and Louvar JF (1990) *Chemical Process Safety: Fundamentals with Applications*. Upper Saddle River, NJ: Prentice Hall.

Perlmutter DD (1986) Self heating and spontaneous combustion. *Proceedings of the Conference on Gas-Solid Reactions in Pyrometallurgy, W. Lafayette, Indiana*.

Perry RH and Green DW (eds.) (1997) *Perry's Chemical Engineers' Handbook*, 7th edn. New York: McGraw-Hill.

Roberge PR (2000) *Handbook of Corrosion Engineering*. New York: McGraw-Hill.

Relevant Websites

http://www.chemexpertwitness.com

http://www.astm.org/Standards/D56.htm; http://www.astm.org/Standards/D93.htm

http://www.astm.org/Standard/index.shtml

http://www.atsdr.cdc.gov

http://www.chemexpertwitness.com

http://www.cpsc.gov

http://www.epa.gov

http://en.wikipedia.org/wiki/Flammability_limit; http://www.engineeringtoolbox.com/fuels-ignition-temperatures-d_171.html

http://en.wikipedia.org/wiki/Flammability_limit

http://www.epa.gov/air/criteria.html

http://www.nfpa.org

http://safety.science.tamu.edu

Materials Analysis and Failure Analysis

AD Micheals, San Jose State University, San Francisco, CA, USA

The Role of Materials Analysis in Determining Causation of Failure

Materials analysis techniques are key tools in the arsenal of the materials failure analyst. Materials analysis seeks to characterize the intrinsic properties of a material in order to understand the extrinsic properties of the material, that is, how the material should behave in a given context. These intrinsic properties include morphology, composition, crystal structure, atomic bonding, elemental distribution, or, indeed, any characteristic that affects the extrinsic properties of the material. Of these, analysis of morphology and composition frequently provides information critical to failure analysis.

Why did a failure occur? This is the fundamental question to be answered by engineering failure analysis. By understanding and quantifying a failed material's properties, and comparing those values with either the specified properties or an exemplar, the materials analyst can gain an understanding of the role the material played in the failure, whether primary, or secondary to another primary failure.

Materials analysis may help the failure analyst determine:

- When a material failed in relation to a sequence of events. Did it fail and cause an event, or did it fail as a result of the event?
- If design or manufacturing was a factor.
- If the choice of material was a factor.
- Whether inadequate maintenance was a factor.

This article focuses on a selection of important materials failure analysis techniques used to determine morphology and composition (Table 1). Selected applications are presented; a list of useful materials analysis references, including sources for analysis protocols, is provided for further background.

Techniques for Determining Morphology

The characteristics of a material that pertain to its form are collectively termed morphology. Morphology may describe both the external and internal structure of a material. The general external form, including the shape, surface features, and surface texture, as well as the segregation of elements into different regions or phases, and even the internal arrangement of atoms, are important to materials analysis because the structure of a material is intimately related to its properties. The most common morphological characterization technique is microscopy. Various types of microscopies are available. Each technique has different strengths and limitations; therefore, the appropriate method must be selected depending on the information required and the feature size to be observed. The two microscopy techniques covered here are optical and scanning electron microscopy.

Microscopy in Materials Analysis

With the techniques of microscopy, external structure can be magnified and examined using light or electrons. The choice of imaging technique is based on the material being examined, the feature size, and the information desired.

Optical Microscopy

In the analysis of materials failures, information about the root cause may be obtained from visual examination. This is especially true when a fracture surface is available. However, magnification is frequently needed to observe the pertinent features of a fracture surface, the surface morphology, or the distribution and morphology of different phases.

In optical microscopy, examination is done using light incident on the specimen, and reflected back into the eye of the investigator, or to a camera. Transmitted light may also be used with appropriately thin or transparent materials. Traditionally, the light used is in the visible spectrum; however, infrared or ultraviolet light frequencies may also be used, in conjunction with appropriate detectors and equipment to display images in a viewable format.

Because of the limitations of their resolving power, the typical magnification range of optical microscopy runs from 1 to 400 times the original size; 1000 times is the upper limit of the magnification range for conventional optical microscopes. When viewing fracture surfaces, which are typically rough, the depth of field, which is the ability of the microscope to keep the entire field of view in focus, is frequently a limiting factor. Depth of field is a function of the optics of the microscope and magnification (depth of field decreases with increasing magnification), as well as of the behavior of light in general.

Optical microscopy is typically performed with physical glass lenses. In common usage, a single-lens microscope is called a 'magnifying glass,' while 'microscope' refers to a compound microscope. Compared to the single-lens microscope, the compound microscope uses multiple lenses along the optical path to achieve a range of specific magnifications as well as improved magnification and optical quality. A compound microscope suitable for viewing solid specimens is shown in Figure 1.

In materials analysis, there are two specific configurations of optical microscope that are commonly used: the inverted microscope (Figure 2) and the stereomicroscope (Figure 3). The inverted microscope is used to image flat, polished specimens. The specimen is placed above the magnifying lenses, in an inverted position. Because the specimen is flat, the limited depth of field is not an issue; magnifications of 1000 times can be achieved with clear focus in the plane of the specimen. An appropriately prepared specimen can evidence transitions between different phases, dislocation motion, history of heat

 http://dx.doi.org/10.1016/B978-0-12-382165-2.00153-7

Table 1 Some materials analysis techniques used to determine morphology and composition

Morphology
Optical microscopy
Scanning electron microscopy
Composition
Energy-dispersive spectroscopy
Wavelength-dispersive spectroscopy
x-Ray fluoroscopy
Absorption spectroscopy
Auger electron spectroscopy
Mass spectrometry
Differential scanning calorimetry
Differential thermal analysis (DTA)
Thermogravimetric analysis

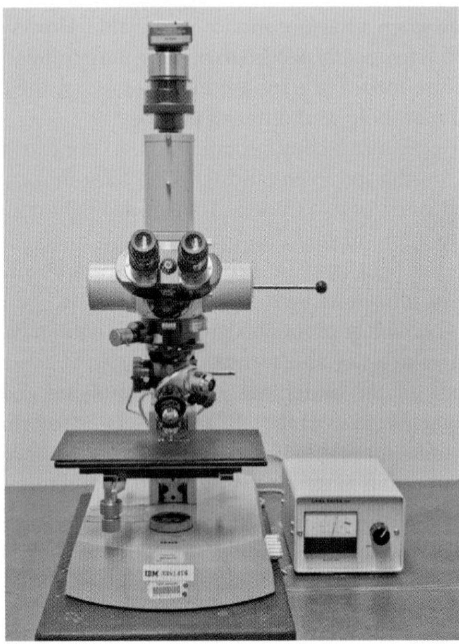

Figure 1 A compound microscope for viewing solid specimens. The optical path goes from the sample through multiple magnifying lenses, and is then split, sending an identical image to each of the dual eyepieces.

treating and mechanical deformation, processing defects, voids, and material composition.

The stereomicroscope consists of two distinct compound microscopes, with offset optical paths terminating at separate eyepieces. The distinct images displayed in the two eyepieces allow for perception of depth. Because the depth of field is inversely related to magnification, magnification is typically limited to 100 times, for the sake of a larger working distance and maintaining an adequate depth of field. Stereomicroscopes are useful for viewing large areas of fracture surface and specimens with large height differences. Stereomicroscopy may often be used to distinguish between various types of fracture, for example, ductile versus brittle fracture, overload fracture, and fatigue fracture.

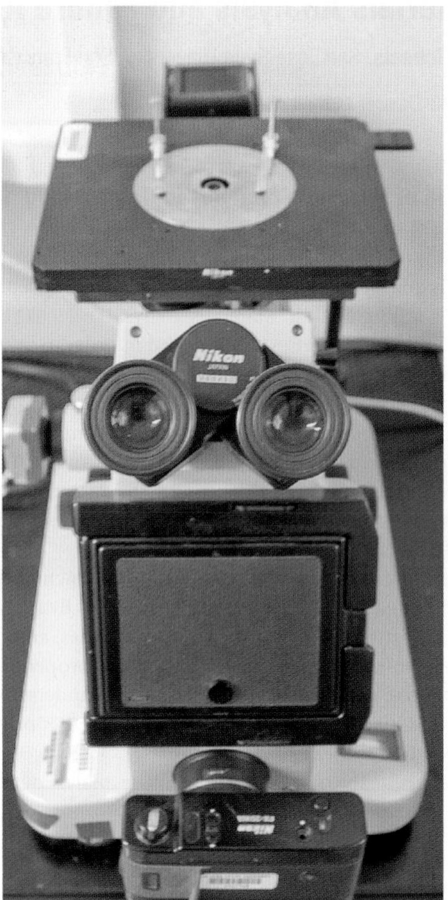

Figure 2 An inverted microscope for examining flat (polished) specimens at high magnifications. Note that the specimen stage is above the optics, or inverted from the 'normal' orientation.

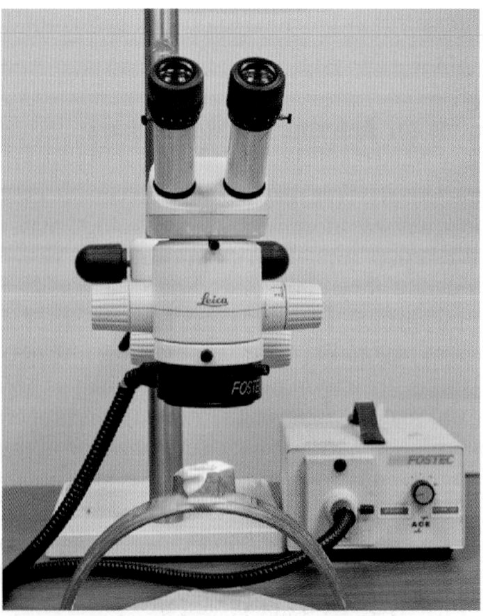

Figure 3 A stereomicroscope used for viewing objects with height differences at low magnification.

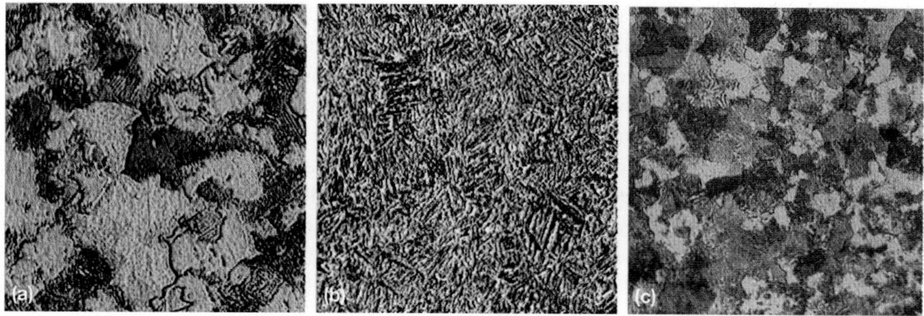

Figure 4 1040 steel, (a) slow cooled, (b) quenched and tempered for 1 h at 205 °C, and (c) failed material of unknown heat treatment. Samples were polished to 0.05 μm alumina abrasive, and then etched for 10 s with 2% Nital etchant (2% nitric acid in ethanol). The micrographs were taken with an inverted microscope at 400 times magnification.

Specimen Preparation for Microstructural Examination

When analyzing a materials failure, it may be of interest to examine the internal microstructure. Microstructure arises from the segregation of different elements or impurities into different regions; these regions form different structures, called phases, within the material. These phases and their relative, spatial configurations have a significant effect on the properties (both desirable and undesirable) of the material. Many of these structures can be observed and identified with an optical or electron microscope. Specimen preparation procedures have been developed to prepare material specimens for examination of their microstructure. The specimen preparation techniques are collectively grouped under the term metallography. Further information can be found in the References section.

Analysis of failed structural steel using optical microscopy

1040 steel in a structural application failed unexpectedly. The failed steel as well as two 1040 steel samples subjected to different heat treatments were prepared for microscopic examination by being polished and chemically etched. The differences brought about by the heat treatments are visible at the relatively low magnification of 400 times. Figure 4(a) shows large grains typical of slow cooling, where time at temperature allows the atoms to move to low-stress positions on the crystal lattice. Figure 4(b), quenched and tempered at a relatively low temperature, is little changed from the fine grain structure typical of martensitic steel; the temperature was too low for the atoms to move and form stress-free grains. The slow cooled sample will have a much lower strength than the quenched sample.

On comparing the failed steel, Figure 4(c), to the samples with known history, it was found that the failed steel had not been strengthened by the appropriate heat treatment.

Scanning Electron Microscopy

For greater magnification, and improved depth of field, an electron microscope can be used. The scanning electron microscope (SEM) is a common instrument, which provides images that are intuitive and easy to understand. Magnification ranges from approximately 20 times to over 20 000 times. Depth of field depends on magnification, but can be as much as 10 mm at low magnification.

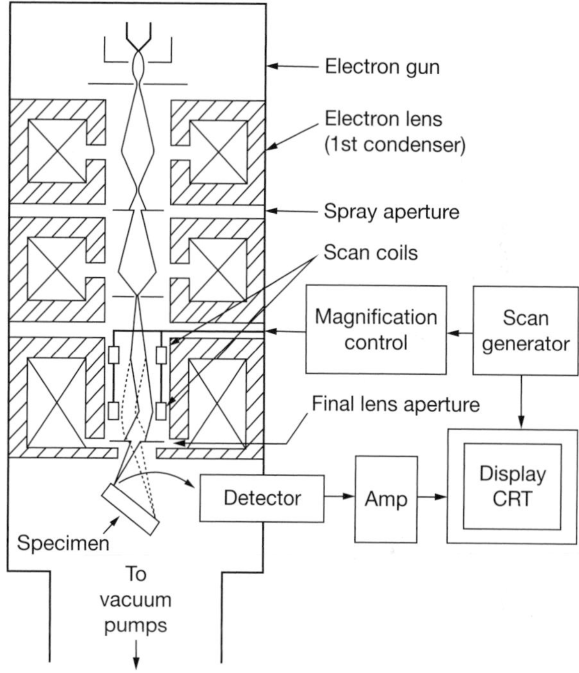

Figure 5 Cross-sectional schematic of the column of a scanning electron microscope. Reprinted from Goldstein J, Newbury D, Joy D, et al. (2003) *Scanning Electron Microscopy and X-Ray Analysis*, p. 23. New York: Springer. Copyright 2003 by Springer Science + Business Media, with kind permission from Springer Science + Business Media B.V.

Whereas an optical microscope illuminates the entire specimen at the same time, and creates an image by focusing the reflected or transmitted light, an SEM image is formed by focusing the electrons used to illuminate the specimen onto a very small area and moving (scanning) the focused beam across the specimen's surface. The 'brightness' of the energy reflected as each small area of the specimen is illuminated is measured and displayed as the brightness of a pixel on an image.

A schematic of an SEM is shown in Figure 5. Electrons are created by heating a filament (tungsten or lanthanum hexaboride), and are then accelerated by an applied voltage of up to 30 kV. The electron beam is focused by electromagnetic lenses to bombard the specimen surface. The beam of these primary electrons (PE) is scanned across the surface of the specimen.

As the beam is scanned, some of those electrons are reflected after scattering, and other additional electrons may be emitted from the specimen. PEs reflected from the specimen are referred to as backscattered electrons (BSEs). BSEs have relatively high energy, up to that of the incident beam. If a PE interacts with a specimen atom, and transfers some of its energy to that atom's electrons, one or more of the atom's electrons may be emitted as secondary electrons (SEs). SEs are low-energy electrons and are distinguished from BSEs as having less than 50 eV of kinetic energy.

Specialized detectors are used to sense the electron signals. The detected electron intensity is converted into an electrical signal that is displayed as a gray scale image where brightness is proportional to the detected electron intensity. The image is sent to a computer, to be displayed, printed, or saved in a digital format. Magnification occurs when the primary electron beam is scanned across a small area of a specimen, and the image of the scanned surface region is displayed on a larger computer screen.

The imaging process usually takes place under high vacuum, around 10^{-6} torr. The vacuum prevents the PE beam from losing its energy in collisions with gaseous atoms, and allows the emitted signal to reach the detectors.

The resolution of the SEM, while theoretically limited by the wavelength of the primary electrons, is more practically dependent on two factors: the incident beam diameter, or spot size, and the region of the specimen that the primary electrons interact with, called the interaction volume (**Figure 6**). The beam diameter is determined by how tightly focused the electron beam is. It is controlled by focusing electromagnetic lenses, and can be adjusted from microns to nanometers. The dimensions of the interaction volume depend strongly on the incident electron energy. The width and depth may range from hundreds of nanometers up to approximately 5 μm. While a high-energy means that the electrons have a shorter wavelength, the electrons in the beam also have high speed and momentum, which drives the electrons farther into the material. The interaction volume also depends on the atomic number Z of the specimen. As Z increases, the number of outer shell electrons in the atom increases and the incident electrons are more strongly repelled by Columbic interaction with the atomic electric field. So, for small Z, as with carbon, the interaction volume is large; for large Z, as with lead, the interaction volume is small.

As can be seen from the interaction volume, SEs are most representative of the specimen surface, while BSEs result from bulk interactions. Therefore, for best resolution of surface features, imaging is typically derived from SEs. For contrast differences derived from elemental composition, the BSE signal is typically used.

Analysis of a ductile iron pipe failure with scanning electron microscopy

A ductile iron pipe failed unexpectedly during a pressure test. Samples from the failed pipe and from a pipe that had survived the pressure test were examined in the SEM. Both specimens were prepared by grinding and polishing to a flat surface. The specimens were chemically etched to create a slight but observable height difference between the iron and carbon phases. In this image, the primary contrast is from the BSE signal. The incident electrons penetrate the low Z carbides, with little BSE emission. The higher Z iron phase reflects more electrons, emitting a higher-intensity signal. Therefore, the iron regions appear bright compared to the carbides.

Ductile iron microstructure typically consists of an iron matrix with distributed spherical carbides. The spherical carbides intercept any cracks in the iron matrix and prevent them from propagating. **Figure 7(a)**, the 'good' pipe, shows the expected ductile iron microstructure. **Figure 7(b)**, the failed pipe, shows poorly formed, nonspherical carbides. As a result, the material of **Figure 7(b)** had a lower-than-expected strength compared to that of **Figure 7(a)**. Additional analysis determined the cause of the poor carbide morphology to be errors in the material composition.

Techniques for Determining Composition

Along with morphology, composition plays an inseparable role in the behavior of a material. While the major elements

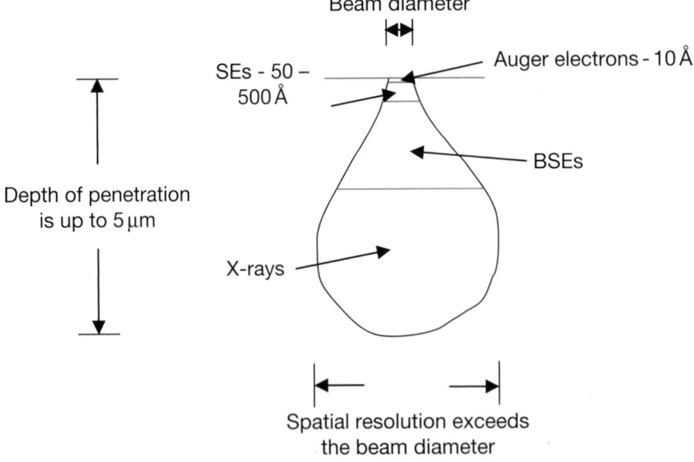

Figure 6 The interaction volume is the three-dimensional portion of the specimen that the primary electrons travel through. Its size varies with the kinetic energy of the primary electrons, and with the atomic number of the specimen.

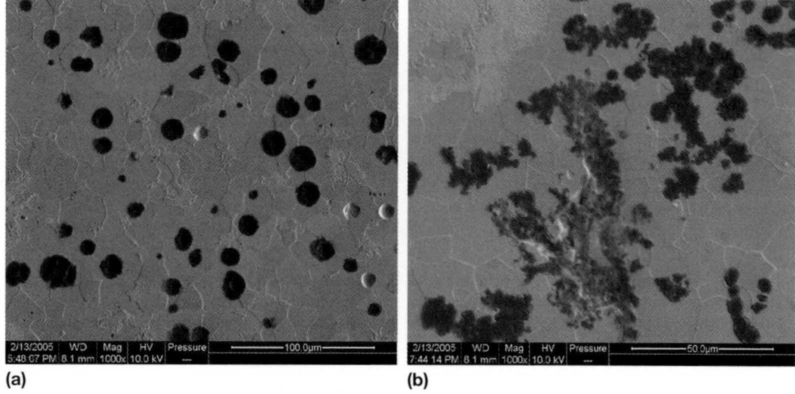

Figure 7 Scanning electron micrographs of two ductile iron specimens. (a) Shows the expected microstructure of the iron matrix with dark spherical carbides; (b) contains poorly formed carbides, which caused lowered material strength.

present in a material obviously affect its macroscopic properties, small amounts may also have a strong effect on properties. An arguably important example of this is carbon steel. Changing the steel carbon content from 0.1% carbon to 0.2% carbon, along with appropriate heat treatment, can increase the tensile strength by orders of 10–100; hardness will increase as well.

The compositional techniques discussed here are x-ray spectroscopy, absorption spectroscopy, mass spectrometry, and thermal and thermogravimetric analysis.

The Physics of Spectroscopy

Phenomena arising from the electronic structure of an atom, and specifically from the arrangements of the electron levels and interactions between them, are unique for each element, and may be used to distinguish the elements present in a specimen. Spectroscopy is the method of detecting the wavelengths of radiation emitted or absorbed by a material and analyzing the results to determine the composition of a specimen. Spectroscopy techniques may determine the types of atoms present, their relative amounts, the type of atomic or molecular bonding, and the ionization state, if any.

Our normal perception of color is a form of spectroscopy that informs us of the composition of what we are viewing, albeit in a limited fashion. While the basis for spectroscopy is rooted in quantum mechanics, it was first described by Newton as he looked at the spectra of the light from the sun separated by a prism. For the purposes of this discussion, however, the shell model of the atom is sufficient to explain the phenomena used in the materials analysis techniques presented.

In the shell model of the atom, a nucleus is surrounded by electrons in specific shells, or orbitals. Each orbital corresponds to a particular energy state. When an inner-shell electron is removed from the atom, the atom is perturbed from its normal state, where all inner shells of the atom are filled. In an attempt to return to the normal, or ground, state, an electron from an outer shell will move to the inner vacant electron position. This position, closer to the nucleus, is a lower energy position; to make the transition, the electron must give up energy. While excess energy can be removed through increased atomic vibration, the electron can also emit electromagnetic radiation

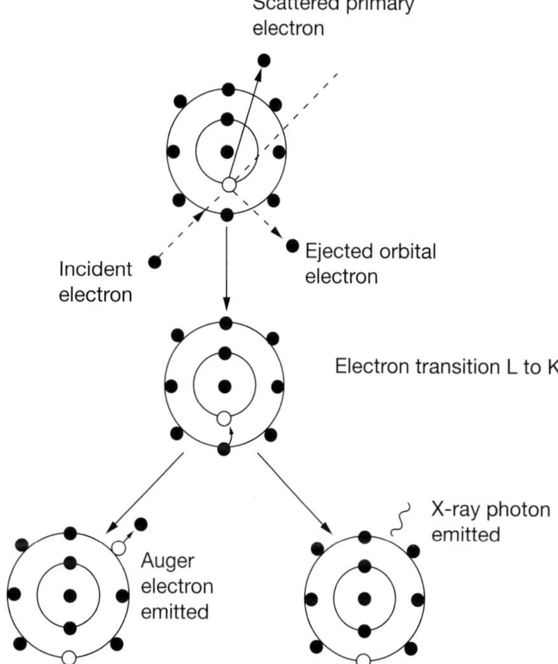

Figure 8 Excitation and relaxation of an atom; excess energy in this case is given off as an x-ray and an Auger electron. Adapted from Goldstein J, Newbury D, Joy D, et al. (2003) *Scanning Electron Microscopy and X-Ray Analysis*, p. 23. New York: Springer. Copyright 2003 by Springer Science + Business Media, with kind permission from Springer Science + Business Media B.V.

(visible light, UV, IR, or x-ray), or transfer a portion of its energy to another electron (Figure 8).

By the quantization of energy theory developed by Planck, the distance between electron energy levels in an atom depends on its atomic number Z, where Z is the number of protons in the nucleus. As Z increases with increasing nuclear charge, the distance between energy levels changes proportionately. For each element, therefore, the energy, or frequency, of the emitted radiation is specific to that element. By detecting and measuring the emitted radiation energy/wavelength, the atomic number can be determined.

The spectroscopic techniques below exploit the relationship between atomic number and emitted radiation frequency to determine composition. To create the emitted radiation, the inner shell electron is removed by a transfer of kinetic energy from an incident particle (a high-energy, high-momentum electron), or from incoming electromagnetic radiation. The method of exciting the emitted signal and the nature of the emitted signal are the primary differences in the techniques.

x-Ray Spectroscopy

When an inner shell electron is stimulated and ejected, and an outer shell electron drops down to fill the hole, an x-ray is emitted. This x-ray is called a characteristic x-ray; it has an energy specific to the element from which it was emitted, and to the specific levels transitioned by the electron.

Two techniques are used to detect the emitted x-rays: energy-dispersive x-ray spectroscopy (EDS) and wavelength-dispersive x-ray spectroscopy (WDS).

There are multiple techniques for stimulating the x-ray emission. In x-ray fluoroscopy, x-rays are used to stimulate x-ray emission. An electron may also be emitted along with an x-ray; this electron is called an Auger electron, and it can also be used to determine element composition. A useful side effect of the electron beam used in electron microscope systems is the stimulation of x-ray emissions. Hence, EDS and WDS detectors are frequently used with electron microscopes.

Each of these techniques has different detection limits and spatial resolution (**Table 2**), which arise from the different incoming and emitted signals exploited by each.

Energy-dispersive x-ray spectroscopy

In EDS, the x-ray photon from the specimen impacts a detector, which may be a lithium-doped silicon semiconductor or a silicon drift detector. An amount of charge proportional to the energy of the x-ray is created in the detector (3.8 eV creates one electron in a silicon–lithium detector). This current is converted to a voltage proportional to the initial x-ray energy. The output spectrum is a histogram displaying the number of x-rays detected with respect to energy (**Figure 9**).

Table 2 Detection limits and spatial resolution for x-ray spectroscopy techniques

Technique	*Elements detected*	*Detection limit (ppm)*	*Minimum spatial resolution*	
			Lateral	*Depth*
Energy-dispersive spectroscopy Wavelength-dispersive spectroscopy	Atomic number > 4 (beryllium and higher)	1000 (EDS), 10 (WDS)	1 μm	1 μm
x-Ray fluoroscopy			10 μm	10 to 100 mm
Auger electron spectroscopy	Atomic number > 3 (lithium and higher)	1000	0.02 μm	0.003 μm

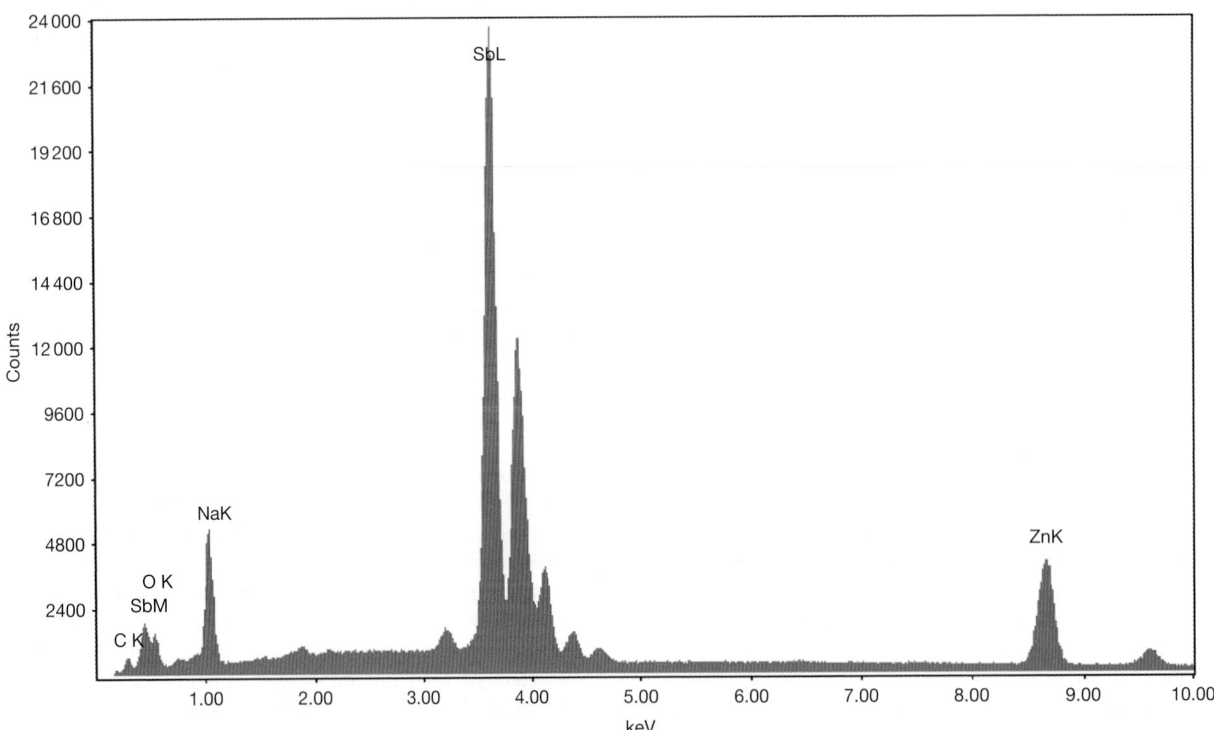

Figure 9 The EDS spectrum of a zinc antimonide semiconductor device.

Wavelength-dispersive x-ray spectroscopy

In WDS, the wave nature of the x-ray is exploited to determine the wavelength. A single crystal, with known atomic plane spacing d, is used as a diffraction grating. An x-ray incident upon the crystal will diffract when it meets conditions set forth by Bragg. When the diffraction crystal is rotated with respect to the specimen, the angle of incidence of the x-ray changes, along with the wavelength needed for diffraction. In this way, a specific range of wavelengths can be scanned and differentiated. Often crystals with different d-spacings are used as needed, depending on the wavelength range to be detected and the sensitivity required. Once x-rays of a given wavelength are being passed by the diffraction crystal, they are counted in a gas proportional counter. The incoming x-ray ionizes the gas in the detector; the resultant free electrons are detected as a current. The current is converted to a voltage; the output is a histogram with number of x-rays versus either wavelength or the corresponding energy.

Choosing between EDS and WDS

EDS measures the energy of the x-ray photon; WDS determines the wavelength of the x-ray. Because the energy of an electromagnetic wave is inversely related to its energy, according to Planck's law, this difference is trivial. The more relevant difference is in the way that each looks at a spectrum. EDS looks across a broad range of energies in the spectrum, while WDS looks at specific regions within the spectrum. With an unknown sample, EDS is more efficient; where the concentration of specific, known elements is desired, WDS is more efficient.

Both EDS and WDS can be accessories to electron microscopes. WDS are primarily found on specialized electron microscopes called electron probe microanalyzers, which are designed to collect very accurate compositional data. Electron microprobe configurations are available with limited or full SEM functionality.

While WDS is slower than EDS for large energy ranges, over a short energy range covered by a single crystal, the total scanning time is reduced. Additionally, WDS detectors have a higher throughput than EDS detectors; so WDS can collect more x-rays than EDS in the same amount of time.

Both EDS and WDS have the same spatial resolution; for the same incident electron energy, the volume of material that is sampled is identical. However, WDS has better spectral resolution; the width of the energy peak with WDS may be as low as 5 eV, compared to around 125 eV with EDS (**Figure 10**). The finer resolution of WDS is useful for eliminating problematic peak overlaps that may occur in EDS, for example, between manganese and iron, between oxygen and vanadium, and between sulfur, molybdenum, and lead. A dedicated WDS system is especially useful for routine examination of specimens containing those elements, such as ferrous alloys.

WDS also can detect smaller elemental fractions than EDS. While the ability to separate overlapping peaks certainly helps sensitivity, the benefit is primarily seen in trace element analysis. In WDS, the wavelength is set to that of the desired element; a fast acquisition rate is then used to obtain a high-intensity peak. The higher the peak, the higher the peak-to-background ratio, and the more accurate the quantification will be.

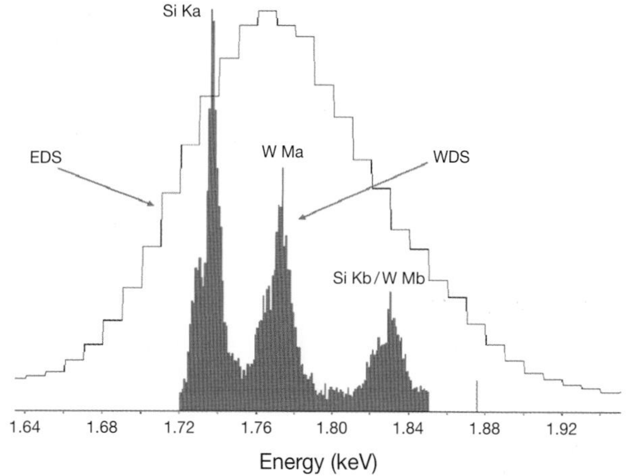

Figure 10 A comparison of the spectral resolutions of EDS and WDS. The blue EDS spectrum shows a single peak of width 260 eV, which identifies the presence of silicon. The superior resolution of WDS reveals the presence of tungsten as well as silicon. The widths of the WDS peaks are less than 40 eV. (Figure courtesy of EDAX Inc.)

Using EDS to identify an unknown material

A small object, found in commercially purchased processed meat, damaged a consumer's tooth. From its appearance, it was suspected that the object was a bit of hard plastic. To differentiate between animal bone, which may be expected in meat, and a foreign object, the object was examined with SEM and EDS. The chemical composition is shown in **Figure 11(a)**. Calcium, expected in bone, was not present, but a high level of sulfur was. For comparison, two known samples, animal bone (**Figure 11(b)**) and two-part epoxy (**Figure 11(c)**), were also analyzed. The unknown object was determined to be a foreign material, a type of glue or epoxy, rather than bone.

x-Ray fluoroscopy

x-Ray fluoroscopy (XRF) determines bulk composition using x-rays to stimulate characteristic x-ray emission. In XRF, the maximum incoming x-ray energy varies with manufacturer and instrument configuration, but typically ranges from 50 to 60 kV. Detection of characteristic x-rays is done by one of the methods described above, either EDS or WDS, and with the same attendant advantages and disadvantages.

In XRF, specimen size, sampling volume, and preparation are additional considerations. XRF instruments typically require a large amount of specimen (1 g or more), with a sampling depth ranging from microns to millimeters, depending on the incident x-ray energy and atomic makeup of the matrix. In the electron microscope, EDS/WDS can be performed on smaller amounts of material, and the x-rays are emitted selectively from the top microns of the specimen surface. However, this selectivity may be disadvantageous in circumstances where the overall composition of an inhomogeneous specimen is needed. Due to the higher sampling depth, XRF is preferred for bulk analysis. In XRF, since morphology is not determined, specimens are commonly ground and pelletized to ensure a homogeneous mixture and a smooth surface.

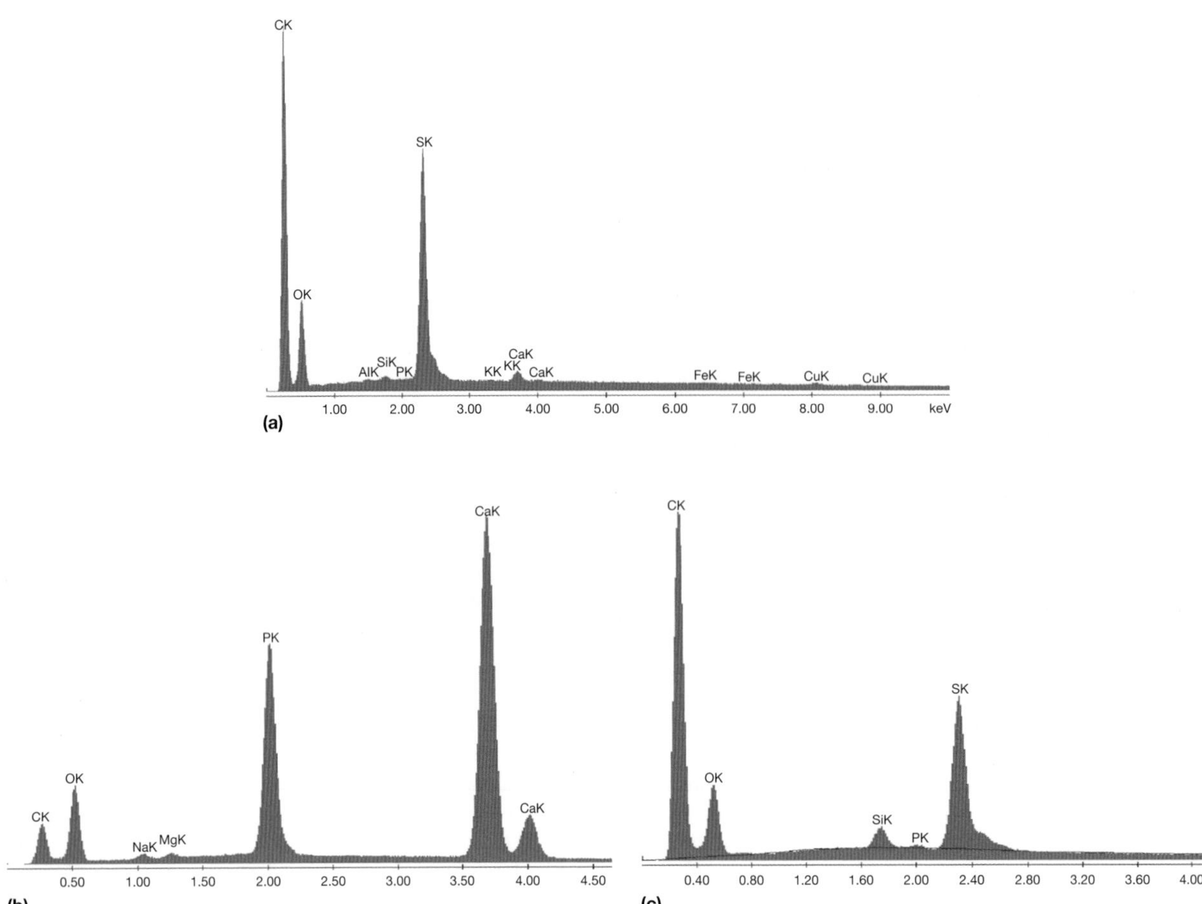

Figure 11 EDS spectra for (a) unknown sample, (b) bone, and (c) two part epoxy.

Auger Electron Spectroscopy

The Auger emission spectroscopy (AES) technique is similar to EDS in signal production, but, instead of x-rays, it detects the low-energy electrons that are emitted during relaxation of an atom after ionization. When an outer shell electron drops down to fill an empty inner shell position, one way it can give up its excess energy is by transferring a portion of that energy to another outer shell electron. This low-energy electron (~20–2500 eV) is then ejected from the atom as an Auger electron.

AES is performed in ultra-high vacuum, around 10^{-9} torr (compared to 10^{-6} torr used in electron microscopy). The ultra-high vacuum keeps the specimen surface clean and allows the low-energy Auger electrons to travel to the detector without colliding with gaseous atoms. An electron beam is directed at the specimen surface, and the surface is oriented so that the emitted Auger electrons are directed into a detector. The most common detector for AES is a cylindrical mirror analyzer (CMA). The CMA consists of two concentric cylinders, each held at a different voltage, creating an adjustable electric field. Fine-tuning of this field directs high-energy electrons away from the detection apparatus, while aiming electrons in the desired low-energy range at an electron multiplier, where they are counted. A typical AES spectrum is shown in **Figure 12**.

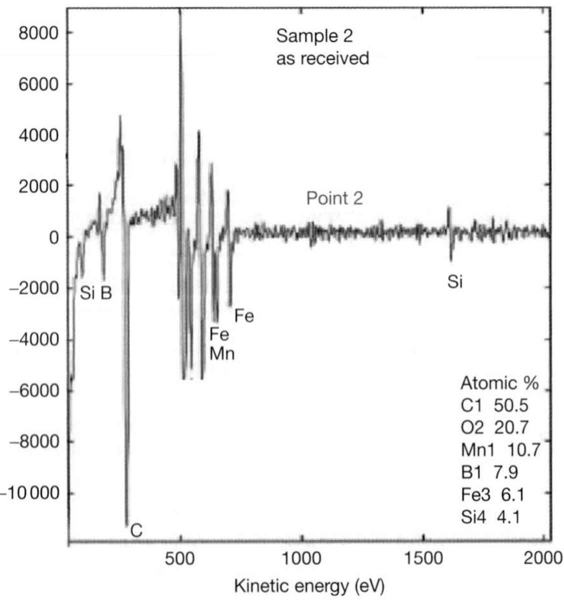

Figure 12 AES spectra of doped silicon nanowires. (Figure courtesy of D. Paul, Physical Electronics USA.)

AES is a true surface analysis technique; weak Auger electrons will not escape from the specimen except at the top

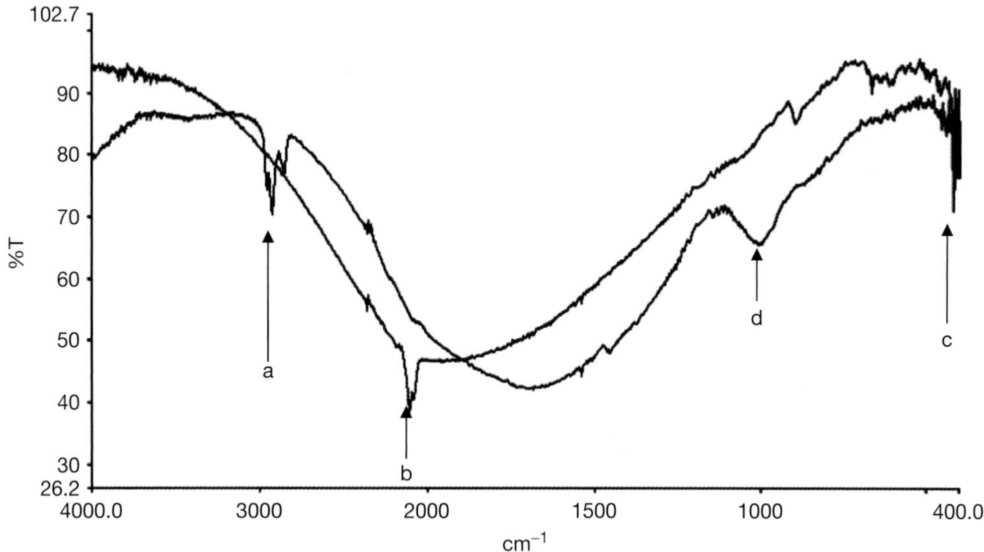

Figure 13 FTIR spectra illustrating 1-octene hydrosilation. The sample is silicon with 1-octene. (a) Octane C–H stretch, (b) Si–H_X stretch X = 1–3, (c) possible Si–O–Si stretch, (d) CH bend. (Figure courtesy of R. Terrill, Department of Chemistry, San Jose State University.)

atomic layers of the surface, that is, the top few nanometers. Coupled with an ion gun for removing surface material, AES is an extremely sensitive technique for determining depth concentration profiles.

Absorption Spectroscopy

In absorption spectroscopy, electromagnetic radiation, generally in the ultraviolet–visible–infrared range of the spectrum, is directed at a specimen. Transmitted, scattered, and/or reflected radiation is detected, and changes in intensity with respect to wavelength are determined. A diminution in intensity signifies atomic absorption (**Figure 13**). As absorption corresponds to quantum-level changes in the specimen, for example, transitions between specific atomic or molecular energy levels, or changes in rotational or vibrational state, the elemental or compound composition may be determined from the specific wavelengths absorbed.

Generally, spectroscopic techniques track changes in light intensity with respect to the incident light intensity (**Figure 14**). The measureable quantities are the incident light intensity I_{Incident} and transmitted light intensity $I_{\text{Transmitted}}$. The fraction of light which is absorbed at a given wavelength is calculated from the measured incident and transmitted light intensity, by

$$I_{\text{Absorbed}}(\lambda) = (1 - I_{\text{Transmitted}}) \times I_{\text{Incident}}$$

Of course, reflected ($I_{\text{Reflected}}$) and scattered ($I_{\text{Scattered}}$) light intensity may also be determined. Various detectors are used depending on the wavelength of light being detected; photodiodes are typically used for visible and ultraviolet light.

Many spectroscopic techniques using infrared, visible, and ultraviolet light are available; these include infrared spectroscopy (IR), inductively coupled plasma atomic emission spectroscopy (ICP-AES), ultraviolet–visible spectroscopy (UV–Vis), Raman spectroscopy, atomic absorption spectroscopy (AAS), and x-ray photoelectron spectroscopy (XPS), also called electron spectroscopy for chemical analysis (ESCA). Further information sources for spectroscopic techniques are provided in the References section.

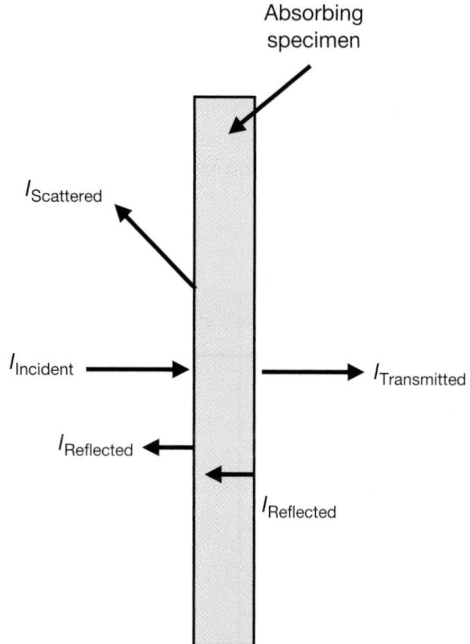

Figure 14 In addition to being absorbed within the specimen, light is reflected from the front and back surface, and scattered at surface imperfections. The amount of absorbed light is the calculated from the incident and transmitted light intensities.

Mass Spectrometry

In mass spectrometry (MS), a gaseous sample is ionized, then analyzed according to the mass-to-charge ratio (m/Z) of its components. Various techniques may be applied for sample vaporization, ionization, and ion detection, depending on the initial specimen and the desired information. In environmental forensics, for example, typical specimens include sorbent from an air sampler, or a material suspected as a source of air contamination. In these cases, the samples are heated in an inert atmosphere, and any resulting effluent gas is ionized by impact with high-energy electrons emitted from a hot tungsten filament. The ions enter the mass spectrometer, and are acted on by a magnetic or an electric field; the resulting change in the speed and trajectory of an ion is due to the applied field strength and the mass, charge, and velocity of the particle. Detecting these changes allows m/Z to be calculated.

For further discrimination of chemical species, a common configuration is the gas chromatograph-mass spectrometer (GC-MS). The effluent is passed through a gas chromatograph, where a column packed with a high-surface-area material absorbs and desorbs chemical species at different rates. The column provides a temporal spread to the species before they enter the mass spectrometer to be enumerated according to their mass-to-charge ratio.

As with spectroscopy, additional spectrometry techniques are available, with different schemes for vaporizing and ionizing the sample, and analyzing the mass-to-charge ratio. These include inductively coupled plasma mass spectrometry (ICP-MS), time-of-flight mass spectrometry (TOF-MS), and secondary ion mass spectrometry (SIMS). Information sources are provided in the References section.

Analysis of process effluents using mass spectrometry

To determine whether blueprint paper could be a source of air contamination during a printing process, a sample of the paper was subjected to testing by heating; the resulting effluent gas was analyzed in the mass spectrometer. The resulting spectrum is shown in **Figure 15**. A number of organic compounds were identified; the largest component was di-propylene glycol.

Thermal and Thermogravimetric Analysis

Differential thermal analysis (DTA) and differential scanning calorimetry (DSC) measure the heat input required to increase a specimen's temperature. The term differential is used since changes in the specimen are measured with respect to a standard reference material. In DTA, the differential temperature change between the specimen and reference for a fixed amount of heat input is measured (**Figure 16**). In DSC, the differential heat input required to increase the temperature of both the specimen and the reference is measured (**Figure 17**). In both cases, the specimen and reference are insulated from the environment in an adiabatic calorimeter.

In the related technique of thermogravimetric analysis (TGA), a small amount of specimen (milligrams) is heated in an inert or reacting atmosphere, and any resulting mass changes are measured with respect to temperature. For example, absorbed water will evaporate by around 100 °C. Bound or adsorbed water will evaporate by around 400 °C, so the degree of hydration may be determined. Decomposition reactions will occur at various temperatures depending on the material composition and atomic bonding.

TGA-DTA/DSC techniques maybe performed simultaneously, to determine the range of thermal characteristics with a single sample/run.

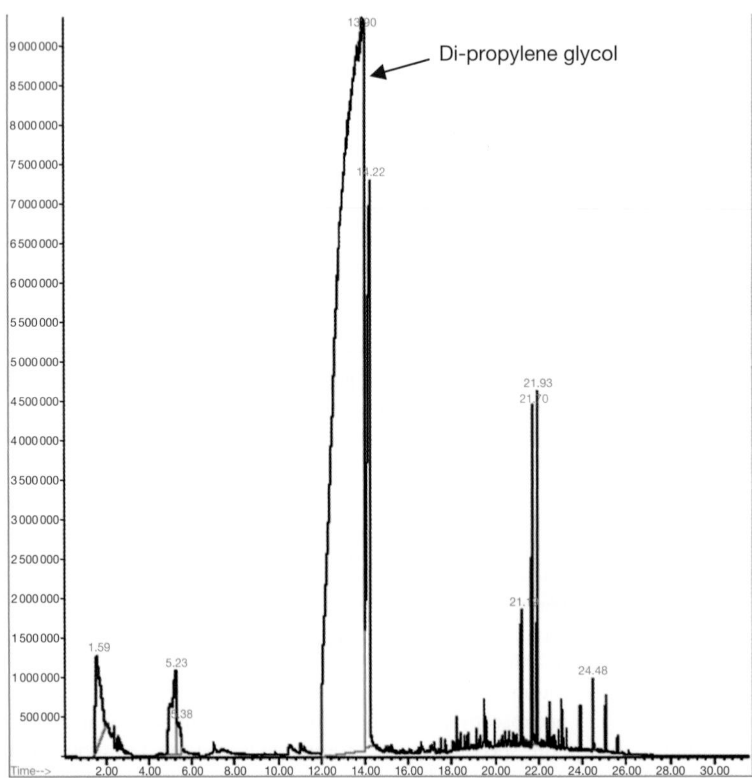

Figure 15 Spectrum obtained via heating and mass spectrometry. The major component of the gaseous effluent was di-propylene glycol.

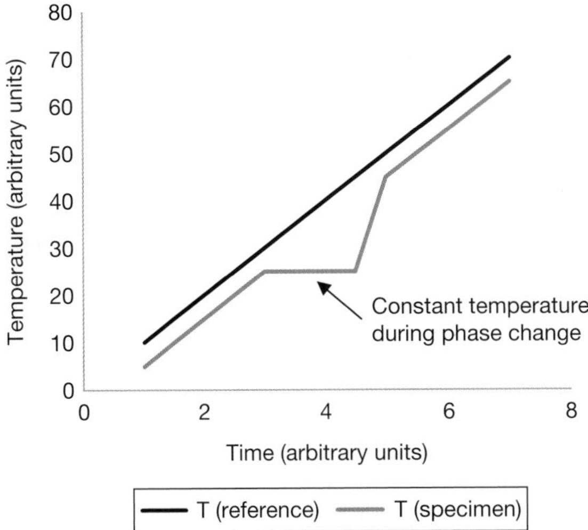

Figure 16 DTA measures the differential temperature change between the specimen and reference for the same amount of heat input. Here the specimen is observed undergoing a phase transition.

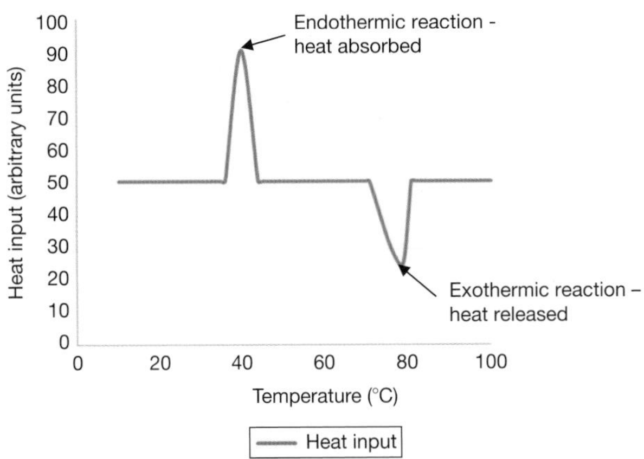

Figure 17 DSC measures the differential heat input required to increase the temperature of both the specimen and the reference. Here the specimen undergoes both an endothermic and an exothermic reaction.

Selecting the Appropriate Technique

Only a small, or limited, selection of useful materials analysis techniques is presented herein; however, many more methods are available, which may be more or less appropriate to a particular investigation. The materials failure analyst must use his or her education, training, and experience to determine which techniques are required. In addition to selecting the appropriate technique, the analyst must give weight to all relevant considerations, including the use of destructive or nondestructive analysis, required specimen size, and specimen composition and characteristics.

See also: **Engineering:** Forensic Engineering/Accident Reconstruction/Biomechanics of Injury/Philosophy, Basic Theory, and Fundamentals; **Methods:** Analytical Light Microscopy; Mass Spectrometry; Microscopy (Electron); Spectroscopic Techniques; Spectroscopy: Basic Principles.

Further Reading

ASM Handbook Committee (1987) *ASM Handbook, vol. 12: Fractography*. Geauga, OH: ASM International.
ASM Handbook Committee (1996) *ASM Handbook, vol. 19: Fatigue and Fracture*. Geauga, OH: ASM International.
Callister W and Rethwisch D (2009) *Materials Science and Engineering: An Introduction*. Chichester: Wiley.
Davis J (ed.) (1998) *Metals Handbook*. Geauga, OH: ASM International.
Goldstein J, Newbury D, and Joy D (eds.) (2003) *Scanning Electron Microscopy and X-ray Microanalysis*. New York: Springer.
Leng Y (2008) *Materials Characterization: Introduction to Microscopic and Spectroscopic Methods*. Chichester: Wiley.
Shipley RJ and Becker WT (eds.) (2002) *ASM Handbook, vol. 11: Failure Analysis and Prevention*. Geauga, OH: ASM International.
Vander Voort G (ed.) (2004) *ASM Handbook, vol. 09: Metallography and Microstructures*. Geauga, OH: ASM International.
Vickerman JC (ed.) (1997) *Surface Analysis – The Principal Techniques*. Chichester: Wiley.
Whan R (ed.) (1986) *ASM Handbook, vol. 10: Materials Characterization*. Geauga, OH: ASM International.

Relevant Websites

http://www.asminternational.org – American Society of Metals International (ASM).
http://www.astm.org – American Society of Testing and Materials (ASTM).
http://www.iso.org – International Organization for Standardization (ISO).

Investigation and Analysis of Electrical Accidents

TP Shefchick, Sunnyvale, CA, USA

Glossary

Arcing A discharge of electricity through a gas.
Burn patterns The damage caused by fire.
Circuit breaker A device designed to open and close a circuit by nonautomatic means, and to open the circuit automatically on a predetermined overload of current.
Conductor A substance or body that allows a current of electricity to pass continuously along/through it.
Electrocution The destruction of life by means of electrical current.
Exemplar Something that serves as a model or example.
Fuse An electrical safety device consisting of or including a wire or strip of fusible metal that melts and interrupts the circuit when the current becomes too high.
Lock out To open an electrical circuit and place a lock on it so that it cannot be closed without removing the lock.
Overhead Aerial utility power supply equipment to buildings or structures.
Panelboard A single panel or a group of panel units containing buses, switches, fuses, and/or circuit breakers for the control of light, heat, and power circuits.
Resistance The physical property of an element or device to rest/oppose the flow of electricity through it.
Service Electrical wires and/or equipment supplying electrical power to buildings or structures.
Specifications The design requirements.
Tripped The position of a circuit breaker's operating handle when it opens due to an overload current.
Underground Subterranean utility power supply wires and/or equipment to buildings or structures.

Investigation

The investigation of electrical phenomena began in Europe in the seventeenth century. The first electrical investigators were called electricians. One of the first electrical investigators was Benjamin Franklin. He made on-site inspections of churches which were struck by lightning. He wrote newspaper articles requesting information about lightning damage, and read articles about lightning damage to churches to determine the effectiveness of church bell ringing, which was believed to disperse lightning. Franklin found that bell ringing during a thunderstorm is a very dangerous occupation. There was no great need for electrical investigations until the inventions of Alexander Graham Bell's telephone in 1876 and Thomas A. Edison's incandescent lamp in 1878. Now we are surrounded by electrical fields, wiring, and devices which can, and do, cause injury or property damage.

The on-scene electrical investigation should be conducted as soon as possible after an event, before evidence is moved, discarded, or altered by repairmen, rescue workers, or first responders. The electrical investigator utilizes the same scene investigation techniques as the crime scene investigator, except that electrical items are the focus of the investigation. As a result, it is imperative that the electrical investigator have substantial practical knowledge about electrical equipment, wiring, and devices. Practical electrical knowledge is obtained through education and experience in designing, installing, maintaining, and repairing electrical devices, appliances, and equipment.

Before visiting the accident scene, any available information about the accident or suspected cause should be obtained from eyewitnesses, private investigators, insurance adjusters, police officers, firemen, first responders, and/or attorneys. The information could be used to confirm or refute what is found at the scene. The suspected cause must be evaluated. Upon arrival at the scene, photographs should be taken of the area surrounding the accident. The electrical power service to the scene should be inspected and documented with photographs and/or diagrams. Is it a residential, commercial, or industrial overhead or underground electrical service? Is there any evidence of recent work and/or repair to the exterior electric service?

Next, the investigator must determine the origin of the electrical accident. Sometimes the origin is where the greatest amount of damage is found. However, combustible materials in the area could cause severe damage remote from the origin. This is where the information obtained from eyewitness accounts might be helpful.

If an area of origin cannot be determined, all the electric lines/wires passing through damaged areas should be inspected. The investigator should be looking for evidence of electrical arcing or short circuiting on the wires. Electrical arcing or short circuiting generates temperatures in the range of 3000–20 000 °C. It is the heat generated by the arcing or short circuiting of electricity that causes most electrical damage and injury. The wires are normally made of copper or aluminum. Copper melts at 1083 °C and aluminum at 570–660 °C. Normally, fires do not generate sufficient heat to cause copper to melt. Therefore, the copper wiring will remain intact except for the insulation, which might have burned away. Evidence of melting on copper wiring indicates that electrical arcing or short circuiting may have occurred at the melted location. Photographs should be taken to document the area surrounding the melted wiring and close-up photographs of the melted wires. Aluminum wiring is quite frequently found melted by a fire, as fires can, and do, generate sufficient heat to melt aluminum. Subsequently, melted aluminum wiring may not be evidence of electrical arcing or short circuiting. Any melted

 http://dx.doi.org/10.1016/B978-0-12-382165-2.00148-3

aluminum wiring should be photographed in place. Wiring suspected of short circuiting or arcing should be retained for further analysis. As much as possible the wiring should be retained, especially undamaged sections which may contain manufacturer's labeling and specifications. All sources of electrical power to the accident area should be inspected and photographed. If damage is found upon power supply components, they should be retained for further analysis. All fuses should be tested with a continuity tester to determine if they have opened. The position of all circuit breakers should be documented as to whether they are 'on/off' or in a middle 'tripped' position. Evidence of overheating on power supply components, a blown fuse, or tripped circuit breaker might aid in the determination of the accident's origin. All electrical devices in the damaged area should be inspected for evidence of internal damage, which could indicate the origin of the problem. In addition, the installation and condition of undamaged electrical equipment in the vicinity of the accident should be inspected. The undamaged equipment might reveal an installation or component problem that caused the electrical accident.

If the area of origin can be determined, it should be photographed from various angles before anything is moved. Everything electrical should be retained from the area of origin and labeled to identify where it was found at the scene. Manufacturer's labels and specifications on electrical equipment should be documented. If a specific electrical device or product is suspected of causing the accident, the accident area should be searched for a similar device, product, or installation.

An exemplar product or installation could reveal what precipitated the accident. The source of electrical power to the origin should be inspected and traced back through the electrical distribution system to where it obtains electrical power. The fuse and/or circuit breaker protecting the distribution system should be inspected and photographed. Any damage to the fuse and/or circuit breaker would require that it/they be retained. They should also be retained if evidence of electrical arcing, short circuiting, or conductor overheating was found in their vicinity. The distance from the fuse and/or circuit breaker to the area of origin should be documented/measured. If the distance is too long, the circuit breaker or fuse will not provide adequate protection. The resistance of a long circuit reduces the fault current through it and impedes the operation of a circuit breaker or fuse.

Electrical conductor overheating is another way electricity can cause damage by igniting combustible materials in contact with it.

Electrical conductor overheating is normally prevented by a fuse or circuit breaker that opens and removes electrical current from the conductor before it overheats. However, sometimes the fuse is too large (mismatched) for the conductor or the circuit breaker fails to properly operate.

The size of the fuses or circuit breakers should be documented, as well as whether any of the fuses opened or circuit breaker positions were 'on/off' or 'tripped.'

The investigation should be conducted with no electrical power feeding into the accident area. The investigator should have a voltage detector to verify that there is no electrical power. A continuity tester would facilitate determining which fuse or circuit breaker fed electrical conductors in the area of origin or if a switch is open or closed. Small digital microscopes that operate with laptop computers provide excellent close-up photographs of electrical devices. A quality 3 charge coupled device progressive scan video camera can provide excellent video of the accident scene and show items from a different perspective than a still photographic camera. It will also bring your audience into the accident scene. Small hand tools are required to open up electrical devices such as panelboards, receptacles, switches, and fixtures. Wire cutters of various sizes are a necessity. A wire caliper would be useful in determining the size of electrical wiring. A very bright light source such as a high-power light-emitting diode flashlight will aid the investigation.

When photographing electrical wiring or components, a dark blue cloth used as a background will produce the best-quality photographs.

Electrical devices retained from the scene should be opened to inspect their internal components for evidence of electrical arcing, short circuiting, or overheating. The exterior of the devices should be photographed before disassembly begins and during various phases of the disassembly. However, if a device cannot be disassembled without altering its appearance, it should be x-rayed to examine its internal components. X-rays will normally show evidence of electrical arcing or short circuiting within the electrical devices. However, the x-rays will not show evidence of overheating. The x-rays will aid in the destructive examination/disassembly of the device.

If the electrical accident involves personal injury or death, the medical records should be obtained to determine the injuries sustained by each victim. Electrical entry and exit wounds, degree of burns, and their locations are normally reported. A low-voltage electrical shock (120 V alternating current or less) might not leave an entry or exit wound, especially if water is involved. The water cools the area and prevents burning of the flesh. The medical records may indicate significantly elevated serum creatine phosphokinase levels due to the muscle contractions caused by the electrical current if the victim remains in the circuit for seconds or minutes while alive. The clothing worn by the victim(s) at the time of the incident should be examined, including their footwear. Any protective clothing and gear should be retained for further examination/analysis. The type of flooring in the accident area should be documented along with the environmental conditions. Architectural plans, construction drawings, and permits of the accident area should be obtained.

An Internet search may reveal videos or photographs of the accident taken by eyewitnesses. Sometimes exemplars, manufacturer's operation manuals, and drawings can be obtained through the Internet. Complaints concerning the product or service might be posted online or at websites such as the Consumer Product Safety Commission.

Analysis

Electrical wiring can melt as a result of a eutectic reaction, which is the lowering of the melting temperature of a metal by a melted metal having a lower melting temperature. The eutectic melted wire can resemble an electrical short circuit or arcing damage. A metal such as aluminum, which melts due to fire exposure, can fall onto copper wiring and cause it to melt, as well. Elemental analysis of the melted areas by scanning electron microscopy/energy dispersive x-ray spectrometry can determine if there is foreign metal present in the melt. If electrical arcing or short circuiting is confirmed, 'arc mapping' can be conducted to aid in the determination of the accident's origin. Arc mapping involves plotting the location of arcs or short circuits on a diagram of the accident area. The arc or short circuit that is found furthest downstream from the source of electrical power most probably is closest to the origin of the problem as it was the first location where the electrical system sustained damage. Upstream electrical short circuits would prevent the occurrence of downstream short circuits, if they occurred first. Consequently, electrical short circuiting or arcing found at the point of the accident's origin downstream from the power source is most probably the initial location of the commencement of the accident. The reason for the arcing or short circuiting should be determined. Did the installation of the wiring meet the requirements of the local electrical codes? In most of the United States, the National Fire Prevention Association's (NFPA) National Electrical Code (NEC) applies to the installation of electrical wiring in residential and commercial buildings. The National Electrical Safety Code (NESC) applies to the installation and maintenance of electric utility wiring and distribution equipment. Many large cities and states have their own electrical codes which follow the requirements of the NEC and the NESC with more stringent requirements.

The x-rays of a suspected defective circuit breaker should be evaluated with design drawings or the x-rays of a properly functioning exemplar circuit breaker. If no discrepancies are found, the circuit breaker should be tested to determine whether it meets the requirements of its certifying laboratory (Underwriters Laboratory, Inc. for low voltage in the United States of America). The National Electrical Manufacturers Association, NEMA, and IEEE have standards which apply to low-voltage and high-voltage circuit breakers that could be of use in an investigation. The testing should be done prior to disassembly of the circuit breaker because it is very difficult to reassemble a circuit breaker exactly as it was prior to disassembly. After testing, the circuit breaker should be disassembled in order to inspect/examine the internal components for evidence of overheating and arcing, which might not be apparent in the x-rays.

Testing should be performed on protective components in electrical equipment and devices to verify that they function as designed. These safety components may be intended to protect against overcurrent, overvoltage, under voltage, temperature limiting, liquid level control, or ground fault protection.

Construction specifications, work invoices, and daily job site reports may be useful in the analysis. The building codes of NFPA, American Society for Testing and Materials, and The International Building Code may also assist in the analysis of the accident scene.

Casework/Examples

The first example involves an electrical accident or more appropriately an electrical incident which occurred at a sporting club. The incident originated at an outdoor racquetball court (Photograph 1). A 12 kV electrical power line had dropped down and made contact with the metal screen around the racquetball court (Photograph 2). The power line continued down and burned a hole in the metal floor of the racquetball court (Photograph 3). Luckily, no one was utilizing the racquetball court at the time of the incident. Severe damage was found underneath the racquetball court where oil heaters and fans were located to heat the court as it was located in a temperate climate location (Photograph 4). None of the fuel ignited even though there was evidence of electrical arcing surrounding the fuel storage tank (Photograph 5). An electrical panelboard near the racquetball court was completely destroyed (Photograph 6). The metal siding on a club house located ~3 m from the court was damaged by electrical arcing (Photograph 7). The ground conductors of various appliances that were plugged in at the time of the incident were burned away. Ground conductors of wiring within the club house were damaged (Photograph 8) and evidence of electrical arcing was found on a fuel line (Photograph 9). Fortunately, the fuel in the line did not ignite.

Photograph 1 Electrical incident at an outdoor racquetball court.

Photograph 2 Electrical power line dropped down and made contact with the metal screen around the racquetball court.

Inspection of the area surrounding the sporting club found that the local utility was installing power line poles and power lines at the time of the incident (Photograph 10). There were

Photograph 3 The power line burned a hole in the metal floor of the racquetball court.

Photograph 4 Severe damage was found underneath the racquetball court.

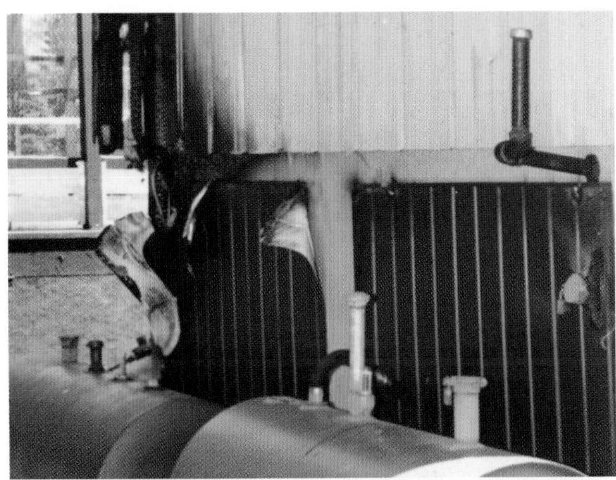

Photograph 5 Evidence of electrical arcing surrounding the fuel storage tank.

Photograph 6 The metal siding on a club house damaged by electrical arcing.

Photograph 7 An electrical panelboard near the racquetball court completely destroyed.

Photograph 8 Ground conductors of wiring within the club house were damaged.

no environmental factors that could have caused the line to fall as the weather was clear at the time of the incident.

Subsequently, the power line most probably fell down as a result of the work activity in the area by the utility company.

The damage was the result of installing an electric power line above the metal racquetball court in violation of electrical code requirements. The NESC requires a vertical clearance of 3 m above the metal racquetball court and a horizontal clearance of 2.4 m.

The next example involves a wildland fire. A wildland fire is a fire which originates in an uninhabited area of land. It might subsequently spread and damage/destroy inhabited buildings and areas of land. Inspection of the burned land areas indicated that the fire originated near a utility electric pole (**Photographs 11** and 12). The utility pole was made of wood (**Photograph** 13). Two levels of power lines were on the utility pole with 69 kV lines at the top (**Photograph** 14). Inspection of the power lines found splices in the power lines (**Photograph** 15). The power lines crossed over a gully where burning was still occurring underneath a 12 cm layer of ash at the time of the investigation (**Photograph** 16). The power lines were traced to the utility substation which controlled them. The wildland fire had destroyed vegetation and buildings in its path as it spread (**Photographs** 17 and 18). Electrical ground conductors were found severely heat-damaged in buildings that were not ignited by the fire as the result of an electrical power surge (**Photographs** 19 and 20).

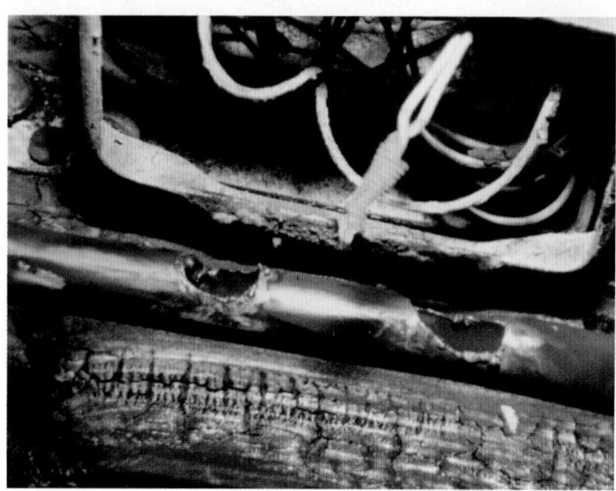

Photograph 9 Evidence of electrical arcing was found on a fuel line.

Photograph 10 Area surrounding the sporting club found that the local utility was installing power line poles and power lines at the time of the incident.

Photograph 11 Inspection of the burned land areas indicated that the fire originated near a utility electric pole.

Photograph 12 Closer perspective of burn patterns near utility poles.

Photograph 13 The utility pole made of wood.

Photograph 14 Two levels of power lines were on the utility pole with 69 kV lines at the top.

Photograph 15 Inspection of the power lines found splices in the power lines.

Photograph 16 The power lines crossed over a gully where burning was still occurring underneath a 12 cm layer of ash at the time of the investigation.

The weather in the area was extremely dry with very little rainfall and at sunset the wind would pick up, sometimes exceeding 100 km h^{-1}.

Photograph 17 The wildland fire had destroyed vegetation and buildings in its path as it spread.

Photograph 18 The contents of some buildings were completely destroyed as the fire spread.

Photograph 19 Electrical ground conductors were found severely heat-damaged in buildings that were not ignited by the fire as the result of an electrical power surge. Arrow in the photograph indicates the ground conductors.

Information was obtained from the utility company concerning protective devices in the utility substation meant to protect the power lines located in the area of the fire's origin. The lines were protected by an electrical recloser. A recloser is a device that senses an electrical problem on a power line such as contact with a tree branch. The recloser will momentarily remove electrical power from the line and then attempt to reclose it in order to restore electrical power if the problem has gone away. The number of attempts the recloser will make is determined by its settings. After a set number of attempts have been tried without success, the recloser will lock out and prevent further power from flowing through the power lines that it protects. To reenergize the power lines, a utility worker must manually reclose the recloser at the utility power substation. The records for the subject recloser indicated that it had locked out and been manually reclosed twice. Depositions of the utility workers revealed that on the night of the fire, one individual was at the utility power substation manually closing the recloser while another worker was on a hill looking to see where the power lines sparked or arced in the darkness. Both utility workers ran from the area after realizing they had ignited a wildland fire.

This fire was the result of the inappropriate action by the utility workers. The utility workers should have walked along the power lines inspecting them until they located the problem with the power lines.

Manually closing the recloser after it had locked out without inspecting the power lines resulted in this fire.

The power line came down because the wind in the area after sunset quite frequently exceeded the capacity of the components on the wooden utility pole in the area of fire origin. The wooden poles were replaced with metal poles that have a higher wind capacity and they look like wooden poles from a distance.

The third case study involves a serious electrical injury to a maintenance worker. The maintenance worker had been assigned the task of cleaning the roof gutters on a large three-story building utilizing a motorized manlift (Photograph 21). The manlift was rented from a local company and they brought the manlift to the building location for the maintenance worker to use. The maintenance worker proceeded to clean the gutters of the roof and while lowering the manlift at one point, his head made contact with a 12 000 V power line. The 12 000 V power line was in close proximity horizontally to the building and ~2 m below the level of the roof gutters. The ground sloped away from the building, which required the manlift to have something to stabilize it when the platform is raised. The manlift had warning labels on it (Photograph 22) which read: 'Danger electrocution hazard.' 'Do not operate this machine unless you have been trained in the safe operation of this machine.' 'Training includes complete knowledge of safety and operating instructions contained in the manufacturer's manuals.' 'This machine is not insulated.' 'You must maintain a clearance of at least 10 feet between any part of the machine or load and any electrical line or apparatus charged up to 50 000 V.'

The tires and base of the manlift were in contact with wet vegetation near the perimeter of the building, which provided a high-resistance current path from the lift's base to the ground (Photograph 23). This manlift did not have outriggers on it. Outriggers are devices which extend from the base of the lift in

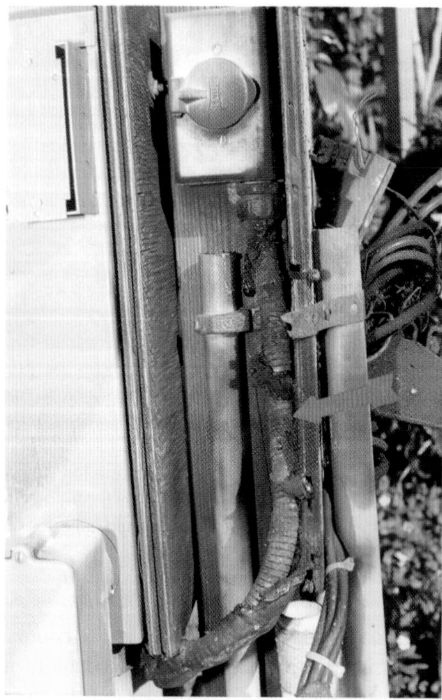

Photograph 20 Heat damaged ground conductors are indicated by the arrow in the photograph.

Photograph 21 The maintenance worker cleaning the roof gutters on a large three-story building utilizing a motorized manlift.

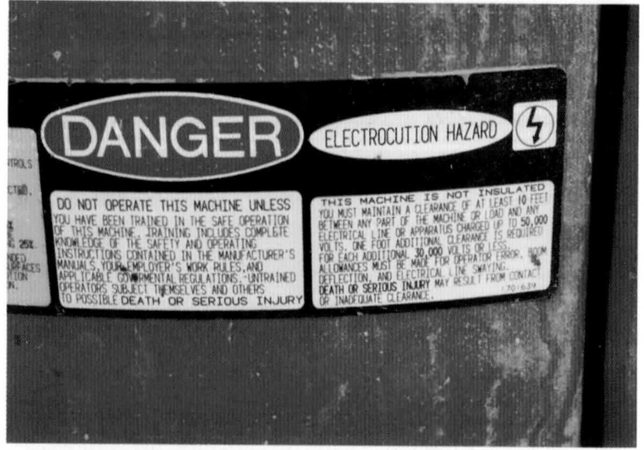

Photograph 22 Warning labels on the manlift.

order to provide stability, particularly when the lift platform is raised. Outriggers are normally made of metal, which would have provided a low-resistance current path from the lift to the ground. The operator's platform could be entered through a metal gate on the platform (Photograph 24). Inspection of the interior side of the entrance gate revealed evidence of burning and clothing material adhering to it (Photograph 25). Evidence of burning was also found on the frame of the platform near the operator's controls (Photograph 26). The operator's controls were covered with spackling materials (Photograph 27). An unlabeled black box was found on the platform which was also covered with spackling materials (Photograph 28). Cleaning the roof gutters did not involve the use of spackling materials. The spackling material covered the latches of the box and verified that it had not been opened by the maintenance worker. The unlabeled black box contained the manlift manufacturer's instruction book/user's manual for the safe operation of the lift.

Evidence of burning found on the interior side of the entrance gate and on the frame near the operator controls indicates that electricity exited the maintenance worker's back

Photograph 23 The tires and base of the manlift were in contact with wet vegetation near the base of the building.

Photograph 24 The operator's platform could be entered through a metal gate on the platform.

Photograph 25 Inspection of the interior side of the entrance gate revealed evidence of burning and clothing material adhering to it.

Photograph 26 Evidence of burning was also found on the frame of the platform near the operator's controls.

Photograph 27 The operator's controls were covered with spackling materials.

Photograph 28 An unlabeled black box was found on the platform which was also covered with spackling materials.

and left hand. Twelve thousand volts contacting the head of a person and exiting out their back and hand would normally electrocute them. However, the tires of the lift provided some isolation (high resistance) to the flow of electricity through the manlift to the ground. A manlift with outriggers should have been supplied by the rental company as the land around the perimeter of the building sloped away from it causing the manlift to be unstable when the platform was raised. However, metal outriggers would have provided a low-resistance path through the manlift to the ground and would have resulted in his electrocution. Instead, the worker was seriously burned and unconscious for more than a month. This incident was the result of the use of inappropriate equipment in a hazardous area by maintenance workers who were not aware of the hazards or not appropriately trained to perform the work.

The next case study is severe burn injuries that a building maintenance worker received from electrical arcing while attempting to change a door on a motor control center.

An electrical contractor had installed capacitors on a motor control center to improve the power factor of the electricity coming into the building (**Photograph 29**). Electric utilities quite frequently charge their customers additional fees for bad electrical power factors. Power factor is the ratio of total watts to the total root-mean-square of volt-amperes. A disconnect switch for the capacitors was installed at the bottom of the motor control center (**Photograph 30**). The electrical contractor did not install the correct door to operate the capacitor disconnect switch in the bottom unit. Subsequently, the contractor asked a maintenance worker of the building to replace the door with the correct unit. The motor control center had warning labels on it.

Photograph 29 An electrical contractor had installed capacitors on a motor control center to improve the power factor of the electricity coming into the building.

One warning label stated: "DANGER: hazard of electrical shock or burn. TURN OFF POWER supplying this equipment before working inside" (**Photograph 31**). Another warning label stated: "TURN OFF POWER AT UTILITY before working behind this cover. The line side bus of any main breaker or switch remains energized when the main is in the off position" (**Photograph 32**). A manufacturer's label on the motor control center indicated that the voltage within it was 277/480 V, three phase, and it had a current rating of 2000 A (**Photograph 33**). The cardboard covering the bottom opening of the motor control center was removed and evidence of burning and arcing was

Photograph 30 A disconnect switch for the capacitors was installed in the bottom of the motor control center.

Photograph 31 Warning labels on the motor control center.

found within it (Photograph 34). The disconnect switch that was previously located in the burned opening had been retained (Photograph 35). Electrical arcing burned a hole through the steel at the top of the unit and through its back (Photograph 36).

The building maintenance worker was not an electrician. He had no knowledge of the hazards involved in working within this motor control center. He was not wearing any personal protective equipment such as eye goggles, face shield, insulating gloves, insulating sleeves, or insulated safety hat. When he was trying to change the door on the capacitor control compartment, his screwdriver slipped and made contact between a charged 277 V component and the grounded enclosure. This caused an arc blast within the unit that vaporized copper and steel components of the compartment. As he was bending over in front of the compartment at the time, he was severely burned from the top of his head to his waist.

Photograph 32 Another warning label.

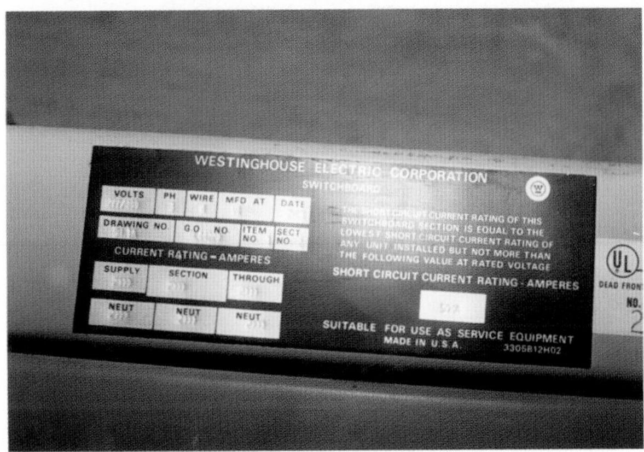

Photograph 33 Manufacturer's label on the motor control center indicating that the voltage within it was 277/480 V, three phase, and it had a current rating of 2000 A.

To safely change the door on the motor control center, electrical power would have to be turned off at the electrical utility's supply point and locked out. The capacitors should be discharged and the power supply conductors grounded to drain off any residual electrical charge within them, prior to attempting maintenance work.

The fifth example/case study is an electrocution which occurred at a luxury hotel. The hotel had four ways of traveling from its registration desk to its guest rooms; walking, golf cart, boat, or electric train (Photograph 37). A maintenance manager at the hotel had found a loose cover over the electric train track which passed through a pedestrian walkway (Photograph 38). The walkway was wet as the canal for the boat system was located in close proximity 2 m away. The maintenance manager was concerned that a guest might slip and fall and hurt themselves. Therefore, he attempted to tighten bolts which held the covers in place (Photograph 39). While reaching underneath the train track cover, he was electrocuted.

Photograph 34 The cardboard covering the bottom opening of the motor control center was removed and evidence of burning and arcing was found within it.

Photograph 35 The disconnect switch that was previously located in the burned opening had been retained.

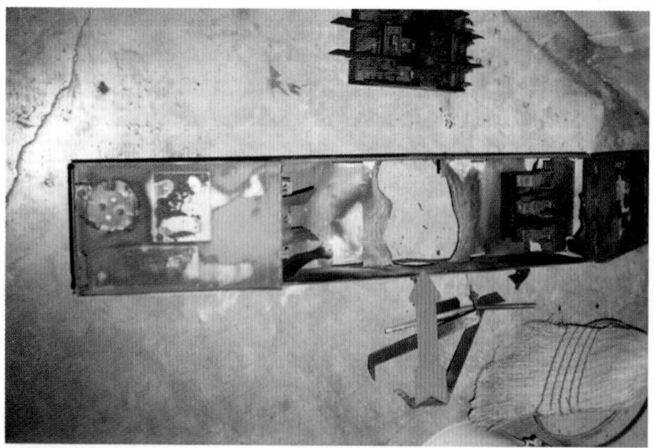

Photograph 36 Electrical arcing burned a hole through the steel at the top of the unit and through its back.

Photograph 37 The hotel had four ways of traveling from its registration desk to its guest rooms: walking, golf cart, boat, or electric train.

Photograph 38 A maintenance manager at the hotel had found a loose cover over the electric train track which passed through a pedestrian walkway.

Photograph 39 The maintenance manager attempted to tighten bolts which held the covers in place.

Examination of the underside of the train revealed that it received electrical power from electrical bus bars energized with 480 V of alternating current beneath it (Photograph 40). Electrical contact shoes (Photograph 41) would slide in a groove of the bus bars as the train moved along its track to obtain power for its traction motors (Photograph 42). An electrical joint compound was utilized to reduce the electrical resistance between the bus bars and electrical shoes (Photograph 43). No evidence was found that the manager made contact with the bus bars. However, an electrical joint compound which conducts electricity was found between the bus bars and bolts that held the train track cover in place. Subsequently, the man was electrocuted when he touched the electrical joint compound while kneeling on the wet concrete walkway which grounded him. Electrical current entered his body through his hand, passed through his heart, and exited out his knees, killing him.

Photograph 40 Examination of the underside of the train revealed that it received electrical power from electrical bus bars.

Photograph 41 Electrical contact shoes.

The sixth and final case study is that of a church fire (Photograph 44). This church was utilized by two different denominations, with differing beliefs, and an arsonist was known to be active in the area. A clockwise inspection of the church exterior found smoke residue around an opening along its base near the northeast corner (Photograph 45). Examination of the burn patterns within the church indicated that the fire originated in the northeast corner below the first pew (Photographs 46 and 47). Electrical copper and aluminum wiring was found passing through the area of fire origin (Photograph 48). Fused disconnect switches located in the

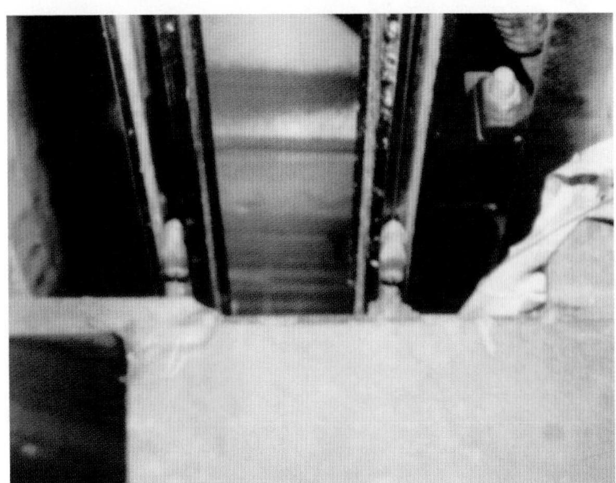

Photograph 42 Electrical contact shoes and energized bus bars.

Photograph 43 An electrical joint compound was utilized to reduce the electrical resistance between the bus bars and electrical shoes.

Photograph 44 The sixth and final case study is that of a church fire.

Photograph 45 A clockwise inspection of the church exterior found smoke residue around an opening along its base near the northeast corner.

basement of the church supplied electrical power to the wiring which passed through the area of origin (**Photograph 49**). One fused disconnect switch was missing its fuses and the aluminum wiring previously attached to it had been cut off (**Photograph 50**). Heat damage was found on the cut-off wires (**Photograph 51**). The manufacturer's label on the inside of the fused disconnect switch was clearly heat-damaged (**Photograph 52**). The aluminum wiring was traced to a second-floor gymnasium attached to the church that was utilized to play basketball. The aluminum wiring was spliced within a junction box in the gymnasium that fed power to an electrical receptacle. When the junction box was opened, a distinct odor of burning electrical insulation was detected and evidence of overheating was found on the spliced wiring (**Photograph 53**). The insulation of the aluminum wiring attached to the receptacle showed evidence of overheating (**Photograph 54**). The receptacle had a room air conditioner plugged into it that did not have the capacity to cool the gymnasium. Therefore, it would draw its maximum rated current when turned on. Testing of the air conditioner found that its compressor motor had shorted out and it would draw more current than rated when turned on. On the day of the fire, there was basketball practice in the gymnasium and the temperature outside the building exceeded 38 °C.

Electricians making repairs in the church were contacted and the fuses previously located in the fused disconnect switch were obtained (**Photograph 55**). The fuses were rated at 100 A and showed evidence of overheating, but they had not opened. The aluminum electrical wiring that they protected was rated at 50 A. The 100 A fuses would not properly protect the 50 A wiring and the resistance of the excessively long circuit limited the fault current. Consequentially, the fire was caused by overheated aluminum wiring that passed through the area of fire origin where heat was entrapped by wooden framing, which eventually ignited.

Photograph 46 Examination of the burn patterns within the church indicated that the fire originated in the northeast corner below the first pew.

Photograph 47 Burn patterns on the north wall beneath the first pew.

Photograph 48 Electrical copper and aluminum wiring was found passing through the area of fire origin.

Photograph 49 Fused disconnect switches located in the basement of the church supplied electrical power to the wiring which passed through the area of origin.

Photograph 51 Heat damage was found on the cut-off wires.

Photograph 50 One fused disconnect switch was missing its fuses and the aluminum wiring previously attached to it had been cut off.

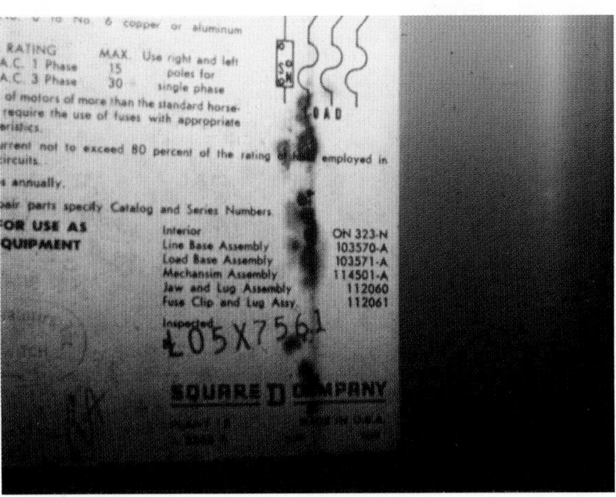

Photograph 52 The manufacturer's label on the inside of the fused disconnect switch was clearly heat-damaged.

Photograph 53 When the junction box was opened, a distinct odor of burning electrical insulation was detected and evidence of overheating was found on the spliced wiring.

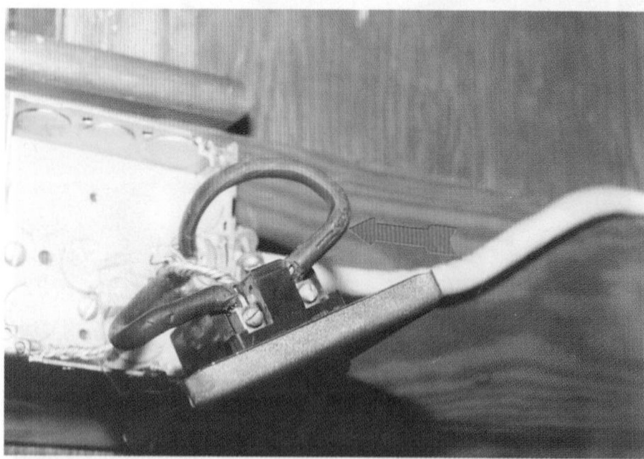

Photograph 54 Insulation of the aluminum wiring attached to the receptacle showed evidence of overheating.

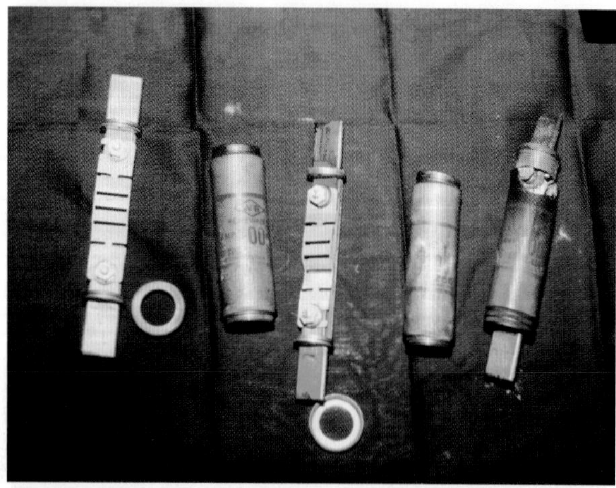

Photograph 55 Electricians making repairs in the church were contacted and the fuses previously located in the fused disconnect switch were obtained.

See also: **Engineering:** Human Factors Investigation and Analysis of Accidents and Incidents; **Forensic Medicine/Clinical:** Electrocution and Lightning Strike.

Further Reading

ASTM (2011) Construction vols. 04.01-04.13, ISBN 978-0-8031-8503-5.

Golde RH (1977) *Lightning*, vol. 1, pp. 170–172. Academic Press.

Franklin B (1753) *Request for Information on Lightning*, Pennsylvania, Gazette, June 1753.

Morse RA (1752) *Benjamin Franklin: Papers on Electricity*, pp. 276–277, 92004, http://www.franklinpapers.org and *Effect of lightning on Captain Waddel's Compass and on the Dutch Church in New York*, from James Bowdoin to Benjamin Franklin, Boston, 2 March 1752.

DeHaan JD (2002) *Kirk's Fire Investigation*, 5th edn. Upper Saddle River, NJ: Prentice Hall 0-13-060458-5.

Encyclopedia Britannica (1978) 15th edn., vol. 6, p. 536. ISBN: 0-85229-330-5.

Encyclopedia Britannica Micropaedia (1978) 15th edn., vol. 3, p. 1006. ISBN: 0-85229-330-5.

Icove DJ and DeHaan JD (2004) *Forensic Fire Scene Reconstruction*. Upper Saddle River, NJ: Pearson Prentice Hall 0-13-094205-7.

IEEE (1978) *Standard Dictionary of Electrical & Electronic Terms*, 2nd edn., LCCN 77-92333.

IEEE (1995) *Circuit Breakers, Switchgear, Substations, and Fuses, C37*, ISBN 1-55937-507-8.

IEEE, National Electrical Safety Code, C2-1997. ISBN: 1-55937-715-1.

International Building Code (2009), 5th printing, Chapters 1–35.

Luther (2008) http://www.Luther.de/en/ and http://chi.gosel.com.net.

Matthews J (1998) Fear and lightning. *Chain Reaction Magazine* 1: 22–23.http://chainreaction.asu.edu.

Nabors RE (1994) *Forensic Electrical Engineering & Liability*. Tucson, AZ: Lawyers & Judges Publishing Company 0-913875-07-4.

Nabors RE, Fish RM, and Hill PF (2004) *Electrical Injuries Engineering, Medical and Legal Aspects*, 2nd edn. Tucson, AZ: Lawyers & Judges Publishing Company, Inc.1-930056-71-0.

National Electrical Manufacturers Association, *ANSI C84.1 Electric Power Systems and Equipment*.

NFPA 921, Guide for Fire and Explosion Investigations (2008) 17.4.5.6, p. 153.

NFPA (1998) *National Fire Codes, A Compilation of NFPA Codes, Standards, Recommended Practices, Manuals and Guides*. Quincy, MA: National Fire Protection Association 0-87765-140-X.

NFPA (2008) *NFPA 921 Guide for Fire & Explosion Investigations*, 2008 edn. Quincy, MA: National Fire Protection Association.

NFPA (2010) *National Electrical Code, International Electrical Code Series, NFPA 70*. Quincy, MA: National Fire Protection Association.

Saferstein R (2011) *Criminalistics*, 10th edn., ch. 2, pp. 28–40. ISBN 13: 978-0-13-504520-6, Upper Saddle River, NJ: Prentice Hall.

Underwriters Laboratories, Inc., *UL 489, Molded-Case Circuit Breakers and Circuit-Breaker Enclosures*.

Wright RK (1997) *Investigation of Electrical Injuries and Death*, p. 8. New York: American Academy of Forensic Science Workshop.

Relevant Websites

www.aafs.org – American Academy of Forensic Sciences.
www.astm.org – American Society of Testing & Materials.
www.cpsc.gov – Consumer Product Safety Commission.
www.craigslist.org – Craigslist.
www.ieee.org/innovate – Institute of Electrical and Electronic Engineers.
www.nafe.org – National Academy of Forensic Engineers.
www.ul.com – Underwriters Laboratory Inc.
www.youtube.com – YouTube.